UNIVERSITY CASEBOOK SERIES

AMERICAN CRIMINAL LAW:

CASES, STATUTES, AND COMMENTS

by

MARKUS D. DUBBER
Professor of Law
SUNY Buffalo School of Law

MARK G. KELMAN
William Nelson Cromwell Professor of Law
Stanford Law School

FOUNDATION PRESS
NEW YORK, NEW YORK
2005

395 Hudson Street
New York, NY 10014
Phone Toll Free 1–877–888–1330
Fax (212) 367–6799
fdpress.com
Printed in the United States of America

ISBN 1–58778–726–1

To Clara, Dora, Maura, & Sophie

MD

To my mother, Sylvia Kelman, one of the pioneer female law professors, and my father, Kurt Kelman, a self-made man of the law (and much else)

MK

*

PREFACE

Criminal law is fun. Whatever challenges await the authors of a civil procedure casebook, putting together a criminal law casebook by comparison is easy: the main job of a criminal law casebook is to stay out of the way of the inherent interest that its subject holds for beginning law students.

The goal of this book, then, is to present a stimulating collection of up-to-date materials that capture the complex reality of modern American criminal law.

The last significant change in the way American criminal law is taught occurred some forty years ago. In 1962, the American Law Institute (ALI) completed its Model Penal Code and Paulsen & Kadish published the first edition of their seminal casebook, Criminal Law and Its Processes (which still covered both substantive and procedural criminal law). Paulsen/Kadish (and later Kadish/Schulhofer) was the first casebook based on the Model Penal Code and has set the standard for American criminal law teaching ever since.

Since then, American criminal law has undergone so many dramatic changes that it is time to reconceptualize American criminal law teaching once again. Some of the more momentous developments since 1962 include:

- The collapse of the rehabilitative project and the renaissance of retribution as a justification for punishment;[1]
- The eventual dominance of incapacitation in a decades-long "war on crime";
- The rise of the "victims' rights" movement, and the concomitant recognition of the victim's significance in all aspects of criminal law, from definition (e.g., hate crimes) to imposition (e.g., victim impact statements) to infliction (e.g., restitution and compensation);
- At the same time, the explosion of so-called victimless crimes, most importantly of drug offenses in a "war on drugs";[2]

1 On the Code's anti-retributivist and pro-treatmentist approach, see Markus Dirk Dubber, "Penal Panopticon: The Idea of a Modern Model Penal Code," 4 Buff. Crim. L. Rev. 53 (2000).

2 The Model Penal Code did not include drug offenses because the "project did not extend to [special topics such as narcotics, alcoholic beverages, gambling and offenses against tax and trade laws]" while "a higher priority on limited time and resources was accorded to branches of the penal law which have not received close legislative scrutiny." See Model Penal Code (Proposed Official Draft) 241 (1962).

- More recently, the enlistment of criminal law in a "war on terror";
- The appearance of internet crime;
- The rise of white collar criminal law;
- The expansion of federal criminal law;
- The growth of administrative, or regulatory, criminal law and the resulting transfer of criminal lawmaking power from the legislature to executive agencies (after the shift from the judiciary to the legislature solidified by the Model Penal Code);
- The emergence of vaguely defined offenses like RICO, money laundering, and stalking that free law enforcement officials from the constraints of legality in the pursuit of elusive "criminal networks" or dangerous individuals;
- The proliferation of inchoate and dangerousness offenses, like possession, solicitation, unilateral conspiracy, facilitation, and reckless endangerment;
- The death and rebirth of loitering statutes;
- The continued expansion of so-called public welfare and malum prohibitum crimes;
- The entrenchment of strict liability offenses throughout the "periphery" (e.g., public welfare offenses) and the "core" of criminal law (e.g., felony murder);
- The reform of the law of sex offenses, including the abandonment of the marital rape exemption and the adoption of rape shield laws;
- The rise and demise (and renaissance?) of constitutional criminal law;
- The curtailment and, in some cases, abandonment of the insanity defense;
- The establishment of plea bargaining as the dominant mode of case disposition and the attendant disappearance of jury trials;
- The emergence of a law of punishment, including the appearance of punishment guidelines as a source of criminal law, the creation of a determinate punishment regime, and the transfer of the power to make the law of punishment to quasi-administrative bodies (sentencing commissions);
- The erosion of the distinction between the treatment of juveniles and the punishment of adults in all aspects of criminal law;
- The expansion of so-called non-punitive measures, including civil forfeiture, indefinite commitment of "sexual predators," and involuntary registration and community notification for sex offenders;
- The rising popularity of so-called alternative punishments, including shaming penalties;
- The widespread adoption of harsh recidivist statutes, including three-strikes laws;
- The demise and rise of capital punishment;

- The privatization of prisons;
- The abolition of parole and the curtailment of probation; and
- Last, but certainly not least, a six-fold increase in the prison population to over two million, resulting in the highest incarceration rate in the world, with particularly disturbing effects on the minority population, with as many as one third of all black males in their twenties under some form of carceral or noncarceral penal control.

General Part (Principles of Liability). The Model Penal Code concerned itself mostly with the general part of criminal law, and today pretty much everyone teaches—and thinks about—the general principles of American criminal law along the lines of the Code. If one takes the MPC as the baseline of American criminal law, as we do in this casebook, the study of the general part should be fairly straightforward, while noting "common law" and "traditional" variations along the way.

To gain a fresh perspective on familiar material, we have frequently adopted a *comparative* approach to the issues covered in the book. Comparative materials include excerpts both from foreign (and, to a lesser extent, international) *criminal* law and from American *civil* law, to highlight parallels between the law of crimes and the law of torts (and, occasionally, contract law and victim compensation law). The ALI's Restatements of Torts make for a particularly convenient point of comparison on common issues, both in the general part (e.g., negligence, recklessness, intention, causation, omission, "privileges") and in the special part, where we consistently explore the availability of civil remedies as alternatives, or supplements, to criminal sanctions. Our discussions of the difficulties in defining when women are "coerced" sexually (in ch. 9, on rape) and in ascertaining when "consent" is "freely given" (see ch. 7, on justification) are explicitly tied to discussions of "coercion" in contract law. This emphasis on parallels among different areas of law will be especially useful to novice law students, who are generally rushed through survey courses covering enormous amounts of material during both semesters of their first year, and find it difficult, without guidance, to notice the relationship among the courses they study.

In another attempt to locate criminal law within a broader conceptual context, we encourage students to explore the constitutional limitations on substantive criminal law. Although substantive criminal law remains far less constitutionalized than does procedural criminal law, constitutional principles can—and in some cases do in fact—place formal and substantive constraints on substantive criminal law as well, including certain aspects of the principle of legality, the source and scope of criminal jurisdiction, double jeopardy, actus reus, mens rea, defenses, burdens of proof, and—perhaps most important—the right of the state to criminalize conduct.[3]

Acknowledging the Model Penal Code as the key to—if not the source of—the general part of American criminal law also allows us to drive

3 See, e.g., Lawrence v. Texas, 123 S. Ct. 2472 (2003) (striking down homosexual "sodomy" statute on due process grounds). Note too that we raise issues about the appropriate reach of the criminal law not merely in relationship to the traditional victimless crimes (e.g., drug use, voluntary sexual contacts) but in relationship to the expansion of white collar crime (e.g., certain forms of securities fraud, money laundering).

home the point that American criminal law is no longer judge-made common law, a point that was still contested in 1962 but no longer warrants extensive discussion. That does not mean, however, that American criminal law is *legislator*-made, as the MPC assumed, and properly so for its time. For even though all of American criminal law is now codified (or at least statutory), much of it has become increasingly insignificant because so much of criminal law today is, in fact, the law of punishment, as opposed to the law of crime: "sentencing" law has become, in a significant sense, the real heart of substantive criminal law. Since sentencing law, however, increasingly is generated by a quasi-administrative—sui generis—body of experts, a sentencing "commission," it appears like an exercise in lawmaking by an executive agency rather than by the judiciary. The executive also makes criminal law through prosecutors, who control sentences through charging decisions, and through other, more traditional, administrative agencies, which promulgate rules and regulations backed by criminal sanctions (generating "regulatory" offenses in the true sense). There is now even a scholarly literature very much *in support* of the shift of criminal lawmaking power to the executive.

The present book deals in some detail with punishment law as criminal law, and sentencing guidelines as codes. The law of punishment—with a now well-developed jurisprudence on sentencing—serves as a convenient point of entry into federal criminal law and the federal guidelines, which turn out to be a de facto federal criminal code, with a general part and a special part, including offense categories and offense definitions.

Special Part (Specific Offenses). The teaching of the special part of criminal law also requires significant updating. The MPC succeeded, by and large, in shaping the big issues of the general part. The special part, though, is another story. If one read the MPC's special part today, one would have no idea what American criminal law—in the special parts of criminal codes, other statutes, and regulations, as well as in courtrooms and in prisons—actually looks like.

Modern criminal law, contrary to the impression left by the MPC, is not about homicide, or theft. It is about the very crimes that appear nowhere in the MPC: drug possession crimes, traffic offenses, and "white collar crime" in its myriad manifestations. If a "traditional" crime deserves emphasis—not only because there is actually some doctrinal development in this area—it is rape, and other sex offenses, not the stagnant homicide, the MPC's central crime.[4]

Homicide used to get more than its share of doctrinal attention, but the trend in modern criminal law has been to generalize once homicide-specific doctrines like self-defense (originally homicide *se defendendo*). Still, an extensive chapter on homicide is included, not only for the sake of continuity but also because the law of homicide remains the most heavily parsed area of the special part and provides a convenient testing ground for student's understanding of the distinctions among various types of mens rea.

4 It's no accident that the blueprint for the MPC first appeared in an article devoted to the law of homicide. Jerome Michael & Herbert Wechsler, "A Rationale of the Law of Homicide (Parts I & II)," 37 Colum. L. Rev. 701, 1261 (1937).

Moreover, the law of provocation/extreme emotional disturbance raises significant theoretical issues that may help students better understand the defenses of excuse and justification, and may help them understand more generally the perils and promises of vaguely defined statutory language, on the one hand, and unduly constrained rules on the other.

The much more common possession offenses by themselves can be used to teach many issues in modern criminal law—actus reus, omission, mens rea, strict liability, conduct offense/result offense, inchoate offenses, complicity, defenses, presumptions (of possession based on something else—like presence—and of something else—like distribution—based on possession). Traffic offenses also generate thoughtful discussion because students are much more likely to be familiar with them through personal experience than they are with, say, homicide. In addition, they raise a host of interesting issues themselves—e.g., actus reus, strict liability, punishment vs. regulation and civil sanction (like suspension of driver's license), and criminal vs. civil negligence.

For similar reasons, white collar crimes receive more attention in the present book than they have in the past. Students—and courts—are less likely to demonize an insider trader, or even a third-party money launderer, than they are a murderer or a rapist, and therefore may be less impatient with the doctrinal niceties of the analysis of criminal liability. What's more, white collar crime is an area of American criminal law that is continuously developing (and expanding) and is much richer, *from the standpoint of criminal law*, than is generally supposed. New white collar crimes nicely illustrate many key issues in criminal law, including, e.g., symbolic legislation, vagueness, legislativity, strict liability, vicarious liability, group criminality, actus reus, complicity, material/non-material elements, federal/state jurisdiction, civil/criminal sanctions/remedies, and in their complicated—and often convoluted—structure, the operation of "the special part" in modern criminal law, be they defined in criminal codes, other codes, or administrative regulations, or—as is often the case—some combination of the three.

We place great emphasis on the effort to have students engage with the doctrinal issues early and often, rather than observe them from afar with the attitude that criminal law is something that happens to other (more precisely, bad) people. To this end, we have included not only cases, statutes, and excerpts from scholarly commentary, but also excerpts from newspaper accounts, jury instructions, and executive materials (like agency regulations, prosecutors' manuals and guidelines, and internal government memoranda) and have supplemented the primary and secondary materials with Problems that allow students to deepen their understanding of an issue or set of issues. The obligatory homicide and rape cases are supplemented—and probably outnumbered—by cases on drug crimes (possession and distribution), gun possession, shoplifting, traffic offenses (DWI, reckless driving, negligent homicide), loitering and trespass, internet crimes, hate crimes, tax evasion, RICO, mail fraud, and money laundering (the crime that opens and closes the casebook).

Form and Function. In implementing the basic approach outlined above, our casebook remains largely within the general structure of a criminal law casebook familiar since Paulsen/Kadish. It begins by exploring justifications for criminal law (ch. 1) and basic formal constraints on the power to make criminal law (ch. 2). Having set out the common structure of the analysis of criminal liability in American criminal law (ch. 3), it covers first the general part (chs. 4–8), and then selected offenses in the special part, rape (ch. 9), homicide (ch. 10), and white collar crimes (ch. 11).

The materials are presented with an eye toward the role of first-year (and often first-semester) criminal law classes as courses on legal thinking, rather than merely on criminal law, on method, rather than merely on substance. A casebook on criminal law—like all first year casebooks—is really two casebooks wrapped into one: a criminal law casebook and a legal methods casebook.

Throughout this book we highlight the materials both for their more straightforward doctrinal significance and for their potential as instances of various repetitive themes that can be traced throughout the doctrine. These themes, we will emphasize, are not limited to particular topics in criminal law, nor are they limited to criminal law in general, but instead are features of legal thought and action that one can detect in all areas of law, and—more to the point—across the first year curriculum.

Among the repetitive themes running through the materials is one of form: the distinction, and tension, between doctrinal rules and standards.[5] The distinction between rules and standards—and recurrent arguments regarding their respective merits—can provide the collection of cases, statutes, and comments in this casebook with a comprehensive formal framework. What's more, it can help connect the course in criminal law to other courses in the first year curriculum, where students encounter similar tensions between rule-like and standard-like tests (as, for instance, the contrast between rules regarding offer and acceptance and standards like the duty to bargain in good faith in the law of contracts).

Aside from these pervasive questions of form, we will also frequently examine the function of particular doctrines, and doctrinal approaches. The complex doctrinal apparatus of the law of possession, for instance, might profitably be understood as part of a general attempt to construct a system of criminal law that is well suited to eliminate criminality through the early detection of potentially dangerous individuals, while ostensibly remaining within the formal limits set by traditional criminal law doctrine. Likewise, it may help to regard the famously self-contradictory capital jurisprudence of the U.S. Supreme Court as part of a system wide effort to shift responsibility for (capital) punishment onto other participants in the criminal justice system.[6]

5 Cf. Mark G. Kelman, "Interpretive Construction in the Substantive Criminal Law," 33 Stan. L. Rev. 591 (1981).

6 Cf. Markus Dirk Dubber, "Policing Possession: The War on Crime and the End of Criminal Law," 91 J. Crim. L. & Criminology 829 (2002); Markus Dirk Dubber, "The Pain of Punishment," 44 Buff. L. Rev. 545 (1996).

But enough about what we tried to do in this book. It's up to you to decide if we succeeded.

MARKUS D. DUBBER
MARK G. KELMAN

* * *

EDITORIAL NOTE

Footnote numbers in cases and other source materials are as in the original, with no renumbering to take account of omitted footnotes. Our footnotes are designated by letters. Most citations in cases have been omitted.

*

ACKNOWLEDGMENTS

This casebook would not have been possible without the many colleagues and friends who provided support and encouragement along the way. It's our pleasure to thank them here. They include Guyora Binder, Mariano-Florentino Cuellar, Anthony Dillof, Charles Ewing, Sara Faherty, Stuart Green, Brian Foley, Wayne Logan, Martha Mahoney, Elizabeth Mensch, David Mills, William Pizzi, Margaret Raymond, Robert Steinfeld, Robert Weisberg, Lois Weithorn, and the members of the Foundation Press Editorial Board. Among our student assistants we would like to thank Andrea von der Empten, Nick Kelman, Bethany Davis Noll, and Eric Tennen. Nicole Ekholm, Linda Kelly, and Deborah Nasisi provided excellent administrative support throughout.

We are grateful for permission to reprint excerpts from the following publications:

Allard, Patricia, & Marc Mauer, Regaining the Vote: An Assessment of Activity Relating to Felon Disenfranchisement Laws (Washington, D.C.: Sentencing Project 2000).

Associated Press, "Child Pornography Writer Gets 10-Year Prison Term," N.Y. Times, July 14, 2001.

——, "Sentencing Opens in Cancer Drug Case," N.Y. Times, Dec. 5, 2002.

Bedau, Hugo Adam, "A Reply to van den Haag," in The Death Penalty in America: Current Controversies 457 (Hugo Bedau ed., New York: Oxford University Press 1997).

Bentham, Jeremy, "An Introduction to the Principles of Morals and Legislation," in The Great Legal Philosophers: Selected Readings in Jurisprudence 262 (Clarence Morris ed., Philadelphia: University of Pennsylvania Press 1959).

Binder, Guyora, "Meaning and Motive in the Law of Homicide," 3 Buff. Crim. L. Rev. 755 (2000).

——, "The Origins of American Felony Murder Rules," 57 Stan. L. Rev. 59 (2004).

——, "The Rhetoric of Motive and Intent," 6 Buff. Crim. L. Rev. 1 (2002).

Blecker, Robert, "Haven or Hell? Inside Lorton Central Prison: Experiences of Punishment Justified," 42 Stan. L. Rev. 1149 (1990).

Bogart, J.H., "Reconsidering Rape: Rethinking the Conceptual Foundations of Rape Law," 9 Can. J.L. & Jurisprudence 159 (1995).

Bucy, Pamela H., "Corporate Ethos: A Standard for Imposing Corporate Criminal Liability," 75 Minn. L. Rev. 1095 (1991).

Butler, Paul, "Racially Based Jury Nullification: Black Power in the Criminal Justice System," 105 Yale L.J. 677 (1995).

Butterfield, Fox, "Freed From Prison, but Still Paying a Penalty," N.Y. Times, Dec. 29, 2002.

Coffee, John C., & Charles K. Whitehead, "The Federalization of Fraud: Mail and Wire Fraud Statutes," in White Collar Crime: Business and Regulatory Offenses § 9.01 (Otto G. Obermaier & Robert. G. Morvillo eds., New York: Law Journal Seminars-Press 1990).

Colb, Sherry F., "South Dakota Proposed Jury Nullification Amendment Should Be Rejected," findlaw.com, Oct. 10, 2002.

Coleman, Doriane Lambelet, "Individualizing Justice Through Multiculturalism: The Liberals' Dilemma," 96 Colum. L. Rev. 1093 (1996).

Dan-Cohen, Meir, "Decision Rules and Conduct Rules: On Acoustic Separation in Criminal Law," 97 Harv. L. Rev. 625 (1984).

Davis, Kenneth Culp, Administrative Law (2d ed., San Diego: K.C. Davis Pub. Co. 1979).

Dubber, Markus Dirk, Criminal Law: Model Penal Code (New York: Foundation Press 2002).

——, "Policing Possession: The War on Crime and the End of Criminal Law," 91 J. Crim. L. & Criminology 829 (2002).

——, "Reforming American Penal Law," 90 J. Crim. L. & Criminology 49 (1999).

——, "Regulating the Tender Heart When the Axe Is Ready to Strike," 41 Buff. L. Rev. 85 (1993).

——, "The Victim in American Penal Law: A Systematic Overview," 3 Buff. Crim. L. Rev. 3 (1999).

——, Victims in the War on Crime: The Use and Abuse of Victims' Rights (New York: New York University Press 2002).

Estrich, Susan, Real Rape: How the Legal System Victimizes Women Who Say No (Cambridge, Mass.: Harvard University Press 1987).

——, "Rape," 95 Yale L.J. 1087 (1986).

Fried, Barbara H., The Progressive Assault on Laissez-Faire: Robert Hale and the First Law and Economics Movement (Cambridge, Mass.: Harvard University Press 1998).

Friedman, Lawrence M., Crime and Punishment in American History (New York: Basic Books 1994).

Gainer, Ronald L., "Federal Criminal Code Reform: Past and Future," 2 Buff. Crim. L. Rev. 45 (1998).

Gardner, John, "The Gist of Excuses," 1 Buff. Crim. L. Rev. 575 (1998).

Greene, Judith A., "Structuring Criminal Fines: Making an 'Intermediate' Penalty More Useful and Equitable," 13 Justice Syst. J. 37 (1988).

Harcourt, Bernard E., "The Collapse of the Harm Principle," 90 J. Crim. L. & Criminology 109 (1999).

Hart, H.L.A., Punishment and Responsibility: Essays in the Philosophy of Law (New York: Oxford University Press 1968).

Henderson, Lynne, "Review Essay: What Makes Rape a Crime?," 3 Berkeley Women's L.J. 193 (1988).

Kahan, Dan M., "Lenity and Federal Common Law Crimes," 1994 Sup. Ct. Rev. 345.

——,"Three Conceptions of Federal Criminal-Lawmaking," 1 Buff. Crim. L. Rev. 5 (1997).

Kahan, Dan M., & Eric A. Posner, "Shaming White-Collar Criminals: A Proposal for Reform of the Federal Sentencing Guidelines," 42 J.L. & Econ. 365 (1999).

Katyal, Neal Kumar, "Conspiracy Theory," 112 Yale L.J. 1307 (2003).

Kay, Julie, "Heat is on Attorneys in Drug Trafficking Cases: Florida Lawyer Is Accused of Taking 'Dirty Money'," Miami Daily Bus. Rev., May 25, 2001.

Kelman, Mark G., "Interpretive Construction in the Substantive Criminal Law," 33 Stan. L. Rev. 591 (1981).

——, "Reasonable Evidence of Reasonableness," 17 Critical Inquiry 798 (1991).

Kennedy, Randall L., "*McCleskey v. Kemp*: Race, Capital Punishment, and the Supreme Court," 101 Harv. L. Rev. 1388 (1988).

Kissinger, Henry A., "The Pitfalls of Universal Jurisdiction: Risking Judicial Tyranny," Foreign Affairs (July/Aug. 2001), at 86.

Kramer, Karen, "Rule by Myth," 47 Stan. L. Rev. 115 (1994).

Lynch, David, "The Impropriety of Plea Agreements: A Tale of Two Counties," 19 Law & Soc. Inquiry 115 (1994).

Lynch, Gerard E., "RICO: The Crime of Being a Criminal," 87 Colum. L. Rev. 661 (1987).

——, "The Sentencing Guidelines As a Not-So-Model Penal Code," 7 Fed. Sentencing Rep. 112 (1994).

Michael, Jerome, & Herbert Wechsler, "A Rationale of the Law of Homicide," 37 Colum. L. Rev. 1261 (1937).

Morris, Herbert, "Persons and Punishment," in On Guilt and Innocence: Essays in Legal Philosophy and Moral Psychology 31 (Berkeley, Cal.: University of California Press 1976).

Morris, Norval, "On 'Dangerousness' in the Judicial Process," 39 Record of the Association of the Bar of the City of New York 102 (1984).

Morse, Stephen J., "Undiminished Confusion in Diminished Capacity," 75 J. Crim. L. & Criminology 1 (1984).

Murphy, Diana E., "The Federal Sentencing Guidelines for Organizations: A Decade of Promoting Compliance and Ethics," 87 Iowa L. Rev. 697 (2002).

Naucke, Wolfgang, "An Insider's Perspective on the Significance of the German Criminal Law Theory's General System for Analyzing Criminal Acts," 1984 BYU L. Rev. 305.

Packer, Herbert L., The Limits of the Criminal Sanction (Stanford: Stanford University Press 1968).

Perkins, Rollin M., Criminal Law (2d ed., New York: Foundation Press 1969).

Pomorski, Stanislaw, "Conspiracy and Criminal Organizations," in The Nuremberg Trial and International Law 213 (George Ginsburgs & V.N. Kudriavtsev eds., Boston: Martinus Nijhoff 1977).

Rashbaum, William, & Shaila Dewan, "Officer Avoids Indictment in Killing on Brooklyn Roof," N.Y. Times, Feb. 18, 2004.

Robinson, Paul H., Peter D. Greene & Natasha R. Goldstein, "Making Criminal Codes Functional: A Code of Conduct and a Code of Adjudication," 86 J. Crim. L. & Criminology 304 (1996).

Ross, Jacqueline E., "Trade-Offs in Undercover Investigations: A Comparative Perspective," 69 U. Chi. L. Rev. 1501 (2002).

Sayre, Francis Bowes, "Public Welfare Offenses," 33 Colum. L. Rev. 55 (1933).

Schulhofer, Stephen J., "Harm and Punishment: A Critique of Emphasis on the Results of Conduct in the Criminal Law," 122 U. Pa. L. Rev. 1497 (1974).

——, Unwanted Sex: The Culture of Intimidation and the Failure of Law (Cambridge, Mass.: Harvard University Press 1998).

Scott, Robert E., & William J. Stuntz, "Plea Bargaining as Contract," 101 Yale L.J. 1909 (1992).

Simons, Kenneth W., "When Is Strict Criminal Liability Just?," 87 J. Crim. L. & Criminology 1075 (1997).

Smith, Patricia, "Legal Liability and Criminal Omissions," 5 Buff. Crim. L. Rev. 69 (2001).

Sokolove, Michael, "Should John Hinckley Go Free?," N.Y. Times, Nov. 16, 2003.

Steiner, Henry J., "Three Cheers for Universal Jurisdiction—Or Is It Only Two?," 5 Theoretical Inquiries in Law 199 (2004).

Stuart, Don, "Supporting General Principles for Criminal Responsibility in the Model Penal Code with Suggestions for Reconsideration: A Canadian Perspective," 4 Buff. Crim. L. Rev. 13 (2000).

Sutherland, Edwin H., "White Collar Criminality," 5 Am. Soc. Rev. 1 (1940).

van den Haag, Ernest, "The Death Penalty Once More," 18 U.C. Davis L. Rev. 957 (1985).

Weiner, Robin D., "Shifting the Communication Burden: A Meaningful Consent Standard in Rape," 6 Harv. Women's L.J. 143 (1983).

Westen, Peter, & James Mangiafico, "The Criminal Defense of Duress: A Justification, Not an Excuse—And Why It Matters," 6 Buff. Crim. L. Rev. 833 (2003).

Whitebread, Charles H., & Christopher Slobogin, Criminal Procedure: An Analysis of Cases and Concepts (4th ed., New York: Foundation Press 2000).

Yuracko, Kimberly A., Perfectionism and Contemporary Feminist Values (Bloomington: Indiana University Press 2003).

*

SUMMARY OF CONTENTS

*

TABLE OF CONTENTS

CHAPTER 11. White Collar Crimes: Larceny, Mail Fraud, Money Laundering 957

*

TABLE OF CASES

Principal cases are in bold type. Non-principal cases are in roman type. References are to Pages.

TABLE OF MODEL PENAL CODE SECTIONS & STATUTES

MODEL PENAL CODE

MODEL PENAL CODE

MODEL PENAL CODE

UNITED STATES

FEDERAL RULES OF EVIDENCE

PROPOSED NEW FEDERAL CRIMINAL CODE (1971)

UNITED STATES CODE ANNOTATED

8 U.S.C.A.—Aliens and Nationality

10 U.S.C.A.—Armed Forces (Uniform Code of Military Justice)

UNITED STATES CODE ANNOTATED

15 U.S.C.A.—Commerce and Trade

18 U.S.C.A.—Crimes and Criminal Procedure

MINNESOTA STATUTES ANNOTATED

MISSISSIPPI CODE

MONTANA CODE ANNOTATED

NEW HAMPSHIRE STATUTES ANNOTATED

NEW JERSEY STATUTES ANNOTATED

NEW YORK, MCKINNEY'S CRIMINAL PROCEDURE LAW

NEW YORK, MCKINNEY'S PENAL LAW

NEW YORK, MCKINNEY'S PENAL LAW

NEW YORK, MCKINNEY'S PENAL LAW

NEW YORK, MCKINNEY'S VEHICLE AND TRAFFIC LAW

NORTH CAROLINA GENERAL STATUTES

NORTH DAKOTA CRIMINAL CODE

OHIO REVISED CODE

OREGON REVISED STATUTES

PENNSYLVANIA CRIMES CODE

SOUTH DAKOTA CODIFIED LAWS

TEXAS CODE OF CRIMINAL PROCEDURE

TEXAS PENAL CODE

UNIFORM VICTIMS OF CRIME ACT

ROME STATUTE OF THE INTERNATIONAL CRIMINAL COURT

STANDARD PENAL CODE FOR LATIN AMERICA

*

AMERICAN CRIMINAL LAW

*

CHAPTER 1

PUNISHMENT AND ITS RATIONALES

The current debate about how, and whether, criminal punishment can be justified is at least as old as the Enlightenment. The question has been around for centuries, if not millennia, and so have the answers. Thinking, and writing, about rationales for punishment today remains within the same conceptual framework of deontological (or, more specifically, retributive) and consequentialist (or, more specifically, utilitarian) theories. While one side (the retributivists) insists that punishment is—and must be—justifiable for its own sake, the other side (the utilitarians, or consequentialists) contends just as vociferously that punishment is—and can be—justifiable only for the sake of some ulterior benefit, or consequence, such as an increase in utility or happiness or some other social good.

Retributivism comes in two forms—positive, or pure, and negative, or limiting. Positive retributivism considers the offender's desert a necessary and a sufficient precondition of punishment; negative retributivism considers desert only a necessary precondition. Consequentialism comes in several varieties. "Crime control" tends to be the end for the sake of which punishment is justified on consequentialist grounds. The various consequentialist theories differ on just how crime is to be prevented. Rehabilitation prevents crime by curing the offender of her abnormal criminal propensities, for her own and the community's sake. Incapacitation prevents the abnormally dangerous offender from committing crime, not by curing her, but by making it impossible for her to (or at least limiting the circumstances in which she can) act on her tendencies. And deterrence prevents crime by scaring the offender away from future crime (specific deterrence) or by making an example of the offender to others, thus scaring them away from crime (general deterrence).

When thinking about the justification of punishment, it's a good idea to differentiate between two aspects of the problem of punishment: why punish in general? and why punish in a particular case? Put another way, we need to justify not only the *institution* of punishment in the abstract, but also the *distribution* of punishment in specific cases.

Note that one of the advantages of splitting the problem of punishment in two is that it makes mixing and matching of theories of punishment possible. Now we can have our cake and eat it too. If we like, we could combine utilitarianism on the general institutional question with retributivism on the specific distributive question. This, in fact, was the view of the scholar who first drew the distinction, the British legal philosopher H.L.A. Hart. See H.L.A. Hart, "Prolegomenon to the Principles of Punishment," in Punishment and Responsibility 1 (1968). And it probably qualifies as the majority view among American commentators, legislators, and judges today.

If we put this distinction in legal doctrinal terms, we might differentiate between the justification of the law of crimes and that of the law of punishments. This doctrinal distinction is reflected in distinctions in the institutional role various participants in the criminal justice system play. Broadly speaking, *legislators* define the rules that *judges* apply to particular cases and that *enforcement officials* execute. In looking at the recent growth of administrative *sentencing commissions*, we must ultimately analyze the degree to which legislatures have unduly delegated the authority to define crimes and the degree to which judges and executive officials have been stripped of the power to exercise discretionary judgment. Each branch of government participates in the practice of punishment and each requires justification for its actions, whether they make the rules, or apply them. See John Rawls, "Two Concepts of Rules," 64 Phil. Rev. 3 (1955); Warren Quinn, "The Right to Threaten and the Right to Punish," 14 Phil. & Pub. Affairs 327 (1985).

Yet another way of thinking about the problem of punishment is to distinguish between the questions of why punish? and how, and how much, to punish? Here the question of distribution is one not of application (to whom?) but of quantity (how much?) and quality (how?).

The law of crimes provides, or at least presumes, answers to the questions of why—and what—to punish. The law of punishments, by contrast, addresses the problem of distribution in both of its variants, the questions whom to punish and how to punish.

The rationales for punishment have received far greater attention in the law of punishments than in the law of crimes. Every day, judges—and sometimes juries—must decide whether a particular person before them deserves punishment, and if so, how much and in what form. To make these decisions, they turn to the various rationales for punishment for guidance. Since the 1980s, a law of *punishments* has evolved as legislatures began to codify the rationales for punishment and—most important—to subject judicial sentencing to more or less mandatory "guidelines." Judges increasingly were required to provide written justifications (rationales) for their sentencing decisions, particularly if the sentence fell outside the range prescribed by the legislature, or by a special commission charged with drafting and updating the guidelines.

In the law of *crimes* the rationales for punishment play a less explicit role. Legislatures tend to assume their power to punish and then proceed to identify, and often to criminalize, conduct they consider objectionable for one reason or another. At any rate their decision to criminalize particular conduct is not subject to legal scrutiny, as long as it remains within the rather wide bounds set by constitutional law. The legislature's general right to punish, as opposed to its invocation in a particular statute, has never been subjected to serious constitutional scrutiny. Courts are content to remark, occasionally, on the presumed origin of the right to punish in the states' "police power," an amorphous governmental power that tends to be treated as synonymous with the power to govern in general. See, e.g., Foucha v. Louisiana, 504 U.S. 71, 80 (1992); Sutton v. New Jersey, 244 U.S.

258 (1917).[a] The power to police, it has been said, "is, and must be from its very nature, incapable of any very exact definition or limitation," and "extends to the protection of the lives, limbs, health, comfort, and quiet of all persons, and the protection of all property." Slaughter–House Cases, 83 U.S. 36, 49–50 (1873). See generally Markus Dirk Dubber, The Police Power: Patriarchy and the Foundations of American Government (2005).

Applying legislative definitions of offenses in particular cases, of course, requires judicial interpretation, even if there are no doubts about their constitutionality. So when a court must decide whether a particular behavior satisfies the definition of a given offense, it will look to the "legislative intent" underlying the statute, including the relevant rationale, or rationales, for punishing the conduct in question. Some criminal codes, in fact, now tell courts to do exactly that (e.g., Model Penal Code § 1.02(3)), in an effort to do away with the rule of "strict construction" used by common law courts to limit the scope of statutory crimes.

Rationales for punishment, however, inform not only the decision about the types of conduct appropriate for criminalization, but also about the basic prerequisites for criminal liability, no matter what the offense might be. Rationales for punishment, in other words, are relevant not only to the special part of criminal law—the law defining specific offenses—but also to its general part—the law defining the necessary conditions of criminal liability, including defenses (or rather their absence).

So, for example, a legislature—or a court—that places particular emphasis on incapacitation might take a different, and more expansive, approach toward the criminalization of attempts to commit a crime than, say, one that favors a retributive, or deterrent, approach to punishment.

From an incapacitative perspective, the criminal law may, in fact must, intervene as soon as a suspect has revealed herself to "constitute a danger to organized society of sufficient magnitude to warrant the imposition of criminal sanctions," People v. Dlugash, 41 N.Y.2d 725, 363 N.E.2d 1155

a. This origin of the power to punish creates problems for federal criminal law. As a government of limited powers, the federal government must derive its power, including its power to punish, from one or another of the powers enumerated in the Federal Constitution. The Constitution, however, makes no reference to a police power. Instead, the power to police is limited to the states. Federal criminal law therefore must rest on other governmental powers, including most notably the power to regulate interstate commerce, a move that only recently has attracted some constitutional attention. See United States v. Lopez, 514 U.S. 549 (1995) (striking down federal gun possession statute as insufficiently related to interstate commerce). Despite increasing Supreme Court scrutiny of the constitutional limits on federal authority to regulate commerce—including increased scrutiny of the authority to use criminal sanctions—there is no doubt that the federal government is more active now then it has historically been in punishing activity that could also be punished at the state level. When we look at RICO and money laundering, see chs. 8 & 11, the predicate offenses are often state crimes; when we look at mail fraud, see ch. 11, we recognize that many defendants who commit classic state property offenses are also vulnerable to federal mail fraud charges. It is important to consider *why* the federal government has chosen (or should choose) to prosecute those who are (at least formally) vulnerable to state prosecution. Similarly, those interested in the growth of international criminal law, particularly regulating human rights abuses, see ch. 2, must consider why international institutions should punish activity that almost inexorably violates domestic law.—EDS.

(1977), even if that means intervening long before the actual commission of an offense, and punishing attempts that had no chance of succeeding, for one reason or another. What's more, the incapacitationist will see no reason to punish unsuccessful attempts any less harshly than successful ones (except to the degree that those who fail to consummate offenses are less dangerous either because they are, and will remain, inept or because their failure bespeaks a certain level of ambivalence in their commitment to criminal ventures); criminal dangerousness has manifested itself in either case.

By contrast, a focus on retributivism might lead a legislature—or a court—to draw the line between innocuous, and unpunished, preparation and punishable attempt far closer to the commission of the offense, if they can justify the punishment of mere attempts at all, on the assumption that the offender's desert turns on both her culpability and the harm she caused in fact. Then again, a retributivist—if we can call her that—who punishes crime as the manifestation of bad character might reach very much the same result as an incapacitationist, the only difference being that one punishes attempts as a tangible symptom of evil, manifest in deed rather than mere thought, and the other as a symptom of criminal abnormality.

Within the consequentialist camp, the deterrence-oriented legislator—or judge—might see no need to provide for punishment of attempts at all. Some deterrence theorists would see no point in threatening sincere attempts to complete a crime with punishment if the completion of the crime already is threatened with punishment. Deterrence theorists, at core, believe that people decide whether to embark on a course of conduct—including a criminal course of conduct—depending in part on its "price." The "price" of engaging in criminal conduct rises if the conduct may be punished. But some deterrence theorists will say that at the decision-making moment, criminals expect to succeed, not fail, in their ventures so their prospective decisions to offend or not will be influenced only by the presence of punishment for consummated crimes. Others might argue that threatening attempts with punishment will deter those who embark on criminal ventures suspecting, or even knowing, *ex ante* that they could fail.

A. Traditional Rationales (Why Punish?)

United States v. Blarek

United States District Court for the Eastern District of New York.
7 F.Supp.2d 192 (1998).

■ WEINSTEIN, SENIOR DISTRICT COURT JUDGE.

Facts

Defendants Blarek and Pellecchia . . . were charged with Racketeering, 18 U.S.C. § 1962(c), Racketeering Conspiracy, 18 U.S.C. § 1962(d), and Conspiring to Launder Monetary Instruments, 18 U.S.C. §§ 371 and 1956(h). . . . Blarek was additionally charged with one count of Interstate

Travel in Aid of Racketeering. 18 U.S.C. § 1952(a)(1). By way of indictment, the government sought the forfeiture of defendants' property traceable to their alleged criminality. Both defendants pleaded not guilty.

Blarek, while operating his own interior design firm in Coconut Grove, Florida, met Pellecchia in 1980. They worked together, and became intimate, cohabitating as homosexual partners. Quickly they established a new decorating company. Blarek was President and Pellecchia Vice–President. The venture was successful. Defendants designed, remodeled, and renovated homes and offices for a broad range of private persons and businesses.

Beginning in the early–1980's, the nature of defendants' operation changed. From that time forward they worked almost exclusively for a single, ill-famed and powerful criminal client—José Santacruz Londoño. Blarek met Santacruz by chance in 1979 during a visit to friends in Colombia. He agreed to work for Santacruz, designing the interior of the drug lord's new ostentatious home....

Other dealings with Santacruz followed. Over a twelve year period, the defendants designed and decorated a number of offices and living spaces for Santacruz, his wife, his mistresses, and his children. * * *

Defendants knowingly laundered tainted cash for Santacruz in the United States in order to continue exercising their own craft and to enhance their own lives.... Both Blarek and Pellecchia knew who José Santacruz was, what he did, and from where his money was derived. Yet, each voluntarily agreed to, and in fact did, "wash" his drug proceeds. * * * Nearly all transactions between Santacruz and defendants were in cash. Defendants traveled to Miami, New York City, and other pre-determined locations to receive large sums of money from Santacruz's couriers. Payments as high as one million dollars at a time were hand-delivered to defendants in piles of fifty and one-hundred dollar bills. Defendants moved the cash between cities, traveling by car or train to avoid airport searches.

Portions of the funds were deposited in defendants' safe deposit boxes, or in bank accounts in amounts of less than $10,000 at a time to avoid federal bank transaction reporting requirements. See 31 C.F.R. § 103.22; see also 31 U.S.C. § 5324. In addition, defendants' own accountant, who pleaded guilty to money laundering and testified as a government witness, converted some one million dollars of the drug cash into checks for the defendants, thus "cleaning" the money for routine use in defendants' business operations. * * *

After a two week trial, in February, 1997, defendants were each found guilty of the Racketeering Conspiracy and Money Laundering Conspiracy counts. The jury also returned a verdict of Blarek's guilt of Interstate Travel in Aid of Racketeering.

Following trial, defendants entered into a stipulation with the government, forfeiting nearly all of their property, including their home in San Francisco worth over two millions dollars, three Harley Davidson motorcycles, a Mercedes Benz automobile, approximately $75,000 worth of jewelry, and hundreds of thousands of dollars in bank accounts and safe deposit boxes.

According to the Presentence Reports prepared by the United States Probation Office, defendants' offense conduct after 1986 involved at least $5.5 million dollars. [E]nhancements were made to the [sentence] based upon defendants' knowledge that the monies received were drug proceeds and for their supervisory role in the crimes....

[Blarek has no prior record.] Taking these factors into account, the Presentence Report indicates Blarek's ... imprisonment range under the United States Sentencing Guidelines would ... be 135 to 168 months. A fine range for Blarek's crimes of $20,000 to $14,473,063, as well as a required period of supervised release of at least two but not more than three years is also indicated.

Pellecchia[, who also has no prior convictions, was assigned] an imprisonment range of 135 to 168 months. The Presentence Report also indicates a fine range of $17,500 to $14,473,063 and a required period of supervised release of at least two but not more than three years. * * *

Law

A. Sentencing Statute: 18 U.S.C. § 3553

1. Sufficient But Not Greater Than Necessary

Congress restructured the federal sentencing law in the 1980's to create the current Guidelines-based system. See Sentencing Reform Act of 1984, Pub. L. No. 98–473, § 211, 98 Stat. 1987, 1989–90 (1984). It expressly stated that courts "shall impose a sentence sufficient, but not greater than necessary," to comply with the purposes of criminal sanctions. 18 U.S.C. § 3553(a). Harshness greater than that required is statutorily prohibited by this portion of the Sentencing Reform Act. Excessive leniency is also forbidden.

2. Seriousness of the Offense, Adequate Deterrence. Protection of the Public, and Correctional Treatment

The Sentencing Reform Act went on to explicitly delineate the purposes of criminal sanctions. Section 3551(a) provides that every defendant "shall be sentenced ... so as to achieve the purposes set forth in subparagraphs (A) through (D) of section 3553(a)(2) to the extent that they are applicable in light of all the circumstances of the case."

Subparagraphs (A) through (D) of section 3553(a)(2) instruct courts to consider the necessity of the sentence imposed:

> (A) to reflect the seriousness of the offense, to promote respect for the law, and to provide just punishment for the offense;
>
> (B) to afford adequate deterrence to criminal conduct;
>
> (C) to protect the public from further crimes of the defendant; and
>
> (D) to provide the defendant with needed educational or vocational training, medical care, or other, correctional treatment in the most effective manner.

... (A) above largely constitutes a summary of the just deserts theory and (B), (C), and (D) encompass utilitarian concerns. In creating the sentencing statutes, "Congress spelled out the four traditional justifications of the criminal sentence—deterrence, incapacitation, retribution and rehabilitation—and expressly instructed the sentencing court to keep these purposes in mind...." Kenneth R. Feinberg, The Federal Guidelines as the Underlying Purposes of Sentencing, 3 Fed. Sent. Rep. 326, 326 (May/June 1991).

When enforcing the complex federal sentencing scheme, courts are required to consider six factors, subsidiary to the traditional sentencing rationales set out above. These are:

(a) "the nature and circumstances of the offense and the history and characteristics of the defendant";

(b) "the kinds of sentences available";

(c) "the kinds of sentence and the sentencing range established" by the Sentencing Guidelines;

(d) "the need to avoid unwarranted sentence disparities among defendants with similar records who have been found guilty of similar conduct";

(e) "any pertinent policy statement issued by the Sentencing Commission"; and

(f) "the need to provide restitution to any victims of the offense."

18 U.S.C. § 3553(a)(1), (3)–(7).

To understand how these statutory provisions should be applied, a brief review of the theory and background of the purposes of criminal sentences is required.

B. Traditional Sentencing Rationales

Sentencing is a critical stage of a criminal prosecution. It represents an important moment in the law, a "fundamental judgment determining how, where, and why the offender should be dealt with for what may be much or all of his remaining life." Marvin E. Frankel, Criminal Sentences vii (1973). It is significant not only for the individual before the court, but for his family and friends, the victims of his crime, potential future victims, and society as a whole.

Four core considerations, in varying degrees and permutations, have traditionally shaped American sentencing determinations: incapacitation of the criminal, rehabilitation of the offender, deterrence of the defendant and of others, and just desert for the crime committed....

Ascertaining priorities among these potentially conflicting notions has long been a point of contention amongst legislators, scholars, jurists, and practitioners. Somewhat oversimplifying, there are two basic camps. Retributivists contend that "just deserts" are to be imposed for a crime committed. Utilitarians, in their various manifestations, suggest that penalties need to be viewed more globally by measuring their benefits against their costs....

Implied in this debate are questions about our basic values and beliefs:

> Why do we impose punishment? Or is it properly to be named "punishment"? Is our purpose retributive? It is to deter the defendant himself

> or others in the community from committing crimes? Is it for reform? rehabilitation? incapacitation of dangerous people? Questions like these have engaged philosophers and students of the criminal law for centuries.

Frankel, supra, at 7.

In the nineteenth and most of the twentieth century American prison and punishment system reforms were designed primarily to rehabilitate the prisoner as a protection against further crime. In more recent years there has been a perception by many that attempts at rehabilitation have failed; a movement towards theoretically-based, more severe, fixed punishments, based upon the nature of the crime gained momentum. Two eighteenth and nineteenth century philosophers set the terms of the current ... debate.

1. Kant's Retributive Just Desert Theory

Immanuel Kant, born in East Prussia in 1724, [famously held that] "the moral worth of an action does not depend on the result expected from it, and so too does not depend on any principle of action that needs to borrow its motive from this expected result. . . ." Immanuel Kant, Groundwork of the Metaphysics of Morals 68–69 (H.J. Paton ed. & trans., Hutchinson Univ. Library 3d ed. 1965) (1785).

. . . . Kant's anti-utilitarian thesis on criminal penalties is reflected in an oft-cited passage from his work, The Metaphysical Elements of Justice:

> Juridical punishment can never be used merely as a means to promote some other good for the criminal himself or for civil society, but instead it must in all cases be imposed on him only on the ground that he has committed a crime; for a human being can never be manipulated merely as a means to the purposes of someone else and can never be confused with the objects of the Law of things ...

Immanuel Kant, The Metaphysical Elements of Justice (Part I of The Metaphysics of Morals) 100 (John Ladd ed. & trans. 1965) (1797). It follows from this position that the sole justification for criminal punishment is retribution or "jus talionis." See Leon Pearl, A Case Against the Kantian Retributivist Theory of Punishment: A Response to Professor Pugsley, 11 Hofstra L. Rev. 273, 274 (1982) ("Immanuel Kant ... held that only a retributivist theory is properly responsive to the criminal's dignity as a rational agent capable of moral conduct, a dignity which he retains despite his commission of a legal offense."). * * *

For Kant and his adherents, "punishment that gives an offender what he or she deserves for a past crime is a valuable end in itself and needs no further justification." Paul H. Robinson & John M. Darley, The Utility of Desert, 91 Nw. U. L. Rev. 453, 454 (1997). "It is not inflicted because it will give an opportunity for reform, but because it is merited." Edmund L. Pincoffs, The Rationale of Legal Punishment 7 (1966). Kantian "just deserts" theory, therefore, focuses almost exclusively on the past to determine the level of punishment that should be meted out to right the wrong that has already occurred as a result of the defendant's delict. * * *

2. Bentham's Utilitarian Theory

Jeremy Bentham, an English philosopher born in 1748, advocated a far different, more prospective approach through his "Principle of Utility." For him, law in general, and criminal jurisprudence in particular, was intended to produce the "greatest happiness for the greatest number," a concept sometimes referred to as the "felicity calculus."

This is not to say that Bentham did not believe in sanctions. It was his view that punishment was sometimes essential to ensure compliance with public laws. See Jeremy Bentham, Bentham's Political Thought 167–68 (Bhikhu Parekh ed. 1973) ("For the most part it is to some pleasure or some pain drawn from the political sanction itself, but more particularly ... to pain that the legislator trusts for the effectuation of his will.").

Unlike his contemporary, Kant, Bentham was not interested in criminal punishment as a way of avenging or canceling the theoretical wrong suffered by society through a deviation from its norms. Rather, a criminal sanction was to be utilized only when it could help ensure the greater good of society and provide a benefit to the community. Bentham's writings in An Introduction to the Principles of Morals and Legislation explain this theory:

> ... all punishment is mischief: all punishment in itself evil. Upon the principle of utility, if it ought at all to be admitted, it ought only to be admitted in as far as it promises to exclude some greater evil ... in the following cases punishment ought not to be inflicted.
>
> I. Where it is groundless: where there is no mischief for it to prevent: the act not being mischievous upon the whole.
>
> II. Where it must be inefficacious: where it cannot act so as to prevent the mischief.
>
> III. Where it is unprofitable, or too expensive: where the mischief it would produce would be greater than what it prevented.
>
> IV. Where it is needless: where the mischief may be prevented, or cease of itself, without it: that is, at a cheaper rate ...

Jeremy Bentham, An Introduction to the Principles of Morals and Legislation, in The Great Legal Philosophers: Select Readings in Jurisprudence 262, 270 (Clarence Morris ed., 1959).

Under the Benthamite approach, deterring crime, as well as correction and reformation of the criminal, are primary aspirations of criminal law. While "the theory of retribution would impose punishment for its own sake, the utilitarian theories of deterrence and reformation would use punishment as a means to [a practical] end—the end being community protection by the prevention of crime." Charles E. Torcia, 1 Wharton's Criminal Law § 1, at 3 (15th ed. 1993).

3. Sanctions in Strict Retributive and Utilitarian Models

Given the divergence in underlying assumptions and theory, the competing retributivist and utilitarian theories suggest opposing methods for ascertaining proper penalties. Under a Kantian model, the extent of punishment is required to neatly fit the crime. "Whoever commits a crime must be punished in accordance with his desert." Pincoffs, supra, at 4.

In the case of murder, some believe that just desert is clear. A taker of life must have his own life taken. Even in the case of killings, however, there are degrees of mens rea, and over large portions of the world capital punishment is outlawed on a variety of just desert and utilitarian grounds. Cf. Alan I. Bigel, Justices William J. Brennan, Jr. and Thurgood Marshall on Capital Punishment: Its Constitutionality, Morality, Deterrent Effect, and Interpretation by the Court, 8 Notre Dame L.J. Ethics & Pub. Pol'y 11, 44 (1994) (statistics show that utilization of death penalty does not significantly lower murder rate).

For lesser offenses, reaching a consensus on the proper "price" for the criminal act under the Kantian approach is even more difficult. As one scholar has written:

> The retributivist can perhaps avoid the question of how we decide that one crime is morally more heinous than another by hewing to his position that no such decision is necessary so long as we make the punishment "equal" to the crime. To accomplish this, he might argue, it is not necessary to argue to the relative wickedness of crimes. But at best this leaves us with the problem of how we do make punishments equal to crimes, a problem which will not stop plaguing retributivists.

Pincoffs, supra, at 16.

Two main theoretical problems are presented by this just deserts approach. The degree of the earned desert—that is to say the extent or length of the appropriate punishment—is subjective. The upper and lower limits of the punishment can be very high or very low, justified on personal views and taste. The "earned" punishment may be quite cruel and do more harm to society, the criminal, and his family, than can be justified on utilitarian grounds.

Determining the appropriateness of sanction differs under Bentham's utilitarian approach, although it too poses challenging theoretical and practical tasks for the sentencer. Under this model, among:

> the factors . . . [to be considered] are the need to set penalties in such a way that where a person is tempted to commit one of two crimes he will commit the lesser, that the evil consequences . . . of the crime will be minimized even if the crime is committed, that the least amount possible of punishment be used for the prevention of a given crime.

See id. at 23. Obviously, one problem with utilizing a system based only upon this approach is that "it is difficult . . . to determine when more good than harm has been achieved . . ." United States v. Concepcion, 795 F.Supp. 1262, 1272 (E.D.N.Y. 1992).

As in the case of Kantian just deserts, the felicity calculation is subject to considerable difficulty and dispute. Another major problem with the utilitarian approach is that the individual criminal can be treated very cruelly, to gain some societal advantage even though the crime is minor—or very leniently, despite the shocking nature of the crime—if that will on balance benefit society.

Given these problems, it may make sense to continue to equivocate, oscillating between these poles, tempering justice with mercy, just deserts with utility calculations, in varying pragmatic ways. "Pragmatism," one of the hallmarks of the American political and legal system, itself suggests a leaning toward utilitarianism. See Webster's New Twentieth Century Dictionary (William Collins ed., 2d ed. 1979) ("in philosophy [pragmatism] . . . tests the validity of all concepts by their practical results").

C. Utility and Retribution Under Sentencing Guidelines

The Sentencing Guidelines, written by the United States Sentencing Commission pursuant to the Sentencing Reform Act, see Pub. L. 98–473, § 217, 98 Stat. 1987, 2019 (1984), purport to comport with the competing theoretical ways of thinking about punishment. The Guidelines state that they [seek to] "further the basic purposes of criminal punishment: deterrence, incapacitation, just punishment, and rehabilitation." See U.S.S.G. Chap. 1, Pt. A(2). A systematic, theoretical approach to these four purposes was not, however, employed by the Commission:

> A philosophical problem arose when the Commission attempted to reconcile the differing perceptions of the purposes of criminal punishment. Most observers of the criminal law agree that the ultimate aim of the law itself, and of punishment in particular, is the control of crime. Beyond this point, however, the consensus seems to break down. Some argue that appropriate punishment should be defined primarily on the basis of the principle of "just deserts." Under this principle, punishment should be scaled to the offender's culpability and the resulting harms. Others argue that punishment should be imposed primarily on the basis of practical "crime control" considerations. This theory calls for sentences that most effectively lessen the likelihood of future crime, either by deterring others or incapacitating the defendant.

Id. at A(3). The Commission decided not to create a solely retributivist or utilitarian paradigm, or "accord one primacy over the other." Id.

It is claimed that, "as a practical matter this choice [between the competing purposes of criminal punishment] was unnecessary because in most sentencing decisions the application of either philosophy will produce the same or similar results." Id. This premise is flawed. In practice, results may vary widely depending upon theory. A penalty imposed based upon pure utilitarian considerations would hardly ever be identical to one that was imposed in a pristine retributive system. While it cannot be said that one is always harsher than the other, seldom would their unrestrained application produce the same sentence.

D. Deference to Sentencing Judge on Guidelines' Critical Sentencing Issues

Since the Sentencing Commission did not say how competing rationales should shape individual sentencing decisions, courts are left to make that judgment. * * *

In writing the initial Guidelines, the Commission "sought to solve both the practical and philosophical problems of developing a coherent sentencing system by taking an empirical approach that used as its starting point data estimating pre-guidelines sentencing practice.'' U.S.S.G. Ch.1, Pt.A(3). It contended that this:

> empirical approach . . . helped resolve its philosophical dilemma. Those who adhere to a just deserts philosophy may concede that the lack of consensus might make it difficult to say exactly what punishment is deserved for a particular crime. Likewise, those who subscribe to a philosophy of crime control may acknowledge that the lack of sufficient data might make it difficult to determine exactly the punishment that will best prevent that crime. Both groups might therefore recognize the wisdom of looking to those distinctions that judges and legislators have, in fact, made over the course of time. These established distinctions are ones that the community believes, or has found over time, to be important from either a just deserts or crime control perspective.

Id. This statistically based foundation has proven inadequate to administer individual criminal litigations except in ''routine'' cases upon which there may be a ''consensus.'' * * *

E. Application of the Guidelines

Until broad-based transformation of the current complex federal system takes place, individual judges have a duty under the statutes to consider all traditional purposes of sentencing when determining an appropriate penalty. Such ''purpose-based analysis by judges may be the best hope for bringing justification to sentences imposed in the federal guideline system.'' Marc Miller, Purposes at Sentencing, 66 S. Cal. L. Rev. 413, 478 (1992).

1. Heartland

The Guidelines [are based on] an assessment of the quantity of punishment required for the ''average'' crime of that sort. As a result, ''sentencing courts [are] to treat each guideline as carving out a 'heartland,' a set of typical cases embodying the conduct that each guideline describes.'' U.S.S.G. Ch.1, Pt.A(4)(b). What this means, the Supreme Court has recently explained, is that ''[a] district judge now must impose on a defendant a sentence falling within the range of the applicable Guideline, if the case is an ordinary one.'' Koon v. United States, 518 U.S. 81, 92 (1996).

The Guidelines, while intended to ensure ''a more honest, uniform, equitable, proportional, and therefore effective sentencing system,'' U.S.S.G. Ch.1, Pt.A(3), must not be interpreted as eliminating judicial sentencing discretion. See Koon, 518 U.S. at 92. The traditional task of imposing a just and fair sentence based upon an independent view integrating all philosophical, statutory, Guidelines and individual particulars of the case at hand remains the job of the . . . judge.

2. Departures

Congress provided for judicial departure from the Sentencing Guidelines whenever a ''court finds that there exists an aggravating or mitigating circumstance of a kind, or to a degree, not adequately taken into consideration by the Sentencing Commission in formulating the guidelines that should result in a sentence different from that described." 18 U.S.C. § 3553(b).

In the same way that the Commission could not have foreseen every type of criminal case, it could not have foretold every potential ground justifying departing from the Guidelines. Except perhaps for a limited few grounds that the Commission has expressly stated should not be considered as reasons for departing, it "does not intend to limit the kind of factors, whether or not mentioned anywhere else in the guidelines, that could constitute grounds for departure in an unusual case." U.S.S.G. Ch.1, Pt.A(4)(b). * * *

Law Applied to Facts

B. Traditional and Statutory Sentencing Rationales

1. Incapacitation

Incapacitation seeks to ensure that "offenders ... are rendered physically incapable of committing crime." Arthur W. Campbell, Law of Sentencing § 2:3, at 27–28 (1991). In colonial America, incapacitation was sometimes imposed in a literal sense. Id. at 28 (loss of organs). With the development of the penitentiary system, incarceration was seen as "a more reliable means of incapacitation." Adam J. Hirsch, The Rise of the Penitentiary: Prisons and Punishment in Early America 44 (1992).

In the instant case, incapacitation is not an important factor. First, these defendants have no prior criminal record indicating any propensity towards crime. Second, their connection to the criminal world, Santacruz, is now deceased. Third, it does not appear that long term restriction is necessary to ensure that defendants do not reenter a life of crime.

Consistent with utilitarian-driven analysis, little would be gained if the sentences emphasized incapacitation.

2. Rehabilitation

Rehabilitation is designed to instill "in the offender proper values and attitudes, by bolstering his respect for self and institutions, and by providing him with the means of leading a productive life ..." Wharton's Criminal Law, supra, at 18. Neither of these men is wayward or in need of special instruction on the mores of civilized society. They have in place strong communal support systems, as evidenced by the many letters submitted to the court by family and friends. They know how to live a law abiding life. It is not required that a penalty be fashioned that teaches them how to be moral in the future. This criterion, rehabilitation, therefore, is not one that is useful in assessing a penalty.

3. Deterrence

Of the two forms of deterrence that motivate criminal penalties—general and specific—only one is of substantial concern here.

Specific deterrence is meant to "disincline individual offenders from repeating the same or other criminal acts." Campbell, supra, at 25. Such dissuasion has likely already occurred. Defendants regret their actions. The ordeal of being criminally prosecuted and publicly shamed by being denominated felons and the imposition of other penalties has taught them a sobering lesson.

General deterrence attempts to discourage the public at large from engaging in similar conduct. It is of primary concern in this case. Defendants' activities have gained a great deal of attention. Notorious cases are ideal vehicles for capturing the attention of, and conveying a message to, the public at large. While it is not appropriate under just desert views for defendants in famous cases to be treated more harshly than defendants in less significant ones simply for the sake of making an example of them, under a utilitarian view the notoriety of a particular defendant may be taken into account by sentencing courts provided the punishment is not disproportionate to the crime.

4. Retribution

Retribution is considered by some to be a barbaric concept, appealing to a primal sense of vengeance. See Wharton's Criminal Law, supra, at 24. It can not, however, be overlooked as an appropriate consideration. When there is a perception on the part of the community that the courts have failed to sensibly sanction wrongdoers, respect for the law may be reduced. This is a notion applicable under both just deserts and utilitarian balancing concepts that has had some resurgence with the current growth of the rights of victims to be heard at sentencing. See, e.g., 18 U.S.C. § 3555 (order of notice to victims). But see Susan Bandes, Empathy, Narrative, and Victim Impact Statements, 63 U. Chi. L. Rev. 361, 365 (1996) ("victim impact statements are narratives that should be suppressed because they evoke emotions inappropriate in the context of criminal sentencing").

Should punishment fail to fit the crime, the citizenry might be tempted to vigilantism. This may be why, according to one group of scholars, "a criminal law based on the community's perceptions of just desert is, from a utilitarian perspective, the more effective strategy for reducing crime." Robinson & Darley, supra, at 454. "White collar" "victimless" offenses, such as the ones committed by these defendants, are harmful to all society, particularly since drugs are involved. It is important, therefore, that the imposition of a penalty in this case captures, to some rational degree, the "worth" of defendants' volitional criminal acts.

5. Sufficient But Not Greater Than Necessary

Mercy is seldom included on the list of "traditional" rationales for sentencing. It is, however, evinced by the federal sentencing statute, 18 U.S.C. § 3553(a), which provides, as noted above, that the lowest possible penalty consistent with the goals of sentencing be imposed. See also United States v. Johnson, 964 F.2d 124, 125 (2d Cir. 1992) ("the United States Sentencing Guidelines do not require a judge to leave compassion and common sense at the door to the courtroom").

The notion that undue harshness should be avoided by those sitting in judgment has long been a part of the human fabric and spirit. Lenity is often the desirable route.

C. Departures

To impose the harsh sentence suggested by Probation and the government under the Guidelines without appropriate downward departures would amount to an act of needless cruelty given the nature of the crimes committed and the personal circumstances of these defendants. Reasoned application of both sets of philosophical considerations—just desert and utilitarian—lead to amelioration.

1. Not a Heartland Case

This case is outside of the heartland of racketeering and money laundering conspiracy cases contemplated by the Guidelines. Under such circumstances the law requires the exercise of a large degree of discretion as bridled and channeled by the sentencing statutes and Guidelines.

Unlike those in most prosecutions in drug money laundering cases, the acts of these defendants were not ones of pure personal greed or avarice. While their manner of living did greatly improve with the receipt of their drug-tainted income, their state of mind was one that was much more complicated—driven largely by excessive artistic pride. So obsessed were defendants with creating art that they lost sight of reality. Abandoned was their previously unblemished law abiding life. In exchange for professional glory and economic freedom to create, they chose to live by the credo of the Cali drug cartel. Cf. Irving Stone, The Agony and the Ecstasy (New American Library 1996) (Medici family's support [of] Michelangelo). Unfortunately for these defendants, in our world Mephistophelean deals are circumscribed by the law.

The unique motivations behind their crimes do make defendants' acts somewhat different from those in the mainstream of criminality. While still morally culpable, the state of mind of these defendants must be taken into account when considering the various rationales behind criminal penalties. Because this and other factors "distinguishes the case from the 'heartland' cases covered by the guidelines in a way that is important to the statutory purposes of sentencing," departure is encouraged. U.S.S.G. § 5K2.0.

2. Vulnerability of Blarek and Pellecchia

The defendants are homosexual lovers in a case that has been broadly publicized. The sexual proclivity of these men will likely be well known to fellow inmates and others in the correctional facilities. Their status will, no doubt, increase their vulnerability in prison.

The Guidelines purport to prohibit sex from being taken into account in the determination of a sentence. See U.S.S.G. § 5H1.10. No mention is made of sexual orientation. See id. Sexual orientation as a basis for departure has been questioned on constitutional grounds. See United States v. Lara, 905 F.2d 599, 603 (2d Cir. 1990) ("That the district court did not base its sentence upon the defendant's bisexual orientation is of some significance because to have done so might have raised serious constitutional concerns."); see also United States v. Wilke, 995 F. Supp. 828 (N.D. Ill. 1998) (collecting cases indicating "one's status as a member of a particular group ... cannot alone provide sufficient reason for departure from the otherwise applicable guideline range").

While sexual orientation may not be an appropriate ground for departure, related ancillary issues presented in some such cases support a reduction in sentence. The reality is that homosexual defendants may need to be removed from the general prison population for their own safety. This would amount to a sentence of almost solitary confinement, a penalty more difficult to endure than any ordinary incarceration. See, e.g., United States v. Lara, 905 F.2d at 603 ("severity of [defendant's] prison term is exacerbated by his placement in solitary confinement as the only means of segregating him from other inmates").

There is ample authority for the proposition that the likelihood of a defendant being abused while in prison supports a downward departure. See Koon v. United States, 518 U.S. at 111–12 (departure based upon "susceptibility to abuse in prison"); United States v. Gonzalez, 945 F.2d 525, 527 (2d Cir. 1991) (departure based upon defendant's small frame and feminine looks resulting in extreme vulnerability in prison). Because these defendants will be especially vulnerable to abuse in prison given their sexual orientation as well as their demeanor and build, downward departure is warranted.

3. Pellecchia's Medical Condition

Defendant Pellecchia is HIV positive and has been for fifteen years. While he currently appears to be in stable condition and has not developed discernable AIDS related symptoms, there is no question that this defendant suffers from a serious medical condition. See Reid J. Schar, Comment, Downward Sentencing Departures for HIV–Infected Defendants: An Analysis of Current Law and a Framework for the Future, 91 Nw. U. L. Rev. 1147, 1154 (1997) ("although the [HIV-positive] individual may feel fine, the infected patient is capable of spreading the disease and the patient's immune system is deteriorating"). This defendant has an extraordinary and unpredictable impairment. See, U.S.S.G. § 5H1.4 ("extraordinary physical impairment may be a reason to impose a sentence below the applicable guidelines range").

Defendant represents that much of his relative well-being is attributable to a special regimen to which he has adhered. He has maintained a strict diet, exercised regularly, received acupuncture frequently, and taken a combination of vitamins and other natural supplements under the close supervision of a medical professional. Following a similar holistic plan within a correctional facility will likely be impossible. Federal prisons do provide appropriate medical care to those who are infected by HIV. Nevertheless, there will be no substitute for his present living arrangements.

While the government may be correct that it can not be proven that defendant's unique treatment has contributed to his stable condition, defendant believes that it has. Since cruelty and its perception is as much a state of mind as a physical reality, he will suffer at least emotionally from the deprivation of his choice of treatment.

The extent to which inmates are exposed to diseases such as tuberculosis in prison is well documented. See Schar, supra, at 1156–57 ("The incidence of TB in prisons has recently been on the rise, and not surprisingly, those who tend to suffer most are HIV-infected prisoners."). Despite federal authorities' concern for prisoners' welfare, incarceration is likely to be detrimental to this defendant's health, resulting in a lessening of his present life expectancy. On this ground a reduction in defendant Pellecchia's sentence is required. * * *

D. Individual Sentences

The final task is weighing the sentencing considerations already delineated, with particular emphasis on general deterrence and imposition of a punishment that can be viewed as deserved in light of the seriousness and danger to society of the crimes. While defendants have [surrendered] most of their property to the government via forfeiture, and do deserve a downward departure from the Guidelines, a stiff fine to eliminate all assets as well as a substantial period of incarceration is required.

1. Blarek

... For reasons already indicated, the sentence imposed should reflect a downward departure.... Blarek is sentenced ... to a concurrent term of 68 months' incarceration for his conviction on the three counts....

In addition, Blarek is fined a total of $305,186, which represents his approximate total net worth after his forfeiture of over $2,000,000 in cash and property to the government, and his payment of attorney's fees.

The maximum period of supervised release, three years, is imposed. During the time that defendant is under supervision, he may not work for any clients or employers outside of the United States to ensure that he is not tempted again into money laundering. A mandatory special assessment of $150 is also imposed.

2. Pellecchia

Pellecchia's ... sentence should reflect ... the same ... departure granted for defendant Blarek with an additional level of downward departure based upon defendant's health as well as his lesser culpability. A concurrent term of incarceration of 48 months ... is imposed for his conviction on two counts....

No fine has been imposed for Pellecchia since he will have a negative net worth of over $100,000 after payment of attorney's fees.

Three years of supervised release is ordered. Like his co-defendant, Pellecchia may not be employed by anyone outside of this country during his period of supervision to minimize chances of his being tempted again into money laundering. A special assessment of $100 is also imposed.

QUESTIONS AND COMMENTS

1. It's unusual, to say the least, to find references to eighteenth century philosophers in judicial opinions, on criminal law or any other area of law. In this case, however, it's also entirely appropriate, since the past two centuries have added little to the subject, despite continued and almost invariably passionate debate. Proponents of retributivism are fond of

claiming the following passage from Exodus 21:24–25 as an early recognition, and perhaps even the source of, their theory of punishment:

> Eye for eye, tooth for tooth, hand for hand, foot for foot,
>
> Burning for burning, wound for wound, stripe for stripe.

Opponents of retributivism are just as fond of citing this passage, often referred to as the lex (or jus) talionis. But see Anthony Phillips, Ancient Israel's Criminal Law: A New Approach to the Decalogue 96–98 (1970) (pre-biblical, possibly Babylonian, origins of the lex talionis). Why do you think that is? And what do you do with one-eyed or toothless assailants, anyway? See G.W.F. Hegel, Philosophy of Right § 101 (1821) (Hegel's answer: what matters is not identity of crime and punishment, but equivalence. See Markus Dirk Dubber, "Rediscovering Hegel's Theory of Crime and Punishment," 92 Mich. L. Rev. 1577 (1994).)

2. The consequentialists cannot quite claim the progressive high road of rationality illuminating the barbaric darkness of un-Enlightened punishment. Their theory, too, has deep historical roots. The general idea of punishment for prevention's, rather than for punishment's, sake is at least as old as Plato—the *Protagoras*, to be precise:

> [N]o one punishes the evil-doer under the notion, or for the reason, that he has done wrong, only the unreasonable fury of a beast acts in that manner. But he who desires to inflict rational punishment does not retaliate for a past wrong which cannot be undone; he has regard to the future, and is desirous that the man who is punished, and he who sees him punished, may be deterred from doing wrong again. He punishes for the sake of prevention....

Protagoras 324a4.

This passage, in a Latin rendition by Seneca, "nemo prudens punit, quia peccatum est, sed ne peccetur" ("no wise man punishes because a wrong has been done, but so that no wrong will be done"), became a much-cited Latin proverb and has provided a convenient framework for debates about the theories of punishment ever since, pitting retributivists, who favor punishment because a wrong *has been* done, against consequentialists, who prefer punishment so that no wrong *will be* done. See Seneca, De Ira, bk. I. XIX. 7.

3. *Traditional Rationales*. The basic ideas underlying the traditional rationales for punishment are as straightforward as they are ancient in origin, and the court in *Blarek* does a good job laying them out. Still, it's worth taking a closer look at their contemporary manifestations, and at their core assumptions about the nature of crime, and punishment.

The reasonable starting point for the discussion of justifications for punishment is that causing pain (or, more generally, disutility) is, at best, suspect, so we oughtn't to do it unless we've got a good reason to do so. But what if punishment is (at least physically) painless? Much of the history of modern punishment can be seen as a continued attempt to remove, or at least to displace, the *physical* pain of punishment. Consider, for instance, the now common practice of executing death sentences by lethal injection.

Cf. Markus Dirk Dubber, "The Pain of Punishment," 44 Buff. L. Rev. 545 (1996). Or is punishment painful by necessity, by definition?

A. *Deterrence.* According to deterrence theory, punishment is justified because it will reduce the number of "unwanted" acts. So, for instance, Y would prefer parking illegally to circling the block in the absence of a sanction, but as the expected cost of so doing rises, she is more likely to circle. Z would love to vandalize, but as the expected cost of so doing rises, he does something else. Deterrence theory is unambiguously connected to an economic/rational actor model of the origin of crime; as a result, some who take issue with it do so by questioning the degree to which would-be criminals calculate rationally, whether explicitly or implicitly.

The basic model is that proscribed conduct is intrinsically desired (by at least some subject to criminal sanctions) but demand for the behavior (like demand for goods generally) drops as the price rises; or, to put it in a property crime (production rather than consumption) context, the economic return to "working" on illicit activities, compared to the return to working on legal activities, must be assessed net of expected punishment costs. Thus, when Q compares the gains to working at a store to the returns to stealing from the store, he is less likely to steal as the net return to theft drops. The function of punishment is to dissuade would-be criminals from engaging in criminal activity, see, e.g., Richard Posner, "An Economic Theory of the Criminal Law," 85 Colum. L. Rev. 1193 (1985), or, in more sophisticated—if not more persuasive—versions, to insure "optimal" levels of crime, see, e.g., Gary S. Becker, "Crime and Punishment: An Economic Approach," 69 J. Pol. Econ. 169 (1968).

This model gives rise to two quite distinct versions of the optimization problem. In one view the legislature recognizes that the costs of suppressing crime are positive—incarceration is costly, so are apprehension and prosecution—and compares the benefits from expected crime reduction with the incremental costs of obtaining that reduction. In the other (less sensible?) view we must prevent punishment levels being set so high that people would not do punishable things even when they're "worth" doing. Most commentators, other than die-hard law & economics scholars, are very skeptical of the usefulness of even talking about the second version since they believe the optimal rate of (most) crimes is zero, because they "launder preferences" so that the utility gains to criminals of, say, assaulting, do not "count" in assessing aggregate social welfare. (One attraction of utilitarian theories of punishment, however, is precisely their commitment to treating offenders equally, by figuring their pleasures and pains into the general utility calculus underlying criminal policy.) See Jeremy Bentham, The Rationale of Punishment 28 (1830) (delinquent's "welfare is proportionately the welfare of the community—his suffering the suffering of the community").

The price of engaging in criminal activity is set by the state both formally (through criminal sentences) and informally (through its capacity to apprehend and convict, which varies in part based on the inputs it channels into those law enforcement activities). Private actors obviously have some impact too; debates over gun control, for instance, often center on the deterrent effect of armed "victims." Cf. John R. Lott, Jr., More

Guns, Less Crime: Understanding Crime and Gun–Control Laws (1998) (data suggest that concealed weapons laws reduce crime); John J. Donohue, "The Impact of Concealed–Carry Laws," in Evaluating Gun Policy: Effects on Crime and Violence 287 (Jens Ludwig & Philip J. Cook eds. 2003) (disputing Lott's findings).

In fact, the expected return to all sorts of criminal activity may be sensitive to "victim" conduct. In thinking about whether there are "rights" that constrain the state from simply following cost-justified decision rules, one might consider whether a victim should be protected by the criminal law even when she has failed to take precautions against crime that are cheaper than the precautions the state could take or, even more starkly, cheaper than the value of the crime to the perpetrator. Imagine in this regard a good worth $5,000 to the perpetrator whose theft could be, but wasn't, prevented for $1. See Louis Michael Seidman, "Soldiers, Martyrs, and Criminals: Utilitarian Theory and the Problem of Crime Control," 94 Yale L.J. 315 (1984). For a discussion of this point from the perspective of German criminal law, see Bernd Schünemann, "The Role of the Victim Within the Criminal Justice System: A Three–Tiered Concept," 3 Buff. Crim. L. Rev. 33, 38–40 (1999) (theory of "Viktimodogmatik").

Even if we know that "demand" for crime is (at least somewhat) price sensitive, we don't know the *location* of demand curves, or whether these are sensitive to conscious social policy: it's clearly a big question whether, say, the move from a one-year to a five-year sentence for assault decreases assaults from 100 to 10/100,000 or whether it decreases them from 1,000 to 100. These are some exemplary views about the location of demand curves for criminal activity:

1. Rates of property crime at a given punishment level are sensitive to unemployment rates (for a review article both examining the conventional claim that the relationship is weak and arguing that the relationship is non-trivial, see Theodore G. Chiricos, "Rates of Crime and Unemployment: An Analysis of Aggregate Research Evidence," 34 Soc. Probs. 187 (1987));

2. Rates of violent crime at a given punishment level are sensitive to the degree of exposure to violence in the mass media (for a review article, see Richard B. Felson, "Mass Media Effects on Violent Behavior," 22 Ann. Rev. Sociology 103 (1996) (suggesting that exposure to TV violence has a small effect on violent behavior by some viewers));

3. Rates of illegal drug use at a given punishment level are sensitive to the availability of counseling (see Robert L. Hubbard et al., Drug Abuse Treatment: A National Study of Effectiveness (1989) (suggesting drug treatment is effective, though not a panacea)).

Simple introspection *seems* to support the deterrence hypothesis; virtually all of us slow down when we spot a police car at the side of the road, ready to give us a ticket, and we do this almost wholly because we fear adverse consequences if we continue to violate the law against speeding. But it is not clear that the presence of the policeman, let alone the existence of speeding statutes generally or the imposition of higher penalties for speeding, actually reduces the amount of speeding. (And ignoring the fact that speeding may be a "crime" whose benefits and costs we calculate more than we calculate the benefits and costs of more emotionally charged, expressive crimes of violence.) The fact that one doesn't speed in the presence of the police officer does not mean that one speeds less over the course of one's journey, even if punishment "works" to reduce crime when it is certain and the punishment process is psychologically proximate.

Naturally, to ascertain whether the existence or level of punishment diminishes crime, we need to be able to compare crime rates across jurisdictions (spatially, over time) with distinct punishment practices; it turns out to be remarkably difficult, though, to ascertain the degree to which punishment practices affect crime rates or are affected by them. (For instance, an increase in crime *may* lead to prison overcrowding that leads to a reduction in punishment.) For a classic discussion of both the theoretical claims and the remarkably muddy empirical evidence on the efficacy of punishment as a deterrent, see Franklin E. Zimring & Gordon J. Hawkins, Deterrence: The Legal Threat in Crime Control (1973). Strong support for the deterrence hypothesis can be found in Isaac Ehrlich, "Crime, Punishment, and the Market for Offenses," 10 J. Econ. Perspectives 43 (1996); a literature review that is far more skeptical that we can be sure of the *existence* of a deterrent effect, much less be certain that the effect is of significant magnitude, can be found in Daniel Nagin, "General Deterrence: A Review of the Empirical Literature," in Estimating the Effects of Criminal Sanctions on Crime Rates 135 (Alfred Blumstein et al. eds., 1978).

Uneasiness about deterrence as a justification for punishment persists. This uneasiness stems not only from doubts about the rational actor model of crime upon which it rests (at least as applied to a large proportion of criminal behavior, and those engaging in it) and the lack of irrefutable empirical support for its efficacy (which is particularly damning for a theory that regards itself as the rational alternative to punishment for its own sake), but also from a longstanding two-pronged attack on its moral justification. As critics of general deterrence have pointed out since Kant, punishing one person for the sake of deterring others amounts to treating him not "as an end" but "simply as a means." Immanuel Kant, Grounding for the Metaphysics of Morals 36 (James W. Ellington trans., 3d ed. 1993) (1785). Plus, critics of deterrence, specific and general, have argued since Hegel that "[t]o base a justification of punishment on threat is to liken it to the act of a man who lifts his stick to a dog. It is to treat a man like a dog instead of according to his freedom and honor." G.W.F. Hegel, Philosophy of Right § 99 (1821). Do you find these criticisms persuasive?

At any rate, to sidestep these empirical and moral concerns—persuasive or not—continental criminal law recently has favored a kinder, gentler variety of deterrence: positive general prevention. The idea here is that punishment is justified as a means toward the end of "maintaining and strengthening trust in the ability of the legal order to exist and to enforce" the law. Claus Roxin, Strafrecht: Allgemeiner Teil 50 (3d ed. 1997). Semantically, this justification of punishment is more attractive because it speaks of "prevention" rather than "deterrence" and "positive" rather than its supposed opposite, "negative," all in an attempt to blunt the canine discipline analogy. To what extent punishment for the sake of enforcing the public's sense of justice, or its trust in the power of the state, steers clear of the Kantian objection is unclear. And the absence of empirical evidence bothers "positive general prevention" no less than "general deterrence," except that its efficacy is even less falsifiable.

B. *Retribution.* Retribution is harder to define than deterrence, but what is relatively clear is that retributivists are nonconsequentialist (that is, they don't base their decisions on an assessment of the quality of the outcomes they expect will occur, prospectively, as a result of the decision to punish), backward-regarding, and that, in some way, they believe we are morally bound to treat people in accord with their "deserts." Sophisticated retributivists reject the oft-presumed nexus between retributivism and vengeance, a presumption that tends to underlie the common claim, cited in *Blarek*, that retributivism is "barbaric." They also distance themselves from the utilitarian argument that criminal law exists to displace, or to provide an outlet for, emotions that might otherwise give rise to private vengeance, believing that punishment should be based more on what the actor does rather than the emotions that were stirred up by the events at issue. (See, e.g., the notorious comment by the influential nineteenth-century British criminal law scholar, judge, and codifier, James Fitzjames Stephen, that "the forms in which deliberate anger and righteous disapprobation are expressed, and the execution of criminal justice is the most emphatic of such forms, stand to [the hatred of criminals] in the same relation in which marriage stands to [sexual passion]." 2 J.F. Stephen, A History of the Criminal Law of England 82 (1883).) In this regard it is interesting that sophisticated retributivists believe it is inappropriate to punish all those who cause the sorts of harm that produce vengeful feelings—exempting, for instance, those who do not act either deliberately or carelessly, or exempting those who lack the "practical reason" to make responsible choices.

Retributivism is associated with the view that the origin of criminal conduct is the freely-willed, intentional behavior of individuals. Some retributivists also stress the "wickedness" of the individual manifesting itself in her criminal conduct, and regard punishment as a response proportional to that moral flaw, or character trait. The latter variety of retributivists faces the difficulty of distinguishing wickedness from, say, dangerousness. If an offender is perceived as no longer dangerous, we might ask ourselves *why* he is not. If we were able to explain *why* he is not dangerous now, and correlatively why he was before, why wouldn't this obviate our sense that he was "wicked" earlier? Consider the following scenario:

> Jack L. has been convicted of three vicious murders and sentenced to life imprisonment. After twenty years in prison, he is up for parole. A model prisoner, L. has won the respect of his fellow inmates and the prison staff, from the guards to the warden, for his acts of kindness toward his fellow man. Having taught himself to read and write, he has composed volumes of breathtakingly beautiful poetry. He also has developed a fascination with mathematics. Writing on his prison issue paper, he has managed to solve several puzzles that have stumped mathematicians for centuries.

> A panel of penologists has determined unanimously that L. no longer represents a danger to the community. Also, a letter has arrived from the chair of the Princeton math department calling for L.'s release, guaranteeing him a chair in theoretical mathematics, and explaining that, with the proper training and in the stimulating and supportive environment of a world class academic institution, he is sure to revolutionize modern mathematics. The Poet Laureate writes a similar letter to the parole board, calling L. "the greatest poetic talent of the last two hundred years."

In a provocative study of the "retributive urge," Michael Moore hypothesizes "that most of us"—except for "saints or moral lepers"—"still feel some inclination, no matter how tentative, to punish" in situations of this sort. Michael S. Moore, "The Moral Worth of Retribution," in Responsibility, Character, and the Emotions: New Essays in Moral Psychology 179, 185 (Ferdinand Schoeman ed. 1988). Do you agree? If so, what follows from the existence of this "inclination"?

How would Jack fare under a version of retributivism that focuses not on the offender's "wickedness," but treats his act of noncompliance with, and even defiance of, the law as a deliberate choice that reflects his personhood? Herbert Morris—and Hegel—have argued that "we have a right to punishment . . . derive[d] from a fundamental right to be treated as a person." Herbert Morris, "Persons and Punishment," in On Guilt and Innocence: Essays in Legal Philosophy and Moral Psychology 31, 32 (1976). Does it make sense to talk about an individual's "right to be punished," as opposed to be treated, or simply ignored as inconsequential? See generally Markus Dirk Dubber, "The Right to Be Punished: Autonomy and Its Demise in Modern Penal Thought," 16 Law & Hist. Rev. 113 (1998).

How would Jack fare under a version of retributivism that stressed the need to restore balance? Criminals are, in a sense, unjustly benefitted by deliberate rule violations and must forfeit their "unfair advantage" by being punished. See, e.g., Morris, supra; George Sher, Desert (1987).

As a final note on retributivism, consider what is generally referred to as the "situationalist" tradition in social psychology. Stated in its strongest form, situationalism holds (a) that "personality" scarcely exists or, more plausibly, (b) that "common sense" vastly overstates the relevance of personality to action and underestimates the role of "situational mediators." See Lee Ross & Richard E. Nisbett, The Person and the Situation: Perspectives on Social Psychology (1991). Consider, in this regard, experiments that show that the tendency to help people in need is very sensitive to mild shifts in situational variables (including group size, the apparent indifference displayed by other group members, and the perceived likelihood of disapproval for one's failure to intervene)[a] and experiments that

a. The classic case here is that of Kitty Genovese who in 1964 was beaten and stabbed to death outside her New York City apartment in front of thirty-eight of her neighbors who watched the crime from their windows but ignored her pleas for help and didn't call the police until it was far too late. A. M. Rosenthal, Thirty-Eight Witnesses (1964); Bibb Latané & Steve A. Nida, "Ten Years of Research on Group Size and Helping," 89 Psych. Bulletin 308–24 (1981).—Eds.

demonstrate that in certain settings, people are quite willing to administer what appear to be painful electric shocks to others.[b]

The mainstream Anglo–American view is that we are deterrence-oriented in "general justifying aim" but retributivists in deciding on the "distribution of punishment." The standard illustration of this view is that we might punish murder to diminish the number of killings but we punish only those who deserve punishment even if punishing some others who don't—e.g., the insane, those wrongly believed to be guilty—might also diminish the number of killings.

C. *Rehabilitation*. Under this view, "correctional" facilities explicitly resocialize offenders in a helpful way, e.g., through job retraining and counseling, and the experience of condemnation may itself reform. Reformation was the dominant ideology of twentieth-century American penal and prison theory through the 1970s. Completed in 1962, the Model Penal Code was heavily reformationist, at least when it came to offenders who displayed curable antisocial tendencies. (The incurable ones were incapacitated, not rehabilitated.) This defense of punishment, however, has nearly disappeared from criminal law texts and public discourse on imprisonment. Cf. Francis A. Allen, The Decline of the Rehabilitative Ideal (1981).

Rehabilitation tends to, but need not, be connected with a non-biologistic determinist view of the origin of crime, which regards crime as caused by social forces, not bad genes, wicked character, or "rational" decisions. At the same time, reformationists must be remarkably optimistic about the efficacy of short-term resocialization in settings where *negative* resocialization appears more *plausible*, if resocialization goes on at all. Naturally, though, some supporters of "new sanctions," such as "reintegrative shaming" and "therapeutic diversion," particularly in drug cases, claim that these sanctions resocialize more effectively.

The decline in the ideology of reformation may well be rooted more in the loss of optimism about the possibility of short-term re-socialization (especially the prospect of accomplishing positive re-socialization in *prisons*) than the loss of faith in the social determinist account of the origin of criminality most typically associated with the ideology. See Robert Martinson, "What Works?—Questions and Answers About Prison Reform," 35 Pub. Interest 22 (1974) (coining "nothing works" slogan); cf. Francis T. Cullen & Paul Gendreau, "The Effectiveness of Correctional Rehabilitation: Reconsidering the 'Nothing Works' Debate," in The American Prison: Issues in Research and Policy 23 (Lynne Goodstein & Doris L. MacKenzie eds., 1989).

b. Stanley Milgram, a Yale psychologist, asked subjects, whom he called "teachers," to administer an electric shock of increasing intensity to a "learner" for each mistake, claiming that the experiment was designed to explore the effects on learning behavior of punishment for incorrect responses. Sixty percent of the "teachers" followed instructions to continue punishing the "learner" up to the maximum 450 volt charge, and all administered at least 300 volts. (The "learners" were played by students or actors feigning increasing levels of discomfort.) Stanley Milgram, The Individual in a Social World (2d ed. 1992).—EDS.

In the academy, the decline of rehabilitation roughly coincided with the revival of retributivism associated with the work of Herbert Morris, among others:

> I want . . . to sketch an extreme version of a set of institutions . . . proceeding on a conception of man which appears to be basically at odds with that operative within a system of punishment. * * *
>
> In this world we are now to imagine when an individual harms another his conduct is to be regarded as a symptom of some pathological condition in the way a running nose is a symptom of a cold. Actions diverging from some conception of the normal are viewed as manifestations of a disease in the way in which we might today regard the arm and legal movements of an epileptic during a seizure. Actions conforming to what is normal are assimilated to the normal and healthy functioning of bodily organs. What a person does, then, is assimilated, on this conception, to what we believe today, or at least most of us believe today, a person undergoes. We draw a distinction between the operation of the kidney and raising an arm on request. This distinction between mere events or happenings and human actions is erased in our imagined system. * * *
>
> Let us elaborate on this assimilation of conduct of a certain kind to symptoms of a disease. First, there is something abnormal in both the case of conduct, such as killing another, and a symptom of a disease such as an irregular heart beat. Second, there are causes for this abnormality in action such that once we know of them we can explain the abnormality as we now can explain the symptoms of many physical diseases. The abnormality is looked upon as a happening with a causal explanation rater than an action for which there were reasons. Third, the causes that account for the abnormality interfere with the normal functioning of the body, or, in the case of killing with what is regarded as a normal functioning of an individual. Fourth, the abnormality is in some way a part of the individual, necessarily involving his body. A well going dry might satisfy our three foregoing conditions of disease symptoms, but it is hardly a disease or the symptoms of one. Finally, and most obscure, the abnormality arises in some way from within the individual. If Jones is hit with a mallet by Smith, Jones may reel about and fall on James who may be injured. But this abnormal conduct of Jones is not regarded as a symptom of disease. Smith, not Jones, is suffering from some pathological condition.
>
> With this view of man the institutions of social control respond not with punishment, but with either preventive detention, in case of "carriers," or therapy in case of those manifesting pathological symptoms. The logic of sickness implies the logic of therapy. And therapy and punishment differ widely in their implications. . . .

Herbert Morris, "Persons and Punishment," in On Guilt and Innocence: Essays in Legal Philosophy and Moral Psychology 31, 36–38 (1976).

How—and why—might "therapy and punishment differ . . . in their implications"? So what if they do? Is the system Morris imagines "basically at odds with that operative within a system of punishment"? So what if it is?

D. *Incapacitation.* Incapacitative punishment seeks to avoid harm to the non-incarcerated population by isolating criminals from (many) potential victims. It's the other, non-rehabilitative, side of "incapacitative and curative-reformative treatment." Jerome Michael & Herbert Wechsler, "A Rationale of the Law of Homicide I," 37 Colum. L. Rev. 701, 759 (1937). Incapacitation is formally consistent with pure "preventive detention," i.e., the incarceration of those predicted to be dangerous, without regard to whether they've been convicted of a crime. Yet, in fact, incapacitationists typically reject it for various reasons. Many adopt a "mixed" theory of punishment requiring punishment be *distributed* only to the blameworthy. Incapacitation, after all, no more precludes an independent commitment to retributivism as a limiting principle for the distribution of punishment than does deterrence. Similarly, they may distrust bureaucratic discretion, and demand that officials act only when certain limited and clearly delineated facts are found. Finally, they may distrust the accuracy of prediction in general, except of course for the implicit prediction made by all incapacitationists that future behavior will tend to mimic past behavior.

Here is one well-known attempt to place principled—retributivist—constraints on incapacitationism. Do you think it succeeds?

> 1) Clinical predictions of dangerousness unsupported by actuarial studies should not be relied on for other than short-term intervention.[a]
>
> 2) The autonomy of the individual should sometimes be restricted because of his predicted dangerousness. The relevant considerations are:
>
> - the extent of the harm that may occur,
> - the likelihood of its occurrence,
> - the extent of individual autonomy to be limited to avoid the harm.
>
> 3) A prediction of dangerousness is a statement of a present condition, not the prediction of a particular result.
>
> 4) It is a mistake to confuse the sufficiency of proof of dangerousness with the decision on whether to require proof beyond a reasonable doubt, or by clear and convincing evidence, or on a balance of probability. . . .
>
> 5) Punishment should not be imposed, nor the term of punishment extended, by virtue of a prediction of dangerousness, beyond that

a. "Clinical" risk assessments are made by a mental health professional, such as a clinical psychologist or psychiatrist, after an interview and/or observation of the offender and draw on any available information about the offender's personality and behavior and the details of her offense. They are notoriously unreliable, being accurate only a third of the time. "Actuarial" assessments, by contrast, consider the extent to which the offender possesses various risk factors associated with recidivism, including education level, employment status, mental disabilities, and criminal history. They are also said to be more accurate, or at least less arbitrary, than clinical assessments. See generally John Monahan et al., Rethinking Risk Assessment (2001).—EDS.

which would be justified as a deserved punishment independently of that prediction.

6) Provided the previous limitation is respected, predictions of dangerousness may properly influence sentencing decisions (and other decisions under the criminal law).

7) The base expectancy rate of criminal violence for the criminal predicted as dangerous must be shown by reliable evidence to be substantially higher than the base expectancy rate for another criminal, with a closely similar criminal record and convicted of a closely similar crime, but not predicted as unusually dangerous, before the greater dangerousness of the former may be relied on to intensify or extend his punishment.

Norval Morris, "On 'Dangerousness' in the Judicial Process," 39 Record of the Association of the Bar of the City of New York 102, 104–05 (1984).

Incapacitation may well be connected with either biological determinist theories of crime, such as life cycle accounts of male violence according to which violence decreases after early adulthood, or socially determinist theories, without the reformationist's optimism about the state's capacity to resocialize. Formally, though rarely in practice, one could also imagine incapacitationists believing in the "wicked person" variety of retributivism, but demanding some forward-looking justification for punishment. For a skeptical review of the efficacy of a variety of incapacitationist strategies, see Franklin E. Zimring & Gordon J. Hawkins, Incapacitation: Penal Confinement and the Restraint of Crime (1995). For a more favorable view, see James Q. Wilson, Thinking About Crime 145–48 (rev. ed. 1983).

E. *Mixed Theories, Multiple Theories*. Few people today hold any single one of these views in its pure form. See *Blarek*. Besides the popularity of mixed theories of various types—mixing one theory for the institution of punishment with another for its distribution—it is also quite commonplace for someone to emphasize different theories in relationship *to distinct crimes*. For instance, a not atypical set of "instincts" for self-identified politically progressive students is to be deterrence-oriented when thinking about white collar crime like securities fraud or tax evasion (or money laundering), retributivist as to sexual assaults, incapacitationist as to "street crime," and rehabilitationist about drug offenses.

4. *Legislature, Judiciary, Executive*. Compare the factors governing sentencing decisions by federal judges set out in 18 U.S.C. § 3553, quoted in *Blarek*, with the factors governing charging decisions by federal prosecutors set out in the U.S. Attorneys' Manual (published by the U.S. Department of Justice), and the factors governing the codification decisions by legislatures, as laid out in the Model Penal Code:

9–27.230 Initiating and Declining Charges—Substantial Federal Interest

1. Federal law enforcement priorities;
2. The nature and seriousness of the offense;
3. The deterrent effect of prosecution;
4. The person's culpability in connection with the offense;

5. The person's history with respect to criminal activity;

6. The person's willingness to cooperate in the investigation or prosecution of others; and

7. The probable sentence or other consequences if the person is convicted.

Model Penal Code § 1.02. Purposes . . .

(1) The general purposes of the provisions governing the definition of offenses are:

(a) to forbid and prevent conduct that unjustifiably and inexcusably inflicts or threatens substantial harm to individual or public interests;

(b) to subject to public control persons whose conduct indicates that they are disposed to commit crimes;

(c) to safeguard conduct that is without fault from condemnation as criminal;

(d) to give fair warning of the nature of the conduct declared to constitute an offense;

(e) to differentiate on reasonable grounds between serious and minor offenses.

5. As an alternative, or a supplement, to self-imposed and self-enforced prosecutorial charging guidelines, courts have the power to dismiss cases that don't fit the traditional rationales for punishment, even though they match the definition of a crime. Consider the Model Penal Code's *de minimis* provision in light of the traditional rationales for punishment:

Model Penal Code § 2.12. De Minimis Infractions.

The Court shall dismiss a prosecution if, having regard to the nature of the conduct charged to constitute an offense and the nature of the attendant circumstances, it finds that the defendant's conduct:

(1) was within a customary license or tolerance, neither expressly negatived by the person whose interest was infringed nor inconsistent with the purpose of the law defining the offense; or

(2) did not actually cause or threaten the harm or evil sought to be prevented by the law defining the offense or did so only to an extent too trivial to warrant the condemnation of conviction; or

(3) presents such other extenuations that it cannot reasonably be regarded as envisaged by the legislature in forbidding the offense.

See generally Stanislaw Pomorski, "On Multiculturalism, Concepts of Crime, and the 'De Minimis' Defense," 1997 BYU L. Rev. 61 (1997).

In many jurisdictions, courts also have the power to dismiss charges "in the interest of justice." See, e.g., N.Y. Crim. Proc. Law § 170.40 (dismissal "in furtherance of justice"). This power is rarely exercised. The following case is an exception:

On February 4, 2002, the defendant was observed on the Mount Vernon East train station platform removing his clothes. Upon investigation by Metropolitan Transportation Authority police officers, a number of "crack pipes" containing residue and two small bags of cocaine were recovered from the defendant's bag. The defendant was thereafter arrested and the misdemeanor charge of criminal possession of a controlled substance in the seventh degree lodged against him. * * *

In a time of diminishing public resources in our state this Court is not prepared to appropriate extensive resources to a jury trial that would potentially ensue little or no benefit to the People. This Court is not unaware of the fact that in order to proceed with the trial a courtroom, Judge, jurors, court officers, court reporters and witnesses must be mobilized and "used" for approximately three full days. Further, the defendant must be transported back and forth and the County will be forced to incur the cost of his counsel. This Court is mindful of the purpose of the Penal Code to "insure the public safety by preventing the commission of offenses through the deterrent influence of the sentences authorized, the rehabilitation of those convicted, and their confinement when required in the interests of public protection," a purpose that would be strained under these circumstances. N.Y. Penal Law § 1.05.

As such, the court hereby dismisses the misdemeanor information lodged against this defendant in the interest of justice. Justice should flow not only to the defendant but also to the people.

People v. Payne, 2002 WL 1769984 (N.Y. City Ct. Mt. Vernon); see also People v. Gragert, 1 Misc.3d 646, 765 N.Y.S.2d 471 (N.Y. Crim. Ct. 2003) (dismissing, in the interest of justice, disorderly conduct information against 17–year-old high school student with no prior criminal record who had participated in a demonstration against the war in Iraq, on the ground that "protest, in its many forms, has a hallowed place in our democracy and is very much a part of our American spirit").

6. *The Process is the Punishment.* The court in *Blarek* remarks that "[t]he ordeal of being criminally prosecuted and publicly shamed by being denominated felons ... has taught [the defendants] a sobering lesson." How is this observation relevant for purposes of determining the appropriate punishment, in this or any other case? What is the purpose of prosecution, trial, and conviction, as opposed to the actual infliction of punishment? What, in other words, is the rationale of the criminal process as punishment? Does it strive to reform? To deter? To "punish"? To incapacitate? Note that judges have the authority to deny bail—in other words, to order pre-trial incarceration—on the basis of the likelihood that the defendant will engage in criminal conduct while out on bail. This preventive detention without, or at least before, a conviction is not punishment, according to the U.S. Supreme Court. Bell v. Wolfish, 441 U.S. 520 (1979).

7. Note that the Model Penal *and Correctional* Code, in § 1.02(2), also lists "general purposes of the provisions governing the sentencing and treatment of offenders," i.e., it explores the applicability of rationales for

punishment not only to the threat, and imposition, of punishment, but also to its execution, arguably the aspect most in need of justification. Does the execution of punishment necessarily serve the some purposes as its threat in criminal codes, and its imposition in criminal courts? Does it require an independent justification, or does its legitimacy derive solely from the fact that it makes good on previous threats of punishment? Contrast the Model Penal Code's purposes provision with that in the South African Correctional Services Act of 1998, and the German Code of Punishment Execution of 1976. What visions of punishment execution—or "correction"—does each provision reflect?

South African Correctional Services Act of 1998

§ 2 Purpose of correctional system

The purpose of the correctional system is to contribute to maintaining and protecting a just, peaceful and safe society by—

(a) enforcing sentences of the courts in the manner prescribed by this Act;

(b) detaining all prisoners in safe custody whilst ensuring their human dignity; and

(c) promoting the social responsibility and human development of all prisoners and persons subject to community corrections.

German Code of Punishment Execution of 1976

§ 2 Purposes of System of Punishment Execution

The execution of a prison sentence shall enable the inmate to lead a life of social responsibility without crime (goal). The execution of a prison sentence also serves to protect the community from further criminal offenses.

§ 3 Organization of the System of Punishment Execution

(1) Life in prison shall be assimilated to the general conditions of life as far as possible.

(2) Detrimental effects of imprisonment shall be averted.

(3) Imprisonment shall be directed toward helping the inmate to enter a life of freedom.

8. *Execution*. The most executive version of the executive aspect of the punishment process, the "execution" of a death sentence, vividly illustrates the need to justify every component of that system, from the definition of crimes, to the imposition of punishments, and eventually to their infliction. The Supreme Court has held that executing a person who turned insane after he had been tried and sentenced for his offense is not only unjustifiable, but unconstitutional. Ford v. Wainwright, 477 U.S. 399 (1986). But is there a theory of punishment that might justify the execution of a person who was insane when he committed the offense? Of a person who turned insane after his crime? After his crime, but before his trial?

The executive end of the criminal process requires justification in a quite literal sense. In criminal law doctrine, to say that someone's conduct is justified is to say that, even though it amounts to criminal conduct in the technical sense of meeting the definition of some criminal offense, it nonetheless is not punishable because its merits outweigh its demerits. (A classic example is burning down a house to save the town from an oncoming fire storm.) Many investigatory acts and pretty much every act of punishment execution satisfies the definition of some criminal offense.[a] The formal reason why they are not punishable is that they are subject to a set of justifications, most importantly that of "execution of public duty."

Model Penal Code § 3.03. Execution of Public Duty.

(1) Except as provided in Subsection (2) of this Section, conduct is justifiable when it is required or authorized by:

(a) the law defining the duties or functions of a public officer or the assistance to be rendered to such officer in the performance of his duties; or

(b) the law governing the execution of legal process; or

(c) the judgment or order of a competent court or tribunal; or

(d) the law governing the armed services or the lawful conduct of war; or

(e) any other provision of law imposing a public duty.

9. *Punishment and Discipline.* Note that the Model Penal Code section on purposes (§ 1.02) makes no reference to "punishment." Instead it refers to "treatment," "correction," and "public control" as the Code drafters set out to replace punishment with "peno-correctional treatment." See Markus Dirk Dubber, "Penal Panopticon: The Idea of a Modern Model Penal Code," 4 Buff. Crim. L. Rev. 53 (2000).

Wardens (and parents[b]) are among those to whom the Code explicitly grants a "right to punish":

§ 303.6. Discipline and Control.

(1) The Warden or other administrative head of each correctional institution shall be responsible for the discipline, control and safe custody of the prisoners therein. No prisoner shall be punished except upon the order of the Warden or other administrative head of the institution or of a deputy designated by him for the purpose; nor shall any punishment be imposed otherwise than in accordance with the provisions of this Section. The right to punish or to inflict punishment shall not be delegated to any prisoner or group of prisoners and no Warden or other administrative head shall permit any such prisoner or

a. Wiretapping looks very much like the crime of "eavesdropping," entrapment like "solicitation" (or even "conspiracy"), searching a suspect's house like "trespass," searching (or frisking) the suspect herself like "assault," arresting her like "battery," seizing her property like "larceny," a drug bust like "possession of narcotics" (with or without intent to distribute), indicting—and convicting—a defendant like "defamation," imprisoning the convict like "false imprisonment," and executing her like "homicide" ("murder," to be precise).—EDS.

b. See Model Penal Code § 3.08(1) (parent's right to discipline "for the purpose of safeguarding or promoting the welfare of the minor, including the ... punishment of his misconduct").—EDS.

group of prisoners to assume authority over any other prisoner or group of prisoners. * * *

The distinction between the two senses of "punishment" implicit in this provision turns out to be of constitutional significance. The warden's "punishment"—or "discipline"—of prisoners to maintain order, etc., is unconstitutional only if it is inflicted "maliciously and sadistically for the very purpose of causing harm"; his infliction of "punishment" as prescribed by a judicial sentence, however, is unconstitutional if it is inflicted "with deliberate indifference" to the prisoner's needs. Hudson v. McMillian, 503 U.S. 1 (1992).

10. The court in *Blarek* discusses not only the standard rationales for punishment, but also their relation—or lack thereof—to the federal sentencing guidelines. What rationales for punishment underlie the statute setting up the federal sentencing commission?

28 U.S.C. § 994. Duties of the Commission.

(c) The Commission, in establishing categories of offenses for use in the guidelines and policy statements ... shall consider whether the following matters, among others, have any relevance to the nature, extent, place of service, or other incidents of an appropriate sentence, and shall take them into account only to the extent that they do have relevance—

(1) the grade of the offense;

(2) the circumstances under which the offense was committed which mitigate or aggravate the seriousness of the offense;

(3) the nature and degree of the harm caused by the offense, including whether it involved property, irreplaceable property, a person, a number of persons, or a breach of public trust;

(4) the community view of the gravity of the offense;

(5) the public concern generated by the offense;

(6) the deterrent effect a particular sentence may have on the commission of the offense by others; and

(7) the current incidence of the offense in the community and in the Nation as a whole.

(d) The Commission in establishing categories of defendants for use in the guidelines and policy statements ... shall consider whether the following matters, among others, with respect to a defendant, have any relevance to the nature, extent, place of service, or other incidents of an appropriate sentence, and shall take them into account only to the extent that they do have relevance—

(1) age;

(2) education;

(3) vocational skills;

(4) mental and emotional condition to the extent that such condition mitigates the defendant's culpability or to the extent that such condition is otherwise plainly relevant;

(5) physical condition, including drug dependence;

(6) previous employment record;

(7) family ties and responsibilities;

(8) community ties;

(9) role in the offense;

(10) criminal history; and

(11) degree of dependence upon criminal activity for a livelihood.

11. Now reconsider the previous question in light of the following two provisions:

28 U.S.C. § 994. Duties of the Commission.

(e) The Commission shall assure that the guidelines and policy statements, in recommending a term of imprisonment or length of a term of imprisonment, reflect the general inappropriateness of considering the education, vocational skills, employment record, family ties and responsibilities, and community ties of the defendant....

(k) The Commission shall insure that the guidelines reflect the inappropriateness of imposing a sentence to a term of imprisonment for the purpose of rehabilitating the defendant or providing the defendant with needed educational or vocational training, medical care, or other correctional treatment.

12. It's easy to overestimate the practical significance of at least some of the lists of purposes of punishment governing various aspects of the criminal justice system. What are lists of purposes directed at legislatures, drafted by the legislatures themselves, other than general pronouncements of policy, or even of good intentions, not unlike the preambles to constitutions in totalitarian states? No court could strike down a statute on the ground that it doesn't comport with the enumerated purposes of criminal law. And the statutory enumeration of purposes of "correction and treatment" may help design a prison system in the abstract, but may have precious little to do with the actual operation of a prison under constraints of security and limited resources.

B. MODES OF PUNISHMENT (HOW TO PUNISH?)

It's useful to distinguish the *quality* of punishment from its *quantity*, or the question of how to punish from that of how much to punish. Today the two questions are often conflated on the assumption that there is one quality of punishment, imprisonment, which is doled out in various quantities. American criminal punishment, however, comes in a wide variety of shapes and sizes, many of which are illustrated by the *Blarek* opinion. Note the full bouquet of sanctions imposed in that case: imprisonment, supervised release, fine, forfeiture, and special assessment.

1. IMPRISONMENT

(a) The extensive prison sentences proposed, and eventually imposed, in *Blarek* are characteristic of American criminal law, though not of criminal law elsewhere. The U.S. prison and jail population stood at 2,100,146 at year-end 2001, up from 501,886 in 1980. Bureau of Justice Statistics, Prisoners in 2001 (U.S. Dep't of Justice, July 2002); Bureau of Justice Statistics, Prisoners in 1994 (U.S. Dep't of Justice, Office of Justice Programs, August 1995). The United States easily has the highest rate of imprisonment among Western countries, and perennially rivals Russia for the highest rate worldwide.

> The United States has the highest prison population rate in the world, some 700 per 100,000 of the national population, followed by Russia (665), the Cayman Islands (600), Belarus (555), the US Virgin Islands (550), Kazakhstan (520), Turkmenistan (490), the Bahamas (480), Belize (460), and Bermuda (445). However, almost two thirds of countries (63%) have rates of 150 per 100,000 or below.

Roy Walmsley, World Prison Population List 1 (London, England, UK: Home Office Research, Development and Statistics Directorate, 3d ed. 2002), http://www.homeoffice.gov.uk/rds/pdfs/r166.pdf (accessed Oct. 12, 2002).

Here are incarceration rates for some other countries: South Africa (410), Mexico (150), UK (125), Egypt (120), Kenya (115), Canada (105), Venezuela (100), Italy (95), Germany (95), France (80), Ireland (80), Japan (45), Iceland (30). Id.

Incarceration rates among black males, and especially young black males, are particularly high.

> Expressed in terms of percentages, 10.0% of black non-Hispanic males age 25 to 29 were in prison on December 31, 2001, compared to 2.9% of Hispanic males and about 1.2% of white males in the same age group. Although incarceration rates drop with age, the percentage of black males age 45 to 54 in prison in 2001 was still nearly 2.7%—only slightly lower than the highest rate (2.9%) among Hispanic males (age 25–29) and more than twice the highest rate (1.3%) among white males (age 30 to 34).

Bureau of Justice Statistics, Prisoners in 2001, at 12 (U.S. Dep't of Justice, July 2002).

> At the start of the 1990s, the U.S. had more Black men (between the ages of 20 and 29) under the control of the nation's criminal justice system than the total number in college. This and other factors have led some scholars to conclude that, "crime control policies are a major contributor to the disruption of the family, the prevalence of single parent families, and children raised without a father in the ghetto, and the 'inability of people to get the jobs still available.' "

Craig Haney & Philip Zimbardo, "The Past and Future of U.S. Prison Policy: Twenty-five Years After the Stanford Prison Experiment," 53 Am. Psychologist 716 (1998).

If one counts not only prison and jail inmates, but also persons under some form of supervised release (such as parole and probation), one in three black men between the ages of 20 and 29 years old is under correctional supervision or control. Marc Mauer & Tracy Huling, Young

Black Americans and the Criminal Justice System: Five Years Later (The Sentencing Project, 1995).

(b) In thinking about the widespread use of incarceration in the United States, it is important to focus on what prison is actually like for prisoners. It is also important to consider the possibility that the experience is *distinct* for different prisoners, and to consider whether we could or should take account of this fact in imposing sentences, or whether we must simply assume that prison terms of equal lengths impose fundamentally equal punishment. (What if a prisoner *prefers* prison life to life outside prison walls?) Consider this excerpt from Robert Blecker, "Haven or Hell? Inside Lorton Central Prison: Experiences of Punishment Justified," 42 Stan. L. Rev. 1149 (1990):

> Of course everyone's "bit"—time spent in prison—is different. One individual feels a loss of freedom more or less than another. A forced separation from home, and the streets, and entrance into a new prison environment can be more or less painful. Losing family ties may cause a criminal to suffer differently at different stages of life. . . .
>
> [A long-time inmate] painted a portrait of maximum suffering inside the joint to frighten a 15-year-old who was hustling in small ways, but who had, as yet, no real criminal record:
>
> "First of all, all first timers do hard time. . . .
>
> Now there are institution administrative rules that you must go by, and there are also institution convict rules that you must go by. Sometimes the two clash. And if you get busted going with the convict rules, then the administration make you pay by sending you to the hole [detention cell] or the wall [maximum security cell block]. . . . If you go with the administration rules and stay on the administration side, then the convicts make you pay: Late at night somebody will come to your bunk while you sleep, hit you in your head or 'shank' [stab] you. If they don't move against you violently, then the verbal abuse is hell. And when you come back from your job or school, all your stuff, your personal letters, clothes, TV, all of your property including your bed, is out on the walk. . . .
>
> Guys will fuck you. They will throw a blanket over your head, grease your ass and fuck you. And have no remorse about it. Once you are fucked, everybody knows about it, and then you can't turn nobody down. Anybody think they can talk you out of your butt will talk you out of your butt, and before long not only are they fucking you but you're sucking dicks and washing people's drawers and socks just like a slave. . . .
>
> Nine out of ten new boys that come in are junkies in less than two years. So when you go on a visit and your mother come down or your girlfriend and you take . . . whatever they can afford to give you . . . grease your butt up before you went into the visiting hall and slide that money up your rectum. And when you get out of the visiting hall, get through shakedown, and back to the dorm, all the money that's not directly taken from you, you give to the dope man. . . .

There's going to come a time that you want to die. And many new boys do die. They hang themselves. They cut their wrists. Most of them make bad attempts at it, or most of them do it for sympathy. . . ."

[The same inmate could present a quite different view to a friend's younger brother, who was about to serve a long sentence at Lorton:]

"It's really not a bad place. . . . If you don't bother nobody, nobody will bother you. . . . You can go to school and if you don't want to, you don't have to do none of that. You don't have to work if you don't want to. You can spend your time keeping yourself in shape, you can spend your time reading and working on whatever you want to work on to take up your time. . . .

The dining hall has a long line to get in, and once you get in it's crowded and it's hot, and for real, the food ain't that good. But for ten dollars a month, you can contract a dude to fix you a meal every day. . . .

Now if you like to get high, all the same things that's available to you on the street is available here at Lorton. . . .

All the TVs in every dormitory is hooked up to a VCR and every weekend they show two movies. . . .

Now if you want to get your dick sucked, you can do that. They got dick-sucking faggots in here that'll suck your dick for two dollars. If men ain't your thing, after you're here for awhile, you'll learn the other things to do. Those little girls will come and see you, and there's ways for you to be with her for ten to fifteen minutes alone. You'll learn all these things within sixty to ninety days of being here. . . .

So be yourself, relax and carry yourself in a manly manner, and everything will work itself out. A month from now you'll be wondering why you ever thought about killing yourself, or why you had so much fear of Lorton. A month from now you'll be running around here like everyone else, having a good time."

Which kid was told it straight? What is the real experience of Lorton? Obviously it depends. Some guys breeze through it; others live in agony. . . .

Almost uniformly the older inmates condemn Lorton Central as a "deathtrap." . . .

Prisoners constantly confront life-threatening situations. If you let someone cut in line in front of you, others will take greater advantage. But if you confront him, you face possible lethal retaliation. . . .

Avoiding deadly confrontations is a never-ending challenge. "I would consider Lorton a 'hell hole' being that life is always on the line. At all times really. I never get to relax," complained [another inmate].

. . . Inmates routinely complain that they have no moments of peace. They must never sleep deeply, never for an instant let the soap cover both eyes while showering. . . .

Some inmates do experience retribution—the infliction of pain and suffering they "deserve" because of the crimes they committed—

> through the fear, uncertainty, and boredom that pervades their daily lives inside Lorton Central. Lorton is for them a "hell hole." However, other inmates' experience of Lorton Central as a "sweet joint," where they play basketball, get high, dress well, work out, have sex, and watch color television is the antithesis of retribution. Moreover, by severing the crime committed outside from the quality of time spent inside, the guards, the prisoners, and the prison's administration further undermine retribution: The short-term, first-time offenders suffer most, while the most hardened criminals—with the best contacts, the best hustles, and the best jobs—enjoy the softest lifestyle. Inside Lorton Central, those who most deserve punishment experience it the least.

Should sentencing take into account differences in how prisoners (might) experience prison? How does *Blarek* resolve this question? Why should a prisoner's "vulnerability" matter for purposes of determining the length of a prison term (as opposed to deciding whether to impose a prison term *at all*), or where to have a prisoner serve his term—in a particular prison (high, medium, low security, in one location rather than another) or in a particular location within the prison (solitary confinement, special housing unit, general population)? The judge in *Blarek* cites Koon v. United States, 518 U.S. 81, 92 (1996), the leading case on the reviewability of sentencing decisions in federal court. There the judge granted the defendants a downward departure because, among other things, he held that they, as (former) police officers, would be vulnerable to prison abuse. Is that justifiable, from the perspective of the various punishment theories, from the perspective of federal sentencing law under the Guidelines? Does it matter, for purposes of your answer, that Koon and his white co-defendants were convicted for "deprivation of rights under color of law," 18 U.S.C. § 242, for beating an African-American motorist, Rodney King?

2. Supervised Release

Traditionally, American criminal law recognized two common types of supervised release: parole (the suspension of the remainder of a prison sentence pending good behavior—i.e., compliance with conditions of parole) and probation (the suspension of the entire prison sentence pending good behavior—i.e., compliance with conditions of probation). The entire "correctional population" (including federal and state prison and jail inmates, parolees, and probationers) by year-end 2001 was 6,594,000, up from 1,840,400 in 1980. Bureau of Justice Statistics, Probation and Parole in the United States, 2001 (U.S. Dep't of Justice, Office of Justice Programs, August 2002); Bureau of Justice Statistics, Probation and Parole Populations, 1995 (U.S. Dep't of Justice, Office of Justice Programs, June 1996).

The federal sentencing commission was charged with achieving "honesty in sentencing," as Congress

> sought to avoid the confusion and implicit deception that arose out of the pre-guidelines sentencing system which required the court to impose an indeterminate sentence of imprisonment and empowered the parole commission to determine how much of the sentence an offender actually would serve in prison. This practice usually resulted in a

> substantial reduction in the effective length of the sentence imposed, with defendants often serving only about one-third of the sentence imposed by the court.

U.S.S.G. ch. 1, pt. A(3).

For the sake of honesty, the commission eliminated parole. It also significantly curtailed the other form of supervised release frequently employed under "the pre-guidelines sentencing system," probation:

> The statute provides that the guidelines are to "reflect the general appropriateness of imposing a sentence other than imprisonment in cases in which the defendant is a first offender who has not been convicted of a crime of violence or an otherwise serious offense. . . ." 28 U.S.C. § 994(j). Under pre-guidelines sentencing practice, courts sentenced to probation an inappropriately high percentage of offenders guilty of certain economic crimes, such as theft, tax evasion, antitrust offenses, insider trading, fraud, and embezzlement, that in the Commission's view are "serious."
>
> The Commission's solution to this problem has been to write guidelines that classify as serious many offenses for which probation previously was frequently given and provide for at least a short period of imprisonment in such cases. The Commission concluded that the definite prospect of prison, even though the term may be short, will serve as a significant deterrent, particularly when compared with pre-guidelines practice where probation, not prison, was the norm.

U.S.S.G. ch. 1, pt. A(4)(d).

The commission, however, didn't do away with supervised release altogether. (See also United States v. Gementera, infra.) It retained it in the form imposed in *Blarek*, as a period of supervision *after* the prison sentence has been served in its entirety, to further the following purposes:

> (1) to protect the public welfare;
>
> (2) to enforce a financial condition;
>
> (3) to provide drug or alcohol treatment or testing;
>
> (4) to assist the reintegration of the defendant into the community; or
>
> (5) to accomplish any other sentencing purpose authorized by statute.

U.S.S.G. § 5D1.1 comment. (n.1)

What rationale(s) for punishment could justify these reforms, including the abolition of parole, the replacement of probation with short prison sentences, and the imposition of supervised release after completion of sentence?

3. FINE

The sentence in *Blarek* is unusual because it includes a "stiff fine." Ordinarily, the fine is a surprisingly insignificant sanction. While U.S. criminal law relies on imprisonment far more heavily than does the criminal law in other countries, the opposite is true of another sanction, the fine. The law of punishment in other countries provides for imprisonment in fewer cases, and for shorter terms of imprisonment in those cases. The fine is the paradigmatic sanction, with imprisonment reserved for exceptional cases.

In the U.S., fines tend to be dismissed as insufficiently serious, as a softer "alternative" to incarceration. What rationale for punishment, if any, underlies this argument? Is the problem that a fine isn't really a "punishment"? There are after all plenty of "civil" fines, imposed for such transgressions as littering or double parking.

Fines are also viewed as economically discriminatory. Why? And how might this argument be addressed? Consider, in this context, the European model of "day fines":

> First developed in Scandinavia in the 1920s and 1930s, and introduced into West Germany during the late 1960s and early 1970s, the day fine system of setting variable rather than fixed fine amounts rests upon a simple two-step [process that embraces both proportionality and equity]. First, the court sentences the offender to a certain number of fine units according to the gravity of the offense, but without regard to his or her means. The value of each unit is then established as a share of the offender's daily income (hence the name "day fine"), and the total fine amount is determined by simple multiplication.

Judith A. Greene, "Structuring Criminal Fines: Making an 'Intermediate' Penalty More Useful and Equitable," 13 Just. Sys. J. 37, 41 (1988).

Day fines can be quite severe. In February 2004, for instance, a Finnish millionaire with an annual net income of $9 million received a $200,000 speeding ticket for driving 50 mph in a 25 mph zone. "Finn Fined Nearly $217,000 for Speeding," N.Y. Times, Feb. 11, 2004.

4. Forfeiture

The fine in *Blarek* might have been stiff. But the "forfeiture" was even stiffer, "over $2,000,000 in cash and property" consisting of the defendants' "home in San Francisco worth over two millions dollars, three Harley Davidson motorcycles, a Mercedes Benz automobile, approximately $75,000 worth of jewelry, and hundreds of thousands of dollars in bank accounts and safe deposit boxes." The relevant criminal forfeiture provision is quite broad; it includes:

18 U.S.C. § 1963. Criminal penalties

(1) any interest the person has acquired or maintained in violation of [the applicable criminal statute];

(2) any—

(A) interest in;

(B) security of;

(C) claim against; or

(D) property or contractual right of any kind affording a source of influence over; any enterprise which the person has established, operated, controlled, conducted, or participated in the conduct of, in violation of section 1962; and

(3) any property constituting, or derived from, any proceeds which the person obtained, directly or indirectly, from racketeering activity or unlawful debt collection....

Like fines, forfeitures too come in a criminal and in a civil variety. The forfeiture in this *Blarek* was clearly "criminal"; after all it appeared in a provision entitled "criminal penalties." "Civil" forfeiture provisions tend to be broader still than their criminal analogues, and easier to secure since, by label, they are not punishment and therefore not subject to traditional—and constitutional—protections limited to criminal proceedings. In civil forfeiture proceedings, there is no requirement of proof beyond a reasonable doubt, nor, for that matter, a requirement of proving the guilt of the property owner. What matters is simply the connection between the property subject to forfeiture (to be proved by a preponderance of the evidence) and some specified criminal activity, not necessarily by its owner. Once that connection has been established, "innocent owners" can avert forfeiture, but only by proving their innocence (also by a preponderance of the evidence). An owner is "innocent" for purposes of the civil forfeiture statute if she "did not know of the conduct giving rise to forfeiture" or "upon learning of the conduct giving rise to the forfeiture, did all that reasonably could be expected under the circumstances to terminate such use of the property." If she purchased the property after it had been used in unlawful activity, she must show that she "did not know and was reasonably without cause to believe that the property was subject to forfeiture." (18 U.S.C. § 983(d)) The "innocent owner" defense was codified in the wake of well-publicized cases such as Bennis v. Michigan, 517 U.S. 1163 (1996), in which the Supreme Court upheld the forfeiture of a car, jointly owned by the petitioner and her husband, "in which her husband," unbeknownst to her, "engaged in sexual activity with a prostitute."

5. Special Assessment

The final, and by far the smallest, component of *Blarek's* punishment package is the special assessment of $150 and $100, respectively. Small it may be, but insignificant it's not. For behind the mandatory special assessment lies one of the most significant developments in American criminal law of the past decades—the rise of victims' rights. Special assessments help fund the federal Crime Victims' Fund, administered by the federal Office for Victims of Crime, and set up by The Victims of Crimes Act of 1984, Pub. L. No. 98–473, Title II, Chap. XIV. By 2002, the fund had accumulated over five billion dollars in fines, asset forfeitures, and special assessments. Office for Victims of Crime, Report to the Nation vi (2003). The bulk of Fund deposits are used to finance victim compensation and assistance programs in every state, and to "improve services to victims of federal crimes." Office for Victims of Crime, Victims of Crime Act Crime Victims Fund 2 (2002). Compensation here should be distinguished from restitution (U.S.S.G. § 5E1.1). Victims receive victim compensation from the state, and restitution directly from the offender. (Why was there no restitution ordered in *Blarek*?) For more on victims' rights in general, and victim compensation law in particular, see section E. infra.

6. DEATH

There is one type of punishment, death, that played no role in *Blarek*. (For further discussion of capital punishment, see ch. 10 infra.) The Supreme Court has stressed repeatedly that the death penalty is of a different *quality* than other punishments, most importantly imprisonment. "Death is different" in fact is one of the cornerstones of the Court's capital punishment jurisprudence. Most of that jurisprudence has been devoted to the procedural aspects of capital punishment, with an eye toward establishing procedural baselines for the nonarbitrary application of the death penalty. Death penalty statutes nowadays use a bifurcated proceeding, consisting of a "guilt phase" and a "sentencing phase." It is during the sentencing phase that both sides have an opportunity to present "aggravating" and "mitigating" factors to the sentencer, which must be a jury, except in cases where the defendant waives his right to jury sentencing.

There are also significant substantive elements in death penalty law, particularly in the law of murder, as legislatures attempt to draw a principled line between capital and noncapital murder. Some common distinctions include the identity of the victim (e.g., police officer, judge), the identity of the offender (e.g., recidivist, prison inmate), the circumstances of the crime (e.g., torture, murder in the course of a felony), or its motive (e.g., financial gain, concealment of another crime).

After the Supreme Court invalidated all existing death penalty statutes in Furman v. Georgia, 408 U.S. 238 (1972), American legislatures, instead of abandoning capital punishment, turned their attention to constructing death penalty statutes that would satisfy the minimum constitutional standards as set out by the Court. By 2001, thirty-eight states, and the federal government, had death penalty statutes on their books. In the seventeen years between 1966 and 1982, nine people were executed in the United States. In 2002 alone, there were 71 executions, with Texas accounting for 33. Executions, however, have not kept pace with death sentences. At year-end 2001, 3,581 people were on death row awaiting execution, all for murder. Murder, however, is not the only capital offense on the books. Others include treason or espionage (California, Colorado, Georgia, Louisiana, U.S.), kidnaping (Georgia, Idaho, Kentucky, South Dakota), aircraft hijacking or piracy (Georgia, Mississippi, U.S.), aggravated sexual battery or assault (Florida, Louisiana, Montana), drug trafficking (Florida), train wrecking (California, U.S.), perjury causing execution (California), and genocide (U.S.). U.S. Department of Justice, Office of Justice Programs, Bureau of Justice Statistics, Capital Punishment 2001 (12/02 NCJ 197020) (Dec. 2001) (http://www.ojp.usdoj.gov/bjs/abstract/cp01.htm) (last visited June 3, 2003).

7. ALTERNATIVE PUNISHMENTS

Some commentators have stressed that punishment is distinctive in its meaning, in what it says about the person subjected to it, or about the persons subjecting her to it. Punishment is said to express "the community's" condemnation of the offender and/or her conduct. Among these expressivists, some have advocated devising "shaming" punishments designed to "reintegrate" the offender into the community and to deter others from offending, so as to avoid being humiliated. Shaming, it is said, should work particularly well among offenders, specifically "white collar criminals," who have strong ties to the community (thus making *re*integration possible) and care about their social status in that community (thus making the prospect of humiliation a deterrent).

> Not long ago Hoboken, New Jersey, suffered from a serious white-collar crime problem: public urination. Unsurprisingly, law enforcement authorities in the city did not initially suspect that this crime was a white-collar one. But when they investigated, they discovered that the people responsible for this heinous offense were not the poor or the homeless but rather well-heeled Wall Street stock brokers and other Manhattan professionals (male and female) who were drawn to Hoboken's trendy bars.
>
> The townspeople were understandably outraged. They responded, however, not by imprisoning these offenders, or by fining them some extraordinary amount, but by *shaming* them: they put the incontinent yuppies on public display, ordered them to mop the city's streets, and for good measure bought ads in the offenders' local newspapers. To be sure, the spectacle of Wall Street brokers scrubbing Hoboken's streets gratified the public demand for retribution. But it also solved the underlying crime problem. Today, Hoboken's streets sparkle. * * *
>
> But as Hoboken's ingenuity attests, fines are not the only alternative to imprisonment. In fact, shame is making a much heralded comeback as a criminal punishment in American law. Judges in numerous states now require offenders to buy newspaper ads, post signs on their property, put bumper stickers on their cars, and even wear distinctive items of clothing announcing their crimes. Such penalties are being used, moreover, not just for petty misdemeanors, such as public urination, but also for more serious common offenses that would otherwise be punished by imprisonment, including drunk driving, larceny, nonaggravated assault, burglary, and drug possession.
>
> Many white-collar offenders—of the conventional variety—are also being shamed. In Cincinnati, for example, a judge ordered a corporate executive to write letters of apology and to publish newspaper ads publicizing his company's contamination of the groundwater with carcinogenic chemicals. In New York, a slumlord was sentenced to house arrest in one of his rat infested buildings (where tenants greeted him with a banner that read, "Welcome, Reptile!").

Dan M. Kahan & Eric A. Posner, "Shaming White–Collar Criminals: A Proposal for Reform of the Federal Sentencing Guidelines," 42 J.L. & Econ. 365, 365–66 (1999).

The use of shaming sanctions has a long tradition in American criminal law. In colonial American law, offenses against religion and morality, like blasphemy and adultery, were punishable—if not by death—by standing in the pillory or sitting on the gallows; more permanent shaming penalties, like branding on the forehead or on the hand, were available for other crimes, including burglary, robbery, manslaughter, and rape. Even in Gov. Thomas Jefferson's 1778 Virginia "Bill for Proportioning Crimes and Punishments," the pillory remained among the prescribed punishments for grand larceny (thirty minutes) and petty larceny (fifteen minutes), and branding was among the punishments for disfigurement. How do these traditional penalties differ from the proposed new shaming penalties?

Are shaming sanctions justifiable under any, or all, of the traditional rationales for punishment? Or do they rely on an independent justification for punishment altogether? Are they constitutional under the Eighth Amendment's prohibition against "cruel and unusual punishments"? What if the alternative is prolonged confinement in prison (perhaps under conditions similar to those described in the Blecker excerpt above), which has largely abandoned any rehabilitative pretense in favor of managing inmates in carceral warehouses and is likely to be considerably more expensive? And isn't punishment shameful by definition and—at least in part—even by design? What's the difference between condemnation and shaming? Are shaming punishments more appropriate for some offenses (and offenders) than others? What if an offender (and/or her victim?) prefers shaming to incarceration? Consider these questions in the context of the following case.

United States v. Gementera

United States Court of Appeals for the Ninth Circuit.
379 F.3d 596 (2004).

■ O'SCANNLAIN, CIRCUIT JUDGE.

We must decide the legality of a supervised release condition that requires a convicted mail thief to spend a day standing outside a post office wearing a signboard stating, "I stole mail. This is my punishment."

I

Shawn Gementera pilfered letters from several mailboxes along San Francisco's Fulton Street on May 21, 2001.... After indictment, Gementera entered a plea agreement pursuant to which he pled guilty to mail theft, *see* 18 U.S.C. § 1708....

The offense was not Gementera's first encounter with the law. Though only twenty-four years old at the time, Gementera's criminal history was lengthy for a man of his relative youth, and it was growing steadily more serious. At age nineteen, he was convicted of misdemeanor criminal mischief. He was twice convicted at age twenty of driving with a suspended license. At age twenty-two, a domestic dispute led to convictions for driving with a suspended license and for failing to provide proof of financial responsibility. By twenty-four, the conviction was misdemeanor battery. Other arrests and citations listed in the Presentence Investigation Report included possession of drug paraphernalia, additional driving offenses (most of which involved driving on a license suspended for his failure to take chemical tests), and, soon after his twenty-fifth birthday, taking a vehicle without the owner's consent.

On February 25, 2003, Judge Vaughn Walker of the United States District Court for the Northern District of California sentenced Gementera. The U.S. Sentencing Guidelines range was two to eight months incarceration; Judge Walker sentenced Gementera to the lower bound of the range, imposing two months incarceration and three years supervised release. He also imposed conditions of supervised release....

[D]efendant [was to] observe postal patrons visiting the "lost or missing mail" window, write letters of apology to any identifiable victims of his crime, ... deliver several lectures at a local school, [and] perform 1 day of 8 total hours of community service during which time he shall either (i) wear a two-sided sandwich board-style sign or (ii) carry a large two-sided sign stating, "I stole mail; this is my punishment," in front of a San Francisco postal facility identified by the probation officer....

II

We first address Gementera's argument that the ... sandwich board condition violates the Sentencing Reform Act. *See* 18 U.S.C. § 3583(d).

The Sentencing Reform Act affords district courts broad discretion in fashioning appropriate conditions of supervised release, while mandating that ... any condition must be "reasonably related" to "the nature and circumstances of the offense and the history and characteristics of the defendant." *See* 18 U.S.C. 3553(a)(1). Moreover, it must be both "reasonably related" to and "involve no greater deprivation of liberty than is reasonably necessary" to "afford adequate deterrence to criminal conduct," *see id.* at 3553(a)(2)(B), "protect the public from further crimes of the defendant," *see id.* at 3553(a)(2)(C), and "provide the defendant with needed educational or vocational training, medical care, or other correctional treatment in the most effective manner." *See id.* at 3553(a)(2)(D). Accordingly, the three legitimate statutory purposes of deterrence, protection of the public, and rehabilitation frame our analysis....

[F]irst, this court must determine whether the sentencing judge imposed the conditions for permissible purposes, and then it must determine whether the conditions are reasonably related to the purposes....

Gementera first urges that the condition was imposed for an impermissible purpose of humiliation. He points to certain remarks of the district court at the first sentencing hearing:

> He needs to understand the disapproval that society has for this kind of conduct, and that's the idea behind the humiliation. And it should be humiliation of having to stand and be labeled in front of people coming and going from a post office as somebody who has stolen the mail.

Reading the record in context, however, we cannot but conclude that the district court's stated rationale aligned with permissible statutory objectives. At the second sentencing hearing, ... the court explained: "Ultimately, the objective here is, one, to deter criminal conduct, and, number two, to rehabilitate the offender so that after he has paid his punishment, he does not reoffend, and a public expiation of having offended is, or at least it should be, rehabilitating in its effect." Although, in general, criminal punishment "is or at least should be humiliating," the court emphasized that "humiliation is not the point." The court's written order similarly stresses that the court's goal was not "to subject defendant to humiliation for humiliation's sake, but rather to create a situation in which the public exposure of defendant's crime and the public exposure of defendant to the victims of his crime" will serve the purposes of "the rehabilitation of the defendant and the protection of the public."....

Read in its entirety, the record unambiguously establishes that the district court imposed the condition for the stated and legitimate statutory purpose of rehabilitation and, to a lesser extent, for general deterrence and for the protection of the public. We find no error in the condition's purpose.

Assuming the court articulated a legitimate purpose, Gementera asserts, under the second prong of our test, that humiliation or so-called "shaming" conditions are not "reasonably related" to rehabilitation....

Gementera involve[s] a defendant who seemingly failed to confront [his] wrongdoing.... [Gementera's] plea decision is unremarkable ... given that he had been apprehended red-handed. Reflecting upon the defendant's criminal history, the court expressed concern that he did not fully understand the consequences of his continued criminality, and had not truly accepted responsibility.... The court also determined that Gementera needed to be educated about the seriousness of mail crimes in particular, given that they might appear to be victimless....

[T]he district court [thus] concluded that public acknowledgment of one's offense—beyond the formal yet sterile plea in a cloistered courtroom—was necessary to his rehabilitation....

Gementera contend[s] that shaming conditions cannot be rehabilitative because such conditions necessarily cause the offender to withdraw from society or otherwise inflict psychological damage, and [he] would erect a per se bar against such conditions. *See* Toni Massaro, *Shame, Culture, and American Criminal Law*, 89 Mich. L. Rev. 1880, 1920–21 (1991) ("When it works, it redefines a person in a negative, often irreversible way" and the "psychological core" it affects cannot thereafter be rebuilt.) Though the district court had no scientific evidence before it, as Gementera complains, we do not insist upon such evidence in our deferential review. Moreover, the fact is that a vigorous, multifaceted, scholarly debate on shaming sanctions' efficacy, desirability, and underlying rationales continues within the academy. By no means is this conversation one-sided....

Criminal offenses, and the penalties that accompany them, nearly always cause shame and embarrassment. Indeed, the mere fact of conviction, without which state-sponsored rehabilitation efforts do not commence, is stigmatic. The fact that a condition causes shame or embarrassment does not automatically render a condition objectionable; rather, such feelings generally signal the defendant's acknowledgment of his wrongdoing. * * *

Finally, we are aware that lengthier imprisonment was an alternative available to the court. The court, however, reasoned that rehabilitation would be better achieved by a shorter sentence, coupled with the additional conditions: "It would seem to me that he's better off with a taste of prison, rather than a longer prison sentence, and some form of condition of release that brings him face-to-face with the consequences of his crime." The judge's reasoning that rehabilitation would better be served by means other than extended incarceration and punishment is plainly reasonable, particularly in light of the significant economic disadvantages that attach to prolonged imprisonment.

... Accordingly, we hold that the condition imposed upon Gementera reasonably related to the legitimate statutory objective of rehabilitation. [In view of this holding, we do not reach the separate issue of whether the condition reasonably relates to the objectives of deterrence and protection of the public.] ...

III

Gementera also urges that the sandwich board condition violates the Constitution....

[T]he Eighth Amendment ... forbids the infliction of "cruel and unusual punishments." U.S. Const. amend. VIII. "The basic concept underlying the Eighth Amendment was nothing less than the dignity of man." *Trop v. Dulles*, 356 U.S. 86, 100, 2 L. Ed. 2d 630, 78 S. Ct. 590 (1958). Consistent with human dignity, the state must exercise its power to punish "within the limits of civilized standards." *Id.*

A particular punishment violates the Eighth Amendment if it constitutes one of "those modes or acts of punishment that had been considered cruel and unusual at the time that the Bill of Rights was adopted." *Ford v. Wainwright*, 477 U.S. 399, 405, 91 L. Ed. 2d 335, 106 S. Ct. 2595 (1986). Shaming sanctions of far greater severity were common in the colonial era, and the parties do not quarrel on this point.

The Amendment's prohibition extends beyond those practices deemed barbarous in the 18th century, however. "The words of the Amendment are not precise, and [ ] their scope is not static. The Amendment must draw its meaning from the evolving standards of decency that mark the progress of a maturing society." *Trop*, 356 U.S. at 100–01....

The parties have offered no evidence whatsoever, aside from bare assertion, that shaming sanctions violate contemporary standards of decency. But the occasional imposition of such sanctions is hardly unusual, particularly in our state courts....

In the absence of any evidence to the contrary, and particularly in comparison with the reality of the modern prison, we simply have no reason to conclude that the sanction before us exceeds the bounds of "civilized standards" or other "evolving standards of decency that mark the progress of a maturing society."

■ HAWKINS, CIRCUIT JUDGE, dissenting.

... There is precious little federal authority on sentences that include shaming components, perhaps indicative of a recognition that whatever legal justification may be marshaled in support of sentences involving public humiliation, they simply have no place in the majesty of a [federal] courtroom. Some state courts have reviewed such sentences and the results have been mixed.

People v. Hackler, 13 Cal. App. 4th 1049, 16 Cal.Rptr.2d 681, 686–87 (Cal. Ct. App. 1993), involved a condition that required a shoplifting offender to wear a court-provided t-shirt whenever he left the house that read: "My record plus two six-packs equals four years" on the front and "I am on felony probation for theft" on the back. Applying a state sentencing regime similar to the federal guidelines—authorizing the imposition of reasonable conditions of probation to foster rehabilitation and to protect public safety—the court struck down the condition. The court held that the relationship between the required conduct (wearing the t-shirt) and the defendant's crime (stealing beer) was so incidental that it was not reasonable and that the true intent behind the condition was to expose Hackler to "public ridicule and humiliation" and not "to foster rehabilitation."

As in Hackler's case, the purpose behind the sandwich board condition was not to rehabilitate Gementera, but rather to turn him into a modern day Hester Prynne.[4] This sort of condition is simply improper under the Sentencing Reform Act.

Ballenger v. State, 210 Ga. App. 627, 436 S.E.2d 793 (Ga. Ct. App. 1993), approved a condition that a convicted drunk driver wear a fluorescent pink identification bracelet identifying him as such. . . .

Just as in *Hackler* and *Ballenger*, the true intention in this case was to humiliate Gementera, not to rehabilitate him or to deter him from future wrongdoing. When the district court initially imposed the sandwich board condition, . . . Gementera filed a motion to correct the sentence by having the sandwich board condition removed. He urged that humiliation was not a legitimate objective of punishment or release conditions. Only at the hearing on Gementera's motion did the district court change its characterization of the shaming punishment, remarking that the punishment was one of deterrence and rehabilitation and not merely humiliation.

. . . To affirm the imposition of such punishments recalls a time in our history when pillories and stocks were the order of the day. To sanction such use of power runs the very great risk that by doing so we instill "a sense of disrespect for the criminal justice system" itself. *Ballenger*, 436 S.E. 2d at 796 (Blackburn, J. dissenting).

I would vacate the sentence and remand for re-sentencing, instructing the district court that public humiliation or shaming has no proper place in our system of justice.

C. PROPORTIONALITY (HOW MUCH TO PUNISH?)

The money laundering statute in *Blarek* did not provide for, and the judge therefore could not have considered imposing, the death penalty. Why would Congress not threaten money laundering with the most severe

4. *See* Hawthorne, *The Scarlet Letter*. . . .

penalty available, given that it is obviously greatly concerned about this offense?

One answer might be that the death penalty would be *disproportionate* to the crime of money laundering. The judge in *Blarek* associates proportionality with retributivism. Why? Must proportionality be limited to retributivism, or might another punishment theory generate a proportionality requirement as well? Bentham, for one, distinguished between various types of proportionality, including "For a Corporal Injury a similar Corporal Injury." Here is his proposed proportional punishment for arson:

> It would be necessary carefully to determine the text of the law, the part of the body which ought to be exposed to the action of the fire; the intensity of the fire; the time during which it is to be applied, and the paraphernalia to be employed to increase the terror of the punishment.

Jeremy Bentham, The Rationale of Punishment 56–62 (1830).

Why might a consequentialist like Bentham care about proportionality? Is retributive proportionality the same as consequentialist proportionality?

The U.S. Supreme Court has struggled to determine what, if any, proportionality limits the federal constitution—and more specifically the Eighth Amendment's prohibition of "cruel and unusual punishments"—places on the relation between crime and punishment.

In the area of capital punishment, the Court has held that proportionality militates against the imposition of the death penalty in cases of rape, Coker v. Georgia, 433 U.S. 584 (1977), as well as in certain unintentional murder cases (e.g., applied to the get-away driver in a robbery during which a death occurs), Enmund v. Florida, 458 U.S. 782 (1982).

In noncapital cases, the Court has been reluctant to strike down statutes imposing harsh prison sentences on proportionality grounds. It has upheld, for example, sentences of forty years and a $20,000 fine for possession and distribution of nine ounces of marijuana, Hutto v. Davis, 454 U.S. 370 (1982), and of life imprisonment without the possibility of parole for simple possession (i.e., possession without the element of intent to distribute) of 672 grams of cocaine, Harmelin v. Michigan, 501 U.S. 957 (1991). Over the years, recidivist statutes have caused the Court particular difficulty. Here is a sample of recent recidivism cases, along with their outcomes:

- mandatory life imprisonment a for recidivist convicted of three fraud-related felonies netting a total of $229.11—*not disproportionate* (Rummel v. Estelle, 445 U.S. 263 (1980));
- life imprisonment without the possibility of parole for seventh felony, writing a "no-account" check for $100—*disproportionate* (Solem v. Helm, 463 U.S. 277 (1983));
- life imprisonment for a third felony conviction under California's "Three Strikes and You're Out" law for stealing three golf clubs worth $399 apiece—*not disproportionate* (Ewing v. California, 538 U.S. 11 (2003));
- mandatory sentence of 25 years to life for a third felony conviction under California's "Three Strikes and You're Out" law for stealing

$150 worth of videotapes—*not disproportionate* (Lockyer v. Andrade, 538 U.S. 63 (2003)).[a]

The following excerpt illustrates the Court's latest foray into proportionality analysis in noncapital cases.

Ewing v. California

Supreme Court of the United States.
538 U.S. 11, 123 S.Ct. 1179 (2003).

■ JUSTICE O'CONNOR announced the judgment of the Court and delivered an opinion in which THE CHIEF JUSTICE and JUSTICE KENNEDY join.

In this case, we decide whether the Eighth Amendment prohibits the State of California from sentencing a repeat felon to a prison term of 25 years to life under the State's "Three Strikes and You're Out" law.

I

A

California's three strikes law reflects a shift in the State's sentencing policies toward incapacitating and deterring repeat offenders who threaten the public safety. The law was designed "to ensure longer prison sentences and greater punishment for those who commit a felony and have been previously convicted of serious and/or violent felony offenses." Cal. Penal Code Ann. § 667(b) (West 1999). * * *

C

On parole from a 9–year prison term, petitioner Gary Ewing walked into the pro shop of the El Segundo Golf Course in Los Angeles County on March 12, 2000. He walked out with three golf clubs, priced at $399 apiece, concealed in his pants leg. A shop employee, whose suspicions were aroused when he observed Ewing limp out of the pro shop, telephoned the police. The police apprehended Ewing in the parking lot. Ewing is no stranger to the criminal justice system....

In October and November 1993, Ewing committed three burglaries and one robbery at a Long Beach, California, apartment complex over a 5–week period. He awakened one of his victims, asleep on her living room sofa, as he tried to disconnect her video cassette recorder from the television in that room. When she screamed, Ewing ran out the front door. On another occasion, Ewing accosted a victim in the mailroom of the apartment complex. Ewing claimed to have a gun and ordered the victim to hand over his wallet. When the victim resisted, Ewing produced a knife and forced the

a. More precisely, the Court held in this case on a writ of habeas corpus that the California Supreme Court's decision that the sentence did *not* violate the Eighth Amendment's prohibition of cruel and unusual punishments did *not* amount to an "unreasonable application of clearly established federal law," the standard of review of state court decisions challenged in a federal habeas corpus proceeding. See generally Markus Dirk Dubber, "Prudence and Substance: How the Supreme Court's New Habeas Retroactivity Doctrine Mirrors and Affects Substantive Constitutional Law," 30 Am. Crim. L. Rev. 1 (1992).

victim back to the apartment itself. While Ewing rifled through the bedroom, the victim fled the apartment screaming for help. Ewing absconded with the victim's money and credit cards.

On December 9, 1993, Ewing was arrested on the premises of the apartment complex for trespassing and lying to a police officer. The knife used in the robbery and a glass cocaine pipe were later found in the back seat of the patrol car used to transport Ewing to the police station. A jury convicted Ewing of first-degree robbery and three counts of residential burglary. Sentenced to nine years and eight months in prison, Ewing was paroled in 1999.

Only 10 months later, Ewing stole the golf clubs at issue in this case. He was charged with, and ultimately convicted of, one count of felony grand theft of personal property in excess of $400. See Cal. Penal Code Ann., § 484 (West Supp. 2002); § 489 (West 1999). As required by the three strikes law, the prosecutor formally alleged, and the trial court later found, that Ewing had been convicted previously of four serious or violent felonies for the three burglaries and the robbery in the Long Beach apartment complex. See § 667(g) (West 1999); § 1170.12(e) (West Supp. 2002).

. . . As a newly convicted felon with two or more "serious" or "violent" felony convictions in his past, Ewing was sentenced under the three strikes law to 25 years to life. * * *

II

A

The Eighth Amendment, which forbids cruel and unusual punishments, contains a "narrow proportionality principle" that "applies to noncapital sentences." Harmelin v. Michigan, 501 U.S. 957, 996–997, 115 L. Ed. 2d 836, 111 S. Ct. 2680 (1991) (Kennedy, J., concurring in part and concurring in judgment). * * *

[In his concurring opinion in *Harmelin*] Justice Kennedy . . . identified four principles of proportionality review—"the primacy of the legislature, the variety of legitimate penological schemes, the nature of our federal system, and the requirement that proportionality review be guided by objective factors"—that "inform the final one: The Eighth Amendment does not require strict proportionality between crime and sentence. Rather, it forbids only extreme sentences that are 'grossly disproportionate' to the crime." Id., at 1001. * * *

B

For many years, most States have had laws providing for enhanced sentencing of repeat offenders. Yet between 1993 and 1995, three strikes laws effected a sea change in criminal sentencing throughout the Nation. . . .

Throughout the States, legislatures enacting three strikes laws made a deliberate policy choice that individuals who have repeatedly engaged in serious or violent criminal behavior, and whose conduct has not been deterred by more conventional approaches to punishment, must be isolated from society in order to protect the public safety. . . .

Our traditional deference to legislative policy choices finds a corollary in the principle that the Constitution "does not mandate adoption of any one penological theory." Harmelin, at 999. A sentence can have a variety of justifications, such as incapacitation, deterrence, retribution, or rehabilitation. Some or all of these justifications may play a role in a State's sentencing scheme. Selecting the sentencing rationales is generally a policy choice to be made by state legislatures, not federal courts.

When the California Legislature enacted the three strikes law, it made a judgment that protecting the public safety requires incapacitating criminals who have already been convicted of at least one serious or violent crime. Nothing in the Eighth Amendment prohibits California from making that choice. . . .

California's justification is no pretext. Recidivism is a serious public safety concern in California and throughout the Nation. According to a recent report, approximately 67 percent of former inmates released from state prisons were charged with at least one "serious" new crime within three years of their release. See U.S. Dept. of Justice, Bureau of Justice Statistics, P. Langan & D. Levin, Special Report: Recidivism of Prisoners Released in 1994, p. 1 (June 2002). In particular, released property offenders like Ewing had higher recidivism rates than those released after committing violent, drug, or public-order offenses. Id., at 8. Approximately 73 percent of the property offenders released in 1994 were arrested again within three years, compared to approximately 61 percent of the violent offenders, 62 percent of the public-order offenders, and 66 percent of the drug offenders. Ibid. * * *

The State's interest in deterring crime also lends some support to the three strikes law. We have long viewed both incapacitation and deterrence as rationales for recidivism statutes. * * *

III

Against this backdrop, we consider Ewing's claim that his three strikes sentence of 25 years to life is unconstitutionally disproportionate to his offense of "shoplifting three golf clubs." Brief for Petitioner 6. We first address the gravity of the offense compared to the harshness of the penalty. At the threshold, we note that Ewing incorrectly frames the issue. The gravity of his offense was not merely "shoplifting three golf clubs." Rather, Ewing was convicted of felony grand theft for stealing nearly $1,200 worth of merchandise after previously having been convicted of at least two "violent" or "serious" felonies. Even standing alone, Ewing's theft should not be taken lightly. . . . [T]he Supreme Court of California has noted the "seriousness" of grand theft in the context of proportionality review. Theft of $1,200 in property is a felony under federal law, 18 U.S.C. § 641, and in the vast majority of States.

In weighing the gravity of Ewing's offense, we must place on the scales not only his current felony, but also his long history of felony recidivism. Any other approach would fail to accord proper deference to the policy judgments that find expression in the legislature's choice of sanctions. In imposing a three strikes sentence, the State's interest is not merely punishing the offense of conviction, or the "triggering" offense: "It is in addition the interest ... in dealing in a harsher manner with those who by repeated criminal acts have shown that they are simply incapable of conforming to the norms of society as established by its criminal law." ...

Ewing's sentence is justified by the State's public-safety interest in incapacitating and deterring recidivist felons, and amply supported by his own long, serious criminal record. Ewing has been convicted of numerous misdemeanor and felony offenses, served nine separate terms of incarceration, and committed most of his crimes while on probation or parole. His prior "strikes" were serious felonies including robbery and three residential burglaries. To be sure, Ewing's sentence is a long one. But it reflects a rational legislative judgment, entitled to deference, that offenders who have committed serious or violent felonies and who continue to commit felonies must be incapacitated.... Ewing's is not "the rare case in which a threshold comparison of the crime committed and the sentence imposed leads to an inference of gross disproportionality." Harmelin, 501 U.S., at 1005 (Kennedy, J., concurring in part and concurring in judgment).

[Affirmed.]

QUESTIONS AND COMMENTS

1. Under the Court's proportionality analysis, what has to be proportional to what? The severity of the crime, the harm caused, the harm threatened, the defendant's culpability, his dangerousness, on the one hand, as compared with the quality of the punishment, its quantity, the way it is inflicted in general, in the particular case, its effect on the particular offender, its effect on the ideal offender?

2. How significant is it that the California three strikes law was enacted both by referendum (as Proposition 184) and by the legislature? What is Ewing being punished for: one offense, several offenses, his dangerousness, his malignity, his incalcitrance?

3. Do you agree with the Court that incapacitation and deterrence support recidivist statutes, and California's statute in particular? What about other theories of punishment? How might one go about designing a recidivist statute under the various theories of punishment? See Markus Dirk Dubber, "Recidivist Statutes as Arational Punishment," 43 Buff. L. Rev. 689 (1995).

4. One of the most controversial characteristics of California's three-strikes law, aside from its broad scope, is the discretion it gives prosecutors to charge "wobblers" as either misdemeanors or felonies. This feature attracted attention at oral argument in *Ewing* before the U.S. Supreme Court (Ewing's crime, grand theft, was a wobbler):

> Justice Ruth Bader Ginsburg asked whether there are standards in California governing prosecutors' discretion in deciding whether to charge wobblers as misdemeanors or felonies. [Counsel for California]

answered that there are no statewide standards, and that it is "unremarkable" that guidelines devised by local prosecutors' offices vary.

"Supreme Court Hears Challenges to California's Three–Strikes Sentencing Law," 72 Crim. L. Rep. no. 7, at 2080 (Nov. 13, 2002).

Are you satisfied with this answer? Could the statute's constitutional problem be fixed by providing statewide standards, to be developed by district attorney's offices across the state, or perhaps codified by the legislature, or perhaps imposed by the judiciary?

5. In contrast to imprisonment, the noncapital sanction of fines recently has come under closer constitutional scrutiny, under the Eighth Amendment's "excessive fines" clause, rather than its "cruel and unusual punishments" clause. See, e.g., United States v. Bajakajian, 524 U.S. 321 (1998) (invalidating criminal forfeiture of $357,144 in currency for failure to declare its transportation outside country). Does it make sense to place constitutional limits on fines, but not on imprisonment?

6. What is left of constitutional proportionality analysis in the wake of *Ewing*? Consider the following case.

United States v. Angelos

United States District Court for the District of Utah, Central Division.
345 F.Supp.2d 1227 (2004).

■ PAUL G. CASSELL, UNITED STATES DISTRICT JUDGE.

Defendant Weldon Angelos ... is a twenty-four-year-old first offender who is a successful music executive with two young children. Because he was convicted of dealing marijuana and related offenses, both the government and the defense agree that Mr. Angelos should serve about six to eight years in prison. But there are three additional firearms offenses for which the court must also impose sentence. Two of those offenses occurred when Mr. Angelos carried a handgun to two $350 marijuana deals; the third when police found several additional handguns at his home when they executed a search warrant. For these three acts of possessing (not using or even displaying) these guns, the government insists that Mr. Angelos should essentially spend the rest of his life in prison. Specifically, the government urges the court to sentence Mr. Angelos to a prison term of no less than 61 1/2 years—six years and a half (or more) for drug dealing followed by 55 years for three counts of possessing a firearm in connection with a drug offense. In support of its position, the government relies on a statute—18 U.S.C. § 924(c)—which requires the court to impose a sentence of five years in prison the first time a drug dealer carries a gun and twenty-five years for each subsequent time. Under § 924(c), the three counts produce 55 years of additional punishment for carrying a firearm.

Mr. Angelos ... argues that his 55–year sentence under § 924(c) violates the Eighth Amendment's prohibition of cruel and unusual punishment....

[T]he court must engage in a proportionality analysis guided by factors outlined in Justice Kennedy's concurrence in Harmelin v. Michigan, 501

U.S. 957 (1991). In particular, the court must examine (1) the nature of the crime and its relation to the punishment imposed, (2) the punishment for other offenses in this jurisdiction, and (3) the punishment for similar offenses in other jurisdictions.

Before turning to these *Harmelin* factors, it is important to emphasize that the criminal conduct at issue is solely that covered by the three § 924(c) counts. Mr. Angelos will be fully and appropriately punished for all other criminal conduct from the sentence on these other counts. Thus, the proportionality question in this case boils down to whether the 55–year sentence is disproportionate to the offense of carrying or possessing firearms three times in connection with dealing marijuana.

The first *Harmelin* factor requires the court to compare the seriousness of the three § 924(c) offenses to the harshness of the contemplated penalty to determine if the penalty would be grossly disproportionate to such offenses. In weighing the gravity of the offenses, the court should consider the offenses of conviction and the defendant's criminal history, as well as "the harm caused or threatened to the victim or society, and the culpability of the offender." ....

The criminal history in this case is easy to describe. Mr. Angelos has no prior adult criminal convictions and is treated as a first-time offender under the Sentencing Guidelines.

The sentence-triggering criminal conduct in this case is also modest. Here, on two occasions while selling small amounts of marijuana, Mr. Angelos possessed a handgun under his clothing, but he never brandished or used the handgun. The third relevant crime occurred when the police searched his home and found handguns in his residence. These handguns had multiple purposes—including recreational activities—but because Mr. Angelos also used the gun to protect himself while dealing drugs, the possession of these handguns is also covered by § 924(c).

Mr. Angelos did not engage in force or violence, or threats of force or violence, in furtherance of or in connection with the offenses for which he has been convicted. No offense involved injury to any person or the threat of injury to any person....

It is relevant on this point that the Sentencing Commission has reviewed crimes like Mr. Angelos' and concluded that an appropriate penalty for all of Mr. Angelos' crimes is no more than about ten years (121 months). With respect to the firearms conduct specifically, the Commission has concluded that about 24 months (a two-level enhancement) is the appropriate penalty. The views of the Commission are entitled to special weight, because it is a congressionally-established expert agency which can draw on significant data and other resources in determining appropriate sentences. Comparing a recommended sentence of two years to the 55–year enhancement the court must impose strongly suggests not merely disproportionality, but gross disproportionality.

The next *Harmelin* factor requires comparing Mr. Angelos' sentence with the sentences imposed on other criminals in the federal system. Generally, "if more serious crimes are subject to the same penalty, or to less serious penalties, that is some indication that the punishment at issue may be excessive." This factor points strongly in favor of finding that the sentence in this case is excessive.... Mr. Angelos will receive a far longer sentence than those imposed in the federal system for such major crimes as aircraft hijacking, second-degree murder, racial beating inflicting life-threatening injuries, kidnapping, and rape. Indeed, Mr. Angelos will receive a far longer sentence than those imposed for three aircraft hijackings, three second-degree murders, three racial beatings inflicting life-threatening injuries, three kidnappings, and three rapes. Because Mr. Angelos is "treated in the same manner as, or more severely than, criminals who have committed far more serious crimes," it appears that the second factor is satisfied.

The final *Harmelin* factor requires the court to examine "sentences imposed for the same crime in other jurisdictions." Evaluating this factor is also straightforward. Mr. Angelos sentence is longer than he would receive in any of the fifty states. The government commendably concedes this point in its brief, pointing out that in Washington State Mr. Angelos would serve about nine years and in Utah would serve about five to seven years. Accordingly, the court finds that the third factor is satisfied.

Having analyzed the three *Harmelin* factors, the court believes that they lead to the conclusion that Mr. Angelos' sentence violates the Eighth Amendment. But before the court declares the sentence unconstitutional, there is one last obstacle to overcome. The court is keenly aware of its obligation to follow precedent from superior courts—specifically the Tenth Circuit and, of course, the Supreme Court. The Supreme Court has considered one case that might be regarded as quite similar to this one. In *Hutto v. Davis,* the Supreme Court held that two consecutive twenty-year sentences—totaling forty years—for possession of nine ounces of marijuana said to be worth $200 did not violate the Eighth Amendment. If *Davis* remains good law, it is hard see how the sentence in this case violates the Eighth Amendment. Here, Mr. Angelos was involved in at least two marijuana deals involving $700 and approximately sixteen ounces (one pound) of marijuana. Perhaps currency inflation could equate $700 today with $200 in the 1980's. But as a simple matter of arithmetic, if 40 years in prison for possessing nine ounces marijuana does not violate the Eighth Amendment, it is hard to see how 61 years for distributing sixteen ounces (or more) would do so.

The court is aware of an argument that the 1982 *Davis* decision has been implicitly overruled or narrowed by [more recent decisions of the Supreme Court.] [Nonetheless,] in light of ... continued references to *Davis* [by the Supreme Court], the court believes it is obligated to follow its holding here. Indeed, in *Davis* the Supreme Court pointedly reminded district court judges that "unless we wish anarchy to prevail within the federal judicial system, a precedent of this Court must be followed by the lower federal courts...." Under *Davis,* Mr. Angelos' sentence is not cruel and unusual punishment. Therefore, his Eighth Amendment challenge must be rejected. * * *

The 55-year sentence mandated by § 924(c) in this case appears to be unjust, cruel, and irrational. But our constitutional system of government requires the court to follow the law, not its own personal views about what the law ought to be. Perhaps the court has overlooked some legal point, and that the appellate courts will find Mr. Angelos' sentence invalid. But applying the law as the court understands it, the court sentences Mr. Angelos to serve a term of imprisonment of 55 years and one day. The court recommends that the President commute this unjust sentence and that the Congress modify the laws that produced it. The Clerk's Office is directed to forward a copy of this opinion with its commutation recommendation to the Office of Pardon Attorney and to the Chair and Ranking Member of the House and Senate Judiciary Committees.

D. COLLATERAL EFFECTS OF PUNISHMENT

To get a sense of the broad and varied landscape of sanctions in American criminal law, it's important to keep in mind that there is a host of so-called "collateral consequences" or "disabilities" (but not "punishments") triggered by criminal punishment "properly speaking."

1. PUBLIC SANCTIONS

Collateral penalties differ from jurisdiction to jurisdiction, from crime to crime, and from punishment to punishment, but here is one, illustrative rather than comprehensive, overview of some collateral consequences set out in federal statutes alone (note the collateral effect on federally funded state programs):

Jury Service Conviction of crime with maximum sentence of over 1 year: disqualified from serving on federal grand or petit jury. 28 U.S.C. § 865(b)(5).	*Immigration* Conviction of aggravated felony or crime involving moral turpitude (e.g., fraud, theft, assault, domestic violence, violation of protection order): deportation. 8 U.S.C. § 1227(a)(2).
Food Stamps and Social Security Drug conviction: ineligible for assistance under state programs funded by Social Security Act or Food Stamp Act. 18 U.S.C. § 862a.	*Misc. Federal Benefits (incl. student loans, small business loans, licenses, & grants)* Drug trafficking conviction: ineligible up to 5 years (1st offense), up to 10 years (2d offense), permanently (3d offense), Drug possession conviction: ineligible up to 1 year (1st offense), up to 5 years (others). 21 U.S.C. § 862.
Registration (Megan's Law) Conviction of crime against a minor, sexually violent offense, or classification as "sexually violent predator": registration of current address. 42 U.S.C. § 14071.	*Firearms Possession* Conviction of crime with maximum sentence of over 1 year or domestic violence crime: firearms possessions punishable with up to 10 years' imprisonment. 18 U.S.C. § 922(g)(1).

For a more complete list, see U.S. Dep't of Justice, Office of the Pardon Attorney, Federal Statutes Imposing Collateral Consequences Upon Conviction (November 2000), http://www.usdoj.gov/pardon/readingroom.htm (accessed Dec. 29, 2002).

Are the various collateral consequences justifiable in light of the traditional rationales for punishment? Consider the following news story.

CHICAGO—Maurice Stewart finally got out of prison last summer after serving 14 years for armed robbery and manslaughter. He needed a place to live, so he called his mother.

Mr. Stewart, a husky 33–year-old, wanted to come home to Stateway Gardens, the decaying public housing project on Chicago's South Side where he had grown up.

It sounded simple enough. But his mother, Pamela Stewart, knew otherwise. Under a little-noticed provision of federal law, anyone convicted of a crime is barred from public housing, and if Mrs. Stewart took her son in, even for a visit, the Chicago Housing Authority could evict her.

The ban on living in public housing is among the penalties for criminals that are not spelled out at sentencing and do not begin until the sentence runs out. Most of the sanctions were passed by Congress and state legislatures in the 1990's to get tough on crime. Now, as the record number of men and women who filled prisons in the last decade are finishing their terms, the consequences of the penalties are being felt.

The penalties also include a lifetime ban on receiving welfare or food stamps for those convicted of drug felonies, prohibitions against getting certain jobs in plumbing, education and other fields, and the loss of the right to vote, for life in some states. [W]omen who serve more than 15 months in prison may be forced to give up their children to foster care. * * *

In one recent case ... a judge with a tough-on-crime reputation allowed an 18–year-old man from El Salvador, who had already pleaded guilty to burglary and nearly completed his prison term, to withdraw his guilty plea and ask for a new trial. The reason for the unusual request ... was that the man faced being deported as a convicted felon. * * *

In recent years the states have also passed legislation lengthening the list of jobs that bar people with a criminal conviction. In New York, there are more than 100 prohibited job categories, including plumbing, real estate, barbering, education, health care and private security.

In Pennsylvania, the Legislature in 1997 passed a sweeping law that prohibits people convicted of a long list of crimes, including the theft of two library books, from working in nursing homes or home health care for the elderly.

The new law caught Earl Nixon by surprise. Mr. Nixon had spent 30 years working in health care, rising to be the administrator of an assisted living center in Pittsburgh. But in 1971, when he was 18, he pleaded guilty to possession of marijuana and received probation.

So when he recently quit his administrator's post and tried to change jobs, he was shocked to discover he could not be rehired, despite a shortage of health care workers. Unable to find a new job, Mr. Nixon moved to Michigan. * * *

Fox Butterfield, "Freed From Prison, but Still Paying a Penalty," N.Y. Times, Dec. 29, 2002; see also Bonnie Miller Rubin, "Denying College Aid Over Drugs Faces Fight," Chi. Trib., Jan. 5, 2004, at 1 (application for federal student aid asks "Have you ever been convicted of selling or possessing drugs?"; affirmative answer results in ineligibility for government grants or federally backed loans).

The widespread disenfranchisement of "felons" has produced particularly troubling results:

- An estimated 3.9 million Americans, or one in fifty adults, have currently or permanently lost the ability to vote because of a felony conviction.
- 1.4 million persons disenfranchised for a felony conviction are ex-offenders who have completed their criminal sentence. Another 1.4 million of the disenfranchised are on probation or parole.
- 1.4 million African American men, or 13 percent of the black adult male population, are disenfranchised, reflecting a rate of disenfranchisement that is seven times the national average. More than one-third (36 percent) of the total disenfranchised population are black men.

Patricia Allard & Marc Mauer, Regaining the Vote: An Assessment of Activity Relating to Felon Disenfranchisement Laws (2000).

Often offenders become aware of the collateral consequences of conviction only after entering a guilty plea. See, e.g., United States v. Gonzalez, 202 F.3d 20 (1st Cir. 2000) (deportation). The American Bar Association recently called for explicitly incorporating "collateral consequences" into the law and practice of sentencing, by (1) collecting all mandatory sanctions for particular offenses in the criminal code, (2) requiring that an offender be informed of the full range of mandatory consequences of the conviction before she pleads guilty, and (3) requiring judges to take collateral sanctions into account at sentencing. 73 Crim. L. Rep. (BNA) 525 (2003). Can these proposals be implemented? If they can, do they address the questions raised by collateral sanctions?

2. PRIVATE SANCTIONS AND CIVIL LIABILITY

Beyond the assortment of public noncriminal sanctions that supplement, but aren't classified as, public criminal sanctions, the imposition of punishment triggers a number of parallel private noncriminal consequences, some formal (e.g., disbarment or loss of license), others less so (e.g., loss of employment, business, or "career"). The *Blarek* court, for instance, refused to consider in mitigation "[s]uch collateral punishment" as the "effect the conviction will have on the ability of the[] defendants to be licensed to practice their profession upon release from prison." See also Koon v. United States, 518 U.S. 81, 109–10 (1996) (anticipated "career loss" as a result of conviction no ground for mitigation).

There is an important, but often forgotten, *alternative* to punishment, which may also, but need not, function as a *supplement*: civil liability in private law (as opposed to public "civil" sanctions like civil forfeiture) and its concomitant civil remedies, financial or equitable. The connection between criminal and civil liability is particularly obvious in the availability of "punitive damages" in tort actions which go beyond the amount needed to compensate the plaintiff for the harm she suffered at the hands of the defendant.

Many crimes have analogues in civil actions in tort and in contract. Here are some examples:

Restatement of Torts (2d) § 13. Battery: Harmful Contact An actor is subject to liability to another for battery if (a) he acts intending to cause a harmful or offensive contact with the person of the other or a third person, or an imminent apprehension of such a contact, and (b) a harmful contact with the person of the other directly or indirectly results.	*Model Penal Code § 211.1. Assault* (1) . . . A person is guilty of assault if he: (a) attempts to cause or purposely, knowingly or recklessly causes bodily injury to another; or (b) negligently causes bodily injury to another with a deadly weapon. . . .
Restatement of Torts (2d) § 35. False Imprisonment (1) An actor is subject to liability to another for false imprisonment if (a) he acts intending to confine the other or a third person within boundaries fixed by the actor, and (b) his act directly or indirectly results in such a confinement of the other, and (c) the other is conscious of the confinement or is harmed by it. * * *	*California Penal Code § 236. False Imprisonment* False imprisonment is the unlawful violation of the personal liberty of another.

These few selections highlight a basic distinction between criminal and tort liability. What is it? Is there an analogue to the crime in *Blarek*, money laundering, in torts (or contracts)?

We will consider parallels between civil and criminal liability—or civil alternatives to criminal punishment, if you like—throughout this book. You may want to keep the following sorts of questions in the back of your mind: Why do we need a criminal law of battery if batterers can be sued by their victims? Why are some torts (including many negligent auto accidents) *not* crimes? Why are some crimes (e.g., treason, perjury) not torts?

We will also need to consider not only the porous line between tort law, conventionally understood, and criminal law, but the porous line between contract law, conventionally understood, and criminal law. Assume that you are my employee and have agreed to be bound by certain work rules in an "employee handbook": Have you stolen something of value from me when you break those rules and I don't receive the performance I contracted for? Does it matter if you *hide* your breach? Arguably, much of the expansion of federal white collar crime law (especially the mail and wire fraud statutes, 18 U.S.C. §§ 1341, 1343) re-located the traditional line between private contract and public criminal law. See ch. 11 infra.

E. THE ROLE OF VICTIMS

The mandatory "special assessment" imposed in *Blarek*, for deposit into the Victims of Crime Act Crime Victims Fund administered by the Office for Victims of Crime, illustrates but one, small, way in which American criminal law has been reformed to take into account the interests of crime victims, even in cases that involve what the judge in *Blarek* called " 'victimless' offenses."

1. VICTIMS AND THE RATIONALES FOR PUNISHMENT

Consider the role of the victim from the perspective of the various traditional rationales for punishment, discussed in the following excerpt. Can a case be made that "victims' rights" generate an entirely new rationale for punishment?

> In the theoretical underpinnings of the substantive criminal law, the so-called theory of punishment, the role of victims differs from theory to theory. Rehabilitation, the reigning ideology in American penal law until the late 1960s, had little use for victims. Punishment or, as the rehabilitationist would have it, peno-correctional treatment, turns on the offender's criminal pathology, as diagnosed by penological experts. Victims are no more relevant to this view of punishment than they are to the medical treatment of any other patient. This is not to say that victims are irrelevant, only that their characteristics or conduct matters merely insofar as they affect the diagnosis and treatment of a particular offender's deviance. So the victim's age might indicate a diagnosis of pedophilia. Similarly, her conduct might help the penologist identify the specific behavioral trigger of the offender's criminal episode, such as in provocation cases, or even constitute strong evidence against a diagnosis of criminal pathology, such as in cases of victim consent. More recently, victim participation has been said also to contribute to the offender's rehabilitative treatment. Victim-offender meetings, for example, may assist the offender's rehabilitation by forcing her to confront the devastating and long-term impact her deviant behavior has on the immediate victim and her community....
>
> By the 1970s, rehabilitationism began to give way to retributivism as the dominant ideology of punishment in the United States....
>
> Retributivism made room for victims insofar as its assessment of desert turned in part on the harm inflicted by the defendant's conduct not only in the abstract, i.e., in the definition of the offense, but also in the particular case, provided the offender displayed an attitude toward the harm that would permit the assignment of blame. The victim's role in retributivism, however, was not uncontested. Many retributivists, after all, rebelled against what they perceived as the rehabilitationists' ill-advised attention to the particular characteristics and circumstances of the offender, rather than to the nature of the offense, for two

reasons. First, such efforts at particularization placed excessive discretion in the hands of those charged with applying penal norms, a discretion which in turn led to non-uniform punishment practices in general, and to discriminatory punishment practices in particular. Second, any offender-based punishment practice risked the degrading stigmatization of its object, who was marked as deviant, rather than judged as having wronged. In its most abstract form, retributivism thus viewed punishment as the vindication of a general penal norm (e.g., against homicide), rather than retribution for the particular harm suffered by a particular victim. The victim's experience was significant only insofar as it established the norm violation. Once the norm violation had been established, the particular sentence imposed on the offender could reflect the particular harm inflicted only insofar as the offender was aware of it (or possessed some other mental state).

This deontological interlude, however, proved short-lived. Certainly in practice, if not in theory, retributivism quickly gave way to its consequentialist analogue, vengeance, and the crudest form of consequentialist penology, incapacitation. The rise of the so-called victims' rights movement in the United States formed an important part of this consequentialist (re)turn. * * *

In the absence of a coherent theory underlying the victims' rights movement ..., one is forced instead merely to identify the symptoms of this sociological phenomenon.... [T]he victims' rights movement can be thought of as the manifestation of a communal self-protective reflex or impulse. The victim would play a central role in such a phenomenology of reflex punishment. It is the injury to a fellow community member by an outsider that triggers the penal impulse. Through identification with the victim, other community members reexperience her suffering. Moreover, they may experience the injury inflicted upon the individual victim as an injury to the community as a whole, and perhaps even as a threat to its continued existence. The victim, in the end, becomes an icon to a community of potential victims. The victim is entitled to an unrestrained manifestation of her pain and confusion, with her fellow community members as empathic onlookers.

In this model, everything would turn on the onlooker's identification with the iconic victim. Without identification, she cannot experience the victim's pain as her own, nor does she consider an injury to the victim as a threat to her own community....

[T]hough based on the perception of fellow community membership with respect to victims, the victims' rights movement, at the same time, has worked to block that identification when it comes to certain offenders. One might even go so far as to say that the victims' rights movement set out to *replace* offender-identification with victim-identification.

The inclusionary-exclusionary nature of the victims' rights movement becomes most obvious in capital cases. Here identification with the victim is said not only to permit but to require differentiation from the offender. By declaring the offender an outsider so alien to the community that identification is simply impossible for lack of even the most basic similarity, the community purges itself of deviant elements and thereby heals itself as it salves the victim's pain. . . .

Once the offender is excluded from the realm of identification, the question 'how could someone like us (or, stronger, like me) have done something like this' no longer arises. To the extent curiosity survives, it does not concern the offender's behavior, but the victim's suffering. Making room for victims thus often amounts to facilitating the search for an answer to the altogether different, passive, question 'how could something like this have happened to someone like us (or me).' The offender and her behavior remains significant only insofar as it can help answer this elusive question, most obviously in the case of victim-offender meetings after conviction.

Markus Dirk Dubber, "The Victim in American Penal Law: A Systematic Overview," 3 Buff. Crim. L. Rev. 3, 4–10 (1999).

2. Community-Based Sanctions

Victim participation plays a central, though ambiguous, role in the use of community-based sanctions, and in "restorative justice" models in general. Consider the following case.

People v. Mooney

County Court of New York, Genesee County.
133 Misc.2d 313, 506 N.Y.S.2d 991 (1986).

■ Glenn R. Morton, J.

The defendant was originally indicted for two counts of attempted manslaughter in the first degree arising out of a single criminal transaction involving the shooting of two separate individuals. Incident thereto, the defendant, with the consent of the People, pleaded guilty to two counts of attempted assault in the first degree as lesser included offenses, and the parties stipulated to a mitigation hearing pursuant to Penal Law § 70.02(5)(b) to determine whether sufficient statutory circumstances existed as would permit the imposition of an alternative community-based sentence in lieu of an indeterminate State prison sentence. * * *

Essentially, the proof here is uncontroverted that the offense is serious, involving the intentional shooting of two people with a .22 caliber semiautomatic rifle in the Village of LeRoy. The nature of the offense is further aggravated here in that it was committed in a sniper-like fashion using a telescopic sight in which the victims received life threatening injuries. However, the proof reflects that the offense was committed under bizarre circumstances across from a police station with little or no rational motive. . . .

The Grand Jury minutes reveal that the defendant also shot himself twice in the head and received similar serious injuries. . . .

. . . The defendant has no criminal history. At the time of the offense he was barely acquainted with one victim and only casually with the other. There had been no immediate contact between them and, at most, the proof would show a weak motive relating to certain misconceptions the defendant and one victim had over statements made to them by a mutual female acquaintance. The defendant was 18 years old at the time of the offense and had been a chronic abuser of a variety of drugs, mainly alcohol and marihuana, over the past five and one-half years. On the night of the offense, the defendant, with two others, consumed a quart of vodka and one ounce of marihuana during the last four hours; and immediately before, the defendant also consumed two "hits" of LSD. Based thereon, the defendant has no recollection of the actual events, and it does appear that an irrational act was involved.

The proof submitted here fails to reflect that the defendant has any psychotic mental illness and principally suffers from a personality disorder. The documentary exhibits and testimony reveal an all too familiar pattern of emotional problems developing from family and social deprivation, which have been severely aggravated by inordinate alcohol and substance abuse. Following the offense, the defendant has participated in extensive personal, social and drug counseling. The expert proof submitted reflects that the defendant has made positive gains during the pretrial period and has remained drug free since December 3, 1984. Currently the expert proof reveals that the defendant, although a polydrug dependent person, does not constitute a community threat so long as he abstains from all mood altering drugs, including alcohol.

Given the pervasive exposure to criminal activity, the Legislature, commencing in 1984, also has established certain standards for the fair treatment of crime victims, which, inter alia, include that the victim and their families be consulted and their views obtained as to the suitability of sentencing alternatives such as community supervision. The victim impact statement submitted here adds a certain amount of sophistication to the legislative intent and provides some objective criteria for consideration as to the effect of the offense, rather than the usual subjective evaluation of the sentencing court. * * *

The victim impact statement includes here a videotape of a victim reconciliation conference conducted on August 17, 1985 approximating four hours in length. Parts one and two consist of a mediated face-to-face confrontation between the defendant and the two immediate victims involved, along with the mother of one victim. Parts three and four consist of an additional confrontation between the same parties, along with other selected representatives of the LeRoy community from law enforcement, the clergy, governmental officials and the citizenry.

The first two parts show, as borne out by the testimony of the victim assistance officer, that both victims, although harboring a great deal of anger as to what happened to them, have from their own life-styles, a large amount of empathy with the defendant's personal plight. A reconciliation was accomplished with one victim during the conference, and he is not opposed to a community-based sentence. The remaining victim continues in a state of reproachment, with strong feelings of anger and revenge. However, it would appear from the probation report that the actual character of the feelings may be adaptive; and at the conference, while supportive of her son, the victim's mother expressed a less hostile attitude and was more receptive to a conciliatory process to eliminate the destructive nature of such feelings to his own future welfare.

Parts three and four relating to the community aspect fail to reveal a discernable sense of outrage; and indicate that a common community understanding exists as to a perceived correlation between the offense and drug abuse. For the most part, those participating were either directly or indirectly involved as a result of the offense in a small cohesive community, and are representative of the attitudes in the immediate area.

The victim impact statement also contains what purports to be a survey of the sentencing attitudes of some 31 other county residents based on a written poll containing a synopsis of the offense and available alternatives. The results would reflect of the 25 persons responding, 23 considered a local community-based sentence appropriate under similar circumstances. No proof as to the particular methodology utilized has been submitted in connection therewith which would permit this court to fairly access whether the survey constituted a representative sample of the extended community. However, considering that it coincides with the prosecutorial discretion exercised here, and is consistent with the narration of the events described by the proof, I find that it does represent a valid expression of community concern.

Considering such, together with the defendant's remorseful attitude, it appears that little purpose would be served here by extended confinement in a State prison for either rehabilitation purposes or to isolate the defendant from the community. Given the described circumstances and the availability of the intensive probation supervision program from the presentence report to closely monitor the defendant, these purposes would be more appropriately served by a community-type sentence. There does remain for consideration whether, for deterrence or retribution purposes, a State prison sentence is warranted. Experience in this area has established that lengthy incarceration is not cost effective to serve these specific purposes where community protection is not a controlling factor. As developed at the two victim reconciliation conferences, the community is supportive and, in the final analysis, no amount of punishment as a practical matter could adequately undo the harm to the actual victims. Significantly, at the community portion of the conference, an expression was made that a more realistic deterrent would be achieved if the defendant served as a living example as to the dangers of drug abuse through an education process. Accordingly, it is determined here that society would be better served by a community-based sentence with more limited incarceration on the defendant's consent to perform 600 hours of community service designed to educate the public to the problems associated through drug abuse.

QUESTIONS AND COMMENTS

1. "Restorative justice" means many things to many people. Consider the following sample.

- Restorative justice is a process of bringing together the individuals who have been affected by an offense and having them agree on how to repair the harm caused by the crime. The purpose is to restore victims, restore offenders, and restore communities in a way that all stakeholders can agree is just. (John Braithwaite, "A Future Where Punishment Is Marginalized: Realistic or Utopian?," 46 UCLA L. Rev. 1727, 1743 (1999).)

• Restorative justice is concerned with the broader relationships between offenders, victims, and communities. All parties are involved in the process of settling the offense and reconciliation. Crime is seen as more than simply the violation of the criminal law. Instead, the key focus is on the damage and injury done to victims and communities and each is seen as having a role to play in responding to the criminal act. As a result of meeting with the victims . . . , offenders are expected to gain an understanding of the consequences of their behavior and to develop feelings of remorse. (Joe Hudson et al., Introduction to Family Group Conferences: Perspectives on Policy and Practice 1, 4 (1996).)

• Restorative justice is a process that brings victims and offenders together to face each other, to inform each other about their crimes and victimization, to learn about each others' backgrounds, and to collectively reach agreement on a "penalty" or "restorative justice sanction." Restorative justice returns the criminal conflict back to the victims and offenders. It empowers them to address sanctioning concerns together. (Russ Immarigeon, "Restorative Justice, Juvenile Offenders and Crime Victims: A Review of the Literature," in Restorative Juvenile Justice: Repairing the Harm of Youth Crime (Gordon Bazemore & Lode Walgrave eds., 1999).)

• Crime is a violation of people and relationships. It creates obligations to make things right. [Restorative] justice involves the victim, the offender, and the community in search for solutions which promote repair, reconciliation, and reassurance. (Howard Zehr, "Changing Lenses: A New Focus for Crime and Justice." 181 (1990).)

Erik Luna, "The Practice of Restorative Justice: Punishment Theory, Holism, and the Procedural Conception of Restorative Justice," 2003 Utah L. Rev. 205, 228–29.

What, if anything, do these accounts of restorative justice have in common? What exactly does restorative justice restore? And what does that restoration have to do with justice?

Does the ideal of restorative justice, whatever it might be, fit with any—or all—of the traditional rationales for punishment? (Does that matter?) Is it an ideal worth pursuing? In all cases, in some, in *Mooney*? (For which defendants, victims, crimes?) Is it an ideal that can be implemented in the "real world"? How? Should participation be voluntary? (For the defendant, the victim, "the community"?) How would you design a restorative justice process?

2. What do you think about involving victims in the punishment of "their" offender? Is that fair? To the victim? To the offender? To "the community"? Do we have less reason to maintain a separate civil system of tort liability if victims participate in determining punishment levels for "their" offender? Is one of the roles of tort law to vindicate the interests of angry, injured parties, as well as to compensate them? See generally

Markus Dirk Dubber, Victims in the War on Crime: The Use and Abuse of Victims' Rights (2002).

What role should community sentiment have played in *Mooney*? What role should it play in the law of punishment? How should a judge go about gauging community sentiment? Does there ever come a point when a crime is so serious that community sentiment against punishment becomes irrelevant? How should conflicts between "victims' rights" and "community sentiment" be resolved?

According to the 1990 census, the Village of LeRoy, which is located in upstate New York, had a population of 4974, with the following racial makeup:

White	4785
Black	161
American Indian, Eskimo, or Aleut	4
Asian or Pacific Islander	24
Other race	0

To what extent did the disposition of the *Mooney* case reflect the size and homogeneity of the community? Who makes up the relevant "community" for purposes of "community-based" sanctions? Is it the community of victims? Is it the "district," represented by the "district attorney"? Or is it the plaintiff, "The People of the State of New York," to quote from the full caption of the case? What about a case involving a defendant who is considered, by the community, as an outsider, for whatever reason (race, nationality, place of birth, place of residence)? Ditto for an outsider-*victim*?

3. Compare the analysis in *Mooney* with the mediation provision in the German Penal Code. What factors influence the judge's sentencing decision under the two schemes? What rationales for punishment do they reflect?

German Penal Code § 46a. Mediation Between the Perpetrator and the Victim, Restitution for Harm Caused.

If the perpetrator has:

1. in an effort to achieve mediation with the aggrieved party (mediation between perpetrator and victim), completely or substantially made restitution for his act or earnestly strived to make restitution; or

2. in a case in which the restitution for the harm caused required substantial personal accomplishments or personal sacrifice on his part, completely or substantially compensated the victim, the court may [reduce the prison sentence] ... or, if the prescribed punishment is imprisonment for up to one year or a fine ..., dispense with punishment.

4. What relevance should victim impact evidence—e.g., in the form of a victim impact statement—play in sentencing? Which rationale for punishment can best accommodate the consideration of victim impact evidence? What about the victim who "continues in a state of reproachment, with strong feelings of anger and revenge"? Is his opinion less (more?) relevant than that of the other victim who reconciled with the offender?

Victim impact evidence has become a common feature in American sentencing law. See, e.g., 18 U.S.C. § 2319(d) (criminal copyright statute authorizing producers, sellers, and copyrights holders of copyrighted works, and their legal representatives, to submit victim impact statements). (Provided, of course, there is a victim. Who would give a victim impact statement in a drug possession case, for instance? A public intoxication case?)

The use of victim impact statements has been particularly controversial in capital cases, where the stakes are high and victim impact testimony often particularly powerful. (Who is the victim of a homicide?) The U.S. Supreme Court prohibited their use in 1987, but reversed itself only four years later. Contrast Booth v. Maryland, 482 U.S. 496 (1987), with Payne v. Tennessee, 501 U.S. 808 (1991). (For a detailed discussion, see the section on capital murder in ch. 10.)

One of the troubling aspects of victim impact evidence is that it may open the door to discriminatory—or at least irrelevant—distinctions among victims. (Is murdering a homeless man with no family or friends and a life expectancy of three months worse than murdering a young and healthy mother of four with a large circle of loving relatives and close friends who helped out at the local soup kitchen three nights a week? Who would give victim testimony in the first case?) Distinctions among victims, however, are not limited to victim impact evidence. Criminal legislation regularly differentiates among offenses on the basis of victim status. Assaulting a police officer is a different—and more serious—crime than "ordinary" assault (so is assaulting a member of a particular racial group, if the assault was motivated by racial animus), rape of a child (and, in some jurisdictions, an older person) is punished more harshly than rape of an adult woman, and so on. Likewise, even if the statute is silent on victim status, sentencing guidelines often are not. See, e.g., U.S. Sentencing Guidelines §§ 3A1.1 & 3A1.2 (providing that the sentence be increased in non-capital cases if the victim had certain characteristics, including race, color, religion, national origin, ethnicity, gender, disability, sexual orientation, unusual vulnerability "due to age, physical or mental condition," particular susceptibility to criminal conduct, or was in government service).

5. Victims' rights tend to be considered in a procedural context, such as the victim's right to attend, or even to participate, in plea negotiations or sentencing. (Why was there no victim impact statement at the *Blarek* sentencing hearing?) That's not to say, however, that victims are irrelevant in substantive criminal law. Keep an eye out for the significance of victims, be it through their conduct, their culpability, their characteristics, or in some other way, as you work your way through the general principles of offender liability (e.g., causation, consent, negligence) and specific offenses (e.g., assault, homicide, and (statutory) rape). See Markus Dirk Dubber, "The Victim in American Penal Law: A Systematic Overview," 3 Buff. Crim. L. Rev. 3, 10–16 (1999); see also Vera Bergelson, "Victims and Perpetrators: An Argument for Comparative Liability in Criminal Law," 8 Buff. Crim. L. Rev. 385 (2005).

3. VICTIM COMPENSATION

Beginning in the 1960s, crime victims have been entitled to claim compensation from the state (as contrasted with restitution from the defendant as part of his sentence) for crime-related injury. While the design of compensation programs varies from jurisdiction to jurisdiction, some consistency has been achieved as a result of the federal government tying federal support for these programs to certain requirements. See 42 U.S.C. § 10602. The following excerpt from the Uniform Victims of Crime Act illustrates the scope of a fairly typical crime victim compensation program.

Uniform Victims of Crime Act § 101. Definitions.

In this [Act]:

(1) "Crime" means an act or omission committed by a person, whether or not competent or an adult, which, if committed by a competent adult, is punishable by [incarceration]. . . .

(6) "Victim" means a person against whom a crime has been committed, but does not include a person who is accountable for the crime or a crime arising from the same conduct, criminal episode, or plan and does not include a government or a governmental subdivision, agency, or instrumentality.

§ 304. Eligibility for Compensation.

The following are eligible to receive compensation under this [Article]:

(1) a victim who has suffered physical, emotional, or psychological injury or impairment as a result of a crime [of violence, including driving while impaired and domestic abuse];

(2) an individual who, as a result of a crime [of violence, including driving while impaired and domestic abuse], has lost care or support from a victim;

(3) an individual who has suffered physical, emotional, or psychological injury or impairment as a result of preventing or attempting to prevent the commission of a crime, apprehending or attempting to apprehend a suspected criminal, aiding or attempting to aid a [law enforcement officer] to apprehend or arrest a suspected criminal, or aiding or attempting to aid a victim of a crime. . . .

§ 305. Award of Compensation.

(a) The [agency] may award compensation for any economic loss directly caused by death or physical, emotional, or psychological injury or impairment, including:

(1) reasonable expenses related to medical care, including prosthetic or auditory devices; ophthalmic care, including eye glasses; dental care, including orthodontic or other therapeutic devices; mental-health care; and rehabilitation;

(2) loss of income;

(3) expenses reasonably incurred in obtaining ordinary and necessary services instead of those the victim, if not injured, would have

performed, not for income but for the benefit of the victim or a member of the victim's family;

(4) loss of care and support; and

(5) reasonable expenses related to funeral and burial or crematory services.

(b) An award may be made whether or not a person is charged, indicted, prosecuted, or convicted of a crime giving rise to the claim.

In addition to (fixed or flexible) surcharges like the "special assessment" in *Blarek*, jurisdictions finance victim compensation programs in various ways, e.g., by collecting a portion of salaries earned by offenders in prison work or while on work release or parole, by contributing forfeited assets from criminal activity, and by allowing taxpayers to designate a part of their income tax refund to be used for victim services.

We will from time to time return to the question of victim compensation throughout the book. The basic underlying question is under what circumstances, and in what sorts of cases, victim compensation can take the place of, or complement, offender punishment.

F. PUNISHMENT VS. SANCTION VS. MEASURE (WHAT IS PUNISHMENT?)

Kansas v. Hendricks

Supreme Court of the United States.
521 U.S. 346, 117 S.Ct. 2072 (1997).

■ JUSTICE THOMAS delivered the opinion of the Court.

The Kansas Legislature enacted the Sexually Violent Predator Act (Act) in 1994 to grapple with the problem of managing repeat sexual offenders.... In the Act's preamble, the legislature explained:

"[A] small but extremely dangerous group of sexually violent predators exist who do not have a mental disease or defect that renders them appropriate for involuntary treatment pursuant to the [general involuntary civil commitment statute].... In contrast to persons appropriate for civil commitment under the [general involuntary civil commitment statute], sexually violent predators generally have anti-social personality features which are unamenable to existing mental illness treatment modalities and those features render them likely to engage in sexually violent behavior. The legislature further finds that sexually violent predators' likelihood of engaging in repeat acts of predatory sexual violence is high. The existing involuntary commitment procedure ... is inadequate to address the risk these sexually violent predators pose to society. The legislature further finds that the prognosis for rehabilitating sexually violent predators in a prison setting is poor, the treatment needs of this population are very long term and the treatment modalities for this population are very different than the traditional treatment modalities for people appropriate for commitment under the [general involuntary civil commitment statute]." Kan. Stat. Ann. § 59–29a01 (1994).

As a result, the Legislature found it necessary to establish "a civil commitment procedure for the long-term care and treatment of the sexually violent predator."

The Act defined a "sexually violent predator" as:

> "any person who has been convicted of or charged with a sexually violent offense and who suffers from a mental abnormality or personality disorder which make the person likely to engage in the predatory acts of sexual violence."

§ 59–29a02(a).

A "mental abnormality" was defined, in turn, as a "congenital or acquired condition affecting the emotional or volitional capacity which predisposes the person to commit sexually violent offenses in a degree constituting such person a menace to the health and safety of others." § 59–29a02(b).

As originally structured, the Act's civil commitment procedures pertained to: (1) a presently confined person who, like Hendricks, "has been convicted of a sexually violent offense" and is scheduled for release; (2) a person who has been "charged with a sexually violent offense" but has been found incompetent to stand trial; (3) a person who has been found "not guilty by reason of insanity of a sexually violent offense"; and (4) a person found "not guilty" of a sexually violent offense because of a mental disease or defect.

The initial version of the Act, as applied to a currently confined person such as Hendricks, was designed to initiate a specific series of procedures. The custodial agency was required to notify the local prosecutor 60 days before the anticipated release of a person who might have met the Act's criteria. The prosecutor was then obligated, within 45 days, to decide whether to file a petition in state court seeking the person's involuntary commitment. If such a petition were filed, the court was to determine whether "probable cause" existed to support a finding that the person was a "sexually violent predator" and thus eligible for civil commitment. Upon such a determination, transfer of the individual to a secure facility for professional evaluation would occur. After that evaluation, a trial would be held to determine beyond a reasonable doubt whether the individual was a sexually violent predator. If that determination were made, the person would then be transferred to the custody of the Secretary of Social and Rehabilitation Services (Secretary) for "control, care and treatment until such time as the person's mental abnormality or personality disorder has so changed that the person is safe to be at large."

In addition to placing the burden of proof upon the State, the Act afforded the individual a number of other procedural safeguards. In the case of an indigent person, the State was required to provide, at public expense, the assistance of counsel and an examination by mental health care professionals. The individual also received the right to present and cross-examine witnesses, and the opportunity to review documentary evidence presented by the State.

Once an individual was confined, the Act required that "[t]he involuntary detention or commitment ... shall conform to constitutional requirements for care and treatment." Confined persons were afforded three different avenues of review: First, the committing court was obligated to conduct an annual review to determine whether continued detention was warranted. Second, the Secretary was permitted, at any time, to decide that the confined individual's condition had so changed that release was appropriate, and could then authorize the person to petition for release. Finally, even without the Secretary's permission, the confined person could at any time file a release petition. If the court found that the State could no longer satisfy its burden under the initial commitment standard, the individual would be freed from confinement. * * *

[Hendricks] contends that where, as here, newly enacted "punishment" is predicated upon past conduct for which he has already been convicted and forced to serve a prison sentence, the Constitution's Double Jeopardy and *Ex Post Facto* Clauses are violated....

The categorization of a particular proceeding as civil or criminal "is first of all a question of statutory construction." We must initially ascertain whether the legislature meant the statute to establish "civil" proceedings. If so, we ordinarily defer to the legislature's stated intent. Here, Kansas' objective to create a civil proceeding is evidenced by its placement of the Sexually Violent Predator Act within the Kansas probate code, instead of the criminal code, as well as its description of the Act as creating a "*civil commitment procedure*." Kan. Stat. Ann., Article 29 (1994) ("Care and Treatment for Mentally Ill Persons"), § 59–29a01 (emphasis added). Nothing on the face of the statute suggests that the legislature sought to create anything other than a civil commitment scheme designed to protect the public from harm.

Although we recognize that a "civil label is not always dispositive," we will reject the legislature's manifest intent only where a party challenging the statute provides "the clearest proof" that "the statutory scheme [is] so punitive either in purpose or effect as to negate [the State's] intention" to deem it "civil." *United States* v. *Ward,* 448 U.S. 242, 248–249 (1980). In those limited circumstances, we will consider the statute to have established criminal proceedings for constitutional purposes. Hendricks, however, has failed to satisfy this heavy burden.

As a threshold matter, commitment under the Act does not implicate either of the two primary objectives of criminal punishment: retribution or deterrence. The Act's purpose is not retributive because it does not affix culpability for prior criminal conduct. Instead, such conduct is used solely for evidentiary purposes, either to demonstrate that a "mental abnormality" exists or to support a finding of future dangerousness. We have previously concluded that an Illinois statute was nonpunitive even though it was triggered by the commission of a sexual assault, explaining that evidence of the prior criminal conduct was "received not to punish past misdeeds, but primarily to show the accused's mental condition and to predict future behavior." In addition, the Kansas Act does not make a criminal conviction a prerequisite for commitment—persons absolved of criminal responsibility may nonetheless be subject to confinement under the Act. An absence of the necessary criminal responsibility suggests that the State is not seeking retribution for a past misdeed. Thus, the fact that the Act may be "tied to criminal activity" is "insufficient to render the statute punitive." *United States* v. *Ursery,* 518 U.S. 267, 292 (1996).

Moreover, unlike a criminal statute, no finding of scienter is required to commit an individual who is found to be a sexually violent predator; instead, the commitment determination is made based on a "mental abnormality" or "personality disorder" rather than on one's criminal intent. The existence of a scienter requirement is customarily an important element in distinguishing criminal from civil statutes. See *Kennedy* v. *Mendoza-Martinez,* 372 U.S. 144, 168 (1963). The absence of such a requirement here is evidence that confinement under the statute is not intended to be retributive.

Nor can it be said that the legislature intended the Act to function as a deterrent. Those persons committed under the Act are, by definition, suffering from a "mental abnormality" or a "personality disorder" that prevents them from exercising adequate control over their behavior. Such persons are therefore unlikely to be deterred by the threat of confinement. And the conditions surrounding that confinement do not suggest a punitive purpose on the State's part. The State has represented that an individual confined under the Act is not subject to the more restrictive conditions placed on state prisoners, but instead experiences essentially the same conditions as any involuntarily committed patient in the state mental institution. Because none of the parties argues that people institutionalized under the Kansas general civil commitment statute are subject to punitive conditions, even though they may be involuntarily confined, it is difficult to conclude that persons confined under this Act are being "punished."

Although the civil commitment scheme at issue here does involve an affirmative restraint, "the mere fact that a person is detained does not inexorably lead to the conclusion that the government has imposed punishment." *United States* v. *Salerno,* 481 U.S. 739, 746 (1987). The State may take measures to restrict the freedom of the dangerously mentally ill. This is a legitimate non-punitive governmental objective and has been historically so regarded. The Court has, in fact, cited the confinement of "mentally unstable individuals who present a danger to the public" as one classic example of nonpunitive detention. *Id.,* at 748–749. If detention for the purpose of protecting the community from harm *necessarily* constituted punishment, then all involuntary civil commitments would have to be considered punishment. But we have never so held.

Hendricks focuses on his confinement's potentially indefinite duration as evidence of the State's punitive intent. That focus, however, is misplaced. Far from any punitive objective, the confinement's duration is instead linked to the stated purposes of the commitment, namely, to hold the person until his mental abnormality no longer causes him to be a threat to others. If, at any time, the confined person is adjudged "safe to be at large," he is statutorily entitled to immediate release. Kan. Stat. Ann. § 59–29a07 (1994).

Furthermore, commitment under the Act is only *potentially* indefinite. The maximum amount of time an individual can be incapacitated pursuant to a single judicial proceeding is one year. If Kansas seeks to continue the detention beyond that year, a court must once again determine beyond a reasonable doubt that the detainee satisfies the same standards as required for the initial confinement. This requirement again demonstrates that Kansas does not intend an individual committed pursuant to the Act to remain confined any longer than he suffers from a mental abnormality rendering him unable to control his dangerousness.

Hendricks next contends that the State's use of procedural safeguards traditionally found in criminal trials makes the proceedings here criminal rather than civil.... The numerous procedural and evidentiary protections afforded here demonstrate that the Kansas Legislature has taken great care to confine only a narrow class of particularly dangerous individuals, and then only after meeting the strictest procedural standards. That Kansas chose to afford such procedural protections does not transform a civil commitment proceeding into a criminal prosecution. * * *

Where the State has "disavowed any punitive intent"; limited confinement to a small segment of particularly dangerous individuals; provided strict procedural safeguards; directed that confined persons be segregated from the general prison population and afforded the same status as others who have been civilly committed; recommended treatment if such is possible; and permitted immediate release upon a showing that the individual is no longer dangerous or mentally impaired, we cannot say that it acted with punitive intent. We therefore hold that the Act does not establish criminal proceedings and that involuntary confinement pursuant to the Act is not punitive. Our conclusion that the Act is nonpunitive thus removes an essential prerequisite for both Hendricks' double jeopardy and *ex post facto* claims.

QUESTIONS AND COMMENTS

1. Which of the types of "sanctions" count—or should count—as "punishment"? This problem has vexed theorists for quite a while. And courts, too, have struggled with it, often in the context of determining the scope of constitutional protections like the Eighth Amendment proscription of "cruel and unusual punishments." Often the difficulty of defining just what makes a punishment a punishment is glossed over by using the noncommittal term "sanction" or the slightly more committal "penalty." It's clear that the type of sanction doesn't help us much here, with the one exception of capital punishment; the death penalty has never been regarded as a civil sanction (neither have other, less drastic, incapacitative sanctions, like cutting off a hand (or tongue, lip, or ear), or, more recently, castration). Fines are neither here nor there; there are "criminal fines" as well as "civil" ones. The same is true of forfeiture. Surprisingly, not even imprisonment is invariably limited to criminal uses, thanks to its availability as a means to break the resistance of someone held in "civil contempt" of a court order, say, to testify despite a grant of immunity. Nonetheless, imprisonment is very rarely classified as non-punitive.

Instead, the Supreme Court has struggled to draw a line between criminal and noncriminal sanctions that runs right through the various types of sanctions in use today. Here is one, oft-cited, attempt to decipher the "punitive nature" of a given sanction (in this case, "forfeiture of citizenship"):

> Whether the sanction involves an affirmative disability or restraint, whether it has historically been regarded as a punishment, whether it comes into play only on a finding of *scienter*, whether its operation will promote the traditional aims of punishment—retribution and deterrence, whether the behavior to which it applies is already a crime, whether an alternative purpose to which it may rationally be connected is assignable for it, and whether it appears excessive in relation to the alternative purpose assigned are all relevant to the inquiry, and may often point in differing directions. Absent conclusive evidence of congressional intent as to the penal nature of a statute, these factors must be considered in relation to the statute on its face.

Kennedy v. Mendoza–Martinez, 372 U.S. 144, 168 (1963).

There are other variations of this test, depending on the constitutional question involved. In *Mendoza-Martinez*, the question was whether the various trial rights guaranteed to criminal defendants in the Fifth and Sixth Amendments applied to a WWII draft evader who had been stripped of his citizenship, including indictment, notice, confrontation, jury trial, assistance of counsel, and compulsory process for obtaining witnesses. In other cases, the "punitive nature" of the sanction affected the availability of the Fifth Amendment protection against successive or multiple punishments ("double jeopardy"), the Fifth and Fourteenth Amendment guarantees of due process and equal protection, or the constitutional prohibition of ex post facto punishment. Under these tests, it turns out, for instance, that "special assessments" like the one imposed in *Blarek* do not count as punishment—neither do similar "civil surcharges," which have become quite popular in recent years, including "presentence investigation fees," "community service participation fees," "local electronic monitoring fees," "custody investigation report fees," "probation supervision fees" (all in New York); "criminal cost fees," "document fees," "marijuana eradication fees," "alcohol and drug services user fees," "law enforcement continuing education fees," "drug abuse, prosecution, interdiction, and correction fees," "alcohol abuse deterrent fees," and "alcohol and drug countermeasures fees," "child abuse prevention fees," "domestic violence prevention fees," "highway work zone fees," and "deferred prosecution fees" (all in Indiana); "criminal justice administration fees" (in California), to name but a few. Cf. Taylor v. Rhode Island Dep't of Corrections, 908 F.Supp. 92 (D.R.I. 1995), rev'd, 101 F.3d 780 (1st Cir. 1996) ("supervision fee").

2. In *Hendricks*, the Supreme Court upheld Kansas's Sexually Violent Predator Act on the ground that it did not constitute "punishment" and therefore was not subject to the constitutional safeguards limited to the criminal law, specifically the proscriptions of double jeopardy and ex post facto legislation. The Court did not, but might have, considered as well whether Hendricks was being sanctioned for the "status" of being a sexual predator, in violation of the Supreme Court's holding in Robinson v. California, 370 U.S. 660 (1962) (California may punish drug use but not the status of being an addict). Does this make sense to you? Can the law be justified under any of the traditional rationales for punishment? Or is that

question irrelevant given the Court's conclusion that the law does not impose punishment?

3. *Hendricks* makes reference, in passing, to another form of non-criminal incarceration that traditionally has not been considered to amount to punishment, the "civil commitment" of the insane. (Note that "sexually violent predators" are *not* insane.) Civil commitment typically is reserved for a person who is mentally ill and:

> (i) who presents a substantial risk of imminent harm to that person or others, as manifested by either recent overt acts or recent expressed threats of violence which present a probability of physical injury to that person or other persons; or
>
> (ii) who is so unable to care for that person's own physical health and safety as to create an imminently life-endangering crisis.

Ga. Code Ann. § 37–3–1(9.1)

Defendants who successfully raise an insanity defense at trial tend to be subject to automatic "civil commitment." See, e.g., 18 U.S.C. § 4243 ("hospitalization" unless, and until, "the person's mental condition is such that his release ... would not create a substantial risk of bodily injury to another person or serious damage to property of another").

4. *Punishment vs. Measure.* The German Penal Code distinguishes carefully between "punishments" and "measures of improvement and protection" (or "rehabilitative and incapacitative measures"). The latter include (according to § 61):

1. placement in a psychiatric hospital;
2. placement in an institution for withdrawal treatment;
3. placement in preventive detention;
4. supervision of conduct;
5. withdrawal of permission to drive;
6. prohibition of engagement in a profession.

The most commonly imposed measure is suspension of driving privileges, which is the collateral sanction of choice in a host of traffic offenses (including DWI and reckless driving). The most controversial one is indefinite preventive detention as a "measure" beyond the prison sentence imposed as a "punishment":

German Penal Code § 66. Placement in Preventive Detention

(1) If someone is sentenced for an intentional crime to a fixed term of imprisonment of at least two years, then the court shall order preventive detention collateral to the punishment, if:

1. the perpetrator has already been sentenced twice, respectively, to imprisonment for at least one year for intentional crimes which he committed prior to the new act;

2. as a result of one or more of these acts prior to the new act he has served a term of imprisonment or deprivation of liberty

pursuant to a measure of reform and prevention for a period of at least two years; and

3. comprehensive evaluation of the perpetrator and his acts reveals that, due to his proclivity to commit serious crimes, particularly those as a result of which the victim suffers serious emotional or physical injury, or serious financial loss is caused, he presents a danger to the general public.

§ 67d. Length of Placement

(3) If ten years of placement in preventive detention have been executed, the court shall declare the measure satisfied if there is no danger that the person under placement will, due to his proclivity, commit serious crimes, as a result of which the victim is seriously harmed emotionally or physically. Supervision of conduct shall commence upon satisfaction of the measure.

§ 67e. Review

(1) The court may review at any time whether the further execution of the placement should be suspended and probation granted. It shall make this review before the expiration of specified terms.

(2) With respect to the various placements, these terms shall be:

. . . .

two years, if in preventive detention.

There is only one limitation upon the imposition of "measures":

§ 62. Principle of Proportionality

A measure of reform and prevention may not be ordered when it is disproportionate to the significance of the acts committed by, or expected to be committed by the perpetrator, as well as to the degree of danger he poses.

Otherwise, measures are exempted from the principles governing the imposition of "punishments," most importantly the nature and extent of her culpability:

§ 46. Principles for Determining Punishment

(1) The guilt of the perpetrator is the foundation for determining punishment. The effects which the punishment will be expected to have on the perpetrator's future life in society shall be considered.

(2) In its determination the court shall counterbalance the circumstances which speak for and against the perpetrator. In doing so consideration shall be given in particular to:

- the motives and aims of the perpetrator;
- the state of mind reflected in the act and the willfulness involved in its commission;
- the extent of breach of any duties;
- the manner of execution and the culpable consequences of the act;

- the perpetrator's prior history, his personal and financial circumstances; as well as
- his conduct after the act, particularly his efforts to make restitution for the harm caused as well as the perpetrator's efforts to achieve mediation with the aggrieved party.

What rationales for punishment underlie the German scheme of punishments and measures? Compare the German scheme with the Kansas statute providing for the indefinite "civil commitment" of "sexually violent predators," reviewed by the Supreme Court in *Hendricks*.

G. THE NATURE OF CRIME (WHAT TO PUNISH?)

Some suggest that punishment is punishment because it, and only it, is punishment for crime. But, then, what is *crime*, or to put it perhaps less ambitiously, what is *a* crime? This turns out to be just as difficult a question. This time, however, we can at least refer to some legislative definitions, such as this one in the New York Penal Law, which lays out a quite elaborate taxonomy of crimehood, including the traditional distinction between misdemeanors and felonies:

N.Y. Penal Law § 10.00 Definitions of terms of general use in this chapter.

1. "Offense" means conduct for which a sentence to a term of imprisonment or to a fine is provided by any law of this state or by any law, local law or ordinance of a political subdivision of this state, or by any order, rule or regulation of any governmental instrumentality authorized by law to adopt the same.

2. "Traffic infraction" means any offense defined as "traffic infraction" by section one hundred fifty-five of the vehicle and traffic law.

3. "Violation" means an offense, other than a "traffic infraction," for which a sentence to a term of imprisonment in excess of fifteen days cannot be imposed.

4. "Misdemeanor" means an offense, other than a "traffic infraction," for which a sentence to a term of imprisonment in excess of fifteen days may be imposed, but for which a sentence to a term of imprisonment in excess of one year cannot be imposed.

5. "Felony" means an offense for which a sentence to a term of imprisonment in excess of one year may be imposed.

6. "Crime" means a misdemeanor or a felony.

N.Y. Veh. & Traf. Law § 155. Traffic infraction.

The violation of any provision of [the Vehicle & Traffic Law] ... or of any law, ordinance, order, rule or regulation regulating traffic which is not declared by this chapter or other law of this state to be a misdemeanor or a felony. *A traffic infraction is not a crime and the punishment imposed therefor shall not be deemed for any purpose a penal or criminal punish-*

ment and shall not affect or impair the credibility as a witness or otherwise of any person convicted thereof.... [emphasis added]

The Model Penal Code originated the notion of a noncriminal offense, the "violation." The substantive significance of the possibility of a noncriminal offense becomes clear in a section that exempts violations from the Code's requirement that "a person is not guilty of an offense unless he acted purposely, knowingly, recklessly or negligently," i.e., with mens rea (or "scienter"). Model Penal Code §§ 2.02, 2.05. Violations are exempt from the "minimum requirements of culpability" because they are not "crimes": they don't "warrant[] the type of social condemnation that is and ought to be implicit in the concept of 'crime.' " Model Penal Code Commentaries § 1.04, at 72–73.

Distinct from the question of the minimum requirements of criminal liability in general (the province of the "general part" of criminal law) is the question of what conduct is classified as criminal in particular (the province of the "special part"). On the latter question, the U.S. Supreme Court, and its state analogues, have had more to say than on the former. Nonetheless, we won't spend much time on it, not least because the constitutionality of the vast bulk of criminal offenses is beyond doubt. No one doubts, for instance, the constitutionality of prohibiting as criminal, and punishing, homicide, assault, theft, rape, and so on. The state's authority to criminalize these traditional offenses is generally thought to derive from its "police power," which is considered "the most essential, the most insistent, and always one of the least limitable of the powers of government." Constitutional Law, 16A Am. Jur. 2d § 317; see generally Markus Dirk Dubber, The Police Power: Patriarchy and the Foundations of American Government (2005).

Just because it tends to have (or tends to be assumed to have) an obvious answer is no reason not to keep asking the question whether the state is permitted to invoke the criminal law—"to punish"—in a particular case. You should keep this question in the back of your mind as you encounter crimes in this book, in your criminal law class, or elsewhere. The state's power to criminalize, and to punish, is all too often simply assumed.

But how should one go about framing, never mind answering, this question when faced with a particular criminal statute? The courts have struggled with this problem; still, two general judicial approaches might be distinguished. The first approach focuses on whether the criminal statute in question violates some more or less "basic" individual right, and pays little, if any, attention to the source of the state's power to criminalize, and whatever inherent limits it might have. First among the basic rights driving the first approach are the rights guaranteed by the First Amendment—free speech in particular, but freedom of religion as well. See, e.g., Beauharnais v. Illinois, 343 U.S. 250 (1952) (criminal libel); R.A.V. v. St. Paul, 505 U.S. 377 (1992) (cross burning); see also Braunfeld v. Brown, 366 U.S. 599 (1961) (blue laws). The right of privacy, based partly on a substantive reading of the constitutional guarantee of "due process," has also attracted judicial attention. Lawrence v. Texas, 539 U.S. 558 (2003) (homosexual "sodomy"); Roe v. Wade, 410 U.S. 113 (1973) (abortion).

The second approach focuses on the police power as the acknowledged source of the state's power to punish, and then asks whether the particular statute falls within its—admittedly broad—scope. The U.S. Supreme Court for some time has been reluctant to vigorously scrutinize states' exercise of their police power. Cf. Lochner v. New York, 198 U.S. 45 (1905) (striking down, as illegitimate exercise of police power, state statute prohibiting bakery owners from "requiring or permitting" their employees to work more than ten hours a day). Unconstrained by federalist concerns about federal courts invalidating state statutes, state courts have been more willing to explore the limits of the police power wielded by their states' legislatures. See Wayne R. LaFave, Substantive Criminal Law § 3.3 (2d ed. 2003).

The following two cases illustrate the different approaches federal and state courts have taken to the question of the constitutional limits upon the legislature's answer to the question "what to punish?" Both strike down criminal possession statutes, but on different grounds.

Stanley v. Georgia

Supreme Court of the United States.
394 U.S. 557, 89 S.Ct. 1243 (1969).

■ MR. JUSTICE MARSHALL delivered the opinion of the Court.

An investigation of appellant's alleged bookmaking activities led to the issuance of a search warrant for appellant's home. Under authority of this warrant, federal and state agents secured entrance. They found very little evidence of bookmaking activity, but while looking through a desk drawer in an upstairs bedroom, one of the federal agents, accompanied by a state officer, found three reels of eight-millimeter film. Using a projector and screen found in an upstairs living room, they viewed the films. The state officer concluded that they were obscene and seized them. Since a further examination of the bedroom indicated that appellant occupied it, he was charged with possession of obscene matter and placed under arrest. He was later indicted for "knowingly hav[ing] possession of . . . obscene matter" in violation of Georgia law. Appellant was tried before a jury and convicted. The Supreme Court of Georgia affirmed.

. . . Appellant argues here, and argued below, that the Georgia obscenity statute, insofar as it punishes mere private possession of obscene matter, violates the First Amendment, as made applicable to the States by the Fourteenth Amendment. For reasons set forth below, we agree that the mere private possession of obscene matter cannot constitutionally be made a crime. * * *

. . . *Roth* [*v. United States,* 354 U.S. 476 (1957)] and its progeny [establish] that the First and Fourteenth Amendments recognize a valid governmental interest in dealing with the problem of obscenity. But the assertion of that interest cannot, in every context, be insulated from all constitutional protections. . . .

It is now well established that the Constitution protects the right to receive information and ideas. "This freedom [of speech and press] . . .

necessarily protects the right to receive. . . ." *Martin v. City of Struthers,* 319 U.S. 141, 143 (1943). This right to receive information and ideas, regardless of their social worth is fundamental to our free society. Moreover, in the context of this case—a prosecution for mere possession of printed or filmed matter in the privacy of a person's own home—that right takes on an added dimension. For also fundamental is the right to be free, except in very limited circumstances, from unwanted governmental intrusions into one's privacy.

"The makers of our Constitution undertook to secure conditions favorable to the pursuit of happiness. They recognized the significance of man's spiritual nature, of his feelings and of his intellect. They knew that only a part of the pain, pleasure and satisfactions of life are to be found in material things. They sought to protect Americans in their beliefs, their thoughts, their emotions and their sensations. They conferred, as against the Government, the right to be let alone—the most comprehensive of rights and the right most valued by civilized man." *Olmstead v. United States, 277 U.S. 438, 478 (1928)* (Brandeis, J., dissenting).

These are the rights that appellant is asserting in the case before us. He is asserting the right to read or observe what he pleases—the right to satisfy his intellectual and emotional needs in the privacy of his own home. He is asserting the right to be free from state inquiry into the contents of his library. Georgia contends that appellant does not have these rights, that there are certain types of materials that the individual may not read or even possess. Georgia justifies this assertion by arguing that the films in the present case are obscene. But we think that mere categorization of these films as "obscene" is insufficient justification for such a drastic invasion of personal liberties guaranteed by the First and Fourteenth Amendments. Whatever may be the justifications for other statutes regulating obscenity, we do not think they reach into the privacy of one's own home. If the First Amendment means anything, it means that a State has no business telling a man, sitting alone in his own house, what books he may read or what films he may watch. Our whole constitutional heritage rebels at the thought of giving government the power to control men's minds.

And yet, in the face of these traditional notions of individual liberty, Georgia asserts the right to protect the individual's mind from the effects of obscenity. We are not certain that this argument amounts to anything more than the assertion that the State has the right to control the moral content of a person's thoughts. To some, this may be a noble purpose, but it is wholly inconsistent with the philosophy of the First Amendment. As the Court said in *Kingsley International Pictures Corp.* v. *Regents,* 360 U.S. 684, 688–689 (1959), "this argument misconceives what it is that the Constitution protects. Its guarantee is not confined to the expression of ideas that are conventional or shared by a majority. . . . And in the realm of ideas it protects expression which is eloquent no less than that which is unconvincing." Nor is it relevant that obscene materials in general, or the particular films before the Court, are arguably devoid of any ideological content. The line between the transmission of ideas and mere entertainment is much too elusive for this Court to draw, if indeed such a line can be drawn at all. Whatever the power of the state to control public dissemination of ideas inimical to the public morality, it cannot constitutionally premise legislation on the desirability of controlling a person's private thoughts.

Perhaps recognizing this, Georgia asserts that exposure to obscene materials may lead to deviant sexual behavior or crimes of sexual violence. There appears to be little empirical basis for that assertion. But more important, if the State is only concerned about printed or filmed materials inducing antisocial conduct, we believe that in the context of private consumption of ideas and information we should adhere to the view that "among free men, the deterrents ordinarily to be applied to prevent crime are education and punishment for violations of the law...." *Whitney v. California,* 274 U.S. 357, 378 (1927) (Brandeis, J., concurring). Given the present state of knowledge, the State may no more prohibit mere possession of obscene matter on the ground that it may lead to antisocial conduct than it may prohibit possession of chemistry books on the ground that they may lead to the manufacture of homemade spirits.

It is true that in *Roth* this Court rejected the necessity of proving that exposure to obscene material would create a clear and present danger of antisocial conduct or would probably induce its recipients to such conduct. But that case dealt with public distribution of obscene materials and such distribution is subject to different objections. For example, there is always the danger that obscene material might fall into the hands of children, or that it might intrude upon the sensibilities or privacy of the general public.[10] No such dangers are present in this case.

Finally, we are faced with the argument that prohibition of possession of obscene materials is a necessary incident to statutory schemes prohibiting distribution. That argument is based on alleged difficulties of proving an intent to distribute or in producing evidence of actual distribution. We are not convinced that such difficulties exist, but even if they did we do not think that they would justify infringement of the individual's right to read or observe what he pleases. Because that right is so fundamental to our scheme of individual liberty, its restriction may not be justified by the need to ease the administration of otherwise valid criminal laws.

We hold that the First and Fourteenth Amendments prohibit making mere private possession of obscene material a crime.[11] ...

State v. Saiez

Supreme Court of Florida.
489 So.2d 1125 (1986).

■ BARKETT, J.

On February 24, 1984, Salvadore Saiez was charged with three violations of section 817.63, Florida Statutes (1983). Under counts 1 and 3 Saiez

10. The Model Penal Code provisions dealing with obscene materials are limited to cases of commercial dissemination. Model Penal Code § 251.4 (Prop. Official Draft 1962); see also Model Penal Code § 207.10 and comment 4 (Tent. Draft No. 6, 1957)....

11. What we have said in no way infringes upon the power of the State or Federal Government to make possession of other items, such as narcotics, firearms, or stolen goods, a crime. Our holding in the present case turns upon the Georgia statute's infringement of fundamental liberties protected by the First and Fourteenth Amendments. No First Amendment rights are involved in most statutes making mere possession criminal....

was charged with the unlawful possession of embossing machines. Under count 2 Saiez was charged with possession of incomplete credit cards. Section 817.63 provided in relevant part:

> Possession of machinery, plates or other contrivance or incomplete credit cards.—... *a person possessing with knowledge of its character any machinery, plates or any other contrivance designed to reproduce instruments purporting to be the credit cards of an issuer who has not consented to the preparation of such credit cards, violates this subsection* and is subject to the penalties set forth in s. 817.67(2).... (Emphasis added.)

Saiez filed a motion to dismiss counts 1 and 3, alleging that the portion of the statute prohibiting the possession of the machinery designed to reproduce instruments purporting to be credit cards was unconstitutional because it prohibited the mere possession of embossing machines regardless of whether they were being used legitimately. The trial court agreed [and] we affirm its decision. * * *

The legislature enacts penal statutes, such as section 817.63, under the state's "police power" which derives from the state's sovereign right to enact laws for the protection of its citizens. Such power, however, is not boundless and is confined to those acts which may be reasonably construed as expedient for protection of the public health, safety, welfare, or morals. The due process clauses of our federal and state constitutions do not prevent the legitimate interference with individual rights under the police power, but do place limits on such interference.

Moreover, in addition to the requirement that a statute's purpose be for the general welfare, the guarantee of due process requires that the means selected shall have a reasonable and substantial relation to the object sought to be attained and shall not be unreasonable, arbitrary, or capricious. *See Nebbia v. New York,* 291 U.S. 502, 525, 54 S. Ct. 505 (1934).

Section 817.63 was obviously an attempt by the legislature to curtail credit card fraud. There is no question that the curtailment of credit card fraud is a legitimate goal within the scope of the state's police power. Having established that the legislative purpose is proper, we must now determine whether the means chosen by the legislature bears a rational relationship to the concededly proper goal. We determine that it does not.

In *Delmonico v. State,* 155 So.2d 368 (Fla. 1963), this Court declared a statute that prohibited the possession of spearfishing equipment in an area of Monroe County to be unconstitutional. The Court explained:

> Fundamental to much of appellants' argument is the contention that the particular section of the statute here involved ... is improper because it fails to require proof of the intent essential to any crime such as a showing that the equipment was possessed with an intent to put it to unlawful use. Instead the law penalizes the mere possession of equipment which in itself is wholly innocent and virtually indispensable to the enjoyment of the presently lawful and unrestricted right of appellants in common with the public at large to engage in spearfishing in waters on all sides of the area covered by the statute....

In order to meet constitutional limitations on police regulation, this prohibition, i.e. against possession of objects having a common and widespread lawful use, must under our previous decisions be reasonably "required as incidental to the accomplishment of the primary purpose of the Act." There is little doubt that the penalty against possession of such equipment will simplify the problem of enforcing the primary prohibition against spearfishing in the area covered by the statute. Expediency, however, is not the test, and we conclude that convenience of enforcement does not warrant the broad restriction imposed by Sec. 370.172(3).

Id. at 369–70 (footnotes omitted). *See also Foster v. State,* 286 So.2d 549, 551 (Fla. 1973) ("it would be an unconstitutional act—in excess of the State's police power—to criminalize the simple possession of a screwdriver"). * * *

In *State v. Walker,* 444 So.2d 1137 (Fla. 2d DCA), the defendant had been charged with violating section 893.13(2)(a)7, Florida Statutes (1981), which prohibited the possession of a lawfully dispensed controlled substance in any container other than that in which the substance was originally delivered. Judge Grimes not[ed] that the prohibited conduct lacked any rational connection to the legislative purpose of controlling drug distribution....

In the instant case ... the legislature has chosen a means which is not reasonably related to achieving its legitimate legislative purpose.... As Judge Grimes phrased it in *Walker*, "without evidence of criminal behavior, the prohibition of this conduct lacks any rational relation to the legislative purpose" and "criminalizes activity that is otherwise inherently innocent." 444 So.2d at 1140. Such an exercise of the police power is unwarranted under the circumstances and violates the due process clauses of our federal and state constitutions.

QUESTIONS AND COMMENTS

1. On what grounds does the U.S. Supreme Court in *Stanley* strike down the possession statute under review? The Florida Supreme Court in *Saiez*? What individual rights do the statutes in *Stanley* and *Saiez* interfere with? Is there a fundamental right to possess embossing machines? Does imprisonment constitute an interference with an individual right that requires justification? For more on possession, see ch. 4 infra.

2. In *Stanley*, the Court dismissed the state's assertion of a link between the consumption of pornography and "deviant sexual behavior or crimes of sexual violence" on the ground that it lacks a sufficient empirical basis. Assume that, in the years since *Stanley*, this empirical basis has been supplied. Would this change the result in *Stanley*? Should it? How close do you think should be the link between a given conduct and future harm before the state may prohibit it, and punish it? Should the nature of the harm matter, aside from the likelihood of its occurrence? Should it matter whether the person engaging in the conduct foresaw the harm, or at least should have foreseen it?

3. In *Saiez*, the Florida Supreme Court found no "rational relationship" between criminalizing the possession of embossing machines and the concededly legitimate goal of preventing credit card fraud. If, as the court also concedes, embossing machines can be—and apparently are—used to perpetrate the very type of criminal conduct (credit card fraud) the legislature intended to prevent by passing the law in question, how can their possession bear no rational relation whatever to the law's purpose? How might the Florida legislature fix the statute to render it constitutional?

4. In *Stanley* and in *Saiez*, what difference did it make that the statutes under review were *criminal* statutes? What if they had been civil in nature—perhaps imposing a requirement that anyone in possession of the items in question register with the government or obtain a license, or employing a presumably civil sanction, including a letter of reprimand, forfeiture, or a small fine? Did the extent or nature of the punishment make a difference? Should it?

5. Based on *Stanley* and *Saiez*, what are the constitutional constraints upon a legislature's power to criminalize in general, and under its police power in particular? Assuming a particular behavior affects "the public health, safety, welfare, or morals," is the legislature free to choose the criminal law to prevent and punish it? Or must it first consider (and exhaust?) less intrusive, non-criminal, means? Assuming criminalization is appropriate, must it use less intrusive, criminal, means? Is it ever appropriate for the state to employ (criminal, non-criminal?) sanctions for "the protection of public ... *morals*," no matter how "expedient" they might be for that purpose?

6. The judge in *Blarek* remarked that the criminal conduct involved in that case was "victimless." What did he mean by that? Who is the victim in *Blarek*? Is the crime in *Blarek* victimless in the same sense as the crimes in *Stanley* and *Saiez*? Can you think of other victimless crimes? Do the decisions in *Stanley* and *Saiez* turn on the issue of victimlessness?

H. The Landscape of Crime (What Is Punishable?)

Modern American criminal law comes in all shapes and sizes, some of which pop up in *Blarek*. *Blarek* is a federal case; it deals with federal criminal law, i.e., crimes defined by the federal legislature, a body of law that has grown exponentially over the past century or so. Although state law continues to account for the vast bulk of criminal law, on the books and in action, crimes can be found on all levels of government, from the international community to the federal government to the states and all smaller governmental entities within each state, including counties, cities, villages, and so on.

Charter of the City of Buffalo, New York

§ 33. Ordinance Powers.

The council shall have power to enact ordinances:

(1) To define and prevent disorderly conduct; to prevent disorderly assemblages; disturbing noises and drunkenness in public

places; to punish vagrants, beggars and disorderly persons as defined by law. . . .

(11) To regulate the use of the public streets, alleys, parks and park approaches, wharves and public grounds. . . .

(14) To protect the public health.

§ 37. Imprisonment.

The council in any ordinance or by general ordinance may provide that any person, upon conviction of a violation thereof, shall be fined or committed to the Erie county penitentiary for such time as the court or magistrate shall fix, not exceeding six months. . . .

While American legislatures have claimed a monopoly on criminal lawmaking for at least fifty years, after centuries of judicial criminal lawmaking, the other two branches of government continue to participate in this task. Although judges are no longer authorized to create new crimes, they continue to make criminal law insofar as every crime defined by the legislature requires interpretation. Some crimes require more judicial filling-in than others. A classic example here is "racketeering" (or RICO), one of the crimes in the *Blarek* case:

> RICO is incomplete on its face. RICO forbids any person to "conduct or participate ... in the conduct of" any "enterprise ... through a pattern of racketeering activity." [18 U.S.C. § 1962(c).] The statute defines the crucial term "enterprise" as "includ[ing] any individual, partnership, corporation, association, or other legal entity, and any union or group of individuals associated in fact." [Id. at § 1961(4).] This formulation literally excludes nothing; any "individual" or any "group of individuals," however constituted, is eligible to be a RICO "enterprise." In truth, the statutory "definition" of "enterprise" is no definition at all, but only a directive to courts not to limit "enterprise" to the formally structured entities that it commonly denotes—such as corporations, partnerships, or associations. But beyond conveying that "enterprise" is not merely one of these entities, the statute affords no clue as to what else an enterprise is (and, more importantly, is not). That task necessarily falls upon the courts.
>
> The meaning of "pattern of racketeering activity" is also incompletely specified. According to the statutory "definition," this element of the offense "requires at least two acts of racketeering activity." [Id. at § 1961(5).] This, too, is not a genuine definition, for it states only a necessary and not a sufficient condition for finding a pattern: there must be at least two racketeering offenses. But while the statute "assumes that there is something to a ... pattern beyond simply the number of predicate acts involved," the text "does not identify ... [what] these additional prerequisites" are; this, too, is for courts to work out.

Dan M. Kahan, "Lenity and Federal Common Law Crimes," 1994 Sup. Ct. Rev. 345, 378–79.

"Money laundering," the central crime at issue in *Blarek*, is another—yet more recent—addition to the federal crimes catalogue. It too is well-known for its flexibility, and vagueness, with the concomitant shift of lawmaking authority from the legislature to other branches of government. (We will take a closer look at money laundering later on in this book, in ch. 11.)

Both RICO and money laundering are good examples of so-called "white collar crimes," a loosely defined category of crimes often distinguished from so-called "street crimes." There is no consensus on just what a "white collar crime" is; it "denotes crimes of high status to some, while to others it refers to either occupational or organizational illegality. Some concentrate on the nature of the offense; others, on its consequences." Stanton Wheeler, "White Collar Crime: History of an Idea," 4 Encyclopedia of Crime and Justice 1652 (1983). Is it a "white collar crime" if a foreman, or a CEO, or a corporation, is criminally liable for negligently causing the death of factory workers in a foreseeable accident on the shop floor? Does it matter?

"White collar crimes," and modern crimes in general, often involve criminal lawmaking by the *executive*. Courts have not been alone in putting meat on RICO's bare bones; federal prosecutors have also played a significant definitional role, by exercising their essentially unreviewable discretion to pick and choose among the myriad of cases that, on their face, might fall under the statutory definition. (More on RICO in ch. 8.)

So-called "regulatory" crimes are in large part defined by the executive branch, i.e., by administrative agencies or officials whose rules and regulations are backed up by the threat of criminal sanction. Consider, for instance, the criminalization provision of the N.Y. Public Health Law:

§ 12–b. Wilful violation of health laws.

1. A person who wilfully violates or refuses or omits to comply with any lawful order or regulation prescribed by any local board of health or local health officer, is guilty of a misdemeanor....

2. A person who wilfully violates any provision of this chapter, or any regulation lawfully made or established by any public officer or board under authority of this chapter, the punishment for violating which is not otherwise prescribed by this chapter or any other law, is punishable by imprisonment not exceeding one year, or by a fine not exceeding two thousand dollars or by both.

The crimes in *Blarek* are all defined, more or less, in the U.S. Code. In fact, they all appear in Title 18 of the U.S. Code, entitled the "Criminal Code." A large number of federal—and state—crimes, however, appear not in the criminal code, but in noncriminal codes devoted to specific policy matters. For instance, the panoply of federal drug crimes—including some punishable by death—can be found, not in Title 18, but in Title 21, dedicated to "Food and Drugs," the first three chapters of which are devoted to "adulterated or misbranded foods and drugs," "teas," and "filled milk," respectively.

Blarek highlights one further example of criminal lawmaking by a branch of government other than the legislature: the federal sentencing guidelines. These highly detailed punishment guidelines are drafted by the federal sentencing commission, a *sui generis* quasi-agency billed as an "independent commission in the judicial branch of the United States," 28 U.S.C. § 991(a). Despite this description, the commission "is not a court and does not exercise judicial power," id., and its rulemaking is subject to the notice and comment requirements of the Administrative Procedure Act, id. § 994(x).

Since the federal legislature never managed to reform its criminal law, which remains scattered among the fifty titles of the U.S. Code and is well-known for being inconsistent, duplicative, and otherwise ill-drafted, the sentencing commission did far more than match punishments to existing, legislatively defined, crimes. It instead dramatically systematized and simplified the federal law of crimes, creating a federal-criminal-code-behind-the-code in the process.

> Because of the failure of code reform, the drafters of the federal sentencing guidelines ... faced ... the task of rationalizing the buzzing confusion of the federal criminal "code," which by then had added to the dense jungle of common-law distinctions and traditional statutes any number of novel genetically-engineered products of the mad legislator's laboratory—RICO, money laundering, carjacking, and a host of jurisdictionally warped variants involving mail, travel and the high seas.
>
> [T]he resulting guidelines bear all the formal attributes of a penal code. Splitting some offenses into what are in effect multiple degrees ..., and combining others under the same guideline provision, the guidelines create, in effect, a simplified codification of the behavior criminalized by federal law. By rendering the offense of conviction ordinarily insignificant for sentencing purposes, and replacing the code offenses for these purposes with comprehensive codified guidelines, the new federal sentencing regime to a considerable extent rationalizes and displaces congressionally-enacted criminal statutes.

Gerard E. Lynch, "The Sentencing Guidelines As a Not–So–Model Penal Code," 7 Fed. Sentencing Rep. 112 (1994).

CHAPTER 2

THE PROCESS OF CRIME AND PUNISHMENT

This is a book about substantive criminal law—or criminal law, for short. It's not about criminal procedure, nor is it about prison law, the other two major components of the law of crime and punishment. The study, and doctrine, of criminal law falls into two parts, the general part and the special part. The general part concerns itself with the general principles of criminal law, including the formal and substantive prerequisites of criminal liability, such as legality, jurisdiction, actus reus, mens rea, and defenses (most importantly, justifications and excuses). The special part includes the definitions of the various types of conduct the commission of which may give rise to criminal liability, provided the basic rerequisites identified in the general part are met.

Criminal procedure, by contrast, concerns itself with the application of the norms of substantive criminal law. It addresses questions raised in the investigation, prosecution, and adjudication of violations of the criminal law.

Prison law, sometimes called the law of corrections, rounds out the law of the criminal process in the broad sense. It concerns itself not with the definition of criminal norms, nor with their application, but with the infliction of sanctions imposed in the criminal process in the narrow sense. The name "prison law" is misleading in that it focuses on one sanction—incarceration—that is common, but by no means the only type of punishment recognized in American criminal law. Other criminal sanctions include capital punishment, fines, supervised release (parole and probation), and forfeiture.

Although our attention will be limited to substantive criminal law, a basic understanding of other aspects of the law of crime and punishment, in particular the law of criminal procedure, will be helpful for several reasons. To begin with, it's important to recognize that the cases collected in this book represent a tiny fraction of the business of American criminal law. The flowchart of the criminal justice system that appears at the end of this book makes clear that much, probably most, criminal activity goes unreported. And even among those relatively few crimes that are reported by private persons or observed by state officials, only a fraction make it past the investigative stage to a prosecution, and fewer yet to an adjudication. Of the cases that are adjudicated, only a very few (less than 10%) make it before a jury, as the vast bulk are disposed through a guilty plea.

Most of the cases in this book are picked from the tiny subset of cases that have made it to a jury trial and then went on to generate a reasoned opinion by an appellate court judge. They are nothing like the norm of cases in American criminal law. By contrast, in German criminal law, for instance, every criminal judgment at trial—of conviction or of acquittal—requires a written judgment setting out its rationale. The judgment of the American criminal trial is more cryptic, and therefore far less susceptible to scrutiny and study: guilty or not guilty.

Note also that, in the United States, the defendant has the right to appeal a conviction, but—unlike in other legal systems, such as, once again in Germany—the prosecution has no corresponding right to appeal an acquittal.[a] (The constitutional protection against double jeopardy is thought to prohibit this.) As a result, the appellate court opinions in this casebook generally will address the question of whether a conviction after a trial before a jury should be reversed for one reason or another, thus necessitating a new trial, should the prosecution decide to try again. Since it's the defendant-appellant who is asking for a reversal, she—and not the prosecution—is the one who bears the burden of convincing the appellate court. Furthermore appellate courts show considerable deference to decisions of the trial court and, most importantly, the ultimate factual determination of a jury. It's thus no surprise that the vast majority of appeals result in an affirmance of the conviction at trial—no matter how many cases *in this book* should go the defendant's way.

Last but not least, it helps to familiarize oneself with the basic procedural postures of a criminal case for the simple reason that otherwise many of the appellate opinions in this book won't make much sense. When a court addresses an appeal, for instance, from a denial of a "demurrer to the indictment," a grant of a motion for a "directed verdict," or a denial of a "petition for habeas corpus," it helps to know a little about what these procedural terms mean.

A. AN OVERVIEW OF CRIMINAL PROCEDURE

A typical case normally begins either with a complaint by a private citizen, or when police directly observe what looks like criminal activity. In the former instance, police usually have time to investigate the complaint through questioning of witnesses and examination of physical evidence. If they decide they have enough evidence to establish "probable cause"[65] that a particular individual committed the crime, they will often approach a magistrate and swear out an arrest warrant on the suspected culprit (as well as, perhaps, a search warrant autho-

a. In jurisdictions that have adopted sentencing guidelines, the prosecution and the defense both can appeal sentences on the ground that they deviate from the prescribed guidelines. See, e.g., 18 U.S.C. § 3742.—EDS.

65. This term ... is found in the Fourth Amendment. ["The right of the people to be secure in their persons, houses, papers, and effects, against unreasonable searches and seizures, shall not be violated, and no warrants shall issue, but upon probable cause, supported by oath or affirmation, and particularly describing the place to be searched, and the persons or things to be seized."]

rizing search of his home). When police observe crime, on the other hand, there is normally no time to secure a warrant. In such cases, if the police have probable cause to believe the individual has committed or is committing a crime, they may arrest him without a warrant; if they do not have probable cause, they may still be able to question him and, if probable cause then develops, arrest him.

During arrest the police may conduct a search of the individual and begin to question him concerning the alleged offense. Soon after arrest, the arrestee is taken to the stationhouse for "booking," which usually involves being fingerprinted and photographed. At this point, when minor charges are involved, the police may release the arrestee on "stationhouse bail." For serious charges, the person usually remains in custody and a more formal interrogation may take place; additionally, the arrestee may be required to participate in a lineup or submit to scientific tests (such as blood tests) if they were not administered in the field, and further searches may also occur.

Fairly soon after arrest and booking (usually within 48 hours) comes the initial appearance in front of a judicial officer (sometimes called an "arraignment on the warrant"). Here the arrestee is informed of the charge (usually written up by the police or prosecutor in the form of a "complaint"), and of his rights to counsel and to remain silent. In many states, if the charges are minor, the magistrate may proceed to try the case at this time as well. In felony cases, if there is no arrest warrant, the magistrate must determine, either at the initial appearance or at a proceeding soon thereafter, whether there is probable cause to detain the individual. If probable cause is found, or there is an arrest warrant, a decision is then made as to whether the arrestee can be released on personal recognizance, subjected to bail conditions, or detained preventively.

In the meantime, the prosecutor formalizes the charges against the arrestee, now more appropriately called the defendant. In some states, the prosecutor need merely file an "information" describing the charges. In other states and the federal system, he must go to a grand jury to obtain an "indictment" stating the charges. In the former jurisdictions, he is usually required to make out a prima facie case on the charges in the information during a preliminary hearing in front of a magistrate. In the latter jurisdictions, he may have to go through the preliminary hearing before he can get to the grand jury.

The Constitution allows the defendant to *demand* counsel only at certain isolated "stages" of the pretrial process such as interrogation or a lineup identification. But in practice counsel is often appointed as early as the initial appearance. Once appointed, counsel can make several different types of pretrial motions, seeking dismissal of the case, change of venue, suppression of illegally obtained evidence, discovery of evidence, or the implementation of a statutory "speedy trial" right. Many of these motions cannot be made after trial or judgment. Defense counsel may also enter into negotiations with the prosecutor with a view to having his client plead guilty in exchange for a reduction in charges or a lenient sentence recommendation.

Sometime before trial, the defendant is brought before the court that will try him. With misdemeanants, as already noted, this is often the initial appearance. With more serious charges, a separate stage, called the "arraignment on the information" (or indictment) occurs, at which the court informs the defendant of his charges and asks him how he pleads. There are three basic pleas: not guilty, guilty and nolo contendere [literally "I don't want to contest"]. If either of the latter two pleas is entered, the court conducts a hearing to ensure the plea is voluntarily and intelligently entered and to discover the terms of any plea agreement that has been reached. Roughly 90 percent of all cases that are not dismissed previously by the police or the prosecutor are adjudicated via plea.

If the defendant pleads not guilty, the case is set for trial. In most cases, the defendant is entitled to a jury, which consists of twelve people in federal court and varies from six to twelve in state courts. In jury cases, voir dire of the jury panel is conduct, during which counsel for both sides, using peremptory and "for cause" challenges, attempt to obtain a jury to their liking. Most states also require that notice of an alibi or insanity defense be made prior to or at this time.

At trial, the prosecution bears the burden of proving each element of the crime beyond a reasonable doubt. After the presentation of evidence, with the defendant's case following the state's case, a verdict is reached and sentence imposed. In jury trials, the judge normally imposes sentence after a separate hearing, although some states permit sentencing by the trial jury.

An appeal may be automatic or discretionary, depending upon the level of the original trial court and the type of crime (misdemeanor or felony) involved. For instance, many states provide for automatic appeal from courts "not of record" [e.g., small claims courts] to a higher court at which a record of the proceedings is kept (and at which the charges will usually be adjudicated *de novo*), but make further appeal to the state supreme court or intermediate appellate court discretionary.... An appeal must usually be taken within a specified time limit. If the defendant does appeal, the bail question may again arise. After sentence and appeal, the defendant may also "collaterally" attack the verdict through a writ of habeas corpus or coram nobis.

A major variation on the [model] described above occurs when the grand jury indictment *precedes* arrest. In these cases, typically involving political corruption or organized crime, the grand jury functions not as a check on charge selection but as an investigative body. When arrest is predicated on an indictment, there is normally no need for a preliminary hearing other than an initial appearance to set bail, advise the defendant of his rights and appoint counsel, if necessary. No probable cause determination is necessary since the grand jury has already found it exists.

Charles H. Whitebread & Christopher Slobogin, Criminal Procedure: An Analysis of Cases and Concepts 12–15 (4th ed. 2000).

B. PLEA BARGAINING

The plea bargaining process is as common as it is controversial. Consider the following excerpts.

> The academic defense of plea-bargaining has generally taken one or more of three forms. First, many have concluded that plea bargaining is indispensable to the system of criminal justice—that without it, the courts would be overwhelmed by a mass of trials they would be unable to handle.[1] A second defense is that plea bargaining is both constitutionally permissible and morally legitimate, since both sides voluntarily engage in and benefit from the practice. Finally, some commentators suggest that the abolition of plea bargaining would be impossible because the parties would continue the practice even if higher authorities tried to curb it.
>
> Although there is a substantial literature on plea bargaining, little of it originates from the vantage point of someone who knows the system from the inside. Plea bargaining, by its very nature, is a closed-door affair that is not readily amenable to observation by outsiders. I bring to this discussion a perspective based on experience with the system: I worked for nearly five and one-half years as a "professional plea bargainer," both as a public defender and as a prosecutor, in the criminal courts of two very different midsized jurisdictions....
>
> In my view, plea bargaining is not an administrative necessity for two reasons. First, most criminal defendants do not want trials and would not choose to go to trial even if they faced no penalty for doing so. Moreover, my experience suggests that with appropriate administrative reforms and changes in attitudes, courts are actually capable of handling substantially more trials than they currently do....
>
> Whether or not plea bargaining is constitutional in the narrow legal sense, I think it is wrong to think of it as a voluntary practice—a deal that makes both sides better off. For the small number of defendants who actually want to go to trial ... plea bargains must be enforced by substantial coercion from judges, prosecutors, and even public defenders. It is these groups who most strongly support plea bargaining and who work the system to their advantage (and to the disadvantage of defendants).
>
> Finally, even though many actors in the judicial system have substantial discretion, I do not believe that this discretion must inevitably be used to sneak plea bargaining back in through the back door when higher authorities try to curb it. My experience suggests that

1. Indeed, this argument was given support by the U.S. Supreme Court itself in a classic statement in Santobello v. New York, 404 U.S. 257, 260 (1971), in which the court claimed: "Properly administered, it [plea bargaining] should be encouraged. If every criminal charge were subjected to a full-scale trial, the states and the federal government would need to multiply by many times the number of judges and court facilities."

when a legal culture develops that allows or encourages trials, all the parties involved find a way to adapt to that legal culture....

It has been my experience that judges, lawyers, and even police officers often love plea bargaining. They love it not because it prevents the breakdown of the criminal justice system but because it helps them avoid work and stress. Defense attorneys universally collected their fees up front,[9] public defenders were paid a set salary, and salaried prosecutors and judges all got paid no differently whether a case was settled in a 60-second negotiation or disposed of by a trial. So, unlike the medical specialist, who is paid handsomely for the stress and work of an intense surgical procedure, and who is rewarded and admired by a professional peer group as well, the attorney pushing for trials received no financial or professional rewards of any kind. Indeed, the opposite was true. Defense attorneys all knew that if they brought too many cases to trial, they would be seen as either unreasonable and worthy of professional ostracism or as a fool who was too weak to achieve "client control."

Many attorneys I knew became masters of the fine art of controlling their clients. Some liked to engage in "chair therapy," in which a client who insists on a trial is made to sit in the hall of the courthouse (or in the courthouse lockup) for days on end during courthouse trial terms, waiting for his day in court, until he accepts a deal. Some (usually unintentionally) resorted to "good cop/bad cop" routines, in which a resistant defendant is subjected to the screams of his or her attorney, followed by the lawyer's associate, who tries to calmly help the accused to see the light. Usually, however, defense attorneys, aware that incredible trial penalties were attached to the "right" to a jury trial, only needed to tell a defendant of the unconscionable sentences that had been meted out to others who dared to create work for a judge.

I quickly learned that prosecutors ... were the real judges when it came to sentencing decisions. By allowing plea bargaining judges successfully dumped the burdens of sentencing most criminal defendants onto prosecutors. How did prosecutors handle this sentencing burden? The answer, I soon learned, was "any way they wanted to." There were no official rules that bound me or my fellow prosecutors in the making of plea-bargaining offers. (The only unwritten rule was to avoid creating bad public relations, either with the press or with the judiciary.) Prosecutors, then, had nearly complete discretion in deciding what offers to make to defense counsel. There were many instances in which prosecutors would decide the appropriate sentence; offer it to defense counsel who then accepted; then search the crimes code for some offense that would produce the "correct" sentence.

This is not to say that prosecutors spent long periods of time agonizing over appropriate sentences. A prosecutor would often work

9. No defense attorney in his or her right mind would ever wait for disposition of a case to attempt to collect a fee. In fact, judges will often grant a continuance on the basis of a defense attorney's vague, in-court reference to "Rule 1" (code for "I haven't been paid yet").

through a pile of cases in machine-gun fashion, making snap decisions as to appropriate punishments in just a few minutes per case. These few minutes (perhaps 3 or so for misdemeanors and 10 for serious felonies) included all the time devoted to (1) examining police reports and all the evidence; (2) reviewing the defendant's prior criminal history; (3) deciding the defendant's fate as to sentencing; and (4) putting the plea offer into a form letter to be sent to defense counsel.

The speed at which assistant district attorneys decide sentences, often involving substantial periods of incarceration, was amazing. But what was also noteworthy was the surprising lack of training we prosecutors received for our sentencing roles. Given no official training, new prosecutors (and almost all prosecutors I encountered were relatively "new" in the sense that most saw the district attorney's office as merely a career steppingstone) were forced to go by their instincts or by the instincts of benighted others around them.

Although quality of defense counsel, in my opinion, never seemed to make much difference during trials (the witnesses, after all, do most of the talking), defense counsel quality seemed to make an enormous difference in plea bargaining. Some attorneys were skillful at power-coercive brinkmanship. Others were completely incompetent at negotiations....

... Although civility and intelligence are usually assets in most professions, plea bargaining tends to exalt the negative traits of human character. Some of the most effective negotiators were arrogant, aggressive, unreasonable, and even ill informed as to the law. These attorney traits formed part of the calculus that prosecutors used in deciding what to offer. Fortunately ... most attorneys chose to be reasonably pleasant, but the more crude, hot tempered, and unreasonable an attorney was, the more many felt obliged to appease him or her with a better deal. Plea bargaining thus made the practice of criminal law one in which legal knowledge and civility took a back seat....

That plea bargaining has little to do with practicing a learned profession can be illustrated in a different way through the story of someone I shall refer to as Bill White, who was the office manager of the ... District Attorney's Office. Although he never attended a day of law school, White was offering plea bargains to defense attorneys just three months into his job. In court, judges would sometimes ask, "Who made that deal?" If a defense attorney answered, "Bill White," it was accepted by all parties as completely legitimate. Ironically, Bill White was one of the most competent people I have ever known and an excellent plea bargainer. The fact that he lacked any legal education or a license to practice law was of little practical consequence. I am convinced that the average car salesman or real estate agent with a few days of instruction could become an adequate plea bargainer....

The danger of convicting an innocent person pursuant to a plea bargain ... is real. For reasons I have never fully understood, many prosecutors are loath to risk losing a case at trial. They will therefore resort to offering incredibly lenient punishments to assure the entry of guilty pleas in those weak cases that probably would and should be lost at trial (in which the reasonable doubt standard would necessarily come into play). For instance, I have witnessed cases in which the charge of rape was ultimately reduced to harassment; armed robbery that should have called for a five-year sentence reduced to a sentence of a few months; and countless cases calling for some jail time reduced to probationary cases. In such situations, no good is done. The guilty get off so easily that they can only lose respect for the system. And the few innocent here and there (those the system was originally designed to protect but probably no longer does) are stigmatized by a criminal conviction and must feel constitutionally abandoned. One might say that the innocent could insist on their day in court. But with their own lawyer forcefully urging them to accept an offer, and given the typically outrageous generosity of the offer coupled with the typically outrageous penalty if they go to trial and lose, only the most courageous among them would refuse this safe but dehumanizing way out. As Albert Alschuler wrote, "to turn a substantial portion of a defendant's punishment on a single tactical decision is ... to assign to the defendant a responsibility that he cannot fairly be required to bear."[24]

David Lynch, "The Impropriety of Plea Agreements: A Tale of Two Counties," 19 Law & Soc. Inquiry 115 (1994).

Most criminal prosecutions are settled without a trial. The parties to these settlements trade various risks and entitlements: the defendant relinquishes the right to go to trial (along with any chance of acquittal), while the prosecutor gives up the entitlement to seek the highest sentence or pursue the most serious charges possible. The resulting bargains differ predictably from what would have happened had the same cases been taken to trial. Defendants who bargain for a plea serve lower sentences than those who do not. On the other hand, everyone who pleads guilty is, by definition, convicted, while a substantial minority of those who go to trial are acquitted.

There is something puzzling about the polarity of contemporary reactions to this practice. Most legal scholars oppose plea bargaining, finding it both inefficient and unjust. Nevertheless, most participants in the plea bargaining process, including (perhaps especially) the courts, seem remarkably untroubled by it. Not only is the practice widespread, but participants generally approve of it. Why is plea bargaining at once so widely condemned and so widely tolerated?

[P]lea bargains are *both* paradigmatic bargains of the sort we routinely enforce in other contexts *and* the product of a seriously flawed bargaining structure. The critics, for their part, have misused or misapplied classical contract arguments for limiting contractual autonomy. Properly understood, classical contract theory supports the freedom to bargain over criminal punishment. At the same time, there are fundamental structural impediments in the plea bargaining context

24. Albert W. Alschuler, "The Changing Plea Bargaining Debate," 69 *Cal. L. Rev.* 652, 668 (1981).

that may underlie the widespread antipathy to the practice. These barriers to efficient bargaining are not, however, grounds for abolition, but instead suggest more focused reforms of current practices....

[A]bolishing plea bargaining would not solve, and might even aggravate, the problem of failing to separate the innocent from the guilty. But abolition is not the only possibility.... By altering the doctrine that governs such issues as when and how bargains are enforced, the consequences of defendants' mistakes, and how background prices (i.e., post-trial sentences) are set, the state can reduce the incentives for strategic bargaining and improve the efficiency and fairness of the plea bargaining process....

[T]he most problematic feature of plea bargaining [is that] the dynamic of the parties' interaction makes it harder for innocent defendants to identify themselves. The normative question is what ought to be done about that problem at the level of legal doctrine.

[A]bolition would likely only worsen innocent defendants' plight. In order to accommodate the dramatic increase in trials, the trial process itself would have to truncated, as Stephen Schulhofer's famous discussion of the Philadelphia process shows. The mini-trials that took the place of bargaining in Philadelphia were brief affairs, most lasting no more than an hour; the pretrial preparation on both sides was minimal. Altering the trial process in this way necessarily increases the error rate (unless our current trial system is nonsensical), meaning that it raises the rate at which innocent defendants are convicted. That, in turn, alters prosecutors' incentives when making decisions about which cases to take to trial. Indeed, it may alter police incentives when making arrests. Police officers and prosecutors alike can afford to be less careful in screening their cases if the trial "backstop" becomes more casual.

In short, prohibiting plea bargaining would likely raise the proportion of innocents who are convicted of crimes. The problem of defendants' inability to use their private information in bargaining would disappear since bargaining would disappear. But if the trial process itself led to a substantially higher rate of conviction of innocent defendants, the ex ante position of those defendants would not improve....

[We instead propose] looking to appropriate contract analogies [to] identify[] opportunities for productive change in the doctrine.

1. Enforceability

When defendants promise to plead guilty in return for government concessions and then do so, they are legally entitled to the concessions. At the same time, if the defendant fails to perform, the prosecutor need not perform either. But while the exchange of promises is, to this extent, supported by legal sanctions, plea bargains are not enforced according to standard, garden-variety contract principles of offer and acceptance. As a consequence, defendants' ability to rely on government promises is much lower than in comparable private settings....

The current regime treats the prosecutor's promise (even if formalized) not as an "offer" that the defendant may "accept" and then enforce, but as an invitation to negotiate, with the deal sealed only when the parties go to court. The prosecutor's proposal, even if accepted, typically does not define the price of the defendant's offense—the only obligation is that the prosecutor mouth the right words at sentencing. The judge sets the price. To put it differently, in contract terms the bargain is not really between the defendant and the prosecutor, since the prosecutor can make only token commitments. The true contracting parties are the defendant and the judge. The prosecutor acts as the judge's negotiating agent, but the judge retains the authority to accept or reject his agent's work. . . .

Enforcing prosecutors' sentencing promises, [however, would] reduce (1) uncertainty, (2) transaction costs, and (3) the disparity between post-plea and post-trial sentences.

These changes would plainly make innocent defendants better off. Currently, if a prosecutor recommends a given sentence in a given case, the judge may either accept the recommendation or ignore it and give the defendant something much worse. Moreover, the innocent defendant may refuse to deal and go to trial, where (if convicted) his sentence will be worse still. Enforcing prosecutors' promises would eliminate the second of these options, and thereby reduce the incidence of the third (by making prosecutors' promises more reliable). Guilty defendants might benefit from enforcement as well, given the reduction in transaction costs. But the biggest winners would be the innocent.

2. Mistake

In all bargains, there is a risk that one party or the other may foolishly agree to terms that do not promote self-interest. This risk affects guilty and innocent defendants alike, but it disproportionately afflicts the innocent. If the defendant is innocent, the probability of conviction must be substantially less than one hundred percent, a fact that the price of the plea bargain ought to take into account. But risk averse innocent defendants may accept bargains that treat them not merely as probably guilty, but as certain to be convicted. Thus, when an innocent defendant's lawyer erroneously prices her client's case, and negotiates a deal that presumes certain conviction, there is a good chance the bad deal will be accepted. In short, mistakes in bargaining surely affect the whole system, but are particularly likely to determine outcomes in cases where guilt is in some question. . . .

But regulating mistake directly is hard, if not impossible. The problem is that one cannot distinguish between good and bad bargaining by looking at the *process* by which the lawyers reached their deal. A two-minute conversation with the prosecutor in the hallway with only slight advance preparation may represent evidence of sloppiness and sloth. Or it may be that defense counsel, who has a great deal of experience in dealing with similar cases, knows the market price, realizes that investigation is extremely unlikely to lead anywhere, and understands how to get to the best offer expeditiously. In a context where bargaining skill depends more on knowledge of information about *other* cases than on case-specific preparation, it is hard to judge a defense attorney's performance by his behavior in any one case.

The only feasible alternative is to review not process but outcomes. A bargained-for sentence that substantially exceeds the norm for the crime is probably due to some kind of defense attorney mistake; at the least, the bargain requires some explaining. The judge is in a poor position to supervise the bargaining process, but he is in a very good position to recognize unusually high sentences. This is particularly true if high sentence recommendations are caused by problems of information revelation that cause defendants' claims of factual innocence to be discounted. Defense attorney mistakes and the innocence problem both argue for treating a bargained-for sentence as a ceiling, but not a floor. Downward judicial revision should be, and generally is, available at the judge's discretion. But the law should go further: downward discretion should be *encouraged* whenever the sentence is substantially above the "market level" in the relevant jurisdiction....

3. Background Prices and Duress

The scenario that most troubles critics of plea bargaining is the innocent defendant who faces a life sentence if convicted at trial and is offered a plea bargain at a recommended sentence of a few years. The huge disparity between the post-trial sentence and the plea sentence presumably leads the defendant, though innocent, to accept the deal. Frank Easterbrook rightly points out that this story is not necessarily a condemnation of plea bargaining. The sentencing differential may simply reflect a low probability of conviction (based on evidence available to the government), or it may stem from limited prison space in the relevant jurisdiction. In either of those cases, the defendant is much better off with the offer than without it: a murder defendant who has a fifty-percent chance of winning at trial *wants* a regime that allows the prosecutor to offer a ten-year sentence with a plea. The situation is a sad one, but preventing the offer only makes it sadder.

The plea offer in such a case does not amount to duress. But there *is* a duress problem with large sentencing differentials in some types of cases, a problem that may disproportionately harm innocent defendants.... [W]here the legislature drafts broad criminal statutes and then attaches mandatory sentences to those statutes, prosecutors have an unchecked opportunity to overcharge and generate easy pleas, a form of strategic behavior that exacerbates the structural deficiencies endemic to plea bargaining. [I]t is possible to avoid [this difficulty by] reducing overbreadth in criminal statutes.... If virtually all of the behavior that falls within a given statute merits the mandatory sentence the legislature attaches, then the strategic problem disappears. But reducing overbreadth has its costs: it occupies prosecutors and courts with detailed elements of detailed crimes, thereby increasing the expense of trial.

Robert E. Scott & William J. Stuntz, "Plea Bargaining as Contract," 101 Yale L.J. 1909, 1909–11, 1949–50, 1953–57, 1959–61, 1965–66 (1992).

Is plea bargaining problematic only because it might disadvantage defendants? What about victims? Should victims be included in the plea bargaining process? What about the public's desire for retribution? Is plea bargaining defensible under any (all?) of the traditional theories of punishment? Cf. Russell L. Christopher, "The Prosecutor's Dilemma: Bargains and Punishments," 72 Fordham L. Rev. 93 (2004).

There is now a large academic literature on American plea bargaining. Here are some further samples: John H. Langbein, "Torture and Plea Bargaining," 46 U. Chi. L. Rev. 3 (1978); Albert W. Alschuler, "Implementing the Criminal Defendant's Right to Trial: Alternatives to the Plea Bargaining System," 50 U. Chi. L. Rev. 931 (1983); Stephen J. Schulhofer, "Is Plea Bargaining Inevitable?," 97 Harv. L. Rev. 1037 (1984); Ronald Wright & Marc Miller, "The Screening/Bargaining Tradeoff," 55 Stan. L. Rev. 29 (2002). For a historical perspective, see George Fisher, Plea Bargaining's Triumph: A History of Plea Bargaining in America (2003).

For a critical discussion of American plea bargaining from a comparative perspective, with proposals for reform, see Markus Dirk Dubber, "American Plea Bargains, German Lay Judges, and the Crisis of Criminal Procedure," 49 Stan. L. Rev. 547 (1997). Once thought to be a peculiarly American practice, plea bargaining is now recognized as a phenomenon in criminal justice systems throughout the world, though at times with considerable embarrassment. The secret use of pre-trial bargaining in Germany, for instance, was not exposed until the publication of a pseudonymous article in 1982. Some German commentators have argued that plea bargaining may be legitimate, or at least no less legitimate than the traditional criminal trial process:

> Based on an account of the traditional German criminal process as an inquisitorial proceeding dominated by a powerful judge whose sole aim is to obtain a confession from the defendant, some German commentators have welcomed plea bargaining. According to this account, the German defendant's role in the proceedings is entirely passive, and is limited to responding to the interrogation by the presiding judge who knows the case file prepared by the prosecution that contains all facts relevant to the resolution of the case. The defendant develops no evidence on her own; she merely motions the court to do the investigating for her. She may request that the court call certain witnesses and appoint certain experts, but she never takes the active role of developing a case and presenting it to the court.
>
> Against the background of this image of the German criminal process, some German commentators regard plea bargaining as an opportunity for the defendant to take a more active role in the process. In this view, plea bargaining strengthens the defendant's position by permitting her to shape the proceedings that will settle her fate. Plea bargaining appears as a process that permits the resolution of disputes in the course of a rational discourse among equals. With an occasional nod in the direction of modern discourse and process theories, it is said that the participation of the defendant in the dialogic process both improves the quality of its resolution and legitimizes it. In this light, plea bargaining appears as the paradigm of a new rational approach to

criminal procedure that seeks to replicate the rational "seminar atmosphere" of certain German white collar trials.

Professor Klaus Lüderssen has gone one step further: he sees the rise of plea bargaining as an important indication of an actual paradigm shift. He calls for the abandonment of traditional substantive and procedural criminal law and advocates the resolution of what are now criminal cases in private tort actions. According to Lüderssen, plea bargaining serves as a model for the rational, dialogic resolution of disputes between victim and offender. Lüderssen views this dialogic resolution as the only way to legitimize the imposition and infliction of sanctions in our modern society of autonomous persons.

Id. at 603–05.

C. PROCEDURAL ORIGINS OF SUBSTANTIVE ISSUES

As soon as the investigatory phase of the criminal process gives way to its prosecutorial phase, and suspicion is converted into accusation through the filing of an indictment (or an information), the American legal system begins to take notice of issues of "substantive criminal law." That's not to say that substantive criminal law has nothing to say about, for instance, the legislative decision whether or not to criminalize a particular behavior or whether or not to do away with this or that traditional prerequisite for criminal liability. All this means is that there won't be any court opinions discussing an issue of substantive criminal law without a criminal case or controversy, i.e., an accusation of criminal conduct.

Once the charging instrument is filed, the defendant (and erstwhile suspect), or rather her counsel, can raise issues of criminal law in her defense. In fact, most of the defense at this point will rest on procedural, rather than substantive, grounds, such as complaints about the illegality of some investigatory method or other (the arrest, or search, was not supported by probable cause, was made without a warrant, or the *Miranda* warnings were given not at all, given incompletely, or subsequently ignored, and so on). But we are in this book talking about substance, not process.

The first procedural move that can give rise to a substantive question is the demurrer, which calls for a dismissal of the case on the simple ground that, even if everything the prosecution alleges in the indictment is true, the defendant would not be guilty of a crime. The demurrer might argue, for instance, that there is no such crime as the prosecution alleges in its indictment, that the defendant's conduct, as alleged in the indictment, does not make out any crime that does exist, or—most dramatically—that whatever crime does exist, and does match the defendant's conduct, is null and void because it violates some constitutional provision. To decide upon any of these matters, the court will have to determine exactly what crimes are in fact on the books, how they are defined, and whether they are constitutional.

Once the trial gets underway (if there is a trial, of course), questions of substantive criminal law generally will not arise until after the prosecution has put on its case. At that time, the defense may decide to file a substantive motion for a directed verdict, asking the judge to decide that on the evidence presented at trial, only an acquittal is possible. At the very end of the trial, after all the evidence is in, and all arguments have been made, the judge lays out the relevant rules of substantive criminal law for the jury (if there is a jury) in the form of "instructions," a major source of substantive issues on appeal. Once the jury (or the judge in the case of a bench trial) has come back with a guilty verdict, the defense can file a motion for a new trial, perhaps renewing its arguments regarding the insufficiency of the indictment or of the evidence. Assuming this motion fails, as it almost inevitably does, the defendant-appellant can decide to try her luck on appeal.

It's worth pointing out at this point that none of the trial-based issues just mentioned arises in the over 90% of cases that are disposed of by plea. In fact, standard plea agreements include a general waiver of the right to appeal one's conviction. The appellate review of guilty pleas is essentially limited to the plea's "voluntariness." (This inquiry is rather perfunctory, as the mere fact of representation by counsel largely predetermines the voluntariness inquiry.) Occasionally cases resolved by plea raise an odd, and apparently easy, question of substantive criminal law: Can a defendant plead guilty to a crime that does not exist? The answer, strangely enough, is "yes." See James E. Bond, Plea Bargaining and Guilty Pleas 3.55(b) (2d ed. 1983). That defendants can plead guilty to a crime while steadfastly maintaining their innocence is taken as a given. Pleas of this sort are called "Alford" pleas, after the Supreme Court's decision in North Carolina v. Alford, 400 U.S. 25 (1970).

After conviction comes sentencing. Thanks to the advent of sentencing guidelines, and more specific statutory constraints on judicial sentencing in general, the sentencing decision has been formalized and, particularly in federal criminal law, subjected to fairly intrusive appellate review. Federal trial judges generate sentencing memoranda of often considerable length, particularly if they decide to deviate from the prescribed guideline sentence. (See, e.g., *United States v. Blarek*, in ch. 1.) And if either side makes use of its right to appeal, the trial court's decision may well generate an appellate court opinion, adding up, eventually, to a full-fledged appellate jurisprudence of punishment.

In addition to "direct" appeals from a conviction and from a sentence, the (now convicted) defendant may pursue "collateral" attacks. They allow convicted persons after their direct appeals are "exhausted" to raise issues that couldn't be raised on direct appeal for one reason or another, e.g., because they rely on facts not contained in the trial record on appeal, most importantly allegations of ineffective assistance of counsel. The form of collateral attack most relevant for our purposes is the petition for a writ of habeas corpus, in which the petitioner asks a court to order the respondent, ordinarily the prison warden or some other state official in charge of the prison system, to release the petitioner from her custody.

D. DISCRETION

Discretion pervades the American criminal justice process, and particularly in its early, investigatory and prosecutorial, stages. Police officers have discretion over which cases they investigate, which suspects they stop, frisk, arrest, and search, and—if they decide to go forward with a case—which crimes they "write up." Next, prosecutors have wide—and largely unreviewed—discretion over which cases they pursue, which cases they pursue but later drop, which counts to include in an indictment (or an information), and how to frame them, which plea offers to make to which defendants represented by which lawyers, which sentence to request upon conviction, and so on. And sentencing guidelines have transferred much of the judge's traditional sentencing discretion onto the prosecutor who can shape the sentencing decision by charging, and accepting pleas to, specific counts that expose the defendant to a predictable sentence range.

Discretion in general, and prosecutorial discretion in particular, tends to be taken as a given in American views of the criminal process. In fact many, perhaps most, observers consider the pervasiveness of discretion to be a good thing. "[T]he good sense of our prosecutors" in particular is often regarded as an important check on legislative vagueness, overreaching, or simple incompetence. United States v. Dotterweich, 320 U.S. 277, 285 (1943).

For a more skeptical view, consider the following excerpt from a leading treatise on administrative law:

> The American legal system—federal, state, and local—is shot through with excessive and unnecessary discretionary power in the hands of miscellaneous and diverse administrators of many kinds, but one kind of discretionary power, representing more than half of all unnecessary such power, is the seemingly ever-present discretionary power not to enforce. . . .
>
> All the regulatory agencies have important power not to enforce—to push a little more or a little less, to be more aggressive or more empathetic, to hold out against pressures for nonenforcement or weak enforcement or to yield to such pressures, to carry out the intent behind the legislation or to allow regulated parties to get the upper hand. Discretion not to enforce is most damaging when it is unevenly exercised from case to case. . . .
>
> Whenever an officer properly applies the law to a private party, he is enforcing the law. And, strangely, any officer having such power to enforce almost always (legally or illegally) has discretionary power not to enforce. Even if a statute provides with clarity and force that the officer "shall" or "must" enforce, or that he has a "duty" to enforce, still the vital practical fact usually is that the officer may exercise a discretion not to enforce.
>
> Furthermore, whether the failure to enforce is legal or illegal may often be of no consequence because of lack of authority elsewhere in the system to compel the officer to perform his mandatory duty to enforce. . . .
>
> But why should we be concerned with the negative power, the power not to enforce? . . . Discretionary power not to enforce is the power to discriminate.

On the question whether the police have a mandatory duty to enforce the law, the formality of the law (what the statutes say) is at one extreme and the reality of the law (what the officers do) is at the opposite extreme. Furthermore, neither of the two extremes has any effect upon the other....

Statutes are quite clear in requiring policemen to arrest for crimes committed in their presence.... The law is not what the statutes provide, because (a) police nullify the statutes by not arresting, and their superiors do not require them to arrest, (b) legislators who are informed take no action against police nullification of the full-enforcement statutes, and (c) legislators participate in the nullification by appropriating only enough for partial enforcement. No one would assert that police nullification of clear statutes is a good system, but anyone who examines the reality is forced to conclude that the effective law is the opposite of what the full enforcement statutes clearly provide.

Whether prosecutors, including those in regulatory agencies, have a mandatory enforcement duty is much more complex. A fact of considerable importance is the pervasive assumption that mandatory prosecution would be impossible. Even though the assumption is strongly dominant, it can be conclusively rebutted. Some discretion is inherent in finding facts and in interpreting law, but other discretion can be eliminated from most enforcement functions (though probably not all). A statute could provide that whenever a prosecutor finds that the evidence is enough to convict for a serious crime he has an enforceable legal obligation to bring the prosecution unless one of a dozen specified reasons for not prosecuting is also found....

Even though compulsory prosecution is exceptional in the United States, we have a substantial amount of it, and American experience shows that it is a viable system. ... [Some] statutes governing transportation agencies, including the Federal Aviation Act, allow compulsory prosecution: "If ... there shall appear to be any reasonable ground for investigating the complaint, it shall be the duty of the administrator or the Board to investigate the matters complained of." ... Under that provision, when a bus company complained of airline family fares, the Civil Aeronautics Board dismissed the complaint without a hearing, but the reviewing court emphasized the "duty" of the Board, held the dismissal reviewable, held that the statute did not vest "anything near absolute discretion in the Board," held that the APA ... required the Board to state grounds for dismissal, and held that "standards for the Board's exercise of discretion must exist." Trailways of New England, Inc. v. CAB, 412 F.2d 926, 931–32 (1st Cir. 1969)....

2 Kenneth Culp Davis, Administrative Law 216–35 (2d ed. 1979)

The principle of compulsory prosecution has long been adopted in continental legal systems, where it is thought to be an indispensable check on arbitrary state power, and of executive power in particular. In German criminal law, for instance, the principle applies to both prosecutors and police:

German Crim. Proc. Code § 152. Indicting Authority; Principle of Compulsory Prosecution

(1) The public prosecution office shall have the authority to prefer public charges.

(2) Except as otherwise provided by law, the public prosecution office shall be obliged to take action in the case of all criminal offenses which may be prosecuted, provided there are sufficient factual indications.

Note that failure to comply with the principle of compulsory prosecution of crime is itself a crime:

German Penal Code § 258. Obstruction of Punishment

(1) Whoever intentionally or knowingly obstructs in whole or in part the punishment of another in accordance with the Penal Code . . . shall be punished with imprisonment for not more than five years or a fine.

§ 258a. Obstruction of Punishment in a Public Office

(1) If the perpetrator is charged in cases under Section 258 subsection (1), as a public official with participation in the criminal proceedings . . . then the punishment shall be imprisonment from six months to five years, in less serious cases, imprisonment for not more than three years or a fine.

Would the German scheme satisfy Davis's concerns? Would it be practicable? Advisable? What danger do you see in a system that purports to eliminate official discretion in the criminal justice process? Do the following provisions (§§ 153 & 153a), which provide for limited exceptions to the "principle of compulsory prosecution" (Legalitätsprinzip) under a countervailing "principle of appropriateness" (Opportunitätsprinzip), address this issue? (The appropriateness principle, by the way, does not apply to police; why do you think that is?)

German Crim. Proc. Code § 153. Non–Prosecution of Petty Offenses

(1) If a less serious criminal offense is the subject of the proceedings, the public prosecution office may dispense with prosecution with the approval of the court . . . if the perpetrator's culpability is considered to be of a minor nature and there is no public interest in the prosecution. . . .

§ 153a. Provisional Dispensing with Court Action; Provisional Termination of Proceedings

(1) In a case involving a less serious criminal offense, the public prosecution office may, with the consent of the court . . . and with the consent of the accused, dispense with preferment of public charges and concurrently impose a condition upon the accused:

1. to make a certain contribution towards reparation for damage caused by the offense,

2. to pay a sum of money to a non-profit-making institution or to the Treasury,

3. to perform some other service of a non-profit-making nature,

4. to comply with duties to pay maintenance at a certain level, or

5. to participate in a seminar pursuant to ... the Road Traffic Act,

if such conditions and instructions are of such nature as to eliminate the public interest in criminal prosecution and if the degree of culpability does not present an obstacle....

Which branch of government most needs to have its discretion curbed—the legislature (through prosecutorial discretion) or the executive (through compulsory prosecution)?

Police officers and prosecutors (and legislators) aren't the only ones exercising discretion in the American process of crime and punishment. If we focus on the heart of the process, the imposition of norms defined by the legislature, the paradigmatic—if rarely employed—fact finder in the American criminal trial, the jury, turns out to enjoy considerable discretion as well. The most dramatic, and controversial, manifestation of that discretion is "jury nullification," where the jury ignores the law as explained to it by the trial judge's instructions, and acquits despite overwhelming evidence. Jury nullification is beyond judicial scrutiny, thanks to the constitutional prohibition of double jeopardy. (The prosecutor gets one bite at the apple: Once you're acquitted, you can't be tried again.) If the jury *convicts* despite insufficient evidence of guilt, the defendant can appeal the verdict on that ground—though she will have a very slim chance of success since appellate courts do not like to disturb a jury's finding of fact.

Theoretically the power to acquit in the teeth of the law and/or the evidence isn't limited to the jury. It applies to anyone charged with rendering a verdict on the question of guilt or innocence, including judges in bench trials, i.e., trials without jury (either because the defendant waived his right to a jury or because the case was too trivial for the jury right to attach in the first place). But judge nullification tends to attract far less attention than does jury nullification.

Jury nullification is far more controversial than is prosecutorial discretion not to charge despite sufficient evidence. The controversy, however, is—strangely enough—not about whether American juries in fact have the power to nullify. Everyone agrees that they do. The dispute instead is about whether American juries should be *informed of* that power.

[A proposed constitutional amendment in South Dakota] would permit a criminal defendant to inform her jurors explicitly of their power to nullify the law and would permit the defense to invite them to exercise this power. It would thus transform the de facto power to nullify the criminal law into an express right to do so—one that could be argued by counsel and referred to in court.

Under a regime in which jurors have the right to nullify, a judge could no longer tell them that they must convict a defendant they find guilty of an offense. To ignore the law would no longer constitute an

> abuse of the jury's power, as long as that disregard inured to the benefit of the defendant.
>
> Under these circumstances, the jury instruction about convicting people when the prosecution proves every element of the offense would become a recommendation rather than an order. If the jury likes the criminal law at issue, it can apply it to the defendant. If it does not, it can acquit the defendant without even considering the evidence.
>
> Sometimes, in an individual case, nullification could yield the best possible result. When a law is patently unjust, but a prosecutor nonetheless chooses to apply it, a jury can use its power to protect a particular defendant from injustice.
>
> Prior to the Civil War in this country, for example, a jury believing the fugitive slave law to be morally repugnant could acquit a defendant charged with its violation, no matter how overwhelming the evidence. It might have been desirable for a defendant to be able to ask explicitly for such an acquittal, rather than having to hope that the jury would, on its own, reject an unjust law.
>
> But consider a much more common scenario involving nullification in the antebellum period. A white man would murder a black man. An unusual prosecutor might charge the white man with the crime and present his evidence to an all-white (and all-male) jury. The jurors—white supremacists who believe that white men should not be prosecuted for killing black men—would find the white defendant not guilty.
>
> Imagine an ... antebellum regime [under the proposed amendment]. The defense lawyer could now explicitly say to the jury that it is unduly harsh and Draconian to convict a white man of "murder" when he kills a black man. Instead of representing an abuse of its absolute discretion to acquit, the jury's disregard for the law would have become an officially sanctioned act of condoning interracial homicide.

Sherry F. Colb, "South Dakota Proposed Jury Nullification Amendment Should Be Rejected," cnn.com, Oct. 10, 2002, http://www.cnn.com/2002/LAW/10/10/findlaw.analysis.colb.nullify/ (accessed Jan. 21, 2003) (The amendment was defeated in Nov. 2002 by 77% to 23%.)

Is there a way to differentiate desirable from undesirable forms of jury nullification? Who determines whether a given exercise of jury nullification is desirable or not? Should the prosecution have the right to appeal an acquittal based on jury nullification? In all cases, in some? How would we even know—and how would we find out—if the acquittal was based on jury nullification or if the jury simply believed the law required an acquittal?

> [F]or pragmatic and political reasons, the black community is better off when some nonviolent lawbreakers remain in the community rather than go to prison. The decision as to what kind of conduct by African–Americans ought to be punished is better made by African–Americans themselves, based on the costs and benefits to their community, than by the traditional criminal justice process, which is controlled by white lawmakers and white law enforcers. Legally, the doctrine of jury nullification gives the power to make this decision to African–American jurors who sit in judgment of African–American

defendants. Considering the costs of law enforcement to the black community and the failure of white lawmakers to devise significant nonincarcerative responses to black antisocial conduct, it is the moral responsibility of black jurors to emancipate some guilty black outlaws.

* * *

My goal is the subversion of American criminal justice, at least as it now exists. Through jury nullification, I want to dismantle the master's house with the master's tools. My intent, however, is not purely destructive; this project is also constructive, because I hope that the destruction of the status quo will not lead to anarchy, but rather to the implementation of certain noncriminal ways of addressing antisocial conduct. Criminal conduct among African–Americans is often a predictable reaction to oppression. Sometimes black crime is a symptom of internalized white supremacy; other times it is a reasonable response to the racial and economic subordination every African–American faces every day. . . .

Paul Butler, "Racially Based Jury Nullification: Black Power in the Criminal Justice System," 105 Yale L.J. 677, 679–80 (1995).

E. The Principle of Legality (Nulla poena sine lege)

In the previous section, we noted the pervasiveness of discretion in the American system of crime and punishment. That prosecutorial discretion in particular is ubiquitous, and is not only tolerated but welcomed, does not mean, however, that American law is totally devoid of limitations on the discretion of state officials in the various branches of government to make or to apply criminal law. Some, but not all, of these limitations even have constitutional status. They traditionally have been grouped under the heading of "the principle of *legality*." The legality principle has several components, targeted at different participants in the criminal justice system. As we'll see, each aspect of the principle of legality will be subject to significant caveats. But for now, let's state the principle before we explore its exceptions.

To begin with there is the principle of *legislativity*, which provides that the power to make criminal law rests solely with the legislature and, which amounts to the same thing, that all criminal law comes in the form of statutes, rather than judicial opinions. Historically, the principle of legislativity in American law arose as an attempt on the part of the legislature to limit the historical discretion of common law judges to recognize nonstatutory offenses, called common law crimes. For that reason, the principle of legislativity has traditionally been referred to as the prohibition of common law crimes.

The principle of *lenity* limits judicial discretion in *interpreting* crimes, rather than in *making* them. Also known as the rule of "strict construction," it originated as an attempt on the part of the judiciary to limit the scope of statutory crimes created by the legislature. Lenity thus doesn't always fit comfortably with legislativity.

The principle of *specificity* limits discretion across all branches of government. It limits the legislature's discretion to define crimes in broad strokes. In this sense, it is the hammer to lenity's trimmer; a court faced with a badly and broadly drawn statute might save the statute by interpreting it narrowly in the name of lenity or invalidate it altogether in the name of specificity. In constitutional law, specificity is known as the constitutional prohibition against vague criminal laws ("void-for-vagueness" doctrine).

Specificity also limits the judiciary's discretion to interpret broadly defined crimes in arbitrary, or at least unpredictable, ways. And, perhaps most important, it limits the discretion of law enforcement officials, primarily the police, to enforce vague criminal laws as they see fit, supplying on the beat whatever content statutory definitions lack on the books.

The principle of *prospectivity* is once again addressed primarily to the legislature, though it also has been held to apply—directly or indirectly—to the judicial interpretations of criminal statutes. It limits the legislature's discretion to provide for the retroactive application of criminal laws, in an effort to prevent *ad hominem* legislation directed at particular people, or groups of people.

The various components of the principle of legality are often said, to a greater or less extent, to implement a right to "fair notice," which would allow citizens to avoid criminal conduct if they so choose while permitting the state to punish those who chose otherwise. The final component of the principle of legality, *publicity*, fits best into this rationale. Here the idea is that criminal laws must be publicized to allow potential offenders to consider the criminal implications of their contemplated course of action.

QUESTIONS AND COMMENTS

1. As you read the following materials on the principle of legality, consider whether any, or all of them, can be justified under the "fair notice" rationale, or any other rationale for that matter. Are there other common threads that connect the various aspects of the legality principle? Also consider the constitutional status of each component of the legality principle: Could a state, or the federal government, do away with any of the elements of the legality principle without running afoul of constitutional law?

2. The legality principle, in its entirety, is often said to be captured by the Latin phrase "nulla poena sine lege," which has been translated as no punishment without *law*, or no punishment without *statute*. (What ambiguity about the scope of the legality principle underlies these alternative translations?) The phrase can be traced back not to Roman law, but to a German criminal law scholar, codifier, and judge, P.J.A. Feuerbach, who coined it in his influential criminal law treatise, first published in 1801.[a]

a. Paul Johann Anselm Feuerbach, the father of the philosopher of religion Ludwig Feuerbach, is considered the founder of modern German criminal law, both through his treatise and the Bavarian Penal Code of 1813, which he drafted based on his—then novel—theory of general deterrence. See G.W.F. Hegel, Philosophy of Right § 99 (1821) (attacking Feuerbach on retributivist grounds).—EDS.

P.J.A. Feuerbach, Textbook of Common Criminal Law in Germany § 20

I. *Every infliction of punishment requires a criminal statute. (Nulla poena sine lege. [No punishment without law.])* Because only the statutory threat of harm justifies the concept and the legal possibility of a punishment.

II. *The infliction of punishment presumes the existence of the conduct threatened with harm. (Nulla poena sine crimine. [No punishment without crime.])* Because only the statute connects the threatened punishment to the act as a legally necessary precondition.

III. *The act subject to the statutory threat of punishment (the statutory precondition) presumes the statutory punishment. (Nullum crimen sine poena legali. [No crime without legal punishment.])* Because the statute connects the specific violation of the law to the harm [of punishment] as a necessary legal consequence.

Feuerbach was a staunch proponent of general deterrence. Consider the legality principle, and each of its components, from the standpoint of general deterrence theory, as well as from that of the other traditional rationales for punishment. Under which rationale can it be justified? Which theory, or theories, of punishment can do without a legality principle?

1. LEGISLATIVITY

Model Penal Code § 1.05. All Offenses Defined by Statute; Application of General Provisions of the Code.

(1) No conduct constitutes an offense unless it is a crime or violation under this Code or another statute of this State.

(2) The provisions of [the General Part] of the Code are applicable to offenses defined by other statutes, unless the Code otherwise provides.

(3) This Section does not affect the power of a court to punish for contempt or to employ any sanction authorized by law for the enforcement of an order or a civil judgment or decree.

California Penal Code § 6.

No act or omission ... is criminal or punishable, except as prescribed or authorized by this Code, or by some of the statutes which it specifies as continuing in force and as not affected by its provisions, or by some ordinance, municipal, county, or township regulation, passed or adopted, under such statutes and in force when this Code takes effect.

Commonwealth v. Keller

Common Pleas Court of Lebanon County, Pennsylvania.
35 Pa. D. & C.2d 615 (1964).

■ GATES, P.J.

[In the space of two years, Ms. Keller twice gave birth to a child out of wedlock while her husband served in the military. Each time, she hid the dead newborn in a box in her house. Since evidence of the cause of death was inconclusive in both cases, she could not be convicted of homicide. She was charged instead with the "common law misdemeanor" of "indecent disposition of a dead body."]

The essential characteristic of the common law, which distinguishes it as a system of law from the civil law, is its flexibility. Under the common law, we are not powerless to cope with novel situations not comprehended or contemplated by the legislators. In his work on the common law, Justice Holmes noted that, "The first requirement of a sound body of law is that it should correspond with the actual feelings and demands of the community, whether right or wrong." The landmark case in this Commonwealth which announces the principle of preserving common law offenses is Commonwealth v. McHale, 97 Pa. 397. After analyzing and determining that common law crimes are preserved, Mr. Justice Paxton, at page 408, asks the question, "What is a common-law offense?"

"The highest authority upon this point is Blackstone. In chap. 13, of vol. 4, of [his Commentaries on the Laws of England (1769)] it is thus defined: 'The last species of offenses which especially affect the Commonwealth are those against the public police or economy. By the public police and economy I mean the due regulation and domestic order of the kingdom, whereby the individuals of the state, like members of a well-governed family, are bound to conform their general behavior to the rules of propriety, good neighborhood and good manners, and to be decent, industrious and inoffensive in their respective stations. This head of offenses must therefore be very miscellaneous, as it comprises all such crimes as especially affect public society, and are not comprehended under any of the four preceding series. These amount some of them to felony, and other to misdemeanors only.' "

Thus, from the McHale case in 1881 down to the present time, our courts have consistently recognized common law offenses under the doctrine set forth in the McHale case. This is so even in the absence of specific common law precedent or statutory declaration....

Ever since the existence of man has been evidenced there is also evidence that there existed a standard of decency and respect for the dead and their resting places. The Holy Scripture discloses that it was a disgrace not to bury the dead: Jeremiah 16:4. See also Genesis 50:1–7. Archaeologists have unearthed graves of prehistoric men indicating that they had a religious, or at least respectful, concern for dead bodies and the way and manner in which they were treated and buried. The renowned pyramids of Egypt are but resting places for the dead and memorials to them. Resort to American Indian lore will reveal a whole body of custom dealing with the Indian's attitude and concept of decency with respect to dead bodies and places of burial. Much of the Indian's day's activities were performed with a view to earning a sacred and hallowed resting place upon their death. The Code of Justinian provided that, "... Directly the body or bones of a dead person, whether slave or free, were buried, the grounds in which they were buried became religious. ..." Carved on the tomb of William Shakespeare is a reflection upon early English people's attitude toward the sanctity of the grave. It says, "Curst be he that moves my bones." ...

It would seem unnecessary for a further extension of this opinion to rationalize the existence in this community of a well-established and known standard of decency and morality with respect to the disposition and treatment of dead bodies. Yet, the importance of this matter commands one further observation. From our childhood, we have all been accustomed to pay a reverential respect to the sepulchres of our fathers and to attach a character of sacredness to the grounds dedicated and enclosed as the cemeteries of the dead. This standard of decency has been recognized by our legislators through the years, and they have made statutory provisions governing cemeteries, cemetery companies, reinterment and abandonment, crypts, burial permits, cremation, mutilation of graves and tombstones, mausoleums and vaults. At both common law and under the statutory law of this Commonwealth, it is an offense to dig up or disturb or desecrate bodies which have been buried. It is an outrage upon the public feelings and torturing to the afflicted relations of the deceased. If it be a crime thus to disturb the ashes of the dead, it must also be a crime to deprive them of a decent burial, by disgracefully exposing or disposing of the body, contrary to usages so long sanctioned by people and which are so grateful to the wounded hearts of friends and mourners, and this is so, irrespective of their religious aspects of burial and life hereafter, be it Christian, Jew, or Agnostic. We thus consider the common law as being sufficiently broad to punish as a misdemeanor, although there may be no exact precedent, any act which directly injures or tends to injure the public to such an extent as to require the state to interfere and punish the wrongdoer, as in the case of acts which injuriously affect public morality or obstruct or pervert public justice, or the administration of government. It is the common law of this Commonwealth that whatever openly outrages decency and is injurious to public morals is a misdemeanor and punishable at law.

We have little difficulty therefore in concluding that this bill of indictment does properly charge the defendant with a crime cognizable under the laws of the Commonwealth, and the court did not err in refusing the defendant's motion to quash the indictment assigning therefor this reason.

Meadows v. State

Supreme Court of Arkansas.
291 Ark. 105, 722 S.W.2d 584 (1987).

■ ROBERT H. DUDLEY, JUSTICE.

The principal issue in this case is whether an unborn viable fetus is a "person" as that term is used in the manslaughter statute. There is little dispute about the facts. The appellant, while intoxicated, drove his car in a reckless manner, veered across the center line of the highway and struck an oncoming car being driven by Randy Waldrip. As a result, Randy Waldrip was killed and an unborn viable fetus, carried by Vanessa Weicht, a passenger in appellant's car, was also killed. The appellant was charged with, and convicted of, two counts of manslaughter; one for killing Randy Waldrip and the other for killing the unborn fetus.

Appellant [argues] that reckless killing of an unborn viable fetus is not included within the purview of the manslaughter statute. The argument has merit. Our statute provides that one commits manslaughter if he "recklessly causes the death of another person." Ark. Stat. Ann. § 41–1504(1)(c). The word "person" is not defined.

The applicable rule of construction is that the common law in force at the time the statute was passed is to be taken into account in construing undefined words of the statute. The quoted statute, which is a part of the Criminal Code, was enacted in 1975, while a pre-code manslaughter statute goes back to the revised statutes which became effective in 1839. The revised statute used the term "human being" rather than the presently used "person," but the terms are synonymous in common law.

In ascertaining the common law, we look not only to our own cases, but to early English cases, early writers on the common law, and cases from other states. In so looking, we find that at common law, in both 1839 and in 1975, an unborn fetus was not included within the definition of a "person" or "human being," and therefore, the killing of a viable unborn child was not murder.

In its brief the State acknowledges that the common law is as set out above, but urges us to alter it. Thus, the critical issue is whether a court ought to create a new common law crime.

... LaFave and Scott discuss at length the issue of whether courts can create new common law crimes. W. LaFave & A. Scott, *Criminal Law* § 67 (1972), at 57–69. They indicate that the modern view finds diminished authority for courts doing so. They conclude:

> It is only natural that judges should create crimes from general principles in medieval England, because such legislature as there was sat only infrequently and legislation was scanty. Today in the United States, as in modern England, the various legislatures meet regularly. The principal original reason for common law crimes has therefore disappeared.

We have recently said, "It is well settled that it is for the legislative branch of a state or federal government to determine the kind of conduct that constitutes a crime and the nature and extent of the punishment which may be imposed." *Sparrow* v. *State*, 284 Ark. 396, 397, 683 S.W.2d 218 (1985).

There are two fundamental policy reasons which make it appropriate for this Court to defer the creation of new crimes to the legislature. First, aside from having the primary authority to create new crimes, the General Assembly is composed of members, proportioned according to population and geography, who are elected at more frequent intervals than are members of this Court. The General Assembly is more closely attuned and more representative of the public will than is this Court. Second, the General Assembly has committees which conduct hearings in a non-adversary manner in order to anticipate all factual situations which may prospectively occur, and it is able to make more distinctions as to the degrees of offenses and to graduate the penalties to match the severity of the offenses. This Court would be limited to making a ruling solely on the adversarily developed facts before it. Accordingly, we decline to create a new common law crime by judicial fiat, but, instead, defer to the legislative branch.

The highest courts of our sister states overwhelmingly agree with our philosophy. Twenty-four states have held, under facts similar to the ones at bar, they would not create new common law crimes. On the other hand, only two states have created a new common law crime under facts similar to those of the case at bar. In its brief the State asks us to follow the holding of those two states. We decline to do so. In *State* v. *Horne*, 282 S.C. 444, 319 S.E.2d 703 (1984), the South Carolina court, without discussing its power to create a new common law crime, prospectively held that the murder of a viable unborn fetus would be a crime. In *Commonwealth* v. *Cass*, 392 Mass. 799, 467 N.E.2d 1324 (1984), the Massachusetts court, by a 4–3 vote, held that a viable fetus was a "person" for purposes of that state's vehicular homicide statute....

Accordingly, we must reverse and dismiss the manslaughter conviction for killing the unborn fetus. * * *

■ STEELE HAYS, JUSTICE, dissenting.

I do not share the majority's concern that this court would be "creating a common law crime" by holding that an unborn, fully viable fetus is a "person" within the meaning of our manslaughter statute.

This is not a "new crime." This court would not in any sense be "creating" a crime. The crime was created legislatively as part of the Revised Statutes, which took effect in 1838. What we would be doing by affirming the trial court is what courts traditionally and necessarily do—interpret an act of the legislature for the purpose of giving effect to what we perceive to be the legislative intent.

The act, Ark. Stat. Ann. § 41–1504(1)(c) (Repl. 1977), is quite clear:

Manslaughter—(1) A person commits manslaughter if: (c) he recklessly causes the death of another person.

.... The issue then is simply whether the legislature intended "person" to include a full term unborn child in 1975 when our current statute was framed to take effect on January 1, 1976. I submit that logic and common sense weigh on the side of the affirmative. * * *

I believe we should ... follow the course taken by the recent cases of *State* v. *Horne*, 282 S.C. 444, 319 S.E.2d 703 (1984); *State* v. *Burrell*, 699 P.2d 499 (Kan. 1985) and *Commonwealth* v. *Cass*, 392 Mass. 799, 467 N.E.2d 1324 (1984), where it was said:

> We think that the better rule is that infliction of prenatal injuries resulting in the death of a viable fetus, before or after it is born, is homicide. If a person were to commit violence against a pregnant woman and destroy the fetus within her, we would not want the death of the fetus to go unpunished. We believe that our criminal law should extend its protection to viable fetuses.

....

Nor would I hold that the appellant is entitled to fair warning that his conduct in this instance should not be criminalized based on a narrow interpretation of "person." . . . The mother whose child was killed and who lived with the appellant at the time of the collision and trial, testified the appellant had been drinking all day and had smoked marijuana cigarettes. Large amounts of beer were consumed and appellant's blood alcohol level was .18 following the collision. While the exact consequences may not have occurred to appellant, the criminality of his conduct could hardly have been in doubt. . . .

QUESTIONS AND COMMENTS

1. Note that Pennsylvania's criminal code was revised on the basis of the Model Penal Code a few years after the decision in *Keller*. The current code explicitly denies courts the power to create common law crimes:

> **Pennsylvania Crimes Code § 107. Application of preliminary provisions.**
>
> (b) Common law crimes abolished.—No conduct constitutes a crime unless it is a crime under this title or another statute of this Commonwealth.

2. For the legitimacy of judicial criminal lawmaking, should it make a difference whether judges are elected (like most state judges), rather than appointed for life (like federal judges)? Would it make a difference if the crime in *Keller* had been created not by a single judge, but by a panel of judges? By an appellate court, rather than a trial court?

Aren't local judges presumably more in tune with the moral sense of their local community than a state legislature in the state capital, or worse yet, a federal legislature in the national capital? Why shouldn't they have the power to create crimes? And aren't judges often far more familiar with the existing law than are legislators who may or may not have enjoyed a legal education and, at any rate, have so many other things on their minds than carefully defining new crimes? How realistic is the image of legislative deliberation (and particularly on the subject of criminal legislation) painted in *Meadows*? On common law crimes, see generally Stanislaw Pomorski, American Common Law and the Principle Nullum Crimen Sine Lege (2d ed. 1975).

3. Or is notice the problem? Do you think that a defendant is more likely to have notice of a legislatively created crime than a judicially created one? Doesn't that depend on the kind of crime? If it is a clear transgression of a noncodified, but clearly established and central, norm of a given community, wouldn't notice be less of a problem than in the case of a violation of some obscure statutory offense, buried in some code? And are statutory compilations necessarily more accessible than case reporters? What about regulatory offenses tucked away in administrative regulations?

Did the defendant in *Keller* have fair notice of the fact that her conduct was wrong? That it was illegal? That it was criminal? Would notice concerns be satisfied only if the defendant realized, at the time of her conduct, that she was committing an act that would be declared a crime at the time of her trial? Or would it be enough if she thought it was wrong, or might expose her to civil liability? Under *Meadows*, would notice require not only that the actor foresee criminal liability in general, but criminal liability for *a particular offense*?

The Model Penal Code, which was specifically designed to do away with common law crimes, includes a provision entitled "abuse of corpse." Model Penal Code § 250.10 ("[A] person who treats a corpse in a way that he knows would outrage ordinary family sensibilities commits a misdemeanor."). Would this provision have applied to Keller's case? Would it have solved the notice problem? (What are "ordinary family sensibilities"?)

4. Or is retroactivity the problem? After all, every time a court creates a new crime in a case, it by necessity applies retroactively to the defendant in that case because her conduct was not a crime when she engaged in it. But what if the court is simply pouring into the form of criminal law firmly held community norms that clearly were around at the time of the defendant's conduct? And what if a court decided to recognize a new crime only prospectively (as did the courts in *State v. Horne* and *Commonwealth v. Cass*, both cited in *Meadows*)?

5. And what about the judicial recognition of *defenses*? Should the judiciary be prohibited from recognizing new defenses as well? Would the following provision violate the principle of legislativity?

Draft Canadian Criminal Code § 17. Common Law Defenses.[a]

> No defense, justification, or excuse shall be unavailable unless contrary to an express provision of the Criminal Code.

6. No one doubts courts' authority to recognize new torts. What's the difference between the law of torts and the law of crimes that would account for the legitimacy of judicial lawmaking in one, but not in the other? Why should tort law—but *not* criminal law—be "subject to continual change by the courts and legislatures to meet the evolving needs of an increasingly mobile, industrialized and technological society"? State ex rel. Atkinson v. Wilson, 175 W.Va. 352, 355, 332 S.E.2d 807, 810 (1984). Given that it "must be forever in progress; and no limits can be assigned to its principles or improvements," isn't the common law—and therefore the judges who make (or rather discover) it—particularly well suited to keep legal doctrine in touch with modern developments and changes in community norms? See id. at 359, 332 S.E.2d at 814 (McHugh, J., dissenting) (quoting Joseph Story, The Miscellaneous Writings of Joseph Story 526 (William W. Story ed. 1852)).

7. The Model Penal Code for all intents and purposes put an end to judicial criminal lawmaking in the United States, as state legislatures passed statutes analogous to Pa. Crimes Code § 107 (see supra comment 1). The movement against judicial criminal lawmaking, however, began much earlier, as new American legislatures started to assert their authority vis-à-vis the judiciary:

> The post-Revolutionary age was an age of reform in criminal justice. The Bill of Rights ... codified ideas about fair trials. Reform of

a. Making Criminal Law Clear and Just: A Criminal Reports Forum (Don Stuart et al. eds., 1999).—EDS.

criminal justice was in the air. Parts of the old system seemed chaotic and barbaric. The republic seemed to need a new system, more rational, more modern, more just and humane. Reformers on the whole, hated the death penalty, and, to a lesser degree, other punishments of the body—whipping, torture, and the like. They hated naked authority. They hated boundless official discretion. They hated institutions of grace and mercy, insofar as they were not governed by principles of law. All these they associated with the defeated monarchy.

They had a point. English criminal justice was a patriarchal jumble, a peculiar mixture of extreme legalism and extreme discretion. The penal code seemed utterly pitiless; anybody who stole so much as a silver spoon or two could be sent to the gallows. But, as Douglas Hay has argued in a brilliant essay, there was an inner and perhaps subconscious logic to the system.[3] Many poor souls were indeed sentenced to death, and many ended up swinging from the gallows. But others escaped death, because some squire or noble put in a word for them, and evoked the king's mercy. This combination of mercy and terror, Hay argues, built a stronger, more efficient structure of social control than terror alone could have done.

This kind of system did not suit the American condition, or the American mind. It appeared (and was) autocratic. It depended on patronage, on the networks that tied together the big landowners in England, the crown, the nobility; on the dependency of poor tenants and farmers who rented or held land on great estates. That system was lacking in America.

A *republican* criminal justice system would look quite different. It would not tolerate cells of uncontrolled discretion, if at all possible. Popular government was supposed to be a government of *laws,* not of grace and favor. This meant that all crimes, and their punishments, should be embodied in a single, clear, definitive code.

Law had to be an open book. "Laws, to be obeyed and administered, must be known; to be known they must be read; to be administered they must be studied and compared. To know them is the right of the people." Edward Livingston wrote those words, introducing his proposed penal code for Louisiana in 1822. In the event, Louisiana did not adopt the code; but the code idea made important conquests in many states, and a reform spirit pruned the criminal law of those features that looked the most irrational.

Codification and the republican idea, for example, were in conflict with the concept of the "common-law crime." This term had two rather different meanings. It referred, in the first place, to traditional crimes—acts recognized as crimes whether or not there was a specific law on the subject, because "everybody" simply *knew* these were crimes. Murder, in other words, was a common-law crime, whether or not some state had a formal text that prohibited murder. Of course,

3. Douglas Hay, "Property, Authority and the Criminal Law," in Albion's Fatal Tree: Crime and Society in Eighteenth-Century England 17 (Douglas Hay et al. eds. 1975).

every state in fact did have a law against murder; this meaning of the term was therefore not very important.

The other sense of the term carried more weight. To put it bluntly, it referred to the power of courts to invent new crimes. A penal code, if it was (in theory) gapless and complete, would put an end to the power of judges to create new common-law crimes. In *United States* v. *Hudson and Goodwin*, [11 U.S. 32 (1812)], the defendants had been indicted for libeling the president and Congress (they had, in print, accused the president and Congress of "having in secret voted $2,000,000 as a present to Bonaparte, for leave to make a treaty with Spain"). The criminal laws passed by Congress did not cover this offense in so many words. The Supreme Court felt this was a crucial—and fatal—flaw. There was no such thing as a federal common-law crime. Unless Congress gave an explicit green light, by passing a law, the courts had no power to punish, no matter what a person may have done.

This was, of course, a federal case; the decision had strong overtones of states' rights. This was early nineteenth-century federalism—a niggardly view of the power of Washington, as compared to the power of the states. The states were, in fact, much slower to rid themselves of the concept of common-law crime.... As late as 1881, the concept cropped up in a Pennsylvania court case. [Commonwealth v. McHale, discussed in *Keller*, supra.] A man named McHale, along with some others, was indicted for stuffing ballot boxes. Nothing in the Pennsylvania code exactly fit the case. The court was willing to stretch a point, reaching into the grab bag of the common law. The issue was not "whether precedents can be found in the books," but whether the acts "injuriously affect the public." McHale's acts shook "the social fabric to its foundations"; the court could not let them go unpunished.

These were, however, isolated cases. The concept of the common-law crime was in retreat throughout the nineteenth century. In Ohio, the high court stated flatly, in 1842, that "With us, there is no such thing as common law crimes." In Indiana, the Revised Statutes of 1852 baldly laid down the rule that "Crimes and misdemeanors shall be defined, and punishment therefor fixed, by statutes of this State, and not otherwise." In practice, too, the concept became less and less important, simply because more and more states passed comprehensive penal codes; by implication, anything not listed was simply not a crime. Judges had too much power, if they could invent new crimes, or extend old ones by analogy.

Lawrence M. Friedman, Crime and Punishment in American History 63–65 (1994)

Is the problem with judicial lawmaking not so much that it is judicial, rather than legislative, but that it does not—and cannot—add up to a code? Is the problem with a common law of crimes, in other words, that it is not as systematic and comprehensive as a code?

8. *The Case of Federal Criminal Law.* At least since United States v. Hudson & Goodwin, 11 U.S. 32 (1812), it's clear that there was to be no

federal common law of crimes. As the Court explained in that case, "powers of the general Government are made up of concessions from the several states—whatever is not expressly given to the former, the latter expressly reserve," and, as it turned out, the federal constitution granted federal courts neither explicitly, nor implicitly, "jurisdiction of crimes against the state."

Yet one commentator has argued that judicial criminal lawmaking, *particularly in federal law*, is not only widespread, but intentional (on the part of the *legislature*) and laudable as well.

> [T]he conventional, legislative-supremacy conception ... is the orthodox view of federal criminal-lawmaking. It's reflected in the principle, established by the Supreme Court early on in United States v. Hudson & Goodwin, that there are and can be no federal "common law" crimes....
>
> In my view, the legislative-supremacy conception obscures much more than it illuminates. It's not literally false, but the truth it contains is partial to the point of material deception. To be sure, Congress must speak before anyone can be convicted of a federal crime, but so long as Congress troubles itself to utter even a single word, the Judiciary will obligingly write the sentence—indeed, the paragraph, the book, and the screen play—that brings a criminal prohibition to life....
>
> Take the federal criminal law of "fraud" as an example. By incorporating "fraud" and its cognates into a host of important statutory offenses—including conspiracy to defraud, and mail and wire fraud—Congress all but guaranteed a central role for courts in constructing federal criminal law. At common-law, fraud was understood to be less a legal rule in its own right than a license to courts to devise new rules on an ad hoc basis. And that's exactly the function that the concept has played in federal criminal law. Chief Justice Burger helpfully described the mail fraud statute as a "first line of defense" against " 'new' frauds" unaddressed by "particularized legislation"—from consumer scams, to blackmail schemes, to illegal lotteries, to public corruption, to misappropriation of confidential information. * * *
>
> Last but by no means least, consider RICO. No one can seriously maintain that Congress defined the elements of this crime. For example, the statutory definition of "enterprise"—which "includes any individual ... and any union or group of individuals associated in fact"—literally excludes nothing from its scope. Other opaque but critical terms—such as "to conduct or participate ... in the conduct of" the affairs of an enterprise—lack any statutory definition whatsoever. Again, it has devolved on courts to fashion mediating doctrines to bring these open-textured statutory formulations into contact with the real world.

Dan M. Kahan, "Three Conceptions of Federal Criminal–Lawmaking," 1 Buff. Crim. L. Rev. 5, 6–8 (1997).

Does judicial participation in putting meat on the bones of skeletal statutes violate the principle of legislativity? (What if the legislature intended it that way?) And what about a statute that prescribes the penalty for a crime, but doesn't define the elements of the crime at all? See, e.g., Mich. Penal Code § 750.321 ("Any person who shall commit the crime of manslaughter shall be guilty of a felony punishable by imprisonment in the state prison, not more than 15 years or by fine of not more than 7,500 dollars, or both, at the discretion of the court.")).

9. The Model Penal Code provides for the imposition of criminal liability for an omission, i.e., for failing to act rather than for acting, if "a duty to perform the omitted act is otherwise imposed by law." Among the sources of duties to act are judicially created, "common law," duties, based on precedent rather than statute (examples include duties based on the relationship of parent to child, husband to wife, captain to sailor, and employer to employee). Does this theory of omission liability violate the principle of legislativity? Consider the following commentary.

> Allowing criminal responsibility to rest not only on breach of statutory duty outside the Criminal Code but on any common law duty such as those found in torts is a fundamental breach of the principle of legality. Duties imposed in the context of civil compensation where the issue is often which party can better bear the risk of harm may well be inappropriate to the issue of just punishment. In a federal system like Canada there is the particular problem that duties imposed in the provincial context, such as the good Samaritan duty imposed in Quebec, may be used in that province to impose criminal responsibility.

Don Stuart, "Supporting General Principles for Criminal Responsibility in the Model Penal Code with Suggestions for Reconsideration: A Canadian Perspective," 4 Buff. Crim. L. Rev. 13, 42 (2000).

10. *Executive Criminal Lawmaking*. The American judiciary lost its power to define new crimes some time ago, first in fact and then in law, although as the *Keller* case illustrates, some courts in some jurisdictions continued their practice of creating common law until well into the second half of the twentieth century.

Today, the executive poses a more credible threat to the legislature's monopoly of criminal lawmaking than does the judiciary. Consider, for instance, the frequent creation of "regulatory crimes" by administrative agencies. (Similarly, executive orders issued by the President create criminal law insofar as their violation may be subject to criminal punishment. See, e.g., United States v. Arch Trading Co., 987 F.2d 1087 (4th Cir. 1993).)

> Today, when a congressional committee adopts new requirements concerning commercial transactions, agricultural acreage allotments, welfare programs, or virtually any other regulated activity, it routinely incorporates at the end of the requirements a statement that any deviation constitutes a federal crime.... Nothing is more distinctive of a mature, modern industrial society than the vast proliferation of minutely specified rules and regulations for the conduct of government, business, unions, and indeed of "private" life, whether it be the manner of driving one's automobile, the character of the wiring and

> plumbing in one's house, or the nature of records and reports required in one's profession.... A not uncommon disposition is "whoever violates any provision of this statute or any rule or regulation thereunder shall be guilty of [a felony or misdemeanor]," although the great majority of the offenses contemplated are likely to be trivial or technical. A noteworthy feature of the legislative process in this connection is that while the Department of Justice initiates and Judiciary Committees must approve of legislation dealing with ordinary crimes, other departments and committees, knowledgeable in the particular field regulated but inexpert and not attuned to the problems of "regulating" human beings, i.e., offenders, or the machinery of penal justice, generally dispose of penal aspects of regulatory law.
>
> [T]here have been found to exist in our federal laws about 1,700 such activities that have been made criminal by statute.... This figure, however, reveals only part of the coverage. Many of the penalty sections authorize the imposition of the specified penalty not only upon a person who violates the provisions described in the statute, but also, as the commission observed in the quoted paragraph, upon one who violates any regulation, rule, or order issued by the agency charged with the administration of the statute. Taking into account the numerous, discrete rules and regulations enforceable under such regulatory statutes (including, for example, those appearing in the 22 pages of OSHA requirements concerning the construction of ladders and scaffolding), it appears that there are more than 10,000 regulatory requirements or proscriptions carrying criminal sanctions under the current federal law.

Ronald L. Gainer, "Federal Criminal Code Reform: Past and Future," 2 Buff. Crim. L. Rev. 45, 72–74 (1998).

Perhaps less obviously, but no less importantly, the drafting of elaborate sentencing "guidelines" by a commission of sentencing experts also represents a form of administrative criminal lawmaking. (On the significance of the federal sentencing guidelines as a source of substantive criminal law, see ch. 1 supra.) While the constitutionality of criminal lawmaking by commission has not been challenged under the principle of legality, the U.S. Supreme Court has considered (and rejected) the claim that the establishment of the federal sentencing commission exceeded Congress's authority to delegate its lawmaking power.

Mistretta v. United States
Supreme Court of the United States.
488 U.S. 361 (1989).

■ JUSTICE BLACKMUN delivered the opinion of the Court.

The [Sentencing] Commission is established "as an independent commission in the judicial branch of the United States." 28 U.S.C. § 991(a). It has seven voting members (one of whom is the Chairman) appointed by the President "by and with the advice and consent of the Senate." "At least three of the members shall be Federal judges selected after considering a list of six judges recommended to the President by the Judicial Conference of the United States." Ibid. No more than four members of the Commission shall be members of the same political party. The Attorney General, or his designee, is an ex officio non-voting member. The Chairman and other members of the Commission are subject to removal by the President "only for neglect of duty or malfeasance in office or for other good cause shown." Ibid. Except for initial staggering of terms, a voting member serves for six years and may not serve more than two full terms. §§ 992(a) and (b).

In addition to the duty the Commission has to promulgate determinative-sentence guidelines, it is under an obligation periodically to "review and revise" the guidelines. § 994(o). It is to "consult with authorities on, and individual and institutional representatives of, various aspects of the Federal criminal justice system." Ibid. It must report to Congress "any amendments of the guidelines." § 994(p). * * *

Petitioner argues that in delegating the power to promulgate sentencing guidelines for every federal criminal offense to an independent Sentencing Commission, Congress has granted the Commission excessive legislative discretion in violation of the constitutionally based nondelegation doctrine. We do not agree. * * *

[O]ur jurisprudence has been driven by a practical understanding that in our increasingly complex society, replete with ever changing and more technical problems, Congress simply cannot do its job absent an ability to delegate power under broad general directives. * * *

■ JUSTICE SCALIA, dissenting.

While the products of the Sentencing Commission's labors have been given the modest name "Guidelines," they have the force and effect of laws, prescribing the sentences criminal defendants are to receive. A judge who disregards them will be reversed. * * *

There is no doubt that the Sentencing Commission has established significant, legally binding prescriptions governing application of governmental power against private individuals—indeed, application of the ultimate governmental power, short of capital punishment. Statutorily permissible sentences for particular crimes cover as broad a range as zero years to life, and within those ranges the Commission was given broad discretion to prescribe the "correct" sentence. Average prior sentences were to be a starting point for the Commission's inquiry, but it could and regularly did deviate from those averages as it thought appropriate. * * *

It should be apparent from the above that the decisions made by the Commission are far from technical, but are heavily laden (or ought to be) with value judgments and policy assessments. This fact is sharply reflected in the Commission's product, as described by the dissenting Commissioner: "Under the guidelines, the judge could give the same sentence for abusive sexual contact that puts the child in fear as for unlawfully entering or remaining in the United States. Similarly, the guidelines permit equivalent sentences for the following pairs of offenses: drug trafficking and a violation of the Wild Free–Roaming Horses and Burros Act; arson with a destructive device and failure to

> surrender a cancelled naturalization certificate; operation of a common carrier under the influence of drugs that causes injury and alteration of one motor vehicle identification number; illegal trafficking in explosives and trespass; interference with a flight attendant and unlawful conduct relating to contraband cigarettes; aggravated assault and smuggling $11,000 worth of fish." Dissenting View of Commissioner Paul H. Robinson on the Promulgation of the Sentencing Guidelines by the United States Sentencing Commission 6–7 (May 1, 1987). * * *
>
> By reason of today's decision, I anticipate that Congress will find delegation of its lawmaking powers much more attractive in the future. If rulemaking can be entirely unrelated to the exercise of judicial or executive powers, I foresee all manner of "expert" bodies, insulated from the political process, to which Congress will delegate various portions of its lawmaking responsibility. How tempting to create an expert Medical Commission (mostly M.D.'s, with perhaps a few Ph.D.'s in moral philosophy) to dispose of such thorny, "no-win" political issues as the withholding of life-support systems in federally funded hospitals, or the use of fetal tissue for research.... The only governmental power the Commission possesses is the power to make law; and it is not the Congress.

11. What's wrong with administrators defining crimes? Aren't they experts in their respective fields? Does the nature of administrative contributions to criminal lawmaking make a difference (e.g., setting criminal pollution levels vs. drafting sentencing guidelines)? Even if the legislature should monopolize the power to make criminal law, why shouldn't it be allowed to delegate that power to the executive branch? Is there a relevant distinction here between criminal law and other types of lawmaking? Consider the following commentary.

> We live, as we all recognize, in an administrative state, in which Congress does and must delegate all manner of technical policymaking responsibility to administrative agencies. But the distinctions being written into law by the Sentencing Commission are not technical matters of how many parts per million of particulate matter are necessary to render the air unfit to breathe. The substantive criminal law concerns some of the most fundamental, and least specialized, questions to be decided in any society, and if it is deemed important to specify more precisely the shades of society's condemnation of different species of crime, is that not a matter for the democratic process—for public legislation, rather than anonymous regulation?
>
> [F]ederal penal code reform failed because the legislative process involved too many procedural hurdles for a truly comprehensive criminal code bill to pass. Yet the guidelines (and their periodic amendments), which accomplish as a practical matter an equally sweeping restructuring of substantive criminal law, swept through Congress without a vote, because under the Sentencing Reform Act of 1984 guidelines become law unless Congress enacts legislation to veto them....
>
> Perhaps this concern is naive: watching Congress' biennial exercise in finger-painting a "comprehensive crime bill" to tout to their

constituents does not inspire one to stand firm for the principle that these folks should play a larger role in sentencing policy. But whether or not Congress would do a better job, making federal criminal law is Congress' job to do.

Gerard E. Lynch, "The Sentencing Guidelines As a Not–So–Model Penal Code," 7 Fed. Sentencing Rep. 112 (1994).

12. What does it mean to say that only the legislature may *make* criminal law? Isn't criminal lawmaking also involved in every act of statutory interpretation, by the judiciary or by the executive in "law enforcement"? Does the following provision, added to the German Penal Code in 1935 (and since repealed), violate the principle of legislativity?

German Penal Code (1935) § 2.

That person will be punished who commits an act which the law declares to be punishable or which deserves punishment according to the fundamental principle of a penal statute and the healthy sentiment of the people.

2. LENITY

Model Penal Code § 1.02. Purposes; Principles of Construction.

(1) The general purposes of the provisions governing the definition of offenses are:

(a) to forbid and prevent conduct that unjustifiably and inexcusably inflicts or threatens substantial harm to individual or public interests;

(b) to subject to public control persons whose conduct indicates that they are disposed to commit crimes;

(c) to safeguard conduct that is without fault from condemnation as criminal;

(d) to give fair warning of the nature of the conduct declared to constitute an offense;

(e) to differentiate on reasonable grounds between serious and minor offenses.

. . .

(3) The provisions of the Code shall be construed according to the fair import of their terms but when the language is susceptible of differing constructions it shall be interpreted to further the general purposes stated in this Section and the special purposes of the particular provision involved. . . .

California Penal Code § 4.

The rule of the common law, that penal statutes are to be strictly construed, has no application to this Code. All its provisions are to be construed according to the fair import of their terms, with a view to effect its objects and to promote justice.

Johnson v. State

Supreme Court of Florida.
602 So.2d 1288 (1992).

■ HARDING, JUSTICE.

The issue before the court is whether section 893.13(1)(c)1, Florida Statutes (1989), permits the criminal prosecution of a mother, who ingested a controlled substance prior to giving birth, for delivery of a controlled substance to the infant during the thirty to ninety seconds following the infant's birth, but before the umbilical cord is severed. * * *

... [T]he [paramount] rules of statutory construction in the criminal context ... [include] the rule of strict construction [and] the rule of lenity. § 775.021(1), Fla.Stat. (1989).

The rules of statutory construction require courts to strictly construe criminal statutes, and that "when the language is susceptible to differing constructions, [the statute] shall be construed most favorably to the accused." § 775.021(1). In strictly construing criminal statutes, we have held that only those terms which are " 'clearly and intelligently described in [a penal statute's] very words, as well as manifestly intended by the Legislature' " are to be considered as included in the statute. We find that the legislative history does not show a manifest intent to use the word "delivery" in the context of criminally prosecuting mothers for delivery of a controlled substance to a minor by way of the umbilical cord. This lack of legislative intent coupled with uncertainty that the term "delivery" applies to the facts of the instant case, compels this Court to construe the statute in favor of Johnson....

Johnson appeals from two convictions for delivering a controlled substance to her two minor children in violation of section 893.13(1)(c)1 (1989).[1] The state's theory of the case was that Johnson "delivered" cocaine or a derivative of the drug to her two children via blood flowing through the children's umbilical cords in the sixty-to-ninety second period after they were expelled from her birth canal but before their cords were severed....

.... On October 3, 1987, Johnson delivered a son. The birth was normal with no complications. There was no evidence of fetal distress either within the womb or during the delivery. About one and one-half minutes elapsed from the time the son's head emerged from his mother's birth canal to the time he was placed on her stomach and the cord was clamped.

1. Section 893.13(1)(c)1 provides as follows:

893.13 Prohibited acts; penalties.—

* * *

(c) Except as authorized by this chapter, it is unlawful for any person 18 years of age or older to deliver any controlled substance to a person under the age of 18 years, or to use or hire a person under the age of 18 years as an agent or employee in the sale or delivery of such a substance, or to use such person to assist in avoiding detection or apprehension for a violation of this chapter. Any person who violates this provision with respect to:

1. A controlled substance ... is guilty of a felony of the first degree....

The obstetrician who delivered Johnson's son testified he presumed that the umbilical cord was functioning normally and that it was delivering blood to the baby after he emerged from the birth canal and before the cord was clamped. Johnson admitted to the baby's pediatrician that she used cocaine the night before she delivered.

A basic toxicology test performed on Johnson and her son was positive for benzoylecgonine, a metabolite or "breakdown" product of cocaine.

In December 1988, Johnson, while pregnant with a daughter, suffered a crack overdose. Johnson told paramedics that she had taken $200 of crack cocaine earlier that evening and that she was concerned about the effects of the drug on her unborn child. Johnson was then taken to the hospital for observation.

Johnson was hospitalized again on January 23, 1989, when she was in labor. Johnson told Dr. Tompkins, an obstetrician, that she had used rock cocaine that morning while she was in labor. With the exception of finding meconium stain fluid in the amniotic sack, there were no other complications with the birth of Johnson's baby daughter. Approximately sixty-to-ninety seconds elapsed from the time the child's head emerged from her mother's birth canal until her umbilical cord was clamped.

The following day, the Department of Health and Rehabilitative Services investigated an abuse report of a cocaine baby concerning Johnson's daughter. Johnson told the investigator that she had smoked pot and crack cocaine three to four times every-other-day throughout the duration of her pregnancy with her daughter.

Johnson's mother acknowledged that Johnson had been using cocaine for at least three years during the time her daughter and son were born. * * *

[I]n [our] view, the primary question in this case is whether section 893.13(1)(c)1 was intended by the Legislature to apply to the birthing process. * * *

In 1982, sections 415.501–514 were enacted to deal with the problem of child abuse and neglect. The Legislature determined that because of the impact that abuse or neglect has on a victimized child, siblings, family structure, and inevitably on all citizens of the state, the prevention of child abuse and neglect is a priority of this state. To further this end, the Legislature required that a comprehensive approach for the prevention of abuse and neglect of children be developed for the state. The statute defined an "abused or neglected child" as a child whose physical or mental health or welfare was harmed, or threatened with harm, by the acts of omissions of the parent or other person responsible for the child's welfare. As originally defined, "harm" included physical or mental injury, sexual abuse, exploitation, abandonment, and neglect.

In 1987, a bill was proposed to broaden the definition of "harm" to include physical dependency of a newborn infant upon certain controlled drugs. However, there was a concern among legislators that this language might authorize criminal prosecutions of mothers who give birth to drug-dependent children. The bill was then amended to provide that no parent of a drug-dependent newborn shall be subject to criminal investigation solely on the basis of the infant's drug dependency. . . .

From this legislative history, it is clear that the Legislature considered and rejected a specific statutory provision authorizing criminal penalties against mothers for delivering drug-affected children who received transfer of an illegal drug derivative metabolized by the mother's body, in utero. In light of this express legislative statement, [we] conclude that the Legislature never intended for the general drug delivery statute to authorize prosecutions of those mothers who take illegal drugs close enough in time to childbirth that a doctor could testify that a tiny amount passed from mother to child in the few seconds before the umbilical cord was cut. * * *

In summary, [we] hold that section 893.13(1)(c)1 does not encompass "delivery" of an illegal drug derivative from womb to placenta to umbilical cord to newborn after a child's birth. If that is the intent of the Legislature, then this statute should be redrafted to clearly address the basic problem of passing illegal substances from mother to child in utero, not just in the birthing process.

. . . . At oral argument the State acknowledged that no other jurisdiction has upheld a conviction of a mother for delivery of a controlled substance to an infant through either the umbilical cord or an in utero transmission; nor has the State submitted any subsequent authority to reflect that this fact has changed. The Court declines the State's invitation to walk down a path that the law, public policy, reason and common sense forbid it to tread. Therefore, we quash the decision below, answer the certified question in the negative, and remand with directions that Johnson's two convictions be reversed.

It is so ordered.

QUESTIONS AND COMMENTS

1. Could *Johnson* have been decided without reference to the principle of lenity? What if the court had found that the legislative intent cut the other way? Would the rule of lenity have made a difference then?

2. Why, do you think, did the Model Penal Code explicitly abolish the rule of lenity? What about the drafters of the California Penal Code? (Here it might be helpful to know that the California Penal Code has nothing to do with the Model Penal Code. The California Penal Code was enacted in 1872; it was based largely on David Dudley Field's draft for a New York Penal Code, which itself was enacted only in 1881.) How would *Johnson* have been resolved under Model Penal Code § 1.02(3)?

3. Can lenity and legislativity be reconciled? Or does legislativity *imply* lenity?

4. Is lenity a constitutional principle? Or merely a canon of statutory interpretation? Should it apply to civil cases, as well as criminal ones? Should it be limited to *federal* criminal law?

5. Dan Kahan has argued that the rule of lenity isn't all that it is cracked up to be, pointing to its "historic underenforcement." Instead of

bemoaning disregard for the rule, however, he suggests that criminal law—and federal criminal law in particular—is better off without it:

> It is a basic axiom of federal criminal jurisprudence that a court should adopt the "harsher" of "two rational readings of a criminal statute only when Congress has spoken in clear and definite language." More than a simple canon of construction, this principle—known as the "rule of lenity"—is considered essential to securing a variety of values of near-constitutional stature. Narrow construction of criminal statutes, it is proclaimed, assures citizens fair notice of what the law proscribes; it constrains the discretion of law enforcement officials; and, most fundamentally, it embodies our legal system's " 'instinctive distaste against men languishing in prison unless the lawmaker has clearly said they should.' "
>
> This is the theory. But it isn't the reality. Judicial enforcement of lenity is notoriously sporadic and unpredictable. As often as not, the "instinctive distaste" for extinguishing individual liberty without clear legislative warrant gives way to other tastes that can be satisfied only by broad readings of federal criminal statutes.... The historic under-enforcement of lenity ... reflects the existence of another largely unacknowledged, but nonetheless well established, rule of federal criminal law: that Congress may delegate criminal lawmaking power to courts.

Dan M. Kahan, "Lenity and Federal Common Law Crimes," 1994 Sup. Ct. Rev. 345, 345–47.

3. SPECIFICITY

Texas Penal Code § 1.02. Objectives of Code.

... [T]he provisions of this code are intended, and shall be construed, to achieve the following objectives:

...

(2) by definition and grading of offenses to give fair warning of what is prohibited and of the consequences of violation;

...

(5) to guide and limit the exercise of official discretion in law enforcement to prevent arbitrary or oppressive treatment of persons suspected, accused, or convicted of offenses ...

People v. Bright

Court of Appeals of New York.
71 N.Y.2d 376 (1988).

■ TITONE, JUDGE.

I.

People v Bright

On the evening of March 19, 1985, a New York City policeman observed defendant Bright displaying an open satchel to a passerby on the

Long Island Railroad Concourse located in Pennsylvania Station. When Bright noticed that the officer was watching him, he quickly closed the satchel. The policeman approached Bright and the following conversation took place:

"Officer: What are you doing here?

"Defendant: Why are you bothering me.

"Officer: Got a ticket to take the train?

"Defendant: No.

"Officer: Are you going to take the train?

"Defendant: No."

Based solely on this exchange, the officer escorted Bright to the Long Island Railroad police office, where he asked Bright to produce identification. When Bright failed to produce any, the officer informed him that he was under arrest for loitering pursuant to Penal Law § 240.35(7). Bright was read his Miranda warnings and asked to empty his pockets. As Bright removed a piece of paper from his trouser pocket, two credit cards and four other identification cards fell to the floor, none of which belonged to him. Bright then told the officer that he had found the various cards and planned to sell them.

Defendant Bright was charged by indictment with two counts of criminal possession of stolen property in the second degree (Penal Law § 165.45[2]), and one count of criminal possession of stolen property in the third degree (Penal Law § 165.40). * * *

People v Clark

On the morning of April 24, 1985, defendant Clark was in the Port Authority Bus Terminal located in New York City when he was approached by a Port Authority police officer. Although the record is not entirely clear as to what occurred next, the officer arrested Clark for loitering in violation of Penal Law § 240.35(7) when he was unable to give a satisfactory explanation regarding his presence in the bus terminal. As an incident to that arrest, the officer searched Clark and found a cellophane envelope containing cocaine and a glass pipe with cocaine residue in the defendant's jacket pocket.

Clark was charged with loitering (Penal Law § 240.35[7]), and criminal possession of a controlled substance in the seventh degree (Penal Law § 220.03). * * *

II.

Penal Law § 240.35(7) is derived from two former enactments. Under former Penal Law § 1990–a(2), a person was guilty of an offense if he loitered or was found sleeping "about any toilet, station or station platform of a subway or elevated railway or of a railroad" and was "unable to give satisfactory explanation of his presence".

The legislative history of Penal Law § 1990–a(2) indicates that the subways and railroad stations had become an attractive place for "fakers, perverts, pickpockets, loiterers, sleepers, flimflam men, etc., [who] infest[ed] these properties, night and day, necessitating constant policing by a large force of special officers and state railway officers." Public officials and railroad authorities sought to prevent "peddlers and loiterers from harassing and annoying people on the railroad properties." The Legislature, aware that the courts were refusing to convict people arrested in the train and subway stations of vagrancy or disorderly conduct, considered the bill necessary to protect the traveling public, especially because of the desire to "clean up" the subways and other railroad facilities in anticipation of the World's Fair held in New York City in 1939.

Former Penal Law § 150(2) made it an offense to loiter "about any toilet, area, station, station platform, waiting room or other appurtenance of an air or bus terminal" unless the loiterer was able "to give satisfactory explanation of his presence". This statute, like its counterpart, Penal Law § 1990–a(2), sought to provide "maximum passenger safety, comfort and convenience" by ridding these facilities of "many undesirable characters" who were loitering, soliciting business and begging in passenger terminals.

In 1965, the Legislature enacted the statute at issue here, Penal Law § 240.35(7), restating in more general terms former Penal Laws §§ 150 and 1990–a(2). Under the statute, one is guilty of a violation if he "[l]oiters or remains in any transportation facility, or is found sleeping therein, and is unable to give a satisfactory explanation of his presence." A "transportation facility" is defined as "any conveyance, premises or place used for or in connection with public passenger transportation, whether by air, railroad, motor vehicle or any other method. It includes aircraft, watercraft, railroad cars, buses, and air, boat, railroad and bus terminals and stations and all appurtenances thereto" (Penal Law § 240.00[2]).

III.

.... In a challenge to the constitutionality of a penal law on the grounds of vagueness, it is well settled that a two-pronged analysis is required. First, the statute must provide sufficient notice of what conduct is prohibited; second, the statute must not be written in such a manner as to permit or encourage arbitrary and discriminatory enforcement (see, Kolender v. Lawson, 461 U.S. 352, 357, 103 S.Ct. 1855, 1858).

The rationale underlying the requirement that a penal statute provide adequate notice is the notion "that no man shall be held criminally responsible for conduct which he could not reasonably understand to be proscribed" (United States v. Harriss, 347 U.S. 612, 617, 74 S.Ct. 808, 812). Consistent with our concept of basic fairness, due process requires that a penal statute be sufficiently definite by its terms so as "to give a person of ordinary intelligence fair notice that his contemplated conduct is forbidden by the statute" (United States v. Harriss, supra, at 617, 74 S.Ct. at 812). For this reason, under our State and Federal Constitutions, the Legislature may not criminalize conduct that is inherently innocent merely because such conduct is "sometimes attended by improper motives," since to do so would not fairly inform the ordinary citizen that an otherwise innocent act is illegal.

The other prong of the test, which requires that a penal law not permit arbitrary or discriminatory enforcement is, perhaps, the more important aspect of the vagueness doctrine (see, Kolender v. Lawson, 461 U.S. 352, 358, 103 S.Ct. 1855, 1858, supra). The Legislature must include in a penal statute "minimal guidelines to govern law enforcement" (id.). The absence of objective standards to guide those enforcing the laws permits the police to make arrests based upon their own personal, subjective idea of right and wrong. A vague statute "confers on police a virtually unrestrained power to arrest and charge persons with a violation" (Lewis v. City of New Orleans, 415 U.S. 130, 135, 94 S.Ct. 970, 973 [Powell, J., concurring]), and "furnishes a convenient tool for 'harsh and discriminatory enforcement by local prosecuting officials, against particular groups deemed to merit their displeasure' " (Papachristou v. City of Jacksonville, 405 U.S. 156, 170, 92 S.Ct. 839, 847).

The term "loiter" or "loitering" has a commonly accepted meaning that has evolved over the years, and connotes the act of remaining about or hanging around a place without any apparent purpose. However, a statute that merely prohibits loitering, without more, is unconstitutionally vague. Such a generalized law fails to distinguish between conduct calculated to cause harm and conduct that is essentially innocent, thereby failing to give adequate notice of what conduct is prohibited. Further, such a statute impermissibly places complete discretion in the hands of the police to determine whom they will arrest.

We have upheld loitering statutes only when they either prohibited loitering for a specific illegal purpose or loitering in a specific place of restricted public access. Thus, statutes making it a crime to loiter for the purpose of using illegal drugs or for the purpose of engaging in prostitution have been upheld. Such laws provide the ordinary citizen with adequate notice of the exact conduct prohibited, and require the officer on-the-scene to objectively observe some definable impermissible act in order to find probable cause to arrest, thereby foreclosing the possibility that the law will be arbitrarily enforced. Similarly, we have held constitutional statutes prohibiting loitering in a specifically restricted place, such as a school or waterfront facility, since these locations were not open to the public, were places where illegal activity was notorious, and were normally frequented only by those who are affiliated with the activity being carried on there.

The thrust of the People's argument on this appeal in support of the statute is twofold. First, the People argue that the "satisfactory explanation" provision in the statute is constitutionally permissible. Second, the People take the position that Penal Law § 240.35(7) falls within the category of statutes prohibiting loitering in specific places of restricted public access. To support these arguments, the People rely on People v. Bell, 306 N.Y. 110, 115 N.E.2d 821, which upheld against constitutional challenge former Penal Law § 1990–a(2), a statute very similar to the one at issue here. In Bell, we held that a provision permitting the police to arrest a person for loitering unless he provides a "satisfactory explanation of his presence" is not a substantive element of the crime, but merely a procedural device to be followed by law enforcement officials in order to prevent the arrest of those who are innocent of any wrongdoing.

We further held that a subway station or railroad station was a place of restricted public access. Nevertheless, we find the People's arguments unpersuasive and in direct opposition to precedents that have emerged since Bell was decided from both this court and the United States Supreme Court.

Regardless of whether one characterizes the "satisfactory explanation" requirement as substantive or procedural, we concluded that a similar provision in a loitering statute that required a person to "identify himself" or "give a reasonably credible account of his conduct and purposes" was unconstitutional. We held that under this provision, "enforcement of the law depends entirely upon whether the arresting officer is satisfied that a suspect has given" an acceptable account of his presence. Similarly, in Kolender v. Lawson, 461 U.S. 352, 103 S.Ct. 1855 supra, the court invalidated a California loitering statute that required a person to provide identification and to account for his presence when requested by a peace officer. The court concluded that the statute contained "no standard for determining what a suspect has to do in order to satisfy the requirement" (Kolender v. Lawson, supra, at 358, 103 S.Ct. at 1858). Thus, the court held that the statute was unconstitutionally vague because it vested "virtually complete discretion in the hands of the police" without any legislative guidelines (id.). The statutory mandate at issue here that a suspect provide the officer with a "satisfactory explanation of his presence" is indistinguishable from these other "credible account" provisions. The determination as to what constitutes a "satisfactory explanation" is left entirely up to the policeman on the scene without any legislative guidance whatsoever, and renders the statute unconstitutional.

Requiring a person suspected of violating the loitering statute provide a "satisfactory explanation" to avoid arrest is also violative of a citizen's right not to answer questions posed by law enforcement officers. Although a police officer may have the right under appropriate circumstances to stop a person in a public place and make inquiry (see, Terry v. Ohio, 392 U.S. 1, 88 S.Ct. 1868), a citizen is under no obligation to provide any explanation regarding his conduct.

He is permitted to remain silent under the Fifth Amendment to the Federal Constitution and article I, section 6 of the State Constitution. However, under Penal Law § 240.35(7), he is faced with the choice of either foregoing his constitutional right to remain silent in the hope that his explanation will satisfy that particular law enforcement official, or invoking his constitutional right to remain silent and being arrested. As we held in People v. Schanbarger, 300 N.Y.S.2d 100, 248 N.E.2d 16, the failure of a suspect to answer an inquiry of a policeman "cannot constitute a criminal act".

Although "an officer may have a right to inquire into suspicious circumstances, a suspect's silence may not be used as a predicate for a separate offense such as loitering." A provision such as this one effectively deprives the citizen of his constitutional right to remain silent, since his failure to speak will result in certain arrest under the statute. It punishes a suspect for exercising his constitutional right to remain silent and impermissibly transforms the invocation of this right into a criminal act.

Even if the statute did not contain the "satisfactory explanation" requirement, however, we would still be compelled to conclude that, as applied, the statute is unconstitutionally vague. Under the Penal Law, a "transportation facility" is defined in such a broad, all-encompassing manner so as to include some facilities that are more analogous to the public street than to a specific area of restricted public access that gives notice of its prohibition against loitering. The statutory definition that embraces "all appurtenances thereto" is also too vague and wide ranging in the context of this case. At the time People v. Bell, 306 N.Y. 110, 115 N.E.2d 821, was decided, railroad stations offered few amenities, serving primarily as a place to purchase a ticket and wait for a train. Since that time, several of our transportation facilities have evolved into large, multipurpose complexes, replete with wide concourses along which numerous retail establishments of all kinds implicitly invite the public to enter, browse and shop.

The two facilities involved here, the Long Island Railroad Station and the Port Authority Bus Terminal, have numerous entrances and exits to the street, the New York City subway lines, as well as to buses, trains and house many other businesses that serve the general public. Thousands of commuters, shoppers and other people enter these terminals for a wide variety of reasons daily. As the Second Circuit has stated, the Port Authority Bus Terminal, "with its many adjuncts, becomes something of a small city." Similarly, Pennsylvania Station is also something of a small, indoor city. These facilities are not places of restricted public access like [a] school or [a] waterfront facility, which gave the loiterer notice that he had no right to be there, but, rather, large, public areas.

Since both transportation facilities at issue here are, in reality, "public places," the statute, as applied, does not satisfy due process, since it fails to give unequivocal notice to the unwary that an activity as innocuous as mere loitering is prohibited. Indeed, facilities such as Pennsylvania Station and Port Authority Bus Terminal are so public in nature, that they actually invite conduct that could be construed as loitering. Thus, in these two cases, the statute has the effect of prohibiting loitering in a public place and cannot withstand constitutional scrutiny.

Moreover, the statute is unconstitutionally vague, since it provides absolutely no legislative "guidelines governing the determination as to whether a person is engaged in suspicious loitering" in places of unrestricted public access. In such large, urban transportation facilities, many people are engaged in activity that is seemingly aimless to the objective observer, such as waiting for a train, strolling about the concourse, or waiting for the rain to stop. Nevertheless, who will be stopped, questioned, and arrested under this statute is left "solely up to the discretion of the police officer" on the scene.

People v. Nelson

Court of Appeals of New York.
69 N.Y.2d 302 (1987).

■ PER CURIAM.

In People v. Nelson et al., each of the defendants was charged with jostling (Penal Law § 165.25)* in Criminal Court informations. Police

* Penal Law § 165.25 provides: "A person is guilty of jostling when, in a public place, he intentionally and unnecessarily:

officers allegedly observed each of them patting down victims' pockets, reaching to purposely touch handbags, putting their hands into other people's pockets or crowding victims or acting as lookouts while their companions took these actions....

On appeal, defendants argue ... that the jostling statute (Penal Law § 165.25) is void for vagueness.... We disagree.

Unlike statutes which have been declared void for vagueness because they provide insufficient warning to the person of ordinary intelligence, Penal Law § 165.25 clearly delineates specific conduct easily avoided by the innocent-minded. It should present no difficulty for a citizen to comprehend that he must refrain from acting with the intent to bring his hand into the proximity of a stranger's pocket or handbag unnecessarily. Moreover, contrary to defendants' claim, the statute is no more difficult to interpret and obey because it does not require larcenous intent. Penal Law § 165.25 prohibits a certain intentional course of conduct regardless of the wrongdoer's underlying purpose or motive.

Defendants concern themselves with possible applications of the word "unnecessarily" which would be outside the statute's intended realm, such as tugging on another's handbag to gain that person's attention. It has often been said, however, that, except in rare circumstances not relevant here, a vagueness challenge must be addressed to the facts before the court. Thus, if the actions of the defendants are plainly within the ambit of the statute, the court will not strain to imagine marginal situations in which the application of the statute is not so clear. Here, defendants do not, nor could they, argue that their own acts should be interpreted as necessary. Therefore, any element of vagueness in this statute has had no effect on these defendants and they have no standing to complain of it. This court cannot consider the possibility that the statute may be vague as applied in other hypothetical situations.

Nor does Penal Law § 165.25 encourage arbitrary or discriminatory application. The law, easily followed by most citizens of this State, provides objective criteria which must be observed by a police officer prior to arrest. It is not dependent upon the subjective conclusions of a complainant or an arresting officer as to what is annoying or suspicious. This is not a statute which casts such a large net that it allows officials to round up those they have concluded to be undesirable. On the contrary, a person may be arrested pursuant to Penal Law § 165.25 if the police have probable cause to believe, based upon observable conduct, that defendant unnecessarily and intentionally placed his hand in the proximity of another's pocket or handbag. * * *

"1. Places his hand in the proximity of a person's pocket or handbag; or

"2. Jostles or crowds another person at a time when a third person's hand is in the proximity of such person's pocket or handbag."

QUESTIONS AND COMMENTS

1. How convincing do you find the first rationale for the principle of specificity, fair notice, in the context of these cases? Do you think the defendants in *Bright* were surprised to find themselves arrested for loitering?

In void-for-vagueness cases, courts tend to focus on the second (discretion) prong of the analysis. (Why do you think that is? What would happen if courts took the notice requirement seriously?) Not so in Botts v. State, 604 S.E.2d 512 (Ga. 2004), which used a notice rationale to strike down Georgia's hate crime penalty statute that enhanced the sentence whenever "the defendant intentionally selected any victim ... as the object of the offense because of bias or prejudice":

> [B]y enhancing all offenses where the victim ... was selected because of any bias or prejudice, [the statute] encompasses every possible partiality or preference. A rabid sports fan convicted of uttering terroristic threats to a victim selected for wearing a competing team's baseball cap; a campaign worker convicted of trespassing for defacing a political opponent's yard signs; a performance car fanatic convicted of stealing a Ferrari—any "bias or prejudice" for or against the selected victim ..., no matter how obscure, whimsical or unrelated to the victim it may be, ... can serve to enhance a sentence. Absent some qualification on "bias or prejudice," [the statute] is left " 'so vague that persons of common intelligence must necessarily guess at its meaning and differ as to its application.' "

The court acknowledged that "persons of ordinary intelligence may understand the dictionary definition of the words 'bias' and 'prejudice.' " So where is the notice problem? (For more on hate crimes, see ch. 5 infra.) Does it help to know that the statute is referred to as a "hate crime penalty statute"?

2. If the problem with loitering statutes is the lack of guidance they provide law enforcement officers, why should it make a difference whether a loitering statute refers to some criminal purpose or other? What if police department policies instructed officers only to arrest loiterers who loiter for a specific selection of criminal purposes, such as prostitution or drug dealing?

3. Can the results in *Bright* and *Nelson* be reconciled? Or is the vagueness inquiry itself hopelessly vague, and arbitrary? After these two opinions, will a legislature have sufficient notice of what it may criminalize without running afoul of the principle of specificity?

4. Could the loitering statute struck down in *Bright* be redrafted to render it constitutional? Would the Model Penal Code "loitering or prowling" statute survive constitutional scrutiny under *Bright*?

> **§ 250.6. Loitering or Prowling.**
>
> A person commits a violation if he loiters or prowls in a place, at a time, or in a manner not usual for law-abiding individuals under circumstances that warrant alarm for the safety of persons or property in the vicinity. Among the circumstances which may be considered in

determining whether such alarm is warranted is the fact that the actor takes flight upon appearance of a peace officer, refuses to identify himself, or manifestly endeavors to conceal himself or any object. Unless flight by the actor or other circumstance makes it impracticable, a peace officer shall prior to any arrest for an offense under this section afford the actor an opportunity to dispel any alarm which would otherwise be warranted, by requesting him to identify himself and explain his presence and conduct. No person shall be convicted of an offense under this Section if the peace officer did not comply with the preceding sentence, or if it appears at trial that the explanation given by the actor was true and, if believed by the peace officer at the time, would have dispelled the alarm.

5. The court in *Bright* makes it clear that not all loitering statutes are unconstitutionally vague. It specifically mentions, as constitutionally unobjectionable, statutes that "either prohibited loitering for a specific illegal purpose or loitering in a specific place of restricted public access." Does the loitering statute considered in the following case pass constitutional muster under this proviso?

Chicago v. Morales
Supreme Court of the United States.
527 U.S. 41 (1999).

■ JUSTICE STEVENS announced the judgment of the Court.

In 1992, the Chicago City Council enacted the Gang Congregation Ordinance, which prohibits "criminal street gang members" from "loitering" with one another or with other persons in any public place....

Before the ordinance was adopted, the city council's Committee on Police and Fire conducted hearings to explore the problems created by the city's street gangs, and more particularly, the consequences of public loitering by gang members. Witnesses included residents of the neighborhoods where gang members are most active, as well as some of the aldermen who represent those areas. Based on that evidence, the council made a series of findings that are included in the text of the ordinance and explain the reasons for its enactment.

The council found that a continuing increase in criminal street gang activity was largely responsible for the city's rising murder rate, as well as an escalation of violent and drug related crimes. It noted that in many neighborhoods throughout the city, "the burgeoning presence of street gang members in public places has intimidated many law abiding citizens." 177 Ill. 2d 440, 445, 687 N.E.2d 53, 58, 227 Ill. Dec. 130 (1997). Furthermore, the council stated that gang members "establish control over identifiable areas ... by loitering in those areas and intimidating others from entering those areas; and ... members of criminal street gangs avoid arrest by committing no offense punishable under existing laws when they know the police are present...." Ibid. It further found that "loitering in public places by criminal street gang members creates a justifiable fear for the safety of persons and property in the area" and that "aggressive action is necessary to preserve the city's streets and other public places so that the public may use such places without fear.'' Moreover, the council concluded that the city ''has an interest in discouraging all persons from loitering in public places with criminal gang members.'' Ibid.

The ordinance creates a criminal offense punishable by a fine of up to $500, imprisonment for not more than six months, and a requirement to perform up to 120 hours of community service. Commission of the offense involves four predicates. First, the police officer must reasonably believe that at least one of the two or more persons present in a ''public place'' is a ''criminal street gang member.'' Second, the persons must be ''loitering,'' which the ordinance defines as ''remaining in any one place with no apparent purpose.'' Third, the officer must then order ''all'' of the persons to disperse and remove themselves ''from the area.'' Fourth, a person must disobey the officer's order. If any person, whether a gang member or not, disobeys the officer's order, that person is guilty of violating the ordinance.[2]

Two months after the ordinance was adopted, the Chicago Police Department promulgated General Order 92–4 to provide guidelines to govern its enforcement.[3] That order purported to establish limitations on the enforcement discretion of police officers ''to ensure that the anti-gang loitering ordinance is not enforced in an arbitrary or discriminatory way.'' Chicago Police Department, General Order 92–4. The limitations confine the authority to arrest gang members who violate the ordinance to sworn ''members of the Gang Crime Section'' and certain other designated officers, and establish detailed criteria for defining street gangs and membership in such gangs. In addition, the order directs district commanders to ''designate areas in which the

2. The ordinance states in pertinent part:

''(a) Whenever a police officer observes a person whom he reasonably believes to be a criminal street gang member loitering in any public place with one or more other persons, he shall order all such persons to disperse and remove themselves from the area. Any person who does not promptly obey such an order is in violation of this section.

''(b) It shall be an affirmative defense to an alleged violation of this section that no person who was observed loitering was in fact a member of a criminal street gang.

''(c) As used in this section:

''(1) 'Loiter' means to remain in any one place with no apparent purpose.

''(2) 'Criminal street gang' means any ongoing organization, association in fact or group of three or more persons, whether formal or informal, having as one of its substantial activities the commission of one or more of the criminal acts enumerated in paragraph (3), and whose members individually or collectively engage in or have engaged in a pattern of criminal gang activity.

. . . .

''(5) 'Public place' means the public way and any other location open to the public, whether publicly or privately owned.

''(e) Any person who violates this Section is subject to a fine of not less than $100 and not more than $500 for each offense, or imprisonment for not more than six months, or both.

''In addition to or instead of the above penalties, any person who violates this section may be required to perform up to 120 hours of community service pursuant to section 1–4–120 of this Code.'' Chicago Municipal Code § 8–4–015.

3. [D]uring the hearings preceding the adoption of the ordinance, ''representatives of the Chicago law and police departments informed the city counsel that any limitations on the discretion police have in enforcing the ordinance would be best developed through police policy, rather than placing such limitations into the ordinance itself.''

presence of gang members has a demonstrable effect on the activities of law abiding persons in the surrounding community," and provides that the ordinance "will be enforced only within the designated areas." Id. at 68a–69a. The city, however, does not release the locations of these "designated areas" to the public.

The Supreme Court struck down the Chicago ordinance because it "fails to give the ordinary citizen adequate notice of what is forbidden and what is permitted" and " 'provides absolute discretion to police officers to determine what activities constitute loitering'." But what about the police department guidelines specifically designed to guide police officer discretion? Aren't detailed expert policies of this sort more likely to actually guide the discretion of officers in the field than necessarily broad statutory guideposts? And what about the council's finding that "a continuing increase in criminal street gang activity was largely responsible for the city's rising murder rate, as well as an escalation of violent and drug related crimes"? And the involvement of "residents of the neighborhoods where gang members are most active, as well as some of the aldermen who represent those areas"?

6. Although loitering statutes have attracted the lion's share of judicial attention, vagueness issues arise throughout the special, and even the general, part of criminal law. Consider the following opinion, which frankly balances the relative merits of "indefiniteness" and "justice."

State v. Maldonado
Supreme Court of New Jersey.
137 N.J. 536, 645 A.2d 1165 (1994).

■ PER CURIAM.

Defendants ... challenge the constitutionality of that portion of the Comprehensive Drug Reform Act of 1986 that imposes strict criminal liability on manufacturers and distributors of certain controlled dangerous substances (CDS) when death results from the ingestion of the CDSs [section 9].[a] ...

Lucy Maldonado obtained heroin for her friend Larry Dunka on May 7, 1988 as an accommodation—she made no profit. Larry's brother John accompanied him in making the purchase and participated in the use of the heroin. After the purchase Larry and John took the

a. N.J. Stat. Ann. § 2C:35–9 (section 9) reads as follows:

a. Any person who manufactures, distributes or dispenses [a] controlled dangerous substance ... is strictly liable for a death which results from the injection, inhalation or ingestion of that substance, and is guilty of a crime of the first degree.

b. ... For purposes of this offense, the defendant's act of manufacturing, distributing or dispensing a substance is the cause of a death when:

(1) The injection, inhalation or ingestion of the substance is an antecedent but for which the death would not have occurred; and

(2) The death was not:

(a) too remote in its occurrence as to have a just bearing on the defendant's liability; or

(b) too dependent upon conduct of another person which was unrelated to the injection, inhalation or ingestion of the substance or its effect as to have a just bearing on the defendant's liability.—EDS.

heroin to another location where Larry injected some of it into his own arm and then into John's arm. When John came to the next morning, he found Larry on the floor dead. [Maldonado pleaded guilty to a violation of section 9 and was sentenced to fifteen years in prison.]

In *Rodriguez*, defendant distributed cocaine to Fred Bennett. Present were Susan Hendricks, defendant's girlfriend, and another man who had accompanied Bennett to defendant's apartment. The cocaine had been weighed and bagged when the police broke into the apartment. In an attempt to hide the evidence, Hendricks and Bennett each swallowed a plastic bag containing cocaine. Within minutes of the police entry, Hendricks collapsed in convulsions on the floor. Emergency medical workers were summoned and, with Bennett looking on, they attempted to resuscitate her. While the medical workers attempted to revive Hendricks, they specifically asked whether anyone else had swallowed drugs. Bennett responded that he had not. Approximately a half hour later, Bennett also went into convulsions and died at the scene. Hendricks subsequently died at the hospital. Rodriguez was charged with violating section 9 for Bennett's death only. [He was convicted at trial and sentenced to eighteen years' imprisonment.]

* * *

The part of section 9 said to be unconstitutionally vague provides that a defendant shall not be convicted unless the State proves beyond a reasonable doubt that the resulting death was "not too remote in its occurrence" and "not too dependent upon conduct of another person . . . as to have a just bearing on the defendant[s'] liability." N.J. Stat. Ann. § 2C:35–9b.

The vagueness charge here does not relate to the first[, notice,] aspect of [the vagueness] doctrine. Necessarily, no drug distributor will be influenced in his conduct, or be able to shape his conduct to conform to the statute since by definition the distributor has no control over the regulated results. No matter how precisely the remoteness factor were defined, no drug distributor could conform his conduct to assure compliance because the law would still punish unintended and unforeseen deaths, even if it were more narrowly circumscribed. A different definition might make a defendant more or less willing not to distribute drugs at all, but that is not the aspect of vagueness that is referred to when it is claimed that vagueness prevents defendants from conforming their conduct to the law. . . . Thus, our "vagueness" analysis focuses on the risk of arbitrary or discriminatory enforcement of section 9. * * *

We concede the basic correctness of defendants' initial contention: exculpation of defendants on the ground that the result for which they would otherwise be liable was too remote to make such liability just is indefinite, indeed considerably so. If the remoteness is expressed in terms of the expiration of time between the act and the result, how long must it be before it is remote; if in terms of space, how far in order to be remote; if in terms of cause and effect, how many other and what kind of causes must there be; and if in terms of difference from what was intended, how much and in what ways must the actual result differ from what was intended? Despite the indefiniteness of the remoteness limitation on liability, however, fairness seems to require some such limitation on a defendant's liability. Thus, a problem arises: how do we limit criminal liability so that defendants are not unjustly punished without creating an intolerable amount of vagueness. * * *

The drafters of the Model Penal Code resolved the conflict between the desirability of limiting criminal liability for results otherwise falling within the law's prohibition but whose occurrence was so far from the ordinary or expectable as to leave doubt about the justice of imposing such liability, and the impossibility of fashioning language to define the extent of such limitation in a way to assure acceptably consistent application by adopting the "too remote to have a just bearing" language. Model Penal Code § 2.03(2)(b), (3)(b) (1985). * * *

The question, then, is whether the law can constitutionally accommodate this conflict in what the most learned of our colleagues have concluded is the best way, or whether, because of the indefiniteness involved, the law must abandon the search. If we choose the latter course, we face an intolerable predicament, for we would be forced either to extend criminal responsibility regardless of remoteness, or to confine it restrictively, severely limiting its scope and effectiveness simply to avoid the possibility of arbitrary application. Therefore, we choose the former—the law is constitutional—and we do so as a matter of our own sense of sound policy. * * *

Th[e] "sense of justice" is clearly involved in many criminal cases. Juries possess not only the unwritten power of nullification,[4] but juries also have the almost-absolute ability to determine life and death in sentencing proceedings under our capital punishment law. The acknowledged power of jurors, seemingly irrationally, certainly not explicitly rationally, to exercise lenity by not convicting of certain charges when the rest of their verdict may clearly indicate guilt is but another example. What other explanation exists for our accommodation of jurors' instincts but our faith in their "sense of justice"? To argue that the benefits of such a rule outweigh its potential detriments, or its actual detriments, is difficult, because some believe that outcomes in criminal cases are wildly unpredictable and that our present system does not afford the consistency that is supposed to be the bedrock of our system of justice. We believe the contrary, but regardless of our belief, we know of no better solution. We realize that given the same set of facts one jury may decide the result is too remote to have a just bearing on defendant's criminal responsibility, and another may not—but the same may be said for almost any submission to juries in criminal cases.

[O]ur trust in juries to understand and apply the "not too remote" element "is indicative of a belief that the jury in a criminal prosecution

4. Indeed, the drafters of the Criminal Code included the "not too remote" exculpation factor partly in anticipation of, and as an accommodation to, the urge of jurors to nullify. "The advantage of putting the issue squarely to the jury's sense of justice is that it does not attempt to force a result which the jury may resist." New Jersey Criminal Law Revision Commission, The New Jersey Penal Code 361 (1971).

serves as the conscience of the community and the embodiment of the common sense and feelings reflective of society as a whole." "[A]nd law in the last analysis must reflect the general community sense of justice." Frances B. Sayre, Public Welfare Offenses, 33 Colum. L. Rev. 55, 70 (1933).

... [W]e have little doubt that remoteness may save a low-level distributor much more often than it will save the manufacturer or kingpin, either because a jury may sense that a manufacturer or kingpin should contemplate the innumerable transactions and occurrences that may follow the original manufacturer or distribution and ultimately led to death whereas the lower level distributor may not, or because the ultimate culpability of one is deemed greater than the other. "Just bearing" allows for consideration of all factors. That is its merit on the side of justice, and its deficit in the expansion of indefiniteness. On balance, we hold that it is constitutional.

7. Federal criminal statutes in general, and white collar crime statutes in particular, have come under vagueness scrutiny. RICO is one, prominent, example.

RICO is a statute of daunting complexity, comprising eight separate lengthy sections. But the length and complexity of the statute helps to mask a certain simplicity in the structure of the criminal prohibitions imposed.

The core of the statute, 18 U.S.C. § 1962, creates four new crimes. Under section 1962(a), it is a crime for any person to "use or invest" any income he has derived "from a pattern of racketeering activity or through collection of an unlawful debt" to establish, operate, or acquire an interest in "any enterprise" engaged in or affecting interstate commerce. Section 1962(b) prohibits acquiring or maintaining an interest in, or control of, any such enterprise "through a pattern of racketeering activity or through collection of an unlawful debt." Subsection (c) of section 1962 makes it a crime for any person "employed by or associated with any enterprise" in or affecting commerce "to conduct or participate, directly or indirectly, in the conduct of such enterprise's affairs through a pattern of racketeering activity or collection of unlawful debt." Finally, section 1962(d) prohibits conspiracies to violate the other three prohibitions. * * *

The argument that RICO is unconstitutionally vague has been uniformly rejected, and on reasoning that is not unappealing. After all, courts have reminded us that, unlike the imprecise loitering statutes that have been found unconstitutionally vague by various courts, RICO does not require citizens to guess at their peril what kinds of conduct they must avoid to conduct their affairs in accordance with law. Since RICO merely imposes additional liability on those who, under certain conditions, commit particular other offenses, all one needs to do to stay out of trouble is to avoid committing murder, mail fraud, narcotics violations, and other predicate acts. Assuming the statutes defining these crimes are not unconstitutionally vague in their own right, RICO provides adequate notice of the prohibited conduct. As one court put it, RICO "may be broad, but it is not vague."

But this answer dodges important problems. It is not clear that the values of legality for guidance of the citizen are adequately served by a scheme in which prohibitions are clearly stated, but unexpectedly severe penalties can be imposed. Without a reasonably clear statement of the penalties that attach to a particular offense, the citizen planning her activities is not really given full notice of what behavior society truly expects from her. The intensity of society's demand, as expressed in the available punishment, is relevant to the actor's understanding of her responsibilities. In some respects, at least, the Constitution protects a citizen's justified expectation that conduct is only punishable to a particular extent in the same way as her expectation that conduct is lawful....

Gerard E. Lynch, "RICO: The Crime of Being a Criminal," 87 Colum. L. Rev. 661, 680–81, 717–18 (1987).

Why might a legislature decide to pass a vague (or a broad) criminal statute? (How does vagueness affect the separation of powers?) What are the merits of vagueness from the perspective of the various rationales for punishment? Should vagueness be balanced against the benefits of more effective law enforcement? For more on RICO, see ch. 11 infra.

8. In the special part of *state* criminal law, stalking laws have faced a series of vagueness challenges, some of which have been successful. Contrast State v. Bryan, 259 Kan. 143, 910 P.2d 212 (1996) (striking down the following statute: "(a) Stalking is an intentional and malicious following ... directed at a specific person when such following or course of conduct seriously alarms, annoys or harasses the person, and which serves no legitimate purpose.") with State v. Asmussen, 668 N.W.2d 725 (S.D. 2003) (upholding the following statute: "Any person: (1) Who willfully, maliciously, and repeatedly follows or harasses another person; or ... (3) Who willfully, maliciously, and repeatedly harasses another person by means of any verbal, electronic, mechanical, telegraphic, or written communication; is guilty of the crime of stalking."). Do these statutes provide sufficient notice about what constitutes stalking? What if the statute included a reference to "*reasonable* fear," or to conduct that "would cause a *reasonable person* to suffer substantial emotional distress"? The New York Court of Appeals upheld that state's stalking statute, N.Y. Penal Law § 120.45 (criminalizing, among other things, "intentionally, and for no legitimate purpose, engag[ing] in a course of conduct directed at a specific person ... likely to cause reasonable fear of material harm to the physical health, safety or property of such person") against a vagueness challenge on these facts:

Although defendant had not previously known his victim, a 22–year-old student, he approached her outside a card store and presented her with a bouquet of flowers on Valentine's Day 2000. Complainant refused the gift, but defendant insisted she take it, introduced himself as "Paul," and shook her hand. Ultimately she took the flowers and walked away.

Later that month, defendant stood "shoulder-to-shoulder" next to complainant at a local coffee shop. He asked her to sit down and have a cup of coffee with him. After she declined, defendant asked her to dinner. She refused, telling him that her boyfriend would not appreciate his advances. Undeterred, defendant presented her with a heart-shaped box of chocolates and a portrait of her that he had drawn. On the portrait defendant had inscribed complainant's first name. Disquieted by this unwanted attention, complainant "made it clear" to defendant that she did not want any further contact with him. After he insisted that complainant accept the gifts, she took them and left the coffee shop to go to a library. Defendant followed her, twice ducking behind trees when complainant looked over her shoulder. When she got to the library, she described defendant to a security guard. A friend then accompanied complainant to the police precinct, where she turned in a written report of the incident. Worried, she spent the night at the friend's house.

A few days later, complainant went to an athletic club on the second floor of a building near her home. From the street below, passersby could see the club's patrons. Defendant positioned himself where he could see complainant and stare at her while she was working out. Increasingly frightened, she called a friend to meet her at the club and accompany her as she left. Once on the street, they saw defendant handing out flyers. Complainant and her friend then went to a bank to withdraw money. Defendant followed and watched them wait in line at the ATM.

The next day, defendant trailed complainant twice. During a break in her classes, he followed her to a delicatessen where she bought lunch. That evening, he followed her home. Rather than go to her dormitory room, complainant took refuge in a delicatessen on the ground floor of her building, where she telephoned her father and stayed for 40 minutes, afraid to leave. During that entire time, defendant paced outside, staring at her through the windows. When complainant left the deli, defendant was still in the area and began walking toward her.

The following day, defendant watched complainant and her friend have lunch and tracked the pair while they shopped, coming within five feet of them. Whenever they looked back at him, defendant would try to hide behind walls or trees. The two friends then walked to the police precinct. Defendant suspended his pursuit only when the two women approached the station house, where complainant filed another report.

For almost every day over the ensuing five weeks, defendant followed complainant to various locations, including her dormitory, school and gymnasium, and to stores and restaurants in the neighborhood. When she caught sight of him, defendant would often duck behind a corner and peek out to leer at her. She was frequently accompanied by her friend, who saw defendant following complainant two to three times a week.

Fearful and distraught, complainant again contacted the police and altered her daily patterns, trying to shake defendant off. His intrusive behavior only intensified, and on April 5, 2000, for the first time, he trailed her outside her neighborhood. On that day, complainant went shopping in uptown Manhattan. When taking the subway

> home, she saw defendant enter her subway car. Defendant did not approach her, but stood several feet away, staring and smirking. Afraid to go home, complainant again spent the night at her friend's house. The following day, she went to the police and filed another report.
>
> The day after that, she saw defendant tracking her once more. For a fifth time, complainant went to the police station, where she broke down in tears. Police arrested defendant the next day and charged him with . . . stalking. . . .

People v. Stuart, 100 N.Y.2d 412 (2003).

9. Although attacks on stalking statutes tend to be framed in vagueness terms, they are often aimed at a different, substantive, issue, e.g., that stalking is already criminalized under existing statutes. See, e.g., People v. Furey, 2 Misc.3d 1011, 784 N.Y.S.2d 922 (Crim. Ct. 2004) (rejecting double jeopardy claim by distinguishing between "harassment"—which includes "stalking-like behavior"—as a public order offense and "stalking" as an offense that inflicts physical and emotional harm on individual victims, and by pointing out that "harassment" requires an "intent to harass, annoy or alarm" on the part of the stalker, while "stalking" focuses on the victim's fear of harm).

This is not unusual in vagueness cases. Is the trouble with vagrancy or RICO really that they are vague, or that they are offensive on substantive grounds because they're "overbroad," i.e., they reach conduct that shouldn't be criminalized in the first place, so that making the statutory proscription more specific wouldn't make it less objectionable? Is vagueness simply a convenient cover for courts unwilling, or unable, to strike down a statute on other grounds? What grounds could those be, in the cases of vagrancy and RICO? Reconsider *Botts*, supra note 1, in this context. Also consider the following excerpt from the U.S. Supreme Court's opinion striking down Jacksonville's vagrancy ordinance, ostensibly on vagueness grounds, in Papachristou v. Jacksonville, 405 U.S. 156 (1972):

> The Jacksonville ordinance makes criminal activities which by modern standards are normally innocent. "Nightwalking" is one. . . . We know . . . from experience that sleepless people often walk at night, perhaps hopeful that sleep-inducing relaxation will result.
>
> Luis Munoz–Marin, former Governor of Puerto Rico, commented once that 'loafing" was a national virtue in his Commonwealth and that it should be encouraged. . . .
>
> "(P)ersons able to work but habitually living upon the earnings of their wives or minor children"—like habitually living "without visible means of support"—might implicate unemployed pillars of the community who have married rich wives. . . . Persons "wandering or strolling" from place to place have been extolled by Walt Whitman and Vachel Lindsay. The qualification "without any lawful purpose or object" may be a trap for innocent acts. Persons "neglecting all lawful business and habitually spending their time by frequenting . . . places where alcoholic beverages are sold or served" would literally embrace many members of golf clubs and city clubs. . . .

The difficulty is that these activities are historically part of the amenities of life as we have known them. They are not mentioned in the Constitution or in the Bill of Rights. These unwritten amenities have been in part responsible for giving our people the feeling of independence and self-confidence, the feeling of creativity. These amenities have dignified the right of dissent and have honored the right to be nonconformists and the right to defy submissiveness. They have encouraged lives of high spirits rather than hushed, suffocating silence.

4. PROSPECTIVITY

United States Constitution art. I.

§ 9. No bill of attainder or ex post facto Law shall be passed.

§ 10. No state shall ... pass any bill of attainder, ex post facto law, or law impairing the obligation of contracts, or grant any title of nobility.

North Dakota Criminal Code § 12.1–01–01.... **Retroactivity—Application**....

2. This title, except as provided in subsection 3, shall not apply to offenses committed prior to its effective date. Prosecutions for such offenses shall be governed by prior law, which is continued in effect for that purpose. For the purposes of this section, an offense was committed prior to the effective date of this title if any of the elements of the offense occurred prior thereto.

3. In cases pending on or after the effective date of this title, and involving offenses committed prior thereto:

a. The provisions of this title according a defense or mitigation shall apply, with the consent of the defendant.

b. The court, with the consent of the defendant, may impose sentence under the provisions of this title which are applicable to the offense and the offender.

Rogers v. Tennessee

Supreme Court of the United States.
532 U.S. 451, 121 S.Ct. 1693 (2001).

■ JUSTICE O'CONNOR delivered the opinion of the Court.

[Wilbert Rogers stabbed a man, who died some 15 months later. After his conviction of second degree murder, he appealed on the basis of the common law "year and a day rule," which provides that no defendant can be convicted of murder unless his victim died by the defendant's act within a year and a day of the act. The Tennessee Supreme Court abolished the rule and applied its decision to petitioner to uphold his conviction.]

This case concerns the constitutionality of the retroactive application of a judicial decision abolishing the common law "year and a day rule." * * *

Although petitioner's claim is one of due process, the Constitution's *Ex Post Facto* Clause figures prominently in his argument. The Clause provides simply that "no State shall ... pass any ... ex post facto Law." Art. I, § 10, cl. 1. The most well-known and oft-repeated explanation of the scope of the Clause's protection was given by Justice Chase, who long ago identified, in dictum, four types of laws to which the Clause extends:

"1st. Every law that makes an action done before the passing of the law, and which was innocent when done, criminal; and punishes such action. 2d. Every law that aggravates a crime, or makes it greater than it was, when committed. 3d. Every law that changes the punishment, and inflicts a greater punishment, than the law annexed to the crime, when committed. 4th. Every law that alters the legal rules of evidence, and receives less, or different, testimony, than the law required at the time of the commission of the offense, in order to convict the offender." *Calder* v. *Bull*, 3 Dallas 386, 390 (1798)

[L]imitations on *ex post facto* judicial decisionmaking are inherent in the notion of due process.... [T]his Court has often recognized the "basic principle that a criminal statute must give fair warning of the conduct that it makes a crime." Deprivation of the right to fair warning, we continued, can result both from vague statutory language and from an unforeseeable and retroactive judicial expansion of statutory language that appears narrow and precise on its face. For that reason, "if a judicial construction of a criminal statute is 'unexpected and indefensible by reference to the law which had been expressed prior to the conduct in issue,' [the construction] must not be given retroactive effect." *Bouie* v. *City of Columbia,* 378 U.S. 347, 354 (1964) (quoting J. Hall, General Principles of Criminal Law 61 (2d ed. 1960)). * * *

Petitioner observes that the Due Process and *Ex Post Facto* Clauses safeguard common interests—in particular, the interests in fundamental fairness (through notice and fair warning) and the prevention of the arbitrary and vindictive use of the laws. While this is undoubtedly correct, petitioner is mistaken to suggest that these considerations compel extending the strictures of the *Ex Post Facto* Clause to the context of common law judging. The *Ex Post Facto* Clause, by its own terms, does not apply to courts. Extending the Clause to courts through the rubric of due process thus would circumvent the clear constitutional text. It also would evince too little regard for the important institutional and contextual differences between legislating, on the one hand, and common law decisionmaking, on the other.

Petitioner contends that state courts acting in their common law capacity act much like legislatures in the exercise of their lawmaking function, and indeed may in some cases even be subject to the same kinds of political influences and pressures that justify *ex post facto* limitations upon legislatures. A court's "opportunity for discrimination," however, "is more limited than [a] legislature's, in that [it] can only act in construing existing law in actual litigation." *James* v. *United States,* 366 U.S. 213, 247, n. 3, 6 L. Ed. 2d 246, 81 S. Ct. 1052 (1961) (Harlan, J., concurring in part and dissenting in part). Moreover, "given the divergent pulls of flexibility and precedent in our case law system," incorporation of the *Calder* categories into due process limitations on judicial decisionmaking would place an unworkable and unacceptable restraint on normal judicial processes and would be incompatible with the resolution of uncertainty that marks any evolving legal system. * * *

[A]t the time of petitioner's crime the year and a day rule had only the most tenuous foothold as part of the criminal law of the State of Tennessee. The rule did not exist as part of Tennessee's statutory criminal code. And while the Supreme Court of Tennessee concluded that the rule persisted at common law, it also pointedly observed that the rule had never once served as a ground of decision in any prosecution for murder in the State. Indeed, in all the reported Tennessee cases, the rule has been mentioned only three times, and each time in dicta. * * *

The judgment of the Supreme Court of Tennessee is accordingly affirmed.

■ JUSTICE SCALIA, dissenting.

The Court today approves the conviction of a man for a murder that was not murder (but only manslaughter) when the offense was committed. It thus violates a principle—encapsulated in the maxim *nulla poena sine lege*—which "dates from the ancient Greeks" and has been described as one of the most "widely held value-judgments in the entire history of human thought." J. Hall, General Principles of Criminal Law 59 (2d ed. 1960). Today's opinion produces, moreover, a curious constitution that only a judge could love. One in which (by virtue of the *Ex Post Facto* Clause) the elected representatives of all the people cannot retroactively make murder what was not murder when the act was committed; but in which unelected judges can do precisely that. One in which the predictability of parliamentary lawmaking cannot validate the retroactive creation of crimes, but the predictability of judicial lawmaking can do so. I do not believe this is the system that the Framers envisioned—or, for that matter, that any reasonable person would imagine. * * *

.... Madison wrote that "*ex-post-facto* laws ... are contrary to the first principles of the social compact, and to every principle of social legislation." The Federalist No. 44, p. 282 (C. Rossiter ed. 1961). I find it impossible to believe, as the Court does, that this strong sentiment attached only to retroactive laws passed by the legislature, and would not apply equally (or indeed with even greater force) to a court's production of the same result through disregard of the traditional limits upon judicial power. Insofar as the "first principles of the social compact" are concerned, what possible difference does it make that "[a] court's opportunity for discrimination" by retroactively changing a law "is more limited than a legislature's, in that it can only act in construing existing law in actual litigation"? The injustice to the individuals affected is no less.

Even if I agreed with the Court that the Due Process Clause is violated only when there is lack of "fair warning" of the impending retroactive change, I would not find such fair warning here. It is not clear to me, in fact, what the Court believes the fair warning consisted of. Was it the mere fact that "the year and a day rule is widely viewed as an outdated relic of the common law"? So are many of the elements of common-law crimes, such as "breaking the close" as an element of burglary, or "asportation" as an element of larceny. See W. LaFave & A. Scott, Criminal Law 631–633, 708–710 (1972). Are all of these "outdated relics" subject to retroactive judicial rescission? Or perhaps the fair warning consisted of the fact that "the year and a day rule has been legislatively or judicially abolished in the vast majority of jurisdictions recently to have addressed the issue." But why not count in petitioner's favor (as giving him no reason to expect a change in law) those even more numerous jurisdictions that have chosen *not* "recently to have addressed the issue"? . . .

In any event, as the Court itself acknowledges, "due process . . . does not require a person to apprise himself of the common law of all 50 States in order to guarantee that his actions will not subject him to punishment in light of a developing trend in the law that has not yet made its way to his State." * * *

QUESTIONS AND COMMENTS

1. *Criminal.* The principle of prospectivity—or the prohibition of retroactivity—seems clear enough, but turns out to be riddled with exceptions. Ever since the 1798 *civil* case of *Calder v. Bull*, the general constitutional provision that "[n]o . . . ex post facto Law shall be passed" applies only to *criminal* laws. Why should that be? What would happen if the constitutional provision meant what it said?

The limitation to criminal law is a familiar one, and places the principle of prospectivity along other constitutional protections that come into play only once the state action in question has been labelled "criminal," "penal," or "punitive." So, for instance, in Kansas v. Hendricks, 521 U.S. 346 (1997), supra ch. 1, the Court rejected both double jeopardy and ex post facto attacks on Kansas's law providing for the indefinite commitment of "sexually violent predators" past completion of their "criminal" sentence because it found the law to be "nonpunitive." Similarly, the Court held in Smith v. Doe, 538 U.S. 84 (2003), that an Alaska statute requiring certain sex offenders to register at their local police stations four times each year for life and posting offenders' personal information—including picture, address, place of employment (if any), race, hair color, height, weight, and date of birth—on the internet (see Alaska Dept. Pub. Safety, Sex Offender Registration, Central Registry, http://www.dps.state.ak.us/nSorcr/asp/) does not impose "punishment" and therefore is not subject to the constitutional prospectivity requirement.

2. *Legislative.* As *Rogers* illustrates, the limitation to *criminal* laws isn't the only one applying to the principle of prospectivity. It's clear that the principle applies to the legislature. There is no reason why it shouldn't also apply to the judiciary, or the executive for that matter, if these branches are involved in making criminal law, or its functional equivalent. Still, the *Rogers* majority suggests why limiting a straightforward proscription of retrospective lawmaking to the legislature might make sense. Do these suggestions convince you? Or does the dissent have the better of this argument?

Apart from making, or changing, the definitions of offenses, or their punishments, as arguably was the case in *Rogers*, courts tend to be active in defining, expanding, and curtailing *defenses*. Even under the limited circumstances set out in *Calder v. Bull*, would the judicial recognition of a new defense, not provided for by statute, violate the principle of prospectivity? What about eliminating a judicially created defense, or limiting it? Or expanding it? Note that, in heavily codified German criminal law, the defense of balance of evils (which justifies the commission of a crime if the benefits of doing so outweigh the harm caused) was first recognized in a judicial decision, in an abortion prosecution, where the doctor performed the abortion to save the life of the mother. RGSt 61, 242 (1927). The defense was not codified until some forty years later, in 1969. See StGB § 34 (necessity as justification); see also Model Penal Code § 3.02.

More generally, does the dissent's distinction between "applying," "changing," and "overruling" the law hold water, particularly in a legal system that remains committed to the ideal of "the common law"? (Reconsider *Meadows*, supra.)

What about the executive? Since the Ex Post Facto Clause applies, on its face, only to a "law," U.S. Const. art. I, § 10, does it apply to agency regulations? This issue has arisen frequently with respect to sentencing guidelines, see, e.g., United States v. Bell, 991 F.2d 1445, 1450 (8th Cir. 1993) (holding that the federal sentencing guidelines were subject to ex post facto analysis because legislature "cannot escape the Constitutional constraints on its power by delegating its lawmaking function to an agency"), and regulations issued by departments of corrections, see, e.g., Smith v. Scott, 223 F.3d 1191 (10th Cir. 2000) (retrospective application of amendment to prison regulation regarding earned time credits violated Ex Post Facto Clause).

3. *Substantive*. *Rogers* also illustrates the different treatment of substantive and procedural rules under the prospectivity principle. The principle is generally thought to apply primarily (if not exclusively) to substantive rules. But see Carmell v. Texas, 529 U.S. 513 (2000) (retrospective elimination of requirement that victim testimony be corroborated violates Ex Post Facto Clause). Is the year and a day rule a doctrine of substance, or of procedure? Is it a prerequisite for murder liability in the same way that "killing of another person" is? Or is it simply an evidentiary rule of convenience about a firm point in time at which it is declared to be impossible—or at least exceedingly difficult—to *prove* that a "killing of another person" has occurred? If it is a rule of substance, is it an offense element? As the majority stresses repeatedly, the rule appeared nowhere in the statutory definition of murder, nor anywhere else in the criminal code for that matter. Would it make a difference if it were an offense element, a defense element, or a "sentencing factor"?

What if a state retroactively extends the statute of limitations for a crime? After expiration of the limitations period? Before? Is that a substantive change or a procedural one? Should it matter? See Stogner v. California, 539 U.S. 607 (2003) (allowing revival of time-barred sex offenses violates Ex Post Facto Clause, but extending unexpired statute of limitations may not).

How about changes pertaining to the consideration of parole eligibility? See, e.g., California Dep't of Corrections v. Morales, 514 U.S. 499 (1995) (retrospective application of a statute permitting a decrease in the frequency of parole reconsideration hearings from every year to every three years does not constitute ex post facto violation; otherwise judiciary would be charged "with the micromanagement of an endless array of legislative adjustments to parole and sentencing procedures, including such innocuous adjustments as changes to the membership of the Board of Prison Terms, restrictions on the hours that prisoners may use the prison law library, reductions in the duration of the parole hearing, restrictions on the time allotted for a convicted defendant's right of allocution before a sentencing judge, and page limitations on a defendant's objections to presentence reports or on documents seeking a pardon from the governor").

4. *Detrimental.* Another distinction that is commonly drawn in the law of prospectivity is that between retrospective changes in the law that are detrimental to the defendant, and those that are beneficial. Only the former are said to violate the principle of prospectivity. So, for instance, if the Tennessee Supreme Court in *Rogers* had *adopted* the year and a day rule, rather than abandoning it, it could have applied its ruling retrospectively. Does that make sense? What rationale for the prospectivity principle could accommodate this distinction between detrimental and beneficial lawmaking?

Standard Penal Code for Latin America[a]

Article 8

If a new statute is enacted after the criminal act was committed, defendant will be prosecuted under the more benign law applicable to the specific case....

Article 9

If a more benign statute is enacted while the convict is serving his sentence, the court with jurisdiction should modify said sentence accordingly.

5. PUBLICITY

Penal Law of Israel § 3.

(a) An enactment creating an offence shall not apply to an act done before the date of its publication in accordance with law or the date it takes effect, whichever is later.

Model Penal Code § 2.04. Ignorance or Mistake.

(3) A belief that conduct does not legally constitute an offense is a defense to a prosecution for that offense based upon such conduct when:

(a) the statute or other enactment defining the offense is not known to the actor and has not been published or otherwise reasonably made available prior to the conduct alleged....

a. Jose M. Canals & Henry Dahl trans., 17 Am. J. Crim. L. 263 (1990).—EDS.

United States v. Casson

United States Court of Appeals for the District of Columbia Circuit.
434 F.2d 415 (1970).

■ MACKINNON, CIRCUIT JUDGE.

At 3:05 P.M. on December 27, 1967, the President affixed his signature to an act for the District of Columbia[2] which, *inter alia*, defined the crime of burglary in the first degree, increased the minimum and maximum punishment therefor, and increased the minimum punishment for robbery by amending the prior laws on both crimes. Between 10 P.M. and 11 P.M. on the same day, appellant Casson in company with another person burglarized a home, stole certain property therein and committed other offenses....

In the absence of any provision fixing an exact time for the law to take effect, it would take effect at the same time as all congressional enactment of criminal laws. The United States Attorney interpreted the statute as having taken effect prior to Casson's crimes, and he was accordingly indicted, convicted and sentenced under the new burglary and robbery statutes, as amended....

Allowing for the difference in time zones between "The Ranch" and the District of Columbia, it is noted that the crimes were committed about six hours after the President signed the bill. Casson was subsequently indicted on four counts: I (First Degree Burglary), with entering a dwelling while persons were present therein, with intent to steal property of another; II (Robbery), by force and violence and against resistance and by putting in fear stealing and taking from the person and from the immediate actual possession of a designated person, property of other persons of a value of about $392.50; III and IV, assaulting two persons with a dangerous weapon, that is a shotgun.

The jury returned guilty verdicts on all counts and defendant was given concurrent sentences as follows: five to fifteen years on Counts I and II, and three to ten years on Counts III and IV. Under the 1967 amendments, for the offense charged in Count I (the burglary count), the penalty of imprisonment was changed by Congress from two to fifteen years to five to thirty years; and under Count II (the robbery count), the minimum punishment was increased from six months to two years imprisonment while the maximum punishment stayed at fifteen years. Thus the actual concurrent sentences adjudged on both counts I and II (5 to 15 years) could have been given under the prior law. * * *

The not too veiled inference in appellant's argument is that he is being prosecuted for disobedience of a law which the Government kept him "from the knowledge of." [Jeremy Bentham, Works 547 (1843)]. Let us see what knowledge of the laws in question was available to Casson in 1967.

2. The endorsement on the enrolled bill preserved in the National Archives is as follows:

Lyndon B. Johnson
3:05 P.M.
December 27, 1967
The Ranch

On December 27, 1967, there was no constitutional or statutory provision expressly requiring that acts passed by Congress had to be published before they became effective.[17] The act establishing the Federal Register made no provision for publishing congressional acts or resolutions, but the Public Printer was required to print copies of all public laws in slip form and in permanent form after the close of each congressional session.

Appellant's claim that he was denied access to knowledge of the law, however, overlooks the widespread publication that Congress gives to the contents of a bill as it journeys through the legislative process. * * *

During the passage of the bill through Congress the news media gave wide publicity to its provisions. In addition, Casson, or any interested person by merely inquiring could easily determine the exact status of the bill and obtain an exact copy in its then form at each stage of its legislative history from its introduction on June 13 until the time of its final passage on December 13. Also, the Congressional Record gave prior notice of all scheduled hearings. * * *

From December 13, 1967 on any person interested in the bill had only to be concerned with one thing, *i.e.*, to be informed of the *time* the President signed the bill—if he signed it. There is no showing here that this information could not have been obtained promptly on request. That staff members of congressional committees accommodate the public, on request, by informing them of the status of bills in various stages of the legislative process is a matter of common knowledge of which we take judicial notice. There is also the possibility, as frequently occurs, that the action the President proposes to take on a bill might be learned in advance by an appropriate inquiry. In the instant case, over six hours transpired from the time the President signed the bill until the offense was committed by Casson. During this period of time there is no showing in this record that it was impossible for an interested person to learn that the President had signed the bill at 3:05 P.M. The fact that the news story on the bill was not released until several hours later in San Antonio does not determine how quickly an inquiry by an interested citizen might have evoked the information. With instantaneous communications as they exist today, it would only take a few minutes for such information to be ascertained. December 27, 1967 was a Wednesday, a regular working day, so it was a working night. [T]he public are charged with knowledge of all the published information concerning a congressional bill that is available during the entire legislative process. Here, the Congressional Record and documents

17. Congress at one time provided for prompt publication of new laws as they were enacted in newspapers of the several states but these provisions were repealed and the Secretary of State was directed to deliver copies to the congressional printer for printing as soon as possible after enactment. There was never any suggestion that the effectiveness of the bill was in any way dependent upon such publication.

Regarding the earlier practice of publishing laws in England, Justice Miller in Gardner v. Collector, 73 U.S., (6 Wall.) 499, 18 L. Ed. 890 (1867), quoted Lord Coke as follows:

> Although proclamation be not made in the county, every one is bound to take notice of that which is done in Parliament, for as soon as Parliament hath concluded anything, the law intends that every person hath notice thereof, for the Parliament represents the body of the whole realm, and therefore it is not requisite that any proclamation be made, seeing the statute took effect before.

published by Congress prove that the bill and all its provisions were in the public domain for over six months, received the widest publicity and full disclosure by Congress and over 100,000 copies of the bill in the exact form in which it passed were printed, distributed and available to the general public over two weeks before the President signed the bill. This is more than adequate notice to the public of the contents of the bill. Actual notice to a particular individual is not a prerequisite. . . .

■ ROBB, CIRCUIT JUDGE (concurring).

I concur in the result and agree that the bill amending the burglary statute became law at 3:05 P.M., December 27, 1967, when the President signed it. I do not agree to the implication . . . that the appellant was not bound by the amended statute unless knowledge of the contents of the bill and of its enactment was in fact available to him. In my opinion this is not the law; certainly it is not so in the case of a statute dealing with a crime *malum in se*, such as burglary. I think the statutory enactment was, in law, notice of its terms to all affected, including the appellant.

QUESTIONS AND COMMENTS

1. Was the law under which Casson was convicted *published* at the time he committed the conduct in question? (Note that Casson committed the acts in question only *after* Johnson had signed the bill.) Judging by the court's discussion, does it really matter one way or the other? Why should it? Does "law" mean "bill"? Does "publish" mean "make available"? Available to whom? Anyone, professional Congress watchers? Potential offenders? The defendant in this case? See Joseph E. Murphy, "The Duty of the Government to Make the Law Known," 51 Fordham L. Rev. 255 (1982).

2. If notice is the rationale for the publicity principle, why isn't actual notice required? Note that the concurring opinion wouldn't even require availability—i.e., the possibility of actual notice. If notice isn't the rationale, what is?

3. The concurring opinion refers to the fact that Casson was convicted of burglary, a *malum in se* crime. Just what makes a *malum in se* crime isn't quite clear. One characteristic of a *malum in se* crime might be that it has been around for a long time in some form, in some jurisdictions, with some attendant punishment. Why should any of this matter in this case, involving this statute, and this defendant? What about the seriousness of the punishment, never mind the historical origins of the crime? Should a different publicity requirement apply to crimes punished by fine than to those punished by imprisonment? Or should it matter whether the law criminalizes previously noncriminal conduct, or changes the quality of the punishment (say, from fine to imprisonment), or merely the quantity of punishment (say, from one year to ten years in prison)? Literally, *malum in se* means "evil in and of itself," in contradistinction to a *malum prohibitum* crime, which is an evil only because it is prohibited, i.e., because the state has declared it so. Should the moral content of the statute matter any more than its pedigree?

What would happen if we really imposed a strict(er) publicity requirement on *malum prohibitum* crimes, considering the constant generation of regulatory offenses by the executive branch of government? This problem is not a new one. It's as old as the modern administrative state. See "Government in Ignorance of the Law—A Plea for Better Publication of Executive Legislation," 48 Harv. L. Rev. 198 (1934)

4. The *Casson* opinion quotes a snippet of a passage from Bentham. Here is the full quote:

> We hear of tyrants, and those cruel ones: but, whatever we may have felt, we have never heard of any tyrant in such sort cruel, as to punish men for disobedience to laws or orders which he had kept them from the knowledge of.

5 Jeremy Bentham, Works 547 (1843).

Does the principle of publicity require the state to publish its laws, to make its laws available to the public, or does it require no more than that the state refrain from making an affirmative effort to "keep [men] from the knowledge of" its laws? At any rate, what's left of the publicity requirement after *Casson*?

F. JURISDICTION

The principle of legality, in its various permutations, is not the only formal prerequisite for a substantive assessment of criminal liability in a particular case. Right at the border between process and substance sits another crucial and complex, though all-too-often overlooked, concept: jurisdiction. Jurisdiction is the power to impose the norms of a given legal system onto a particular person. It attracts great attention in civil law, where entire courses are devoted to studying the question of whether a Texas court has jurisdiction over a California corporation that had the misfortune of selling defective toothpaste somewhere in the Lone Star State. In criminal law, and usually in criminal procedure as well, jurisdiction tends to receive little, if any, attention. (The leading article on criminal jurisdiction stems from 1935, "Jurisdiction with Respect to Crime," 29 Am. J. Int'l L. 435, 467 (Supp. 1935).) This makes some sense because in Anglo–American law, the question of jurisdiction tended to have a simple answer: jurisdiction was exclusively a territorial matter. If you committed a crime in state A, then you were subject to the criminal jurisdiction of state A. The only question that might come up was what, exactly, it meant for a crime to be committed "in" a given state. What if you hatched the plan in state B, met your partner in crime in state C, bought your gun in state D, then dragged the victim across state lines into state E, and so on? Recently, however, questions of jurisdiction have become a great deal more interesting and visible, as American criminal law has begun to move away from the territoriality principle as the sole basis of jurisdiction.

As you read the following materials, consider the following questions:

What view of the nature of crime and the function of punishment underlies the various approaches to criminal jurisdiction? Why should it matter, for instance, *where* a crime was committed? Why should criminal jurisdiction reach a tourist, an illegal immigrant, a resident alien? Does notice matter at all?

What role does, or should, consent play in the law of criminal jurisdiction? More broadly yet, must I have participated—or at least have had the (meaningful?) opportunity to participate—in the making of a criminal statute, or criminal law in general, in order to be punishable for having violated it? May slaves be punished by a state that completely precluded them from forming law, or ignored their interests generally? Can a non-democratic government ever legitimately punish? Can a democratic government ever *illegitimately* punish?

1. The Territorial Principle

Texas Penal Code § 1.04. Territorial Jurisdiction

(a) This state has jurisdiction over an offense that a person commits by his own conduct or the conduct of another for which he is criminally responsible if:

(1) either the conduct or a result that is an element of the offense occurs inside this state;

(2) the conduct outside this state constitutes an attempt to commit an offense inside this state;

(3) the conduct outside this state constitutes a conspiracy to commit an offense inside this state, and an act in furtherance of the conspiracy occurs inside this state; or

(4) the conduct inside this state constitutes an attempt, solicitation, or conspiracy to commit, or establishes criminal responsibility for the commission of, an offense in another jurisdiction that is also an offense under the laws of this state.

(b) If the offense is criminal homicide, a "result" is either the physical impact causing death or the death itself. . . .

(c) An offense based on an omission to perform a duty imposed on an actor by a statute of this state is committed inside this state regardless of the location of the actor at the time of the offense.

(d) This state includes the land and water and the air space above the land and water over which this state has power to define offenses.

German Penal Code § 3. Applicability to acts within the country.

German penal law is applicable to acts committed within the country.

Confederated Tribes of the Colville Reservation Code § 1–1–430. Implied Consent.

Entrance by any person or his property into the Reservation or Tribal Court jurisdiction shall be deemed equivalent to and construed to be . . . a consent to criminal jurisdiction of the Tribes . . .; provided, however, that criminal jurisdiction of the Tribal Court shall not extend to trial of non-Indians.

STATEMENT OF MINNESOTA ATTORNEY GENERAL ON INTERNET JURISDICTION[a]

WARNING TO ALL INTERNET USERS AND PROVIDERS

THIS MEMORANDUM SETS FORTH THE ENFORCEMENT POSITION OF THE MINNESOTA ATTORNEY GENERAL'S OFFICE WITH RESPECT TO CERTAIN ILLEGAL ACTIVITIES ON THE INTERNET.

PERSONS OUTSIDE OF MINNESOTA WHO TRANSMIT INFORMATION VIA THE INTERNET KNOWING THAT INFORMATION WILL BE DISSEMINATED IN MINNESOTA ARE SUBJECT TO JURISDICTION IN MINNESOTA COURTS FOR VIOLATIONS OF STATE CRIMINAL AND CIVIL LAWS.

The following discussion sets out the legal basis for this conclusion. Minnesota's general criminal jurisdiction statute provides as follows:

> A person may be convicted and sentenced under the law of this State if the person:
>
> (1) Commits an offense in whole or in part within this state; or
>
> (2) Being without the state, causes, aids or abets another to commit a crime within the state; or
>
> (3) Being without the state, intentionally causes a result within the state prohibited by the criminal laws of this state.
>
> It is not a defense that the defendant's conduct is also a criminal offense under the laws of another state or of the United States or of another country.

Minnesota Statute § 609.025.

This statute has been interpreted by the Minnesota Supreme Court. In State v. Rossbach, 288 N.W.2d 714 (Minn. 1980), the defendant appealed his conviction for aggravated assault. The defendant, standing inside the border of an Indian Reservation, had fired a rifle across the boundary line at a person outside the border. The defendant claimed that Minnesota courts did not have jurisdiction because his act took place off of Minnesota lands. Applying Minnesota Statute § 609.025 and the common law, the Minnesota Supreme Court affirmed the conviction, holding that the intentional impact within Minnesota land created jurisdiction....

The above principles of Minnesota law apply equally to activities on the Internet. Individuals and organizations outside of Minnesota

a. Available at http://cyber.law.harvard.edu/ilaw/Jurisdiction/Minnesota_Full.html (last accessed Dec. 14, 2004).—EDS.

who disseminate information in Minnesota via the Internet and thereby cause a result to occur in Minnesota are subject to state criminal . . . laws.

An Example of Illegal Activity on the Internet—Gambling

Gambling appears to be an especially prominent aspect of criminal activity on the Internet. There are a number of services outside of Minnesota that offer Minnesota residents the opportunity to place bets on sporting events, purchase lottery tickets, and participate in simulated casino games. These services are illegal in Minnesota.

Lotteries

A lottery is defined as "a plan which provides for the distribution of money, property or other reward or benefit to persons selected by chance from among participants some or all of whom have given a consideration for the chance of being selected." § 609.75(1)(a).

Generally, it is unlawful in Minnesota to sell or transfer a chance to participate in a lottery. § 609.755(2). It is also unlawful to disseminate information in Minnesota about a lottery, except a lottery conducted by an adjoining state, with intent to encourage participation therein. § 609.755(3). Acts in Minnesota in furtherance of a lottery conducted outside of Minnesota are included, notwithstanding its validity where conducted. § 609.75(1)(c). Violation of these provisions is a misdemeanor, punishable by up to 90 days in jail, or a fine of up to $700, or both. §§ 609.755, 609.02(3). It is a gross misdemeanor under Minnesota law to conduct a lottery. § 609.76(1)(3). A gross misdemeanor is punishable by up to one year in jail, or a $3,000 fine, or both. § 609.02(4).

Sports Bookmaking

Sports bookmaking is defined as "the activity of intentionally receiving, recording or forwarding within any 30–day period more than five bets, or offers to bet, that total more than $2,500 on any one or more sporting events." § 609.75(7). Engaging in sports bookmaking is a felony, which is punishable by more than one year imprisonment. §§ 609.76(2), 609.02(2). Intentionally receiving, recording, or forwarding bets or offers to bet in lesser amounts is a gross misdemeanor. § 609.76(1)(7).

Accomplice Liability

Minnesota's accomplice statute provides that one who intentionally aids, advises, counsels, or conspires with another to commit a crime is equally liable for that crime. § 609.05(1). Therefore, persons or organizations who knowingly assist Internet gambling organizations in any unlawful activity may themselves be held liable for that unlawful activity. Thus, for example, Internet access providers and credit card companies that continue to provide services to gambling organizations after notice that the activities of the organizations are illegal would be subject to accomplice liability.

Placing a Bet through Internet Gambling Organizations

Minnesota residents should be aware that it is unlawful to make a bet through Internet gambling organizations. Minnesota law makes it a misdemeanor to place a bet unless done pursuant to an exempted, state-regulated activity, such as licensed charitable gambling or the state lottery. §§ 609.75(2)–(3), 609.755(1). Internet gambling organizations are not exempted. Therefore, any person in Minnesota who places a bet through one of these organizations is committing a crime....

Gambling is just one example of illegal activity on the Internet. However, the same jurisdictional principles apply with equal force to any illegal activity.

QUESTIONS AND COMMENTS

1. Why should territory determine jurisdiction? Is the point of criminal law to protect—or to "pacify"—territory as a medieval patriarch might seek to protect the "peace" (or *mund*) of his household? It is generally acknowledged that "[t]he common law regarded the interests of a sovereign as both absolute within its territorial limits and circumscribed by those limits." People v. Stokes, 88 N.Y.2d 618 (1996). Even today, courts insist that "[t]he general rule is that jurisdiction is proper only over 'offenses as may be committed within its jurisdiction.' " People v. Blume, 443 Mich. 476, 505 N.W.2d 843 (1993).

Increasingly, however, courts have recognized that this "rule against extraterritorial jurisdiction" is subject to certain "exceptions" (to be explored in detail below). What has changed? Why have courts abandoned their "blind adherence to a purely territorial concept of jurisdiction" (*Blume*, supra)? Have the "exceptions" swallowed the "rule"? Cf. Wendell Berge, "Criminal Jurisdiction and the Territorial Principle," 30 Mich. L. Rev. 238 (1931) ("[m]odern criminals have little concern for political boundaries except as such boundaries are an aid in effecting a criminal purpose"); Daniel L. Rotenberg, "Extraterritorial Legislative Jurisdiction and the State Criminal Law," 38 Tex. L. Rev. 763 (1960) ("interstate population centers, organized crime, mobility, and recidivism reveal that each state has an interest in crimes committed in other states").

2. Can territorial jurisdiction claim any link to the principle of consent? Does entering a jurisdiction imply consenting to its laws, or at least consenting to their application? But do I really have any idea what laws govern a political community I'm entering, be it a village (with its ordinances), a city (with its charter), a county (with its code), a state (with its statutes), or a country? Or should I be presumed not only to consent to these laws, but also to be familiar with them? (See ch. 5, on ignorance of law as a defense.)

In this context, what's the significance of the fact that the Minnesota Attorney General Office's "statement" was posted on its website? Does posting it provide notice to (potential? past?) internet gamblers that they may be subject to Minnesota criminal law? If they continue (begin?) their internet gambling after reading the notice (or even after its posting?), have they consented to the application of Minnesota criminal law to them? Note that the statement sets out not only the basis for criminal jurisdiction, but also includes a summary of Minnesota criminal law on gambling. What, if anything, would this consent have to do with territorial jurisdiction? Could criminal jurisdiction be based on the mere announcement of criminal jurisdiction, coupled with (actual or constructive) notice and (actual or constructive) consent? What, in fact, is left of territorial jurisdiction if Minnesota criminal law is applied to someone sitting at a computer terminal in Florida who accesses a website housed on a server in New Jersey and maintained by a resident of California? Cf. Terrence Berg, "www.wildwest.gov: The Impact of the Internet on State Power to Enforce the Law," 2000 BYU L. Rev. 1305.

What, at any rate, is the precise statutory basis of the Minnesota's AG's assertion of criminal jurisdiction over internet gambling? If it's subsection (3), what is the "result" that the offender has "intentionally cause[d] within the state"?

3. The Sixth Amendment to the U.S. Constitution provides that "the accused shall enjoy the right to a speedy and public trial, by an impartial jury of the state and district wherein the crime shall have been committed." Is the territoriality principle meant to insure that the defendant is subject to the judgment not of (potentially hostile or at least unsympathetic) foreigners but of members of her community, thus providing for a measure of (indirect) self-government, which in turn might lend some legitimacy to the jury's verdict? But what if the defendant is not a member of the community where the crime is committed? In highly mobile modern society, what is the connection between the locus of the crime and the alleged perpetrator's community membership?

4. It's important to recognize that the U.S. Constitution—thanks to the so-called dual sovereignty exception to the double jeopardy prohibition—would not stand in the way of two (or more) states asserting criminal jurisdiction over the same course of conduct, and subjecting the actor to independent, and cumulative, punishment. Assuming both states, or sovereigns, have taken offense (and have decided that jurisdiction lies, say, because—as in *Rossbach*—the conduct element occurred in one, and the result element in the other) each is entitled to respond through its criminal law as it sees fit. See Heath v. Alabama, 474 U.S. 82 (1985); see also the discussion of *United States v. Lara,* infra. Would it make sense to leave cross-border cases to federal criminal law? (Under current law, federal criminal law would apply not instead of, *but in addition to*, whatever state criminal law applies, thanks once again to the dual sovereignty rule.)

2. THE PERSONALITY PRINCIPLE

Personal jurisdiction is as straightforward as territorial jurisdiction, but comes in two varieties, one focusing on the status of the offender (active), the other on that of the victim (passive).

a. Active Personality (Nationality)

Uniform Code of Military Justice

Art. 2. Persons subject to this chapter

(a) The following persons are subject to this chapter:

(1) Members of a regular component of the armed forces . . .; volunteers . . .; inductees . . .; and other persons lawfully called or ordered into, or to duty in or for training in, the armed forces. . . .

(2) Cadets, aviation cadets, and midshipmen.

(3) Members of a reserve component while on inactive-duty training. . . .

(4) Retired members of a regular component of the armed forces who are entitled to pay.

(5) Retired members of a reserve component who are receiving hospitalization from an armed force.

(6) Members of the Fleet Reserve and Fleet Marine Corps Reserve.

(7) Persons in custody of the armed forces serving a sentence imposed by a court-martial.

(8) Members of the National Oceanic and Atmospheric Administration, Public Health Service, and other organizations, when assigned to and serving with the armed forces.

(9) Prisoners of war in custody of the armed forces.

(10) In time of war, persons serving with or accompanying an armed force in the field. * * *

Art. 5. Territorial applicability of this chapter

This chapter applies in all places.

Poarch Band of Creek Indians Code § 4–1–2. Personal Jurisdiction—Criminal

The Tribal Court shall have criminal jurisdiction over [a]ll enrolled Tribal members, or other federally recognized Indians for any violation of a criminal offense contained in the Tribal Criminal Code . . . when the criminal offense is alleged to have occurred on . . . the reservation. . . .

German Penal Code § 7. Applicability to acts outside the country in other cases.

(II) German penal law is applicable to . . . acts committed outside the country, if the act is threatened with punishment at the place of the act or the place of the act is not subject to any penal power and if the actor

1. was a German at the time of the act or became a German after the act. . . .

b. Passive Personality

18 U.S.C. § 2332. Criminal penalties

(a) Homicide.—

Whoever kills a national of the United States, while such national is outside the United States, shall—

(1) if the killing is murder . . ., be fined under this title, punished by death or imprisonment for any term of years or for life, or both. . . .

(b) Attempt or Conspiracy With Respect to Homicide.—

Whoever outside the United States attempts to kill, or engages in a conspiracy to kill, a national of the United States shall—

(1) in the case of an attempt to commit a killing that is a murder . . . be fined under this title or imprisoned not more than 20 years, or both; and

(2) in the case of a conspiracy by two or more persons to commit a killing that is a murder . . ., if one or more of such persons do any overt act to effect the object of the conspiracy, be fined under this title or imprisoned for any term of years or for life, or both so fined and so imprisoned.

(c) Other Conduct.—

Whoever outside the United States engages in physical violence—

(1) with intent to cause serious bodily injury to a national of the United States; or

(2) with the result that serious bodily injury is caused to a national of the United States;

shall be fined under this title or imprisoned not more than ten years, or both.

(d) Limitation on Prosecution.—

No prosecution for any offense described in this section shall be undertaken by the United States except on written certification of the Attorney General or the highest ranking subordinate of the Attorney General with responsibility for criminal prosecutions that, in the judgment of the certifying official, such offense was intended to coerce, intimidate, or retaliate against a government or a civilian population.

German Penal Code § 7. Applicability to acts outside the country in other cases.

(I) German penal law is applicable to acts committed outside the country against a German, if the act is threatened with punishment at the place of the act or the place of the act is not subject to any penal power. * * *

United States v. King

United States Court of Appeals for the Ninth Circuit.
552 F.2d 833 (1976).

■ CHOY, CIRCUIT JUDGE.

Appellants King ... and Powell ... were both convicted of unlawful distribution in Japan of heroin intended for importation into the United States in violation of 21 U.S.C. § 959 [Manufacture or distribution for purposes of unlawful importation]. Adopted in 1970, the statute is expressly aimed at having extraterritorial effect, but King and Powell protest that its attempted reach exceeds the legislative power vested in Congress by the Constitution.

There is no constitutional bar to the extraterritorial application of penal laws....

Both sides cite the same five principles of extraterritorial authority generally recognized under international law: the territorial, nationality, protective, universality, and passive personality principles. Appellants argue that only the territorial principle (determining jurisdiction by reference to the place where the offense is committed) and the protective principle (determining jurisdiction by reference to the national interest injured by the offense) have been accepted as valid bases of authority by American courts....

We think this argument fails. In upholding statutes with extraterritorial impact, courts have recognized that the territorial concept of jurisdiction is neither exclusive nor a full and accurate characterization of the powers of states to exercise jurisdiction beyond the confines of their geographical boundaries....

Thus, [appellants] have not established that authority under one of the other three principles would not be acceptable. Since both appellants are United States citizens, the nationality principle would apply: American authority over them could be based upon the allegiance they owe this country and its laws if the statute concerned as does § 959, evinces a legislative intent to control actions within and without the United States.

United States v. Lara

Supreme Court of the United States.
541 U.S. 193, 124 S.Ct. 1628 (2004).

■ JUSTICE BREYER delivered the opinion of the Court.

Respondent Billy Jo Lara is an enrolled member of the Turtle Mountain Band of Chippewa Indians in north-central North Dakota. He married a member of a different tribe, the Spirit Lake Tribe, and lived with his wife and children on the Spirit Lake Reservation, also located in North Dakota. After several incidents of serious misconduct, the Spirit Lake Tribe issued an order excluding him from the reservation. Lara ignored the order; federal officers stopped him; and he struck one of the arresting officers.

The Spirit Lake Tribe subsequently prosecuted Lara in the Spirit Lake Tribal Court for "violence to a policeman." Lara pleaded guilty and, in respect to that crime, served 90 days in jail.

After Lara's tribal conviction, the Federal Government charged Lara in the Federal District Court for the District of North Dakota with the federal crime of assaulting a federal officer. 18 U.S.C. § 111(a)(1) [punishable by up to 20 years in prison]. Key elements of this federal crime mirror elements of the tribal crime of "violence to a policeman." And this similarity between the two crimes would *ordinarily* have brought Lara within the protective reach of the Double Jeopardy Clause. U.S. Const., Amdt. 5 (the Government may not "subject" any person "for the same offense to be twice put in jeopardy of life or limb"). But the Government, responding to Lara's claim of double jeopardy, pointed out that the Double Jeopardy Clause does not bar successive prosecutions brought by *separate sovereigns*, and it argued that this "dual sovereignty" doctrine determined the outcome here.

The Government noted that this Court has held that an Indian tribe acts as a separate sovereign when it prosecutes its *own members*. The Government recognized, of course, that Lara is not one of the Spirit Lake Tribe's *own* members; it also recognized that, in *Duro* v. *Reina, 495 U.S. 676, 110 S. Ct. 2053*, this Court had held that a tribe no longer possessed *inherent or sovereign authority* to prosecute a "nonmember Indian." But it pointed out that, soon after this Court decided *Duro*, Congress enacted new legislation specifically authorizing a tribe to prosecute Indian members of a different tribe. That new statute, in permitting a tribe to bring certain tribal prosecutions against nonmember Indians, does not purport to delegate the Federal Government's own *federal* power. Rather, it enlarges the *tribes'* own " 'powers of self-government' " to include "the inherent power of Indian tribes, hereby recognized and affirmed, to exercise criminal jurisdiction over *all* Indians," including nonmembers. 25 U.S.C. § 1301(2) (emphasis added).

In the Government's view, given this statute, the Tribe, in prosecuting Lara, had exercised its own inherent *tribal* authority, not delegated *federal* authority; hence the "dual sovereignty" doctrine applies; and since the two prosecutions were brought by two different sovereigns, the second, federal, prosecution does not violate the Double Jeopardy Clause.

[We agree.]

[This case] concerns a power similar in some respects to the power to prosecute a tribe's own members—a power that this Court has called "inherent." In large part it concerns a tribe's authority to control events that occur upon the tribe's own land. See *United States* v. *Mazurie*, 419 U.S. 544, 557, 95 S. Ct. 710 (1975) ("Indian tribes are unique aggregations possessing attributes of sovereignty over both their members and *their territory*" (emphasis added)). * * *

That being so, the Spirit Lake Tribe's prosecution of Lara did not amount to an exercise of federal power, and the Tribe acted in its capacity of a separate sovereign. Consequently, the Double Jeopardy Clause does not prohibit the Federal Government from proceeding with the present prosecution for a discrete *federal* offense. The contrary judgment of the Eighth Circuit is reversed.

■ JUSTICE KENNEDY, concurring in the judgment.

* * * Lara ... is a citizen of the United States. To hold that Congress can subject him, within our domestic borders, to a sovereignty outside the basic structure of the Constitution is a serious step. The Constitution is based on a theory of original, and continuing, consent of the governed.... There is a historical exception for Indian tribes, but only to the limited extent that a member of a tribe consents to be subjected to the jurisdiction of his own tribe. * * * Perhaps the Court's holding could be justified by an argument that by enrolling in one tribe Lara consented to the criminal jurisdiction of other tribes, but the Court does not mention the point. And, in all events, we should be cautious about adopting that fiction.

The present case, however, does not require us to address these difficult questions of constitutional dimension. Congress made it clear that its intent was to recognize and affirm tribal authority to try Indian nonmembers as inherent in tribal status. The proper occasion to test the legitimacy of the tribe's authority, that is, whether Congress had the power to do what it sought to do, was in the first, tribal proceeding. There, however, Lara made no objection to the tribe's authority to try him. In the second, federal proceeding, because the express rationale for the tribe's authority to try Lara—whether legitimate or not—was inherent sovereignty, not delegated federal power, there can be no double jeopardy violation. For that reason, I concur in the judgment.

QUESTIONS AND COMMENTS

1. Note that *Lara* illustrates both active and passive personality; the active personality principle underlies Indian tribes' jurisdiction over insiders, while the federal statute criminalizing assault on a federal officer protects an insider against harm, regardless whether that harm is inflicted by a fellow insider or not. Is the Spirit Lake Tribe's jurisdiction over Lara (Lara's conduct?) based on personality or on territoriality, or both?

Is a national's (a resident's?) duty of allegiance to her country and its laws (see *King*) a sufficient ground for punishing her for extraterritorial (or for that matter *intra*territorial) conduct?

2. Why would the military and Indian tribes have personal jurisdiction over their members? Why might state criminal law and federal criminal law rely on territorial jurisdiction instead? What sort of (self-)conception of a political community is reflected in a theory of personal jurisdiction? What role does consent play? How does consent manifest itself in personal jurisdiction? What do I have to consent to: joining a political community, submitting myself to the (criminal, civil) jurisdiction of its laws, its courts, in general, in a particular case? What did Lara consent to?

3. *Lara* addresses a double jeopardy issue that frequently arises in cases where tribal jurisdiction and federal jurisdiction overlap. Central to the Court's analysis is the "dual sovereignty" doctrine, which permits criminal prosecutions for the same act for identical or significantly similar offenses by separate sovereigns, including states, the federal government, and Indian tribes. The origins of (and justification for?) the dual sovereignty doctrine are set out in Heath v. Alabama, 474 U.S. 82, 88–90 (1985):

The dual sovereignty doctrine is founded on the common-law conception of crime as an offense against the sovereignty of the government. When a defendant in a single act violates the "peace and dignity" of two sovereigns by breaking the laws of each, he has committed two distinct "offences." As the Court explained in Moore v. Illinois, 14 How. 13, 19 (1852), "[a]n offence, in its legal signification, means the transgression of a law." Consequently, when the same act transgresses the laws of two sovereigns, "it cannot be truly averred that the offender has been twice punished for the same offence; but only that by one act he has committed two offences, for each of which he is justly punishable."

In applying the dual sovereignty doctrine, then, the crucial determination is whether the two entities that seek successively to prosecute a defendant for the same course of conduct can be termed separate sovereigns. This determination turns on whether the two entities draw their authority to punish the offender from distinct sources of power. Thus, the Court has uniformly held that the States are separate sovereigns with respect to the Federal Government because each State's power to prosecute is derived from its own "inherent sovereignty," not from the Federal Government....

The States are no less sovereign with respect to each other than they are with respect to the Federal Government. Their powers to undertake criminal prosecutions derive from separate and independent sources of power and authority originally belonging to them before admission to the Union and preserved to them by the Tenth Amendment....

The cases in which the Court has applied the dual sovereignty principle outside the realm of successive federal and state prosecutions illustrate the soundness of this analysis. [In] United States v. Wheeler, 435 U.S. 313, ... the Court ... reiterated the principle that the sovereignty of two prosecuting entities for these purposes is determined by "the ultimate source of the power under which the respective prosecutions were undertaken." On the basis of this reasoning, the Court held that the Navajo Tribe, whose power to prosecute its members for tribal offenses is derived from the Tribe's "primeval sovereignty" rather than a delegation of federal authority, is an independent sovereign from the Federal Government for purposes of the dual sovereignty doctrine.

3. The Protective Principle

Protective jurisdiction, like the passive variety of personal jurisdiction, focuses on the victim. Except this time the victim is not a person, but the state (whose sovereign dignity has been offended by the crime).

N.Y. Crim. Proc. L. § 20.20. Geographical jurisdiction of offenses.

[A] person may be convicted in the criminal courts of this state of an offense defined by the laws of this state ... when:

1. Conduct occurred within this state ...; or

2. Even though none of the conduct constituting such offense may have occurred within this state:

(b) The statute defining the offense is designed to prevent the occurrence of a particular effect in this state and the conduct constituting the offense committed was performed with intent that it would have such effect herein....

German Penal Code § 5. Acts outside the country against legal interests within the country.

German penal law is applicable, independent of the law of the place of the act, to the following acts committed outside the country:

1. Preparation for a war of aggression ...;
2. High treason ...;
3. Endangering the democratic law state ...;
4. Treason against the country and endangering external security ...;
5. Offenses against the defense of the country....

United States v. Rodriguez

United States District Court for the Southern District of California.
182 F.Supp. 479 (1960).

■ CARTER, DICTRICT JUDGE.

The present case raises this question: May aliens, found within the United States, be prosecuted here for the commission of crimes allegedly committed outside the territorial limits of the United States, when the crimes charged concern the use of false statements to secure the documents necessary for admission into the United States?

[The defendants are charged with making false statements in an immigration application, in violation of 18 U.S.C. § 1546 ("fraud and misuse of visas, permits, and other documents"), for trying to obtain immigrant visas at American consulates and embassies abroad on the basis of sham marriages with American citizens.]

A Harvard research project, Research in International Law, considered various problems of international criminal jurisdiction, reporting its conclusions in 1935 (see Research on International law, Part II, Jurisdiction with Respect to Crime, 29 Am.J.Int'l L.Supp. 435 (1935)). The reporter for that portion of the project, Professor E. D. Dickinson, summarized their findings concerning five general principles of international jurisdiction:

> "These five general principles are: first, the territorial principle, determining jurisdiction by reference to the place where the offence is committed; second, the nationality principle, determining jurisdiction by reference to the nationality or national character of the person committing the offence; third, the protective principle, determining jurisdiction by reference to the national interest injured by the offence; fourth, the universality principle, determining jurisdiction by reference to the custody of the person committing the offence; and fifth, the passive personality principle, determining jurisdiction by reference to

> the nationality or national character of the person injured by the offence. Of these five principles, the first is everywhere regarded as of primary importance and of fundamental character * * *. The third is claimed by most states, regarded with misgivings in a few, and generally ranked as the basis of an auxiliary competence." Id. at 445. * * *
>
> The protective principle was codified by the Harvard group in Article 7 of their report:
>
> > "A state has jurisdiction with respect to any crime committed outside its territory by an alien against the security, territorial integrity or political independence of that state, provided that the act or omission which constitutes the crime was not committed in exercise of a liberty guaranteed the alien by the law of the place where it was committed." Id. at 543.

It is clear that international law recognizes not only the territorial theory of jurisdiction, but also the protective principle and several others as well. Having these principles in mind, it is now necessary for us to consider their effect upon the potential exercise of jurisdiction by our constitutionally created government.

A state might seek to exercise its jurisdiction in two general localities: First, it can attempt to impose its laws upon those found within its boundaries, holding these persons, whoever they may be, liable for acts committed within or without the territorial limits of the State. Second, the state might seek to control the actions of those physically in some other sovereign nation....

.... Entry by an alien into the United States secured by means of false statements or documents is an attack directly on the sovereignty of the United States. The effect of such an entry in connection with espionage or subversive activities clearly pinpoints the great impact such an entry could have on sovereignty.

To put it in more general terms, the concept of essential sovereignty of a free nation clearly requires the existence and recognition of an inherent power in the state to protect itself from destruction. This power exists in the United States government absent express provision in the Constitution, and arises from the very nature of the government which was created by the Constitution....

Possessing this power of protection, Congress is entitled to utilize it to the full extent. From the body of international law, the Congress may pick and choose whatever recognized principle of international jurisdiction is necessary to accomplish the purpose sought by the legislation. The mere fact that, in the past, Congress may not have seen fit to embody in legislation the full scope of its authorized powers is not a basis for now finding that those powers are lacking. Disuse, or even misuse of power inherent in the federal government, or given to it by the Constitution, is not a valid basis for us to hold that this power may not later be employed in a proper fashion.

QUESTIONS AND COMMENTS

1. If the protective theory extends criminal jurisdiction to any "crime against the sovereignty of the state," who gets to decide which act falls

under the state's criminal jurisdiction? Could a court decide whether a particular offense in a particular case offends the state's dignity? In that case, might this basis for criminal jurisdiction not be applied to *intra*territorial acts, given that any offense by definition offends the authority of the state?

Could the legislature simply codify a general principle of criminal jurisdiction providing that "any act that threatens the sovereignty of the state falls within the criminal jurisdiction of the state"? Alternatively, must it identify which theory of jurisdiction justifies bringing which offense within extraterritorial criminal jurisdiction—as the German Penal Code does? Or is it enough to list any and all offenses that fall within the criminal jurisdiction of the respective political entity and then leave it to the courts to determine which theory of jurisdiction supports criminal jurisdiction in each particular case? Why is codification of any kind required, given that the protective principle "arises from the very nature of government"?

2. Both the passive personality principle and the protective ("injured forum") principle base jurisdiction on the status of the victim. And yet they differ in one important respect: while one protects individual members of a given political community, the other protects the community (the "forum") itself. The protective principle applies *only* if the community as a whole is threatened; acts that merely affect one or more individual members, rather than "the well being of the community as a whole," aren't significant enough to trigger criminal jurisdiction. See, e.g., In re Taub, 3 N.Y.3d 30, 814 N.E.2d 799, 781 N.Y.S.2d 492 (2004). Does this distinction reflect different views of crime, and of criminal victimhood?

3. One noteworthy limitation on the reach of the protective principle is the common requirement that the extraterritorial conduct be *intended* to harm the state-sovereign in question. See, e.g., People v. Blume, 443 Mich. 476, 505 N.W.2d 843 (1993) (no extraterritorial criminal jurisdiction where defendant knew—but did not intend—that his criminal conduct would "have a detrimental effect within the state"). This importation of a mens rea requirement (and a strict one at that, as compared to, say, requiring that the actor have considered, but ignored, the possibility that her conduct might reach the state seeking criminal jurisdiction or that she reasonably *should have* been aware of this eventuality) as to what the Model Penal Code would call a "nonmaterial element" (see ch. 4 infra) may well reflect the continued unease with which American legislatures and courts approach extraterritorial criminal jurisdiction. (On the various types of mens rea, see ch. 5 infra.)

4. THE UNIVERSAL PRINCIPLE

Under universal jurisdiction, the location of the crime is as irrelevant as the status of the victim or of the offender.

Rome Statute of the International Criminal Court

Art. 1. The Court

An International Criminal Court ("the Court") is hereby established. It shall be a permanent institution and shall have the power to exercise its jurisdiction over persons for the most serious crimes of international concern, as referred to in this Statute, and shall be complementary to national criminal jurisdictions. The jurisdiction and functioning of the Court shall be governed by the provisions of this Statute.

Art. 5. Crimes within the jurisdiction of the Court

1. The jurisdiction of the Court shall be limited to the most serious crimes of concern to the international community as a whole. The Court has jurisdiction in accordance with this Statute with respect to the following crimes:

(a) The crime of genocide;

(b) Crimes against humanity;

(c) War crimes;

(d) The crime of aggression.

2. The Court shall exercise jurisdiction over the crime of aggression once a provision is adopted ... defining the crime and setting out the conditions under which the Court shall exercise jurisdiction with respect to this crime. . . .

Art. 8. War crimes

1. The Court shall have jurisdiction in respect of war crimes. . . .

2. For the purpose of this Statute, "war crimes" means ...

(b) ... [S]erious violations of the laws and customs applicable in international armed conflict, within the established framework of international law, namely, any of the following acts:

(i) Intentionally directing attacks against the civilian population as such or against individual civilians not taking direct part in hostilities;

(ii) Intentionally directing attacks against civilian objects, that is, objects which are not military objectives;

(iii) Intentionally directing attacks against personnel, installations, material, units or vehicles involved in a humanitarian assistance or peacekeeping mission in accordance with the Charter of the United Nations, as long as they are entitled to the protection given to civilians or civilian objects under the international law of armed conflict;

(iv) Intentionally launching an attack in the knowledge that such attack will cause incidental loss of life or injury to civilians or damage to civilian objects or widespread, long-term and severe damage to the natural environment which would be clearly excessive in relation to the concrete and direct overall military advantage anticipated;

(v) Attacking or bombarding, by whatever means, towns, villages, dwellings or buildings which are undefended and which are not military objectives;

(vi) Killing or wounding a combatant who, having laid down his arms or having no longer means of defence, has surrendered at discretion....

German Penal Code § 6. Acts outside the country against internationally protected legal interests.

German penal law ... is applicable, independent of the law of the place of the act, to the following acts committed outside of the country:

1. Genocide;
2. Crimes involving atomic energy, explosives and radiation ...;
3. Attacks on air and sea traffic ...;
4. Traffic in human beings ...;
5. Unauthorized distribution of narcotics;
6. Dissemination of pornography ...;
7. Forgery of currency and securities ..., [and] of credit cards ...;
8. Economic subsidy fraud....

QUESTIONS AND COMMENTS

1. What assumptions about the nature of international law, and of human rights, underlie the principle of universal jurisdiction? Does it make a difference whether it is a national court exercising universal jurisdiction—as provided for in German law—or an international court? Does the domestic model of international jurisdiction become obsolete with the establishment of an international criminal court?

2. The principle of universal jurisdiction has been quite controversial, both as an extension of the jurisdiction of domestic criminal courts and as the source of the jurisdiction of an international criminal court.

Proponents of universal jurisdiction argue that it is needed to prevent safe havens for crimes of international concern, to give victims of these crimes an opportunity to document their suffering, and to provide the international community with a forum. See, e.g., Kenneth Roth, "The Case for Universal Jurisdiction," Foreign Affairs (Sept./Oct. 2001), at 150.

Critics argue that the international criminal court poses a threat to the rights of those criminal defendants who are most in need of procedural safeguards against rash condemnation, and express concern about the potential for abuse of a quasi-legal process for political ends and even as an instrument of "judicial tyranny."

Consider the following two excerpts, one a cautious endorsement of universal criminal jurisdiction, the other a vigorous critique.

> [U]niversal jurisdiction involves the application by a state judiciary of that state's criminal law to a prosecution bearing no significant relationship to the state's territory, citizens, or security. In its contemporary form, universal jurisdiction involves broadly ranging criminal investigations and prosecutions for the commission of serious interna-

tional crimes that have been incorporated into state law. For example, the judiciary of state X applies its criminal law to a citizen of state Y in a prosecution based on the charge that this citizen committed a serious international crime in Y against citizens of Y and state Z....

Since World War II, international law in its conventional and customary forms has greatly expanded the scope of its criminalization of individual conduct. Those crimes range from airplane hijacking (an update of the old law on piracy) or traffic in drugs or prostitution to serious violations of the basic international human rights norms that have developed since the Universal Declaration of Human Rights of 1948, particularly those involving the killing, injuring, or persecution of people.

Even in the age of the new International Criminal Court ("ICC") and other international tribunals of limited jurisdiction, the use of universal jurisdiction for state prosecutions may help to reduce the historic impunity of the perpetrators. That will be particularly the case when other, more concerned states will not or cannot prosecute. Universal jurisdiction may then be essential to bringing gross violators to justice. But its expanded substantive reach brings new difficulties to the scene.

A strong consensus among states approved the arrest and conviction of the pirate. That consensus will sometimes but not always obtain with respect to identifying those who should be brought to criminal judgment because of their conduct in authoritarian, repressive regimes or in the many internal and international armed conflicts of the last half-century. The villain or tyrant to some states and peoples may represent the hero to others. One ethnic or ideological group may understand a particular historical record or interpret concrete events radically differently from another. A particular state may be viewed in a bright light by some, but critically by others.

In such circumstances, a criminal prosecution based on universal jurisdiction in a relatively "unconcerned" state may well raise issues of fairness and prejudice and, in the end, raise doubts in other states and peoples about the legitimacy of a trial and conviction. Such attitudes may stem partly from the arbitrary or random identity of the unrelated forum, which may gain custody of the defendant and decide to prosecute even in absence of a broad international consensus that the defendant merits prosecution and condemnation....

A primary argument justifying universal jurisdiction focuses on the contributions of courts relying on it to advance a community interest in punishing the commission of serious international crimes, promoting accountability and dissuading others from threatening peace and world order. In some sense, the state court acts as an international tribunal; it is performing an international function in bringing violators to justice under international norms incorporated in domestic law. At the same time, that court may be the sole avenue of hope for victims who are blocked for one or another reason from other strategies like seeking prosecution in the territorial state or state of defendant's nationality....

But not infrequently the territorial state may also constitute an impossible forum for a prosecution . . ., or at least be unavailable . . . for a long period of time after the violence stops. Its judiciary may be destroyed, its internal security insufficient to protect courts and witnesses, its potential for again erupting in massive violence too acute to permit prosecutions, its political situation likely to produce ongoing stalemate over the issue of prosecutions. Moreover, an amnesty in the territorial state may be imposed by the more powerful party without recourse to popular debate and participation in that decision. * * *

What then are my basic concerns about universal jurisdiction? Piracy serves as a useful point of departure. The image of a piracy prosecution is one of condemning an international outlaw, *hostis humani*, a criminal who offends all states and threatens their common interest in a peaceful regime of the high seas for purposes of commerce and transportation. There is no room within this image for divisions among states, for some states being sympathetic to the effects of piracy in the play of interests and power among states (although there was no doubt some historical room, and major seafaring powers were more concerned than other states). There is no place, as it were, for ideological or political divisions, for double images of the pirate as villain and hero.

The same could be said for other crimes subject or potentially subject to universal jurisdiction—for example, the slave trade, or today international crimes like trafficking in women for prostitution or the drug trade. Of course rogue regimes may support the states and nonstate actors that are conducting these activities, and sharp divisions among states may develop about the most effective way of attacking the problems. But criminal prosecutions based on universal jurisdiction are unlikely to generate sharp differences among states about how these activities, engaged in dominantly by nonstate actors, are to be evaluated.

. . . [By contrast, consider a] political leader or military figure [who] could be understood or imagined within one state or group as hero, in another as villain, within one state or group as freedom fighter, in another as terrorist. In such circumstances, it could be possible to predict with some degree of certainty that a given person would be more likely to be prosecuted and convicted in one state or group than another. . . . The differences between attitudes in the two states or groups that bear on the probability of prosecution and conviction could stem from a distinctive character of the conflict producing sharp divisions among states and cultures about how it and its parties would be viewed—perhaps the ideological character of the conflict, perhaps the religious or ethnic divisions involved, perhaps the political alliances and traditional relationships between the conflict's parties and a given state or group, perhaps any of a broad range of other factors.

Whatever the explanations that would surely vary from conflict to conflict, the double images of hero and criminal would displace the relatively broad consensus over the pirate as an evildoer. If the putative defendant were a former head of state or high-ranking official, the rift in opinion could grow, for the state itself would symbolically be on trial in a forum that was in a formal sense unrelated, but in a political or ideological sense leaning toward an image of the conflict and defendant that could heighten the likelihood of prosecution and conviction. The goal of protecting the defendant by assuring a fair trial could be prejudiced.

Consider the leading political figures—Ariel Sharon, Yasser Arafat, Fidel Castro and an impressive number of former Presidents including George Bush, Saddam Hussein (Iraq), Hissène Habré (Chad) and Hashemi Rafsanjani (Iran)—who have been the subject of one or another proceeding in Belgium (a number of these cases were not actively pursued). Prosecutions of some of these figures based on universal jurisdiction would provoke different or even polar reactions from different states or groups. Far from representing a common effort of judiciaries everywhere to vindicate common goals, universal jurisdiction could be understood as a partisan enterprise in which states seeing the villain would reach out to prosecute, while those holding the image of hero would not. . . .

Henry J. Steiner, "Three Cheers for Universal Jurisdiction—Or Is It Only Two?," 5 Theoretical Inquiries in Law 199 (2004).

The doctrine of universal jurisdiction asserts that some crimes are so heinous that their perpetrators should not escape justice by invoking doctrines of sovereign immunity or the sacrosanct nature of national frontiers. Two specific approaches to achieve this goal have emerged recently. The first seeks to apply the procedures of domestic criminal justice to violations of universal standards, some of which are embodied in United Nations conventions, by authorizing national prosecutors to bring offenders into their jurisdictions through extradition from third countries. The second approach is the International Criminal Court (ICC). . . .

The very concept of universal jurisdiction is of recent vintage. The sixth edition of Black's Law Dictionary, published in 1990, does not contain even an entry for the term. The closest analogous concept listed is hostes humani generis ("enemies of the human race"). Until recently, the latter term has been applied to pirates, hijackers, and similar outlaws whose crimes were typically committed outside the territory of any state. * * *

[A]ny universal system should contain procedures not only to punish the wicked but also to constrain the righteous. It must not allow legal principles to be used as weapons to settle political scores. Questions such as these must therefore be answered: What legal norms are being applied? What are the rules of evidence? What safeguards exist for the defendant? And how will prosecutions affect other fundamental foreign policy objectives and interests? * * *

It is an important principle that those who commit war crimes or systematically violate human rights should be held accountable. But the consolidation of law, domestic peace, and representative government in a nation struggling to come to terms with a brutal past has a claim as well. The instinct to punish must be related, as in every constitutional democratic political structure, to a system of checks and balances that includes other elements critical to the survival and expansion of democracy. * * *

When discretion on what crimes are subject to universal jurisdiction and whom to prosecute is left to national prosecutors, the scope for arbitrariness is wide indeed. So far, universal jurisdiction has involved the prosecution of one fashionably reviled man of the right [Augusto Pinochet] while scores of East European communist leaders—not to speak of Caribbean, Middle Eastern, or African leaders who inflicted their own full measures of torture and suffering—have not had to face similar prosecutions.

Some will argue that a double standard does not excuse violations of international law and that it is better to bring one malefactor to justice than to grant immunity to all. This is not an argument permitted in the domestic jurisdictions of many democracies—in Canada, for example, a charge can be thrown out of court merely by showing that a prosecution has been selective enough to amount to an abuse of process. In any case, a universal standard of justice should not be based on the proposition that a just end warrants unjust means, or that political fashion trumps fair judicial procedures.

The ideological supporters of universal jurisdiction also provide much of the intellectual compass for the emerging International Criminal Court. * * *

The doctrine of universal jurisdiction is based on the proposition that the individuals or cases subject to it have been clearly identified. In some instances, especially those based on Nuremberg precedents, the definition of who can be prosecuted in an international court and in what circumstances is self-evident. But many issues are much more vague and depend on an understanding of the historical and political context. It is this fuzziness that risks arbitrariness on the part of prosecutors and judges years after the event and that became apparent with respect to existing tribunals.

For example, can any leader of the United States or of another country be hauled before international tribunals established for other purposes? This is precisely what Amnesty International implied when, in the summer of 1999, it supported a "complaint" by a group of European and Canadian law professors to Louise Arbour, then the prosecutor of the International Criminal Tribunal for the Former Yugoslavia (ICTY). The complaint alleged that crimes against humanity had been committed during the NATO air campaign in Kosovo. Arbour ordered an internal staff review, thereby implying that she did have jurisdiction if such violations could, in fact, be demonstrated. Her successor, Carla Del Ponte, in the end declined to indict any NATO official because of a general inability "to pinpoint individual responsibilities," thereby implying anew that the court had jurisdiction over NATO and American leaders in the Balkans and would have issued an indictment had it been able to identify the particular leaders allegedly involved. * * *

Distrusting national governments, many of the advocates of universal jurisdiction seek to place politicians under the supervision of magistrates and the judicial system. But prosecutorial discretion without accountability is precisely one of the flaws of the International Criminal Court. Definitions of the relevant crimes are vague and highly susceptible to politicized application. Defendants will not enjoy due process as understood in the United States.

Any signatory state has the right to trigger an investigation. As the U.S. experience with the special prosecutors investigating the executive branch shows, such a procedure is likely to develop its own momentum without time limits and can turn into an instrument of political warfare. * * *

Henry A. Kissinger, "The Pitfalls of Universal Jurisdiction: Risking Judicial Tyranny," Foreign Affairs (July/Aug. 2001), at 86.[a]

3. When all is said and done, what is the point of the various theories of criminal jurisdiction? Assuming that a political entity is authorized to pass a criminal statute (in the U.S., on the basis of the police power in the case of the individuals states, or on the basis of, say, the commerce clause in the case of the federal government), are there any constraints on how far it can extend the reach of its criminal jurisdiction? Do notions of individual rights or political legitimacy have any relevance to this issue at all, or is it simply a matter of international relations? Can the extension of criminal jurisdiction ever be unjust, or merely impolitic or perhaps undiplomatic? (Note the inapplicability, in American constitutional law, of the double jeopardy proscription to prosecutions brought by separate sovereigns for the same act.)

a. It should be noted that there have been calls for the initiation of criminal proceedings under universal jurisdiction against Kissinger himself, for his conduct as National Security Advisor (1969–75) and Secretary of State (1973–77). See, e.g., Christopher Hitchens, The Trial of Henry Kissinger (2001); Application for a Warrant for the Arrest of Henry Alfred Kissinger (London, Apr. 22, 2002), International Campaign Against Impunity (ICAI), http://www.icai-online.org/56478,46136.html (accessed Feb. 17, 2004).—EDS.

CHAPTER 3

THE BASIC STRUCTURE OF AMERICAN CRIMINAL LAW

The study of "American criminal law" faces a serious difficulty: it's surprisingly hard to say just what "American criminal law" encompasses. There once was a time when American law in general, and American criminal law in particular, was conceived of as part of the grand system of "The Common Law," whose origins were lost in the mist of Anglo–Saxon dooms and whose doctrines encompassed the entire Civilized World, i.e., the British Empire. Oddly enough, this conception of American law as a subspecies of English common law survived the American Revolution and, at least in the area of criminal law, flourished well into the twentieth century.

The nineteenth century did produce a growing number of American criminal statutes and of American court opinions interpreting them, but a sense of a distinctly American criminal law was slow to develop. Even textbooks (and casebooks) on American criminal law initially relied mostly on English cases. Until the mid-twentieth century, American criminal law survived as a hodgepodge of "common law" and "statutory law."

All that changed with the drafting of the Model Penal Code in the 1950s. Since then the Model Penal Code has replaced the Common Law as the common denominator of American criminal law. Comprehensive codes—based more or less on the Model Code—have replaced collections of statutes that were thought of as supplements, or modest amendments, to The Common Law, rather than as authoritative statements of a system of criminal law. The Model Penal Code also worked a fairly dramatic shift of criminal lawmaking power from the judiciary to the legislature. While the judiciary today retains a "common law" power of adjudication, that discretion is limited to the interpretation of legislatures' criminal codes (and criminal statutes strewn throughout other codes). But "the notion of a common-law crime is utterly anathema today." Rogers v. Tennessee, 532 U.S. 451, 476 (2001) (Scalia, J., dissenting). For a more detailed discussion of the power to make, and to apply, criminal law, see ch. 2.

Today, American criminal law consists of fifty-two American criminal *laws*—the systems of criminal law defined by the criminal codes of the fifty states, the federal government, and the District of Columbia. It would be foolhardy to attempt an overview of this cornucopia of criminal law doctrines. We will instead focus on those features of American criminal law that are most widely shared among the various American jurisdictions. This means paying particular attention to the *general part* of criminal law (and, not coincidentally, of criminal codes). The general part deals with the general principles of criminal liability. It sets out the conditions that must be met before a particular person can be convicted of a crime, and addresses questions such as: Did the defendant in a vehicular homicide case act voluntarily, intentionally, or at least negligently, or was her running over the pedestrian just an accident? Does she have some sort of defense available to her? Perhaps she was speeding because she was rushing to get her ailing husband to the hospital for a life-saving operation? Or perhaps she was being held hostage by a gun toting bank robber who commandeered her car? Or perhaps she had fallen asleep at the wheel after a long night's drive? After taking a cold pill with an undisclosed side effect of extreme drowsiness?

There is considerable overlap on questions of the general part across American jurisdictions. That's not to say—as we'll see—that no significant differences remain. At any rate, there is considerably *more* overlap in the general part than there is in the *special part* of criminal law. The special part deals with the types and definitions of crimes which will trigger criminal liability, assuming the general preconditions laid out in the general part are met. So the special part will consider questions like, How is vehicular homicide defined, exactly? Does it require operating, driving, or occupying, a vehicle, a motor vehicle, an automobile, a car, a truck, a bicycle, with recklessness, just negligence, or no mental state whatsoever? How does its definition differ from that of other, similar, crimes, like speeding, reckless driving, vehicular assault, homicide, or just plain assault? And what about my attitude toward the death of the pedestrian—does it matter? If so, must I have acted with the purpose of killing him, or just accepted, or taken a chance, that he might die? And what does "death" mean anyway? Brain death? If so, when does brain death occur?

There are commonalities in the special part of American criminal law as well—just as there are commonalities across the special parts of non-U.S. criminal laws. There is, for instance, some consensus on what type of conduct ought to be criminalized, and what sorts of interests the criminal law should protect. But apart from these general structural commonalities, there are simply too many crimes, and too many *different* crimes, to make an overview of the special part of American criminal law feasible in an introductory casebook.

The distinction between the general part and the special part, and much of the content of the general part, is an achievement of the Model Penal Code. The present section provides, first, a general introduction to the Model Code and, second, an overview of the structure of the general part as laid out by the Code, and as adopted, with the inevitable variations, across American criminal jurisdictions.

A. THE MODEL PENAL CODE

Today the Model Penal Code, published by the American Law Institute in 1962, is acknowledged as "the principal text in criminal law teaching" and "the point of departure for criminal law scholarship." Sanford H. Kadish, "The Model Penal Code's Historical Antecedents," 19 Rutgers L.J.

521, 521 (1988). The Model Code will make frequent, and more or less explicit, appearances throughout this book, in cases, statutes, and in questions and comments, despite the fact that it is just that, a *model* code that no single jurisdiction has adopted in its entirety. To make sense of the Code excerpts strewn about the book, and to help students understand why the Code matters, notwithstanding its mere model status, an introduction to the Code will be helpful.

> An important reason why the Model Code is the key to American criminal law in fact, and not only in theory, is that so much of American criminal law derives from it, one way or another. Most obvious is the Code's influence in the forty or so jurisdictions that recodified their criminal law on its basis, including New York, Texas, Illinois, Pennsylvania, and New Jersey. Even though none of these revisions adopted the Code as a whole, all of them were influenced by it to a greater or lesser extent....
>
> The Code continues to influence the criminal law in "non-MPC" jurisdictions as well. These include two important jurisdictions where the national recodification effort triggered by the Code failed miserably, California and federal criminal law. As evidence of its nationwide impact, the Code has been cited in over 2,000 opinions from every American jurisdiction. Courts in non-MPC jurisdictions frequently draw on the Code's analysis to elucidate unsettled issues, such as the mental state requirements of particular offenses, even if they end up rejecting the particular solution proposed by the Code drafters. By last count, the Code has been cited in over 100 California and over 500 federal opinions, including more than 100 Supreme Court opinions....
>
> *Origins: The ALI, Legal Process, and Treatmentism*
>
> To get a handle on the Model Penal Code, it helps to know something about where it came from and who drafted it. Although it was drafted between 1952 and 1962, the origins of the Code lie in the 1930s. That's when the American Law Institute decided to tackle criminal law and criminal procedure. An organization of distinguished jurists founded in 1923 "to promote the clarification and simplification of the law and its better adaptation to social needs, to secure the better administration of justice, and to encourage and carry on scholarly and scientific legal work," the ALI took a look at American criminal law and procedure at the time and was so appalled by what it saw that it decided that, unlike in other areas like torts or contracts, more than a mere "restatement" of the law was called for. What was needed was a fresh start in the form of *model codes*. The Model Code of Criminal Procedure was completed in 1930. The Model Penal Code was next, but its drafting was postponed until after World War II.
>
> After the war, Herbert Wechsler, a Columbia law professor, was put in charge of the Model Penal Code project. Wechsler had laid out the plans for a comprehensive reform of American criminal law in a monumental 1937 article, entitled modestly and somewhat misleadingly "A Rationale for the Law of Homicide." Jerome Michael & Herbert

Wechsler, A Rationale of the Law of Homicide (Parts I & II), 37 Colum. L. Rev. 701, 1261 (1937). * * *

.... Wechsler was a leading proponent of what came to be known as the Legal Process school—a moniker derived from the phenomenally influential and, until recently, remarkably unpublished, casebook of the same name by Henry Hart and Albert Sacks. Henry M. Hart & Albert M. Sacks, The Legal Process: Basic Problems in the Making and Application of Law (William N. Eskridge, Jr. & Phillip P. Frickey eds., 1994). Its Legal Process pedigree accounts for several features of the Model Code.

First, the Code is a model piece of *legislation*. Its goal was to transfer the power to make criminal law from the common-law making judiciary to the statute-law making legislature. "No conduct constitutes an offense unless it is a crime or violation under this Code or another statute of this State." Model Penal Code § 1.05(1). Common law crimes were no more.

Second, the Code is *comprehensive*. In its effort to guide the courts' discretion in applying the rules generated by the legislature, the Code left little to chance. Given too much wiggling room, ingenious judges might try to circumvent the prohibition of common law crimes. That's why the Code reads—and looks—as much like a criminal law textbook as it does like a code.[17] It was meant to teach criminal law to criminal justice professionals.

Third, the Code is a *code*. It attempted to construct a rational system of criminal law, rather than a compendium of existing rules. This system served certain "purposes," which the drafters, in an unusual step, made explicit. Id. § 1.02. Those purposes were then implemented in the "principles," "provisions," and "definitions" that make up the bulk of the Code.

Fourth, the Code is *pragmatic*. Legal Process was a way of making policy first and a theory of law second. Now there's no point to a policy that's not implemented. And implemented the Code was, more or less completely, in the majority of American jurisdictions. * * *

Wechsler was not only committed to the Legal Process way of doing things. He also subscribed to another orthodoxy of his time: treatmentism. Growing out of the beginnings of the new science of criminology at the turn of the twentieth century, treatmentism called for the replacement of punishment with treatment. According to treatmentism, crime was a disorder that required diagnosis and treatment. Penal treatment was prescribed based on a penological diagnosis that roughly distinguished between two types of offender: those who could be cured and those who couldn't. The former were subjected to rehabilitative, the latter to incapacitative, treatment.

17. This feature of the Code distinguishes it from other influential modern criminal codes, and makes it a much better teaching vehicle. The German Penal Code, for instance, doesn't define actus reus, mens rea, causation, or consent.

In the treatmentist model, criminal law was not a matter of meting out just punishments, but a matter of administering indicated treatments. A rational system of criminal law, or rather of criminal administration, was a system that prescribed and then administered the proper treatment based on a correct diagnosis. This was precisely the sort of policy challenge that the Legal Process school was designed to meet. And meet it the Model Penal Code did.

Criminal Propensities

That the Model Code wholeheartedly endorsed the then-orthodoxy of treatmentism is not of merely theoretical interest. The Code as a whole doesn't make sense unless one keeps the centrality of treatmentism in mind. Moreover, when confronted with a particularly ornery Code provision, it helps to remind oneself that all the drafters were doing was "describe the character deficiencies of those subjected to [the criminal law] in accord with the propensities that they manifest."[21] * * *

Penal treatment supplements the Code's primary goal, the prevention of crime. The Code pursues its preventive goal in two steps. First, it tries to deter crime. § 1.02(1)(a). Second, if that attempt fails it *treats* those it couldn't deter, that is, it "subject[s] to public control persons whose conduct indicates that they are disposed to commit crimes." § 1.02(1)(b). The attempt at deterrence of course fails untold times every day. And so it turns out in fact that treatment, despite its officially supplementary status, appears as the tail that wags deterrence's dog.

Once diagnosed as disposed to commit crimes under the Code's first half, offenders are sent on for treatment according to the elaborate set of correctional guidelines laid out in the Code's second, and much neglected, correctional half: parts III & IV. The Code's first half gets all the attention in criminal law classes, and rightly so since it's there that we find the stuff of substantive criminal law, including general principles of liability (part I) and specific offenses (part II). But the first half is merely a set up for the second. The first half (the "Penal Code" proper) provides the tools for diagnosing the criminal disposition which is then treated according to the second half (the "Correctional Code"). Put both halves together and you have the "Penal and Correctional Code" that the Model Penal Code set out to be. § 1.01(1). * * *

The Structure of the Model Penal Code

In a sense, the Model Penal Code's structure *is* the Model Penal Code. The Code wears its conceptual coherence on its sleeve. So comprehensive and integrated is the Code's conceptual structure that its table of contents could easily serve as the outline for a criminal law exam. Try doing that with codes untouched by the Model Code, like the federal criminal code, or the California penal code.

21. Model Penal Code Commentaries §§ 220.1 to 230.5, at 157 n.99.

The Model Code drafters imposed structure on chaos wherever they turned. For example, the Code systematized the special part of criminal law by categorizing offenses by the interests and institutions they are designed to protect, such as the state, the person, property, or the family. Before the Code, the preferred method of organization in American criminal codes was the alphabet. In 1948, four years before the Model Code project began in earnest, Congress decided to revise the vast body of federal criminal statutes that had accumulated over a century and a half. That revision, "for which the spadework was done by the hired hands of three commercial law-book publishers, on delegation from a congressional committee desirous of escaping the responsibility of hiring and supervising its own staff,"[28] consisted of placing the existing statutes in alphabetical order. The federal criminal code, Title 18, has retained this ordering to this day, more or less.[29] Efforts to recodify federal criminal law on the basis of the Model Penal Code failed in the early 1980s.

The Code's greatest structural contribution, however, came not in the special part, but in the general part of criminal law. Before the Model Penal Code, American criminal codes had no general parts to speak of. Central concepts like actus reus or mens rea remained undefined. Defenses were treated in the context of particular offenses, chief among them homicide and larceny, rather than as general principles of criminal liability that applied to any and all offenses. The federal criminal code, to return to our example, is still without a general part worth its name. Title 18 contains no general provision on jurisdiction, voluntariness, actus reus, mens rea, causation, mistake, entrapment, duress, infancy, justification, self-defense, or inchoate offenses.

... [T]he Code's structure bears within it a roadmap for the analysis of criminal liability in every case that an American lawyer, judge, or law student might come across.

Once again, the Model Penal Code consists of two parts, the general and the special part:

Part I. General Provisions

Part II. Definition of Specific Offenses

The general part includes general principles that apply across the board to all offenses defined in the special part. These principles are divided into five articles.

Art. 1 Preliminary

Art. 2 General principles of liability

Art. 3 General principles of justification

28. Henry M. Hart, Jr., The Aims of the Criminal Law, 23 Law & Contemp. Probs. 401, 432 n.70 (1958).

29. *Less* because, in its continuous generation of federal crimes, Congress on occasion has found even the alphabet too demanding a structural device. So, for instance, the chapter on "child support" (18 U.S.C. ch. 11A) precedes that on "chemical weapons" (ch. 11B), and "importation of explosive materials" comes after "explosives" but before "extortion," (chs. 39–41)....

Art. 4 Responsibility

Art. 5 Inchoate crimes

Article 1 deals with a number of issues at the boundary between criminal law and criminal procedure, including jurisdiction and venue,[32] the statute of limitations,[33] double jeopardy,[34] and proof requirements.[35] [I]t spells out the purposes of the Code,[36] establishes the principle of legality (in the sense that the legislature holds the monopoly in criminal law making)[37] and defines certain key concepts.[38]

Article 2 is the heart of the Code's general part. Here we find provisions on the core principles of criminal liability, including

§ 2.01 actus reus

§ 2.02 mens rea (& § 2.05)

§ 2.03 causation

§ 2.04 mistake (§ 2.04(1))

§ 2.06 complicity

In addition, the drafters began addressing possible defenses to criminal liability, such as

§ 2.04 ignorance (§ 2.04(3))

§ 2.08 intoxication

§ 2.09 duress

§ 2.10 military orders

§ 2.11 de minimis

§ 2.12 entrapment

The treatment of defenses begins in earnest in article 3, dedicated to "general principles of justification." The justification defenses covered include

§ 3.02 necessity

§ 3.03 public duty

§ 3.04 self-defense

§ 3.05 defense of another

§ 3.06 defense of property

§ 3.07 law enforcement

§ 3.08 special responsibility

Article 4 concludes the Code's consideration of defenses, completing the list of excuse defenses begun in art. 2 with excuses based on the actor's nonresponsibility due to incapacity:

§ 4.01 insanity

32. § 1.03.

33. § 1.06.

34. §§ 1.07–.11.

35. § 1.12.

36. § 1.02.

37. § 1.05.

38. §§ 1.04 & 1.13.

§ 4.10 immaturity

Finally, article 5 deals with inchoate crimes. It's a code within a code, specifying the general principles of inchoate liability, including possible defenses, and defining both inchoate crimes and quasi-inchoate—possession related—crimes at the same time.

§ 5.01 attempt

§ 5.02 solicitation

§ 5.03 conspiracy

§ 5.06 possession of dangerous instruments (& § 5.07)

By defining specific offenses, rather than setting out general principles of liability, the article on inchoate crimes already stands with one foot in the special part.[39] That part, the second half of the Penal Code, is devoted exclusively to the definition of offenses. It's here that we find the stuff of criminal law, the crimes that make the criminal law what it is. These are divided into the following categories of criminally protected interests,

Offenses against the existence or stability of the state[40]

Offenses involving danger to the person

Offenses against property

Offenses against the family

Offenses against public administration

Offenses against public order and decency

Miscellaneous offenses[41]

Narcotics

Alcoholic beverages

Gambling

Offenses against tax and trade laws

Markus D. Dubber, Criminal Law: Model Penal Code 6–22 (2002).

B. THE BUILDING BLOCKS OF CRIMINAL LIABILITY

The general part of American criminal law shares certain structural features that are worth keeping in mind while trying to make sense of the variety of approaches to the analysis of criminal liability developed in the fifty-two criminal jurisdictions, complete with criminal codes and a growing body of judicial interpretation, that make up American criminal law. This structural backbone is laid out with useful clarity in the Model Penal Code.

39. In fact, several criminal codes revised on the basis of the Model Code place the definition of inchoate offenses not at the end of the general part, but at the beginning of the special part. See, e.g., N.Y. Penal Law arts. 110–115.

40. Model Penal Code 123 (Proposed Official Draft 1962).

41. Id. at 241.

If the Model Penal Code is the key to American criminal law, then section 1.02 is the key to the key. Section 1.02 is the Model Penal Code in a nutshell. It compresses the Code's elaborate analytic structure into a single statement of the prerequisites of criminal liability. And that's precisely what one would expect from a self-consciously systematic statement of criminal law, a *code*: Section 1.02 lays out the "purposes" that the remainder of the Model Penal Code works out in detail, applying them to particular issues in the analysis of criminal liability. * * *

.... It tells us not only what sort of conduct is criminal, but also what sort of person is to be punished (or rather treated) for having engaged in it. Right at the outset, it defines both the crime and the criminal, or the offense and the offender.

This is a crime:

conduct that

unjustifiably and inexcusably

inflicts or threatens

substantial harm to

individual or public interests.[46]

And this is a criminal:

a "person[] whose conduct indicates that [he is] disposed to commit crimes."[47]

The rest of the Code merely puts meat on these general definitions, and on the definition of crime in particular. Likewise, the bulk of this book unfolds the doctrinal rules packed into section 1.02's definition of the prerequisites of criminal liability.

At the outset, however, it's important to get clear on the relation between the definitions of crimes and criminals contained in section 1.02. [T]he Code is committed to the idea that no one should be punished unless and until she has committed a crime, no matter how disposed to committing crimes she may be. The concept of crime, in this sense, is prior to that of a criminal: one must commit a crime before one can be labeled a criminal. At the same time, it's not as though the two questions are entirely unrelated. [T]he entire Code is designed to diagnose criminal dangerousness. Rules about whether a crime has been committed, therefore, will try to weed out those who lack that predisposition and even to differentiate between different levels of that predisposition. And that's why our exploration of the Code's definition of crimes will also have to keep in mind its definition of criminals.

The criminal law—and the Model Penal Code—is concerned first and foremost with general rules governing the question whether a crime has been committed. These general rules provide an analytic framework of criminal liability that is applied to particular cases, in

46. § 1.02(1)(a).

47. § 1.02(1)(b).

order to determine whether a particular person is criminally liable for a particular crime, i.e., whether he is guilty....

The Model Code defines a crime as "conduct that unjustifiably and inexcusably inflicts or threatens substantial harm to individual or public interests." Criminal liability thus has these three components:

1. conduct
2. without justification and
3. without excuse

To count as a crime, "conduct" must, however, meet several additional criteria, namely it must:

a. inflict or threaten
b. substantial harm to individual or public interests

And if we put the two together, we get the Model Penal Code's complete scheme of criminal liability:

A person is criminally liable if he engages in

1. conduct that
   a. inflicts or threatens
   b. substantial harm to individual or public interests
2. without justification and
3. without excuse.

The Model Penal Code ... does no more than elaborate on this basic structure of criminal liability.

[There are] other schemes of criminal liability, such as the one said to underlie the "common law." It's difficult to crystallize a single liability scheme from hundreds of years of Anglo–American common law. Still, it seems clear enough that a crime in the common law sense consists of two "offense" elements

1. actus reus (the guilty act) and mens rea (the guilty mind).

Actus reus and mens rea are necessary, but not sufficient, prerequisites of criminal liability under the common law. Owing to the hopelessly confused common law concept of mens rea, which after centuries of judicial expansion and contraction came to encompass everything and nothing, it's difficult to say what else is needed for criminal liability, exactly. It's safe to say, however, that courts from early on recognized that criminal liability required both a criminal "offense" (consisting of actus reus and mens rea) and the absence of "defenses." Particularly in the law of homicide, which has always managed to attract the lion's share of doctrinal attention, courts generally divided these defenses into two types, justifications and excuses.[48] Criminal liability thus attached to an offense committed

48. 4 William Blackstone, Commentaries on the Laws of England 178–88 (1769) (justifiable and excusable homicide)....

2. without justification and
3. without excuse.

The analytic schemes of the Model Penal Code and the common law are more or less interchangeable depending on how one views the connection between conduct and mens rea. The Model Code defines conduct as encompassing both: conduct is "an action or omission and its accompanying state of mind."[49] Replacing "actus reus and mens rea" with "conduct," the common law scheme of criminal liability therefore looks like this:

1. conduct
2. without justification and
3. without excuse

The "common law" and the Model Penal Code thus do not differ in their general analysis of criminal liability. That's why the Model Penal Code serves as the analytic backbone of American criminal law, common law or not. Where the two differ on occasion is at the level of particular rules. . . .

Markus D. Dubber, Criminal Law: Model Penal Code 23–24, 26–31 (2002).

More specifically, the common backbone of the general part of American criminal law looks something like this (with citations to the Model Penal Code):

1. Criminality (arts. 1–2, 5): Does the behavior constitute criminal conduct?
   A. What are the elements of the offense as defined? (§ 1.13(9))
      1. Conduct (§ 1.13(5))
      2. Circumstances
      3. Result
      4. Mode of Culpability (as to each element)
         —purpose, knowledge, recklessness, negligence (§ 2.02)
         —none (strict liability, § 2.05)
         —rules of interpretation (§§ 2.02(3), (4), 2.05)
   B. Does the behavior satisfy each element of the offense?
      1. Conduct
         —act (§ 2.01)
         —voluntariness (§ 2.01)
         —omission (§ 2.01)
         —complicity (§ 2.06)
      2. Circumstances
         —consent (§ 2.11)
      3. Result

49. § 1.13(5).

—causation (§ 2.03)

—but for (§ 2.03(1)(a))

—proximate (§ 2.03(1)(b)–(4))

4. Mode of Culpability (as to each element)

—mistake (§ 2.04(1))

—intoxication (§ 2.08)

—diminished capacity (§ 4.02(1))

5. Inchoate Crimes (art. 5)

—attempt (§ 5.01)

—solicitation (§ 5.02)

—conspiracy (§ 5.03)

2. Illegality (Justification) (art. 3): Is the criminal conduct unlawful generally speaking?

A. Necessity (choice of evils) (§ 3.02)

B. Self-defense (§ 3.04); defense of another (§ 3.05); defense of property (§ 3.06)

C. Law enforcement (§ 3.07)

D. Public duty (§ 3.03)

E. Special responsibility (§ 3.08)

F. Consent (§ 2.11)

3. Guilt (Excuse) (arts. 2, 4): Is the accused blameworthy for her criminal and unlawful conduct?

A. Duress (§ 2.09)

B. Military orders (§ 2.10)

C. Entrapment (§ 2.13)

D. Ignorance of Law (§ 2.04(3))

E. Provocation and Diminished Capacity (§ 210.3(1)(b))

F. Insanity and Infancy (§§ 4.01, .10)

—involuntary intoxication (§ 2.08(4))

Markus D. Dubber, Criminal Law: Model Penal Code 284–86 (2002).

In sum, the general part of American criminal law breaks the general question, who is criminally liable for what?, into three subsidiary questions: (1) Did the defendant engage in criminal conduct?, (2) If so, was she justified in doing so?, and (3) If she wasn't justified, was she excused?

In its basic outline, the general part of American criminal law bears a certain resemblance to the "General System for Analyzing Criminal Acts" in German criminal law. Wolfgang Naucke illustrates how the German three-step analysis of criminal liability operates:

> German courts are time and again confronted by the following set of facts: A group of young people has difficulty gaining public attention for their political views, and to remedy this problem they decide to

"advertise": They have some posters printed and paste them up as firmly as possible in as many locations as they see fit. The modern glues are quite permanent, and the material is often bonded to the surface to which it is attached. It is usually a tremendous inconvenience to remove the posters or fliers, and is sometimes impossible.

Under German criminal law, the question is whether the foregoing conduct is sufficient to constitute the crime of damaging property under section 303 of the German Criminal Code.[a] There are conflicting opinions, and the courts and scholars defend their views with numerous arguments. It is unsettled whether firmly pasting a flier or poster on an object damages that object. Those who believe that it does must turn to further questions. Conceivably, such property damage is justified by the right to freedom of speech. Even someone who does not accept the argument that free speech rights legitimize property damage might still argue that the young people should not be punished because they (mistakenly) thought that their right to freedom of speech justified their actions. * * *

.... In [the general system for analyzing criminal acts] are collected those features of crime that are common to all crimes, whether it be damaging property, theft, murder, or anything else. If, therefore, unauthorized advertising is to be punishable under German law, it must be found to exhibit the general paradigmatic features of crime as determined by German criminal theory, as well as the particular elements of section 303 established by statute. * * *

The general analytical system describes the main features of criminal action with the German terms *Tatbestandsmässigkeit* (definition of the offense), *Rechtswidrigkeit* (wrongfulness), and *Schuld* (culpability). Whatever the governing code provision may be, every criminal act must be wrongful and culpable conduct that conforms to (i.e., is violative of) the definition of the offense. Unauthorized advertising can only be punished if it violates the definition, is wrongful, and is culpable. These central elements are discussed with much effort and pomp in Germany. The discussion ... has not achieved a conclusive result. A few main points, however, are undisputed.

a. The definition of an offense. The word *Tatbestandsmässigkeit* embraces all of the elements of a particular crime that are found in the applicable code section. A rough American equivalent would be the phrase "elements of the offense." There is a *Tatbestand* or definition of theft, homicide, fraud, and so on. The problems ... with applying section 303 to "wild postering" are questions about whether such conduct fits within the scope of the definition of damaging property. A German law student writing an exam on the issue, or for that matter, a German judge deciding a "wild postering" case, would be regarded as engaging in improper analysis if he or she tried to treat these question

a. § 303. Damaging Property

(1) Whoever unlawfully damages or destroys the property of another shall be punished with imprisonment for not more than two years or a fine.—EDS.

at a different stage of the analysis—i.e., as an issue of wrongfulness or culpability.

Demanding that the problem of determining which legal interest is protected by section 303 be treated as a problem of the definition of damaging property affects more that the mere formal ordering of legal analysis. This demand also aids the decision of substantive issues. The content of the definition of a crime cannot be extended beyond that formulated by the legislature. In the context of section 303, for example, the authority of the property owner to determine what may happen to his property is protected only to the extent this authority is asserted to prevent damage to, or destruction of, the property. From this perspective it would take a strained interpretation to hold unauthorized advertising to be a violation of section 303, since such conduct leaves the property intact and intrudes solely upon the owner's authority.... If however, the definition of the crime of damaging property were tied to the authority of the owner to control his property, the determination of whether a particular act satisfied the element of the definition would be dependent upon whether the property owner viewed the act as an incursion upon his authority....

b. Wrongfulness. Rechtswidrigkeit, or wrongfulness, embraces all the statutory and extra statutory general grounds for holding that conduct which is violative of the definition may still be found to be justified, thereby escaping punishment. Self-defense is a classic justification that negates the wrongfulness of an act. The right to free speech, which some "wild posterers" cite as the source of the legitimacy of their activity, is a doubtful justification in their case. But it is in any event an argument that must be legally analyzed under the heading of wrongfulness. The category of wrongfulness in the general analytical system not only proves the proper place for the discussion of such justifications but also provokes the discussion of doubtful justification.

c. Culpability. The first task of the element of *Schuld* or culpability in the general analytical system is to secure the status of culpability as an indispensable prerequisite to punishment. A result of the culpability requirement is that the lawyer must carefully consider possible grounds for excusing the actor, even though his conduct is violative of the definition of the crime and is wrongful. Insanity and duress are illuminating examples of the doctrines that serve to negate culpability in this manner. A party availing himself of either of these defenses typically claims that while he has engaged in conduct specified in the definition of some crime, and though he has done so without justification, he cannot fairly be held responsible for what he did.

Legal discussions of unauthorized advertising commonly encounter the view that this conduct conforms to the definition of damaging property and is wrongful. Those who defend this position are not, however, finished with their analysis. They must take up the further problem presented by the possibility that the actor thought he had a right to paste up posters, In the terms of the theory of the general analytical system, this is a problem of culpability. A perhaps overly simplistic formulation is that the category of culpability marshals all of the arguments favoring a finding of not guilty that are based on the subjective state of the accused and insures that they are considered in every case.

Wolfgang Naucke, "An Insider's Perspective on the Significance of the German Criminal Law Theory's General System for Analyzing Criminal Acts," 1984 BYU L. Rev. 305, 308–09, 310–14.

QUESTIONS AND COMMENTS

1. What are the advantages of applying a uniform sequential approach to the analysis of criminal liability? What are its disadvantages?

2. The German three-step approach was developed by criminal law scholars around the beginning of the twentieth century and is now applied as a matter of course by all German courts. Does it matter who devises—or who adopts—the framework for the analysis of criminal liability? Should it be codified? If it isn't codified, does it violate the principle of legality (more specifically, the principle of legislativity)? What if a judge decided to deviate from it, in a particular case, in all cases?

Is the German approach consistent with the structure of the Model Penal Code's general part? With the Model Code's treatmentist orientation?

3. *Justification and Excuse*. The distinction between offense elements and defense elements seems straightforward enough. There are some things—called offense elements—that the prosecution must prove, and there are others—called defense elements—that the defendant must prove. (As we'll see in the next chapter, it's not quite so simple.) But what is the distinction between a justification and an excuse? This question we'll get a chance to explore in greater detail in ch. 7. For our purposes—to get a general sense of the lay of the land of American criminal law—it's enough to get the basic gist of the distinction. On one hand, consider someone who exceeds the posted speed limits to get a heart attack victim to the hospital. She may argue that her conduct, though criminal on its face because it violated a statute backed by criminal sanctions (speeding), was *justified*, i.e., that it is affirmatively good (or at least not affirmatively bad), something we'd want to encourage, rather than punish, even though behavior "like it" is ordinarily bad (and, presumably for that very reason also criminal). On the other hand, consider the same speeder—only that this time around she exceeds the speed limit because a bank robber has jumped into her car and, with a gun to her head, tells her to speed off to evade a police cruiser in hot pursuit. In this case, she may argue that her conduct is *excused*, i.e., that it is so difficult to avoid usually punishable behavior that punishment is inappropriate (perhaps because she could not have been deterred or because she is not blameworthy or dangerous, but rather merely unlucky to have been caught in the circumstances she was caught in). What distinction between justification and excuse is implied in the German scheme of criminal liability, as summarized by Naucke?

4. *The Analysis of Victim Compensability*. The analysis of victim compensation claims mirrors the analysis of criminal liability in interesting

ways. Compensation law and punishment law both provide a legal analysis of crime from the perspectives of the two persons who constitute it: the victim and the offender. One seeks to determine the compensability of a "claimant," the other the punishability of a "defendant." Along the way, they struggle with identical issues from diametrically opposed, yet complimentary, viewpoints, beginning with the question of jurisdiction and ending with that of responsibility, i.e., of (victim) innocence or (offender) guilt.

Compensation and punishment, the law of victimhood and of offenderhood, represent complimentary responses by the state through law to the fact of crime. In any given case of crime, the crucial question is which, if any, of these responses is appropriate. Sometimes compensation may be sufficient; other times punishment may be necessary as well. In other cases no state response of any kind is called for because the persons constituting the crime ("victim" and "offender") are perfectly capable of dealing with its effects on their own, as persons possessed with the power of self-determination who require the state's assistance only in extraordinary cases where that very power has been compromised or destroyed altogether. Here then are the general outlines of the analysis of victim compensability:

> The kernel of a general account of victimhood lies ... in the general definition of victimhood [such as the one found in the New York victim compensation statute]: a victim is "a person who suffers personal physical injury as a direct result of a crime." N.Y. Exec. Law § 620. To receive compensation, however, mere victimhood is not enough. Not victims, but *innocent* victims trigger the legislature's empathy ..., as the "declaration of policy and legislative intent" at the very beginning of New York's victim compensation statute makes clear:
>
> > The legislature recognizes that many *innocent* persons suffer personal physical injury or death as a result of criminal acts. Such persons or their dependents may thereby suffer disability, incur financial hardships, or become dependent upon public assistance. The legislature finds and determines that there is a need for government financial assistance for such victims of crime. Accordingly, it is the legislature's intent that aid, care and support be provided by the state, as a matter of grace, for such victims of crime (emphasis added).
>
> Combining the definition of "victim" and the declaration of legislative intent, we end up with the following test of compensability: To qualify for victim compensation a claimant must be
>
> > (i) "a person who suffers personal physical injury as a direct result of a crime" and
> >
> > (ii) "innocent."
>
> A compensable victim [thus] is *an innocent person who suffers personal physical injury as a direct result of a crime.*
>
> [Based on a review] of victims legislation from throughout the country, we can construct the outline of a general law of compensability. The analysis of compensability falls into two stages:

(1) At the first stage, the victim's general eligibility for compensation is determined. To be facially eligible for compensation in the abstract, a "claimant" must establish

(a) that she falls within the scope of the relevant compensation statute ("jurisdiction") and

(b) that she is capable of being a victim ("an innocent *person* who suffers personal physical injury as a direct result of a crime").

Assuming she is eligible in the abstract, she must establish that she is eligible in particular, by showing

(c) that she was in fact the victim of a crime ("an innocent person *who suffers personal physical injury as a direct result of a crime*") and

(d) that she was in fact not responsible for that crime ("an *innocent* person who suffers personal physical injury as a direct result of a crime").

If she succeeds on all four counts, and she bears the burden of proof on all of them [by a preponderance of the evidence], she is compensable.

(2) The inquiry then proceeds to the second stage, where the amount of compensation is determined. That amount will depend on various factors, including

(a) her responsibility for the crime, if any,

(b) the actual harm suffered, and

(c) her neediness.

Markus Dirk Dubber, Victims in the War on Crime: The Use and Abuse of Victims' Rights 9–10, 234–35 (2002).

C. An Illustration: *Dudley and Stephens*

It might be helpful to see how the various levels of inquiry into criminal liability shape the analysis of a particular case.

The Queen v. Dudley and Stephens

Queen's Bench Division.
14 Q.B.D. 273 (1884).

INDICTMENT for the murder of Richard Parker on the high seas....

At the trial before Huddleston, B., at the Devon and Cornwall Winter Assizes, November 7, 1884, the jury, at the suggestion of the learned judge, found the facts of the case in a special verdict which stated "that on July 5, 1884, the prisoners, Thomas Dudley and Edward Stephens, with one Brooks, all able-bodied English seamen, and the deceased also an English boy, between seventeen and eighteen years of age, the crew of an English yacht [the Mignonette], a registered English vessel, were cast away in a storm on the high seas 1600 miles from the Cape of Good Hope, and were compelled to put into an open boat belonging to the said yacht. That in this boat they had no supply of water and no supply of food, except two 1 lb. tins of turnips, and for three days they had nothing else to subsist upon. That on the fourth day they caught a small turtle, upon which they subsisted for a few days, and this was the only food they had up to the twentieth day when the act now in question was committed. That on the twelfth day the turtle were entirely consumed, and for the next eight days they had nothing to eat. That they had no fresh water, except such rain as they from time to time caught in their oilskin capes. That the boat was drifting on the ocean, and was probably more than 1000 miles away from land. That on the eighteenth day, when they had been seven days without food and five without water, the prisoners spoke to Brooks as to what should be done if no succour came, and suggested that some one should be sacrificed to save the rest, but Brooks dissented, and the boy, to whom they were understood to refer, was not consulted. That on the 24th of July, the day before the act now in question, the prisoner Dudley proposed to Stephens and Brooks that lots should be cast who should be put to death to save the rest, but Brooks refused consent, and it was not put to the boy, and in point of fact there was no drawing of lots. That on that day the prisoners spoke of their having families, and suggested it would be better to kill the boy that their lives should be saved, and Dudley proposed that if there was no vessel in sight by the morrow morning the boy should be killed. That next day, the 25th of July, no vessel appearing, Dudley told Brooks that he had better go and have a sleep, and made signs to Stephens and Brooks that the boy had better be killed. The prisoner Stephens agreed to the act, but Brooks dissented from it. That the boy was then lying at the bottom of the boat quite helpless, and extremely weakened by famine and by drinking sea water, and unable to make any resistance, nor did he ever assent to his being killed. The prisoner Dudley offered a prayer asking forgiveness for them all if either of them should be tempted to commit a rash act, and that their souls might be saved. That Dudley, with the assent of Stephens, went to the boy, and telling him that his time was come, put a knife into his throat and killed him then and there; that the three men fed upon the body and blood of the boy for four days; that on the fourth day after the act had been committed the boat was picked up by a passing vessel, and the prisoners were rescued, still alive, but in the lowest state of prostration.... That if the men had not fed upon the body of the boy they would probably not have survived to be so picked up and rescued, but would within the four days have died of famine. That the boy, being in a much weaker condition, was likely to have died before them. That at the time of the act in question there was no sail in sight, nor any reasonable prospect of relief. That under these circumstances there appeared to the prisoners every probability that unless they then fed or very soon fed upon the boy or one of themselves they would die of starvation. That there was no appreciable chance of saving life except by killing some one for the others to eat...."

The learned judge then adjourned the assizes until the 25th of November at the Royal Courts of Justice. On the application of the Crown they were again adjourned to the 4th of December, and the case ordered to be argued before a Court consisting of five judges. * * *

Dec. 9.

■ The judgment of the Court (Lord Coleridge, C.J., Grove and Denman, JJ., Pollock and Huddleston, B–B.) was delivered by LORD COLERIDGE, C.J.

The two prisoners, Thomas Dudley and Edwin Stephens, were indicted for the murder of Richard Parker on the high seas on the 25th of July in the present year. They were tried before my Brother Huddleston at Exeter on the 6th of November, and under the direction of my learned Brother, the jury returned a special verdict, the legal effect of which has been argued before us, and on which we are now to pronounce judgment.

... From the[] facts, stated with the cold precision of a special verdict, it appears sufficiently that the prisoners were subject to terrible temptation, to sufferings which might break down the bodily power of the strongest man and try the conscience of the best.... But nevertheless this is clear, that the prisoners put to death a weak and unoffending boy upon the chance of preserving their own lives by feeding upon his flesh and blood after he was killed, and with the certainty of depriving him of any possible chance of survival. The verdict finds in terms that "if the men had not fed upon the body of the boy they would probably not have survived," and that, "the boy being in a much weaker condition was likely to have died before them." They might possibly have been picked up next day by a passing ship; they might possibly not have been picked up at all; in either case it is obvious that the killing of the boy would have been an unnecessary and profitless act. It is found by the verdict that the boy was incapable of resistance, and, in fact, made none; and it is not even suggested that his death was due to any violence on his part attempted against, or even so much as feared by, those who killed him. * * *

... [T]he real question in the case [is] whether killing under the circumstances set forth in the verdict be or be not murder. ... First it is said that it follows from various definitions of murder in books of authority, which definitions imply, if they do not state, the doctrine, that in order to save your own life you may lawfully take away the life of another, when that other is neither attempting nor threatening yours, nor is guilty of any illegal act whatever towards you or any one else. But if these definitions be looked at they will not be found to sustain this contention....

Now it is admitted that the deliberate killing of this unoffending and unresisting boy was clearly murder, unless the killing can be justified by some well-recognised excuse admitted by the law. It is further admitted that there was in this case no such excuse, unless the killing was justified by what has been called "necessity." But the temptation to the act which existed here was not what the law has ever called necessity. Nor is this to be regretted. Though law and morality are not the same, and many things may be immoral which are not necessarily illegal, yet the absolute divorce of law from morality would be of fatal consequence; and such divorce would follow if the temptation to murder in this case were to be held by law an absolute defence of it. It is not so. To preserve one's life is generally speaking a duty, but it may be the plainest and the highest duty to sacrifice it. War is full of instances in which it is a man's duty not to live, but to die. The duty, in case of shipwreck, of a captain to his crew, of the crew to the passengers, of soldiers to women and children, ... these duties impose on men the moral necessity, not of the preservation but of the sacrifice of their lives for others, from which in no country, least of all, it is to be hoped, in England, will men ever shrink as indeed, they have not shrunk....

It is not needful to point out the awful danger of admitting the principle which has been contended for. Who is to be the judge of this sort of necessity? By what measure is the comparative value of lives to be measured? Is it to be strength, or intellect, or what? It is plain that the principle leaves to him who is to profit by it to determine the necessity which will justify him in deliberately taking another's life to save his own. In this case the weakest, the youngest, the most unresisting, was chosen. Was it more necessary to kill him than one of the grown men? The answer must be "No"—

> "So spake the Fiend, and with necessity,
>
> The tyrant's plea, excused his devilish deeds."[a]

It is not suggested that in this particular case the deeds were devilish, but it is quite plain that such a principle once admitted might be made the legal cloak for unbridled passion and atrocious crime. There is no safe path for judges to tread but to ascertain the law to the best of their ability and to declare it according to their judgment; and if in any case the law appears to be too severe on individuals, to leave it to the Sovereign to exercise that prerogative of mercy which the Constitution has intrusted to the hands fittest to dispense it.

... It is therefore our duty to declare that the prisoners' act in this case was wilful murder, that the facts as stated in the verdict are no legal justification of the homicide; and to say that in our unanimous opinion the prisoners are upon this special verdict guilty, of murder.

THE COURT then proceeded to pass sentence of death upon the prisoners. [This sentence was afterwards commuted by the Crown to six months' imprisonment.]

QUESTIONS AND COMMENTS

1. At the first level of inquiry, the court addresses the question whether the defendants have committed a crime. Does their behavior fit all the elements of the relevant crime, murder?

Let's start with the *actus reus.* Dudley did in fact stab Parker. But did he kill him, or more precisely, did he cause his death? See, e.g., Model Penal Code § 210.1(1) ("A person is guilty of criminal homicide if he purposely, knowingly, recklessly or negligently causes the death of another human being."). Assuming that Parker was about to die anyway, does hastening his inevitable and imminent death amount to causing it? (The

a. Milton, Paradise Lost (bk. iv, l. 393).—EDS.

answer is yes—if you think about it, every homicide does no more than hasten the inevitable.)

There is no question that stabbing Parker counts as an act (since it constitutes a bodily movement), but was it voluntary? Under criminal law's limited view of voluntariness, the answer is clearly yes. Dudley might have been parched, and starving, and weak, but his act of stabbing was not brought on by an epileptic seizure, nor was he sleepwalking, two typical cases of involuntary acts.

And so Dudley's behavior meets every objective element of the offense of murder. He "caused" the death of another human being, as we just saw. (If he hadn't caused the death, but tried to, he might be liable for attempted murder. Model Penal Code § 5.01.) He caused the "death" of another human being, as opposed to merely causing some nonfatal physical harm. (That would be an assault. See Model Penal Code § 211.1.) He caused the death of "another" human being, rather than his own death. (Suicide is no longer a crime, though assisting suicide still is. Model Penal Code § 210.5.) And he caused the death of another "human being," rather than that, says of an animal. (Killing an animal may be a crime, but it wouldn't be murder. See Model Penal Code § 250.11 ("cruelty to animals").) See ch. 10 for an in-depth discussion of murder and other types of homicide.

What about Brooks? Can't he be held liable for Parker's death for failing to come to his aid? Is not participating in the planning and execution of the killing enough to avoid criminal liability for it? The answer is yes—absent a specific duty to aid another person, the failure to come to his aid is not punishable. If anyone had a duty toward Parker, it was Dudley, as the ship's captain, who traditionally has been charged with the welfare of sailors under his command. Since Dudley blatantly violated this duty, was it upon Brooks to assume it in his stead? (But what if Dudley hadn't done anything at all to save the lives of Stephens—and Brooks, as it turns out? What if he had just sat there and let the boat drift along, until eventually Stephens, Brooks, and Parker had died? Could he be held liable for their deaths since he was *their* captain, too?)

Mens rea is not quite so easily dismissed. The defendants claim that they lacked the proper mens rea for murder, more specifically that they did not act "wilfully" (or with "malice") in killing the cabin boy because they did so not out of ill will but out of necessity. The court rejects this argument. Mens rea is not the symptom of an "evil mind," or a "malignant heart," and murder is merely intentionally causing the death of another person. As long as Dudley sought to kill Parker, or at least knew that stabbing him would lead to his death, he is guilty of murder, no matter how laudable (or at least non-evil) his motives for doing so might be have been.

Note that only Dudley commits the act of killing, but that Stephens nonetheless is held liable for the murder as well. Given Stephen's intimate involvement in the events culminating in the actual killing, Dudley's conduct is "imputed" to Stephens; Stephens is treated as though he had wielded the knife himself. He is punished as Dudley's accomplice.

Once again, why does Brooks escape punishment? Can he be liable as an "accessory after the fact," who benefits from Dudley's criminal conduct, without participating in it? Mere presence near criminal conduct, however, clearly is not enough to be held legally accountable for that conduct.

Finally, and still at the first level of inquiry, it's worth considering whether Dudley and Stephens are guilty of conspiracy, a separate offense that consists of an agreement to commit a crime—apart from the commission of the crime itself. The answer would be yes, since a conspiracy need not be based on a written, or even an explicit, agreement. And the two clearly did agree to have Dudley kill Parker. It's unlikely that Brooks would count as a co-conspirator since he repeatedly registered his objection to the plan. Here it's worth noting that in many American jurisdictions today, Dudley and Stephens could be convicted of—though not necessarily punished for—both the conspiracy to commit murder and the murder itself.

2. Having determined that "the deliberate killing of this unoffending and unresisting boy was clearly murder," the court moves on to consider whether the defendants have any *defenses* available that would bar, or at least mitigate, their liability for their concededly criminal conduct.

It begins by looking at justifications, and *self-defense* in particular. Self-defense does not apply, however, because Parker was "unoffending and unresisting." In modern terms, Dudley had no right to defend himself against Parker for the simple reason that Parker did not threaten him "with unlawful force." Parker might have posed a threat to Dudley's existence, but self-defense does not come into play until and unless Parker himself behaved unlawfully when he posed the threat. It's the unlawfulness of the threat that makes self-defense against it lawful.

But perhaps "the killing was justified by what has been called 'necessity' "? The court answers no, because killing an innocent person to save one's life is wrong, no matter how understandable it might be. But what is wrong cannot be justified. Today we would split the necessity inquiry into two parts. First, we would ask ourselves whether Dudley's act was truly *necessary*. Did he have no other options available to him at the time? Could he have waited a minute, an hour, a day? Could he have tried to catch more turtles, or fish? Second, did he make the right choice, i.e., did he avoid greater harm by inflicting the harm of killing Parker? The court in *Dudley* takes the position that it is never right to take one (innocent) person's life to save the lives of others—so that necessity could never be a defense to murder. Contemporary American law does not necessarily take quite so strict a position. See, e.g., Model Penal Code Commentaries § 3.02, at 15 ("numerical preponderance in the lives saved compared to those sacrificed"). (For a more detailed exploration of necessity as a justification in *Dudley*, see ch. 7.)

If self-defense and necessity do not apply, perhaps another justification defense—consent—might. While the court does not explore this possibility, it's worth considering whether the drawing of lots—or some other process of selection involving all potential victims—might have allowed Dudley to argue consent. Even today, however, the justification of consent is controversial, and particularly in cases involving the infliction of serious physical injury or even death. (Note, for instance, the continued criminalization of assisted suicide. Cf. Washington v. Glucksberg, 521 U.S. 702 (1997); Vacco v. Quill, 521 U.S. 793 (1997).)

3. Assuming that Dudley satisfies the elements of an offense (murder) and that he has no justification defenses available to him, it's time to consider the question of *excuses*. Once again, necessity is Dudley's best hope. But, the court asks itself, can necessity ever *excuse* murder, even if it cannot justify it? Can the pressure of the situation ever be so overwhelming, the circumstances so extenuating, that committing a crime, including murder, is excused, even if it remains the wrong thing to do? The court's answer is, once again, no. There is no defense of necessity as an excuse, period, whether to murder or to any other defense. It is charged with deciding questions of law, the court reasons, not of mercy. The latter are reserved for the chief executive, the Queen. And, in fact, the defendants' sentences were commuted.

Modern criminal law relies less on executive pardon, and instead attempts to incorporate the availability of excuses into the doctrinal analysis of criminal liability. That doesn't mean, however, that Dudley would in fact be excused. For starters, many jurisdictions do not recognize necessity as an excuse—also known as circumstantial, or situational, duress. Unbearable threats must emanate from a person to count as an excuse. And so, here too, Dudley remains without a defense. Other jurisdictions do not extend the defense of duress—personal or circumstantial—to murder cases, finding that killing another person can never be without punishment, no matter what the reason.

What about insanity, finally? This defense wasn't raised in *Dudley*, and for good reason, for it would have had no chance of success. For at that time, English criminal law followed the so-called *M'Naghten* insanity test, which limited insanity to persons who, because of a mental defect, were unable to tell right from wrong. No one suggested that Dudley was mentally ill—though he surely was quite exhausted—nor that he, because of a mental defect, wrongly believed that killing Parker wasn't wrong. (He might have believed that killing Parker wasn't wrong, but that belief was not the manifestation of a mental disease.) Many American jurisdictions today recognize another type of insanity, which excuses persons who acted on an "irresistible impulse." While the impulse to kill Parker might have been strong indeed, it too could not be said to spring from a mental disease, but instead from the desire to survive.

CHAPTER 4

CRIMINAL CONDUCT (OBJECTIVE OFFENSE ELEMENTS)

Under the English common law, criminal liability required both the presence of an offense, and the absence of defenses. For behavior to qualify as an offense in the first place, two things were required, a guilty act (*actus reus*) and a guilty mind (*mens rea*). A mens rea without an actus reus was no crime, only an evil thought. An actus reus without a mens rea likewise did not a crime make, as the maxim "actus non est reus, nisi mens sit rea" ("an act is not guilty without a guilty mind") proclaimed. Now, as we'll see, there were so many exceptions to these norms, or at least so many interpretations of them, that many people came to wonder whether it made any sense to keep invoking them. Whatever its substantive merits—or even its accuracy—the notion that a common law crime consisted of both an actus reus and a mens rea remains a useful way of thinking about the minimum requirements for criminal liability in American criminal law.

A. INTRODUCTION: OFFENSE ELEMENTS IN CONTEXT

1. OBJECTIVE ELEMENTS VS. SUBJECTIVE ELEMENTS

One modern way of understanding the traditional distinction between actus reus and mens rea is to think of the first as referring to the *objective* elements of an offense and the latter as referring to its *subjective* elements. The elements of an offense are objective in the sense that they refer to states of affairs, or facts, that exist independently of how they might be perceived by someone, most importantly the person who stands accused of having committed an offense. They are subjective if they refer to a person's—the alleged offender's—perception of a state of affairs. (The victim's perception may also be relevant as, for instance, in the perception of a threat posed by the offender. See, e.g., People v. Thompson, 72 N.Y.2d 410 (1988), infra ch. 9 (in sex crimes, whether threats amount to "forcible compulsion" depends on "the state of mind produced in the victim by the defendant's conduct").) For example, the imaginary crime of intentionally eating breakfast in bed consists of the objective elements of eating, breakfast, and in bed, along with the subjective element of intention. To commit this crime I must not only in fact be eating, breakfast, in bed, but must also do this with the intention of doing just that, as opposed to, say, ordering breakfast in bed, or eating dinner in bed, or eating breakfast on the balcony. Much of criminal law concerns itself with determining just what it means to eat, breakfast, in bed and—even more so—what it means to do this intentionally. The former set of questions is addressed in the present chapter. The latter is addressed in the next.

Not much rides on the distinction between objective and subjective offense elements. For our purposes at least, it's simply a convenient structuring device, more convenient—and less arcane—than the traditional distinction between actus reus and mens rea. One thing you might like to do as you go through the materials in this book is to ask yourself whether a particular topic deals with an objective or a subjective element of criminal liability. You'll see that even *defenses* have objective and subjective elements, for instance. (To qualify for self-defense, do you have to use force for the *purpose* of defending yourself, or is it enough that you were *in fact* threatened with an unlawful attack? See ch. 7.) Often you may wonder whether it's possible—or useful—to separate objective from subjective aspects of criminal liability, as for instance in the case of the requirement that behavior cannot be subject to punishment unless it qualifies as a *voluntary* act. Imagine that you knock over an expensive vase during an epileptic seizure. What, you may (and should) wonder, distinguishes the actus reus notion of voluntariness from the mens rea notion of knowledge, for instance? See, e.g., In re Ronnie L., 121 Misc.2d 271 (N.Y. Fam. Ct. 1983), infra ch. 5. Then there is the tricky question of causation, which is difficult to classify as either objective or subjective. (For my actions to qualify as the cause of some criminal harm, do I have to *know* that they would—or foresee that they might—have the precise effect in the precise way at the precise time in which it occurred, or is it enough that they had that effect *as a matter of fact*? See ch. 6.) Just because it's hard to classify something, though, shouldn't keep you from trying to parse out its various aspects, some of which may look more objective, others more subjective. Very few doctrinal distinctions will be neat. If they appear that way, this should raise your suspicion. Much of what "thinking like a lawyer" consists of is muddling up distinctions that everyone thought were clearly drawn. The rest is being able to draw the distinction at a different point that makes more sense (or favors your client).

Within the general category of objective offense elements, several further distinctions can be drawn, some of which are more contested, and doctrinally significant, than others, but all of which are useful in getting a sense of the lay of the land.

2. TYPES OF OFFENSE ELEMENTS (MODEL PENAL CODE)

Beginning with the Model Penal Code, it has become common to differentiate between three types of offense elements: *conduct*, *attendant circumstance*, and *result*.

> The "circumstances" of the offense refer to the objective situation that the law requires to exist, in addition to the defendant's act or any results that the act may cause. The elements of "nighttime" in burglary, "property of another" in theft, "female not his wife" in rape, and "dwelling" in arson are illustrations. "Conduct" refers to "breaking and entering" in burglary, "taking" in theft, "sexual intercourse" in rape and "burning" in arson. Results, of course, include "death" in homicide.

Model Penal Code Commentaries § 5.01, at 301 n.9.

Not every offense will have every type of offense element. Conduct is the only type of offense element that every offense will have—otherwise there would be no act, which we just saw is a minimum requirement for criminal liability. Attendant circumstances may not be required, but they are nonetheless useful in defining proscribed behavior with sufficient specificity (a matter of constitutional importance, given the principle of legality, supra ch. 2) and in differentiating among different types, and grades, of criminal conduct. Homicide, as defined in the Model Penal Code, "causing the death of another human being," sets out no attendant circumstances specifying the time, place, and manner of the killing. Yet even homicide doesn't quite manage to do without attendant circumstances altogether. It may make no difference when, where, and how you cause the death of another human being, but "another human being" it must be, meaning—at least in the Model Code's view of things—that it cannot be yourself (that would be suicide, which once was, but no longer is, a crime), a fetus (that would be abortion),[a] a corpse (that would be impossible, since the corpse is already dead), or an animal (that may be mistreatment of an animal or destruction of property).

Result offenses vs. conduct offenses. Homicide may not feature many attendant circumstances, but it does include another type of element, result ("death"). Homicide, in fact, is the paradigmatic *result offense*, as distinguished from a *conduct offense*, which contains no result element and criminalizes conduct alone. Driving while intoxicated is a good example of a conduct offense. It makes no difference whether the intoxicated driver caused an accident or any specific harm to anyone. Her driving under the influence alone makes out the crime.

The distinction between conduct and result offenses has some doctrinal implications. Causation questions arise only with respect to result offenses; unless the offense contains a result element, the question whether the defendant's conduct caused the result does not come up. Similarly, some jurisdictions permit inchoate liability (e.g., attempt) when an actor is merely reckless or negligent only in the case of conduct offenses, because they find the notion of attempting to bring about a result nonintentionally nonsensical. See ch. 6.

The distinction between the three types of offense elements is significant at several levels, most importantly under the Model Penal Code scheme. As we will see, the Model Code at various places assigns different subjective elements (i.e., types of mens rea) to different types of objective elements. For instance, the law of attempt requires purpose with respect to conduct, purpose or belief with respect to result, and something altogether different with respect to attendant circumstances. Model Penal Code Commentaries § 5.01, at 301–05. Moreover, the Model Code *defines* the various types of mens rea (purpose, knowledge, recklessness, negligence) differently depending on the type of objective offense element they're accompanying. See ch. 5. Purpose, for instance, means something different when it's

a. Model Penal Code § 210.0(1) (" 'human being' means a person who has been born and is alive"). Not all jurisdictions limit homicide in this way. See ch. 10.—EDS.

attached to a conduct or result element, on one hand, and to an attendant circumstance, on the other: To engage in *conduct* (say, "breaking and entering") purposely, it must be my "conscious object" to do so, but to act purposely with respect to an *attendant circumstance* (say, "nighttime") requires merely that I'm "aware" of its existence. § 2.02(2)(a).

Given its structural and doctrinal significance, it's somewhat problematic that categorizing a given offense element as conduct, attendant circumstance, or result isn't always easy. The Code drafters did not define the types of offense elements. (How, for instance, would you classify the elements of the Code's very own "Recklessly Endangering Another Person" (§ 211.2): "A person commits a misdemeanor if he recklessly engages in conduct which places or may place another person in danger of death or serious bodily injury"? See State v. Lambert, 280 Mont. 231, 929 P.2d 846 (1996).)

Offense analysis vs. element analysis. In the end, however, it's good to keep in mind that, in the words of the Code drafters, "[w]hile these terms [the three types of offense elements] are not airtight categories, they have served as a helpful analytical device in the development of the Code." Commentaries § 5.01, at 301 n.9. Most important, the distinction between the types of offense elements should be seen within the larger context of the Code drafters' attempt to replace the common law's *offense analysis* of mens rea with *element analysis*. The drafters felt that the common law's attempt to treat each offense as though it had only one subjective element, or mens rea, was misguided. They instead suggested that each *element* of an offense could have a type of mens rea attached to it. The significance of this change in approach will not become clear until we discuss mens rea, in the next chapter. Briefly, though, one might note that a person surely could have the purpose to start a fire (conduct), while being merely reckless as to whether the structure would be destroyed (result) and negligent as to whether the structure belonged to another person (attendant circumstance). For now, we mention it only to give you a better sense of what the Code drafters had in mind when they differentiated between different types of offense elements.

Material elements vs. nonmaterial elements. Another structural distinction among objective offense elements is also driven by concerns about subjective offense elements, that between *material* and *nonmaterial* elements. Material elements of an offense include the three types of offense elements (conduct, attendant circumstance, result) that appear "in the description of the forbidden conduct in the definition of the offense." They do not, however, include "an element that ... relate[s] exclusively to the statute of limitations, jurisdiction, venue or to any other matter similarly unconnected with (i) the harm or evil, incident to conduct, sought to be prevented by the law defining the offense, or (ii) the existence of a justification or excuse for such conduct." § 1.13(10). The distinction between material and nonmaterial elements allows the Code drafters to require that the state prove every *element* of an offense beyond a reasonable doubt (§ 1.12(1)) while at the same time limiting the requirement that each and every element of an offense be accompanied by some type of mens rea (§ 2.02(1)) to *material elements*. The drafters were concerned that, without thus restricting "the minimum requirements of culpability" to material elements, much of federal criminal law in particular would become bogged down in what they considered to be misguided litigation regarding a defendant's awareness of the presence of purely jurisdictional offense elements that had nothing to do with the substance of the crime in question.[a] Does a defendant have to know, for instance, that his gun had at some point crossed state lines in order to be liable for criminal possession of a firearm under the following federal statute?

> It shall be unlawful for any person—
>
> (3) who is an unlawful user of or addicted to any controlled substance . . .
>
> to ship or transport in interstate or foreign commerce, or possess in or affecting commerce, any firearm or ammunition; or to receive any firearm or ammunition which has been shipped or transported in interstate or foreign commerce.

18 U.S.C. § 922(g)(3).

More significant than the distinctions between objective and subjective offense elements and among different objective offense elements is that between offense elements and *defense elements*.

3. OFFENSE ELEMENTS DISTINGUISHED

The distinction between what counts as an offense element and what doesn't has come to play an important role in the law of criminal procedure, and of *constitutional* criminal procedure in particular. Since we are mostly concerned with substantive criminal law, we will touch only briefly on this topic. If nothing else, the distinction between offense and non-offense elements illustrates how a doctrine of substantive criminal law can shape procedural criminal law.

a. Offense Elements vs. Defense Elements

At the outset, it might be helpful to distinguish between four types of defenses: *element-negating defenses, affirmative defenses, justifications,* and *excuses.*

(1) The first type of defenses—*element-negating* (or *failure-of-proof*) defenses—in a way are not "defenses" at all. They consist of the claim that the behavior in question does not satisfy one or more of the elements laid out in the definition of an offense. A common example of this type of defense is the claim that the defendant lacked the requisite knowledge (or some other subjective offense element) for commission of the offense because she was intoxicated—she was too drunk, for example, to realize that the bicycle she rode home after a party was her friend's, not her own.

(2) Element-negating defenses are often contrasted with *affirmative defenses.* In the case of an affirmative defense, the defendant bears some, or all, of the burden of proof regarding an issue. Affirmative defenses may place only the *burden of production* on the defendant, allowing her to raise

a. Commentaries § 1.13, at 210–11.—EDS.

the defense only if she can come forward with some evidence to support it. Alternatively, they may shift the entire burden of proof onto the defendant, including the *burden of persuasion*. The burden of persuasion on an affirmative defense may range from low (preponderance of the evidence) to medium (clear and convincing evidence) to high (beyond a reasonable doubt).

(3) The distinction between element-negating and affirmative defenses can be misleading, however. From a *substantive* standpoint, the distinction is more properly drawn between element-negating defenses and *justifications* and *excuses*. (For a preliminary discussion of the distinction between justifications—which assert that the conduct is not unlawful, although it satisfies the elements of an offense—and excuses—which assert that the defendant is not responsible for her unlawful conduct—see ch. 3. Justifications and excuses are explored in detail in ch. 7.) While it may be true as a doctrinal fact that justifications and excuses are often affirmative defenses, this need not be so. (Whether an affirmative defense can be anything but a justification or an excuse is another question.) As you go through the materials on burdens of proof and various conceptions of justification and excuse, keep this point in mind.

The following materials explore the constitutional constraints on the legislature's classification of certain facts as elements of an offense, as opposed to elements of a defense.

(i) Burdens of Proof

The constitutional law of burdens of proof is quickly summed up. In 1970, the Supreme Court decided that due process requires that the state prove "beyond a reasonable doubt . . . every fact necessary to constitute the crime . . . charged." In re Winship, 397 U.S. 358, 364 (1970). Since then, the Court has declared that "every fact necessary to constitute the crime . . . charged" includes every element of the offense, and only every element of the offense. Specifically, it does not include any element of a *defense*, no matter how the defense is classified, as a justification or an excuse.

Patterson v. New York

Supreme Court of the United States.
432 U.S. 197, 97 S.Ct. 2319 (1977).

■ MR. JUSTICE WHITE delivered the opinion of the Court.

After a brief and unstable marriage, the appellant, Gordon Patterson, Jr., became estranged from his wife, Roberta. Roberta resumed an association with John Northrup, a neighbor to whom she had been engaged prior to her marriage to appellant. On December 27, 1970, Patterson borrowed a rifle from an acquaintance and went to the residence of his father-in-law. There, he observed his wife through a window in a state of semiundress in the presence of John Northrup. He entered the house and killed Northrup by shooting him twice in the head.

[Patterson was convicted of second-degree murder, which in New York has two elements: (1) "intent to cause the death of another person"; and

(2) "caus(ing) the death of such person or of a third person." N.Y. Penal Law § 125.25 (McKinney 1975). A person accused of murder may raise an affirmative defense that he "acted under the influence of extreme emotional disturbance for which there was a reasonable explanation or excuse." If successful, this defense reduces the defendant's liability to manslaughter.]

We cannot conclude that Patterson's conviction under the New York law deprived him of due process of law....

[The affirmative defense of] extreme emotional disturbance ..., which the [New York] Court of Appeals described as permitting "the defendant to show that his actions were caused by a mental infirmity not arising to the level of insanity, and that he is less culpable for having committed them," does not serve to negative any facts of the crime which the State is to prove in order to convict of murder. It constitutes a separate issue on which the defendant is required to carry the burden of persuasion....

This view may seem to permit state legislatures to reallocate burdens of proof by labeling as affirmative defenses at least some elements of the crimes now defined in their statutes. But there are obviously constitutional limits beyond which the States may not go in this regard. * * *

QUESTIONS AND COMMENTS

1. What, according to *Patterson,* constitutes an offense element? What are the "obvious[] constitutional limits beyond which the States may not go in" classifying elements as defense elements or, more generally, in defining the elements of an offense? May the state, for instance, define homicide as "causing death," turning all other matters into defense elements—so that the defendant would have to prove (or at least introduce evidence) that she did not cause the death intentionally, recklessly or negligently, that she did not kill a person, that she did not kill *another* person? Could the state go one extra step and simply declare any or all of these matters *irrelevant* for purposes of homicide liability? See Montana v. Egelhoff, 518 U.S. 37 (1996) (upholding statute rendering evidence of intoxication irrelevant to proof of requisite mental state).

2. Under *Patterson*, could the New York legislature simply drop the defense of extreme emotional disturbance? What about other defenses, like self-defense or insanity? Would it make sense to distinguish between established and new defenses, so that the legislature would have a free hand when it comes to defining new defenses, but not when it comes to changing (increasing?) the burden of proof regarding established ones? Why? (The dissent in *Patterson* suggests that this distinction would be a good idea because it would remove a disincentive for legislatures to adopt new defenses. 432 U.S. at 226 (Powell, J., dissenting). Is that a good (the only?) reason?) Sensible or not, could such a change be retroactively applied, under the principle of legality (see ch. 2)?

Does the fact that the legislature could eliminate a defense altogether mean that they can shift the procedure for proving the absence of a defense? Assume that the legislature *could* make negligent, rather than knowing, receipt of stolen property a crime. Could it then say instead that, while knowledge is required, the defendant must prove he did *not* know the property he received was stolen? More generally, once the legislature recognizes a defense, even one it is not constitutionally required to recognize, should it be entirely free to attach whatever conditions it chooses on the operation of that defense? Could it limit the defense to middle-aged defendants, to "virtuous" ones, to state residents, or to those with no prior record? Could it force defendants to prove the defense beyond the shadow of a doubt, without assistance of counsel, or on the basis of the testimony of at least two eyewitnesses?

3. How would you classify the defense of provocation, or of extreme emotional disturbance—as a justification or as an excuse? Would it make sense to treat justifications and excuses differently in the constitutional law of evidentiary burdens?

4. Here is how the Model Penal Code deals with the question of who must prove what, and by what standard, based on its definition of "offense element," in § 1.13(9):

Model Penal Code § 1.12. Proof Beyond a Reasonable Doubt; Affirmative Defenses; Burden of Proving Fact When Not an Element of an Offense; Presumptions.

(1) No person may be convicted of an offense unless each element of such offense is proved beyond a reasonable doubt. In the absence of such proof, the innocence of the defendant is assumed.

(2) Subsection (1) of this Section does not:

(a) require the disproof of an affirmative defense unless and until there is evidence supporting such defense; or

(b) apply to any defense which the Code or another statute plainly requires the defendant to prove by a preponderance of evidence.

(3) A ground of defense is affirmative, within the meaning of Subsection (2)(a) of this Section, when:

(a) it arises under a section of the Code which so provides; or

(b) it relates to an offense defined by a statute other than the Code and such statute so provides; or

(c) it involves a matter of excuse or justification peculiarly within the knowledge of the defendant on which he can fairly be required to adduce supporting evidence.

What role does this provision assign to the distinction between offenses and defenses, and between justifications and excuses? Would the result in *Patterson* have been different, had the Supreme Court constitutionalized this approach? What is the significance of subsection (2)(b)? And why does the Code speak of an assumption, rather than a presumption, of innocence?

5. Affirmative defenses come in different forms, depending on what aspect of the burden of proof they shift to the defendant. Contrast the Model Code's definition of an affirmative defense, in § 1.12(2)(a), with that found in the New York Penal Law:

New York Penal Law § 25.00 Defenses; burden of proof

1. When a "defense," other than an "affirmative defense," defined by statute is raised at a trial, the people have the burden of disproving such defense beyond a reasonable doubt.

2. When a defense declared by statute to be an "affirmative defense" is raised at a trial, the defendant has the burden of establishing such defense by a preponderance of the evidence.

(ii) Presumptions

Even on an issue that has not been declared an "affirmative defense," i.e., one that clearly counts as an offense element, modern criminal codes ease the burden on the prosecution through another procedural device, the "presumption." The Supreme Court has placed some limits on the propriety of this convenient burden-easing (if not technically burden-shifting) technique. These limits are explored in the following case.

People v. Leyva

Court of Appeals of New York.
38 N.Y.2d 160 (1975).

■ FUCHSBERG, JUDGE.

All three defendants appeal from separate orders affirming their convictions for criminal possession of dangerous drugs rendered after a joint jury trial. All three were apprehended while they were together inside an automobile which also contained a large quantity of cocaine, stored in a manila envelope underneath the front seat. Their arrest stemmed from information received by police from an informer.

At trial, after the arresting officers testified to finding both the defendants and the drugs in the same car, the prosecution utilized the statutory presumption of possession authorized by section 220.25 of the Penal Law to complete its prima facie case against defendants. That statute reads: "The presence of a dangerous drug in an automobile, other than a public omnibus, is presumptive evidence of knowing possession thereof by each and every person in the automobile at the time such drug was found."

Defendant Low testified in his own behalf. He attempted to explain that he was in the car by accident and did not know the drugs were there. Defendants Leyva and Garcia put in no evidence and did not take the stand.

Each defendant now challenges the use of the presumption of possession. * * *

Statutory presumptions, particularly when used in criminal cases, have occasioned much comment among judges and scholars. The debate centers on the tensions produced by attempts to balance prosecutorial necessity against the basic jurisprudential requirement that no liability be imposed upon a defendant until every element of the case against him has been proved beyond a reasonable doubt.

On the one hand, a statutory presumption of possession which operated to shift the burden of proof to a defendant unless he produced rebuttal evidence might well be unconstitutional. On the other hand, denying the prosecution the use of any inferential tool in cases like the present one would lead to the "practical impossibility of proving ... actual participation in the illegal activities." In the absence of a legislative presumption in drug cases, for example, many drug traffickers could operate with impunity simply by ensuring that the contraband was in some part of the transporting vehicle and not on their persons.

In a series of cases, the United States Supreme Court has provided some guidelines for use in effecting a proper balance. The guidelines [set out] the requirement that there be a rational connection between the facts which are proved and the one which is to be inferred with the aid of the presumption. [Tot v. United States, 319 U.S. 463, 63 S.Ct. 1241 (1943); Leary v. United States, 395 U.S. 6, 36, 89 S.Ct. 1532, 1548 (1969)].... [N]o amount of prosecutorial necessity would serve to validate a presumption. Practical, prosecutorial need is a necessary ingredient but it is not, in and of itself, sufficient to justify the use of a presumption.

.... Given the peculiar and unique circumstance an automobile provides, ... it cannot be said that statutory recognition of the likelihood that all persons inside a car carrying quantities of drugs know about them are involved in their transport is irrational. Indeed, the 1972 Interim Report of the Temporary State Commission to Evaluate the Drug Laws states it very well:

> We do not believe that persons transporting dealership quantities of contraband are likely to go driving around with innocent friends or that they are likely to pick up strangers. We do not doubt that this can and does in fact occasionally happen, but because we find it more reasonable to believe that the bare presence in the vehicle is culpable, we think it reasonable to presume culpability in the direction which the proven facts already point. Since the presumption is an evidentiary one, it may be offset by any evidence including the testimony of the defendant, which would negate the defendant's culpable involvement.

[O]ver a pound of cocaine was found in the car with these defendants. Moreover, ... the presumption is evidentiary and rebuttable, whether by defendants' own testimony or by any other evidence in the case, including the inherent or developed incredibility of the prosecution's own witnesses. A jury is not to be told that it *must* find defendants guilty if the prosecution proves that they and drugs were present in a car together; it is only to be told that it *may* so find. This affords added protection against the possibility that a presumption might operate to direct a verdict.

Low ... asserts that any testimony or evidence produced by a defendant which is directed toward negation of the presumption should serve to remove it from the jury altogether. We do not agree....

According to Low, he had been working in Florida as a cook until the day before the arrest, when, he said, he had driven up from that State in a friend's car. He did not explain what happened to the friend's car, but said that, while on his way to the bus terminal to go to New Jersey, he met a man named Cepero, whom he knew slightly from Florida. Cepero, Low stated, offered him a ride, but indicated that he had an errand to do first. Low testified that he agreed to the ride and the errand and drove, with Cepero, to a nearby hotel, where Cepero went inside. After a good while, Cepero returned with Leyva and Garcia and asked Low, as a favor, to drive the other two defendants to Brooklyn. Low testified that he did not know his precise destination in Brooklyn, but took directions from Leyva from time to time. He found himself arrested at the bridge exit.

Thus Low asked the jury to believe that, though he was arrested in a car bearing Florida license plates, he had no prior connection with that car, and that his trip to New York from Florida only the day before was pure coincidence. He also asked the jury to believe that, for no apparent reason, he consented, at the behest of a very casual acquaintance whom he had just chanced to encounter, to drive Garcia and Leyva to Brooklyn, a destination opposite to his own New Jersey-bound one. He offered no explanation as to why they could not have driven themselves. He further asked the jury to believe that Cepero had either failed entirely to provide for the driving of the car used to transport the large and very expensive quantity of cocaine here involved or had, on mere impulse, decided to entrust it to a near-stranger who was completely unaware of his undertaking. Moreover, he offered no explanation as to why he was, on the first day of his arrival after his long trek from Florida, willing to be so readily detoured by the offer of a ride that turned into four hours of waiting for Garcia and Leyva to appear at the hotel. Yet Low suggests that this testimony should have been sufficient to deny the prosecution the use of the presumption as a matter of law. * * *

None of the defendants here disputed the fact that they were in the car, nor did they argue that drugs were not found in it. These were the two underlying facts which the statute requires be proved before the presumption applies. Once the prosecution had proved them, it was entitled to rely on the presumption as a part of its prima facie case....

It might be possible, of course, that a defendant's evidence will prove the truth of his choice of inferences so conclusively that reasonable persons could no longer believe the inference authorized by the statute. There is nothing arcane about such a situation; where a defendant's proof is conclusive and reasonable persons cannot disagree about the matter at issue, our courts always have the power to issue a trial order of dismissal or direct the jury's finding on an element of a crime....[4] * * *

... Low's story ... was not sufficient to achieve such a result....

So applied, the presumption here is completely consonant with the constitutional requirement that the burden of proving guilt beyond a reasonable doubt stay with the People.... [T]he court expressly advised the jury ... that the presumption did not result "in a shifting of the burden at all" [and] that the burden of proof, remaining with the People, requires the establishment of guilt beyond a reasonable doubt....

4. [According to the Model Penal Code,] the issue of the existence of the presumed fact must be submitted to the jury unless the court is satisfied that the evidence as a whole clearly negatives the presumed fact. Model Penal Code § 1.12, subd. (5), par. (a)....

QUESTIONS AND COMMENTS

1. What role should prosecutorial convenience play in assessing the constitutionality, or the wisdom, of setting up evidentiary presumptions of the sort at issue in *Leyva*?

2. For purposes of the constitutionality—or wisdom—of a presumption, should the quantity of drugs (or weapons or other contraband) matter, as the *Leyva* court suggests it does? What about the quality of the drug (heroin, cocaine, marijuana)? Does the New York presumption draw these distinctions?

3. The *Leyva* court relies on commonly made distinctions among types of presumptions. If a presumption is an inference from the truth of one proposition (A) to that of another (B), presumptions differ (1) in whether they require or merely permit the inference from A to B (mandatory vs. permissible) and (2) in whether or not they allow for the disproof of B in the face of A (rebuttable vs. irrebuttable (or conclusive)). The constitutionally significant distinction is that between mandatory and permissible presumptions. Permissible presumptions are not as constitutionally suspect as are mandatory presumptions. They are constitutional as long as the two propositions they connect by inference are "rationally related," i.e., as long as they simply direct the factfinder to a particular inference that she might have drawn on her own.

Mandatory presumptions are unconstitutional if they amount to an unconstitutional shift of the burden of proof from the state onto the defendant. Since, following *Patterson*, these shifts are unconstitutional if—and only if—they relate to an element of the offense, mandatory presumptions are unconstitutional if—and only if—they relate to an element of the offense.

But what difference do you think, does it really make in a real trial, with real jurors, whether a presumption is, technically speaking, permissible, rather than mandatory, and rebuttable, rather than irrebuttable? Do you think jurors can tell the difference between the various types of presumptions? Between a presumption, an inference, and a conclusion? Do you think it matters if they can?

Are irrebuttable (or conclusive) presumptions really "rules of substantive law masquerading as rules of proof"? Jerome A. Hoffman, "Thinking About Presumptions: The 'Presumption' of Agency from Ownership as Study Specimen," 48 Ala. L. Rev. 885, 898 (1997). And if they are, what difference would that make for purposes of constitutional scrutiny? The California Supreme Court upheld a statute providing that "possession of immediate precursors sufficient for the manufacture of ... hydriodic acid ... shall be deemed to be possession of the derivative substance" on the ground that it "creates no presumption at all, but is simply a valid exercise of the Legislature's power to create substantive law and define crimes." People v. McCall, 32 Cal.4th 175, 82 P.3d 351, 8 Cal.Rptr.3d 337 (2004). The statute, according to the court, "tells us that 'possession of hydriodic acid,' the conduct made criminal ..., does not ... merely carry its lay meaning, but is a term of art that *includes* the possession of hydriodic acid's essential chemicals," red phosphorus and iodine in this case. Possession of these chemicals thus doesn't establish a presumption of possession of hydriodic acid, the controlled substance. Instead, "the possession of red phosphorus and iodine ... is the *legal equivalent* of possession of hydriodic acid...." The legislature's "power to select the elements of crimes, and to define one thing in terms of another," however, is "broad."

4. How likely do you think it is that a defendant will actually be able to rebut the theoretically rebuttable presumption at issue in *Leyva*? What if it turns out that the likelihood is close to zero? Should this matter for constitutional purposes? When does a presumption shift, rather than merely lighten, the burden of proof? What if the judge specifically instructs the jury—as in *Leyva*—that the burden of proof on the issue remains with the state?

b. Offense Elements vs. Sentencing Factors

In recent years, courts have paid considerably more attention to the distinction between offense elements and *sentencing factors* than to that between offense elements and *defense elements*. Classifying an issue as a sentencing factor, rather than as an offense element, doesn't shift the burden of proof (or at least of production) onto the defendant, nor does it establish a presumption. Instead, it streamlines the criminal process by moving the issue from the guilt phase of the trial into the sentencing phase. Unlike offense elements, sentencing factors (such as, for instance, the exact amount of drugs the defendant was convicted of possessing) need not be set out in the indictment; the burden of proving them is lower than that at trial (ordinarily, by a preponderance of the evidence); and they are found by a judge, rather than by a jury.

Originally, the Supreme Court took very much the same approach to the distinction between offense elements and sentencing factors that it has to that between offense elements and defense elements. A sentencing factor was a sentencing factor if the legislature said so, or at least made its intentions fairly clear (say, by setting it out in a separate part of the statute). See McMillan v. Pennsylvania, 477 U.S. 79 (1986) (mandatory enhancement for possession of firearm during commission of felony).

More recently, however, the Court has begun to look beyond—or beneath—legislative classification. Paying particular attention to the (Sixth Amendment) right to a jury trial, the Court has found fault with a number of provisions that require judges to increase the sentence based on facts not proved beyond a reasonable doubt to a jury. See Apprendi v. New Jersey, 530 U.S. 466 (2000) (striking down state hate crime statute providing for increased sentence if trial court finds, by a preponderance of the evidence, that defendant acted out of racial animus); Blakely v. Washington, ___ U.S. ___, 124 S.Ct. 2531 (2004) (under *Apprendi*, striking down state sentencing guidelines providing for increased sentence if trial court finds, by a preponderance of the evidence, that defendant acted with deliberate cruelty); United States v. Booker, ___ U.S. ___, 125 S.Ct. 738 (2005) (under *Apprendi*, declaring federal sentencing guidelines advisory, rather than mandatory).

QUESTIONS AND COMMENTS

1. The dissent in *Patterson* proposed—and the majority rejected—the principle that the prosecution must prove beyond a reasonable doubt any "factor [that] makes a substantial difference in punishment and stigma" 432 U.S. at 226 (Powell, J., dissenting). Can *Apprendi* and its progeny be explained as an application of this principle? What's left of *Patterson* after *Apprendi*? See *Blakely*, supra (holding that, under *Apprendi*, "every defendant has the right to insist that the prosecutor prove to a jury all facts legally essential to the punishment").

2. What effect does the classification of a "sentencing factor" as an "offense element" under *Apprendi* have on substantive criminal law? The Court, in *Apprendi* and its progeny, focused on the procedural significance of the classification (e.g., jury, indictment, burden of proof). Now saddled with the burden of proving an element beyond a reasonable doubt (as opposed to by a preponderance of the evidence) does the state have to prove not only that the element was present, but also that the defendant was *aware of* its presence (or had some other type of mens rea)? Does the defendant charged with possessing a controlled substance have to know what drug he is possessing, once the identity of the drug is reclassified as an offense element under *Apprendi*? See United States v. Barbosa, 271 F.3d 438 (3d Cir. 2001) (no).

B. ACTS

Formally speaking, behavior amounts to a criminal offense if it satisfies each element, objective and subjective, of the offense. No matter what other elements an offense might have, it must contain a conduct element. An offense without a conduct element would criminalize something other than an act, in violation of the time honored principle of Anglo–American criminal law that only acts may be punished.

Why do we have an *act requirement* in the criminal law? In thinking about how to answer this question, one might distinguish between several implicit *contrasts*: (a) acts vs. thoughts (e.g., killing vs. really wishing someone dead; to some degree, we deal with this issue in talking about the line between (non-punishable) preparation and (punishable) attempt in ch. 6); (b) acts vs. statuses (drug use vs. addiction; begging vs. pauperism); (c) voluntary vs. involuntary acts; (d) acts vs. omissions; and (e) acts vs. possession.

There are some purely *procedural interpretations* of the act requirement. That is to say that one might not want to punish anything but acts even if one thought it were substantively desirable to do so because administering laws attempting to punish non-acts would lead to a host of unwanted effects. Note that these explanations apply more to situations in which we are contrasting act and thought rather than act and status.

1. Fair notice concerns may come into play. Here the idea is that the state can't communicate proscriptions of thoughts adequately clearly to alert citizens when they will run afoul of the law. How *badly* must one want someone dead before one has violated a law against

wishing someone dead? (A fourteenth century statute defined treason as, among other things, "compass[ing] or imagin[ing] the death of our lord the King." 25 Edw. 3 stat. 5 c. 2.)

2. The vagueness problem also gives rise to concerns with restraining discretion. How do we avoid giving officials (too much) room to make undisciplined judgments about whom to punish if legislation is not mechanically administrable?

3. Moreover thoughts, one might think, can only be known through confession. Anglo–American law, however, traditionally has been skeptical of both the accuracy and legitimacy of confession, unless the defendant's confession enables us to corroborate, or imagine corroborating, the externally verifiable facts she confesses to. Accuracy fears are a function of the fear of over-confession (the neurotically guilt-ridden, the coerced) and under-confession (by the naturally wily or the well-counseled), while legitimacy fears presumably spring from fear of the "spectacle" of "undue" selflessness.

There are also some *substantive interpretations* of the act requirement, which provide reasons we might not punish thoughts even if we clearly knew precisely what people thought, i.e., on the assumption that it's not *procedurally* troublesome to ascertain thoughts, say, because we had access to a foolproof truth serum.

1. Deeds are chosen, while thoughts, fantasies, and statuses are outside people's control, and hence neither capable of being deterred nor blameworthy.

2. Moreover, it is not uncommon to believe that only acts can harm others in ways a properly limited state will think are worth preventing (deterrence-oriented approach) or worth punishing (retributivist approach), though, clearly, "heretical" *beliefs* are hardly universally deemed harmless.

3. Punishing internal states, as opposed to external acts, intrudes upon the individual's substantial zone of privacy (including the life of the imagination) and is the hallmark of an overreaching state.

It is hard to translate these general concerns into positions on concrete issues. For instance, is it permissible, given the act requirement, to punish homosexual acts but not the "status" of "being homosexual"? Note that there are interesting questions here about figuring out what that even means. Consider, in the quasi-criminal context of military discharge, soldiers who think of themselves/perform as "straight" people, despite the fact that they've had sexual relations with someone who is of the same gender. Military regulations, which ostensibly punish only conduct, permit military personnel to raise such "identity" defenses, blurring the line between "status" and "conduct" inquiries. For a discussion, see Janet E. Halley, Don't: A Reader's Guide to the Military's Anti–Gay Policy (1999); see also Lawrence v. Texas, 539 U.S. 558, 579 (2003) (O'Connor, J., concurring). Similarly, would the act requirement forbid punishing addiction but not drug use, even if we believe a factually inexorable concomitant of addiction is drug use? See, e.g., S.D. Codified Laws § 22–42–15 ("Ingesting substance, except alcoholic beverages, for the purpose of becoming intoxicated").

1. ACTS VS. THOUGHTS

> The stories that Brian Dalton wrote in his journal about torturing and molesting children were so disturbing that grand jurors asked a detective to stop reading after about two pages.
>
> The stories, though, were also completely fictional. Even so ... Mr. Dalton was sentenced to 10 years in prison. * * *
>
> Mr. Dalton, who was on probation from a 1998 conviction involving pornographic photographs of children, was charged after his probation officer found the journal in a routine search of his home.
>
> The 14–page journal contained fictional stories about three children, ages 10 and 11, being caged in a basement, molested and tortured.
>
> Mr. Dalton, 22, pleaded guilty last week to pandering obscenity involving a minor. As part of the plea bargain, a second count was dropped in exchange for five fewer years in prison. * * *
>
> Mr. Dalton was charged under Ohio's 1989 child pornography law, which bans possession of obscene material involving children. * * *
>
> Janet LaRue, senior director of legal studies at the Family Research Council in Washington, which fights child pornography, said Mr. Dalton's tales could be extremely dangerous because they could entice him to seduce children. "It's like an arsonist with matches," Ms. LaRue said. * * *

"Child Pornography Writer Gets 10–Year Prison Term," N.Y. Times, July 14, 2001, at A12, col. 5.[a]

QUESTIONS AND COMMENTS

1. What act did Dalton commit? What acts did he *not* commit? What if Dalton had destroyed *handwritten* journal entries moments after writing them, but that we were able to tell what he had written because his pen had left impressions in the papers beneath the pages he had written on? What if he had spoken the tales into a tape recorder and destroyed the tape? Spoken them to his psychiatrist? Should the psychiatrist be obliged to (permitted to?) report him to the police?

2. The statute to which Dalton pled guilty makes it a felony to, among other things, "buy, procure, possess, or control any obscene material, that has a minor as one of its participants." Ohio Rev. Code Ann. § 2907.321. Does the statute apply to Dalton's case? Can it be squared with *Stanley v. Georgia*, supra ch. 1?

a. Two years later, Dalton's conviction was reversed on the ground that his lawyer had provided him with ineffective assistance by not informing him of the legal implications of his guilty plea. "Court Dismisses Guilty Plea By Sex Writer," N.Y. Times, July 18, 2003, at A15, col. 1.—EDS.

3. Assume Dalton had integrated his entries into messages that he exchanged with participants in an internet chat room who are known—to some extent—to be merely *posing* as sexually explicit, smart-mouthed minors. If Dalton half-knew the people he was exchanging messages with weren't minors, even though he—and they—pretended they were, did he commit an act?

4. Should it make a difference that Dalton already was on probation for a related offense? What if it turned out that he had acted out his fantasies on a previous occasion? What if he was just someone who has a tendency to make elaborate plans before he does anything—go on a trip, bake a cake, build a doghouse? What if it turns out that a child molester is *less* likely to act out his fantasies if he writes them down? What if Dalton's therapist (his probation officer?) had encouraged him to do so for that purpose?

2. ACT VS. STATUS

People v. Davis

Court of Appeals of New York.
33 N.Y.2d 221 (1973).

■ JASEN, JUDGE.

Wilbert Davis, a heroin addict, has been convicted of criminal possession of a dangerous drug in the sixth degree and criminal possession of a hypodermic instrument.... * * *

The facts are undisputed. On February 4, 1971, the landlord of the premises at 34 Fort Green Place, Brooklyn, approached a uniformed patrolman on duty in the area. He led the officer to that address, a three story "walk up", and permitted him to enter. The officer ascended one flight of stairs and observed the defendant standing in a bathroom, about to inject himself with a syringe later determined to contain heroin. When approached by the officer, the defendant pleaded with him to be allowed to take the injection. In effecting the arrest, the officer observed fresh needle marks on defendant's right arm. Defendant admitted that he had been using heroin for about a year and one half.

At trial, the defendant offered evidence designed to show the nature of narcotic addiction and that he was, in fact, a narcotic addict. The defendant conceded his addiction to heroin and this concession was amply supported by medical testimony not disputed by the People.

The argument for reversal is predicated on Robinson v. California, 370 U.S. 660, 82 S.Ct. 1417 and Powell v. Texas, 392 U.S. 514, 88 S.Ct. 2145. In Robinson, the petitioner was convicted under a California statute making it a criminal offense for a person to be addicted to narcotics. The Trial Judge instructed the jury that it was a misdemeanor under the statute "either to use narcotics, or to be addicted to the use of narcotics", that the "portion of the statute referring to 'addicted to the use' of narcotics is based upon a condition or status", and that "(i)t is a continuing offense" which "subjects the offender to arrest at any time before he reforms."

The Supreme Court reversed. Implicitly recognizing that narcotic addiction is a disease, the court held that a State law making the "status" of narcotic addiction a criminal offense inflicted cruel and unusual punishment in violation of the Eighth and Fourteenth Amendments. By way of rationale, the court emphasized the absence of an actus reus, that under the statute the criminal sanction was imposed even though a person has "never touched any narcotic drug within the State or been guilty of any irregular behavior there." The court was careful to point out, however, that the States retained broad power to regulate narcotic drugs traffic within their borders. Such regulation, it said, could take a variety of valid forms, citing, by way of example, the power to impose criminal sanctions against the unauthorized sale, manufacture, purchase or possession of narcotics.

In dissent, Justice White voted to affirm the conviction, being of the view that the appellant was not being punished on the basis of status, illness or condition, but for the regular and habitual use of narcotics in violation of California law. In dicta, particularly pertinent here, he observed: "If it is 'cruel and unusual punishment' to convict appellant for addiction, it is difficult to understand why it would be any less offensive to the Fourteenth Amendment to convict him for use on the same evidence of use which proved he was an addict. It is significant that in purporting to reaffirm the power of the States to deal with the narcotics traffic, the Court does not include among the obvious powers of the State the power to punish for the use of narcotics. I cannot think that the omission was inadvertent."

In Powell v. Texas, supra, the Supreme Court ... was asked to extend Robinson by prohibiting a State from punishing a chronic alcoholic for public drunkenness. Leroy Powell was convicted of violating a Texas statute declaring it unlawful to "get drunk or be found in a state of intoxication in any public place." The Trial Judge, sitting without a jury, made certain "findings of fact": that "chronic alcoholism is a disease which destroys the afflicted person's will power to resist the constant, excessive consumption of alcohol"; that "a chronic alcoholic does not appear in public of his own volition but under a compulsion symptomatic" of his disease; and that Powell was afflicted with disease as described.

The Supreme Court affirmed. The plurality opinion per Justice Marshall, rejecting the trial court's findings of fact, observed that one could not "conclude, on the state of this record or on the current state of medical knowledge, that chronic alcoholics in general, and Leroy Powell in particular, suffer from such an irresistible compulsion to drink and to get drunk in public that they are utterly unable to control their performance of either or both these acts and thus cannot be deterred at all from public intoxication." Robinson was distinguished on the ground that Powell was not convicted for being a chronic alcoholic, but for being in public while drunk. Unlike Robinson, the sanctions of the Texas statute were not directed at "mere status", but at socially offensive behavior: appearing in public drunk.

In a dissent joined by three Justices, Justice Fortas adopted the trial court's findings and viewed the Texas statute as imposing punishment for the "mere condition of being intoxicated in public" and read Robinson as barring the imposition of criminal sanctions "upon a person for being in a condition he is powerless to change." As a corollary, Justice Fortas declared that "a person may not (consistent with the Eighth Amendment) be punished if the condition essential to constitute the defined crime is part of the pattern of his disease and is occasioned by a compulsion symptomatic of the disease." Justice White ... observed: "If it cannot be a crime to have an irresistible compulsion to use narcotics, Robinson v. California, 370 U.S. 660, 82 S.Ct. 1417 (1962), I do not see how it can constitutionally be a crime to yield to such a compulsion. Punishing an addict for using drugs convicts for addiction under a different name. Distinguishing between the two crimes is like forbidding criminal conviction for being sick with flu or epilepsy but permitting punishment for running a fever or having a convulsion. Unless Robinson is to be abandoned, the use of narcotics by an addict must be beyond the reach of the criminal law. Similarly, the chronic alcoholic with an irresistible urge to consume alcohol should not be punishable for drinking or for being drunk." * * *

Implicit in the defendant's argument that it constitutes cruel and unusual punishment to impose a criminal penalty upon an addict who possesses narcotics and associated paraphernalia for his own use, is an appeal for judicial recognition of a drug dependence defense to criminal responsibility, an argument better addressed, at this juncture, to the Legislature.* Doubtless, the argument is logically appealing that if an addict cannot, consistent with the Federal and State Constitutions, be punished for being in the status or condition of addiction, he cannot be punished for the acts of possessing for his personal use narcotics and associated instruments, the necessary incidents of his condition, which acts are realistically inseparable from the status or condition itself.

There is, however, no square holding for defendant's position that acts incident to addiction may not be punished. Robinson did not so hold. Indeed it is authority for the proposition that actual behavior may be punished but not the condition or status of addiction itself.... [Moreover,] it is unmistakably clear that the majority in Powell recoiled from the asserted Eighth Amendment claim and the recognition of new lines of defense to criminal accountability by reason of the compulsions attributable to alcoholism, and presumably narcotic addiction, conditions from which it is still widely assumed, rightly or wrongly, that the victim retains some capacity to extricate himself....

.... The ramifications of recognizing the asserted cruel and unusual punishment defense, and impliedly the defense of drug dependence, are startling. The difficulty lies in knowing where to stop. The obvious danger is that the defense will be extended to other crimes—robberies, burglaries and the like—which can be shown to arise from the compulsive craving for drugs. And if "mere purchase or possession" by the addict for his own use is protected, what of the "mere sale" to the same addict by an obliging trafficker in illicit drugs? Could not the sale to the addict who is driven to

* The drug dependence defense would appear to be premised on the theory that addiction involves a compelling propensity to use narcotics, amounting to a loss of self control, depriving the addict's acts of possession and use, etc., of volition, a theory about which debate rages.

acquire drugs by his compulsive craving be defended as a humane act inflicting no harm on other members of society?

Moreover, any attempted limitation on the availability of the drug dependence defense to those acts such as purchase, possession or receipt of narcotics for the addict's personal use, finds little justification in the cruel and unusual punishment clause with which it intertwines. For example, assuming the drug dependence defense be recognized, is it somehow less offensive to contemporary concepts of human decency, as embodied in the constitutional proscription of cruel and unusual punishment (Trop v. Dulles, 356 U.S. 86, 101) to punish an addict who, out of a compulsive craving for drugs, steals to fund his habit than it is to punish an addict who, out of the same craving, merely purchases or possesses illicit drugs for his own use? If the compulsion is the same, why is the one act blameworthy and not the other? Such a distinction smacks of limitation by fiat and invites accusations of arbitrariness. * * *

[W]hile it may be that the policy of rehabilitation would be well served by affording addicts a cruel and unusual punishment and drug dependence defense to possession for their own use, we should not lose sight of the utility of such penalties to law enforcement. For example, these possible penalties may, through the exercise of prosecutorial discretion, enable law enforcement to enlist addict informers in ferreting out the wholesalers of illicit drugs, thereby facilitating the policy of elimination of the drug traffic. Then, too, punishment may persuade some addicts to undertake rehabilitation through various State or private programs. On the other hand, recognition of the defense might conceivably make the addict the witting or unwitting tool of the drug trafficker.

In sum, recognition of defendant's constitutional claim and implicitly, at least, the drug dependence defense, does not follow inexorably from the Robinson and Powell decisions and, indeed, strong reasons of public policy militate against any such recognition by this court.

The order of the Appellate Term should be affirmed.

Pottinger v. City of Miami

United States District Court, Southern District of Florida.
810 F.Supp. 1551 (1992).

■ ATKINS, SENIOR DISTRICT JUDGE.

Plaintiffs ("plaintiffs" or "class members") filed this action in December of 1988 on behalf of themselves and approximately 6,000 other homeless people living in the City of Miami. Plaintiffs' complaint alleges that the City of Miami ("defendant" or "City") has a custom, practice and policy of arresting, harassing and otherwise interfering with homeless people for engaging in basic activities of daily life—including sleeping and eating—in the public places where they are forced to live. Plaintiffs further claim that the City has arrested thousands of homeless people for such life-sustaining conduct under various City of Miami ordinances and Florida Statutes....

Plaintiffs allege, pursuant to 42 U.S.C. § 1983,[1] that the property destruction and arrests, which often result in no criminal charges, prosecutions or convictions, violate their rights under the United States and Florida Constitutions.... [P]laintiffs do not challenge the facial validity of the ordinances or statutes under which they are arrested. Rather, they contend that the City applies these laws to homeless individuals as part of a custom and practice of driving the homeless from public places. Accordingly, plaintiffs do not argue that any of the ordinances should be stricken; instead, they ask that the City be enjoined from arresting homeless individuals for inoffensive conduct, such as sleeping or bathing, that they are forced to perform in public. * * *

Plaintiffs contend that the City's arrests of class members under various ordinances prohibit them from lying down, sleeping, standing, sitting or performing other essential, life-sustaining activities in any public place at any time. Plaintiffs argue that their status of being homeless is involuntary and beyond their immediate ability to alter and that the conduct for which they are arrested is inseparable from their involuntary homeless status. Consequently, plaintiffs argue, application of these ordinances to them is cruel and unusual in violation of the eighth amendment.

The judicial prohibition of status-based abuse of police power under the eighth amendment is not without precedent. In a leading United States Supreme Court case addressing the issue, the Court held that punishment of a person for his involuntary status of being an addict was cruel and unusual in violation of the eighth amendment. Robinson v. California, 370 U.S. 660, 82 S.Ct. 1417 (1962)....

Based on Robinson, courts have overturned vagrancy laws because they punish status or condition.... [I]n Headley v. Selkowitz, 171 So.2d 368 (Fla.1965), the Florida Supreme Court stated that a vagrancy statute, even if facially valid, should not be applied to "innocent victims of misfortune" who appear to be vagrants, but "who are not such either by choice or intentional conduct." Id. at 370; see also Parker v. Municipal Judge, 83 Nev. 214, 427 P.2d 642, 644 (1967) ("It is simply not a crime to be unemployed, without funds, and in a public place. To punish the unfortunate for this circumstance debases society."); Alegata v. Commonwealth, 353 Mass. 287, 231 N.E.2d 201, 207 (1967) ("Idleness and poverty should not be treated as a criminal offense."). Again, voluntariness of the status or condition is the decisive factor.

Although the law is well-established that a person may not be punished for involuntary status, it is less settled whether involuntary conduct that is inextricably related to that status may be punished. An initial reading of Powell suggests that all conduct is outside the rule of Robinson.... However, the Powell plurality was not confronted with a critical distinguishing factor that is unique to the plight of the homeless plaintiffs in this

1. Section 1983 provides as follows:

Every person who, under color of any statute, ordinance, regulation, custom, or usage, of any State, or Territory, or the District of Columbia, subjects, or causes to be subjected, any Citizen of the United States or any other persons within the jurisdiction thereof to the deprivation of any rights, privileges or immunities secured by the Constitution and laws, shall be liable to the person injured in an action of law, suit in equity, or other proper proceedings for redress.

case: that they have no realistic choice but to live in public places.... [T]he record in the present case amply supports plaintiffs' claim that their homeless condition compels them to perform certain life-sustaining activities in public.

As a number of expert witnesses testified, people rarely choose to be homeless. Rather, homelessness is due to various economic, physical or psychological factors that are beyond the homeless individual's control.

Professor Wright testified that one common characteristic of homeless individuals is that they are socially isolated; they are part of no community and have no family or friends who can take them in. Professor Wright also testified that homelessness is both a consequence and a cause of physical or mental illness. Many people become homeless after losing their jobs, and ultimately their homes, as a result of an illness. Many have no home of their own in the first place, but end up on the street after their families or friends are unable to care for or shelter them. Dr. Greer testified that once a person is on the street, illnesses can worsen or occur more frequently due to a variety of factors such as the difficulty or impossibility of obtaining adequate health care, exposure to the elements, insect and rodent bites, and the absence of sanitary facilities for sleeping, bathing or cooking. * * *

[C]lass members ... become homeless due to a variety of factors that are beyond their control. In addition, plaintiffs do not have the choice, much less the luxury, of being in the privacy of their own homes. Because of the unavailability of low-income housing or alternative shelter, plaintiffs have no choice but to conduct involuntary, life-sustaining activities in public places. The harmless conduct for which they are arrested is inseparable from their involuntary condition of being homeless. Consequently, arresting homeless people for harmless acts they are forced to perform in public effectively punishes them for being homeless. This effect is no different from the vagrancy ordinances which courts struck because they punished "innocent victims of misfortune" and made a crime of being "unemployed, without funds, and in a public place." Therefore, just as application of the vagrancy ordinances to the displaced poor constitutes cruel and unusual punishment, arresting the homeless for harmless, involuntary, life-sustaining acts such as sleeping, sitting or eating in public is cruel and unusual.

The City suggests, apparently in reference to the aftermath of Hurricane Andrew, that even if homelessness is an involuntary condition in that most persons would not consciously choose to live on the streets, "it is not involuntary in the sense of a situation over which the individual has absolutely no control such as a natural disaster which results in the destruction of one's place of residence so as to render that person homeless." The court cannot accept this distinction. An individual who loses his home as a result of economic hard times or physical or mental illness exercises no more control over these events than he would over a natural disaster. Furthermore, as was established at trial, the City does not have enough shelter to house Miami's homeless residents. Consequently, the City cannot argue persuasively that the homeless have made a deliberate choice to live in public places or that their decision to sleep in the park as opposed to some other exposed place is a volitional act. [T]he lack of reasonable alternatives should not be mistaken for choice.

For plaintiffs, resisting the need to eat, sleep or engage in other life-sustaining activities is impossible. Avoiding public places when engaging in this otherwise innocent conduct is also impossible.... [P]laintiffs have no place else to go and no place else to be. This is so particularly at night when the public parks are closed. As long as the homeless plaintiffs do not have a single place where they can lawfully be, the challenged ordinances, as applied to them, effectively punish them for something for which they may not be convicted under the eighth amendment—sleeping, eating and other innocent conduct. Accordingly, the court finds that defendant's conduct violates the eighth amendment ban against cruel and unusual punishment and therefore that the defendant is liable....

QUESTIONS AND COMMENTS

1. Can the holdings in *Robinson* and *Powell* be reconciled? To what extent is *Robinson* simply a case about a nonmaterial element present in any federalist system—jurisdiction—rather than a general jurisprudential principle? Is the problem in *Robinson* merely that one can be an addict *in California* even though one's never used drugs *in California* at all? To what extent does the Supreme Court in *Robinson* and *Powell* protect the *appearance*, rather than the *reality*, of safeguarding defendants against punishment when they are choiceless? An addict may—in practice—be unable to avoid running afoul of what the Court sees as constitutionally legitimate criminal prohibitions. But *formally*, as long as only narcotics use, not addict status, is proscribed, he *could* wake up each day and, prospectively, avoid committing a crime. To what extent might the Court in *Robinson* rely on the act/thought (not the act/status) distinction? Is addiction merely a very strong desire or propensity to take drugs? Has Dalton revealed in his pornographic writings more than a very strong desire or propensity to molest?

2. Do the holdings in *Robinson* and *Powell* compel the holding in *Davis*? Is the issue in *Davis* closer to that in *Robinson* or to that in *Powell*?

3. What crimes was Davis convicted of? Did he ask the court to strike down the statutes, or did he ask that they not be applied to his case? How about Robinson and Powell?

4. The court claims that Davis "implicitly" asked it to recognize a "drug dependence" defense? Do you agree? Could his claim have been framed more narrowly? If so, would it be more likely to succeed? Is Davis seeking recognition for a "defense" or does he argue that he committed no crime in the first place, so that he wouldn't need a defense?

5. The Court in *Robinson* claimed that punishing a person for being addicted to drugs is like punishing him for the " 'crime' of having a common cold." Robinson v. California, 370 U.S. 660, 667 (1962). Is that true? And what's wrong, anyway, with punishing someone for having a cold? Is the seriousness of the disease significant? Its communicability? Its

preventability? Perhaps we find it peculiar to talk of blaming people for *being* sick, but is it invariably troublesome to blame people for *getting* sick?

6. What about quarantines? What about civil commitment? How much turns (or should turn) on the distinction between "punishment" and "treatment"? See In re De La O, 59 Cal.2d 128, 378 P.2d 793, 28 Cal.Rptr. 489 (1963) (holding *Robinson* did not preclude mandatory civil commitment of addicts, but precluded only *punishment*).

7. If all addicts take drugs, and if to take drugs they must possess them, then what's the difference between punishing an addict for being an addict and punishing him for possessing drugs? What about *taking* drugs, as opposed to *possessing* them?

8. Is "homelessness" (or "vagrancy") a status? An involuntary status? May voluntary status be punished in keeping with the act requirement?

9. Can *Pottinger* be distinguished from *Powell*?

10. If a person is homeless in New York City, where rents are high, is it fair for the state to argue that he is not "involuntarily" homeless if he *could* move upstate (to Buffalo, say), where rents are far lower? What if doing so would force him to abandon whatever social or familial ties he had? Preclude him from having a reasonable chance to rehabilitate himself?

11. What constraints, if any, does the "act requirement" in general, and the (constitutional?) rule against punishing status in particular, place on the judicial interpretation of criminal statutes? Consider the following case.

> The defendant is charged with driving while intoxicated, N.Y. Veh. & Traf. Law § 1192(2) ["Operating a motor vehicle while under the influence of alcohol or drugs"]. [T]he only issue to be determined is whether the defendant was "operating the vehicle".
>
> It is undisputed that the vehicle was a two-seater, 1977 Corvette, and that it was parked on Lawrence Avenue in Franklin Square while the defendant ... attended a rock concert at the Plattdeutsche Park Restaurant.
>
> Defendant and his witness, Rich Loiacano [the car's owner], both testified that the defendant was not expected to drive the vehicle and that the vehicle did not move. Further, that Mr. Loiacano had to start the vehicle routinely as on this occasion by using a screw driver on the starter and that Mr. Loiacano requested the defendant sit in the driver seat and push the gas pedal to prevent stalling of the engine after Mr. Loiacano started the car by first inserting the key, turning it to the "on" position and then starting the car by using the screw driver under the hood of the car....
>
> [There are several] cases in which operation was established based upon the defendant sitting behind the wheel with the car running but without the observation of defendant driving:
>
> People v. Domagala, 123 Misc. 757, 206 N.Y.S. 288 (1924). Defendant was observed attempting to start his motor vehicle six times, and every time he attempted to put it into gear the motor stalled.... The

Court found that defendant "violate[d] the law the instant he began to manipulate the machinery of the motor for the purpose of putting the automobile into motion."

People v. Marriott, 37 A.D.2d 868, 325 N.Y.S.2d 177 (1971). Defendant was alone in a car in a remote area. He was observed sitting behind the wheel with the engine stopped, and later with the engine running.

Matter of Prudhomme v. Hults, 27 A.D.2d 234, 278 N.Y.S.2d 67 (1967). Defendant was stopped on the center mall of the Thruway with the motor running, the lights on, but the car was not in gear and the defendant was slumped over the steering wheel. A ticket was found indicating that he entered the Thruway 7.5 miles away.

It has been recognized that the definition of "operation" for purposes of § 1192 is broader than the ordinary definition of driving. It includes the act of "[using] the mechanism of the automobile for the purpose of putting the automobile in motion even though [the vehicle does not move]." *Prudhomme*, supra.

[T]his definition . . . is included in the jury charges for violations of § 1192. The reason for such a charge is to allow the jury to draw a fair inference that the defendant was sitting behind the wheel with the motor running because he had been driving or was about to drive. Where there exists a logical, credible explanation such an inference can be defeated. The definition of operation cannot so alter its ordinary meaning as to create a new crime not intended by the legislature. In People v. DeSantis, Appellate Term 9th & 10th Jud. Dist., N.Y.L.J. 5/21/90 p. 32, col. 4, the court found that based upon the defendant's testimony he started the vehicle solely to keep warm and not for the purpose of putting the automobile in motion and, therefore, was not operating the vehicle within the meaning of § 1192.

Accordingly, the Court finds that the defendant did not operate the motor vehicle in question and the charge is hereby dismissed.

People v. O'Connor, 159 Misc.2d 1072 (N.Y. Dist. Ct. 1994).

Are you convinced that O'Connor didn't satisfy the conduct element of the offense, as interpreted by the courts? Does this interpretation satisfy the act requirement, or does it amount to punishing the status of being intoxicated while in the driver's seat of a car? Would punishing this status be unconstitutional in light of *Robinson* and *Powell*, (a) in general, (b) in O'Connor's case? Does the judicial interpretation of the DWI statute comport with the various aspects of the principle of legality (see ch. 2)?

3. VOLUNTARY VS. INVOLUNTARY ACTS

One attempt to reconcile *Robinson* and *Powell* has focused on a distinction between two aspects of the act requirement, one requiring an act, the other requiring *voluntariness*. The idea is that *Robinson* stands for the proposition that non-acts (and more specifically, statuses) cannot be punished. *Powell*, however, makes clear that an act, in order to be punishable, need not be (unambiguously) voluntary. Do you find this reading persuasive? Wholly apart from the question of reconciling *Robinson* and *Powell*, does it even make sense to talk about an involuntary act? Consider the following excerpts from the Model Penal Code and Restatement (Second) of Torts.

Model Penal Code § 2.13. General Definitions.

In this Code, unless a different meaning plainly is required:

(2) "act" or "action" means a bodily movement whether voluntary or involuntary;

(3) "voluntary" has the meaning specified in Section 2.01;

§ 2.01. Requirement of Voluntary Act.

(1) A person is not guilty of an offense unless his liability is based on conduct which includes a voluntary act or the omission to perform an act of which he is physically capable.

(2) The following are not voluntary acts within the meaning of this Section:

(a) a reflex or convulsion;

(b) a bodily movement during unconsciousness or sleep;

(c) conduct during hypnosis or resulting from hypnotic suggestion;

(d) a bodily movement that otherwise is not a product of the effort or determination of the actor, either conscious or habitual.

Restatement (Second) of Torts § 2. Acts.

The word "act" is used throughout the Restatement of this Subject to denote an external manifestation of the actor's will and does not include any of its results....

Comment:

a. Necessity of volition. There cannot be an act without volition. Therefore, a contraction of a person's muscles which is purely a reaction to some outside force, such as a knee jerk or the blinking of the eyelids in defense against an approaching missile, or the convulsive movements of an epileptic, are not acts of that person. So too, movements of the body during sleep when the will is in abeyance are not acts. Since some outward manifestation of the defendant's will is necessary to the existence of an act which can subject him to liability, it is not enough that a third person has utilized a part of the defendant's body as an instrument to carry out his own intention to cause harm to the plaintiff. In such case, as in the case of the knee jerk, the actor is the third person who has used the defendant's body as an instrument to accomplish some purpose of his own, or who has struck the defendant's leg so as to have caused the knee jerk.

b. Freedom of actor's will. If the actor's will is in fact manifested by some muscular contraction, including those which are necessary to the speaking of words, it is not necessary that his will operate freely and without pressure from outside circumstances. Indeed, the fact that the pressure is irresistible in the sense that it is one which reasonable men cannot be expected to resist, does not prevent its manifestation from being an act, although it may make the act excusable. A muscular reaction is always an act unless it is a purely reflexive reaction in which the mind and will have no share. Thus, if A, finding himself about to fall, stretches his hand out to seize some object, whether a fellow human being or a mere inanimate object, to save himself from falling, the stretching out of his hand and the grasping of the object is an act in the sense in which that word has heretofore been used, since the defendant's mind has grasped the situation and has dictated a muscular contraction which his rapidly formed judgment leads him to believe to be helpful to prevent his fall. While the decision is formed instantaneously, none the less the movement of the hand is a response to the will exerted by a mind which has already determined upon a distinct course of action. The exigency in which the defendant is placed, the necessity for a rapid decision, the fact that the decision corresponds to a universal tendency of mankind, may be enough to relieve the defendant from liability, but it is not enough to prevent his grasping of the object from being his act.

Penal Law of Israel § 34G.

A person shall bear no criminal liability for an act done by him while unable to choose between doing and not doing it, due to lack of control over his bodily movements for such act, such as an act done in consequence of physical coercion which he cannot overcome or by way of reflectory or spasmodic reaction or while asleep or in a state of hypnosis.

The Model Code drafters rejected the Restatement definition of an act so as not to "inject into the criminal law questions about determinism or free will." (Commentaries § 2.01, at 215). Did they succeed? Could they? Should they? What in the end is the difference between the Model Code and Restatement definitions of a voluntary act? Should there by a difference between the notion of a voluntary act in criminal law and the law of torts? Would a definition of voluntariness not in terms of the actor's will but her ability to choose between acting and not acting, as used in the Israeli Penal Law, be preferable?

Note also that the Code, in the end, requires a voluntary act, rather than merely an act, for criminal liability. In fact, most of the rationale for the Code's act requirement focuses on the illegitimacy of punishing (or "correcting") *involuntary* acts:

> It is fundamental that a civilized society does not punish for thoughts alone. Beyond this, the law cannot hope to deter involuntary movement or to stimulate action that cannot physically be performed; the sense of personal security would be undermined in a society where such movement or inactivity could lead to formal social condemnation of the sort that a conviction necessarily entails. People whose involuntary movements threaten harm to others may present a public health

or safety problem, calling for therapy or even for custodial commitment; they do not present a problem of correction.

Commentaries § 2.01, at 214–15.

But what is the difference between "correction" (or treatment) and "therapy" or "custodial commitment"? Why does one require a voluntary act, while the other does not?

State v. Tippetts

Court of Appeals of Oregon.
180 Ore. App. 350, 43 P.3d 455 (2002).

■ Kistler, J.

Defendant appeals from a judgment of conviction for supplying contraband. He argues that the trial court should have granted his motion for a judgment of acquittal because he did not voluntarily introduce marijuana into the Washington County Jail....

In October 1998, police officers obtained a warrant to search defendant's house. The officers located the house and, after knocking on the door and announcing their presence, forced the door open. Once inside, the officers saw defendant running towards the back of the house. They followed and subdued him. They placed him in handcuffs, read him his Miranda rights, and searched him. The officers found no drugs or other contraband on defendant. The officers then searched defendant's home, where they found methamphetamine and a weapon.

The officers formally placed defendant under arrest and took him to the Washington County Jail, where they turned him over to Officer Morey. Before searching him, Morey asked defendant whether he had any knives, needles, or drugs on him that he was bringing into the jail. Morey then searched defendant and found a small bag of marijuana in his pants pocket. Based on the marijuana Morey found, the state charged defendant with supplying contraband. A person commits the crime of supplying contraband if "the person knowingly introduces any contraband into a correctional facility, youth correction facility or state hospital[.]" Ore. Rev. Stat. § 162.185(1)(a).[1]

At trial, defendant moved for a judgment of acquittal on the charge of supplying contraband. [H]e argued that he could be found guilty of that crime only if he voluntarily introduced the contraband into the jail. Defendant contended that no reasonable juror could find that he acted voluntarily. He argued that, once he was arrested, he could not avoid taking the marijuana with him into the jail. The trial court denied defendant's motion, reasoning that defendant could have avoided the charge by admitting to possession of the marijuana before the officer discovered it.

On appeal, defendant renews his argument [based] on Ore. Rev. Stat. § 161.095(1), which provides:

1. The state also brought other charges against defendant. Those charges are not relevant to the issue that defendant raises on appeal.

> "The minimal requirement for criminal liability is the performance by a person of conduct which includes a voluntary act or the omission to perform an act which the person is capable of performing."

The state, for its part, does not defend the trial court's ruling on the ground that the court articulated,[2] nor does the state argue that there is evidence in this case from which a reasonable juror could find that defendant chose to take the marijuana into the jail with him.[3] . . .

. . . . By its terms, [Ore. Rev. Stat. § 161.095(1)] requires (1) that the act that gives rise to criminal liability be performed or initiated by the defendant and (2) that the act be voluntary. Ore. Rev. Stat. § 161.085(2), in turn, defines the phrase "voluntary act." It means "a bodily movement performed consciously[.]" Ore. Rev. Stat. § 161.085(2).

The texts of Ore. Rev. Stat. §§ 161.095(1) and 161.085(2) support defendant's position. Applied to the charge of supplying contraband, they require (1) that defendant either initiate the introduction of contraband into the jail or cause it to be introduced and (2) that he do so consciously. Defendant, however, did not initiate the introduction of the contraband into the jail or cause it to be introduced in the jail. Rather, the contraband was introduced into the jail only because the police took defendant (and the contraband) there against his will.

The state argues, however, that the use of the word "consciously" in the definition of the phrase "voluntary act" somehow changes that conclusion. The state reasons that the word consciously means "aware" and that an act will be voluntary as long as the defendant is aware that it is occurring. In explaining its position at oral argument, the state reasoned that, under its interpretation, if the police forcibly took a minor who was intoxicated out of his or her house and brought the minor into a public area, he or she could be convicted of public intoxication. In the state's view, the police's movement of the person into a public area would be a "voluntary act" that would satisfy Ore. Rev. Stat. § 161.095(1), as long as the person was aware that he or she was being moved. * * *

[A] voluntary act requires something more than awareness. It requires an ability to choose which course to take—i.e., an ability to choose whether to commit the act that gives rise to criminal liability. Conversely, a person may be aware that a particular act is being committed during a seizure or during a reflexive act, but that fact alone does not make the act voluntary.

2. The state does not dispute that, without a sufficient promise of immunity, Article I, section 12, of the Oregon Constitution and the Fifth Amendment to the United States Constitution prevent the state from forcing defendant to choose between admitting to possession of a controlled substance and being charged with introducing that substance into a correctional facility. There is no evidence in this record that defendant was promised immunity from criminal liability if he admitted to possessing controlled substances.

3. The state does not argue that, even if defendant's interpretation of the statute were correct, we may affirm the trial court's ruling because there is circumstantial evidence that would permit a reasonable juror to infer that defendant made a conscious choice to take the contraband with him into the jail. For example, the state does not argue that there is any evidence that would permit a reasonable juror to find that defendant could have disposed of the contraband after he was arrested but chose not to do so.

.... The state does not argue that there is any evidence from which a reasonable juror could find that defendant had such a choice, and we turn to the alternative basis that the state advances for upholding the trial court's ruling.

[In the alternative], the state argues that, even if the introduction of the drugs into the jail was not itself a "voluntary act," Ore. Rev. Stat. § 161.095(1) requires only "the performance by a person of conduct which includes a voluntary act[.]" The state reasons that, even if defendant did not voluntarily introduce the marijuana into the jail after the police arrested him, he voluntarily possessed it before he was arrested. The earlier voluntary act of possession, the state concludes, is sufficient to hold defendant criminally liable for the later involuntary act of introducing the marijuana into the jail. Defendant responds that Ore. Rev. Stat. § 162.185(1)(a) punishes the act of introducing the contraband into a correctional facility; it does not punish the act of possessing drugs. Defendant reasons that turning the voluntary act of possession into the predicate for holding him liable for involuntarily introducing marijuana into the jail stretches the word "includes" too far. * * *

Ore. Rev. Stat. § 161.095(1) derives from the Model Penal Code. The commentary to the analogous section of the Model Penal Code explains:

> "It will be noted that the formulation does not state that liability must be based on the voluntary act or the omission simpliciter, but rather upon conduct which includes such action or omission. The distinction has some analytical importance. If the driver of an automobile loses consciousness with the result that he runs over a pedestrian, none of the movements or omissions that accompany or follow this loss of consciousness may in themselves give rise to liability. But a prior voluntary act, such as the act of driving, or a prior omission, such as failing to stop as he felt illness approaching, may, under given circumstances, be regarded as sufficiently negligent for liability to be imposed. In that event, however, liability is based on the entire course of conduct, including the specific conduct that resulted in the injury."

American Law Institute, Model Penal Code § 2.01, 120 (Tentative Draft No. 4 1955).

The commentary to the Model Penal Code makes clear that the mere fact that defendant voluntarily possessed the drugs before he was arrested is insufficient to hold him criminally liable for the later act of introducing the drugs into the jail. Rather, to satisfy Ore. Rev. Stat. § 161.095(1), the involuntary act must, at a minimum, be a reasonably foreseeable or likely consequence of the voluntary act on which the state seeks to base criminal liability. On these facts, no reasonable juror could find that the introduction of contraband into the jail was a reasonably foreseeable consequence of possessing it. Moreover, the state does not dispute that, in this case, the police's act of arresting defendant and transporting him to the jail was an intervening cause that resulted in the marijuana's being introduced into the jail....

Conviction for supplying contraband reversed.

United States v. Tucker

United States Court of Appeals for the Tenth Circuit.
305 F.3d 1193 (2002).

■ MURPHY, CIRCUIT JUDGE.

The appellant, Jeffrey Tucker, was convicted of one count of possession of child pornography, 18 U.S.C. § 2252A(a)(5)(B), and sentenced to sixty months' imprisonment. * * *

On the evening of June 11, 1998, ... several Salt Lake City police officers searched Tucker's residence. * * * Using specialized software, [Special Agent Daniel Hooper of the Utah Department of Public Safety] recovered some 27,000 images stored on Tucker's computer. He estimated that of the .jpg images which were viewable, ninety to ninety-five percent were child pornography. Some of those images were very small, called "thumbnail" images, but many were larger images. Hooper recovered files containing child pornography from different parts of the hard drive. Some were located in the Web browsers' cache files. Others were located in the computer's recycle bin and in "unallocated" hard drive space. Hooper testified that the forensic examination revealed that Tucker accessed the cache files and manually deleted images in the files by dragging them to the computer recycle bin. Hooper rejected the suggestion that Tucker had accidentally run across these images, citing Web browser history files which showed that Tucker repeatedly visited the same sites. * * *

After a bench trial, the district court found the defendant guilty. It found that Tucker visited Web sites that displayed child pornography as thumbnail images. Tucker would often select thumbnail images to enlarge them. The district court found that upon visiting a site displaying thumbnail images or upon selecting a thumbnail for enlargement, the images were automatically cached on Tucker's hard drive. The district court found that Tucker had admitted that he routinely accessed the cached images on his hard drive and deleted them after an Internet session.

The district court concluded that Tucker possessed child pornography under the meaning of 18 U.S.C. § 2252A(a)(5)(B) because he had control over the images cached on his hard drive. The court reasoned that Tucker's habit of manually deleting images from the cache files established that he exercised control over them. The district court also rejected Tucker's argument that since the Web browsers automatically cached image files without his input, he did not voluntarily possess the images. The district court reasoned that Tucker visited Web sites for the purpose of viewing child pornography, and that "[t]he images would not have been saved to his cache file had Tucker not volitionally reached out for them." Finally, the district court concluded that Tucker's possession was knowing, since he purposefully visited Web sites containing child pornography knowing that the images would be stored on his computer's hard drive. * * *

Tucker maintains that he did not possess child pornography but merely viewed it on his Web browser. He concedes, however, that he knew that when he visited a Web page, the images on the Web page would be sent to his browser cache file and thus saved on his hard drive. Yet, Tucker contends that he did not desire the images to be saved on his hard drive and deleted the images from his cache file after each computer session. There is no merit to this argument.

18 U.S.C. § 2252A(a)(5)(B) provides that any individual who "knowingly possesses any book, magazine, periodical, film, videotape, computer disk, or any other material that contains 3 or more images of child pornography that has been ... transported in interstate ... commerce ... shall be punished."

The statute does not define possession, but in interpreting the term, we are guided by its ordinary, everyday meaning. Possession is defined as "the holding or having something (material or immaterial) as one's own, or in one's control." Oxford English Dictionary (2d ed. 1989); see also United States v. Simpson, 94 F.3d 1373, 1380 (10th Cir. 1996) (defining "knowing possession" in drug context as encompassing situations in which an individual "knowingly hold[s] the power and ability to exercise dominion and control" over the narcotics). Tucker contends that because he did not personally save, or "download," the images to his hard drive, he had no control over them. We agree with the district court, however, that Tucker had control over the files present in his Web browser cache files.

Customs Agent Daufenbach testified that an individual could access an image in a cache file, attach it to an email, post it to a newsgroup, place it on a Web site, or print a hard copy. He stated, "Just like as with any other data file, you could do almost anything with it." Agent Hooper similarly testified that an individual could "view [an image in the cache]. He could rename it. He could copy it to a floppy disk. He could email it to somebody. He could modify the file.... Anything he could do with any other file he could do with these files." This unrebutted testimony conclusively demonstrates Tucker had control over images stored in his cache and thus possessed them.

[Nonetheless,] Tucker argues ... that he did not voluntarily cache the files. Rather, he maintains, his Web browser "sav[ed] the images against his will." ... Tucker, however, intentionally sought out and viewed child pornography knowing that the images would be saved on his computer. Tucker may have wished that his Web browser did not automatically cache viewed images on his computer's hard drive, but he concedes he knew the Web browser was doing so. Tucker continued to view child pornography knowing that the pornography was being saved, if only temporarily, on his computer. In such circumstances, his possession was voluntary. Since he knew his browser cached the image files, each time he intentionally sought out and viewed child pornography with his Web browser he knowingly acquired and possessed the images.[16]

Tucker's conviction is AFFIRMED.

16. We offer no opinion on whether the mere viewing of child pornography on the Internet, absent caching or otherwise saving the image, would meet the statutory definition of possession. We likewise do not address the question whether an individual could be found guilty of knowingly possessing child pornography if he viewed such images over the Internet but was ignorant of the fact that his Web browser cached such images.

QUESTIONS AND COMMENTS

1. The court's opinion in *Tippetts* contains a veiled reference to the well-known case of Martin v. State, 31 Ala.App. 334, 17 So.2d 427 (1944), in which the Alabama Court of Appeals overturned the public intoxication conviction of a man on the ground that he had not acted voluntarily.

> Appellant was convicted of being drunk on a public highway, and appeals. Officers of the law arrested him at his home and took him onto the highway, where he allegedly committed the proscribed acts, viz., manifested a drunken condition by using loud and profane language.
>
> The pertinent provisions of our statute are: "Any person who, while intoxicated or drunk, appears in any public place where one or more persons are present, * * * and manifests a drunken condition by boisterous or indecent conduct, or loud and profane discourse, shall, on conviction, be fined", etc. Code 1940, Title 14, Section 120.
>
> Under the plain terms of this statute, a voluntary appearance is presupposed. The rule has been declared, and we think it sound, that an accusation of drunkenness in a designated public place cannot be established by proof that the accused, while in an intoxicated condition, was involuntarily and forcibly carried to that place by the arresting officer.
>
> Conviction of appellant was contrary to this announced principle and, in our view, erroneous. It appears that no legal conviction can be sustained under the evidence, so, consonant with the prevailing rule, the judgment of the trial court is reversed and one here rendered discharging appellant.
>
> Of consequence, our original opinion of affirmance was likewise laid in error. It is therefore withdrawn.
>
> Reversed and rendered.

2. Note that the statute in *Martin*, unlike that in *Tippetts*, requires *two* acts, the drunken public appearance and "boisterousness." (Also contrast the intoxication statute in *Powell*: "get drunk or be found in a state of intoxication in any public place.")

a. Assume, at least for argument's sake, that the public appearance by the defendant in *Martin* was wholly *involuntary*. Since the statute is conjunctive, the appeals court must take it as given that the fact finder believed that the defendant violated both elements of the statute (that is to say that he should not have been convicted if he'd simply been drunk in public, but that he also was "boisterous"). The court's (undefended) conclusion is that both elements of the offense must be committed *voluntarily* (though the court never mentions the second element so this isn't an explicit conclusion) or that Martin's boisterousness isn't voluntary either. The judges seem to believe the former in saying, quite cryptically, "a voluntary appearance is presupposed." It would be far easier to maintain this position if there were some universal principle that *all* elements of an offense must be "committed" voluntarily, or be "acts" in any sense at all. (Had the defendant in *Tippetts* enlisted the aid of a friend to smuggle the marijuana into prison, could he defend himself by noting that he was not in prison voluntarily?) But do the strong, straightforward arguments against punishing involuntary conduct apply to cases in which there are two (or more) elements, one of which is committed voluntarily? Is boisterousness, once drunk, involuntary? Is it involuntary in the same sense as, say, a reflex action, or "unstoppable" like a stuck tape recorder blaring obscenities might be? Is it involuntary in any sense cognizable by the criminal law, given that we readily punish, say, drunken assailants though the probability of assault is dramatically raised by drinking as well?

b. Now assume that the public appearance were *voluntary* (certainly the more common scenario). Would it make Martin's punishment for boisterous public intoxication any less bothersome if boisterousness, once drunk, were not voluntary? If all drunks are boisterous in public, the second part of the statute is redundant (i.e., one wouldn't have to make it illegal to be drunk and boisterous, being drunk would be sufficient since all who drink would be boisterous). If only some drunks are involuntarily boisterous once drunk (must Martin prove this about himself to be exonerated?)—or if all drunks are involuntarily boisterous some of the time—then the statute makes distinctions that are quite troublesome, punishing some, but not all, drunks on the basis of a factor outside their control (in effect, the statute permits being drunk in public unless one happens to be boisterous, though being boisterous or not is a morally arbitrary distinction between persons). More pointedly, it would make convictions in these routine cases problematic given the holding of this case (that all elements of an offense must be voluntary acts) since in the routine case, we would have declared that the second element (boisterousness) was not a voluntary act and, by extension from the holding, "voluntary boisterousness is presupposed."

c. By paying no attention to the second part of the statute, the court in *Martin* is able to evade two recurring issues in criminal jurisprudence: (1) how committed must the court remain to the "rule-boundedness" of criminal law norms (a decision that the defendant didn't have "enough" opportunity to avoid the offense, because it's "difficult" to avoid being boisterous once drunk, or once agitated by the arrest, is less "rule-like" than one that says one cannot convict when there is no act)?, and (2) how committed must the court remain to the "intentionalist" model that dominates criminal law (we can treat all action as freely willed and hence blameworthy except in extreme circumstances in which we can declare, for instance, that there's been no act)? See Mark Kelman, "Interpretive Construction in the Substantive Criminal Law," 33 Stan. L. Rev. 591 (1981). (Avoiding the view that boisterousness is "excused" because responsive to pressure serves these same functions. How?) How does the court in *Tippetts* deal with this issue?

3. *Rules vs. Standards*. One of the formal themes that we will trace as we work our way through the materials in this book is the distinction between rules and standards. In criminal law, this distinction is often quite explicit. Take, for instance, the U.S. Supreme Court's jurisprudence on the constitutionality of the death penalty. The Court began by banning unguided standards for determining death-worthiness (Furman v. Georgia, 408

U.S. 238 (1972)), then banned non-discretionary rules (Woodson v. North Carolina, 428 U.S. 280 (1976)), and eventually moved back to rules with standards that capital juries were required to "balance." (Lockett v. Ohio, 438 U.S. 586 (1978)). (Murderers are vulnerable to capital punishment if and only if they have committed murder under certain reasonably precisely delineated "special circumstances." Those who are "vulnerable" to capital punishment should be sentenced to death only if more vaguely defined aggravating circumstances outweigh vaguely defined mitigating ones. See ch. 10.) Often the issue may remain implicit, as when courts (and legislators and commentators) ponder the respective merits of negligence and strict liability.

But the distinction between rules and standards appears in other first-year classes as well. In contracts, for instance, the doctrine of "acceptability" fluctuates between rules (nominal consideration), standards (unconscionability), and various intermediate positions (status disqualifications like infancy and incompetence, duress, fraud, and the relevance of "unequal bargaining power"). Doctrinal accounts of contract "formation" likewise draw on rules (offer, acceptance, mirror image terms), standards (duty to bargain in good faith), and intermediate positions (interpret terms in light of past dealings, commercial practice, or market prices, promissory estoppel when a plaintiff "reasonably relied" on the defendant's action).

Not only the *distinction* between rules and standards can be traced through the doctrine of criminal law (and of other first-year courses), so can recurrent arguments about their merits. So it is often said that rules are objectionable because they are both under- and overinclusive. At the same time, they clearly do manage to clarify obligations (something of particular importance in the criminal law) and to reduce discretion. Standards, by contrast, are criticized insofar as they are enforced in a random (at best) or bigoted (at worst) fashion. Still, they allow us to act on our desire to see substantive justice done in each case on the basis of all the relevant facts rather than having to rely on "proxies" (such as implicit and explicit presumptions or various objective indicators) for the salient facts. While it is true that standards don't give adequate notice for planning and may lead to unfair surprise, if people expect good faith dealings and don't know the applicable rules, it's the strict enforcement of rules that may yield surprise.

Another argument often raised against rules is that they allow people to "walk the line" (e.g., a competent infant can enter a contract knowing he'll void it if it turns out unfavorably). This sort of behavior is not only intrinsically undesirable, so the argument goes, but also means that rules become more inapt over time since the "natural" amount of counter-purposive behavior will grow if people tailor their behavior to avoid harsh legal consequences. Finally, it is often argued that rules reduce litigation by making outcomes more predictable. Yet they have the opposite effect if they lead to such unfair results that there are pressures to find exceptions, waivers, etc. Moreover, "clear rules" may be less clear than they appear because (a) two facially clear rules cover the same material but there is no meta-rule to say which governs and/or (b) in the presence of incomplete enforcement, the "real" rule isn't the nominal rule at all, but the "standard" that determines when the state actually intervenes. (Think about speeding laws. Drivers may not be ticketed unless they exceed the rule-like limits, but there is no "rule" to determine which of the large number of speeders will be stopped.) One could make a fairly strong argument that the growth areas in the criminal law are "crimes" in which the "rules" are clear but we *expect* radically incomplete enforcement. This is especially prominent, historically and today, in relationship to "vice" crimes like gambling, prohibition of drugs and alcohol, and prostitution. This may well be a *problem*—it may not be good that legislators feel free to prohibit a class of activity on the assumption that only a subset of that activity will be effectively criminalized. Sometimes, however, it is hard to imagine how the legislature could have specified the "bad" versions of what they were genuinely worried about with adequate specificity. Radically incomplete enforcement is the norm not only in "drug prohibition" but also in the white collar crime area, where those who breach fiduciary disclosure duties, for instance, may—but only on rare occasions—be said to "defraud" the parties who could have made use of the undisclosed information. For more on white collar crime, see ch. 11 infra.

4. What if Tippetts had been charged with possessing contraband in prison, rather than supplying it?

5. Does it matter whether Tippetts knew that he had the marijuana in his pocket? What if the police had put it there on the way to the jail? What if they had put it there *with the purpose* of having Tippetts charged with supplying contraband? What if Tippetts had been charged with no other crime?

6. The *Tippetts* court distinguishes its decision from a case in which the defendant had reason to believe that he would engage in some involuntary act in the future. Why should this matter? What would the foreseeability of an involuntary act have to do with its involuntariness? Is foreseeability a question of the presence or absence of an act, or rather of the presence or absence of some mental state regarding the act? If so, why should it matter what knowledge—or foresight—I might have had at time T_1, if my criminal liability depends on the act I committed at T_2? Or is it not a matter of awareness at all, but of *causation*? Must my voluntary (but non-criminal) act at time T_1 have caused my involuntary (but criminal) act at T_2? How could that be? What could that mean? Consider the following case.

> [The defendant suffered from an epileptic seizure while driving his car down Delaware Avenue in Buffalo on "a bright, sunny day" in March of 1955. His car jumped the curb and ran into a group of six schoolgirls, killing four of them. He had suffered several seizures in the previous years, including one in September of 1954, and took daily medication to help prevent seizures.]
>
> Defendant was indicted and charged with violating section 1053–a of the Penal Law.[a] . . .

a. § 1053–a (Criminal negligence in the operation of a vehicle resulting in death) applies to any "person who operates or drives any vehicle of any kind in a reckless or culpably negligent manner, whereby a human being is killed."—EDS.

[Defendant argues] that his demurrer should have been sustained, since the indictment here does not charge a crime. The indictment states essentially that defendant, knowing "that he was subject to epileptic attacks or other disorder rendering him likely to lose consciousness for a considerable period of time", was culpably negligent "in that he consciously undertook to and did operate his Buick sedan on a public highway" and "while so doing" suffered such an attack which caused said automobile "to travel at a fast and reckless rate of speed, jumping the curb and driving over the sidewalk" causing the death of 4 persons. In our opinion, this clearly states a violation of section 1053–a of the Penal Law. The statute does not require that a defendant must deliberately intend to kill a human being, for that would be murder. Nor does the statute require that he knowingly and consciously follow the precise path that leads to death and destruction. It is sufficient, we have said, when his conduct manifests a "disregard of the consequences which may ensue from the act, and indifference to the rights of others." . . .

Assuming the truth of the indictment, as we must on a demurrer, this defendant knew he was subject to epileptic attacks and seizures that might strike at any time. He also knew that a moving motor vehicle uncontrolled on public highway is a highly dangerous instrumentality capable of unrestrained destruction. With this knowledge, and without anyone accompanying him, he deliberately took a chance by making a conscious choice of a course of action, in disregard of the consequences which he knew might follow from his conscious act, and which in this case did ensue. . . .

To hold otherwise would be to say that a man may freely indulge himself in liquor in the same hope that it will not affect his driving, and if it later develops that ensuing intoxication causes dangerous and reckless driving resulting in death, his unconsciousness or involuntariness at that time would relieve him from prosecution under the statute. . . . To have a sudden sleeping spell, an unexpected heart or other disabling attack, without any prior knowledge or warning thereof, is an altogether different situation, and there is simply no basis for comparing such cases with the flagrant disregard manifested here.

People v. Decina, 2 N.Y.2d 133, 138 N.E.2d 799, 157 N.Y.S.2d 558 (1956).

7. Is *Decina* consistent with *Martin*?

8. Did Decina act any less involuntarily than did Martin? Decina was an epileptic; there is no evidence that Martin was an alcoholic. Is an act any less involuntary if it is triggered by a medical condition—that Decina apparently tried to contain by taking medication—than if it is triggered by another person (the police officers in *Martin*)? Is the problem in *Martin* not (only) that Martin's act was not voluntary, but that the officers' act *was*?

What might Martin have done that induced (caused?) the police to drag him into public? If he should have foreseen that his conduct would lead to his being taken into public, is his public appearance truly involuntary? A person jumps from an airplane: is the fall through space involuntary?

9. In a well-publicized case, South Dakota Congressman Bill Janklow, an insulin-dependent diabetic, ran a stop sign at a rural intersection with his car and killed a motorcyclist. In defense, Janklow argued that his blood sugar dropped just prior to the crash, making him disoriented and confused. The diabetic reaction, he said, was brought on by the fact that he had not eaten for eighteen hours after taken his insulin that morning. Janklow was aware of the risk associated with not taking insulin as well as with the risk associated with taking insulin and not eating, but testified that a tight meeting schedule had prevented him from eating that day. Assuming Janklow did suffer from the diabetic reaction, what voluntary act—or omission—did he commit, if any? Janklow was convicted of manslaughter, speeding, running a stop sign, and reckless driving, and sentenced to 100 days in jail (plus a fine of $5,450, $574 in court costs, $85 for a blood test, and $50 dollars a day for his incarceration). Kirk Semple, "Judge Sentences Janklow to 100 Days in Jail," N.Y. Times, Jan. 22, 2004.

10. In *Decina*, the majority implies that the defendant is guilty of reckless driving—and of reckless homicide if he causes a death in the course of driving recklessly—any time he gets behind the wheel of a car. If you were defending Decina against this charge, what might you argue? What counterarguments should you expect?

Today, most states issue driver's licenses to epileptics only if they have been seizure free for a specified period of time (ranging from three months to two years, six months in most cases). "Driving and the Law," http://www.epilepsy.com/epilepsy/rights driving (accessed Sept. 17, 2004). If the driver has a seizure while driving, however, all insurance is void and her license is revoked. Should an epileptic (or a diabetic) be immunized from ongoing reckless driving charges if licensed (or at least if licensed under a licensing system that purports to assess the risks he poses and trades off such risks against the desirability of protecting his mobility)? Is the relevant question at core a question of substance or one of process (allocation of decision making authority): that is to say, is the question whether such a driver "is" reckless, or whether the judgment of whether he is reckless should be left to juries or should be decided by a central authority? Must we always retain residual rules against reckless driving to deal with the fact that a central authority inevitably possesses imperfect information: what do we do if the epileptic's condition *changes*, and he knows that, during the period he remains licensed? Is he (then and only then?) not the person the licensing authority adjudged to be taking risks that were not unduly substantial and unjustified?

11. Are sleep and voluntariness compatible? Anyone who has ever taken a long road trip is familiar with the sleepiness that may overtake a driver. What if the sleepiness turns into sleeping at the wheel? What if the defendant charged with reckless driving (or reckless homicide if a fatal accident results) was aware of the risk that she might be nodding off (at some point in the future, right away)? See Beatty v. Kelly, 9 A.D.2d 1001 (N.Y. App. Div. 1959) (reckless driving); Commonwealth v. Huggins, 836 A.2d 862 (Pa. 2003) (reckless homicide). But how can I be said to have engaged in a voluntary act while asleep? What sort of warning signs of fatigue are enough to justify criminal liability? Studies suggest that, in a recent year, about half of all drivers felt drowsy and about twenty percent actually fell asleep while driving. John P. McAlpin, "State Giving Tired

Drivers Wake-up Call," The Record (Bergen County, N.J.), Sept. 28, 2003, at A3.

12. Are sleep and action compatible? Cf. Chip Brown, "The Man Who Mistook His Wife For a Deer," N.Y. Times, Feb. 2, 2003, sec. 6, at 34, col. 1. Sleepwalking is a textbook example of action—even highly complex bodily movement—without voluntariness. In Fain v. Commonwealth, 78 Ky. 183 (1879), the court overturned the manslaughter conviction of a defendant for shooting and killing another man who had tried to wake him from a deep slumber. The court dismissed the fact that the defendant had only recently borrowed the pistol as having no "legitimate bearing" on the resolution the case. While the court condemned the defendant's behavior, it could find no reason to punish it:

> If the prisoner ... knew, as he no doubt did, his propensity to do acts of violence when aroused from sleep, he was guilty of a grave breach of social duty in going to sleep in the public room of a hotel with a deadly weapon on his person, and merits, for that reckless disregard of the safety of others, some degree of punishment, but we know of no law under which he can be punished. Our law only punishes for overt acts done by responsible moral agents. If the prisoner was unconscious when he killed the deceased, he cannot be punished for that act, and as the mere fact that he had the weapon on his person and went to sleep with it there did no injury to any one, he cannot be punished for that.

Is *Fain* consistent with *Decina*? What alternatives to criminal punishment might the state explore in cases like *Decina* and *Fain*?

13. In what sense do Tippetts and Martin look like an involuntary "batterer," who gets picked up and tossed at the victim? Are their acts better described as justified? Excused? Does it matter that the police are involved? What if their conduct were compelled by natural causes—a flood, a snowstorm, an earthquake? How inevitable, or "uncontrollable" must their behavior be?

14. Is *Tucker* consistent with *Tippetts*? *Martin*? What, exactly, was the act of possession in *Tucker*? Visiting the sites, viewing the images, downloading them, viewing them again after having downloaded them, moving them into the recycle bin, emptying the recycle bin, etc.? Does it matter whether Tucker knew that images viewed on the Web are automatically stored on his computer? What if he had used a library computer instead? At any rate, is the problem in *Tucker* that he didn't act, that he didn't act voluntarily, or that he didn't act voluntarily and knowingly?

C. OMISSIONS

1. DUTIES

State v. Miranda

Supreme Court of Connecticut.
245 Conn. 209, 715 A.2d 680 (1998).

■ KATZ, J.

.... The defendant commenced living with his girlfriend and her two children in an apartment in September, 1992. On January 27, 1993, the defendant was twenty-one years old, his girlfriend was sixteen, her son was two, and her daughter, the victim in this case, born on September 21, 1992, was four months old. Although he was not the biological father of either child, the defendant took care of them and considered himself to be their stepfather. He represented himself as such to the people at Meriden Veteran's Memorial Hospital where, on January 27, 1993, the victim was taken for treatment of her injuries following a 911 call by the defendant that the child was choking on milk. Upon examination at the hospital, it was determined that the victim [suffered from multiple injuries].... [T]he trial court found that the injuries, many of which created a risk of death, had been caused by great and deliberate force [and] that the defendant had been aware of [the injuries]....

The trial court ... found the defendant guilty of one count of § 53–21[a] and six counts of § 53a–59(a)(3).[b] The trial court found the defendant not guilty of nineteen counts of assault in the first degree. Those counts had charged him with either personally inflicting the injuries or not preventing the child's mother from inflicting the injuries.[4] The court imposed a total effective sentence of forty years imprisonment.

The defendant appealed to the Appellate Court, which ... reversed the assault convictions concluding that the defendant had no legal duty to act under the circumstances of this case....

I

Before addressing the ... issue of whether the facts and circumstances of this case were sufficient to create a legal duty to protect the victim from parental abuse pursuant to § 53a–59(a)(3), we turn our attention to the question of whether, even if we assume such a duty exists, the failure to act can create liability under that statute. In other words, by failing to act in accordance with a duty, does a defendant commit a crime, such as assault in the first degree in violation of § 53a–59(a)(3), that is not specifically defined by statute in terms of an omission to act but only in terms of cause and result?....

a. General Statutes § 53–21. Injury or risk of injury to, or impairing morals of, children.

Any person who (1) wilfully or unlawfully causes or permits any child under the age of sixteen years to be placed in such a situation that the life or limb of such child is endangered, the health of such child is likely to be injured or the morals of such child are likely to be impaired, or does any act likely to impair the health or morals of any such child, ... shall be guilty of a class C felony.—EDS.

b. General Statutes § 53a–59. Assault in the first degree: Class B felony.

"(a) A person is guilty of assault in the first degree when ... (3) under circumstances evincing an extreme indifference to human life he recklessly engages in conduct which creates a risk of death to another person, and thereby causes serious physical injury to another person...."—EDS.

4. Although the trial court never stated who actually had caused the injuries, we take judicial notice that the child's mother entered a plea of nolo contendere to the crimes of intentional assault in the first degree and risk of injury to a minor. She received a sentence of twelve years incarceration suspended after seven years.

The trend of Anglo–American law has been toward enlarging the scope of criminal liability for failure to act in those situations in which the common law or statutes have imposed an affirmative responsibility for the safety and well-being of others. Criminal liability of parents based on a failure to act in accordance with common-law affirmative duties to protect and care for their children is well recognized in many jurisdictions. See, e.g., People v. Stanciel, 153 Ill. 2d 218, 606 N.E.2d 1201, 180 Ill. Dec. 124 (1992) (mother guilty of homicide by allowing known abuser to assume role of disciplinarian over child); State v. Williquette, 129 Wis. 2d 239, 385 N.W.2d 145 (1986) (mother guilty of child abuse for allowing child to be with person known previously to have been abusive and who subsequently abused child again). * * *

[C]riminal conduct can arise not only through overt acts, but also by an omission to act when there is a legal duty to do so. "Omissions are as capable of producing consequences as overt acts. Thus, the common law rule that there is no general duty to protect limits criminal liability where it would otherwise exist. The special relationship exception to the 'no duty to act' rule represents a choice to retain liability for some omissions, which are considered morally unacceptable." State v. Williquette, supra, 129 Wis. 2d 253. Therefore, had the defendant been the victim's parent—someone with an undisputed affirmative legal obligation to protect and provide for his minor child—we would conclude that his failure to protect the child from abuse could constitute a violation of § 53a–59(a)(3).

II

We next turn to the issue of whether the duty to protect can be imposed on the defendant, an adult member of the household unrelated to the child. . . .

The defendant argues that there is no statutory or common-law precept "authorizing the expansion of assault under § 53a–59(a)(3)." The state argues that there is both. We conclude that, based on the trial court's findings that the defendant had established a family-like relationship with the mother and her two children, that he had voluntarily assumed responsibility for the care and welfare of both children, and that he had considered himself the victim's stepfather, there existed a common-law duty to protect the victim from her mother's abuse, the breach of which can be the basis of a conviction under § 53a–59(a)(3). Therefore, we need not decide whether General Statutes §§ 46b–38a, 17–101 and 17a–103 create an express statutory duty as well.[12]

12. General Statutes § 46b–38a provides: "Family violence prevention and response: Definitions. For the purposes of sections 46b–38a to 46b–38f [dealing with 'family violence prevention and response'], inclusive:

"(1) 'Family violence' means an incident resulting in physical harm, bodily injury or assault, or an act of threatened violence that constitutes fear of imminent physical harm, bodily injury or assault between family or household members. Verbal abuse or argument shall not constitute family violence unless there is present danger and the likelihood that physical violence will occur.

"(2) 'Family or household member' means (A) spouses, former spouses; (B) parents and their children; (C) persons eighteen years of age or older related by blood or marriage; (D) persons sixteen years of age or older other than those persons in subpara-

There are many statutes that expressly impose a legal duty to act and attach liability for the failure to comply with that duty. With other statutes, however, the duty to act can be found outside the statutory definition of the crime itself, either in another statute; or in the common law.

We note initially that the question of whether a duty, and thus, liability for the breach of that duty, should be recognized in this state is not foreclosed by our penal code.... Section 53a–4 of the code provides: "The provisions of this chapter shall not be construed as precluding any court from recognizing other principles of criminal liability or other defenses not inconsistent with such provisions." The official commentary to that provision states: "The purpose of this savings clause is to make clear that the provisions of §§ 53a–5 to 53a–23, which define the principles of criminal liability and defenses, are not necessarily exclusive. A court is not precluded by sections 53a–5 to 53a–23 from recognizing other such principles and defenses not inconsistent therewith." Commission to Revise the Criminal Statutes, Penal Code Comments, Conn. Gen. Stat. Ann. (West 1985) § 53a–4, p. 196.

We do not believe that the principle of imposing a common-law duty in and of itself is inconsistent with any other principle of criminal liability provided in the code. "Failure to act when there is a special relationship does not, by itself, constitute a crime. The failure must expose the dependent person to some proscribed result. The definition of proscribed results constitutes the substantive crime, and it is defined in the criminal code...." State v. Williquette, supra, 129 Wis. 2d 254....

.... Although one generally has no legal duty to aid another in peril, even when the aid can be provided without danger or inconvenience to the provider, there are four widely recognized situations in which the failure to act may constitute breach of a legal duty: (1) where one stands in a certain relationship to another; (2) where a statute imposes a duty to help another; (3) where one has assumed a contractual duty; and (4) where one voluntarily has assumed the care of another. 1 W. LaFave & A. Scott, supra, § 3.3

graph (C) presently residing together or who have resided together; and (E) persons who have a child in common regardless of whether they are or have been married or have lived together at any time." * * *

General Statutes § 17a–101 provides in pertinent part: "Protection of children from abuse. Mandated reporters. Training program for identification and reporting of child abuse and neglect. (a) The public policy of this state is: To protect children whose health and welfare may be adversely affected through injury and neglect; to strengthen the family and to make the home safe for children by enhancing the parental capacity for good child care; to provide a temporary or permanent nurturing and safe environment for children when necessary; and for these purposes to require the reporting of suspected child abuse, investigation of such reports by a social agency, and provision of services, where needed, to such child and family. ..."

General Statutes § 17a–103 provides: "Reports by others. Any person ... having reasonable cause to suspect or believe that any child under the age of eighteen is in danger of being abused, or has been abused or neglected ... may cause a written or oral report to be made to the Commissioner of Children and Families or his representative or a law enforcement agency. The Commissioner of Children and Families or his representative shall use his best efforts to obtain the name and address of a person who causes a report to be made pursuant to this section."

(a) (1)–(4), pp. 284–87.[14] The state argues that this case falls within both the first and fourth situations, or some combination thereof.

We begin with the duty based upon the relationship between the parties. One standing in a certain personal relationship to another person has some affirmative duties of care with regard to that person. "Legal rights and duties ... may arise out of those complex relations of human society which create correlative rights and duties the performance of which is so necessary to the good order and well-being of society that the state makes their observance obligatory." Annot., 100 A.L.R.2d 483, 488 (1965).

It is undisputed that parents have a duty to provide food, shelter and medical aid for their children and to protect them from harm. "The inherent dependency of a child upon his parent to obtain medical aid, i.e., the incapacity of a child to evaluate his condition and summon aid by himself, supports imposition of such a duty upon the parent." Commonwealth v. Konz, 498 Pa. 639, 644, 450 A.2d 638 (1982). Additionally, " 'the commonly understood general obligations of parenthood entail these minimum attributes: (1) express love and affection for the child; (2) express personal concern over the health, education and general well-being of the child; (3) the duty to supply the necessary food, clothing, and medical care; (4) the duty to provide an adequate domicile; and (5) the duty to furnish social and religious guidance.' " In re Adoption of Webb, 14 Wash. App. 651, 653, 544 P.2d 130 (1975)....

In addition to biological and adoptive parents and legal guardians, there may be other adults who establish familial relationships with and assume responsibility for the care of a child, thereby creating a legal duty to protect that child from harm. "Recognizing the primary responsibility of a natural parent does not mean that an unrelated person may not also have some responsibilities incident to the care and custody of a child. Such duties may be regarded as derived from the primary custodian, i.e., the natural parent, or arise from the nature of the circumstances." People v. Berg, 171 Ill. App. 3d 316, 320, 525 N.E.2d 573, 121 Ill. Dec. 515 (1988).

Most courts deciding whether, under a particular set of facts, liability for an omission to act may be imposed under a statute that does not itself impose a duty to act, have looked to whether a duty to act exists in another statute, in the common law or in a contract. Of those courts acting outside the context of a statutory or contractual duty that have held a defendant criminally liable for failing to protect a child from injury, most have relied on a combination of both the first and fourth situations described by Professors LaFave and Scott to establish a duty as the predicate for the defendant's conviction. More specifically, these courts have examined the nature of the relationship of the defendant to the victim and whether the

14. A leading case first outlining these four situations added a requirement to the fourth that appears to have been omitted in recent years. See *Jones* v. *United States*, 113 U.S. App. D.C. 352, 308 F.2d 307, 310 (D.C. App. 1962) ("where one has voluntarily assumed the care of another and *so secluded the helpless person as to prevent others from rendering aid*" [emphasis added]). This refinement would not seem applicable to an infant, or for that matter a child of tender years, because a child is *always* dependent on others for care and intervention when sick or in danger.

defendant, as part of that relationship, had assumed a responsibility for the victim.[15] * * *

In State v. Orosco, 113 N.M. 789, 833 P.2d 1155 (1991), the court examined whether the defendant, who lived with the victim and his mother and who failed to intervene when one of his friends sexually abused the victim, could be held criminally liable for the abuse. [T]he court held that, by assuming the care and welfare of the child, the defendant stood in the position of a parent.[16]

In Leet v. State, 595 So. 2d 959 (Fla. App. 1991), the court examined whether the defendant could be held criminally responsible for abuse of a child by his mother although he was not the child's father.... Although the defendant had argued that he was not financially responsible for the child and could not have authorized his medical treatment, the court, nevertheless, concluded that he had the authority, and indeed, the duty to prevent the mother's conduct.

In People v. Wong, 182 A.D.2d 98, 588 N.Y.S.2d 119 (1993), the court examined whether the defendants, who had been babysitters for the child victim's parents, could be convicted of manslaughter for harming the child and for failing to provide him with necessary medical care. To support a conviction based upon their failure to provide medical attention, the prosecution relied on two theories: (1) that the defendants had contracted with the child's parents to care for the child while the parents worked; and (2) that the defendants voluntarily had assumed care for the child....

As these cases demonstrate, the traditional approach in this country is to restrict the duty to save others from harm to certain very narrow categories of cases. We are not prepared now to adopt a broad general rule covering other circumstances.[17] We conclude only that, in accordance with the trial court findings, when the defendant, who considered himself the victim's parent, established a familial relationship with the victim's mother and her children and assumed the role of a father, he assumed, under the common law, the same legal duty to protect the victim from the abuse as if he were, in fact, the victim's guardian.... That duty does not depend on an ability to regulate the mother's discipline of the victim or on the defendant having exclusive control of the victim when the injuries oc-

15. As we have stated, some courts in other jurisdictions have held that liability can flow from the breach of a duty created by contract; see, e.g., *Commonwealth* v. *Pestinikas*, 421 Pa. Super. 371, 617 A.2d 1339 (1992) (because there was evidence that victim's death had been caused by appellant's failure to provide food and medical care that he had agreed by oral contract to provide, omission to act was sufficient to support conviction for criminal homicide). The state is not relying on that theory as a basis for conviction and, therefore, we express no opinion as to whether that relationship can serve as a theory of liability.

16. As an additional basis for its decision, the court reasoned that the defendant's failure to protect the child could be regarded by the attacker as support of the abusive conduct and, therefore, made him an aider and abettor.

17. Many other countries have adopted a more inclusive view in determining what classes of persons shall have a duty to rescue another from harm when they can do so without unreasonable risk to themselves. See J. Dawson, "Negotiorum Gestio: The Altruistic Intermeddler," 74 Harv. L. Rev. 1073, 1101–1106 (1961); see also L. Frankel, "Criminal Omissions: A Legal Microcosm," 11 Wayne L. Rev. 367, 368–69 (1965).

curred. Nor is the duty contingent upon an ability by the state or the mother to look to the defendant for child support. Moreover, whether the defendant had created a total in loco parentis relationship with the victim by January, 1993, is not dispositive of whether the defendant had assumed a responsibility for the victim. "If immediate or emergency medical attention is required from a child's custodian it should not matter that such custodian is not the primary care provider or for that matter a legally designated surrogate." People v. Berg, supra, 171 Ill. App. 3d 320.

Nor should we reject the concept of a duty in this case because the defendant might not have been able to authorize medical treatment for the victim had he taken her to the hospital. The status required to impose the legal duty to safeguard the victim is not coextensive with the status that permits one to authorize treatment....

Finally, we recognize the continuing demographic trend reflecting a significant increase in nontraditional alternative family arrangements. Consequently, more and more children will be living with or may depend upon adults who do not qualify as a natural or adoptive parent.... To distinguish among children in deciding which ones are entitled to protection based upon whether their adult caregivers have chosen to have their relationships officially recognized hardly advances the public policy of protecting children from abuse. * * *

The judgment of the Appellate Court is reversed and the case is remanded to that court for consideration of the defendant's remaining claims.

■ PALMER, J., with whom MCDONALD, J., joins, concurring.

I join the opinion of the majority. A serious question remains, however, as to whether the defendant, Santos Miranda, had fair warning that his failure to act, in the particular circumstances of this case, could give rise to the crime of assault in the first degree in violation of General Statutes § 53a–59(a)(3). The legal duty that we recognize today has never before been expressly recognized in this state; indeed, the Appellate Court, upon consideration of the defendant's appeal, unanimously concluded that no such duty existed. In such circumstances, it is by no means clear that the due process clauses of the federal and state constitutions permit such a duty to be imposed on this defendant for purposes of criminal liability under the assault statute.[1] Since the defendant will have the opportunity to raise a due process claim on remand, however;[2] and because I agree with the analysis and conclusions of the majority, I join the opinion of the majority.

1. There is, of course, a difference between the recognition of an existing duty, on the one hand, and the creation of an altogether new duty, on the other. Whether that distinction is significant for due process purposes under the specific facts of this case remains to be seen.

2. The importance of this issue to the defendant cannot be overstated in view of the fact that he received a cumulative sentence of thirty years imprisonment on the six counts of assault in the first degree. Because the defendant also received a consecutive ten year prison term on the one count of risk of injury to a child, his total effective sentence is forty years imprisonment. By contrast, the child's mother, who, it appears, actually caused the child's injuries, received a total effective sentence of only seven years imprisonment.

■ BERDON, J., dissenting.

The majority's determination that the facts in this case were sufficient to create a legal duty on the part of the defendant to protect the child from parental abuse pursuant to § 53a–59(a)(3) is premised on its unsupported conclusion that had the defendant been the victim's parent, he would have had an undisputed affirmative legal obligation to protect the child from assault pursuant to § 53a–59(a)(3). There is an affirmative obligation on the defendant and the parent, under the circumstances of this case, to protect the child, but that duty does not arise under § 53a–59(a)(3). Rather, in this state, the obligation to act arises under § 53–21, entitled "injury or risk of injury to, or impairing the morals of, children," which was enacted by the legislature many years ago to address the failure to act with respect to the welfare of a child.... Here, the trial court found the defendant guilty of risk of injury with respect to the child, for which he was sentenced to the maximum term of ten years. The defendant's conviction under § 53–21, however, is not before us....

II

The majority addresses [the] issue ... whether the "conduct" referred to in § 53a–59(a)(3) includes the failure to act.... Section 53a–59(a) provides in part that "[a] person is guilty of assault in the first degree when ... (3) under circumstances evincing an extreme indifference to human life he recklessly engages in conduct which creates a risk of death to another person, and thereby causes serious physical injury to another person...." Although "conduct" can include the failure to act under circumstances when there is a duty to act; 1 W. LaFave & A. Scott, Substantive Criminal Law (1986) § 3.3, p. 282; the majority points to nothing in the text of § 53a–59(a)(3), or its legislative history, to support its conclusion that conduct under § 53a–59(a)(3) includes the failure to act. In fact, both the common definition of assault—"a violent attack with physical means"; Webster's Third New International Dictionary; and the legal definition of assault—"any wilful attempt or threat to inflict injury upon the person of another"; Black's Law Dictionary (6th Ed. 1990); belie the majority's claim.

Moreover, by construing § 53a–59(a)(3) to include the duty to act, the majority stands a long-standing and fundamental principle of statutory construction on its head: Penal statutes "are to be expounded strictly against an offender, and liberally in his favor. This can only be accomplished, by giving to them a literal construction, so far as they operate penally...." Daggett v. State, 4 Conn. 60, 63 (1821).... While a criminal statute is not to be defeated by an unreasonably strict construction of its language, it must be rather strictly construed so that the conduct made criminal will be ascertainable with reasonable certainty from a careful reading of the statute.... A careful reading of § 53a–59(a)(3) would never lead a rational reader to believe that a person was subject to criminal liability under the statute for the failure to act-whether the person is a stranger, a live-in boyfriend, or a parent. * * *

III

Nevertheless, even if the majority were correct that one person can assault another person under § 53a–59(a)(3) by failing to act, the defendant's conviction in this case cannot stand. By superimposing on § 53a–59(a)(3) a common-law duty on the part of a person to act in order to protect a child from harm when that third person voluntarily assumes responsibility for the care and the welfare of the child and considers himself to have a stepfather-stepchild relationship with the child, the majority has created a new crime. In crafting this new crime, the majority ignores the fact that it is the legislature that defines substantive crimes. This division between the legislature and the court was established in 1971 when the legislature adopted the penal code and repealed General Statutes (Rev. to 1968) § 54–117, which recognized common-law crimes. * * *

The majority argues that it may recognize a duty to protect a child from abuse under § 53a–59(a)(3) because it is merely applying a long-standing principle of liability consistent with the principles of liability permitted by § 53a–4. Even if we assume that it is merely applying a principle of liability rather than creating a substantive crime, the majority, however, ... fails to cite any cases in which this court has applied this principle of liability for acts of omission.

Moreover, the majority makes no attempt to explain why the "principle of imposing a common-law duty" to protect a child from abuse is not inconsistent with the [general] principles of liability set forth in ... the penal code. Indeed, the majority ignores the fact that the recognition of this new duty under § 53a–59(a)(3) is inconsistent with the notion of accessory liability.... For example, this court consistently has held that one cannot be held liable under a theory of aiding and abetting, for merely being present at the time of the crime and acquiescing to the commission of the crime....

IV

The legislature will be very much surprised to discover that we have in place, under § 53a–59(a)(3), a law that provides that the failure to act is punishable criminal conduct. Although the legislature recently has grappled with the issue of imposing an affirmative obligation on the part of a parent and an unrelated adult to protect children from abuse; see Substitute House Bill No. 5283 (1988) (H.B. No. 5283), entitled "An Act Concerning Facilitation of Abuse of a Child"; it did not enact the proposed legislation. Nevertheless, the majority of this court, without any understanding of the implications of its decision today and without the aid of expert advice that is available to the legislature through the public hearing process, impetuously and presumptuously crafts a crime of assault that was never intended by the legislature. Clearly, if the legislature agreed with the majority that, pursuant to § 53a–59(a)(3), parents as well as unrelated adults had an affirmative legal obligation to protect children from abuse, it never would have had a need to consider H.B. No. 5283, a bill that explicitly criminalizes the conduct with which the defendant was charged in the present case.

The representatives of several state agencies and several non-profit groups created to support victims of abuse spoke out against H.B. No. 5283 at the public hearing before the legislature's select committee on children....

First, those who testified before the committee expressed unanimous concern that holding persons liable for not protecting children from abuse actually would cause more harm than it would prevent. They testified that if the legislature wants to accomplish its goal of preventing children from being injured as a result of violence, it must first consider ways to improve the delivery of services to at risk families under the state's present child welfare system. For example, Diane Edell, program director of the Aetna Foundation Children Center at Saint Francis Hospital and Medical Center, testified that "this law ... will [not] do anything to protect children. There are other things ... prevention programs, specialized mental health programs, helping mothers to leave abusive relationships that will help us help our children better."

Furthermore, several speakers testified that, if the legislature imposed liability on persons who fail to protect a child from abuse, it would discourage persons who are in the best position to know whether a child has been abused from informing the appropriate authorities after the abuse occurs. "If we want to help these children we need to find ways to make these parents stronger, not create laws that will result in fewer parents coming forward with their suspicions." Remarks of Edell, supra. Finally, according to chief public defender Gerard A. Smyth, H.B. No. 5283 would "discourage people from acting as 'caretakers' " of children, and, consequently, would affect the level of care received by children in this state.

Second, nearly every speaker at the public hearing before the select committee on children testified that the legislature did not need to enact H.B. No. 5283 because "the situation that [it] is intended to address is already covered by" § 53–21, the risk of injury to a child statute....

Third, the speakers at the public hearing before the select committee on children agreed that, even if the committee approved H.B. No. 5283, the bill would have to be made more specific in order to set forth the effort that must be extended to satisfy the duty to protect children from abuse. According to Smyth, for example, it was unclear whether parents, guardians and caretakers could satisfy the duty established in H.B. No. 5283, to act to protect such child from physical abuse, by reporting a risk of abuse to the department of children and families; or whether such persons would be required "to take more active measures, such as concealing a child from a custodial parent if necessary ... or ... withholding a child from a parent suspected of abuse."

Clearly, all of these delineated issues are best left for the legislature's consideration, not ours.

V

Finally, in crafting this new common-law crime, the majority acknowledges constitutional problems in attempting to apply it in this case. For example, the majority has created an ex post facto law in its classic sense. Furthermore, there is at least a question as to whether the defendant's convictions for assault and risk of injury violate the constitutional prohibition against double jeopardy.... I would affirm the judgment of the Appellate Court.

Accordingly, I dissent.

State ex rel. Kuntz v. Montana Thirteenth Judicial District

Supreme Court of Montana.
298 Mont. 146, 995 P.2d 951 (2000).

■ JUSTICE JAMES C. NELSON delivered the opinion of the court.

The alleged facts indicate that [Bonnie] Kuntz and [Warren] Becker ... were in the process of ending what is described as a stormy relationship. When Kuntz arrived at the[ir] mobile home ..., she discovered that many of her personal belongings had been destroyed, the interior of the home "trashed," and the phone ripped from the wall. Kuntz told the deputies that she then went into the kitchen. There, allegedly, Becker physically attacked her, and at one point grabbed her by the hair, shook her, and slammed her into the stove. [Kuntz then stabbed Becker with a knife.]

... Kuntz was charged with negligent homicide for causing the death of Warren Becker by stabbing him once in the chest ... and by failing to call for medical assistance. Although she admitted stabbing Becker and causing his death, Kuntz entered a plea of not guilty based on the defense of justifiable use of force. * * *

Applying the foregoing to the facts here, we conclude that Kuntz and Becker, having lived together for approximately six years, owed each other the same "personal relationship" duty as found between spouses .... This duty, identified as one of "mutual reliance" by LaFave and Scott, would include circumstances involving "two people, though not closely related, [who] live together under one roof." LaFave & Scott, § 3.3(a)(1), at 285–286. To hold otherwise would result in an untenable rule that would not ... impose a legal duty to summon medical aid on persons in a relationship involving cohabitation. Nevertheless, this holding is far from dispositive in establishing a legal duty under the facts presented.

We agree with the District Court that the duty based on "creation of the peril" is far more closely aligned with the factual circumstances here. Undoubtedly, when a person places another in a position of danger, and then fails to safeguard or rescue that person, and the person subsequently dies as a result of this omission, such an omission may be sufficient to support criminal liability. * * *

.... The State contends that even if Kuntz's use of force was justified, a proven subsequent failure by her to summon aid could constitute a gross deviation from ordinary care.... Although the use of force may be justified, to not hold such a person criminally accountable for the subsequent omission would, according to the State, "encourage revenge and retaliation."

Whether inflicted in self-defense or accidentally, a wound that causes a loss of blood undoubtedly places a person in some degree of peril, and therefore gives rise to a legal duty to either 1) personally provide assistance; or 2) summon medical assistance. Even so, the performance of this legal duty . . . does not require that a person place herself at risk of serious bodily injury or death. * * *

[T]he duty to summon aid may in fact be "revived" as the State contends, but only after the victim of the aggressor has fully exercised her right to seek and secure safety from personal harm. Then, and only then, may a legal duty be imposed to summon aid for the person placed in peril by an act of self-defense. . . .

[A] person, who is found to have used justifiable force, but who nevertheless fails to summon aid in dereliction of the legal duty as defined here, may be found criminally negligent only where the failure to summon aid is the cause-in-fact of death, rather than the use of force itself. * * *

For these reasons, the District Court's order denying Kuntz's motion to amend or strike the amended information is affirmed, and this case is remanded for further proceedings consistent with this opinion.

■ JUSTICE TERRY N. TRIEWEILER concurring and dissenting.

[A] person is justified in the use of deadly force only when necessary to prevent imminent death or serious bodily harm to herself or another, or to prevent commission of a forcible felony. It severely limits the circumstances under which deadly force is justified. However, it specifically recognizes that under those circumstances, the amount of force necessary may be deadly. It is inherently contradictory to provide by statute that under certain circumstances deadly force may be justified, but that having so acted, a victim has a common law duty to prevent the death of her assailant.

[T]he majority opinion . . . predicates criminal liability on a finding that the failure to summon aid is the cause in fact of death. However, where a person is placed in peril by another's justified use of force it can never be said that the failure to summon aid, rather than the original act of force, is the cause in fact of death, because presumably death would never have occurred but for the original act of self-defense. * * *

. . . . A person driven to the point of having to violently defend herself from a violent attack should not, at the risk of criminal punishment, be required to know that at some undefined point in time she has a duty to save that same person. A normal person under those circumstances is incapable of undertaking such an intellectual process. To require her to do so is inconsistent with the traditional notion that when criminal liability is based on the failure to perform a duty, it must be a plain duty which leaves no doubt as to its obligatory force.

QUESTIONS AND COMMENTS

1. The majority in *Miranda* bases its decision exclusively on the defendant's common law duty. Could it have found a statutory duty, based

on the statutes cited in n. 12? How explicit—and how closely related—does a statutory duty have to be to count as the basis for criminal punishment?

2. Is Miranda being punished for violating a duty or for committing an assault, or both? One way of thinking about omission liability is to differentiate between direct (or express) and indirect (or implied) omissions.

Model Penal Code § 2.01. Omission as Basis of Liability.

(3) Liability for the commission of an offense may not be based on an omission unaccompanied by action unless:

(a) the omission is expressly made sufficient by the law defining the offense; or

(b) a duty to perform the omitted act is otherwise imposed by law.

German Penal Code § 13. Commission by Omission.

(1) Whoever fails to avert a result, which is an element of a penal norm, shall only be punishable under this law, if he is legally responsible for the fact that the result does not occur, and if the omission is equivalent to the realization of the statutory elements of the crime through action.

Indirect omission liability is best thought of as a theory of liability, by which the failure to act is treated as "equivalent" to an act. As such, it applies to every offense which requires an affirmative act in its definition (like homicide). Direct omission liability, by contrast, refers to a group of crimes, which in their definition make reference to a failure to act (like failing to file an income tax return). Unlike implied omission liability, express omission crimes do not expand the reach of ordinary commission crimes. Is one type of omission liability more troubling than the other? Could—and should—all omission liability be made explicit? Should liability under a *direct* omission statute preclude liability under an *indirect* omission theory for another crime? (Look carefully in this regard at Judge Berdon's dissent and his remarks about § 53–21 of the Connecticut Code.) In other words, can a single omission be punished twice?

3. Is it desirable as matter of policy, even if it is fair, to punish someone because he has violated a duty that he "voluntarily assumed"? (Imagine prosecuting paid lifeguards and by-standers at the community pool for manslaughter if they fail to save a drowning child they are all capable of saving. It might seem *fairer* to prosecute the lifeguard—if she didn't want to be held accountable for saving people, she didn't have to take the job—but is it sensible? In terms of the purposes of punishment? In terms of insuring that we'll have enough people willing to be lifeguards?) In what sense can Miranda be said to have voluntarily assumed the child's care? Did he assume the duty upon voluntarily associating himself with the child's mother? Can mere presence in the household, or mere financial support, create a duty of care? Can the duty ever arise based on the *child's* perception of her relationship with, or her reliance upon, the adult?

4. What about the additional requirement that the defendant "so secluded the helpless person as to prevent others from rendering aid,"

which the majority in *Miranda* dismissed with the remark that it "appears to have been omitted in recent years"? What was the point of this requirement and how would it have cut in *Miranda*? If the defendant "actively harms" the victim, it is apparent that the world would have been a better place for the victim had the defendant never been around. Arguably, if the defendant starts to rescue a victim and third parties forego their own rescue efforts because they think the defendant is "taking care of it," the defendant *worsens* the victim's prior position. How attenuated a counterfactual of this sort should we employ though in ascertaining whether a "failure to act" harms the victim? If the local doctor refuses to give life-sustaining emergency care, do we imagine another doctor would have come along had the defendant doctor not established a practice? Would someone more protective of the child have displaced the defendant in *Miranda*? Or do we impose liability because it is so deeply morally objectionable for a caretaker to fail to protect the child, whether we can readily describe this failure to protect as "harming" the child or not?

5. *Miranda* mentions four common sources of duties whose violation can give rise to criminal omission liability. *Kuntz* mentions a fifth: duties based on the creation of the need for assistance in the first place ("creation of the peril"). You have just hit a man who has wandered onto the highway in the middle of the night. Assume you bear no responsibility for the accident whatsoever (you were driving carefully, your lights were on, etc.). Do you have a duty to come to the accident victim's aid? If he dies, are you liable for murder, assuming you knew that he would die if you didn't call for help? Does it matter whether he was responsible for the accident? Whether he was drunk, disoriented, on the run from an armed robber, or an armed robber on the run from the police? See, e.g., "Woman Is Sentenced to 50 Years In Case of Man in Windshield," N.Y. Times, June 28, 2003, at A10, col. 5 (former nurse's aide convicted of murder after accidentally hitting homeless man with her car, driving home with his body stuck in the windshield, and then leaving him to die in her garage); see also People v. Woodruff, 4 A.D.3d 770, 771 N.Y.S.2d 620 (N.Y. App. Div. 2004) (experienced hunter charged with manslaughter after accidentally shooting someone and then driving home without reporting the accident or responding to victim's cry for help).

6. Should it matter, in cases like *Kuntz*, whether the use of (deadly?) force was justified or merely excused? What if Kuntz turned out have been mistaken in her perception that she had to stab Becker to protect herself? What if she's wrong about the risk of coming to Becker's aid after having stabbed him? What if she turns out to have been neither justified nor excused? Would she have a duty to come to Becker's aid then? Why doesn't the court simply rely on Kuntz's quasi-spousal duty? Consider, in this context, People v. Robbins, 83 A.D.2d 271, 443 N.Y.S.2d 1016 (1981), where a married woman, after a religious revelation that she was healed of epilepsy, stopped taking her medication. As a result, she had several seizures and died. A negligent homicide indictment against the husband for failing to summon medical aid was dismissed on the ground that the wife made a "rational decision" to exercise her right to refuse medical treatment.

7. How significant do you think the defendant's character, most importantly the lack of empathy, is in omission cases? What if Kuntz had stayed with Becker until his last breath, crying inconsolably and muttering "sorry" over and over again, instead of calling an ambulance? What if she instead calmly made herself a sandwich? See State v. Morgan, 86 Wn. App. 74, 936 P.2d 20 (1997) (doubling the sentence for manslaughter by omission for "egregious lack of remorse").

8. Consider the following hypotheticals. In each case, V is elderly and immobile and dies of starvation when unable to get food that D could readily get him.

1. D1 is a neighbor, aware of V's plight; assume that D1 has a longstanding grudge against V (or some other motive to see V dead) that animates his decision not to bring V the food.
2. D2 is a storeowner: a) with an ongoing food delivery contract with V which he breaches b) who took an order over the phone and failed to fill the order after he promised he would, aware of V's plight.
3. D3 is a welfare worker who fails to check on V's need for homemaking services despite the presence of administrative regulations that define that as part of his job.
    a. Note the routine direct omission liability cases in which Ds have statutory duties to act: e.g., duty of young men to register for the draft; duties of teachers/health care workers to report suspected abuse or neglect of children.
    b. Note, too, that somewhat more general care duties are imposed by common law or statute on people in certain status positions (e.g., ship and plane captain to passengers and crew (United States v. Knowles, 26 Fed. Cas. 800 (N.D. Cal. 1864)); innkeeper to inebriated customer (State v. Reitze, 86 N.J.L. 407, 92 A. 576 (1914); see also Territory v. Manton, 8 Mont. 95, 19 P. 387 (1888) (husband to wife); Regina v. Smith, 8 Carr. & P. 153 (Eng. 1837) (master to apprentice).
4. D4 is V's husband but they've long been separated, though not divorced, and utterly out of touch.

Compare the status relationships that give rise to duties to aid with those that give rise to the right to use force (see, e.g., Model Penal Code § 3.08 (Use of Force by Persons with Special Responsibility for Care, Discipline or Safety of Others)). Is "special responsibility" the common foundation for these duties and rights? Could we have the duties without the rights, or vice versa? Note that these duties are generally not reciprocal (with the exception—in modern criminal law, though not originally—of interspousal duties). See, e.g., People v. Sanford, 777 N.Y.S.2d 595 (2004) (child owes no common law duty to parent); Billingslea v. State, 780 S.W.2d 271 (Tex. Crim. App. 1989) (child owes no statutory duty to parent). (Historically the householder's patriarchal authority over members of his household functioned as the source of both his vicarious liability for their actions and his power to discipline them. See Markus Dirk Dubber, The

Police Power: Patriarchy and the Foundations of American Government (2005).)

Should it matter whether these duties are derived from common law precedent or from statutes? Compare Tex. Penal Code § 6.01 ("a person who omits to perform an act does not commit an offense unless a statute provides that the omission is an offense or otherwise provides that he has a duty to perform the act") and N.Y. Penal Law § 15.00(3) (defining omission as "a failure to perform an act as to which a duty of performance is imposed by law").

From criminal or civil statutes? Compare People v. Steinberg, 79 N.Y.2d 673 (1992) (affirming manslaughter conviction for failure to summon medical aid based on parent's duty to child derived from definition of "neglected child" in Family Court Act) with Don Stuart, "Supporting General Principles for Criminal Responsibility in the Model Penal Code with Suggestions for Reconsideration: A Canadian Perspective," 4 Buff. Crim. L. Rev. 13, 42 (2000) (arguing that basing omission liability on any source other than a criminal statute violates principle of legality).

9. Most American jurisdictions do not use the criminal law to enforce a general duty to aid. They instead regard omission liability as limited to certain exceptions to the general rule against omission liability. Vermont and Wisconsin are two states that do have general omission liability statutes.

12 Vt. Stat. Ann. § 519. Emergency medical care

(a) A person who knows that another is exposed to grave physical harm shall, to the extent that the same can be rendered without danger or peril to himself or without interference with important duties owed to others, give reasonable assistance to the exposed person unless that assistance or care is being provided by others.

(b) A person who provides reasonable assistance in compliance with subsection (a) of this section shall not be liable in civil damages unless his acts constitute gross negligence or unless he will receive or expects to receive remuneration. Nothing contained in this subsection shall alter existing law with respect to tort liability of a practitioner of the healing arts for acts committed in the ordinary course of his practice.

(c) A person who willfully violates subsection (a) of this section shall be fined not more than $100.00.

Wis. Stat. § 940.34. Duty to aid victim or report crime [; misdemeanor].

(2)(a) Any person who knows that a crime is being committed and that a victim is exposed to bodily harm shall summon law enforcement officers or other assistance or shall provide assistance to the victim.

. . .

(d) A person need not comply with this subsection if any of the following apply:

1. Compliance would place him or her in danger.

2. Compliance would interfere with duties the person owes to others.

3. In the circumstances described under par. (a), assistance is being summoned or provided by others.

. . .

(3) . . . Any person who provides . . . reasonable assistance under this section is immune from civil liability for his or her acts or omissions in providing the assistance. This immunity does not apply if the person receives or expects to receive compensation for providing the assistance.

How do these statutes differ? What legislative concerns do they reflect? These statutes are very rarely enforced. Why do you think that is? Given the expansion of duties documented in *Miranda* and *Kuntz*, do you think it still makes sense to claim that omission liability remains the exception? Or has it become the rule, even in states that do not have a general omissions statute?

Now compare the Vermont and Wisconsin statutes with the analogous provision in German criminal law. See generally Alberto Cadoppi, "Failure to Rescue and the Continental Criminal Law," in The Duty to Rescue 93 (Michael A. Menlowe et al., eds. 1993).

German Penal Code § 323c. Failure to Render Assistance

Whoever does not render assistance during accidents or common danger or need, although it is required and can be expected of him under the circumstances and, especially, is possible without substantial danger to himself and without violation of other important duties, shall be punished with imprisonment for not more than one year or a fine.

Note that the precursor to this provision was inserted into the German criminal code in 1935. After 1945, it was heavily criticized on the ground that it reflected a National Socialist view of law, and criminal law in particular, as a means of reflecting and strengthening communal life, at the expense of individual rights and without regard to the distinction between legal obligations and moral norms. The original version of the provision read as follows:

German Penal Code § 330c. Failure to Render Assistance

Whosoever, in case of accident or common danger, or necessity, does not render assistance, even though this is his duty according to sound popular sentiment and, in particular, does not comply with the request for assistance of a police agent, even though he could comply with the request without serious danger and without the infringement of other important duties, is punishable with prison for up to two years or with a fine.

10. Consider arguments for and against a duty to aid from the perspectives of the various traditional theories of punishment. Or are these arguments beside the point since existing duty-to-aid statutes are so rarely enforced that one should instead analyze the dispute as a purely symbolic

battle between those who believe the law should remain committed to a position of individualistic self-reliance, with strong protection for free action, and those who believe the law ought to (at least seem to) demand a certain level of altruism?

11. Two other arguments against a duty to aid, not based on the rationales for punishment, are also worth mentioning. One might object, for instance, that duties should be fully realizable and that the duty to save isn't: While one can go through life never killing, one can't fully realize a duty to save all those who could be easily saved. Now there are probably two quite distinct arguments imbedded in this single proposition; to wit, either that (i) duty-to-aid statutes are vague (this must be part of the implicit argument because the duty as stated, "save people in X circumstances only," is fully realizable) or (ii) to the degree the statute isn't vague, it draws morally arbitrary lines, that is, it is either too narrow or too broad (why should we have to save the particular subset of people the statute directs us to save?). In the end, the first argument may well fold into the second as complaints about the vagueness of a rule are often in fact complaints about its reach, in which case the critic would have to produce a different argument directed at the rule's substance, rather than our ability to abide by it. (For more on vagueness, see ch. 2.)

Furthermore, it might be argued that duty-to-aid statutes are unfair since they expose different people to the "risk" of liability on a fortuitous basis: whether they happen to encounter readily remediable suffering. Of course, though, at the purely "factual" level, the "risk" of disobeying "ordinary" *commission*-based criminal law rules is highly sensitive to distinct life circumstances as well. Even at the more closely analogous formal level, we've got plenty of statutes that only some can violate—and therefore only some are at risk of violating; for example, only men have to register for the draft; many immigration statutes can be violated only by non-citizens.

12. Tort law treats the duty to aid in very much the same way as does criminal law, with a similar relationship between rule and exception and even a similar progressive expansion of the exception at the expense of the "older rule."

Restatement (Second) of Torts § 314. Duty To Act For Protection Of Others

The fact that the actor realizes or should realize that action on his part is necessary for another's aid or protection does not of itself impose upon him a duty to take such action.

Comment:

a. The general rule stated in this Section should be read together with other sections which follow. Special relations may exist between the actor and the other, . . . which impose upon the actor the duty to take affirmative precautions for the aid or protection of the other. The actor may have control of a third person, or of land or chattels, and be under a duty to exercise such control. . . . The actor's prior conduct, whether tortious or innocent, may have created a situation of peril to the other, as a result of which the actor is under a duty to act to prevent harm.... The actor may have committed himself to the performance of an undertaking, gratuitously or under contract, and so may have assumed a duty of reasonable care for the protection of the other or even of a third person....

c. ... The result of the rule has been a series of older decisions to the effect that one human being, seeing a fellow man in dire peril, is under no legal obligation to aid him, but may sit on the dock, smoke his cigar, and watch the other drown. Such decisions have been condemned by legal writers as revolting to any moral sense, but thus far they remain the law. It appears inevitable that, sooner or later such extreme cases of morally outrageous and indefensible conduct will arise that there will be further inroads upon the older rule.

Would you expect tort liability for inaction to be narrower than criminal liability? Broader? Why? Note that tort law doesn't distinguish between innocent and tortious conduct giving rise to a situation of peril. Why? Does that make sense for criminal law as well (e.g., in *Kuntz*)?

2. OMISSIONS VS. COMMISSIONS

Vacco v. Quill

Supreme Court of the United States.
521 U.S. 793, 117 S.Ct. 2293 (1997).

■ CHIEF JUSTICE REHNQUIST delivered the opinion of the Court.

In New York, as in most States, it is a crime to aid another to commit or attempt suicide,[1] but patients may refuse even lifesaving medical treatment.[2] The question presented by this case is whether New York's prohibition on assisting suicide therefore violates the Equal Protection Clause of the Fourteenth Amendment. * * *

The Equal Protection Clause commands that no State shall "deny to any person within its jurisdiction the equal protection of the laws." This provision ... embodies a general rule that States must treat like cases alike but may treat unlike cases accordingly. If a legislative classification or distinction "neither burdens a fundamental right nor targets a suspect class, we will uphold [it] so long as it bears a rational relation to some legitimate end." Romer v. Evans, 517 U.S. 620, ___, 116 S.Ct. 1620, 1627, 134 L.Ed.2d 855 (1996). * * *

1. N.Y. Penal Law § 125.15 (McKinney 1987) ("Manslaughter in the second degree") provides: "A person is guilty of manslaughter in the second degree when ... (3) He intentionally causes or aids another person to commit suicide. Manslaughter in the second degree is a class C felony." Section 120.30 ("Promoting a suicide attempt") states: "A person is guilty of promoting a suicide attempt when he intentionally causes or aids another person to attempt suicide. Promoting a suicide attempt is a class E felony."

2. "It is established under New York law that a competent person may refuse medical treatment, even if the withdrawal of such treatment will result in death." Quill v. Koppell, 870 F.Supp. 78, 84 (S.D.N.Y.1994).

On their faces, neither New York's ban on assisting suicide nor its statutes permitting patients to refuse medical treatment treat anyone differently than anyone else or draw any distinctions between persons. Everyone, regardless of physical condition, is entitled, if competent, to refuse unwanted lifesaving medical treatment; no one is permitted to assist a suicide....

The Court of Appeals, however, concluded that some terminally ill people—those who are on life-support systems—are treated differently than those who are not, in that the former may "hasten death" by ending treatment, but the latter may not "hasten death" through physician-assisted suicide. This conclusion depends on the submission that ending or refusing lifesaving medical treatment "is nothing more nor less than assisted suicide." Unlike the Court of Appeals, we think the distinction between assisting suicide and withdrawing life-sustaining treatment, a distinction widely recognized and endorsed in the medical profession and in our legal traditions, is both important and logical; it is certainly rational.

* * *

New York is a case in point. The State enacted its current assisted-suicide statutes in 1965.[10] Since then, New York has acted several times to protect patients' common-law right to refuse treatment. In so doing, however, the State has neither endorsed a general right to "hasten death" nor approved physician-assisted suicide. Quite the opposite: The State has reaffirmed the line between "killing" and "letting die." * * *

[W]e disagree with respondents' claim that the distinction between refusing lifesaving medical treatment and assisted suicide is "arbitrary" and "irrational." Granted, in some cases, the line between the two may not be clear, but certainty is not required, even were it possible. Logic and contemporary practice support New York's judgment that the two acts are different, and New York may therefore, consistent with the Constitution, treat them differently. By permitting everyone to refuse unwanted medical treatment while prohibiting anyone from assisting a suicide, New York law follows a longstanding and rational distinction. * * *

The judgment of the Court of Appeals is reversed.

QUESTIONS AND COMMENTS

1. The entire enterprise of limiting omission liability to "exceptional" cases makes sense only if omissions and commissions can be meaningfully distinguished. This problem, however, is notoriously difficult. For what looks like an omission from one perspective may look like a commission from another. Does a father who raises his children in a dilapidated rat-infested home without heat or running water fail to perform his parental obligation or is he actively endangering the welfare of his children or perhaps engaging in child abuse? See Commonwealth v. Wallace, 817 A.2d 485 (Pa.Super.2002). Is filing a tax return without a required supplementa-

10. It has always been a crime, either by statute or under the common law, to assist a suicide in New York.

ry form failing to supply information or supplying false information? See Siravo v. United States, 377 F.2d 469 (1st Cir. 1967). One way of expanding omission liability, then, is to redefine omissions as commissions, thus circumventing the additional constraints placed on omission liability (most importantly, the requirement of a duty). Given these concerns, does it make sense to assign constitutional significance to the line between omission and commission?

2. In *Quill*, apart from the constitutional issue and apart from the questions of causation and intent, does it make a difference—from the standpoint of the actus reus and for purposes of criminal liability—whether I (1) fail to provide life support, (2) fail to continue providing life support, (3) turn off life support, (4) hasten death, (5) assist suicide, (6) commit murder? Should it?

3. In Bronston v. United States, 409 U.S. 352 (1973), the Supreme Court held that a witness could not be convicted of perjury for an answer that is literally true but not responsive to the question asked and arguably misleading by negative implication. (The witness first answered that he did not have a Swiss bank account. When then asked, "Have you ever?," he replied, "The company had an account there for about six months...." That was true; what he neglected to volunteer was that *he* had had a personal account as well.) Is it more accurate to say that such witnesses "lie" or that they "omit to correct fact-finder misimpression"? Does the Court's distinction between lying and non-responsiveness rest on an artificial view of how we communicate with one another? Or does nothing in the case turn on the "omission-commission" distinction at all? Is it instead a case about the responsibility of advocates to clarify ambiguity and the difficulty of administering a rule forbidding nonresponsive, misleading answers?

D. POSSESSION

Possession offenses have been notoriously difficult to reconcile with the act requirement:

> Possession is not a conduct offense. As commentators have pointed out for centuries, possession is not an act, it is a state of being, a status.[287] To possess something is to *be* in possession of it.
>
> To dismiss possession simply on the ground that it violates the so-called act requirement of Anglo–American criminal law, however, would be premature. The act requirement, from the outset, applied to common law offenses only, i.e., to offenses that traced their origins back through a grand chain of common law precedents, rather than to a specific statute that created a new offense.... English judges from very early on threw out possession indictments as violative of the act requirement only if they alleged a common law offense of possession, rather than invoked a statutory possession provision. Once it was settled that the possession indictment was brought under one of the

287. *E.g.*, Regina v. Dugdale, 1 El. & Bl. 435, 439 (1853) (Coleridge, J.).

increasing number of possession statutes, the common law's act requirement was no longer an issue.[288] The act requirement was as irrelevant to statutory possession as the mens rea requirement was to "statutory" rape.[289]

The common law's act requirement, therefore, does not stand in the way of modern possession statutes. And the thin slice of the act requirement constitutionalized by the U.S. Supreme Court in ... *Robinson v. California*[290] also can do little, by itself, to challenge possession offenses. The constitutional act requirement merely prohibits the criminalization of addiction in particular, and of sickness in general (or at least "having a common cold"). Possession doesn't criminalize an illness, at least not directly. The Supreme Court in *Robinson* went out of its way to reassure legislatures that they remained free to "impose criminal sanctions ... against the unauthorized manufacture, prescription, sale, purchase, or possession of narcotics."

Then there is the general uneasiness regarding omission offenses characteristic of American criminal law. Absent a clear duty to act, the failure to act is not criminal. If possession isn't an act, perhaps one should think of it as an omission, the omission to get rid of the item one possesses. But what is the duty that compels me to drop the shiny new pistol that my friend has just bought himself at the local gun store, or to toss out the baggie of cocaine I noticed in the glove compartment of my rental car? If one looked hard enough, perhaps one could find such a duty nestled in the criminalization of a possession that is defined as the failure to end it. But the point of requiring a specific duty for omission liability, the significance of the general unwillingness to criminalize omission, is precisely to reject omission liability absent specific and unambiguous provisions to the contrary.

Markus Dirk Dubber, "Policing Possession: The War on Crime and the End of Criminal Law," 91 J. Crim. L. & Criminology 829, 915–16 (2002).

Despite the well-recognized tension between possession offenses and the act requirement, possession offenses have come to occupy a central position in American criminal law:

Possession offenses ... are everywhere in modern American criminal law, on the books and in action. They fill our statute books, our arrest statistics, and, eventually, our prisons. By last count, New York law recognized no fewer than 153 possession offenses; one in every five prison or jail sentences handed out by New York courts in 1998 was imposed for a possession offense. That same year, possession offenses accounted for over 100,000 arrests in New York State, while drug possession offenses alone resulted in over 1.2 million arrests nationwide. * * *

288. *See, e.g.,* Rex v. Lennard, 1 Leach 90 (1772) (applying 8 & 9 Will. 3, c. 26 (Eng.)).

289. *See* Regina v. Prince, 2 L.R. Cr. Cas. Res. 154 (1875).

290. Robinson v. California, 370 U.S. 660 (1962).

> So broad is the reach of possession offenses, and so easy are they to detect and then to prove, that possession has replaced vagrancy as the sweep offense of choice. Unlike vagrancy, however, possession offenses promise more than a slap on the wrist. Backed by a wide range of penalties, they can remove undesirables for extended periods of time, even for life. . . .
>
> New York boasts no fewer than 115 felony possession offenses, all of which require a minimum of one year in prison; eleven of them provide for a maximum sentence of life imprisonment.

Markus Dirk Dubber, "Policing Possession: The War on Crime and the End of Criminal Law," 91 J. Crim. L. & Criminology 829, 834–35, 859 (2002).

QUESTIONS AND COMMENTS

1. What makes possession offenses such popular crime fighting tools? Why do police officers like them? Prosecutors? Many possession convictions arise out of traffic stops. Why? How else might evidence of possession be discovered? Think about everyday interactions between police and suspects.

2. Legislatures tend to offer a definitional solution to the problem of possession liability. Compare the following approaches. Are they convincing? Consistent? What sort of "bodily movement" is possession? Is it an act? Is it a voluntary act?

Model Penal Code § 2.01. Possession as an Act.

(4) Possession is an act . . . if the possessor knowingly procured or received the thing possessed or was aware of his control thereof for a sufficient period to have been able to terminate his possession.

Texas Penal Code § 1.07. Definitions.

(39) "Possession" means actual care, custody, control, or management.

Texas Penal Code § 6.01. Requirement of Voluntary Act or Omission.

(a) A person commits an offense only if he voluntarily engages in conduct, including an act, an omission, or possession.

(b) Possession is a voluntary act if the possessor knowingly obtains or receives the thing possessed or is aware of his control of the thing for a sufficient time to permit him to terminate his control.

Proposed New Federal Criminal Code § 301 (1971). Basis of Liability for Offenses.

(1) Conduct. A person commits an offense only if he engages in conduct, including an act, an omission, or possession, in violation of a statute which provides that the conduct is an offense.

3. Perhaps possession functions not so much as a culpable omission, or a punishable status, but as an *implicit* presumption:

> One way of thinking of possession offenses is to view them as criminalized presumptions of some other offense. In criminalizing possession, the legislature really criminalizes import, manufacture, purchase. Or forward-looking, the legislature really criminalizes use, sale, or export. In the latter variety, the prospective presumption resembles an implicit inchoate offense. So possession really is an attempt to use, sell, or export, or more precisely, possession is an attempt to attempt to use, sell, or export, that is, an inchoate inchoate offense....
>
> [T]he implicit presumption inherent in the concept of a possession offense reveals the modus operandi of possession, the secret of its success as a policing tool beyond legal scrutiny. Possession succeeds because it removes all potentially troublesome features to the level of legislative or executive discretion, an area that is notoriously difficult to scrutinize. In its design and its application, possession is, in doctrinal terms, a doubly inchoate offense, one step farther from the actual infliction of personal harm than ordinary inchoate offenses like attempt. In practical terms, it is an offense designed and applied to remove dangerous individuals even before they have had an opportunity to manifest their dangerousness in an ordinary inchoate offense. On its face, however, it does not look like an inchoate offense, nor does it look like a threat reduction measure targeting particular types of individuals.

Markus Dirk Dubber, "Policing Possession: The War on Crime and the End of Criminal Law," 91 J. Crim. L. & Criminology 829, 907–08 (2002).

4. Is it a problem that the legislature would set up an *implicit* presumption? Why doesn't the legislature, instead of defining a separate offense A (possession) that's really a presumption of some other offenses B (e.g., acquisition) or C (e.g., use), simply set up explicit presumptions of offenses B or C? Is this an attempt to circumvent whatever constitutional limitations might have been placed on the propriety of presumptions? Is it more difficult to disprove an implicit presumption than (non-conclusive) explicit ones?

5. As you read through the following materials, think about whether the implicit presumption of use or acquisition is appropriate. What happens if you add to the implicit presumption inherent in every possession case various explicit presumptions (e.g., from presence to possession, or from possession to possession with intent to use)? More generally, if possession is conceptualized as an inchoate offense (like attempt), can it—in the cases that follow—be justified in terms of the function of inchoate offenses, i.e., the identification and removal of abnormally dangerous individuals? Does the possessor "constitute a danger to organized society of sufficient magnitude to warrant the imposition of criminal sanctions" (People v. Dlugash, 41 N.Y.2d 725 (1977))?

6. It might be helpful to distinguish among distinct possession offenses if we consider possession an (implicit?) inchoate offense. In drug

possession cases, for instance, it seems likely that we believe the person charged with possession *intends* an (unobserved) future crime (sale, use). In that sense, possession is related to attempt law. In weapons possession cases, though, we may think the accused has created a risk, regardless of his future intentions. (A weapon may go off accidentally; it may be seized and used by someone with bad intentions; it may change the probability that the possessor will choose to use lethal force.) *All* risk creation offenses are subject to criticism: does it make sense to punish reckless driving rather than to punish only those drivers who cause vehicular accidents? But the important point for now is that in some cases, the possession offense is (in part) more akin to a risk-creation than an attempt offense.

Think too about international agreements designed to limit weapons proliferation that proscribe the possession, say, of certain forms of fissionable material. The possession of such material may be banned *both* because we believe that those nations observed to possess such material will, at some future date, deliberately transform them into weapons, and also because it is risky for such material to be around, regardless of the possessor's intentions, because it may inadvertently wind up in the hands of dangerous parties wholly unconnected to the initial possessor.

1. SIMPLE VS. COMPOUND POSSESSION

Possession offenses come in all shapes and sizes. It's particularly important to keep in mind the distinction between *simple* and *compound* possession, most notably possession with the intent to use the item possessed in some way. Drug criminal law, for instance, distinguishes between simple possession and possession with the intent to distribute. Although the distinction between simple and compound possession is often overlooked, it can make a difference, as in the following case.

People v. Lee

Court of Appeals of New York.
58 N.Y.2d 491, 448 N.E.2d 1328 (1983).

■ JONES, JUDGE.

On June 15, 1981 defendant was arrested and charged with violation of section 39–3 of the Village of Monticello Code which provides: "No person shall have in his possession, within the Village of Monticello, an open or unsealed bottle or container of an alcoholic beverage while such person is in any public place, including but not limited to any public highway, public street, public sidewalk, public alley, public parking lot or area, except for locations licensed for the sale of alcoholic beverages by the State of New York and the De Hoyos Park pavillion area, when such area is being used with the approval of the village authorities involved." Following denial by the Village Justice Court of defendant's motion to dismiss the charge on the ground that section 39–3 of the code is unconstitutional, defendant pleaded guilty. On appeal Sullivan County Court affirmed the judgment of conviction. * * *

.... The Village Justice Court upheld the statute as a reasonable exercise of the municipal police power ... Apparently recognizing the insufficiency of that analysis, County Court sustained the ordinance by reading the section "to prohibit possession *with the intent* of the possessor or another to consume in one of the proscribed public places" (emphasis in original). Whatever might be judged to be the constitutionality of an ordinance so drafted, it suffices for present purposes to note that the provision now before us prescribes no such element of intent. We are called on to pass on the constitutionality of the provision as enacted, not as it might have been drafted.

.... While reasonable regulation of the possession of alcoholic beverages might be upheld, outright proscription as criminal of possession only of a container of an alcoholic beverage has not been shown to bear a reasonable relation to the public good. Consumption in public may be an activity subject to criminal proscription but no reasonable argument could be advanced to support a proscription against public possession alone which, if uniformly enforced, would effectively foreclose the acquisition of all alcoholic beverages for all purposes.

Nor is the ordinance in this case saved by the fact that all that is proscribed is possession of alcoholic beverages in "open or unsealed" containers. The condition of openness in itself in no way threatens the public good, as the County Court recognized when it imported an intent to consume in public. While, of course, a container must be opened or unsealed to permit consumption, it cannot be presumed that every opening or unsealing is for the purpose of direct human consumption or least of all for the purpose of direct human consumption in a public place.

Absent any legislative findings or other demonstration that there exists a reasonable relation between mere possession of an opened or unsealed container of an alcoholic beverage and the public good, we conclude that the Monticello ordinance cannot withstand constitutional scrutiny. The proscription strikes down what may well be innocuous behavior and undertakes to make criminal conduct which would not carry the slightest taint of corruption or impropriety and which a person of ordinary intelligence would not perceive as criminal (cf. *Papachristou v. City of Jacksonville*, 405 U.S. 156).

Accordingly, the order of the County Court should be reversed, the judgment of conviction vacated, and the accusatory instrument dismissed.

■ CHIEF JUDGE COOKE (dissenting).

The majority errs ... in holding the ordinance unconstitutional as lacking a rational basis....

[T]he village enacted an ordinance proscribing only the possession of open containers of alcohol in public places. The regulation, designed to promote public order, is narrowly drawn. Inasmuch as licensed liquor stores are prohibited from selling liquor in unsealed containers and bars and restaurants may not sell open containers of alcohol for off-premises consumption, the ordinance does not affect the ability of persons to consume alcohol in licensed establishments or to purchase such beverages for consumption at home. The ordinance merely prohibits a person who buys a sealed container of an alcoholic beverage from opening it in the proscribed public places.

The majority concedes that a municipality may criminally prohibit the public consumption of alcohol. The ordinance here goes one small step further by proscribing the possession in public of an open container of alcohol. If a prohibition against public consumption is constitutional as a valid exercise of the police power, so must a ban on possession of open containers be valid. Both proscriptions have a rational basis in the same public policy—avoidance of disorders and related problems created by the consumption of alcoholic beverages in unlicensed public places. As with the ban on public consumption, the prohibition against possessing an open container punishes a discrete act, rather than a person's status. * * *

Finally, it should be emphasized that there is no evidence in the record that the ordinance has been enforced in an arbitrary or discriminatory manner against only certain portions of the citizenry.

QUESTIONS AND COMMENTS

1. The majority cites a well-known case (Papachristou v. City of Jacksonville, 405 U.S. 156 (1972)), in which the Supreme Court struck down a vagrancy statute on vagueness grounds (see ch. 2). The statute provided, among other things, that "rogues and vagabonds, or ... disorderly persons ... shall be deemed vagrants." What do possession statutes have in common with vagrancy statutes? How do they differ? Is the statute in *Lee* vague? Does it invite arbitrary enforcement?

2. Does possession punish status in fact, if not on its face? Are drug and gun possession in particular so common that possession statutes are bound to be enforced only against certain people, say, in "high crime areas"? Cf. Illinois v. Wardlow, 528 U.S. 119 (2000) (gun and drug possession searches in "high crime areas"); see generally Markus Dirk Dubber, "Policing Possession: The War on Crime and the End of Criminal Law," 91 J. Crim. L. & Criminology 829 (2002). This focus on status—and the distinction between who may, and who may not, possess—is occasionally made explicit. See, e.g., N.J. Stat. § 2C:39–7(b) ("Certain Persons Not to Have Weapons"); United States v. Leviner, 31 F.Supp.2d 23, 26–27 (D. Mass. 1998) (federal felon-in-possession (of a firearm) statute "the prototypical status offense"). Are explicitly status-based possession offenses less troubling than general possession offenses? More troubling? How about statutes that criminalize possession by anyone, and then grant certain persons an "exemption" from liability? Consider the following statute:

N.Y. Penal Law § 265.20. Exemptions

a. Sections 265.01, 265.02, 265.03, 265.04, 265.05, 265.10, 265.11, 265.12, 265.13, 265.15 and 270.05 [weapons offenses] shall not apply to:

1. Possession of any of the weapons, instruments, appliances or substances ... by the following:

(a) Persons in the military service of the state of New York....

(b) Police officers....

(c) Peace officers....

(d) Persons in the military or other service of the United States....

(e) Persons employed in fulfilling defense contracts with the government of the United States....

2. Possession of a machine-gun, firearm, switchblade knife, gravity knife, pilum ballistic knife, billy or blackjack by a warden, superintendent, headkeeper or deputy of a state prison, penitentiary, workhouse, county jail or other institution for the detention of persons....

11. Possession of a pistol or revolver by a police officer or sworn peace officer of another state while conducting official business within the state of New York.

b. Section 265.01 [criminal possession of a weapon] shall not apply to possession of that type of billy commonly known as a "police baton" which is twenty-four to twenty-six inches in length and no more than one and one-quarter inches in thickness by members of an auxiliary police force....

Note that this statute exempts all covered persons (including off-duty police officers) from liability not only for simple possession offenses, but also for compound possession offenses, including possession of a deadly instrument with the intent to use it unlawfully. People v. Desthers, 73 Misc.2d 1085, 343 N.Y.S.2d 887 (Crim. Ct. 1973).

3. How significant is the difference between possessing an open container and possessing an open container with the intent to drink from it? Why else would one open a beer bottle? A soda can? A juice bottle? What if the defendant intends to transport an open bottle from one place in which it could be legally consumed (for instance, one's private home) to another (a friend's home)? What about a half-full glass of beer?

4. Why would a legislature criminalize the possession of alcohol, rather than its possession with intent to consume it? Its possession with intent to consume it, rather than its actual consumption? Its consumption rather than its excessive consumption? Its excessive consumption rather than intoxication? Intoxication rather than behavior while intoxicated? Behavior while intoxicated rather than harm caused by that behavior? What is lost and what is gained as one moves from the criminalization of possession to the criminalization of harm?

2. ACTUAL VS. CONSTRUCTIVE POSSESSION

Another important distinction in the criminal law of possession is that between *actual* (or *physical*) and *constructive* possession. Constructive possession derives from a person's control over an area, or over another person in actual possession of an item. Possession is defined as "dominion or control" (or "dominion *and* control") over an item, with actual and constructive possession representing two ways in which dominion or control can manifest itself.

People v. Rivera

Supreme Court of New York, Appellate Division, First Department.
77 A.D.2d 538, 430 N.Y.S.2d 88 (1980).

Judgment of conviction, after non-jury trial, Supreme Court, New York County rendered June 21, 1979, affirmed. During a street altercation between members of two families, the Riveras and the Guadalupes, defendant Felix Rivera called to his brother Raul: "Get the gun!" Raul ran to his own home and returned with a loaded weapon. William Guadalupe advanced on Raul and Felix yelled to his brother to kill William. Raul fired and William fell dead. Felix then indicated German Guadalupe and told Raul to shoot him. The latter complied, wounding his victim. Defendant was convicted only of possession of the weapon with intent to use it unlawfully against another (Penal Law § 265.03).

On this appeal, defendant raises claimed repugnance of the verdict, as well as absence of actual possession. There was no repugnance evidence in the court's verdict which, acquitting defendant of homicide and assault counts, convicted of possession of the gun with intent to commit the assault of which acquitted. The court, while engaging in some discussion with counsel at the close of the case, did not articulate the reasons for the verdict. We cannot speculate why the court did not convict defendant-appellant of either the homicide or the assault count, whether it was because the evidence was not believed, or whether this was exercise of a prerogative to convict of a lesser crime because the victim "deserved what he got" a rough but not unknown form of justice. There was no repugnance in this verdict, inconsistency perhaps, but that is always within the scope of authority of a trier of the fact. . . .

As to whether this defendant had possession of the weapon, as defined in Penal Law § 10.00(8), while it is true that brother Felix never had the gun in his hand, he had complete "dominion" and "control" over it, commanding brother Raul to get it and bring it and to pull the trigger. Raul's act was that of Felix as though Felix had used his muscles instead of his voice and his will. Possession was in both and the requisite intent resided in the mind of each.

People v. Valot

Court of Appeals of Michigan.
33 Mich.App. 49, 189 N.W.2d 873 (1971).

■ CHURCHILL, JUDGE.

Defendant, Harold Valot, was charged with having had possession and control of marijuana contrary to the provisions of Mich. Comp. Laws § 335.153. He was convicted by nonjury trial. . . .

Three Redford Township policemen went to a motel in their township in response to a call from a motel employee. Upon answering they learned from the motel manager that he was concerned about the continued use of one of the motel rooms by a number of "hippie-type people". . . .

[When the police entered the motel room they observed five persons all apparently asleep. There were four marijuana cigarettes on a desk. There was also a water pipe, with marijuana residue in the pipe near where Valot and his girl friend were sleeping. Next to the water pipe was a marijuana cigarette butt. On another bed a man was sleeping and near him on the floor was another marijuana cigarette butt. Sprawled on the floor somewhere was another man and another woman. Valot had paid the rent for the room for one day. His girl friend paid the rent for the second day; he offered to reimburse her but she refused. The rent for the third day had not been paid.] * * *

The legislature used the words "possession" and "control" in the narcotics statute in their commonly understood sense, and not in a restricted, technical sense. The trial judge conceded the possibility that someone, unbeknownst to defendant, brought the marijuana into the room, but nevertheless did not have a reasonable or fair doubt as to defendant's control thereof. It was a fact question. There was strong circumstantial evidence to support the court's findings. Defendant's control of the marijuana in the room was a fact reasonably inferred from the evidence.

Upon timely motion of either party, or on its own initiative, the trial court may correct the judgment to disclose that defendant was convicted of control rather than possession of marijuana. His conviction is affirmed.

■ LEVIN, J. (dissenting).

I dissent because it is not a crime to be in control of a room where marijuana is found and because the people failed to prove that the defendant, Harold Eugene Valot, Jr., was in possession or control of marijuana.

* * *

One or more of the persons in the room possessed or controlled the marijuana that was in it. There was, however, no evidence as to who brought the marijuana into the room or who used it. The people did not prove by direct or circumstantial evidence that Valot, rather than another person or persons in the room, was himself in actual possession of the marijuana found in the room. There was no evidence, direct or circumstantial, that Valot ever used marijuana or did so on this occasion....

If Valot did not bring the marijuana into the room or smoke it—and, again, there was no evidence that he had—then someone else did. It is not reasonable to infer from Valot's control of the room and his knowledge that others in the room possessed or were using marijuana, and I quote from the majority opinion, that Valot, rather than one or another of the other persons in the room, was in "control of the marijuana in the room".

* * *

[U]nless the trier of fact has the discretion to convict any one who was in the room essentially of the crime of being in a room where marijuana is in use, knowing that it is in use, then there must be some independent evidence of the joint enterprise—evidence in addition to the evidence that the persons charged were all present in the room when the marijuana was used.

The rented motel room bore the earmarks of a crash pad. The ebb and flow of humanity in and out of the room indicates a somewhat unconventional living style. Conventional notions as to control and possession are simply inapplicable to crash-pad communal life. I think we should know a great deal more about such societal patterns than we do before we declare our satisfaction that it is reasonable to infer that whoever happens to have paid the rent for a motel room occupied by a number of persons is in control or possession of marijuana or other property belonging to the persons moving in and out of the room.

But, even if we apply conventional notions of control and possession, Valot's conviction should not be affirmed. * * *

I recognize that leaving the matter at large so that prosecutors can charge whomever they wish and judges and juries can convict those who seem culpable without differentiable proof facilitates law enforcement.

The legislature may, if it wishes, amend the statute to make presence in a room where marijuana is in use a crime.[9] In the meantime, enforcement of the law prohibiting possession and control of marijuana is not, in my opinion, of sufficient overriding public importance to justify departure from fundamental principles long established.

The legislature made possession and control of marijuana a crime. It is not a crime for one in possession or control of a motel room to invite or allow hippy types in the room or to fail to evict guests smoking marijuana. The legislature has not yet made a citizen responsible for the indulgence of others in his presence.

QUESTIONS AND COMMENTS

1. Possession offenses often function as convenient fall-back offenses. If other charges don't stick or are thought to be inappropriate for some reason, there is a good chance that a possession case can be made. What function does the possession offense serve in *Rivera*? Also consider the following case (People v. Young, 94 N.Y.2d 171 (1999) (rejecting claim of vindictive sentencing)).

> Defendant was charged with burglarizing two houses in April 1991 and stealing, among other things, two 12–gauge shotguns, ammunition, two diamond rings and a stereo set. After a jury trial, he was convicted of first–degree robbery, first– and second–degree burglary, criminal possession of stolen property in the fourth and fifth degrees, and grand larceny in the fourth degree. Supreme Court sentenced defendant, as a persistent violent felony offender, to concurrent indeterminate prison terms of 25 years to life on the first–degree robbery and first–degree burglary counts, to run consecutively to a sentence of 20 years to life on the second–degree burglary count. In addition, the court sentenced

9. The Massachusetts legislature has so enacted. See 3A Annotated Laws of Massachusetts, 1970 Cum Supp, C 94, § 213A, which provides:

"Whoever is present at a place where he knows a narcotic drug is illegally kept or deposited, or whoever is in the company of a person, knowing that said person is illegally in possession of a narcotic drug, or whoever conspires with another person to violate the narcotic drugs law, may be arrested without a warrant by an officer or inspector whose duty it is to enforce the narcotic drugs law, and may be punished by imprisonment in the state prison for not more than five years, or by imprisonment in a jail or house of correction for not more than two years or by a fine of not less than five hundred dollars nor more than five thousand dollars."

defendant, as a second felony offender, to concurrent two–to–four year terms on the fourth–degree possession of stolen property and grand larceny counts. Finally, defendant received a one–year sentence on the fifth–degree possession of stolen property count. Defendant's aggregate sentence totaled 45 years to life. * * *

The Appellate Division reversed defendant's conviction, holding that his confession was the product of an unlawful arrest. Following retrial before a different Judge ..., defendant was convicted of criminal possession of stolen property in the fourth degree and acquitted of the remaining counts.[a] ...

The Judge then sentenced defendant, as a persistent felony offender, to an indeterminate prison term of 25 years to life, stating that he was not "imposing any sentence upon [defendant] for a crime for which [defendant was] acquitted." Rather, the sentence was based "solely and exclusively [on] those convictions that I have already referred to, not only presently, but those I have found in your past to be determinative of this sentence." The court continued:

> "[B]ased upon everything I have considered * * * there is no question in my mind that you require a lengthy period of incarceration, including possible lifetime supervision. There is also no question in my mind, since I have had the opportunity to review all the papers before me and make the findings * * * that you are a scourge to the community. I don't have any question whatsoever on that particular point."

2. Assuming the facts were as stated in *Rivera*, how could Felix be guilty of possession but not of homicide and assault? Could he constructively possess Raul's weapon without also constructively using it? Could Raul possess it actually and Felix constructively? Could Raul be guilty of assault and homicide if Felix is not?

3. *Rivera* and *Valot* illustrate two varieties of constructive possession: (i) dominion and control over a person (who was in actual possession of item in question) and (ii) dominion and control over an area (where the item in question is present).

Did Felix in fact have control over his brother? Can a person have control over another person as she would over an area? How does control over a person manifest itself? Did Raul commit an act? A voluntary act? What if Felix (who, let's assume, is ten years older and 100 pounds heavier) instead had picked Raul up and dropped him on top of one of the Guadalupes, causing serious injury?

Valot was in control of the drugs because he was in control of the motel room (and, less clearly, of the people in it). Does (or should) anything turn in *Valot* on the fact that the defendant paid for the room? Is the court (implicitly) asserting that someone who "owns" a space has a duty that a "mere guest" would not have to stop others from bringing marijuana into

a. Possession of stolen property in the fourth degree is a class E felony, with a sentence range of 1–4 years. N.Y. Penal Law § 70.00. A "persistent felony offender" may be sentenced to between 15 and 25 years to life. N.Y. Penal Law § 70.10.—EDS.

the space? Because it is socially less awkward for the "owner" to do so than another guest? Could *that* give rise to a duty? Would the court have found any and all of Valot's *guests* to be guilty?

4. Am I in dominion or control of substances in my bloodstream or in my urine? Can a possession conviction rest solely on the results of a blood test? State v. Flinchpaugh, 232 Kan. 831, 659 P.2d 208 (1983) (no). Of a urinalysis? State v. Schroeder, 674 N.W.2d 827 (S.D. 2004) (yes). Are the test results evidence of prior, or of present, possession? What is the *voluntary act* in having traces of a controlled substance in my blood? (Once an intoxicant has entered the bloodstream, am I in control of it, or is it in control of me?) How about cases in which the defendant has ingested balloons filled with drugs?

5. Consider the function of the doctrine of constructive possession in modern possession law in light of its role in the historical development of the law of larceny, which prohibits interfering with another person's *possession* (rather than ownership) of a thing (see ch. 11, infra):

> Originally, servants could not steal objects entrusted to them by their lord for the simple reason that they had legally acquired possession of them. What they already possessed they couldn't steal, since larceny was the interference with someone else's possession. This loophole was eventually closed to better protect the lord's property against disloyal—but not yet thieving—servants. So the courts invented the concept of constructive possession. The servant, it was decided in the eighteenth century, had only "custody" of the objects handed to him by his lord, while possession, constructive possession, remained with the master. Hence, when the servant ran away, or otherwise misappropriated the objects constructively possessed by his lord, he committed larceny.

Markus Dirk Dubber, "Policing Possession: The War on Crime and the End of Criminal Law," 91 J. Crim. L. & Criminology 829, 938–39 (2002).

Note that ownership likewise is not a prerequisite for liability for a possession offense:

> There is no requirement that the prosecution prove that an accused has title to the contraband since guilt may be established regardless of whether it belongs to someone else. Indeed, there is a marked distinction between possession and ownership, to the extent that one may possess a chattel or thing without being its owner and, conversely, may own something without possessing it. Parenthetically, although proof of title, interest or even equity in or claim to the [contraband] is not essential, testimony in that direction might be relevant to the subject of possession, particularly where it is constructive in nature.

People v. Sierra, 45 N.Y.2d 56, 61 (1978).

6. Is "being in control of" an act, or more—or less—of an act than "being in possession of"? What about "being in the presence of"?

The dissent in *Valot* points out that the Michigan legislature had not criminalized mere presence, but implies that it could do just that if it were so inclined. But what about the constitutional proscription against criminalizing status, where presence—unlike possession—isn't even *defined* in terms of an act (acquisition) or an omission (failure to divest)? Or might we define presence likewise as the act of placing oneself within the drug's presence or as the failure to discontinue it (by removing oneself from the drug's presence, i.e., as the absence of nonpresence, or the absence of absence, for short)?

The Massachusetts general drug presence statute cited by the *Valot* dissent has been replaced by a narrower heroin presence statute (Mass. Gen. Laws ch. 94C, § 35), which now reads (emphasis added):

> Any person who is knowingly present at a place where heroin is kept or deposited ..., or *any person who is in the company of a person, knowing that said person is in possession of heroin* ..., shall be punished by imprisonment for not more than one year or by a fine of not more than one thousand dollars, or both....

Being in the presence of drugs other than heroin thus no longer exposes one to criminal liability in Massachusetts. Commonwealth v. Camerano, 42 Mass.App. 363, 677 N.E.2d 678 (1997) (marijuana). In fact, courts have overturned some constructive possession convictions on the ground that upholding them would "come[] perilously close to endorsing guilt by presence at the scene of contraband." Commonwealth v. Sespedes, 442 Mass. 95, 810 N.E.2d 790 (2004) (no constructive possession where defendant had access to, and was briefly present in, vacant apartment where hidden drugs were found).

Note, however, that it is possible to be liable for both "being in the presence of" *and* "possessing" the same heroin. Commonwealth v. Fernandez, 48 Mass.App. 530, 723 N.E.2d 527 (2000) (presence is not a lesser included offense of possession, because I can be present without possessing, and vice versa).

7. *Sentencing.* Possession is not only a separate offense, but also increases criminal liability for other offenses. In some offenses, gun possession appears as an offense element. For instance, one variety of first degree trespass in the New York Penal Law requires that the offender "[p]ossesses, or knows that another participant in the crime possesses, an explosive or a deadly weapon." N.Y. Penal Law § 140.17(1). See also N.Y. Penal Law § 120.55 (stalking in the second degree); see generally Markus Dirk Dubber, "Policing Possession: The War on Crime and the End of Criminal Law," 91 J. Crim. L. & Criminology 829, 902 (2002).

More commonly, gun possession is an aggravating factor considered at sentencing. The first major case on so-called "sentencing factors"—which, unlike offense elements, didn't have to be proved beyond a reasonable doubt at trial, but could be found at sentencing under a preponderance of the evidence standard—involved a provision that imposed a mandatory minimum sentence on anyone who "visibly possessed a firearm" while committing certain felonies. McMillan v. Pennsylvania, 477 U.S. 79, 106 S.Ct. 2411 (1986). The federal sentencing guidelines contain several provisions dealing with gun possession as an aggravating factor. See, e.g., U.S.S.G. § 2D1.1(b) (enhancement if "a dangerous weapon ... was possessed"); U.S.S.G. § 5C1.2(2) (no downward departure if defendant "possess[ed] a firearm or other dangerous weapon ... in connection with the offense"). Courts have struggled to differentiate between these provisions. See, e.g., United States v. Zavalza–Rodriguez, 379 F.3d 1182 (10th Cir. 2004) (contrasting § 2D1.1(b), which requires mere presence—i.e., "a temporal and spatial relation ... between the weapon, the drug trafficking activity, and the defendant"—with § 5C1.2(2), which requires "active possession"). The harshest possession aggravator, however, is 18 U.S.C. § 924(c), which imposes mandatory minimum sentences between five years and life imprisonment without release for possession of a firearm "during and in relation to any crime of violence or drug trafficking crime." (See *United States v. Angelos*, ch. 1 supra.)

8. *Presumptions.* The state's burden of proving constructive possession, particularly in drug and weapon possession cases, is significantly lightened by means of presumptions arising from the defendant's presence near the item in question. Common presumptions of drug or weapon possession attach to presence in a car or a room that is found to contain the item whose possession is prohibited. (See *People v. Leyva*, supra.) Once possession is established, further presumptions may permit *forward* inferences to transform strict possession into *knowing* possession, simple possession into compound possession (e.g., possession with intent to distribute or to use the item possessed), or *backward* inferences to transform possession into another offense altogether, such as importation, manufacture, transfer, or larceny (or other forms of illegal acquisition).

Among the more controversial presumptions in the law of possession is the presumption of constructive possession. Should a presumption of possession attach in the following scenario?

> Rivas, the front-seat passenger, [was convicted] of the offense of possession ..., based on a theory of constructive possession. [T]he only evidence upon which the government relied to implicate Rivas is that he had been seated in the front passenger seat next to a center console upon which the police discovered two ziplock bags of cocaine while Rivas was outside of the car speaking to an acquaintance on the sidewalk several feet away from the car. There was no evidence presented on the length of time that Rivas had been in the car or whether Rivas was engaged in an ongoing drug venture with Melgar, the driver, or with the two passengers in the backseat.

Rivas v. United States, 734 A.2d 655 (D.C. 1999) (presumption attaches because sufficient evidence that defendant "knew of the location of the [contraband] and that he had both the power and the intention to exercise dominion or control over it"). Is the driver (the owner?) of a car in control of items found in the trunk? See State v. Smith, 374 Md. 527, 823 A.2d 664 (2003) (lessee/driver presumed to know contents of rental vehicle, including weapon found in trunk under passenger's jacket).

9. *Sole vs. Joint Possession.* Another convenient feature of constructive possession is that it permits *joint* possession, which is distinguished from *sole* (or *exclusive*) possession. If an item is under the "dominion and control" of several persons (say because it is within their reach), then each person can be found to constructively possess it. This means, as a matter of

criminal procedure, that each occupant of a car is under suspicion of being in constructive possession of contraband detected in the car and is subject to arrest on that ground (provided none comes forward and admits to sole possession). See Maryland v. Pringle, 540 U.S. 366 (2003).

In the typical "joint possession" case, does the legislature believe that all of the occupants of the car *really* jointly acquired the contraband or intend to use it together? Or does the legislature simply worry that all will "get away" with a crime that *one* of them must have committed? Is it just to convict a particular defendant of possessing marijuana because a friend bought or intended to use it? So long as he had adequate opportunity to dissociate himself from the friend's activity? In the end, is joint possession an instance of group, rather than individual, liability? Of liability based on presence alone?

What to do with a constructive possession case against one person where another person is in sole (and actual) possession of the item in question? Consider the following case.

> Shortly after midnight on August 31, 1990, two police officers on Amsterdam Avenue in Manhattan, near the intersection of West 156th Street, heard gunshots from across the street and saw Felix Sanchez and Ricardo Agostini firing handguns at an unarmed black male. As the officers ran toward the scene, Sanchez attempted to shoot one of them, but his pistol jammed. Sanchez fled through an alley one block ... and entered a van driven by the defendant.... The van ... was stopped shortly thereafter ... two blocks away from where Sanchez had entered it. When defendant and Sanchez were removed from the van, a .32 calibre pistol was found on a bag in the space between the front bucket seats, the pistol still warm from a recent firing and still jammed with a spent bullet in the chamber.
>
> In a joint indictment, ... Sanchez and the defendant were charged with criminal possession of a weapon in the third degree....
>
> Defendant moved to dismiss the indictment for insufficiency. He contended that the possession count, based on the presumption contained in Penal Law § 265.15(3), was insufficient because, inasmuch as the gun had been seen in Sanchez's possession, the exception contained in paragraph (a) of that section applied. * * *
>
> Penal Law § 265.15(3)(a) provides that the presence in an automobile of "any firearm ... is presumptive evidence of its possession by all persons occupying such automobile at the time such weapon ... is found, except ... if such weapon ... is found upon the person of one of the occupants therein."
>
> [B]y the terms of the statute, the exception applies only where the weapon is found on the person of another citing, as illustrative, instances where the weapon was found under one person's shirt or other items of clothing or in a pocket. The exception may also apply where an officer observes a person remove a weapon from his or her person immediately prior to arrest in an attempt to hide it somewhere inside an automobile. However, where the officer does not observe the

weapon in the exclusive possession of any one person immediately prior to or at the time of arrest, the exception is inapplicable.

In this case, the weapon was found between the front bucket seats of the van and there was no testimony from [the arresting officer] indicating he had observed either Sanchez or defendant in possession of the weapon immediately prior to arrest. The exception is, therefore, inapplicable. . . .

■ CIPARICK, JUDGE (concurring).

While I am constrained to agree with the result reached by the majority, the injustice created under the facts of this case by a literal reading of the exception that the weapon be found on the person of an occupant in a motor vehicle merits consideration.

Here, the facts clearly demonstrate that the seized weapon had been carried into a waiting van by the individual who attempted to shoot the police officers in his pursuit. The fleeing shooter was then apprehended in the passenger seat of that van minutes after the shooting incident, and the warm pistol jammed with a spent bullet was found between the seats occupied by him and the driver of the van, who by all accounts was in the driver's seat throughout the incident. Certainly, under these circumstances, the efficacy of attributing possession of the weapon to the defendant driver by way of a rebuttable presumption is dubious and compels a result at odds with the legislative impetus for this exception (see, People v. Lemmons, 40 N.Y.2d 505, 510–512, 387 N.Y.S.2d 97, 354 N.E.2d 836 [statute prompted by the frequency of cases in which the People were unable to secure any conviction when a weapon was concealed in an automobile with more than one occupant]). In this regard, I believe it would be useful for the Legislature to consider an amendment to Penal Law § 265.15(3)(a) to remedy this statutory injustice.

People v. Verez, 83 N.Y.2d 921 (1994).

How could the legislature amend the presumption of possession statute to address the concurrence's concerns?

3. "INNOCENT" POSSESSION AND OTHER DEFENSES

Courts have been reluctant to recognize general defenses in possession cases that go beyond attempts to negate elements of the offense. For instance, it has been held that the justification of self-defense is not available in a possession prosecution. As a result, someone who shoots and kills an attacker in justifiable self-defense may nonetheless be liable for unlawful possession of the weapon used in her lawful defense:

> The essence of the illegal conduct defined in sections 265.01–265.05 of the Penal Law is the act of possessing a weapon unlawfully. . . . Once the unlawful possession of the weapon is established, the possessory crime is complete and any unlawful use of the weapon is punishable as a separate crime. * * * [A] person either possesses a weapon lawfully or he does not and he may not avoid the criminal charge by claiming that he possessed the weapon for his protection. Justification may

> excuse otherwise unlawful use of the weapon but it is difficult to imagine circumstances where it could excuse unlawful possession of it.

People v. Almodovar, 62 N.Y.2d 126 (1984); see also People v. Pons, 68 N.Y.2d 264 (1986) (self-defense cannot be defense to weapons possession because self-defense applies to *use of physical force*, not simple possession of a weapon or even possession with the intent to use it).

Courts that do recognize self-defense as a limited defense in possession cases, disagree about how to frame the defense (element-negating vs. justification), and relatedly, about who bears the burden of proving (or disproving) it. See United States v. Deleveaux, 205 F.3d 1292 (11th Cir. 2000); see also State v. Harmon, 104 N.J. 189, 516 A.2d 1047 (1986) (self-defense justification may be available in possession cases "[o]nly in those rare and momentary circumstances where an individual arms himself spontaneously to meet an immediate danger"); cf. United v. Gomez, 92 F.3d 770 (9th Cir. 1996) (recognizing limited *necessity* defense to federal felon-in-possession statute where defendant-informer was in fear for his life after his identity had been revealed in an indictment).

Given the unavailability of general defenses, some courts have tried to graft a narrow defense of "innocent" (or "temporary") possession onto apparently absolute possession prohibitions, as the following case illustrates.

People v. E.C.

Supreme Court of New York, Criminal Term, Queens County.
195 Misc.2d 680, 761 N.Y.S.2d 443 (2003).

■ JOEL L. BLUMENFELD, J.S.C.

The issue presented in this case is whether ... the temporary and lawful possession of one-eighth of an ounce of cocaine is a defense to criminal possession of a controlled substance in the fourth degree (Penal Law § 220.09 [1]). * * *

.... [T]he defendant ... was employed by Primo Security to work as a bouncer at a bar, was told to confiscate illegal contraband before anyone was allowed inside, and that their policy was that if anything was confiscated, he should contact Primo who would turn in the contraband to the police. On the night in question, the defendant confiscated 14 packets of cocaine from a patron on his way into the bar. Prior to his having an opportunity to contact Primo, the police responded to noise outside the bar at which time the defendant gave the police the 14 packets of cocaine. * * *

The foundation for the common law defense [of temporary and lawful possession] originates with the possession of a weapon. In *People v. Persce,* 204 N.Y. 397, 97 N.E. 877, 27 N.Y. Cr. 41 (1912), the defendant possessed a "slungshot." The court, in dicta, recognized that the possession of a weapon as part of a criminal act did not mean mere possession. In *Persce,* the court mentioned two exceptions: (1) "legal ownership of a weapon in a collection of curious and interesting objects" and (2) possession "which might result temporarily and incidentally from the performance of some lawful act, as disarming a wrongful possessor."

The Common Law defense was followed in *People v. La Pella,* 272 N.Y. 81, 4 N.E.2d 943 (1936), in which the defendant found a firearm in a public toilet, put it in his pocket and intended to give it to the police after meeting his wife on a nearby street corner. Apparently, some 20 minutes after picking up the firearm, the defendant saw a detective and without any request, gave the detective the firearm. The court held that it was error for the trial court not to instruct the jury as to the common law defense: "that if this defendant found this pistol as claimed by him, and if he thereafter took this gun for the purpose of delivering it to an officer or to a police station, that he was performing a civic duty, and that such possession was not the possession intended by section 1897." . . .

The People do not dispute the existence of this common law defense with respect to weapons, rather they argue against applying it to other possessory crimes such as criminal possession of a controlled substance. . . .

The People seem to be taking an absolutist position to the temporary and innocent possession of a controlled substance. This position makes little sense in real life and runs contrary to public policy considerations. It also allows for certain factual situations to be criminalized where it is clear that the state would not want to punish people doing the right thing. While many real life situations come to mind, three intriguing ones came up in oral argument.

First, if a parent discovers illegal drugs in their child's bedroom and decided to confront the child with these drugs—just like we see on the public service announcements on television—the parent would be guilty of a degree of criminal possession of a controlled substance under the People's absolutist position.

Second, if a teacher, dean, guidance counselor or principal in a school came into possession of a controlled substance by either taking it from a student or finding it in a desk, open locker, the hall or any other part of the school, the teacher, dean, guidance counselor or principal would be guilty of a degree of criminal possession of a controlled substance under the People's absolutist position.

The third example might be the most intriguing especially in drug cases. During the trial, like other drugs cases, after the People entered into evidence the 14 packets of cocaine, they published them to the jury. The jurors, one-by-one, took the cocaine into their hands and looked at it and then passed them to the next juror. The last juror returned the 14 packets to the court. Under this situation, each juror would be guilty of a degree of criminal possession of a controlled substance under the People's absolutist position.

The same policy consideration for weapons are equally valid for controlled substances. We want people, not just law enforcement, to confiscate illegal drugs from their children and students and turn them in to the proper authorities. We want people who find drugs on the street to pick them up and turn them in to the proper authorities. We want jurors to be able to examine evidence without fear of prosecution. It makes no sense whatsoever to criminalize this type of behavior. It runs contrary to public policy....

Accordingly, the jury will be instructed [on the temporary and lawful possession defense.] [I]t will be up to the jury to decide whether the defendant was telling the truth and whether the defense applies.

QUESTIONS AND COMMENTS

1. How could "innocent" possession *not* be a defense? How would you characterize the defense of "innocent possession"? Element-negating (what offense element would it be negating)? Justification? Excuse? If it is a justification or an excuse, should it be an affirmative defense? (Justifications and excuses are affirmative defenses under the Model Penal Code.) If it is a justification or excuse, why wouldn't it be covered by general defenses (like self-defense or duress)? Note that New York does not permit justification defenses in possession cases. See People v. Almodovar, 62 N.Y.2d 126 (1984).

In United States v. Teemer, 394 F.3d 59 (1st Cir. 2005), the court refused to recognize an innocent possession defense to the federal felon-in-possession statute, 18 U.S.C. § 922(g). Teemer had claimed that his only contact with the weapon in question had consisted of once moving it off a sofa at his friend's house "so he could watch a football game." "The statute," the panel pointed out, "bans possession outright without regard to how great a danger exists of misuse in the particular case," adding that it was meant " 'to prevent the crook and gangster, racketeer and fugitive from justice from being able to ... in any way come in contact with firearms of any kind.' " Rather than set out an innocent possession defense, the court preferred relying upon juries to detect "circumstances that arguably come within the letter of the law but in which conviction would be unjust ... for common sense is the touchstone in situations of innocent contact, and the occasions that might warrant leniency are myriad and hard to cabin in advance."

2. Does possession become any less of a possession when it is temporary, or innocent? Why aren't temporary possession cases covered by the definition of possession? See, e.g., N.Y. Penal Law § 15.00(2) (voluntary act "includes the possession of property if the actor was aware of his physical possession or control thereof for a sufficient period to have been able to terminate it").

3. If the real purpose behind at least some possession statutes is to criminalize (retrospectively) the illicit—but inevitably unobserved—acquisition of contraband or (prospectively) the illicit future use of the contraband, then punishing "innocent" possession meets no obvious legislative purpose. Can we understand the meaning of the legal term "possession" without reference to the purposes of punishing "possession"? Would it be better if legislatures made explicit reference to the fact that the defendant should be exonerated if he lacked the capacity to terminate control but also should be exonerated if he had not purposely acquired control, and did not intend to make future use of the contraband?

4. *E.C.* extends the innocent possession defense from weapons possession to drug possession. But might not the scope of "innocent possession" be different in drug and weapons cases because possession prosecutions serve different roles in these cases? Should it be *easier* for the drug possessor to negate the (implicit) presumption of future use or sale than it is for the weapons possessor to negate the accusation that he is responsible for creating an undue risk, by permitting a weapon to be present in a dangerous place for longer than is absolutely necessary? See, in this regard, Bieder v. United States, 707 A.2d 781 (D.C. App. 1998). Bieder, who was licensed to carry a pistol in New York, had engaged in some legal recreational shooting in Virginia. Driving back to New York, he stopped in the District of Columbia to show his daughter the Capitol. A handbook issued by New York authorities had cautioned him against leaving firearms in unattended vehicles, so Bieder removed the gun from the trunk, loaded it with ammunition, placed it in a pouch, and voluntarily handed it to a police officer at the Capitol for safekeeping. The court sustained his conviction for carrying a pistol he was not licensed to carry in D.C. The opinion was in part fact specific (focusing on the defendant's decision to *load* the gun) but stated, more broadly, that a defense of "innocent possession" requires that "an accused must show not only an absence of criminal purpose but also that his possession was excused and justified as stemming from an affirmative effort to aid and enhance social policy underlying law enforcement." Could E.C. meet that standard? Could the confrontational parent the court discusses in *E.C.*? There are certainly cases, though, that reject the proposition that the scope of the "innocent possession" defense is different in drug and weapons cases. See, e.g., People v. Hurtado, 47 Cal.App.4th 805, 54 Cal.Rptr.2d 853 (1996).

5. *Agency Defense*. Another defense that does not apply to possession offenses is the "agency" defense recognized in some jurisdictions in drug distribution cases. For a classic agency defense case, see People v. Roche, 45 N.Y.2d 78 (1978), where the court stressed the defendant's "nonentrepreneurlike" behavior and the absence of proof of a profit motive on the defendant's part:

> [A]n undercover police officer, Sylvio Lugo, . . . struck up a friendship with the defendant, Antonio Roche, after initially encountering him as a fellow patron at various bars. In the course of one of their later meetings, Lugo mentioned that he was interested in making a purchase of narcotics. Roche indicated that he might be of assistance in doing so. . . . [Two months later,] after Lugo's subsequent attempts to follow up were unsuccessful, he telephoned Roche to tell him that he was in a hurry to make an immediate purchase. [T]hey proceeded . . . to Les Nannettes Bar in Manhattan, using Lugo's car. There Roche entered the premises alone, presumably to [see] the seller. Upon returning to Lugo . . ., he reported that things had been arranged and that the price would be $4,000. Lugo thereupon handed that sum in cash to Roche who, again alone, re-entered Les Nanettes with it and in a few minutes was back to advise Lugo that the actual delivery of the drugs would take place at a discotheque called the Cheetah. [There Roche received the drugs from a third person and passed them on to Lugo.]

Note that New York punishes "selling" drugs and "possessing" them. Would the agency defense apply in jurisdictions that criminalize "distributing" drugs, rather than selling them? (The agency defense is often raised along with the defense of entrapment, discussed in ch. 7.)

It's no surprise that the agency defense doesn't apply in possession cases. It was, after all, designed to reduce liability for distribution to liability for (simple) possession, by treating the defendant as the purchaser's, rather than the seller's, "agent":

> [According to the agency defense,] "one who acts on behalf of a purchaser of drugs cannot be convicted of criminal sale of a controlled substance, or of criminal possession thereof with intent to sell." The underlying theorization is that a person, who acts solely on behalf of the recipient of the drugs in a transaction, performs as an extension of the recipient and cannot be guilty of a sale, since that person is merely transferring to the recipient that which the recipient already owns or that to which he is entitled, there being no sale, exchange, gift or disposal of the drugs to the recipient.
>
> Conceptually, the theory does not fit within the ambit of mere possession, as distinguished from possession with intent to sell, since the former contains no element pertaining to or any exception in respect to an agent or person possessing on behalf of another....

People v. Sierra, 45 N.Y.2d 56 (1978).

The agency defense assumes that drug possession is punished less harshly than drug distribution. But what if simple possession of sufficiently large quantities is itself subject to severe penalties? See, e.g., N.Y. Penal Law § 220.21 (simple possession classified as A–I felony, punishable by life imprisonment). If (all? some?) simple possession statutes are justified on the ground that they are "really" inchoate distribution (or other use) statutes, then why wouldn't the agency defense apply to them?

CHAPTER 5

MENTAL STATE (SUBJECTIVE OFFENSE ELEMENTS)

The voluntariness (or "actness") of physical conduct is rarely an issue. People don't often defend against a homicide charge by saying, "I ran over V involuntarily." A case like *People v. Decina* (ch. 4) is very much the exception that proves the rule. Distinctions in mental state, by contrast, are quite frequently germane. So a defendant is more likely to argue something like, "I am responsible for the physical motions that killed him, but I didn't mean those physical motions to kill. . . ." Even young children are quick to defend themselves by pointing out that they whacked their sibling over the head "by accident," and not "on purpose." (Only a suspiciously precocious six-year-old, by contrast, will lead with "*I* didn't *really* hit her; it was a reflex. . . .")

In fact, it's not much of an exaggeration to say that mens rea is *the* central issue in criminal law. Actus reus issues rarely arise and defenses rarely apply. But again and again, a defendant's guilt or innocence turns on the question whether she intended, foresaw, contemplated, or desired to engage in proscribed conduct or to cause a proscribed result. Even if mens rea doesn't mean the difference between guilt and innocence, it often will determine the amount of punishment that will be meted out. (Defendants with distinct mental states may be guilty of different crimes or different *grades* of the same crime.) The typical example here is homicide, which uses mental states to differentiate between murder (purpose, knowledge, gross recklessness, extreme indifference to the value of human life), manslaughter (ordinary recklessness), and negligent homicide (negligence). At the same time, many crimes require no mental states of any kind. These so-called strict (or absolute) liability offenses require an actus reus, but no mens rea. If you are pulled over for speeding, it makes no difference whatsoever whether you "knew how fast you were going," no matter what the police officer might ask you as you stand by the side of the road.

Just where "voluntariness" ends, and "mental state" begins is not always easy to tell. (Remember that even in *Decina*, much of the discussion was not about voluntariness, but about negligence and recklessness, two paradigmatic mental states, or modes of culpability.) After exploring the line between actus reus and mens rea, we'll take a close look at the basic mental state categories, paying particular attention to the influential Model Penal Code scheme. At the same time, we'll encourage you to think about why the lines between adjacent categories may be much less clear than one might expect. To illustrate the mental state categories, we'll mostly use homicide examples for convenience's sake.

A. VOLUNTARINESS VS. MENTAL STATES

In the Matter of Ronnie L.

Family Court, New York County.
121 Misc.2d 271 (1983).

■ BRUCE M. KAPLAN, JUDGE.

[The present juvenile delinquency petition alleges that Respondent Ronnie L criminally possessed a loaded weapon in violation of N.Y. Penal Law § 265.02(4) ("A person is guilty of criminal possession of a weapon in the third degree when: . . . (4) Such person possesses any loaded firearm.")]

On the morning of February 3, 1982 Respondent was observed . . . with Gregory P, a non-student, on the first floor of Park West High School. Since P was considered an intruder, both youths were taken to Mr. Jefferson's office in accordance with school security policy. At that juncture, Respondent was wearing a black leather jacket, and Gregory P was wearing a maroon sheepskin coat.

In Mr. Jefferson's office, confusion arose as to which boy owned which jacket. Gregory P's mother advised Mr. Jefferson that Gregory owned a black leather jacket, and did not own a maroon sheepskin coat. This fact was confirmed by Respondent's testimony that he and Gregory had switched jackets while on the fourth floor.

While the youths were in his office, Mr. Jefferson first patted down Gregory P, and then patted down the Respondent about five minutes later. Mr. Jefferson testified that as he patted down the Respondent, he felt a hard object, and asked the Respondent to remove whatever it was from his coat pocket. Mr. Jefferson further testified that when he felt the hard object, and before he removed the object from Respondent's pocket, Respondent said "It's not mine, Mr. Jefferson." The object which Respondent removed from his pocket was a holstered and loaded .22 caliber pistol. Respondent's testimony differed in that he claimed that he did not discover that he had a gun until he was removing it from his jacket pocket and, out of surprise, said "It's not mine, Mr. Jefferson."

Respondent claimed that the petition cannot be sustained because he was not in knowing possession of a loaded weapon.

The court cannot accept this argument since the offense is one of strict liability. However, even a strict liability offense must be the result of a voluntary act. If that fact is not established by proof beyond a reasonable doubt the petition cannot be sustained.

Penal Law section 15.10 contains the definition of strict liability. It provides:

> The minimal requirement for criminal liability is the performance by a person of conduct which includes a voluntary act or the omission to perform an act which he is physically capable of performing. If such conduct is all that is required for commission of a particular offense, or if

an offense or some material element thereof does not require a culpable mental state on the part of the actor, such offense is one of "strict liability." If a culpable mental state on the part of the actor is required with respect to every material element of an offense, such offense is one of "mental culpability."

The concept of a voluntary act is central to this definition. It is defined by Penal Law section 15.00, subd. 2 in the following manner:

"Voluntary act" means a bodily movement performed consciously as a result of effort or determination, and includes the possession of property if the actor was aware of his physical possession or control thereof for a sufficient period to have been able to terminate it.

A crime of strict liability stands in contrast to one requiring a culpable mental state.

The description of the latter is set forth in Penal Law section 15.15 subd. 1 which provides:

1. When the commission of an offense defined in this chapter, or some element of an offense, requires a particular culpable mental state, such mental state is ordinarily designated in the statute defining the offense by use of the terms "intentionally," "knowingly," "recklessly" or "criminal negligence," or by use of terms, such as "with intent to defraud" and "knowing it to be false," describing a specific kind of intent or knowledge.

These culpable mental states are set out in Penal Law section 15.05. We need only concern ourselves with the term "intentionally" which is defined as follows:

1. "Intentionally." A person acts intentionally with respect to a result or to conduct described by a statute defining an offense when his conscious objective is to cause such result or to engage in such conduct.

We face a conundrum when we attempt to draw a meaningful distinction between "voluntary act" (P.L. section 15.00 subd. 2) and, acting "intentionally" (P.L. section 15.05 subd. 1) in the context of an offense whose gravamen is mere possession.

In the first instance the law speaks of a voluntary act as one "consciously performed as a result of effort or determination." It includes possession of property if the actor was aware of his physical possession, and had hold of it sufficiently long to terminate that possession.

In the second the law speaks of acting intentionally "when one's conscious objective is to cause a result or engage in particular conduct."

These definitions are substantially similar....

.... The same volitional processes are involved in the offense of possessing a firearm, a strict liability offense, as would be implicated if the statute were one of mental culpability and required that the firearm be possessed either "intentionally" or "knowingly".

If conduct necessarily involves a culpable mental state—is there any reason not to expressly make it a material element of the offense?

* * *

Nonetheless the court concludes that there was a legislative intent to make P.L. section 265.02 subd. 4 a strict liability crime. Article 265 of the Penal Law deals with firearms and other dangerous weapons. Criminal possession of a weapon in the third degree (P.L. section 265.02), a class D felony, prohibits possession of a loaded firearm without regard to a culpable mental state.

In contrast, criminal possession of a weapon in the second degree (P.L. section 265.03), a class C felony, requires that a person possess a loaded firearm with intent to use the same unlawfully against another. It is the addition of a culpable mental state that distinguishes the two offenses, makes the latter a more serious one, and clearly establishes that the former (265.02 subd. 4) was clearly intended to be a strict liability offense. * * *

In similar situations other Courts have considered what degree of volition a Defendant must exhibit before he can be convicted of a crime.... [I]n People v. Davis, 112 Misc.2d 138, 446 N.Y.S.2d 159 (Crim.Ct., Bronx Co., 1981), the Court, in ruling that P.L. section 265.05[a] was a crime of strict liability, stated "[t]he doing of an act such as possession of a weapon may by statute be made criminal per se without regard to the doer's intent or knowledge, but nevertheless the act of possessing must not be involuntary as an involuntary act is not criminal. These two concepts are not the same. They are mutually exclusive." * * *

The court credits Mr. Jefferson's testimony, and concludes that respondent was aware that he possessed the gun before he started to remove it from his pocket. Respondent was wearing the coat in which the gun was found from the time he and P. exchanged coats on the fourth floor until it was removed approximately five minutes after they entered Mr. Jefferson's first floor office.... The holstered revolver is both bulky and weighty. Respondent had navigated four flights of stairs with the gun in the side pocket of a waist-length jacket. It is inconceivable that he would not feel it bumping against him as he descended the staircase, and not investigate what was in his pocket. * * *

Probation is ordered to conduct an investigation, prepare a report and be prepared to recommend an appropriate disposition....

QUESTIONS AND COMMENTS

1. What's the point of distinguishing voluntariness from mental states? What's the difference between voluntariness, and knowledge and intention, using the definitions in *Ronnie L.*? Does the difficulty of distinguishing voluntariness from mens rea arise only in possession cases? Would it make more sense simply to distinguish between the objective element of a crime (the act understood as bodily movement) and its subjective element

a. "It shall be unlawful for any person under the age of sixteen to possess any air-gun, spring-gun ..., or any gun or any instrument or weapon in or upon which any loaded or blank cartridges may be used, or any loaded or blank cartridges or ammunition therefor, or any dangerous knife...."—EDS.

(which would include voluntariness and mens rea, if any)? See generally Paul H. Robinson, "Should the Criminal Law Abandon the Actus Reus/ Mens Rea Distinction?," in Action and Value in Criminal Law 187 (Stephen Shute et al. eds., 1996).

2. What about strict liability crimes? If the statute does not require, for instance, that the actor be aware of what she was doing, whom she was harming and how, or what she was possessing, must she still have acted voluntarily?

3. How about the court's efforts at statutory interpretation? Does the fact that § 265.03 requires an intent to *use* the firearm speak to the question of whether both §§ 265.02(4) and 265.03 require *awareness* that one possesses a firearm? Has the court taken adequate account of the requirement in § 15.00(2) that an actor voluntarily possesses property only if aware of his control over the item? Do the facts support a finding that Ronnie L., the "person alleged to be a juvenile delinquent" (the "defendant" in an adult criminal case), was aware that he possessed a (loaded) firearm, or just that he possessed something?

B. THE MODEL PENAL CODE SCHEME IN CONTEXT

The Model Penal Code drafters undertook an ambitious—and, as it turned out, highly influential—effort to construct an integrated framework for the American law of mens rea. They thought of themselves as revising and systematizing what they considered to be a hopelessly confused body of rules assembled by previous generations of common law judges, legislators, and scholars. It therefore makes sense to approach their scheme from a historical perspective. (For a brief historical account of common law mens rea, see Francis B. Sayre, "Mens Rea," 45 Harv. L. Rev. 974 (1932)).

Queen v. Tolson

Queen's Bench Division.
23 Q.B.D. 168 (1889).

■ STEPHEN, J.

. . . Though this phrase (non est reus, nisi mens sit rea) is in common use, I think it most unfortunate, and not only likely to mislead, but actually misleading, on the following grounds. It naturally suggests that apart from all particular definitions of crimes, such a thing exists as a "mens rea", or "guilty mind", which is always expressly or by implication involved in every definition. This is obviously not the case, for the mental elements of different crimes differ widely. "Mens rea" means, in the case of murder, malice aforethought; in the case of theft, an intention to steal; in the case of rape, an intention to have forcible connection with a woman without her consent; and in the case of receiving stolen goods, knowledge that the goods were stolen. In some cases it denotes mere inattention. For instance, in the case of manslaughter by negligence it may mean forgetting to notice a signal. It appears confusing to call so many dissimilar states of mind by one name. It seems contradictory indeed to describe a mere absence of mind as a "mens rea", or guilty mind. The expression again is likely to and often does mislead. To an unlegal mind it suggests that by the law of England no act is a crime which is done from laudable motives, in other words, that immorality is essential to crime.

Herbert L. Packer, The Limits of the Criminal Sanction 104–05 (1968)

When we speak of Arthur's having the *mens rea* of murder, we may mean any one or more of the following things: that he intended to kill Victor; or that he was aware of the risk of his killing Victor but went ahead and shot him anyhow; or (more dubiously) that he ought to have known but didn't that there was a substantial risk of his killing Victor or that he knew it was wrong to kill a fellow human being, or that he ought to have known it; or that he didn't really think that Victor was trying to kill him; or that he did think that, but only a fool would have thought it; or that he was not drunk to the point of unconsciousness when he killed Victor; or that even though he was emotionally disturbed he wasn't grossly psychotic, etc., etc.

Cal. Penal Code § 7. [1872]

1. The word "willfully," when applied to the intent with which an act is done or omitted, implies . . . a purpose or willingness to commit the act, or make the omission referred to. . . .

2. The words "neglect," "negligence," "negligent," and "negligently" import a want of such attention to the nature or probable consequences of the act or omission as a prudent man ordinarily bestows in acting in his own concerns.

3. The word "corruptly" imports a wrongful design to acquire or cause some pecuniary or other advantage to the person guilty of the act or omission referred to, or to some other person.

4. The words "malice" and "maliciously" import a wish to vex, annoy, or injure another person, or an intent to do a wrongful act, established either by proof or presumption of law.

5. The word "knowingly" imports . . . a knowledge that the facts exist which bring the act or omission within the provisions of this code. . . .

La. Crim. Code § 10. Criminal intent. [1942]

Criminal intent may be specific or general:

(1) Specific criminal intent is that state of mind which exists when the circumstances indicate that the offender actively desired the prescribed criminal consequences to follow his act or failure to act.

(2) General criminal intent is present whenever there is specific intent, and also when the circumstances indicate that the offender, in the ordinary course of human experience, must have adverted to the prescribed criminal consequences as reasonably certain to result from his act or failure to act.

La. Crim. Code § 11. Criminal intent; how expressed.

The definitions of some crimes require a specific criminal intent, while in others no intent is required. Some crimes consist merely of criminal negligence that produces criminal consequences. However, in the absence of qualifying provisions, the terms "intent" and "intentional" have reference to "general criminal intent."

La. Crim. Code § 12. Criminal negligence.

Criminal negligence exists when, although neither specific nor general criminal intent is present, there is such disregard of the interest of others that the offender's conduct amounts to a gross deviation below the standard of care expected to be maintained by a reasonably careful man under like circumstances.

Model Penal Code § 2.02. General Requirements of Culpability. [1962]

(2) *Kinds of Culpability Defined.*

(a) *Purposely.*

A person acts purposely with respect to a material element of an offense when:

(i) if the element involves the nature of his conduct or a result thereof, it is his conscious object to engage in conduct of that nature or to cause such a result; and

(ii) if the element involves the attendant circumstances, he is aware of the existence of such circumstances or he believes or hopes that they exist.

(b) *Knowingly.*

A person acts knowingly with respect to a material element of an offense when:

(i) if the element involves the nature of his conduct or the attendant circumstances, he is aware that his conduct is of that nature or that such circumstances exist; and

(ii) if the element involves a result of his conduct, he is aware that it is practically certain that his conduct will cause such a result.

(c) *Recklessly.*

A person acts recklessly with respect to a material element of an offense when he consciously disregards a substantial and unjustifiable risk that the material element exists or will result from his conduct. The risk must be of such a nature and degree that, considering the nature and purpose of the actor's conduct and the circumstances known to him, its disregard involves a gross deviation from the standard of conduct that a law-abiding person would observe in the actor's situation.

(d) *Negligently.*

A person acts negligently with respect to a material element of an offense when he should be aware of a substantial and unjustifiable risk that the material element exists or will result from his conduct. The risk must be of such a nature and degree that the actor's failure to perceive it, considering the nature and purpose of his conduct and the circumstances known to him, involves a gross deviation from the standard of care that a reasonable person would observe in the actor's situation.

QUESTIONS AND COMMENTS

1. Did the Model Penal Code address the concerns expressed in the *Tolson* and Packer excerpts? Is the Model Penal Code mens rea scheme more specific, accessible, sensible, scientific than its predecessor(s)? Note that the Model Penal Code drafters attempted to separate out the various issues covered by the traditional notion of mens rea and assign them to different doctrinal categories. For instance, knowledge of the illegality (and criminality) of one's conduct is now handled under the excuse of ignorance of law or, if the defendant suffers from a mental disease or defect, under the excuse of insanity; laudable motives are dealt with—if at all—under the heading of justification; intoxication is addressed in a special section on, well, intoxication; the belief that one is defending oneself against another's (unlawful) attack is covered under a separate defense of self-defense; and so on. Does this differentiation simplify, or complicate, the law of culpability? Does it capture more, or fewer (or different), intuitions about who deserves (more, less, any) punishment? Is there a comprehensive notion of culpability (or mens rea, or intent) that is worth preserving but gets lost in the Model Penal Code's differentiated approach? For a detailed discussion of the Model Penal Code's mens rea scheme, see Markus D. Dubber, Criminal Law: Model Penal Code § 4.2 (2002); Paul H. Robinson & Jane A. Grall, "Element Analysis in Defining Criminal Liability," 35 Stan. L. Rev. 681 (1983).

2. Compare the Model Penal Code scheme to the California and Louisiana schemes. How do they differ? Are these differences significant?

3. How does the traditional distinction between general and specific intent, as laid out in the Louisiana Criminal Code, map onto the distinctions between the various mental states under the Model Penal Code scheme? Some jurisdictions draw the general/specific intent line at recklessness (rather than at knowledge), so that specific intent encompasses purpose and knowledge, and general intent includes recklessness and negligence. See, e.g., State v. Cameron, 104 N.J. 42, 514 A.2d 1302 (1986).

Secondary (or cumulative) intent crimes are also often classified as "specific intent" crimes. In that case burglary would qualify as a specific intent crime in that it requires both unlawfully entering a house and the intent to commit a crime (ordinarily, but not necessarily, a theft) once inside. (Another, more common, example is possession with intent to distribute.)

Then again, some courts have distinguished between general intent as an intent to commit an *act* and specific intent as an intent to achieve a forbidden *result*. (The Model Penal Code captures this distinction by differentiating among types of offense elements (conduct, attendant circumstances, result), and between conduct and result in particular, each of which could be accompanied by a different mental state; see ch. 4.)

Finally, the distinction might serve to differentiate between someone who acts with the intent of causing harm to someone, anyone, and one who acts with the intent of causing harm to a specific individual, at a specific time. (This issue nowadays tends to be dealt with in the law of causation; see ch. 8.)

The Model Code drafters abandoned the distinction between general and specific intent as hopelessly confused. Does this mean that the distinction—or the set of distinctions it represents—is *pointless* as well? Or does a distinction between general and specific intent (or some other broader distinction among mental states) capture some intuition about the subjective element of crime? Or are all mental states—four, by the Model Penal Code's count—so distinct that they cannot profitably be grouped in some way?

The doctrinal significance of the distinction between general and specific intent lies in the fact that intoxication could negate only specific, but not general, intent. As one might suspect, the Model Penal Code instead ties the relevance of intoxication evidence to specific mental states (so that it can negate purpose or knowledge, but not recklessness or negligence). See section G, infra.

4. Compare the distinction between general and specific intent, and the Model Penal Code's mens rea default rule, with the general distinction between intentional and nonintentional (negligent) acts in German and Israeli criminal law.

German Penal Code § 15. Intentional and negligent conduct.

Only intentional conduct is punishable, unless the statutory law expressly threatens negligent conduct with punishment.

German Penal Code (Alternative Draft)[a] § 17. Intention.

(1) He acts intentionally whoever knowingly and wilfully causes a statutorily proscribed harm to occur.

(2) He also acts intentionally whoever seriously considers the accomplishment of a crime to be possible and who takes that into account.

(3) He acts knowingly whoever knows that the circumstances which the statute requires in order to establish voluntary conduct are present, or whoever foresees as certain the occurrence of these circumstances.

German Penal Code (Alternative Draft) § 18. Negligence.

He acts negligently whoever fails to exercise the care to which he is obligated and of which he is capable, and who thereby causes a statutorily proscribed harm to occur.

Penal Law of Israel § 20.

(a) Mens rea means awareness of the nature of the act, of the existence of the circumstances and of the possibility of the conse-

a. Sections 17 and 18 were not included in the final version of the Code. They nonetheless provide a useful summary of a commonly drawn distinction between intention and negligence in German criminal law.—EDS.

quences of the act being brought about, such nature, circumstances and consequences being ingredients of the offence, and as regards the consequences, means also one of the following:

(1) "intention" to bring about the consequences;

(2) "Recklessness," being one of:

(i) "indifference" to the possibility of bringing about the consequences;

(ii) "rashness"—assumption of an unreasonable risk as to the possibility of bringing about the consequences hoping that it will be possible to prevent them.

(b) For the purposes of intention, foreseeing the consequences as almost certain to occur shall be deemed to be an intention to bring them about.

How do these schemes compare to the Model Code's? Do they draw similar distinctions? Apply the various mens rea schemes to the cases in this chapter. Do the results differ? Does the analysis?

5. *Mental States and Element Types*. One of the most striking features of the Model Penal Code mens rea scheme is that it differentiates between definitions of mental states for the various types of offense elements (conduct, attendant circumstance, result). The danger here is to lose the forest for the trees, and replacing one bewildering variety of mental states (mens rea, scienter, intent (general and specific), malice, and so on) with another. It's well worth taking a moment to get the gist of the various mental state definitions in the Code.

(a) *Purpose*. The core concept here is "conscious object." And the one definition that's most likely to matter in actual cases is that with respect to a result element. The Restatement of Torts makes this explicit:

> "Intent," as it is used throughout the Restatement of Torts, has reference to the consequences of an act rather than the act itself. When an actor fires a gun in the midst of the Mojave Desert, he intends to pull the trigger; but when the bullet hits a person who is present in the desert without the actor's knowledge, he does not intend that result.

Restatement of Torts (Second) § 8A cmt. a.

The Code drafters, by contrast, attempted a definition of purpose with respect to conduct and attendant circumstances as well. Note that purpose with respect to an attendant circumstance doesn't require that you're aware of its existence (though it's sufficient if you *are* aware). Your belief or even hope is enough, even if it turns out to be mistaken. So, assuming purposely destroying another's property is a crime (and "purposely" attaches to the attendant circumstance of "another's"), then you're guilty as long as you believe—or hope—that the bike you're twisting up into a pretzel belongs not to you, but to your ex-boyfriend.

(b) *Knowledge*. The core concept here is "awareness." It applies to all types of offense elements, except result. (Why doesn't it apply to result?) This means, among other things, that it's possible to act purposely with respect to an attendant circumstance, say, without also acting knowingly with respect to it (since purpose would be satisfied as long as I believed or hoped that the attendant circumstance were present). The more important question is whether it's possible to act purposely—but not knowingly—with respect to a *result*. See People v. Steinberg, 79 N.Y.2d 673 (1992), infra.

(c) *Recklessness and Negligence.* Note first that both recklessness and negligence differ from knowledge in the magnitude of the risk—knowledge requires practical certainty; recklessness and negligence require only substantial risk. Later on, we'll explore the difficulty of drawing this quantitative distinction. For now, it's enough to recognize that criminal liability for recklessness, unlike knowledge, requires *more* than actual awareness of a risk of harm. The conscious disregard of that (lower) risk must also deviate from the norms of the relevant control group ("law-abiding" persons in the case of the Model Penal Code, or plain "reasonable" persons in most codes based on the Model Penal Code, see, e.g., N.Y. Penal Law § 15.00(3)).

Recklessness and negligence don't differ depending on what type of objective offense element they accompany. They are the conscious disregard and culpable ignorance of a substantial risk, respectively. Once again, the definition with respect to result, and attendant circumstances, is clear enough. There's a question, though, how recklessness or negligence might be defined with respect to one's conduct. How can one be reckless or negligent regarding one's conduct—i.e., disregard a risk, or even be unaware of a risk—that one might be engaging in a certain behavior? Can I be merely negligent about the fact that I'm driving, for instance, and yet be said to drive *voluntarily*? How clueless about—or mystified by—my conduct must I be for it not to count as *mine*?

6. And why do we punish negligence at all? Negligence has long been the basis for civil liability in the law of torts. But does it warrant punishment? How can punishing negligent conduct be justified under the traditional rationales for punishment? Does it reflect a character flaw (lack of care? callousness?) that deserves punishment? A dangerousness that needs incapacitating? Or is punishing negligence about encouraging people to be less careless (or frightening them into being more careful)?

7. *Exercise.* It's important to recognize that the definitions in Model Penal Code § 2.02 (and analogous provisions in other codes) are just that, definitions. They have nothing to do with questions of fact, or proof. They help us figure out what the elements of an offense are; they don't help us figure out whether a defendant's behavior satisfies these elements. Think of "purpose," "knowledge," "recklessness," and "negligence" as shorthand for descriptions of mental states that may differ depending on the offense element type to which they are attached. As an exercise, answer the following questions. (a) What are the definitions of "purposely," "knowingly," "recklessly," and "negligently" in the Model Penal Code's homicide provisions (§§ 210.1–.4)?; (b) What are the definitions of "knowingly" and "recklessly" in the Code's interference with custody provision (§ 212.4(1))?

C. STATUTORY INTERPRETATION: WHAT MENS REA IS REQUIRED (IF ANY)?

Arguably the Code maintains the distinction between general and specific intent in fact, if not in theory. For instance we'll see that the distinction continues to play a role in the Code's treatment of intoxication evidence, which used to be limited to specific intent crimes, and is now—under the Code—limited to offense elements with a subjective element of purpose or knowledge.

Another way in which the Code can be seen as trying to retain the substance of the general/specific intent distinction, without retaining the distinction itself is through its general mens rea *default* rule:

Model Penal Code § 2.02. General Requirements of Culpability.

(3) *Culpability Required Unless Otherwise Provided.* When the culpability sufficient to establish a material element of an offense is not prescribed by law, such element is established if a person acts purposely, knowingly or recklessly with respect thereto.

On the face of it, this section sets out a rule for the interpretation of statutes that do not identify a mental state for each objective element. In substance, it reflects an indirect way of capturing the general principle that each offense requires some general mens rea, unless the statute provides otherwise, either by doing away with mens rea or by requiring some specific mens rea beyond what is ordinarily required (as, for instance, in the case of burglary, which traditionally required general intent with respect to the entering, but specific intent with respect to the stealing). See Model Penal Code Commentaries § 2.02, at 244. The underlying assumption would be that general intent requires at least recklessness, whereas specific intent requires "more"—i.e., knowledge or purpose, in the terminology of the Model Penal Code. (Analogous default provisions can be found in many American codes, though the default mental state is not always recklessness. See, e.g., N.Y. Penal Law §§ 15.15(2) & 15.00(6) (criminal negligence); Mo. Rev. Stat. § 562.021 (purpose or knowledge); see generally Guyora Binder, "Felony Murder and Mens Rea Default Rules: A Study in Statutory Interpretation," 4 Buff. Crim. L. Rev. 399, 416–30 (2000)).

Note that the Code speaks in terms of the "culpability sufficient to establish a material element of an offense," rather than the offense as a whole. In the Code, modes of culpability attach to (material) elements, not to offenses. (On the distinction between element analysis and offense analysis, see ch. 4.) This also means that the mere fact that one element features a mental state requirement doesn't mean that another element also features that mental state requirement, or any other mental state requirement, for that matter. It is perfectly possible, for instance, for one objective element (like stealing) to require a mental state (say, purpose), while another element (like entering) does not, or requires a different mental state (say, knowledge). To figure out which element requires which mental state, if any, the Code sets out another rule of interpretation:

Model Penal Code § 2.02. General Requirements of Culpability.

(4) *Prescribed Culpability Requirement Applies to All Material Elements.* When the law defining an offense prescribes the kind of culpability that is sufficient for the commission of an offense, without distinguishing among the material elements thereof, such provision shall apply to all the material elements of the offense, unless a contrary purpose plainly appears.

Note that this *one-for-all* rule of interpretation includes a significant exception for cases in which the legislature makes it clear that it didn't mean a mental state to cover elements other than the one to which it is attached. The following cases illustrate the application of the one-for-all and default rules:

People v. Ryan

Court of Appeals of New York.
82 N.Y.2d 497, 626 N.E.2d 51, 605 N.Y.S.2d 235 (1993).

■ KAYE, CHIEF JUDGE.

Penal Law § 220.18(5) makes it a felony to "knowingly and unlawfully possess ... six hundred twenty-five milligrams of a hallucinogen." The question of statutory interpretation before us is whether "knowingly" applies to the weight of the controlled substance. We conclude that it does and that the trial evidence was insufficient to satisfy that mental culpability element. * * *

[Defendant asked a friend, David Hopkins, to order a shipment of hallucinogenic mushrooms on his behalf.] [T]he police chemist testified that the total weight of the mushrooms in Hopkins' package was 932.8 grams (about two pounds), and that a 140–gram sample of the package contents contained 796 milligrams of psilocybin, a hallucinogen. He did not know, however, ... how much psilocybin would typically appear in two pounds of mushrooms.

At the close of the People's case, defendant moved to dismiss for insufficient proof that he knew the level of psilocybin in the mushrooms, and also requested a charge-down to seventh degree attempted criminal possession, which has no weight element. Both applications were denied, defendant was convicted as charged, and he was sentenced as a second felony offender to 10 years-to-life. * * *

.... Penal Law § 220.18(5) provides:

> A person is guilty of criminal possession of a controlled substance in the second degree when he knowingly and unlawfully possesses: ...
>
> 5. six hundred twenty-five milligrams of a hallucinogen.

It is undisputed that the knowledge requirement of the statute applies to the element of possession (see also, Penal Law § 15.00), and that defendant must also have "actual knowledge of the nature of the possessed substance." At issue is whether defendant must similarly know the weight of the material possessed. That is a question of statutory interpretation....

In effectuating legislative intent, we look first of course to the statutory language. Read in context, it seems evident that "knowingly" does apply to the weight element. Indeed, given that a defendant's awareness must extend not only to the fact of possessing something ("knowingly ... possesses") but also to the nature of the material possessed ("knowingly ... possesses ... a hallucinogen"), any other reading would be strained. Inasmuch as the knowledge requirement carries through to the end of the sentence, eliminating it from the intervening element—weight—would rob the statute of its obvious meaning. We conclude, therefore, that there is a mens rea element associated with the weight of the drug.

That reading is fortified by two rules of construction ordained by the Legislature itself. First, a "statute defining a crime, unless clearly indicating a legislative intent to impose strict liability, should be construed as defining a crime of mental culpability" (Penal Law § 15.15). If any material element of an offense lacks a mens rea requirement, it is a strict liability crime (Penal Law § 15.10). Conversely, a crime is one of "mental culpability" only when a mental state "is required with respect to every material element of an offense" (id.). * * *

In a similar vein, the Legislature has provided in Penal Law § 15.15(1):

> Construction of statutes with respect to culpability requirements.
>
> 1. When the commission of an offense defined in this chapter, or some element of an offense, requires a particular culpable mental state, such mental state is ordinarily designated in the statute defining the offense by use of the terms "intentionally," "knowingly," "recklessly" or "criminal negligence," or by use of terms, such as "with intent to defraud" and "knowing it to be false," describing a specific kind of intent or knowledge. When one and only one of such terms appears in a statute defining an offense, it is presumed to apply to every element of the offense unless an intent to limit its application clearly appears.

Accordingly, if a single mens rea is set forth, as here,[2] it presumptively applies to all elements of the offense unless a contrary legislative intent is plain.

We discern no "clear" legislative intent to make the weight of a drug a strict liability element, as is required before we can construe the statute in that manner. * * *

State v. Lozier

Supreme Court of Ohio.
101 Ohio St.3d 161, 803 N.E.2d 770 (2004).

■ PFEIFER, J.

On February 14, 2001, the Holmes County Grand Jury indicted defendant-appellee, Chad A. Lozier, for trafficking in drugs in violation of Ohio Rev. Code § 2925.03(A). All . . . counts against appellee contained a specification that appellee sold drugs within the vicinity of a school, which enhances the penalty under Rev. Code § 2925.03(C)(5)(b). . . .

The sales at issue occurred at appellee's former home, which is located approximately 745 feet from the Holmes County Job and Family Services building. That building housed, on its third floor, a remedial education program known as "Project Stay." The state stipulated that it had no

2. "Unlawfully" is not a term of mental culpability but means "in violation of article thirty-three of the public health law" (Penal Law § 220.00).

evidence that appellee knew of the existence of Project Stay and that there was nothing to mark it or to identify it as a school to the public.

The trial court ruled that Project Stay was, in fact, a school. The court also ruled that whether appellee knew that he was selling drugs in the vicinity of the school was irrelevant, since the specification for trafficking within the vicinity of a school is written in terms of strict liability. Appellee was convicted on four counts of trafficking with the sentence-enhancement specifications.

Appellee appealed from his convictions to the Fifth District Court of Appeals, arguing that the trial court had erred in finding that Rev. Code § 2925.03(C)(5)(b) imposes strict liability. The appellate court agreed and reversed the judgment of the trial court, concluding that the culpable mental state associated with Rev. Code § 2925.03(C)(5)(b) is "knowingly."

The sole issue raised in this appeal is whether Rev. Code § 2925.03(C)(5)(b), which elevates trafficking in LSD to a fourth degree felony if the offense is committed "in the vicinity of a school," imposes strict criminal liability on a defendant. We make our determination against the backdrop of Rev. Code § 2901.04(A), which states that "sections of the Revised Code defining offenses or penalties shall be strictly construed against the state, and liberally construed in favor of the accused."

The case against appellee begins with his violation of Rev. Code § 2925.03(A), which itself requires a mental state of "knowingly":

No person shall knowingly do any of the following:

"(1) Sell or offer to sell a controlled substance. . . ."

Rev. Code § 2925.03(C)(5)(b) is in play because appellee was selling LSD, and because he was selling that substance in the vicinity of a school. The relevant statutory language is as follows:

> (C) Whoever violates division (A) of this section is guilty of one of the following: . . .
>
> (5) If the drug involved in the violation is L.S.D. or a compound, mixture, preparation, or substance containing L.S.D., whoever violates division (A) of this section is guilty of trafficking in L.S.D. The penalty for the offense shall be determined as follows: . . .
>
> (b) . . . . If the offense was committed in the vicinity of a school or in the vicinity of a juvenile, trafficking in L.S.D. is a felony of the fourth degree. . . .

The mental state of the offender is a part of every criminal offense in Ohio except for those plainly imposing strict liability. Rev. Code § 2901.21(A)(2) requires that, in order to be found guilty of a criminal offense, a person must have "the requisite degree of culpability for each element as to which a culpable mental state is specified by the section defining the offense."

Rev. Code § 2901.21(B) addresses strict liability statutes and those statutes that do not address a culpable mental state. That statute reads:

> When the section defining an offense does not specify any degree of culpability, and plainly indicates a purpose to impose strict criminal

> liability for the conduct described in the section, then culpability is not required for a person to be guilty of the offense. When the section neither specifies culpability nor plainly indicates a purpose to impose strict liability, recklessness is sufficient culpability to commit the offense.

Thus, recklessness is the catchall culpable mental state for criminal statutes that fail to mention any degree of culpability, except for strict liability statutes, where the accused's mental state is irrelevant. However, for strict liability to be the mental standard, the statute must plainly indicate a purpose to impose it. * * *

Here, we are dealing with a[] pair of discrete clauses separated by "or." The phrase at issue in Rev. Code § 2925.03(C)(5)(b) reads:

> "If the offense was committed *in the vicinity of a school* or *in the vicinity of a juvenile*, trafficking in L.S.D. is a felony of the fourth degree, and division (C) of section 2929.13 of the Revised Code applies in determining whether to impose a prison term on the offender." (Emphasis added.)

Standing alone, "in the vicinity of a school or in the vicinity of a juvenile" does not indicate any required degree of mental culpability. However, each clause, "in the vicinity of a school" and "in the vicinity of a juvenile," is separately defined in the chapter's definitional section. "In the vicinity of a juvenile," as defined in Rev. Code § 2925.01(BB), employs strict liability terms:

> (BB) An offense is "committed in the vicinity of a juvenile" if the offender commits the offense within one hundred feet of a juvenile or within the view of a juvenile, regardless of whether the offender knows the age of the juvenile, whether the offender knows the offense is being committed within one hundred feet of or within view of the juvenile, or whether the juvenile actually views the commission of the offense.

Rev. Code § 2925.01(BB) makes it abundantly clear that the offender's mental state is irrelevant in determining whether the offender has committed an offense "in the vicinity of a juvenile." An offender is liable whether or not he knows the age of the juvenile, or whether he realizes that a juvenile is in the vicinity.

By contrast, the definition of "in the vicinity of a school," contained in Rev. Code § 2925.01(P), lacks the express strict liability language of Rev. Code § 2925.01(BB). That definition reads:

> (P) An offense is "committed in the vicinity of a school" if the offender commits the offense on school premises, in a school building, or within one thousand feet of the boundaries of any school premises.

The General Assembly, in imposing the strict liability requirement for drug sales "in the vicinity of a juvenile," perfectly illustrates what Rev. Code § 2901.21(B) calls a "purpose to impose strict liability." Additionally, the stark contrast between the definition of "committed in the vicinity of a school" and the definition of "committed within the vicinity of a juvenile" indicates that the General Assembly did not intend to impose strict liability for selling LSD in the "vicinity of a school" section.

[I]f one part of a clause explicitly sets forth a mental state, that mental state does not apply to another discrete clause within that subsection. In fact, it is an indication that the General Assembly is attaching differing mental states as to the two distinct clauses. . . . We find that the language employed by the General Assembly in the Rev. Code § 2925.01(P) and (BB) definitions establishes differing levels of culpability for offenses committed "in the vicinity of a juvenile" and "in the vicinity of a school," plainly indicating that the General Assembly's purpose was to impose strict liability for acts committed "in the vicinity of a juvenile" but not for acts committed "in the vicinity of a school."

Moreover, we find that the differing degrees of mental culpability for offenses committed near a school as opposed to near a juvenile are consistent with a coherent legislative policy.

The distance requirement for an act to be committed within "the vicinity of a juvenile" is only 100 feet or "within view of the juvenile." Drug trafficking is a dangerous activity. Beyond the psychic danger of seeing drugs being sold, there is a very real physical danger surrounding a drug transaction, even for nonparticipants. Thus, a child, whether in view or not, could become a part of the collateral damage of a failed transaction. The threat to a child is real and imminent.

On the other hand, to be "in the vicinity of a school," an offender could, by definition, be 1,000 feet away from a school. A child may not necessarily be nearby, or even in the school. The transaction could occur in the late evening hours, or in summer, or during any other period of the year that the school is closed.

The difference between the potential peril of a transaction that occurs "in the vicinity of a school" and "in the vicinity of a juvenile" is significant. "In the vicinity of a school" addresses danger that can be theoretical; "in the vicinity of a juvenile" addresses a real, present danger. Because the "vicinity of a juvenile" offense is so much more dangerous, the General Assembly has determined that the offender's knowledge that a juvenile is nearby is irrelevant. Also, since "in the vicinity of a juvenile" includes being in view of a juvenile, its parameters can expand well beyond 100 feet. Thus, if an offense occurs within 1,000 feet of a school, the offender still can be subject to strict criminal liability if there is a juvenile within view. As the danger to children becomes more real, the culpable mental state gets stricter.

Having determined that the General Assembly's purpose was to impose differing culpable mental states for acts committed "in the vicinity of a juvenile" and "in the vicinity of a school," we must determine what culpable mental state applies to offenses that occur "in the vicinity of a school." Since the definition of "in the vicinity of a school" includes no culpable mental state, we employ Rev. Code § 2901.21(B) to provide the requisite culpability for the offense in question. We therefore hold that the culpable mental state of recklessness applies to the offense of trafficking in LSD "in the vicinity of a school" under Rev. Code § 2925.03(C)(5)(b).

Although the court of appeals found that the requisite mental state is "knowingly," and we conclude that recklessness is the appropriate standard, we nevertheless affirm. A reviewing court is not authorized to reverse a correct judgment merely because it was reached for the wrong reason.

Accordingly, we affirm the judgment of the court of appeals and remand the cause to the trial court for further proceedings.

■ O'CONNOR, J., dissenting.

... Rev. Code § 2901.21(B) cannot operate to supply the mental element of recklessness to Rev. Code § 2925.03(C)(5)(b) because Rev. Code § 2925.03 includes a mental element in defining Lozier's offense. Rev. Code § 2925.03(A) requires the mens rea of *knowingly* selling or offering to sell a controlled substance. Rev. Code § 2925.03(C)(5)(b) then provides a sentencing enhancement "if the offense [of knowingly selling or offering to sell LSD] was committed in the vicinity of a school...." Although the statute's enhancement provision does not specify a degree of culpability, the section defining Lozier's offense does. Thus, Rev. Code § 2925.03(A)'s knowledge requirement precludes imputing recklessness to Rev. Code § 2925.03(C)(5)(b) via R.C.2901.21(B).

Having resolved that Rev. Code § 2901.21(B) is inapplicable here, we still must determine the degree of culpability required for a sentencing enhancement under Rev. Code § 2925.03(C)(5)(b)....

[A] mental element cannot be imputed from one discrete clause to another and ... the exclusion of a mental element from a discrete clause indicates the applicability of strict liability where the section defining the offense includes a mental element. I would ... hold that the knowledge requirement of Rev. Code § 2925.03(A) cannot be imputed to Rev. Code § 2925.03(C)(5)(b), and that the exclusion of a mental element from Rev. Code § 2925.03(C)(5)(b), in light of Rev. Code § 2925.03(A)'s knowledge requirement, subjects the described conduct to strict liability. * * *

I find further support for my position that Rev. Code § 2925.03(C)(5)(b) describes a strict liability offense in *United States v. Falu* (C.A.2, 1985), 776 F.2d 46, which resolved the same issue presented herein within the context of former Section 845(a), Title 21, U.S.Code, a federal statute that was analogous to Rev. Code § 2925.03. In *Falu*, the district court resolved that Section 845(a) imposed strict liability. [T]he universal purpose of enhancing penalties for trafficking in drugs in the vicinity of schools is to protect children from the pariahs that are drug dealers. Thus, the *Falu* court found, "[A] requirement that the dealer know that a sale is geographically within the prohibited area would undercut this unambiguous legislative design." I wholeheartedly agree, and I believe that the same rationale applies to requiring recklessness.

QUESTIONS AND COMMENTS

1. In the wake of *Ryan,* the New York legislature amended the statute to read as follows:

> A person is guilty of criminal possession of a controlled substance in the second degree when he knowingly and unlawfully possesses: ...

5. a hallucinogen and said hallucinogen weighs six hundred twenty-five milligrams or more.

Would this change the result in *Ryan*? Should it?

2. Who has the better of the argument in *Lozier*, the majority or the dissent? How might the *Ryan* court (the Model Penal Code?) have resolved the question of statutory interpretation in *Lozier*? What is the relevance of "legislative policy" in *Lozier*? What if the majority—or dissent—had discovered that "legislative policy" didn't support their interpretation of the statutory language?

3. As the dissent in *Lozier* argues, and the legislative response to *Ryan* makes clear, sometimes legislatures mean just what they say (or rather don't say). If an element of an offense has no mental state attached to it, then it is meant not to have a mental state attached to it. It is, in other words, meant to be a strict liability element.

The Model Penal Code, though it launched a "frontal assault" on strict liability, Model Penal Code Commentaries § 2.05, at 282, provided for an exception to the general rule in § 2.02 that "a person is not guilty of an offense unless he acted purposely, knowingly, recklessly or negligently, as the law may require, with respect to each material element of the offense":

Model Penal Code § 2.05. When Culpability Requirements Are Inapplicable to Violations and to Offenses Defined by Other Statutes; Effect of Absolute Liability in Reducing Grade of Offense to Violation.

(1) The requirements of culpability prescribed by Sections 2.01 and 2.02 do not apply to:

(a) offenses which constitute violations . . .; or

(b) offenses defined by statutes other than the Code, insofar as a legislative purpose to impose absolute liability for such offenses or with respect to any material element thereof plainly appears.

(2) Notwithstanding any other provision of existing law and unless a subsequent statute otherwise provides:

(a) when absolute liability is imposed with respect to any material element of an offense defined by a statute other than the Code and a conviction is based upon such liability, the offense constitutes a violation; and

(b) although absolute liability is imposed by law with respect to one or more of the material elements of an offense defined by a statute other than the Code, the culpable commission of the offense may be charged and proved, in which event negligence with respect to such elements constitutes sufficient culpability. . . .

Model Penal Code § 1.04. Classes of Crimes; Violations.

(1) An offense defined by this Code or by any other statute of this State, for which a sentence of [death or of] imprisonment is authorized,

constitutes a crime. Crimes are classified as felonies, misdemeanors or petty misdemeanors. * * *

(5) An offense defined by this Code or by any other statute of this State constitutes a violation if it is so designated in this Code or in the law defining the offense or if no other sentence than a fine, or fine and forfeiture or other civil penalty is authorized upon conviction or if it is defined by a statute other than this Code which now provides that the offense shall not constitute a crime. A violation does not constitute a crime and conviction of a violation shall not give rise to any disability or legal disadvantage based on conviction of a criminal offense.

According to the Model Code, under what circumstances is an element to be interpreted as a strict liability element? And what effect does that interpretation have on the liability of someone who has been convicted under the statute in question?

Given the considerable, and constantly growing, number of criminal offenses found in statutes other than criminal codes and in administrative regulations, see ch. 1 supra, what sort of limitation does the Code place on strict liability offenses? Under the terms of the Code provisions on culpability, would a legislature be prevented from providing for strict liability *crimes*? As *Lozier* and *Ryan* (and *Ronnie L.*) make clear, legislatures that followed the Code's general approach to statutory interpretation regarding ambiguous mental state requirements did not necessarily follow the Code's attempt to limit strict liability to noncriminal offenses. Serious possession offenses are only one common type of strict liability crimes; the most notorious one is felony murder (assuming one follows a common interpretation of the felony murder doctrine as imposing strict liability for deaths resulting from intentional felonies). See infra ch. 11.

4. *Interpretative rules vs. evidentiary rules, again.* What did the *Lozier* and *Ryan* courts hold? That the defendant lacked the requisite mental state with respect to an offense element? That the statute requires that the state prove that the defendant had the requisite mental state? That the statute requires *the defendant* to prove that he *lacked* the requisite mental state?

The rules of statutory interpretation regarding ambiguous mental state requirements resemble the definitions of these mental states in Model Penal Code § 2.02 (and analogous provisions in other codes) in that they help us determine the requirements for liability under a particular offense definition. They are, in fact, yet one step further removed from the application of the offense definition to a particular case than are the provisions in § 2.02, for they only help us determine which of the four subjective mental states (purpose, knowledge, recklessness, negligence) is meant to attach to each objective element of an offense definition. Once the match between mental state and offense element has been made, we can turn to § 2.02 to find out exactly how that mental state is defined. (In particular, they should not be confused with the doctrine of "transferred intent," section E, infra.)

Revisit the exercise in question 7, p. 288, supra. Using the rules of statutory interpretation regarding ambiguous mental state requirements, which mental state attaches to the various offense elements in the Model Code's provisions on homicide and interference with custody?

D. AMBIGUITIES IN THE MODEL PENAL CODE'S MENS REA SCHEME

The best way to get a handle on the various modes of culpability under the Model Penal Code is to take a close look at the lines that are meant to separate them. Focusing on the borderlines is only fair. After all, the Model Code drafters explicitly set out to develop a set of mens rea categories that—unlike traditional Anglo–American criminal law—draw distinctions between offenses and offenders that were both clear, and therefore predictable, and appropriate. Why is it important that mental states, as well as objective offense elements, be predictable? At the end of the day, did the drafters achieve their goal?

It helps to keep in mind that, to the drafters, "appropriate" meant reflective of the offender's level and type of dangerousness. The proper mens rea classification thus contributed to the overall diagnosis that was to form the basis for the assignment of the correct duration and form of peno-correctional treatment to the offender. As you work through the materials on mens rea, think about how the Code's scheme of mental states reflects this focus on treatmentist penology. Of course other measures of appropriateness are possible. What are they? How do they relate to the various theories of punishment? And how are they reflected in the Code's mens rea scheme?

1. PURPOSE VS. KNOWLEDGE

a. Conscious Object vs. Awareness

People v. Steinberg

Court of Appeals of New York.
79 N.Y.2d 673 (1992).

■ KAYE, JUDGE.

In the evening of November 1, 1987, defendant and Hedda Nussbaum[a] were at home in their one-bedroom Greenwich Village apartment, with their two "adopted"[b] children, Lisa, then six years old, and Mitchell, 16 months old. Nussbaum was in the kitchen with Lisa while defendant dressed in the bedroom for his dinner appointment with a friend. Lisa went

a. Although both Steinberg and Nussbaum were originally charged in Lisa's death, charges against Nussbaum were dropped when she agreed to testify against Steinberg. According to Nussbaum, who had been the victim of severe domestic abuse by Steinberg, Steinberg had struck Lisa because "he could not stand the girl staring at him." Campbell Robertson, "Steinberg to Be Freed Today, 16 Years After Killing Girl," N.Y.Times, June 30, 2004, at B3, col. 1.—EDS.

b. Steinberg had illegally adopted Lisa from her biological mother, who eventually obtained a $15 million civil judgment against him for the girl's death. Id.—EDS.

into the bedroom to ask defendant to take her with him. Moments later, defendant carried Lisa's limp body out to Nussbaum, who was then in the bathroom, and they laid the child on the bathroom floor. Lisa was unconscious, having experienced blunt head trauma of great force, and her breathing was raspy. According to Nussbaum, defendant later admitted that he had "knocked [Lisa] down and she didn't want to get up again."

While Nussbaum attempted to revive Lisa, defendant continued dressing. Defendant told Nussbaum to let her sleep, promised to awaken the child upon his return, and then left for dinner. Nussbaum did not seek medical care for Lisa because she believed defendant had supernatural healing powers, and felt that calling for assistance would be considered a sign of disloyalty.

Defendant returned about three hours later, at 10:00 P.M., retrieved a file relating to his oil well investments, and left again. When he came back a few minutes later, Nussbaum urged him to revive the still-unconscious child. Defendant declined—explaining that they "ha[d] to be relating when she wakes up"—and he instead freebased cocaine for the next several hours. Finally, at 4:00 A.M., after Nussbaum's repeated urgings, defendant carried Lisa from the bathroom floor to the bedroom, where her breathing seemed to sound better. Defendant rested his arm on Lisa, and continued talking to Nussbaum.

At 6:00 A.M., when Nussbaum left the room, defendant called out that Lisa had stopped breathing. Defendant initially rejected Nussbaum's offer to call 911, but finally acceded when his attempts to resuscitate the child failed. Police and paramedics arrived shortly after being summoned, administered oxygen, and rushed Lisa to the hospital.

At the hospital, defendant explained that Lisa had gone to bed complaining of a stomach ache, and had vomited during the night, but that he believed she was otherwise all right until he checked on her around 6:00 A.M. and discovered that her breathing was coarse. In fact, the doctors determined that Lisa, who was in a coma, was suffering from severe head injuries—a result of blunt trauma—and placed her on life support equipment. Lisa's condition did not improve, and neurological tests performed on November 3 indicated that she was brain dead. Life support was discontinued on November 5.

Defendant was indicted for second degree (depraved indifference) murder,[c] first degree manslaughter, and seven charges that were severed or dismissed. Defendant was acquitted of murder but convicted of manslaughter, and the Appellate Division affirmed the conviction....

First degree manslaughter requires proof that defendant, with intent to cause serious physical injury,* caused death (Penal Law § 125.20[1])....

c. Section 125.25 Murder in the second degree

A person is guilty of murder in the second degree when: 2. Under circumstances evincing a depraved indifference to human life, he recklessly engages in conduct which creates a grave risk of death to another person, and thereby causes the death of another person.... —EDS.

* "Serious physical injury" is "physical injury which creates a substantial risk of death, or which causes death or serious and protracted disfigurement, protracted impairment of health or protracted loss or impair-

Defendant contends that failure to obtain medical care for a child cannot, as a matter of law, support the mens rea element of first degree manslaughter—intent to cause serious physical injury—unless defendant has medical expertise, and would thereby know that serious injury will result from a lack of medical attention. That contention—which he characterizes as the core question on this appeal—is meritless. * * *

The revised Penal Law, in accord with the modern trend, distinguishes between "intent" and "knowledge." A person acts intentionally when there is a "conscious objective" to cause the result proscribed by statute (Penal Law § 15.05[1]). By contrast, a person acts knowingly when there is an awareness that a particular element of a crime is satisfied (see, Penal Law § 15.05[2]). Thus, if intent is the governing mens rea (as it is here), the focus is on the defendant's conscious aim or purpose—the objective—in doing particular acts. Defendant's knowledge or awareness that the result will occur—while a factor the jury may take into consideration to infer intent—is itself not a prerequisite of intent.

Contrary to defendant's claim, even a person without specialized medical knowledge can have the intent to cause serious physical injury by withholding medical care. If the objective is to cause serious physical injury, the mental culpability element of first degree manslaughter is satisfied—whether or not defendant had knowledge that the omission would in fact cause serious injury or death.

Defendant argues that "everyone" knows that failure to supply food to a child will lead to death, and thus intentional homicide is a proper charge under those circumstances, but that the need for medical care is often a matter of opinion, and a layperson could not be expected to know the gravity of the situation. The distinction defendant would have us draw, as a matter of law, between defendants who have a medical background and those who do not, is unsupportable.

[We reject] defendant's attempt to import a knowledge requirement into a statute that has none. . . .

QUESTIONS AND COMMENTS

1. Historically, purpose and knowledge were rarely distinguished, as both fit comfortably under the broad concept of intent.[a] (Though some courts—and statutes—might distinguish between purpose as *specific*, and knowledge as one form of *general* intent. See La. Crim. Code § 10. Confusingly, other codes—particularly more modern ones—refer to purpose as intent, distinguishing it from knowledge. See N.Y. Penal Law § 15.05.) Even in jurisdictions that draw the distinction, liability rarely requires purpose. There are some exceptions, though. To be guilty of treason, one must not simply know that one's giving aid and comfort to the enemy but it must be one's purpose to do so. In most jurisdictions (though as we'll see

ment of the function of any bodily organ." (Penal Law § 10.00[10].)

a. See also Restatement of Torts (Second) § 8A (" 'intent' denote[s] that the actor desires to cause consequences of his act, or that he believes that the consequences are substantially certain to result from it").—EDS.

later on, not all), an accomplice must have the purpose to aid the principal, not simply take steps that he knows will help the principal attain her criminal end. See ch. 8. Plus, attempt liability (i.e., liability for trying to commit a crime, but falling short for one reason or another) also requires purpose (again, subject to limitations which we'll get to later, in ch. 6). So does liability for other inchoate offenses, including conspiracy and solicitation—though not for facilitation.

2. *Objective vs. Awareness*. Requiring purpose rather than knowledge tends to be seen as *limiting* the scope of criminal liability. Why? Does requiring purpose necessarily limit the scope of criminal liability? Compared with knowledge, or even with recklessness? Is it true that proving purpose implies having proved knowledge, as section 2.02(5) suggests?

> **Model Penal Code § 2.02. General Requirements of Culpability.**
>
> (5) Substitutes for Negligence, Recklessness and Knowledge. When the law provides that negligence suffices to establish an element of an offense, such element also is established if a person acts purposely, knowingly or recklessly. When recklessness suffices to establish an element, such element also is established if a person acts purposely or knowingly. When acting knowingly suffices to establish an element, such element also is established if a person acts purposely.

Assume the court in *Steinberg* is right to find that Steinberg acted with purpose. Does that imply Steinberg also acted with knowledge? If not, is it fair to punish someone more harshly for purposeful, than for knowing or even reckless conduct, both of which would require at least awareness?

3. Does it make sense to distinguish between purpose and knowledge? What should one make of a claim that one didn't *want* something to happen though one proceeded to do something that would make it happen, knowing full well that it would occur? What's the point of drawing the distinction? From the perspective of the Model Code's treatmentism? From any of the traditional rationales of punishment?

b. Conditional Purpose

Assuming that we can distinguish purpose from knowledge, how about the difference between knowledge and *conditional* purpose? Is there even such a thing as conditional purpose? Consider the following case.

Holloway v. United States

Supreme Court of the United States.
526 U.S. 1, 119 S.Ct. 966 (1999).

■ Justice Stevens delivered the opinion of the Court.

Carjacking "with the intent to cause death or serious bodily harm" is a federal crime.[1] The question presented in this case is whether that phrase

1. "Whoever, *with the intent to cause death or serious bodily harm* takes a motor vehicle that has been transported, shipped, or received in interstate or foreign commerce

requires the Government to prove that the defendant had an unconditional intent to kill or harm in all events, or whether it merely requires proof of an intent to kill or harm if necessary to effect a carjacking. [We conclude] that Congress intended to criminalize the more typical carjacking carried out by means of a deliberate threat of violence, rather than just the rare case in which the defendant has an unconditional intent to use violence regardless of how the driver responds to his threat.

A jury found petitioner guilty on three counts of carjacking.... In each of the carjackings, petitioner and an armed accomplice identified a car that they wanted and followed it until it was parked. The accomplice then approached the driver, produced a gun, and threatened to shoot unless the driver handed over the car keys. The accomplice testified that the plan was to steal the cars without harming the victims, but that he would have used his gun if any of the drivers had given him a "hard time." When one victim hesitated, petitioner punched him in the face, but there was no other actual violence.

The District Judge instructed the jury that the Government was required to prove beyond a reasonable doubt that the taking of a motor vehicle was committed with the intent "to cause death or serious bodily harm to the person from whom the car was taken." After explaining that merely using a gun to frighten a victim was not sufficient to prove such intent, he added the following statement over petitioner's objection:

> "In some cases, intent is conditional. That is, a defendant may intend to engage in certain conduct only if a certain event occurs.
>
> "In this case, the government contends that the defendant intended to cause death or serious bodily harm if the alleged victims had refused to turn over their cars. If you find beyond a reasonable doubt that the defendant had such an intent, the government has satisfied this element of the offense...." * * *

The specific issue in this case is what sort of evil motive Congress intended to describe when it used the words "with the intent to cause death or serious bodily harm" in the 1994 amendment to the carjacking statute. More precisely, the question is whether a person who points a gun at a driver, having decided to pull the trigger if the driver does not comply with a demand for the car keys, possesses the intent, at that moment, to seriously harm the driver. In our view, the answer to that question does not depend on whether the driver immediately hands over the keys or what the offender decides to do after he gains control over the car. At the relevant moment, the offender plainly does have the forbidden intent. * * *

from the person or presence of another by force and violence or by intimidation, or attempts to do so, shall—

"(1) be fined under this title or imprisoned not more than 15 years, or both,

"(2) if serious bodily injury ... results, be fined under this title or imprisoned not more than 25 years, or both, and

"(3) if death results, be fined under this title or imprisoned for any number of years up to life, or both, or sentenced to death." 18 U.S.C. § 2119 (1994 ed. and Supp. III) (emphasis added).

[I]t is reasonable to presume that Congress was familiar with the cases and the scholarly writing that have recognized that the "specific intent" to commit a wrongful act may be conditional. The facts of the leading case on the point are strikingly similar to the facts of this case. In People v. Connors, 253 Ill. 266, 97 N.E. 643 (1912), the Illinois Supreme Court affirmed the [assault] conviction of a union organizer who had pointed a gun at a worker and threatened to kill him forthwith if he did not take off his overalls and quit work. The court held that the jury had been properly instructed that the "specific intent to kill" could be found even though that intent was "coupled with a condition" that the defendant would not fire if the victim complied with his demand. That holding has been repeatedly cited with approval by other courts and by scholars. Moreover, it reflects the views endorsed by the authors of the Model [Penal] Code.[11] The core principle that emerges from these sources is that a defendant may not negate a proscribed intent by requiring the victim to comply with a condition the defendant has no right to impose; "[a]n intent to kill, in the alternative, is nevertheless an intent to kill."

■ JUSTICE SCALIA, dissenting.

I think ... that in customary English usage the unqualified word "intent" does not usually connote a purpose that is subject to any conditions precedent except those so remote in the speaker's estimation as to be effectively nonexistent—and it *never* connotes a purpose that is subject to a condition which the speaker hopes will not occur. (It is this last sort of "conditional intent" that is at issue in this case....) "Intent" is "[a] state of mind in which a person seeks to accomplish a given result through a course of action." Black's Law Dictionary 810 (6th ed.1990). One can hardly "seek to accomplish" a result he hopes will not ensue. * * *

[I]t is *not* common usage—indeed, it is an unheard-of usage—to speak of my having an "intent" to do something, when my plans are contingent upon an event that is not virtually certain, and that I hope will not occur. When a friend is seriously ill, for example, I would not say that "I intend to go to his funeral next week." I would have to make it clear that the intent is a conditional one: "I intend to go to his funeral next week if he dies." The carjacker who intends to kill if he is met with resistance is in the same position: He has an "intent to kill if resisted"; he does not have an "intent to kill."

QUESTIONS AND COMMENTS

1. Should we (at least do our best) to adopt a general determinate rule about conditional intent? Scalia thinks he does adopt just such a rule, by saying that conditional intent *never* suffices. Does this work? Note that

11. Section 2.02(6) of the Model Penal Code provides:

"Requirement of Purpose Satisfied if Purpose is Conditional.

"When a particular purpose is an element of an offense, the element is established although such purpose is conditional, unless the condition negatives the harm or evil sought to be prevented by the law defining the offense." American Law Institute, Model Penal Code (1985).

Of course, in this case the condition that the driver surrender the car was the precise evil that Congress wanted to prevent.

he confesses that virtually all intention is conditional on the non-occurrence of certain *unexpected* events. Would it be more persuasive to say that we don't intend things when we intend them only if something happens that we *wish* didn't happen, and that the probability or improbability (i.e., the unexpectedness) of the event is of no moment in defeating the notion that one possesses an intent so long as one *wishes* for the event on which the event is conditioned? Thus, if a defendant enters a house—arguably—"intending" to steal, *if the house contains valuable jewels*, wouldn't we say he intended to steal regardless of whether he thought there were a 90% or a 10% chance that the jewels were actually there?

2. The Model Penal Code also purports to set up a determinate rule about conditional intent, by providing that conditional intent *always* suffices. Does this work? Note the exception for cases in which the "condition negatives the harm or evil sought to be prevented by the law defining the offense." What did the drafters have in mind here? (According to the Commentaries, "it would not be an assault with the intent to rape, if the defendant's purpose was to accomplish the sexual relation only if the mature victim consented; the condition negatives the evil with which the law was framed to deal." Model Penal Code Commentaries § 2.02, at 247. In this case, did the defendant ever have even a conditional intent to rape?)

3. The alternative, of course, is to make case-by-case judgments about how to treat conditional intent. We might, for instance, divide the intentions in terms of time, i.e., treat the defendant—in some cases—as not having a criminal intent *yet.* Or we might treat defendants—in some cases—as having an intent only given unusual or unexpected, rather than expected, or wanted rather than unwanted, circumstances. How would *Holloway* come out under this approach? What if the actor doesn't *want* but might *expect* resistance, or at least finds it reasonably likely? Should conditional intent suffice if the condition is *either* desired or anticipated?

c. Purpose vs. Motive

State v. Wyant

Supreme Court of Ohio.
64 Ohio St.3d 566, 597 N.E.2d 450 (1992).

■ HERBERT R. BROWN, JUSTICE.

The principal issue before us is the constitutionality of the ethnic intimidation statute, Ohio Rev. Code § 2927.12 . . .:

"(A) No person shall violate section 2903.21, 2903.22, 2909.06, or 2909.07, or division (A)(3), (4), or (5) of section 2917.21 of the Revised Code by reason of the race, color, religion, or national origin of another person or group of persons.

"(B) Whoever violates this section is guilty of ethnic intimidation. Ethnic intimidation is an offense of the next higher degree than the offense the commission of which is a necessary element of ethnic intimidation."

The statute creates enhanced criminal penalties for some people who commit aggravated menacing (Rev. Code § 2903.21), menacing (Rev. Code

§ 2903.22), criminal damaging or endangering (Rev. Code § 2909.06), criminal mischief (Rev. Code § 2909.07), or certain types of telephone harassment (Rev. Code § 2917.21[A][3], [4], or [5]).

The predicate offenses to ethnic intimidation are already punishable acts under other statutes. [T]he enhanced penalty results solely from the actor's reason for acting, or his motive. We must decide whether a person's motive for committing a crime can support either a separate, additional crime, or an enhanced penalty for an existing crime.

Motive, in criminal law, is not an element of the crime. In their textbook, 1 Substantive Criminal Law (1986) 318, Section 3.6, LaFave and Scott argue that if defined narrowly enough, motive is not relevant to substantive criminal law, although procedurally it may be evidence of guilt, or, in the case of good motive, may result in leniency. Other thought-related concepts such as intent and purpose are used in the criminal law as elements of crimes or penalty-enhancing criteria, but motive itself is not punished.

There is a significant difference between why a person commits a crime and whether a person has intentionally done the acts which are made criminal. Motive is the reasons and beliefs that lead a person to act or refrain from acting. The same crime can be committed for any of a number of different motives. Enhancing a penalty because of motive therefore punishes the person's thought, rather than the person's act or criminal intent. * * *

Culpable mental state, or intent, is usually required to find one guilty of a crime. "Intent" refers to the actor's state of mind or volition at the time he acts. Did A intend to kill B when A's car hit B's, or was it an accident? This is not the same as A's motive, which is why A intentionally killed B. When A murders B in order to obtain B's money, A's intent is to kill and the motive is to get money. One can have motive without intent, or intent without motive. For instance, the wife of a wealthy but disabled man might have a motive to kill him, and yet never intend to do so. A psychopath, on the other hand, may intend to kill and yet have no motive.

Purpose to commit an additional criminal act is frequently seen in criminal statutes as a basis for enhanced penalty or as creating a separate, more serious crime. For example, burglary is a trespass "with purpose" to commit a theft offense or felony. Purpose in this context is not the same as motive. What is being punished is the act of trespass, plus the additional act of theft, or the intent to commit theft. Upon trespassing, A's intent is to commit theft, but the motive may be to pay debts, to buy drugs, or to annoy the owner of the property. The object of the purpose is itself a crime. Thus the penalty is not enhanced solely to punish the thought or motive.

Criminal penalties are often enhanced using the concept of an aggravating circumstance. These also are distinguishable from motive. For example, under Rev. Code § 2929.04, any of a number of aggravating circumstances can increase the penalty for aggravated murder to death. Among these is murder committed "for the purpose of" escaping another offense. The basis for enhancing the penalty in this case is once again an additional act or intent. Escaping another offense is in itself a crime. The enhanced penalty for murder does not stem from motive (i.e., preference of life on the street to life in prison), but from the additional act of escape, or the intent to escape.

Rev. Code § 2929.04(A)(2) declares murder for hire to be an aggravating circumstance. This is not properly seen as enhancing the penalty for a mercenary motive. Hiring is a transaction. The greater punishment is for the additional act of hiring or being hired to kill. The motive for the crime (such as jealousy, greed or vengeance) is not punished.

Some aggravating circumstances involve the identity of the victim, such as a peace officer or governmental official. Rev. Code § 2929.04(A)(1), (6). The legislature has decided, in these instances, that acts against certain individuals are more serious criminal acts. Imposing a higher penalty for killing the Governor than for killing an ordinary citizen is similar to imposing a higher penalty for stealing a painting worth $1,000 than for stealing one worth only $5.

Under the above analysis, the legislature could decide that blacks are more valuable than whites, and enhance the punishment when a black is the victim of a criminal act. Such a statute would pass First Amendment analysis because the motive or the thought which precipitated the attack would not be punished. However, Rev. Code § 2927.12 could not have been written that way because such a statute would not survive analysis under the Equal Protection Clause of the Fourteenth Amendment to the United States Constitution. * * *

Based upon the foregoing authorities and our analysis of the statute, we find that the effect of Rev. Code § 2927.12 is to create a "thought crime." This violates Section 11, Article I of the Ohio Constitution, and the First and Fourteenth Amendments to the United States Constitution.

Conduct motivated by racial or religious bigotry can be constitutionally punished under the criminal code without resort to constructing a thought crime. In fact, the behavior which is alleged in each case before us can be punished under the criminal statutes identified in Rev. Code § 2927.12.

QUESTIONS AND COMMENTS

1. It is often said, and the *Wyant* court clearly agrees, that "hardly any part of the penal law is more definitely settled than that motive is irrelevant." Jerome Hall, General Principles of Criminal Law 153 (1947). Yet the U.S. Supreme Court in *Holloway* appeared to be very much concerned with motive; it took the issue raised in the case to be "what sort of *evil motive* Congress intended to describe when it used the words 'with the intent to cause death or serious bodily harm' " (emphasis added). Was the Supreme Court unaware of the irrelevance of motive? Or is the old maxim not as "definitely settled" as it might appear, or as it once was? Consider the following excerpt.

> It has often been said that the criminal law is concerned only with intent, not motive.... [U]nderstanding the motive/intent distinction and the irrelevance of motive maxim requires understanding the changing context in which these rhetorical constructions have been

invoked.... [T]he original point of the irrelevance-of-motive maxim was to urge courts to apply formal offense definitions and to encourage legislatures to supply them. Legal reformers associated "intentions" with behavior, which could be compared to rules of conduct. By contrast, they associated "motives" with character, which could only be evaluated by discretionary moral judgment. Thus, the irrelevance of motive maxim implied that courts should assess behavior by applying conduct rules rather than by engaging in discretionary moral judgment. An intention was supposed to be somehow more *legal* than a motive and the irrelevance of motive connoted fidelity to the principle of legality. The motive/intent distinction was part of the rhetoric of the rule of law in criminal law, and stood for a particular allocation of discretion among courts and legislatures. * * *

[W]hen twentieth century lawyers encountered the irrelevance of motive maxim in older cases and treatises, ... they interpreted the distinction between motive and intent as a psychological distinction, among the kinds of mental states that should inculpate offenders. But here they faced the difficulty that the terms "intent" and "motive" are used interchangeably in ordinary language. These terms could only be distinguished as technical terms of art.

Twentieth century legal scholars came up with three different candidates for such a technical distinction between intent and motive. According to one version, intentions were cognitive states of mind, like expectations or perceptions of risk. Motives, by contrast, were desiderative states—desires, purposes, or ends. The difficulty with this version of the distinction was that it seemed to render the motive-is-irrelevant maxim descriptively false, since criminal law often conditioned liability on these desiderative states.

A second version of the distinction divided desiderative states into immediate and remote goals, identifying intention with the former and motive with the latter. The difficulty with this version of the distinction was that any act might be explained by not just two, but perhaps a very great number of goals. Any goal might be denominated an intention when compared to a more remote goal, and a motivation when compared to a more immediate goal.

In an effort to sort goals into just two categories, some commentators suggested that intentions were only those goals that were offense elements, while motives were any more remote goals. This version of the motive/intent distinction certainly accorded with the motive-is-irrelevant maxim, but at the price of reducing it to an empty tautology, true by definition.

If the motive-is-irrelevant maxim is true by definition, it has no normative bite. If the only identifying characteristic of motives is that they are not offense elements, the irrelevance of motive maxim can tell us nothing about how to define offenses. It can have no implications regarding hate crimes, mercy killing, transferred intent, necessity, provocation, or criminal negligence. On the other hand, the irrelevance of motive maxim will have law reform implications if we take it to mean that criminal liability should never be predicated on desiderative

> states. But this version of the irrelevance of motive maxim has law reform implications only because it is (and has long been) at odds with so much criminal law doctrine. . . .

Guyora Binder, "The Rhetoric of Motive and Intent," 6 Buff. Crim. L. Rev. 1, 1–5 (2002).

Is Binder right to argue that the irrelevance of motive has outlived its usefulness, now that criminal offenses are codified? Are there reasons for disregarding motive even now? Does it make sense to limit the consideration of motive to sentencing (as is often suggested)? Could we exclude motive as an aggravating factor, while retaining it as a mitigating factor (as in cases that raise justification (excuse?) defenses, such as those involving the use of force in self-defense or perhaps mercy killings)? Or should consideration of motive be excluded altogether from the analysis of criminal liability and the assessment of sanctions, and limited to questions of fact (did X do it, or did Y)? Assuming the (complete or partial) exclusion of motive is desirable, is it *feasible*—given that it's difficult to distinguish between motives and intentions (do you a think a jury could tell the difference?) and that everyday speech (and, as *Holloway* illustrates, the U.S. Supreme Court) doesn't ordinarily draw this distinction? Would that be a reason to abandon other notoriously contested—and frequently ignored or misunderstood—distinctions, such as that between recklessness and negligence? Is there something unique about the indeterminacy of the distinction between motive and intent that would explain why we cannot tolerate it?

Or is the point not the difficulty of telling motive from intent, but rather that—even if we can draw the distinction—we *should* consider motive because motive is no less (more?) relevant to culpability than is intent (and recklessness and so on)? What rationale(s) for punishment would be consistent with taking motive into account? Is the fact that, in everyday moral judgment, we consider motive (if it is a fact), a sufficient reason for considering it in the legal assessment of criminal liability?

2. What if the statute in *Wyant* had simply made reference to a result worse than the "usual" result for the non-enhanced crime? What, in other words, if the statute had enhanced punishment not for otherwise punishable acts committed "by reason of the race, color, religion, or national origin of another person or group of persons," but for committing these acts with "awareness"—or "purpose"—that they will intimidate such a person or group of persons? Does (should?) this distinction make a difference? Are we punishing motive in one, but not the other case? Would the statute have been better or worse off had it included an explicit reference to "motive" as an offense element? The idea that "hate crime" enhancements impermissibly distinguish defendants who have committed the same act by virtue solely of their motivation (and perhaps their character?) is a powerful one. See, e.g., Heidi Hurd, "Why Liberals Should Hate 'Hate Crime' Legislation," 20 Law & Phil. 215 (2001). It may depend, though, on the notion that there is a single, uncontroversial account of the act each has committed. Consider two defendants who apply spray paint to a building: one paints a swastika on a synagogue, the other paints "Tiffany Luvs Jake" on a school. Arguably, the same act has occurred: defacing public property and

compromising the interests we would wish to protect by prohibiting such defacement. Arguably, not, though, in terms of impact on victims. (Who counts as a victim here? The property owner? Passersby? Members of a particular (ethnic) group? The public? "Public peace"? See In re B.C., 680 N.E.2d 1355 (Ill. 1997) (upholding hate crime conviction for "displaying patently offensive depictions of violence toward African Americans in such an unreasonable manner as to alarm and disturb James Jeffries," who was not African American, on the ground that "individual persons, but more importantly our entire community, are harmed by a defendant's bias-motivated criminal conduct").) Think, now, about two defendants who each assault people, only one committing the prototypical hate crime. Are their *acts* the same?

3. The *Wyant* court concludes that the statute created a "thought crime," and therefore violates the First Amendment. Is the statute also inconsistent with the act requirement?

4. Is the court in *Wyant* persuasive when it argues that punishment aggravation for those "hired" to kill is based not on their atypically bad (shallow pecuniary) motive but on the "act of being hired"? What's troublesome about the "act of being hired" except as an expression of motive? Is the court's point instead that motive may be relevant (to the legislature), but it can only be assessed by particular fact finders directed to look at precisely defined acts, acts that are proxies for motive? (That is to say, the legislature cares about murdering because one was hired solely because it bespeaks bad motive, but fact finders are restrained by rules that alert them only to look for "hiring," not more general "pecuniary motives"?) But if that's right, should we address more directly *how to find*, say, "racist" motivation rather than its relevance? And is it right that we should only find such motivation through prototypical conduct forms that could be encapsulated in rules (no burning crosses; no assaults accompanied by a list of racist epithets) or is it better to rely only on vaguer standards to guide fact finders?

2. KNOWLEDGE VS. RECKLESSNESS

a. Certainty vs. Likelihood

People v. Sanchez

Court of Appeals of New York.
98 N.Y.2d 373, 777 N.E.2d 204, 748 N.Y.S.2d 312 (2002).

■ LEVINE, J.

Defendant was convicted, after a jury trial, of "depraved indifference" murder (Penal Law § 125.25[2]) for the shooting death of Timothy Range....

Range and defendant were the boyfriends of two sisters, Monon Washington and Candace Johnson.... The occasion for their being together on the day of the fatal shooting was a party celebrating the third birthday of Candace's daughter at the family's apartment in Brooklyn....

The People's case rested upon the testimony of Monon Washington and her mother, Rose Liburd. Monon testified ... that Range and defendant got along and used to lift weights together. That evening, however, harsh words were exchanged in a hallway near the foyer entrance of the apartment when Range implied that defendant was unfaithful to Candace.... Liburd ... observed defendant walking through the entrance doorway from the hallway ... to the foyer, away from Range, who was behind the partially opened door. Then she saw defendant abruptly turn around, fire a gun pointed at Range's chest and flee. The entire incident was over in a matter of seconds. Range collapsed after phoning 911 from the kitchen. He was taken by ambulance to a hospital where he expired.

The forensic evidence ... indicated that the gun was fired not more than 12–18 inches from his chest. * * *

The indictment charged defendant with one count each of intentional murder (Penal Law § 125.25[1]) and depraved indifference murder, and various weapons possession offenses.... Defendant was acquitted of intentional murder but convicted of depraved indifference murder and criminal possession of a weapon in the second degree. The Appellate Division affirmed defendant's conviction.

Under Penal Law § 125.25(2), a person commits murder in the second degree when "[u]nder circumstances evincing a depraved indifference to human life, he [or she] recklessly engages in conduct which creates a grave risk of death to another person, and thereby causes the death of another person." ... [Defendant] argues that the People's proof was consistent only with an intentional killing and, thus, that there was no reasonable view of the evidence under which he could have been found not guilty of intentional murder and guilty of causing Range's death recklessly—the culpable mental state required under Penal Law § 125.25(2)....

Viewing the evidence in the light most favorable to the People, as we must, a rational jury could harbor a reasonable doubt that the homicide of Range was intentional—i.e., that defendant's "conscious objective [was] to cause [Range's death]" (Penal Law § 15.05[1]). * * *

Although the gun was discharged at point blank range, the bullet only struck Range in his upper left chest. The trajectory of the bullet through Range's body indicated that the gun was fired at an angle toward Range, a fact consistent with Rose Liburd's description of defendant's movements and Range's position behind the door. The jury may also have taken into account the pre-existing good relations between defendant and Range, and concluded that this was an instantaneous, impulsive shooting—perhaps to disable or frighten Range, rather than to kill him. Thus, a jury reasonably could have found that defendant's homicidal level of mental culpability was reckless rather than intentional. * * *

Alternatively, defendant argues ... that there was no reasonable view of the evidence to support a finding that defendant acted under circumstances evincing a depraved indifference to human life. We are unpersuaded. To the contrary, accepting the jury's determination that the killing of Range was not intentional (see supra), defendant's shooting into Range's torso at point blank range presented such a transcendent risk of causing his death that it readily meets the level of manifested depravity needed to establish murder under Penal Law § 125.25(2). Here, once it rejected intentional murder, the jury (which concededly was properly instructed) could reasonably conclude that defendant's conduct was so manifestly destined to result in Range's death as to deserve the same societal condemnation as purposeful homicide. . . .

. . . . The meaning of the phrase ["under circumstances evincing a depraved indifference to human life"] was directly debated in People v. Register, 60 NY2d 270 [1983]. There, the proof was that defendant arrived at a crowded bar room with a loaded handgun, drank continuously for four hours and announced several times that he was "going to kill somebody tonight" (60 NY2d at 275). After his companion got into an argument with another patron named Mitchell, defendant fired at Mitchell but missed, striking another patron. He then shot Mitchell in the stomach at close range, injuring but not killing him, and turned and fired at yet a third patron, resulting in that person's death.

. . . . The dissenters in *Register* construed the phrase as referring to a mens rea element additional to recklessness. . . . The *Register* majority, however, focused on the first words of the phrase, referring to "circumstances evincing" depraved indifference, and concluded that "[t]his additional requirement refers to neither the mens rea nor the actus reus. If it states an element of the crime at all, it is not an element in the traditional sense but rather a definition of the factual setting in which the risk creating conduct must occur—objective circumstances which are not subject to being negatived by evidence of defendant's intoxication".

Thus, the *Register* majority explained that the requirement of circumstances evincing a depraved indifference to human life under Penal Law § 125.25(2) murder focuses not on the subjective intent of the defendant, "but rather upon an objective assessment of the degree of risk presented by defendant's reckless conduct". As *Register* instructs, objective circumstances of exceptionally high, unjustified risk of death constitute the primary means by which the Legislature differentiated between the reckless state of mind sufficient to establish the mental culpability of manslaughter and the extreme recklessness of murder under Penal Law § 125.25(2).

. . . *Register* does not hold that "ordinary recklessness" is sufficient to establish depraved indifference murder. *Register* requires a significantly heightened recklessness, distinguishing it from manslaughter in two ways. First, "in a depraved mind murder the actor's conduct must present a grave risk of death whereas in manslaughter it presents the lesser substantial risk of death" (60 NY2d at 276). Then, it also requires proof of circumstances manifesting a depraved indifference to human life, focusing the inquiry, as we have seen, "on an objective assessment of the degree of risk" which "converts the substantial risk present in manslaughter into a very substantial risk" (id. at 277). Thus, *Register* concludes, extreme recklessness—the conscious disregard of circumstances revealing the exceptional risk of death from the defendant's conduct—was the predominant means chosen by the Legislature to distinguish murder under Penal Law

§ 125.25(2) from manslaughter and make it equivalent in grade to intentional murder....

Later cases have consistently followed and by now have made settled law of *Register*'s conclusion that the crux of murder under Penal Law § 125.25(2) is recklessness exaggerated by indifference to the circumstances objectively demonstrating the enormity of the risk of death from the defendant's conduct. * * *

There may, of course, be other circumstances manifesting depravity—including the brutal, barbaric or savage nature of a defendant's reckless conduct.... That would be especially relevant where the risk of death merely meets the statutory threshold of being grave. These, however, are only "collateral to the basic proposition of known risk" of death (Gegan, A Case of Depraved Mind Murder, 49 St. John's L Rev 417, 450 [1974]). They are not necessary when the risk of death is manifestly extreme and unjustified. Then, a defendant's disregard of the risk elevates and magnifies the degree of recklessness, itself establishing the required circumstances evincing depraved indifference to human life.

Register's focus on an objective assessment of an exceedingly high degree of risk that the defendant created and ignored, which differentiates reckless murder from reckless manslaughter, is completely consistent ... with modern criminal law theory.... W.R. LaFave and A.W. Scott, Jr. posit a continuum of risks from homicidal behavior, forming the basis to distinguish lower grades of homicide from murder (2 LaFave and Scott, Substantive Criminal Law § 7.4, at 200):

> "Grossly negligent conduct, or reckless conduct, which results in death may serve as the basis for manslaughter liability, but it will not do for murder.
>
> "For murder the degree of risk of death ... must be more than a mere unreasonable risk, more even than a high degree of risk. Perhaps the required danger may be designated a 'very high degree' of risk to distinguish it from those lesser degrees of risk which will suffice for other crimes."

The American Law Institute's Model Penal Code is especially instructive. Our Penal Law Revision Commission, having drafted and proposed the 1967 revised Penal Law, acknowledged its special debt to the Model Code, pointing out that the Code's chief reporter, Professor Herbert Wechsler, was also a member of the Commission (see New York State Temporary Commission on Revision of the Penal Law and Criminal Code, Proposed New York Penal Law, Commission Foreword, at v-vi [1964]). The Model Penal Code's version of reckless murder is a homicide "committed recklessly under circumstances manifesting extreme indifference to the value of human life" (Model Penal Code § 210.2 [1980]).

As the commentary to the Model Penal Code explains, the culpability for non-intentional murder is extreme recklessness—i.e., the disregard of such a high degree of risk created by the actor's conduct that it "cannot fairly be distinguished in grading terms from homicides committed purposely or knowingly" (Model Penal Code § 210.2, Comment 4, at 21). That is because "purposeful or knowing homicide demonstrates precisely such

indifference to the value of human life. Whether recklessness is so extreme that it demonstrates similar indifference is not a question, it is submitted, that can be further clarified. It must be left directly to the trier of fact under instructions which make it clear that recklessness that can fairly be assimilated to purpose or knowledge should be treated as murder and that less extreme recklessness should be punished as manslaughter" (id. at 22).
* * *

For all of the foregoing reasons, the order of the Appellate Division should be affirmed.

■ ROSENBLATT, J. (dissenting).

To be guilty of depraved indifference murder, the defendant must evince more than mere indifference to human life. The indifference must be so extreme—so wicked and mischievous—as to constitute a depraved indifference. That inhuman frame of mind is what equates the crime's blameworthiness with intentional murder. * * * [T]he killer [must] exhibit such utter indifference to human life as to constitute depravity—that the killing, although not intentional, reflects the defendant's uncommonly evil and morally perverse frame of mind. * * *

To the extent that it endorses *Register*, the majority ... conflates depraved indifference murder with reckless manslaughter.... In concluding that depraved indifference murder has a mens rea of ordinary recklessness, the Court in *Register* essentially took the "depraved" out of depraved indifference, so that depraved indifference murder is virtually indistinguishable from reckless manslaughter. According to *Register*, depraved indifference murder and reckless manslaughter have the identical mens rea element of recklessness. The only difference between the two crimes lies in the so-called "objective circumstances" surrounding the criminal act. If the defendant's conduct created a "substantial" risk of death, the crime is second degree manslaughter. If, however, the defendant's conduct created a "grave" risk of death, the crime is depraved indifference murder.

Register conflates the two crimes not only by giving them the same mens rea, but also by seeking to differentiate them only in terms of "objective circumstances" that are all but indistinguishable. For the factfinder, everything turns on whether the defendant's conduct created a "grave" risk of death as opposed to a "substantial" risk of death. I think it is too much to ask of any juror. The difference between reckless manslaughter, which carries a minimum punishment of 1 year in prison, and depraved indifference murder, which carries a minimum punishment of 15 years in prison, should not turn on the razor-thin distinction between "substantial" and "grave."

Indeed, the *Register* Court's formulation has the effect of treating defendants with the exact same mental culpability unequally by giving them vastly different sentences even though their moral culpability is identical. This consequence violates a fundamental principle of the criminal law, which seeks to punish defendants in proportion to the blameworthiness of their offense.... As one harsh critic of *Register* has asked, "How can it be just to punish for murder, one offender whose mental culpability is no greater than that of another guilty only of manslaughter—thereby exposing the former to an additional fifteen years of imprisonment?" (Gegan, More Cases of Depraved Mind Murder: The Problem of Mens Rea, 64 St John's L Rev at 435).

QUESTIONS AND COMMENTS

1. *Risk*. Assume that we follow the Model Penal Code (and the New York Penal Law) in defining knowledge regarding a result (death, in the case of homicide) as subjective awareness of a practical certainty and recklessness as conscious disregard of a substantial and unjustifiable risk. In that case, the line between recklessness and knowledge is essentially *quantitative* (high probability vs. practical certainty) yet lacks a clearly demarcated quantitative border. See Model Penal Code Commentaries § 2.02, at 236 n.13.

What's left of the distinction after *Sanchez*? How exceptional, egregious, gross, or exceedingly high can recklessness be before it becomes knowledge? Is the line between substantial risk and practical certainty any easier to draw than that between substantial risk and grave risk? If we can distinguish meaningfully between substantial and grave risk, can we then distinguish between grave risk and practical certainty? Could the New York legislature solve the problem in *Sanchez* by making it clear that the mens rea of depraved indifference murder is knowledge?

2. *Awareness*. Knowledge and recklessness resemble each other not only in that they both turn on awareness of some *risk*, but also in that they require actual, subjective, *awareness* of that risk. (Is *Sanchez* consistent with this requirement?) Note, however, that the standard definition of recklessness (including the one in the Model Penal Code) is ambiguous in the following sense: the defendant must be subjectively aware that she's taking a risk, and the risk she's taking must *in fact* be both substantial and unjustified, but it's not clear whether or not she must be subjectively aware that the risk is substantial or unjustified. What about a case in which a surgeon knows she's taking a substantial risk but believes unambivalently, contrary to the fact finder, that the risk is *justified*? Can you be reckless and yet think you're right? Or does recklessness imply not only the fact, but also the recognition, that you're risking a wrong?

3. *Acceptance and Indifference*. Is there another dimension to the distinction between recklessness and knowledge? How significant is the requirement that the actor consciously *disregard* the risk? To act recklessly with respect to a result must she *accept*, or *reconcile herself* to, the fact that her conduct may result in the proscribed harm? Does acceptance make a difference when it comes to knowledge (or recklessness)? *Should* acceptance matter? For knowledge? Does thinking about "acceptance" also help us better understand the purpose/knowledge line? Does the defendant in *Steinberg accept* that he might kill (or seriously harm) his victim? Cf. Alan C. Michaels, "Acceptance: The Missing Mental State," 71 S. Cal. L. Rev. 953 (1998).

If conscious disregard implies acceptance, what happens to the court's attempt in *Sanchez* to distinguish between depraved indifference and recklessness? How does acceptance differ from indifference? Does that difference affect culpability?

German criminal law distinguishes sharply between a case in which the actor *hopes* that her behavior will not result in the proscribed harm, or perhaps even that she will be able to *avoid* that result, and a case in which she has no similar qualms and is happy to take her chances, and thus *accepts* the harmful result, should it occur. Even though the risk of harm I'm aware of is the same in both cases, German criminal law treats only the second case as an instance of intentional conduct.

Let's say I'm eager to try out my new high powered rifle. I drive to a large abandoned lot across town and take aim at the windows of a dilapidated burnt out building some distance away. I end up shooting and seriously wounding a homeless person asleep in the building. I was aware all along that this might happen, though I wasn't sure it would. In one case, though, I sincerely hope that the building is unoccupied and that, even if it isn't, I won't end up hitting whoever is in it. In the other, I couldn't care less if someone gets hurt—what was the victim doing trespassing anyway?

Imagine too that the defendant *behaves* differently as a result of his distinct attitudes. One defendant checks the building on Sunday to see that it is unoccupied before going shooting on Monday. We might still believe that the check is *inadequate*—the risk of killing remains too high—and that he is subjectively aware of the risk.

Would the Model Penal Code's concept of recklessness allow us to differentiate between these two cases? Should it? Cf. Israeli Penal Law § 20 (supra).

4. *Depravity*. The dissent in *Sanchez* claims that the majority read depravity out of depraved indifference. Assuming that's correct (is it?), is that necessarily a bad thing? What relevance does depravity have to the assessment of criminal liability—as opposed to moral condemnation (is it even relevant there?)? Is the line between intentional murder and depraved indifference murder—and that between depraved indifference murder and reckless manslaughter—any easier to draw if we interpret depravity as an "uncommonly evil and morally perverse frame of mind," as the dissent would have it? In fact, wouldn't that instead conflate the two offenses, by turning liability for both on the presence of a "perverse frame of mind," which manifests itself either in intentional or in depravedly indifferent action? How would we go about assessing "uncommon evil and moral perversion," and how would we know it once we saw it? What would a jury deliberation on this question look like? Would this not amount to punishing character—in violation of the act requirement?

Does the dissent nonetheless highlight a weakness in the Model Penal Code approach to the distinction between recklessness, on one hand, and purpose (or intention, in the language of the New York Penal Law) and knowledge, on the other? Perhaps one should think of the statutory reference to "depraved indifference" as an attempt to add another, subjective, dimension to the recklessness inquiry which, under the Model Penal Code, focuses on the type and magnitude of *risks*. Is there a meaningful distinction between ordinary indifference (which arguably is required for ordinary recklessness) and depraved (or gross) indifference (which would be required for gross recklessness, such as that required for depraved indifference murder)? Might we think of gross indifference as callousness (or acceptance)?

b. Willfulness

The Model Penal Code mens rea scheme has a hard time accommodating mental states other than the quartet of purpose, knowledge, recklessness, and negligence. That's not really a surprise; the point of the scheme, after all, was to *replace* the traditional mens rea concepts altogether. The concept of willfulness has proved particularly meddlesome. It appears in none of the Code's offense definitions. Yet it remains in scores of real-life criminal statutes, and therefore in judicial opinions trying to make sense of them. Most recently, it has proved particularly popular as a device for turning otherwise civil provisions into criminal statutes. And, so "because it is such a dreadful word and so common in the regulatory statutes," the Code drafters decided "to superimpose some norm of meaning on it." ALI Proceedings 160 (1955).

Model Penal Code § 2.02. General Requirements of Culpability.

> (8) *Requirement of Wilfulness Satisfied by Acting Knowingly*. A requirement that an offense be committed wilfully is satisfied if a person acts knowingly with respect to the material elements of the offense, unless a purpose to impose further requirements appears.

This provision, however, has done little to guide judicial attempts to interpret a mental state that finds no room in the Model Penal Code scheme. (Why?) Two lines of cases struggling with willfulness might be distinguished. One deals with the problem of *willful ignorance* (or conscious—or deliberate—avoidance), the other with *willfulness and knowledge of illegality*.

(i) Willful Ignorance and Conscious Avoidance

Knowledge, as actual awareness, is often difficult to prove. Faced with a defendant who steadfastly denies any knowledge of the relevant facts, a prosecutor might ask the judge to give an "ostrich" instruction.

United States v. Jewell

United States Court of Appeals for the Ninth Circuit.
532 F.2d 697 (1976).

■ BROWNING, CIRCUIT JUDGE.

[Appellant was convicted of] possession of a controlled substance, prohibited by 21 U.S.C. § 841(a)(1).... [He] argues that it was reversible error to instruct the jury that the defendant could be convicted upon proof beyond a reasonable doubt that if he did not have positive knowledge that a controlled substance was concealed in the automobile he drove over the border, it was solely and entirely because of a conscious purpose on his part to avoid learning the truth....

It is undisputed that appellant entered the United States driving an automobile in which 110 pounds of marihuana worth $6,250 had been concealed in a secret compartment between the trunk and rear seat. Appellant testified that he did not know the marihuana was present. There was circumstantial evidence from which the jury could infer that appellant had positive knowledge of the presence of the marihuana, and that his contrary testimony was false. On the other hand there was evidence from which the jury could conclude that appellant spoke the truth—that although appellant knew of the presence of the secret compartment and had knowledge of facts indicating that it contained marihuana, he deliberately avoided positive knowledge of the presence of the contraband to avoid responsibility in the event of discovery. * * *

.... The court told the jury that the government must prove beyond a reasonable doubt that the defendant ... "knowingly" possessed the marihuana. The court continued:

> The Government can complete their burden of proof by proving, beyond a reasonable doubt, that if the defendant was not actually aware that there was marijuana in the vehicle he was driving when he entered the United States his ignorance in that regard was solely and entirely a result of his having made a conscious purpose to disregard the nature of that which was in the vehicle, with a conscious purpose to avoid learning the truth.

The legal premise of these instructions is firmly supported by leading commentators here and in England.... Professor Glanville Williams states, on the basis of both English and American authorities, "To the requirement of actual knowledge there is one strictly limited exception. ... [The] rule is that if a party has his suspicion aroused but then deliberately omits to make further enquiries, because he wishes to remain in ignorance, he is deemed to have knowledge." Professor Williams concludes, "The rule that wilful blindness is equivalent to knowledge is essential, and is found throughout the criminal law."[7]

The substantive justification for the rule is that deliberate ignorance and positive knowledge are equally culpable. The textual justification is that in common understanding one "knows" facts of which he is less than absolutely certain. To act "knowingly," therefore, is not necessarily to act only with positive knowledge, but also to act with an awareness of the high

7. G. Williams, Criminal Law: The General Part, § 57 at 159 (2d ed. 1961). Mr. Williams' concluding paragraph reads in its entirety:

> The rule that wilful blindness is equivalent to knowledge is essential, and is found throughout the criminal law. It is, at the same time, an unstable rule, because judges are apt to forget its very limited scope. A court can properly find wilful blindness only where it can almost be said that the defendant actually knew. He suspected the fact; he realised its probability; but he refrained from obtaining the final confirmation because he wanted in the event to be able to deny knowledge. This, and this alone, is wilful blindness. It requires in effect a finding that the defendant intended to cheat the administration of justice. Any wider definition would make the doctrine of wilful blindness indistinguishable from the civil doctrine of negligence in not obtaining knowledge.

probability of the existence of the fact in question. When such awareness is present, "positive" knowledge is not required.

This is the analysis adopted in the Model Penal Code. Section 2.02(7) states: "When knowledge of the existence of a particular fact is an element of an offense, such knowledge is established if a person is aware of a high probability of its existence, unless he actually believes that it does not exist." As the Comment to this provision explains, "Paragraph (7) deals with the situation British commentators have denominated 'wilful blindness' or 'connivance,' the case of the actor who is aware of the probable existence of a material fact but does not satisfy himself that it does not in fact exist."[9] * * *

No legitimate interest of an accused is prejudiced by such a standard, and society's interest in a system of criminal law that is enforceable and that imposes sanctions upon all who are equally culpable requires it.

The conviction is affirmed.

■ KENNEDY, CIRCUIT JUDGE, dissenting.

The majority opinion justifies the conscious purpose jury instruction as an application of the wilful blindness doctrine recognized primarily by English authorities. A classic illustration of this doctrine is the connivance of an innkeeper who deliberately arranges not to go into his back room and thus avoids visual confirmation of the gambling he believes is taking place. The doctrine is commonly said to apply in deciding whether one who acquires property under suspicious circumstances should be charged with knowledge that it was stolen.

.... English authorities seem to consider wilful blindness a state of mind distinct from, but equally culpable as, "actual" knowledge.[6] When a statute specifically requires knowledge as an element of a crime, however, the substitution of some other state of mind cannot be justified even if the court deems that both are equally blameworthy.

Finally, the wilful blindness doctrine is uncertain in scope. There is disagreement as to whether reckless disregard for the existence of a fact constitutes wilful blindness or some lesser degree of culpability. Some cases have held that a statute's scienter requirement is satisfied by the constructive knowledge imputed to one who simply fails to discharge a duty to inform himself. There is also the question of whether to use an "objective" test based on the reasonable man, or to consider the defendant's subjective belief as dispositive.

9. Model Penal Code 129–30 (Tent. Draft No. 4, 1955). Comment 9 reads in full as follows:

Paragraph (7) deals with the situation British commentators have denominated "wilful blindness" or "connivance," the case of the actor who is aware of the probable existence of a material fact but does not satisfy himself that it does not in fact exist. Whether such cases should be viewed as instances of acting recklessly or knowingly presents a subtle but important question.

6. The use of the term "actual knowledge" in this manner is misleading in suggesting the possibility of achieving a state of total certainty, and that only such knowledge is "actual." In fact, we commonly act on less than complete information and in this world may never know one-hundred-percent certainty.

The approach adopted in section 2.02(7) of the Model Penal Code clarifies, and, in important ways restricts, the English doctrine.... This provision requires an awareness of a high probability that a fact exists, not merely a reckless disregard, or a suspicion followed by a failure to make further inquiry. It also establishes knowledge as a matter of subjective belief, an important safeguard against diluting the guilty state of mind required for conviction. It is important to note that section 2.02(7) is a *definition* of knowledge, not a substitute for it....

In light of the Model Penal Code's definition, the "conscious purpose" jury instruction is defective in three respects. First, it fails to mention the requirement that Jewell have been aware of a high probability that a controlled substance was in the car. It is not culpable to form "a conscious purpose to avoid learning the truth" unless one is aware of facts indicating a high probability of that truth. To illustrate, a child given a gift-wrapped package by his mother while on vacation in Mexico may form a conscious purpose to take it home without learning what is inside; yet his state of mind is totally innocent unless he is aware of a high probability that the package contains a controlled substance. Thus, a conscious purpose instruction is only proper when coupled with a requirement that one be aware of a high probability of the truth.

The second defect in the instruction as given is that it did not alert the jury that Jewell could not be convicted if he "actually believed" there was no controlled substance in the car. The failure to emphasize, as does the Model Penal Code, that subjective belief is the determinative factor, may allow a jury to convict on an objective theory of knowledge—that a reasonable man should have inspected the car and would have discovered what was hidden inside....

Third, the jury instruction clearly states that Jewell could have been convicted even if found ignorant or "not actually aware" that the car contained a controlled substance. This is unacceptable because true ignorance, no matter how unreasonable, cannot provide a basis for criminal liability when the statute requires knowledge. A proper jury instruction based on the Model Penal Code would be presented as a way of defining knowledge, and not as an alternative to it. * * *

QUESTIONS AND COMMENTS

1. Note how the willful ignorance cases further help to blur the line between knowledge and recklessness, by holding that suspicion—which is, in essence, subjective awareness of a possibility—followed by failure to ascertain the actual state of affairs is tantamount to knowledge, at least so long as one is *deliberate* in avoiding the knowledge. But what does it mean for a defendant to be "deliberate" (or, even more vexing, "conscious") in *not* knowing? What exactly is required for a finding of deliberateness (or consciousness) in this context? Is the failure to make inquiries enough? Or is an affirmative act of avoidance required? In United States v. Giovannetti, 919 F.2d 1223 (7th Cir. 1990) (Posner, J.), a case involving a defendant who was convicted as an accomplice for renting premises to gamblers, the willful ignorance instruction was disallowed because the defendant did *not* "act"

not to find out the premises he rented were being used by gamblers—as opposed to taking affirmative steps to avoid learning about how the room was being used. But how would we determine what he ordinarily would have found out living a life uninfluenced by the desire not to know?

2. One reason why (some) courts are eager to avoid framing conscious avoidance as a failure to act, rather than as an affirmative act, is that otherwise conscious avoidance might slip not merely from actual knowledge into constructive knowledge into recklessness, but into a form of criminal, or even of civil, negligence (i.e., a failure to exercise reasonable care, or to comply with some duty; what duty?):

> "The danger in giving the instruction where there is evidence of direct knowledge but no evidence of avoidance of knowledge is that the jury could still convict a defendant who merely should have known about the criminal venture." Conviction because the defendant "should have known" is tantamount to conviction for negligence.... *See United States v. Pacific Hide & Fur Depot, Inc.*, 768 F.2d 1096, 1098 (9th Cir. 1985) ("It is not enough that defendant was mistaken, recklessly disregarded the truth, or negligently failed to inquire."). *Accord See United States v. Murrieta–Bejarano*, 552 F.2d 1323, 1326 (9th Cir. 1977) (Kennedy, J., dissenting) ("The danger is that juries will avoid questions of scienter and convict under the standards analogous to negligence ... wholly inconsistent with the statutory requirement of scienter."); *United States v. Hanlon*, 548 F.2d 1096, 1101–02 (2d Cir. 1977) (condemning the use of the word "reckless" in deliberate ignorance jury instructions); *United States v. Bright*, 517 F.2d 584, 587 (2d Cir. 1975) ("A negligent or a foolish person is not a criminal when criminal intent is an ingredient.").
>
> In addition, courts must studiously guard against the danger of shifting the burden to the defendant to prove his or her innocence. *See Murrieta–Bejarano*, 552 F.2d at 1325 ("The effect of a [deliberate ignorance] instruction in a case in which no facts point to deliberate ignorance may be to create a presumption of guilt.").

United States v. de Francisco–Lopez, 939 F.2d 1405, 1410–11 (10th Cir. 1991).

Trial courts tend to deal with this anxiety by giving an instruction along the following lines: "The necessary knowledge cannot be established by showing that the defendant you are considering was careless, negligent or foolish." Do you think this blunt approach is likely to be effective? Do you agree with Judge Posner's suggestion, in *Giovannetti*, supra, that concerns about ostrich instructions smuggling in a negligence standard can be allayed by "thinking carefully about just what it is that real ostriches do (or at least are popularly supposed to do)"?

> They do not just fail to follow through on their suspicions of bad things. They are not merely *careless* birds. They bury their heads in the sand so that they will not see or hear bad things. They *deliberately* avoid acquiring unpleasant knowledge. The ostrich instruction is designed for cases in which there is evidence that the defendant, knowing or strongly suspecting that he is involved in shady dealings, takes steps

> to make sure that he does not acquire full or exact knowledge of the nature and extent of those dealings. A deliberate effort to avoid guilty knowledge is all the guilty knowledge the law requires.

919 F.2d at 1228.

Would it be helpful, then, to encourage jurors to consider to what extent the defendant's behavior matched that of an ostrich (real or metaphorical)?

(ii) Willfulness and Knowledge of Illegality

The concept of willfulness problematizes the boundaries of knowledge in another way. The Model Penal Code provides that "[n]either knowledge nor recklessness or negligence as to whether conduct constitutes an offense or as to the existence, meaning or application of the law determining the elements of an offense is an element of such offense, unless the definition of the offense or the Code so provides." § 2.02(9). At the same time, we've already seen that the Code equates willfulness with knowledge. § 2.02(8). And yet courts frequently hold that willfulness requires more than knowledge of the nature or results of one's conduct *and* that the "more" consists precisely in knowledge of the illegality of the conduct in question.

People v. Coe

Court of Appeals of New York.
71 N.Y.2d 852, 522 N.E.2d 1039 (1988).

Defendant, a registered nurse employed at the Isabella Geriatric Center in Manhattan, was convicted under Public Health Law § 12–b(2), after a bench trial, of wilfully violating a provision of the Public Health Law and regulations adopted thereunder (see, Public Health Law § 12–b[2]) in connection with the alleged abuse or mistreatment of an elderly resident (see, Public Health Law § 2803–d[7]; 10 N.Y. Comp. Codes R. & Regs. § 81.1[a], [b]).... Public Health Law § 2803–d(7) proscribes acts of physical abuse, neglect or mistreatment of residents or patients in facilities such as the Isabella Geriatric Center. Under 10 N.Y. Comp. Codes R. & Regs. § 81.1(a) the term "abuse" is defined as "inappropriate physical contact with a patient or resident of a residential health care facility ... Inappropriate physical contact includes, but is not limited to, striking ... shoving". Under 10 N.Y. Comp. Codes R. & Regs. § 81.1(b) "mistreatment" is defined as, among other things, "inappropriate use of physical ... restraints on ... a patient or resident of a residential health care facility".

According to the evidence adduced at trial defendant—attempting to locate two missing $5 bills—forcibly searched an 86-year-old resident who had a history of heart disease. Despite the resident's repeated objections, defendant went through his pockets while an attendant pinned his arms behind him. Shortly after the incident, the resident died.... On appeal, after a unanimous affirmance by the Appellate Division, defendant contends that the People did not make the required showing that she wilfully violated a provision of the Public Health Law or a Public Health Law regulation.

We decline to adopt the People's contention that for criminal liability under Public Health Law § 12–b(2) it need only be shown that the defendant acted deliberately and voluntarily, as opposed to accidentally. This construction requires reading the word "wilfully"—not as modifying "violates", the word which immediately follows it in the statute—but rather as describing the manner in which the underlying act was committed. In short, the People would have us read the statute as stating that any person who consciously performs an act, when such act happens to contravene some provision or regulation of the public health laws, is guilty of a misdemeanor. * * *

We also reject defendant's contention, however, that for liability under Public Health Law § 12–b it must be shown that defendant acted with an "evil motive, bad purpose or corrupt design". We hold that the Legislature, in using the term "wilfully" in Public Health Law § 12–b, intended a culpable mental state generally equivalent to that required by the term "knowingly" (see, Model Penal Code § 2.02[8]). To require proof of an evil motive or intent to injure—higher culpable mental states appropriate for intentional crimes classified as felonies—for conduct in violation of a statute or regulation which the Legislature has seen fit to classify under Public Health Law § 12–b(2) as a misdemeanor would be impermissible judicial legislation. It would also be inconsistent with the legislative purpose of protecting the public against Public Health Law violations by criminalizing a broad range of conduct under Public Health Law § 12–b but, at the same time, treating such regulatory or statutory violations as crimes of less serious degree.

Nor were the People required, as defendant impliedly argues, to demonstrate that she knew she was violating a specific statute or regulation. Rather, the People were required to show only that defendant was aware that her conduct was illegal. Here, defendant admitted receiving a copy of the patient's bill of rights (codified in Public Health Law § 2803–c) and attending lectures regarding its contents. The bill of rights mandates, among other things, that residents must be free from having their personal privacy invaded; being physically or mentally abused; and being forced to do anything against their will. Moreover, defendant admitted that she knew that it would be inappropriate to search a patient who physically resisted. There is ample support in the record for the Trial Judge's undisturbed finding that the People established "a knowing violation ... of the statute."

QUESTIONS AND COMMENTS

1. Why might the legislature require willfulness—in the sense set out in *Coe*—for "regulatory" crimes such as the one at issue in *Coe*? Why would the willfulness requirement have been redundant under the state's proposed interpretation? What, exactly, did the defendant have to "know" to be criminally liable? What, exactly, was the crime that Coe committed (be sure to assemble all objective and subjective elements)?

2. The willfulness requirement plays a key role in many areas of white collar criminal law. Tax evasion is criminal, for instance, only if it's done willfully. And willfulness, in tax criminal law, requires nothing less than a "voluntary, intentional violation of a known legal duty." This means, among other things, that a defendant may not be precluded from arguing that he truly did not know that the Internal Revenue Code treats

wages as income, and therefore as subject to income tax. See Cheek v. United States, 498 U.S. 192 (1991), infra.

3. Note the structure of Coe's crime. The court explains that she was "convicted under" Public Health Law § 12–b(2). That section, however, merely provides that willful violations of the Public Health Law or any regulation adopted thereunder are punishable as misdemeanors. The specific provision of the Public Health Law she violated, § 2803–d(7), proscribes, among other things, "physical abuse, neglect or mistreatment" of patients. To learn what constitutes "abuse" or "mistreatment," one must consult two regulations issued by the Public Health Commissioner, 10 N.Y. Comp. Codes R. & Regs. §§ 81.1(a) & (b). When the court in *Coe* mentions that Coe needn't have known that she was violating a "specific statute or regulation," which specific statute or regulation did it have in mind? Could one draw a distinction between awareness of the (substantive) provision describing illegal conduct and the (formal) provision declaring that this conduct amounts to a crime, under certain circumstances (here that it was engaged in willfully)? Or would it be enough if the defendant were aware of the norm underlying the (substantive) provision (if you're a nurse, don't abuse patients), no matter where—and in what form—she might have encountered this norm?

3. Recklessness vs. Negligence

The line between recklessness and negligence is particularly significant, and one that it would be particularly nice to draw clearly and predictably. For it's often the line that separates criminal liability from civil liability, or no liability at all. Recklessness, after all, is the default mental state in the Model Penal Code. As a result, negligence crimes are quite rare—though, interestingly, strict liability crimes (i.e., crimes with *no* mental state with respect to at least one element) aren't. In the Model Penal Code, for instance, there are all of three: negligent homicide, assault (with a deadly weapon), and criminal mischief (with dangerous means). §§ 210.4, 211.1(b), 220.3. In the New York Penal Law, four offenses explicitly require no more than negligence: negligent homicide, assault (with a deadly weapon), vehicular assault, and vehicular manslaughter. §§ 120.00(3), 120.03(1), 125.10, 125.12. (Note, however, that in New York, the default mental state is negligence, not recklessness, so that quite a few more crimes *implicitly* require negligence. N.Y. Penal Law §§ 15.15(2) & 15.00(6).)

Of course defendants may be guilty of serious crimes when they are "merely" negligent as to a critical element of the offense. For instance, in most jurisdictions, a rape defendant who negligently believes that the victim has consented is culpable: the state need not prove he was subjectively aware of the substantial and unjustifiable risk that the victim did not consent. See ch. 9.

People v. Strong

Court of Appeals of New York.
37 N.Y.2d 568, 338 N.E.2d 602, 376 N.Y.S.2d 87 (1975).

■ Jasen, Judge.

Defendant was charged, in a one-count indictment, with manslaughter in the second degree (Penal Law, § 125.15) for causing the death of

Kenneth Goings. At the trial, the defense requested that the court submit to the jury, in addition to the crime charged, the crime of criminally negligent homicide (Penal Law, § 125.10). The court refused, and the jury found defendant guilty as charged.

The sole issue upon this appeal is whether the trial court erred in refusing to submit to the jury the lesser crime of criminally negligent homicide. [W]here a reasonable view of the evidence supports a finding that a defendant committed this lesser degree of homicide, but not the greater, the lesser crime should be submitted to the jury.... If there is no reasonable view of the evidence which would support such a finding, the court may not submit such lesser offense.*

"The essential distinction between the crimes of manslaughter, second degree, and criminally negligent homicide", we said in People v. Stanfield, 36 N.Y.2d 467, 369 N.Y.S.2d 118, 330 N.E.2d 75, "is the mental state of the defendant at the time the crime was committed." (People v. Haney, 30 N.Y.2d 328, 333, 333 N.Y.S.2d 403, 407, 284 N.E.2d 564, 565.) In one, the actor perceives the risk, but consciously disregards it. (Penal Law, § 15.05, subd. 3.) In the other, he negligently fails to perceive the risk. (Penal Law, § 15.05, subd. 4.) The result and the underlying conduct, exclusive of the mental element, are the same." Although in Stanfield we pointed out that "criminal recklessness and criminal negligence ... may ... be but shades apart on the scale of criminal culpability", it would be incorrect to infer from Stanfield that in every case in which manslaughter, second degree, is charged, a defendant is entitled also to an instruction as to criminally negligent homicide.

In determining whether the defendant in this case was entitled to the charge of the lesser crime, the focus must be on the evidence in the record relating to the mental state of the defendant at the time of the crime. The record discloses that the defendant, 57 years old at the time of trial, had left his native Arabia at the age of 19, emigrating first to China and then coming to the United States three years later. He had lived in Rochester only a short time before committing the acts which formed the basis for this homicide charge. He testified that he had been of the Sudan Muslim religious faith since birth, and had become one of the sect's leaders, claiming a sizable following. Defendant articulated the three central beliefs of this religion as "cosmetic consciousness, mind over matter and psysiomatic psychomatic consciousness." He stated that the second of these beliefs, "mind over matter", empowered a "master", or leader, to lie on a bed of nails without bleeding, to walk through fire or on hot coals, to perform surgical operations without anesthesia, to raise people up off the ground, and to suspend a person's heartbeat, pulse, and breathing while that person remained conscious. In one particular type of ceremony, defendant, purportedly exercising his powers of "mind over matter", claimed he could stop a follower's heartbeat and breathing and plunge knives into his chest without any injury to the person. There was testimony

* If the court is authorized to submit a lesser included offense and either party requests that it do so, it must submit the lesser offense.

from at least one of defendant's followers that he had successfully performed this ceremony on previous occasions. Defendant himself claimed to have performed this ceremony countless times over the previous 40 years without once causing an injury. Unfortunately, on January 28, 1972, when defendant performed this ceremony on Kenneth Goings, a recent recruit, the wounds from the hatchet and three knives which defendant had inserted into him proved fatal.

We view the record as warranting the submission of the lesser charge of criminally negligent homicide since there is a reasonable basis upon which the jury could have found that the defendant failed to perceive the risk inherent in his actions. The defendant's conduct and claimed lack of perception, together with the belief of the victim and defendant's followers, if accepted by the jury, would justify a verdict of guilty of criminally negligent homicide. There was testimony, both from defendant and from one of his followers, that the victim himself perceived no danger, but in fact volunteered to participate. Additionally, at least one of the defendant's followers testified that the defendant had previously performed this ritual without causing injury. Assuming that a jury would not believe that the defendant was capable of performing the acts in question without harm to the victim, it still could determine that this belief held by the defendant and his followers was indeed sincere and that defendant did not in fact perceive any risk of harm to the victim.

That is not to say that the court should in every case where there is some subjective evidence of lack of perception of danger submit the lesser crime of criminally negligent homicide. Rather, the court should look to other objective indications of a defendant's state of mind to corroborate, in a sense, the defendant's own subjective articulation. Thus, in Stanfield, there was evidence from which the jury could have reasonably concluded that the victim herself did not view Stanfield's actions as creating any risk of harm. Here, the evidence supporting defendant's claimed state of mind is, if anything, stronger.

Therefore, on the particular facts of this case, we conclude that there is a reasonable view of the evidence which, if believed by the jury, would support a finding that the defendant was guilty only of the crime of criminally negligent homicide, and that the trial court erred in not submitting, as requested, this lesser offense to the jury.

Accordingly, we would reverse and order a new trial.

■ Gabrielli, Judge (dissenting).

[T]he evidence established defendant's awareness and conscious disregard of the risk his ceremony created and is entirely inconsistent with a negligent failure to perceive that risk. Testimony was adduced that just prior to being stabbed, Goings, a voluntary participant up to that point, objected to continuance of the ceremony saying "No, father" and that defendant, obviously evincing an awareness of the possible result of his actions, answered, "It will be all right, son". Defendant testified that after the ceremony, he noticed blood seeping from the victim's wounds and that he attempted to stop the flow by bandaging the mortally wounded Goings. Defendant further stated that when he later learned that Goings had been removed to another location and had been given something to ease the pain, he became "uptight", indicating, of course, that defendant appreciated the risks involved and the possible consequences of his acts. * * *

Can it be reasonably claimed or argued that, when the defendant inflicted the several stab wounds, one of which penetrated the victim's heart and was four and three-quarter inches deep, the defendant failed to perceive the risk? The only and obvious answer is simply "no".

Moreover, the record is devoid of evidence pointing toward a negligent lack of perception on defendant's part. The majority concludes otherwise by apparently crediting the testimony of defendant, and one of his followers, that at the time defendant was plunging knives into the victim, the defendant thought "there was no danger to it". However, it is readily apparent that the quoted statement does not mean, as the majority assert, that defendant saw no risk of harm in the ceremony, but, rather, that he thought his powers so extraordinary that resultant injury was impossible. Thus, the testimony does not establish defendant's negligent perception for even a grossly negligent individual would perceive the patent risk of injury that would result from plunging a knife into a human being; instead, the testimony demonstrates defendant's conscious disregard of the possible consequences that would naturally flow from his acts.

This case might profitably be analogized to one where an individual believing himself to be possessed of extraordinary skill as an archer attempts to duplicate William Tell's feat and split an apple on the head of another individual from some distance. However, assume that rather than hitting the apple, the archer kills the victim. Certainly, his obtuse subjective belief in his extraordinary skill would not render his actions criminally negligent. Both, in the context of ordinary understanding and the Penal Law definition (s 15.05, subd. 3), the archer was unquestionably reckless and would, therefore, be guilty of manslaughter in the second degree. The present case is indistinguishable.

Commonwealth v. Pierce

Supreme Judicial Court of Massachusetts.
138 Mass. 165 (1884).

■ HOLMES, J.

The defendant has been found guilty of manslaughter, on evidence that he publicly practised as a physician, and, being called to attend a sick woman, caused her, with her consent, to be kept in flannels saturated with kerosene for three days, more or less, by reason of which she died. There was evidence that he had made similar applications with favorable results in other cases, but that in one the effect had been to blister and burn the flesh as in the present case. * * *

The court instructed the jury, that "it is not necessary to show an evil intent;" that, "if by gross and reckless negligence he caused the death, he is guilty of culpable homicide;" that "the question is whether the kerosene (if it was the cause of the death), either in its original application, renewal, or continuance, was applied as the result of foolhardy presumption or gross negligence on the part of the defendant".... In other words, that ... he was bound at his peril to do no grossly reckless act when ... he intermeddled with the person of another. * * *

[R]ecklessness in a moral sense means a certain state of consciousness with reference to the consequences of one's acts. No matter whether defined as indifference to what those consequences may be, or as a failure to consider their nature or probability as fully as the party might and ought to have done, it is understood to depend on the actual condition of the individual's mind with regard to consequences, as distinguished from mere knowledge of present or past facts or circumstances from which some one or everybody else might be led to anticipate or apprehend them if the supposed act were done. We have to determine whether recklessness in this sense was necessary to make the defendant guilty of felonious homicide, or whether his acts are to be judged by the external standard of what would be morally reckless, under the circumstances known to him, in a man of reasonable prudence.

More specifically, the question[] raised [is] whether the defendant's ignorance of the tendencies of kerosene administered as it was will excuse the administration of it.

So far as civil liability is concerned, at least, it is very clear that what we have called the external standard would be applied, and that, if a man's conduct is such as would be reckless in a man of ordinary prudence, it is reckless in him. Unless he can bring himself within some broadly defined exception to general rules, the law deliberately leaves his idiosyncrasies out of account, and peremptorily assumes that he has as much capacity to judge and to foresee consequences as a man of ordinary prudence would have in the same situation....

If this is the rule adopted in regard to the redistribution of losses, which sound policy allows to rest where they fall in the absence of a clear reason to the contrary, there would seem to be at least equal reason for adopting it in the criminal law, which has for its immediate object and task to establish a general standard, or at least general negative limits, of conduct for the community, in the interest of the safety of all. * * *

Exceptions overruled.

QUESTIONS AND COMMENTS

1. Unlike knowledge and recklessness, recklessness and negligence do not differ quantitatively in the Model Penal Code scheme. The level of risk is the same in both cases.

Also unlike knowledge and recklessness, recklessness and negligence *do* differ in the actor's subjective awareness of that risk. The negligent actor is unaware of the risk (that the victim might die, for instance), but a reasonable person in her position would have been aware of the unduly high probability that death would result from her conduct. The reckless actor is aware of the risk, and goes ahead anyway.

(Note, however, that mere failure to perceive the risk isn't enough for negligence; the failure must be unreasonable. Cf. People v. Boutin, 75

N.Y.2d 692 (1990) (in fatal car accident, failure to see stopped vehicle not sufficient for negligent homicide liability without "any other misconduct that created or contributed to a 'substantial and unjustifiable' risk of death").)

The line between recklessness and negligence thus is only as clear as that between subjective awareness and objective awareness, or between the particular defendant and the reasonable person. The most central insight to hold in mind in this regard is that fact finders may well infer what the particular defendant believed on the basis of what *most* similarly situated people would believe, so that a defendant who is "in fact" merely negligent may be adjudged reckless.

2. One reason that "criminal recklessness and criminal negligence ... may ... be but shades apart on the scale of criminal culpability" (*Strong*) is that traditionally courts have considered recklessness as a type of negligence. The law of torts—which first developed the concepts of recklessness and negligence, while the criminal law still pondered the meaning of mens rea—has long struggled to differentiate between the two. There recklessness has been little more than an aggravated form of negligence, or that-which-isn't-quite-intention-yet-is-no-longer-mere-negligence. Consider the definition of recklessness in the Restatement of Torts and compare it to the Model Penal Code definition (can you explain the difference in terms of the different functions of the law of torts and the law of crimes?):

> **Restatement of Torts (Second) § 500. Reckless Disregard of Safety Defined.**
>
> The actor's conduct is in reckless disregard of the safety of another if he does an act ..., knowing or having reason to know of facts which would lead a reasonable man to realize, not only that his conduct creates an unreasonable risk of physical harm to another, but also that such risk is substantially greater than that which is necessary to make his conduct negligent.

Note that the difficulty of distinguishing recklessness from negligence in criminal law is compounded by the fact that negligence itself is not supposed to give rise to criminal liability unless it is "gross" or, well, "criminal." See, e.g., La. Crim. Code § 12; N.Y. Penal Law § 15.05(4). The following passage illustrates the difficulty:

> A persistent problem, faced by the courts and legislatures alike, has been the formulation of the "extra" qualities that distinguish unintended homicides, which give rise to criminal liability, from those which, at most, produce civil liability for negligence. The Model Penal Code (Tent. Draft No. 4 (April 25, 1955), Comments to § 2.02, at p. 128) observes, concerning the judicial and statutory definitions of conduct causing death which is criminal, although unintentional: "Thus under statutes, as at common law, the concept of criminal negligence has been left to judicial definition and the definitions vary greatly in their terms. As Jerome Hall has put it, the 'judicial essays run in terms of 'wanton and wilful negligence,' 'gross negligence,' and more illuminating yet, 'that degree of negligence that is more than the

negligence required to impose tort liability.' The apex of ambiguity is 'wilful, wanton negligence' which suggests a triple contradiction—'negligence' implying inadvertence; 'wilful,' intention; and 'wanton,' recklessness." * * *

Since the criminally negligent offender's liability arises only from a culpable failure to perceive the risk, his culpability is obviously less than that of the reckless offender who consciously disregards the risk. It is, however, "appreciably greater than that required for ordinary civil negligence by virtue of the 'substantial and unjustifiable' character of the risk involved and the factor of 'gross deviation' from the ordinary standard of care." (Commission Staff Notes, Gilbert Criminal Code and Penal Law (1971), cf. Prosser, Law of Torts (4th ed.), § 31; Restatement, Torts, § 282.)

People v. Haney, 30 N.Y.2d 328, 332–33 (1972).

If tort law has trouble telling the difference between ordinary negligence and recklessness, and in fact has used recklessness and gross negligence interchangeably, how can criminal law hope to draw a clear line between *gross* negligence and recklessness? How does *Pierce* deal with this question? What remains of the distinction between recklessness and negligence if the *awareness of the risk* in recklessness is judged by an objective (reasonableness) standard, rather than requiring *actual awareness* of the risk on the part of the actor? Is negligence—i.e., the *utter failure* to even recognize the risk one's actions pose to the interests of others—"obviously" (*Haney*) less culpable than recklessness, or even knowledge?

3. The Model Penal Code attempts to further differentiate recklessness from negligence by distinguishing between the relevant reference group to whom we compare the actor—"law-abiding" persons in one case, "reasonable" persons in the other. This distinction has been largely ignored, as codes tend to invoke the reasonable person in both cases. See, e.g., N.Y. Penal Law § 15.05(3) & (4); N.J. Crim. Code § 2C:2–2(b)(3) & (4); Pa. Crimes Code § 302(b)(3) & (4); see also Tex. Penal Code § 6.03(c) & (d) ("ordinary person"). What might the drafters have had in mind? George Fletcher has suggested an answer:

> If there is a reason for this shift, it is that the culpability of disregarding a risk derives from a conscious departure from a level of legally permissible risk-taking. In contrast, the culpability of failing to perceive the risk derives not from the choice to violate a legal imperative, but from the failure to meet reasonable standards of attentiveness.

George Fletcher, Rethinking Criminal Law 262 (1978).

4. NEGLIGENCE VS. STRICT LIABILITY

Francis Bowes Sayre, "Public Welfare Offenses," 33 Colum. L. Rev. 55 (1933).

Blackstone, ... summarizing the classical conception of a crime, declared that "to constitute a crime against human laws, there must be first a vicious will, and secondly an unlawful act consequent upon such vicious will." "There can be no crime large or small without an evil mind," says

Bishop. "It is therefore a principle of our legal system, as probably it is of every other, that the essence of an offense is the wrongful intent, without which it cannot exist."

In the face of an almost unbroken line of authorities to similar effect we are witnessing today a steadily growing stream of offenses punishable without any criminal intent whatsoever. Convictions may be had for the sales of adulterated or impure food, violations of the liquor laws, infractions of anti-narcotic acts, and many other offenses based upon conduct alone without regard to the mind or intent of the actor. . . .

What does this ... movement portend?. . . . Are we to look forward to a day when criminality will be based upon external behavior alone irrespective of intent?

No such conclusion is warranted. Criminality is and always will be based upon a requisite state of mind as one of its prime factors. . . . "Public welfare offenses," if one may coin the phrase, constitute, however, a noteworthy exception. . . .

All criminal law is a compromise between two fundamentally conflicting interests—that of the public which demands restraint of all who injure or menace the social well-being and that of the individual which demands maximum liberty and freedom from interference. . . . During the nineteenth century it was the individual interest which held the stage; the criminal law machinery was overburdened with innumerable checks to prevent possible injustice to individual defendants. The scales were weighted heavily in his favor, and, as we have found to our sorrow, the public welfare often suffered. In the twentieth century came reaction. We are thinking today more of the protection of social and public interests; and coincident with the swinging of the pendulum in the field of legal administration in this direction modern criminologists are teaching the objective underlying correctional treatment should change from the barren aim of punishing human beings to the fruitful one of protecting social interests. * * *

[S]wamped with ... inundations of cases of petty violations, the lower criminal courts would be physically unable to examine the subjective intent of each defendant, even were such determination desirable. As a matter of fact it is not; for the penalty in such cases is so slight that the courts can afford to disregard the individual in protecting the social interest.

The ready enforcement which is vital for effective petty regulation on an extended scale can be gained only by a total disregard of the state of mind. * * *

How then can one determine practically which offenses do and which do not require *mens rea*, where the statute creating the offense is entirely silent as to requisite knowledge? Although no hard and fast lines can be drawn, two cardinal principles stand out upon which the determination must turn.

The first relates to the character of the offense. All criminal enactments in a sense serve the double purpose of singling out wrongdoers for the purpose of punishment or correction and of regulating the social order. But often the importance of the one far outweighs the other. Crimes created primarily for the purpose of singling out individual wrongdoers for punishment or correction are the ones commonly requiring *mens rea*; police offenses of a merely regulatory nature are frequently enforceable irrespective of a guilty intent.

The second criterion depends upon the possible penalty. If this be serious, particularly if the offense be punishable by imprisonment, the individual interest of the defendant weighs too heavily to allow conviction without proof of a guilty mind. To subject defendants entirely free from moral blameworthiness to the possibility of prison sentences is revolting to the community sense of justice; and no law which violates this fundamental instinct can long endure.

Morissette v. United States

Supreme Court of the United States.
342 U.S. 246, 72 S.Ct. 240 (1952).

■ MR. JUSTICE JACKSON delivered the opinion of the Court.

[Morissette was convicted of "converting" $84 worth of federal property, by selling spent bomb casings as scrap metal, under the following statute in the federal criminal code (title 18):

> Whoever embezzles, steals, purloins, or knowingly converts to his use or the use of another, or without authority, sells, conveys or disposes of any record, voucher, money, or thing of value of the United States or of any department or agency thereof, or any property made or being made under contract for the United States or any department or agency thereof ... shall be fined not more than $10,000 or imprisoned not more than ten years, or both; but if the value of such property does not exceed the sum of $100, he shall be fined not more than $1,000 or imprisoned not more than one year, or both. (18 U.S.C. § 641)

Morissette defended on the ground that he believed the bomb casings had been abandoned. He had found them on a practice bombing range while hunting. Despite the presence of signs reading "Danger—Keep Out—Bombing Range," the range "was known as good deer country and was extensively hunted."

In a lengthy opinion, the Supreme Court reversed the conviction, reading an "intent" requirement into the statute because it did not define a "public welfare" offense. Instead the Court held that "[s]tealing, larceny, and its variants and equivalents, were among the earliest offenses known to the law that existed before legislation; they are invasions of rights of property which stir a sense of insecurity in the whole community and arouse public demand for retribution, the penalty is high and, when a sufficient amount is involved, the infamy is that of a felony, which, says Maitland, is 'as bad a word as you can give to man or thing.' "]

The contention that an injury can amount to a crime only when inflicted by intention is no provincial or transient notion ..., although a few exceptions ... came to be recognized.[8] ... [There is] a category of ... crimes ... that depend on no mental element but consist only of forbidden acts or omissions. This ... is made clear from examination of a century-old but accelerating tendency, discernible both here and in England, to call into

8. Exceptions came to include sex offenses, such as [statutory] rape, in which the victim's actual age was determinative despite defendant's reasonable belief that the girl

existence new duties and crimes which disregard any ingredient of intent. The industrial revolution multiplied the number of workmen exposed to injury from increasingly powerful and complex mechanisms, driven by freshly discovered sources of energy, requiring higher precautions by employers. Traffic of velocities, volumes and varieties unheard of came to subject the wayfarer to intolerable casualty risks if owners and drivers were not to observe new cares and uniformities of conduct. Congestion of cities and crowding of quarters called for health and welfare regulations undreamed of in simpler times. Wide distribution of goods became an instrument of wide distribution of harm when those who dispersed food, drink, drugs, and even securities, did not comply with reasonable standards of quality, integrity, disclosure and care. Such dangers have engendered increasingly numerous and detailed regulations which heighten the duties of those in control of particular industries, trades, properties or activities that affect public health, safety or welfare.

[L]awmakers . . . have sought to make such regulations more effective by invoking criminal sanctions to be applied by the familiar technique of criminal prosecutions and convictions. This has confronted the courts with a multitude of prosecutions, based on statutes or administrative regulations, for what have been aptly called "public welfare offenses." These cases do not fit neatly into any of such accepted classifications of common-law offenses, such as those against the state, the person, property, or public morals. Many of these offenses are not in the nature of positive aggressions or invasions, with which the common law so often dealt, but are in the nature of neglect where the law requires care, or inaction where it imposes a duty. Many violations of such regulations result in no direct or immediate injury to person or property but merely create the danger or probability of it which the law seeks to minimize. While such offenses do not threaten the security of the state in the manner of treason, they may be regarded as offenses against its authority, for their occurrence impairs the efficiency of controls deemed essential to the social order as presently constituted. In this respect, whatever the intent of the violator, the injury is the same, and the consequences are injurious or not according to fortuity. Hence, legislation applicable to such offenses, as a matter of policy, does not specify intent as a necessary element. The accused, if he does not will the violation, usually is in a position to prevent it with no more care than society might reasonably expect and no more exertion than it might reasonably exact from one who assumed his responsibilities. Also, penalties commonly are relatively small, and conviction does not grave damage to an offender's reputation.

State v. Wingate

Court of Appeal of Louisiana, First Circuit.
668 So.2d 1324 (1996).

■ KUHN, JUDGE.

Relator, Edwin Wingate, was charged by bill of information with one count of possession of undersized catfish, in violation of La. Rev. Stat.

had reached age of consent. . . . Most extensive inroads upon the requirement of intention, however, are offenses of negligence, such as involuntary manslaughter or criminal negligence and the whole range of crimes arising from omission of duty.

56:326 A(7)(b).... Relator pled not guilty and, after a bench trial on July 11, 1995, was found guilty as charged [and] was sentenced to 60 days in the parish jail and was fined $400, or 30 days in the parish jail in default of payment of the fine.

On December 4, 1994, relator's tractor-trailer was stopped by Wildlife and Fisheries agents on I–10 in St. Tammany Parish just before the Mississippi state line. A search of the truck, which contained a large shipment of frozen catfish, revealed that a very high proportion of the shipment consisted of undersized channel catfish. Relator, a truck driver for Bennett Seafood, which is located in Bainbridge, Georgia, was arrested and cited for the above violations. * * *

Relator stated ... he furnished a tractor-truck, and Bennett Seafood provided the trailer. He explained Bennett Seafood placed orders for the catfish, and he only picked them up, wrote a check for the purchase, and transported the fish back to Bennett Seafood. He testified he did not open the boxes, and he did not know what size fish were in the boxes....

In this assignment of error, relator contends that the trial court erred in finding him guilty of possession of undersized catfish. Specifically, he urges there was no showing of knowledge or scienter. Relator states he "did not know what size catfish he picked up and was transporting and had no way of knowing except to rip open each sealed box" and defrost the fish therein. He requests this Court to "read into the law scienter or knowledge." We decline to do so. * * *

It is well established that some crimes have no intent element. We note the Legislature could have placed an intent requirement into La. Rev. Stat. § 56:326 A, but it did not do so. We believe there is an important reason why. To judicially read into this statute the requirement of scienter or guilty knowledge as urged by relator would further hamper the already strained enforcement efforts of Wildlife and Fisheries agents. An intent requirement might not significantly reduce the apprehension and prosecution of commercial fishermen who take and/or possess undersized fish, but it would make the prosecution of wholesale and retail dealers virtually impossible. A dealer could simply claim to have no knowledge of the number, size, or species of fish which had been cleaned, frozen or packaged, which would be almost an absolute defense. While we are not unsympathetic to relator's argument that an unknowing and otherwise innocent person might be convicted of a violation of this statute simply by doing his job as a truck driver, we note that all persons (hunters, recreational fishermen, commercial fishermen, seafood dealers, etc.) must familiarize themselves with all applicable Wildlife and Fisheries laws or risk prosecution for violations thereof....

QUESTIONS AND COMMENTS

1. Could the Supreme Court have decided *Morissette* without reference to the question of strict liability? See Henry M. Hart, Jr., "The Aims of the Criminal Law," 23 Law & Contemp. Probs. 401, 431–32 (1958)

(*Morissette* raises simple question of "claim of right," which traditionally has been held to negative the requisite intent for larceny and similar property offenses).

How would *Morissette* be resolved under the Model Penal Code rules regarding the general requirement of culpability and the interpretation of statutes with ambiguous mental state requirements?

Note that in the wake of *Morissette*, federal courts have differentiated between knowing that the converted property belonged to the United States and knowing that it belonged to another (i.e., someone other than the defendant). After initially holding that 18 U.S.C. § 641 required the former knowledge, courts are now satisfied that the latter, more general, knowledge is enough. See, e.g., United States v. Speir, 564 F.2d 934 (10th Cir. 1977) ("thing of value of the United States" is jurisdictional element).

2. What, at any rate, is the distinction between "public welfare offenses" and "real" (or "traditional" or "common law") crimes? Is it the *stigma* attached to a conviction (or perhaps the infliction of the punishment—think of the pillory or modern shaming penalties like John TV, where the pictures and names of persons convicted of soliciting prostitution are shown on television)? How is that measured? Doesn't the stigma change over time? *Shouldn't* it change, if we're serious about punishing, say, heavy polluters who ruin the environment? Isn't stigmatization a necessary (a desirable?) aspect of all punishment? Does it matter how the *defendant* perceives the stigma of (another?) conviction? Why should it matter for purposes of strict liability how traditional a crime is? Is strict liability more, or *less*, appropriate for new crimes that extend criminal liability in novel ways? For new crimes that criminalize behavior that is not *malum in se* (wrong in itself), but punished merely because it is a *malum prohibitum*, i.e., *because* the state prohibits it? Or is the problem not with strict liability, but with public welfare offenses—or more generally, overcriminalization—in the first place? Would public welfare offenses be unobjectionable if they required all the mens rea in the world?

When does a new offense become a "traditional" offense? Would a public welfare offense in 1952 be a traditional offense today? Don't all offenses punish a *malum prohibitum*? Isn't one of the reasons for punishing murder, say, that the "offender" offended against the authority of the state, "violated" a state statute, "disobeyed" the state's order to refrain from killing other people, etc.? Why does it matter whether a crime amounts to a *malum in se*? Since when is the law in general, and the criminal law in particular, concerned with moral wrongs as such? Doesn't a moral wrong become a legal wrong precisely because it violates a legal proscription, in the form of a state statute? Isn't that what the principle of legality is all about (see ch. 2)?

Assuming we can distinguish *malum prohibitum* offenses from those that are *malum in se*, can their punishment be justified in light of the traditional rationales for punishment? If there is nothing intrinsically wrong about the conduct, what justifies its punishment in the first place, with or without a mental state requirement? Is there something objectionable about not playing by the rules because it's wrong (?) to violate norms while benefiting from everyone else's compliance with them (think of driving on the designated side of the road), or because it's bad (?) to think of oneself as being above norms designed to police the (unintentional) behavior of others less skilled, smart, and otherwise competent (think of speeding)? See Stuart Green, "Why It's a Crime to Tear the Tag Off a Mattress: Overcriminalization and the Moral Content of Regulatory Offenses," 46 Emory L.J. 1533 (1997) (fair play); R.A. Duff, "Crime, Prohibition, and Punishment," 19 J. Applied Phil. 97, 104 (2002) ("civic arrogance").

Sayre, in his 1933 article (supra) that introduced the term "public welfare" into American criminal law and continues to be cited extensively today, draws two distinctions between public welfare and other offenses. One is based on the "character" of the offense, the other on the penalty. As to character, how helpful is it to contrast "crimes created primarily for the purpose of singling out individual wrongdoers for punishment or correction" with "police offenses of a merely regulatory nature"? Recall (from ch. 1) that, at bottom, every crime is a police offense given that the power to punish as a whole is said to derive from the power to police, which "extends to the protection of the lives, limbs, health, comfort, and quiet of all persons, and the protection of all property." Slaughter–House Cases, 83 U.S. 36, 49–50 (1873).

What about the quantity (or the quality) of (the threatened, the imposed, the inflicted?) punishment? Should this matter for purposes of deciding whether strict liability is appropriate (whether a court should read a mental state requirement into an ambiguous statute; whether the state may constitutionally do away with a mental state requirement)? Are you convinced by the Model Penal Code's attempt to limit strict liability to "non-criminal" offenses called "violations," that are punishable by (any!) fine, but not by imprisonment? Model Penal Code § 2.05. While courts often generally refer to the fact that public welfare offenses tend not to be "serious," in fact they (and particularly the U.S. Supreme Court) have not limited strict liability to nonserious offenses (offenses that aren't punishable by prison, or misdemeanors, or violations, etc.). See, e.g., United States v. Balint, 258 U.S. 250 (1922) (strict liability narcotics offense punishable by up to five years' imprisonment); United States v. Dotterweich, 320 U.S. 277 (1943) (strict liability offense of shipping mislabeled drugs punishable by up to one year's imprisonment); see also In re Ronnie L., 121 Misc. 2d 271 (N.Y. Fam. Ct. 1983), supra (strict liability weapons possession, a D felony, punishable by up to seven years' imprisonment, N.Y. Penal Law § 70.00(2)(d)).

3. *Morissette* held that the statute required "intent," but did not specify just what sort was needed. Would a negligence standard satisfy the Court? How, exactly, would negligence differ from strict liability? Instead of thinking of strict liability (and, perhaps even negligence) as doing away with a mental state requirement altogether, does it make sense to think of strict liability as an irrebuttable (conclusive) presumption of negligence, which takes certain fact finding issues away from juries for certain reasons? Would a requirement of negligence necessarily be *preferable* to strict liability?

Mark Kelman has challenged the traditional distinction between (certain forms of) negligence and strict liability, calling for a more differentiated, case-by-case assessment of the respective merits of negligence and strict liability:

> In essence, the legislative "policy" decision whether to condemn a defendant only where negligence is shown or to condemn whenever harm is caused is simply a perfectly traditional "balancing" of interests between rules and standards. If the legislature enacts a negligence standard, so that, *e.g.*, a manufacturer is liable for sending out adulterated food only if he acted unreasonably, or a liquor license holder is liable for selling to underage customers only if he screened customers unreasonably, two rather poor, though different, sets of bad consequences can result. If the negligence standard is vaguely defined, so that each jury is simply instructed to determine whether the particular defendant was reasonable, jury verdicts will be inconsistent, unpredictable and biased—classic problems of standards. Moreover, if the particular jury equates reasonable behavior with ordinary behavior, an entire industry may free itself of responsibility by uniformly acting less carefully than the legislature would like. On the other hand, the legislature may *predefine* "reasonable care," setting out a precise series of steps which the defendant must take to be found nonnegligent. The problem is that this centralized command may be imperfectly tuned to the precise circumstances each potential defendant is in. Each defendant may know a cheaper, more effective way of averting harm. But it may be in the defendant's selfish interest to adopt the legislature's technique, even if it will cause more social harm.
>
> Strict liability—that is, conclusively presuming that causing harm is blameworthy—has its costs too. Like all conclusive presumptions, it is inaccurate in particular cases. There will be cases where someone gets blamed whom, on closer analysis, we should not have blamed. Of course, that is true in the "rule-like" form of negligence too, where we demand that actors take predefined steps. And what may be worse, the "rule-like" form of negligence may induce socially irrational behavior. The standard-like form of negligence may convict some innocents, too. But it may convict innocents for *bad* reasons (*e.g.*, race prejudice of juries) rather than for *no* reason (*i.e.*, the accidental overinclusiveness of the conclusive presumption).

Mark G. Kelman, "Interpretive Construction in the Substantive Criminal Law," 33 Stan. L. Rev. 591, 609–10 (1981).

In response, Kenneth Simons has proposed a new analysis of strict liability from an explicitly retributive perspective:

> Kelman seems to believe that ... the distinction between negligence and strict liability [is] illusory in every case.... If his analysis were correct, then we could characterize any strict liability prohibition as an acceptable rule-like form of negligence. But, to take an extreme case, it surely is not consistent with retributive blame to replace our current homicide statutes with a simple prohibition on causing the death of another person, on the theory that such a prohibition is

merely the "rule-like" form of prohibitions against murder, manslaughter, and negligent homicide.

On the other hand, Kelman's challenge is an important one. Why is it permissible for a state to pass a law requiring two forms of identification before one sells liquor to any person, in lieu of a law simply prohibiting the sale of liquor to a person one should know is a minor? And why are these two laws (the rule-like and standard-like forms of negligence, respectively) justifiable on a retributive theory, while a prohibition on selling liquor to a minor without regard to fault is not so justifiable?

... To satisfy retributivist ideals fully, a legislature would ... adopt a form of criminal legislation which, as foreseeably applied, would result in the conviction of a class of offenders only a very small proportion of whom would be nonculpable. With respect to the choice between a rule-like and standard-like form of negligence, it would, all other things equal, adopt that form that would result in the punishment of a class of offenders of which a smaller proportion would be nonculpable. But all other things are not equal. Concerns about fair notice and about bias and inconsistency in the application of criminal norms by juries (and judges) are legitimate. On a pluralist view of the permissible goals of legislation, these concerns properly constrain the full implementation of the retributivist ideal. * * *

Thus, to return to an earlier example, it is permissible for a state to pass a law requiring two forms of identification before one sells liquor to any person, in lieu of a law simply prohibiting the sale of liquor to a person one should know is a minor. The rule-like form of negligence here appears reasonably accurate in excluding those who should not know that the buyer is a minor, provides much clearer notice than the standard-like form, and is relatively easy for the judge or jury to apply. By contrast, a prohibition on selling liquor to a minor without regard to fault is not justifiable, if (as likely) a substantial proportion of those whom the law would punish are not culpable.

Kenneth W. Simons, "When Is Strict Criminal Liability Just?," 87 J. Crim. L. & Criminology 1075, 1128–31 (1997).

4. If strict liability is morally objectionable, why not negligence? In both cases, criminal liability is assessed without proof of subjective awareness. But without awareness, how can there be the opportunity for choice, which—according to *Morissette*—undergirds "our substantive criminal law"? But without even the opportunity for choice, how can there be blame—and punishment—for "choosing freely to do wrong"? Cf. Jerome Hall, "Negligent Behavior Should Be Excluded from Penal Liability," 63 Colum. L. Rev. 632 (1963). Do we exercise meaningful control over the degree to which we *become* aware? Do we, at least to some degree, choose (over time) whether or not we will be unaware *at a particular time*?

5. In thinking about the relative merits of strict liability and negligence and the "public welfarenesss" of offenses, consider the case of United States v. Hanousek, 176 F.3d 1116 (9th Cir. 1999). On Hanousek's watch as "roadmaster" of a stretch of railroad, a backhoe operator struck a pipeline,

spilling thousands of gallons of oil into an Alaskan river. Hanousek was convicted of "negligently discharging a harmful quantity of oil into a navigable water of the United States" in violation of the federal Clean Water Act (CWA), and sentenced to six months' imprisonment, six months in a halfway house, six months' supervised release, and a $5,000 fine. The court first decided that Congress intended that ordinary civil negligence, defined as "the failure to use reasonable care," be sufficient for criminal liability under the CWA. It then held that the creation of a civil negligence crime did not violate due process because the CWA's criminal provisions "are clearly designed to protect the public at large from the potentially dire consequences of water pollution and as such fall within the category of public welfare legislation." What does the "as such" mean here—is it the protection of the public at large that makes the difference, or the potentially dire consequences, or the nature of the consequences (water pollution)? What if it turned out the Act was intended to protect the purity of the water in the river, or the flora and fauna living within it, or the beauty of unspoiled nature for the enjoyment by the public at large? What exactly *are* the dire consequences of polluting a river? If we do away with criminal negligence, should we require at least some evidence as to the likelihood of harm, e.g., that the spill would affect the drinking water supply—of lone hunters, of cities, of states?

6. The statute under which Wingate was convicted contains the following provision, dealing with the possession of undersized crabfish:

> [A] wholesale or retail dealer and a commercial fisherman may be subject to the penalties provided by law for the possession of undersized crabs. If the wholesale or retail dealer can provide to wildlife and fisheries agents at the time of discovery the identity of the commercial fisherman who harvested the undersized crabs and subsequently sold such crabs to the wholesale or retail dealer, the dealer shall not be subject to the penalties.

La. Rev. Stat. § 56:326(F)(1).

How should we classify this provision? Is it a defense? An exemption? Or an instruction directed at law enforcement officials, prosecutors, judges? Does it bar conviction, or only punishment? Is it proper to limit it to the possession of undersized crabfish (but not catfish)? Even if Wingate had been caught possessing undersized crabfish, could he have benefited from the provision—does a trucker qualify as a "wholesale or retail dealer"?

What does this provision, in substance and form, tell you about the function and role of possession offenses (in *Wingate*, in general) and of strict liability offenses? For a detailed discussion of possession offenses, see ch. 4.

7. Note that *Morissette* did not address the *constitutionality* of the federal conversion statute. The Supreme Court was merely interpreting a federal statute, in its capacity as the highest federal court in the land, rather than as the ultimate arbiter of federal constitutional questions. In fact, the Court went out of its way to clarify that "[c]onsequences of a general abolition of intent as an ingredient of serious crimes . . . [o]f course . . . would not justify judicial disregard of a clear command to that effect

from Congress." Accordingly there appears to be no (federal) constitutional bar to doing away with mens rea for even the most serious of offenses. This observation is subject to two narrow exceptions. First, the Court presumably would object to the imposition of capital punishment for a strict liability crime, because "death is different." See Enmund v. Florida, 458 U.S. 782 (1982) (capital punishment to be proportionate to blameworthiness). Second, the Court has been more receptive to constitutional attacks on strict liability in cases implicating free speech rights, on account of the "firstness of the first amendment." See, e.g., United States v. X–Citement Video, Inc., 513 U.S. 64 (1994). On these issues, see generally Herbert L. Packer, "Mens Rea and the Supreme Court," 1962 Sup. Ct. Rev. 107, 107 (concluding that "mens rea is an important requirement, but it is not a constitutional requirement, except sometimes"). Packer's classic article is updated in Richard Singer & Douglas Husak, "Of Innocence and Innocents: The Supreme Court and Mens Rea Since Herbert Packer," 2 Buff. Crim. L. Rev. 859, 943 (1999) ("we can say with Packer: mens rea is not constitutionally mandated, except sometimes"). For an attempt to expose a consistent rationale underlying the Supreme Court's jurisprudence on the constitutional status of the mens rea requirement, see Alan C. Michaels, "Constitutional Innocence," 112 Harv. L. Rev. 828 (1999) (strict liability unconstitutional if, and only if, "the other elements of the crime, with the strict liability element excluded, could not themselves be made a crime"); cf. R.A. Duff, "Strict Liability, Legal Presumptions, and the Presumption of Innocence," in Appraising Strict Liability (A.P. Simester ed. 2005) (proposing similar test for the legitimacy—as opposed to the constitutionality—of strict liability); see also Markus Dirk Dubber, "Toward a Constitutional Law of Crime and Punishment," 55 Hastings L.J. 509, 549 (2004) (mens rea requirement as manifestation of autonomy).

8. Best known among the "few exceptions" to the general mens rea requirement acknowledged in *Morissette* are "sex offenses, such as rape, in which the victim's actual age was determinative despite defendant's reasonable belief that the girl had reached age of consent." Besides the felony of "statutory" rape—which was called "statutory" precisely because it was defined by statute, and therefore not subject to the common law presumption of mens rea—there was also bigamy, another felony. A well-known nineteenth century Massachusetts case held, for instance, that "if a woman, who has a husband living, marry another person, she is punishable, though her husband has voluntarily withdrawn from her, and remained absent and unheard of, for any term of time less than seven years, and though she honestly believes, at the time of her second marriage, that he is dead." Commonwealth v. Mash, 48 Mass. (7 Metc.) 472 (1844). (Does this amount to strict liability, or a temporary conclusive presumption of negligence?) The court explained, in an opinion by Chief Justice Shaw, that "in a matter of this importance, so essential to the peace of families and the good order of society, it was not the intention of the law to make the legality of a second marriage, whilst the former husband or wife is in fact living, depend upon ignorance of such absent party's being alive, or even upon an honest belief of such person's death." (Does this mean that the more *serious* the offense, the *better* the case for strict liability?) To what degree are we evaluating instead how readily the ignorant defendant could

have avoided the offense? It might "chill" less behavior that we want to encourage if we tell people they simply may not marry for seven years after their spouse disappears than if we told merchants they'd be strictly liable for receiving stolen property any time property they dealt in turned out to be stolen.

9. The statutory rape and bigamy cases highlight the connection between the problem of strict liability and that of mistake. Mistakes serve to negate a subjective offense element: "I didn't *know* that my wife was dead and therefore lacked the requisite mental state attached to the attendant circumstance of the first spouse being alive at the time of my second marriage." (Or, in *Morissette*, I *thought* the bomb casings had been abandoned, so I couldn't have *intended* to convert them.) But if there is no subjective offense element, then mistakes are beside the point. The "strict liability" cases involving statutory rape thus are really about the relevance of a mistake regarding an offense element, more specifically the attendant circumstance of the victim's age. (Mistakes are discussed in greater detail later on in this chapter.)

10. Another issue that often confuses discussions of strict liability is the distinction between strict liability *offenses* and strict liability *elements*. Earlier judicial decisions focused on the question of whether the offense as a whole featured *some* mental state requirement, no matter to which element(s) it might attach.

Consider, for instance, *Regina v. Prince*, a well-known nineteenth century English case:

> By sect. 55 of the Offences against the Person Act, 1861: "Whosoever shall unlawfully take . . . any unmarried girl, being under the age of sixteen years, out of the possession and against the will of her father or mother, or of any other person having the lawful care or charge of her, shall be guilty of a misdemeanour . . ."
>
> At the assizes for Surrey held at Kingston-on-Thames on Mar. 24, 1875, Henry Prince was tried before Denman, J., on the charge of having unlawfully taken one Annie Phillips, an unmarried girl being under the age of sixteen years, out of the possession, and against the will of her father, contrary to sect. 55 of the Offences against the Person Act, 1861. [T]he defendant pleaded in defence that the girl Annie Phillips, though proved by her father to be fourteen years old on April 6, 1875, looked very much older than sixteen. [T]he jury found upon reasonable evidence that before the defendant took her away she had told him that she was eighteen, that the defendant bona fide believed that statement, and that such belief was reasonable. . . .
>
> ■ BRAMWELL, B. [I]t is said . . . the statute . . . must be read as though the word "knowingly" or some equivalent word was in it. The reason given is that as a rule mens rea is necessary to make any act a crime or offence, and that, if the facts necessary to constitute an offence are not known to the alleged offender, there can be no mens rea. . . .
>
> The legislature has enacted that if anyone does this wrong act he does it at the risk of the girl turning out to be under sixteen. This

> opinion gives full scope to the doctrine of mens rea. If the taker believed he had the father's consent, though wrongly, he would have no mens rea. So if he did not know she was in anyone's possession, nor in the care or charge of anyone. In those cases he would not know he was doing the act forbidden by the statute, an act which, if he knew she was in the possession and care or charge of anyone, he would know was a crime or not according as she was under sixteen or not.

Regina v. Prince, L.R. 2 C.C.R. 154 (1875).

Consistent with its element analysis (see ch. 4), the Model Penal Code instead focuses on offense elements without mental state requirements, so that any offense that contains a strict liability *element* violates the basic principle that "a person is not guilty of an offense unless he acted purposely, knowingly, recklessly or negligently, as the law may require, *with respect to each material element of the offense.*" Model Penal Code § 2.02(1) (emphasis added).

The modern approach is illustrated by *State v. Guest*:

> The question presented in the State's petition for review is whether an honest and reasonable mistake of fact regarding a victim's age may serve as a defense to a charge of statutory rape.
>
> On April 7, 1977, the respondents, Moses Guest and Jacob Evan, were charged with the statutory rape of T.D.G., age fifteen, in violation of Alaska Stat. § 11.15.120.[1] The parties entered into a stipulation that "the evidence expected to be presented at trial will support a reasonable belief on the part of each defendant that the alleged victim, age 15, was sixteen years of age or older at the time of the alleged act of sexual intercourse." In light of that stipulation, the court ordered that it would [give an instruction on reasonable mistake of age.] The state brings a petition for review from that order.
>
> Respondents concede that in most jurisdictions a reasonable mistake of age is not a defense to a charge of statutory rape....
>
> We recognized in Speidel v. State, 460 P.2d 77 (Alaska 1969), that consciousness of wrongdoing is an essential element of penal liability. "It is said to be a universal rule that an injury can amount to a crime only when inflicted by intention that conduct cannot be criminal unless it is shown that one charged with criminal conduct had an awareness or consciousness of some wrongdoing."....
>
> Our opinion in Speidel stated that there are exceptions to the general requirement of criminal intent which are categorized as "public welfare" offenses.... Statutory rape may not appropriately be categorized as a public welfare offense. It is a serious felony. If the offender is less than nineteen years of age, he may be imprisoned for up to twenty years. If he is nineteen years of age or older, he may be punished by imprisonment for any term of years.

1. Section 11.15.120 provides in relevant part:

Rape. (a) a person who ... (2) being 16 years of age or older, carnally knows and abuses a person under 16 years of age, is guilty of rape.

> [W]e hold that a charge of statutory rape is defensible where an honest and reasonable mistake of fact as to the victim's age is shown.

State v. Guest, 583 P.2d 836 (Alaska 1978).

Why is statutory rape *not* a public welfare offense? What (or who) is offended in a statutory rape if not the public welfare? What aspect of the public welfare is offended in a crime like statutory rape? In a violation of the Clean Water Act? The possession of undersized catfish? Who (or what) is the victim in *Prince*?

Can the following Model Penal Code provisions dealing with mistakes as to age in sex offenses be squared with Model Penal Code §§ 2.02(1) & 2.05?

Model Penal Code § 213.1. Rape and Related Offenses.

(1) *Rape*. A male who has sexual intercourse with a female ... is guilty of rape if:

(d) the female is less than 10 years old.

Rape is a felony in the second degree....

Model Penal Code § 213.6. Provisions Generally Applicable to Article 213.

(1) *Mistake as to Age*. Whenever in this Article the criminality of conduct depends on a child's being below the age of 10, it is no defense that the actor did not know the child's age, or reasonably believed the child to be older than 10. When criminality depends on the child's being below a critical age other than 10, it is a defense for the actor to prove by a preponderance of the evidence that he reasonably believed the child to be above the critical age.

E. CONCURRENCE

Cal. Penal Code § 20.

In every crime or public offense there must exist a union, or joint operation of act and intent, or criminal negligence.

Regina v. Faulkner

Court of Crown Cases Reserved, Ireland.
13 Cox Crim. Cas. 550 (1877).

At the Cork Summer Assizes, 1876, the prisoner was indicted for setting fire to the ship Zemindar, on the high seas, on the 26th day of June, 1876.... It was proved that the Zemindar was on her voyage home with a cargo of rum, sugar, and cotton, worth 50,000£. That the prisoner was a seaman on board, that he went into the bulk head ... for the purpose of stealing some rum, that he bored a hole in the cask with a gimlet, that the rum ran out, that when trying to put a spile in the hole out of which the rum was running, he had a lighted match in his hand; that the rum caught fire; that the prisoner himself was burned on the arms and neck; and that the ship caught fire and was completely destroyed....

At the second hearing of the case before the Court for Crown Cases Reserved, the learned judge made the addition of the following paragraph to the case stated by him for the court.

"It was conceded that the prisoner had no actual intention of burning the vessel, and I was not asked to leave any question to the jury as to the prisoner's knowing the probable consequences of his act, or as to his reckless conduct."

The learned judge told the jury that although the prisoner had no actual intention of burning the vessel, still if they found he was engaged in stealing the rum, and that the fire took place in the manner above stated, they ought to find him guilty. The jury found the prisoner guilty on both counts, and he was sentenced to seven years penal servitude. The question for the court was whether the direction of the learned judge was right, if not, the conviction should be quashed. * * *

■ BARRY, J.

A very broad proposition has been contended for by the Crown, namely, that if, while a person is engaged in committing a felony, or, having committed it, is endeavouring to conceal his act, or prevent or spoil waste consequent on that act, he accidently does some collateral act which if done wilfully would be another felony either at common law or by statute, he is guilty of the latter felony.... No express authority either by way of decision or *dictum* from judge or text writer has been cited in support of it.... I shall consider myself bound for the purpose of this case by the authority of *Reg. v. Pembliton* (12 Cox C. C. 607). That case must be taken as deciding that to constitute an offence under the Malicious Injuries to Property Act, sect. 51, the act done must be in fact intentional and wilful, although the intention and will may (perhaps) be held to exist in, or be proved by, the fact that the accused knew that the injury would be the probable result of his unlawful act, and yet did the act reckless of such consequences. The present indictment charges the offence to be under the 42nd section of the same Act, and it is not disputed that the same construction must be applied to both sections.... The jury were ... directed to give a verdict of guilty upon the simple ground that the firing of the ship, though accidental, was caused by an act done in the course of, or immediately consequent upon, a felonious operation, and no question of the prisoner's malice, constructive or otherwise, was left to the jury. [T]hat direction was erroneous, and ... the conviction should be quashed.

■ FITZGERALD, J.

[T]o establish the charge of felony under sect. 42, the intention of the accused forms an element in the crime to the extent that it should appear that the defendant intended to do the very act with which he is charged, or that it was the necessary consequence of some other felonious or criminal act in which he was engaged, or that having a probable result which the defendant foresaw, or ought to have foreseen, he, nevertheless, persevered in such other felonious or criminal act. The prisoner did not intend to set fire to the ship; the fire was not the necessary result of the felony he was attempting; and if it was a probable result, which he ought to have foreseen, of the felonious transaction in which he was engaged, and from which a malicious design to commit the injurious act with which he is charged might have been fairly imputed to him, that view of the case was not submitted to the jury. On the contrary, it was excluded from their consideration on the requisition of the counsel for the prosecution. Counsel for the prosecution in effect insisted that the defendant, being engaged in the commission of, or in an attempt to commit a felony, was criminally responsible for every result that was occasioned thereby, even though it was not a probable consequence of his act or such as he could have reasonably foreseen or intended. No authority has been cited for a proposition so extensive, and I am of opinion that it is not warranted by law. . . .

■ O'BRIEN, J.

. . . . With respect to *Reg. v. Pembliton* (12 Cox C. C. 607), it appears to me there were much stronger grounds in that case for upholding the conviction than exist in the case before us. In that case the breaking of the window was the act of the prisoner. He threw the stone that broke it; he threw it with the unlawful intent of striking some one of the crowd about, and the breaking of the window, was the direct and immediate result of his act. And yet the Court unanimously quashed the conviction upon the ground that, although the prisoner threw the stone intending to strike some one or more persons, he did not intend to break the window. The courts above have intimated their opinion that if the jury (upon a question to that effect being left to them) had found that the prisoner, knowing the window was there, might have reasonably expected that the result of his act would be the breaking of the window, that then the conviction should be upheld. During the argument of this case the Crown counsel required us to assume that the jury found their verdict upon the ground that in their opinion the prisoner may have expected that the fire would be the consequence of his act in stealing the rum, but nevertheless did the act recklessly, not caring whether the fire took place or not. But at the trial there was not even a suggestion of any such ground, and we cannot assume that the jury formed an opinion which there was no evidence to sustain, and which would be altogether inconsistent with the circumstances under which the fire took place. The reasonable inference from the evidence is that the prisoner lighted the match for the purpose of putting the spile in the hole to stop the further running of the rum, and that while he was attempting to do so the rum came in contact with the lighted match and took fire. . . .

Regina v. Cunningham

Court of Criminal Appeal.
[1957] 2 Q.B. 396, [1957] 2 All E.R. 412 (1957).

■ BYRNE, J.

The appellant was convicted at Leeds Assizes on an indictment framed under s. 23 of the Offences against the Person Act, 1861, which charged that he unlawfully and maliciously caused to be taken by Sarah Wade a certain noxious thing, namely, coal gas, so as thereby to endanger the life of the said Sarah Wade. The facts were that the appellant was engaged to be married, and Mrs. Wade, his prospective mother-in-law, was the tenant of a house, No. 7a, Bakes Street, Bradford, which was unoccupied but which was to be occupied by the appellant after his marriage. Mrs. Wade and her husband, an elderly couple, lived in the house next door.

At one time the two houses had been one, but when the building was converted into two houses a wall had been erected to divide the cellars of the two houses, and that wall was composed of rubble loosely cemented. On the evening of Jan. 17 last, the appellant went to the cellar of No. 7a, Bakes Street, wrenched the gas meter from the gas pipes and stole it, together with its contents. In a second indictment he was charged with the larceny of the gas meter and its contents; to that indictment he pleaded guilty, and was sentenced to six months' imprisonment. In respect of that matter he does not appeal. The facts were not really in dispute, and in a statement to a police officer the appellant said: "All right I will tell you, I was short of money, I had been off work for three days, I got 8s. from the gas meter. I tore it off the wall and threw it away". Although there was a stop tap within two feet of the meter, the appellant did not turn off the gas, with the result that a very considerable volume of gas escaped, some of which seeped through the wall of the cellar and partially asphyxiated Mrs. Wade, who was asleep in her bedroom next door, with the result that her life was endangered. * * *

The act of the appellant was clearly unlawful and, therefore, the real question for the jury was whether it was also malicious within the meaning of s. 23 of the Offences against the Person Act, 1861.

.... Section 23 provides as follows:

"Whosoever shall unlawfully and maliciously administer to or cause to be administered to or taken by any other person any poison or other destructive or noxious thing, so as thereby to endanger the life of such person, or so as thereby to inflict upon such person any grievous bodily harm, shall be guilty of felony ..."

Counsel argued first that mens rea of some kind is necessary. Secondly, that the nature of the mens rea required is that the appellant must intend to do the particular kind of harm that was done, or alternatively that he must foresee that that harm may occur, yet nevertheless continue recklessly to do the act. Thirdly, that the learned judge misdirected the jury as to the meaning of the word "maliciously".

We have considered [the relevant] cases, and we have also considered, in the light of those cases, the following principle which was propounded by the late Professor C.S. Kenny in the first edition of his *Outlines of Criminal Law* published in 1902, and repeated in the sixteenth edition, edited by Mr. J.W. Cecil Turner, and published in 1952 (ibid., at p. 186):

> "... in any statutory definition of a crime 'malice' must be taken not in the old vague sense of 'wickedness' in general, but as requiring either (i) an actual intention to do the particular kind of harm that in fact was done, or (ii) recklessness as to whether such harm should occur or not (i.e., the accused has foreseen that the particular kind of

harm might be done, and yet has gone on to take the risk of it). It is neither limited to, nor does it indeed require, any ill-will towards the person injured."

.... In our opinion, the word "maliciously" in a statutory crime postulates foresight of consequence.

In his summing-up, the learned judge directed the jury as follows:

"You will observe that there is nothing there about 'with intention that that person should take it'. He has not got to intend that it should be taken; it is sufficient that by his unlawful and malicious act he causes it to be taken. What you have to decide here, then, is whether, when he loosed that frightful cloud of coal gas into the house which he shared with this old lady, he caused her to take it by his unlawful and malicious action.

" 'Unlawful' does not need any definition. It is something forbidden by law. What about 'malicious'? 'Malicious' for this purpose means wicked—something which he has no business to do and perfectly well knows it. 'Wicked' is as good a definition as any other which you would get." * * *

With the utmost respect to the learned judge, we think it is incorrect to say that the word "malicious" in a statutory offence merely means wicked. We think the learned judge was, in effect, telling the jury that if they were satisfied that the appellant acted wickedly—and he had clearly acted wickedly in stealing the gas meter and its contents—they ought to find that he had acted maliciously in causing the gas to be taken by Mrs. Wade so as thereby to endanger her life. In our view, it should have been left to the jury to decide whether, even if the appellant did not intend the injury to Mrs. Wade, he foresaw that the removal of the gas meter might cause injury to someone but nevertheless removed it....

Palani Goundan v. Emperor[a]

1920 Madras 862 (India).

... The accused struck his wife a blow on her head with a ploughshare, which, though not known to be a blow likely to cause death, did, in fact, render her unconscious and believing her to be dead, in order to lay the foundation of a false defence of suicide by hanging, the accused hanged her on a beam by a rope and thereby caused her death by strangulation, and it was held by the Full Bench that the accused was not guilty of either murder or culpable homicide not amounting to murder as the original intention was not to cause death but only to cause injury and the second intention was only to dispose of a supposedly dead body in a way convenient for the defence which the accused was about to set up....

Thabo Meli v. Regina

Judicial Committee, Privy Council.
1 All Eng. Rep. 373 (1954).

The four appellants in this case were convicted of murder....

a. This case and the next are taken from Steven Lowenstein, Materials on Comparative Criminal Law as Based Upon the Penal Codes of Ethiopia and Switzerland (1965).—EDS.

It is established by evidence, which was believed and which is apparently credible, that there was a preconceived plot on the part of the four accused to bring the deceased man to a hut and there to kill him; and then to fake an accident, so that the accused should escape the penalty for their act. The deceased man was brought to the hut. He was there treated to beer and was at least partially intoxicated; and he was then struck over the head in accordance with the plan of the accused.

.... The accused took out the body, rolled it over a low krantz or cliff, and dressed up the scene to make it look like an accident. Obviously they believed at that time that the man was dead, but it appears from the medical evidence that the injuries which he received in the hut were not sufficient to cause the death and that the final cause of his death was exposure where he was left at the foot of the krantz.

The point of law which was raised in this case can be simply stated. It is said that two acts were necessary and were separable: first, the attack in the hut; and, secondly, the placing of the body outside afterwards. It is said that, while the first act was accompanied by mens rea, it was not the cause of death; but that the second act, while it was the cause of death, was not accompanied by mens rea; and on that ground it is said that the accused are not guilty of any crime except perhaps culpable homicide.

It appears to their Lordships impossible to divide up what was really one transaction in this way. There is no doubt that the accused set out to do all these acts in order to achieve their plan and as parts of their plan; and it is much too refined a ground of judgment to say that, because they were under a misapprehension at one stage and thought that their guilty purpose had been achieved before in fact it was achieved, therefore they are to escape the penalties of the law.... [T]here could be no separation such as that for which the accused contend, as to reduce the crime from murder to a lesser crime, merely because the accused were under some misapprehension for a time during the completion of their criminal plot.

[T]his appeal should be dismissed.

QUESTIONS AND COMMENTS

1. The doctrine of concurrence provides that act and mental state, actus reus and mens rea, must "concur." But what does that mean? (Is it helpful to think of concurrence as requiring that there exist, in the words of Cal. Penal Code § 20, supra, "a union, or joint operation" between actus reus and mens rea?)

Here are three preliminary ways of making sense of the concurrence requirement. (1) It's not enough to engage in the requisite conduct at one time, and then to harbor the requisite intent at another. Just because I very much wish you ill, at least for a few seconds, after you cut me off on the freeway doesn't mean that I'll be guilty of vehicular assault when I accidentally rearend you ten minutes later, without even knowing it's you. (At T_1, I had the intent to cause physical injury, but didn't engage in any conduct to bring about that result. At T_2, I did engage in conduct that causes physical injury, but I no longer had the requisite intent.)

(2) Mental state and actus reus must concur not only in time, but also by offense. Just because you had the requisite mental state with respect to one offense doesn't mean that you had it with respect to another offense as well. It's not permissible to "transfer" intent from one offense onto another, even if the two concur, or at least overlap, in time. Just because I intended to steal your minivan doesn't mean I'm guilty of kidnapping if it turns out your three-year-old was playing hide and seek in the backseat.

(3) Recall that the Model Penal Code rejected the notion that each offense, taken as a whole, required some sort of mens rea. Instead, mental states attached to each element. In light of the Code's element analysis, the concurrence requirement thus would mean that mental fault can't be transferred from one element to another within the same offense. Just because I intended to pull the trigger doesn't mean I intended to kill you (because I didn't know you were standing behind the door, I thought the gun was unloaded, you were impervious to bullets, etc.). Contrast this version of the concurrence requirement (or its flipside, the transfer prohibition) with the "one-for-all" rule in Model Penal Code § 2.02(4).

2. Apply the concurrence requirement to *Cunningham, Palani, Thabo Meli*, and the following hypotheticals. What intent is being transferred to what?

- A, en route to buy a gun to kill V, accidentally runs him over.
- B deliberately burns a field (the crime of malicious damage) and an unforeseeable wind spreads the fire so that a house burns down (actus reus of arson).
- C shoots at V and misses; the bullet hits an unforeseeably present gas main that explodes and burns a structure.
- D shoots at V and misses, but the bullet she fired hits and kills X, an unforeseeably present bystander, killing him.

Several standard *exceptions* to the concurrence doctrine have been developed.

- E punches V (battery) and inadvertently destroys his vision (mayhem).
- F inadvertently kills V in the course of deliberately committing a burglary. (This, the felony-murder rule, is the prime exception to the concurrence doctrine; we'll come back to study it at some length, in ch. 10.)
- G intentionally shoots and kills V, not realizing that V is a police officer. Murdering a police officer is an "aggravating" factor that turns ordinary murder into capital murder.
- H sells drugs, not noticing that he's within 100 yards of a school. Selling drugs close to school is a more serious crime than drug sale generally.

Are any of these exceptions to the concurrence doctrine defensible? Are G and H more defensible than E and F because they aggravate punishment for the same crime, rather than creating liability for another?

3. In *Cunningham*, assume that the second crime (poisoning) can be committed negligently, then assume it can be committed recklessly. What's the best argument that Cunningham was non-negligent, or non-reckless? What's the defendant's situation? How do we decide if the risk that he has taken is reasonable or not? What's the relevant reference group? Does his prior, intentional, commission of a criminal act affect our judgment of his reasonableness vis-à-vis his subsequent act? Imagine two defendants who engage in conduct with an equal risk of poisoning another: one is Cunningham, another is a nurse administering dangerous medication to a patient. Is *any* risk that Cunningham takes of poisoning so *unduly* "substantial and unjustifiable" that he could (should?) be judged negligent? Given our flexibility in making the reasonableness judgment, how much bite does concurrence doctrine really have? How much bite *ought* it to have?

4. Is the fact that Faulkner was engaged in a crime while he committed another at all relevant for purposes of determining his liability for the latter? Consider in particular the various alternatives laid out in Fitzgerald's opinion. How could these be framed in terms of the Model Penal Code mens rea scheme? Are they consistent with that scheme? Is *Pembliton* distinguishable?

5. Malice is a key concept in both *Faulkner* and *Cunningham*. Along with willfulness, it is among the traditional mens rea concepts that were abandoned by the Model Penal Code drafters. Cf. Rollin M. Perkins & Ronald N. Boyce, Criminal Law 860 (3d ed. 1982) ("The Model Penal Code does not use 'malice' because those who formulated the Code had a blind prejudice against the word. This is very regrettable because it represents a useful concept...."). Also like willfulness, malice nonetheless has not entirely disappeared from American criminal statutes and court opinions, particularly in the law of homicide (where courts continue to ponder "malice aforethought"), though it is no accident that *Faulkner* and *Cunningham* are (older) English cases. (Looking at the opinions in these two cases, how does malice fit into the Model Penal Code mens rea scheme? Where does the "necessary result" language fit in?) Is malice inconsistent with the concurrence requirement? Can it be interpreted so as to avoid any such inconsistency? (Do *Faulkner* and *Cunningham* succeed in this regard?) Or must it be abandoned altogether? What is it about malice that makes it so problematic? Just how problematic is malice from the perspective of the various traditional rationales for punishment? What if malice were a character trait, revealed by the first offense? In that case, would we even need to "transfer" anything from the first to the second offense?

The *Cunningham* court rejects the equation of malice with general wickedness. How about particularized wickedness? Is it a crime to *be* "wicked"? Is the difference between a crime and a tort that only a crime is *committed wickedly*, though harm is inflicted—or threatened—in both cases? Or is there no place for a term like wickedness in a system of criminal law committed to the principle of legality?

6. Unlawfulness also figures prominently in *Faulkner* and *Cunningham*. Like malice, it too runs into problems with the concurrence doctrine: The basic idea is that once you commit one "unlawful" act, then there is no need to prove intent (or any mental state?) with respect to any of its "direct and immediate" (or even probable) results. To the extent that

unlawfulness implies not only actus reus but also mens rea, then "transferred unlawfulness" (if we can call it that) implies transferred intent. See generally Rollin M. Perkins & Ronald N. Boyce, Criminal Law 914–20 (3d ed. 1982). Needless to say, the Model Penal Code did away with unlawfulness as a mental state ("unlawful intent," *Faulkner*), not to mention a mental state that can be transferred from one crime to another.

The concept of unlawfulness appears throughout the criminal law, and throughout these materials. It has been construed not only as a type of mental state (see *Cunningham*), but also as an attendant circumstance with its very own mental state (see the discussion of mistake in section F, infra), and as an element of various defenses of justification and excuse (see ch. 7).

F. MISTAKE

Having explored the subjective elements of an offense, and the *absence* of subjective elements in strict liability offenses, we now turn to two common ways in which the subjective element of an offense may be found to be lacking in a particular case: mistake and intoxication. As the Model Penal Code puts it, "[i]gnorance or mistake as to a matter of fact or law is a defense if . . . the ignorance or mistake negatives the purpose, knowledge, belief, recklessness or negligence required to establish a material element of the offense." § 2.04(1)(a); see also § 2.08(1) ("intoxication . . . not a defense unless it negatives an element of the offense"). This provision is so straightforward it might be considered redundant. Surely, *anything* that negatives a subjective offense element would count as a defense. Of course, if no mental state is required in the first place then the fact that the defendant didn't act with that mental state is beside the point. So claims of mistake or intoxication make no difference in a strict liability offense.

As we'll see, however, both mistake and intoxication also come in another, excuse, variety. As *excuses*, mistake and intoxication no longer claim to be negating mental states—instead denying responsibility, or blameworthiness, despite conceding the mental state issue—and therefore would apply to strict liability offenses as well.

The difficulties in the law of mistake arise when one tries to draw lines between the different varieties of mistake. What sorts of mistake counts as a defense in what cases? When does a mistake disprove a subjective offense element? Under what circumstances does a mistake constitute a defense even if it doesn't negate a mental state requirement? (The question of how to treat mistakes as to subjective *defense* elements—"I *thought* he was coming at me with a knife" (in a self-defense case) or "I *thought* the gun he held to my head was loaded" (in a duress case)—will be addressed when we discuss justification and excuse defenses, in ch. 7.)

1. INTRODUCTION

4 William Blackstone, Commentaries on the Laws of England 27 (1769)

Ignorance or mistake is another defect of will; when a man, intending to do a lawful act, does that which is unlawful. For here the deed and the will acting separately, there is not that conjunction between them, which is necessary to form a criminal act. But this must be an ignorance or mistake of fact, and not an error in point of law. As if a man, intending to kill a thief or housebreaker in his own house, by mistake kills one of his own family, this is no criminal action: but if a man thinks he has a right to kill a person excommunicated or outlawed, wherever he meets him, and does so; this is willful murder. For a mistake in point of law, which every person of discretion is bound and presumed to know, is in criminal cases no sort of defence.

Model Penal Code § 2.02(9). Culpability as to Illegality of Conduct.

Neither knowledge nor recklessness or negligence as to whether conduct constitutes an offense or as to the existence, meaning or application of the law determining the elements of an offense is an element of such offense, unless the definition of the offense or the Code so provides.

Model Penal Code § 2.04(3). Ignorance or Mistake.

A belief that conduct does not legally constitute an offense is a defense to a prosecution for that offense based upon such conduct when:

(a) the statute or other enactment defining the offense is not known to the actor and has not been published or otherwise reasonably made available prior to the conduct alleged;

(b) he acts in reasonable reliance upon an official statement of the law, afterward determined to be invalid or erroneous, contained in (i) a statute or other enactment; (ii) a judicial decision, opinion or judgment; (iii) an administrative order or grant of permission; or (iv) an official interpretation of the public officer or body charged by law with responsibility for the interpretation, administration, or enforcement of the law defining the offense.

QUESTIONS AND COMMENTS

1. Blackstone—and Model Penal Code § 2.02(9)—state (more formally) the familiar aphorism, "Ignorance of the law is no excuse." But Model Penal Code § 2.04(3) then describes some conditions in which ignorance of the law *is* an excuse. How might these views be reconciled? Perhaps the particular defendant's ignorance of the law he is charged with violating is not, standing alone, an excuse, but reasonable ignorance of the governing law is an excuse—and the Code *defines* (exhaustively? suggestively?) a "reasonable" error in § 2.04(3). But if that view were correct, then why does § 2.02(9) say explicitly that negligence (or recklessness) as to whether conduct constitutes an offense is not an element of the offense? Cf. § 1.13(16) (reasonable belief is non-reckless or non-negligent belief). Alternatively, one might point to the fact that § 2.02(9) merely provides that awareness of the law is not an *element* of an offense (which the prosecution would have to prove beyond a reasonable doubt), unless the statute says so (e.g., by requiring that the defendant acted "unlawfully" or "willfully"), but leaves open the possibility that ignorance of law might still constitute an *excuse*, properly speaking (which the defendant may have to prove, or at

least to support with some evidence). Cf. § 2.09(4) (defendant must prove "ignorance of law" defense set out in § 2.09(3) by preponderance of the evidence). But then why should ignorance of law be merely an excuse (and a rather limited one at that, with not only the burden of production on the defendant, but the burden of persuasion as well)? Why shouldn't knowledge of the law be treated like an offense element? Why should we treat mistakes about offense elements so differently from other mistakes?

2. The conventional position is that as to pure mistakes of law—mistakes about whether one's conduct is proscribed, mistakes about the existence or meaning of the governing law one is charged with violating—courts have historically dispensed with the need to find the defendant blameworthy, holding that ignorance of law is simply irrelevant no matter how blameless it might be, no matter how hard the defendant tried to find out what the law is. The vast majority of commentators find this practice indefensible.

An alternative view is that those who take the conventional view simply misunderstand the function of strict liability. In this alternative view, what we mean when we say that defendants are strictly liable with respect to their awareness of the law is that we, first, conclusively presume that defendants who are unaware of (some suitable subset of) laws *are* negligent in being unaware and, second, do not permit fact finders in these cases to make particularized inquiries into reasonableness. Generally, of course, there are both constitutional and prudential limits on the use of presumptions. See ch. 2 supra. Note, however, that what's at stake here are presumptions about whether a *reasonable* person would know (at least some) laws, rather than presumptions about whether a *particular* defendant knew a law.

Imagine, for instance, that the legislature *defines* (is entitled to define?) a belief as reasonable only if it is statistically commonplace: is it then fair for the legislature to assert that *anyone* who doesn't know that, say, kidnapping or failing to file a tax return is against the law has been unreasonable? Is there any issue of fact for a fact finder to resolve if a defendant claims that he made a reasonable mistake about the existence of a criminal norm against kidnapping? Note that at the *formal* level, the Model Penal Code does not use the language of presumptions: instead, the Code states that it is simply not an element of an offense that the actor is negligent as to, or subjectively aware of, the illegality of his conduct. Thus, the Code does not formally relieve the prosecutor of the burden of proving knowledge or negligence as to illegality. Does this formal distinction matter?

3. Blackstone distinguishes mistakes of fact from mistakes of law. There is yet a third "category" of errors we will need to attend to: these could be called mistakes of non-governing law (or what the Model Penal Code calls "legal circumstances attendant to the definition of the offense").

It might be helpful to take a first crack at illustrating the distinction among these categories by thinking about the following sort of example: (1) a person charged with larceny says that she does not know that larceny is a crime (mistake of governing law); (2) a person takes an umbrella from the cloak room that has sat there for six months, incorrectly believing such property is abandoned so that, as far as she knew, she did not take property that belonged to another (mistake of non-governing law); (3) a person takes an umbrella that physically resembles the one that he brought to the restaurant from the cloak room, believing that it is his, though it in fact belonged to another patron (mistake of fact). (Note that the third defendant, like the second, reaches an erroneous conclusion that could be termed legal: both defendants mistakenly believe that the property they are taking is not property belonging to another. Why, then, is the third defendant's mistake nonetheless considered *factual*? Consider, too, a defendant in a statutory rape case who mistakenly believes the person with whom he has had sexual relations is seventeen though she is in fact less than sixteen: would we describe this mistake as factual whether or not we say that he has made a mistake about her age or a mistake about her legal capacity to consent? Why?)

We need to attend to three broad issues in relationship to these sorts of errors: First, can we *categorize* a particular mistake claim? Second, how have courts conventionally *treated* each sort of error? Finally, to what degree are the distinctions between the categories *sensible*? Most particularly, are there reasons to treat all instances of each category identically? Why might we decide that we should prove knowledge, or at least negligence, in some, but not all, circumstances in which a defendant claims to have made a mistake of governing law? Why might we treat some mistakes that could be categorized as mistakes of non-governing law the way we would treat cognate mistakes of fact and why might we treat some the way we would treat cognate mistakes of law? Does it (and should it) matter whether the defendant is claiming that his ignorance either justifies or excuses his misdeed or is claiming instead that his mistake negates an offense element?

4. Why should we ever differentiate the treatment of mistakes of law and fact? If it is unjust to punish someone who does not know (or is reasonable in not knowing) that what he is doing is wrongful, why does it matter if he doesn't know it is wrongful because he doesn't understand the precise quality of his act or because he doesn't know the precise contours of the criminal law? One person doesn't know that he is carrying a sharp pair of scissors on to an airplane but knows it would be illegal to do so; the other has no idea that the act is illegal. Are there any reasons to treat them differently from one another, except to the extent that one has formed his belief more carelessly?

5. Should every mistake of fact be a defense?

(1) *Unreasonable mistakes*. Statute A makes it a *felony* (punishable by one year's imprisonment) to "knowingly sell alcohol to anyone under the age of 16." Assuming my customer is in fact 15, should I escape liability if I honestly thought he was 19? Or should it matter whether my belief was also "reasonable"? How can I "know" something that I'm mistaken about? What would it mean for my (mistaken) belief to be reasonable? That I should have taken certain precautions to prevent my mistake (ask the customer's age, check ID, check ID for obvious (sophisticated?) forgery, consider height, weight, dress, demeanor, etc.)? Or that most (many) people (like me?) in my situation would have made the same mistake? Or should

the unreasonableness of a mistake only matter when the mental state attached to the offense element in question is recklessness or negligence? See Model Penal Code § 1.12(13) (reasonable belief is "a belief which the actor is not reckless or negligent in holding"); see also id. § 2.02(2)(c) & (d) (defining recklessness and negligence in terms of law-abidingness and reasonableness, respectively). What about a statute that is *defined* in terms of reasonable belief? See, e.g., Minn. Stat. § 609.352(2) (solicitation of "a child or someone the person reasonably believes is a child"); N.J. Stat. § 2C:35–11 (possession of "any substance which is not a controlled dangerous substance ... [u]nder circumstances which would lead a reasonable person to believe that the substance is a controlled dangerous substance").

(2) *Non-exculpatory reasonable mistakes.* Same facts, except there is another law, Statute B, which makes it a *misdemeanor* (punishable by a $500 fine) to "sell alcohol to anyone between the ages of 16 and 20." Should I be liable under the more serious statute (Statute A), even though under the facts as I (reasonably) believed them to be I would only have violated the less serious one (Statute B)? Traditional Anglo–American criminal law says yes, for various reasons.

(a) One traditional view is that I'm precluded from raising a mistake defense as to Statute A so long as I would have committed a (legal or moral) *wrong* had things been as I thought they were. (How would this approach apply to malum prohibitum offenses? What relevance does the moral status of conduct have for an assessment of its criminality? Does it matter whether I *realized* that, under the circumstances as I supposed them to be, I was committing a *moral* wrong, but not a legal one? Could the various aspects of the principle of legality, discussed in ch. 2 supra, be squared with this approach? Do I *forfeit* my defense because I'm wicked, morally speaking?)

(b) Another, less sweeping, rule ignores a mistake claim if I would have committed an *unlawful* act (where unlawful acts encompass both civilly illegal—e.g., tortious—acts and criminal offenses, but not merely immoral conduct). (If, under circumstances as I supposed them to be, I was not committing a crime, why should I be subject to criminal—as opposed to civil—liability? Is (hypothetical) civil liability a better reason to forfeit a defense than (hypothetical) immorality? Under the various theories of punishment, am I just as wicked, dangerous, blameworthy, etc. as the defendant who doesn't make a mistake and is fully aware of the fact that he is selling alcohol to a fifteen-year-old?)

(c) The narrowest—and most recent—view allows the mistake defense unless I would have committed a *criminal* act had I been right. The Model Penal Code, in § 2.04(2), takes this position, denying the defense if (and only if) "the defendant would be guilty of another offense had the situation been as he supposed." The Code, however, then adds a twist, by providing for an "incomplete" mistake-of-fact defense even in these cases: "the grade and degree of the offense of which he may be convicted [shall be reduced] to those of the offense of which he would be guilty had the situation been as he supposed." Cf. State v. Peña, 839 A.2d 870 (N.J. 2004) (defendant charged with drug possession defends on the ground that he thought he was in possession of stolen property—fur coats—a much less serious offense).

Would I be guilty of having violated Statute A under any (or all) of the three approaches? Are they (equally?) justifiable under the various rationales for punishment? (If so, shouldn't we also convict defendants of the offense they thought they were committing when that offense is *more* serious than the one they did in fact commit?) At any rate, how could we simply declare evidence irrelevant that goes to negate an offense element? Why does the Model Penal Code *convict* the mistaken defendant of the crime he did commit in fact and then *punish* him as though he had been convicted of the crime he thought he committed? Consider the Model Penal Code Commentaries:

> Section 2.04(2) is addressed to a limited problem that may produce distortion in the law, namely where the defendant claims mistake but where a criminal offense still would have occurred had the situation been as the defendant believed it to be. If the defense were denied altogether, an actor culpable in respect to one offense could be convicted of a much more serious offense. On the other hand, the defendant should not go free, for on either view—the facts as they occurred or as the defendant believed them to be—a criminal offense was committed.
>
> The offense of burglary will illustrate the problem. Burglary is defined generally by Section 221.1 to include entry into any building or occupied structure for the purpose of committing a crime therein, and is graded normally as a felony of the third degree. It is a felony of the second degree, however, if the building is a dwelling house. If the defendant believed, and formed his belief in a manner that could not be characterized as reckless, that the building was a store, he could be convicted only of a third degree felony.
>
> To deny the relevance of the defense of mistake in this situation would be in effect to re-characterize, for this special purpose, the culpability level normally required by the Code for the material element of the more serious offense. Presumably a considered judgment led to the inclusion as a material element the requirement that the building be a dwelling in order to aggravate the offense to a second degree felony; measuring the defendant's culpability toward that element should be an important exercise in grading the extent of the criminality involved. The doctrine that when one intends a lesser crime he may be convicted of a graver offense committed inadvertently leads to anomalous results if it is generally applied in the penal law....
>
> Even if the defendant in the circumstances supposed is not to be convicted of the graver crime, it seems clear that he should not be acquitted. One possibility is that the case could go to the jury as an attempt to commit the lesser offense. Another possibility would be to permit a conviction of the lesser offense, the one which he would have committed had the facts been as he supposed them to be. A third possibility, which is the one embraced in Section 2.04(2), is to deny the defense in these circumstances, but to limit the classification of the offense and the available dispositions of the defendant to those that would have been available upon conviction of the lesser offense.

> These three alternative approaches were published as such in Tentative Draft No. 4 at 17 (1955). The Advisory Committee and the Council selected the approach reflected in [§ 2.04(2)], largely on the ground that it avoided a procedural objection to the other alternatives, namely, that they might lead to a conviction of a crime that the indictment or the information did not charge. The important point, whichever of these solutions is adopted, is that the effective measure of defendant's liability should be his culpability, not the actual consequences of his conduct. This is the result obtained here, through the denial of a defense that otherwise would be available.

Model Penal Code Commentaries § 2.04, at 272–74.

2. Mistakes of Governing Law

a. The Traditional Principle: Ignorance Is No Excuse, Nor Is Culpable Ignorance or Subjective Awareness a Presumptive Element of Offenses

United States v. Baker, 807 F.2d 427 (5th Cir. 1986)

[Historically, trademark counterfeiting was addressed solely by the civil penalties found in the Lanham Act. In 1984, Congress, finding that the civil penalties inadequately deterred counterfeiting, enacted the Trademark Counterfeiting Act of 1984, criminalizing much of the conduct that had only been subject to civil penalties.]

Paul Baker was convicted under this new statute for dealing in counterfeit watches. He does not dispute that he intentionally dealt in the watches. He also admits that he knew the "Rolex" watches he sold were counterfeit.... He asserts that he did not know that trafficking in counterfeit goods is criminal and that he would not have done so had he known he was committing a crime. The district court ... refused to instruct the jury that Baker could not be convicted if he did not have the purpose to "disobey or disregard the law." Baker's sole contention on appeal is that the statute requires knowledge that the conduct is criminal....

The statute clearly sets out the elements of the crime and the mental state required for each element. The defendant must intentionally deal in goods and he must knowingly use a counterfeit mark in connection with these goods. There is no ambiguity in this language and nothing in the statute suggests that any other mental state is required for conviction....

Baker's claim is merely that, even though he had the mental state required by the face of the statute, he should not be convicted because he did not know that Congress had passed a law criminalizing his conduct. This clearly is not the law.

Commonwealth v. Doane, 55 Mass. 5 (1848)

[The defendant was indicted and tried for stealing half a ton of pig iron from a shipment that he had helped unload. The defendant "called a witness, who had been at sea for seven years" and asked him, "Whether the officers of a vessel considered themselves entitled to any part of the cargo, under any circumstances" in order to show "a custom for the officers of ships to appropriate to themselves a small part of the cargo." When that question was ruled inadmissible, the defendant proposed to ask the witness, "Whether he had known instances of mates having appropriated parts of cargo under a claim of right." That question, too, was ruled inadmissible. The court first noted that the defendant was not an officer, and on that ground alone, not entitled to ask questions about the custom of officers, but noted further . . .]

[Such] a custom could not be sustained as a legal custom. It wants the element of a legal custom. A custom to take another man's property and convert it to one's own use, without consent, or giving an equivalent, is a custom bad on its face, and cannot be supported. Nor was the second question proposed to be put to the witness competent evidence.... It surely will not be contended, that the fact, that similar offences have been committed by others, would constitute any legal defense for the parties charged in the present case....

QUESTIONS AND COMMENTS

1. Should it have made a difference, for purposes of cases like *Baker*, if the conduct in question had not been subject to any penalties, not even civil ones, before Congress provided for criminal penalties? What if the conduct had been criminalized (only) under state law? Subject to civil penalties (only) under state law? Even if Baker had a notice argument, wouldn't it be enough if there were *some* norm against his conduct ("don't sell counterfeit watches"), no matter where it appears and what form it takes (a moral norm, an executive order, a regulation, an appellate opinion, a statute)?

2. The court in *Doane* treats it as self-evident that it would not excuse an actor to demonstrate that (nearly) everyone in his position does just what he did, believing it was perfectly proper. Why don't we reserve something as severe as criminal punishment for *atypical* conduct, so that we should be wary of punishing a person for doing what others do, even if they all know what they are doing violates existing law? And if "strict liability" serves as a conclusive presumption of *negligent* ignorance, isn't it inappropriate to make that presumption when many people are ignorant? Or is it enough to rely on the discretion of system participants (including police officers, prosecutors, and—perhaps most important—jurors, with their inherent power to nullify the law) to weed out technical, but not atypical, violations of criminal statutes? See Model Penal Code § 2.12 (de minimis violations).

b. Limitations on the Traditional Principle: Due Process

In looking at these cases, think about whether it would be accurate to say that defendants are strictly liable to know governing law *except* when it would be so inaccurate to assume that those who are ignorant are *unreasonably* ignorant that it would violate Due Process norms to make that assumption:

Lambert v. California, 355 U.S. 225 (1957)

[The defendant was convicted of violating a Los Angeles ordinance that required any "convicted person" to register with the police within five days of arriving in the city. The Court reversed her conviction stating:] We do not go with Blackstone in saying that "a vicious will" is necessary to constitute a crime, for conduct alone without regard to the intent of the doer is often sufficient. There is wide latitude in the lawmakers to declare an offense and to exclude elements of knowledge and diligence from its definition. But we deal here with conduct that is wholly passive—mere failure to register. It is unlike the commission of acts, or the failure to act under circumstances that should alert the doer to the consequences of his deed. The rule that "ignorance of the law will not excuse" is deep in our law.... On the other hand, due process places some limits on its exercise. Engrained in our concept of due process is notice.... [A]ppellant on first becoming aware of her duty to register was given no opportunity to comply with the law and avoid its penalty even though her default was entirely innocent.... We believe that actual knowledge of the duty to register or proof of the probability of such knowledge and subsequent failure to comply are necessary before a conviction under the ordinance can stand.

State v. Leavitt, 107 Wash.App. 361, 27 P.3d 622 (2001)

[In 1998, the defendant pleaded guilty to one count of violation of a domestic violence protective order. The court imposed a one-year suspended sentence, conditional in relevant part on not possessing firearms, but the court did not inform him that he would not be permitted to possess firearms beyond the one-year period without first petitioning for restoration of that privilege. Leavitt kept his gun permit but relinquished his firearms by delivering them to his brother in Utah; at the end of the one-year period, he retrieved them. He was later found in possession of the retrieved weapons, after arrest on another domestic violence complaint in 1999. The court reversed his conviction.] ...

Rev. Code Wash. § 9.41.047(1) provides in pertinent part:

> At the time a person is convicted of an offense making the person ineligible to possess a firearm, ... *the convicting ... court shall notify* the person, orally and in writing, that the person must immediately surrender any concealed pistol license and *that the person may not possess a firearm unless his or her right to do so is restored by a court of record.*

[Emphasis added.] Conviction of a misdemeanor no-contact order against a family member falls within the class of crimes for which the Legislature has prohibited firearm possession. After Leavitt was convicted ... Rev. Code Wash. § 9.41.047(1) required the sentencing court to advise him that he could no longer possess a firearm. This the sentencing court did not do....

What are the consequences of a sentencing court's failure to comply? ...

The law is clear that knowledge of the *illegality* of firearm possession is not an element of the crime. Rather, the State must prove only that the defendant knew he possessed the firearm. . . .

[T]he court . . . failed to advise Leavitt that he lost his right to possess firearms for an indefinite period as required by statute, gave Leavitt written notice of an apparently one-year firearm-possession restriction, and implicitly allowed Leavitt to retain his concealed weapon permit. These combined actions and inactions of the predicate-sentencing court misled Leavitt reasonably to understand that his firearm possession restriction was limited to one year. . . .

Under these unique circumstances, it would be a denial of due process to require Leavitt to speculate about additional firearm-possession restrictions beyond his one-year probation where the sentencing court did not inform him otherwise, in spite of the legislature's clear requirement to do so.

QUESTIONS AND COMMENTS

1. The Court in *Lambert* seems to imply that it is especially problematic to impose an affirmative duty on the defendant when she has no reason to be aware of her duty. Does anything really turn on the act/omission distinction here? What if the statute at issue forbade convicted felons from shopping in stores in Los Angeles that sold any tools that could be used in burglaries and the defendant was arrested at the first hardware store she went into? How might one reformulate the holding in *Lambert* to avoid focusing on the fact that the particular statute at issue imposed a duty to act?

2. What's the significance of the fact that the statute in *Lambert* was a strict liability offense? Would the statute violate due process even if it required some mens rea (say regarding the fact that the defendant qualified as a "convicted person" or that she was within the Los Angeles city limits)? Is the Court placing limits on strict liability offenses by implying that due process may require that defendants have been aware of their existence?

3. What is it exactly that accounts for the due process violation in *Leavitt*? Is the problem that the sentencing court didn't do what it was supposed to do, or that—even if it had followed statutory instructions—Leavitt didn't know he was barred from possessing a firearm indefinitely? What if there hadn't been a "clear requirement"—but merely a suggestion—that the sentencing judge inform Leavitt of the full extent of his disqualification from firearm possession? What if the court just hadn't mentioned this collateral penalty, instead of also giving Leavitt "written notice of an apparently one-year firearm-possession restriction"? Why was there a due process violation even though the court never explicitly told Leavitt that he was *not* barred indefinitely from possessing a firearm (which clearly would have been erroneous)? Compare section d. infra.

c. Limitations on the Traditional Principle: Statutory Interpretation

It is plain that the legislature is *entitled*, even if it isn't constitutionally required, to predicate criminal liability on a defendant's knowing the law she is charged with having violated. Statutory language, and legislative intent, may often be ambiguous, though. Consider the following cases.

Cheek v. United States

Supreme Court of the United States.
498 U.S. 192, 111 S.Ct. 604 (1991).

■ MR. JUSTICE WHITE delivered the opinion of the Court.

Title 26, § 7201 of the United States Code provides that any person "who willfully attempts in any manner to evade or defeat any tax imposed by this title or the payment thereof" shall be guilty of a felony. Under 26 U.S.C. § 7203, "[a]ny person required under this title ... or by regulations made under authority thereof to make a return ... who willfully fails to ... make such return" shall be guilty of a misdemeanor. This case turns on the meaning of the word "willfully" as used in § 7201 and 7203.

Petitioner John L. Cheek has been a pilot for American Airlines since 1973. He filed federal income tax returns through 1979 but thereafter ceased to file returns. He also claimed an increasing number of withholding allowances—eventually claiming 60 allowances by mid-1980—and for the years 1981 to 1984 indicated on his W-4 forms that he was exempt from federal income taxes....

At trial, the evidence established that between 1982 and 1986, petitioner was involved in at least four civil cases that challenged various aspects of the federal income tax system. In all four of those cases, the plaintiffs were informed by the courts that many of their arguments, including that they were not taxpayers within the meaning of the tax laws, that wages were not income, that the Sixteenth Amendment does not authorize the imposition of an income tax on individuals, and that the Sixteenth Amendment is unenforceable, were frivolous or had been repeatedly rejected by the courts....

Cheek represented himself at trial and testified in his defense. He admitted that he had not filed personal income tax returns during the years in question. He testified that as early as 1978, he had begun attending seminars sponsored by, and following the advice of a group that believes, among other things, that the federal income tax is unconstitutional. Some of the speakers at these meetings were lawyers who purported to give professional opinions about the invalidity of the federal income tax laws. Cheek produced a letter from an attorney stating that the Sixteenth Amendment did not authorize a tax on wages and salaries but only a gain on profit. Petitioner's defense is that, based on the indoctrination he received from this group and from his own study, he sincerely believed that the tax laws were unconstitutionally enforced and that his actions during the 1980-86 period were lawful. He therefore argued that he had acted without the willfulness required for conviction of the various offenses with which he is charged.

In the course of the instructions, the trial court advised the jury that to prove "willfulness" the Government must prove the voluntary and intentional violation of a known legal duty, a burden that could not be proved by showing mistake, ignorance or negligence. The court further advised the jury that an objectively reasonable good-faith misunderstanding of the law would negate willfulness but mere disagreement with the law would not. The court described Cheek's beliefs about the income tax system and instructed the jury that if it found that Cheek "honestly and reasonably believed that he was not required to pay income taxes or to file tax returns," a not guilty verdict should be returned.

[After several rounds of questions from the jury] the District Court gave the jury an additional instruction ... that "an honest but unreasonable belief is not a defense and does not negate willfulness," and that "advice or research resulting in the conclusion that wages of a privately employed person are not income or that the tax laws are unconstitutional is not objectively reasonable and cannot serve as the basis for a good faith misunderstanding of the law defense." The court also instructed the jury that "persistent refusal to acknowledge the law does not constitute a good faith misunderstanding of the law." ...

Petitioner appealed his conviction, arguing that the District Court erred by instructing the jury that only an objectively reasonable misunderstanding of the law negates the statutory willfulness requirement....

The proliferation of statutes and regulations has sometimes made it difficult for the average citizen to know and comprehend the extent of the duties and obligations imposed by the tax law. Congress has accordingly softened the impact of the common-law presumption [that every person know the law, so that ignorance of the law is no defense] by making specific intent to violate the law an element of certain federal criminal tax offenses. Thus, the Court almost 60 years ago interpreted the term "willfully" as used in the federal criminal tax statutes as carving out an exception to the traditional rule. This special treatment is largely due to the complexity of the tax laws. In United State v. Murdock, 290 U.S. 389 (1933), the Court recognized that:

> Congress did not intend that a person by reason of a bona fide misunderstanding as to his liability for the tax, as to his duty to make a return, or as to the adequacy of the records he maintained, should become a criminal by his mere failure to measure up to the prescribed standard of conduct....

Willfulness, as construed by our prior decisions in criminal tax cases, requires the Government to prove that the law imposed a duty on the defendant, that defendant knew of this duty and that he voluntarily and intentionally violated that duty....

In this case, if Cheek asserted that he truly believed that the Internal Revenue Code did not purport to treat wages as income, and the jury believed him, the Government would not have carried its burden to prove willfulness....

Of course the more unreasonable the asserted belief or misunderstandings are, the more likely the jury will consider them to be nothing more than simple disagreements with known legal duties ... and will find that the Government has carried its burden of proving knowledge ...

Claims that some of the provisions of the tax code are unconstitutional are of a different order. They do not arise from innocent mistakes caused by the complexity of the Internal Revenue Code. Rather, they reveal full knowledge of the provisions at issue and a studied conclusion, however wrong, that those provisions are invalid and unenforceable....

We do not believe that Congress contemplated that such a taxpayer, without risking criminal prosecution, could ignore the duties imposed on him by the Internal Revenue Code and refuse to utilize the mechanisms provided by Congress to present his claims of invalidity to the courts and to abide by their decisions. There is no doubt that Cheek, from year to year, was free to pay the tax that the law purported to require, file for a refund, and, if denied, present his claims of invalidity, constitutional or otherwise, to the courts....

We thus hold [it] was ... not error in this case for the District Judge to instruct the jury not to consider Cheek's claims that the tax laws were unconstitutional. However, it was error for the court to instruct the jury that petitioner's asserted beliefs that wages are not income and that he was not a taxpayer within the meaning of the Internal Revenue Code should not be considered by the jury in determining whether Cheek had acted willfully.

[Cheek was convicted on remand: the court instructed the jurors that they could consider their view of the reasonableness of Cheek's belief in "deciding whether he held the belief in good faith." United States v. Cheek, 3 F.3d 1057 (7th Cir. 1993).]

Ratzlaf v. United States, 510 U.S. 135 (1994)

[Federal law requires banks and other financial institutions to file reports with the Secretary of the Treasury whenever they are involved in a cash transaction that exceeds $10,000. It is illegal to "structure" transactions—i.e., to break up a single transaction above the reporting threshold into two or more separate transactions for the purpose of evading a financial institution's reporting requirement. See 31 U.S.C. §§ 5322, 5324. The defendant first tried to pay $100,000 of casino gambling debt in cash; when informed that the cash transaction would be reported, he procured a number of cashier's checks from local banks, all in amounts less than $10,000, to pay the debt.] ...

The trial judge instructed the jury that the Government had to prove defendant's knowledge of the banks' reporting obligation and his attempt to evade the obligation, but did not have to prove defendant knew the structuring was unlawful ... We ... reverse....

... Ratzlaf admits that he structured cash transactions, and that he did so with knowledge of, and a purpose to avoid, the banks' duty to report currency transactions in excess of $10,000. The statutory formulation under which Ratzlaf was prosecuted, however, calls for proof of "willfulness" on the actor's part.... [While most provisions of the Bank Secrecy Act have been interpreted to require a purpose to disobey the law], the United States urges that § 5324 violators, by their very conduct, exhibit a purpose to do wrong, which suffices to show "willfulness." ...

Undoubtedly, there are bad men who attempt to elude official reporting requirements in order to hide from Government inspectors such criminal activity as laundering drug money or tax evasion. But currency structuring is not inevitably nefarious.... [U]nder the government's construction an individual would commit a felony against the United States by making cash deposits in small doses, fearful that the bank's reports would increase the likelihood of burglary, or in an endeavor to keep a former spouse unaware of his wealth....

We do not dishonor the venerable principle that ignorance of the law generally is no defense to a criminal charge. In particular contexts, however, Congress may decree otherwise. That, we hold, is what Congress has done.

[The Court may well have read congressional intent incorrectly: Congress overturned the decision in *Ratzlaf* almost immediately. Under the Money Laundering Suppression Act of 1994, Pub. L. No. 103–325, Tit. IV. § 411, 108 Stat. 22533, the defendant can be convicted so long as it is her purpose to prevent the filing of the required report.]

Bryan v. United States, 524 U.S. 184 (1998)

[The 1968 Omnibus Crime Control and Safe Streets Act imposed criminal penalties on every unlicensed dealer in firearms. In 1986, Congress enacted the Firearms Owners' Protection Act (FOPA), "to add a scienter requirement as a condition to the imposition of penalties."]

[The] evidence proved that petitioner did not have a federal license to deal in firearms; that he used so-called "straw purchasers" in Ohio to acquire pistols that he could not have purchased himself; that the straw purchasers made false statements when purchasing the guns; that petitioner assured the straw purchasers that he would file the serial numbers off the guns; and that he resold the guns on Brooklyn street corners known for drug dealing. The evidence was unquestionably adequate to prove that petitioner was dealing in firearms, and that he knew that his conduct was unlawful. There was, however, no evidence that he was aware of the federal law that prohibits dealing in firearms without a federal license....

Petitioner ... argues that we must read § 924(a)(1)(D) to require knowledge of the law because of our interpretation of "willfully" in two other contexts. In certain cases involving willful violations of the tax laws, we have concluded that the jury must find that the defendant was aware of the specific provisions of the tax code that he was charged with violating. See, e.g., *Cheek v. United States*.... Similarly, in order to satisfy a willful violation in *Ratzlaf*, we concluded that the jury had to find that defendant knew that his structuring of cash transactions to avoid a reporting requirement was unlawful.... Those cases, however, are readily distinguishable. Both the tax cases and *Ratzlaf* involved highly technical statutes that presented the danger of ensnaring individuals engaged in apparently innocent conduct.... The danger of convicting individuals engaged in apparently innocent activity that motivated our decisions in the tax cases and *Ratzlaf* is not present here because the jury found that this petitioner knew that his conduct was unlawful....

In his dissent, Justice Scalia wrote:

The jury apparently found, and the evidence clearly shows, that Bryan was aware in a general way that some aspect of his conduct was unlawful.... The issue is whether that general knowledge of illegality is enough to sustain the conviction, or whether a "willful" violation of the licensing provision requires proof that the defendant knew that his conduct was unlawful specifically because he lacked the necessary license. On that point the statute is, in my view, genuinely ambiguous.... Everyone agrees that § 924(a)(1)(D) requires some knowledge of the law; the only real question is *which* law? The Court's answer is that knowledge of *any* law is enough—or, put another way, that the defendant must be ignorant of *every* law violated by his course of conduct to be innocent of willfully violating the licensing requirement....

I do not believe that the Court's approach makes sense of the statute that Congress enacted. I have no quarrel with the Court's assertion that "willfully" in § 924(a)(1)(D) requires only "general" knowledge of illegality—in the sense that the defendant need not be able to recite chapter and verse from Title 18 of the United States Code. It is enough, in my view, if the defendant is generally aware that the *actus reus* punished by the statute—dealing in firearms without a license—is illegal. But the Court is willing to accept a *mens rea* so "general" that it is entirely divorced from the *actus reus* this statute was enacted to punish.... Bryan would be guilty of "willfully" dealing in firearms without a federal license even if, for example, he had never heard of the licensing requirement but was aware that he had violated the law by using straw purchasers or filing the serial numbers off the pistols....

In the face of [the statute's] ambiguity, I would invoke the rule that "ambiguity concerning the ambit of criminal statutes should be resolved in favor of lenity."

QUESTIONS AND COMMENTS

1. The Court in *Cheek* focuses a good deal on the complexity of the tax laws: is the law that Cheek himself purports to be ignorant of (treating wages as taxable income) an especially complex one? Does the fact that the Court held in *Murdock* that taxpayers who *miscompute* tax liability should not be held criminally liable unless they did so willfully necessarily dictate the holding in *Cheek*?

Assume, first, solely for argument's sake, that Cheek is culpable if he is unreasonable in his beliefs about the law. Is there an issue of fact in the case that needs to be resolved by the jury about whether he is unreasonable?

Assume, instead, as the Court ultimately found, that the statute requires that he *know* his legal duty. Was there an issue of fact even on *this* issue, given Cheek's testimony, which would mandate a jury instruction on this question? Given the fact that willful ignorance is tantamount to knowledge? See *United States v. Jewell*, supra. Does Cheek ever claim to believe that the Internal Revenue Service shared his views that wages were not income? Or only that the IRS is wrong not to? The Court dismissed the relevance of his mistaken constitutional claims, but how can *that* be right if it accepts the relevance of (what the Court constructs) as his purely statutory claim: isn't he really testifying that the *reason* he believes that wages are not income is that it would be unconstitutional to treat them as income? Since willfulness implies the violation of a "known legal duty," how can Cheek be said to have acted willfully if he was convinced that he was under no legal obligation to pay taxes no matter what the reason (that wages aren't treated as income *or* that treating wages as income is unconstitutional)?

Isn't the real effect—if any—of the *Cheek* decision to permit tax protesters to elicit the sympathy of the occasional juror who wishes to nullify by identifying himself as an ideological opponent of the federal tax system? Are there really any non-hypothetical cases in which tax protesters don't believe there is at least some strong risk that the IRS does not share their views, a risk that would require them to check further were they to avoid being deemed willfully ignorant? Certainly, one can *imagine* someone raised in an isolated community of tax protesters who truly did not know (and was not even "negligent" if we permit him to compare himself to members of his sub-cultural community, rather than the community more generally) that one is obliged to pay income taxes when one earns a salary, but should we frame a legal rule in response to a far-fetched hypothetical?

Reliance on one's lawyer's advice (or, for that matter, on information disseminated at anti-tax seminars) about the legality of one's conduct is never enough to make out an ignorance of law defense, *except* in willfulness cases like *Cheek*. Legal advice may be relevant to counter the claim of a violation of a known legal duty. See Bursten v. United States, 395 F.2d 976 (5th Cir. 1968) (another tax evasion case).

2. The willfulness requirement, with its room for ignorance-of-law claims, is common in white-collar criminal law. (Why?) The law of criminal securities fraud recognizes an interesting statutory ignorance-of-law defense that precludes imprisonment, but not noncarceral sanctions (mostly fines, but also revocation of licenses):

> Any person who willfully violates any provision of this chapter, or any rule or regulation thereunder the violation of which is made unlawful or the observance of which is required under the terms of this chapter, ... shall upon conviction be fined not more than $10,000, or imprisoned not more than two years, or both, ...; but no person shall be subject to imprisonment under this section for the violation of any rule or regulation if he proves that he had no knowledge of such rule or regulation.
>
> 15 U.S.C. § 78ff(a) (Securities Exchange Act of 1934).

Note that the burden of proof as to this partial defense is on the defendant. Cf. United States v. Lilley, 291 F.Supp. 989 (S.D. Tex. 1968) (general awareness of the illegality of securities fraud, without knowledge of the specific rule violated, is enough).

d. Limitations on the Traditional Principle: Good Faith Reliance on Official Pronouncements

Hopkins v. State, 69 A.2d 456 (Md. 1949)

[Appellant was convicted for violation of a statute making it unlawful to erect or maintain any sign intended to aid in the solicitation or performance of marriages. The Act under consideration had been passed to curb a thriving business among "unethical ministers" that had built up following the passage of more stringent marriage laws in nearby states. Appellant erected two signs, illuminated at night, with the name Rev. W.F. Hopkins on one and the words "W.F. Hopkins, Notary Public, Information" on the other. The court sustained the conviction.]

Defendant contended that the judge erred in excluding testimony offered to show that the State's Attorney advised him in 1944 before he erected the signs that they would not violate the law. It is generally held that the advice of counsel, even though followed in good faith, furnishes no excuse for a person violating the law and cannot be relied upon as a defense in a criminal action. Moreover, advice given by a public official, even a State's Attorney, that a contemplated act is not criminal will not excuse an offender if, as a matter of law, the act performed did amount to a violation of the law. These rules are founded upon the maxim that ignorance of the law will not excuse its violation. If an accused could be exempted from punishment for crime by reason of the advice of counsel, such advice would become paramount to the law.

Cox v. Louisiana, 379 U.S. 559 (1965)

[Defendant was convicted of violating a Louisiana statute prohibiting "pickets or parades in or near a building housing a court of the State of Louisiana" with intent to interfere with the administration of justice. Defendant led a civil rights rally of 200 persons on the far side of the street from the courthouse, about 100 feet from the courthouse steps, with the permission of the city's police chief and sheriff, who were the city officials present at the demonstration. The Court reversed the convictions stating:]

[T]he statute, with respect to the determination of how near the courthouse a particular demonstration can be, foresees a degree of on-the-spot administrative interpretation of how "near" the courthouse a particular demonstration might take place. [Permitting police to regulate the time, place and manner of regulations does not] constitute a waiver of law.... Obviously telling demonstrators how far from the courthouse steps is "near" the courthouse for purposes of a permissible peaceful demonstration is a far cry from allowing one to commit, for example, murder or robbery.... [T]o sustain appellant's ... conviction for demonstrating where they told him he could "would be to sanction an indefensible form of entrapment by the State—convicting a citizen for exercising a privilege which the State had clearly told him was available to him...."

In his dissent, Justice Clark wrote:

One hardly needed an on-the-spot administrative decision that the demonstration was "near" the courthouse.... Reading the facts in a way most favorable to the appellant would, in my opinion, establish only that the Chief of Police consented to the demonstration at that location.... I never knew until today that a law enforcement official—city, state or national—could forgive a breach of the criminal laws.

People v. Marrero

New York Court of Appeals.
69 N.Y.2d 382, 507 N.E.2d 1068 (1987).

■ BELLACOSA J.

[Defendant was arrested for possession of a loaded .38 caliber pistol, in violation of N.Y. Penal Law § 265.02. Under § 265.20(a)(1)(c), defendant would have been entitled to an "exemption" from various weapons offenses, including § 265.02, if he were a "peace officer." Peace officers are defined in N.Y. Crim. Proc. Law §§ 1.20 (defining "peace officer" as "a person listed in section 2.10") & 2.10 ("peace officers" include "correction officers of any state correction facility or of any penal correctional institution"). At the time of his arrest, defendant insisted that he was exempt from the possession charge because he was a federal corrections officer (at a federal prison in Danbury, Connecticut). His pre-trial motion to quash the indictment was granted, but the indictment was reinstated by the Appellate Division, which held, 3–2, that he was not a "peace officer" within the meaning of the statute. He was convicted upon trial. . . .]

The common-law rule on mistake of law was clearly articulated in Gardner v. People, 69 N.Y. 299. In *Gardner*, the defendants misread a statute and mistakenly believed that their conduct was legal. The court insisted, however, that the "mistake of law" did not relieve the defendants of criminal liability. . . .

The desirability of the *Gardner*-type outcome ... is underscored by Justice Holmes' statement: "It is no doubt true that there are many cases in which the criminal could not have known that he was breaking the law, but to admit the excuse at all would be to encourage ignorance where the lawmaker has determined to make men know and obey, and justice to the individual is rightly outweighed by the larger interests on the other side of the scales." (Holmes, The Common Law at 48 [1881]).

The revisors of New York's Penal Law intended no fundamental departure from the common-law rule in Penal Law § 15.20, which provides in pertinent part:

> 2. A person is not relieved of criminal liability for conduct because he engaged in such conduct under a mistaken belief that it does not, as a matter of law, constitute an offense, unless such mistaken belief is founded upon an official statement of the law contained in (a) a statute or other enactment ... (d) an interpretation of the statute or law relating to the offense, officially made or issued by a public servant, agency, or body legally charged or empowered with the responsibility or privilege of administering, enforcing, or interpreting such statute or law.

The defendant claims as a first prong of his defense that he is entitled to raise the defense of mistake of law under section 15.20(2)(a) because his mistaken belief that his conduct was legal was founded upon an official statement of the law contained in the statute itself. Defendant argues that his mistaken interpretation of the statute was reasonable in view of the alleged ambiguous wording of the peace officer exemption statute. . . .

The prosecution ... counters ... by asserting that one cannot claim the protection of mistake of law under section 15.20(2)(a) simply by misconstruing the meaning of a statute but must instead establish that the statute relied on actually permitted the conduct in question and was only later found to be erroneous. . . .

It was early recognized that the "official statement" mistake of law defense was a statutory protection against prosecution based on reliance on a statute that did *in fact* authorize certain conduct. While providing a narrow escape hatch, the idea was simultaneously to encourage the public to read and rely on official statements of the law, not to have individuals conveniently and personally question the validity and interpretation of the law and act on that basis. If later the statute was invalidated, one who mistakenly acted in reliance on the authorizing statute would be relieved of criminal liability. This makes sense and is fair. To go further does not make sense and would create legal chaos. . . .

If defendant's argument were accepted . . . [m]istakes about the law would be encouraged, rather than respect for and adherence to law. There would be an infinite number of mistake of law defenses which could be devised from a good-faith, perhaps reasonable, but mistaken interpretation of criminal statutes, many of which are concededly complex. . . .

QUESTIONS AND COMMENTS

1. How might one justify the traditional rule that ignorance of governing law does not excuse the defendant?

Note that the court in *Hopkins* expresses concern that those who (mis)interpret law will illegitimately displace the legislature as sources of authority. Is that concern realistic? How would the Attorney General's statements to Hopkins about what he was permitted to do have become "like" legislation? How would they differ?

Note that the court in *Marrero* observes that it is important to give people incentives to know the law. Why wouldn't we give adequate incentives to know the law if we convicted defendants who were *negligently* ignorant?

The *Marrero* court seems, too, to treat the traditional rule as trading off fairness to individuals for collective gains or efficiency. Why is the rule more socially efficient? Would it be inefficient to litigate claims that a particular defendant did not know the law? That she was reasonable in her ignorance? On the other hand, why is the rule unfair? Did the defendant in *Baker* make adequate efforts to know the law?

2. Dan Kahan argues that the mistake of law defense should be available only to those defendants who are in some deep sense morally innocent, who attempt to be virtuous citizens generally, not to those who try to discover precisely what the criminal law lets them get away with. See Dan Kahan, "Ignorance of Law Is an Excuse—but Only for the Virtuous," 96 Mich. L. Rev. 127 (1997). This view seems to support the explicit holding in *Bryan* and may help us make sense of the court's hostility to the defendant in *Marrero*, a person who had furnished guns to family members who *plainly* did not qualify as corrections officers and who carried a gun despite his employer's official policy against carrying such guns, on or off

the job. Isn't Justice Scalia, dissenting in *Bryan*, right, though, to worry about punishing people because they are not in some sense virtuous, or even, "generally law-abiding"? Isn't that what the constitutional prohibition of punishing status, not conduct, is meant to protect against? See ch. 4, supra. Should the criminal law be in the business of separating the virtuous from the not-so-virtuous? Is it?

At the same time, what does Justice Scalia imagine a trial in *Bryan* would look like if the Court had resolved the case as he wished? How would the government establish that Bryan, or practically anyone else, knew that gun sellers needed licenses? How would Bryan, or practically anyone else, rebut a presumption that they knew that such licenses were required?

3. Does the argument between the dissent and majority in *Cox* turn only on whether the statute was clear on its face? Do (must?) both sides acknowledge that a defendant is not culpable if he seeks an authoritative interpretation of an *ambiguous* term? Is it unambiguous that the signs Hopkins posted violate a statute directed at "promoting and soliciting marriage"?

Does the court in *Leavitt* suggest that the court in *Hopkins* violated the defendant's Due Process rights? Or is the *Leavitt* court merely trying to give teeth to a particular legislative command, directing judges to inform defendants of an important collateral consequence of conviction (gun possession rights)?

4. Has Marrero made a mistake of governing law or non-governing law? Does he not know that persons other than peace officers are forbidden to carry weapons (is *that* the governing law?) or does he not know whether he is a peace officer (is that non-governing law defining an attendant circumstance or part of the definition of this offense)? Consider that question again after reading section 3 (on mistakes of non-governing law), below, not just for *Marrero*, but for all of the cases you have looked at. Does the defendant in *Doane*, for instance, not know that it is illegal to steal or does he not know that what he is doing is stealing? Are those questions really distinguishable in *Doane*? In other cases?

What difference does it make whether a defendant is mistaken about governing or non-governing law? Don't we have an interest in getting citizens to familiarize themselves with all laws, criminal or not, governing or not? Should it matter what *type* of governing law the defendant is mistaken about? Should courts distinguish between mistakes about malum prohibitum and malum in se offenses? About public welfare and common law offenses? Complex or straightforward offenses? New and traditional offenses?

e. Limitations on the Traditional Principle: Cultural Defenses

Should the law excuse foreigners who violate the law by taking actions that are acceptable in their own cultures? Should it do so out of respect for cultural diversity? Should it do so because the presumption that we ordinarily might make that a person who took reasonable steps to learn our laws *would* learn those laws is an unreasonable presumption to make for a defendant who—simply patterning himself after those he has observed around him—would have learned that the behavior proscribed here was permissible or mandatory in his culture-of-origin?

Consider the following case.

United States v. Tomono

United States Court of Appeals for the Eleventh Circuit.
143 F.3d 1401 (1998).

■ PER CURIAM.

Defendant Kei Tomono is a Japanese national who operates a commercial reptile import/export business called Amazon International. In April 1996, Tomono entered the United States at San Francisco on a flight from Japan. He carried in his luggage approximately 60 ... "Fly River" turtles ... and 113 ... "Snake–Neck" turtles.... Upon entry to the United States, Tomono completed a standard Customs Declaration Form 6059B, which he was able to read and understand. A statement on the form read, "I am ... bringing fruits, plants, meats food, soil, birds, snails, other live animals, wildlife products, farm products, or have been on a farm or ranch outside the U.S." Tomono checked the box marked "No" in response to this statement....

In August 1997, Tomono again flew into San Francisco from Japan. On this trip, he had six "Red Mountain Racer" snakes and two Mandarin Rat snakes in his luggage. On his Customs form he again indicated that he was not bringing any live animals into the United States. Tomono intended to sell these snakes to a reptile collector in Florida, and boarded a plane to Orlando. Unbeknownst to Tomono, government agents had conducted a border search of his luggage in San Francisco and found the snakes....

[Tomono pleaded guilty to violating an anti-smuggling statute, 18 U.S.C. § 545, prohibiting the fraudulent or knowing importation of goods contrary to law, and the Lacey Act, forbidding the importation of fish and wildlife taken in violation of federal, state or foreign law.]

At the sentencing hearing, ... Tomono moved for a downward departure ..., alleging that because of the cultural differences between the United States and Japan, he was unaware of the serious consequences of his actions, and that these cultural differences constituted a factor not considered by the Sentencing Commission that should be taken into account in calculating his sentence. The district court agreed with Tomono.... The Government appeals the downward departure....

[W]e have held that a district court granting a downward departure must articulate the specific mitigating circumstances upon which it relies and the reasons why these circumstances take a case out of the guidelines' heartland....

[The judge] elaborated on her reasoning in her order denying the Government's Motion to Correct Sentence, concluding:

> Even though ignorance of the laws of a country is generally not sufficient to justify a downward departure, the cultural differences between the Defendant's culture and the laws of the U.S. are signifi-

> cant. For example, in Japan, snakeneck turtles and flyriver turtles are not endangered species and are common. Regulations are not as stringent and, as a result, Defendant would not have been arrested in Japan for keeping the animals. . . .

[After rejecting other grounds for the downward departure, the court continued:] This leaves us with Tomono's claimed ignorance, presumably arising from "cultural differences" of the consequences of his actions under United States law. Tomono's business was the importation and exportation of wildlife. Although he may not have been an expert in United States customs law, Tomono testified that he knew that United States regulations forbid the importation of turtles with a carapace length of less than four inches, and that he was aware of "other rules" regarding the importation of animals. . . . Section 2Q2.1 of the guidelines, under which Tomono was sentenced, specifically applies to crimes involving the illegal importation and exportation of wildlife. . . . By definition, imported wildlife comes from other countries: presumably, a significant portion of illegally imported wildlife will be imported by people from other countries, many of whom will have an imperfect understanding of United States customs law. The record before us does not support the conclusion that the circumstances surrounding Tomono's crime were very different from the heartland of cases considered by the Sentencing Commission in drafting § 2Q2.1. We hold that the district court abused its discretion in concluding that the circumstances of this case were sufficiently unusual to justify granting Tomono a downward departure. . . .

QUESTIONS AND COMMENTS

1. Though the case obviously does not use the modern language, does the defendant in *Doane* actually raise something very much like what we would now call a "cultural defense"?

2. Does the defendant in *Tomono* claim that his punishment should be mitigated because he did not know the American law (since he was not exposed to it), or because his acts do not reveal as bad a character or as anti-social a disposition, given his background, as they would reveal if they had been committed by an American? Or does he claim in some sense that it is disrespectful to Japanese culture for American courts to ignore the fact that within that culture, what the defendant did is not criminal? What if the conduct isn't criminal in the defendant's culture, but is subject to a civil fine, exposes the actor to civil liability (torts, contracts, etc.), or is considered wrongful, though not illegal?

In United States v. Yu, 954 F.2d 951 (3d Cir. 1992), the court considered sympathetically, but ultimately did not find it necessary to rule on, the government's claim that if a trial judge were to consider cultural differences in granting downward departures, the judge would violate the anti-discrimination provision in the sentencing guidelines that forbids accounting for "national origin" in setting sentences. In *Yu*, the defendant was convicted of bribing his income tax auditor, and claimed, among other things, that such "bribes" might be described as "honoraria" in his native Korea, and that the failure to offer such a payment to an official with whom one had theses sorts of dealings would be considered an insult. Is the government's argument persuasive?

3. In a number of the most-debated cases in which defendants might raise "cultural defenses," male defendants claim that they should be exonerated (or punished less harshly) because some acts widely considered to violate women's autonomy rights in this culture are permissible within their culture of origin: for instance, Hmong defendants accused of rape have argued that they are engaging in the traditional practice of "bride capture." See, e.g., Deirdre Evans–Pritchard & Alison Dundes Renteln, "The Interpretation and Distortion of Culture: A Hmong 'Marriage by Capture' Case in Fresno, California," 4 S. Cal. Interdisciplinary L.J. 1 (1994). (Note that the defense might be offered *either* as a "mistake of law" excuse or as a "mistake of fact"—that the defendant subjectively believed a woman was consenting despite the presence of what the defendant construed as "ritual protests," and that it was reasonable to do so given his background. Should one version of the defense be more likely to succeed than the other?) The dilemma posed by these cases is captured well by Doriane Coleman:

> Allowing sensitivity to a defendant's culture to inform the application of laws to that individual is good multiculturalism. It also is good progressive criminal defense philosophy, which has as a central tenet the idea that the defendant should receive as much individualized (subjective) justice as possible.... [But] the use of cultural defenses is anathema to another fundamental goal of the progressive agenda, namely the expansion of legal protections for some of the least powerful members of American society: women and children.

Doriane Lambelet Coleman, "Individualizing Justice Through Multiculturalism: The Liberals' Dilemma," 96 Colum. L. Rev. 1093 (1996).

4. "Cultural defenses" are not necessarily framed as mistakes of law (or of fact). In State v. Kargar, 679 A.2d 81 (Me. 1996), the defendant, an Afghani refugee, was convicted of gross sexual assault (defined as, among other things, engaging in a sexual act with another person under fourteen years of age) for kissing his infant son's penis. In defense, Kargar produced several witnesses who testified that kissing a young son's penis is accepted as common practice in Afghanistan to show love for the child. The trial court imposed a suspended sentence on the grounds that there was "no sexual gratification" and that the conduct occurred in the open, with Kargar's wife present. Maine's Supreme Judicial Court held, however, that sentence mitigation was not enough (noting that collateral consequences of conviction included registration as a sex offender and possible deportation) and overturned the conviction, explaining that the trial court should have dismissed the case under the state's *de minimis* statute which authorizes dismissal where the defendant's conduct "presents such ... extenuations that it cannot reasonably be regarded as envisaged by the Legislature in defining the crime." In its opinion, the court cautioned that "although it may be difficult for us as a society to separate Kargar's conduct from our notions of sexual abuse, that difficulty should not result in a felony conviction in this case" and emphasized that "Kargar does not argue that

he should now be permitted to practice that which is accepted in his culture."

In People v. Romero, 69 Cal.App.4th 846, 81 Cal.Rptr.2d 823 (1999), the defendant argued that he had stabbed the victim to death in order to defend his younger brother and moved to introduce expert testimony on "the role of honor, paternalism, and street fighters in the Hispanic culture," including that

> (1) street fighters have a special understanding of what is expected of them; (2) for a street fighter in the Hispanic culture, there is no retreat; (3) the Hispanic culture is based on honor, and honor defines a person; and (4) in this culture a person "would be responsible to take care of someone," i.e., defendant had a strong motivation to protect his younger brother.

In upholding the trial court's denial of the motion, the appellate court rejected what it termed Romero's attempt to create "a reasonable street fighter standard."

3. MISTAKES OF NON-GOVERNING LAW

a. Mistakes of Non–Governing Law Treated like Mistakes of Governing Law

State v. Woods

Supreme Court of Vermont.
107 Vt. 354, 179 A. 1 (1935).

■ BUTTLES, SUPERIOR JUDGE.

The respondent was convicted in Orleans county court of a violation of P.L. 8602, commonly known as the Blanket Act [an Act that established criminal penalties for "A man with another man's wife, or a woman with another woman's husband, found in bed together, under circumstances affording presumption of an illicit intention . . ."]. . . .

. . . [T]he respondent, a single woman, with her three children, in company with one Leo Shufelt . . . motored in the summer of 1933 to Reno, Nevada. . . . Leo Shufelt, who was a married man, instituted divorce proceedings against his wife, then living in Vermont; . . . process in said divorce proceedings was served upon the said wife; . . . she never accepted service of same, did not go to Nevada, and had no appearance entered on her behalf in said cause.

It further appears that after hearing, a decree was granted which purported to be a decree of divorce to the said Shufelt, and thereupon he and the respondent went through a marriage ceremony in Reno. . . . [H]e subsequently went to Lowell, Vt., where the respondent later joined him and where the offense herein charged is alleged to have been committed.

The respondent does not challenge . . . the invalidity of the attempted Nevada divorce. . . .

The respondent contends . . . that an honest belief in the validity of the Reno divorce and of her subsequent marriage to Shufelt would be a defense to this prosecution. There is much diversity of view as to whether a mistaken belief as to a fact, upon reasonable grounds, may or may not constitute a defense in a criminal action of a nature similar to this one. In State v. Ackerly, 79 Vt. 69, 64 A. 450, this court held that an honest belief that his wife was dead was not a defense in a prosecution for bigamy, the respondent having attempted to remarry.

But in State v. Audette, 81 Vt. 400, 70 A. 833, it was held that, under the circumstances of the case, ignorance of the fact that the woman whom the respondent attempted to marry had a husband living was available as a defense in a prosecution for adultery, he having been misled by her false statements as to that fact.

Here, the respondent relies upon a mistake of law rather than a mistake of fact. Her presence in Reno and her marriage to Shufelt immediately after the supposed divorce was granted by the judge who granted the decree indicate that she must have known all about the facts and circumstances of that proceeding. No claim is made that she did not know the facts. Her mistake, if one she made, was to the legal effect in Vermont of the Nevada decree. The maxim *Ignorantia legis non excusat*, and the corresponding presumption that every one is conclusively presumed to know the law, are of unquestioned application in Vermont as elsewhere, both in civil and in criminal cases. . . .

It remains to consider whether this presumption is applicable in this case in view of the phraseology of P.L. 8602, under which the respondent was prosecuted. Clearly it does apply if the words "under circumstances affording presumption of an illicit intention" mean that the act which the respondent intends to is forbidden and not that the respondent must have acted with a guilty mind.

. . . Our public policy as evidenced by our divorce statutes and our refusal to recognize the validity of attempted foreign divorces under certain circumstances would have little force if people could use such attempted foreign divorce coupled with a plea of ignorance of the law as a defense to prosecution for sexual offenses. . . .

b. Mistakes of Non–Governing Law Treated like Cognate Mistakes of Fact

People v. Bray

California Court of Appeal.
52 Cal.App.3d 494, 124 Cal.Rptr. 913 (1975).

■ GERALD BROWN, PRESIDING JUSTICE.

James Eugene Bray appeals the judgment following his jury conviction on two counts of being a felon in possession of a concealable firearm. . . .

Bray's meritorious contention is the trial court should have instructed the jury that ignorance or mistake of fact is a defense to the crime.

In 1969 Bray pled guilty to being an accessory after the fact.... At sentencing, the Kansas prosecutor recommended Bray be granted probation because he had no previous criminal record, he had been unwilling to participate in the crime but had gotten involved by driving a friend away from the scene and he had cooperated with the district attorney's office....

In January 1972, Bray filled out an application to vote in the State of California. He discussed the problems he had had in Kansas with the Deputy of the Registrar of Voters and asked if would be allowed to vote. The Deputy could not answer the question and suggested he say on the registration form that he had been convicted of a felony and fill out a supplementary information form to find out if he, in fact, had committed a felony. This Bray did; he was allowed to vote.

In early July of 1973, Bray applied for a part-time job as a guard with ADT Sterling Security Company. On the application he answered that he had been arrested or charged with a crime but had not been convicted of a felony. At the bottom of the page Bray explained the circumstances surrounding his arrest and period of probation. In September he received a notice from the Bureau of Collection and Investigative Services that he had been registered as a guard or patrolman.

Later in July of 1973 Bray bought a .38 caliber revolver from a pawn shop ... to use in guard assignments requiring an armed patrolman. On one of the required forms he said he had not been convicted of a felony; on another he said he had not been convicted of a crime with a punishment of more than one year. After the statutory five-day waiting period, the gun was delivered to him....

In order to gain a conviction under section 12021, the prosecutor must prove: (1) conviction of a felony and (2) ownership, possession, custody or control of a firearm capable of being concealed on their person.... There was no question here that Bray had been in possession of a concealable firearm; there was no question he had been convicted of the crime, "accessory after the fact" in Kansas. Bray says there must be proof he knew he was a felon....

[K]nowledge that one is a felon becomes relevant where there is doubt the defendant knew he had committed a felony. Here, even the prosecution had substantial difficulty in determining whether the offense was considered a felony in Kansas. In arguing to the court the necessity of a Kansas attorney's expert testimony, the district attorney said, ".... even in our own jurisdiction, let alone a foreign jurisdiction such as the State of Kansas, it's extremely difficult to determine whether a sentence was a felony or a misdemeanor."

Although the district attorney had great difficulty in determining whether the Kansas offense was a felony or a misdemeanor, he expects the layman Bray to know its status easily. There was no doubt Bray knew he had committed an offense; there was, however, evidence to the effect he did not know the offense was a felony. Without this knowledge Bray would be ignorant of the facts necessary for him to come within the prescription of the statute....

This decision should not be interpreted to mean that instructions on mistake or ignorance of fact and knowledge of the facts are required every time a defendant claims he did not know he was a felon. Here Bray had been convicted in Kansas of what for California is an unusual crime, "accessory after the fact" and even the prosecutor claimed difficulty in knowing whether it was a felony. In addition, Bray on more than one occasion had been led to believe by state regulatory agencies that he was not a felon: he was allowed to vote, he was registered in an occupation allowing him to carry a gun, and he was allowed to buy and register the gun. Throughout the trial, Bray laid the proper foundation for the instructions and he requested them. It is only in very unusual circumstances such as these that the giving of these instructions is necessary.

Model Penal Code and Commentaries § 2.02, at 250 (1985)

It should be noted that the general principle that ignorance or mistake of law is no excuse is greatly overstated: it has no application, for example, when the circumstances made material by the definition of the offense include a legal element. Thus it is immaterial in theft, when claim of right is adduced in defense, that the claim involves a legal judgment as to the right of property. Claim of right is a defense because the property must belong to someone else for the theft to occur and the defendant must have culpable awareness of that fact.... The law involved is not the law defining the offense; it is some other legal rule that characterizes the attendant circumstances that are material to the offense.

QUESTIONS AND COMMENTS

1. A typical application of the "principle" embodied in the Model Penal Code can be seen in *Regina v. Smith*, [1974] 2 Q.B. 354. Defendant had installed ceiling, floorboard, and wall panels in the apartment he rented when putting in stereo wires; while removing the wires he destroyed parts of the ceiling and floorboard. The court reversed his conviction for "damaging the property of another" because he was not aware that the property he had earlier installed was a "fixture" under English property law, belonging to the landlord rather than the tenant, so that he had destroyed property of another.

Frequently, commentators refer to mistakes of non-governing law as mistakes of *non-criminal law*; while that is an apt characterization of *Smith*, is it an apt characterization of *Bray*? Should the cases be treated differently? Is there any distinction between the mistakes the defendant made in *Smith* and the mistake a hypothetical defendant who smashed a guitar that looked just like his, that he mistook for his, might make? Even if they can be distinguished, should they be treated differently?

2. Does the Court in *Woods* decide that violators of the Blanket Act need not know they are in bed with a married man, but merely know that they are in bed with a man who in fact turns out to be married, so that the crime is, in traditional terms, a "general intent" crime rather than a crime that requires what was traditionally called a crime requiring some "specific

intent" (here, to commit adultery)? If so, how does one explain the *Audette* case cited in *Woods*? Is it plausible to say, as the court does, that Woods was found in bed under circumstances permitting us to infer her *illicit* intention?

Assume that one defendant believes that the man she is sleeping with is unmarried because he has handed her a forged divorce decree and the other because, like Woods, she believes he has received a valid divorce that the state of Vermont does not actually recognize. Is there any reason to treat these cases differently? Does it depend *solely* on the reasonableness of each belief? What if the forgery is a very bad one, one which most people would discern as a forgery, and Vermont's treatment of out-of-state *ex parte* divorces obscure and hard to discern?

3. Does the court in *Bray* believe the state must prove that the defendant knew of his felon status because he was *reasonable* in believing he was not a felon? Why doesn't the court then simply require the State to prove he made an unreasonable error?

Re-read the last paragraph of the court's decision in *Bray* and think back to the decision in *Cheek*. Is the *Bray* court right to restrict the number of situations in which defendants are entitled to jury instructions on mistake?

4. Are there ever any reasons to treat mistakes of governing law differently than mistakes of fact, and, if there are, should we treat *all* mistakes of non-governing law more like mistakes of fact (as the Model Penal Code suggests)? Think about the following cases: First, a hypothetical third defendant in a Blanket Act case believes that the man she is sleeping with is unmarried because he has been separated from, and out of contact with for more than two decades, a woman he married some 25 years earlier, and she believes that they are thus no longer married.

Second, imagine that a defendant has taken an umbrella from a cloakroom that he knows was brought to the restaurant by some stranger. He says, though, that he needed the umbrella a lot, because he has been ill, and that he genuinely believed he was entitled to take something that he badly needed but that is of little value to another. Is this best *classified* as a mistake about whether theft is illegal or as a mistake about what property "belongs to another"? Is the distinction the Model Penal Code draws between mistakes of governing law and mistakes as to legal rules that characterize attendant circumstances *analytically* tenable? Isn't the statement, "I cannot take property of another" just a short-hand for the statement, "I cannot take property that has been left in the cloakroom for a substantial amount of time, but not so long that it would be considered abandoned in my jurisdiction; I cannot take property of little value to others that I badly need; I cannot keep property entrusted to me as a bailee; I cannot take fixtures I have installed in the apartment I have rented" etc.? If it is, isn't a mistake about, say, whether one can take fixtures a mistake about the governing law of theft, *thoroughly explicated*? If there is no sharp *analytical* distinction between defining an offense and applying it to predictable fact patterns, is there nevertheless a *pragmatic* distinction that might rescue us in trying to decide cases?

If we look at this more pragmatically, does it matter whether we characterize a mistake about whether long-separated spouses are free to remarry as a mistake of governing law or non-governing law? Whether we say that the person who thinks she can take the umbrella she needs is making a mistake about what is hers (and call *that* a non-governing law mistake) or is making a mistake about whether she is legally privileged to take what is not hers (and call that a mistake of governing law)? Whether we characterize her mistake as a mistake about some element of the offense (larceny) or about the availability of a justification (or excuse) defense—namely that she has a right to take things she needs more than their owner (or that no one is accountable for crimes committed in situations of dire need)? (Reconsider whether it is even worth figuring out in *Doane* whether to describe the defendants as making a mistake of non-governing law. Obviously their mistake—that one can take a small portion of an employer's goods in the absence of a formal contract to do so—displays less of a misunderstanding of the property/larceny regime than the mistake of the hypothetical defendant who claims an entitlement to most everything he needs, but his misunderstanding is fairly deep nonetheless.)

Finally, most realistically, imagine two groups of federal agents, each charged with violating 18 U.S.C. § 241 (making it a crime if "two or more persons conspire to injure, oppress, threaten or intimidate any citizen in the free exercise or enjoyment of any right or privilege secured to him by the constitution . . ."). Each group of agents has engaged in an illegal search, violating the victims' Fourth Amendment rights to be free from unreasonable searches. Group One made a classic factual mistake: they had a search warrant to search 500 Elm Street and searched 50 Elm Street instead. Group Two made (some sort of) legal error. They incorrectly believed that they were authorized to search the victims' homes as they had received executive branch authorization to conduct a warrantless search because of national security concerns. (Do they know that they can't violate constitutional rights, but make a mistake of non-governing law in determining what these rights are? Or do they not really know the governing law, fully explicated? Does their mistake negate an offense element or is it a mistake about the scope or existence of the offense?) Assume, too, that in some sense, one could describe the error that Group One made as more "unreasonable" than the error made by the agents in Group Two. (The warrant describing 500 Elm Street made it clear that it was a commercial space and 50 Elm Street was clearly in an all-residential neighborhood. The question of whether the executive could waive the warrant requirement in the class of cases the agents acted in was a close one.) Are there reasons to believe that any defendants who have made (wholly) factual errors in violating constitutional rights should not be criminally punished, while believing that liability should be "stricter" (punish the negligent? use strict liability?) when government agents interpret the law in a fashion that expands their own power relative to the power courts ultimately declare them to have? Does the Model Penal Code's suggestion that mistakes of non-governing law be treated like cognate mistakes of fact preclude that result? Or does it determine nothing because the line between mistakes of governing and non-governing law is too unstable to dictate *any* results? For a discussion of some of these issues in the context of Watergate-era trials of defendants who had acted on what were determined to be overreaching interpretations of their search powers, see United States v. Barker, 546 F.2d 940 (D.C. Cir. 1976).

5. Can we classify a mistake as a mistake of non-governing law if the "law" about which the defendant is mistaken has no meaning outside the governing law? (If that is the case, must we describe the mistake as a mistake about the meaning of an offense element?) Think about the following: A defendant shoots and kills an unarmed burglar posing no imminent threat of death or grievous bodily harm in a jurisdiction that forbids the use of deadly force to stop burglars under these circumstances. See, e.g., N.H. Stat. § 627:4. The defendant makes a plausible claim that he has lived his whole life in a jurisdiction that would permit the use of deadly force to thwart any burglary. See, e.g., Ky. Rev. Stat. § 503.080(2)(b). Has he made a mistake of non-governing law ("I know I can't kill unless I am justified but I wrongly thought I was justified") or governing law? Is it a mistake about governing law (solely) because the rule against using deadly force against unarmed burglars has no application outside the homicide statute? Do we need to consider, once again, whether we *want* to treat legal and factual errors differently regardless of their "reasonableness"? (Imagine, once more, comparing a defendant whose self-defense claim is authentic but factually unreasonable—few in his position would have felt threatened—with the defendant whose lack of knowledge of the deadly force law in his jurisdiction appears both less idiosyncratic and less careless.)

But should *everything* (anything?) turn on whether a legal norm has secondary applications? A defendant, charged with bigamy, believes his wife, who had disappeared on a camping trip, is dead. Though at first blush that may sound like a purely factual question, it could be effectively converted by statute into a legal question: a section of the Family Law Code states that one cannot treat one's spouse as dead unless a coroner has issued a death certificate or she has been missing for five years. Does this become a "mistake of governing law" if this "presumption of spousal death law" is used *only* in determining whether someone has committed bigamy, while it becomes a mistake of non-governing law (about whether one is still married) if it has other uses (e.g., in deciding when to probate a will; when life insurance policies must be paid off, etc.)? Could that make sense? Compare Mich. Comp. Laws § 750.439 (polygamy penalties not applicable to party who marries when his or her spouse has been absent for five years) and Mich. Comp. Laws § 700.1208(2) (for purposes of estate code, spouse is presumed dead if missing for five years) with 720 Ill. Comp. Stat. 5/11–12 (affirmative defense to bigamy in Illinois that prior spouse has been absent for five years during which defendant did not know him or her to be alive; no other statutory presumption of spousal death).

6. What, in the end, is the point of distinguishing between mistakes of fact and mistakes of law, particularly since it has proved so difficult to draw? Assuming the distinction can be drawn consistently, why should mistakes of fact exculpate, but not mistakes of law? Isn't the relevant distinction between mistakes as to an *element* of the offense and mistakes as to the *existence* of the offense? Can we draw that distinction? Assuming it's clear why mistakes as to an offense element should exculpate, why

should a mistake as to the criminality of my conduct have the same effect? Would simply not knowing that I'm committing a crime be enough to excuse my facially criminal behavior? Would reliance on an official (mis)statement of the law be the only reason for excusing my conduct? Should my "good-faith" efforts to find and interpret the relevant (criminal?) law be enough? What about the avoidability of my mistake? Consider the treatment of ignorance of law in Israeli and German criminal law.

Penal Law of Israel § 34A

For the purposes of criminal liability, it is immaterial whether a person, owing to a mistake as to the existence or meaning of a penal enactment, imagines that his act is not prohibited, unless the mistake could not reasonably have been avoided.

German Penal Code § 16. Mistake about Circumstances of the Act.

(1) Whoever upon commission of the act is unaware of a circumstance which is a statutory element of the offense does not act intentionally. Punishability for negligent commission remains unaffected.

(2) Whoever upon commission of the act mistakenly assumes the existence of circumstances which would satisfy the elements of a more lenient norm, may only be punished for intentional commission under the more lenient norm.

German Penal Code § 17. Mistake of Law.

If upon commission of the act the perpetrator lacks the appreciation that he is committing a wrong, he acts without guilt if he was unable to avoid this mistake. If the perpetrator could have avoided the mistake, the punishment may be mitigated....

G. INTOXICATION

Intoxication works very much like mistake. It too can negate mens rea—as a simple matter of evidence. It too can function as an excuse, even if doesn't (or can't, because we're faced with a strict liability crime) negate mens rea. It too, in its excuse version, has met sufficient hostility to have resulted in general maxims ("ignorance of the law is no excuse" in one case, "drunkenness is no excuse" in the other).

People v. Walker, 38 Mich. 156 (1878): While it is true that drunkenness cannot excuse crime, it is equally true that when a certain intent is a necessary element in a crime, the crime cannot have been committed when the intent did not exist. In larceny the crime does not consist in the wrongful taking of the property, for that might be a mere trespass; but it consists in the wrongful taking with felonious intent; and if the defendant, for any reason whatever, indulged no such intent, the crime cannot have been committed.

State v. Cameron

Supreme Court of New Jersey.
104 N.J. 42, 514 A.2d 1302 (1986).

■ CLIFFORD, J.

This appeal presents a narrow, but important, issue concerning the role that a defendant's voluntary intoxication plays in a criminal prosecution. The specific question is whether the evidence was sufficient to require the trial court to charge the jury on defendant's intoxication, as defendant requested. The Appellate Division reversed defendant's convictions, holding that it was error not to have given an intoxication charge. We granted the State's petition for certification and now reverse.

Defendant, Michele Cameron, age 22 at the time of trial, was indicted for second degree aggravated assault, in violation of N.J. Stat. Ann. § 2C:12–1(b)(1)[a]; possession of a weapon, a broken bottle, with a purpose to use it unlawfully, contrary to N.J. Stat. Ann. § 2C:39–4(d)[b]; and fourth degree resisting arrest, a violation of N.J. Stat. Ann. § 2C:29–2.[c] A jury convicted defendant of all charges. After merging the possession count into the assault charge, the trial court imposed sentences aggregating seven years in the custody of the Commissioner of the Department of Corrections, with a three year period of parole ineligibility and certain monetary penalties.

The charges arose out of an incident of June 6, 1981, on a vacant lot in Trenton. The unreported opinion of the Appellate Division depicts the following tableau of significant events:

The victim, Joseph McKinney, was playing cards with four other men. Defendant approached and disrupted the game with her conduct. The participants moved their card table to a new location within the lot. Defendant followed them, however, and overturned the table. The table was righted and the game resumed. Shortly thereafter, defendant attacked McKinney with a broken bottle. As a result of that attack he sustained an injury to his hand, which necessitated 36 stitches and caused permanent injury.

Defendant reacted with violence to the arrival of the police. She threw a bottle at their vehicle, shouted obscenities, and tried to fight them off. She had to be restrained and handcuffed in the police wagon.

The heart of the Appellate Division's reversal of defendant's conviction is found in its determination that voluntary intoxication is a defense when

a. 2C:12–1(b). Aggravated assault.

A person is guilty of aggravated assault if he (1) [a]ttempts to cause serious bodily injury to another, or causes such injury purposely or knowingly or under circumstances manifesting extreme indifference to the value of human life recklessly causes such injury.—EDS.

b. 2C:39–4(d). Possession of weapons for unlawful purposes.

Any person who has in his possession any weapon, except a firearm, with a purpose to use it unlawfully against the person or property of another is guilty of a crime of the third degree.—EDS.

c. 2C:29–2. Resisting Arrest; Eluding Officer.

[A] person is guilty of a crime of the fourth degree if he, by flight, purposely prevents or attempts to prevent a law enforcement officer from effecting an arrest.—EDS.

it negates an essential element of the offense—here, purposeful conduct. We agree with that proposition. Likewise are we in accord with the determinations of the court below that all three of the charges of which this defendant was convicted—aggravated assault, the possession offense, and resisting arrest—have purposeful conduct as an element of the offense; and that a person acts purposely "with respect to the nature of his conduct or a result thereof if it is his conscious object to engage in conduct of that nature or to cause such a result"....

Under the common law intoxication was not a defense to a criminal charge.... [T]he early cases nevertheless held that in some circumstances intoxication could be resorted to for defensive purposes—specifically, to show the absence of a specific intent. "The exceptional immunity extended to the drunkard is limited to those instances where the crime involves a specific, actual intent. When the degree of intoxication is such as to render the person incapable of entertaining such intent, it is an effective defence. If it falls short of this it is worthless." [Warner v. State, 56 N.J.L. 686, 690 (1894).]

The principle ... developed from the foregoing approach, that intoxication formed the basis for a defense to a "specific intent" crime but not to one involving only "general" intent....

N.J. Stat. Ann. § 2C:2–8 provide[s]:

> a. Except as provided in subsection d. of this section, intoxication of the actor is not a defense unless it negatives an element of the offense.
>
> b. When recklessness establishes an element of the offense, if the actor, due to self-induced intoxication, is unaware of a risk of which he would have been aware had he been sober, such unawareness is immaterial.
>
> c. Intoxication does not, in itself, constitute mental disease....
>
> d. Intoxication which (1) is not self-induced or (2) is pathological is an affirmative defense if by reason of such intoxication the actor at the time of his conduct lacks substantial and adequate capacity either to appreciate its wrongfulness or to conform his conduct to the requirement of law.
>
> e. Definitions. In this section unless a different meaning plainly is required:
>
> > (1) "Intoxication" means a disturbance of mental or physical capacities resulting from the introduction of substances into the body;
> >
> > (2) "Self-induced intoxication" means intoxication caused by substances which the actor knowingly introduces into his body, the tendency of which to cause intoxication he knows or ought to know, unless he introduces them pursuant to medical advice or under such circumstances as would afford a defense to a charge of crime;

(3) "Pathological intoxication" means intoxication grossly excessive in degree, given the amount of the intoxicant, to which the actor does not know he is susceptible.

As is readily apparent, self-induced intoxication is not a defense unless it negatives an element of the offense. Under the common-law intoxication defense ... intoxication could either exculpate or mitigate guilt "if the defendant's intoxication, in fact, prevents his having formed a mental state which is an element of the offense and if the law will recognize the proof of the lack of that mental state." [U]nder pre-Code law, intoxication was admissible as a defense to a "specific" intent, but not a "general" intent, crime.

The original proposed Code rejected the specific/general intent distinction, choosing to rely instead on the reference to the four states of culpability for offenses under the Code: negligent, reckless, knowing, and purposeful conduct.... In essence, "[t]hat which the cases now describe as a 'specific intent' can be equated, for this purpose, with that which the Code defines as 'purpose' and 'knowledge.' See § 2C:2–2b. A 'general intent' can be equated with that which the Code defines as 'recklessness,' or criminal 'negligence.' " Code Commentary at 68....

N.J. Stat. Ann. § 2C:2–8 was modeled after the Model Penal Code (MPC) § 2.08. The drafters of the MPC, as did the New Jersey Commission, criticized the specific-general intent distinction, and adopted instead the same four states of culpability eventually enacted in the Code. In the commentary, the drafters of the MPC expressly stated their intention that intoxication be admissible to disprove the culpability factors of purpose or knowledge, but that for crimes requiring only recklessness or negligence, exculpation based on intoxication should be excluded as a matter of law.

The drafters explicitly determined that "intoxication ought to be accorded a significance that is entirely co-extensive with its relevance to disprove purpose or knowledge, when they are the requisite mental elements of a specific crime.... [W]hen the definition of a crime or a degree thereof requires proof of such a state of mind, the legal policy involved will almost certainly obtain whether or not the absence of purpose or knowledge is due to the actor's ... intoxication or to some other cause." [*MPC Commentaries*, § 2.08 at 357.]

The policy reasons for requiring purpose or knowledge as a requisite element of some crimes are that in the absence of those states of mind, the criminal conduct would not present a comparable danger, or the actor would not pose as significant a threat. Moreover, the ends of legal policy are better served by subjecting to graver sanctions those who consciously defy legal norms. It was those policy reasons that dictated the result that the intoxication defense should be available when it negatives purpose or knowledge. The drafters concluded: "If the mental state which is the basis of the law's concern does not exist, the reason for its non-existence is quite plainly immaterial." Id. at 358.

Thus, when the requisite culpability for a crime is that the person act "purposely" or "knowingly," evidence of voluntary intoxication is admissible to disprove that requisite mental state....

The foregoing discussion establishes that proof of voluntary intoxication would negate the culpability elements in the offenses of which this defendant was convicted.

The charges—aggravated assault, possession of a weapon with a purpose to use it unlawfully, and resisting arrest—all require purposeful conduct (aggravated assault uses "purposely" or "knowingly" in the alternative). The question is what level of intoxication must be demonstrated before a trial court is required to submit the issue to a jury....

The guiding principle is simple enough of articulation. We need not here repeat the citations to authorities already referred to in this opinion that use the language of "prostration of faculties such that defendant was rendered incapable of forming an intent." * * *

So firmly fixed in our case law is the requirement of "prostration of faculties" as the minimum requirement for an intoxication defense that we feel secure in our assumption that the legislature intended nothing different in its statutory definition of intoxication: "a disturbance of mental or physical capacities resulting from the introduction of substances into the body." N.J. Stat. Ann. § 2C:2–8(e)(1). In order to satisfy the statutory condition that to qualify as a defense intoxication must negative an element of the offense, the intoxication must be of an extremely high level. * * *

Measured by the foregoing standard and evidence relevant thereto, it is apparent that the record in this case is insufficient to have required the trial court to grant defendant's request to charge intoxication.... True, the victim testified that defendant was drunk, and defendant herself said she felt "pretty intoxicated," "pretty bad," and "very intoxicated." But these are no more than conclusory labels, of little assistance in determining whether any drinking produced a prostration of faculties. * * *

Ordinarily, of course, the question of whether a defendant's asserted intoxication satisfies the standards enunciated in this opinion should be resolved by the jury. But here, viewing the evidence and the legitimate inferences to be drawn therefrom in the light most favorable to defendant, the best that can be made of the proof of intoxication is that defendant may have been extremely agitated and distraught. It may even be that a fact-finder could conclude that her powers of rational thought and deductive reasoning had been affected. But there is no suggestion in the evidence that defendant's faculties were so prostrated by her consumption of something less than a pint of wine as to render her incapable of purposeful or knowing conduct. The trial court correctly refused defendant's request.

QUESTIONS AND COMMENTS

1. Can intoxication negate negligence? How can intoxication—assuming it's sufficient to "prostrate the faculties"—be relevant to the presence of purpose and knowledge, but *not* recklessness? How can intoxication not even be relevant to *knowledge*? See Alaska Stat. § 11.81.900(2) ("[A] person who is unaware of conduct or a circumstance of which the person would have been aware had that person not been intoxicated acts knowingly with respect to that conduct or circumstance."). How can intoxication

not be relevant to any mental state whatsoever? See Mont. Code Ann. § 45–2–203 ("A person who is in an intoxicated condition is criminally responsible for his conduct and an intoxicated condition is not a defense to any offense and may not be taken into consideration in determining the existence of a mental state which is an element of the offense unless the defendant proves that he did not know that it was an intoxicating substance when he consumed, smoked, sniffed, injected, or otherwise ingested the substance causing the condition.").

In Montana v. Egelhoff, 518 U.S. 37 (1996), the U.S. Supreme Court upheld the Montana statute against a constitutional attack, based in part on the following rendition of "the historical record":

> By the laws of England, wrote Hale, the intoxicated defendant "shall have no privilege by this voluntarily contracted madness, but shall have the same judgment as if he were in his right senses." 1 M. Hale, Pleas of the Crown *32–33. According to Blackstone and Coke, the law's condemnation of those suffering from dementia affectata was harsher still: Blackstone, citing Coke, explained that the law viewed intoxication "as an aggravation of the offence, rather than an excuse for any criminal misbehaviour." 4 W. Blackstone, Commentaries *25–26. This stern rejection of inebriation as a defense became a fixture of early American law as well.... In an opinion citing the foregoing passages from Blackstone and Hale, Justice Story rejected an objection to the exclusion of evidence of intoxication as follows:
>
> "This is the first time, that I ever remember it to have been contended, that the commission of one crime was an excuse for another. Drunkenness is a gross vice, and in the contemplation of some of our laws is a crime; and I learned in my earlier studies, that so far from its being in law an excuse for murder, it is rather an aggravation of its malignity." United States v. Cornell, 25 F. Cas. 650, 657–658 (No. 14,868) (CC R.I. 1820).
>
> The historical record does not leave room for the view that the common law's rejection of intoxication as an "excuse" or "justification" for crime would nonetheless permit the defendant to show that intoxication prevented the requisite mens rea. Hale, Coke and Blackstone were familiar, to say the least, with the concept of mens rea, and acknowledged that drunkenness "deprive[s] men of the use of reason," Hale, supra, at *32; see also Blackstone, supra, at *25. It is inconceivable that they did not realize that an offender's drunkenness might impair his ability to form the requisite intent; and inconceivable that their failure to note this massive exception from the general rule of disregard of intoxication was an oversight.

Should intoxicated offenders, then, be punished *more* severely, rather than less severely, than sober ones? Would *that* be unconstitutional?

2. Or is the claim *not* that intoxication can't disprove recklessness, but *proves* it? Is the act of drinking (or taking some other intoxicant) reckless itself? By definition? Most of the time? Presumptively? Rebuttably? Irrebuttably? Or should a court have to inquire into the *actual* mental state of the defendant *at the time* she drank (started to drink, became "intoxicat-

ed")? Either way, how can she be punished for committing a criminal act at time T_2 on the ground of her having the requisite mental state at time T_1? Wouldn't that violate the concurrence doctrine?

Alternatively, should a defendant be liable even for knowledge and purpose crimes if she intoxicated herself *knowing* or *with the conscious object* that she would commit the (some?) crime? Or should it be enough that she simply thought that drinking would make it more likely that she would commit it?

3. Assuming intoxication evidence should be relevant without limitation—based on the proposition that the *reason* for the absence of an offense element is beside the point—should the intoxicated person escape criminal liability altogether? Or should she be liable for getting drunk in the first place? If so, should that liability be tied to the crimes she actually ended up committing in her intoxicated state? What, in the end, is the difference between, on one hand, *exculpating* the intoxicated offender for the offense whose objective elements she satisfies and then *punishing* her for the offense of having committed an offense while intoxicated, and, on the other hand, simply punishing her for the original offense?

German Penal Code § 323a. Total Intoxication.

(1) Whoever intentionally or negligently gets intoxicated with alcoholic beverages or other intoxicants, shall be punished with imprisonment for not more than five years or a fine, if he commits an unlawful act while in this condition and may not be punished because of it because he lacked the capacity to be adjudged guilty due to the intoxication, or this cannot be excluded.

(2) The punishment may not be more severe than the punishment provided for the act which was committed while intoxicated.

In the case of a continuing offense, like possession, what is the relevant point in time at which a requisite mental state—if any—can be negated by evidence of intoxication?

Defendant appeals from a judgment convicting him following a jury trial of two counts of criminal possession of a weapon in the third degree (Penal Law § 265.02[1], [4]).... [R]eversal is required based on the court's refusal to charge the jury on the issue of his intoxication. Penal Law § 15.25 provides that "evidence of intoxication of the defendant may be offered by the defendant whenever it is relevant to negative an element of the crime charged." ... Here, intoxication was relevant to defendant's knowing possession of the firearm and defendant's awareness that the firearm was loaded....

Although the People correctly note that there is no dispute that defendant was not intoxicated when he came into possession of the weapon, that is not the relevant time period at issue here. The indictment does not charge defendant with criminal possession of a weapon at any time other than on January 19, 2001, at a certain bar in Genesee Falls....

People v. Ressler, 302 A.D.2d 921, 754 N.Y.S.2d 485 (2003).

But isn't possession defined in terms of acquisition, and of the failure to discontinue possession? See Model Penal Code § 2.01(4).

4. The Model Penal Code, and the N.J. Criminal Code, distinguish between voluntary and involuntary intoxication, and impose restrictions on raising the former as a defense that do not apply to the latter. Does that make sense? Isn't a voluntarily intoxicated person just as intoxicated as an involuntarily intoxicated one? What does "voluntary" mean in this context? Does it mean the same thing as in the context of actus reus? Can *involuntary* intoxication negate a mental state?

Note that involuntary intoxication operates as a defense not only against specific and general intent elements. It also constitutes a separate defense even if it doesn't negate a mental state, provided it results in an incapacity of the kind and degree otherwise required for a finding of insanity, i.e., if "by reason of such intoxication the actor at the time of his conduct lacks substantial capacity either to appreciate its criminality [wrongfulness] or to conform his conduct to the requirements of law." Model Penal Code § 2.08(4).

In "pathological" intoxication cases, see MPC § 2.08(5)(c); N.J. Stat. § 2C:2–8(e)(3), how do we go about determining the actor's expectations regarding her susceptibility to a substance's intoxicating effect? Is the defense unavailable to a defendant who has consumed (any? the same? similar?) intoxicants in the past? See, e.g., State v. Sette, 259 N.J.Super. 156, 611 A.2d 1129 (1992) (in a murder case, no pathological intoxication instruction where defendant argued that his behavior was the result of an exaggerated intoxication caused by the combined impact of cocaine, marijuana, and Co–Tylenol—all taken voluntarily—and the chemicals he was exposed to in his work as a landscaper, "an intoxication on a level wholly out of line with his reasonable expectations based upon his experience as a cocaine drug user").

5. What's the point of requiring that intoxication "prostrate the faculties"? Obviously, intoxication evidence is relevant only insofar as it negates some mental state. Does requiring "prostration" mean that it's not enough to have lacked the requisite awareness, and that one must have lacked some other capacity as well? If that's so, why shouldn't intoxication qualify as a mental disease or defect? How can we simply *declare* that intoxication doesn't constitute a mental disease? What about drug addicts? Alcoholics?

CHAPTER 6

CRIMINAL HARM: CAUSATION AND ATTEMPT

When people think of crime, they often think of violent crime, committed by one person upon another. Someone has been killed (beaten up, robbed, burglarized, etc.) by someone else. The criminal law is about categorizing these different types of injury, and specifying the general conditions under which the person who caused them is punished for them, and how much. That's true enough, but oversimplifies the matter. For it turns out that criminal law expends quite a lot of doctrinal energy not only on who should be punished how much for inflicting some harm on another person, but also on what counts as criminal harm in the first place and, even more generally, whether criminal punishment presupposes the infliction of harm at all, or at least, what relevance the harm actually inflicted (as opposed to that contemplated or desired) has for the assignment of blame (or a regimen of "peno-correctional treatment").

One way of thinking about the issue of whether the actual infliction of harm matters is to frame it in terms of whether criminal punishment should turn on luck or fortuities: Compare five different defendants:

The first defendant shoots his victim with homicidal intent, and the victim dies on the spot from the gunshot wound. The second fires his gun in precisely the same way, with the same skill and the same intent, but the victim does not die. (The bullet lodges in the proverbial book in the victim's breast pocket; extraordinary ER surgeons save the day.) Should we punish these defendants differently? Should we punish the second defendant at all if the victim is neither wounded nor scared by the attack? Should we punish him because he has in some sense "breached the peace"—causing harm to the "social fabric" if not to a particular individual—or because he has shown himself to be dangerous (in need of incapacitation or reform) or displayed that he is so wicked in both thought and deed (or so willing to violate the law's commands) that he simply merits punishment?

A third defendant also shoots the victim; the victim ultimately dies, and he might well not have died but-for the fact that the defendant shot him, but the causal link between defendant conduct and death is arguably somewhat attenuated. (The victim dies en route to the hospital because the ambulance, speeding through red lights to get to the extraordinary ER surgeons as quickly as possible, gets into a fatal crash; the defendant survives surgery but dies of incompetently treated post-surgery complications.) If we have decided that we should punish our first defendant more severely than our second, how do we ascertain whether those "like" the third defendant are more similar (and along what policy-relevant dimensions?) to the first defendant (whose victim died on the spot) or our second (whose victim remains alive)? This is, at core, the subject of the material on causation.

The fourth defendant's gun misfires as he pulls the trigger. Is he as punishable as the person who shoots and misses? Whose shot lodges in the vest-pocket book? How about a defendant who "merely" took aim, but never pulled the trigger because a policeman subdued him before he had the opportunity to pull the trigger? Do we *know* he would have pulled the trigger had the policeman not intervened? Do we know that he is just like the person who shoots and kills except that he was "lucky" enough to be interrupted by the policeman before he consummated the offense? What about a defendant who was stopped driving, gun in hand, to the place where he expected the victim to be? What about a defendant who put the gun down after he gripped the trigger to fire and took aim? How about a person who shoots someone who is already dead? These, and related, questions are central to our inquiry into the law of attempt.

Finally, imagine a fifth defendant who shoots her victim, intending to kill, but fails to do so. This defendant, though, mistakenly and unreasonably believes the victim was threatening her in a fashion that would justify the use of deadly self-defensive force. Is this fifth defendant like the fourth defendant? Or does the fact that she did not intend to murder but rather intended to commit a justified homicide differentiate her? Even if one were in a jurisdiction in which making an unreasonable error about the need to use self-defensive force would not even mitigate the punishment she would face if she in fact killed the victim? This question is also dealt with in the material on attempts.

Questions about the relevance of harm inevitably raise questions about the point of criminal law. Here the contrast with the law of torts may be instructive. There is no doubt that civil tort liability requires harm. Without "damages" there is no need for a "remedy." Is the point of criminal law to remedy particularly egregious harms—egregious not only because they are more serious but also because they are accompanied by some sort of culpable intent—or is it to accomplish some other purpose? Perhaps to maintain the public peace (what used to be—and in England still is—known as the King's peace)? To uphold the law? To punish disobedience of state commands (it is after all a matter between the state and the individual, rather than between two individuals, as in a civil tort case)? To identify the dangerous (in order to rehabilitate or incapacitate them)?

Keep these issues in mind as you think about the following materials, which highlight some of the more obvious ways in which American criminal law deals with the problem of harm. In this chapter, we'll first focus some attention on the degree to which criminal sanctions are premised on locating particular "victims." We then focus most, though not all, of our attention on *causation* (assuming an offense definition requires the infliction of harm, *and that harm actually occurs*, when can that harm be attributed to the person who has engaged in the conduct proscribed by the offense?) and *attempt* (assuming an offender sets out to inflict criminal harm, but for some reason doesn't succeed, so that *the harm does not occur*, when can she be punished for trying?).

That's not to say that the question of harm doesn't arise in other doctrinal contexts as well. Attempt, for instance, is only one of a group of so-called "inchoate" (or incomplete, preparatory, or anticipatory) offenses, each of which criminalizes conduct that falls short of committing a completed offense—a more complete list would also include conspiracy (entering into an agreement to commit the offense), solicitation (importuning someone else to commit the offense), and possession (possessing items that might be used, or might have been used, in committing the offense).[a] As another example, consider consent. Does the victim's consent to the infliction of (what we'd generally see as) harm mean that no harm—or at least no *criminal* harm—was done? Or, to put it another way, is the victim who consents to something the criminal law generally considers harmful (e.g., a battery) still a "victim"?[b] Does it depend on whether the victim consents to the "battery" in a socially conventional setting (a football game, a boxing ring) rather than a socially "underground" one (sado-masochistic sex)?

A. THE GENERAL RELEVANCE—AND DEFINITION—OF HARM

N.Y. Veh. & Traf. Law § 1192. Operating a motor vehicle while under the influence of alcohol or drugs.

(3) Driving while intoxicated. No person shall operate a motor vehicle while in an intoxicated condition....

A violation of subdivision three ... of section eleven hundred ninety-two ... shall be a misdemeanor....

N.Y. Veh. & Traf. Law § 1212. Reckless driving.

Reckless driving shall mean driving or using any motor vehicle, motorcycle or any other vehicle propelled by any power other than muscular power or any appliance or accessory thereof in a manner which unreasonably interferes with the free and proper use of the public highway, or unreasonably endangers users of the public highway. Reckless driving is prohibited. Every person violating this provision shall be guilty of a misdemeanor.

N.Y. Penal Law § 120.03. Vehicular assault in the second degree.

A person is guilty of vehicular assault in the second degree when:

(1) with criminal negligence he causes serious physical injury to another person, and ...

(2) causes such serious physical injury by operation of a vehicle in violation of subdivision ... three ... of section eleven hundred ninety-

a. More on conspiracy and solicitation in ch. 8, on possession in ch. 4.—EDS.

b. More on consent in chs. 7 & 9.—EDS.

two of the vehicle and traffic law.... Vehicular assault in the second degree is a class E felony.

Commonwealth v. Slaney

Supreme Judicial Court of Massachusetts, Middlesex.
345 Mass. 135, 185 N.E.2d 919 (1962).

■ Kirk, Justice.

For a year and half to two years before the alleged offence, the defendant, a married man, and [Mary] Bowen, a married woman separated from her husband, had frequently been in one another's company. Shortly before the alleged offence there was a change in Mrs. Bowen's attitude toward the defendant. On the night of August 2, 1961, the defendant went to the Oxford Grille, a restaurant and bar in Cambridge owned by [Joseph A.] DeVincentis, where Mrs. Bowen was employed as a waitress. He persistently asked Mrs. Bowen to wait on him and to see him after work. She refused. The defendant remained on the premises. Toward closing time (midnight) DeVincentis asked the defendant not to bother Mrs. Bowen and to leave the place. The defendant left. At 1:15 a.m. when DeVincentis and Mrs. Bowen left the restaurant and were crossing the street toward a lot where DeVincentis's car was parked, a car driven by the defendant emerged from a nearby alley at high speed and stopped in front of the entrance to the lot. The defendant got out of his car, approached Mrs. Bowen and DeVincentis, and demanded that Mrs. Bowen go with him. During the talk which followed, DeVincentis explained that he merely was going to take Mrs. Bowen to a nearby taxi stand. The defendant "threw a punch," which just touched the top of DeVincentis's head. The defendant then pulled out a gun, pointed it "right at" DeVincentis, and advised him to start praying because he was going to shoot Mrs. Bowen, DeVincentis, and himself. The defendant was seven or eight feet away from DeVincentis. Mrs. Bowen pleaded with him to put the gun away.

DeVincentis told him he was "silly," and tried to move closer to the defendant in order to maneuver into a position to take the gun away from him. The defendant backed away and, while doing so, the gun was discharged. The bullet pierced Mrs. Bowen's handbag and dress. She felt a breeze on her right leg but she was not wounded. Police on foot patrol heard the shot, went to the scene, disarmed the defendant, and placed him under arrest.

DeVincentis testified that he was not afraid at any time; that when he tried to get closer to the defendant to maneuver to get the gun he was not afraid that he was going to be shot. However, he did not think it was a joke; he was trying to devise some plan to get the gun; he did not go up to him and grab the gun because the defendant would have "shot and let go."

The defendant's contention that he was entitled to a finding of not guilty on the charge of assault with a dangerous weapon on DeVincentis is based on his thesis that fear on the part of the victim is an essential element of the crime of assault, and that DeVincentis's testimony conclusively eliminates that element from the Commonwealth's case....

With respect to the crime of assault, as is frequently the case in our statutes relating to common law crimes, the Legislature has prescribed the penalty for the crime but has not defined the crime itself. For the definition of the crime of assault, resort must be had to the common law.

The defendant, in support of the proposition that proof of fear on the part of the victim is necessary to sustain a conviction of the crime of assault at common law, cites the definition given by a text writer.[1] This definition expresses a concept of common law assault which, as applied to the criminal law, is at variance with that held by the overwhelming number of authorities, both old and recent, who define the essentials of a common law assault in such familiar terms as: an attempt (or offer) to do bodily harm to another by force and violence; or simply, an attempt to commit a battery.... The criminal law is designed primarily to preserve the public peace. The imperturbability or fortitude of a victim, or the unawareness of an intended victim, should not afford a defence to the criminal prosecution of the wrongdoer. The guilt or innocence of a person charged with assault "depends entirely upon what the wrongdoer does and intends and not at all upon what the other apprehends, or does not apprehend." Perkins on Criminal Law (1957) 89. It follows from what we have said that in this Commonwealth neither fear, nor terror nor apprehension of harm is an essential ingredient of the common law crime of assault.

QUESTIONS AND COMMENTS

1. Can the (ir)relevance of harm be justified in light of the traditional rationales of punishment? Or is harm "a vestige of the criminal law's early role as instrument of official vengeance," or perhaps, earlier still, of the blood feud?

> The criminal law attributes major significance to the harm actually caused by a defendant's conduct, as distinguished from the harm intended or risked. If, for example, a person attacks his wife and tries to kill her, he will be guilty of assault and attempted murder even if she escapes unharmed. He will also commit a battery if she is injured, mayhem if the injury is of certain especially serious types, and murder if she dies. The applicable penalties generally increase accordingly.
>
> Yet both the defendant's state of mind and his actions may have been identical in all four of the cases supposed. The precise location of a knife or gunshot wound, the speed of intervention by neighbors or the police, these and many other factors wholly outside the knowledge or control of the defendant may determine the ultimate result. Accordingly, the differences in legal treatment would seem at first blush inconsistent with such purposes of the criminal law as deterrence, rehabilitation, isolation of the dangerous, and even retribution—in the sense of punishment in accordance with moral blame....
>
> Emphasis on the harm caused can, of course, be understood as a vestige of the criminal law's early role as instrument of official ven-

1. 1 Bishop's New Criminal Law (8th ed., 1892) 337 defines "Assault" as including "a reasonable apprehension of immediate bodily harm."

geance. Actual damage was once prerequisite to the existence of a crime, and the doctrine that an attempt to commit a crime was in itself criminal developed slowly. . . .

Stephen J. Schulhofer, "Harm and Punishment: A Critique of Emphasis on the Results of Conduct in the Criminal Law," 122 U. Pa. L. Rev. 1497, 1498–1500 (1974).

Does Schulhofer's criticism take into account offenses that are not defined in terms of (serious) harm to individuals? What if harm were defined broadly to include threats to "public interests," "public welfare," "state authority," or "the proper functioning of government"?

There are at least two ways of thinking about abandoning a harm requirement. One is to think of offenses the definition of which requires the infliction of harm and then to punish attempts to commit them (or some other inchoate version of the offense, like agreeing to commit them (conspiracy)). Another is not to require that offenses be defined as requiring the infliction of individual harm, or even of any harm whatever. Either way, abandoning the harm requirement expands the power of the state by widening the scope of criminal law, both by adding new offenses and increasing the reach of existing ones.

2. What's the harm in driving while intoxicated, reckless driving, vehicular assault, the crime of assault, and the tort of assault? Is endangerment a harm? See Claire Finkelstein, "Is Risk a Harm?," 151 U. Pa. L. Rev. 963 (2003) (yes; arguing that a person who inflicts a risk of harm on another damages that person's "legitimate interest in avoiding unwanted risks," and distinguishing "risk harm" from "ordinary, tangible" or "outcome harm"). Does DWI punish endangerment? Does reckless driving? DWI and reckless endangerment both criminalize risk creation. Note, however, that DWI, unlike reckless endangerment, does not require a showing that the defendant's conduct in fact created a risk of harm. Put another way, DWI is an *abstract* endangerment offense, and reckless endangerment a *specific* (or *actual*) endangerment offense. Vehicular assault, by contrast, is a harm offense. See generally Markus Dirk Dubber, "The Possession Paradigm: The Special Part and the Police Power Model of the Criminal Process," in Defining Crimes (R.A. Duff & Stuart P. Green eds. 2005).

3. Contrast the varieties of assault laid out in the Model Penal Code. What harm(s) do they proscribe?

Model Penal Code § 211.1. Assault.

(1) *Simple Assault.* A person is guilty of assault if he:

(a) attempts to cause or purposely, knowingly or recklessly causes bodily injury to another; or

(b) negligently causes bodily injury to another with a deadly weapon; or

(c) attempts by physical menace to put another in fear of imminent serious bodily injury.

Simple assault is a misdemeanor unless committed in a fight or scuffle entered into by mutual consent, in which case it is a petty misdemeanor.

4. Does it make sense to punish *everyone* who takes (undue? unjustified?) risks of causing physical injury or death, or only to punish (far more severely?) the sub-set consisting of those who actually cause the harms that every member of the larger group risks? Will people be deterred more by the somewhat more remote prospect of very serious punishment or the more likely prospect of less serious punishment? Do we "waste" punishment (needlessly inflicting pain and expending money and resources building more prisons) if we punish all unjustified risk-takers if people would be (adequately) deterred by the threat of punishment if they actually caused harms? Do those who risk harm reveal different things about their moral character or dangerousness than those who cause it (albeit unintentionally)?

5. We all, rather regularly, feel as if we've barely escaped a car crash, and doubtless witness (or engage in) a good deal of really bad driving, both in these "just-miss" situations and situations in which, despite the bad driving, there was no near-accident. But, arguably, the image of the bad driving quickly escapes our attention when "nothing happened." If we are hit, though, or a loved one killed or injured, the event (and the prior risk-taking) may remain persistently salient. Should the criminal law account for that reaction? Could a legal system composed of people who've all had this reaction *help* but take account of the reaction, whether it "should" or not?

6. There are certainly a number of "white collar" crimes in which there is a particular victim (or set of victims), quite like conventional victims of larceny. (On white collar crimes, see generally ch. 11 infra.) The victim(s) of a classic fraud, induced to part with money only because misinformed about the qualities of the goods or services they are buying, seem unambiguously *harmed* as individuals. There are a number of other situations, though, in which the "harms" associated with the white collar criminal's conduct are either considerably more diffuse or, arguably, ephemeral. There are undoubtedly public corruption cases in which governments (and by extension taxpayers) overpay for goods and services as a result of the defendant's scheme, but others in which the defendant has (done no more than?) arguably tarnished the political process in a fashion that may be far harder to specify.

The issue arises in relationship to the criminalization of "insider trading" under statutes and executive rules that proscribe securities *fraud*.[a] See, e.g., Constance L. Hays, "U.S. Prosecutors Ask Judge to Keep Stewart Charges Intact," N.Y. Times, Nov. 7, 2003, at C9, col. 1 (Martha Stewart charged with securities fraud for "falsely proclaiming her innocence as a means of shoring up the share price of her own company,

a. Securities Exchange Act of 1934 § 10(b) ("any manipulative or deceptive device or contrivance in contravention of such rules and regulations as the [Securities and Exchange] Commission may prescribe"); Securities and Exchange Commission Rule 10b–5 ("any act, practice, or course of business which operates or would operate as a fraud or deceit upon any person in connection with the purchase or sale of any security").—EDS.

Martha Stewart Living Omnimedia, once she had been publicly linked with [an] insider-trading investigation" regarding her sale of shares in another company, ImClone). The issue is a complex one, and may require a grounding in corporate law and economics to appreciate more fully.

As a general introduction, though, it is important to recognize that insider trading cases are prosecuted under two distinct theories.

In the "classical" insider trading scheme, a corporate insider breaches her fiduciary duty to the shareholders by trading with a shareholder while in possession of "material, nonpublic information." The insider could discharge his duty to the shareholders either by disclosing the information or by abstaining from trading on it. The cases decided on this theory typically recognize that there must be some classic form of fraud—the particular shareholder was concretely injured because she would not have bought (or sold) the security had there not been some material misrepresentation of the actual value of the security that the fiduciary duty-holder was bound to correct. See, in this regard, earlier cases rejecting the notion that the "market" generally could be victimized, such as Dirks v. SEC, 463 U.S. 646 (1983); Chiarella v. United States, 445 U.S. 222 (1980) (corporate insiders must be prevented "from ... taking unfair advantage of uninformed stockholders").[b]

Under the second theory, generally labeled the "misappropriation theory," a "person commits fraud 'in connection with' a securities transaction ... when he misappropriates confidential information for securities trading purposes, in breach of a duty owed to the source of the information," Unites States v. O'Hagan, 521 U.S. 642 (1997). In this second class of cases, the person using the inside information has no duty to the person with whom she is trading to disclose the misappropriated information, but rather "misuses" information from another source (to whom she does have a duty of loyalty and confidentiality). In *O'Hagan*, for example, the defendant was a member of a law firm retained by the company Grand Met to help with a bid for common stock of Pillsbury Company. O'Hagan was involved in the bid with Grand Met, but during the time this bid was being negotiated he bought call options for Pillsbury stock (i.e., options that permit him to buy the stock at a particular price, presumably lower than the price Pillsbury stock will sell for once the Grand Met bid becomes common knowledge). He did not have a fiduciary duty to the Pillsbury shareholders to disclose the nonpublic information (he is not *their* agent), and in fact these shareholders are not entitled to the information at all. Indeed, if the Pillsbury shareholders had not sold to O'Hagan, they would have sold to some other party at the same or perhaps even a lower price, so it is difficult to say that they—the potential fraud victims under the classic insider trading theory—were injured.

b. It is worth noting as well that in these classic corporate insider cases, one might also argue that the insider is deriving a form of undeserved compensation from the firm—stock-trading profits grounded in information that she gets by virtue of her position that she was not contractually entitled to. It is not clear that she gains that compensation *at the expense* of the management group that directly employs her, but if she gains it at the expense of some sub-set of shareholders, for whom management acts as an agent, she may be cheating her "true" employer.—EDS.

According to the Supreme Court, however, O'Hagan breached his duty to his law firm and its client Grand Met by defrauding them of the exclusive use of nonpublic information. *Assuming* that it is true that the parties to the security transaction itself were not actually defrauded, the case must rest on the idea that O'Hagan caused a far more diffuse harm, jeopardizing the honesty and integrity of the market more generally. (Otherwise, O'Hagan would have simply committed mail fraud, victimizing the law firm and its client, rather than *securities* fraud.) See *O'Hagan*, 521 U.S. at 745 (although informational disparity is inevitable in the securities markets, investors likely would hesitate to venture their capital in a market where trading based on misappropriated nonpublic information is unchecked by law); see also, in this regard, the 2000 revisions by the Securities and Exchange Commission to Rule 10b–5–2:

> The prohibitions against insider trading in our securities laws play an essential role in maintaining the fairness, health, and integrity of our markets. We have long recognized that the fundamental unfairness of insider trading harms not only individual investors, but also the very foundations of our markets, by undermining investor confidence in the integrity of markets.

If "all" the insider is doing, then, is undermining (some? many?) investors' general sense that markets are "fair," that everyone has pretty much the same chance to make or lose money, has the defendant caused the sort of "harm" either to individuals or the "social fabric" that the criminal law ought to proscribe?

7. Think also about two of the questions raised in the *Walters* case, below. First, when we think of the ways in which an ordinary thief harms his victim, we think that he transfers property from the victim to himself: in that regard, the usual defendant in a fraud case causes the victim to give him something he would not have given to him absent the deceit. What happens, though, if the victim loses something, but the defendant does not (at least obviously) gain something? Second, how careful must we be to make sure that the "victim" was *entitled* to the property that she lost before we construe her "loss" as a criminally cognizable harm?

United States v. Walters

United States Court of Appeals for the Seventh Circuit.
997 F.2d 1219 (1993).

■ EASTERBROOK, CIRCUIT JUDGE.

Norby Walters, who represents entertainers, tried to move into the sports business. He signed 58 college football players to contracts while they were still playing. Walters offered cars and money to those who would agree to use him as their representative in dealing with professional teams. Sports agents receive a percentage of the players' income, so Walters would profit only to the extent he could negotiate contracts for his clients. The athletes' pro prospects depended on successful completion of their collegiate careers. To the NCAA, however, a student who signs a contract with an agent is a professional, ineligible to play on collegiate teams. To avoid jeopardizing his clients' careers, Walters dated the contracts after the end of their eligibility and locked them in a safe. He promised to lie to the universities in response to any inquiries. Walters inquired of sports lawyers at Shea & Gould whether this plan of operation would be lawful. The firm rendered an opinion that it would violate the NCAA's rules but not any statute.

Having recruited players willing to fool their universities and the NCAA, Walters discovered that they were equally willing to play false with him. Only 2 of the 58 players fulfilled their end of the bargain; the other 56 kept the cars and money, then signed with other agents. They relied on the fact that the contracts were locked away and dated in the future, and that Walters' business depended on continued secrecy, so he could not very well sue to enforce their promises. When the 56 would neither accept him as their representative nor return the payments, Walters resorted to threats. . . .

There is a . . . problem with the theory of this prosecution [charging the defendant with mail fraud, rather than extortion]. The United States tells us that the universities lost their scholarship money. Money is property; this aspect of the prosecution does not encounter a problem under *McNally v. United States*, 483 U.S. 350, 97 L. Ed. 2d 292 (1987) [mail fraud statute protects property rights, not intangible rights]. Walters emphasizes that the universities put his 58 athletes on scholarship long before he met them and did not pay a penny more than they planned to do. But a jury could conclude that had Walters' clients told the truth, the colleges would have stopped their scholarships, thus saving money. So we must assume that the universities lost property by reason of Walters' deeds. Still, they were not out of pocket *to Walters;* he planned to profit by taking a percentage of the players' professional incomes, not of their scholarships. Section 1341 [mail fraud] condemns "any scheme or artifice to defraud, or *for obtaining* money or property" (emphasis added). If the universities were the victims, how did he "obtain" their property?, Walters asks.

According to the United States, neither an actual nor a potential transfer of property from the victim to the defendant is essential. It is enough that the victim lose; what (if anything) the schemer hopes to gain plays no role in the definition of the offense. We asked the prosecutor at oral argument whether on this rationale practical jokes violate § 1341. A mails B an invitation to a surprise party for their mutual friend C. B drives his car to the place named in the invitation. But there is no party; the address is a vacant lot; B is the butt of a joke. The invitation came by post [thus satisfying the "mail" element of mail fraud]; the cost of gasoline means that B is out of pocket. The prosecutor said that this indeed violates § 1341, but that his office pledges to use prosecutorial discretion wisely. Many people will find this position unnerving (what if the prosecutor's policy changes, or A is politically unpopular and the prosecutor is looking for a way to nail him?). Others, who obey the law out of a sense of civic obligation rather than the fear of sanctions, will alter their conduct no matter what policy the prosecutor follows. . . .

Practical jokes rarely come to the attention of federal prosecutors, but large organizations are more successful in gaining the attention of public officials. In this case the mail fraud statute has been invoked to shore up the rules of an influential private association. Consider a parallel: an association of manufacturers of plumbing fixtures adopts a rule providing that its members will not sell "seconds" (that is, blemished articles) to the public. The association proclaims that this rule protects consumers from shoddy goods. To remain in good standing, a member must report its sales monthly. These reports flow in by mail. One member begins to sell "seconds" but reports that it is not doing so. These sales take business away from other members of the association, who lose profits as a result. So we have mail, misrepresentation, and the loss of property, but the liar does not get any of the property the other firms lose. Has anyone committed a federal crime? The answer is yes—but the statute is the Sherman Act, 15 U.S.C. § 1,[a] and the perpetrators are the firms that adopted the "no seconds" rule. The trade association we have described is a cartel, which the firm selling "seconds" was undermining. Cheaters depress the price, causing the monopolist to lose money. Typically they go to great lengths to disguise their activities, the better to increase their own sales and avoid retaliation. The prosecutor's position in our case would make criminals of the cheaters, would use § 1341 to shore up cartels.

Fanciful? Not at all. Many scholars understand the NCAA as a cartel, having power in the market for athletes.... The NCAA depresses athletes' income—restricting payments to the value of tuition, room, and board, while receiving services of substantially greater worth. The NCAA treats this as desirable preservation of amateur sports; a more jaundiced eye would see it as the use of monopsony power to obtain athletes' services for less than the competitive market price.[b] Walters then is cast in the role of a cheater, increasing the payments to the student athletes. Like other cheaters, Walters found it convenient to hide his activities. If, as the prosecutor believes, his repertory included extortion, he has used methods that the law denies to persons fighting cartels, but for the moment we are concerned only with the deceit that caused the universities to pay stipends to "professional" athletes. For current purposes it matters not whether the NCAA *actually* monopsonizes the market for players; the point of this discussion is that the prosecutor's theory makes criminals of those who consciously cheat on the rules of a private organization, even if that organization is a cartel. We pursue this point because any theory that makes criminals of cheaters raises a red flag....

But what is it about § 1341 that labels as a crime all deceit that inflicts any loss on anyone? Firms often try to fool their competitors, surprising them with new products that enrich their treasuries at their rivals' expense. Is this mail fraud because large organizations inevitably use the mail? "Any scheme or artifice to defraud, or for obtaining money or property by means of false or fraudulent pretenses, representations, or promises" reads like a description of schemes to get money or property by fraud rather than methods of doing business that incidentally cause losses. * * *

a. 15 U.S.C. § 1 prohibits any "contract, combination in the form of trust or otherwise, or conspiracy, in restraint of trade or commerce among the several States, or with foreign nations."—EDS.

b. A monopsony is a market with only one buyer, i.e., the buying-side equivalent of a selling-side monopoly.—EDS.

Walters is by all accounts a nasty and untrustworthy fellow, but the prosecutor did not prove that his efforts to circumvent the NCAA's rules amounted to mail fraud.

8. To what extent does Judge Easterbrook's opinion in *Walters* rest on what he sees as the illegitimacy of the NCAA's "cartel-imposed" restrictions on college athlete's "salaries"? If the charges had been brought against the *athletes* themselves for defrauding the schools by lying about their professional status, wouldn't they plainly have been guilty of defrauding the schools absent a finding that the universities are not entitled to withhold scholarship funds to "professionals"? Hasn't Walters, though, at the very least aided and abetted that scheme to defraud so that the question of whether he is the direct beneficiary or not of the university's payments is beside the point? Wouldn't we describe someone as an embezzler (a species of thief) if he directed money from the victim's account to a third party's? Moreover, doesn't Walters *want* the universities to give scholarship money to the athletes so that they will be more likely to develop into professional-quality athletes? On the other hand, doesn't it seem that the prosecutor's decision to charge Walters for mail fraud must actually have turned on the fact that he ultimately threatened the young men with violence? For more on mail fraud, see ch. 11 infra.

B. CAUSATION

1. THE BASIC STRUCTURE OF CAUSATION INQUIRIES: ACTUAL AND PROXIMATE CAUSE

Model Penal Code § 2.03. Causal Relationship Between Conduct and Result; Divergence Between Result Designed or Contemplated and Actual Result or Between Probable and Actual Result.

(1) Conduct is the cause of a result when:

(a) it is an antecedent but for which the result in question would not have occurred; and

(b) the relationship between the conduct and result satisfies any additional causal requirements imposed by the Code or by the law defining the offense.

(2) When purposely or knowingly causing a particular result is an element of an offense, the element is not established if the actual result is not within the purpose or the contemplation of the actor unless:

(a) the actual result differs from that designed or contemplated, as the case may be, only in the respect that a different person or different property is injured or affected or that the injury or harm designed or contemplated would have been more serious or more extensive than that caused; or

(b) the actual result involves the same kind of injury or harm as that designed or contemplated and is not too remote or accidental in its occurrence to have a [just] bearing on the actor's liability or on the gravity of his offense.

(3) When recklessly or negligently causing a particular result is an element of an offense, the element is not established if the actual result is not within the risk of which the actor is aware or, in the case of negligence, of which he should be aware unless:

(a) the actual result differs from the probable result only in the respect that a different person or different property is injured or affected or that the probable injury or harm would have been more serious or more extensive than that caused; or

(b) the actual result involves the same kind of injury or harm as the probable result and is not too remote or accidental in its occurrence to have a [just] bearing on the actor's liability or on the gravity of his offense.

(4) When causing a particular result is a material element of an offense for which absolute liability is imposed by law, the element is not established unless the actual result is a probable consequence of the actor's conduct.

Robertson v. Commonwealth

Supreme Court of Kentucky.
82 S.W.3d 832 (2002).

■ COOPER, JUSTICE.

Michael Partin, a police officer employed by the city of Covington, Kentucky, was killed when he fell through an opening between the roadway and the walkway of the Clay Wade Bailey Bridge and into the Ohio River while in foot pursuit of Appellant Shawnta Robertson. Following a trial by jury in the Kenton Circuit Court, Appellant was convicted of manslaughter in the second degree for [recklessly][a] causing Partin's death, Ky. Rev. Stat. § 507.040(1), and was sentenced to imprisonment for six years.

At about 2:00 a.m. on January 4, 1998, Officer Brian Kane of the Kenton County Police Department attempted to arrest Appellant in Covington for possession of marijuana. Appellant broke free of Kane's grasp and began running north on Fourth Street toward the Clay Wade Bailey Bridge which spans the Ohio River between Covington and Cincinnati, Ohio. Kane radioed for assistance and pursued Appellant on foot "at a sprint." When Appellant reached the bridge, he vaulted over the concrete barrier between the roadway and the walkway and began running north on the walkway toward Cincinnati. Kane, who, at that point, was running on top of the concrete barrier jumped down to the walkway and continued his pursuit.

Meanwhile, Partin and two other Covington police officers, Steve Sweeney and Cody Stanley, responded to Kane's request for assistance and

a. The Kentucky Criminal Code follows the Model Penal Code definitions of recklessness and negligence, but then renames recklessness "wantonness" and negligence "recklessness." To avoid confusion, the Model Penal Code terminology has been reinserted into the opinion.—EDS.

arrived at the bridge almost simultaneously in three separate vehicles. What was later determined to be Partin's police cruiser proceeded past the point where Appellant was running and stopped. Appellant then also stopped, reversed course, and began running back toward Kane. Kane ordered Appellant to "get down," whereupon, Appellant raised both hands above his head and fell to his knees in apparent submission. Kane got on top of Appellant and pulled his hands behind his back so as to apply handcuffs. While doing so, Kane thought he saw a shadowy movement or a flash in his peripheral vision. He then heard a voice say that "somebody's off the bridge."

... Sweeney and Stanley ... saw Partin exit his vehicle, proceed to the concrete barrier, place his left hand on the barrier, then vault over the barrier "as if he had done it a million times before," and disappear.... Partin fell ... into the river ninety-four feet below. His body was recovered four months later.

No one will ever know why Partin fell through the opening between the concrete barrier and the pedestrian walkway. Perhaps, he did not realize the opening was there. Perhaps, he knew it was there and miscalculated his vault. Either way, however, his death resulted from his own volitional act and not from any force employed against him by Appellant. Whether Appellant's act of resisting arrest by unlawful flight from apprehension was a legal cause of Partin's death requires application of the [following] provisions: * * *

Ky. Rev. Stat. § 501.060

(1) Conduct is the cause of a result when it is an antecedent without which the result in question would not have occurred.

...

(3) When [recklessly or negligently] causing a particular result is an element of the offense, the element is not established if the actual result is not within the risk of which the actor is aware or, in the case of [negligence], of which he should be aware unless:

(a) The actual result differs from the probable result only in the respect that a different person or different property is injured or affected or that the probable injury or harm would have been more serious or more extensive than that caused; or

(b) The actual result involves the same kind of injury or harm as the probable result and occurs in a manner which the actor knows or should know is rendered substantially more probable by his conduct.

(4) The question of whether an actor knew or should have known the result he caused was rendered substantially more probable by his conduct is an issue of fact.

Obviously, Appellant's unlawful act of resisting arrest by fleeing from apprehension was a "but for" cause of Partin's fatal attempt to pursue him by vaulting from the roadway of the bridge to the walkway....

Once an act is found to be a cause in fact of a result and a substantial factor in bringing about that result, it is recognized as the proximate cause unless another cause, independent of the first, intervenes between the first and the result. And even then the first cause is treated as the proximate cause if the harm or injury resulting from the second is deemed to have been reasonably foreseeable by the first actor.

Thus, the fact that Partin vaulted over the concrete barrier of his own volition does not exonerate Appellant if Partin's act was either foreseen or foreseeable by Appellant as a reasonably probable result of his own unlawful act of resisting arrest by fleeing from apprehension. And Ky. Rev. Stat. § 501.060(3)(a) clarifies that it is immaterial that it was Partin, as opposed to Kane or one of the other police officers, who fell from the bridge if such was a reasonably foreseeable consequence of the pursuit. * * *

Analogous to this set of facts is the case where a person pursued by the police in a high speed motor vehicle chase is held criminally liable for the death of an innocent bystander accidentally struck by a pursuing police vehicle. E.g., People v. Schmies, 44 Cal. App. 4th 38, 51 Cal.Rptr.2d 185 (Cal. Ct. App. 1996). In People v. Schmies, the California Court of Appeal directly addressed the effect of the police officers' conduct vis-à-vis the criminal liability of the defendant.

> The negligence or other fault of the officers is not a defense to the charge against defendant. The fact that the officers may have shared responsibility or fault for the accident does nothing to exonerate defendant for his role. In short, whether the officers' conduct could be described with such labels as negligent, careless, tortious, cause for discipline, or even criminal, in an action against them, is not at issue with respect to the defendant here. In this sense the "reasonableness" of the officers' conduct, focused upon their point of view and their blameworthiness for the death, is not relevant.
>
> The issue with respect to defendant focuses upon his point of view, that is, whether the harm that occurred was a reasonably foreseeable consequence of his conduct at the time he acted. Since the officers' conduct was a direct and specific response to defendant's conduct, the claim that their conduct was a superseding cause of the accident can be supported only through a showing that their conduct was so unusual, abnormal, or extraordinary that it could not have been foreseen.

Id. at 193–94. Although California does not have a statutory equivalent of Ky. Rev. Stat. § 501.060, this common law analysis of causation is consistent with the principles embodied in our statute. Did the defendant commit an illegal act that induced the officer's response? If so, was that response reasonably foreseeable by the defendant at the time that he acted? The fault or negligence of the officer is not determinative of the defendant's guilt. However, the reasonableness of the officer's response is relevant in determining whether the response was foreseeable by the defendant. The more reasonable the response, the more likely that the defendant should have foreseen it. It is immaterial that the ultimate victim was the officer, himself, as opposed to an innocent bystander.

Here, the conduct that supports Appellant's conviction is not, as the Commonwealth suggests, his own act of vaulting over the concrete barrier. Partin was not present when that act occurred; thus, it was not reasonably foreseeable that he would have vaulted over the barrier in reliance on the fact that Appellant had done so without incident. (That analysis might have been appropriate if Officer Kane had fallen from the bridge when he followed Appellant onto the walkway.) The conduct that supports Appellant's conviction is the continuation of his unlawful flight when he obviously knew that Partin intended to pursue him (as evidenced by the fact that when he saw Partin's vehicle stop, he reversed course and began running in the opposite direction), and that, to do so, Partin would be required to cross the open space between the roadway and the walkway and thereby risk falling to his death....

QUESTIONS AND COMMENTS

1. In *Robertson,* the trial court gave the following instruction:

Second–Degree Manslaughter

You will find the Defendant guilty of Second–Degree Manslaughter under this Instruction if, and only if, you believe from the evidence beyond a reasonable doubt that in this county on or about January 4, 1998 and before the finding of the Indictment herein, he caused the death of Michael Partin by unlawfully fleeing from police apprehension,

and

A. That the Defendant was aware of and consciously disregarded a substantial and unjustifiable risk that his conduct would result in Michael Partin's death, and that his disregard of that risk constituted a gross deviation from the standard of conduct that a reasonable person would have observed in the same situation;

or

B. That the death of Michael Partin occurred in a manner that the Defendant knew was rendered substantially more probable by his conduct.

Is proximate cause an *alternative* theory of liability, or is it a *supplement* to the ordinary requirements of liability, including objective and subjective offense elements? How would *Robertson* have been resolved under the Model Penal Code? What exactly is the relationship between causation and mens rea in the Model Code scheme? Recall that a defendant who is not deemed to have caused a particular harm is generally nonetheless guilty of committing an alternative offense (either a risk creation offense or an attempt): does that suggest that causation is (or should be thought to be) akin to an aggravating offense element?

2. *Tort vs. Crime.* Criminal courts are very anxious to differentiate cause in criminal law from cause in tort law. While there is consensus on the point that there is a difference, and that the difference matters greatly, it's not so clear what the difference is. What is it?

Restatement (Second) of Torts § 9. Legal Cause.

The words "legal cause" ... denote the fact that the causal sequence by which the actor's tortious conduct has resulted in an invasion of some legally protected interest of another is such that the law holds the actor responsible for such harm unless there is some defense to liability.

Comment:

b. In order that a particular act or omission may be the legal cause of an invasion of another's interest, the act or omission must be a substantial factor in bringing about the harm....

Note that causation inquiries tend to be more important in tort law than in criminal law—and, for that reason, they tend to get more attention. This is true at the purely formal, doctrinal level: In torts, the plaintiff must prove causation as part of his prima facie case; on the other hand, a criminal prosecutor needs to prove causation only in result offense cases, i.e., in cases involving an offense that features a result element (like homicide). (For the distinction between conduct and result offenses, see ch. 4.) Perhaps less obviously, this is true conceptually as well: In torts, causation issues are conceptualized as directly connected to the central question of the standard of care. If you ask whether a defendant could have averted more harm by taking a particular precaution than the precaution cost her to take, you're in part asking a (comparative) causation question: What effects will arise if the defendant engages in the activity *without* taking the precaution, and how does that effect differ from the effect that would occur if she engaged in the activity *with* the precaution? Alternatively, and even more importantly, if one instead views tort law as a corrective justice system seeking to restore injured plaintiffs to some *status quo ante*, then the two basic questions are: What is the baseline of entitlements, and how do we determine the degree to which the defendant caused a decline in the value of the plaintiff's "legitimate" holdings (that is, those holdings that he's entitled to)? Criminal law, by contrast, tends to pay far closer attention to the defendant's mental state (often without an inquiry into standards of care, except of course in cases of "criminal" negligence), without having to rely quite as much on the doctrine of causation to differentiate between punishable and nonpunishable conduct.

3. Note that the cause-in-fact rule may be underinclusive. Consider, for instance, two non-conspiring shooters who simultaneously fire a shot at their victim. Assuming that each shot would have been sufficient to kill, in what sense is each shot the but-for cause of the death? There are two formal answers: (1) They both are but-for causes, taken together (but for one *or the other* shot, the death wouldn't have occurred), (2) Each is the but-for cause of the particular way in which the death occurred, namely through two simultaneous and independently fatal shots. Are you convinced? Is one answer preferable to the other?

Overinclusiveness tends to be the far bigger problem, since any given act is the but-for cause of any number of results. (Think about it. What *wouldn't* have happened had you *not* gotten up this morning? Had you not gone to law school? This law school? At this time?) To what extent can (or should) this problem be "corrected" for with vague proximate cause standards (see, e.g., Model Penal Code § 2.03(2)(b) & (3)(b)) ("not too accidental or remote as to have a [just] bearing on the actor's liability")?

The Model Code drafters explained that their "not too remote" standard was designed to "put[] the issue squarely to the jury's sense of justice." Commentaries § 2.03, cmt. Is this standard useful? It may well be the case that courts have developed "rules of thumb" that are somewhat more rule-like than the "not too remote" standard to deal with certain issues that recurringly raise thorny causation issues: e.g., bad medical treatment or victim risk-taking. (See section 3 infra.)

Is the Model Penal Code's "not too remote" standard so vague as to be unconstitutional? Consider the following case, State v. Maldonado, 137 N.J. 536, 645 A.2d 1165 (1994). (For the facts of this case, see p. 137 supra.)

> Our strong "sense of justice" requires us to consider the remoteness of ... adventitious outcomes when determining criminal liability, but our inability to express what feature of unusual or extended causal chains affects our sense of justice makes developing a precise and definite standard that will accommodate our sense of justice difficult, and we have found none better than the "too remote to have a just bearing" standard.... The only practical standard is the jury's sense of justice. * * *
>
> Despite the vagueness of the "not too remote" standard ... the authors of the Model Penal Code ultimately decided that it represented the best solution, concluding that what was really involved was a communal determination by a jury about how far criminal responsibility should go in cases of this kind: a community's sense of justice on whether a defendant, otherwise clearly responsible under the criminal law, should be relieved of punishment because the result appeared too distant from his act. * * *
>
> The question, then, is whether the law can constitutionally accommodate this conflict [between the desirability of limiting criminal liability for results otherwise falling within the law's prohibition but whose occurrence was so far from the ordinary or expectable as to leave doubt about the justice of imposing such liability, and the impossibility of fashioning language to define the extent of such limitation in a way to assure acceptably consistent application] in what the most learned of our colleagues have concluded is the best way, or whether, because of the indefiniteness involved, the law must abandon the search. If we choose the latter course, we face an intolerable predicament, for we would be forced either to extend criminal responsibility regardless of remoteness, or to confine it restrictively, severely limiting its scope and effectiveness simply to avoid the possibility of arbitrary application. Therefore, we choose the former—the law is constitutional—and we do so as a matter of our own sense of sound policy.
>
> In many, many other areas the law cannot be precise but must be practical. Even in the fashioning of rules of liability, this Court bluntly has acknowledged that its sense of sound policy and justice may be the ultimate touchstone....
>
> This "sense of justice" is clearly involved in many criminal cases. Juries possess not only the unwritten power of nullification, but juries

also have the almost-absolute ability to determine life and death in sentencing proceedings under our capital punishment law. The acknowledged power of jurors, seemingly irrationally, certainly not explicitly rationally, to exercise lenity by not convicting of certain charges when the rest of their verdict may clearly indicate guilt is but another example. What other explanation exists for our accommodation of jurors' instincts but our faith in their "sense of justice"? . . .

As we said about our acceptance of jury nullification, our trust in juries to understand and apply the "not too remote" element "is indicative of a belief that the jury in a criminal prosecution serves as the conscience of the community and the embodiment of the common sense and feelings reflective of society as a whole." "[A]nd law in the last analysis must reflect the general community sense of justice."

4. What's the point of subsections (2)(a) and (3)(a) in the Model Penal Code's causation provision? And what do they have to do with causation? Here the Code is disposing of two familiar scenarios in which the actual victim or harm differ from the victim or harm intended (contemplated, etc.). If I, gun at the ready, set out to kill Joe, my archenemy, but end up hitting Calvin, my best friend, who is standing behind him because Joe unexpectedly bends down to tie his shoelaces, did I murder Calvin? Subsections (2)(a) and (3)(a) say yes. But why? After all, I didn't intend to kill Calvin at all, in fact that was the farthest thing from my mind. So how can I be said to have intended to cause his death? The traditional answer is that my intent vis-à-vis Joe is "transferred" onto Calvin. Here then we would be transferring intent from one victim onto another, rather than from one element to another, or even one offense to another. Compare the discussion of the concurrence requirement in ch. 5. What does "transferring" mean in this context? Does it mean, simply, that I won't be allowed to argue that I should be treated as if I never harbored, and acted upon, criminal intent, simply because I was unlucky—or simply clumsy—enough to have harmed the "wrong" person? Am I not just as dangerous, or blameworthy, or wicked, if I shoot a gun at Joe but hit Calvin as I would be if I hit Joe?

However this may be, the "transferred intent" theory is, as its name suggests, about intent. It is not about causation. The Code drafters, by contrast, frame the different-victim problem as a causation issue. Does that make sense? Isn't it clear that I did cause Calvin's death? Is it as odd to say that I *caused* Calvin's death as it is to say that I *intended* his death?

Another way of thinking about this problem is to consider it in terms of (one version of) the traditional distinction between general and specific intent. What counts, under this view, is that I had the (general) intent to cause the death of a "human being," which is all that the homicide statute requires and that I didn't need the (specific) intent to cause the death of a particular human being. As long as I did cause the death of a human being in a foreseeable manner (pulling the trigger, discharging a firearm, firing a bullet), I am guilty of homicide. But isn't causation all about the specifics of the situation? Isn't that what distinguishes causation analysis from mens rea analysis—that I not only have the requisite mental state with respect to the abstract result element laid out in the statute (death of another human being), but also that I foresaw (or contemplated, or should have foreseen, etc.) the particular way in which a particular human being came to his death?

Why not convict me of attempted murder (of Joe)—which requires intent (see the discussion of attempt, infra)—*and* of reckless (or negligent) homicide (of Calvin), depending on whether I was aware of a risk that Calvin might get killed or not? If I, with the intent to kill both Joe and Calvin, fired a single bullet that first hits Joe and then hits Calvin, killing both, wouldn't I be guilty of two murders?

Subsections (2)(a) and (3)(a) also specify that, like differences in the victim harmed, so differences in the harm inflicted too are irrelevant for purposes of causation, provided the harm I contemplated (intended, etc.) was more serious than the harm I managed to inflict. So I can't defend against an assault charge by arguing that I didn't mean (merely) to injure the victim, but to kill her (assuming I can kill without injuring). This makes intuitive sense, but—again—why is this a matter of causation, as opposed to mens rea? Couldn't I simply be convicted of attempted homicide, rather than assault?

5. *Omission vs. Commission*. Can an omission function as a cause? The Model Penal Code—and American criminal law generally—assumes that it can. See, e.g., Model Penal Code § 1.13(5) (defining "conduct" as "an action or omission and its accompanying state of mind") & § 2.03 (setting out "causal relationship between conduct and result"). But how? How can a nonact (a nonevent?) set in motion a chain of events that eventually results in some proscribed harm? If nonacts can cause harm, how do we differentiate between nonacts that are causes and nonacts that aren't? Consider the following hypothetical posed by Patricia Smith:

> Suppose that a train switchman, Charlie, and his buddy, Frank, are about to watch a playoff basketball game when Charlie says to Frank, "I have to pull that switch at 9:02. Don't let me forget or the L & W will crash straight into the Boston Flyer." The game is riveting, and at 9:03 the L & W crashes straight into the Boston Flyer. Charlie is responsible for the crash. No question about it. But what should be said about the cause?
>
> One possibility is that Charlie didn't really cause the wreck. (It was just an omission, after all—only the absence of action.) So we just say that he caused it because we want to hold him responsible. That, however, seems clearly wrong. If Charlie's grossly negligent omission didn't cause the train wreck, what did? . . .
>
> [T]he second possibility is that Charlie did cause the train wreck—by his negligent omission. But if that is admitted, then it should be noticed that there is no causal difference between Charlie and Frank. Both of them sit side by side on the couch, five feet from the switch, and watch the ball game until 9:03 when the trains crash. Both have full knowledge that the trains will crash if the switch is not pulled. Both have ample opportunity and ability to pull it. Of course, one has a duty (and thus, a responsibility) to pull the switch and the other does not, but what difference can that make causally? If either one had

jumped up at the last second and pulled the switch, the wreck would not have happened. So in fact either one was necessary and sufficient in the circumstances.

Patricia Smith, "Legal Liability and Criminal Omissions," 5 Buff. Crim. L. Rev. 69, 101–02 (2001).

2. Cause-in-Fact

KANSAS CITY, Mo. (AP)—Tearful witnesses told a judge Thursday that Robert R. Courtney's cancer drug dilution scheme had cost them precious days with their loved ones and vowed that the rogue pharmacist's ultimate punishment would come after his death. * * *

Federal prosecutors requested the maximum of 30 years for a "cold-blooded" crime they say hastened at least one patient's death and, as Courtney has admitted, was motivated by greed.

Courtney, who was arrested in August 2001, pleaded guilty in February to 20 counts of adulterating, misbranding and tampering with the cancer drugs Taxol and Gemzar. Those counts stem from his dilution of 158 chemotherapy doses he prepared last year for 34 patients of a Kansas City doctor. * * *

For Courtney, using less than the prescribed doses of medications he prepared was a way to make money. Federal authorities said he could pocket $780 on a single dose of Gemzar, for example, by putting only a small fraction of the prescribed amount into an intravenous solution.

While saying that diluting the cancer drugs probably hastened some deaths and may have caused others, prosecutors acknowledge it would be difficult to prove in court that Courtney's crimes killed patients.

In a statement to prosecutors, Courtney cited pressure to pay a $600,000 tax bill and the final one-third of a $1 million pledge to his church as a reason for diluting the drugs.

"Sentencing Opens in Cancer Drug Case," N.Y. Times, Dec. 5, 2002.

Commonwealth v. Atencio

Supreme Judicial Court of Massachusetts.
345 Mass. 627, 189 N.E.2d 223 (1963).

■ Wilkins, Chief Justice.

Each defendant has been convicted upon an indictment for manslaughter in the death of Stewart E. Britch and upon an indictment for illegally carrying a firearm. * * * The cases ... arose out of a "game" of "Russian roulette." * * *

Facts which the jury could have found are these. On Sunday, October 22, 1961, the deceased, his brother Ronald, and the defendants spent the day drinking wine in the deceased's room in a rooming house in Boston. At some time in the afternoon, with reference to nothing specific so far as the record discloses, Marshall said, "I will settle this," went out, and in a few minutes returned clicking a gun, from which he removed one bullet. Early in the evening Ronald left, and the conversation turned to "Russian roulette."

The evidence as to what happened consisted of testimony of police officers, who took statements of the defendants, and testimony of one defendant, Atencio. The evidence did not supply all the facts. For example, the source and ownership of the revolver were not made clear. The jury could have found that it was produced by the deceased and that he suggested the "game," or they might have found neither to be the fact. There was evidence that Marshall earlier had seen the revolver in the possession of the deceased, and that the latter handed it to Marshall, who put it in the bathroom under the sink. Later when the deceased accused him of stealing it, he brought it back from the bathroom, and gave it to the deceased. Any uncertainty is not of prime importance. The "game" was played. The deceased and Atencio were seated on a bed, and Marshall was seated on a couch. First, Marshall examined the gun, saw that it contained one cartridge, and, after spinning it on his arm, pointed it at his head, and pulled the trigger. Nothing happened. He handed the gun to Atencio, who repeated the process, again without result. Atencio passed the gun to the deceased, who spun it, put it to his head, and pulled the trigger. The cartridge exploded, and he fell over dead.

There is no controversy as to definition. Involuntary manslaughter may be predicated upon wanton or reckless conduct. * * *

We are of opinion that the defendants could properly have been found guilty of manslaughter. This is not a civil action against the defendants by the personal representative of Stewart Britch. In such a case his voluntary act, we assume, would be a bar. Here the Commonwealth had an interest that the deceased should not be killed by the wanton or reckless conduct of himself and others. Such conduct could be found in the concerted action and coöperation of the defendants in helping to bring about the deceased's foolish act. The jury did not have to believe testimony that the defendants at the last moment tried to dissuade the deceased from doing that which they had just done themselves.

The defendants argue as if it should have been ruled, as a matter of law, that there were three "games" of solitaire and not one "game" of "Russian roulette." That the defendants participated could be found to be a cause and not a mere condition of Stewart Britch's death. It is not correct to say that his act could not be found to have been caused by anything which Marshall and Atencio did, nor that he would have died when the gun went off in his hand no matter whether they had done the same. The testimony does not require a ruling that when the deceased took the gun from Atencio it was an independent or intervening act not standing in any relation to the defendants' acts which would render what he did imputable to them. It is an oversimplification to contend that each participated in something that only one could do at a time. There could be found to be a mutual encouragement in a joint enterprise. In the abstract, there may have been no duty on the defendants to prevent the deceased from playing. But there was a duty on their part not to coöperate or join with him in the "game." Nor, if the facts presented such a case, would we have to agree that if the deceased, and not the defendants, had played first that they could not have been found guilty of manslaughter. The defendants were much more than merely present at a crime. It would not be necessary that the defendants force the deceased to play or suggest that he play.

We are referred in both briefs to cases of manslaughter arising out of automobiles racing upon the public highway. When the victim is a third person, there is no difficulty in holding the drivers, including the one whose car did not strike the victim. * * *

In two cases the driver of a noncolliding car has been prosecuted for the death of his competitor, and in both cases an appellate court has ruled that he was not guilty of manslaughter. In Commonwealth v. Root, 403 Pa. 571, 170 A.2d 310, the competitor drove on the wrong side of the road head-on into an oncoming truck and was killed. The court held that "the defendant's reckless conduct was not a sufficiently direct cause of the competing driver's death to make him criminally liable therefor." In Thacker v. State, 103 Ga.App. 36, 117 S.E.2d 913, the defendant was indicted for the involuntary manslaughter of his competitor in a drag race who was killed when he lost control of his car and left the highway. The court said that the indictment "fails to allege any act or acts on the part of the defendant which caused or contributed to the loss of control of the vehicle driven by the deceased, other than the fact that they were engaged in a race at the time."

Whatever may be thought of those two decisions, there is a very real distinction between drag racing and "Russian roulette." In the former much is left to the skill, or lack of it, of the competitor. In "Russian roulette" it is a matter of luck as to the location of the one bullet, and except for a misfire (of which there was evidence in the case at bar) the outcome is a certainty if the chamber under the hammer happens to be the one containing the bullet.

The judgments on the indictments for manslaughter are affirmed.

QUESTIONS AND COMMENTS

1. In the *Courtney* case, why would the prosecutor have a hard time establishing causation? Wouldn't it be sufficient if the prosecutor could prove that the defendant's conduct had shortened *someone's* life, even if that victim would have died soon anyway? Think of a deliberate "mercy killer" in that regard who "merely" ends a terminal patient's life a few days earlier than it would otherwise have ended. Does the fact that the identifiable victim was dying anyway matter at all? Or is the problem that the victims in *Courtney* die of cancer, no matter when they die, while the mercy killer changes the cause of death? If a victim were bleeding to death and the defendant administered an anti-coagulant to accelerate the death from bleeding, would it be difficult to find he had caused a death? Think as well about a case in which it is trickier to identify victims: When we say that cigarette smoking causes lung cancer deaths, do we mean that it raises the probability of premature death from lung cancer or that, in a particular autopsy, we can ascertain whether smoking caused the disease that killed the particular victim? If there is no such autopsy evidence, is it appropriate to say that we don't know that smoking causes lung cancer?

Imagine a case in which multiple witnesses identify two members of rival gangs, X and Y, who each fired shots at one another on a crowded street corner. (Because they are rivals, they did not conspire with one another.) Ten people die, five each killed by bullets from two different weapons. The police never recover the weapons so it is never clear whether any particular person died as a result of X's stray gunshots or Y's. Does it (should it) matter that we cannot, with certainty, attribute any particular decedent's death to a particular defendant's conduct? Does it (should it) matter that we cannot attribute any particular cancer death to Courtney's conduct? Can we distinguish Courtney's case from this gang shooting case? In ways that should matter?

2. What do you think of the resolution of the *Courtney* case through a plea agreement? Is it fair to Courtney, given the difficulties of proving causation? Should criminal liability ever be based on insufficient proof? Is it fair to the victims?

Is the problem that the proof of causation would be speculative (i.e., not beyond a reasonable doubt)? What if there are several independent alternative theories of but-for cause, but it's impossible to prove the single actual cause? In such a case, does the prosecution establish causation as long as the defendant foresaw—or could have foreseen—each of the alternative courses of events? See, e.g., People v. Warner–Lambert Co., 51 N.Y.2d 295 (1980) (prosecution speculating as to various possible causal explanations for factory explosion, without settling on one). Is it enough to prove that the defendant—rather than someone else—was the but-for cause of harm, even if we cannot establish which of his acts in fact caused the harm?

3. Set aside for the moment the fact (emphasized by both the court and defendants) that the victim in *Atencio* kills himself (such intervention by an arguably responsible victim would generally be thought to raise a proximate cause issue). Can we say beyond a reasonable doubt that any particular participant in the game is a but-for cause of the death? In the sense that if he withdrew from the game, the game would not have gone on? Is it more sensible to say that each defendant "encouraged" or "facilitated" the game of Russian roulette, without needing to conclude that any of them *caused* it? See the material on accomplice liability, ch. 8 infra.

3. Proximate Cause

a. Victim Action and Traits

(i) Subsequent Victim Intervention: Deliberate Victim Self-Destruction

People v. Campbell

Court of Appeals of Michigan.
124 Mich.App. 333, 335 N.W.2d 27 (1983).

■ HOEHN, JUDGE.

Defendant, Steven Paul Campbell, was charged with open murder, Mich. Comp. Laws § 750.316 [defined as murder "perpetrated by means of poison, lying in wait, or any other willful, deliberate, and premeditated killing"], in connection with the suicide death of Kevin Patrick Basnaw. Following a preliminary examination in district court on March 10, 1981, defendant was bound over to circuit court for trial. Defendant moved to quash the information ... on the ground that providing a weapon to a person, who subsequently uses it to commit suicide, does not constitute the crime of murder. The motion to quash was denied by the circuit court, and this Court granted leave to appeal. * * *

On October 4, 1980, Kevin Patrick Basnaw committed suicide. On the night in question, Steven Paul Campbell went to the home of the deceased. They were drinking quite heavily.

The testimony indicates that late in the evening the deceased began talking about committing suicide. He had never talked about suicide before.

About two weeks before, the defendant, Steven Paul Campbell, caught the deceased in bed with defendant's wife, Jill Campbell. Some time during the talk of suicide, Kevin said he did not have a gun. At first the defendant, Steven Paul Campbell, indicated Kevin couldn't borrow or buy one of his guns. Then he changed his mind and told him he would sell him a gun, for whatever amount of money he had in his possession. Then the deceased, Kevin Basnaw, indicated he did not want to buy a gun, but Steve Campbell continued to encourage Kevin to purchase a gun, and alternately ridiculed him.

The defendant and the deceased then drove to the defendant's parent's home to get the weapon, leaving Kimberly Cleland, the deceased's girlfriend, alone. Even though she knew of the plan, she did not call anyone during this period of time. She indicated she thought the defendant was saying this to get a ride home.

The defendant and the deceased returned in about fifteen minutes with the gun and five shells. The deceased told his girlfriend to leave with the defendant because he was going to kill himself. He put the shells and the gun on the kitchen table and started to write a suicide note.

The defendant and the deceased's girlfriend left about 3 to 3:30 a.m. When they left, the shells were still on the table.

Steven, out of Kevin's presence and hearing, told Kimberly not to worry, that the bullets were merely blanks and that he wouldn't give Kevin real bullets. Kimberly and Steven prepared to leave.

On the way home, Kimberly asked Steven if the bullets he had given Kevin were really blanks. Steven said that they were and said "besides, the firing pin doesn't work". The girlfriend indicated that both defendant and deceased were about equally intoxicated at this point. The deceased's blood alcohol was found to be .26 percent.

The deceased's girlfriend drove herself to the defendant's home and remained there overnight. * * *

Next morning, one Billy Sherman arrived at about 11:30 a.m. and he and the deceased's roommate found the deceased slumped at the kitchen table with the gun in his hand. Dr. Kopp, the county Pathologist, listed the cause of death as suicide; self-inflicted wound to the temple. No autopsy was performed. No time of death was established.

The prosecutor argues that inciting to suicide, coupled with the overt act of furnishing a gun to an intoxicated person, in a state of depression, falls within the prohibition, "or other wilful, deliberate and premeditated killing". * * *

The term suicide excludes by definition a homicide. Simply put, the defendant here did not kill another person.

A second ground militates against requiring the defendant to stand trial for murder.

Defendant had no present intention to kill. He provided the weapon and departed. Defendant hoped Basnaw would kill himself but hope alone is not the degree of intention requisite to a charge of murder.

The common law is an emerging process. When a judge finds and applies the common law, hopefully he is applying the customs, usage and moral values of the present day. It is noted that in none of the cases decided since 1920 has a defendant, guilty of incitement to suicide, been found guilty of murder. Instead, they have been found guilty of [lesser types of homicide, including negligent and reckless homicide]. * * *

A number of legislatures have considered the problem and have enacted legislation which may be accepted as evidence of present day social values in this area. A number of states have made, or proposed making, incitement to suicide a crime. The penalties imposed by some of these states include:

Arkansas	— 10 years
Colorado	— Manslaughter
Florida	— 15 years
Maine	— 1 year
Minnesota	— 15 years
Missouri	— 15 years
Oregon	— 10 years
Wisconsin	— 5 years
Michigan proposed	— 10 years

Incitement to suicide has not been held to be a crime in two-thirds of the states of the United States. In the states where incitement to suicide has been held to be a crime, there has been no unanimity as to the nature or severity of the crime.

Most certainly, Michigan's imposition of a mandatory life sentence, without parole, for this type of conduct stands as the most severe punishment afforded.

No Legislature has classified such conduct as murder. * * *

While we find the conduct of the defendant morally reprehensible, we do not find it to be criminal under the present state of the law.

The remedy for this situation is in the Legislature.

People v. Kevorkian

Supreme Court of Michigan.
447 Mich. 436, 527 N.W.2d 714 (1994).

■ CAVANAGH, C.J. and BRICKLEY and GRIFFIN, J.J.

[A year before Michigan enacted a statute criminally sanctioning assisted suicide, the defendant was indicted for murdering two patients: the defendant had strapped a "suicide machine" to the arms of two patients suffering from conditions that were both extremely painful and arguably terminal in the short-term, each of whom had sought his assistance in ending their lives. The "suicide machine" permitted the patients, by lifting their hands, to release a fast-acting anesthetic that would put the patient to sleep rapidly; upon falling asleep, the patient's second hand would drop, releasing a toxic chemical. The trial court dismissed the charges, but was reversed on appeal. The Michigan Supreme Court in turn reversed the intermediate appellate court, noting . . .]

The Court of Appeals majority relied principally on People v. Roberts, 211 Mich. 187, 178 N.W. 690 (1920). In *Roberts*, the defendant's wife was suffering from advanced multiple sclerosis and in great pain. She previously had attempted suicide and . . . requested that he provide her with poison. He agreed, and placed a glass of poison within her reach. She drank the mixture and died. The defendant was charged with murder. He pleaded guilty, and the trial court determined the crime to be murder in the first degree. . . .

After discussing a similar Ohio case, Blackburn v. State, 23 Ohio. St. 146 (1872), the *Roberts* Court concluded:

> We are of the opinion that when defendant mixed the paris green with water and placed it within reach of his wife to enable her to put an end to her suffering by putting an end to her life, he was guilty of murder by means of poison within the meaning of the statute, even though she requested him to do so. By this act he deliberately placed within her reach the means of taking her own life, which she could have obtained in no other way by reason of her helpless condition.

We must determine further whether *Roberts* remains viable, because, as noted in People v. Stevenson, 416 Mich. 383, 390, 331 N.W.2d 143 (1982):

> This Court has often recognized its authority, and indeed its duty, to change the common law when change is required.

. . . . To convict a defendant of criminal homicide, it must be proven that death occurred as a direct and natural result of the defendant's act. . . . Recent decisions draw a distinction between active participation in a suicide and events leading up to the suicide, such as providing the means. * * * [In In re Joseph G., 34 Cal.3d 429, 194 Cal.Rptr. 163, 667 P.2d 1176 (1983), the California Supreme Court] explained that a conviction of murder is proper if a defendant participates in the final overt act that causes death, such as firing the gun or pushing the plunger on the hypodermic needle [but not] where the defendant is involved merely "in the events leading up to the commission of the final overt act, such as furnishing the means...."

[We] overrule *Roberts* to the extent that it can be read to support the view that the common-law definition of murder encompasses the act of intentionally providing the means by which a person commits suicide. Only where there is probable cause to believe that death was the direct and natural result of a defendant's act can the defendant be properly bound over on a charge of murder. [In a footnote, the court then pointed out that a defendant who recklessly or negligently provides the means by which another commits suicide could be found guilty of a lesser offense, such as involuntary manslaughter (i.e., reckless or negligent homicide).]

State v. Bauer

Court of Appeals of Minnesota.
471 N.W.2d 363 (1991).

■ SHORT, JUDGE.

In these consolidated appeals, Justin Bauer challenges his conviction for aiding a suicide and his conviction and sentence for fetal (felony) homicide. The state challenges the downward departure on the homicide sentence. We affirm. * * *

Eighteen-year-old Rachelle Cazin died of a single gunshot wound to the head. Justin Bauer, then 17, was with Cazin when she died. At the time of her death, Cazin was pregnant with a six to six-and-one-half month old fetus. Bauer did not deny paternity, but testified he did not believe Cazin was pregnant. There was testimony at trial that Bauer made threats against Cazin because she was spreading rumors she was pregnant with his child. Bauer admitted he was angry with Cazin.

On April 9, Cazin asked Bauer to meet her in the woods near their home and to bring his gun. The couple met as planned and agreed to commit suicide together. Bauer testified Cazin put the gun in her mouth and he counted to three, but nothing happened. Bauer claims he then tried to talk Cazin out of shooting herself. As he walked away from her, he heard a gunshot. Bauer hid Cazin's body under a layer of brush, ran home, changed his clothes, unloaded the gun, threw the remaining shells outside and cleaned the gun. * * *

The jury found Bauer not guilty of second degree (intentional) murder and fetal homicide. He was found guilty of aiding a suicide and of felony fetal homicide. * * *

The trial court gave notice of its intent to consider a downward durational departure on the felony fetal homicide conviction. The state opposed the departure, and argued for consecutive sentencing. The trial court sentenced Bauer to concurrent sentences of 24 months for aiding a suicide and 60 months for felony fetal homicide, approximately a 50 percent downward durational departure. * * *

Bauer also challenges the state's proof of causation on the fetal homicide offense. Bauer was convicted of [murder of an unborn child in the second degree, defined as]

> caus[ing] the death of an unborn child, without intent to effect the death of any unborn child or person, while committing or attempting to commit a felony offense.

Minn.Stat. § 609.2662(2) (1988). Expert testimony established that the fetus died from asphyxiation caused by cessation of blood flow from its mother. This death was certainly a foreseeable consequence of her suicide. Although Bauer testified he did not know Cazin was pregnant, there was much evidence from which the jury could have inferred otherwise. Nor are we persuaded Cazin's decision to commit suicide was an intervening independent force. In *State v. Schaub,* 231 Minn. 512, 517, 44 N.W.2d 61, 64 (1950), the court held a manslaughter conviction could be upheld if the defendant's act was the "proximate cause [of death] without the intervention of an efficient independent force in which defendant did not participate or which he could not reasonably have foreseen." Cazin's suicide was not an "intervening cause," as Bauer argues, because he participated in it and could reasonably have foreseen it. * * *

[In support of its decision to grant defendant a 50 percent downward departure, the] trial court cited the "type of conduct involved" in aiding a suicide as compared to other felonies involved in felony [murder] charges [such as robbery, burglary, kidnapping, arson, or rape], and stated the 60–month sentence was more "proportionate" to the severity of the offense. The trial court questioned whether the guidelines commission or legislature anticipated the causation problem presented by using aiding a suicide as an underlying felony for felony murder.

We find no causation problem with applying the felony murder rule to these facts. However, the trial court was well within its discretion in finding Bauer's conduct less serious than the typical felony murder (or feticide) offense. Moreover, the legislature enacted a separate statute for fetal homicide in the course of a less serious felony. *See* Minn.Stat. § 609.268, subd. 1 (1988) ["Death of an unborn child. Whoever, in the commission of a felony . . . causes the death of an unborn child is guilty of a felony. . . ."]. Bauer could have been charged under this statute, which clearly includes an underlying felony of aiding a suicide, and which provides a less severe range of punishment. *Compare id.* (up to 15 years) *with* Minn.Stat. § 609.2662, supra (up to 40 years). In 1987, the presumptive sentence for this offense was 54 months, six months *less* than the sentence Bauer received. The trial court in its discretion found aiding a suicide less serious than the conduct typically involved in a felony murder (or feticide) offense. For example, aiding a suicide, although an intentional offense, relies heavily on the suicide's own resolve to commit the criminal act. *Cf.* Minn. Sent. Guidelines II.D.2.a.(2) (defendant's minor or passive role may be considered in mitigation). * * *

QUESTIONS AND COMMENTS

1. Is *Campbell* a case about causation or about mental state? *Kevorkian*? (Note that the courts in both cases did not preclude criminal liability

for (lesser) types of homicide other than murder.) Does it make sense to say that Campbell might have caused the death of another person *negligently* if he had *carelessly* left a gun lying around the house of a depressed and suicidal friend but not that he caused it deliberately if he handed the person the gun, hoping he would die? Courts have, on occasion, held that it is negligent to furnish someone with a gun, knowing the person one has armed is suicidal. See, e.g., City of Akron v. Head, 73 Ohio Misc.2d 67, 657 N.E.2d 1389 (Ohio Mun. 1995). In People v. Duffy, 79 N.Y.2d 611 (1992), the defendant, "tired" of hearing his friend complain about wanting to die, handed him a gun and some bullets. The deceased then loaded the gun and shot himself. The New York Court of Appeals upheld the defendant's manslaughter conviction on the ground that he had engaged in "reckless conduct which results in another person's committing suicide," even though he had been acquitted of the separate crime of "intentionally caus[ing] or aid[ing] another person to commit suicide," N.Y. Penal Law § 125.15(3).

When the *Campbell* court says that the defendant lacked the *present intention to kill,* what does it mean? Had he left an odorless and invisible poison in a glass of water before leaving the house with Basnaw's girlfriend, which Basnaw might or might not have ingested, would he lack a present intention to kill then?

2. Why isn't Campbell guilty of murder simply for lying to Kimberly Cleland, the girlfriend of the deceased, about whether he had left Basnaw with a weapon capable of inflicting lethal damage? If a defendant misdirected ambulance workers to the wrong part of the house so they wouldn't find where a heart attack victim was actually lying, hoping to stop the rescue workers from saving the victim, wouldn't he be guilty of murder? (Why) are Campbell's efforts to deflect a potential rescuer different?

3. Is the *Kevorkian* court right to imply that we should consider the defendant more culpable if the deceased consents to a defendant's homicidal acts rather than killing himself with means the defendant furnishes? What if we think the two victims differ from one another only because one is still physically *capable* of moving enough to use the means the defendant furnishes and the other is not? Or do we worry that those who act upon (consenting) victims do not give them the last opportunity to reflect upon, and renounce, their decision to end their lives? Wouldn't we worry in either case that the defendant unduly influenced the victim's decision to choose death? That if we tried to restrict the "right to die" to situations in which those who chose death were "terminally ill" or in "desperate pain" that we could not confine or define these terms with adequate specificity?

Is the distinction between "active participation in a suicide" and "events leading up to the suicide, such as providing the means" relevant to the *causation* question or to the question of whether the defendant performed a punishable *act*? See ch. 4. Can providing the means to a person who intends to commit suicide (and requests them) be recast as failing to prevent that person from committing suicide? Is the problem that the participation isn't *active* or that it isn't a participation *in the suicide*, as opposed to some preparations? Is the problem the absence of an act on the defendant's part or the presence of an act on the victim's? Does it make a difference, for purposes of the questions of causation, whether the defendant owed the victim a duty to come to her aid? Reconsider *Roberts*, *Kevorkian*, and *Bauer* in this light.

4. Consider *Campbell* and *Kevorkian* in light of the legality principle. (See ch. 2.) In *Campbell*, the intermediate Michigan appellate court remarks that the decision whether or not to criminalize assisted suicide is for the legislature to make. At the same time, it expresses the hope that, "[w]hen a judge finds and applies the common law, ... he is applying the customs, usage and moral values of the present day," and then adopts a different (and narrower) definition of murder. This change is then affirmed in *Kevorkian* by the Michigan Supreme Court, along the way overruling its previous decision holding that assisted suicide qualifies as murder. Is the decision to criminalize a decision for the legislature, but the decision to decriminalize for the courts?

5. Note that the court in *Bauer* grants a downward sentencing departure because the intervening actor bore independent responsibility for the death of the fetus: the finding, of course, implies that she bore some responsibility for the suicide that caused the death of the fetus. Is it appropriate to adjust sentences to account for the belief that some defendants are causally responsible enough to be held accountable for committing a result crime but not as causally responsible as those who typically cause that result? Should we stop trying to make all-or-nothing causation judgments in all of these cases? If we decide to make an all-or-nothing judgment, is it possible to square (one interpretation of) the judgment in *Kevorkian* (defendant is not responsible for the death of the person who commits suicide) with the judgment in *Bauer* (defendant is causally responsible for a second death that results from a suicide)?

(ii) Subsequent Victim Intervention: Risk-Taking

People v. Kern

Supreme Court of New York, Appellate Division, Second Department.
149 A.D.2d 187, 545 N.Y.S.2d 4 (1989).

■ MOLLEN, PRESIDING JUSTICE.

This appeal arises out of the highly publicized confrontation between a group of white teenagers and three black men during the early morning hours of December 20, 1986, in Howard Beach, Queens County, which resulted in the death of one of the black men, Michael Griffith, and the severe beating of his companion, Cedric Sandiford. The three defendants involved in this appeal, Scott Kern, Jon Lester and Jason Ladone, were convicted, after a joint jury trial, of manslaughter in the second degree.[a] * * * On appeal, the defendants contend, *inter alia,* that the evidence adduced at trial was legally insufficient to support their manslaughter ... convictions. * * *

a. N.Y. Penal Law § 125.15(1) ("A person is guilty of manslaughter in the second degree when ... [h]e recklessly causes the death of another person....").—EDS.

During the early evening hours of December 19, 1986, Michael Griffith, Curtis Sylvester, Cedric Sandiford and Timothy Grimes left Brooklyn in a car driven by Sylvester and traveled to the home of Grimes' brother located in St. Albans, Queens County. Upon reaching their destination, they found that Grimes' brother was not at home and the foursome then set out to return to Brooklyn. As they were traveling westbound on the Belt Parkway, their car began to overheat, forcing them to leave the parkway at the Cross Bay Boulevard exit in Queens. The group drove in a southerly direction on Cross Bay Boulevard through Howard Beach and continued for approximately 10 minutes towards the Rockaways. The car eventually came to a halt on the shoulder of Cross Bay Boulevard. Sandiford, Grimes and Griffith left Sylvester with the car, walked to a nearby bridge toll plaza and eventually returned to the disabled car with a container of water. Despite their efforts, the car remained inoperable and the men agreed that Griffith, Grimes and Sandiford would summon assistance and then return to Brooklyn. Sylvester intended to remain with the car and wait for a tow truck. Grimes, Griffith and Sandiford proceeded on foot northbound along Cross Bay Boulevard in search of a gas station and the train. The trio arrived in Howard Beach at approximately midnight.

Meanwhile, in Howard Beach, a birthday party was being held which was attended by approximately 30 teenagers including Scott Kern, Jon Lester, Jason Ladone and Robert Riley. At approximately 12:20 A.M., Kern's girlfriend, Claudia Calogero, who had a 12:30 A.M. curfew, left the party and was driven home by Salvatore DeSimone. They were accompanied by Jon Lester and a fourth youth. As DeSimone was turning the corner from Cross Bay Boulevard onto 157th Avenue, Griffith, Grimes and Sandiford started to cross the street towards the New Park Pizzeria. According to Calogero's testimony, three black men darted in front of the car forcing DeSimone to stop the car suddenly. An argument ensued between the pedestrians and the occupants of the car. According to Calogero's testimony, Sandiford stuck his head in the car window and stared at the teenagers. According to Sandiford's testimony, however, the occupants of DeSimone's car stuck their heads out the window and yelled "Nigger[s], get [out of] the neighborhood". Following that confrontation, the three black men crossed the street and entered the pizzeria. The youths continued on their way. After bringing Calogero home, DeSimone, Lester and the other youth returned to the party.

Robert Riley was sitting on the outside steps of the house where the party was being held, when DeSimone, Lester and the other youth arrived. Lester shouted, "There were some niggers on the boulevard, let's go up there and kill them". A few minutes later, a number of youths, including Kern, Lester, Ladone and Pirone, left the party to track down the three black men. * * *

Meanwhile, at approximately 12:45 A.M., Grimes, Sandiford and Griffith, who had finished eating their pizza in the New Park Pizzeria, exited the restaurant. At that point, the several vehicles containing the teenagers pulled into the parking lot outside the pizzeria and the youths, with the exception of Laura Castagna, emerged from the cars. The group, wielding bats and sticks, confronted Griffith, Grimes and Sandiford outside the pizzeria and shouted, "Niggers get * * * out of the neighborhood". Riley testified that Kern was banging a baseball bat on the ground as the teenagers formed a semicircle around the three black men who, according to Riley, were each holding a knife. According to Grimes, several of the youths were carrying bats and sticks, and one youth held "something that looked like an iron pipe". Sandiford testified that he did not have a weapon and that he did not observe whether Griffith or Grimes displayed any weapons. Grimes testified that he pulled out a knife and held it in front of him as the youths approached. At that point, Sandiford was struck in the back by a bat. Although Riley never saw Kern swing the bat that he had been holding, he did testify that after Sandiford was struck, Riley grabbed the bat from Kern because he (Riley) said he could swing it "harder". As the three black men began to flee across Cross Bay Boulevard, Riley, Kern, Ladone, Lester, Pirone, and several other youths gave chase.

Griffith, Grimes and Sandiford ran in different directions. Grimes headed north on Cross Bay Boulevard and managed to escape his attackers. Sandiford was struck several times with bats and tree limbs by his assailants as they continued to chant, "Niggers, get * * * out of the neighborhood". * * *

[After a long chase] Griffith jumped over the guardrail and ran onto the Belt Parkway. When the youths reached the guardrail, Riley observed Griffith run across the three eastbound lanes of the highway, jump the center median and enter the westbound lanes, where he was struck by a vehicle being driven by Dominic Blum. * * *

The results of the autopsy performed on Michael Griffith established that he was killed almost instantaneously upon being struck by Blum's vehicle. Additionally, expert testimony was presented to establish that, based upon an analysis of Griffith's urine and brain tissue, Griffith had ingested cocaine at least 10 hours prior to his death and that, since the effects of cocaine last no longer than six hours, Griffith was not under the influence of cocaine at the time of his death. [A defense expert disputed this finding, testifying that based upon his review of the autopsy and toxicological reports "Griffith had ingested cocaine approximately 15 minutes to two hours before his death" and that he therefore "was under the influence of the drug at the time of his death."]

The defendants maintain that the evidence adduced at trial [on the issue of causation] was legally insufficient.... The defendants assert that their actions, insofar as Griffith was concerned, amounted to no more than a chase through the streets of Howard Beach while screaming racial epithets which ended when Griffith jumped over the barricade at the end of 90th Street.... We disagree. * * *

[In] the case at bar, the only reasonable alternative left open to Griffith while being persistently chased and threatened by the defendants and their friends, several of whom were carrying weapons, was to seek safety by crossing the parkway where he unfortunately met his death. Clearly, on the basis of these facts, it cannot be said that the defendants' despicable conduct was not a sufficiently direct cause of Griffith's death. The defendants will not be heard to complain that, in desperately fleeing their murderous assault, Griffith chose the wrong escape route.

Commonwealth v. Root

Supreme Court of Pennsylvania.
403 Pa. 571, 170 A.2d 310 (1961).

■ CHARLES ALVIN JONES, CHIEF JUSTICE.

The appellant was found guilty of involuntary manslaughter for the death of his competitor in the course of an automobile race between them on a highway.... The testimony, which is uncontradicted in material part, discloses that, on the night of the fatal accident, the defendant accepted the deceased's challenge to engage in an automobile race; that the racing took place on a rural 3–lane highway; that the night was clear and dry, and traffic light; that the speed limit on the highway was 50 miles per hour; that, immediately prior to the accident, the two automobiles were being operated at varying speeds of from 70 to 90 miles per hour; that the accident occurred in a no-passing zone on the approach to a bridge where the highway narrowed to two directionally-opposite lanes; that, at the time of the accident, the defendant was in the lead and was proceeding in his right hand lane of travel; that the deceased, in an attempt to pass the defendant's automobile, when a truck was closely approaching from the opposite direction, swerved his car to the left, crossed the highway's white dividing line and drove his automobile on the wrong side of the highway head-on into the oncoming truck with resultant fatal effect to himself.

This evidence would of course amply support a conviction of the defendant for speeding, reckless driving and, perhaps, other violations of The Vehicle Code....

While precedent is to be found for application of the tort law concept of "proximate cause" in fixing responsibility for criminal homicide, the want of any rational basis for its use in determining criminal liability can no longer be properly disregarded.... Proximate cause, as an essential element of a tort founded in negligence, has undergone in recent times, and is still undergoing, a marked extension. More specifically, this area of civil law has been progressively liberalized in favor of claims for damages for personal injuries to which careless conduct of others can in some way be associated. To persist in applying the tort liability concept of proximate cause to prosecutions for criminal homicide after the marked expansion of civil liability of defendants in tort actions for negligence would be to extend possible criminal liability to persons chargeable with unlawful or reckless conduct in circumstances not generally considered to present the likelihood of a resultant death. * * *

.... [T]he action of the deceased driver in recklessly and suicidally swerving his car to the left lane of a 2–lane highway into the path of an oncoming truck was not forced upon him by any act of the defendant; it was done by the deceased and by him alone, who thus directly brought about his own demise. * * *

In the case now before us, the deceased was aware of the dangerous condition created by the defendant's reckless conduct in driving his automobile at an excessive rate of speed along the highway but, despite such knowledge, he recklessly chose to swerve his car to the left and into the path of an oncoming truck, thereby bringing about the head-on collision which caused his own death. * * *

■ EAGEN, JUSTICE (dissenting).

The opinion of the learned Chief Justice admits, under the uncontradicted facts, that the defendant, at the time of the fatal accident involved, was engaged in an unlawful and reckless course of conduct. Racing an automobile at 90 miles per hour, trying to prevent another automobile going in the same direction from passing him, in a no-passing zone on a two-lane public highway, is certainly all of that. Admittedly also, there can be more than one direct cause of an unlawful death. To me, this is self-evident. But, says the majority opinion, the defendant's recklessness was not a direct cause of the death. With this, I cannot agree.

If the defendant did not engage in the unlawful race and so operate his automobile in such a reckless manner, this accident would never have occurred. He helped create the dangerous event. He was a vital part of it. The victim's acts were a natural reaction to the stimulus of the situation. The race, the attempt to pass the other car and forge ahead, the reckless speed, all of these factors the defendant himself helped create. He was part and parcel of them. That the victim's response was normal under the circumstances, that his reaction should have been expected and was clearly foreseeable, is to me beyond argument. That the defendant's recklessness was a substantial factor is obvious. All of this, in my opinion, makes his unlawful conduct a direct cause of the resulting collision. * * *

While the victim's foolhardiness in this case contributed to his own death, he was not the only one responsible and it is not he alone with whom we are concerned. It is the people of the Commonwealth who are harmed by the kind of conduct the defendant pursued. Their interests must be kept in mind.

I, therefore, dissent and would accordingly affirm the judgment of conviction.

QUESTIONS AND COMMENTS

1. Did the defendants in *Kern* force the deceased to elect between two risks? How about the defendant in *Root*? Would it matter if the deceased in *Kern* had elected an option that seems manifestly imprudent? Would it matter if the imprudence were a function of having consumed drugs (or alcohol, see *Kibbe*, infra)? (Why wouldn't that be a victim vulnerability case, like *Frazier* or *Stamp*, infra?) Would it matter if the deceased had ingested drugs that did not make him *imprudent* in electing among risks, but made him self-destructive or a thrill seeker?

Contrast *Root* not only with *Kern* but with *Robertson*. Does it matter whether the victim was under some duty to respond to the defendant's behavior—in some way, or in the specific way he did?

2. It might be worth anticipating some of the problems in formulating cases like *Root* or *Atencio*, alternatively, as accomplice liability cases rather than "causation" cases. Cf. People v. Abbott, 84 A.D.2d 11, 445 N.Y.S.2d 344 (App. Div. 1981). We cannot convict a defendant of aiding and abetting

a party unless that party had himself committed a crime. Suicide—self-murder—is not a crime (though it once was, with suicides being buried at crossroads with a stake driven through their heart, see 4 William Blackstone, Commentaries on the Laws of England 189–90 (1769); see also State v. Levelle, 13 S.E. 319 (S.C. 1891) (suicide a felony)), nor is self-manslaughter. (That's why assisting suicide is now a separate crime, whereas before it could be punished as aiding and abetting the crime of suicide. See, e.g., N.Y. Penal Law § 125.15(3).) So, for instance, if the more reckless drag racer kills himself, rather than a by-stander, the party who encouraged the reckless behavior (by challenging the more reckless person to the race, by speeding up himself, etc.) cannot be guilty of aiding and abetting another's criminal offense. And, of course, it is difficult to know, given the requirement that an accomplice must intend his aid to support the principal, whether one can aid and abet a result crime when one is merely reckless as to that result. But if we think of *Root* (or *Atencio*) as an accomplice liability case, we need not decide that the defendant is the cause-in-fact or proximate cause of the harm (though complicity raises causation questions of its own). For more on accomplice liability, see ch. 8.

(iii) Prior Victim Vulnerability

State v. Frazier

Supreme Court of Missouri.
339 Mo. 966, 98 S.W.2d 707 (1936).

■ ELLISON, JUDGE.

The appellant was convicted of manslaughter and his punishment assessed at a fine of $400 and 6 months in the county jail, for the killing of Daniel I. Gross.... The deceased was a hemophiliac, or "bleeder." The appellant struck him on the jaw once with his fist. A slight laceration on the inside of the mouth resulted which produced a hemorrhage lasting ten days and ending in death.... The evidence for the appellant was that ... Gross' death was not caused by the blow struck, but by his disease, aforesaid....

[The deceased] was 36 years old and had been afflicted with hemophilia since birth. He had been under treatment for that disease about 2 years before when he bumped his knee on a table, and was in the Veterans' Hospital in St. Louis for a short time. He was below the average in height and overweight, or fat, as some of the witnesses said, and rather pale or anemic. He walked with a slow draggy or hobbling gait....

Dr. Barron, the attending physician, gave it as his professional opinion that the death of Gross was caused by hemorrhage from the laceration in his mouth, and the evidence is clear that the laceration was produced by the blow struck by appellant. But it was the doctor's further opinion that the blow on the jaw would not have caused the deceased to bleed to death if he had not been a hemophiliac. He also testified the hemorrhages from hemophilia might occur spontaneously, and admitted that he had learned the patient was bleeding rather freely from the kidneys, and, it seems, also through the intestinal tract, during the last 3 days of his sickness. He made no examination of these parts, and the foregoing information came to him only as it was communicated with the case history. He found no evidence of violence in the region of these organs, and stated blood from the wound in the mouth when swallowed might find its way into the intestines. He also said the mere fact that a person might pass blood wouldn't be an indication of bleeding at the kidneys. And yet the record shows that, when asked on cross-examination whether the hemorrhage that caused Gross' death was from the intestines, the kidneys, or the mouth, he said he didn't know....

Remembering the appellant was convicted of manslaughter, two questions remain: (1) Was it an adequate defense that the appellant did not know the deceased was a hemophiliac, and struck only one moderate blow with his first, which ordinarily would not have been dangerous to life? (2) Is he to be excused because the blow producing the hemorrhage would not have resulted fatally if deceased had not been a hemophiliac? Both these questions must be answered in the negative. Section 3988, Rev. Stat. Mo.1929, provides that "every killing of a human being by the act, procurement or culpable negligence of another, not herein declared to be murder or excusable or justifiable homicide, shall be deemed manslaughter." If one commits an unlawful assault and battery upon another without malice and death results, the assailant is guilty of manslaughter, although death was not intended and the assault was not of a character likely to result fatally.

Neither is it an excuse that appellant did not know the deceased was a hemophiliac, and that death would not have resulted but for that affliction. On this point 13 R.C.L. § 55, p. 750, says: "The law declares that one who inflicts an injury on another and thereby accelerates his death shall be held criminally responsible therefor, although death would not have resulted from the injury but for the diseased or wounded condition of the person so injured." And the doctrine is more fully set out in 29 C.J. § 57, p. 1082, as follows: "If the deceased was in feeble health and died from the combined effects of the injury and of his disease, or if the injury accelerated the death from the disease, he who inflicted the injury is liable, although the injury alone would not have been fatal. The same rule applies, although the disease itself would probably have been fatal, if the injury accelerated death. It is immaterial that defendant did not know that the deceased was in the feeble condition which facilitated the killing, or that he did not reasonably anticipate that his act would cause death."

People v. Stamp

Court of Appeal of California, Second District.
2 Cal.App.3d 203, 82 Cal.Rptr. 598 (1969).

■ Cobey, Acting P.J.

Defendants appeal their conviction of the murder of Carl Honeyman who, suffering from a heart disease, died between 15 and 20 minutes after Koory and Stamp held up his business, [the General Amusement Company]. * * *

[D]uring the hours before the robbery Honeyman had appeared to be in normal health and good spirits. The victim was an obese, 60–year-old man, with a history of heart disease, who was under a great deal of pressure due to the intensely competitive nature of his business. Additionally, he did not take good care of his heart. * * *

Appellant's contention that the felony-murder rule is inapplicable to the facts of this case is . . . without merit. Under the felony-murder rule of section 189 of the Penal Code, a killing committed in either the perpetration of or an attempt to perpetrate robbery is murder of the first degree. This is true whether the killing is wilfull, deliberate and premeditated, or merely accidental or unintentional, and whether or not the killing is planned as a part of the commission of the robbery. . . . * * *

The doctrine is not limited to those deaths which are foreseeable. Rather a felon is held strictly liable for all killings committed by him or his accomplices in the course of the felony. As long as the homicide is the direct causal result of the robbery the felony-murder rule applies whether or not the death was a natural or probable consequence of the robbery. So long as a victim's predisposing physical condition, regardless of its cause, is not the only substantial factor bringing about his death, that condition, and the robber's ignorance of it, in no way destroys the robber's criminal responsibility for the death. So long as life is shortened as a result of the felonious act, it does not matter that the victim might have died soon anyway. In this respect, the robber takes his victim as he finds him.

QUESTIONS AND COMMENTS

1. Glanville Williams (tracking a good deal of case law) notes that we treat intervening *intentional* human action as a superseding cause, at least so long as the intervening human actor is sane and categorically responsible rather than, say, an infant or insane. In his article, "*Finis* for *Novus Actus*?," 48 Camb. L.J. 391, 391–92 (1989), he notes:

> The legal attitude . . . rests on what is known to philosophers as the principle of autonomy. . . . The autonomy doctrine, expressing itself through its corollary the doctrine of *novus actus interveniens*, teaches that the individual's will is the autonomous (self-regulating) prime cause of behavior.

Can we square this observation with the Model Penal Code's efforts to tie causation judgments to foreseeability? Defendant One hands a gun to a three-year-old who is *very* unlikely to be able to shoot himself, but he drops the gun in such a way that he *is* in fact able to shoot himself. Defendant Two hands a gun to a despondent, albeit sane, person who has been talking for hours about suicide. The death in the second case is far more foreseeable (at least by hypothesis), but only Defendant One will be deemed causally responsible. Does foreseeability matter at all or is it relevant to mental state (a subjective offense element) rather than cause (an objective offense element)? Would it make sense to limit a requirement of foreseeability to cases involving intervening actors? See Rollin M. Perkins & Ronald N. Boyce, Criminal Law 813 (3d ed. 1982); see generally H.L.A. Hart & Tony Honoré, Causation in the Law 325–40 (2d ed. 1985).

It is possible that intervening human actors are merely an *exception* to the general rule connecting foreseeability and cause. See, in that regard, Sanford Kadish, Blame and Punishment: Essays in the Criminal Law 144–45 (1987). It is also possible that inquiries into causation are *always* backward-regarding, rather than forward-regarding. We trace *back* from the existence of the dead body until we find someone to attribute the death to. (Is this account more plausible in some cases—murder, say—than in others?) Foreseeability is present (or not) at the moment of action (not consequence); it seemingly better explains culpability than the viability of a punishment-enhancing vengeance motive. Think about *Stamp*: the court explicitly holds that foreseeability is not necessary. Is that a defensible judgment or an outlier case? A reflection of the fact that it is a felony-murder case in which we could dispense with an inquiry into culpability because malice is conclusively presumed when a killing occurs during a felony? But how do we find that a killing (rather than a death) occurred during the course of a felony unless, working back from the dead body, we reach the defendant *before* we reach the victim's predisposing condition?

2. What's left of proximate cause in a case like *Stamp*? Is the proximate cause requirement simply inapplicable in a serious case, like a felony murder? Would that make sense (assuming that felony murder is a strict liability offense)? How would this issue be resolved under the Model Penal Code approach to causation, an approach that ties causation to mental state?

3. What's the difference between the *Stamp* causation requirement and causation in torts? Does the criminal defendant take her victim as she finds him (in all cases, in egregious cases, in cases involving physical violence)? (Is that the gist of *Frazier*?) In Smith v. Leech Brain & Co. Ltd., [1962] 2 Q.B. 405, the plaintiff suffered a burn on his lip during the course of his employment. The tissues on his lips were prone to cancer. Smith died when the burn developed into a cancer. The court rejected the employer-defendant's argument that he wasn't liable because it wasn't foreseeable that the burn would cause cancer, which in turn would cause Smith's death: "The test is not whether these defendants could reasonably have foreseen that a burn would cause cancer and that S would die. The question is whether these defendants could reasonably foresee the type of injury which he suffered, namely, the burn. What, in the particular case, is the amount of damage which he suffers as a result of that burn, depends on the characteristics and constitution of the victim."

4. Should it matter whether the victim is partly responsible for his atypical vulnerability? For exposing himself to the injury that, he knows (or suspects), will result in atypically serious injury? What if the victim in *Frazier* had failed to take drugs prescribed to control his hemophilia because he didn't think he needed them, because he couldn't afford them, because he didn't like their taste? What if the victim in *Stamp* had simply forgotten to take his medicine that day, or had absentmindedly taken the wrong medicine, or had decided to stop taking the medicine altogether because he was tired of living and struggling to make it in his business?

Should it matter whether the defendant knew of (or suspected) the victim's condition? Whether the victim warned (or tried to warn) the defendant of his condition? Whether the *victim* was aware of his condition?

b. Third Party Intervention

(i) Medical Interveners

Williams v. State

Court of Appeals of Indiana, Second District.
782 N.E.2d 1039 (2003).

■ MATHIAS, JUDGE.

Jerome Williams ("Williams") was convicted of murder.[1] * * *

On December 17, 1999, Frank Townsend ("Townsend") was using his car to provide taxi services to earn extra money for the holidays. At approximately 11:00 p.m., Williams and his cousin, Cleve Williams ("Cleve"), left a friend's house and walked to a gas station. At the gas station, Williams used a payphone to call a cab. Both Williams and Cleve had handguns; Cleve had received one earlier that day from Williams. When Townsend arrived at the gas station, Williams sat in the front seat and Cleve sat in the back seat. Williams told Townsend to keep his hands on the steering wheel and drive.

A few minutes later, the car stopped near the intersection of North Beville and Coyner. Williams's and Cleve's aunt lived across the street from that location. Almost immediately after the car stopped, shooting started from the front seat area of the car. Cleve then pulled out his gun and started shooting. * * * The ambulance arrived shortly and took care of Townsend. * * *

On January 19, 2000, Townsend underwent major surgery, and his gallbladder was removed. For part of his hospitalization Townsend had a trach tube inserted to assist him with breathing. On March 4, 2000, Townsend was in pain and was disoriented. He had an elevated fever and high white blood cell count. On March 5, 2000, Townsend, while sitting in a chair, went into cardiac arrest when his trach tube became blocked by mucus. He did not recover from the lack of oxygen to his brain, and he was taken off of life support on March 8. * * *

Williams argues that there was insufficient evidence to support his conviction for murder because there was ample evidence presented that Townsend's death was caused by the intervening cause of medical malpractice. Williams contends that because no one was present in Townsend's room when his trach tube became plugged and because there was no indication that any of the hospital staff saw a call light from Townsend's room the intervening cause of medical malpractice actually caused Town-

1. Ind. Code § 35–42–1–1(2) ("A person who ... kills another human being while committing or attempting to commit arson, burglary, child molesting, consumer product tampering, criminal deviate conduct, kidnapping, rape, robbery, or carjacking ... commits murder....").

send's death. "An intervening cause is an independent force that breaks the causal connection between the actions of the defendant and the injury." *Wooley v. State,* 716 N.E.2d 919, 928 (Ind. 1999). Usually, a defendant is responsible for the death of the decedent if the injuries inflicted contributed either mediately or immediately to the death. In order for an intervening cause to break the chain of criminal responsibility, it must be so extraordinary that it would be unfair to hold the defendant responsible for the actual result.

In the present case, Townsend was shot multiple times by Williams and Cleve when they attempted to rob Townsend on December 17, 1999. Because of the injuries Townsend sustained, he was taken to the hospital, where he was treated and remained for several months until he died on March 8, 2000. The medical examiner testified to the fact that Townsend had been shot five times and to the extensive damage done to Townsend's body by the bullets. The medical examiner also stated that the cause of Townsend's death had been multiple gunshot wounds. * * *

Had it not been for Williams shooting Townsend several times, Townsend would not have been in the hospital nor would he have needed the trach tube. Any problems that occurred with the trach tube were therefore the result of the hospitalization and treatment necessitated by the injuries inflicted when Williams shot Townsend, and the use of the trach tube was not extraordinary. *See Wilson v. State,* 537 N.E.2d 1185, 1187 (Ind.1989) (insertion of tubes into victim's body not an intervening cause because it was necessitated by the injury inflicted on victim by defendant); *Gibson v. State,* 515 N.E.2d 492, 496 (Ind.1987) (staph infection was a direct result of the surgery and hospitalization necessitated by the injuries inflicted by defendant on the victim).

Williams's expert witness testified that she believed that there had been a breach of the standard of nursing care because no one was monitoring Townsend when his trach tube became plugged and because no one responded if Townsend called for help. No testimony was given that Townsend had called for help or that he had used his call light and received no response. Because Williams caused Townsend's injuries, which necessitated the insertion of the trach tube that became plugged, the plugging of the trach tube was not extraordinary and did not constitute an intervening cause. Sufficient evidence was presented to support Williams's conviction for murder.

People v. Stewart

Court of Appeals of New York.
40 N.Y.2d 692, 358 N.E.2d 487, 389 N.Y.S.2d 804 (1976).

■ WACHTLER, J.

The defendant was charged with stabbing and killing Daniel Smith. There is no doubt that the defendant stabbed Smith and that Smith later died at a hospital. However at trial one of the principal issues was whether the stab wound caused the death, or whether death was caused solely by medical malpractice at the hospital or by other intervening effective medical cause. The jury after being charged to consider several alternative counts of assault and homicide found the defendant guilty of manslaughter in the first degree. On this appeal the defendant urges that the evidence was only sufficient to establish assault because the People failed, as a matter of law, to prove that the stab wound caused Smith's death beyond a reasonable doubt.

The stabbing occurred when the defendant arrived unexpectedly at his former girlfriend's Brooklyn apartment on the evening of October 8, 1971. He found Daniel Smith there and ordered him to leave at knife point. When Smith suggested that they talk it over, the defendant rejected the idea and stabbed him in the stomach. Smith was then taken to a Brooklyn hospital where he was operated on later that evening. The following day the defendant was arrested and charged with assault. On November 8, 1971 Smith died in the hospital and the defendant was charged with murder.

At the trial the People called Dr. Dominck Di Maio, the Deputy Chief Medical Examiner for the Borough of Brooklyn, to establish the cause of death.... Di Maio stated that when Smith entered the hospital he had a single knife wound in the abdomen which had punctured the stomach. Prior to the operation he was given "a substance which is commonly called Curare" which paralyzes the chest muscles making it impossible for the patient to breathe on his own. As a result, the anesthesiologist had to "breathe" for him by squeezing a bag of oxygen into the lungs, a procedure called ventilation. During the initial stages of the operation, the surgeons discovered that Smith also had an incarcerated hernia. After they had sutured the wounds and completed the operation on the stomach, the surgeons proceeded to correct the hernia. During this phase of the operation "it was noted that the body was turning blue and there was no pulse, which means the person went into cardiac arrest." Smith then suffered a loss of oxygen to the brain and massive brain damage. He died a month later without ever regaining consciousness. At the time of death, the stomach wound had completely healed. Nevertheless at the trial, and in his autopsy report, Di Maio stated that in his opinion death was caused by "a stab wound of the abdomen, stomach, cardiac arrest during surgical correction of the stab wound and another operation which was indicated during the surgical procedure with sepsis, which means infection, and kidney shut down."

At the conclusion of the trial the court submitted various counts to the jury including common-law murder, manslaughter in the first degree[1] and assault in the first degree.[2] As indicated they found the defendant guilty of manslaughter in the first degree on the theory that he assaulted Daniel

1. On this count the court charged the jury under subdivision 1 of section 125.20 of the Penal Law which states: "A person is guilty of manslaughter in the first degree when * * * [with] intent to cause serious physical injury to another person, he causes the death of such person".

2. On this count the charge was pursuant to subdivision 1 of section 120.10 of the Penal Law which states: "A person is guilty of assault in the first degree when * * * [with] intent to cause serious physical injury to another person, he causes such injury to such person * * * by means of a deadly weapon or a dangerous instrument".

Smith to inflict serious physical injury and, without intending to do so, caused his death. * * *

One accused of homicide, of course, cannot be convicted unless it is shown that he "cause[d] the death of a person" (Penal Law, § 125.00). No matter what degree of homicide is charged this is always an essential element which the People must prove beyond a reasonable doubt. This means that the prosecutor must, at least, prove that the defendant's conduct was an actual cause of death, in the sense that it forged a link in the chain of causes which actually brought about the death. But something more is required before his conduct will be recognized as a legal cause of death warranting criminal sanctions. The requirement here is that "the defendant's actions must be *a sufficiently direct cause* of the ensuing death before there can be any imposition of criminal liability" *(People v. Kibbe,* 35 N.Y.2d 407, 413). Thus an "obscure or merely probable connection between an assault and death will, as in every case of alleged crime, require acquittal of the charge of any degree of homicide." *(People v. Brengard,* 265 N.Y. 100, 108).

We have held that "direct" does not mean "immediate". The defendant may be held to have caused the death even though it does not immediately follow the injury. Neither does "direct" mean "unaided" for the defendant will be held liable for the death although other factors, entering after the injury, have contributed to the fatal result. Thus if "felonious assault is operative as a cause of death, the causal co-operation of erroneous surgical or medical treatment does not relieve the assailant from liability for homicide" *(People v. Kane,* 213 NY 260, 270). But if "the death is solely attributable to the secondary agency, and not at all induced by the primary one * * * its intervention constitutes a defense" *(Kane, supra,* at p. 270).

In the *Kane* case the defendant shot a pregnant woman, Anna Klein, inflicting two "serious pistol-shot wounds"—one bullet lodged in the back three inches from the spine and the other fractured a rib and lodged in one of the lungs. The wounds caused a miscarriage; the miscarriage caused septic peritonitis and that led to death. The defendant argued that the miscarriage and the blood poisoning had been caused by improper medical treatment. We held that there was no testimony that the miscarriage or the septic condition "was or could have been developed" as the defendant claimed. On the other hand the evidence that was introduced was "sufficient to warrant the finding that the wounds inflicted by the defendant operated as causes of death even though the medical treatment may also have had some causative influence" *(Kane, supra,* at p. 277).

In *Kane* however we observed that if one of the interns at the hospital "had carelessly killed Anna Klein by the negligent administration of a deadly poison, the defendant would not have been liable for her death" *(Kane, supra,* at pp. 270–271). Thus despite the fact that the defendant had inflicted serious wounds, he could not have been convicted if the death was solely attributable to grossly negligent treatment. This often presents a delicate question. Later in the *Kane* opinion we cited with approval a case *(Commonwealth v. Eisenhower,* 181 Pa. 470) in which the defendant was held liable for homicide although there was evidence that a surgeon operating on the wound forgot to remove a drainage tube which later found its way into the spinal cord "and thus caused death." The Pennsylvania court said that even if this had occurred " 'the prisoner cannot escape by showing that death was the result of an accident occurring in an operation which his felonious act made necessary.' "

One of the problems in the case now before us is that there is some question as to whether the operation on the hernia was made necessary by the defendant's act. According to the testimony it was "medically correct", arguably necessary, clearly incidental—but the hernia itself was absolutely unrelated to the stab wound. Dr. Di Maio conceded that the chances were that if it had not been performed, the patient would have survived. This type of necessity is obviously of a different order than is normally required to fix responsibility for homicide. It is, we believe, a factor we must consider in determining whether the causal relationship is sufficiently direct. * * *

The other difficulty in the case is that it was never determined what actually caused the cardiac arrest. Dr. Di Maio acknowledged several possibilities which individually or combined could have created the condition. Most of the factors cited would indicate that the defendant's act was responsible either because it created a physical strain or shock or created the need for an operation which had the same effect. But Dr. Di Maio conceded that there was some evidence that the anesthesiologist failed to provide oxygen to the patient and that this alone could have been the cause of death. In our view if this occurred it was a grave neglect, perhaps gross negligence, but in any event sufficient to break whatever tenuous causal relationship existed at the time of this incidental operation. There is of course no showing that this was in fact the cause of death but on this record it cannot be ruled out as a possibility, certainly not beyond a reasonable doubt. * * *

Accordingly, the order of the Appellate Division should be modified by reducing the conviction from manslaughter in the first degree to assault in the first degree....

State v. Shabazz

Supreme Court of Connecticut.
246 Conn. 746, 719 A.2d 440 (1998).

■ BORDEN, ASSOCIATE JUSTICE.

[The defendant stabbed Michael Stewart with a knife in the course of a fight over the use of a pay phone on the New Haven green. Stewart was rushed to the hospital, where he died twelve hours later. Shabazz was convicted of murder under Conn. Gen. Stat. § 53a–54a(a) ("A person is guilty of murder when, with intent to cause the death of another person, he causes the death of such person").]

The defendant ... claims that the trial court improperly precluded him from introducing evidence that the gross negligence of the hospital caused the victim's death. We disagree. * * *

This claim is controlled by our decision in *State v. Jacobs,* 194 Conn. 119, 479 A.2d 226 (1984). In that case, we [held that] "*[g]ross maltreatment by attending physicians constitutes a defense only in the exceptional case where that maltreatment is the sole cause of the victim's death.*" *Id.*, at 125–26, 479 A.2d 226 (emphasis added).

In the present case, there was no evidence from which the jury rationally could have inferred that the hospital's gross negligence was the sole cause of the victim's death. [Defendant's experts both conceded that] the stab wounds inflicted by the defendant would have been fatal in the absence of any medical treatment. At the most, the purported gross negligence would have been a contributing cause of the death, not the sole cause. This would be insufficient under *Jacobs*. * * *

■ BERDON, ASSOCIATE JUSTICE, dissenting.

... I write separately because I ... disagree with the majority's conclusion that the trial court properly excluded relevant evidence tending to show that the gross negligence of Yale–New Haven Hospital (hospital) was the cause of the victim's death.

If the trial court had allowed the defendant, Abdullah Shabazz, to introduce all of the evidence relevant to the cause of death of the victim, Michael Stewart, the jury could have found that the negligence of the hospital was an intervening act that caused the victim's death. Specifically, the jury could have found that the proximate cause of the victim's death was not the stab wound inflicted upon him by the defendant, but, rather, the hospital's gross negligence in: (1) failing to monitor him in an intensive care setting; (2) failing to discover and suture a stab wound to his liver; and (3) administering anticoagulant medication to him—conduct that resulted in his bleeding to death. * * *

At the hearing in limine to determine the admissibility of evidence, the defendant proffered the testimony of two leading physicians that would have provided a basis upon which the jury could have found that the gross negligence of the hospital was the efficient, intervening cause of the victim's death. First, the defendant proffered the testimony of William Martin Stahl, a physician specializing in trauma surgery. Stahl testified that the victim's major injury was a stab wound to his liver that was treated properly and that after the operation no further bleeding was indicated. Stahl further testified, however, that the hospital breached the standard of care for a trauma patient because it failed to place the victim in a monitored environment for at least twenty-four hours after his operation and that, instead, hospital personnel sent the victim to an unmonitored hospital bed (floor).

Specifically, Stahl testified that: "This is not the type of patient with that degree of bleeding requiring four units of blood, liver lacerations are notorious for rebleeding, and he had a severe metabolic acidosis for a period of time, you don't send this patient to the floor.... He goes to the [intensive care unit (ICU)] or a monitored environment...."

In addition, Stahl testified that hospital personnel deviated from the standard of care by administering 5000 units of heparin, an anticoagulant, to the victim when he first arrived on the floor. Such treatment, according to Stahl, was totally contraindicated and predisposed the patient to further bleeding.... Stahl testified that if the victim's vital signs, urine output and blood gases had been monitored properly, the bleeding "would have been detected before he died and could have been corrected."

.... According to Stahl, the victim had "a better than 90 percent chance of surviving" the liver wound, and "this chance was taken away [by the hospital] ... in the postoperative period."

The defendant also proffered the testimony of Cyril H. Wecht, a physician specializing in anatomic, clinical and forensic pathology. Wecht testified that the hospital's negligent care following the victim's removal from the postoperative recovery room caused his death. In Wecht's opinion, the victim had recovered well from surgery, despite the hospital's negligence in completely missing one stab wound in the liver and failing to diagnose a laceration in one of his lungs. According to Wecht, [the victim should have been sent to an intensive care unit where he would be very carefully monitored also because he was] "known to be a drug addict. That alone is a big red flag. These people can have all kinds of problems including withdrawal." * * *

The majority opinion confuses sole proximate cause with intervening cause as a result of dicta from *State v. Jacobs,* 194 Conn. 119, 479 A.2d 226 (1984). In *Jacobs,* this court stated in dicta that "[g]ross maltreatment by attending physicians constitutes a defense only in the exceptional case where that maltreatment is the sole cause of the victim's death." *Id.*, at 125–26. The negligence in *Jacobs* was not gross negligence and the court found that "[a]t best, the defendant's offer [tended] to show that the victim might have recovered if greater skill and care had been employed in his care and treatment." *Id.*, at 123–24 n.2. Thus, *Jacobs* was not a gross negligence case, and to rely on dicta from that case that is contrary to the law of intervening cause is inappropriate.

.... In their treatise, Professors LaFave and Scott, discussing causation, wrote: "Intervening Cause: Acts of a Third Person. The most common case involves the negligent treatment of wounds by a doctor or nurse. A, intending to kill B, merely wounds him; but the doctor so negligently treats the wound that B dies. It is generally held that A is guilty of murdering B, i.e., that A's act legally caused B's death, unless the doctor's treatment *is so bad as to constitute gross negligence* or intentional malpractice." * * *

In the present case, whether the hospital's treatment of the victim constituted gross negligence of the nature that would constitute an intervening cause was an issue that the defendant was entitled to have the jury decide. The testimony of Stahl and Wecht should have been admitted and the jury should have been instructed on intervening causation....

QUESTIONS AND COMMENTS

1. *Medical Interveners.* Among potentially intervening causes, medical (mal)treatment is particularly common. Consider the following hypotheticals. In each, the Defendant D intends to kill the Victim V and runs him over with her car, but V does not immediately die; instead, his ankle is broken:

1. V goes to the hospital and dies of an infection that's prevalent there; he is no more susceptible to infection as a result of the broken ankle.
2. V is given phenylbutazone to reduce inflammation and develops fatal aplastic anemia; the treatment of V's wounds with the anti-inflammatory drug is non-negligent and death from this *particular* cause is quite rare, though death from the non-negligent treatment of the sorts of wounds that V received is, in general, considerably less rare (mostly because of deaths from anesthesia during surgery).
3. V develops a wound-related infection and is *negligently* given antibiotics to which he develops a fatally adverse reaction.
4. V is killed by a surgeon (a nurse) who has it in for him and who realizes he has a better chance of getting away with murder once he's got V on the operating table (on life support).

Is D causally responsible for the deaths in any or all of these cases? Under the standards articulated in *Williams*? *Stewart*? *Shabazz*? The *Shabazz* dissent?

2. Does it matter (does anything else matter?) how the autopsy would be written: does the fact that the autopsy report in hypothetical 2 would state that the patient died of aplastic anemia mean that the defendant is not causally responsible for the death, even though one could readily say that V died as a result of *non-negligent* treatment of the wound D inflicted?

Consider in this regard the holding in a British case, Regina v. Cheshire, [1991] 3 All E.R. 670:

> If at the time of death the original wound is still an operating cause and a substantial cause, then the death can properly said to be the result of the wound, albeit that some other cause of death is also operating. Only if it can be said that the original wounding is merely the setting in which another cause operates can it be said that the death does not result from the wound.

Did Williams die of the wound the defendant inflicted or did he suffocate? Did he suffocate because he required treatment for the wound that leads to an atypical risk of suffocation? Did the hypothetical V who died of aplastic anemia die from the wound or was the wound merely the setting in which he developed a disease? If you were explaining how the hypothetical V died to an aggrieved family member, would you emphasize his atypical reaction to a common drug or emphasize the defendant's role in putting him in harm's way? Does that judgment depend on the foreseeability of the particular mode of death, and if so, how do we decide at what level of particularity to describe the "mode of death"?

See, in this regard, Mark G. Kelman, "Interpretive Construction in the Substantive Criminal Law," 33 Stan. L. Rev. 591, 640–42 (1981), and Michael S. Moore, "Foreseeing Harm Opaquely," in Action and Value in Criminal Law 125–27 (Stephen Shute et al. eds. 1993): Kelman and Moore each argues that the concept of foreseeability is inherently arbitrary and subject to manipulation because each harm-causing event can be described in many different ways, at different levels of generality, and that at higher levels of generality, the event will seem more foreseeable. Death from aplastic anemia (relatively unforeseeable?) can be readily characterized as "death from complications arising from routine non-negligent medical care" and *that* is foreseeable.

3. Does it matter to the *Williams* court whether or not nurses ignored a call button? Why? Does it matter to the *Stewart* court whether the stabbing *necessitated* the hernia operation? Why? What if it were merely safer to have the operation *now*, given that the patient was, as a stabbing victim, at marginally greater risk in surgical situations so that the number of separate surgeries should be minimized?

4. The *Stewart* court and the *Shabazz* majority plainly hold that a defendant is causally responsible if the wound kills in fact, no matter how it is treated. But doesn't that do away with proximate cause altogether? Or should there be some rule that bad medical treatment has no effect on foreseeability because such bad treatment is always within the zone of foreseeable risk?

5. Compare the tests invoked in *Stewart*, supra, and *Kern*, infra. Does it make sense to use one test to determine the sufficiency of all intervening causes? Or is there something about medical professionals that would require/justify a different (a higher? a lower?) standard in their case? Could it be that so many of potential interveners are doctors—particularly in homicide cases? In that case, should we have a different test for certain sub-sets of medical professionals, such as EMTs or ER doctors and nurses? Is it *unfair* to medical professionals, given that they are so much more likely to be placed in situations where their errors might cause (serious, greater) harm and/or that they engaged in a "helping profession" and "treatment" (as opposed to the potential interveners in *Kern* and *Kibbe,* infra, who hit someone while driving down the street)? Would it deter people from entering the medical profession, from entering emergency medicine? Should any of this matter for purposes of determining whether the defendant's conduct caused the proscribed result?

(ii) Other Third Party Intervention

People v. Kibbe

Court of Appeals of New York.
35 N.Y.2d 407 (1974).

■ GABRIELLI, JUDGE.

The factual setting of the bizarre events of a cold winter night of December 30, 1970, as developed by the testimony, including the voluntary statements of the defendants, reveal the following: During the early evening the defendants were drinking in a Rochester tavern along with the victim, George Stafford. The bartender testified that Stafford was displaying and "flashing" one hundred dollar bills, was thoroughly intoxicated and was finally "shut off" because of his inebriated condition. At some time between 8:15 and 8:30 p.m., Stafford inquired if someone would give him a ride to Canandaigua, New York, and the defendants, who, according to their statements, had already decided to steal Stafford's money, agreed to drive him there in Kibbe's automobile. The three men left the bar and proceeded to another bar where Stafford was denied service due to his condition. The defendants and Stafford then walked across the street to a third bar where they were served, and each had another drink or two.

After they left the third bar, the three men entered Kibbe's automobile and began the trip toward Canandaigua. Krall drove the car while Kibbe demanded that Stafford turn over any money he had. In the course of an exchange, Kibbe slapped Stafford several times, took his money, then compelled him to lower his trousers and to take off his shoes to be certain that Stafford had given up all his money; and when they were satisfied that Stafford had no more money on his person, the defendants forced Stafford to exit the Kibbe vehicle.

As he was thrust from the car, Stafford fell onto the shoulder of the rural two-lane highway on which they had been traveling. His trousers were still down around his ankles, his shirt was rolled up towards his chest, he was shoeless and he had also been stripped of any outer clothing. Before the defendants pulled away, Kibbe placed Stafford's shoes and jacket on the shoulder of the highway. Although Stafford's eyeglasses were in the Kibbe vehicle, the defendants, either through inadvertence or perhaps by specific design, did not give them to Stafford before they drove away. It was some time between 9:30 and 9:40 p.m. when Kibbe and Krall abandoned Stafford on the side of the road. The temperature was near zero, and, although it was not snowing at the time, visibility was occasionally obscured by heavy winds which intermittently blew previously fallen snow into the air and across the highway; and there was snow on both sides of the road as a result of previous plowing operations. The structure nearest the point where Stafford was forced from the defendants' car was a gasoline service station situated nearly one half of a mile away on the other side of the highway. There was no artificial illumination on this segment of the rural highway.

At approximately 10:00 p.m. Michael W. Blake, a college student, was operating his pickup truck in the northbound lane of the highway in question. Two cars, which were approaching from the opposite direction, flashed their headlights at Blake's vehicle. Immediately after he had passed the second car, Blake saw Stafford sitting in the road in the middle of the northbound lane with his hands up in the air. Blake stated that he was operating his truck at a speed of approximately 50 miles per hour, and that he "didn't have time to react" before his vehicle struck Stafford. After he brought his truck to a stop and returned to try to be of assistance to Stafford, Blake observed that the man's trousers were down around his ankles and his shirt was pulled up around his chest. A deputy sheriff called to the accident scene also confirmed the fact that the victim's trousers were around his ankles, and that Stafford was wearing no shoes or jacket.

At the trial, the Medical Examiner of Monroe County testified that death had occurred fairly rapidly from massive head injuries. In addition, he found proof of a high degree of intoxication with a .25%, by weight, of alcohol concentration in the blood.

For their acts, the defendants were convicted of murder, robbery in the second degree and grand larceny in the third degree. However, the defendants basically challenge only their convictions of murder, claiming that the People failed to establish beyond a reasonable doubt that their acts "caused the death of another", as required by the statute (Penal Law, § 125.25, subd. 2)[a].... In answering this question, we are required to determine whether the defendants may be convicted of murder for the occurrences which have been described. They contend that the actions of Blake, the driver of the pickup truck, constituted both an intervening and superseding cause which relieves them of criminal responsibility for Stafford's death. There is ... no statutory provision regarding the effect of an intervening cause of injury as it relates to the criminal responsibility of one who sets in motion the machinery which ultimately results in the victim's death; and there is surprisingly little case law dealing with the subject. Moreover, analogies to causation in civil cases are neither controlling nor dispositive, since, as this court has previously stated: "A long distance separates the negligence which renders one criminally liable from that which establishes civil liability" (People v. Rosenheimer, 209 N.Y. 115, 123, 102 N.E. 530, 533); and this is due in large measure to the fact that the standard or measure of persuasion by which the prosecution must convince the trier of all the essential elements of the crime charged, is beyond a reasonable doubt (In re Winship, 397 U.S. 358, 361, 90 S.Ct. 1068, 25 L.Ed.2d 368). Thus, actions which may serve as a predicate for civil liability may not be sufficient to constitute a basis for the imposition of criminal sanctions because of the different purposes of these two branches of law.... However, to be a sufficiently direct cause of death so as to warrant the imposition of a criminal penalty therefor, it is not necessary that the ultimate harm be intended by the actor. It will suffice if it can be said beyond a reasonable doubt, as indeed it can be here said, that the ultimate harm is something which should have been foreseen as being reasonably related to the acts of the accused. * * *

We subscribe to the requirement that the defendants' actions must be a sufficiently direct cause of the ensuing death before there can be any imposition of criminal liability, and recognize, of course, that this standard is greater than that required to serve as a basis for tort liability. Applying these criteria to the defendants' actions, we conclude that their activities on the evening of December 30, 1970 were a sufficiently direct cause of the death of George Stafford so as to warrant the imposition of criminal sanctions. In engaging in what may properly be described as a despicable course of action, Kibbe and Krall left a helplessly intoxicated man without his eyeglasses in a position from which, because of these attending circumstances, he could not extricate himself and whose condition was such that he could not even protect himself from the elements. The defendants do not dispute the fact that their conduct evinced a depraved indifference to human life which created a grave risk of death, but rather they argue that it was just as likely that Stafford would be miraculously rescued by a good

a. N.Y. Penal Law § 125.25(2) ("A person is guilty of murder in the second degree when ... [u]nder circumstances evincing a depraved indifference to human life, he recklessly engages in conduct which creates a grave risk of death to another person, and thereby causes the death of another person.").—EDS.

samaritan. We cannot accept such an argument. There can be little doubt but that Stafford would have frozen to death in his state of undress had he remained on the shoulder of the road. The only alternative left to him was the highway, which in his condition, for one reason or another, clearly foreboded the probability of his resulting death.

Under the conditions surrounding Blake's operation of his truck (i.e., the fact that he had his low beams on as the two cars approached; that there was no artificial lighting on the highway; and that there was insufficient time in which to react to Stafford's presence in his lane), we do not think it may be said that any supervening wrongful act occurred to relieve the defendants from the directly foreseeable consequences of their actions. In short, we will not disturb the jury's determination that the prosecution proved beyond a reasonable doubt that their actions came clearly within the statute and "cause(d) the death of another person".

People v. Warner–Lambert Co.

Court of Appeals of New York.
51 N.Y.2d 295 (1980).

■ JONES, JUDGE.

[An explosion in a Warner–Lambert factory killed six workers. The corporation and various of its officers were charged with manslaughter in the second degree in violation of section 125.15 of the Penal Law and criminally negligent homicide in violation of section 125.10 of the Penal Law.]

There can be no doubt that there was competent evidence before the Grand Jury here which, if accepted as true, would have been sufficient to establish the existence of a broad, undifferentiated risk of explosion from ambient MS dust which had been brought to the attention of defendants.[a] . . .

[The prosecution presented three theories as to the actual cause of the explosion.] [T]he proof with respect to the actual cause of the explosion is speculative only, and as to at least one of the major hypotheses—that involving oxygen liquefaction—there was no evidence that that process was foreseeable or known to any of the defendants. In sum, there is no proof sufficient to support a finding that defendants foresaw or should have foreseen the physical cause of the explosion. This being so there was not legally sufficient evidence to establish the offenses charged. . . .

It has been the position of the People that but-for causation is all that is required for the imposition of criminal liability. Thus, it is their submission, reduced to its simplest form, that there was evidence of a foreseeable and indeed foreseen risk of explosion of MS dust and that in consequence of defendants' failure to remove the dust a fatal explosion occurred. The chain of physical events by which the explosion was set off, i.e., its particular

a. "[M]agnesium stearate (MS) [is] a dry, dustlike lubricant which was applied by hand, then into a die-cut punch (a Uniplast machine) which was sprayed with a cooling agent (liquid nitrogen), where the gum was formed into the square tablets. . . . Both MS and liquid nitrogen are considered safe and are widely used in the industry."—EDS.

cause, is to them a matter of total indifference. On oral argument the People contended that liability could be imposed if the cause of the explosion were the lighting of a match by an uninvited intruder or the striking of a bolt of lightning. In effect they would hold defendants to the status of guarantors until the ambient dust was removed. It thus appears that the People would invoke an expanded application of proximate cause principles lifted from the civil law of torts.

We have rejected the application of any such sweeping theory of culpability under our criminal law, however.... The critical issue in People v. Kibbe [supra] was whether the defendants should be held criminally liable for murder when the particular cause of death was vehicular impact rather than freezing. Under the theory now advanced by the People it would have been irrelevant that death had been the consequence of one particular chain of causation rather than another; it would have been enough that the defendants exposed their victim to the risk of death and that he died.... To analogize the actual situation in the case now before us to that in Kibbe it might be hypothesized that the abandoned victim in Kibbe instead of being either frozen to death or killed when struck by a passing motor vehicle was killed when struck by an airplane making an emergency landing on the highway or when hit by a stray bullet from a hunter's rifle—occasions of death not reasonably to have been foreseen when the defendants abandoned their victim.

People v. Kern

Supreme Court of New York, Appellate Division, Second Department.
149 A.D.2d 187, 545 N.Y.S.2d 4 (1989).

■ MOLLEN, PRESIDING JUSTICE.

[The facts of this case are reproduced on p. 418 of the casebook.]

The defendants' ... assertion that Blum's alleged negligent operation of his vehicle was an intervening proximate cause of Griffith's death is ... without merit.

Blum testified that, as he was driving on the highway in the vicinity of the Cross Bay Boulevard exit, he was in the left westbound lane of the highway. The car in front of him slowed down and instead of applying his brakes, Blum proceeded to move over to the middle lane. At that point, Blum heard a "bang". Noticing that his windshield was cracked, Blum pulled over onto the right shoulder of the highway. Unaware of what he had hit, Blum looked back onto the highway and, after he observed that the traffic appeared to be flowing normally, he resumed his trip to Brooklyn. Blum explained that he had never considered the possibility that he had struck a person. When he arrived home, Blum realized the full extent of damage to his car and, after speaking with his father, Blum and his father returned to the scene of the accident where they spoke to the police. * * *

Based on the circumstances surrounding the incident, including the dark early morning hour, it cannot be said that an intervening wrongful act occurred to relieve the defendants from the directly foreseeable consequences of their actions. * * * Moreover, even if we assume that Blum was less than cautious in the operation of his vehicle, the facts demonstrate that his actions were not the *sole* cause of Griffith's ensuing death since it was the defendants' wrongful conduct which forced Griffith to seek refuge from his assailants by crossing the highway.

QUESTIONS AND COMMENTS

1. Two years after the New York Court of Appeals' decision in *Kibbe* excerpted above, a federal appellate court granted Kibbe's federal habeas petition on the ground that "the trial judge's instructions permitted the jury . . . to disregard Kibbe's colorable claim that, as to the murder charge, his actions had not caused the death of a decedent and thus violated Kibbe's constitutional right to have every element of the crime with which he was charged proven beyond a reasonable doubt" under In re Winship, 397 U.S. 358 (1970). Kibbe v. Henderson, 534 F.2d 493 (2d Cir. 1976), rev'd, 431 U.S. 145 (1977). Here is the Second Circuit's rendition of Blake's fatal collision with Stafford:

> About half an hour after Kibbe and Krall had abandoned Stafford, Michael Blake, a college student, was driving his pickup truck northbound on the highway at 50 miles an hour, ten miles per hour in excess of the posted speed limit. A car passed Blake in a southbound direction and the driver flashed his headlights at Blake. Immediately thereafter, Blake saw Stafford sitting in the middle of the northbound lane with his hands in the air. Blake testified that he "went into a kind of shock" as soon as he saw Stafford, and that he did not apply his brakes. Blake further testified that he did not attempt to avoid hitting Stafford because he "didn't have time to react."

Now do you think that Kibbe had a "colorable" claim that Blake's conduct constituted an intervening cause? What if Blake had been drunk? What's the relevance of Stafford's intoxication? Does it mitigate Blake's responsibility? Kibbe's?

2. The courts in *Kibbe* and *Kern* mention that the defendants' conduct was "despicable." What relevance does (should) the despicability of the defendant's conduct have for the determination of whether that conduct caused the proscribed result?

3. Analyze *Kibbe* under the Model Penal Code's causation provision. Distinguish the Model Penal Code analysis from that set out in *Kibbe*.

4. In People v. Arzon, 92 Misc.2d 739, 401 N.Y.S. 156 (N.Y.Sup.Ct. 1978), the court sustained the murder conviction of a defendant who had set a fire on the fifth floor of his apartment building. Firemen perished, largely because in the course of escaping the building after failing in their efforts to subdue the fire the defendant had set, they were overcome by smoke emanating from another fire that had broken out independently on the second floor. Remarking that "the defendant's conduct need not be the sole and exclusive factor in the victim's death," the court held that "an individual is criminally liable if his conduct was a sufficiently direct cause of the death, and the ultimate harm is something which should have been foreseen as being reasonably related to his acts." The firemen's death was

foreseeable because fire is "nonselective and uncontrollable in its destructiveness."

Assume that we will never know precisely what set off the explosion in *Warner-Lambert*. Imagine, then, that the defense is permitted to hypothesize any story it wants about what triggered the explosion that suits its purposes best. Is there any story that it could tell about what caused the explosion that would relieve it of liability, given the *Arzon* holding? Assume that the explosion occurred as a result of deliberate arson by a third party: would that relieve the company of causal responsibility? Is it important that the triggering mechanism have been foreseeable, or merely that the company have foreseen that—in the event that any sort of triggering mechanism occur—the dust would intensify an explosion?

5. Is *Kern* consistent with *Kibbe* and *Warner-Lambert*? What is the connection between the "sole cause" and "foreseeability" tests as applied to intervening causes?

C. ATTEMPT

The law of causation deals with a specific harm-related problem—the connection between harm and conduct. Assuming the defendant's behavior matches every element set out in the definition of the offense, objective and subjective, the law of causation answers the question whether the *particular* result that occurred in a *particular* way was caused by the defendant's *particular* conduct. In a typical homicide causation case, for instance, we have a dead body, but must decide whether the defendant's actions (in fact? or merely in the sense that we find it reasonable to attribute responsibility to him?) caused the death.

The law of attempt deals with another harm-related issue—*its absence.* In an attempt, the defendant hasn't managed to satisfy each element of the completed offense. Though she did her best, she has fallen short for some reason. The question is whether she should be punished for trying, and if so, whether she should be punished as harshly as she would have been punished had she succeeded. In a typical homicide *attempt* case, then, we don't have a dead body, but must decide whether the defendant tried hard enough to come up with one to warrant punishment nonetheless.

1. GRADING

Model Penal Code § 5.05. Grading of Criminal Attempt.

Except as otherwise provided ... attempt [is a crime] of the same grade and degree as the most serious offense that is attempted.... An attempt ... to commit a [capital crime or a] felony of the first degree is a felony of the second degree.

Model Penal Code Commentaries § 5.05, at 489–90.

The theory of the grading system may be stated simply. To the extent that sentencing depends upon the antisocial disposition of the actor and the demonstrated need for a corrective sanction, there is likely to be little difference in the gravity of the required measures depending on the consummation or the failure of the plan. It is only when and insofar as the severity of sentence is designed for general deterrent purposes that a distinction on the ground is likely to have reasonable force. It is doubtful ... that the threat of punishment for the inchoate crime can add significantly to the net deterrent efficacy of the sanction threatened for the substantive offense that is the actor's object which he, by hypothesis, ignores.

Cal. Penal Code § 664. Attempts; punishment.

Every person who attempts to commit any crime, but fails, or is prevented or intercepted in its perpetration, shall be punished where no provision is made by law for the punishment of those attempts, as follows:

(a) If the crime attempted is punishable by imprisonment in the state prison, the person guilty of the attempt shall be punished by imprisonment in the state prison for one-half the term of imprisonment prescribed upon a conviction of the offense attempted. However, if the crime attempted is willful, deliberate, and premeditated murder, ... the person guilty of that attempt shall be punished by imprisonment in the state prison for life with the possibility of parole....

The California scheme—in which attempts are punished less harshly across the board than the consummated object offense would be punished—is the traditional, and more commonplace, one, though the Model Penal Code approach has had modest influence. See, e.g., Del. Code tit. 11 § 531; Pa. Stat. Ann. tit. 18 § 905. The following excerpts consider the merits of the traditional grading scheme.

H.L.A. Hart, Punishment and Responsibility: Essays in the Philosophy of Law 129–31 (1968)

[E]ven from the point of view of the general deterrent, the skeptical argument which suggested that there is no case for punishing an attempt is ... mistaken. It is perfectly true that those who commit crimes intend to succeed, but this does not show that punishing a man for an unsuccessful attempt will not increase the efficacy of the law's threats.... [F]irst, there must be many who are not completely confident that they will succeed in their criminal objective, but will be prepared to run the risk of punishment if they can be assured that they have to pay nothing for attempts which fail.... [There must also] be many cases where men might with good or bad reason believe that if they succeed in committing some crime they will escape, but if they fail they may be caught. Treason is only the most obvious of such cases....

A more difficult question concerns the almost universal practice of legal systems of fixing a more severe punishment for the completed crime than for the mere attempt.... [A] retributive theory in which severity of punishment is proportional to the allegedly evil intentions of the criminal is in grave difficulty; for there seems to be no difference in wickedness, though there may be in skill, between the successful and the unsuccessful attempt in this respect.... [From a deterrent perspective, there are crimes] whose consummation occupies a considerable space of time so that the criminal may have time between the attempt and its consummation to think again.... He might desist, but if he is already involved in the full penalty by virtue of merely having attempted to commit the crime, he may have no motive for desisting. Similar reasoning is presented when it is pointed out that if a man shoots and misses there is no reason why he should not shoot again if he is already liable to the full penalty for his unsuccessful attempt.

Stephen J. Schulhofer, "Attempt," in 1 Encyclopedia of Crime and Justice 91, 97 (1st ed. 1983)

[T]he most plausible explanation for more lenient treatment of attempts is that the community's resentment and demand for punishment are not aroused to the same degree when serious harm has been averted. This explanation, however, raises further questions.... To what extent should the structure of penalties serve to express intuitive societal judgments that cannot be rationalized in terms of such instrumental goals as deterrence, isolation, rehabilitation, and even retribution—that is, condemnation reflecting the moral culpability of the act?

QUESTIONS AND COMMENTS

1. *Why Punish Attempts?* The question of *how* attempts should be punished—particularly in relation to punishment for the consummated offense—doesn't arise, of course, until it is settled *whether* they should be punished at all. At the very least, the answer to the latter question would inform the answer to the former.

Hart finds the grading question "more difficult" than the justifiability question. Do you agree? Can you make a case *against* punishing attempts from the perspectives of the various traditional rationales for punishment? The Model Penal Code drafters were quite clear about "the primary purpose of punishing attempts": "to neutralize dangerous individuals." Commentaries § 5.01, at 323. The attempt serves as an "indication that the actor is disposed toward [criminal] activity, not alone on this occasion but on others." Commentaries art. 5, at 294 (intro.). The drafters saw no point in punishing attempts as a matter of deterrence. What would be the point of threatening attempts with punishment if the consummated offense is already proscribed? If a person ignores the threat of punishment for a successful attempt, why would she pay any attention to the threat of punishment for an unsuccessful one? If she didn't *intend* to succeed in her attempt, then—under traditional attempt law—she wouldn't be liable for an attempt in the first place. See section 3 (mens rea) infra.

Consider two other possible justifications for punishing attempts. Perhaps attempts ought to be punished because even an attempt can inflict (psychological) harm upon the intended victim. The target of an attempted murder surely will experience some distress, assuming, of course, she was aware of the attempt at the time—or perhaps learned about it after the fact. Attempts, in other words, would be punishable as a form of assault. See *Commonwealth v. Slaney,* part A, supra; cf. R.A. Duff, Criminal Attempts (1996) (attempts as attacks on legally protected interests). Unlike in tort law, however, victim awareness of the attempt is *not* a prerequisite for criminal liability. Cf. Restatement (Second) of Torts § 22 ("An attempt to inflict a harmful or offensive contact or to cause an apprehension of such contact does not make the actor liable for an assault if the other does not become aware of the attempt before it is terminated."). Then again, perhaps attempts are punishable insofar as the harm of criminal law is not personal, but public. And, as *Slaney* points out, an attempt can disturb the "public peace" too. (Consider, for instance, the facts in *Slaney*, where a shot is fired outside a restaurant.)

At any rate, do we have to punish all attempts? Or would it make sense to punish attempts only for certain crimes? Serious ones, perhaps? Or those "whose consummation occupies a considerable space of time," in Hart's words? American criminal law punishes attempts for all offenses, from violations to misdemeanors to felonies. German criminal law, by contrast, punishes attempts only for felonies and for selected misdemeanors. German Penal Code § 23(1).

2. Take the case of a defendant who sticks his hand in one pocket, expecting to snatch a wallet, only to find the first pocket he sticks his hand in empty. If we punish attempted larceny and larceny identically, does the defendant have any selfish incentive not to stick his hand in the other pocket, hoping to find the wallet there? Why not? What if we punished *each* attempt separately: must we punish (as California does) the attempted pickpocket half as much as the successful one to give incentives to desist or could we get the same effect by punishing the person who made two distinct efforts to steal the wallet twice as much as the one who made but one effort? Are attempted murderers different, because we cannot really do any more than send someone to jail for life, much less do more than put them to death?

3. Those who drafted the Model Penal Code (and Schulhofer) apparently assume that those who are guilty of attempting a crime are indistinguishable from those who consummate offenses except for distinctions in luck, and that these distinctions in luck are of no moment morally or in terms of assessing the offender's dangerousness. (If that's so, why differentiate between the punishment of attempts and consummated offenses (only) in the most serious cases? Why would the difference between attempted murder and murder matter, but not between attempted burglary and burglary (at most a second degree felony in the Model Penal Code)?) There is another possible distinction: those who fail may be (relatively or very) *inept*. Should (mild or severe) ineptitude matter to an incapacitationist? A retributivist?

Can there be any doubt about the intuition that someone who tries, but fails, to inflict harm deserves less punishment than someone who succeeds? From the victim's perspective, do I feel the same resentment if you take a swing at me and miss as I would if your aim had been better?

From the offender's perspective, do I feel the same guilt if I try to shoot you dead as I would if I succeeded? Should we disregard these intuitions as irrational (and therefore irrelevant?) or should we try to construct a law of attempt that reflects them?

And what about the possibility that (at least some of) those who fail are more *ambivalent* than those who succeed and fail because of that ambivalence? Might someone fail to kill her (more-or-less?) intended victim in part because she has (some) moral hesitations that interfere with her prowess?

Is the problem that we are trying to establish a general rule that tells us how to punish attempts when people fail to consummate crimes for quite different reasons: (i) the person whose expertly-shot victim is saved by the dazzling skill of the emergency room doctors, (ii) the person who shoots the shoulder instead of the head or the heart, ostensibly aiming to kill, but perhaps bedeviled by some degree of gnawing moral doubt, and (iii) the person who is thrown to the ground by police, before he has either had the chance to shoot or to repent and decide never to shoot, may all have committed an attempt. But can a general law of attempt deal with the fact that some attempts are, at core, *unfinished* and others, at core, are *unsuccessful*? That some of the unsuccessful ones fail because the defendant's conduct was deficient and others because victims (or their allies) foil the most perfect plans? For a rough distinction between unfinished and unsuccessful attempts, compare Model Penal Code § 5.01(1)(a), (b) (unsuccessful, but complete, attempt) with § 5.01(1)(c) (unfinished attempt).

Or is the problem that we are trying to resolve the grading question ex ante, as a matter of legislation? Would it be preferable to leave the differentiation among types of attempt, and between attempt and consummated offense, to the sentencing judge? Consider the U.S. Sentencing Guidelines provision on attempts.

U.S. Sentencing Guidelines § 2X1.1. Attempt . . .

(a) Base Offense Level: The base offense level from the guideline for the substantive offense. . . .

(b) Specific Offense Characteristics

(1) If an attempt, decrease by 3 levels, unless the defendant completed all the acts the defendant believed necessary for successful completion of the substantive offense or the circumstances demonstrate that the defendant was about to complete all such acts but for apprehension or interruption by some similar event beyond the defendant's control.

Background: In most prosecutions for . . . attempts, the substantive offense was substantially completed or was interrupted or prevented on the verge of completion by the intercession of law enforcement authorities or the victim. In such cases, no reduction of the offense level is warranted. Sometimes, however, the arrest occurs well before the defendant . . . has completed the acts necessary for the substantive offense. Under such circumstances, a reduction of 3 levels is provided under § 2X1.1(b)(1). . . .

2. ACT

a. Distinguishing Non-punishable Preparation from Punishable Attempts

Why do we need to differentiate "mere" (non-punishable) preparation from punishable attempts? Surely, there are cases in which a defendant who has (arguably) attempted one crime has already committed some separate crime in so doing. For instance, in situations in which a victim fights off her assailant before he is able to rape her, the assailant will almost certainly be guilty of another crime or crimes (e.g., battery, sexual battery, perhaps kidnapping) whether or not we decide that he has attempted rape. But if this is the case, we should plainly punish him for committing *that* crime without regard to attempt law.

More typically, though, when we're dealing with attempts, we're considering situations in which the defendant's conduct is not harmful in and of itself. Thus, we wouldn't punish her unless we were convinced that she was going to do something *else* that we thought *was* harmful. To the extent this proposition is true, we may well distinguish preparation from attempt not to determine when harm has occurred but to have some test (and associated set of jury instructions) to guide the following inquiry: when are we adequately sure that the defendant firmly intended to commit a crime, and would have done so but for circumstances outside her control, looking just at her conduct (rather than things that we know about her more generally—of the form, "the defendant's the sort of person to have intended...") or things that we know (or more accurately, *could* know) because the defendant has confessed them?

One way of "testing" the intuition that we're not trying to distinguish harms from non-harms is to note that we wouldn't punish most things that we call attempts if we believed that the defendant were not going to do anything more than he'd already done (or, in the case of impossible attempts, see *People v. Dlugash*, infra, something *different* than what he has already done, rather than something *further*). Another way of testing this intuition is to note that defendants accused of attempt have posed no "objective" risk of causing harm (in the sense that shooting bullets up in the air poses a risk of harm, even before they come down and hit someone, or that driving drunk poses a risk of harm, regardless of the defendant's subsequent efforts to avoid such harm); rather it is because we believe people who do certain things typically go on to do certain other, harmful, things that we might picture the *defendant* as "risky." Thus, attempt is *not* a "risk creation" crime either in the way that reckless or drunk driving is or in the way that leaving a loaded gun in the presence of small children might be.

It is vital to note that when we come back to discuss voluntary renunciation or abandonment, see subsection b., infra, we have to deal with the possibility that abandonment appears a reasonable defense only on the supposition that the attempt itself was not culpable, but was only culpable as an *indicator of expected future conduct*, an indicator that proved false or misleading when the defendant voluntarily abandoned her attempt.

(i) Some Traditional Tests Distinguishing Preparation From Attempt

King v. Barker

New Zealand Court of Appeal.
[1924] N.Z.L.R. 865.

That the common law has recognized the distinction between acts of attempt and acts of preparation ... is undoubted.... The rule ... suggested in R. v. Eagleton [169 E.R. 826 (1855)] was that in order to constitute a criminal attempt, as opposed to mere preparation, the accused must have taken the last step he was able to take along the road of his criminal intent. He must have done all he intended to do and was able to do for the purpose of effectuating his criminal purpose. When he has stopped short of this, whether because he has repented, or because he has been prevented, or because the time or occasion for going further has not arrived ... [he] still remains within the region of innocent preparation....

Subsequent authorities make it clear that the [*Eagleton*] test is not the true one. [R. v. White [1910] 2 K.B. 124] held that the first administration of poison in a case of intended slow poisoning by repeated doses amounted in itself to attempted murder. It is said by the Court: "The completion of one of a series of acts intended by a man to result in killing is an attempt to murder, even though the completed act would not, unless followed by other acts, result in killing...."

An act done with intent to commit a crime is not a criminal attempt unless it is of such a nature as to be itself sufficient evidence of the criminal intent with which it is done. A criminal attempt is an act which shows criminal intent on the face of it. The case must be one in which *res ipsa loquitur*. An act, on the other hand, which is in its own nature and on the face of it innocent is not a criminal attempt. It cannot be brought within the scope of criminal attempt by evidence aliunde [e.g., through admission or confession] as to the criminal purpose with which it is done.... That a man's unfulfilled criminal purposes should be punishable they must be manifested not by his words, merely, or by acts which are in themselves of innocent or ambiguous significance, but by overt acts which are sufficient in themselves to declare and proclaim the guilty purpose with which they are done....

To buy a box of matches with intent to use them in burning a haystack is not an attempt to commit arson, for it is in itself and in appearance an innocent act, there being many other reasons than arson for buying matches. The act does not speak for itself of any guilty design.... But he who takes matches to a haystack and there lights one of them and blows it out on finding that he is observed has done an act which speaks for itself, and he is guilty of criminal attempt accordingly.... The purchaser of matches would not be guilty of attempted arson even if he declared to the vendor or to any other person the guilty purpose with which he bought them. Such evidence is relevant for the purpose of satisfying the jury that the requisite criminal intent existed, but it is not relevant in determining the prior question of law whether the act charged amounts in law to an attempt or is too remote for that purpose.

People v. Murray

Supreme Court of California.
14 Cal. 159 (1859).

■ FIELD, C. J.

The evidence in this case entirely fails to sustain the charge against the defendant of an attempt to contract an incestuous marriage with his niece. It only discloses declarations of his determination to contract the marriage, his elopement with the niece for that avowed purpose, and his request to one of the witnesses to go for a magistrate to perform the ceremony. It shows very clearly the intention of the defendant, but something more than mere intention is necessary to constitute the offense charged. Between preparation for the attempt and the attempt itself, there is a wide difference. The preparation consists in devising or arranging the means or measures necessary for the commission of the offense; the attempt is the direct movement toward the commission after the preparations are made. To illustrate: a party may purchase and load a gun, with the declared intention to shoot his neighbor; but until some movement is made to use the weapon upon the person of his intended victim, there is only preparation, and not an attempt. For the preparation, he may be held to keep the peace; but he is not chargeable with any attempt to kill. So in the present case, the declarations, and elopement, and request for a magistrate, were preparatory to the marriage; but until the officer was engaged, and the parties stood before him, ready to take the vows appropriate to the contract of marriage, it cannot be said, in strictness, that the attempt was made. The attempt contemplated by the statute must be manifest by acts which would end in the consummation of the particular offense, but for the intervention of circumstances independent of the will of the party.

Commonwealth v. Kennedy

Supreme Judicial Court of Massachusetts.
170 Mass. 18, 48 N.E. 770 (1897).

■ HOLMES, J.

[It is alleged] that the defendant feloniously, wilfully, and maliciously attempted to murder [Albert F.] Learoyd by placing a quantity of deadly poison known as "rough on rats," known to the defendant to be a deadly poison, upon, and causing it to adhere to [a] cup, the cup being then empty, with the intent that Learoyd should thereafter use the cup for drinking while the poison was there, and should swallow the poison....

[W]e assume that an act may be done which is expected and intended to accomplish a crime, which is not near enough to the result to constitute an attempt to commit it, as in the classic instance of shooting at a post supposed to be a man. As the aim of the law is not to punish sins, but is to prevent certain external results, the act done must come pretty near to accomplishing that result before the law will notice it. But, on the other hand, ... it is not necessary that the act should be such as inevitably to accomplish the crime by the operation of natural forces, but for some casual and unexpected interference. It is none the less an attempt to shoot a man that the pistol which is fired at his head is not aimed straight, and therefore in the course of nature cannot hit him. Usually acts which are expected to bring about the end without further interference on the part of the criminal are near enough, unless the expectation is very absurd.

In this case the acts are alleged to have been done with intent that Learoyd should swallow the poison, and, by implication, with intent to kill him.... Intent imports contemplation, and more or less expectation, of the intended end as the result of the act alleged. If ... the habits of Learoyd and the other circumstances were such that the defendant's expectation that he would use the cup and swallow the poison was well grounded, there could be no doubt that the defendant's acts were near enough to the intended swallowing of the poison, and, if the dose was large enough to kill, that they were near enough to the accomplishment of the murder....

The cup belonged to Learoyd, and the defendant expected that he would use it. To allow him immunity, on the ground that this part of his expectation was ill grounded, would be as unreasonable as to let a culprit off because he was not warranted in thinking that his pistol was pointed at the man he tried to shoot.

A more important point is that ... the dose [is said not to have been] large enough to kill.... Every question of proximity[, however,] must be determined by its own circumstances.... Any unlawful application of poison is an evil which threatens death, according to common apprehension, and the gravity of the crime, the uncertainty of the result, and the seriousness of the apprehension, coupled with the great harm likely to result from poison even if not enough to kill, would warrant holding the liability for an attempt to begin at a point more remote from the possibility of accomplishing what is expected than might be the case with lighter crimes....

In the case of crimes exceptionally dealt with or greatly feared, acts have been punished which were not even expected to effect the substantive evil unless followed by other criminal acts; e.g., in the case of treason[a].... A familiar statutory illustration of this class is to be found in the enactments with regard to having counterfeit bills in one's possession with intent to pass them....

Exceptions overruled.

Commonwealth v. Peaslee

Supreme Judicial Court of Massachusetts, Essex.
177 Mass. 267 (1901).

■ HOLMES, C.J.

This is an indictment for an attempt to burn a building and certain goods therein, with intent to injure the insurers of the same....

a. See, e.g., Treason Act of 1350, 25 Edw. 3 stat. 5 c. 2 (defining treason as, among other things, "compass[ing] or imag-in[ing] the death of our lord the King").—EDS.

The evidence was that the defendant had constructed and arranged combustibles in the building in such a way that they were ready to be lighted, and if lighted would have set fire to the building and its contents. To be exact, the plan would have required a candle which was standing on a shelf six feet away to be placed on a piece of wood in a pan of turpentine and lighted. The defendant offered to pay a younger man in his employment if he would go to the building, seemingly some miles from the place of the dialogue, and carry out the plan. This was refused. Later the defendant and the young man drove towards the building, but when within a quarter of a mile the defendant said that he had changed his mind, and drove away. This is as near as he ever came to accomplishing what he had in contemplation.

The question on the evidence, more precisely stated, is whether the defendant's acts come near enough to the accomplishment of the substantive offense to be punishable. The statute does not punish every act done towards the commission of a crime, but only such acts done in an attempt to commit it. The most common types of an attempt are either an act which is intended to bring about the substantive crime, and which sets in motion natural forces that would bring it about in the expected course of events, but for the unforeseen interruption, as, in this case, if the candle had been set in its place and lighted, but had been put out by the police, or an act which is intended to bring about the substantive crime, and would bring it about but for a mistake of judgment in a matter of nice estimate or experiment, as when a pistol is fired at a man, but misses him, or when one tries to pick a pocket which turns out to be empty. In either case the would-be criminal has done his last act.

Obviously new considerations come in when further acts on the part of the person who has taken the first steps are necessary before the substantive crime can come to pass. In this class of cases there is still a chance that the would-be criminal may change his mind. In strictness, such first steps cannot be described as an attempt, because that word suggests an act seemingly sufficient to accomplish the end, and has been supposed to have no other meaning. That an overt act, although coupled with an intent to commit the crime, commonly is not punishable if further acts are contemplated as needful, is expressed in the familiar rule that preparation is not an attempt. But some preparations may amount to an attempt. It is a question of degree. If the preparation comes very near to the accomplishment of the act, the intent to complete it renders the crime so probable that the act will be a misdemeanor, although there is still a locus poenitentiae, in the need of a further exertion of the will to complete the crime. * * *

.... A mere collection and preparation of materials in a room for the purpose of setting fire to them, unaccompanied by any present intent to set the fire, would be too remote. If the accused intended to rely upon his own hands to the end, he must be shown to have had a present intent to accomplish the crime without much delay, and to have had this intent at a time and place where he was able to carry it out.... We assume, without deciding, that that is the meaning of the indictment; and it would have been proved if, for instance, the evidence had been that the defendant had been frightened by the police as he was about to light the candle....

Exceptions sustained.

McQuirter v. State

Court of Appeals of Alabama.
36 Ala.App. 707, 63 So.2d 388 (1953).

■ PRICE, JUDGE.

Appellant, a Negro man, was found guilty of an attempt to commit an assault with intent to rape, under an indictment charging an assault with intent to rape. The jury assessed a fine of $500.

About 8:00 o'clock on the night of June 29, 1951, Mrs. Ted Allen, a white woman, with her two children and a neighbor's little girl, were drinking Coca–Cola at the "Tiny Diner" in Atmore. When they started in the direction of Mrs. Allen's home she noticed appellant sitting in the cab of a parked truck. As she passed the truck appellant said something unintelligible, opened the truck door and placed his foot on the running board.

Mrs. Allen testified appellant followed her down the street and when she reached Suell Lufkin's house she stopped. As she turned into the Lufkin house appellant was within two or three feet of her. She waited ten minutes for appellant to pass. When she proceeded on her way, appellant came toward her from behind a telephone pole. She told the children to run to Mr. Simmons' house and tell him to come and meet her. When appellant saw Mr. Simmons he turned and went back down the street to the intersection and leaned on a stop sign just across the street from Mrs. Allen's home. Mrs. Allen watched him at the sign from Mr. Simmons' porch for about thirty minutes, after which time he came back down the street and appellant went on home. * * *

" 'An attempt to commit an assault with intent to rape,' ... means an attempt to rape which has not proceeded far enough to amount to an assault". Burton v. State, 8 Ala.App. 295, 62 So. 394, 396. Under the authorities in this state, to justify a conviction for an attempt to commit an assault with intent to rape the jury must be satisfied beyond a reasonable doubt that defendant intended to have sexual intercourse with prosecutrix against her will, by force or by putting her in fear. Intent is a question to be determined by the jury from the facts and circumstances adduced on the trial, and if there is evidence from which it may be inferred that at the time of the attempt defendant intended to gratify his lustful desires against the resistance of the female a jury question is presented.

In determining the question of intention the jury may consider social conditions and customs founded upon racial differences, such as that the prosecutrix was a white woman and defendant was a Negro man. After considering the evidence in this case we are of the opinion it was sufficient to warrant the submission of the question of defendant's guilt to the jury, and was ample to sustain the judgment of conviction. * * *

Tremaine v. State

Supreme Court of Mississippi.
245 Miss. 512, 148 So.2d 517 (1963).

■ McGehee, Chief Justice.

The appellant was indicted, tried, convicted, and sentenced to serve a term of three years in the state penitentiary for an alleged attempt to rape the prosecutrix....

On the occasion complained of, at about 2:30 in the afternoon, the appellant is alleged to have gone ... to the home of the prosecutrix. When he arrived at the home of the prosecutrix, driving a "salmon-pink 1955 Ford", he inquired of her where he could locate the owner of the horses that were for sale, and requested of her that he be permitted to use her telephone. [The prosecutrix allowed him to use her telephone in the kitchen. She then invited him into the yard to give him directions. When she went back into the house, appellant followed her.] She testified that he then asked her if her house was air-conditioned and she told him, yes. And when she was walking from her kitchen into the dining room, he started walking toward her, "and grabbed my bathrobe and yanked it up, and then I don't know what I did, but he grabbed both of my arms like this (indicating) and—you know—held me like that (indicating); so I said, 'My children and my mother are back there asleep'." That she then somehow broke away from him and "went out the back door by the side of my car and he ran around in front of me and I said 'you better go on because I am going to scream and I am going to get your license and report you to the police'." And he said, "If you scream, I will silence you in one blow". She says that she then saw a car coming....

We think that under the foregoing facts and circumstances there is a strong probability that appellant intended at the time to use force against the prosecutrix, but ... we do not think there is any proof of any overt act in that behalf.

It will be noted that the prosecutrix did not contend that the appellant undertook to lure her into a bedroom or to otherwise molest her in any manner. She does not contend that he made any lewd or lascivious remark to her or committed any overt act which would amount to an attempt to rape. * * *

In the case of Green v. State, 67 Miss. 356, 7 So. 326, where the prosecuting witness was riding a horse along a public road and stopped at a train crossing, she saw a negro man near. As she proceeded on her way, the negro ran after her and caught hold of her riding skirt. She screamed and struck her horse and got away from him. [H]e was convicted of the crime of attempted rape and appealed to this Court, where it was held: "The evidence is insufficient to support the verdict of the jury. We may conjecture the purpose of the defendant to have been to commit a rape, but, on the facts disclosed, it is conjecture only, and not an inference reasonably drawn from the evidence. The probabilities may be greater that a rape was intended rather than robbery or murder, but mere probability of guilt of a particular crime, and that, too, springing more from instinct than from proved facts, cannot support a verdict of guilty. There is great danger of improper convictions in cases of this character, and, while the court should not for that reason invade the province of the jury, the danger admonishes us of the necessity of standing firmly upon the right and duty of proper supervision and control of them." This was during the year 1890, when it was almost inconceivable that a negro man would catch hold of the clothing of a white woman under such circumstances for any purpose other than to attempt the crime charged. * * *

Reversed and judgment here for appellant.

(ii) "Substantial Steps" and the Model Penal Code Approach

Model Penal Code § 5.01. Criminal Attempt.

(1) *Definition of Attempt.* A person is guilty of an attempt to commit a crime if, acting with the kind of culpability otherwise required for commission of the crime, he:

(a) purposely engages in conduct which would constitute the crime if the attendant circumstances were as he believes them to be; or

(b) when causing a particular result is an element of the crime, does or omits to do anything with the purpose of causing or with the belief that it will cause such result without further conduct on his part; or

(c) purposely does or omits to do anything which, under the circumstances as he believes them to be, is an act or omission constituting a substantial step in a course of conduct planned to culminate in his commission of the crime.

(2) *Conduct Which May Be Held Substantial Step Under Subsection (1)(c).* Conduct shall not be held to constitute a substantial step under Subsection (1)(c) of this Section unless it is strongly corroborative of the actor's criminal purpose. Without negativing the sufficiency of other conduct, the following, if strongly corroborative of the actor's criminal purpose, shall not be held insufficient as a matter of law:

(a) lying in wait, searching for or following the contemplated victim of the crime;

(b) enticing or seeking to entice the contemplated victim of the crime to go to the place contemplated for its commission;

(c) reconnoitering the place contemplated for the commission of the crime;

(d) unlawful entry of a structure, vehicle or enclosure in which it is contemplated that the crime will be committed;

(e) possession of materials to be employed in the commission of the crime, which are specially designed for such unlawful use or which can serve no lawful purpose of the actor under the circumstances;

(f) possession, collection or fabrication of materials to be employed in the commission of the crime, at or near the place contemplated for its commission, where such possession, collection or fabrication serves no lawful purpose of the actor under the circumstances;

(g) soliciting an innocent agent to engage in conduct constituting an element of the crime.

Commonwealth v. Donton

Superior Court of Pennsylvania.
439 Pa.Super. 406, 654 A.2d 580 (1995).

Originally, conviction for criminal attempt required proof that a defendant committed an overt act with the intent of completing a crime, but fell short of actually completing it. In 1972, with the enactment of the crimes code, the legislature broadened the definition of attempt by defining it as follows:

> A person commits an attempt when, with the intent to commit a specific crime, he does any act which constitutes a substantial step toward the commission of that crime.

18 Pa. Cons. Stat. Ann. § 901(a). This definition has been interpreted by this court as an expansion of the crime of attempt in that it no longer concentrates on the acts that remain to be done by the defendant but instead focuses on the acts the defendant has completed.

People v. Hawkins

Appellate Court of Illinois, Fourth District.
311 Ill.App.3d 418, 723 N.E.2d 1222 (2000).

■ MYERSCOUGH, JUSTICE.

After a bench trial in July 1997, defendant, Shavun M. Hawkins, was convicted of ... attempt (criminal sexual assault) (720 Ill. Comp. Stat. 5–8/4(a), 12–13(a)(2))[a]. . . .

S.G. was ... a student at Eastern Illinois University. In May 1996, she was living in a townhouse at 950 Edgar, No. 7, in Charleston.... The front door to the house was commonly left unlocked because friends of the residents frequently came and went.

S.G. testified she did homework until about 11:30 p.m. on May 30, 1996, then went to Mother's Bar. After she returned home, she did more schoolwork before retiring between 2 and 2:30 a.m....

[At approximately 5 a.m., defendant] entered S.G.'s residence and proceeded to her bedroom. After fumbling around in the dark, defendant grabbed S.G.'s foot. He turned the light switch on and off. Defendant then sat on the edge of S.G.'s bed and removed his shoes. He started to get under the covers until he was interrupted by S.G.'s urgent request for an explanation. Defendant then put his arm on S.G.'s shoulder and told her he was there to "kick it" with her. [S.G. sprung out of bed and turned on the

a. § 720 Ill. Comp. Stat. 5/12-13. Criminal Sexual Assault.

(a) The accused commits criminal sexual assault if he or she:

(1) commits an act of sexual penetration by the use of force or threat of force; or

(2) commits an act of sexual penetration and the accused knew that the victim was unable to understand the nature of the act or was unable to give knowing consent....—EDS.

light. She saw defendant, still sitting on the bed, wearing black pants and a white shirt, but with his shoes off. She asked him who he was and what he was doing there. He said his name was Shavun and someone had sent him to the house.] Defendant did not leave until S.G. went upstairs screaming. [S.G. had no recollection of having seen defendant before.]

With these facts in evidence, the judge could reasonably conclude that defendant had crossed the line where preparation ends and actual execution of a criminal act begins. That defendant was merely preparing to commit a criminal sexual assault would be a reasonable conclusion had he been interrupted while looking for S.G.'s house; or upon entering the residence, in the absence of additional evidence corroborating his intent to commit a sexual assault. However, defendant's acts, specifically, sitting on S.G.'s bed, taking off his shoes, crawling between the sheets, and announcing his sexual objective to "kick it" with her, were not only corroborative of his intent, but brought him within a "dangerous proximity of success" as well. Depending on what S.G. was wearing at the time (a fact not in the record), defendant may have been dangerously close to achieving sexual penetration....

An attempt crime is one "that falls short of completion through means other than the defendant's voluntary relenting." People v. Dogoda, 9 Ill. 2d 198, 203, 137 N.E.2d 386, 389 (1956). Defendant's "attempt" ended when S.G. stopped it by removing herself from the situation, not by defendant's volition. The trier of fact could reasonably conclude that, when defendant got into bed with S.G., he was past the point where he was likely to experience a change of heart.

Defendant calls our attention to all the actions he did not take, in an attempt to persuade us that his conduct did not amount to a substantial step. Defendant points out that he did not take off any of his clothes but his shoes; he did not touch or fondle S.G.'s genitals or breasts; he did not act "aggressively" toward S.G.; he did not demand that she remove her clothes; and he did not demand sexual contact. We are not persuaded. Defendant's conduct did amount to a substantial step toward the commission of a sexual assault. Defendant does not have to remove his clothing, remove S.G.'s clothing, act "aggressively," or "demand" sexual contact to commit criminal sexual assault under section 12–13(a)(2). * * *

Defendant relies upon People v. Montefolka, 287 Ill. App. 3d 199, 678 N.E.2d 1049 (1997). In Montefolka, the victim was awakened in the night by her whining dog. When she went downstairs to check on the dog, she discovered the defendant inside the house. She ran for the door but defendant grabbed her. He wrestled her to the floor and, while holding her in a "choke hold," twice ordered her to take off her underpants. The victim refused and eventually, through conversation, was able to calm the defendant and he left the house with some cash. The First District Appellate Court reversed the defendant's attempt (criminal sexual assault) conviction, finding he had not taken a substantial step toward the forced act of penetration.

Montefolka is inapplicable here ... because the case is factually distinguishable from the case at hand. Defendant took more steps clearly indicative of an intent to commit a sexual assault than did the defendant in

Montefolka. Defendant entered S.G.'s home and bedroom as she slept, he located S.G. in the bed, removed his shoes, got into bed under the covers with her, put his arm around her, and told her that he had come to "kick it" with her.

Affirmed.

United States v. Ramos–Palomino

United States Court of Appeals for the Tenth Circuit.
51 Fed. Appx. 814 (2002).

■ SEYMOUR, CIRCUIT JUDGE.

On January 11, 2001, a special undercover agent with the Kansas Bureau of Investigation [and a confidential informer, Armando Martinez,] met with Palomino and negotiated the purchase of one pound of meth.... Palomino said he had tried unsuccessfully to obtain the pound of meth but he would have it the next day. He explained he had an approximately one-ounce sample he would sell, which the agent agreed to purchase....

When Martinez called the next day, Palomino told him the meth would be available for purchase after 3:00 p.m. When Martinez and the agent arrived at the tavern at 3:30 p.m., Palomino was there with another man who identified himself as Mr. Palomino's partner and said the meth was coming. After a long wait, Palomino offered to sell the agent some cocaine and went home to get it. When Palomino returned, he told Martinez and the agent that the meth deal would take place at another tavern. The men left to go to the second tavern and on the way Palomino handed the agent a plastic sack containing five one-ounce baggies of cocaine. Palomino wanted $3000 for the drug but told the agent he could pay for the cocaine along with the meth when it arrived.

Martinez and the agent arrived at the second tavern and waited outside for Palomino. After a while, ... Palomino came out of the tavern, told the agent he wanted to be paid for the cocaine, and was arrested. * * *

The government charged Palomino with [various] drug offenses.... Count Three, which Palomino challenges as unsupported by sufficient evidence, was based on his unsuccessful effort to sell the agent a pound of meth. That count alleged that Palomino attempted to possess with the intent to distribute 450 grams or more of a mixture containing meth, in violation of 21 U.S.C. §§ 841(a)(1) and 846....

The crime of attempt requires proof of the requisite criminal intent, and commission of an act constituting a substantial step toward commission of the substantive offense.... Palomino ... maintains the government presented no evidence he contacted anyone in an attempt to obtain a pound of meth prior to his meeting with the agent at the tavern the afternoon of January 12. However, the record reveals testimony by Martinez that Palomino told him on January 11 he had tried without success to obtain the pound of meth but would have it the next day, and testimony by Martinez that after Palomino sold the agent the cocaine on January 12 outside the tavern, Palomino "was trying to obtain the pound of methamphetamine for the agent[,] ... trying to call other people, trying to communicate with other persons." Although his efforts were unsuccessful, his failure was a matter beyond his control rather than a decision on his part to abandon the venture. Accordingly, this evidence of Palomino's efforts to obtain the meth to sell to the agent allowed a reasonable jury to find beyond a reasonable doubt that he took a substantial step toward possessing with the intent to distribute the meth.

United States v. Presto

Court of Military Appeals.
24 M.J. 350 (1987).

■ EVERETT, CHIEF JUDGE.

After Presto sold 567.59 grams of marijuana to two acquaintances who turned out to be a confidential source and an agent of the Criminal Investigation Command (CID), the two buyers asked about purchasing an additional 10 kilograms of marijuana from him. He agreed to try to obtain the requested amount but warned that he doubted if he could get more than 2 or 3 kilograms. * * *

Appellant explained in the stipulation of fact that [after making some unsuccessful phone inquiries regarding the availability of the larger quantity of marijuana] he had decided ... not to consummate the large sale but, instead, was acting only to persuade his buyers of his good efforts in order to get the remaining money owed him from the first sale....

"[T]o be guilty of an attempt, a 'defendant must have engaged in conduct which constitutes a substantial step toward commission of the crime' and that '[a] substantial step must be conduct strongly corroborative of the firmness of the defendant's criminal intent." United States v. Jackson, 560 F.2d 112, 116 (2d Cir.)....

Although placing a call to a potential source in order to determine the availability of drugs tends to corroborate appellant's criminal intent, we are unconvinced that the statutory requirement of "more than mere preparation" has been met. [A]ppellant had not received from the prospective buyers the money for the purported purchase. In fact, he was still owed money from a prior transaction with these buyers. The phone calls from appellant had not located drugs available for purchase. Moreover, if a supply of the desired drugs had been located, then Presto would have had to negotiate a price for his own purchase and thereafter would have had to go to the source and pick up the drugs.

When the military judge asked trial counsel about the act on which the Government was relying, the response made clear that this act was the placing of phone calls.... The act is simply too ambiguous; and too many other steps remained before the distribution could be consummated.

Reversed.

QUESTIONS AND COMMENTS

1. Recall the preliminary observation that attempt liability will lie even if the defendant has posed no "objective" risk of causing harm—in the

sense that putting poison in water that some might drink poses a risk of harm, even before anyone drinks the water, without regard to any future acts the defendant intends to take or might take, or in the sense that blocking the fire exits at a crowded club poses a risk of harm, regardless of the defendant's subsequent efforts to avoid the harm. (Unfinished) attempts instead are punished because we believe that people who do certain things typically go on to do certain other things that are harmful, that the *people* are risky, even if their specific attempt is not.

Is this consistent with the act requirement, and with the prohibition of punishing status in particular? Is it critical that we find that their objective acts *reveal* them to be risky, not that we believe them to be risky? But what about *Palomino*? Would we know that someone who claimed to be trying to get drugs would consummate a drug sale, absent external impediments, unless we believed his *status* was that of a drug dealer?

2. It may be useful to align the tests that distinguish preparation from attempt along a spectrum, beginning with the most bright-line "rule-like" tests and ending with "standards," decisions with little value as precedent that present little more than restatements of the purpose of regulating the area. Where do the attempt cases in this chapter and the Model Penal Code fall along this spectrum?

RULE				STANDARD
A	B	C	D	E

A. The defendant is preparing until she has taken the last possible step in her control to consummate the crime.

B. The defendant is preparing until her acts are, on their face, unequivocally directed towards the consummation of the offense (*res ipsa loquitur*). (One way to think of this is to imagine that the fact finder "freeze frames" at the point the defendant stopped and "knows" what *must* happen next.)

C. The defendant is preparing until her acts are in "dangerous" or "physical" proximity to harm.

D. The defendant is attempting so long as she has taken a "substantial step" towards consummation of the offense and the act or acts that constitute substantial steps "strongly corroborate" her intent. (What work does the word "strongly" do here?) Many types of acts that were historically categorically excluded from the class of acts that could be dubbed attempts are not categorically ruled out (e.g., lying in wait; casing the joint; purchasing useful materials), leaving it up to the fact finder to assess their corroborative value.

E. The defendant is attempting when the fact finder believes that she has a criminal intention and that she has taken steps ("overt acts") that are not only not inconsistent with that intention but would in fact further her criminal scheme.

Now consider some of the problems faced by rule-like and standard-like tests in this area. The rule-like "last possible step" tests plainly suffer from under-inclusiveness. Why, after all, does it matter *when* evidence of dangerousness manifests itself? Shouldn't the criminal law interfere—to neutralize the risky, or evil, person—at that point, wherever it might fall along the way to consummation? Isn't it simply impossible to attempt certain crimes (e.g., rape, some forms of larceny) if we refuse to convict the defendant of attempt until he has done everything in his power to consummate the offense? At the same time, the last possible step test may (more rarely) prove over-inclusive. The metaphoric slow fuse cases raise the question of what to do when the defendant needn't do more, but still has plenty of opportunity to prevent the proscribed harm. (The defendant has lit the fuse that will cause the fire without her taking any more steps, but the fuse will burn for hours and she could step on it, readily, at any point.) In such cases, are we adequately sure that she will commit the offense—and that she in fact poses an exceptional danger?

The standard-like tests, in their indefiniteness, leave room for arbitrariness, and even prejudice. (What best explains the holding in *McQuirter*? Are *McQuirter* and *Tremaine* consistent? *Hawkins* and *Montefolka*?) At the same time, they are potentially over-inclusive. In theory, the criminal intent that the defendant's acts must strongly corroborate is the intent to commit a particular crime, not the intent to commit crime in some broader sense. But what if there is considerable evidence of lawbreaking (say, selling drugs)—or of general dangerousness—but much weaker evidence that the defendant intended to commit the particular crime he's charged with (that drug sale, to those undercover agents, that day)? Are *Palomino* and *Presto* consistent with one another, or do they merely reveal the distinctions between judges who are especially scrupulous about not accounting for more general information about a defendant and focusing narrowly on whether he attempted the particular crime in question, and those judges who are more wary of letting unambiguous drug dealers go free because deals with undercover agents are often incomplete? In any case, is the firm intention to commit an offense sufficient evidence of dangerousness? What if someone has a habit of breaking as many firm commitments as he keeps?

3. Two hours before he entered S.G.'s bedroom, the defendant in *Hawkins* had had sexual intercourse with another sleeping female student, B.H., in a different house near the Eastern Illinois University campus. Is it possible to judge whether the defendant had taken substantial steps towards raping S.G. (*either* by having intercourse through the use of force or with an unconscious victim) without knowing what had happened earlier that evening? On the other hand, is it *permissible* to take account of that other incident—for which he will be separately punished—in judging whether he should be convicted for attempting to assault S.G. sexually? If we do so, are we punishing Hawkins in significant part for his status as a "sexual predator" rather than for his specific acts?

4. Consider the merits of the Model Penal Code test. It allows police officers to interfere at an earlier stage of criminal planning, which is a good thing if you agree with the Code drafters that criminal law is a tool for harm prevention—and danger management. Advocates of the test in fact worry that any test that demands that defendants take steps more proximate to harm put police to an unacceptable election between two legitimate

goals of police work: on the one hand, it is appropriate for police to want to arrest (and ultimately incarcerate) dangerous persons, while at the same time they rightly want to prevent the consummation of harm. But if you tell police that would-be bank robbers will go scot-free if they are arrested outside the bank, about to put on masks, with a getaway car with covered plates across the street, they may be tempted to let them enter the bank, where thwarting the robbery may pose considerably more risks. For a classic discussion, see Glanville Williams, "Police Control of Intending Criminals," [1955] Crim. L. Rev. 66, 69.

But can the Model Penal Code be squared with retributivist concerns regarding individual blameworthiness and liberal worries about extending police authority in the name of public safety? The Model Code test also tries to connect the preparation vs. attempt inquiry more closely, and explicitly, to what the Code drafters considered to be the function of criminal law in general and the law of attempt in particular (identifying dangerous individuals). But what happens to the act requirement, and the prohibition of criminalizing thought, once we relegate the actus reus of attempt to evidentiary significance? (An act is an attempt if it is a substantial step, and a step is substantial if "it is strongly corroborative of the actor's criminal purpose.") Is the increase in public safety worth abandoning a focus on acts in favor of a focus on thoughts (and those who harbor them)?

5. Note that the Model Penal Code differentiates between three types of attempt, in subsection (a), (b), and (c), depending on which type of offense element the actor didn't quite manage to satisfy. The first two categories are versions of a "complete" attempt, or what we have called an "unsuccessful" attempt, i.e., an attempt where the actor has done everything she thought necessary to consummate the offense. Subsection (a) deals with cases where the *attendant circumstances* turned out to be different than anticipated. (It's attempted murder if I stab a corpse with murderous intent in the belief that he was still "another human being.") Attempts that fail to achieve the requisite *result* are handled in subsection (b). (It's also attempted murder if I shoot to kill another person, but miss.) "Incomplete" (or what we've called "unfinished") attempts fall under subsection (c), where my *conduct* left something to be desired to match the offense definition. (Attempted murder, once more, if I decide to kill my ex-wife, pick up my rifle, attach a scope to it, and drive to her house.) The preparation vs. attempt question comes up only in cases under subsection (c). Try to classify the cases in this chapter according to this scheme. The scheme hasn't caught on, as many legislatures have preferred to stick with their traditional attempt definitions. Why? Does the Model Penal Code scheme have any advantages? See, e.g., Cal. Penal Code § 21a ("An attempt to commit a crime consists of two elements: specific intent to commit the crime, and a direct but ineffectual act done toward its commission."); N.Y. Penal Law § 110.00 ("A person is guilty of an attempt to commit a crime when, with intent to commit a crime, he engages in conduct which tends to effect the commission of such crime.").

6. *Punishable pre-preparation and quasi-inchoate consummated offenses.* The line between attempt and preparation may be hard to draw, but

everyone agrees that it coincides with the line between punishable and nonpunishable conduct. Differentiating punishable from nonpunishable conduct is, after all, *the point* of differentiating between attempt and preparation. And yet it turns out the criminal law repeatedly reaches beyond the line between attempt and preparation to punish conduct that *falls short* of preparation. See, e.g., 18 U.S.C. § 1503 ("endeavoring" to obstruct justice); N.Y. Penal Law § 165.25 ("jostling" as inchoate larceny; see *People v. Nelson*, ch. 2 supra). As a result, attempts are punished, and so are acts that don't amount to a preparation, yet preparation remains nonpunishable. Does this make any sense? What does that say about the project of differentiating between attempt and preparation? Is punishing pre-preparatory conduct consistent with any of the rationales for punishing attempts? Are there any limits on how far back the state can push the borders of punishability?

The most important exception to the nonpunishability of pre-attempt conduct is the widespread criminalization of possession, ranging from simple possession to compound possession (i.e., possession with the intent to use). On possession generally, see ch. 4 supra. The continuum from dangerousness at the one end to its manifestation at the other begins with simple possession. Here we are farthest removed from the harm that the use of the object may cause. In the strict liability variety of simple possession, the inference from the dangerousness of the item possessed to its possessor is most tenuous—since she must not even be aware of any or all aspects of her possession, including its quality (anything? drugs? a machine gun?) or quantity (1 kilo? of drug and/or of carrier (blotter paper, mushrooms)?). Compound possession at least requires the intent to use the item possessed in a way that may or may not be harmful. Only then comes the (nonpunishable) preparation to use the item possessed in some particular way, followed by the (punishable) attempt to use it, and eventually its actual use. See Markus Dirk Dubber, "Policing Possession: The War on Crime and the End of Criminal Law," 91 J. Crim. L. & Criminology 829, 860–61 (2002).

Defendants who commit certain (formally consummated) substantive offenses are actually punished predominantly for the same reason as (formally) inchoate offenders are punished—because we believe they would have gone on to commit some other dangerous acts had they not been apprehended when they were—though to some extent we impose penalties for these offenses because the defendant's conduct has already breached the peace or alarmed a particular victim. Common law burglary, for instance—defined as breaking and entering a dwelling at night with the further intent to commit a felony inside—doubtless partly sanctioned the defendant because surreptitious nighttime entries into dwellings were themselves alarming and dangerous. But the serious punishment for burglary also served to insure that people who intended to commit crimes—larcenies, robberies—were punished severely though they had not yet "attempted" larceny or robbery, assuming they were apprehended while "merely" breaking into a dwelling. Whether this rationale still applies, after the development of a general law of attempt, the expansion of attempt liability—under the Model Penal Code—far beyond last proximate acts, and the imposition of serious punishment for attempt (even to the point of punishing attempts as harshly as consummated offenses), is another question. See People v. Gaines, 74 N.Y.2d 358, 361–62 (1989). On burglary, see ch. 11 infra.

Similarly, it is possible to describe (more recently enacted) anti-stalking statutes as proscribing behavior both because it is intrinsically alarming *and* because it is thought to signal (the unduly strong) probability of future violence. These statutes, designed to sanction harassing conduct that terrorizes and torments others, were passed largely in response to widespread harassment (especially of women) both by grudge holders and (ostensible) "admirers." See, e.g., People v. Stuart, 100 N.Y.2d 412 (2003) (upholding anti-stalking statute against vagueness challenge); see also Nick Zimmerman, "Attempted Stalking: An Attempt-to-Almost–Attempt-to-Act," 20 N. Ill. U. L. Rev. 219 (2000).

It is interesting to contemplate the degree to which existing or proposed anti-stalking statutes violate whatever principles animate the judgment that "mere" preparation should go unpunished and the degree to which they can, in theory or practice, be squared with (at least certain versions of) the commitment to eradicate gender discrimination. Consider the following Problem.

* * *

Problem

Kelly King is a twenty-one year-old college senior who became obsessed with Pat Parris, a sophomore at her school who is an Olympic gymnast. He is enrolled in one of her literature classes and she has sat near him in class on several occasions, but until her arrest, he did not know her name nor have any sense of who she was. She made thirty "contacts" with him over a forty-five day period in March and April of her senior year. The following five contact-types should suffice to give you a sense of the strengths and weaknesses of the case: there were no contacts that were either more "threatening" or "crude" than these.

On two occasions, she left gifts, in gift-wrapped boxes, outside his dorm room. The first came in early March: it was an expensive sweater with a note attached, "This would look great on you. Like what wouldn't?" The second one, which came a month later, was an expensive early edition of Dickens' "Great Expectations" with a note, "My personal favorite, K."

She left a message on his phone answering machine in late March: "I'm going crazy not seeing you. Thank God I'll see you soon." She did not leave a name or phone number.

She sent him a dozen e-mails, starting the second week of March, none of them traceable to her account, but all were signed. Half were signed "K" and half were signed "Kelly" though he knew no one named Kelly and did not ascertain her identity till the police looked into the matter in mid-April, after the psychotherapist he started to see after his third contact from Kelly finally convinced him that he should seek help from the police. The following two e-messages are fairly typical: "Why do you have everything? Sometimes I feel like screaming you're so perfect, and I'm just not sure whether I'm screaming in rage or ecstasy." "I know I'm invisible to you. I so want you to see me, but I know that if you could see me, you'd stop me from seeing you, so close, so often."

She slipped a CD that she had burned into his backpack one day at the end of class. He played the song she had downloaded (Ani DiFranco's "Untouchable Face"), curious to find out more about the person who kept contacting him. The chorus of the song was: "Fuck you, and your untouchable face. And fuck you, for existing in the first place. And who am I, that I should be vying for your touch? Said who am I, I bet you can't even tell me that much." Pat told police that while he rarely, if ever, uses crude or profane language, most of his friends do frequently, and it doesn't ordinarily bother him at all.

Four times, she sent him photos in the mail that she had taken of him in public spaces. In one of them, he was kissing a friend of the opposite sex, and Kelly had drawn a circle around the young woman's face and written the words, "Way beneath you."

You are assisting a District Attorney who wants you to assess whether to bring misdemeanor harassment charges against Kelly King under the following statute:

> § 1. A person commits misdemeanor harassment if, with purpose to harass another, he or she (a) makes a telephone call without purpose of legitimate communication; or (b) insults, taunts, or challenges another in a fashion likely to provoke a violent or disorderly response; or (c) makes repeated communications anonymously or at extremely inconvenient hours or in offensively crude language; or (d) subjects another to an offensive touching; or (e) engages in any other course of alarming conduct serving no legitimate purpose of the actor.
>
> § 2. A person commits felonious harassment if he or she harasses another person and, in the course of so doing, makes credible threats to that person, such that the person he or she harasses is placed in reasonable fear for his or her safety.
>
> § 3. For the purposes of this act, a person "harasses" another when he or she engages in conduct which seriously alarms, annoys, torments or terrorizes the person, and the conduct serves no legitimate purpose. The course of conduct must be such as would cause a reasonable person in the position of the object of the harassment to suffer substantial emotional distress.
>
> § 4. For the purposes of this act, a "credible threat" means a threat which causes the person who is the target of the threat to reasonably fear for his or her safety. A threat may be communicated verbally, or in writing, or be implied by a pattern of conduct or a combination of verbal or written statements and conduct.

What are the best arguments that Kelly is guilty of misdemeanor harassment? That she is not?

For purposes of the following two questions, assume that Kelly is a young man and Pat a young woman. Change nothing else about the interaction between the parties, though.

Assume that Kelly (female) would have been guilty of *misdemeanor* harassment. Make the best case that you can that Kelly (male) should nonetheless be guilty of *felony* harassment.

Assuming that the case for felony harassment is *stronger* if brought against Kelly (male) than Kelly (female), does this imply that we are applying "different sets of laws" to male and female defendants? Why and why not? That we are punishing Kelly (male) in (significant) part not for his acts but for the status of being male?

b. Renunciation (Abandonment)

(i) (Why) Should Abandonment Be a Defense?

Model Penal Code § 5.01. Criminal Attempt.

(4) *Renunciation of Criminal Purpose.* When the actor's conduct would otherwise constitute an attempt under Subsection (1)(b) or (1)(c) of this Section, it is an affirmative defense that he abandoned his effort to commit the crime or otherwise prevented its commission, under circumstances manifesting a complete and voluntary renunciation of his criminal purpose. The establishment of such defense does not, however, affect the liability of an accomplice who did not join in such abandonment or prevention.

Within the meaning of this Article, renunciation of criminal purpose is not voluntary if it is motivated, in whole or in part, by circumstances, not present or apparent at the inception of the actor's course of conduct, which increase the probability of detection or apprehension or which make more difficult the accomplishment of the criminal purpose. Renunciation is not complete if it is motivated by a decision to postpone the criminal conduct until a more advantageous time or to transfer the criminal effort to another but similar objective or victim.

People v. Staples

Court of Appeal of California, Second District.
6 Cal.App.3d 61, 85 Cal.Rptr. 589 (1970).

■ REPPY, J.

Defendant was charged in an information with attempted burglary (Pen. Code, §§ 664, 459). . . .

In October 1967, while his wife was away on a trip, defendant, a mathematician, under an assumed name, rented an office on the second floor of a building in Hollywood which was over the mezzanine of a bank. Directly below the mezzanine was the vault of the bank. Defendant was aware of the layout of the building, specifically of the relation of the office he rented to the bank vault. Defendant paid rent for the period from October 23 to November 23. The landlord had 10 days before commencement of the rental period within which to finish some interior repairs and painting. During this prerental period defendant brought into the office certain equipment. This included drilling tools, two acetylene gas tanks, a blow torch, a blanket, and a linoleum rug. The landlord observed these items when he came in from time to time to see how the repair work was progressing. Defendant learned from a custodian that no one was in the building on Saturdays. On Saturday, October 14, defendant drilled two groups of holes into the floor of the office above the mezzanine room. He stopped drilling before the holes went through the floor. He came back to the office several times thinking he might slowly drill down, covering the holes with the linoleum rug. At some point in time he installed a hasp lock on a closet, and planned to, or did, place his tools in it. However, he left the closet keys on the premises. Around the end of November, apparently after November 23, the landlord notified the police and turned the tools and equipment over to them. Defendant did not pay any more rent. It is not clear when he last entered the office, but it could have been after November 23, and even after the landlord had removed the equipment....

.... There was definitely substantial evidence entitling the trial judge to find that defendant's acts had gone beyond the preparation stage. Without specifically deciding where defendant's preparations left off and where his activities became a completed criminal attempt, we can say that his "drilling" activity clearly was an unequivocal and direct step toward the completion of the burglary....

.... Usually the actors in cases falling within [the] category of ["incomplete"] attempts are intercepted or caught in the act. Here, there was no direct proof of any actual interception. But it was clearly inferable by the trial judge that defendant became aware that the landlord had resumed control over the office and had turned defendant's equipment and tools over to the police. This was the equivalent of interception.

The inference of this nonvoluntary character of defendant's abandonment was a proper one for the trial judge to draw. However, it would seem that the character of the abandonment in situations of this type, whether it be voluntary (prompted by pangs of conscience or a change of heart) or nonvoluntary (established by inference in the instant case), is not controlling. The relevant factor is the determination of whether the acts of the perpetrator have reached such a stage of advancement that they can be classified as an attempt. Once that attempt is found there can be no exculpatory abandonment. "One of the purposes of the criminal law is to protect society from those who intend to injure it. When it is established that the defendant intended to commit a specific crime and that in carrying out this intention he committed an act that caused harm[5] or sufficient danger of harm, it is immaterial that for some collateral reason he could not complete the intended crime."

QUESTIONS AND COMMENTS

1. *The current status of the renunciation defense*. In some jurisdictions (e.g., California), there is no abandonment defense; in others, the defense appears in the attempt statute itself, see Model Penal Code § 5.01(4),

5. In the instant case defendant's drilling was done without permission and did cause property damage.

German Penal Code § 24, or elsewhere in the criminal code, see, e.g., New York Penal Law § 40.10 (among "other defenses involving lack of culpability"). In still other jurisdictions, courts have allowed the defense despite the absence of statutory guidance. See, e.g., People v. Kimball, 109 Mich.App. 273, 311 N.W.2d 343 (1981).

2. Why might we have such a defense? Attempts, after all, are crimes and most crimes can't be "undone." Why might we allow defendants to undo this one?

Deterrence oriented commentators might believe we should allow the defense in order to give defendants incentives to desist (from the "consummated" offense, though obviously *not* from the attempt, since that line has already been crossed). See Martin Wasik, "Abandoning Criminal Intent," [1980] Crim. L. Rev. 785, 793. But isn't that a reason to punish attempts less severely than consummated crimes, rather than providing a complete defense to attempts? Or is the (latent) argument that distinctions in the magnitude of punishment are less psychologically salient than the distinction between (any?) punishment and no punishment?

Also, this incentives argument doesn't fully explain what's special about attempts: Why don't we give parallel incentives to undo the ill effects of completed crimes, especially in cases in which effects can be undone to a significant extent (e.g., give these sorts of incentives to return stolen property)?

3. Perhaps, instead, the argument is that abandoned attempts are not the sure-fire indicators of bad character (or "dangerousness" for incapacitationists) that consummated crimes (or non-abandoned attempts, for that matter) are. Abandonment would then allow the defendant to rebut the presumption of dangerousness that ordinarily attaches to crossing the preparation/attempt line with the requisite criminal purpose. See Model Penal Code Commentaries § 5.01, at 359. This approach to the defense of abandonment, however, has wider implications. At core, it is an attack on an inapt conclusive presumption that could readily be made in other settings (are thieves who make full restitution to victims really the same, in terms of character or dangerousness, as those who don't voluntarily give property back?).

So the big question appears to be why don't we tolerate the fact that all rules and conclusive presumptions are inapt *here*, if we tolerate it elsewhere? Is it because attempt law is already so unrule-like that it would seem silly to deprive jurors of relevant facts? When we declare that we are substantially certain that those who have passed the preparation line really would go on to consummate offenses but for external intervention, we must know we're (at least partly) kidding ourselves: we may have no good choice but to punish those who've been intercepted, both because so many of them really are committed to consummating offenses and because we need to give police incentives for early intervention. At the same time, we realize that we've made a murky judgment about future dangerousness (or bad character). We also know our presumption may be proven wrong in some cases (by the existence of voluntary abandonment). Moreover, we typically are comfortable using conclusive presumptions only when individualized determinations are difficult, and yet it's relatively easy for fact finders to distinguish abandoned from unabandoned attempts.

4. Even critics of the abandonment defense agree that abandonment (or more generally, renunciation of criminal purpose) should be taken into account at sentencing. But why? If abandonment makes no sense as a statutory defense *ex ante*, why would it make sense as a discretionary sentencing discount *ex post*? And, once again why should a sentencing discount for abandonment or renunciation be limited to attempt cases? Consider the following provisions from the U.S. Sentencing Guidelines in light of the various traditional rationales for punishment in general, and for the abandonment defense in particular.

§ 3E1.1. Acceptance of Responsibility

(a) If the defendant clearly demonstrates acceptance of responsibility for his offense, decrease the offense level by 2 levels. . . .

Commentary:

1. In determining whether a defendant qualifies under subsection (a), appropriate considerations include, but are not limited to, the following:
   (a) truthfully admitting the conduct comprising the offense(s) of conviction. . . . [A] defendant who falsely denies, or frivolously contests, relevant conduct that the court determines to be true has acted in a manner inconsistent with acceptance of responsibility;
   (b) voluntary termination or withdrawal from criminal conduct or associations;
   (c) voluntary payment of restitution prior to adjudication of guilt;
   (d) voluntary surrender to authorities promptly after commission of the offense;
   (e) voluntary assistance to authorities in the recovery of the fruits and instrumentalities of the offense;
   (f) voluntary resignation from the office or position held during the commission of the offense;
   (g) post-offense rehabilitative efforts (*e.g.*, counseling or drug treatment); and
   (h) the timeliness of the defendant's conduct in manifesting the acceptance of responsibility.

§ 5K2.16. Voluntary Disclosure of Offense (Policy Statement)

If the defendant voluntarily discloses to authorities the existence of, and accepts responsibility for, the offense prior to the discovery of such offense, and if such offense was unlikely to have been discovered otherwise, a departure below the applicable guideline range for that offense may be warranted. For example, a downward departure under this section might be considered where a defendant, motivated by remorse, discloses an offense that otherwise would have remained undiscovered. This provision does not apply where the motivating factor is the defendant's knowledge that discovery of the offense is likely or imminent, or where the defendant's disclosure occurs in connection with the investigation or prosecution of the defendant for related conduct.

(ii) Is the Renunciation "Voluntary" and "Complete"?

Assuming abandonment should matter, what should count as abandonment? Why must an abandonment have been "voluntary" and "complete"?

Voluntariness. Isn't one (the?) point of criminal law to encourage people not to engage in criminal conduct by communicating to them that if they do, they will get caught and punished? Does that make refraining from criminal conduct, or abandoning thoughts of criminal conduct, insufficiently "voluntary" because it is responsive to the threat of punishment? Why does it matter whether a decision not to commit a crime was voluntary? Isn't that the difference between law and morality, that law doesn't care *why* you follow rules, just *that* you do? If it doesn't matter why you commit crimes (see the irrelevance of motive doctrine, ch. 5), why should it matter why you don't?

Consider four attempted shoplifters, each of whom has already put the fancy sweater on underneath his clothes. A gives up the sweater when the beepers go off; B when he sees the sign, "one way mirrors monitored by security personnel"; C when he sees the sign, "shoplifters will be prosecuted"; and D when he sees another customer being led to a back room by the store detective. In each case, is the abandonment voluntary? Are the cases different?

Completeness. Must you abandon all future criminal activity in order to qualify as having abandoned the plan to engage in a specific crime? Look carefully at Model Penal Code § 5.01(4): how do the drafters define a "complete" renunciation? If you're being punished for posing a risk of particular criminal conduct, why should you have to establish that you're not posing a risk of (similar?) criminal conduct in the future? *How* would you make this case? What sort of evidence would you introduce? If you are a professional bank robber (or a person with a long rap sheet), can you ever qualify for the abandonment defense? (See also ch. 8 on entrapment: can such people ever qualify for an entrapment defense that requires that the defendant not have a propensity to commit the offense?)

Le Barron v. State

Supreme Court of Wisconsin.
32 Wis.2d 294, 145 N.W.2d 79 (1966).

■ CURRIE, CHIEF JUSTICE.

On March 3, 1965 at 6:55 p.m., the complaining witness, Jodean Randen . . . was walking home across a fairly well-traveled railroad bridge in Eau Claire. She is a slight woman whose normal weight is 95 to 100 pounds. As she approached the opposite side of the bridge she passed a man who was walking in the opposite direction. The man turned and followed her, grabbed her arm and demanded her purse. She surrendered her purse and at the command of the man began walking away as fast as she could. Upon discovering that the purse was empty, he caught up with her again, grabbed her arm and told her that if she did not scream he would not hurt her. He then led her—willingly, she testified, so as to avoid being hurt by him—to the end of the bridge. While walking he shoved her head down and warned her not to look up or do anything and he would not hurt her.

On the other side of the bridge along the railroad tracks there is a coal shack. As they approached the coal shack he grabbed her, put one hand over her mouth, and an arm around her shoulder and told her not to scream or he would kill her. At this time Mrs. Randen thought he had a knife in his hand. He then forced her into the shack and up against the wall. As she struggled for her breath he said, "You know what else I want," unzipped his pants and started pulling up her skirt. She finally succeeded in removing his hand from her mouth, and after reassuring him that she would not scream, told him she was pregnant and pleaded with him to desist or he would hurt her baby. He then felt her stomach and took her over to the door of the shack, where in the better light he was able to ascertain that, under her coat, she was wearing maternity clothes. He thereafter let her alone and left after warning her not to scream or call the police, or he would kill her. * * *

The material portions of the controlling statutes provide:

> Sec. 944.01(1). "Any male who has sexual intercourse with a female he knows is not his wife, by force and against her will, may be imprisoned not more than 30 years."
>
> Sec. 939.32(2). "An attempt to commit a crime requires that the actor have an intent to perform acts and attain a result which, if accomplished, would constitute such crime and that he does acts toward the commission of the crime which demonstrate unequivocally, under all the circumstances, that he formed that intent and would commit the crime except for the intervention of another person or some other extraneous factor."

The thrust of defendant's argument, that the evidence was not sufficient to convict him of the crime of attempted rape, is [that] the factor which caused him to desist, viz., the pregnancy of complainant, was intrinsic and not an "extraneous factor" within the meaning of sec. 939.32(2). * * *

The argument, that the pregnancy of the instant complainant which caused defendant's desistance does not qualify as an "extraneous factor" within the meaning of sec. 939.32 is in conflict with our holding in State v. Damms, 9 Wis. 2d 183, 100 N.W.2d 592 (1960). There we upheld a conviction of attempt to commit murder where the accused pulled the trigger of an unloaded pistol intending to kill his estranged wife thinking the pistol was loaded. It was held that the impossibility of accomplishment due to the gun being unloaded fell within the statutory words, "except for the intervention of some other extraneous factor." Particularly significant is this statement in the opinion:

> An unequivocal act accompanied by intent should be sufficient to constitute a criminal attempt. Insofar as the actor knows, he has done everything necessary to insure the commission of the crime intended,

> and he should not escape punishment because of the fortuitous circumstance that by reason of some fact unknown to him it was impossible to effectuate the intended result.

The unloaded condition of the gun was every bit as much a part of the intrinsic fact situation in the *Damms* case as was complainant's pregnancy in the instant case. We determine that such pregnancy constituted the intervention of an "extraneous factor" within the meaning of sec. 939.32(2).

QUESTIONS AND COMMENTS

1. Consider as well some hypothetical cases that alter the facts of *Le Barron*: Defendant desists at the same point in time that the defendant in *Le Barron* desists because (a) he has moralistic hesitations about sexually assaulting pregnant women; alternatively, he has "revulsion" reactions to sex with pregnant women; (b) the victim is atypically articulate for someone in the incredibly stressful situation that the victim finds herself in and is able to bring home to the defendant the enormity of his contemplated crime (this is one way to describe the facts in People v. McNeal, 152 Mich.App. 404, 393 N.W.2d 907 (1986)); (c) when the defendant first sees the victim in the light, he realizes that she physically reminds him of his sister.

2. The Model Penal Code explicitly notes that we ought not to credit the defendant if he abandoned only the specific *instance* of the crime, but not the category. But how do we move from an instance to a category? We know the defendant abandoned *this* crime, in *this* setting, but what else can we *know*?

Perhaps any renunciation that occurs because the (objective?) cost-benefit calculation that a (reasonable?) defendant would have made when he started has changed by the time he stops, is especially suspect. Yet in some sense, every situation in which a defendant abandons is (at least somehow) distinct from the situation he imagined when he began, or now imagines would be more ideal. Abandonment cases at least appear relatively easy when the costs of proceeding have plainly risen beyond those the defendant would have initially anticipated (a hypothetical Le Barron runs when he hears the police sirens right outside the shack) or when the benefits of the crime have plainly fallen (a person abandons a larceny when he realizes the "diamond bracelet" he was about to remove from the safe is just glass beads). But it is hardly clear that the "new circumstances" (pregnancy in *Le Barron* or a moving plea by an articulate victim in *McNeal*) are of this sort. If there is to be an abandonment defense at all, how could we reject the defendant's claim in *McNeal*? And if the point of the abandonment defense is that we sometimes need to rethink *our* commitment to the notion that those defendants who cross the preparation/attempt line are themselves committed to a course of conduct that will culminate in a proscribed outcome, how can we apply it in a case (like the case in which the police are approaching) in which we have no reason to rethink our commitment?

3. *Intentionalism vs. Determinism.* If we *punish* only those whose acts are viewed as (adequately morally) voluntary, so ought we *credit* only (generally praiseworthy) acts we'd describe as voluntary. But haven't we then entered the trickiest domain in criminal jurisprudence? Ascertaining what is to "count" as adequately morally voluntary in situations in which the defendant's conduct is clearly voluntary in a "muscular-willed" sense is inevitably difficult. The *probability* that a sexual attacker will desist when he learns his victim is pregnant doubtless increases (as the probability of committing assaults increases when drunk, as the probability of committing property offenses rises when poor), but one would hardly describe desistance in these cases as incontrovertibly determined or *inevitable*, much less unchosen.

4. Should we care at all about the *general* moral quality of the defendant's reasons for change or just ask whether the change is excessively situation specific: In this sense, is the hypothetical defendant who is revolted by pregnancy significantly differentiable, in terms of abandonment defenses, from the defendant who is morally "moved" by protectiveness for fetuses? Could we make this distinction even if we wanted to: if the externally verifiable facts are equally consistent with good and bad motivation, won't a well-counseled or naturally wily defendant know just how to explain what he has done?

5. In evaluating the general acceptability of the defense in light of the discussion of "voluntariness" and "completeness," the following thought experiment might be helpful: Imagine that there are 25,000 citizens, 24,000 of whom never pass the preparation/attempt line. Of those 1,000 who pass it, 900 consummate the offense, 80 get stopped by purely external forces, 15 "abandon" for reasons that we think anyone would abandon for (and we view these 95 as non-differentiable from those who complete the offenses, as the "same people in different circumstances"), and 5 "abandon" because of something we might call a "true change of heart." Should we compare the 5 to the 24,000 who never start or to the 995 who succeed, get stopped, or stop for reasons "anyone would stop for"?

6. Note that the *Le Barron* court speaks about the defendant's discovery, in cases like the misfiring gun case (*Damms)*, of the impossibility of achieving his objective: was it *impossible* for Le Barron to rape the victim, Mrs. Randen?

c. Impossibility

In the classic impossible attempts case, the defendant has done all she is going to do (we are not talking about inferring what a defendant might do *next*) but still has not consummated the offense. In some sub-set of these cases, the defendant has tried her best to commit a crime, but because of a *mistake* about some attendant circumstance not only didn't consummate the offense, but *couldn't have* consummated it. (She has—arguably—tried to receive stolen property, but the property she has arranged to get her hands on has been recovered by the police so that it is no longer stolen; she has—arguably—tried to bribe a juror but handed the cash-filled envelope and instructions to a courtroom by-stander who was seated near the jury box.)

In other circumstances, one would not so readily describe the defendant as having made a mistake about the presence or absence of an offense element, but rather, a mistake about the efficacy of her conduct in reaching a particular result. (She has not tried to kill an already-dead person—that's at least arguably better described as a mistake about an offense element—but shoots an unloaded gun. Or she has stuck her hand in an empty pocket, thinking she can steal something.)

What all these cases have in common, it seems, is that the course of the defendant's conduct is temporally complete and that if all we could infer about a defendant is that she intended to do precisely what she did, none of the defendants in these cases intended to commit a crime. So we need to establish some sort of structure to ascertain when we are (adequately) sure what the defendant intended to do *instead* of the precise things she actually did. Does the distinction between (inculpatory) mistakes about offense elements and inculpatory mistakes about the possibility of consummating an offense help guide that inquiry?

People v. Dlugash

Court of Appeals of New York.
41 N.Y.2d 725, 363 N.E.2d 1155, 395 N.Y.S.2d 419 (1977).

■ Jasen, Judge.

The criminal law is of ancient origin, but criminal liability for attempt to commit a crime is comparatively recent. At the root of the concept of attempt liability are the very aims and purposes of penal law. The ultimate issue is whether an individual's intentions and actions, though failing to achieve a manifest and malevolent criminal purpose, constitute a danger to organized society of sufficient magnitude to warrant the imposition of criminal sanctions. * * *

On December 22, 1973, Michael Geller, 25 years old, was found shot to death in the bedroom of his Brooklyn apartment.... Defendant stated that, on the night of December 21, 1973, he, [Joe] Bush and Geller had been out drinking. Bush had been staying at Geller's apartment.... When Geller ... pressed his demand for rent money, Bush drew his .38 caliber pistol, aimed it at Geller and fired three times. Geller fell to the floor. After the passage of a few minutes, perhaps two, perhaps as much as five, defendant walked over to the fallen Geller, drew his .25 caliber pistol, and fired approximately five shots in the victim's head and face. Defendant contended that, by the time he fired the shots, "it looked like Mike Geller was already dead"....

[Officer] Carrasquillo ... asked the defendant why he would do such a thing. According to Carasquillo, the defendant said, "gee, I really don't know." Carasquillo repeated the question 10 minutes later, but received the same response. After a while, Carasquilllo asked the question for a third time and defendant replied, "well, gee, I guess it must have been because I was afraid of Joe Bush." * * *

[T]he evidence did not establish, beyond a reasonable doubt, that Geller was alive at the time defendant fired into his body. To sustain a homicide conviction, it must be established, beyond a reasonable doubt, that the defendant caused the death of another person.[a] The People were required to establish that the shots fired by defendant Dlugash were a sufficiently direct cause of Geller's death. While the defendant admitted firing five shots at the victim approximately two to five minutes after Bush had fired three times, all three medical expert witnesses testified that they could not, with any degree of medical certainty, state whether the victim had been alive at the time the latter shots were fired by the defendant.... Whatever else it may be, it is not murder to shoot a dead body. * * *

The modern concept of attempt has been said to date from Rex v. Scofield (Cald 397), decided in 1784. In that case, Lord Mansfield stated that "(t)he intent may make an act, innocent in itself, criminal; nor is the completion of an act, criminal in itself, necessary to constitute criminality. Is it no offence to set fire to a train of gunpowder with intent to burn a house, because by accident, or the interposition of another, the mischief is prevented?"....

The most intriguing attempt cases are those where the attempt to commit a crime was unsuccessful due to mistakes of fact or law on the part of the would-be criminal. A general rule developed in most American jurisdictions that legal impossibility is a good defense but factual impossibility is not. Thus, for example, it was held that defendants who shot at a stuffed deer did not attempt to take a deer out of season, even though they believed the dummy to be a live animal. The court stated that there was no criminal attempt because it was no crime to "take" a stuffed deer, and it is no crime to attempt to do that which is legal. (State v. Guffey, 262 S.W.2d 152 (Mo.App.); see, also, State v. Taylor, 345 Mo. 325, 133 S.W.2d 336 (no liability for attempt to bribe a juror where person bribed was not, in fact, a juror).) These cases are illustrative of legal impossibility. A further example is Francis Wharton's classic hypothetical involving Lady Eldon and her French lace. Lady Eldon, traveling in Europe, purchased a quantity of French lace at a high price, intending to smuggle it into England without payment of the duty. When discovered in a customs search, the lace turned out to be of English origin, of little value and not subject to duty. The traditional view is that Lady Eldon is not liable for an attempt to smuggle. (1 Wharton, Criminal Law (12th ed.), § 225, p. 304, n.9)

On the other hand, factual impossibility was no defense. For example, a man was held liable for attempted murder when he shot into the room in which his target usually slept and, fortuitously, the target was sleeping elsewhere in the house that night. (State v. Mitchell, 170 Mo. 633, 71 S.W. 175.) Although one bullet struck the target's customary pillow, attainment of the criminal objective was factually impossible....

The New York cases can be parsed out along similar lines. One of the leading cases on legal impossibility is People v. Jaffe, 185 N.Y. 497, 78 N.E. 169, in which we held that there was no liability for the attempted receipt of stolen property when the property received by the defendant in the belief that it was stolen was, in fact under the control of the true owner. Similarly, in People v. Teal, 196 N.Y. 372, 89 N.E. 1086, a conviction for

a. N.Y. Penal Law § 125.00 ("Homicide means conduct which causes the death of a person").—EDS.

attempted subornation of perjury was overturned on the theory that the testimony attempted to be suborned was irrelevant to the merits of the case. Since it was not subornation of perjury to solicit false, but irrelevant, testimony, "the person through whose procuration the testimony is given cannot be guilty of subornation of perjury and, by the same rule, an unsuccessful attempt to that which is not a crime when effectuated, cannot be held to be an attempt to commit the crime specified." (196 N.Y., at p. 377, 89 N.E. at p. 1088.) Factual impossibility, however, was no defense. Thus, a man could be held for attempted grand larceny when he picked an empty pocket.

As can be seen from even this abbreviated discussion, the distinction between "factual" and "legal" impossibility was a nice one indeed and the courts tended to place a greater value on legal form than on any substantive danger the defendant's actions posed for society. The approach of the draftsmen of the Model Penal Code was to eliminate the defense of impossibility in virtually all situations. Under the code provision, to constitute an attempt, it is still necessary that the result intended or desired by the actor constitute a crime. However, the code suggested a fundamental change to shift the locus of analysis to the actor's mental frame of reference and away from undue dependence upon external considerations. The basic premise of the code provision is that what was in the actor's own mind should be the standard for determining his dangerousness to society and, hence, his liability for attempted criminal conduct.

In the belief that neither of the two branches of the traditional impossibility arguments detracts from the offender's moral culpability, the Legislature substantially carried the code's treatment of impossibility into the 1967 revision of the Penal Law. Thus, a person is guilty of an attempt when, with intent to commit a crime, he engages in conduct which tends to effect the commission of such crime. (Penal Law, § 110.00.) It is no defense that, under the attendant circumstances, the crime was factually or legally impossible of commission, "if such crime could have been committed had the attendant circumstances been as such person believed them to be." (Penal Law, § 110.10.) Thus, if defendant believed the victim to be alive at the time of the shooting, it is no defense to the charge of attempted murder that the victim may have been dead.

Turning to the facts of the case before us, we believe that there is sufficient evidence in the record from which the jury could conclude that the defendant believed Geller to be alive at the time defendant fired shots into Geller's head. Defendant admitted firing five shots at a most vital part of the victim's anatomy from virtually point blank range. Although defendant contended that the victim had already been grievously wounded by another, from the defendant's admitted actions, the jury could conclude that the defendant's purpose and intention was to administer the coup de grace.

Commonwealth v. Henley

Supreme Court of Pennsylvania.
504 Pa. 408, 474 A.2d 1115 (1984).

■ PAPADAKOS, JUSTICE.

Appellant is the owner of the Henley Brothers Jewelry Store located at 740 Samson Street in the City of Philadelphia. On December 22, 1980, an informant, wired with a tape recording device, was given five specially coated chains by the police, and sent to Appellant's jewelry store. The informant entered the store and offered to sell the gold chains to Appellant. He represented to Appellant that the chains were stolen. Appellant, believing them to be stolen, purchased the chains for $30.00....

Appellant was charg[ed] with the crime of theft by receiving stolen goods and receiving stolen property as a business. 18 Pa. Cons. Stat. § 3925. These charges were later amended to attempted theft by unlawful taking or disposition, 18 Pa. Cons. Stat. §§ 901, 3925, and he was tried on this charge at a non-jury trial....

At the conclusion of the Commonwealth's case, Appellant demurred to the evidence, arguing that the chains were not stolen property because they were in police custody, and that, therefore, he could not be found guilty of an attempt to receive stolen property which was not stolen. The trial court found this defense of legal impossibility persuasive and granted the demurrer.

A defense based on the old legal or factual impossibility argument ... is no longer available. [However,] an intent to commit an act which is not characterized as a crime by the laws of the subject jurisdiction can not be the basis of a criminal charge and conviction even though the actor believes or misapprehends the intended act to be proscribed by the criminal laws. An example of this is where a fisherman believes he is committing an offense in fishing on a certain lake without a license when a fishing license is, in fact, not required in the subject jurisdiction. Since the conduct here would be perfectly legal, the actor could not be held accountable for any attempted crime.

Since the defense of legal impossibility has been abrogated, it was not available to Appellant and the demurrer was improperly granted. This matter must, therefore, be remanded to the Court of Common Pleas for trial.

■ Nix, Chief Justice, concurring.

I join the opinion and write in an attempt to further clarify an area which has proven over the years to be one elusive of satisfactory explication.

[A] prosecution for an attempt, without regard to the impossibility of achieving the intended result, [is allowed] where the conduct would constitute the crime, if the attendant circumstances were as the actor believed them to be. However, ... we must be careful to distinguish situations where the intended conduct is not a crime. The mere fact that one thinks his conduct is criminal, but it is in fact lawful conduct, does not provide a basis for attaching criminal liability. The actor's willingness to perform an act which society has not deemed criminal does not reflect the dangerous disposition that would warrant a criminal sanction.

Up to this point in the development of our law, we have not accepted a willingness to break the law as the sole criterion for attaching criminal liability. The abstract inclination to violate the law must be concretized into an intent to engage in specific conduct which, if completed as intended, would amount to a violation of the criminal law. In both instances there is a subjective willingness to engage in the activity regardless of its legality. The justification for criminal sanction in the latter is that the conduct intended and entered upon is in fact a crime.

Candor requires the acknowledgement that [this] distinction . . . is not beyond question. Experience may prove that this approach will produce its own problems in its application. Since I am not willing to accept the position that intent to break the law should be the sole criterion,* and the former approach [of differentiating between factual and legal impossibility] has demonstrated its gross deficiencies, I applaud this . . . change.

QUESTIONS AND COMMENTS

1. *Impossibility and Mistake*. The law of mistake (see ch. 5) deals with situations in which the defendant wrongly believed that her conduct was legal. The law of impossible attempts deals with cases in which the defendant wrongly believed that her conduct was *illegal*. When do we hold someone responsible for attempting to violate a law when they mistakenly believe they have violated one? Traditional American criminal law doctrine allowed "legal impossibility" as a defense, but not "factual impossibility." This rule was closely related to traditional mistake of law doctrine: mistake of law doctrine tells us that defendants do not get to define what *isn't* criminal through their mistaken beliefs about what is legal. Legal impossibility doctrine tells us that they don't get to define what *is* criminal either. More recently, under the influence of the Model Penal Code, impossibility is said *not* be a defense when the defendant's actual intent, not limited by true facts unknown to him, was to do an act or bring about a result proscribed by law.

Why is modern doctrine—and the Model Penal Code in particular—hostile to impossibility claims? How do the various traditional rationales of punishment view the impossibility defense? Is the line between impossible attempts to commit non-crimes and impossible attempts to commit crimes more sensible than that between legally and factually impossible attempts? In terms of dangerousness, is there necessarily a difference between a person who attempts to commit a non-crime and one who attempts to commit a crime, assuming in both cases they *think* they're attempting to commit a crime (or a wrong, or to inflict harm)?

2. In what sense is impossibility a *defense*? Does it negate an offense element? Does it excuse—or justify—otherwise punishable conduct? Who should bear the burden of proof on impossibility?

3. Many American impossibility cases involve the crime of receiving stolen property (see, e.g., *Henley* and the classic case of *Jaffe*, summarized in *Dlugash*). Assume the crime of receiving stolen property is defined as "purposely receiv[ing] . . . movable property of another knowing that it has

* We should not rush to generalize proclivities beyond the proclivity to commit a specific recognized crime. To do otherwise would allow the law of attempt to manufacture crimes not previously defined by the legislature.

been stolen, or believing that it has probably been stolen." Model Penal Code § 223.6(1). Why wouldn't someone like Jaffe, say, be guilty of receiving stolen property, never mind of *attempting* to receive stolen property? Is it impossible for him to receive stolen property that isn't in fact stolen, or is it impossible for him to *attempt* to receive stolen property that isn't in fact stolen? What difference does this make if an attempted crime is punished at the same level as a consummated one? Consider the following case.

People v. Thousand
Supreme Court of Michigan.
465 Mich. 149, 631 N.W.2d 694 (2001).

■ YOUNG, J.

On December 8, 1998, while using the screen name "Bekka," [Deputy William] Liczbinski was approached by defendant, who was using the screen name "Mr. Auto–Mag," in an Internet chat room. Defendant described himself as a twenty-three-year-old male from Warren, and Bekka described herself as a fourteen-year-old female from Detroit. Bekka indicated that her name was Becky Fellins, and defendant revealed that his name was Chris Thousand. During this initial conversation, defendant sent Bekka, via the Internet, a photograph of his face.

From December 9 through 16, 1998, Liczbinski, still using the screen name "Bekka," engaged in chat room conversation with defendant. During these exchanges, the conversation became sexually explicit. Defendant made repeated lewd invitations to Bekka to engage in various sexual acts, despite various indications of her young age. * * *

The two then planned to meet at an area McDonald's restaurant at 5:00 p.m. on the following Thursday.... Liczbinski and other deputy sheriffs were present at the specified McDonald's restaurant when they saw defendant inside a vehicle matching the description given to Bekka by defendant. Defendant ... entered the restaurant [and] was ... taken into custody.... Following a preliminary examination, defendant was bound over for trial on charges of solicitation to commit third-degree criminal sexual conduct, Mich. Cons. Laws §§ 750.157b(3)(a) and 750.520d(1)(a) [and] attempted distribution of obscene material to a minor, Mich. Cons. Laws §§ 750.92 and 722.675.[3]

Defendant brought a motion to quash the information, arguing that, because the existence of a child victim was an element of each of the charged offenses, the evidence was legally insufficient to support the charges. The circuit court agreed and dismissed the case.... The Court of Appeals affirmed ... conclud[ing] that it was legally impossible for defendant to have committed the charged offense of attempted distribution of obscene material to a minor. The panel held that, because "Bekka" was, in fact, an adult, an essential requirement of the

3. [A]lthough the original information charged defendant with the *completed* offense of distribution of obscene material to a minor, the circuit court subsequently granted the prosecution's motion to amend the charge to *attempted* distribution of obscene material to a minor.

underlying substantive offense was not met (dissemination to a minor), and therefore it was legally impossible for defendant to have committed the crime. * * *

Defendant in this case is not charged with the substantive crime of distributing obscene material to a minor in violation of Mich. Cons. Laws § 722.675.[16] It is unquestioned that defendant could not be convicted of that crime, because defendant allegedly distributed obscene material not to "a minor," but to an adult man. Instead, defendant is charged with the distinct offense of attempt, which requires only that the prosecution prove intention to commit an offense prohibited by law, coupled with conduct toward the commission of that offense. The notion that it would be "impossible" for the defendant to have committed the *completed* offense is simply irrelevant to the analysis. Rather, in deciding guilt on a charge of attempt, the trier of fact must examine the unique circumstances of the particular case and determine whether the prosecution has proven that the defendant possessed the requisite specific intent and that he engaged in some act "towards the commission" of the intended offense.

What would happen to undercover police work if impossibility were a defense? The classic American legal impossibility case features a police informant who tries to get a suspect to buy property the suspect (wrongly) thinks is stolen. See, e.g., *Jaffe* (cloth); Booth v. State, 398 P.2d 863 (Ct. Crim. App. Okla. 1964) (coat); *Henley* (jewelry); United States v. Hsu, 155 F.3d 189 (3d Cir. 1998) (trade secrets).

4. *Types of Impossibility*. Impossibility cases can be divided into some formal categories. These divisions may not be particularly analytically helpful, but they may help to explain some aspects of existing practice (and the Model Penal Code drafters' decision to do away with the distinction between legal and factual impossibility altogether).

A. Pure legal impossibility

1. Examples: D possesses liquor after Prohibition is repealed, wrongly believing it's still in force; in a custodial interference case, D mistakenly believes it's illegal for him, the non-custodial parent, to take his child, though it turns out in his jurisdiction that all biological parents are immune from custodial

16. At the time of the alleged offense, Mich. Cons. Laws § 722.675 provided, in relevant part:

(1) A person is guilty of distributing obscene matter to a minor if that person does either of the following:

(a) Knowingly disseminates to a minor sexually explicit visual or verbal material that is harmful to minors.

* * * (2) A person knowingly disseminates sexually explicit matter to a minor when the person knows both the nature of the matter and the status of the minor to whom the matter is disseminated.

(3) A person knows the nature of matter if the person either is aware of the character and content of the matter or recklessly disregards circumstances suggesting the character and content of the matter.

(4) A person knows the status of a minor if the person either is aware that the person to whom the dissemination is made is under 18 years of age or recklessly disregards a substantial risk that the person to whom the dissemination is made is under 18 years of age.

interference *criminal charges* (though they may face court orders to return children, be held criminally liable if they violate such court orders, etc.).

2. These cases—involving attempts to commit non-crimes—rarely reach the courts (though see *Henley*) because it would plainly undercut the legislature's monopoly on criminal law-making if we punished the defendant for attempting a crime that the legislature abolished or never enacted. How, in fact, would one even name (or charge in an indictment) the crime the defendant "attempted" to commit? It might be true that defendants in these cases demonstrate a general willingness to violate "the law" broadly construed, but they don't demonstrate a willingness to violate any particular law that is in force, and in a legal regime committed to Rule of Law values, the statement that a person is a "willing law violator" rather than a demonstrated willing violator of a specific statute is a troubling one.

B. Traditional legal impossibility

1. Examples: in a forgery case, D changes the numbers on a check, unaware that he's not making a "material" alteration, because—as it turns out—the written amount prevails (see Wilson v. State, 85 Miss. 687, 38 So. 46 (1905)); in a custodial interference case, D doesn't realize that both parents have joint custody pending finalization of divorce decree, even if the child is living with one spouse pursuant to a separation agreement.

2. These cases involve general mistakes about a legal condition necessary to consummate the offense; they are made at the same fairly high level of abstraction as in cases of mistakes of non-governing law (e.g., what is a "material alteration" in forgery?). That is to say, the person knows the particulars of her situation but has trouble drawing a legal conclusion even with that knowledge. Just as the defendant in *Woods*, ch. 5 supra, knew that Leo Shufelt had gotten an *ex parte* divorce in Nevada but did not know whether he was nonetheless still married in Vermont, and just as the defendant in *Smith*, ch. 5 supra, knows that he installed fixtures in his landlord's apartment but does not know that when he leaves, the fixtures remain the property of the landlord, so defendants in these impossible attempts cases know what happened, but not its legal meaning.

C. Legal/factual impossibility

1. Examples: D receives property wrongly believing it's "stolen" (*Jaffe*); in a custodial interference case, D's lawyer reads her the wrong divorce decree over the phone so that she wrongly believes she doesn't have custody.

2. These mistakes (like mistakes of fact with a legal aspect) are about a legal condition needed to consummate the offense, but the defendant's error is particular and drawing a conclusion if

particulars are known would be easy. Thus, like the defendant in the classic mistake case who wrongly believes he is unmarried because his wife gave him a forged divorce decree, defendants in this class of impossibility cases could readily draw a legal conclusion (about the presence or absence of an offense element) if they only knew precisely what had happened.

D. Pure factual impossibility

1. Examples: D picks an empty pocket; in a custodial interference case, D carries off a life-like doll from his child's bed wrongly believing it's his child.
2. The mistake that precludes the defendant from consummating the offense has no obvious legal element at all.
3. The ready capacity to distinguish these last two classes of cases depends in significant part on whether it is appropriate to say that all elements of offenses are "legal" elements: thus, a person who hands money to a non-juror has made a legal/factual mistake if we emphasize that bribing a *juror* (rather than non-juror) is an element of the bribery statute and hence a *legal* fact, but it will look more like a purely factual error if we emphasize that (unlike the error made by the defendant in *Jaffe*) the recipient's status as "juror" has no apparent legal quality in the way that a good's status as "stolen" does. What may be even more bothersome, the question of whether the person who hands money and instructions to the "non-juror" is making an error about an offense element or purely about a fact, also seems to depend on the precise wording of the statute she is charged with violating: If she is charged with attempting to obstruct justice, we would tend to focus on the fact that she had not taken action likely to effectuate her desired result (obstructing justice) rather than that she had mistakenly thought an absent offense element was present. Similarly, the defendant who shoots the pillow (see *Mitchell*, discussed in *Dlugash*) might be seen as making a mistake about an offense element (the thing he shot is not a human being and an element of the homicide statute is—or at least may be—that one must kill a human being) or as making a factual error (choosing factually inefficacious means to achieve the end of killing). In *Thousand*, we can describe the defendant as mistakenly believing that the person he distributed the material to was less than eighteen (sounds factual), that he mistakenly thought the person was ineligible to receive the material he distributed (sounds more legal/factual) or simply note that he mistakenly thought an offense element was present. *Dlugash* is similar: did he think his victim was alive, not dead (a non-legal fact) or that an element of the homicide offense (causing the death of a living person) was present?

Traditionally, courts were clear on two things. Only A. and B. transparently counted as viable defenses, under the heading of "legal impossibility," where D., as an instance of "factual impossibility," did not. Trouble traditionally arose in category C., as courts found it difficult (or at least complained about finding it difficult) to differentiate between legal and factual impossibility in borderline cases. For instance, assuming—in our custodial interference case—I am allowed to take my child with the custodial parent's consent, if I pick up the child unaware that the custodial parent has left a phone message granting me consent, am I making a factual or a legal factual mistake? Am I mistaken about the fact of the phone message, or about its legal significance, or about the absence of consent as an element of the offense of custodial interference? Or, to quote a fairly typical recent opinion (United States v. Hsu, 155 F.3d 189, 199 (3d Cir. 1998)):

> The ... distinction between factual and legal impossibility is essentially a matter of semantics, for every case of legal impossibility can reasonably be characterized as a factual impossibility. For instance, the fact that A shoots a corpse, rather than a person, is also a product of circumstances beyond A's control; A did not commit murder because the person he intended to kill was already dead.

But is the line between factual and legal impossibility really that hard to draw? Or is the (far more significant? only?) problem not that it's hard to draw, but that it's beside the point? In the classic factual impossibility case of picking an empty pocket, what's the mistake? What's the element (the "attendant circumstance") the thwarted pickpocket was mistaken about, assuming theft is defined as unlawfully taking property of another with purpose to deprive him thereof? Can't a *legal* impossibility case be a case where the defendant makes an (inculpatory) mistake about an offense element (thinking it's there when it really isn't), while a *factual* impossibility case is one where the defendant is wrong about something external to the definition of the offense? Would that distinction explain the cases? Would it make sense? Or is it wholly irrelevant?

Think about the following: Defendant One (as in *Mitchell* and *Dlugash*) thinks he is shooting at a live person, though he is not. At the formal level, one certainly *could* describe him as mistakenly believing an offense element is present when it is not. (It is a formal element in virtually all homicide statutes that one causes the death of another human being.) Defendant Two tries to defraud (through phone and e-mail messages, for instance) a person who is actually already dead by the time the messages arrive. Fraud statutes usually don't explicitly state (as an offense element) that one must try to acquire property of another live person, so one might well be more prone—if using this categorical scheme—to describe what the Defendant Two sought to do as *factually* impossible to achieve. But is it sensible to believe that the cases should be treated differently simply because one error is (marginally) related to an offense element?

The modern trend is to reject "legal impossibility" and recognize only A. as a defense (generally without recourse to the now disfavored label "legal impossibility"). This avoids the familiar difficulty of distinguishing legal and factual impossibility within category C. Put another way, this move shifts the crucial line-drawing exercise to another point along the spectrum, namely the line between A. and B.

5. Consider the connection between the distinction between preparation and attempt and the impossibility question, explored in the following case.

United States v. Oviedo
United States Court of Appeals for the Fifth Circuit.
525 F.2d 881 (1976).

The facts before us are ... simple—Oviedo sold a substance he thought to be heroin, which in reality was an uncontrolled substance. The legal question before us is likewise simple—are these combined acts and intent cognizable as a criminal attempt under 21 U.S.C. § 846.[a] The answer, however, is not so simple.

Oviedo and the government both agree the resolution of this case rests in an analysis of the doctrines of legal and factual impossibility as defenses to a criminal attempt.... The traditional analysis recognizes legal impossibility as a valid defense, but refuses to so recognize factual impossibility.

These definitions [of legal and factual impossibility] are not particularly helpful here, for they do nothing more than provide a different focus for the analysis. In one sense, the impossibility involved here might be deemed legal, for those *acts* which Oviedo set in motion, the transfer of the substance in his possession, were not a crime. In another sense, the impossibility is factual, for the *objective* of Oviedo, the sale of heroin, was proscribed by law, and failed only because of a circumstance unknown to Oviedo. * * *

When the question before the court is whether certain conduct constitutes mere preparation which is not punishable, or an attempt which is, the possibility of error is mitigated by the requirement that the objective acts of the defendant evidence commitment to the criminal venture and corroborate the *mens rea.* To the extent that this requirement is preserved it prevents the conviction of persons engaged in innocent acts on the basis of a *mens rea* proved through speculative inferences, unreliable forms of testimony, and past criminal conduct.

Courts could have approached the preparation-attempt determination in another fashion, eliminating any notion of particular objective facts, and simply could have asked whether the evidence at hand was sufficient to prove the necessary intent. But ... conviction upon proof of mere intent provides too great a possibility of speculation and abuse. * * *

When the defendant sells a substance which is actually heroin, it is reasonable to infer that he knew the physical nature of the substance, and to place on him the burden of dispelling that inference. However, if we convict the defendant of attempting to sell heroin for the sale of a non-narcotic substance, we eliminate an objective element that has major evidentiary significance and we increase the risk of mistaken conclusions that the defendant believed the goods were narcotics.

a. 21 U.S.C. § 846 ("Any person who attempts or conspires to commit any offense defined in this subchapter [dealing with 'drug abuse prevention and control'] shall be subject to the same penalties as those prescribed for the offense, the commission of which was the object of the attempt or conspiracy"). There is no general federal criminal attempt statute.—EDS.

Thus, we demand that in order for a defendant to be guilty of a criminal attempt, the objective acts performed, without any reliance on the accompanying *mens rea*, mark the defendant's conduct as criminal in nature. The acts should be unique rather than so commonplace that they are engaged in by persons not in violation of the law.

Here we have only two objective facts. First, Oviedo told the agent that the substance he was selling was heroin, and second, portions of the substance were concealed in a television set. If another objective fact were present, if the substance were heroin, we would have a strong objective basis for the determination of criminal intent and conduct consistent and supportive of that intent. The test set out above would be met, and, absent a delivery, the criminal attempt would be established. But when this objective basis for the determination of intent is removed, when the substance is not heroin, the conduct becomes ambivalent.... We cannot conclude that the objective acts of Oviedo apart from any indirect evidence of intent mark his conduct as criminal in nature. Rather, those acts are consistent with a noncriminal enterprise. Therefore, we will not allow the jury's determination of Oviedo's intent to form the sole basis of a criminal offense.

What's the connection between the preparation/attempt issue and the impossibility issue? Can both issues be reduced to the same inquiry? Is motive relevant to (required for?) attempt liability? How does *Oviedo's* approach fit into the spectrum of traditional approaches to impossibility laid out above? For a case applying *Oviedo*, see United States v. Reeves, 794 F.2d 1101 (6th Cir. 1986) (holding that the fact the defendant possessed not cocaine, but an innocuous substance, was irrelevant to the defendant's conviction for attempt to possess cocaine because "the Congressional intent in fashioning the attempt provision as part of an all-out effort to reach all acts and activities related to the drug traffic was all inclusive and calculated to eliminate technical obstacles confronting law enforcement officials").

How does *Oviedo* work and what problems should we expect in trying to implement it? At core, one might argue the case holds that fact finders should convict only if they believe beyond a reasonable doubt that what the defendant intended to do was specifically proscribed by the criminal law. (It is not enough that the defendant intended to violate "the law" in some more general sense, a fact that might be revealed beyond a reasonable doubt by, e.g., furtiveness; thus, for instance, someone who believes it is illegal to "smuggle" in currency or sugar, though there are no actual prohibitions against bringing currency or sugar into the country, might act like someone who thinks he's got to conceal what he's doing.) The basis of this belief must be that fact finders are able to find beyond a reasonable doubt, solely by observing the defendant's conduct, that he must have failed to meet all his subjective ends, and believe that he'd have violated some in-force statute had he met these ends. It is *crucial* that the fact finder know this looking only at the defendant's conduct, without regard to any extrinsic confessional evidence; if he's satisfied to have accomplished what he did, the fact that he thought it had a different legal quality will be knowable only by confession. Failure or ineptness is more readily inferable from externally verifiable facts while the legal quality of the act is typically not.

What "principles" are at stake in making this judgment? Why might we think it inappropriate to convict a defendant when the *only* potential source of inculpatory material is confession? Confessions, after all, are used when the material confessed corroborates externally verifiable facts or leads us to know what *could* have been seen (even if no one actually saw it). And second, what principles are at stake in making the judgment that it is not appropriate to punish the defendant simply for revealing a general anti-social disposition?

Note that none of the "formal" lines we drew will do much good if this is the approach: Wilson looks guilty (what else was he trying to do but *forge* a check? try out his new pen? number fetishism?) while none of the people in the custodial interference cases seems guilty (except, perhaps, the doll-baby snatcher); Dlugash looks innocent, though: there *are* facially plausible reasons to shoot a dead body—e.g., to scare off others in the same room—whether those are Dlugash's authentic reasons or not. (But the hypothetical defendant who sent out e-mail and phone messages attempting to defraud someone who is already dead—assuming she has also passed the preparation/attempt line—would probably not be exonerated by virtue of the fact that one cannot defraud the dead: it is plain on the face of the conduct that the person sought to do something different.)

Look at an "attempted bigamy" prosecution in which the defendant is not in fact married though he may believe, incorrectly, that he is, or at an "attempted statutory rape" prosecution in which the defendant wrongly thinks the victim is underage although she is in fact overage. How would we *know* that the defendant thought he was married (or that he had not met his subjective ends marrying *now*, whether or not that constituted an illicit second marriage), and how would we tell how old the defendant thought the person he had sex with was, or whether he wanted to sleep with *her*, rather than have sex with an underage girl, unless he tells us?

It might be hardest to deal with (atypical) cases, in which *most* people "attempting" the crime the defendant arguably attempted have done nothing to corroborate, externally, an illicit intention, but the particular defendant has. Think first about the "attempted" statutory rapist who has "demonstrated" he hasn't met his subjective ends by picking girls up at a junior high (and happens to pick up an 18-year-old who says she's 14). Think, too, about more realistic cases like *Thousand*: does entering a chat room that is labeled as a chat room for teens show, on its face and without regard to confession, both that the defendant subjectively believed he was talking to a teen and that he did not meet his subjective ends if she turned out not to be a teenager?

Thinking about *Thousand* raises two other tricky issues, though: One, to which we return in ch. 7, is whether it is appropriate for a government agent to engage in (arguably provocative) sexual "chats" with the defendant. Is it particularly bothersome if the agent is more persistent, or more sexually explicit, or more prone to imply that "she" is willing to engage in sexual activity than actual teenagers in such chat rooms typically are? (This raises an entrapment issue.) The second is how to evaluate a claim by defendants in the position of Thousand who never set up a "meet" with their "chat" partner but are charged, instead, *solely* with attempting to distribute pornographic material to minors. Assume that some such defendants say that they (at least partly) *know* that they are (at least very likely) to be chatting with adult men posing as young girls. They don't *focus* on that fact, but are partly aware of it (in a cognitive sense). Might Thousand describe himself as intending to engage in sexual "chat" with (or distribution of pornographic images and words to) someone who does not contradict his *fantasy* that he is "chatting" with a teenage girl? Is that (sufficiently) distinct from intending to "chat" with (send sexual materials to) a teenage girl? See Donald S. Yamagami, Comment, "Prosecuting Cyber–Pedophiles: How Can Intent Be Shown in a Virtual World in Light of the Fantasy Defense?," 41 Santa Clara L. Rev. 547 (2001). Factfinders have generally, but not invariably, rejected defendants' claims that they believed they were "chatting" with adults posing as children, and courts have left these findings undisturbed. See, e.g., United States v. Bailey, 228 F.3d 637 (6th Cir. 2000); People v. Scott, 740 N.E.2d 1201 (Ill. App. 2000).

Perhaps the fullest, most revealing picture of an Internet "sting" operation can be seen in People v. Biagini, 2003 WL 21246774 (Cal. App.). The case also raises with particular clarity a preparation vs. attempt issue that always arises in less clear form whenever alleged pedophiles arrange "meets" with people who turn out to be agents: how sure can we be that they would have had sex with an actual teenager they had to confront in real life? In *Biagini*, as the dissenters note, the defendant never even drove his car to the alleyway behind the pizza restaurant at which he was slated to meet "Christina"—an actual teen who had been, with the advice of a police officer, engaged in explicit sexual chat with the defendant after he had met her and sexually propositioned her earlier. Biagini had gone first to the restaurant behind which he was supposed to meet his victim and admitted to police officers that he had looked to see if she was inside that restaurant. When he found out he could not buy single slices at the first restaurant, he went to a second pizza place where he was arrested. He was convicted of attempting unlawful sexual intercourse with a minor more than three years younger than himself.

6. Does absence of causation imply presence of attempt liability? Consider *Dlugash*.

7. Justice Holmes, in *Kennedy* (supra), makes a special exception for "absurd" attempts. Just how absurd must an attempt be not to be punishable? Is it enough if it has no chance of success—say because of the intended victim's superior strength or wit? Or because of the harmless nature of the act itself—imagine sticking pins in a doll resembling the victim, or painting Satanic symbols on the victim's house, or poisoning someone with artificial sweetener? Model Penal Code § 5.05(2) provides for a reduction in punishment or dismissal if the actor's conduct is "so inherently unlikely to result or culminate in the commission of a crime that neither such conduct nor the actor presents a public danger." Doesn't this amount to a (factual) impossibility defense after all?

3. MENTAL STATE

The question of the mens rea of attempt traditionally has had a more straightforward answer than that of its actus reus. Nothing less than *intent* will do. (Why? Think about the rationales for punishing attempt in the first place.)

But intent with respect to what? (And, as always when it comes to "intent": what exactly does intent mean? Purpose, knowledge, recklessness? General intent? Specific intent?)

With its emphasis on element, rather than offense, analysis, the Model Penal Code further complicates matters by raising the question of what mental state is required with respect to what type of offense element—conduct, attendant circumstance, result? See Model Penal Code § 5.01, supra. Similar to its detailed and rather complex treatment of the actus reus of attempt, the Model Code's differentiated approach to the mens rea of attempt has not caught on among American legislatures, see, e.g., Cal. Penal Code § 21a, supra, N.Y. Penal Law § 110.00, supra, though it is worth considering whether courts nonetheless employ it, if only implicitly, as they interpret the broadly phrased attempt provisions in their respective criminal codes.

Under the Model Code scheme, what is the mens rea of attempt with respect to the result element of the consummated crime? When I aim a gun at another person must I pull the trigger *with the purpose* of killing her, or is it enough if I merely think that pulling the trigger will kill her? What about attendant circumstances? And conduct? Will the mens rea required in the definition of the object offense suffice? Or is intent required in all cases, with respect to all offense elements?

a. Mental State With Respect to Result and Conduct

Smallwood v. State

Court of Appeals, Maryland.
343 Md. 97, 680 A.2d 512 (1996).

■ MURPHY, CHIEF JUDGE.

On August 29, 1991, Dwight Ralph Smallwood was diagnosed as being infected with the Human Immunodeficiency Virus (HIV). According to medical records from the Prince George's County Detention Center, he had been informed of his HIV-positive status by September 25, 1991. In February 1992, a social worker made Smallwood aware of the necessity of practicing "safe sex" in order to avoid transmitting the virus to his sexual partners, and in July 1993, Smallwood told health care providers at Children's Hospital that he had only one sexual partner and that they always used condoms. Smallwood again tested positive for HIV in February and March of 1994.

On September 26, 1993, Smallwood and an accomplice robbed a woman at gunpoint, and forced her into a grove of trees where each man alternately placed a gun to her head while the other one raped her. On September

28, 1993, Smallwood and an accomplice robbed a second woman at gunpoint and took her to a secluded location, where Smallwood inserted his penis into her with "slight penetration." On September 30, 1993, Smallwood and an accomplice robbed yet a third woman, also at gunpoint, and took her to a local school where she was forced to perform oral sex on Smallwood and was raped by him. In each of these episodes, Smallwood threatened to kill his victims if they did not cooperate or to return and shoot them if they reported his crimes. Smallwood did not wear a condom during any of these criminal episodes.

Based upon his attack on September 28, 1993, Smallwood was charged with, among other crimes, attempted first-degree rape, robbery with a deadly weapon, assault with intent to murder, and reckless endangerment. In separate indictments, Smallwood was also charged with the attempted second-degree murder of each of his three victims. On October 11, 1994, Smallwood pled guilty in the Circuit Court for Prince George's County to attempted first-degree rape and robbery with a deadly weapon. The circuit court (Nichols, J.) also convicted Smallwood of assault with intent to murder and reckless endangerment based upon his September 28, 1993 attack, and convicted Smallwood of all three counts of attempted second-degree murder. * * *

Smallwood asserts that the trial court lacked sufficient evidence to support its conclusion that Smallwood intended to kill his three victims. Smallwood argues that the fact that he engaged in unprotected sexual intercourse, even though he knew that he carried HIV, is insufficient to infer an intent to kill. The most that can reasonably be inferred, Smallwood contends, is that he is guilty of recklessly endangering his victims by exposing them to the risk that they would become infected themselves. The State disagrees, arguing that the facts of this case are sufficient to infer an intent to kill. The State likens Smallwood's HIV-positive status to a deadly weapon and argues that engaging in unprotected sex when one is knowingly infected with HIV is equivalent to firing a loaded firearm at that person.[3]

In *Faya v. Almaraz,* 329 Md. 435, 438–440, 620 A.2d 327 (1993), we discussed HIV and the Acquired Immune Deficiency Syndrome (AIDS) in detail. There, we described HIV as a retrovirus that attacks the human immune system, weakening it, and ultimately destroying the body's capacity to ward off disease. We also noted that

> [t]he virus may reside latently in the body for periods as long as ten years or more, during which time the infected person will manifest no symptoms of illness and function normally. HIV typically spreads via genital fluids or blood transmitted from one person to another through sexual contact, the sharing of needles in intravenous drug use, blood

3. Smallwood also argues that the legislature preempted the crimes of assault with intent to murder and attempted murder with respect to transmission of HIV when it enacted Maryland Code §§ 18–601.1 of the Health General Article, which makes it a criminal offense to knowingly transfer or attempt to transfer HIV to another individual and sets a maximum sentence of three years imprisonment. Because we reverse Smallwood's convictions of attempted murder and assault with intent to murder on other grounds, it is unnecessary to address this argument.

> transfusions, infiltration into wounds, or from mother to child during pregnancy or birth.

Id. at 439, 620 A.2d 327. In *Faya,* we also described AIDS and its relationship to HIV:

> AIDS, in turn, is the condition that eventually results from an immune system gravely impaired by HIV. Medical studies have indicated that most people who carry the virus will progress to AIDS. AIDS patients by definition are profoundly immunocompromised; that is, they are prone to any number of diseases and opportunistic infections that a person with a healthy immune system might otherwise resist. AIDS is thus the acute clinical phase of immune dysfunction.... AIDS is invariably fatal.

Id. at 439–40, 620 A.2d 327. In this case, we must determine what legal inferences may be drawn when an individual infected with the HIV virus knowingly exposes another to the risk of HIV-infection, and the resulting risk of death by AIDS.

As we have previously stated, "[t]he required intent in the crimes of assault with intent to murder and attempted murder is the specific intent to murder, i.e., the specific intent to kill under circumstances that would not legally justify or excuse the killing or mitigate it to manslaughter." *State v. Earp,* 319 Md. 156, 167, 571 A.2d 1227 (1990). * * *

Smallwood ... was properly found guilty of attempted murder and assault with intent to murder only if there was sufficient evidence from which the trier of fact could reasonably have concluded that Smallwood possessed a specific intent to kill at the time he assaulted each of the three women. * * *

An intent to kill may be proved by circumstantial evidence. "[S]ince intent is subjective and, without the cooperation of the accused, cannot be directly and objectively proven, its presence must be shown by established facts which permit a proper inference of its existence." *Earp, supra,* 319 Md. at 167, 571 A.2d 1227. Therefore, the trier of fact may infer the existence of the required intent from surrounding circumstances such as "the accused's acts, conduct and words." *State v. Raines,* 326 Md. 582, 591, 606 A.2d 265 (1992). As we have repeatedly stated, "under the proper circumstances, an intent to kill may be inferred from the use of a deadly weapon directed at a vital part of the human body." *Raines, supra,* 326 Md. at 591, 606 A.2d 265.

In *Raines, supra,* we upheld the use of such an inference. In that case, Raines and a friend were traveling on a highway when the defendant fired a pistol into the driver's side window of a tractor trailer in an adjacent lane. The shot killed the driver of the tractor trailer, and Raines was convicted of first degree murder. The evidence in the case showed that Raines shot at the driver's window of the truck, knowing that the truck driver was immediately behind the window. We concluded that "Raines's actions in directing the gun at the window, and therefore at the driver's head on the other side of the window, permitted an inference that Raines shot the gun with the intent to kill." *Id.* at 592–93, 606 A.2d 265.

The State argues that our analysis in *Raines* rested upon two elements: (1) Raines knew that his weapon was deadly, and (2) Raines knew that he was firing it at someone's head. The State argues that Smallwood similarly knew that HIV infection ultimately leads to death, and that he knew that he would be exposing his victims to the risk of HIV transmission by engaging in unprotected sex with them. Therefore, the State argues, a permissible inference can be drawn that Smallwood intended to kill each of his three victims. The State's analysis, however, ignores several factors.

First, we must consider the magnitude of the risk to which the victim is knowingly exposed. The inference drawn in *Raines, supra,* rests upon the rule that "[i]t is permissible to infer that 'one intends the natural and probable consequences of his act.'" *Ford v. State,* 330 Md. 682, 704, 625 A.2d 984 (1993). Before an intent to kill may be inferred based solely upon the defendant's exposure of a victim to a risk of death, it must be shown that the victim's death would have been a natural and probable result of the defendant's conduct.... When a deadly weapon has been fired at a vital part of a victim's body, the risk of killing the victim is so high that it becomes reasonable to assume that the defendant intended the victim to die as a natural and probable consequence of the defendant's actions.

Death by AIDS is clearly one *natural* possible consequence of exposing someone to a risk of HIV infection, even on a single occasion. It is less clear that death by AIDS from that single exposure is a sufficiently *probable* result to provide the sole support for an inference that the person causing the exposure intended to kill the person who was exposed. While the risk to which Smallwood exposed his victims when he forced them to engage in unprotected sexual activity must not be minimized, the State has presented no evidence from which it can reasonably be concluded that death by AIDS is a probable result of Smallwood's actions to the same extent that death is the probable result of firing a deadly weapon at a vital part of someone's body. Without such evidence, it cannot fairly be concluded that death by AIDS was sufficiently probable to support an inference that Smallwood intended to kill his victims in the absence of other evidence indicative of an intent to kill.

In this case, we find no additional evidence from which to infer an intent to kill. Smallwood's actions are wholly explained by an intent to commit rape and armed robbery, the crimes for which he has already pled guilty. For this reason, his actions fail to provide evidence that he also had an intent to kill. As one commentator noted, in discussing a criminal case involving similar circumstances, "[b]ecause virus transmission occurs simultaneously with the act of rape, that act alone would not provide evidence of intent to transmit the virus. Some additional evidence, such as an explicit statement, would be necessary to demonstrate the actor's specific intent." * * *

The cases cited by the State demonstrate the sort of additional evidence needed to support an inference that Smallwood intended to kill his victims. The defendants in these cases have either made explicit statements demonstrating an intent to infect their victims or have taken specific actions demonstrating such an intent and tending to exclude other possible intents. In *State v. Hinkhouse,* 139 Or.App. 446, 912 P.2d 921 (1996), for example, the defendant engaged in unprotected sex with a number of women while knowing that he was HIV positive. The defendant had also actively concealed his HIV-positive status from these women, had lied to several of them by stating that he was not HIV-positive, and had refused the women's requests that he wear condoms. There was also evidence that he had told at least one of his sexual partners that "if he were [HIV-]positive, he would spread the virus to other people." *Id.* at 924. The Oregon Court of Appeals found this evidence to be sufficient to demonstrate an intent to kill, and upheld the defendant's convictions for attempted murder.

In *State v. Caine,* 652 So.2d 611 (La.App. 1995), a conviction for attempted second degree murder was upheld where the defendant had jabbed a used syringe into a victim's arm while shouting "I'll give you AIDS." The defendant in *Weeks v. State,* 834 S.W.2d 559 (Tex.App.1992), made similar statements, and was convicted of attempted murder after he spat on a prison guard. In that case, the defendant knew that he was HIV-positive, and the appellate court found that "the record reflects that [Weeks] thought he could kill the guard by spitting his HIV-infected saliva at him." *Id.* at 562. There was also evidence that at the time of the spitting incident, Weeks had stated that he was "going to take someone with him when he went," that he was "medical now, and that he was 'HIV–4.' "
* * *

In contrast with these cases, the State in this case would allow the trier of fact to infer an intent to kill based solely upon the fact that Smallwood exposed his victims to the risk that they might contract HIV. Without evidence showing that such a result is sufficiently probable to support this inference, we conclude that Smallwood's convictions for attempted murder and assault with intent to murder must be reversed.

QUESTIONS AND COMMENTS

1. The *Smallwood* holding is certainly typical in one regard: to be guilty of attempted murder in most jurisdictions, the defendant must have a purpose (or "specific intent") to kill, even though he might be convicted of murder had he simply been (grossly) reckless in engaging in conduct that risked and actually caused death. See Merritt v. Commonwealth, 164 Va. 653, 180 S.E. 395 (1935) ("To commit murder, one need not intend to take life; but to be guilty of an attempt to murder, he must so intend. It is not sufficient that his act, had it proved fatal, would have been murder."). Thus, in People v. Acevedo, 32 N.Y.2d 807, 298 N.E.2d 691, 345 N.Y.S.2d 555 (1973), the court overturned the attempted murder conviction of a defendant who had fired a rifle from the rooftop of a building, wounding several people, because the jury had not been instructed that he could not be convicted absent an intent to kill. The murder statute in force would have permitted conviction for murder if the defendant had killed a human being by taking "an act imminently dangerous to others" if that act evinced "a depraved mind, regardless of human life, although without a premeditated design to effect the death of any individual."

2. Insofar as attempt is said to require "specific intent" with respect to the result element of the consummated offense, attempt cases raise the line-drawing problems familiar from our discussion of mens rea (see ch. 5). Look carefully at the *Smallwood* opinion: which of the following statements appear to reflect the court's view (or which do you find convincing)?

The court believes that for a person to be guilty of attempted murder, she must have a true purpose that her conduct causes death: mere knowledge, or belief, that it might do so does not suffice.

The court believes that we can (best?) infer such purpose from "confessional" statements: thus, an HIV+ person *could* be convicted of attempted murder for having unprotected sex with someone, even if the probability that such a single sexual act would cause death is low or even nearly non-existent. (Look in this regard at the *Caine* and *Weeks* cases cited in *Smallwood*.)

The court believes that we can often infer (in the absence of confessional statements) that someone has the specific intent that a certain result come about because he knows that it will, but the HIV+ person cannot possibly "know" that it will because it is *not*, in fact, substantially certain that an HIV+ person will transmit the HIV virus to people when one has unprotected sex with them.

The court's inability to infer purpose from gross recklessness is inconsistent with its willingness to infer it from knowledge: once one recognizes that the defendant could choose to have consensual sex (or for that matter, as in this case, choose to rape) for reasons disconnected from the *desire* to kill, one must decide whether to account for the disconnect between "acceptance" of a result and "desire" for that result and the substantial certainty/probability line has *nothing* to do with that.

Knowledge that one's actions will cause a particular result is neither a necessary nor sufficient condition for finding purpose to cause that result. That it is not *necessary* can be seen if one reflects on the possibility of conviction based on confessing the desire to cause harm, or reflects on the case in which a defendant shoots her enemy from a distance, in circumstances that make it unlikely that she will succeed in hitting her. See *People v. Steinberg*, ch. 5, supra. (Note that if it becomes unlikely *enough*, we may have to face, once more, the problem of what to do about inept attempts. Would we ever classify a shooter as making an inept attempt to kill, no matter how improbable success is, or do we reserve that label for those who take steps to kill, like casting spells, that seem categorically disconnected from harm-causing?) That it is not *sufficient* can be seen if one reflects on the possibility that the defendant might be pretty sure he will cause a certain result, but would prefer not to; the result is simply (ordinarily) ancillary to the achievement of his primary goal (in the sense that risking spreading AIDS is ancillary to having sex).

We allow the state to infer intent from knowledge, or to prove intent "by circumstantial evidence," all the time, not just in attempt cases. How else could we hope to prove intent, or any other subjective state of mind, other than through the defendant's admission? (And what would happen to the privilege against self-incrimination—or to conviction rates—if conviction required self-incrimination?) Would it make sense to make it harder (easier?) for the state to prove intent in attempt cases, compared to cases involving consummated offenses? Would it make a difference whether attempted offenses are punished on a par with consummated ones?

3. Note that the Model Penal Code would convict of attempted murder even if the offender did *not* act with the purpose of bringing about the result proscribed in the definition of the consummated offense (death)—provided, of course, he acted with at least the kind of culpability required for the completed offense. Though purpose would be sufficient, it would not be necessary; a "belief" that his actions "will cause such result without further conduct on his part" will do. Model Penal Code § 5.01(1)(b); see also People v. Krovarz, 697 P.2d 378 (Colo. 1985) (relying on Model Penal Code in holding that knowledge as to result suffices for attempt liability). According to the Code drafters, the inclusion of belief was not inconsistent with the traditional rule that attempts require intent (at least as to result), if only the concept of intent is interpreted broadly enough—as it traditionally, if inconsistently, has—to include not only purpose, but knowledge as well. ("Knowledge" here becomes "belief." One can hardly *know* some result will come about when, by hypothesis, it did not; otherwise, it wouldn't be a case of attempt.) Substantively, the drafters felt that in the case of a person who firmly believes his conduct will bring about the statutorily proscribed result, "the manifestation of the actor's dangerousness is just as great—or very nearly as great—as in the case of purposive conduct." Model Penal Code Commentaries § 5.01, at 305. If there is no distinction between purpose and knowledge in attempts, then why should we draw a distinction between these two mental states in other contexts? And how would Smallwood fare under the Model Penal Code test?

4. *Impossible attempts, again.* Occasionally courts are called upon to decide whether an attempt to commit a particular crime is "logically possible" or "legally cognizable." The idea here is that attempt requires intent; some offenses don't; therefore it's "impossible" to attempt these offenses. An example is People v. Campbell, 72 N.Y.2d 602, 535 N.Y.S.2d 580, 532 N.E.2d 86 (1988). There the court decided that an attempted assault "is an impossibility" where the assault statute imposed strict liability for an unintended injury. (The statute provided that a "person is guilty of assault in the second degree when ... [w]ith intent to prevent a peace officer ... from performing a lawful duty, he causes physical injury to such peace officer...." N.Y. Penal Law § 120.05(3).) In the court's words, "[b]ecause the very essence of a criminal attempt is the defendant's intention to cause the proscribed result, it follows that there can be no attempt to commit a crime which makes the causing of a certain result criminal even though wholly unintended." What if the strict liability offense element is not the result (as in *Campbell*), but conduct (or an attendant circumstance, such as the victim's being a peace officer in a case under the statute at issue in *Campbell*)? What if it's not a strict liability element, but one that requires some mental state less than intent (such as recklessness or negligence)?

And what does it mean to say that "the very essence of a criminal attempt" implies intent? Is this a point about everyday language use ("when we say that we attempt to accomplish something, we always mean that we intend to succeed")? But then shouldn't attempt liability require *purpose* (rather than mere belief, as in the Model Penal Code) with respect to result? Are there no half-hearted attempts? Or is it a point about criminal law doctrine? If that's the case, then couldn't (shouldn't?) we redefine the "essence" of attempt? Or should we call nonintentional attempts something else—like "endeavors" or "efforts" or "tries"?

Here is another, more prosaic, way of thinking about logical impossibility. Assume there are two crimes, one criminalizing the intentional, the other the nonintentional infliction of harm (murder and involuntary manslaughter, for instance). In that case would an attempt to commit the lesser—nonintentional—version of the crime amount to an attempt to commit the greater—intentional—version? Would attempted involuntary manslaughter be "impossible" because it would amount to attempted murder?

The issue of logical impossibility (as opposed to the more familiar factual or legal variety) arises most frequently in homicide cases. There the question is whether it's possible to attempt nonintentional homicide (i.e., reckless homicide (involuntary manslaughter) or negligent homicide). Most jurisdictions answer "no" (based on the above-mentioned talk about the essence of attempt). See, e.g., People v. Hernandez, 44 Colo.App. 161, 614 P.2d 900, 901 (1980) ("An attempt to commit criminal negligent homicide . . . requires proof that the defendant intended to perpetrate an unintended killing—a logical impossibility. The words 'attempt' and 'negligence' are at war with one another; they are internally inconsistent and cannot sensibly co-exist.") The Model Penal Code drafters give the same answer, but for a different reason: "[T]he scope of the criminal law would be unduly extended if one could be liable for an attempt whenever he recklessly or negligently created a risk of any result whose actual occurrence would lead to criminal responsibility." Model Penal Code Commentaries § 5.01, at 304. How can we tell where the due extension of the scope of the criminal law ends, and where its undue extension begins? Does this rule make sense from the perspective of the Model Penal Code's treatmentist approach to criminal law? From that of the other traditional rationales for punishment?

Should someone who engages in reckless behavior but, through sheer luck, manages not to harm anyone (say someone picks up a stack of kitchen knives and, just for fun, tosses the lot at a startled party guest, who miraculously remains unhurt) escape criminal liability altogether? To cover these cases, the Model Penal Code provides for a misdemeanor of reckless endangerment. Model Penal Code § 211.2 ("recklessly engag[ing] in conduct which places or may place another person in danger of death or serious bodily injury"). If reckless endangerment is a quasi-attempt offense, should attempted reckless endangerment be punishable? (The Model Code drafters thought so; reckless endangerment, they explained, "aimed at the prohibition of particular reckless *behavior*, rather than the prohibition of a particular *result*." Model Penal Code Commentaries § 5.01, at 304 n.16 (emphasis added). Why wouldn't *that* unduly extend the scope of criminal law? What difference should it make whether we're dealing with a conduct offense, rather than a result offense (like homicide)? If I attempt a somersault, isn't it my intent to succeed in doing a somersault just as much as it would be my intent to cause your death if I attempted to kill you?)

5. In People v. Thomas, 729 P.2d 972 (Colo. 1986), the Colorado Supreme Court sustained a conviction for "attempted reckless manslaughter" where the defendant fired at, but did not kill, a fleeing man he believed to have raped a former girlfriend. He claimed that two of the shots were merely "warning shots" (not intended to kill) and that the third had been fired accidentally when the man kicked him on the staircase where he was chasing him. The court relied on Colorado's attempt provision, Colo. Rev. Stat. § 18–2–101(1), which reads, in its entirety, "[a] person commits criminal attempt if, acting with the kind of culpability otherwise required for the commission of an offense, he engages in conduct constituting a substantial step toward commission of the offense." The court argued that the mens rea for manslaughter is recklessness, that Thomas had acted recklessly, and that he had taken substantial steps towards killing the victim. The court argued that the defendant need only intend to "engage in and complete the risk-producing act or omission"; he need not intend "that death occur even though the underlying crime, reckless manslaughter, has death as an essential element."

Is the Colorado court correct? Are there significant distinctions between the Colorado statute and Model Penal Code § 5.01? Would it help to distinguish between what we labeled "unfinished" and "unsuccessful" attempts in considering this question? Is every badly reckless driver guilty of "attempted reckless manslaughter" if Thomas is, so long as they would be guilty of reckless manslaughter if someone died as a result of their bad driving? If it is sufficient to convict the reckless driver of a risk-creation crime (like reckless driving), should it be sufficient to convict Thomas of either a risk-creation crime (see, e.g., Model Penal Code § 211.2) or the other crime he was in fact convicted of, first degree assault? Is *Thomas* different because, as the concurring judge in the case suggested, "the defendant came close enough to intending harm that he can be convicted." Or is it that he came close enough to *causing* harm and failed to do so for more obviously fortuitous reasons than the reckless driver who never even gets into an accident?

b. Attendant Circumstances

United States v. Langley

U.S. Court of Military Appeals.
33 M.J. 278 (1991).

■ EVERETT, SENIOR JUDGE.

Contrary to his pleas, a general court-martial with officer and enlisted members convicted appellant of assault with intent to commit rape, as charged, in violation of Article 134, Uniform Code of Military Justice, 10 U.S.C. § 934. [While there may be some difference under certain fact

patterns between attempted rape and assault with intent to commit rape, typically where an assault is the predicate act, as here, the offenses are the same. Accordingly, the requisite intent involved ... would be the same.[a]]
* * *

We granted appellant's petition for review to consider whether ... the military judge erred by instructing the members that appellant's claimed mistake of fact as to the victim's consent must be both honest and reasonable rather than merely honest. We conclude that he did.

Essentially, Langley defended against the charge on the basis of voluntary intoxication and mistake of fact as to the victim's lack of consent.
* * *

The issue before us first was addressed by this Court nearly four decades ago in *United States v. Short,* 4 U.S.C.M.A. 437, 16 C.M.R. 11 (1954).... There, as here, the accused was charged with assault with intent to rape under circumstances where the assault stopped before actual penetration. He did not deny the incident at his trial, but he explained that he had "thought she was a prostitute" and that they had negotiated agreement on a business arrangement. At the conclusion of the evidence, defense counsel requested but was denied the following instruction:

> In order to constitute an offense, the accused must think victim is not consenting because he must intend not only to have carnal knowledge of the woman but to do so by force.

[This Court held that the instruction was properly denied and affirmed the conviction.] Judge Brosman dissented from that portion of the lead opinion which concerns us here. He wrote:

> Rape—like unpremeditated murder—has ordinarily been treated as requiring only a general criminal intent. Thus, drunkenness, even in excessive degree, would probably not constitute a defense to this crime—that is, as serving to belie the accused's necessary intent. However, assault with intent to commit rape would seem to occupy a quite different position.... Clearly, then, drunkenness could operate to negate the intent required for conviction of such an assault. An *unreasonable* mistake of fact could perhaps not serve to deny criminal liability for a consummated rape. But could it negative the prerequisites for a finding of guilt of assault with intent to commit rape—just as an unreasonable mistake of fact is said to destroy liability for larceny by false pretenses? * * *
>
> It may be regarded as anomalous to conclude that an accused may be exonerated from guilt of assault with intent to commit rape because of an unreasonable mistake, whereas he could have been convicted lawfully of rape had penetration been effected under the same misapprehension. It is to be observed, however, that the anomaly is no greater than that involved in holding that an assault with intent to murder requires a specific intent to kill, whereas the crime of murder

a. Attempt is defined as follows: "An act, done with specific intent to commit an offense under this chapter, amounting to more than mere preparation and tending, even though failing, to effect its commission, is an attempt to commit that offense." 10 U.S.C. § 880.—EDS.

> may be made out with a lesser intent. The fact of the matter is that a specific intent is, by definition, required for the present finding. The evidence, in my view, raised the possibility that a mistake of fact on the accused's part precluded that intent.

Id. at 446–47.

Rape is defined in Article 120, U.C.M.J., 10 U.S.C. § 920, as "an act of sexual intercourse with a female not his wife, by force and without her consent." No specific intent is mentioned in the statute—only general criminal *mens rea* is involved. Accordingly, if an accused mistakenly believed that his victim consented to intercourse, that is not enough. Instead, because the "mistake goes to ... [an] element requiring only general intent or knowledge, the ignorance or mistake must have existed in the mind of the accused and must have been reasonable under all the circumstances." R.C.M. 916(j), Manual.

By contrast, assault with intent to commit rape contains as an expressed element "[t]hat, at the time of the assault, the accused ... intended to commit rape...." Para. 64b(2). "In assault with intent to commit rape, the accused must have intended to overcome any resistance by force, and to complete the offense. Any lesser intent will not suffice." Para. 64c(4). More than a general criminal *mens rea* is involved; instead, the prosecution must affirmatively prove that, at the time of the assault, the accused specifically intended to forcibly accomplish sexual intercourse. * * *

Accordingly, we hold that, in a prosecution for assault with intent to commit rape, at some point during the assault, the accused must have had the specific intent to commit each element of rape. Accordingly, the Court of Military Review erred in affirming the military judge's ruling that appellant's claimed mistake of fact as to his victim's consent must have been both honest and reasonable, instead of just honest. [The court nonetheless affirmed the conviction believing there was no evidence adduced that the defendant had made either an honest or an honest and reasonable error.]

Commonwealth v. Dunne

Supreme Judicial Court of Massachusetts.
394 Mass. 10, 474 N.E.2d 538 (1985).

[The defendant was convicted of assault on a child under sixteen with intent to commit a rape, which the court determined "is attempted statutory rape." At the time of the offense, the victim was fifteen years and four months old. The court rejected the defendant's argument that conviction required proof of his knowledge of the victim's age, an element not charged in the indictment or proven at trial.]

The Commonwealth need only prove two elements to support a conviction ... for statutory rape: "(1) sexual intercourse or unnatural sexual intercourse, with (2) a child under sixteen years of age." *Commonwealth* v. *Miller*, 385 Mass. 521, 522 (1982). In that case, we held that in a prosecution for statutory rape "it is immaterial that the defendant reasonably believed that the victim was sixteen years of age or older." This is the rule in most jurisdictions.... As the Supreme Court of New Hampshire has held, "[t]he fact that the defendant was ignorant of the age of [the victim] or that he did not intend the intercourse to be with a [person] of nonage would not prevent his act from constituting rape if completed, or an attempt, if it failed." *State* v. *Davis*, 108 N.H. 158, 160–161 (1967).... Indeed, it would be incongruous for us to posit one rule for the completed act and another for the attempt.... This is simply a matter of common sense for the policies underlying the rules in both cases are identical.

QUESTIONS AND COMMENTS

1. Consider three defendants. Each has engaged in sufficient conduct to be guilty of attempting a crime, but has not consummated the offense; furthermore, each is mistaken as to the existence of some attendant circumstance. The mistake, though, that each has made would *not* be exculpatory in the jurisdiction in which the defendant's conduct occurred had the crime been consummated.

Thus, Defendant One (see *Dunne*) has taken sufficient steps that he would plainly be guilty of attempting statutory rape if his victim were indeed underage and he knew that. He is also in a jurisdiction in which he would be guilty of statutory rape had he had sexual relations with the victim, even if he mistakenly believed her to be old enough to consent and his mistakes about her age were, in the eyes of the finder of fact, "reasonable." Should he be guilty of attempted statutory rape, though, if he is subjectively unaware of the victim's age at the time his efforts to have sex with her are thwarted?

Defendant Two has taken sufficient steps to be guilty of attempted rape (see *Langley*). At the time his efforts are thwarted (e.g., by victim resistance or third party intervention) he negligently believes she is consenting to sexual relations. Only reasonable errors about consent, though, would exonerate a defendant charged with rape. Is Defendant Two guilty of attempted rape?

Defendant Three shoots her victim, subjectively, but unreasonably, believing that he was threatening her. Had the victim died, she would be guilty of murder because "imperfect self-defense" is non-exculpatory in the particular jurisdiction (see ch. 7). However, the victim is saved by the extraordinary efforts of fabulous surgeons. Is she guilty of attempted murder, given that she believed (however unreasonably) that she was not committing murder but justified homicide when she shot the victim?

2. Why, as a purely *verbal* matter, might each of these three defendants say "I have not attempted [statutory rape; rape; criminal homicide, respectively] but [sex with a woman capable of granting consent; consensual sex; and non-criminal justified killing, respectively]". In purely verbal terms, can the prosecutor successfully counter the defendant's claim by arguing that each defendant intended to engage in conduct that we would describe as statutory rape (or rape, or murder)?

3. In *policy* terms, what is the argument that the defendants in each case are guilty? What is the argument that the cases are differentiable? Can we ever solve the problem we have raised on several occasions: "attempt" law covers (at least) two very different sorts of scenarios—ones in which the defendant's attempt is unfinished and ones in which it is unsuccessful? Does the historical requirement of "specific intent" make more sense in the context of the unfinished than the unsuccessful? Generally? In relationship to attendant circumstances? Do we know (at what level of certainty?) what Defendants One and Two would do if they "learned" of their victim's age or her non-consent prior to consummating the offense? Does it matter how many opportunities each has already had to learn? How many he might still have? Does it matter that Defendant Three has completed her course of conduct?

4. Note too that courts face distinct options in terms of "legal form" in regulating these sorts of cases. A court might announce one of two opposite *rules*—always treat the mental state for each element of the offense the same way in attempt as in the completed offense, or always require knowledge/purpose as to each material element of the offense in attempt cases. Alternatively, it could announce a vaguer *standard*: instruct the fact finders to convict if and only if the defendant demonstrated beyond a reasonable doubt an intent to do acts that we would characterize as the consummated offense.

5. The Model Penal Code section on attempt is clear about what mental state is required with respect to conduct (purpose) and result (purpose or belief). Model Penal Code § 5.01(1)(a) & (b), supra. What mental state, though, is required with respect to attendant circumstances? The Commentaries explain that, in the absence of specific provisions setting out what mental state is required with respect to an offense element type (like subsections (a) and (b), dealing with conduct and result, respectively), the general provision at the outset of § 5.01(1) applies. Model Penal Code Commentaries § 5.01, at 301–02. The mental state required as to attendant circumstances thus would be "the kind of culpability otherwise required for commission of the crime." This would mean, for instance, that strict liability attendant circumstance elements in the consummated offense would remain strict liability elements in the attempted offense as well. See *Dunne*. Why this special treatment of attendant circumstances? Does it make sense in jurisdictions that don't follow the Model Penal Code's rejection of strict liability (except for violations and in certain sex offenses involving underage victims)? Or is *Langley* right to insist on the differential approach to the mens rea of attempted and consummated offenses?

CHAPTER 7

Justification and Excuse

A. Introduction

4 William Blackstone, Commentaries on the Laws of England 177–78, 182 (1769)

Now homicide, or the killing of any human creature, is of three kinds: *justifiable*, *excusable*, and *felonious*. The first has no share of guilt at all; the second very little; but the third is the highest crime against the law of nature, that man is capable of committing. * * *

In these instances of *justifiable* homicide, you will observe that the slayer is in no kind of fault whatsoever, not even in the minutest degree.... But that is not quite the case in *excusable* homicide, the very name whereof imports some fault, some error, some omission; so trivial however, that the law excuses it from the guilt of felony....

United States v. Lopez

United States District Court for the Northern District of California.
662 F.Supp. 1083 (1987).

Justification defenses are those providing that, although the act was committed, it is not wrongful. For example, a forest fire is burning toward a town of 10,000 residents. An actor burns a field of corn located between the fire and the town in order to set up a firebreak. By setting fire to the field with the intent to destroy it, the actor satisfies all the elements of the crime of arson; however, he most likely will have a complete defense because his conduct is justified. Burning the field avoided a greater societal harm; therefore, the act is not a crime.

When a defense is categorized as an excuse, however, the result is that, although the act is wrongful, the actor will not be held accountable. "Where the actor is not blameworthy, for reasons of either incapacity or extreme pressure, there is not criminal liability." Comment, *Necessity Defined: A New Role in the Criminal Defense System*, 29 UCLA L. Rev. 409, 414 (1981). Thus, an insane person who robs a bank will be excused from liability.

Simply stated, when a defendant prevails on a justification defense, no wrongful act occurred; the act itself becomes lawful. If a defendant succeeds on a defense classified as an excuse, a wrongful act occurred; however, no criminal liability is attached to the actor.

The classification of a defense as a justification or an excuse has an important effect on the liability of one who aids and abets the act. A third party has the right to assist an actor in a justified act. Therefore, a third party could not be held liable for aiding and abetting the arson described in the hypothetical above. In contrast, a sane getaway driver could be convicted of aiding and abetting an insane person's bank robbery. Excuses are always personal to the actor.

Spunaugle v. State

Court of Criminal Appeals of Oklahoma.
946 P.2d 246 (1997).

Spunaugle attempted to raise a duress defense to the charge of first degree malice murder. Duress has never been recognized in Oklahoma as a defense to that crime. * * *

The Oklahoma approach to duress contrasts sharply with the common law which has been hostile to the defense. One nineteenth century writer, J. Stephen, noted, "Compulsion by threats ought in no case whatever be admitted as an excuse for crime." *A History of the Criminal Law in England* 108 (1883). While the common law does recognize the defense, it limits application of the duress defense considerably by grounding it in the so-called "choice of evils" moral philosophy of justification. Under this philosophy, one is not morally justified to commit a greater harm to avoid a lesser one. Thus, where harm is unavoidable, one may not choose to commit an equal or greater harm to avoid harm himself. J. Hall, *General Principles of Criminal Law* 422 (2d ed. 1947).

When this theory is applied to malice murder, the defense of duress is precluded, for when threatened by harm, a person "ought rather die himself than escape by the murder of an innocent." *4 W. Blackstone's Commentaries* 30.... States which follow this rationale limit the application of the duress defense to certain crimes.

Justification is but one of two legal theories supporting the defense of duress. The other foundation, wholly separate and distinct from the theory of justification, is the doctrine of excuse. Finkelstein, *Duress: A Philosophical Account of the Defense in Law,* 37 Ariz. L. Rev. 251–283 (1995).

Under this legal doctrine, a person may be excused for committing a crime, even murder, if "men of ordinary firmness" would have acted in the same way to save their own lives. Model Penal Code § 2.09. The legal theory of excuse focuses on the *actor* and "represents the legal conclusion that the conduct is wrong, ... but that criminal liability is inappropriate because some characteristics of the actor vitiates society's desire to punish him." Robinson, *Criminal Law Defenses: A Systematic Analysis,* 83 Colum. L. Rev. 199, 229 (1982). LaFave and Scott acknowledge a majority of the modern codes take this approach, and that a significant number of the modern statutory schemes make the duress defense available "whatever the charge against the defendant." W. LaFave & A. Scott, *Criminal Law* 437 (2d ed. 1986).

Simply put, if the defense of duress is based on the legal theory of excuse in Oklahoma, it is available to answer a charge of first degree malice murder; if it is based on the legal theory of justification, it is not. To determine which theoretical underpinning supports the defense of duress in Oklahoma, we look ... to the plain language of the defining statutes.

Section 152(7) focuses on the actor, defining the person under duress as not capable of committing a crime.[a] Section 155 focuses on the actor, and exonerates him if he acts under duress.[b] Section 156[c] ... entitles a person to the defense if that person acted as a result of a reasonable belief "there was imminent danger of death or great bodily harm" to himself, his spouse, or his child. All of the defining statutory language focuses on the *actor,* while none of it focuses on the act, or justification of the act.

In light of this clear and consistent statutory language, we conclude Oklahoma did not adopt the "choice of evils" theory of justification. Rather our defense of duress is based on the legal theory of excuse.... We find the defense of duress is available in Oklahoma to a defendant charged with the crime of first degree malice murder.

State v. Leidholm

Supreme Court of North Dakota.
334 N.W.2d 811 (1983).

[We] begin with an explanation of the basic operation of the law of self-defense as set forth in Chapter 12.1–05 of the North Dakota Century Code.

Our criminal code is the product of a massive revision which began in 1971 and culminated in 1973.... Although remnants of the "old code" survived revision and remain in the present code, most of its provisions are in substantial part modeled after the Proposed New Federal Criminal Code, which in turn relies heavily on the American Law Institute Model Penal Code. Both the Proposed Code and the Model Penal Code are highly integrated codifications of the substantive criminal law which exhibit close interrelationships between their respective parts. This integration is especially apparent in Chapter 12.1–05 of the North Dakota Century Code, which is an almost complete adoption of Chapter 6 of the Proposed Code dealing with defenses involving justification and excuse....

Conduct which constitutes self-defense may be either justified[a] or

a. § 152. Persons capable of committing crimes ...

All persons are capable of committing crimes, except those belonging to the following classes:

....

7) Persons who committed the act, or make the omission charged, while under involuntary subjection to the power of superiors.—EDS.

b. § 155. Subjection to superior exonerates

The involuntary subjection to the power of a superior which exonerates a person charged with a criminal act or omission from punishment therefor, arises from duress.—EDS.

c. § 156. Duress defense

A person is entitled to assert duress as a defense if that person committed a prohibited act or omission because of a reasonable belief that there was imminent danger of death or great bodily harm from another upon oneself, one's spouse or one's child.—EDS.

a. § 12.1–05–03. Self-defense.

A person is justified in using force upon another person to defend himself against danger of imminent unlawful bodily injury, sexual assault, or detention by such other person....—EDS.

excused.[b] Although the distinction between justification and excuse may appear to be theoretical and without significant practical consequence, because the distinction has been made in our criminal statutes we believe a general explanation of the difference between the two concepts—even though it requires us to venture briefly into the pathway of academicism—is warranted.

A defense of justification is the product of society's determination that the actual existence of certain circumstances will operate to make proper and legal what otherwise would be criminal conduct. A defense of excuse, contrarily, does not make legal and proper conduct which ordinarily would result in criminal liability; instead, it openly recognizes the criminality of the conduct but excuses it because the actor believed that circumstances actually existed which would justify his conduct when in fact they did not. In short, had the facts been as he supposed them to be, the actor's conduct would have been justified rather than excused.

In the context of self-defense, this means that a person who believes that the force he uses is necessary to prevent imminent unlawful harm is justified in using such force if his belief is a correct belief; that is to say, if his belief corresponds with what actually is the case. If, on the other hand, a person reasonably but incorrectly believes that the force he uses is necessary to protect himself against imminent harm, his use of force is excused.

QUESTIONS AND COMMENTS

1. How do Blackstone, *Lopez*, *Spunaugle,* and *Leidholm*, distinguish justification from excuse? Are the distinctions they draw compatible?

2. Under *Leidholm's* approach to the distinction between justification and excuse, why should it make a difference whether I was correct in thinking that I was justified in defending myself? Why can a mistaken belief never justify? What if I believe that I am *excused*? What if I'm incorrect in holding that belief?

3. What difference does it make in *Spunaugle* that the defense is classified as a justification or as an excuse? Is there something about the nature of excuses that would require that they be of general application, while justifications may be applicable only to certain offenses, but not to others? Wouldn't you expect the opposite—that justifications, not excuses, are necessarily general? Can I *ever* be justified, as opposed to excused, in killing another to save my life? Reconsider *Leidholm*.

4. Would it (should it) make a difference whether the criminal law in general, or a criminal trial in particular, characterizes a defense as a justification or an excuse? What does an acquittal on the ground of

b. § 12.1–05–08. Excuse.

A person's conduct is excused if he believes that the facts are such that his conduct is necessary and appropriate for any of the purposes which would establish a justification or excuse under this chapter, even though his belief is mistaken. However, if his belief is negligently or recklessly held, it is not an excuse in a prosecution for an offense for which negligence or recklessness, as the case may be, suffices to establish culpability....—EDS.

justification say about the accused, as compared to an acquittal on the ground of excuse? What does it say about the victim? Does the accused have an interest (or even a right?) to have a defense recognized as a justification rather than as an excuse? Does the victim? Should jury verdicts, rather than simply—and mysteriously—declaring the defendant "guilty" or "not guilty," specify whether the behavior was criminal but justified or criminal but excused or neither? See George P. Fletcher, With Justice For Some: Victims' Rights in Criminal Trials (1995).

Is the question of whether a defendant is justified similar to the question of whether "objective offense elements" (see ch. 4) are present, while the question of whether a defendant is excused is more similar to the question of whether "subjective offense elements" (see ch. 5) are present? Think about the question of victim perceptions of trial outcomes in relationship not only to justification vs. excuse, but objective and subjective offense elements more generally. Assume that the jury in a rape trial believes that the victim did not consent to sex but that the defendant should be exonerated because he reasonably mistakenly believed she did (see ch. 9). Should the verdict simply be "not guilty" or should we require juries to state the victim was raped but that the defendant must be exonerated because a subjective offense element was lacking? Why?

5. Should a finding of justification in a criminal case bar a finding of liability in a civil case? What about a successful excuse defense?

Does the fact that the hypothetical arson defendant in *Lopez* did a publicly beneficial thing mean that the cornfield owner should go *uncompensated*? Uncompensated by the defendant? If the defendant burned the field because he was under duress, should the cornfield owner go uncompensated? What if the source of the duress is judgment-proof? Should the defendant or the cornfield owner bear the loss?

6. Now think about the legality principle (ch. 2). Should justifications be codified? Excuses? Should excuses be subject to the principle of publicity? Should justifications or excuses be subject to the principle of specificity? Legislativity? Prospectivity? Meir Dan–Cohen distinguishes between conduct rules and decision rules, and explores the implications of the absence of what he calls "acoustic separation" between the two:

> The distinction I intend to draw between conduct rules and decision rules can best be understood through a simple thought experiment. Imagine a universe consisting of two groups of people—the general public and officials. The general public engages in various kinds of conduct, while officials make decisions with respect to members of the general public. Imagine further that each of the two groups occupies a different, acoustically sealed chamber. This condition I shall call "acoustic separation." Now think of the law as a set of normative messages directed to both groups. In such a universe, the law necessarily contains two sets of messages. One set is directed at the general public and provides guidelines for conduct. These guidelines are what I have called "conduct rules." The other set of messages is directed at the officials and provides guidelines for their decisions. These are "decision rules."

> The specific conduct rules that such a system would maintain would depend upon what conduct lawmakers deemed desirable—desirable, that is, in terms of the policies underlying the legal system. Similarly, the content of the decision rules of the system would be determined by the kinds of decisions that were deemed desirable in this sense.
>
> The categories of conduct rules and decision rules, as defined in our imaginary universe, will help us to analyze real legal systems as well. In the real world, too, we may speak of messages that convey normative information regarding conduct to the general public, and we may distinguish such messages from ones aimed at guiding the decisions of officials. A fundamental difference exists, however, between the imagined universe and the real world: the condition of acoustic separation, which obtained in the former by definition, seems to be absent from the latter. In the real world, the public and officialdom are not in fact locked into acoustically sealed chambers, and consequently each group may "hear" the normative messages the law transmits to the other group.
>
> .... [One] difference between the real world and our imaginary universe is that, in the imaginary universe, acoustic separation ensures that conduct rules cannot, as such, affect decisions; similarly, decision rules cannot, as such, influence conduct. The two sets of rules are independent. Not so in the real world. Here, officials are aware of the system's conduct rules and may take them into account in making decisions. By the same token, because individuals are familiar with the decision rules, they may well consider those rules in shaping their own conduct. We may say, therefore, that reality differs from the imagined world in that real-world decision rules are likely to have conduct side effects, just as real-world conduct rules are likely to have decisional side effects.
>
> .... [T]he possibility that conduct or decision rules may have ... unintended side effects creates the potential for conflict between decision rules and conduct rules in the absence of acoustic separation. A decision rule conflicts with a conduct rule if the decision rule conveys, as a side effect, a normative message that opposes or detracts from the power of the conduct rule. Conversely, a conduct rule conflicts with a decision rule when the messages it sends decision-makers contradict the decision rule. Such conflicting messages are impossible under conditions of acoustic separation. Because officials and the public each receive only the messages specifically directed to them and meant to guide their respective activities, neither group is in danger of receiving conflicting messages addressed to the other.

Meir Dan–Cohen, "Decision Rules and Conduct Rules: On Acoustic Separation in Criminal Law," 97 Harv. L. Rev. 625, 630–32 (1984).

Are justifications conduct or decision rules? Excuses? Is acoustic separation worth establishing? If so, how might we do it? Paul Robinson has proposed distinguishing between a code of conduct and a code of adjudication:

A traditional criminal code performs several functions. It announces the law's commands to those whose conduct it seeks to influence. It also defines the rules to be used in deciding whether a breach of the law's commands will result in criminal liability and, if so, the grade or degree of liability. In serving the first function, the code addresses all members of the public. In performing the second function, it addresses lawyers, judges, jurors, and others who play a role in the adjudication process.

In part because of these different audiences, the two functions call for different kinds of documents. To effectively communicate to the public, the code must be easy to read and understand. It must give a clear statement, in objective terms if possible, of the conduct that the law prohibits and under what conditions it is prohibited. Readability, accessibility, simplicity, and clarity characterize a code that most effectively articulates and announces the criminal law's rules of conduct.

The adjudicators, on the other hand, can tolerate greater complexity. Clarity and simplicity are always a virtue, but the judgments required of adjudicators necessarily limit how simple the adjudication rules can be. While the public can be told rather easily and clearly that "you may not cause bodily injury or death to another person," when a prohibited injury or death does occur, the adjudicators need rules to determine whether the injurer ought to escape liability because he or she had no culpability, was insane, believed mistakenly but reasonably that the force used was necessary for self-defense, or for any number of other reasons. If liability is appropriate, the adjudication rules must determine the appropriate degree of liability, taking account of the actor's level of culpability, the extent of the injury, and a variety of other mitigating and aggravating circumstances. Many, if not most, of these liability and grading factors require complex and sometimes subjective criteria.

The current practice of using a single code to perform both functions means that neither function is performed as well as it could be. Is it possible to draft two codes—a code to articulate the rules of conduct, written for lay persons, and a code to govern the adjudication process, written for criminal justice professionals? If one were to pull out of a current criminal code only those provisions that a lay person must know in order to remain law-abiding, what would such a document contain and what would it look like? If one were to organize a code to capture the decisional process for criminal adjudication, what would such a document contain and what would it look like? This Article attempts to answer these questions. We tentatively conclude that distinct codes of conduct and of adjudication can be drafted and can allow the criminal law to perform both functions more efficiently and successfully.

The possibility of creating separate codes for separate functions is made feasible in part because each doctrine of criminal law typically serves one or the other function. For example, to communicate effectively to the members of the public the rules needed to conform their

> conduct to the requirements of law, a code need not clearly communicate the subtleties of the insanity defense, the detailed definitions of culpable states of mind, or the operation of the entrapment doctrine. That is, a code of conduct and a code of adjudication can be created by segregating the doctrines of criminal law into one or the other code according to the function that each doctrine performs.

Paul H. Robinson, Peter D. Greene, & Natasha R. Goldstein, "Making Criminal Codes Functional: A Code of Conduct and a Code of Adjudication," 86 J. Crim. L. & Criminology 304 (1996).

"Justified Violations of the Criminal Law" appear in the code of conduct. "Excuses" (along with "Minimum Requirements for Liability," including actus reus and mens rea) appear in the code of adjudication. Is Robinson's codification proposal consistent with the principle of legality?

7. To what degree do we establish a justification defense because of the inevitable over-inclusiveness of the criminal law's basic conduct rules? Is it possible for a legislature to identify prospectively, with precision, forms of conduct that will *always* be harmful? Would it be possible for a legislature to identify prospectively, with precision, the situations in which the general prohibitions on a type of conduct should *not* apply?

8. Can I have a right to raise an excuse defense? A justification defense? If a legislature (or a court?) decided to do away with a defense altogether, should it make a difference whether the defense is an excuse or a justification? Reconsider *Patterson*, ch. 4 supra; see also Markus Dirk Dubber, "Toward a Constitutional Law of Crime and Punishment," 55 Hastings L.J. 509 (2004).

9. Could (or should) the consideration of excuses be limited to sentencing, rather than influencing whether, and of what, a defendant is convicted in the first place? What about justifications? Assume a defendant unsuccessfully raises a justification or excuse defense at trial; should the judge be *allowed* to consider evidence of justification or excuse at sentencing?

10. Are excuses properly left to the exercise of executive pardon? What should a police officer do who has sufficient evidence to suspect that a crime has been committed *and* that the offender has a justification defense available to her? An excuse? Should a prosecutor pursue such a case? Who should determine the availability of a justification or excuse defense in a particular case?

11. *Excuses and Character.* In what sense are excuses "personal"? Just what personal characteristics of the actor are relevant when it comes to deciding whether she—or her conduct?—is excused? John Gardner explores the relevance of character in the law of excuse:

> It is often said that the criminal law judges actions, not character. That is true, but misleading. It is true that, barring certain exceptional and troubling examples, crimes are actions, and being a crime is therefore a property of actions. Nevertheless, the criminality of an action frequently falls to be determined, in part, according to standards of character—according to standards of courage, carefulness, honesty, self-discipline, diligence, humanity, good will, and so forth....

> [S]tandards of character figure ... in many of the criminal law's excusatory doctrines. Now a link between character and excuse has often been forged by those interested in the philosophical foundations of the criminal law. On one familiar view, ... we should grant an excuse to somebody in respect of what he did if and only if what he did was no manifestation of his character. This view proceeds from the sound thought that excuses matter because a person's excused actions do not reflect badly on him—do not show him, personally, in a bad light. That being so, the thinking goes, an excuse must be something that blocks the path from an adverse judgment about an action to a correspondingly adverse judgment about the person whose action it is. The action is cowardly, say, but since this person does not otherwise tend towards cowardly actions, she herself is no coward. Her cowardly action is "out of character." And that, according to [this] view, is the gist of excuses.
>
> [T]he gist of an excuse[, however,] is not that the action was "out of character," in the sense of being a departure from what we have come to expect from the person whose action it is. Quite the contrary, in fact. The gist of an excuse ... is precisely that the person with the excuse lived up to our expectations. On first encounter, this claim may give the misleading impression that people's wrongful actions are excused so long as they continue to live up to the character standards that they have always lived up to, however appalling. One may have an image of someone excusing themselves by saying: "I've always been spiteful and malicious, so how did you expect me to behave?".... So the question, for excusatory purposes, is obviously not whether the person claiming the excuse lived up to expectations in the predictive sense of being true to form or true to type or even true to our disappointing experience of human beings in general. The question is whether that person lived up to expectations in the normative sense. Did she manifest as much resilience, or loyalty, or thoroughness, or presence of mind as a person in her situation should have manifested? In the face of terrible threats, for example, did this person show as much fortitude as someone in his situation could properly be asked to show? In the face of constant taunts, did this person exhibit as much self-restraint as we have a right to demand of someone in her situation? The character standards which are relevant to these and other excuses are not the standards of our own characters, nor even the standards of most people's characters, but rather the standards to which our characters should, minimally, conform.

John Gardner, "The Gist of Excuses," 1 Buff. Crim. L. Rev. 575 (1998).

12. *Defenses and Victim Compensation.* Mirroring the criminal law, the law of victim compensation also takes into account victim behavior that may amount to a defense in a criminal case against the offender. Victim behavior that mitigates, or precludes, the offender's criminal liability may mitigate, or preclude, the victim's compensability. What are the criminal law analogues to the grounds for reducing, or denying, victim compensation in the following excerpt from the Uniform Victims of Crime Act? Is there a reason to distinguish between justifications and excuses as grounds for

reducing compensability? See generally Markus Dirk Dubber, Victims in the War on Crime: The Use and Abuse of Victims' Rights pt. II (2002).

Uniform Victims of Crime Act § 309. Limit on Compensation Because of Claimant's Conduct.

(a) The [agency] may reduce or deny compensation to a claimant ... who is accountable for the crime or a crime arising from the same conduct, criminal episode, or plan....

(c) The [agency] may reduce or deny compensation to the extent that the victim or claimant engaged in a violation of law, misconduct, or unreasonably dangerous behavior that contributed to the claimant's loss.

Comment

Under subsection (c), compensation otherwise payable to the claimant may be reduced or denied to the extent that the agency determines that the loss is the result of certain contributory conduct of the victim or claimant. Individuals like police officers whose occupations are inherently dangerous remain eligible because their conduct is not "unreasonably" dangerous. Similarly, the agency should avoid reducing or denying compensation for "good Samaritan" conduct. *Compare* Mich. Comp. Laws Ann. § 18.361(11)(5) ("The board may disregard the responsibility of the claimant for his or her own injury where the record shows that the injury was attributable to efforts by the claimant to apprehend a person who had committed a crime in his or her presence.")....

The agency may establish guidelines for implementation of this section. Several States currently address the issue of contributory conduct by guidelines or rules, in addition to statutes. For example, Florida's Guideline 10L–4.02 specifies:

> While there is no set formula for calculating the percentage of contribution to be assessed, the following factors should serve as a guideline:
>
> (1) If it appears that the victim was provoked by the defendant in a manner threatening bodily harm to the victim, and the victim acted in self defense, no contribution should be assessed.
>
> (2) If it appears that the victim was provoked by the defendant in a manner where bodily harm to the victim appeared unlikely, and the victim used poor judgment because of intoxication or other drug involvement, a 25% contribution factor should be assessed.
>
> (3) If it appears that the defendant was provoked by the victim in a manner where bodily harm appeared unlikely, a 50% contribution factor should be assessed.
>
> (4) If the victim is injured as a result of his conduct not being that of a prudent person, a 50% contribution factor should also be assessed.

> (5) If it appears that the defendant was provoked by the victim in a manner where bodily harm to the defendant appears intentional, a 75% contribution factor should be assessed.
>
> (6) If it appears that the defendant was provoked by the victim in a manner where bodily harm to the defendant is unquestionable, a 100% contribution factor shall be assessed and the claim denied.
>
> (7) If the victim is not wearing protective equipment as prescribed by law, a 25% contribution factor shall be assessed. This includes helmets, seat belts, etc.
>
> (8) If the victim was involved in drugs, as verified by the police report or other official documents, a 100% contribution factor should be assessed and the claim denied.

Somewhat similarly, Minn. R. 7505.2900 specifies:

> The board shall reduce, by a minimum of 25%, any claim submitted by or on behalf of a person who the board finds has engaged in any of the following acts or behavior that contributed to the injury for which the claim is filed:
>
> A. used fighting words, obscene or threatening gestures, or other provocation;
>
> B. knowingly and willingly been in a vehicle operated by a person who is under the influence of alcohol or a controlled substance;
>
> C. consumed alcohol or other mood-altering substances; or
>
> D. failed to retreat or withdraw from a situation where an option to do so was readily available.

Finally, Montana Policy & Procedure Manual, which covers contributory conduct at considerable length, provides in part:

> Contribution results in denial or reduction of benefits. A victim contributed to the infliction of death or injury with respect to which a claim is made if the victim's actions brought about to any degree the resulting injuries and such injuries were reasonably foreseeable by the victim at the time of his or her contributing actions. . . .
>
> Contribution concerns the victim's illegal or wrongful actions. Contribution is not stupidity, but gross stupidity can be contribution, that is, *no* reasonable person would have done what the victim did.
>
> Some situations are 100% contribution, [such as when] the victim issues or accepts a challenge to fight. Beware of moral judgments. It is inappropriate to deny benefits on a moral issue and may be unconstitutional and illegal as well, since the decision maker is using an arbitrary standard.

B. SELF-DEFENSE

1. INTRODUCTION

Joseph H. Beale, "Retreat from a Murderous Assault," 16 Harv. L. Rev. 567, 568 (1903)

From the beginning of the jurisdiction of the king's courts over crime to the reign of Edward I. homicide could be justified only when done in execution of the king's writ, or by authority of a custom by which a thief [caught red-handed], an outlaw, or perhaps other manifest felons, might be taken by force without a warrant; in short, in cases were the homicide was committed in execution of the law. In all other cases, whether of misadventure or of necessary self-defense, the defendant could set up no justification but must be convicted; to use the words of Pollock and Maitland, he deserved but needed a pardon....

4 William Blackstone, Commentaries on the Laws of England 182 (1769)

Excusable homicide is of two sorts; either *per infortunium,* by misadventure [where a man ..., without any intention of hurt, unfortunately kills another]; or *se defendendo,* upon a principle of self-preservation.... Homicide in *self-defence*, or *se defendendo*, upon a sudden affray, is excusable rather than justifiable.... This species of self-defence must be distinguished from that [which is] calculated to hinder the perpetration of a capital crime; which is not only a matter of excuse but of justification. But the self-defence, which we are now speaking of, is that whereby a man may protect himself from an assault, or the like, in the course of a sudden brawl or quarrel, by killing him who assaults him.... This right of natural defence does not imply a right of attacking: for, instead of attacking one another for injuries past or impending, men need only have recourse to the proper tribunals of justice. They cannot therefore legally exercise this right of preventive defence, but in sudden and violent cases; when certain and immediate suffering would be the consequence of waiting for the assistance of the law.

Martin v. Ohio

Supreme Court of the United States.
480 U.S. 228, 107 S.Ct. 1098 (1987).

■ JUSTICE WHITE delivered the opinion of the Court.

The Ohio Code provides that "[t]he burden of going forward with the evidence of an affirmative defense, and the burden of proof by a preponderance of the evidence, for an affirmative defense, is upon the accused." Ohio Rev. Code Ann. § 2901.05(A) (1982). ... The Ohio courts have "long determined that self-defense is an affirmative defense," and that the defendant has the burden of proving it as required by § 2901.05(A).

As defined by the trial court in its instructions in this case, the elements of self-defense that the defendant must prove are that (1) the defendant was not at fault in creating the situation giving rise to the argument; (2) the defendant had an honest belief that she was in imminent danger of death or great bodily harm, and that her only means of escape from such danger was in the use of such force; and (3) the defendant did not violate any duty to retreat or avoid danger. The question before us is whether the Due Process Clause of the Fourteenth Amendment forbids placing the burden of proving self-defense on the defendant when she is charged by the State of Ohio with committing the crime of aggravated murder, which, as relevant to this case, is defined by the Revised Code of Ohio as "purposely, and with prior calculation and design, caus[ing] the death of another." Ohio Rev. Code Ann. § 2903.01 (1982).

.... On July 21, 1983, petitioner Earline Martin and her husband, Walter Martin, argued over grocery money. Petitioner claimed that her husband struck her in the head during the argument. Petitioner's version of what then transpired was that she went upstairs, put on a robe, and later came back down with her husband's gun which she intended to dispose of. Her husband saw something in her hand and questioned her about it. He came at her, and she lost her head and fired the gun at him. Five or six shots were fired, three of them striking and killing Mr. Martin. * * *

In re Winship, 397 U.S. 358, 364, 90 S.Ct. 1068, 1072, 25 L.Ed.2d 368 (1970), declared that the Due Process Clause "protects the accused against conviction except upon proof beyond a reasonable doubt of every fact necessary to constitute the crime with which he is charged." * * *

[T]he jury was here instructed that to convict it must find, in light of all the evidence, that each of the elements of the crime of aggravated murder has been proved by the State beyond reasonable doubt, and that the burden of proof with respect to these elements did not shift. * * *

It would be quite different if the jury had been instructed that self-defense evidence could not be considered in determining whether there was a reasonable doubt about the State's case, i.e., that self-defense evidence must be put aside for all purposes unless it satisfied the preponderance standard. Such an instruction would relieve the State of its burden and plainly run afoul of *Winship's* mandate....

We are ... not moved by assertions that the elements of aggravated murder and self-defense overlap in the sense that evidence to prove the latter will often tend to negate the former. It may be that most encounters in which self-defense is claimed arise suddenly and involve no prior plan or specific purpose to take life. In those cases, evidence offered to support the defense may negate a purposeful killing by prior calculation and design, but Ohio does not shift to the defendant the burden of disproving any element of the state's case....

Affirmed.

■ JUSTICE POWELL, with whom JUSTICE BRENNAN, JUSTICE MARSHALL, and JUSTICE BLACKMUN join, dissenting.

In its willingness to defer to the State's legislative definitions of crimes and defenses, the Court apparently has failed to recognize the practical effect of its decision. Martin alleged that she was innocent because she acted in self-defense, a complete justification under Ohio law. Because she had the burden of proof on this issue, the jury could have believed that it was just as likely as not that Martin's conduct was justified, and yet still have voted to convict. In other words, even though the jury may have had a substantial doubt whether Martin committed a crime, she was found guilty under Ohio law. . . .

People v. McManus

Court of Appeals of New York.
67 N.Y.2d 541 (1986).

■ HANCOCK, JUDGE.

Defendant was indicted on one count each of intentional murder (Penal Law § 125.25[1]) and depraved indifference murder (Penal Law § 125.25[2]) for firing a shot into a group of youths and fatally wounding one of them. Defendant never denied firing the shot. Rather, he insisted that he did so to "scare off" the five youths who were robbing and assaulting his companion.

In a written statement, given at the station house on the night of the incident, defendant told the police that he and his companion were approached by five males. One put a pistol to his friend's stomach and, when defendant attempted to intervene, another drew a pistol on him. Defendant was ordered to give up his money but instead turned and ran. When he looked back, defendant saw his friend being beaten and robbed. The group began to chase defendant and he fled to his home, locked the door and retrieved his uncle's rifle. The group stood outside, yelling for defendant and brandishing their pistols. Defendant opened the door and, when they saw his rifle, the group fled. Defendant gave chase. During the chase, the group came upon defendant's friend and began assaulting him again. At his friend's desperate urging, defendant fired the rifle, hitting someone in the group. * * *

The court . . . instructed [the jury] on justification . . . with respect to the intentional murder count. The court gave no such charge, however, concerning depraved indifference murder and, at the conclusion of the court's instructions, counsel requested that the charge of justification be repeated for that offense. The following exchange ensued:

"THE COURT: You want me to charge justification twice and I'm not going to do it.

"COUNSEL: If the jury has reasonable doubt as to whether or not the district attorney disproved the defense of justification, then they must acquit on all charges.

"THE COURT: No, that's not necessarily true here.

"COUNSEL: I take an exception.

"THE COURT: Depraved justification is not a defense as [to] depraved indifference.

* * *

"THE COURT: You see, let me explain something to you [counsel], as one lawyer to another. In order for you to have justification, you must have intent. You are admitting that you killed somebody. You did it because you were justified. How can you have a reckless depraved indifference and say you were justified. I don't think it applies. I decline your request."

The jury acquitted defendant of intentional murder, failed to reach a verdict on the lesser included charge of manslaughter under extreme emotional disturbance, but convicted defendant of depraved indifference murder.

The Appellate Division unanimously affirmed. ... The court reasoned that a depraved mind murder, by its very definition, cannot be justified and hence, that the defense is necessarily precluded. The argument is that justification and depraved indifference are incompatible concepts: that the defense cannot excuse a reckless disregard of an unjustified risk. Such reasoning, we believe, misconceives the essential nature of the defense. Justification does not make a criminal use of force lawful; if the use of force is justified, it cannot be criminal at all.

The defense of justification affirmatively permits the use of force under certain circumstances. Pursuant to Penal Law § 35.15, a person "may" use physical force to defend himself or a third person, and his conduct, which would otherwise constitute an offense, is simply not criminal.[1] The defense does not operate to excuse a criminal act, nor does it negate a particular element of a crime. Rather, by recognizing the use of force to be privileged under certain circumstances, it renders such conduct entirely lawful. * * *

This right to defend oneself or another was early codified in this State as an integral part of the murder statutes, and this court has long held the People have the burden of disproving beyond a reasonable doubt a defendant's claim that he was acting in the exercise of that right. Accordingly, justification under the Penal Law is an ordinary defense rather than an affirmative one. As such, whenever justification is sufficiently interposed by the defendant, the People must prove its absence to the same degree as any element of the crime charged.

1. Section 35.15 outlines the circumstances under which the use of physical force in defense of a person is justified. Subdivision (1) of that section provides, in part: "A person may, subject to the provisions of subdivision two, use physical force upon another person when and to the extent he reasonably believes such to be necessary to defend himself or a third person from what he reasonably believes to be the use or imminent use of unlawful physical force by such other person." (See also, Penal Law § 35.05[2] and § 35.10[6].)

Subdivision (1) provides a limitation upon the foregoing where the force used is deadly. A person may only use such force upon another in certain specified situations, including where:

"(a) He reasonably believes that such other person is using or about to use deadly physical force * * * or

"(b) He reasonably believes that such other person is committing or attempting to commit a kidnapping, forcible rape, forcible sodomy or robbery".

From the foregoing, it follows that there is no basis for limiting the application of the defense of justification to any particular mens rea or to any particular crime involving the use of force. Indeed, the Legislature has clearly not done so. The introductory provision to article 35 of the Penal Law evinces an intent to give the justification defense the broadest possible scope. It states without qualification that the defense is available "[i]n *any* prosecution for an offense" (Penal Law § 35.00 [emphasis added]). Likewise, section 35.15, the provision specifically at issue in this case which outlines the circumstances under which the use of physical force and deadly physical force are justified, is devoid of any such limiting language. * * *

.... The apparent conceptual difficulty in reconciling the defense of justification with a "wanton indifference to human life or a depravity of mind" which is essential to depraved indifference murder is of no moment. The defense must not be viewed as one that operates to negate or refute an aspect of the crime charged. Rather, if the People fail to disprove justification, the use of force is deemed lawful and the defendant is entitled to an acquittal.

Model Penal Code § 3.04. Use of Force in Self–Protection.

(1) *Use of Force Justifiable for Protection of the Person.* [T]he use of force upon or toward another person is justifiable when the actor believes that such force is immediately necessary for the purpose of protecting himself against the use of unlawful force by such other person on the present occasion.

(2) *Limitations on Justifying Necessity for the Use of Force.*

....

(b) The use of deadly force is not justifiable under this Section unless the actor believes that such force is necessary to protect himself against death, serious bodily harm, kidnapping or sexual intercourse compelled by force or threat; nor is it justifiable if:

(i) the actor, with the purpose of causing death or serious bodily harm, provoked the use of force against himself in the same encounter; or

(ii) the actor knows that he can avoid the necessity of using such force with complete safety by retreating or by surrendering possession of a thing to a person asserting a claim of right thereto or by complying with a demand that he abstain from any action which he has no duty to take, except that:

(1) the actor is not obliged to retreat from his dwelling or place of work, unless he was the initial aggressor or is assailed in his place of work by another person whose place of work the actor knows it to be....

QUESTIONS AND COMMENTS

1. In *Martin*, the Court distinguishes between the issues of mens rea and of self-defense. (Why? See *Patterson v. New York*, ch. 4, supra.) Having drawn the distinction, however, the Court then concedes that evidence of

self-defense is relevant to both issues. Was that necessary? Is a killing any less intentional because it was committed in self-defense? Is it less premeditated (or, in the words of the Ohio statute, done "with prior calculation and design")? Reconsider *Dudley & Stephens*, ch. 2, supra. Is *McManus* consistent with *Martin* on this point?

Assume Martin killed her husband only to keep him from killing her. Did she commit a murder with justification, or no crime at all? Is someone who kills in self-defense "innocent"? As compared to someone who didn't actually do the killing (say because she had an alibi)? As compared to someone who acted under duress?

2. If self-defense doesn't negate mens rea, is it a justification or an excuse? Do we grant the defense because "[d]etached reflection cannot be demanded in the presence of an uplifted knife," Brown v. United States, 256 U.S. 335, 343, 41 S.Ct. 501, 502 (1921)? What if the person claiming self-defense did have an opportunity for detached reflection, say, because the uplifted knife is still several feet away? Is reflection—or at least the opportunity for reflection, or the passage of time between recognizing an impending attack and responding to it—inconsistent with an excuse? Compare the role of reflection and deliberation in the distinction between first and second degree murder, discussed in ch. 10 infra.

What balance of rights underlies the defense of self-defense? Does the attacker forfeit his right to life—and to physical integrity—altogether? Or do his rights count less than his victim's? Because the victim is "innocent"? (What does that mean?) Because the attacker is *more* culpable (or less innocent) than his victim? How do we figure out who is "victim" and who "attacker" in cases where the latter responds to the former's provocation, or where the roles of victim and attacker change rapidly and frequently, as in a prolonged struggle? Or is it best to think of self-defense as a form of private law enforcement, by focusing not on the fact that the person claiming self-defense uses force to prevent an attack against himself, but to prevent a crime? To incapacitate a dangerous individual? But then, how do we determine who is the more dangerous of the two, the "attacker" or the "victim"? See generally Claire Oakes Finkelstein, "On the Obligation of the State to Extend a Right of Self–Defense to its Citizens," 147 U. Pa. L. Rev. 1361 (1999).

Note that homicide in self-defense initially was no defense at all, but at best excusable and therefore a possible ground for pardon, but not for outright acquittal. See J.H. Baker, An Introduction to English Legal History 601 (3d ed. 1990) (homicide se defendendo only "excusable," not "justifiable" because any homicide deprives the king of a subject). Does contemporary American criminal law continue to bear traces of these origins of self-defense as a discretionary exception to the rule that any killing is punishable (or blameworthy)?

3. Even if self-defense is a justification or an excuse—rather than relevant to mens rea—why is the "conceptual difficulty" of claiming self-defense as a defense against a non-intentional crime only "apparent"? Other courts have agreed with the trial court and the intermediate appellate court in *McManus* and reached the opposite conclusion. See, e.g., Duran v. State, 990 P.2d 1005 (Wyo. 1999) (self-defense no defense in

reckless homicide case). Is *McManus* more consistent with viewing self-defense as a justification or as an excuse?

4. Should self-defense be a defense to all crimes? Recall that originally, it was limited to homicide cases. What about offenses that include unlawfulness, illegality, or criminality (as in "unlawful possession of a weapon") as an element? See, e.g., People v. Laramore, 1 Misc.3d 5, 764 N.Y.S.2d 299 (N.Y. App. Term 2003) ("We cannot conceive of a situation where an intent to use a kitchen knife *unlawfully* can ever be justified."); People v. Almodovar, 62 N.Y.2d 126 (1984) (self-defense inapplicable to weapons possession because "a person either possesses a weapon lawfully or he does not and he may not avoid the criminal charge by claiming that he possessed the weapon for his protection"). But see People v. King, 22 Cal.3d 12, 15–16, 148 Cal.Rptr. 409, 410, 582 P.2d 1000, 1001 (1978) (self-defense may be defense to unlawful possession of weapon where accused in emergency arms himself to face immediate danger). (Possession offenses are discussed in detail in ch. 4.)

What about offenses that do not proscribe the use of force? See People v. Pons, 68 N.Y.2d 264 (1986) (self-defense inapplicable to weapons possession because that offense "does not involve the use of physical force").

What about offenses that require the (secondary) intent to commit a crime (like burglary)? Cf. People v. Bess, 107 A.D.2d 844 (N.Y. App. Div. 1985) (no necessity defense to burglary because "defendant either entered or remained in the building intending to commit a crime therein or was lacking that guilty intent"). What if I break into a house with the intent of grabbing a weapon so that I can defend myself against someone who is chasing me down the street?

5. Assume that the defendant is being attacked in a crowded bar by someone with a gun. The defendant himself is armed and decides to shoot at his attacker before he is shot first. He knows that if he shoots, he will risk the lives of at least a half dozen patrons of the bar. Should he be permitted to raise a self-defense claim? If he kills the attacker? If he kills a patron? Does the answer depend on whether we conceive of self-defense as a justification or an excuse? Or should we analyze the question of what crime (if any) he has committed if he shoots a patron by direct reference to the issue of whether he is reckless or negligent in killing the patron? But couldn't we argue, instead, if he killed a patron that he is guilty of *murder*, through the transferred intent doctrine (ch. 6 supra), unless he would have been exonerated had he killed the attacker?

6. *Unlawful Force.* Many modern codes make it clear that self-defensive force may be used only against "unlawful" force. See, e.g., Model Penal Code § 3.04(1), N.Y. Penal Law § 35.15(1). But what makes an attack unlawful? What if I'm attacked by someone whose conduct is *excused*, e.g., by a child, by someone who would qualify for an insanity defense, or by someone acting under duress? Should it matter whether I recognized, or should have recognized, that the attacker was "irresponsible" or "innocent"? See Restatement (Second) of Torts §§ 64, 66 caveat.

What if I'm attacked by a sleepwalker or an epileptic—i.e., by someone who did not engage in a voluntary act? What if I'm attacked by someone whose conduct doesn't qualify as criminal because she lacked the requisite mens rea?

Assume I'm crossing the street and see a car coming toward me. Can I use force in self-defense, say, by shooting the driver, if the driver is obeying the speed limit and all other travel laws, and isn't negligent in any way, but is blinded by the sunlight (or suffers an epileptic seizure)? What if the driver is in fact speeding (a strict liability offense) but neither is nor should have been aware of that fact?

If I cannot claim self-defense in these cases, may I use a necessity (balance of evils) defense? See part C infra.

Note that the law of torts generally limits the use of self-defense to *intentional* attacks. See Restatement (Second) of Torts §§ 63, 65. In cases of negligent attacks, the actor has a duty to retreat, id. § 64, except if the negligent attack poses a fatal threat, id. § 66. (Can an *attack* ever be negligent?)

Consider the Model Penal Code's definition of unlawful force (do you find this definition helpful?):

> "unlawful force" means force, including confinement, which is employed without the consent of the person against whom it is directed and the employment of which constitutes an offense or actionable tort or would constitute such offense or tort except for a defense (such as the absence of intent, negligence, or mental capacity; duress; youth; or diplomatic status) not amounting to a privilege to use the force. Assent constitutes consent, within the meaning of this Section, whether or not it otherwise is legally effective, except assent to the infliction of death or serious bodily harm.

Model Penal Code § 3.11(1).

Why is the use of force in self-defense limited to unlawful attacks? Does the requirement of unlawfulness fit better with viewing self-defense as a justification or as an excuse? Isn't the point of justification that certain conduct that matches the definition of an offense—and therefore is facially criminal—is not unlawful, generally speaking?

Might one, then, not simply replace the concept of "unlawful force" with that of *unjustified* force? The use of self-defensive force—a nominal violation of any number of criminal statutes, including assault and homicide, depending on the force used—would be justified, then, as long as it's not used against an attack that is itself justified. Self-defense, for instance, would be no justification for using force against another's justified self-defense. Cf. Restatement (Second) of Torts § 72 ("The actor is not privileged to defend himself against any force or confinement which the other is privileged for any purpose to inflict upon the actor except where the other's privilege is based upon a reasonable mistake of fact not caused by the fault of the actor."). Could it still be an excuse, assuming the actor *believed* she was justified (say, because she didn't realize that her attacker acted in justified self-defense)?

7. *Unlawful Arrest.* Do I have a right to defend myself against "unlawful" arrest (say, one not based on probable cause, or one made

without a warrant, where probable cause, or a warrant, is required)? See Model Penal Code § 3.04 (use of force in self-defense not justifiable "to resist an arrest which the actor knows is being made by a peace officer, although the arrest is unlawful"); N.Y. Penal Law § 35.27 ("A person may not use physical force to resist an arrest, whether authorized or unauthorized, which is being effected or attempted by a police officer or peace officer when it would reasonably appear that the latter is a police officer or peace officer."). What about an arrest that's made with *excessive* force? Am I justified in using force to protect myself against the excessive force, if not the underlying arrest (which may or may not be unlawful)? Even if the arrest is lawful, can the force used to effect it be unlawful?

8. *Defense of Others*. Originally defense of others was limited to force used to protect one's relatives, or members of one's household. See, e.g., N.Y. Penal Code § 262(2) (1865) ("husband, wife, parent, child, master, mistress or servant"). Today it applies to any "person." Model Penal Code § 3.05. The basic idea is that I should be able to avail myself of a defense if the person I'm protecting would have been entitled to defend herself. (Is this approach more consistent with self-defense as a justification or as an excuse?) What if I misjudge the situation, though? Assume I had come up the street just as McManus pulled out his rifle. Not seeing his friend on the ground, I concluded that McManus was about to shoot into the group of youths for no good reason. If I tackle McManus to prevent him from firing a shot, am I guilty of assault? Contrast Model Penal Code § 3.05(1)(b) with Wood v. State, 128 Ala. 27 (1900) (third party defender "enter[s] combat at his own peril").

2. IMMINENCE VS. IMMEDIACY

State v. Buggs

Court of Appeals of Arizona.
167 Ariz. 333, 806 P.2d 1381 (1990).

■ KLEINSCHMIDT, JUDGE.

The defendant, Johnny Frank Buggs, was convicted upon a trial by jury of aggravated assault. He was sentenced to a maximum term of imprisonment of twenty years. . . .

The defendant's version of the facts is as follows. The defendant became involved in a fight with two women, Shirley Hall and Verna Brown, in a pool hall in a neighborhood notorious for the prevalence of illegal drugs. The fight spilled outside to the parking lot, and the defendant tripped over a cement curb. When the defendant fell down, three men with whom he had had a prior "incident" began kicking him. While this was going on, one of the women the defendant had been fighting stabbed him in the back. A friend of the defendant's grabbed him and picked him up.

The defendant went to the side of the building, and his friend put a pistol in his hand and told him to take care of himself. The defendant went back to the area in front of the pool hall where there were a number of people standing around. Two of the men who had assaulted the defendant were present. The defendant believed they were members of the Crips gang and assumed, because of their reputations, that they had firearms. The defendant also saw one of the women he had been fighting, Verna Brown, and she had a knife in her hand, although she did not then threaten him with it. The defendant was afraid of the men, and he fired his pistol at them. He missed the men but hit Verna Brown in the leg.

At various points in his testimony, the defendant elaborated on his fear of the Crips. When asked why he felt he was in danger when he returned to the parking lot, he said: "Because I know the Crips, I know what they do. You have to get them before they get you." He explained that when he was on the side of the building and his friend handed him the pistol, he returned to the front of the building because he was afraid that if he left the area by another route, he would be ambushed. He explained: "Well, see, I've been on the streets a long time, I have seen how the Crips act, I know what they do, and they get you in a position where you don't know no protection, they will wipe you."

When asked why he fired at the two men he said:

> I guess if you haven't—well, you wouldn't understand it but once you get into it with one of them they going to retaliate on you, I don't know where you are at, they all pack, they all holding a gun. So, you want to stay alive the best thing to do is get them when you see them.

The defendant went on to explain that, because they had set upon him just shortly before, he believed that the two men were about to kill him. * * *

Under Ariz. Rev. Stat. § 13–404(A), self-defense constitutes justification for conduct if: (1) a reasonable person would believe (2) that physical force is *immediately* necessary (3) to protect oneself against another's use or attempted use of unlawful physical force. . . .

The aspect of this case which gives us concern is that, at the time the defendant shot in the direction of the Crips, they were not advancing upon or physically menacing him in any way. Characterized most strongly for the defendant, all that the evidence showed was that the defendant thought the men he shot at were highly dangerous individuals who meant to do him harm, and who he decided had to be eradicated right away to prevent them from gaining an advantage over him and injuring him at some later time. The question is, does this kind of threat justify the defendant's action? We believe it does not. The defendant's action was not immediately necessary to prevent the harm he feared.

The Arizona case most closely on point is *State v. Reid*, 155 Ariz. 399, 747 P.2d 560 (1987). There, the defendant shot and killed her father while he was asleep. The defendant testified that she feared her father because he had a long history of having abused her sexually and physically. She also said that she could detect a change in personality when one of the victim's fits of violence was approaching and, by inference, apparently believed that such a fit was imminent.

The defendant was convicted of murder and appealed. The state cross-appealed, claiming that the trial court erred in instructing the jury on self-defense. The supreme court agreed with the state, but indicated that in some circumstances knowledge of the victim's violent reputation *may* warrant a less restrictive definition of what is "immediately necessary" for self-defense than is usually applied. It noted the following language from a

Kansas case, *State v. Hundley*, 236 Kan. 461, 467–68, 693 P.2d 475, 479 (1985):

> "[I]mmediate," in the instruction on self-defense places undue emphasis on the immediate action of the deceased, and obliterates the nature of the buildup of terror and fear which had been systematically created over a long period of time.

The Arizona Supreme Court then went on to say that even *if* it were to hold that a history of violence could be a factor in supporting a self-defense instruction, the facts in the case before it did not rise to that level.

Arizona is one of several states whose statutes relating to self-defense are couched in terms of the immediate need to use force. Most statutes speak in terms of allowing the use of force against the threat of imminent attack by another. W.R. LaFave & A.W. Scott, Jr., Substantive Criminal Law, § 5.7(d) (1986). This difference in terms and the structure of the statutes does not seem to result in any practical distinction in the application of the law. LaFave and Scott bring the problem into sharp focus with the following discussion:

> As a general matter, the requirement that the attack reasonably appear to be imminent is a sensible one. If the threatened violence is scheduled to arrive in the more distant future, there may be avenues open to the defendant to prevent it other than to kill or injure the prospective attacker; but this is not so where the attack is imminent. But the application of this requirement in some contexts has been questioned. "Suppose A kidnaps and confines D with the announced intention of killing him one week later. D has an opportunity to kill A and escape each morning as A brings him his daily ration. Taken literally, the *imminent* requirement would prevent D from using deadly force in self-defense until A is standing over him with a knife, but that outcome seems inappropriate. * * * The proper inquiry is not the immediacy of the threat but the immediacy of the response necessary in defense. If a threatened harm is such that it cannot be avoided if the intended victim waits until the last moment, the principle of self-defense must permit him to act earlier—as early as is required to defend himself effectively."

Id. at 656 (quoting 2 P. Robinson, Criminal Law Defenses § 131(c)(1) (1984)).

The authors go on to acknowledge that a debate exists, usually discussed in the context of the battered wife, between those who urge that the "imminency" requirement be abolished or loosely construed and those who argue that it remain in place....

While we agree that a victim's past acts and reputation for violence will often be relevant on the question of the reasonableness of a defendant's use of force in self-defense, it would be inappropriate in a case such as this to dispense with or dilute the requirement that one may resort to deadly force only if it is necessary to prevent immediate harm. The defendant's "self-defense" in this case was nothing other than a "preemptive strike" against the men he feared. While there may be some circumstances imaginable that would allow for a defense based on that concept, this case does not present them. This case, for instance, does not present the same dire need as does the example used by LaFave and Scott of the kidnapper who plans to kill his victim in a week. Here, when the defendant returned to the area of the confrontation and fired his pistol at the men who had kicked him, he was not under their domination and control, and they gave no signal that they intended to renew their attack. Our conclusion is in line with settled authority to the effect that after a fight has broken off, one cannot pursue and kill merely because he once feared for his life.

[T]he defendant [therefore] was not entitled to an instruction on self-defense. . . .

QUESTIONS AND COMMENTS

1. What's the point of limiting self-defense to protection against "imminent" harm? Is that more consistent with a view of self-defense as a justification or as an excuse? Is the imminence of the anticipated harm part of the *reason* why we permit a defense of self-defense or is it a *limitation* on the scope of the defense, which is based on other considerations (such as weighing costs and benefits, or competing rights)?

2. Distinguish between three possible interpretations of the imminence requirement: (a) is the harm imminent?, (b) is there an imminent need to act in self-defense?, and (c) is there a need to act in self-defense at some point? Why might the second and third inquiries be harder for the jury? Is the difficulty of fact-finding (i.e., a problem of "procedure") driving the common hesitation to adopt the latter two substantive standards?

Is it possible, instead, that the key to self-defense law is the defendant's impulsiveness and *lack* of reflection, rather than a proper (or at least reasonable) analysis of the need to act in self-defense? In fact, under this conception of self-defense, would reflection on the part of the self-defender be *inconsistent* with the defense?

3. Proportionality

a. Deadly vs. Nondeadly Force

People v. Bradley

Supreme Court of New York, Appellate Division, Second Department.
297 A.D.2d 640, 747 N.Y.S.2d 48 (2002).

According to the evidence adduced at the trial by the prosecution, the defendant and his two codefendants entered a Queens grocery store, and proceeded to a refrigerated display case, from which they removed 40–ounce bottles of malt liquor which they concealed in their pants. When they attempted to leave the store without paying for the malt liquor, they were met by the proprietor of the store, who demanded that the three men either pay for the bottles or surrender them. One of the codefendants reached into his pocket, apparently as if to obtain money, and removed his hand in a closed fist. He punched the proprietor in the left eye, fracturing the left orbital bone. . . .

According to the testimony of the codefendant Sherwin Bowen, the store proprietor instigated the assault by handling an old wooden handsaw in a menacing manner, and by expressing a racial epithet while the trio waited to pay for their purchases. Under this version of events, the proprietor attacked one of the codefendants with the saw, prompting the melee.

Facing various charges of robbery, assault, and gang assault, the defendant asserted a justification defense (see Penal Law § 35.15[1]) on the theory that any physical force used against the proprietor of the store was in defense of the proprietor's unjustified threatened use of the saw. The trial court granted the defendant's request for a simple justification charge concerning the use of ordinary physical force. However, the trial court determined that based upon what it perceived to be the serious physical injury sustained by the proprietor, i.e., the fractured orbital bone that required surgical repair, and the proprietor's alleged use of the saw, that a deadly physical force justification charge was also warranted. . . .

Deadly physical force is defined as "physical force which, under the circumstances in which it is used, is readily capable of causing death or other serious physical injury" (Penal Law § 10.00[11]). Serious physical injury is defined as "physical injury which creates a substantial risk of death, or which causes death or serious and protracted disfigurement, protracted impairment of health or protracted loss or impairment of the function of any bodily organ" (Penal Law § 10.00[10]). Even if the proprietor of the store sustained serious physical injury, it does not automatically follow that deadly physical force was used. A non-deadly push could cause a fall that might result in unintended serious injury or death, but that does not transform the use of ordinary force into the use of deadly force was used. The People's proof established only that one of the codefendants threw a single, albeit crushing punch. This was a use of ordinary, not deadly, physical force.

Pursuant to the unambiguous language of Penal Law § 35.15(2)(a), under the circumstances of the instant case, deadly physical force could not be used if retreat could be made in complete safety; the trial court so charged the jury. Retreat, however, is not a condition precedent of the use of ordinary physical force in self-defense. . . .

Because the evidence of the defendant's guilt was not overwhelming, we conclude that the above charge error deprived the defendant of a fair trial.

b. Retreat

Commonwealth v. Toon

Appeals Court of Massachusetts.
55 Mass. App. Ct. 642, 773 N.E.2d 993 (2002).

■ GRASSO, J.

In the early morning of Saturday, July 11, 1998, the defendant Troy A. Toon stabbed Gary Moreis on Warwick Avenue in the Oak Bluffs section of

Martha's Vineyard. Moreis bled to death. A jury found the defendant guilty upon indictments charging murder in the second degree and assault and battery by means of a dangerous weapon, a knife. On appeal, the defendant [complains of an erroneous instruction on self-defense.] We conclude that the defendant was not entitled to a self-defense instruction at all. * * *

With the victim was his cousin, Evelyn Larkin. With the defendant were his brother, Ducas Matthews, and two female companions, Maria Gomes and Megan Jennings. As might be expected, Larkin presented an account more favorable to Moreis. Matthews, Jennings, and Gomes presented accounts more favorable to the defendant. From their testimony emerged uncontroverted facts, as well as diametrically different views of what transpired.

Minor inconsistencies aside, the testimony established that at about 10:45 P.M. on Friday, July 10, Moreis, who was thirty-six years old and lived on Martha's Vineyard, had a chance encounter with his cousin Larkin. They socialized for about two hours at the Atlantic Connection, a local bar. There, Larkin observed Moreis consume one drink.[7]

The defendant, who was twenty-four, had come to Martha's Vineyard to visit his father and his brother, Ducas Matthews. Prior to the fatal altercation, the defendant, Matthews, and Gomes had been together all evening, first at a private residence where Gomes had consumed a considerable amount of alcohol. At about 11:30 P.M. they proceeded to the Lamp Post, another local bar. Because, at nineteen, Matthews was underage, he could not accompany the defendant and Gomes inside the Lamp Post. He remained outside, where he encountered Jennings. As the bars began to close, each group headed off.

Larkin set out to drive Moreis to a campground where he lived with his girlfriend, Andrea Hayden. En route, Moreis asked Larkin to stop briefly at Warwick Avenue, where he owned a garage. Coincidentally, the defendant, Matthews, Jennings, and Gomes were headed toward Warwick Avenue to locate a man named Robert Correia, some marijuana, and a party.

At this point, the specifics diverge.... According to the defendant's companions, Moreis had encountered the defendant, Matthews, Gomes, and Jennings around 1:00 A.M. on Warwick Avenue. Moreis approached the group and yelled epithets, directed particularly toward the defendant, asking what the defendant was doing on Moreis's street. Moreis, who was five feet seven inches tall, 190 pounds, and well built, was acting "crazy."....

According to Jennings, the confrontation began when Moreis approached and, amidst a barrage of profanities, called the defendant a "pretty boy." The defendant responded that he wasn't looking for trouble, but for Rob (Correia). Meanwhile, Matthews sought to defuse the situation. Ignoring Matthews's attempts at diplomacy, Moreis continued to yell and called the defendant a "pretty boy" and told the defendant that he would

7. Moreis died at the hospital some five hours after the fight. An autopsy established that Moreis had consumed cocaine within six hours of his death.

"whip [his] ass." According to Jennings, the defendant said, "If you want to fight we fight, but I am not going to back off because you are an older man.... Knock it off, or I'll doink [stab] you." Jennings did not see a knife in the defendant's hand as he said this. Moreis told the defendant to go ahead and "doink" him "if that's going to make you a bigger man." Jennings was unequivocal ... that Moreis struck the first blow.

Jennings testified that Moreis grabbed the defendant by the shirt and pushed him back against the van, but that the defendant was able to push Moreis off him. The defendant told Moreis to back off him, but Moreis did not and continued to call the defendant a "punk" and a "pretty boy," and told the defendant to leave the area. Jennings stated that when Moreis stepped back, she saw blood on Moreis's shirt.

Jennings (and all the witnesses) testified that Moreis continued to fight with the defendant even after he had been stabbed. Moreis ripped off his shirt, grabbed the defendant by the throat, and threw him against a van. He pummeled the defendant, who fell against a car and onto the ground, skinning his knees. At this point, Gomes and Matthews intervened and pulled the combatants apart. Moreis leaned against a black pickup truck and grabbed a lawnchair from its open cab. Seeing this, Matthews armed himself with a table leg. Before the combatants could inflict further damage, a neighbor appeared, took the chair from Moreis, and declared an end to the fight.

Jennings related that later that night, the defendant said to her: "I don't know why this even happened, because I don't know him and he came in my face was [sic] starting with me, and I warned him to back off and he wouldn't back off." The defendant told her that when they started fighting "I didn't feel the knife come out.... I only got him once."

* * *

[A]ll the evidence suggested that the reason for the altercation and ultimately for the stabbing was the defendant's intent to defend his manhood against a perceived challenge by a combative and unruly stranger.... Even in the light most favorable to the defendant, it was unmistakable that Moreis did not want the defendant and his friends on Warwick Avenue and that the defendant and his friends did not wish to leave. The confrontation occurred on a public street, with both access and opportunity to retreat in the face of Moreis's threats and insults. The defendant could have walked away at any time. There was simply no evidence that an avenue of escape was unavailable to the defendant at the start of the confrontation. Nor was there any evidence that the defendant availed himself of all means to avoid combat before resorting even to nondeadly force.

While the defendant may have had an equal right to remain on the public street, the measure of a duty to retreat is not equality of right to remain in the face of an unreasonable demand, but the ability to retreat. A stubborn unwillingness to walk away, even in the face of a perceived affront to the defendant's manhood, does not equate with an inability to retreat any more than it manifests a concern for personal safety. We need not decide whether under different circumstances, not present here, a right to remain might justify an unwillingness to back down in the face of an unreasonable demand to leave. Suffice to say, here the only proffered reason the defendant and his friends were there, and remained, was to buy marijuana. Before either nondeadly force or deadly force may be invoked the duty to retreat must be observed. See Commonwealth v. Niemic, 427 Mass. 718, 722, 696 N.E.2d 117 (1998) (if a defendant has an opportunity to retreat, but fails to do so, he has no privilege to use force in self-defense). Even were we to accept the dubious proposition advanced by the defendant that the defendant's threat to stab Moreis may be viewed as a way of avoiding a confrontation by conveying to Moreis the wisdom of backing down or facing serious injury, there remains, nevertheless, a duty to retreat, if possible, before resorting to force, whether nondeadly or deadly. * * *

Judgment affirmed.

c. Initial Aggressor

Rowe v. United States

Supreme Court of the United States.
164 U.S. 546, 17 S.Ct. 172 (1896).

■ MR. JUSTICE HARLAN delivered the opinion of the Court.

[T]he evidence on both sides was to the effect that the deceased used language of an offensive character for the purpose of provoking a difficulty with the accused, or of subjecting him to the indignity of a personal insult. [To be more precise, the deceased, a white man by the name of Frank Bozeman, had used a racial epithet against the accused, a Cherokee.] The offensive words did not, it is true, legally justify the accused in what he did—the evidence of the government tending to show that "he kicked at deceased, hitting him lightly on the lower part of the leg". . . . According to the evidence of the defence, the accused then "stepped back, and leaned up against the counter," indicating thereby, it may be, that he neither desired nor intended to pursue the matter further. If the jury believed the evidence on behalf of the defence, they might reasonably have inferred from the actions of the accused that he did not intend to make a violent or dangerous personal assault upon the deceased, but only, by kicking at him or kicking him lightly, to express his indignation at the offensive language of the deceased.

It should have been submitted to the jury whether the act of the accused in stepping back and leaning against the counter, not in an attitude for personal conflict, was intended to be, and should have been reasonably interpreted as being, a withdrawal by the accused in good faith from further controversy with the deceased. On the contrary, the court, in effect, said that if, because of words used by the deceased, the accused kicked at or kicked the deceased, however lightly, and no matter how offensive those words were, he put himself in a position to make the killing manslaughter, even if the taking of life became, by reason of the suddenness, rapidity and fierceness of the assault of the deceased, absolutely necessary to save his own. [T]he court . . . pressed upon the jury the proposition that "a person who has slain another cannot urge in justification of the killing a necessity produced by his own unlawful and wrongful acts." But that abstract principle has no application to this case, if it be true—as the evidence on behalf of the defence tended to show—that the first real provocation came from the deceased when he used towards the accused language of an offensive character, and that the accused immediately after kicking at or lightly kicking the deceased, signified by his conduct that he no longer desired controversy with his adversary; whereupon the deceased, despite the efforts of the accused to retire from further contest, sprang at the latter, with knife in hand, for the purpose of taking life, and would most probably have accomplished that object, if the accused had not fired at the moment he did.

Under such circumstances, did the law require that the accused should stand still, and permit himself to be cut to pieces, under the penalty that if he met the unlawful attack upon him and saved his own life, by taking that of his assailant, he would be guilty of manslaughter? We think not.

If a person, under the provocation of offensive language, assaults the speaker personally, but in such a way as to show that there is no intention to do him serious bodily harm, and then retires under such circumstances as show that he does not intend to do anything more, but in good faith withdraws from further contest, his right of self-defence is restored when the person assaulted, in violation of law, pursues him with a deadly weapon and seeks to take his life or do him great bodily harm. In Parker v. The State, 88 Alabama, 4, 7, the court, after adverting to the general rule that the aggressor cannot be heard to urge in his justification a necessity for the killing which was produced by his own wrongful act, said: "This rule, however, is not of absolute and universal application. An exception to it exists in cases where, although the defendant originally provoked the conflict, he withdraws from it in good faith, and clearly announces his desire for peace. If he be pursued after this, his right of self-defence, though once lost, revives. 'Of course,' says Mr. Wharton, in referring to this modification of the rule, 'there must be a real and bona fide surrender and withdrawal on his part; for, if there be not, then he will continue to be regarded as the aggressor.' 1 Wharton's Cr. Law, (9th ed.) § 486. The meaning of the principle is that the law will always leave the original aggressor an opportunity to repent before he takes the life of his adversary. Bishop's Cr. Law, (7th ed.) § 871." Recognizing this exception to be a just one, the court properly said, in addition: "Due caution must be observed by courts and juries in its application, as it involves a principle which is very liable to abuse. The question of the good or bad faith of the retreating party is of the utmost importance, and should generally be submitted to the jury in connection with the fact of retreat itself, especially where there is any room for conflicting inferences on this point from the evidence." Both parties to a mutual combat are wrong-doers, and the law of self-defence cannot be invoked by either, so long as he continues in the combat. But, as said by the Supreme Court of Iowa in State v. Dillon, 74 Iowa, 653, 659, if one "actually and in good faith withdraws from the combat, he ceases to be a wrong-doer; and if his adversary have reasonable ground for holding that he has so withdrawn, it is sufficient, even though the fact is not clearly evinced." In Wharton on Homicide, § 483, the author says that "though the defendant may have thus provoked the conflict, yet, if he withdrew from it in good faith and clearly announced his desire for peace, then, if he be pursued, his rights of self-defence revive.''

QUESTIONS AND COMMENTS

1. What sort of *proportionality* between protective force and protected-against force should we require? Is requiring necessity—and proportionality—more in keeping with self-defense as a justification or as an excuse?

2. In *Rowe*, the Court mentions in passing that the ''offensive words did not . . . legally justify'' Rowe's initial kick. Can words ever provide the basis for a self-defense justification?

3. It's useful to distinguish the general requirements for the use of force in self-defense from the additional requirements for the use of *deadly force*. Why do we need special requirements for the use of deadly force? Wouldn't a general requirement of proportionality between protective and protected-against force suffice? What does the *retreat* requirement add to the general necessity requirement?

Is it more sensible to say that *no* force (let alone deadly force) is *ever* ''necessary'' if harm could be averted by retreat, or is it the case instead that rules limiting the amount of force a self-defender is permitted to use (to proportional and necessary force) are premised on the prior notion that he may stand his ground? (If we require retreat, have we (implicitly) permitted the aggressor to violate the victim's prior right to stay where she was entitled to be?)

4. Note that, in *Bradley* (and in the Model Penal Code, § 3.11(2)), deadly force is not force that causes death in fact, but merely force that *may* cause death *or* serious physical injury. The supplemental requirements triggered by the use of deadly force therefore are not limited to homicide (or even attempted homicide) cases. Other cases apply a more limited definition of deadly force. See, e.g., Miller v. Clark County, Wash., 340 F.3d 959 (9th Cir. 2003) (use of police dog trained to ''bite and hold,'' which bit suspect for between 45 to 60 seconds and caused ''severe injury,'' doesn't qualify as use of deadly force, defined as ''force reasonably likely to kill''). What's the point of drawing a distinction between deadly and nondeadly *force*, as opposed to, say, one between certain types of harm (death, physical injury) and/or between different types of mental state regarding death (intent, knowledge, recklessness, etc.)?

In *Bradley,* why was the trial court wrong to think that since the force used did result in serious physical injury it must have been ''readily capable'' of inflicting that injury? Is a ''single, albeit crushing, punch'' to the face analogous to a ''nondeadly push''? What's the danger of inferring—retrospectively—the capacity to inflict a certain type of harm from the actual infliction of that harm?

Why was *Bradley* so interested in *not* getting a deadly force self-defense instruction?

5. Why should we have a retreat requirement in the first place? If I have a right to be where I am and do what I do, why should I have to yield

to an unlawful aggressor, even if I can do so in complete safety? (In *Toon*, should it matter whether the defendant was motivated by an "intent to defend his manhood," rather than by an unwillingness to give in to Moreis's unjustified and unprovoked demands that he leave "Moreis's street"?) Is this way of thinking only appropriate for "the border-ruffian, who walks about the earth with one hand in his hip-pocket, and shoots each similar gentleman in sight"? See Joseph H. Beale, "Retreat from a Murderous Assault," 16 Harv. L. Rev. 567, 582 (1903). Or is it really based on a wrongheaded concern with protecting one's "honor," where a "really honorable man, a man of truly refined and elevated feeling, would perhaps always regret the apparent cowardice of a retreat, but he would regret ten times more after the excitement of the contest was past, the thought that he had the blood of a fellow-being on his hands." Id. at 581. Is the retreat requirement more compatible with viewing self-defense as a justification, or as an excuse?

If we decide in favor of a retreat requirement, why should it be limited to *deadly* force (as it is in the Model Penal Code and many other jurisdictions, including New York)? Note that the law of torts imposes a retreat requirement even on the use of nondeadly self-defensive force. Restatement (Second) of Torts § 63.

6. The retreat requirement does not apply to attacks within one's own home. Why? Can the use of force in self-defense ever be "necessary" if a retreat in complete safety is possible, even from one's home? There is a difference of opinion on whether the home exception to the retreat requirement is itself subject to an exception—if one inhabitant is attacked by another. While some jurisdictions impose a duty to retreat even in this situation, most do not. What effect would recognizing the duty to retreat in cases of attacks by a co-habitant have on intrafamilial violence? See Weiand v. State, 732 So.2d 1044 (Fla. 1999).

7. In *Rowe,* does it matter why the defendant kicked Bozeman? What if he had kicked Bozeman just because he felt like it? Was *Bozeman* the one who provoked Rowe so that he could kill or seriously injure him in "self-defense"? Should the initial assailant ever be permitted to use deadly force against his victim, once that victim turns around and defends herself? Wouldn't the initial assailant have forfeited his right to self-defense, since he after all is responsible for his claimed need to defend himself in the first place, *by forcing another person to defend herself*? What if he provoked his victim not with the "*purpose* of causing death or serious bodily harm," Model Penal Code § 3.04(2)(b)(i), but merely *knowing* or *expecting* that the victim would respond in a way that would allow him to use deadly force in "self-defense"? (How would the Model Penal Code resolve the issue in *Rowe*?)

Instead of granting the initial aggressor a full-fledged (justification?) defense, would it be more appropriate to mitigate his sentence? Consider the following provision of the United States Sentencing Guidelines.

U.S. Sentencing Guidelines § 5K2.10. Victim's Conduct (Policy Statement).

If the victim's wrongful conduct contributed significantly to provoking the offense behavior, the court may reduce the sentence . . . to reflect the nature and circumstances of the offense. In deciding the extent of a sentence reduction, the court should consider:

(a) the size and strength of the victim, or other relevant physical characteristics, in comparison with those of the defendant;

(b) the persistence of the victim's conduct and any efforts by the defendant to prevent confrontation;

(c) the danger reasonably perceived by the defendant, including the victim's reputation for violence;

(d) the danger actually presented to the defendant by the victim; and

(e) any other relevant conduct by the victim that substantially contributed to the danger presented.

Victim misconduct ordinarily would not be sufficient to warrant application of this provision in the context of offenses [involving] Criminal Sexual Abuse. In addition, this provision usually would not be relevant in the context of non-violent offenses. There may, however, be unusual circumstances in which substantial victim misconduct would warrant a reduced penalty in the case of a non-violent offense. For example, an extended course of provocation and harassment might lead a defendant to steal or destroy property in retaliation.

8. Who's the victim? In self-defense cases, it's often hard to tell who counts as the victim and who as the offender, and therefore who is entitled to use (what?) force against whom, at various points during the course of a violent confrontation. The retreat and provocation rules try to provide some help on this point. Who's the victim in *Rowe*? In *Toon*?

4. Self-Defense and Property Interests

a. Property as the Object of the Criminal Conduct to Be Justified

Boget v. State

Court of Criminal Appeals of Texas.
74 S.W.3d 23 (2002).

■ KEASLER, J.

James Boget was charged with criminal mischief for damaging a truck. At his trial, Boget introduced evidence that the vehicle was damaged while he was defending himself from its driver. Boget's requested jury instruction on self-defense was denied. The State argues that Boget was not entitled to the instruction because self-defense is not available unless a defendant is charged with an offense involving force against another, and criminal mischief is not such an offense. We disagree and hold that self-defense is available in a prosecution for criminal mischief where the mischief arises out of the accused's use of force against another. * * *

[According to Boget], he saw [a] truck driving around the parking lot [of his apartment complex] and suspected the driver[, Maria Palacios,] was responsible for causing [a] disturbance at the complex. Boget said that when he approached the vehicle, the truck "took off" toward him and hit him. The impact caused Boget to hit the front windshield, flip over the top of the truck, and land in the truck bed. According to Boget, he then began hitting the back windshield and rear windows with his flashlight. He got out of the truck when it stopped before exiting the complex. * * *

Section 9.31 of the Penal Code provides that "a person is justified in using force against another when and to the degree he reasonably believes the force is immediately necessary to protect himself against the other's use or attempted use of unlawful force."

According to the State, self-defense "by its own terms" involves the use of force against another person. The State argues that criminal mischief, on the other hand, requires the intentional or knowing damage or destruction of another's tangible property. It concludes that because the offense Boget was charged with did not involve force against another, he was not entitled to a charge on self-defense. * * *

When we interpret statutes we seek to effectuate the collective intent or purpose of the legislators who enacted the legislation. At issue is not the definition of the word "another", but rather what it means to direct force "against" another. The plain language of the statute fails to give us an answer.

Self-defense is popularly thought of as the natural right of individuals to act in concert against the threat of others. The assumption is that there is a natural right to preserve oneself from any kind of threat made against person or property with whatever force seems necessary at the time. As Blackstone said of self-defense:

> Both the life and limbs of a man are of such high value, in the estimation of the law of England, that it pardons even homicide if committed se defendendo, or in order to preserve them. For whatever is done by a man, to save either life or member, is looked upon as done with the highest necessity or compulsion.[22]

The commentators have differing views concerning whether self-defense is an appropriate defense to any crime committed in defending oneself. [S]elf-defense has generally been limited to situations in which the defendant is charged with an assaultive crime. This is largely because the rules of self-defense evolved from the law on homicide. The connection of self-defense to assaultive crimes is clear in light of the fact that even some modern penal codes limit discussion of self-defense to the sections on homicide and assault and battery. This factor weighs against extending self-defense to offenses other than offenses against the person.

Texas followed this model until 1974, when the entire Penal Code was rewritten. The Legislature removed self-defense from the section of the Penal Code involving offenses against the person and placed the defense in Title 2 of the Code entitled "General Principles of Criminal Responsibility.".... In his commentary to the draft concerning the new chapter on justification, Dean Keeton explained:

22. 1 William Blackstone, Commentaries *130.

> With the inclusion of proposed ch. 3 in the new Texas Penal Code our written law will for the first time specify in one place every variety of conduct otherwise criminal that is justified. Unlike the present penal code, which distinguishes types of justifiable conduct mainly on the basis of whether it causes death or injury, ch. 3 creates a comprehensive series of descriptive categories—for example, protection of persons, law enforcement, special relationships—and then deals with problems of justification peculiar to each category....

As Dean Keeton pointed out in his commentary, the general rule is that force is justified when necessary to protect against another person's threat or use of unlawful force. The law recognizes that the right of self-preservation entitles a person to defend himself even to the point of taking the life of his assailant if necessary. * * *

The duty of this Court is to effectuate the intent of the statute. In this case, that means encouraging the use of restraint in defensive situations. A rule that allows a charge on self-defense where a person kills another, but prohibits the defense when a person merely damages the other's property is inconsistent with the purposes of the statute.

For instance, assume a person is about to be run down by a speeding car. If she brandishes her pistol and fires at the front tires of the car to stop the vehicle, she will not receive a charge on self-defense should she be indicted for criminal mischief. On the other hand, if she shoots the driver she is entitled to a charge on self-defense in a murder prosecution. This result is contrary to the object of the statute because it punishes the individual who used the least force possible in self-preservation.

In Boget's case, had his flashlight gone through the window and hit Palacios, he would be entitled to a charge on self-defense in an assault prosecution. It would be illogical to deny him the instruction simply because his force didn't actually land on Palacios. The relevant inquiry is whether he directed his force against another. We find that under Boget's version of the facts, his force was directed against Palacios. * * *

b. Property as the Interest to Be Protected

People v. Petronio

County Court of New York, Nassau County.
192 Misc.2d 240, 746 N.Y.S.2d 781 (2002).

■ DONALD P. DERIGGI, J.

The Defendant was convicted after trial of Murder in the Second Degree.... Before the charge the defendant had requested that the jury be instructed [regarding] justification in defense of a dwelling during a burglary[a] and the Court refused to so instruct.

During the trial the evidence showed that the Defendant and the deceased, Jeffrey Walters, had arranged the sale and purchase of a substan-

a. In New York, burglary is defined as "knowingly enter[ing] or remain[ing] unlawfully in a building with intent to commit a crime therein." N.Y. Penal Law § 140.20. Burglary is discussed in ch. 11 infra.—EDS.

tial amount of ecstasy at the Defendant's house, 20 Kelly Street, Valley Stream. The victim arrived and, when he showed the Defendant the drugs, the Defendant protested that he was being cheated. Defendant said that this was certainly not 14 thousand ecstasy pills and that not only was the quantity insufficient but that some of the pills were fake. The Defendant testified that the victim then pushed him and a fight ensued. The Defendant said the victim pushed him to the ground, the victim being on top of the Defendant, when the Defendant sprayed the victim in the eyes with pepper spray and then managed to get up, push the victim to the ground, face down, hit his face into the floor several times and then brought his foot down twice on the victim's neck, thereby killing him.

The Defendant requested and the jury was charged under the justification statute, Section 35.15 of the Penal Law, on the use of deadly physical force. The Court's charge included the provisions of Section 35.15(2)(a), i.e., that the use of deadly physical force is permissible when one reasonably believes that the other person is using or is about to use deadly physical force. With regard to the justification charge related to deadly physical force to terminate a burglary [under Section 35.20(3)], the facts do show that the incident occurred in the Defendant's dwelling and while there was no evidence presented to show that the Defendant directly ordered the victim out of his dwelling, there is a view of the evidence which shows that the victim began the aggressive acts by pushing or punching the Defendant.

.... The Defendant argues that ... a license or privilege to enter a dwelling is automatically terminated by the aggressor's criminal act and that he is then "remaining unlawfully" in the dwelling and since he is committing a crime, in this case Assault, he is actually therefore perpetrating a Burglary, warranting the use of deadly force against him to terminate the Burglary....

Perhaps the best and clearest language on this issue is found in a trial court decision People v. Crowell 122 Misc 2d 133, 470 N.Y.S.2d 306 (Oswego Co. Ct. 1983). In that case, the Defendant was given permission to enter the premises for the purpose of painting it. The Court found that the privilege to be within the premises is not negated by the formulation of a criminal intent or even the undertaking of a criminal action therein. The Court went on to state that "the doctrine remains that a licensed or privileged entry or remaining is not transformed into an unlawful one upon the occurrence of criminal conduct on the part of the licensee. To rule to the contrary would mean that an intoxicated houseguest who loses his temper and intentionally smashes a vase becomes a burglar. Innumerable like examples can be imagined...."

The controlling law in this area is People v. Godfrey 80 N.Y. 2d 860, 587 N.Y.S.2d 594, 600 N.E.2d 225 (1992). In that case, two individuals agreed to have a fight in the Defendant's residence. They had a fight. The Defendant then told the victim to leave his house. The victim refused to leave and again attacked the Defendant. The Defendant shot the victim.

The Court held as follows ...

> Section 35.20 Subdivision 3 of the Penal Law authorizes a person to use deadly physical force against another person if he or she reason-

ably believes that such force is necessary to terminate a burglary of his or her own home.... The People contend that even if the (victim) could "technically" be considered to have been committing a burglary when he was killed, the Defendant should nevertheless not be permitted to rely on Section 35.20 Subdivision 3 as authorizing his use of deadly physical force. Specifically, they maintain that an individual, who, like the defendant invites another on to his or premises and then actively and willingly joins in that person's criminal conduct, should not be permitted to kill that person merely because he or she does not promptly cease pursuing the criminal endeavor upon being ordered to leave the premises. Section 35.20 Subdivision 3, as its legislative history makes clear, was intended to protect those individuals who suddenly find themselves the victim of an intrusion upon their premises by one bent on a criminal end. There is nothing in that provision's legislative history or otherwise which suggests that it was also meant to protect one who, like the Defendant, invites another person into his home, fully aware that such person intends to commit a crime once inside. Such an individual is no less responsible for any ensuing invasion of his own security than the would be burglar and therefore cannot claim the protections of 35.20 Subdivision 3.

The Godfrey case is parallel and similar to the case before this Court. In both cases the Defendant and the victim went to the Defendant's house for the purpose of committing a crime. In Godfrey, the Defendant argued that he had at some point ordered the victim out of the house and when the victim again attacked him he shot the victim. In the Petronio case, the Defendant did not order the victim out of the house but contends that the invitation was automatically terminated by the subsequent assault. Under either scenario, according to Godfrey, the Defendant cannot avail himself of the justification statute permitting deadly physical force to be used to terminate a burglary. In both cases, the Defendants were no less responsible for the ensuing invasion of their security than the would be burglars and therefore cannot claim the protections of Penal Law Section 35.20(3).

QUESTIONS AND COMMENTS

1. Why should defendants have a justification for committing property offenses in self-defense? Do you agree with the *Boget* court's answer to this question? How does granting someone a complete defense to criminal conduct "encourag[e] the use of restraint in defensive situations"? Wouldn't *denying* the defense provide that much more encouragement? To avoid the difficulty in *Boget* wouldn't it make sense to formulate self-defense not in terms of the use of "force against another," but more generally in terms of the commission of facially criminal conduct that is justifiable as an act of self-defense?

Note that in cases like *Boget* the object of the facially criminal conduct I'm trying to justify differs from the source of the threat. (Or are all property offenses ultimately also offenses against the person—i.e., the owner or possessor?) Who (or what) is the attacker in cases where the defendant claims to use self-defense by damaging, or destroying, an inanimate object? An animate, but nonhuman, object—like a dog? If my neighbor's miniature Schnauzer attacks me as I take a walk around the block, does it make sense to say that I'm using self-defense when I give it a kick? (Would it make a difference if it was a stray dog? A wolf?) If, on the same walk, I suddenly see another neighbor's unoccupied car (whose brakes had suddenly given out) roll down the hill toward me at a frightening—and ever-increasing—pace, am I using self-defense if I shoot out its tires? Can I use self-defense in cases where it's a stretch to say that I'm using force "against another"? At what point is it more appropriate to think of cases involving the justification of property offenses as raising issues of *necessity* (see infra) rather than of self-defense?

2. Dwellings have long enjoyed a position of privilege in Anglo–American criminal law, as evidenced by the home exception to the retreat requirement in the law of self-defense. The law of defense of property generally strikes the balance in favor of life over property, so that the use of deadly force to protect one's property is not justifiable. The criminal law, however, is far less likely to force me to abandon or sacrifice my home to preserve the life of the arsonist or the trespasser who drives me out of my house at gunpoint. See, e.g., N.Y. Penal Law § 35.20(1); Model Penal Code § 3.06(3)(d)(i).

Lesser interferences with one's property—e.g., through larceny, criminal mischief, or ordinary trespass—may be averted only through the use of nondeadly force. See Ayers v. State, 60 Miss. 709 (1883) ("No man is required by law to yield possession of his property to the unlawful claim of another. He may defend his possession; and while he may not kill to prevent the trespass, he may kill to protect his own person against a deadly assault made by the trespasser on him."); N.Y. Penal Law § 35.25. On the recovery of stolen property, see ch. 11, infra.

What about burglary? Burglary traditionally has been defined as trespass with the intent to commit a crime (most often larceny). To the extent that burglary is a property offense that does not threaten the destruction or dispossession of one's home, it would appear that I would not be justified in using deadly force to prevent it. That is the position of the Model Penal Code. Model Penal Code § 3.06(3)(d) (deadly force justified to avert burglary only in case of danger to persons, and not only to property). Many jurisdictions, including New York, however, take the opposite view. N.Y. Penal Law § 35.20(3) (deadly force justified to avert burglary). See *Petronio*.

Critics of the Model Penal Code approach have invoked the age-old right of the "householder" to defend himself and "the members of his household" against intruders, a right that finds support in the "basic sentiments of the community" and "popular sentiment." Note, "The Use of Deadly Force in the Protection of Property Under the Model Penal Code," 59 Colum. L. Rev. 1212, 1216, 1223 n.56, 1224 (1959). The Code drafters, for their part, maintained that their approach reflected "[t]he basic judgment ... that 'the preservation of life has such moral and ethical standing in our culture and society, that the deliberate sacrifice of life merely for the protection of property ought not to be sanctioned by law.' "

Model Penal Code Commentaries § 3.06, at 72; see also People v. Ceballos, 12 Cal.3d 470 (1974) (spring gun).

Do these different approaches to the defense reflect different attitudes toward the defense of self-defense in general (including the defense of one's person and one's property)? Is the Model Penal Code provision more consistent with a view of self-defense as justification, and that of its critics more with a view of self-defense as excuse?

Consider the interplay of the rules governing use of deadly force in defense of one's person and of one's property (real and moveable) in light of the facts in United States v. Peterson, 483 F.2d 1222 (D.C. Cir. 1973):

> Charles Keitt, the deceased, and two friends drove in Keitt's car to the alley in the rear of Peterson's house to remove the windshield wipers from the latter's wrecked car. While Keitt was doing so, Peterson came out of the house into the back yard to protest. After a verbal exchange, Peterson went back into the house, obtained a pistol, and returned to the yard. In the meantime, Keitt had reseated himself in his car, and he and his companions were about to leave.
>
> Upon his reappearance in the yard, Peterson paused briefly to load the pistol. "If you move," he shouted to Keitt, "I will shoot." He walked to a point in the yard slightly inside a gate in the rear fence and, pistol in hand, said, "If you come in here I will kill you." Keitt alighted from his car, took a few steps toward Peterson and exclaimed, "What the hell do you think you are going to do with that?" Keitt then made an about-face, walked back to his car and got a lug wrench. With the wrench in a raised position, Keitt advanced toward Peterson, who stood with the pistol pointed toward him. Peterson warned Keitt not to "take another step" and, when Keitt continued onward shot him in the face from a distance of about ten feet. Death was apparently instantaneous.

3. What if I use deadly force against a burglar in my apartment in the *mistaken* belief that I am justified—or, for that matter, excused—in doing so, say, because I have just moved from New York to a state that follows the Model Penal Code on this point? What if I am mistaken in my assessment of the *lawfulness* of force used against me, or by me against another? Cf. Model Penal Code § 3.09(1).

4. Why was Petronio so interested in getting the defense-of-property instruction, given that ordinarily life is valued more highly than is property? Why might he have qualified under the defense-of-property provision, but not under the defense-of-person one?

5. Is *Petronio* consistent with *Rowe*? Why isn't Petronio entitled to raise a defense-of-property justification? Did he forfeit his right to defend his home (because he is a drug dealer, because he dealt drugs in his home, because he consented to some criminal activity in his home)? Did he breach the peace of his home by conducting a criminal transaction there, so that there was no peace left to protect by the time the drug deal went bad? Would he have been justified in using *nondeadly* force to evict Walters?

On the notion of a house peace, which the householder strove to keep and which could be broken in any number of ways (from burglary to weapons possession to an affray), see 1 Frederick Pollock & Frederic William Maitland, The History of English Law Before the Time of Edward I 454 (2d ed. 1898) ("The sheriff has his peace, the lord of a soken has his peace; nay, every householder has his peace; you break his peace if you fight in his house, and, besides all the other payments that you must make to atone for your deed of violence, you must make a payment to him for the breach of his *mund*.") German criminal law retains several offenses explicitly defined as breaches of various peaces: *Hausfriedensbruch* (breach of the peace of the house), § 123 StGB; *Landfriedensbruch* (breach of the peace of the country), § 125 StGB; and *Störung des öffentlichen Friedens* (disturbance of the public peace), § 126 StGB.

6. Consider the self-defense provision in the German Penal Code. Is this provision too general to pass muster under the legality principle? Note that this section does not differentiate among protected interests (person, property), nor among the interests violated for the sake of protection (again person, property), nor among defense of one's own interest and that of another. Should it matter *why* someone exceeds the bounds of justified self-defense? Should behavior covered under § 33 still count as a justification? Should § 33 exculpate completely or only mitigate punishment?

German Penal Code § 32. Self–Defense.

(1) Whoever commits an act in necessary self-defense does not act unlawfully.

(2) Necessary self-defense is the defense which is required to avert an imminent unlawful assault from oneself or another.

§ 33. Excessive Self–Defense.

If the perpetrator exceeds the limits of necessary self-defense due to confusion, fear or fright, then he shall not be punished.

5. Reasonableness and Mistake

State v. Kelly

Supreme Court of New Jersey.
97 N.J. 178, 478 A.2d 364 (1984).

■ WILENTZ, C.J.

On May 24, 1980, defendant, Gladys Kelly, stabbed her husband, Ernest, with a pair of scissors. He died shortly thereafter at a nearby hospital. The couple had been married for seven years, during which time Ernest had periodically attacked Gladys. According to Ms. Kelly, he assaulted her that afternoon, and she stabbed him in self-defense, fearing that he would kill her if she did not act.

Ms. Kelly was indicted for murder. At trial, she did not deny stabbing her husband, but asserted that her action was in self-defense. To establish the requisite state of mind for her self-defense claim, Ms. Kelly called Dr. Lois Veronen as an expert witness to testify about the battered-woman's syndrome. After hearing a lengthy voir dire examination of Dr. Veronen, the trial court ruled that expert testimony concerning the syndrome was inadmissible on the self-defense issue. . . .

Ms. Kelly was convicted of reckless manslaughter. * * *

The Kellys had a stormy marriage. Some of the details of their relationship, especially the stabbing, are disputed. The following is Ms. Kelly's version of what happened. . . .

The day after the marriage, Mr. Kelly got drunk and knocked Ms. Kelly down. Although a period of calm followed the initial attack, the next seven years were accompanied by periodic and frequent beatings, sometimes as often as once a week. During the attacks, which generally occurred when Mr. Kelly was drunk, he threatened to kill Ms. Kelly and to cut off parts of her body if she tried to leave him. Mr. Kelly often moved out of the house after an attack, later returning with a promise that he would change his ways. . . .

[The day of the stabbing, Ms. Kelly went to a friend's house] with her daughter, Annette, to ask Ernest for money to buy food. He told her to wait until they got home, and shortly thereafter the Kellys left. After walking past several houses, Mr. Kelly, who was drunk, angrily asked "What the hell did you come around here for?" He then grabbed the collar of her dress, and the two fell to the ground. He choked her by pushing his fingers against her throat, punched or hit her face, and bit her leg.

A crowd gathered on the street. Two men from the crowd separated them, just as Gladys felt that she was "passing out" from being choked. Fearing that Annette had been pushed around in the crowd, Gladys then left to look for her. Upon finding Annette, defendant noticed that Annette had defendant's pocketbook. Gladys had dropped it during the fight. Annette had retrieved it and gave her mother the pocketbook.

After finding her daughter, Ms. Kelly then observed Mr. Kelly running toward her with his hands raised. Within seconds he was right next to her. Unsure of whether he had armed himself while she was looking for their daughter, and thinking that he had come back to kill her, she grabbed a pair of scissors from her pocketbook. She tried to scare him away, but instead stabbed him. * * *

In the past decade social scientists and the legal community began to examine the forces that generate and perpetuate wife beating and violence in the family. What has been revealed is that the problem affects many more people than had been thought and that the victims of the violence are not only the battered family members (almost always either the wife or the children). There are also many other strangers to the family who feel the devastating impact, often in the form of violence, of the psychological damage suffered by the victims.

Due to the high incidence of unreported abuse (the FBI and other law enforcement experts believe that wife abuse is the most unreported crime in the United States), estimates vary of the number of American women who are beaten regularly by their husband, boyfriend, or the dominant male figure in their lives. One recent estimate puts the number of women beaten yearly at over one million. See California Advisory Comm'n on Family Law, Domestic Violence app. F at 119 (1st report 1978). The state police statistics show more than 18,000 reported cases of domestic violence in New Jersey during the first nine months of 1983, in 83% of which the victim was female. It is clear that the American home, once assumed to be the cornerstone of our society, is often a violent place.

While common law notions that assigned an inferior status to women, and to wives in particular, no longer represent the state of the law as reflected in statutes and cases, many commentators assert that a bias against battered women still exists, institutionalized in the attitudes of law enforcement agencies unwilling to pursue or uninterested in pursuing wife beating cases.

Another problem is the currency enjoyed by stereotypes and myths concerning the characteristics of battered women and their reasons for staying in battering relationships. Some popular misconceptions about battered women include the beliefs that they are masochistic and actually enjoy their beatings, that they purposely provoke their husbands into violent behavior, and, most critically, as we shall soon see, that women who remain in battering relationships are free to leave their abusers at any time.

As these cases so tragically suggest, not only do many women suffer physical abuse at the hands of their mates, but a significant number of women kill (or are killed by) their husbands. In 1978, murders between husband and wife or girlfriend and boyfriend constituted 13% of all murders committed in the United States. Undoubtedly some of these arose from battering incidents. Federal Bureau of Investigation, Crime in the United States 1978 (1978). Men were the victims in 48% of these killings. Id.

As the problem of battered women has begun to receive more attention, sociologists and psychologists have begun to focus on the effects a sustained pattern of physical and psychological abuse can have on a woman. The effects of such abuse are what some scientific observers have termed "the battered-woman's syndrome," a series of common characteristics that appear in women who are abused physically and psychologically over an extended period of time by the dominant male figure in their lives. Dr. Lenore Walker, a prominent writer on the battered-woman's syndrome, defines the battered woman as one who is repeatedly subjected to any forceful physical or psychological behavior by a man in order to coerce her to do something he wants her to do without concern for her rights. Battered women include wives or women in any form of intimate relationships with men. Furthermore, in order to be classified as a battered woman, the couple must go through the battering cycle at least twice. Any woman may find herself in an abusive relationship with a man once. If it occurs a second time, and she remains in the situation, she is defined as a battered woman.

According to Dr. Walker, relationships characterized by physical abuse tend to develop battering cycles. Violent behavior directed at the woman occurs in three distinct and repetitive stages that vary both in duration and intensity depending on the individuals involved.

Phase one of the battering cycle is referred to as the "tension-building stage," during which the battering male engages in minor battering incidents and verbal abuse while the woman, beset by fear and tension, attempts to be as placating and passive as possible in order to stave off more serious violence.

Phase two of the battering cycle is the "acute battering incident." At some point during phase one, the tension between the battered woman and the batterer becomes intolerable and more serious violence inevitable. The triggering event that initiates phase two is most often an internal or external event in the life of the battering male, but provocation for more severe violence is sometimes provided by the woman who can no longer tolerate or control her phase-one anger and anxiety.

Phase three of the battering cycle is characterized by extreme contrition and loving behavior on the part of the battering male. During this period the man will often mix his pleas for forgiveness and protestations of devotion with promises to seek professional help, to stop drinking, and to refrain from further violence. For some couples, this period of relative calm may last as long as several months, but in a battering relationship the affection and contrition of the man will eventually fade and phase one of the cycle will start anew.

The cyclical nature of battering behavior helps explain why more women simply do not leave their abusers. The loving behavior demonstrated by the batterer during phase three reinforces whatever hopes these women might have for their mate's reform and keeps them bound to the relationship.

Some women may even perceive the battering cycle as normal, especially if they grew up in a violent household. Or they may simply not wish to acknowledge the reality of their situation. T. Davidson, Conjugal Crime, at 50 (1978) ("The middle-class battered wife's response to her situation tends to be withdrawal, silence and denial . . .").

Other women, however, become so demoralized and degraded by the fact that they cannot predict or control the violence that they sink into a state of psychological paralysis and become unable to take any action at all to improve or alter the situation. There is a tendency in battered women to believe in the omnipotence or strength of their battering husbands and thus to feel that any attempt to resist them is hopeless.

In addition to these psychological impacts, external social and economic factors often make it difficult for some women to extricate themselves from battering relationships. A woman without independent financial resources who wishes to leave her husband often finds it difficult to do so because of a lack of material and social resources.

Even with the progress of the last decade, women typically make less money and hold less prestigious jobs than men, and are more responsible for child care. Thus, in a violent confrontation where the first reaction might be to flee, women realize soon that there may be no place to go. Moreover, the stigma that attaches to a woman who leaves the family unit without her children undoubtedly acts as a further deterrent to moving out.

In addition, battered women, when they want to leave the relationship, are typically unwilling to reach out and confide in their friends, family, or the police, either out of shame and humiliation, fear of reprisal by their husband, or the feeling they will not be believed.

Dr. Walker and other commentators have identified several common personality traits of the battered woman: low self-esteem, traditional beliefs about the home, the family, and the female sex role, tremendous feelings of guilt that their marriages are failing, and the tendency to accept responsibility for the batterer's actions.

Finally, battered women are often hesitant to leave a battering relationship because, in addition to their hope of reform on the part of their spouse, they harbor a deep concern about the possible response leaving might provoke in their mates. They literally become trapped by their own fear. Case histories are replete with instances in which a battered wife left her husband only to have him pursue her and subject her to an even more brutal attack.

The combination of all these symptoms—resulting from sustained psychological and physical trauma compounded by aggravating social and economic factors—constitutes the battered-woman's syndrome. Only by understanding these unique pressures that force battered women to remain with their mates, despite their long-standing and reasonable fear of severe bodily harm and the isolation that being a battered woman creates, can a battered woman's state of mind be accurately and fairly understood.

The voir dire testimony of Dr. Veronen, sought to be introduced by defendant Gladys Kelly, conformed essentially to this outline of the battered-woman's syndrome. . . .

Dr. Veronen described the various psychological tests and examinations she had performed in connection with her independent research. These tests and their methodology, including their interpretation, are, according to Dr. Veronen, widely accepted by clinical psychologists. Applying this methodology to defendant (who was subjected to all of the tests, including a five-hour interview), Dr. Veronen concluded that defendant was a battered woman and subject to the battered-woman's syndrome.

In addition, Dr. Veronen was prepared to testify as to how, as a battered woman, Gladys Kelly perceived her situation at the time of the stabbing, and why, in her opinion, defendant did not leave her husband despite the constant beatings she endured.

Whether expert testimony on the battered-woman's syndrome should be admitted in this case depends on whether it is relevant to defendant's claim of self-defense, and, in any event, on whether the proffer meets the standards for admission of expert testimony in this state. We examine first the law of self-defense and consider whether the expert testimony is relevant.

.... The use of force against another in self-defense is justifiable "when the actor reasonably believes that such force is immediately necessary for the purpose of protecting himself against the use of unlawful force by such other person on the present occasion." N.J. Stat. Ann. § 2C:3–4(a). Further limitations exist when deadly force is used in self-defense. The use of such deadly force is not justifiable unless the actor reasonably believes that such force is necessary to protect himself against death or serious bodily harm.... [N.J. Stat. Ann. § 2C:3–4(b)(2)].

Self-defense exonerates a person who kills in the reasonable belief that such action was necessary to prevent his or her death or serious injury, even though this belief was later proven mistaken. "Detached reflection cannot be demanded in the presence of an uplifted knife," Justice Holmes aptly said, Brown v. United States, 256 U.S. 335, 343, 41 S.Ct. 501, 502, 65 L.Ed. 961, 963 (1921); and the law accordingly requires only a reasonable, not necessarily a correct, judgment.

While it is not imperative that actual necessity exist, a valid plea of self-defense will not lie absent an actual (that is, honest) belief on the part of the defendant in the necessity of using force. While no case in New Jersey has addressed the point directly, the privilege of self-defense does not exist where the defendant's action is not prompted by a belief in its necessity: "He has no defense when he intentionally kills his enemy in complete ignorance of the fact that his enemy, when killed, was about to launch a deadly attack upon him." W. LaFave & A. Scott, Criminal Law § 53, at 394 (1972).[7] ...

Honesty alone, however, does not suffice. A defendant claiming the privilege of self-defense must also establish that her belief in the necessity to use force was reasonable. As originally proposed, the new Code of Criminal Justice would have eliminated the reasonableness requirement, allowing self-defense whenever the defendant honestly believed in the imminent need to act. This proposed change in the law was not accepted by the Legislature. N.J. Stat. Ann. § 2C:3–4 as finally enacted retains the requirement that the defendant's belief be reasonable.[8]

Gladys Kelly claims that she stabbed her husband in self-defense, believing he was about to kill her. The gist of the State's case was that Gladys Kelly was the aggressor, that she consciously intended to kill her husband, and that she certainly was not acting in self-defense.

The credibility of Gladys Kelly is a critical issue in this case. If the jury does not believe Gladys Kelly's account, it cannot find she acted in self-defense. The expert testimony offered was directly relevant to one of the critical elements of that account, namely, what Gladys Kelly believed at the time of the stabbing, and was thus material to establish the honesty of her stated belief that she was in imminent danger of death.[10] * * *

7. See also Restatement of Torts 2d § 63 (1965) at 101. Under principles of self-defense as a justification for the torts of assault and battery—which closely parallel criminal self-defense principles—no privilege of self-defense exists for one acting in ignorance of another's intent to inflict harm on him.

8. The rejected form of § 2C:3–4 was patterned after § 3.04 of the Model Penal Code. The purpose of the proposed Code and M.P.C. provisions was to prevent one who killed in the honest but mistaken and unreasonable belief in the necessity of the action from being convicted of a crime like murder, which is premised on an act motivated by unlawful purpose.

10. The factual contentions of the parties eliminated any issue concerning the duty to retreat. If the State's version is accepted, defendant is the aggressor; if defendant's version is accepted, the possibility of retreat is excluded by virtue of the nature of the attack that defendant claims took place. We do not

... Dr. Veronen would have bolstered Gladys Kelly's credibility. Specifically, by showing that her experience, although concededly difficult to comprehend, was common to that of other women who had been in similarly abusive relationships, Dr. Veronen would have helped the jury understand that Gladys Kelly could have honestly feared that she would suffer serious bodily harm from her husband's attacks, yet still remain with him. This, in turn, would support Ms. Kelly's testimony about her state of mind (that is, that she honestly feared serious bodily harm) at the time of the stabbing.

On the facts in this case, we find that the expert testimony was relevant to Gladys Kelly's state of mind, namely, it was admissible to show she honestly believed she was in imminent danger of death....

We also find the expert testimony relevant to the reasonableness of defendant's belief that she was in imminent danger of death or serious injury. [T]he expert's testimony, if accepted by the jury, would have aided it in determining whether, under the circumstances, a reasonable person would have believed there was imminent danger to her life.

At the heart of the claim of self-defense was defendant's story that she had been repeatedly subjected to "beatings" over the course of her marriage. While defendant's testimony was somewhat lacking in detail, a juror could infer from the use of the word "beatings," as well as the detail given concerning some of these events (the choking, the biting, the use of fists), that these physical assaults posed a risk of serious injury or death. When that regular pattern of serious physical abuse is combined with defendant's claim that the decedent sometimes threatened to kill her, defendant's statement that on this occasion she thought she might be killed when she saw Mr. Kelly running toward her could be found to reflect a reasonable fear; that is, it could so be found if the jury believed Gladys Kelly's story of the prior beatings, if it believed her story of the prior threats, and, of course, if it believed her story of the events of that particular day.

The crucial issue of fact on which this expert's testimony would bear is why, given such allegedly severe and constant beatings, combined with threats to kill, defendant had not long ago left decedent. ... The expert could clear up [this issue], by explaining that one of the common characteristics of a battered wife is her inability to leave despite such constant beatings; her "learned helplessness"; her lack of anywhere to go; her feeling that if she tried to leave, she would be subjected to even more merciless treatment; her belief in the omnipotence of her battering husband; and sometimes her hope that her husband will change his ways.

People v. Goetz

Court of Appeals of New York.
68 N.Y.2d 96 (1986).

■ CHIEF JUDGE WACHTLER.

A Grand Jury has indicted defendant on attempted murder, assault, and other charges for having shot and wounded four youths on a New York

understand that the State claims defendant breached that duty under any version of the facts. If, however, the duty becomes an issue on retrial, the trial court will have to determine the relevancy of the battered-woman's syndrome to that issue.

City subway train after one or two of the youths approached him and asked for $5. The lower courts, concluding that the prosecutor's charge to the Grand Jury on the defense of justification was erroneous, have dismissed the attempted murder, assault and weapons possession charges. We now reverse and reinstate all counts of the indictment.

The precise circumstances of the incident giving rise to the charges against defendant are disputed, and ultimately it will be for a trial jury to determine what occurred. We feel it necessary, however, to provide some factual background to properly frame the legal issues before us. Accordingly, we have summarized the facts as they appear from the evidence before the Grand Jury. We stress, however, that we do not purport to reach any conclusions or holding as to exactly what transpired or whether defendant is blameworthy. The credibility of witnesses and the reasonableness of defendant's conduct are to be resolved by the trial jury.

On Saturday afternoon, December 22, 1984, Troy Canty, Darryl Cabey, James Ramseur, and Barry Allen boarded an IRT express subway train in The Bronx and headed south toward lower Manhattan. The four youths rode together in the rear portion of the seventh car of the train. Two of the four, Ramseur and Cabey, had screwdrivers inside their coats, which they said were to be used to break into the coin boxes of video machines.

Defendant Bernhard Goetz boarded this subway train at 14th Street in Manhattan and sat down on a bench towards the rear section of the same car occupied by the four youths. Goetz was carrying an unlicensed .38 caliber pistol loaded with five rounds of ammunition in a waistband holster....

It appears from the evidence before the Grand Jury that Canty approached Goetz, possibly with Allen beside him, and stated "give me five dollars". Neither Canty nor any of the other youths displayed a weapon. Goetz responded by standing up, pulling out his handgun and firing four shots in rapid succession. The first shot hit Canty in the chest; the second struck Allen in the back; the third went through Ramseur's arm and into his left side; the fourth was fired at Cabey, who apparently was then standing in the corner of the car, but missed, deflecting instead off of a wall of the conductor's cab. After Goetz briefly surveyed the scene around him, he fired another shot at Cabey, who then was sitting on the end bench of the car. The bullet entered the rear of Cabey's side and severed his spinal cord. * * *

On December 31, 1984, Goetz surrendered to police in Concord, New Hampshire, identifying himself as the gunman being sought for the subway shootings in New York nine days earlier. Later that day, after receiving Miranda warnings, he made two lengthy statements, both of which were tape recorded with his permission. In the statements, which are substantially similar, Goetz admitted that he had been illegally carrying a handgun in New York City for three years. He stated that he had first purchased a gun in 1981 after he had been injured in a mugging. Goetz also revealed that twice between 1981 and 1984 he had successfully warded off assailants simply by displaying the pistol.

According to Goetz's statement, the first contact he had with the four youths came when Canty, sitting or lying on the bench across from him, asked "how are you," to which he replied "fine". Shortly thereafter, Canty, followed by one of the other youths, walked over to the defendant and stood to his left, while the other two youths remained to his right, in the corner of the subway car. Canty then said "give me five dollars". Goetz stated that he knew from the smile on Canty's face that they wanted to "play with me". Although he was certain that none of the youths had a gun, he had a fear, based on prior experiences, of being "maimed".

Goetz then established "a pattern of fire," deciding specifically to fire from left to right. His stated intention at that point was to "murder [the four youths], to hurt them, to make them suffer as much as possible". When Canty again requested money, Goetz stood up, drew his weapon, and began firing, aiming for the center of the body of each of the four. Goetz recalled that the first two he shot "tried to run through the crowd [but] they had nowhere to run". Goetz then turned to his right to "go after the other two". One of these two "tried to run through the wall of the train, but * * * he had nowhere to go". The other youth (Cabey) "tried pretending that he wasn't with [the others]" by standing still, holding on to one of the subway hand straps, and not looking at Goetz. Goetz nonetheless fired his fourth shot at him. He then ran back to the first two youths to make sure they had been "taken care of". Seeing that they had both been shot, he spun back to check on the latter two. Goetz noticed that the youth who had been standing still was now sitting on a bench and seemed unhurt. As Goetz told the police, "I said '[y]ou seem to be all right, here's another' ", and he then fired the shot which severed Cabey's spinal cord. Goetz added that "if I was a little more under self-control * * * I would have put the barrel against his forehead and fired." He also admitted that "if I had had more [bullets], I would have shot them again, and again, and again."

After waiving extradition, Goetz was brought back to New York and arraigned on a felony complaint charging him with attempted murder and criminal possession of a weapon. The matter was presented to a Grand Jury in January 1985, with the prosecutor seeking an indictment for attempted murder, assault, reckless endangerment, and criminal possession of a weapon. ... On January 25, 1985, the Grand Jury indicted defendant on one count of criminal possession of a weapon in the third degree (Penal Law § 265.02), for possessing the gun used in the subway shootings, and two counts of criminal possession of a weapon in the fourth degree (Penal Law § 265.01), for possessing two other guns in his apartment building. It dismissed, however, the attempted murder and other charges stemming from the shootings themselves.

Several weeks after the Grand Jury's action, the People, asserting that they had newly available evidence, moved for an order authorizing them to resubmit the dismissed charges to a second Grand Jury. Supreme Court, Criminal Term, after conducting an in camera inquiry, granted the motion. Presentation of the case to the second Grand Jury began on March 14, 1985....

On March 27, 1985, the second Grand Jury filed a 10–count indictment, containing four charges of attempted murder (Penal Law §§ 110.00,

125.25 [1]), four charges of assault in the first degree (Penal Law § 120.10[1]), one charge of reckless endangerment in the first degree (Penal Law § 120.25), and one charge of criminal possession of a weapon in the second degree (Penal Law § 265.03 [possession of loaded firearm with intent to use it unlawfully against another]). Goetz was arraigned on this indictment on March 28, 1985, and it was consolidated with the earlier three-count indictment.

On October 14, 1985, Goetz moved to dismiss the charges contained in the second indictment alleging ... that the prosecutor's instructions to that Grand Jury on the defense of justification were erroneous and prejudicial to the defendant so as to render its proceedings defective. * * *

In an order dated January 21, 1986, Criminal Term granted Goetz's motion to the extent that it dismissed all counts of the second indictment, other than the reckless endangerment charge.... The court ... held ... that the prosecutor, in a supplemental charge elaborating upon the justification defense, had erroneously introduced an objective element into this defense by instructing the grand jurors to consider whether Goetz's conduct was that of a "reasonable man in [Goetz's] situation". The court ... concluded that the statutory test for whether the use of deadly force is justified to protect a person should be wholly subjective, focusing entirely on the defendant's state of mind when he used such force.[2] * * *

Penal Law article 35 recognizes the defense of justification, which "permits the use of force under certain circumstances". One such set of circumstances pertains to the use of force in defense of a person, encompassing both self-defense and defense of a third person (Penal Law § 35.15). Penal Law § 35.15(1) sets forth the general principles governing all such uses of force: "[a] person may ... use physical force upon another person when and to the extent he reasonably believes such to be necessary to defend himself or a third person from what he *reasonably believes* to be the use or imminent use of unlawful physical force by such other person" (emphasis added).

Section 35.15(2) sets forth further limitations on these general principles with respect to the use of "deadly physical force": "A person may not use deadly physical force upon another person under circumstances specified in subdivision one unless (a) He *reasonably believes* that such other person is using or about to use deadly physical force ... or (b) He *reasonably believes* that such other person is committing or attempting to commit a kidnapping, forcible rape, forcible sodomy or robbery" (emphasis added).

Thus, consistent with most justification provisions, Penal Law § 35.15 permits the use of deadly physical force only where requirements as to triggering conditions and the necessity of a particular response are met. As

2. The court did not dismiss the reckless endangerment charge because, relying on the Appellate Division decision in People v. McManus, 108 A.D.2d 474, 489 N.Y.S.2d 561, it held that justification was not a defense to a crime containing, as an element, "depraved indifference to human life." As our reversal of the Appellate Division in McManus holds, justification is a defense to such a crime. [See *McManus,* supra.] Accordingly, had the prosecutor's instructions on justification actually rendered the Grand Jury proceedings defective, dismissal of the reckless endangerment count would have been required as well.

to the triggering conditions, the statute requires that the actor "reasonably believes" that another person either is using or about to use deadly physical force or is committing or attempting to commit one of certain enumerated felonies, including robbery. As to the need for the use of deadly physical force as a response, the statute requires that the actor "reasonably believes" that such force is necessary to avert the perceived threat.

Because the evidence before the second Grand Jury included statements by Goetz that he acted to protect himself from being maimed or to avert a robbery, the prosecutor correctly chose to charge the justification defense in section 35.15 to the Grand Jury. ... When the prosecutor had completed his charge, one of the grand jurors asked for clarification of the term "reasonably believes". The prosecutor responded by instructing the grand jurors that they were to consider the circumstances of the incident and determine "whether the defendant's conduct was that of a reasonable man in the defendant's situation". It is this response by the prosecutor—and specifically his use of "a reasonable man"—which is the basis for the dismissal of the charges by the lower courts.

As expressed repeatedly in the Appellate Division's plurality opinion, because section 35.15 uses the term "he reasonably believes", the appropriate test, according to that court, is whether a defendant's beliefs and reactions were "reasonable to him". Under that reading of the statute, a jury which believed a defendant's testimony that he felt that his own actions were warranted and were reasonable would have to acquit him, regardless of what anyone else in defendant's situation might have concluded. Such an interpretation defies the ordinary meaning and significance of the term "reasonably" in a statute, and misconstrues the clear intent of the Legislature, in enacting section 35.15, to retain an objective element as part of any provision authorizing the use of deadly physical force.

Penal statutes in New York have long codified the right recognized at common law to use deadly physical force, under appropriate circumstances, in self-defense. These provisions have never required that an actor's belief as to the intention of another person to inflict serious injury be correct in order for the use of deadly force to be justified, but they have uniformly required that the belief comport with an objective notion of reasonableness. * * *

In 1961 the Legislature established a Commission to undertake a complete revision of the Penal Law and the Criminal Code. The impetus for the decision to update the Penal Law came in part from the drafting of the Model Penal Code by the American Law Institute, as well as from the fact that the existing law was poorly organized and in many aspects antiquated. Following the submission by the Commission of several reports and proposals, the Legislature approved the present Penal Law in 1965 and it became effective on September 1, 1967. The drafting of the general provisions of the new Penal Law, including the article on justification, was particularly influenced by the Model Penal Code. While using the Model Penal Code provisions on justification as general guidelines, however, the drafters of the new Penal Law did not simply adopt them verbatim.

The provisions of the Model Penal Code with respect to the use of deadly force in self-defense reflect the position of its drafters that any culpability which arises from a mistaken belief in the need to use such force should be no greater than the culpability such a mistake would give rise to if it were made with respect to an element of a crime. Accordingly, under Model Penal Code § 3.04(2)(b), a defendant charged with murder (or attempted murder) need only show that he "*believe[d]* that [the use of deadly force] was necessary to protect himself against death, serious bodily injury, kidnapping or [forcible] sexual intercourse" to prevail on a self-defense claim (emphasis added). If the defendant's belief was wrong, and was recklessly, or negligently formed, however, he may be convicted of the type of homicide charge requiring only a reckless or negligent, as the case may be, criminal intent (see, Model Penal Code § 3.09[2]).

The drafters of the Model Penal Code recognized that the wholly subjective test set forth in section 3.04 differed from the existing law in most States by its omission of any requirement of reasonableness. The drafters were also keenly aware that requiring that the actor have a "reasonable belief" rather than just a "belief" would alter the wholly subjective test. . . .

New York did not follow the Model Penal Code's equation of a mistake as to the need to use deadly force with a mistake negating an element of a crime, choosing instead to use a single statutory section which would provide either a complete defense or no defense at all to a defendant charged with any crime involving the use of deadly force. The drafters of the new Penal Law adopted in large part the structure and content of Model Penal Code § 3.04, but, crucially, inserted the word "reasonably" before "believes". * * *

We cannot lightly impute to the Legislature an intent to fundamentally alter the principles of justification to allow the perpetrator of a serious crime to go free simply because that person believed his actions were reasonable and necessary to prevent some perceived harm. To completely exonerate such an individual, no matter how aberrational or bizarre his thought patterns, would allow citizens to set their own standards for the permissible use of force. It would also allow a legally competent defendant suffering from delusions to kill or perform acts of violence with impunity, contrary to fundamental principles of justice and criminal law.

We can only conclude that the Legislature retained a reasonableness requirement to avoid giving a license for such actions. . . . [T]he drafters of section 35.15 were proposing a single section which, for the first time, would govern both the use of ordinary force and deadly force in self-defense or defense of another. Under the 1909 Penal Law and its predecessors, the use of ordinary force was governed by separate sections which, at least by their literal terms, required that the defendant was in fact responding to an unlawful assault, and not just that he had a reasonable ground for believing that such an assault was occurring. Following the example of the Model Penal Code, the drafters of section 35.15 eliminated this sharp dichotomy between the use of ordinary force and deadly force in defense of a person. Not surprisingly then, the integrated section reflects the wording of Model Penal Code § 3.04, with the addition of "reasonably" to incorporate the long-standing requirement of "reasonable ground" for the use of deadly force and apply it to the use of ordinary force as well. * * *

Statutes or rules of law requiring a person to act "reasonably" or to have a "reasonable belief" uniformly prescribe conduct meeting an objective standard measured with reference to how "a reasonable person" could have acted. * * *

Goetz ... argues that the introduction of an objective element will preclude a jury from considering factors such as the prior experiences of a given actor and thus, require it to make a determination of "reasonableness" without regard to the actual circumstances of a particular incident. This argument, however, falsely presupposes that an objective standard means that the background and other relevant characteristics of a particular actor must be ignored. To the contrary, we have frequently noted that a determination of reasonableness must be based on the "circumstances" facing a defendant or his "situation". Such terms encompass more than the physical movements of the potential assailant. [T]hese terms include any relevant knowledge the defendant had about that person. They also necessarily bring in the physical attributes of all persons involved, including the defendant. Furthermore, the defendant's circumstances encompass any prior experiences he had which could provide a reasonable basis for a belief that another person's intentions were to injure or rob him or that the use of deadly force was necessary under the circumstances.

Accordingly, a jury should be instructed to consider this type of evidence in weighing the defendant's actions. The jury must first determine whether the defendant had the requisite beliefs under section 35.15, that is, whether he believed deadly force was necessary to avert the imminent use of deadly force or the commission of one of the felonies enumerated therein. If the People do not prove beyond a reasonable doubt that he did not have such beliefs, then the jury must also consider whether these beliefs were reasonable. The jury would have to determine, in light of all the "circumstances", as explicated above, if a reasonable person could have had these beliefs. * * *

Order reversed.

[After a jury trial, Goetz was acquitted of assault and attempted murder, but convicted of possession of an illegal weapon, for which he served eight-and-a-half months.]

QUESTIONS AND COMMENTS

1. Assuming self-defense is a justification, what if I think I have to defend myself, but turn out to be mistaken (because I wasn't in immediate danger, because I could have retreated (in homicide cases), etc.)? Would I be excused? Or still justified? Compare *Leidholm*, supra, with Model Penal Code § 3.09.

2. In a homicide case, what happens if I'm not only mistaken about having to defend myself, but *unreasonably* so? What, if any, crime will I be liable for? Under New York law (see *Goetz*)? Under the Model Penal Code (see §§ 1.13(16); 2.02(10); 3.09)?

3. *Imperfect Self-Defense*. As an alternative to the Model Penal Code and the New York approach, some jurisdictions recognize a doctrine of

"imperfect self-defense," which in homicide cases reduces liability from murder to manslaughter if the offender honestly, but unreasonably, believed she had to use *deadly force* to protect herself. The basic idea here is that the presence of a belief in the need to protect oneself is inconsistent with the "malice" required for murder liability in these jurisdictions. See, e.g., People v. Flannel, 25 Cal.3d 668, 160 Cal.Rptr. 84, 603 P.2d 1 (1979). As one commentator put it more generally:

> Since manslaughter is a "catch-all" concept, covering all homicides which are neither murder nor innocent, it logically includes some killings involving other types of mitigation, and such is the rule of the common law. For example, if one man kills another intentionally, under circumstances beyond the scope of innocent homicide, the facts may come so close to justification or excuse that the killing will be classified as voluntary manslaughter rather than murder.

Rollin M. Perkins, Criminal Law 69–70 (2d ed. 1969).

In homicide cases, is this solution preferable to the Model Penal Code or New York approach? More particularly, how does it differ from the Model Penal Code approach? Does it make sense to limit certain varieties of self-defense to homicide cases? Is imperfect self-defense more like a justification or an excuse? Is imperfect self-defense a "defense" at all? If the state decided to place the burden of proving imperfect self-defense on the defendant, would it run afoul of the due process clause, as interpreted in *Patterson v. New York*, supra ch. 2? If a court, rather than the legislature, recognizes the defense of imperfect self-defense, is it violating the principle of legality (and of legislativity in particular)? See, e.g., State v. Bowens, 108 N.J. 622, 532 A.2d 215 (1987) (yes).

In what ways is the person who deliberately kills another, wrongly and unreasonably believing herself to be justified, like the person who engages in conduct that causes death, negligently unaware that her conduct will do so? In what ways is she different? What about people who (unreasonably) see threats all around them—people who are atypically prone to believe that strangers in bars are about to fight or attack them? Are they more morally culpable than the person who never recognizes that she is risking another's death? More dangerous (from the vantage point of an incapacitationist or reformationist)?

4. What does the requirement of reasonableness add to a merely subjective test if, as the court in *Goetz* insists, the reasonableness inquiry is to consider "any relevant knowledge the defendant had about" the potential assailant, "the physical attributes of all persons involved, including defendant," and "the defendant's circumstances," including "any prior experiences he had which could provide a reasonable basis for a belief that another person's intentions were to injure or rob him"? See also State v. Leidholm, 334 N.W.2d 811 (N.D. 1983) (in a battered woman's syndrome case, explaining that "an accused's actions are to be viewed from the standpoint of a person whose mental and physical characteristics are like the accused's and who sees what the accused sees and knows what the accused knows").

What factors will we allow to be considered: Why battered woman's syndrome but not pre-marriage depression? Can Goetz present himself as a part of a sub-group of previous mugging victims? (Reconsider *People v. Romero*, in ch. 5 supra.) How about racists (Goetz was white, his victims black)? And if he can't use racists, why not? Must the "cause" of one's misperceptions be at least morally neutral? Or is the problem with the racist that he is too likely to be wrong, i.e., to overestimate the likelihood (or severity) of an attack and therefore to overreact in erroneously presumed self-defense? See generally Jody Armour, "Race Ipsa Loquitur: Of Reasonable Racists, Intelligent Bayesians, and Involuntary Negrophobes," 46 Stan. L. Rev. 781 (1994); Mark Kelman, "Reasonable Evidence of Reasonableness," 17 Critical Inquiry 798 (1991).

What, at any rate, is so objectionable about a purely subjective test that would allow the defense as long as I honestly believed I had to defend myself? Is this a proof problem—because we would have to take a defendant's word for whether he did or didn't hold this belief? But why wouldn't that be a problem with subjective beliefs in other areas of criminal law, most notably the law of mens rea (which deals with mental states attaching to *offense* elements, rather than *defense* elements)?

Is the Model Penal Code's test purely subjective, as the court in *Goetz* seems to think? Or does the Model Code implicitly consider reasonableness by providing that unreasonable beliefs will expose a defendant to liability for reckless or negligent offenses, depending on whether she was recklessly or only negligently mistaken? Model Penal Code §§ 1.13(16) & 3.09(2).

5. Can Kelly's defense be construed as a justification, rather than an excuse? Was she mistaken in her assessment of the likelihood, imminence, and severity of an attack and the necessity of using (deadly) force? Or was she simply better able to make this assessment in light of her previous experiences with her husband? What significance should we ascribe to statistical generalizations about domestic violence, such as "the police don't take domestic violence seriously, protective court orders don't work, men who hit make up and then hit harder," Mark Kelman, "Reasonable Evidence of Reasonableness," 17 Critical Inquiry 798, 813 (1991). Does it matter whether Kelly subjectively relied on these statistics?

Should our assessment of the reasonableness of Goetz's assessment rely on statistics regarding black crime, black-on-white crime, black-on-white robberies, black-on-white robberies in New York City, by young men, in groups, on the subway, etc.? What if it turns out that "the rate of robbery arrests among blacks is roughly twelve times the rate of nonblacks (that is, it would be twelve times more probable that a particular black person is a robber than a nonblack, if one had to make a purely race-based estimate)," so that even after accounting for racially discriminatory arrest practices "it is nonetheless implausible that actual rates of robbery by race are even close," see id. at 814 n.20? Again, does it matter whether Goetz in fact relied on these statistics, rather than on racial prejudice? Can *Kelly* be distinguished from *Goetz* because she had particularized knowledge of her potential attacker, and of the effectiveness of alternative responses to *his* threats, where Goetz—at best—could cite statistical generalizations?

6. "It is most persuasive to ... reject the subway killer's proffered evidence not because he 'inaccurately' assessed risks (though he might well have), but because the consequences of acting as he did, given his perception of risk, are so horrible. This would be true even if his judgment were not in part race based; it is even more dramatically true given the fact that it is. Assume, perhaps counterfactually, that the battered woman was in no greater danger of death or serious bodily harm than the subway killer was. Assume that we could be assured that of twenty subway killers we must judge, one was correct in asserting that he would have died or been grievously wounded unless he used deadly force, and of twenty abused women who kill, the same one in twenty needed to use force to prevent the same dire consequences. The nineteen mistaken subway killers have executed some combination of absolute innocents, taunters, and relatively nonviolent robbers, while the battered wives killed nineteen established assaulters." Kelman, supra, at 815.

Look carefully at how the Model Penal Code, in § 2.02(d), defines negligence. Are the risks Kelly and Goetz take equally *justified,* even if we assume that they are equally *substantial*?

7. Race played a central—if not always acknowledged—role in the *Goetz* case. At the trial, the defense referred to the black victims as "savages," "vultures," and "predators on society." According to one observer of the trial, "[t]hese verbal attacks signaled a perception of the four youths as representing something more than four individuals committing an act of aggression against a defendant. That 'something more' requires extrapolation from their characteristics to the class of individuals for which they stand. There is no doubt that one of the characteristics that figures into this implicit extrapolation is their blackness." George P. Fletcher, A Crime of Self-Defense: Bernhard Goetz and the Law on Trial 206 (1988). Given the obvious salience of race in cases of this nature, does an inquiry into "objective" reasonableness invite judgment on the basis of shared fears and prejudices, rather than on the reasonableness of the risk assessment?

8. In 1996, a civil jury awarded Darrell Cabey, who was paralyzed and suffered brain damage as a result of being short by Goetz, $43 million. Tina Kelley, "Still Seeking Payment From Bernard Goetz," N.Y. Times, Sept. 10, 2000, at 39, col. 1. The privilege of self-defense in tort law is remarkably similar to the defense of self-defense in criminal law:

Restatement (Second) of Torts § 65. Self-Defense by Force Threatening Death or Serious Bodily Harm.

(1) Subject to the statement in Subsection (3), an actor is privileged to defend himself against another by force intended or likely to cause death or serious bodily harm, when he reasonably believes that

(a) the other is about to inflict upon him an intentional contact or other bodily harm, and that

(b) he is thereby put in peril of death or serious bodily harm or ravishment, which can safely be prevented only by the immediate use of such force....

(3) The privilege stated in Subsection (1) does not exist if the actor correctly or reasonably believes that he can with complete safety avoid the necessity of so defending himself by

(a) retreating if attacked in any place other than his dwelling place, or in a place which is also the dwelling of the other, or

(b) relinquishing the exercise of any right or privilege other than his privilege to prevent intrusion upon or dispossession of his dwelling place or to effect a lawful arrest.

How, then, can Goetz be civilly, but not criminally, liable?

C. NECESSITY

The Queen v. Dudley and Stephens

Queen's Bench Division.
14 Q.B.D. 273 (1884).

[text of opinion at supra p. 191]

4 William Blackstone, Commentaries on the Law of England 186 (1769)

There is one species of homicide *se defendendo*, where the party slain is equally innocent as he who occasions his death: and yet this homicide is also excusable from the great universal principle of self-preservation, which prompts every man to save his own life preferably to that of another, where on of them must inevitably perish. As, among others, in that cases mentioned by Lord Bacon, where two persons, being shipwrecked, and getting on the same plank, but finding it not able to save them both, one of them thrusts the other from it, whereby he is drowned. He who thus preserves his own life at the expense of another man's, is excusable through unavoidable necessity, and the principle of self-defence; since their both remaining on the same weak plank is a mutual, though innocent, attempt upon, and an endangering of, each other's life.

People v. Craig

Court of Appeals of New York.
78 N.Y.2d 616, 585 N.E.2d 783, 578 N.Y.S.2d 471 (1991).

■ HANCOCK, JUDGE.

Defendants were arrested on May 7, 1985 and charged with the violation of trespass (Penal Law § 140.05[a]) when they refused to leave the office of a United States Representative after conducting a peaceful demonstration in which they voiced their opposition to the policy of the United States in imposing an embargo of Nicaragua. In a nonjury trial, Rochester City Court rejected the defense of justification under Penal Law § 35.05(2), which, under certain circumstances, provides that conduct that would

a. N.Y. Penal Law § 140.05 ("A person is guilty of trespass when he knowingly enters or remains unlawfully in or upon premises. Trespass is a violation.").—EDS.

otherwise be illegal may be justified as necessary to avoid a greater evil. County Court affirmed and defendants have appealed to this Court by leave. . . .

City Court . . . precluded defendants from offering testimony of expert witnesses to substantiate their contentions concerning the imminence and seriousness of the injuries allegedly resulting from the Government's policies. The court reasoned that Penal Law § 35.05(2) called for a subjective, state-of-mind standard of proof and that the only relevant question was whether a defendant's "intent or state of mind was such that it raises itself to the defense of justification". It, therefore, excluded expert opinions of third parties as irrelevant.

In a written decision, City Court found that the prosecution had disproved the defense of justification beyond a reasonable doubt[1] and had established defendants' guilt of trespass under Penal Law § 140.05. . . . On appeal, defendants' primary argument is that City Court erred in its interpretation of Penal Law § 35.05(2) as establishing a subjective rather than an objective standard and in its exclusion of defendants' proffered expert testimony. . . .

The general notion that conduct which would otherwise be criminal may be justified as necessary to avoid a greater harm, now codified in New York in Penal Law § 35.05(2), may be traced to cases in the early English common law. In the older English cases, it was a defense to a criminal charge that a defendant committed an act to save a life or to put out a fire. And prisoners might escape from a burning jail without violating the law. In the United States, early Federal cases also recognized the defense of necessity (see, e.g., United States v. Ashton, 24 Fed. Cas. No. 14,470 [C.C.D.Mass.1834] [sailors charged with mutiny justified their refusal to obey captain's orders on ground that ship was not seaworthy]). Where the defense was permitted in the common law, the cases generally required the existence of an "impending danger, present, imminent and not to be averted" (Note, Necessity as a Defense, 21 Colum. L. Rev. 71, 72–73).

The view that necessity for avoiding a greater evil might afford a justification for prohibited conduct was adopted in 1962 by the American Law Institute in Model Penal Code § 3.02. Section 3.02 reflects the judgment that a "choice of evils" defense "like the general requirements of culpability, is essential to the rationality and justice of the criminal law, and is appropriately addressed in a penal code". The essential concept of the Model Code provision is that conduct which "the actor believes to be necessary to avoid a harm or evil to himself or to another" is justifiable, provided that "the harm or evil sought to be avoided" is greater than that "sought to be prevented by the law" being broken (§ 3.02[a]). The provision is not, by its terms, limited to cases involving imminent danger. Nevertheless, the examples given in the commentaries to section 3.02 are of emergency situations involving immediate threat of harm reminiscent of the older common-law cases—e.g., destroying property to prevent spread of

1. Justification is a defense, not an affirmative defense. If a defendant's conduct is justified on the ground of necessity or choice of evils under Penal Law § 35.05(2), it is not unlawful. When the defense is raised, the People must prove beyond a reasonable doubt that defendant's conduct was not justified.

a fire, entering a vacant cabin as refuge in a mountain blizzard and using provisions, jettisoning cargo or violating an embargo to save a vessel.

New York's first recognition of the defense of necessity came in 1965 with the adoption of Penal Law § 35.05(2) as part of the revised Penal Law. Section 35.05, insofar as pertinent, provides that:

> "conduct which would otherwise constitute an offense is justifiable and not criminal when . . .
>
> "2. Such conduct is necessary as an emergency measure to avoid an imminent public or private injury which is about to occur by reason of a situation occasioned or developed through no fault of the actor, and which is of such gravity that, according to ordinary standards of intelligence and morality, the desirability and urgency of avoiding such injury clearly outweigh the desirability of avoiding the injury sought to be prevented by the statute defining the offense in issue."

Although derived from Model Code § 3.02, section 35.05(2) is more limited than the Model Code provision and contains restrictive language not found in section 3.02 (e.g., in the requirements that conduct to be justified must be "necessary as an *emergency measure* to avoid an *imminent* public or private injury which *is about to occur*" and that "the desirability and *urgency* of avoiding such injury clearly outweigh the desirability of avoiding" the prohibited conduct [emphasis added]). The Staff Notes of the Temporary State Commission on Revision of the Penal Law and Criminal Code indicate that section 35.05(2) was envisioned as providing a defense of justification "in rare and highly unusual circumstances". As illustrative of conduct which would be justifiable under the section, the Staff Notes cite, inter alia, the "burning of real property of another in order to prevent a raging forest fire from spreading into a densely populated community".

Section 35.05(2) differs from the Model Code provision in another significant particular. Unlike the Model Code which contains a standard for justifiability that is partially subjective (i.e., "[c]onduct that the actor *believes to be necessary* to avoid a harm or evil to himself or to another" [§ 3.02(1)] [emphasis added]), the New York statutory standard is, by its terms, objective. There is no reference in section 35.05(2) to what the actor intends, or believes to be necessary. In this respect, the section is also unlike Penal Law § 35.15 which bases justification for the use of physical force on the actor's reasonable belief that such force is necessary to defend himself or a third person (§ 35.15) and for the use of deadly force on the actor's reasonable belief that the other person is using or about to use deadly physical force (§ 35.15[a]).

In People v. Goetz, 68 N.Y.2d 96, 506 N.Y.S.2d 18, 497 N.E.2d 41, we emphasized that the words "reasonably believes" in Penal Law § 35.15 embody in the justification standard for self-defense elements which are subjective (i.e., what the actor believes) as well as objective (i.e., whether a reasonable person could have had these beliefs). From the plain wording of section 35.05(2) and the omission of any language suggesting that justification was intended to depend on any belief held by the actor, we agree with defendants' contention that the statute sets forth a standard that is, by its terms, objective only.[3]

Section 35.05(2) specifies that whenever "evidence relating to the defense of justification under this subdivision is offered by the defendant, the court shall rule as a matter of law whether the claimed facts and circumstances would, if established, constitute a defense". Thus, the court must decide, as a threshold legal question, whether the defense will lie. We turn to whether under the objective standard in section 35.05(2), the avoidance of the harm resulting from the Government's actions in Nicaragua, as postulated by the defendants, could be the basis for a justification defense under the statute. Put another way, the question is: does the harm which defendants sought to avoid by conducting a protest in an effort to change governmental policy constitute an "imminent public or private injury" (§ 35.05) which, as intended by the Legislature, could justify their conduct as a "necessary [preventative] ... emergency measure"?

To ascertain the type of situation envisioned by the Legislature in enacting section 35.05(2), we, of course, look first to the statute, giving the words their natural and obvious meaning. It is apparent that the language of the statute bears both on the nature of the conduct to be justified and the harm to be avoided. The conduct must be "necessary as an emergency measure to avoid an imminent public or private injury which is about to occur" (§ 35.05). The requirement that the conduct be "necessary as an emergency measure" to avoid the injury contemplates conduct which is not only warranted by the circumstances as an emergency response but is also reasonably calculated to have an actual effect in preventing the harm. It rules out conduct that is tentative or only advisable or preferable or conduct for which there is a reasonable, legal alternative course of action. And the requirement that the impending injury must be "imminent" and "about to occur" denotes an impending harm which constitutes a present, immediate threat—i.e., a danger that is actual and at hand, not one that is speculative, abstract or remote.

From the foregoing analysis, we conclude that the harm resulting from governmental actions in Nicaragua, as described by defendants, lacks the immediacy required by the statute. Moreover, the actions of defendants in committing a trespass in Congressman Eckert's office cannot be viewed as an emergency measure reasonably calculated to avoid the harm or as a necessary choice over alternative, legal courses of action designed to effect a change in the policy of the Administration. We conclude that the claimed facts and circumstances offered by defendants would not, if established, constitute a defense under section 35.05(2)....

3. Although the operative standard is objective, it would seem virtually inevitable that a defendant who acted under circumstances which made the defense applicable would have done so with the subjective intention of avoiding the greater evil of the imminent injury. We need not address the hypothetical situation where actual necessity existed but the actor did not have the intention of avoiding the greater evil. Here, unquestionably, defendants believed that their conduct would in some way avoid the greater evil in Nicaragua. Nor need we address the situation where—under an objective/reasonable person standard—the action was necessary but necessity-in-fact did not exist.

We note that courts in other jurisdictions in cases arising out of protest demonstrations have reached similar conclusions, applying the common law or analogous statutes (see, e.g., Andrews v. People, 800 P.2d 607, 609–610 [Colo.1990] [rejecting "choice of evils defense" where defendants blocked road leading to nuclear weapons plant, under statute virtually identical to New York's, because conduct was not effective to achieve the purpose or necessary in the face of available legal alternatives and the threatened harm was long-term and speculative, not definite and imminent]; People v. Stiso, 93 Ill.App.3d 101, 48 Ill.Dec. 687, 416 N.E.2d 1209 [1981] [no defense of necessity under statute similar to Model Penal Code for obstructing clinic performing abortions]).

Inasmuch as the claimed facts and circumstances pertaining to the situation in Nicaragua would not, if established, constitute a justification defense, we do not reach defendants' contention that the court erred in excluding their proffered expert testimony.

Model Penal Code § 3.02. Justification Generally: Choice of Evils.

(1) Conduct which the actor believes to be necessary to avoid a harm or evil to himself or to another is justifiable, provided that:

(a) the harm or evil sought to be avoided by such conduct is greater than that sought to be prevented by the law defining the offense charged; and

(b) neither the Code nor other law defining the offense provides exceptions or defenses dealing with the specific situation involved; and

(c) a legislative purpose to exclude the justification claimed does not otherwise plainly appear.

(2) When the actor was reckless or negligent in bringing about the situation requiring a choice of harms or evils or in appraising the necessity for his conduct, the justification afforded by this Section is unavailable in a prosecution for any offense for which recklessness or negligence, as the case may be, suffices to establish culpability.

QUESTIONS AND COMMENTS

1. Why did Dudley and Stephens have to raise any defense at all? Why can't we distinguish between their conduct and "real" murder without having recourse to defenses? Are Dudley and Stephens murderers? Does that matter?

2. The court dismisses Dudley and Stephens's self-defense argument. Why? Conversely, could the defendant in *Boget*, supra, have availed himself of a necessity defense?

3. If self-defense is viewed as an excuse, aren't self-defense and the sort of necessity defense arguably raised in *Dudley & Stephens* pretty similar? In each sort of case, it appears, the defendant is claiming that she should be exonerated if she reasonably believed she would die or suffer grievous bodily harm unless she killed the victim. Note that the *Dudley &*

Stephens court remarked that the defendants may not have an *ideal* excuse case (though the court rules that even an ideal case would be legally insufficient) because killing Parker might have been futile or needless. But isn't it equally true that some defendants who raise successful self-defense claims have killed in situations in which their conduct might have proven futile? (Imagine shooting one of multiple armed attackers....) Isn't it equally true that some such defendants have killed in situations in which their conduct might have proven needless? (Imagine an attacker with a defective gun....) Is the distinction that self-defenders act impulsively while Dudley and Stephens acted deliberately? But look again at the disputes over the imminence requirement in self-defense. See *Buggs*, supra.

4. Similarly, if self-defense is viewed as a justification, does it make drawing the distinction between it and necessity any easier? If one focuses on the *unlawfulness* (rather than the imminence) of the force against which I am defending myself and the *proportionality* of the self-defensive force (rather than its necessity), does it make sense to regard self-defense as covering situations that have been determined in advance by the legislature to *justify* the commission of a crime in order to avoid the greater "harm or evil" (of becoming the victim of an unlawful attack)? If that's so, why do we even need a separate justification of self-defense?

5. How might one argue that self-defenders are justified, while Dudley and Stephens are, at best, "merely" excused (for giving in to pressures a more heroic person might withstand)? Is the key that self-defenders elect to end a more "culpable" life rather than an "innocent" one, or that "the necessity for response always stems from [the victim's] *wrong* to [the defendant]" (Richard A. Epstein, Torts 59 (1999) (emphasis added))? But what about those who defend themselves against "irresponsible" attackers (infants, insane persons)?

What about those who reasonably, but mistakenly, believe they are being attacked? Should we distinguish the excuse highlighted in *Leidholm*, supra—an excuse grounded in mistakes about whether one is justified—from the excuses highlighted in *Lopez*, supra? If the idea is that the person who mistakenly believes he is justified has a more praiseworthy motive (and character) than the person who merely tries to save his own life, what do we do if we believe that many (if not most) self-defenders are actually motivated by the selfish desire to save themselves, not by the (socially acceptable) desire to minimize the loss of (relatively) innocent life?

Is the key instead that the victim in a self-defense case "causes" the defendant's peril? But how is it morally relevant that someone causes peril if he does not do so culpably? And can we really distinguish those who cause peril from those whose death serves the defendant's ends? Compare the following victims: V1 is the heaviest person on the lifeboat; the boat will sink unless he is tossed overboard. Does it matter if he is uniquely situated (that is, if the boat would stay afloat if some other passenger were tossed off)? V2 is non-negligently about to toss debris from a skyscraper construction site on to the place where you are (non-negligently) walking (the person who removed the pedestrian barriers and warning signs is the bad guy here). Does it matter if he is about to throw the debris or is operating a debris-disposal machine that will turn off if you shoot him dead? V3 is on the life boat and is about to eat some of the small amount of food that is left. Does it matter if he is just as entitled to the food as you are? Does it matter, and if so how much, that Dudley and Stephens would be no better off if we simply removed Parker from the scene? Does it matter, and if so how much, that the overweight person on the lifeboat is completely "passive" and the debris thrower "active"?

Should our reactions to the defendants' conduct turn in significant part on the fact that they actively killed Parker? Assume that they had merely waited for him to be the first to die and then used his flesh and blood for sustenance; assume, too, that they might have *saved* Parker by taking other steps that harmed, but did not kill someone else on the boat (e.g., amputate a body part in a fashion that would not lead them to bleed to death). Would Parker have been treated more morally (less criminally?) had they "merely" let him die (though he could have been saved) because we treat the "natural lottery" as unproblematic, or should we condemn the others for not selecting the least life-destructive option from the array of horrific options that were available to them?

6. The necessity defense is of fairly recent origin. Until the Model Penal Code, American criminal codes as a rule did not recognize a necessity defense. (Even German criminal law didn't codify what the courts—and commentators—originally referred to as "supralegal necessity" until the 1960s.) Why is necessity a defense at all? Isn't the defendant who claims necessity simply second-guessing the legislature? If necessity is to be a defense, should it be codified?

7. The court in *Dudley & Stephens* explains that, no matter how sympathetic it might find the defendants' claim, it could not grant them relief. Its hands were tied because courts decide questions of law only. Mercy, by contrast, was not a judicial, but an executive, matter; it was the Queen's prerogative to grant—or to withhold—mercy as she saw fit. While the institution of executive pardon persists to this day in American criminal law, excuses are no longer considered beyond the pale of legal—and therefore judicial—analysis. (See *Spunaugle v. State*, part A, supra.) Why is that? And what view of crime and punishment does this trend reflect?

8. Why, exactly, did the court reject Dudley and Stephens's necessity argument? How would they have fared under the Model Penal Code? Under the New York necessity statute?

9. What if the defendant is mistaken about any of the elements of the necessity defense? What if he believes—mistakenly—that it's *necessary* to commit a crime to avoid greater harm? (Was it necessary for Dudley to kill Parker, at that time?) That the harm he's trying to avoid is *greater* than the harm he's causing? (What if Dudley thought his life was worth more than anyone else's, and Parker's in particular?) What if he's unreasonable in his belief? Does it make sense to treat these mistakes (about necessity and balance) differently?

What if he *didn't* think he needed to commit a crime to prevent—or didn't *intend* to prevent—greater harm, but it turns out that he did in fact (see n.3 in *Craig*)? What if the hiker breaks into a remote mountain hut to get something to eat, without realizing that he is hopelessly lost and will not be found until two weeks later?

10. What's the point of the *necessity* requirement? Why isn't it enough that the balance of evils comes out in favor of committing the crime, rather than standing by idly and letting the greater occur? If I made the right choice, what does it matter whether I had to act on it right away?

11. What if the defendant contributed to the situation that gives rise to the necessity? Should he be allowed to turn around and claim the necessity as a defense? Or has he forfeited his right to do so? What if I start a brush fire precisely so that I would end up in a situation where I had to set fire to my enemy's house to "save" the town? What if I set the fire knowing that this would happen, expecting that it might, or ignoring obvious signs that it may? What if Dudley—who was the captain of the Mignonette—would have had sufficient supplies, had he properly rationed them before the ship wreck? Compare the necessity provisions in the Model Penal Code and the N.Y. Penal Law (quoted in *Craig*) on this point. (Also compare to the defendant who contributes to the situation that gives rise to a self-defense claim. *Rowe,* supra.)

12. In *Craig*, why isn't the necessity defense unsuccessful simply because the defendants had other—legal—alternatives available to them, by means of the ordinary democratic process? The New York Penal Law provision on necessity (in a portion not reproduced in the *Craig* opinion) makes it clear that "[t]he necessity and justifiability of such conduct may not rest upon considerations pertaining only to the morality and advisability of the statute, either in its general application or with respect to its application to a particular class of cases arising thereunder." Can civil disobedience ever be justified on necessity grounds? Should the likelihood of success make a difference?

In Commonwealth v. Leno, 415 Mass. 835 (1993), the Massachusetts Supreme Judicial Court upheld convictions for unauthorized possession of instruments to administer controlled substances and unlawful distribution of an instrument to administer controlled substances of a "fifty-five year old grandfather" who ran a needle exchange program in a "high drug area" to "stem the spread of AIDS." The court explained that "prevention of possible future harm does not excuse a current systematic violation of the law in anticipation of the eventual over-all benefit to the public" and pointed out that "[c]itizens who disagree with the Legislature's determination of policy are not without remedies," notably "the popular initiative." At any rate, the court concluded, "[t]he defendants' argument raises the issue of jury nullification, not the defense of necessity." Is the defense of necessity an invitation to jury nullification? If so, is that a bad thing? (On jury nullification, see supra ch. 2.)

For a rare example of a successful necessity defense in a civil disobedience case, see People v. Gray, 150 Misc.2d 852 (N.Y. Crim. Ct. 1991). The defendants in *Gray* had participated in a demonstration on a New York City bridge organized by "Transportation Alternatives" ("an organization devoted to the promotion of non-vehicular, ecologically sound means of transportation") and were charged with disorderly conduct for disobeying a police order to move. They successfully raised a necessity defense, arguing that their criminal conduct was designed to prevent grave harm, to wit the " 'asphyxiation of New York' by automobile-related pollution."

13. Do we really need a full-fledged necessity defense, or would it be preferable to convict of the crime the defendant concededly committed, and then mitigate the sentence? Would this solution address the anxiety about jury nullification?

U.S. Sentencing Guidelines § 5K2.11. Lesser Harms (Policy Statement)

Sometimes, a defendant may commit a crime in order to avoid a perceived greater harm. In such instances, a reduced sentence may be appropriate, provided that the circumstances significantly diminish society's interest in punishing the conduct, for example, in the case of a mercy killing. Where the interest in punishment or deterrence is not reduced, a reduction in sentence is not warranted. For example, providing defense secrets to a hostile power should receive no lesser punishment simply because the defendant believed that the government's policies were misdirected.

14. What's the significance of Dudley's not having everyone draw lots? Does this affect the availability of the necessity defense? Should they have held a vote? For purposes of the necessity defense, do I need to obtain the permission of the person against whom I'm committing the crime I'm charged with? Should I at least have to make an effort to get his permission?

15. Let's assume that the balance of evils doesn't come out in Dudley's favor—that taking one life to save three is not the right thing to do. Should he have a defense available simply because he had no other choice but to kill Parker? In other words, is necessity enough? Compare the two versions of the necessity defense in the German Penal Code.

German Penal Code § 34. Necessity as Justification.

Whoever, faced with an imminent danger to life, limb, freedom, honor, property or another legal interest which cannot otherwise be averted, commits an act to avert the danger from himself or another, does not act unlawfully, if, upon weighing the conflicting interests, in particular the affected legal interests and the degree of danger threatening them, the protected interest substantially outweighs the one interfered with. This shall apply, however, only to the extent that the act is a proportionate means to avert the danger.

German Penal Code § 35. Necessity as Excuse.

(1) Whoever, faced with an imminent danger to life, limb or freedom which cannot otherwise be averted, commits an unlawful act to avert the danger from himself, a relative or person close to him, acts without guilt. This shall not apply to the extent that the perpetrator could be expected under the circumstances to assume the risk, in particular, because he himself caused the danger or stood in a special legal relationship; however the punishment may be mitigated....

(2) If upon commission of the act the perpetrator mistakenly assumes that circumstances exist, which would excuse him under

subsection (1), he will only be punished, if he could have avoided the mistake. The punishment shall be mitigated....

Penal Law of Israel § 34K.

A person shall bear no criminal liability for an act required to have been done immediately by him to save his or another's life, freedom, body or property from an imminent danger of serious injury deriving from the circumstances at the time of the act, and for which no alternative act was available.

Penal Law of Israel § 34L.

A person shall bear no criminal liability for an act he was ordered to do by a threat with grave and imminent injury to his or another's life, freedom, body or property and was coerced to do the act.

Necessity as excuse is also sometimes referred to as circumstantial (or "situational") duress, as distinguished from personal duress, which—as the name suggests—originates not from circumstances, but from another person. The Model Penal Code does not recognize a defense of circumstantial duress. Commentaries § 2.09, at 383. For Dudley and Stephens, and others in similar circumstances, this means that they will either satisfy the requirements for a full-fledged necessity defense (necessity *plus* correct balance of evils) or have no defense at all. (For more on duress, see infra part F.)

16. What's balanced? In cases raising the necessity defense, it's important to get clear on what exactly is supposed to be balanced. Is it the harm the legislature intended to prevent by passing the statute the defendant has violated? Or is it the harm the defendant actually inflicted in the particular case? Or should we focus instead on the defendant's conduct, rather than on the harm that he did, or didn't, inflict? How should we deal with harmless (or "victimless") offenses, like possession or speeding? And do we take into account the likelihood that harm might have resulted, even if it didn't result in fact? Should we balance that against the likelihood that the defendant would succeed in averting another harm? Compare the Model Penal Code, the New York Penal Law, and the German Penal Code on this point. Also consider the following case.

At 4:20 on a Saturday morning, after consuming alcohol, defendant was involved in a minor traffic accident on a New York City street. According to defendant, the driver of the second vehicle became belligerent when defendant attempted to exchange license and insurance information with him and the driver reached into the back seat of his car. Believing that the driver was about to produce a weapon, defendant returned to his own car and fled the scene. A short distance from the first accident defendant struck and killed a pedestrian, Frank Flotteron, crossing West Street.

.... The jury convicted defendant of ... criminally negligent homicide and driving while impaired ...; as to the ... leaving the scene [of an accident] count, the jury found defendant not guilty "with justification." Defendant now seeks reversal of the homicide conviction.... Defendant does not contest the driving while impaired conviction. * * *

> [W]e conclude that the jury should have been instructed on justification with respect to the manslaughter and vehicular homicide counts.
>
> Upon defendant's request, and with no objection by the People, the trial court instructed the jury on the justification defense as to the leaving the scene count. The court refused defendant's request that the jury be given the justification charge with respect to the ... homicide count[], concluding that defendant could have left the scene with his car door locked or could have driven at a safe speed to a police or service station. In concluding that the charge was not warranted as to those counts, the trial court also noted defendant's testimony that he did not see the car following him after defendant went through a red light some time prior to the second accident. * * *
>
> Defendant asserts that he chose to engage in certain conduct (speeding) in avoidance of a perceived attack—intentional conduct on his part that formed the basis for the charge of criminally negligent homicide. Indeed, the trial court charged the jury that it could not find defendant guilty of criminally negligent homicide unless it concluded that he was speeding at the time of the fatal accident. In these circumstances, we agree with defendant that he was entitled to have the jury consider whether his speeding was justified.
>
> If on any reasonable view of the evidence, the jury might have decided that defendant's actions were justified, the failure to charge the defense constitutes reversible error. It is not for the trial court to hypothesize other reasonable alternatives to the course of action chosen by the defendant. By giving the charge to the jury on the leaving the scene charge, the Judge concluded that one reasonable view of the evidence justified that conduct. Defendant argues, and we agree, that under these circumstances he was entitled to have the jury determine if the manner in which he fled the scene was also justified.

People v. Maher, 79 N.Y.2d 978 (1992).

17. Defendants cannot raise a justification defense if the legislature contemplated (and rejected) the very sort of justification the defendant is raising. See Model Penal Code § 3.02(1)(b) & (c). Even if the Code did not codify this "principle," wouldn't it follow from the common basic understanding of the purpose of the justification defense: to correct the overinclusiveness of prospective rules that cannot contemplate every precise situation in which defendants might act? In every justification case, isn't the defendant claiming, at core, that the legislature would have permitted (or even encouraged) him to do just what he did had they had his precise case in mind? Isn't he claiming that they forbade a broad category of cases of which his conduct is an instance solely because legislation must be general and imprecise?

The big problem, of course, is how to *implement* the principle that one cannot raise a justification defense if the legislature has already assessed the benefits and costs of your conduct. How do we determine when the legislature did and did not contemplate the situation the defendant is in? Reconsider *Leno* (note 12, supra): Is the core of the court's claim that the legislature has clearly weighed the pros and cons of clean needle programs (is that true because a bill establishing such programs was introduced and rejected? because public debate has been vigorous? because laws in other jurisdictions differ?) Can we ever *know* that the legislature has rejected the claim that the benefits of such programs do not outweigh the costs in *situations that are indistinguishable from the situation the defendant is in*? See also Murphy v. Commonwealth, 521 S.E.2d 301 (Va. App. 1999) (rejecting necessity claim by a defendant who used marijuana to treat debilitating migraines, noting that the Virginia legislature, by expressly *permitting* medical marijuana use in a specific set of cases—glaucoma and cancer—implicitly rejected it in other cases). But might a defendant still argue that the legislators contemplated *most* migraine cases, but not ones of my severity?

A second possible problem is that one could believe that juries *should* (have the right to) supplant legislative judgments about the relative costs and benefits of particular conduct and refuse to convict those defendants who convince them that the benefits of their conduct substantially outweighed the costs.

* * *

Problem

Consider the following Justice Department memorandum on the use of torture in light of the above discussion of self-defense and necessity. The relevant federal statutes are reproduced below.

18 U.S.C. § 2340.—Definitions

As used in this chapter—

(1) "torture" means an act committed by a person acting under the color of law specifically intended to inflict severe physical or mental pain or suffering (other than pain or suffering incidental to lawful sanctions) upon another person within his custody or physical control;

(2) "severe mental pain or suffering" means the prolonged mental harm caused by or resulting from—

(A) the intentional infliction or threatened infliction of severe physical pain or suffering;

(B) the administration or application, or threatened administration or application, of mind-altering substances or other procedures calculated to disrupt profoundly the senses or the personality;

(C) the threat of imminent death; or

(D) the threat that another person will imminently be subjected to death, severe physical pain or suffering, or the administration or application of mind-altering substances or other procedures calculated to disrupt profoundly the senses or personality. . . .

18 U.S.C. § 2340A.—Torture

(a) Offense.—

Whoever outside the United States commits or attempts to commit torture shall be fined under this title or imprisoned not more than 20 years, or both, and if death results to any person from conduct prohibited by this subsection, shall be punished by death or imprisoned for any term of years or for life.

(b) Jurisdiction.—

There is jurisdiction over the activity prohibited in subsection (a) if—

(1) the alleged offender is a national of the United States; or

(2) the alleged offender is present in the United States, irrespective of the nationality of the victim or alleged offender. . . .

U.S. Department of Justice
Office of Legal Counsel

Office of the Assistant Attorney General Washington, D.C. 20530
August 1, 2002

Memorandum for Alberto R. Gonzales
Counsel to the President

Re: Standards of Conduct for Interrogation under 18 U.S.C. §§ 2340–2340A

You have asked for our Office's views regarding the standards of conduct under the Convention Against Torture and Other Cruel, Inhuman and Degrading Treatment or Punishment, as implemented by Sections 2340–2340A of title 18 of the United States Code. As we understand it, this question has arisen in the context of the conduct of interrogations outside of the United States. We conclude below that Section 2340A proscribes acts inflicting, and that are specifically intended to inflict, severe pain or suffering, whether mental or physical. Those acts must be of an extreme nature to rise to the level of torture within the meaning of Section 2340A and the Convention. We further conclude that certain acts may be cruel, inhuman, or degrading, but still not produce pain and suffering of the requisite intensity to fall within Section 2340A's proscription against torture. * * *

Even if an interrogation method, however, might arguably cross the line drawn in Section 2340 . . ., we believe that under the current circumstances certain justification defenses might be available that would potentially eliminate criminal liability.

Standard criminal law defenses of necessity and self-defense could justify interrogation methods needed to elicit information to prevent a direct and imminent threat to the United States and its citizens.

A. Necessity

* * * It appears to us that under the current circumstances the necessity defense could be successfully maintained in response to an allegation of a Section 2340A violation. On September 11, 2001, al Qaeda launched a surprise covert attack on civilian targets in the United States that led to the deaths of thousands and losses in the billions of dollars. According to public and governmental reports, al Qaeda has other sleeper cells within the United States that may be planning similar attacks. Indeed,

al Qaeda plans apparently include efforts to develop and deploy chemical, biological and nuclear weapons of mass destruction. Under these circumstances, a detainee may possess information that could enable the United States to prevent attacks that potentially could equal or surpass the September 11 attacks in their magnitude. Clearly, any harm that might occur during an interrogation would pale to insignificance compared to the harm avoided by preventing such an attack, which could take hundreds or thousands of lives.

Under this calculus, two factors will help indicate when the necessity defense could appropriately be invoked. First, the more certain that government officials are that a particular individual has information needed to prevent an attack, the more necessary interrogation will be. Second, the more likely it appears to be that a terrorist attack is likely to occur, and the greater the amount of damage expected from such an attack, the more that an interrogation to get information would become necessary. Of course, the strength of the necessity defense depends on the circumstances that prevail, and the knowledge of the government actors involved, when the interrogation is conducted. . . .

B. Self–Defense

Even if a court were to find that a violation of Section 2340A was not justified by necessity, a defendant could still appropriately raise a claim of self-defense. * * *

The threat of an impending terrorist attack threatens the lives of hundreds if not thousands of American citizens. Whether such a defense will be upheld depends on the specific context within which the interrogation decision is made. If an attack appears increasingly likely, but our intelligence services and armed forces cannot prevent it without the information from the interrogation of a specific individual, then the more likely it will appear that the conduct in question will be seen as necessary. If intelligence and other information support the conclusion that an attack is increasingly certain, then the necessity for the interrogation will be reasonable. The increasing certainty of an attack will also satisfy the imminence requirement. Finally, the fact that previous al Qaeda attacks have had as their aim the deaths of American citizens, and that evidence of other plots have had a similar goal in mind, would justify proportionality of interrogation methods designed to elicit information to prevent such deaths.

To be sure, this situation is different from the usual self-defense justification, and, indeed, it overlaps with elements of the necessity defense. Self-defense as usually discussed involves using force against an individual who is about to conduct the attack. In the current circumstances, however, an enemy combatant in detention does not himself present a threat of harm. He is not actually carrying out the attack; rather, he has participated in the planning and preparation for the attack, or merely has knowledge of the attack through his membership in the terrorist organization. Nonetheless, leading scholarly commentators believe that interrogation of such individuals using methods that might violate Section 2340A would be justified under the doctrine of self-defense, because the combatant by aiding and promoting the terrorist plot "has culpably caused the situation where someone might get hurt. If hurting him is the only means to prevent the death or injury of others put at risk by his actions, such torture should be permissible, and on the same basis that self-defense is permissible." Michael S. Moore, Torture and the Balance of Evils, 23 Israel L. Rev. 280, 323 (1989) (symposium on Israel's Landau Commission Report).

Thus, some commentators believe that by helping to create the threat of loss of life, terrorists become culpable for the threat even though they do not actually carry out the attack itself. They may be hurt in an interrogation because they are part of the mechanism that has set the attack in motion, *id.* at 323, just as is someone who feeds ammunition or targeting information to an attacker. Under the present circumstances, therefore, even though a detained enemy combatant may not be the exact attacker—he is not planting the bomb, or piloting a hijacked plane to kill civilians—he still may be harmed in self-defense if he has knowledge of future attacks because he has assisted in their planning and execution.

Further, we believe that a claim by an individual of the defense of another would be further supported by the fact that, in this case, the nation itself is under attack and has the right to self-defense. This fact can bolster and support an individual claim of self-defense in a prosecution, according to the teaching of the Supreme Court in *In re Neagle*, 135 U.S. 1 (1890). In that case, the State of California arrested and held deputy U.S. Marshal Neagle for shooting and killing the assailant of Supreme Court Justice Field. In granting the writ of habeas corpus for Neagle's release, the Supreme Court did not rely alone upon the marshal's right to defend another or his right to self-defense. Rather, the Court found that Neagle, as an agent of the United States and of the executive branch, was justified in the killing because, in protecting Justice Field, he was acting pursuant to the executive branch's inherent constitutional authority to protect the United States government. *Id.* at 67 ("We cannot doubt the power of the president to take measures for the protection of a judge of one of the courts of the United States who, while in the discharge of the duties of his office, is threatened with a personal attack which may probably result in his death."). That authority derives, according to the Court, from the President's power under Article II to take care that the laws are faithfully executed. In other words, Neagle as a federal officer not only could raise self-defense or defense of another, but also could defend his actions on the ground that he was implementing the Executive Branch's authority to protect the United States government.

If the right to defend the national government can be raised as a defense in an individual prosecution, as *Neagle* suggests, then a government defendant, acting in his official capacity, should be able to argue that any conduct that arguably violated Section 2340A was undertaken pursuant to more than just individual self-defense or defense of another. In addition, the defendant could claim that he was fulfilling the Executive Branch's authority to protect the federal government, and the nation, from attack. The September 11 attacks have already triggered that authority, as recognized both, under domestic and international law. Following the example of *In re Neagle*, we conclude that a government defendant may also argue that his conduct of an interrogation, if properly authorized, is justified on the basis of protecting the nation from attack.

There can be little doubt that the nation's right to self-defense has been triggered under our law. The Constitution announces that one of its purposes is "to provide for the common defense." U.S. Const., Preamble. Article I, § 8 declares that Congress is to exercise its powers to "provide for the common Defence." *See also* 2 Pub. Papers of Ronald Reagan 920, 921 (1988–89) (right of self-defense recognized by Article 51 of the U.N. Charter).

The President has a particular responsibility and power to take steps to defend the nation and its people. *In re Neagle*, 135 U.S. at 64. *See also* U.S. Const., art. IV, § 4 (The United States shall ... protect [each of the States] "against Invasion"). As Commander-in-Chief and Chief Executive, he may use the armed forces to protect the nation and its people. *See, e.g., United States v. Verdugo–Urquidez*, 494 U.S. 259, 273 (1990). And he may employ secret agents to aid in his work as Commander-in-Chief. *Totten v. United States*, 92 U.S. 105, 106 (1876).... The September 11 events were a direct attack on the United States, and ... the President has authorized the use of military force with the support of Congress....

If a government defendant were to harm an enemy combatant during an interrogation in a manner that might arguably violate Section 2340A, he would be doing so in order to prevent further attacks on the United States by the al Qaeda terrorist network.

In that case, we believe that he could argue that his actions were justified by the executive branch's constitutional authority to protect the nation from attack.

This national and international version of the right to self-defense could supplement and bolster the government defendant's individual right.
* * *

Jay S. Bybee

Assistant Attorney General

D. LAW ENFORCEMENT, PUBLIC DUTY, AND SPECIAL RESPONSIBILITY

Model Penal Code § 3.07. Use of Force in Law Enforcement.

(1) *Use of Force Justifiable to Effect an Arrest.* [T]he use of force upon or toward the person of another is justifiable when the actor is making or assisting in making an arrest and the actor believes that such force is immediately necessary to effect a lawful arrest.

(2) *Limitations on the Use of Force.*

....

(b) The use of deadly force is not justifiable under this Section unless:

(i) the arrest is for a felony; and

(ii) the person effecting the arrest is authorized to act as a peace officer or is assisting a person whom he believes to be authorized to act as a peace officer; and

(iii) the actor believes that the force employed creates no substantial risk of injury to innocent persons; and

(iv) the actor believes that:

(1) the crime for which the arrest is made involved conduct including the use or threatened use of deadly force; or

(2) there is a substantial risk that the person to be arrested will cause death or serious bodily harm if his apprehension is delayed.

Tennessee v. Garner

Supreme Court of the United States.
471 U.S. 1, 105 S.Ct. 1694 (1985).

■ JUSTICE WHITE delivered the opinion of the Court.

At about 10:45 p.m. on October 3, 1974, Memphis Police Officers Elton Hymon and Leslie Wright were dispatched to answer a "prowler inside call." Upon arriving at the scene ... Hymon ... saw someone run across the backyard. The fleeing suspect, ... Edward Garner, stopped at a 6–feet-high chain link fence at the edge of the yard. With the aid of a flashlight, Hymon was able to see Garner's face and hands. He saw no sign of a weapon, and, though not certain, was "reasonably sure" and "figured" that Garner was unarmed. He thought Garner was 17 or 18 years old and about 5′5″ or 5′7″ tall.[2] While Garner was crouched at the base of the fence, Hymon called out "police, halt" and took a few steps toward him. Garner then began to climb over the fence. Convinced that if Garner made it over the fence he would elude capture, Hymon shot him. The bullet hit Garner in the back of the head. Garner was taken by ambulance to a hospital, where he died on the operating table. Ten dollars and a purse taken from the house were found on his body.

In using deadly force to prevent the escape, Hymon was acting under the authority of a Tennessee statute and pursuant to Police Department policy. The statute provides that "[i]f, after notice of the intention to arrest the defendant, he either flee or forcibly resist, the officer may use all the necessary means to effect the arrest." Tenn. Code Ann. § 40–7–108 (1982). The Department policy was slightly more restrictive than the statute, but still allowed the use of deadly force in cases of burglary. The incident was reviewed by the Memphis Police Firearm's Review Board and presented to a grand jury. Neither took any action.

2. In fact, Garner, an eighth-grader, was 15. He was 5′4″ tall and weighed somewhere around 100 or 110 pounds.

Garner's father then brought this action in the Federal District Court for the Western District of Tennessee, seeking damages under 42 U.S.C. § 1983 for asserted violations of Garner's constitutional rights. ... After a 3–day bench trial, the District Court entered judgment for all defendants. It dismissed the claims against the Mayor and the Director for lack of evidence. ... The Court of Appeals reversed and remanded. It reasoned that the killing of a fleeing suspect is a "seizure" under the Fourth Amendment,[6] and is therefore constitutional only if "reasonable." ... Officers cannot resort to deadly force unless they "have probable cause ... to believe that the suspect [has committed a felony and] poses a threat to the safety of the officers or a danger to the community if left at large."[7] ....

A police officer may arrest a person if he has probable cause to believe that person committed a crime. ... To determine the constitutionality of a seizure "[w]e must balance the nature and quality of the intrusion on the individual's Fourth Amendment interests against the importance of the governmental interests alleged to justify the intrusion." * * *

The intrusiveness of a seizure by means of deadly force is unmatched. The suspect's fundamental interest in his own life need not be elaborated upon. The use of deadly force also frustrates the interest of the individual, and of society, in judicial determination of guilt and punishment. Against these interests are ranged governmental interests in effective law enforcement. It is argued that overall violence will be reduced by encouraging the peaceful submission of suspects who know that they may be shot if they flee....

Without in any way disparaging the importance of these goals, we are not convinced that the use of deadly force is a sufficiently productive means of accomplishing them to justify the killing of nonviolent suspects. The use of deadly force is a self-defeating way of apprehending a suspect and so setting the criminal justice mechanism in motion. If successful, it guarantees that that mechanism will not be set in motion. And while the meaningful threat of deadly force might be thought to lead to the arrest of more live suspects by discouraging escape attempts,[9] the presently available

6. "The right of the people to be secure in their persons ... against unreasonable searches and seizures, shall not be violated...." U.S. Const., Amdt. 4.

7. The Court of Appeals concluded that the rule set out in [section 3.07 of] the Model Penal Code "accurately states Fourth Amendment limitations on the use of deadly force against fleeing felons."

9. We note that the usual manner of deterring illegal conduct—through punishment—has been largely ignored in connection with flight from arrest. Arkansas, for example, specifically excepts flight from arrest from the offense of "obstruction of governmental operations." The commentary notes that this "reflects the basic policy judgment that, absent the use of force or violence, a mere attempt to avoid apprehension by a law enforcement officer does not give rise to an independent offense." Ark.Stat.Ann. § 41–2802(3)(a) (1977) and commentary. In the few States that do outlaw flight from an arresting officer, the crime is only a misdemeanor. Even forceful resistance, though generally a separate offense, is classified as a misdemeanor.

This lenient approach does avoid the anomaly of automatically transforming every fleeing misdemeanant into a fleeing felon—subject, under the common-law rule, to apprehension by deadly force—solely by virtue of his flight. However, it is in real tension with the harsh consequences of flight in cases where deadly force is employed. For example, Tennessee does not outlaw fleeing from ar-

evidence does not support this thesis. The fact is that a majority of police departments in this country have forbidden the use of deadly force against nonviolent suspects....

.... Where the suspect poses no immediate threat to the officer and no threat to others, the harm resulting from failing to apprehend him does not justify the use of deadly force to do so. It is no doubt unfortunate when a suspect who is in sight escapes, but the fact that the police arrive a little late or are a little slower afoot does not always justify killing the suspect. ...

[By contrast,] where the officer has probable cause to believe that the suspect poses a threat of serious physical harm, either to the officer or to others, it is not constitutionally unreasonable to prevent escape by using deadly force. Thus, if the suspect threatens the officer with a weapon or there is probable cause to believe that he has committed a crime involving the infliction or threatened infliction of serious physical harm, deadly force may be used if necessary to prevent escape, and if, where feasible, some warning has been given....

It is insisted that the Fourth Amendment must be construed in light of the common-law rule, which allowed the use of whatever force was necessary to effect the arrest of a fleeing felon, though not a misdemeanant.... Most American jurisdictions also imposed a flat prohibition against the use of deadly force to stop a fleeing misdemeanant, coupled with a general privilege to use such force to stop a fleeing felon. * * *

It has been pointed out many times that the common-law rule is best understood in light of the fact that it arose at a time when virtually all felonies were punishable by death.[11] "Though effected without the protections and formalities of an orderly trial and conviction, the killing of a resisting or fleeing felon resulted in no greater consequences than those authorized for punishment of the felony of which the individual was charged or suspected." American Law Institute, Model Penal Code § 3.07, Comment 3, p. 56 (Tentative Draft No. 8, 1958). Courts have also justified the common-law rule by emphasizing the relative dangerousness of felons.

Neither of these justifications makes sense today. Almost all crimes formerly punishable by death no longer are or can be. And while in earlier times "the gulf between the felonies and the minor offences was broad and deep," 2 Pollock & Maitland 467, n. 3, today the distinction is minor and often arbitrary. Many crimes classified as misdemeanors, or nonexistent, at common law are now felonies. These changes have undermined the concept,

rest. The Memphis City Code does, § 22–34.1 (Supp.17, 1971), subjecting the offender to a maximum fine of $50, § 1–8 (1967). Thus, Garner's attempted escape subjected him to (a) a $50 fine, and (b) being shot.

11. The roots of the concept of a "felony" lie not in capital punishment but in forfeiture. 2 F. Pollock & F. Maitland, The History of English Law 465 (2d ed. 1909) (hereinafter Pollock & Maitland). Not all felonies were always punishable by death. Nonetheless, the link was profound. Blackstone was able to write: "The idea of felony is indeed so generally connected with that of capital punishment, that we find it hard to separate them; and to this usage the interpretations of the law do now conform. And therefore if a statute makes any new offence felony, the law implies that is shall be punished with death, viz. by hanging, as well as with forfeiture...." 4 W. Blackstone, Commentaries * 98.

which was questionable to begin with, that use of deadly force against a fleeing felon is merely a speedier execution of someone who has already forfeited his life. They have also made the assumption that a "felon" is more dangerous than a misdemeanant untenable. Indeed, numerous misdemeanors involve conduct more dangerous than many felonies.[12]

There is an additional reason why the common-law rule cannot be directly translated to the present day. The common-law rule developed at a time when weapons were rudimentary. Deadly force could be inflicted almost solely in a hand-to-hand struggle during which, necessarily, the safety of the arresting officer was at risk. Handguns were not carried by police officers until the latter half of the last century. Only then did it become possible to use deadly force from a distance as a means of apprehension. As a practical matter, the use of deadly force under the standard articulation of the common-law rule has an altogether different meaning—and harsher consequences—now than in past centuries. * * *

The District Court concluded that Hymon was justified in shooting Garner because state law allows, and the Federal Constitution does not forbid, the use of deadly force to prevent the escape of a fleeing felony suspect if no alternative means of apprehension is available. This conclusion made a determination of Garner's apparent dangerousness unnecessary. The court did find, however, that Garner appeared to be unarmed, though Hymon could not be certain that was the case. Restated in Fourth Amendment terms, this means Hymon had no articulable basis to think Garner was armed.

... [T]he fact that Garner was a suspected burglar could not, without regard to the other circumstances, automatically justify the use of deadly force. Hymon did not have probable cause to believe that Garner, whom he correctly believed to be unarmed, posed any physical danger to himself or others.

.... While we agree that burglary is a serious crime, we cannot agree that it is so dangerous as automatically to justify the use of deadly force. The FBI classifies burglary as a "property" rather than a "violent" crime. Although the armed burglar would present a different situation, the fact that an unarmed suspect has broken into a dwelling at night does not automatically mean he is physically dangerous. This case demonstrates as much. In fact, the available statistics demonstrate that burglaries only rarely involve physical violence. During the 10-year period from 1973–1982, only 3.8% of all burglaries involved violent crime.

People v. Peña

Supreme Court of New York, Bronx County.
169 Misc.2d 75, 641 N.Y.S.2d 794 (1996).

■ William C. Donnino, Justice.

[The evidence before the Grand Jury indicates that the defendant was robbed at gunpoint in his family bodega on February 18, 1995, at about

12. White-collar crime, for example, poses a less significant physical threat than, say, drunken driving.

7:45 p.m. When the two robbers left the store, Peña went outside and fired several shots at two men whom he mistook for the robbers, killing one of them.]

The applicable statute, Penal Law § 35.30(4)(b), reads as follows:

> 4. A private person acting on his own account may use physical force, other than deadly physical force, upon another person when and to the extent that he reasonably believes such to be necessary to effect an arrest or to prevent the escape from custody of a person whom he reasonably believes to have committed an offense and who in fact has committed such offense; and he may use deadly physical force for such purpose when he reasonably believes such to be necessary to:
>
> ....
>
> (b) Effect the arrest of a person who has committed murder, manslaughter in the first degree, robbery, forcible rape or forcible sodomy and who is in immediate flight therefrom.

To understand the full meaning of that statute, it is necessary to review its history. The current Penal Law went into effect on September 1, 1967. Shortly thereafter, the justification provisions engendered a serious public debate. ... In ... 1968 ..., section 35.30 of the then revised Penal Law was repealed and a new section 35.30, containing a number of substantive changes, was enacted. Two of those changes bear on the issue presented.

First, the provisions authorizing the justifiable use of deadly force by a police or peace officer to make an arrest were considered too restrictive and they were expanded. For current purposes, the substance of those changes is not important. What is important is that the expanded authorization for the justifiable use of deadly physical force by a police or peace officer was qualified by a provision that made the officer who justifiably used deadly physical force to effect an arrest criminally responsible for the reckless assault or homicide of an innocent person from the exercise of such force.[2]

Second, the law governing the justifiable use of force by a citizen to make an arrest was expanded. That law was expanded by adding the above-quoted provision that authorized under the specified circumstances the use of deadly physical force to effect an arrest where one of the specified crimes (including robbery) was committed and the perpetrator was in immediate flight....[3]

Under the former Penal Law and initially in the revised Penal Law the citizen was not authorized to use deadly force to effect an arrest except

2. Penal Law § 35.30(2): The fact that a police officer or a peace officer is justified in using deadly physical force under circumstances prescribed in paragraphs (a) and (b) of subdivision one [of section 35.30] does not constitute justification for reckless conduct by such police officer or peace officer amounting to an offense against or with respect to innocent persons whom he is not seeking to arrest or retain in custody

3. Other substantive changes also expanding the justifiable use of force by a citizen were made in the provisions dealing with the justifiable use of force in defense of premises and in defense of a person in the course of a burglary in Penal Law § 35.20.

upon reasonable belief that the person sought to be arrested was using or about to use deadly force against the citizen or another.

"That rule [explained the Penal Law commentators of that time] was grounded in an aversion to the picture of an ordinary citizen stalking an alleged criminal in bounty hunting style with the intention of capturing him dead or alive. Though logical and sound from that viewpoint, the doctrine has frequently been criticized in its application to arrests made or attempted immediately after the commission of particularly heinous crimes. The criticism may be illustrated by considering the case of a man who, immediately after a burglary of his home during which he was robbed and his wife raped, seizes a gun, looks out the window and sees the culprit fleeing down the street. Under the [former law], he would not be justified in using the gun for apprehension purposes. With cases of that nature in mind," the Legislature amended the law. Denzer and McQuillan, Practice Commentary, McKinney's Cons Laws of NY, Book 39, Penal Law § 35.30, 1974 Pocket Part, page 76.

Most importantly, the amended law contained no provision—similar to the one included for an officer—expressly making the citizen criminally responsible for reckless assault or homicide of an innocent person during the otherwise justified use of deadly force to effect the arrest of a rapist or robber.

Given the setting within which this legislation was drawn, it is plain, as we shall see, that the Legislature acted deliberately in including the qualified liability provision for an officer and not for the citizen.

Initially, the justification article was in substance and in structural format influenced by the Model Penal Code. The Model Penal Code justification sections were written to provide justification for certain uses of force irrespective of the result of that force, and any restrictions as to the result of that use were separately provided for in a different section. In fact, New York's provision [Penal Law § 35.30(2)] qualifying the extent of an officer's authority to use justifiable force to effect an arrest of certain felons was drawn from Model Penal Code section 3.09(3).[a] [T]hat section was separate and apart from the sections of the Model Penal Code that set forth the justification rules, and the Model Code Provision made that qualification applicable to all its justification provisions dealing with the use of force upon or toward the person of another [including self-defense, defense of another, and defense of property]. So, New York ... followed the Model Penal Code structure ... of setting forth its justification provisions without qualification, and then, in the one instance where it decided to accept one of the Model Penal Code qualifications, New York plainly made a conscious decision not to extend the Model Penal Code's qualification on the use of force upon or toward the person of another beyond a police or peace officer effecting an arrest. * * *

a. § 3.09(3) When the actor is justified ... in using force upon or toward the person of another but he recklessly or negligently injures or creates a risk of injury to innocent persons, the justification ... is unavailable in a prosecution for such recklessness or negligence towards innocent persons.—EDS.

With that history in mind, common sense and the normal rules of statutory construction dictate that the inclusion of a qualification on the justifiable use of such force by an officer and its exclusion in the justifiable use of such force by a citizen in the same statute be read as deliberate expression of the legislative will to qualify the justification provisions as applied to an officer but not as applied to a citizen. * * *

In People v. Jacobs, 105 Misc.2d 616, 432 N.Y.S.2d 614 (Sup.Ct.1980), the court held that it was "inconceivable" that the Legislature deliberately chose to excuse reckless conduct in the use of deadly physical force to effect the arrest of a robber who was in immediate flight from the crime because such a law could lead to "absurd" results in excusing those who recklessly injure or kill others under such circumstances. To reach its conclusion the *Jacobs* court posited an atypical, admittedly horrifying, hypothetical of a person robbed in Yankee Stadium who fired recklessly in the pursuit of the robber and killed a dozen people. Because that result was a theoretically possibility under the statute as written, the *Jacobs* court judged that the Legislature could not have intended that and held that the citizen was liable for reckless conduct in effecting the arrest of a robber in immediate flight from the crime. * * *

[W]hen the statutory meaning and legislative intent of a statute is clear, [however,] that "a" result may in a court's view be absurd is not by itself sufficient to permit a court not to follow the legislative direction. In the end, therefore, the difficulty with the *Jacobs* conclusion is that the evidence is overwhelming that the Legislature did intend what *Jacobs* found unacceptable. * * *

While the Legislature did not explain why it drew a distinction between a police and peace officer and a citizen, there is one explanation to be found in part in the statute itself. The officer need not be correct in his/her reasonable belief that the person the officer is seeking to arrest committed an enumerated felony; nor is the officer restricted to using the deadly physical force to effect the arrest of a person who is in immediate flight from the commission of the felony. Before using deadly physical force, the citizen must be correct in his/her reasonable belief that the person he/she is seeking to arrest committed an enumerated felony and that such person is in immediate flight from the commission of the enumerated felony. Given that the police and peace officer is specially trained, inter alia, in the responsible use of firearms under trying circumstances, and that he/she was being authorized to use that deadly physical force on a much broader scale than the citizen, the Legislature wanted some statutory incentive for the police to act responsibly in the use of their broad power to use deadly physical force by holding them responsible for reckless conduct. . . . For the citizen who could not be presumed to have had training in the use of deadly physical force, and who would be acting often under stress, on the spur of the moment, in response to the commission of an enumerated felony and while the felon was in immediate flight from that felony, and who would often otherwise be a responsible member of the community, the Legislature chose not to hold that citizen accountable for an otherwise justifiable use of force that resulted in injury or death to the wrong person.

QUESTIONS AND COMMENTS

1. Note two things about the Model Penal Code provision on the use of force to arrest. First, the Model Penal Code does not restrict the law enforcement defense to police officers. Only the use of *deadly* force is limited to someone who is "authorized to act as a peace officer or is assisting a person whom he believes to be authorized to act as a peace officer." The important point here is that, at least in theory, it is not the case that a person's *status* as a police officer authorizes her to use force, or to engage in other facially criminal conduct, including, for instance, speeding. But see N.Y. Veh. & Traf. Law § 1104(d) (police cars "may exceed the maximum speed limits for the purpose of calibrating such vehicles' speedometer"). Likewise, facially criminal conduct committed by a police officer "during an emergency operation" is not justified (merely) because it is committed by a police officer, but because it falls within the purview of the necessity defense, or some other more specific provision. See, e.g., id. ("police, sheriff or deputy sheriff bicycle operated as an authorized emergency vehicle shall not be prohibited from using any sidewalk, highway, street or roadway during an emergency operation").

Second, arrests without the use of deadly force also require justification. For even the most ordinary arrest involves the use of force by one person against another, and as such constitutes facially criminal conduct, e.g., assault, kidnapping, imprisonment. In theory, if not in practice, if a person engages in conduct that matches the definition of some offense, she is criminally liable unless she has a defense available to her, even if she is a police officer. The use of nondeadly force is subject to far looser constitutional constraints than is the use of deadly force. Graham v. Connor, 490 U.S. 386 (1989) (calling for general reasonableness inquiry based on "careful attention to the facts and circumstances of each particular case, including the severity of the crime at issue, whether the suspect poses an immediate threat to the safety of the officers or others, and whether he is actively resisting arrest or attempting to evade arrest by flight").

2. *Special Responsibility.* The law enforcement defense should be distinguished not only from self-defense (and defense of another and defense of property), which aim to prevent crime, not to facilitate its punishment, but also from defenses that *do* turn on the actor's status, more specifically her status vis-à-vis the victim. So under the Model Penal Code prison guards, for instance, are authorized to use force against inmates "for the purpose of enforcing the lawful rules or procedures of the [correctional] institution." Parents too may use force "for the purpose of safeguarding or promoting the welfare" of their child. Others specifically authorized to use force to discharge certain "special responsibilities" toward others include teacher-student, guardian-incompetent person, captain/pilot/conductor-passenger. See Model Penal Code § 3.08.

On the constitutional limits—or lack thereof—on the use of force by teachers upon students, see Ingraham v. Wright, 430 U.S. 651 (1977) (Eighth Amendment prohibition against cruel and unusual "punishments" doesn't apply to "disciplinary" corporal punishment in schools). In 1999–2000, almost ten percent of public school students in the state of Mississippi were struck by their teachers. In 2003–04, over ten percent of Memphis, Tenn., public school students were corporally punished, as 28,000 "paddlings" were administered among the school district's 118,000 students. (Paddling involves the use of a wooden paddle shaped like a slim oar, wrapped with duct tape or perforated to minimize wind resistance.) See Ellen Barry, "In Memphis, a Battle Won, the Paddle Lost," L.A. Times, Nov. 24, at A14 (reporting Nov. 2004 decision—by 5–4—of the Memphis school board to ban corporal punishment).

3. *Public Duty*. Law enforcement also resembles, but differs from, the defense of public duty. This defense applies to facially criminal conduct committed for the purpose not of preventing criminal conduct or *facilitating* its punishment; it instead justifies the infliction of punishment itself, the most executive—and final—aspect of the process of crime and punishment that begins with the definition of criminal norms, continues with their application in the criminal process, and ends with the infliction of punishment for their violation. Why is the hangman not a murderer?

Model Penal Code § 3.03. Execution of Public Duty.

(1) [C]onduct is justifiable when it is required or authorized by:

(a) the law defining the duties or functions of a public officer or the assistance to be rendered to such officer in the performance of his duties; or

(b) the law governing the execution of legal process; or

(c) the judgment or order of a competent court or tribunal; or

(d) the law governing the armed services or the lawful conduct of war; or

(e) any other provision of law imposing a public duty.

4. Note that the defenses of law enforcement and public duty supplement, but do not replace, the general defense of self-defense. In fact, self-defense is defined more broadly when it comes to police conduct. See, e.g., Model Penal Code §§ 3.04(2)(a)(ii)(1) (claim of right) & 3.04(2)(b)(ii)(2) (duty to retreat).

5. Do we need all these particularized defenses? Or would a general necessity defense be enough?

6. *Garner* was a civil case. If we disregard questions of Officer Hymon's belief regarding the constitutionality (or even the legality) of his conduct, and assuming that Tennessee law had adopted the Model Penal Code position on the defense of law enforcement, what was Hymon's criminal liability, if any? Of course, the absence of a defense (justification or excuse) doesn't imply criminal liability. The elements of a crime must also have been met. And criminal liability doesn't imply criminal prosecution, or conviction. Compare Hymon's case with the following report of a police shooting in New York City:

> A grand jury declined to indict a police officer yesterday in the fatal shooting of an unarmed 19-year-old man on the roof of a Brooklyn housing project last month, officials said.

Officials have said that prosecutors in the office of the Brooklyn district attorney, Charles J. Hynes, asked the jury to consider charging the officer with criminally negligent homicide and manslaughter in the shooting, which Police Commissioner Raymond W. Kelly said appeared to be unjustified.

Indictments of police officers in such cases are rare, but some legal experts had suggested that there might be an indictment in this politically charged case, in part because the victim, Timothy Stansbury Jr., who was black, was not carrying a weapon or committing a crime. Also, the experts noted, no words were exchanged before the shot was fired between the officer, Richard S. Neri Jr., who is white, and Mr. Stansbury. * * *

Officer Neri, a housing officer with nearly 12 years on the force who had never before fired his weapon while on duty, was patrolling the roof of the Louis Armstrong Houses with his partner about 1 a.m. on Jan. 24 when they approached a rooftop door to check the stairway inside. At almost the same moment, Mr. Stansbury and two friends were approaching the door from the inside, intending to use the roof as a shortcut to a party in an adjoining building.

When the door opened, Officer Neri fired once.... Officer Neri told the panel that he had been startled and had not intended to fire.... He said ... that he had his gun pointed down and his finger on the side of the barrel, in accordance with police training, and could not remember raising his arm and moving his finger to the trigger. After Officer Neri fired, ... Mr. Stansbury fled back into the building, and Officer Neri did not know "if he shot his partner or any other individual" until he saw Mr. Stansbury in a pool of blood in the lobby....

The officer was later criticized by some, including the president of 100 Blacks in Law Enforcement Who Care, for having his gun drawn while patrolling even though no specific danger had been reported. But there are no police guidelines telling officers when to draw their guns; it is a decision that rests largely on the officer's own assessment of danger, and housing project rooftops are often havens for drug dealers and other criminals. * * *

Unlike manslaughter, in which the perpetrator must display a reckless disregard of the risk of his actions, a person can be guilty of criminally negligent homicide even if he "fails to perceive a substantial and unjustifiable risk" of a tragic result.

"The grand jury, in interpreting this rather general language, is bringing to bear the conscience of the community on the police officer's conduct," said Stephen Gillers, a professor of legal ethics at New York University School of Law....

The panel's decision seemed to underscore the unwillingness of grand juries, like juries in criminal trials, to find fault in cases where officers make mistakes—even egregious ones—in settings where they said they had reasons to be fearful and their actions were in good faith. In the case of Amadou Diallo, an unarmed West African immigrant

> slain in 1999, four officers were acquitted after they testified that they initially fired on him, unleashing 41 shots, because they believed he was reaching for a gun, when in fact it was his wallet.

Shaila K. Dewan & William K. Rashbaum, "Officer Avoids Indictment in Killing on Brooklyn Rooftop," N.Y. Times, Feb. 18, 2004, at B1, col. 2.

7. *Bystanders*. One of the problems associated with the use of deadly force, and particularly deadly force by means of a firearm, has nothing to do with either the officer or the suspect. Ideally injury to bystanders will be prevented by adopting restrictive deadly force regulations that require the officer to consider, among other things, the risk of harm to third parties—and backing them up with constitutional law, as in *Garner*. But what happens if a bystander does get hurt? Does the New York statute, as interpreted in *Peña*, make any sense? Should it matter whether you are yourself the victim of the crime whose perpetrator you are trying to arrest by deadly force? What other defenses might Peña have raised?

E. CONSENT

1. ELEMENT-NEGATING DEFENSE VS. JUSTIFICATION VS. EXCUSE

Model Penal Code § 2.11. Consent.

(1) *In General.* The consent of the victim to conduct charged to constitute an offense or to the result thereof is a defense if such consent negatives an element of the offense or precludes the infliction of the harm or evil sought to be prevented by the law defining the offense.

(2) *Consent to Bodily Harm.* When conduct is charged to constitute an offense because it causes or threatens bodily harm, consent to such conduct or to the infliction of such harm is a defense if:

(a) the bodily harm consented to or threatened by the conduct consented to is not serious; or

(b) the conduct and the harm are reasonably foreseeable hazards of joint participation in a lawful athletic contest or competitive sport; or

(c) the consent establishes a justification for the conduct under Article 3 of the Code.

(3) *Ineffective Consent.* Unless otherwise provided by the Code or by the law defining the offense, assent does not constitute consent if:

(a) it is given by a person who is legally incompetent to authorize the conduct charged to constitute the offense; or

(b) it is given by a person who by reason of youth, mental disease or defect or intoxication is manifestly unable or known by the actor to be unable to make a reasonable judgment as to the nature or harmfulness of the conduct charged to constitute the offense; or

(c) it is given by a person whose improvident consent is sought to be prevented by the law defining the offense; or

(d) it is induced by force, duress or deception of a kind sought to be prevented by the law defining the offense.

§ 3.08. Use of Force by Persons with Special Responsibility for Care, Discipline or Safety of Others.

The use of force upon or toward the person of another is justifiable if:

. . . .

(4) the actor is a doctor or other therapist or a person assisting him at his direction, and:

(a) the force is used for the purpose of administering a recognized form of treatment which the actor believes to be adapted to promoting the physical or mental health of the patient; and

(b) the treatment is administered with the consent of the patient or, if the patient is a minor or an incompetent person, with the consent of his parent or guardian or other person legally competent to consent in his behalf, or the treatment is administered in an emergency when the actor believes that no one competent to consent can be consulted and that a reasonable person, wishing to safeguard the welfare of the patient, would consent;

N.Y. Penal Law § 165.05. Unauthorized Use of a Vehicle in the Third Degree.

A person is guilty of unauthorized use of a vehicle in the third degree when:

1. Knowing that he does not have the consent of the owner, he takes, operates, exercises control over, rides in or otherwise uses a vehicle. A person who engages in any such conduct without the consent of the owner is presumed to know that he does not have such consent.

State v. George

Court of Appeals of Missouri.
937 S.W.2d 251 (1996).

■ REINHARD, JUDGE.

Defendant appeals after he was convicted by a jury of one count of second degree assault, § 565.060, Rev. Stat. Mo. 1994, and one count of third degree assault, § 565.070, Rev. Stat. Mo. 1994. . . .

The evidence reveals that on December 2, 1993, defendant was a patient at the psychiatric intensive care unit at St. Anthony's Hospital in South St. Louis County. About mid-day defendant became angry, agitated, and upset. . . . Hospital security was notified. When Dusty Barnes and Mary Ann Erger, security personnel within the hospital, responded to the call, defendant was moving up and down the hallway saying that "somebody was going to get hurt." . . . When he screamed that he wanted a light for his cigarette, Barnes approached defendant and offered him a light. As defendant leaned forward, Barnes dropped his lighter and brought defendant to the floor.

Defendant punched Barnes in the eye.... While Erger was helping to control and hold down defendant, he bit her leg through her trousers.... The bite later became infected, and she had to have an incision to remove a hematoma. Erger was able to work only part-time for approximately two months....

Section 565.080, Rev. Stat. Mo. 1986, provides:

1. When conduct is charged to constitute an offense because it causes or threatens physical injury, consent to that conduct or to the infliction of the injury is a defense only if:

(1) The physical injury consented to or threatened by the conduct is not serious physical injury; or

(2) The conduct and the harm are reasonably foreseeable hazards of

(a) The victim's occupation or profession; or

(b) Joint participation in a lawful athletic contest or competitive sport; or

(3) The consent establishes a justification for the conduct....

2. The defendant shall have the burden of injecting the issue of consent.[2]

* * *

Defendant urges that because of the nature of the guards' job, they consented to assaultive behavior. The state, however, argues that the security officers did not consent to defendant's conduct, and although they may have consented to "minor physical injuries which arise out of ordinary interactions" by virtue of their occupation, defendant exceeded the scope of any such consent.

When the Missouri legislature adopted a version of the Model Penal Code, it included a provision that was not in the model code. Our research reveals that few states, which adopted statutes similar to the Model Penal Code, have included a provision setting forth consent as a defense by nature of one's occupation. See e.g., Me.Rev.Stat.Ann. Tit. 17–A, § 109 (West 1995); N.D.Cent.Code § 12.1–17–08 (1995); Tex. Penal Code Ann. § 22.06 (West 1996). * * *

The trial court in this case also relied upon § 10.13 of the new Missouri Criminal Code: A Manual for Court Related Personnel (n.d.). This manual discusses § 565.080 and provides "if the injury is a reasonably

2. .... The Comment to the 1973 proposed code provides:

Because some physical injuries are not criminal if consented to, a section dealing with consent is needed. This section allows consent as a defense if the physical injury is not serious. Where serious physical injury is involved consent as a defense is limited to the situations covered by subsections (2) and (3). The major area under the justification sections will be medical treatment where serious physical injury can lawfully be consented to.

Mo.Ann.Stat. § 565.080 (Vernon 1979).

foreseeable hazard of the victim's employment he may be deemed to consent to the risk of injury by accepting the employment. An example would be military or police training exercises."

In Tanksley v. State, 656 S.W.2d 194, 195 (Tex.Ct.App.1983), an imprisoned defendant called a jailer to the holding cell window. The defendant, while holding a sharpened toothbrush handle, stated that he would stab the jailer in the eye when the holding cell door was opened. The defendant was convicted of aggravated assault. At trial, the jailer admitted that "inmates are sometimes belligerent, that while he was rarely threatened, he had been insulted 'verbally' and abused a few times while working in the jail." Id.

On appeal, the defendant argued that "by the nature of the jailer's employment he consented ... to any assault as a risk of his occupation, within the meaning of Tex.Pen.Code Ann. § 22.06(2)(A) (1974)."[4] The court found that the provisions of the Texas Code "do not define effective consent to mean engaging in an occupation having a risk of assault." Although a "victim's express or apparent assent to an accused's conduct is effective as a defense if the victim knew that such conduct was a risk of his occupation," the court found the jailer did not assent to the defendant's conduct.

In the case at hand, defendant relies upon the literal reading of § 565.080 to support his contention that he was entitled to the consent defense. Defendant ... relies upon ... cases ... involving the issue of assumption of risk. We do not find either case to be persuasive. Assumption of risk cases are civil matters involving money damages, an award of which will benefit the victim. These matters differ from criminal cases, which involve not only the defendant and the victim, but also the public.

For example, in State v. Fransua, 85 N.M. 173, 510 P.2d 106 (App. 1973), defendant and victim were in a bar drinking heavily. After an argument, defendant stated that if he had a gun, he would shoot victim. The victim then brought defendant a gun and told him "if he wanted to shoot me to go ahead." Defendant shot victim, and at trial, defendant argued that victim consented to the shooting. The court disagreed ...:

> It is generally conceded that a state enacts criminal statutes making certain violent acts crimes for at least two reasons: One reason is to protect the persons of its citizens; the second, however, is to prevent a breach of the public peace. While we entertain little sympathy for either the victim's absurd actions or the defendant's equally unjustified act of pulling the trigger, we will not permit the defense of consent to be raised in such cases.... [T]he public has a stronger and overriding interest in preventing and prohibiting acts such as these.

4. Section 22.06 of the Texas Penal Code provides:

> The victim's effective consent ... to the actor's conduct is a defense to prosecution under Section 22.01 (Assault) [or] 22.02 (Aggravated Assault) ... if:
>
> * * *
>
> (2) the victim knew the conduct was a risk of:
>
> (A) his occupation.

An intentional assault which occurs while working as a hospital guard differs from participating in military or police training exercises. In the latter example, an individual has consented to reasonably foreseeable injuries that may occur. In this case, however, there was no evidence that the security officers consented to the assault. Defendant said he was glad he had punched Barnes in the face, and then he bit Erger. This was an intentional assault.

By enacting the consent statute, the legislature did not intend to legalize intentional criminal assaults on persons engaged in the security profession. Rather, the legislature intended to "accommodate the assault law to reality, in that many acts which our society considers to be quite acceptable, and even desirable, are technically assaults by whatever rational definition that term may be given." State v. Floyd, 466 N.W.2d 919, 922 (Iowa.Ct.App.1990).

For instance, in State v. Floyd, supra, a fight erupted during an aggressive basketball game. The court discussed the issue of consent to an assault occurring during a sporting event and found that the legislature "contemplated a person who commits acts during the course of play, and the exception seeks to protect those whose acts otherwise subject to prosecution are committed in furtherance of the object of the sport." The court found at the time of the altercation, defendant and his victims were not "voluntary participants in a sport." The court added, however, that even if the defendant and his victims were sport participants, "[i]t strains the imagination and contorts the concept of foreseeability beyond recognition to assert that the brutal assaults carried out by defendant ... could have been 'reasonably foreseeable incident[s].' "

In the present case, it would be illogical to condone defendant's intentional assault of two guards simply because of the victims' profession. The consent statute was intended to protect acceptable acts committed during employment that would otherwise be subject to prosecution but which are committed in furtherance of one's employment. Authorizing a person to assault a worker who attempts to calm a person's abusive or disruptive behavior would not further the statute's intention. Rather, allowing the consent statute to legalize intentional assaults would thwart the purpose of Missouri's statutes criminalizing assaultive behavior. * * *

Furthermore, ... [c]ommon sense suggests that while the statute's terms insinuate consent is a defense to foreseeable and intentional assaults occurring within the victim's occupation, the statute cannot reasonably be construed to provide a defense to such conduct. We can infer that a security guard at a hospital or other business who is aware of previous assaults against his or her co-workers does not consent to future assaults against him or her. Without such an inference, it is foreseeable that convenience store workers, service station attendants, or bank tellers, who are working where previous assaults have occurred, would be assaulted, and the assailant would go unpunished for such behavior. We do not think the legislature intended the consent defense to encompass such situations.

We conclude that the trial court did not err. * * *

Judgment affirmed.

People v. Schacker

District Court of New York, Suffolk County.
175 Misc.2d 834, 670 N.Y.S.2d 308 (1998).

■ LAWRENCE DONOHUE, J.

The defendant is charged with assault in the third degree in violation of Penal Law § 120.00(1). The factual portion of the information reads as follows: "[A]t the Superior Ice Rink ... the defendant Robert Schacker during an ice hockey game and after a play was over and the whistle had blown, did come up behind Andrew Morenberg who was standing near the goal net and did strike him on the back of the neck and caused him to strike his head on the crossbar of the net, causing him to sustain a concussion, headaches, blurred vision, and memory loss. Injuries had been treated at St. John's Hospital, Smithtown."

The deposition of the complainant parallels the factual portion of the information. At the hearing [on the motion to dismiss], the hospital records of the complainant were admitted. Both an X-ray and a CAT scan showed no damage. The final diagnosis was "Contusion Forehead". Thus the medical records show only minor injuries....

As Chief Judge Benjamin Cardozo said in *Murphy v. Steeplechase Amusement Co.* (250 NY 479, 482–483):

> One who takes part in ... a sport accepts the dangers that inhere in it so far as they are obvious and necessary, just as a fencer accepts the risk of a thrust by his antagonist or a spectator at a ball game the chance of contact with the ball....
>
> A different case would be here if the dangers inherent in the sport were obscure or unobserved ... or so serious as to justify the belief that precautions of some kind must have been taken to avert them.

Persons engaged in athletic competition are generally held to have legally assumed the risk of injuries which are known, apparent and reasonably foreseeable consequences of participation. Hockey players assume the risk of injury by voluntarily participating in a hockey game at an ice rink.

This tort rule states a policy "intended to facilitate free and vigorous participation in athletic activities." This policy would be severely undermined if the usual criminal standards were applied to athletic competition, especially ice hockey. If cross checking, tripping and punching were criminal acts, the game of hockey could not continue in its present form.

The complainant does not assume the risk of reckless or intentional conduct. However, it must be recognized that athletic competition includes intentional conduct that has the appearance of criminal acts. In fact, in many sporting events, physical injuries are caused by contact with other players. However, the players are "legally deemed to have accepted personal responsibility for" the risks inherent in the nature of sport. This includes intentional acts which result in personal injury. Thus, in order to allege a criminal act which occurred in a hockey game, the factual portion of the information must allege acts that show that the intent was to inflict physical injury which was unrelated to the athletic competition. Although play may have terminated, the information herein does not show that the physical contact had no connection with the competition. Furthermore, the injuries must be so severe as to be unacceptable in normal competition, requiring a change in the nature of the game. That type of injury is not present in this case. Firstly, the physical injury resulted from hitting the net, not from direct contact with the defendant. Secondly, the hospital records do not indicate severe trauma to the complainant.

The idea that a hockey player should be prosecuted runs afoul of the policy to encourage free and fierce competition in athletic events. The People argued at the hearing that this was a nonchecking hockey league. While the rules of the league may prohibit certain conduct, thereby reducing the potential injuries, nevertheless, the participant continues to assume the risk of a strenuous and competitive athletic endeavor. The normal conduct in a hockey game cannot be the standard for criminal activity under the Penal Law, nor can the Penal Law be imposed on a hockey game without running afoul of the policy of encouraging athletic competition.

For the foregoing reasons, the interest of justice requires a dismissal of this charge. . . .

QUESTIONS AND COMMENTS

1. The Model Penal Code distinguishes between two versions of the consent defense. First, consent can function as an element-negating defense if it negatives an offense element. So if an offense is defined explicitly in terms of the absence of consent, then the presence of consent bars conviction. Second, even if the absence of consent isn't part of the offense definition, consent can operate as a general defense. In that case, the "victim's" consent wouldn't stand in the way of the "offender's" engaging in the statutorily proscribed conduct, but it would preclude the infliction of the "harm or evil" that the statute—and the criminal law—was designed to proscribe and prevent. Compare this formulation with the Model Penal Code's formulation of the necessity defense. § 3.02. Can the consent defense be viewed as a(nother) particular manifestation of the necessity defense?

What if the victim's consent goes beyond acquiescence, or even a request, and becomes a plea? Consider the case of the wife who, after years of caring for her ailing and incapacitated husband finally breaks down and gives in to his insistent pleas to end his life.

2. What difference does it make whether consent is classified as an element-negating "defense," or a justification? Should a defendant bear the burden of proof on consent? Is consented-to conduct criminal in any sense? Or are certain types of nominally criminal, but consented-to, conduct so desirable (rather than merely not unlawful) that it makes little sense to describe them as criminal but justified? Is a surgeon, who regularly cuts open his patients on the operating table, committing an assault that requires a defense? How about the hockey player applying a check, the football player making a tackle, the boxer throwing a punch (or biting an ear)? Does the characterization of a behavior as "criminal but justified"

affect the willingness of people to engage in that behavior, even if they are in no danger of prosecution?

Note that, in rare cases, the judge—under the Model Penal Code—has the authority to dismiss a case even if it doesn't qualify for either variant of the consent defense.

Model Penal Code § 2.12. De Minimis Infractions.

The Court shall dismiss a prosecution if, having regard to the nature of the conduct charged to constitute an offense and the nature of the attendant circumstances, it finds that the defendant's conduct:

(1) was within a customary license or tolerance, neither expressly negatived by the person whose interest was infringed nor inconsistent with the purpose of the law defining the offense....

Here the Code drafters were thinking of daily bumps on the subway, which technically may qualify as assaults.

3. Why shouldn't consent be a defense in every crime? What view of the criminal law underlies the notion that consent is not a defense? Under this view, who—or what—is the victim of a crime, and therefore in a position to consent to its commission?

Is the problem that it is just too difficult to determine whether consent is present in a given case, or type of cases? (Assessing the presence of consent in a specific case can prove rather difficult. For a detailed exploration of this issue in the law of rape, see ch. 9.) Or is the problem that there are certain types of people who are incapable of consent? The very young? The very old? The mentally incompetent? But why can't we simply limit the defense to cases that don't involve victims of this type—after all, how can I claim that someone consented to my conduct if that person is in fact incapable of giving consent?

Or is it that we think no one "in her right mind" would consent to certain conduct, notably conduct involving the infliction of serious physical harm, or even death? But what about tattooing, cosmetic surgery, or circumcision? How should the law deal with assisted suicide—i.e., consent to homicide? See Washington v. Glucksberg, 521 U.S. 702 (1997) ("consent of a homicide victim is 'wholly immaterial to the guilt of the person who cause[d] [his death]' "). Should the defendant in *Strong* (the sect leader who killed a follower in a "religious ordeal"), supra ch. 5, have been allowed to raise a consent defense? If so, should he have succeeded? If not, why not?

What do we do when we think even ordinary, perfectly sane people are "inter-temporally" inconsistent in their preferences? Your friend tells you that he is going on a diet and will beg you for cake later in the day, but you should turn him down. Later that day, he begs for the cake, and explains that the person who told you not to give him the cake was too vain, or just not hungry enough, to think straight. If you give him the cake, did he consent to that? If you withhold the cake, did he consent to *that*? Does his last choice govern? The most "considered"? The one *you* think serves his well-being best? What if we think people who make certain sorts of choices frequently express regret about having made them, or would (as in the case of those who beg to be killed) express regret if they could? Does it matter how good people's foresight is? (Do people who take certain narcotic drugs at eighteen consent to a lifetime of addiction?)

Even if we believe that the presence of consent connotes the absence of harm, don't we believe that we expect distinct *manifestations* of consent, and sobriety of judgment, in some situations more than others? A person consents to the exchange of $1 for a pen with little thought and we may accept that he is not harmed by the exchange; if a person casually says, "I'm depressed, shoot me and put me out of my misery," we wouldn't think the person who shot her was as justified as the person who took a dollar and gave back a pen. But why?

And what do we do about the fact that people may consent to something because their option set is restricted in ways that don't seem ideal. So one victim consents to be beaten because he is a committed masochist; another because he is broke (or desperate for narcotics) and the sadistic batterer offers him money or drugs if he'd submit. Do we care *why* the victim consents if we are trying to judge the defendant's conduct? Certainly, we wouldn't say a person "consented" to battery if her alternative were to be shot. Should we say she has consented to battery if her alternative is to be homeless? (We discuss at length this ambiguity in deciding when someone "consents" or has been "coerced" in ch. 9, on rape.) For a further discussion of these issues, see Mark Kelman, A Guide to Critical Legal Studies 126–37 (1987).

4. Consider the following English case involving consensual sado-masochistic sex. Regina v. Brown, House of Lords, [1994] 1 A.C. 212.

> [The defendants], with several other men, were charged with a series of offences, including assault and wounding, relating to sado-masochistic activities that had taken place over a 10–year period.... The acts consisted in the main of maltreatment of the genitalia (with, for example, hot wax, sandpaper, fish hooks and needles) and ritualistic beatings either with the assailant's bare hands or a variety of implements, including stinging nettles, spiked belts and a cat-o'-nine tails. There were instances of branding and infliction of injuries which resulted in the flow of blood and which left scarring.
>
> These activities were consensual and were conducted in private for no apparent purpose other than the achievement of sexual gratification. The infliction of pain was subject to certain rules including the provision of a code word to be used by any "victim" to stop an "assault", and did not lead to any instances of infection, permanent injury or the need for medical attention.
>
> The activities took place at a number of locations, including rooms equipped as torture chambers. Video cameras were used to record events and the tapes copied and distributed amongst members of the group. The prosecution was largely based on the contents of those video tapes. There was no suggestion that the tapes had been sold or used other than by members of the group.

The applicants pleaded guilty to the assault charges after the trial judge ruled that they could not rely on the consent of the "victims" as an answer to the prosecution case.[a]

Lord Templeman (writing for the majority).

[T]he authorities dealing with the intentional infliction of bodily harm do not establish that consent is a defence to a charge under the Act of 1861.[b] They establish that consent is a defence to the infliction of bodily harm in the course of some lawful activities. The question is whether the defence should be extended to the infliction of bodily harm in the course of sado-masochistic encounters....

Counsel for the appellants argued that consent should provide a defence ... because it was said every person has a right to deal with his own body as he chooses. I do not consider that this slogan provides a sufficient guide to the policy decision which must now be taken. It is an offence for a person to abuse his own body and mind by taking drugs. Although the law is often broken, the criminal law restrains a practice which is regarded as dangerous and injurious to individuals and which if allowed and extended is harmful to society generally. In any event the appellants in this case did not mutilate their own bodies. They inflicted harm on willing victims.... In principle there is a difference between violence which is incidental and violence which is inflicted for the indulgence of cruelty. The violence of sado-masochistic encounters involves the indulgence of cruelty by sadists and the degradation of victims. Such violence is injurious to the participants and unpredictably dangerous. I am not prepared to invent a defence of consent for sado-masochistic encounters which breed and glorify cruelty....

Society is entitled and bound to protect itself against a cult of violence. Pleasure derived from the infliction of pain is an evil thing. Cruelty is uncivilised.

How (why) do we distinguish consent to sado-masochistic sex from consent to boxing blows? Capacity of the participants to consent? History and pedigree? Public acceptability?

5. Presumably, the putative victims in *George* did not consent to the precise act that the defendant took. Presumably, those who agree to surgery affirmatively *want* the surgeon to commit an assault and those who

a. The facts are taken from the European Court of Human Rights' opinion in the case. Laskey v. United Kingdom, (1997) 24 E.H.R.R. 39 (convictions upheld as proper means for "protection of health").

b. Section 20 of the Offences Against the Person Act 1861:

Whosoever shall unlawfully and maliciously wound or inflict any grievous bodily harm upon any other person, either with or without any weapon or instrument, ... shall be liable ... to [imprisonment] ... for not more than five years.

According to the case law, to constitute a wound for the purposes of the section, the whole skin must be broken, not merely the outer layer or epidermis.

Section 47:

Whosoever shall be convicted on indictment of any assault occasioning actual bodily harm shall be liable ... to imprisonment for not more than five years.

Actual bodily harm is defined as "any hurt or injury calculated to interfere with health or comfort."—EDS.

agree to play hockey want contact (or believe the game of hockey would be different, and worse, without it). But perhaps that makes the contrast seem too readily drawn: a prison guard or psychiatric hospital worker might not affirmatively desire that there will be some scuffling in the context of maintaining control over an unruly population, but we still may adjust our sense of when a certain level of contact is impermissible based on the ordinary expectations (if not the most optimistic fantasies) about the job. Thus, the acceptability of (a certain amount) of physical contact from Marine drill sergeants may not depend on the affirmative desire of each trainee for each contact.

6. What about assumption of risk? Should a defense of assumption of risk be limited to "civil matters involving money damages" (*George*)? Or is it appropriate to import tort notions of assumption of risk into the analysis of criminal liability (*Schacker*)? What about criminal matters involving fines? What about civil matters involving punitive damages? Why would we allow a defense in civil cases, which may result in a damage award and—in theory—carry no condemnation, but not in criminal ones, which may result in *punishment*, including fines, imprisonment, or even death? Assume your law library puts up a sign that reads "A thief is operating in the law library. Guard your laptops, book bags, briefcases, etc. Don't let that thief take your things!" If your laptop is stolen while you leave it unattended for ten minutes to grab a book from another floor, does the "thief" have a consent, or assumption of risk, defense? What if you leave your car door unlocked, ajar, wide open, with the keys on the passenger seat, in the ignition, with the motor running?

2. Constitutional Limitations

One obvious way to obviate the need for a consent defense is not to criminalize consensual behavior in the first place. The following cases explore the question whether constitutional law places any limitations on the state's power to criminalize consensual conduct.

Lawrence v. Texas

Supreme Court of the United States.
539 U.S. 558, 123 S.Ct. 2472 (2003).

■ Justice Kennedy delivered the opinion of the Court.

In Houston, Texas, officers of the Harris County Police Department were dispatched to a private residence in response to a reported weapons disturbance. They entered an apartment where one of the petitioners, John Geddes Lawrence, resided. The right of the police to enter does not seem to have been questioned. The officers observed Lawrence and another man, Tyron Garner, engaging in a sexual act. The two petitioners were arrested, held in custody over night, and charged and convicted before a Justice of the Peace.

The complaints described their crime as "deviate sexual intercourse, namely anal sex, with a member of the same sex (man)." App. to Pet. for Cert. 127a, 139a. The applicable state law is Tex. Penal Code Ann.

§ 21.06(a) (2003). It provides: "A person commits an offense if he engages in deviate sexual intercourse with another individual of the same sex." The statute defines "deviate sexual intercourse" as follows:

"(A) any contact between any part of the genitals of one person and the mouth or anus of another person; or

"(B) the penetration of the genitals or the anus of another person with an object." § 21.01(1). * * *

The petitioners were adults at the time of the alleged offense. Their conduct was in private and consensual. * * *

At the outset it should be noted that there is no longstanding history in this country of laws directed at homosexual conduct as a distinct matter.... Laws prohibiting sodomy do not seem to have been enforced against consenting adults acting in private. A substantial number of sodomy prosecutions and convictions for which there are surviving records were for predatory acts against those who could not or did not consent, as in the case of a minor or the victim of an assault.... Instead of targeting relations between consenting adults in private, 19th-century sodomy prosecutions typically involved relations between men and minor girls or minor boys, relations between adults involving force, relations between adults implicating disparity in status, or relations between men and animals. * * *

[F]or centuries there have been powerful voices to condemn homosexual conduct as immoral. The condemnation has been shaped by religious beliefs, conceptions of right and acceptable behavior, and respect for the traditional family. For many persons these are not trivial concerns but profound and deep convictions accepted as ethical and moral principles to which they aspire and which thus determine the course of their lives. These considerations do not answer the question before us, however. The issue is whether the majority may use the power of the State to enforce these views on the whole society through operation of the criminal law. "Our obligation is to define the liberty of all, not to mandate our own moral code." *Planned Parenthood of Southeastern Pa.* v. *Casey,* 505 U.S. 833, 850 (1992).

.... In *Casey,* the Court ... confirmed that our laws and tradition afford constitutional protection to personal decisions relating to marriage, procreation, contraception, family relationships, child rearing, and education. In explaining the respect the Constitution demands for the autonomy of the person in making these choices, we stated as follows:

"These matters, involving the most intimate and personal choices a person may make in a lifetime, choices central to personal dignity and autonomy, are central to the liberty protected by the Fourteenth Amendment. At the heart of liberty is the right to define one's own concept of existence, of meaning, of the universe, and of the mystery of human life. Beliefs about these matters could not define the attributes of personhood were they formed under compulsion of the State."

Persons in a homosexual relationship may seek autonomy for these purposes, just as heterosexual persons do. * * *

As an alternative argument in this case, counsel for the petitioners . . . contend that . . . the Texas statute [is] invalid under the Equal Protection Clause. That is a tenable argument, but . . . [w]ere we to hold the statute invalid under the Equal Protection Clause some might question whether a prohibition would be valid if drawn differently, say, to prohibit the conduct both between same-sex and different-sex participants. * * *

The present case does not involve minors. It does not involve persons who might be injured or coerced or who are situated in relationships where consent might not easily be refused. It does not involve public conduct or prostitution.... The case does involve two adults who, with full and mutual consent from each other, engaged in sexual practices common to a homosexual lifestyle. The petitioners are entitled to respect for their private lives. The State cannot demean their existence or control their destiny by making their private sexual conduct a crime. Their right to liberty under the Due Process Clause gives them the full right to engage in their conduct without intervention of the government. "It is a promise of the Constitution that there is a realm of personal liberty which the government may not enter." *Casey, supra*, at 847. The Texas statute furthers no legitimate state interest which can justify its intrusion into the personal and private life of the individual.

Had those who drew and ratified the Due Process Clauses of the Fifth Amendment or the Fourteenth Amendment known the components of liberty in its manifold possibilities, they might have been more specific. They did not presume to have this insight. They knew times can blind us to certain truths and later generations can see that laws once thought necessary and proper in fact serve only to oppress. As the Constitution endures, persons in every generation can invoke its principles in their own search for greater freedom. * * *

■ JUSTICE O'CONNOR, concurring in the judgment.

.... I agree with the Court that Texas' statute banning same-sex sodomy is unconstitutional. See Tex. Penal Code Ann. § 21.06 (2003). Rather than relying on the substantive component of the Fourteenth Amendment's Due Process Clause, as the Court does, I base my conclusion on the Fourteenth Amendment's Equal Protection Clause.

The Equal Protection Clause of the Fourteenth Amendment "is essentially a direction that all persons similarly situated should be treated alike." *Cleburne* v. *Cleburne Living Center, Inc.*, 473 U.S. 432, 439 (1985). Under our rational basis standard of review, "legislation is presumed to be valid and will be sustained if the classification drawn by the statute is rationally related to a legitimate state interest." *Cleburne* v. *Cleburne Living Center*, *supra*, at 440. * * *

The statute at issue here makes sodomy a crime only if a person "engages in deviate sexual intercourse with another individual of the same sex." Tex. Penal Code Ann. § 21.06(a) (2003). Sodomy between opposite-sex partners, however, is not a crime in Texas. That is, Texas treats the same conduct differently based solely on the participants. Those harmed by this law are people who have a same-sex sexual orientation and thus are more likely to engage in behavior prohibited by § 21.06.

The Texas statute makes homosexuals unequal in the eyes of the law by making particular conduct—and only that conduct—subject to criminal sanction. It appears that prosecutions under Texas' sodomy law are rare.... [W]hile the penalty imposed on petitioners in this case was relatively minor, the consequences of conviction are not. [P]etitioners' convictions, if upheld, would disqualify them from or restrict their ability to engage in a variety of professions, including medicine, athletic training, and interior design. See, *e.g.*, Tex. Occ. Code Ann. § 164.051(a)(2)(B) (2003 Pamphlet) (physician); § 451.251 (a)(1) (athletic trainer); § 1053.252(2) (interior designer). Indeed, were petitioners to move to one of four States, their convictions would require them to register as sex offenders to local law enforcement. See, *e.g.*, Idaho Code § 18–8304 (Cum. Supp. 2002); La. Stat. Ann. § 15:542 (West Cum. Supp. 2003); Miss. Code Ann. § 45–33–25 (West 2003); S. C. Code Ann. § 23–3–430 (West Cum. Supp. 2002)....

Texas attempts to justify its law, and the effects of the law, by arguing that the statute satisfies rational basis review because it furthers the legitimate governmental interest of the promotion of morality.... Moral disapproval of a group cannot be a legitimate governmental interest under the Equal Protection Clause because legal classifications must not be "drawn for the purpose of disadvantaging the group burdened by the law." *Romer* v. *Evans*, 517 U.S. 620, 633 (1996). Texas' invocation of moral disapproval as a legitimate state interest proves nothing more than Texas' desire to criminalize homosexual sodomy. But the Equal Protection Clause prevents a State from creating "a classification of persons undertaken for its own sake." *Id.*, at 635. And because Texas so rarely enforces its sodomy law as applied to private, consensual acts, the law serves more as a statement of dislike and disapproval against homosexuals than as a tool to stop criminal behavior. The Texas sodomy law "raises the inevitable inference that the disadvantage imposed is born of animosity toward the class of persons affected." *Id.*, at 634. * * *

Commonwealth v. Bonadio

Supreme Court of Pennsylvania.
490 Pa. 91 (1980).

■ OPINION OF THE COURT.

This is an appeal from an Order of the Court of Common Pleas of Allegheny County granting appellees' Motion to Quash an Information on the ground that the Voluntary Deviate Sexual Intercourse Statute[1] is unconstitutional. Appellees were arrested at an "adult" pornographic the-

1. The relevant portions of the statute are the following:

"A person who engages in deviate sexual intercourse under circumstances not covered by section 3123 of this title (related to involuntary deviate sexual intercourse) is guilty of a misdemeanor of the second degree." Act of December 6, 1972, P.L. 1482, No. 334 § 1, 18 Pa.C.S.A. § 3124 (1973).

" 'Deviate sexual intercourse.' Sexual intercourse per os or per anus between human beings who are not husband and wife, and any form of sexual intercourse with an animal." Act of December 6, 1972, P.L. 1482, No. 334, § 1, 18 Pa.C.S.A. § 3101 (1973).

ater on charges of voluntary deviate sexual intercourse and/or conspiracy to perform the same.

The Commonwealth's position is that the statute in question is a valid exercise of the police power pursuant the authority of states to regulate public health, safety, welfare, and morals. Yet, the police power is not unlimited, as was stated by the United States Supreme Court in Lawton v. Steele, 152 U.S. 133, 137, 14 S.Ct. 499, 501, 38 L.Ed. 385 (1894).

> "To justify the State in thus interposing its authority in behalf of the public, it must appear, first, that the *interests of the public generally*, as distinguished from those of a particular class, require such interference; and, second, that the means are reasonably necessary for the accomplishment of the purpose, and *not unduly oppressive upon individuals*." (Emphasis added.)

The threshold question in determining whether the statute in question is a valid exercise of the police power is to decide whether it benefits the public generally. The state clearly has a proper role to perform in protecting the public from inadvertent offensive displays of sexual behavior, in preventing people from being forced against their will to submit to sexual contact, in protecting minors from being sexually used by adults, and in eliminating cruelty to animals. To assure these protections, a broad range of criminal statutes constitute valid police power exercises, including proscriptions of indecent exposure, open lewdness, rape, involuntary deviate sexual intercourse, indecent assault, statutory rape, corruption of minors, and cruelty to animals. The statute in question serves none of the foregoing purposes.... The Voluntary Deviate Sexual Intercourse Statute has only one possible purpose: to regulate the private conduct of consenting adults. Such a purpose, we believe, exceeds the valid bounds of the police power while infringing the right to equal protection of the laws guaranteed by the Constitution of the United States and of this Commonwealth.

With respect to regulation of morals, the police power should properly be exercised to protect each individual's right to be free from interference in defining and pursuing his own morality but not to enforce a majority morality on persons whose conduct does not harm others.

> "No harm to the secular interests of the community is involved in atypical sex practice in private between consenting adult partners."

Model Penal Code § 207.5—Sodomy & Related Offenses. Comment (Tent. Draft No. 4, 1955).

Many issues that are considered to be matters of morals are subject to debate, and no sufficient state interest justifies legislation of norms simply because a particular belief is followed by a number of people, or even a majority. Indeed, what is considered to be "moral" changes with the times and is dependent upon societal background. Spiritual leadership, not the government, has the responsibility for striving to improve the morality of individuals. Enactment of the Voluntary Deviate Sexual Intercourse Statute, despite the fact that it provides punishment for what many believe to be abhorrent crimes against nature and perceived sins against God, is not properly in the realm of the temporal police power.

The concepts underlying our view of the police power in the case before us were once summarized as follows by the great philosopher, John Stuart Mill, in his eminent and apposite work, ON LIBERTY (1859):

> [T]he sole end for which mankind are warranted, individually or collectively, in interfering with the liberty of action of any of their number, is self-protection.... [T]he only purpose for which power can be rightfully exercised over any member of a civilised community, against his will, is to prevent harm to others. His own good, either physical or moral is not a sufficient warrant. He cannot rightfully be compelled to do or forbear because it will be better for him to do so, because it will make him happier, because, in the opinions of others, to do so would be wise, or even right. These are good reasons for remonstrating with him, or reasoning with him, or persuading him, or entreating him, but not for compelling him, or visiting him with any evil in case he do otherwise. To justify that, the conduct from which it is desired to deter him must be calculated to produce evil to some one else. *The only part of the conduct of any one, for which he is amenable to society, is that which concerns others. In the part which merely concerns himself, his independence is, of right, absolute. Over himself, over his own body and mind, the individual is sovereign.*
>
> It is, perhaps, hardly necessary to say that this doctrine is meant to apply to human beings in the maturity of their faculties....
>
> But there is a sphere of action in which society as distinguished from the individual, has, if any, only an indirect interest; comprehending all that portion of a person's life and conduct which affects only himself, or if it also affects others, only with their free, voluntary, and undeceived consent and participation....
>
> This, then, is the appropriate region of human liberty. It comprises, first, the inward domain of consciousness; demanding liberty of conscience, in the most comprehensive sense; liberty of thought and feeling; absolute freedom of opinion and sentiment on all subjects, practical or speculative, scientific, *moral, or theological* ... Secondly, the principle requires liberty of tastes and pursuits; of framing the plan of our life to suit our own character; of doing as we like, subject to such consequences as may follow: without impediment from our fellow-creatures, *so long as what we do does not harm them, even though they should think our conduct foolish, perverse, or wrong*. Thirdly, from this liberty of each individual, follows the liberty, within the same limits of combination among individuals; freedom to unite, for any purpose not involving harm to others: the persons combining being supposed to be of full age, and not forced or deceived.
>
> No society in which these liberties are not, on the whole, respected, is free, whatever may be its form of government;....
>
> *The only freedom which deserves the name, is that of pursuing our own good in our own way, so long as we do not attempt to deprive others of theirs*, or impede their efforts to obtain it. Each is the proper guardian of his own health, whether bodily, or mental or spiritual. Mankind are greater gainers by suffering each other to live as seems

good to themselves, than by compelling each to live as seems good to the rest. (Emphasis Supplied)

This philosophy, as applied to the issue of regulation of sexual morality presently before the Court, or employed to delimit the police power generally, properly circumscribes state power over the individual. * * *

Order affirmed.

QUESTIONS AND COMMENTS

1. Are *Lawrence* and *Bonadio* about privacy or about consent? Would the state be entitled to criminalize public sexual conduct? Compare *Lawrence* and *Bonadio* with *Regina v. Brown*, supra p. 586.

In what sense are the "crimes" in *Lawrence* and *Bonadio* "victimless"? Are they better thought of as "harmless"? What, in other words, is the harm in consensual conduct between two people? Or is the claim that only certain types of sexual conduct (still widely designated as "deviate," see, e.g., Model Penal Code § 213.0(3); N.Y. Penal Law § 13000(2)) are harmful?

2. Can victims be harmed regardless of their consent or ostensible consent (which is a function of exploitation or some subtler coercion)? Consider in this context the criminalization of prostitution, non-violent incest (with underage or adult victims), or usury (charging excessive interest on a loan, e.g., N.Y. Penal Law § 190.40 (more than 25% per annum)). What if the "offender" is also the "victim," as in the case of (certain?) drug offenses? Even if the victim—or the offender—isn't harmed, what about "third party spillovers"? Is there a distinction, for instance, between criminalizing adultery and certain types of non-adulterous sexual contact? How might one go about recognizing or evaluating third party impacts, particularly when they're said not so much to fall on particular victims but on some broader "social fabric," or the "moral health" (or simply the "morals") of "the community," or "the public"? Is the protection of the public's moral health in the name of the police power a legitimate state interest? How clearly must an interest be defined to count as a legitimate reason for invoking the criminal sanction? Is "public health"—or "public welfare"—sufficiently defined? Who is the victim in offenses designed to protect the public health? Is it particular people or "the public"? Who—or what—is harmed by offenses against "the environment"? Is the consent defense ever available in cases affecting public—rather than individual—interests?

Markus Dubber argues that the war on crime is, in fact, a war on victimless crimes, such as possession, in which the state has replaced the individual as the victim of crime:

> [T]he notion of the state as the only victim is nothing new to modern American criminal law. Since the middle ages, English criminal law has been conceived of as a system of enforcing the king's peace. And the king's peace in turn was nothing other than the peace attached to every householder, his *grið* or *mund*. Since the king's household eventually covered the entire realm, rather than his court,

any attack within the realm against one of *his* subjects (an odd, but all too common, oxymoron) also disturbed *his* peace. In Pollock and Maitland's words, "[b]reach of the king's peace was an act of personal disobedience," a personal affront, daring him to exercise his power to keep his house in order.

And yet again, the modern American state makes an entirely different victim than did the English king, much as it makes a different kind of *pater patriae*. The significant difference here lies in the fact that a breach of the king's peace amounted to a personal challenge to the king, as a person and not merely as an institution. Every man within the king's *mund* was beholden to him personally by an oath of fealty, as every man to his lord, ever since William the Conqueror "decree[d] that every freeman shall affirm by oath and compact that he will be loyal to king William both within and without England, that he will preserve with him his lands and honor with all fidelity and defend him against his enemies."

The state, unlike the king, has no personal identity. As a total institution, not merely an abstraction but an abstraction precisely from particular persons and their conflicting interests, the state has only an institutional identity. So counterfeiting is not an offense against the king, but "a contempt of and misdemeanor against the United States."

.... Although a violation of state commands constitutes, technically speaking, an act of abstract disobedience against the state, as opposed to one of personal disobedience against the king, yet it is always also an act of disobedience against the officials constituting the state and one of *personal* disobedience against the particular official issuing the command or enforcing it. The modern American system of governance thus turns out to be just like the historical English one, except it has no head, or rather its head is not a person, but a deliberately apersonal abstraction.

Markus Dirk Dubber, Victims in the War on Crime: The Use and Abuse of Victims' Rights 116–17 (2002).

3. The *Bonadio* court implies that the permissible scope of legislation will be significantly restricted if we insist that others be harmed by conduct. But can't the legislature always make claims that any sort of conduct harms third parties, especially if the causal link between conduct and result need not be *proven* and if we needn't identify the particular third party who was harmed? Consider the following remarks by Bernard Harcourt:

During the past two decades, the proponents of regulation and prohibition of a wide range of human activities—activities that have traditionally been associated with moral offenses—have turned to the harm argument. Catharine MacKinnon has focused on the multiple harms to women and women's sexuality caused by pornography. The broken windows theory of crime prevention has emphasized how minor crimes, like prostitution and loitering, cause major crimes, neighborhood decline, and urban decay.

Bernard E. Harcourt, "The Collapse of the Harm Principle," 90 J. Crim. L. & Criminology 109 (1999); see also Dana M. Tucker, "Preventing the Secondary Effects of Adult Entertainments: Is Zoning the Solution?," 12 J. Land Use & Envtl. L. 383 (1997) (exploring restrictions on porn shops justified not as protection of public morals, but as prevention of "secondary effects," including "spread of HIV," "increased crime, prostitution, rape, and neighborhood deterioration").

Think about "private" prostitution (a publicly invisible, discreet "call girl" service). On the one hand, one could argue that the john and prostitute each consent to the exchange of money for sex. But, first, are we sure that the prostitute is unharmed? That she is not making a choice she will deeply regret? That she is not just choosing the best option from an unduly restricted option set? And are third parties harmed? Because of the increased risk of the spread of STDs to future sexual partners? Because in a more causally ambiguous, diffuse sense, the existence of prostitution encourages the sexual objectification of women (in a fashion that harms women generally)?

4. What if Texas retained its sodomy statute, but permitted a defense of consent? Is the problem in *Lawrence* (and *Bonadio*) the statute or the unavailability of a consent defense? Must the state show why a general consent defense is *not* applicable to a specific offense? If a consent defense is recognized, would the state be entitled to shift the burden of proof onto the defendant? In general? In the case of sodomy statutes? Can *Lawrence* and *Bonadio* be read as recognizing a right to a consent defense, at least in certain cases? In what cases?

5. The dissent in *Lawrence* argues that the majority's opinion calls into question "laws against bigamy, same-sex marriage, adult incest, prostitution, masturbation, adultery, fornication, bestiality, and obscenity." Is that true? If so, is that a bad thing? Why should these types of conduct be criminalized? Is criminalization more defensible in some cases than in others? On what ground? Cf. Tatjana Hörnle, "Penal Law and Sexuality: Recent Reforms in German Criminal Law," 3 Buff. Crim. L. Rev. 639 (2000) (decriminalization of adultery and bestiality in Germany in 1969).

6. Crimes may be thought of as "victimless" in what is ultimately a *procedural* sense if we believe that no complaining witness will come forward to report defendants' violations, so that enforcement will be based on the (arguably problematic) use of police decoys, surveillance, and informers. From the vantage point of anti-abortion activists, abortion is not a *substantively* victimless crime (because the fetus is a person). But it is still "procedurally" victimless because neither the abortionist nor the woman who sought the abortion will complain that a crime has been committed: enforcement is thus dependent on, say, undercover police women posing as pregnant. To what extent should the content of the substantive criminal law be driven by decisions about the acceptability of the means needed to enforce it?

7. Crimes may also be described as "victimless" when there is only limited social consensus that the prohibited conduct is harmful. What differentiates the prohibition of homosexual conduct from the prohibition of battery in this view is not that battery is "intrinsically" harmful (and

homosexual conduct "intrinsically" good, benign, or at least no worse than permitted heterosexual conduct) but that there is little disagreement about the wrongfulness of battery (even among those who batter?). The criminal law should not, perhaps, be used to enforce "bare majority" values or encode the (contested) morality of a politically ascendant sub-group. Once more, though, a crime could be viewed to be victimless in this sense even if its proponents thought the conduct unquestionably harmful. Again, the case of abortion is instructive. One could believe, personally, that abortion plainly harms what should be the protected interests of the fetus but that there is inadequate social consensus that that is the case to justify the use of criminal sanctions, rather than ongoing political persuasion, to "deter abortions." There may be particular reasons, given church-state separation values, to be especially suspicious of criminal statutes (against abortion? against homosexuality?) that embody not just generic religion-based morality, but the sectarian beliefs of some, but not all, religious groups. (For instance, religious doctrine on the moral acceptability of abortion differs sharply by sect.)

F. DURESS

Model Penal Code § 2.09. Duress.

(1) It is an affirmative defense that the actor engaged in the conduct charged to constitute an offense because he was coerced to do so by the use of, or a threat to use, unlawful force against his person or the person of another, which a person of reasonable firmness in his situation would have been unable to resist.

(2) The defense provided by this Section is unavailable if the actor recklessly placed himself in a situation in which it was probable that he would be subjected to duress. The defense is also unavailable if he was negligent in placing himself in such a situation, whenever negligence suffices to establish culpability for the offense charged.

United States v. Bailey

Supreme Court of the United States.
444 U.S. 394, 100 S.Ct. 624 (1980).

■ MR. JUSTICE REHNQUIST delivered the opinion of the Court.

In the early morning hours of August 26, 1976, respondents Clifford Bailey, James T. Cogdell, Ronald C. Cooley, and Ralph Walker, federal prisoners at the District of Columbia jail, crawled through a window from which a bar had been removed, slid down a knotted bedsheet, and escaped from custody. Federal authorities recaptured them after they had remained at large for a period of time ranging from one month to three and one-half months. Upon their apprehension, they were charged with violating 18 U.S.C. § 751(a), which governs escape from federal custody.[1] At their trials,

1. Title 18 U.S.C. § 751(a) provides: Whoever escapes or attempts to escape from the custody of the Attorney General or his authorized representative, or from any

each of the respondents adduced or offered to adduce evidence as to various conditions and events at the District of Columbia jail, but each was convicted by the jury. . . .

In reaching our conclusion, we must decide the state of mind necessary for violation of § 751(a) and the elements that constitute defenses such as duress and necessity. . . .

Respondents' defense of duress or necessity centered on the conditions in the jail during the months of June, July, and August 1976, and on various threats and beatings directed at them during that period. In describing the conditions at the jail, they introduced evidence of frequent fires in "Northeast One," the maximum-security cellblock occupied by respondents prior to their escape. Construed in the light most favorable to them, this evidence demonstrated that the inmates of Northeast One, and on occasion the guards in that unit, set fire to trash, bedding, and other objects thrown from the cells. According to the inmates, the guards simply allowed the fires to burn until they went out. Although the fires apparently were confined to small areas and posed no substantial threat of spreading through the complex, poor ventilation caused smoke to collect and linger in the cellblock.

Respondents Cooley and Bailey also introduced testimony that the guards at the jail had subjected them to beatings and to threats of death. Walker attempted to prove that he was an epileptic and had received inadequate medical attention for his seizures.

Consistently during the trial, the District Court stressed that, to sustain their defenses, respondents would have to introduce some evidence that they attempted to surrender or engaged in equivalent conduct once they had freed themselves from the conditions they described. . . . Only respondent Walker suggested that he had attempted to negotiate a surrender. Like Cooley and Bailey, Walker testified that the FBI had told his "people" that they would kill him when they recaptured him. Nevertheless, according to Walker, he called the FBI three times and spoke with an agent whose name he could not remember. That agent allegedly assured him that the FBI would not harm him, but was unable to promise that Walker would not be returned to the D.C. jail. Walker testified that he last called the FBI in mid-October. He was finally apprehended on December 13, 1976.

At the close of all the evidence, the District Court rejected respondents' proffered instruction on duress as a defense to prison escape. * * *

Common law historically distinguished between the defenses of duress and necessity. Duress was said to excuse criminal conduct where the actor was under an unlawful threat of imminent death or serious bodily injury,

institution or facility in which he is confined by direction of the Attorney General, or from any custody under or by virtue of any process issued under the laws of the United States by any court, judge or magistrate, or from the custody of an officer or employee of the United States pursuant to lawful arrest, shall, if the custody or confinement is by virtue of an arrest on a charge of felony, or conviction of any offense, be fined not more than $5,000 or imprisoned not more than five years, or both; or if the custody or confinement is for extradition or by virtue of an arrest or charge of or for a misdemeanor, and prior to conviction, be fined not more than $1,000 or imprisoned not more than one year, or both.

which threat caused the actor to engage in conduct violating the literal terms of the criminal law. While the defense of duress covered the situation where the coercion had its source in the actions of other human beings, the defense of necessity, or choice of evils, traditionally covered the situation where physical forces beyond the actor's control rendered illegal conduct the lesser of two evils. Thus, where A destroyed a dike because B threatened to kill him if he did not, A would argue that he acted under duress, whereas if A destroyed the dike in order to protect more valuable property from flooding, A could claim a defense of necessity.

Modern cases have tended to blur the distinction between duress and necessity. In the court below, the majority discarded the labels "duress" and "necessity," choosing instead to examine the policies underlying the traditional defenses. In particular, the majority felt that the defenses were designed to spare a person from punishment if he acted "under threats or conditions that a person of ordinary firmness would have been unable to resist," or if he reasonably believed that criminal action "was necessary to avoid a harm more serious than that sought to be prevented by the statute defining the offense." The Model Penal Code redefines the defenses along similar lines. See Model Penal Code § 2.09 (duress) and § 3.02 (choice of evils).

We need not speculate now, however, on the precise contours of whatever defenses of duress or necessity are available against charges brought under § 751(a). Under any definition of these defenses one principle remains constant: if there was a reasonable, legal alternative to violating the law, "a chance both to refuse to do the criminal act and also to avoid the threatened harm," the defenses will fail. Clearly, in the context of prison escape, the escapee is not entitled to claim a defense of duress or necessity unless and until he demonstrates that, given the imminence of the threat, violation of § 751(a) was his only reasonable alternative.

In the present case, the Government contends that respondents' showing was insufficient on two grounds. First, the Government asserts that the threats and conditions cited by respondents as justifying their escape were not sufficiently immediate or serious to justify their departure from lawful custody. Second, the Government contends that, once the respondents had escaped, the coercive conditions in the jail were no longer a threat and respondents were under a duty to terminate their status as fugitives by turning themselves over to the authorities.

Respondents, on the other hand, argue that the evidence of coercion and conditions in the jail was at least sufficient to go to the jury as an affirmative defense to the crime charged. As for their failure to return to custody after gaining their freedom, respondents assert that this failure should be but one factor in the overall determination whether their initial departure was justified. . . .

We need not decide whether such evidence as that submitted by respondents was sufficient to raise a jury question as to their initial departures. This is because we decline to hold that respondents' failure to return is "just one factor" for the jury to weigh in deciding whether the initial escape could be affirmatively justified. . . .

First, we think it clear beyond peradventure that escape from federal custody as defined in § 751(a) is a continuing offense and that an escapee can be held liable for failure to return to custody as well as for his initial departure. Given the continuing threat to society posed by an escaped prisoner, "the nature of the crime involved is such that Congress must assuredly have intended that it be treated as a continuing one." * * *

The Anglo–Saxon tradition of criminal justice, embodied in the United States Constitution and in federal statutes, makes jurors the judges of the credibility of testimony offered by witnesses. It is for them, generally, and not for appellate courts, to say that a particular witness spoke the truth or fabricated a cock-and-bull story. An escapee who flees from a jail that is in the process of burning to the ground may well be entitled to an instruction on duress or necessity, " 'for he is not to be hanged because he would not stay to be burnt.' " United States v. Kirby, 7 Wall. 482, 487, 19 L.Ed. 278 (1869). And in the federal system it is the jury that is the judge of whether the prisoner's account of his reason for flight is true or false. But precisely because a defendant is entitled to have the credibility of his testimony, or that of witnesses called on his behalf, judged by the jury, it is essential that the testimony given or proffered meet a minimum standard as to each element of the defense so that, if a jury finds it to be true, it would support an affirmative defense—here that of duress or necessity.

We therefore hold that, where a criminal defendant is charged with escape and claims that he is entitled to an instruction on the theory of duress or necessity, he must proffer evidence of a bona fide effort to surrender or return to custody as soon as the claimed duress or necessity had lost its coercive force. We have reviewed the evidence ... and find the case not even close, even under respondents' versions of the facts, as to whether they either surrendered or offered to surrender at their earliest possible opportunity. Since we have determined that this is an indispensable element of the defense of duress or necessity, respondents were not entitled to any instruction on such a theory. * * *

.... The requirement of a threshold showing on the part of those who assert an affirmative defense to a crime is by no means a derogation of the importance of the jury as a judge of credibility. Nor is it based on any distrust of the jury's ability to separate fact from fiction. On the contrary, it is a testament to the importance of trial by jury and the need to husband the resources necessary for that process by limiting evidence in a trial to that directed at the elements of the crime or at affirmative defenses. If, as we here hold, an affirmative defense consists of several elements and testimony supporting one element is insufficient to sustain it even if believed, the trial court and jury need not be burdened with testimony supporting other elements of the defense.

These cases present a good example of the potential for wasting valuable trial resources. [T]he jury in the trial of Bailey, Cooley, and Walker heard five days of testimony. It was presented with evidence of every unpleasant aspect of prison life from the amount of garbage on the cellblock floor, to the meal schedule, to the number of times the inmates were allowed to shower. ... Were we to hold, as respondents suggest, that the jury should be subjected to this potpourri even though a critical element of the proffered defenses was concededly absent, we undoubtedly would convert every trial under § 751(a) into a hearing on the current state of the federal penal system.

State v. Toscano

Supreme Court of New Jersey.
74 N.J. 421, 378 A.2d 755 (1977).

■ PASHMAN, J.

On April 20, 1972, the Essex County Grand Jury returned a 48–count indictment alleging that eleven named defendants and two unindicted co-conspirators had defrauded various insurance companies by staging accidents in public places and obtaining payments in settlement of fictitious injuries. . . .

Dr. Joseph Toscano, a chiropractor, was named as a defendant in the First Count and in two counts alleging a conspiracy to defraud the Kemper Insurance Company. . . . [According to the indictment,] William Leonardo . . . and his cohorts . . . would stage an accident or feign a fall in a public place.[2] A false medical report for the "injured" person, together with a false verification of employment and lost wages, would then be submitted to the insurer of the premises. . . . The insurance companies made cash payments to resolve the claims under their "quick settlement" programs, usually within a few weeks after the purported accidents. * * *

Defendant first met Richard Leonardo in 1953 as a patient and subsequently knew him as a friend. Defendant briefly encountered [Richard's] brother, William, in the late 1950's. . . . Richard told him many times that William was "on junk," that he had a gang, that "they can't keep up with the amount of money that they need for this habit," and that he himself stayed away from William.

Thus, when William first called the defendant at his office, asking for a favor, he immediately cut off the conversation on the pretext that he was with a patient. . . . [D]efendant testified that he was "nauseated" by "just his name." A few days later, on a Thursday evening, he received another call in his office. This time Leonardo asked defendant to make out a report for a friend in order to submit a bill to a claims adjuster. He was more insistent, stating that defendant was "going to do it," but defendant replied that he would not and could not provide the report. Once again the doctor ended the conversation abruptly by claiming, falsely, that he was with other persons.

The third and final call occurred on Friday evening. Leonardo was "boisterous and loud" repeating, "You're going to make this bill out for me." Then he said: "Remember, you just moved into a place that has a very dark entrance and you leave there with your wife. . . . You and your wife are going to jump at shadows when you leave that dark entrance."

2. The mishaps occurred in supermarkets, discount stores, movie theaters and a factory. On two occasions, Leonardo and others deliberately caused an accident while road testing a used car from a dealer. There were three incidents in 1968, five in 1969, three in 1970 and one in 1971.

Leonardo sounded "vicious" and "desperate" and defendant felt that he "just had to do it" to protect himself and his wife. He thought about calling the police, but failed to do so in the hope that "it would go away and wouldn't bother me any more."

In accordance with Leonardo's instructions, defendant left a form in his mailbox on Saturday morning for Leonardo to fill in with the necessary information about the fictitious injuries. It was returned that evening and defendant completed it. * * *

After defendant testified, the trial judge granted the State's motion to exclude any further testimony in connection with defendant's claim of duress, and announced his decision not to charge the jury on that defense. * * *

Since New Jersey has no applicable statute defining the defense of duress,[a] we are guided only by common law principles which conform to the purposes of our criminal justice system and reflect contemporary notions of justice and fairness.

At common law the defense of duress was recognized only when the alleged coercion involved a use or threat of harm which is "present, imminent and pending" and "of such a nature as to induce a well grounded apprehension of death or serious bodily harm if the act is not done." Nall v. Commonwealth, 208 Ky. 700, 271 S.W. 1059 (1925).

It was commonly said that duress does not excuse the killing of an innocent person even if the accused acted in response to immediate threats. Aside from this exception, however, duress was permitted as a defense to prosecution for a range of serious offenses, [including treason, kidnapping, arson], and many lesser crimes, [such as robbery, breaking and entering with intent to steal, forgery, and perjury].

To excuse a crime, the threatened injury must induce "such a fear as a man of ordinary fortitude and courage might justly yield to." United States v. Haskell, 26 Fed.Cas. 207 (Pa.Cir.Ct.1823). Although there are scattered suggestions in early cases that only a fear of death meets this test, see Respublica v. M'Carty, 2 U.S. 86, 2 Dall. 86, 1 L.Ed. 300 (Pa.Supr.Ct.1781) (treason),[8] an apprehension of immediate serious bodily harm has been considered sufficient to excuse capitulation to threats. Thus, the courts have assumed as a matter of law that neither threats of slight injury nor threats of destruction to property are coercive enough to overcome the will of a person of ordinary courage. See People v. Ricker, 45 Ill.2d 562, 262 N.E.2d 456 (1970) (loss of job); D'Aquino v. United States, supra (denial of food rations). Cf. State v. Gann, N.D., 244 N.W.2d 746 (1976) (economic need); United States v. Palmer, 458 F.2d 663 (9 Cir. 1972) (prospect of

a. New Jersey has since adopted the duress provision quoted in n. 12 infra.—EDS.

8. Several states, by statute, continue to require that the actor have reasonable cause to believe that his life was in danger. See, e. g., Arizona Rev.Stat.Ann., Tit. 13-134 (1956); Arkansas Stat.Ann. § 41-117 (1947); Deering's California Penal Code § 26(8) (1960); Colorado Rev.Stat.Ann. Ch. 40-1-11 (1960); Idaho Code, § 18-101 (1947); Montana Rev.Code Ann., Tit. 94-201 (1947). Minnesota limits the defense to situations in which "instant death" is threatened. Minn. Stat. 609.08 (1965).

"financial ruin"). A "generalized fear of retaliation" by an accomplice, unrelated to any specific threat, is also insufficient.

More commonly, the defense of duress has not been allowed because of the lack of immediate danger to the threatened person. When the alleged source of coercion is a threat of "future" harm, courts have generally found that the defendant had a duty to escape from the control of the threatening person or to seek assistance from law enforcement authorities.

Assuming a "present, imminent and impending" danger, however, there is no requirement that the threatened person be the accused. Although not explicitly resolved by the early cases, recent decisions have assumed that concern for the well-being of another, particularly a near relative, can support a defense of duress if the other requirements are satisfied. See United States v. Gordon, 526 F.2d 406 (9 Cir. 1975) (friends imperiled); United States v. Stevison, 471 F.2d 143 (7 Cir. 1972) (suicide threat by defendant's daughter); Koontz v. State, 204 So.2d 224 (Fla.App. 1967) (threats to mother and sister). Cf. State v. Gann, supra (need to support family).

A less rigorous standard has been imposed in a few cases involving relatively minor, non-violent crimes. [For instance,] in Commonwealth v. Reffitt, 149 Ky. 300, 148 S.W. 48 (1912) a tenant farmer entered into an illegal transaction after being threatened with physical harm and destruction of his crop. Although there was no clear-cut threat of immediate danger, the court emphasized the inability of the civil and military authorities to prevent acts giving rise to the illegal coercion.

For the most part, however, the same test has been utilized to assess the sufficiency of the defendant's allegations for the purpose of charging the jury, regardless of the nature of the crime.

The insistence under the common law on a danger of immediate force causing death or serious bodily injury may be ascribed to its origins in early cases dealing with treason, to the proclivities of a "tougher-minded age," or simply to judicial fears of perjury and fabrication of baseless defenses. We do not discount the latter concern as a reason for caution in modifying this accepted rule, but we are concerned by its obvious shortcomings and potential for injustice. Under some circumstances, the commission of a minor criminal offense should be excusable even if the coercive agent does not use or threaten force which is likely to result in death or "serious" bodily injury.[10] Similarly, it is possible that authorities might not be able to prevent a threat of future harm from eventually being carried out.... Warnings of future injury or death will be all the more powerful if the prospective victim is another person, such as a spouse or child, whose safety means more to the threatened person than his own wellbeing.

10. If the only consideration were the maximization of social benefits in a single instance, there would undoubtedly be situations in which even the destruction of property or of a person's reputation would constitute a greater evil than the commission of an act proscribed by the criminal law. Both the Model Penal Code and the proposed New Jersey Penal Code established a general principle of justification as a defense, which would encompass many of those cases. See Model Penal Code § 3.02, Comment (Tent. Draft No. 8, 1958); New Jersey Penal Code § 2C:3–1 (1971). Under present law, however, such a defense is limited to self-defense or defense of another.

Finally, as the drafters of the Model Penal Code observed, "long and wasting pressure may break down resistance more effectively than a threat of immediate destruction." § 2.09, Comment at 8 (Tent.Draft No. 10, 1960).

Commentators have expressed dissatisfaction with the common law standard of duress. Stephen viewed the defense as a threat to the deterrent function of the criminal law, and argued that "it is at the moment when temptation is strongest that the law should speak most clearly and emphatically to the contrary." Stephen, 2 History of the Criminal Law in England 107 (1883). A modern refinement of this position is that the defense should be designed to encourage persons to act against their self-interest if a substantial percentage of persons in such a situation would do so. Hall, General Principles of Criminal Law (2d ed. 1960), 446–47. This standard would limit its applicability to relatively minor crimes and exclude virtually all serious crimes unless committed under threat of imminent death.[11]

Others have been more skeptical about the deterrent effects of a strict rule. As the Alabama Supreme Court observed in an early case:

That persons have exposed themselves to imminent peril and death for their fellow man, and that there are instances where innocent persons have submitted to murderous assaults, and suffered death, rather than take life, is well established; but such self-sacrifice emanated from other motives than the fear of legal punishment. (97 Ala. 5, 12, 12 So. 301, 303 (1893))

Building on this premise, some commentators have advocated a flexible rule which would allow a jury to consider whether the accused actually lost his capacity to act in accordance with "his own desire, or motivation, or will" under the pressure of real or imagined forces. The inquiry here would focus on the weaknesses and strengths of a particular defendant, and his subjective reaction to unlawful demands. Thus, the "standard of heroism" of the common law would give way, not to a "reasonable person" standard, but to a set of expectations based on the defendant's character and situation.

The drafters of the Model Penal Code and the New Jersey Penal Code sought to steer a middle course between these two positions by focusing on whether the standard imposed upon the accused was one with which "normal members of the community will be able to comply...." They stated:

[L]aw is ineffective in the deepest sense, indeed it is hypocritical, if it imposes on the actor who has the misfortune to confront a dilemmatic choice, a standard that his judges are not prepared to affirm that they should and could comply with if their turn to face the problem should arise. Condemnation in such case is bound to be an ineffective threat; what is, however, more significant is that it is divorced from any moral base and is injust. Where it would be both "personally and socially debilitating" to

11. This approach goes considerably beyond the common law in severity. See State v. St. Clair, 262 S.W.2d 25, 27 (Mo.1953) ("coercion does not excuse taking the life of an innocent person, yet it does excuse in all lesser crimes"). However, several states have distinguished between capital and non-capital crimes, and felony and non-felony offenses. See, e. g., Texas Stat.Ann.-Penal Code § 8.05 (1970).

accept the actor's cowardice as a defense, it would be equally debilitating to demand that heroism be the standard of legality. (Model Penal Code s 2.09, Comment at 7 (Tent.Draft No. 10, 1960), quoting Hart, "The Aims of the Criminal Law," 23 Law & Contemp.Prob. 401, 414 and n. 31 (1958); New Jersey Model Penal Code s 2C:2–9, Commentary at 71 (1971).)

Thus, they proposed that a court limit its consideration of an accused's "situation" to "stark, tangible factors which differentiate the actor from another, like his size or strength or age or health," excluding matters of temperament. They substantially departed from the existing statutory and common law limitations requiring that the result be death or serious bodily harm, that the threat be immediate and aimed at the accused, or that the crime committed be a non-capital offense. While these factors would be given evidential weight, the failure to satisfy one or more of these conditions would not justify the trial judge's withholding the defense from the jury.

Both the Prosecutor and the Attorney General substantially approve of the modifications suggested by the drafters of the model codes. However, they would allow the issue to be submitted to the jury only where the trial judge has made a threshold determination that the harm threatened was "imminent." Defendant ... advocates leaving the question of immediacy to the jury.

For reasons suggested above, a per se rule based on immediate injury may exclude valid claims of duress by persons for whom resistance to threats or resort to official protection was not realistic. While we are hesitant to approve a rule which would reward citizens who fail to make such efforts, we are not persuaded that capitulation to unlawful demands is excusable only when there is a "gun at the head" of the defendant. We believe that the better course is to leave the issue to the jury with appropriate instructions from the judge.

Although they are not entirely identical, under both model codes defendant would have had his claim of duress submitted to the jury.[12]

12. The most significant difference between the two provisions is the treatment of duress as a defense to murder. The Model Penal Code permits it as an affirmative defense, while the New Jersey Penal Code allows it only to reduce a crime from murder to manslaughter. The relevant portions of the two provisions are set forth below:

Model Penal Code § 2.09

(1) It is an affirmative defense that the actor engaged in the conduct charged to constitute an offense because he was coerced to do so by the use of, or a threat to use, unlawful force against his person of another, which a person of reasonable firmness in his situation would have been unable to resist.

(2) The defense provided by this Section is unavailable if the actor recklessly placed himself in a situation in which it was probable that he would be subjected to duress. The defense is also unavailable if he was negligent in placing himself in such a situation, whenever negligence suffices to establish culpability for the offense charged.

New Jersey Penal Code § 2C:2–9

a. Subject to Subsection b of this Section, it is an affirmative defense that the actor engaged in the conduct charged to constitute an offense because he was coerced to do so by the use of, or a threat to use, unlawful force against his person or the person of another, which a person of reasonable firmness in his situation would have been unable to resist.

b. The defense provided by this Section is unavailable if the actor recklessly placed

Defendant's testimony provided a factual basis for a finding that Leonardo threatened him and his wife with physical violence if he refused to assist in the fraudulent scheme. Moreover, a jury might have found from other testimony adduced at trial that Leonardo's threats induced a reasonable fear in the defendant. Since he asserted that he agreed to complete the false documents only because of this apprehension, the requisite elements of the defense were established. Under the model code provisions, it would have been solely for the jury to determine whether a "person of reasonable firmness in his situation" would have failed to seek police assistance or refused to cooperate, or whether such a person would have been, unlike defendant, able to resist.

.... Henceforth, duress shall be a defense to a crime other than murder if the defendant engaged in conduct because he was coerced to do so by the use of, or threat to use, unlawful force against his person or the person of another, which a person of reasonable firmness in his situation would have been unable to resist. * * *

We recognize that in other instances where the initial burden of producing evidence in support of an affirmative defense has been placed on the defendant, the burden of disproving the defense beyond a reasonable doubt has remained with the State. See, e. g., State v. Stein, 70 N.J. 369, 393, 360 A.2d 347 (1976) (entrapment); State v. Abbott, supra, 36 N.J. at 71–72, 174 A.2d 881 (self-defense). In this case, however, we think it more appropriate as a matter of public policy to follow the practice utilized in insanity cases and to require the defendant to prove the existence of duress by a preponderance of the evidence.

The peculiar nature of duress, which focuses on the reasonableness of the accused's fear and his actual ability to resist unlawful demands, is not completely offset by the "person of reasonable firmness" standard. While the idiosyncracies of an individual's temperament cannot excuse an inability to withstand such demands, his attributes (age, health, etc.) are part of the "situation" which the jury is admonished to consider. We think that the admittedly open-ended nature of this standard, with the possibility for abuse and uneven treatment, justifies placing the onus on the defendant to convince the jury.

Defendant's conviction of conspiracy to obtain money by false pretenses is hereby reversed and remanded for a new trial.

■ CONFORD, P. J., concurring in part and dissenting in part.

.... I do not regard the defense [of duress] as any more subject to "abuse" and "uneven treatment" than any of the other criminal affirmative defenses such as self-defense, entrapment or the like. If the defense of duress is true in a particular case the defendant is innocent as having been free from culpable intent. Ordinarily a defendant cannot be convicted unless the jury finds his criminal intent beyond a reasonable doubt. Yet the

himself in a situation in which it was probable that he would be subjected to duress. The defense is also unavailable if he was criminally negligent in placing himself in such a situation, whenever criminal negligence suffices to establish culpability for the offense charged. In a prosecution for murder, the defense is only available to reduce the degree of the crime to manslaughter.

rule today adopted by the Court would permit the jury to convict even if they entertained a reasonable doubt that the defendant (as a person of reasonable firmness) had been free from the coercive effect of duress when he committed the indicted act.

The fact that evidence of duress is peculiarly within the knowledge of the defendant is no justification for the Court's position. That situation is more or less true of all affirmative defenses a circumstance which explains why the standard rule imposes on the defendant the initial burden of coming forward with some evidence of the defense (unless the State's case supplies it). There is no reason to believe a jury less capable, in duress cases as compared with other affirmative defenses, of appraising credibility of witnesses and weighing proofs and accordingly concluding they have no reasonable doubt that the defense is untrue in a particular case.

QUESTIONS AND COMMENTS

1. Note that the Model Penal Code deals with duress in Article 2 (General Principles of Liability) rather than in Article 3 (General Principles of Justification) or 4 (Responsibility). Is duress an element-negating "defense," a justification, or an excuse? Contrast Peter Westen & James Mangiafico, "The Criminal Defense of Duress: A Justification, Not an Excuse—And Why It Matters," 6 Buff. Crim. L. Rev. 833 (2003), with Joshua Dressler, "Exegesis of the Law of Duress: Justifying the Excuse and Searching for Its Proper Limits," 62 S. Cal. L. Rev. 1331 (1989).

Does the limitation, in the Model Penal Code and elsewhere, of duress to cases of "unlawful force" imply a view of duress as a justification? What does it matter whether the force is unlawful or not, if the force is strong enough to compel a choice the actor otherwise wouldn't have made? Or is the gist of duress that it deprives the actor of choice altogether, rather than forcing him to make the wrong (criminal) one? In this regard, contrast duress with involuntariness (ch. 4).

2. The Model Penal Code limits duress to personal duress, i.e., to duress created by the threats made by one person upon another, rather than by the circumstances or the situation (circumstantial or situational duress). (See *Dudley & Stephens*, supra.) The limitation to "unlawful force" was apparently intended to exclude cases of situational duress. (But couldn't this have been done without reference to unlawfulness?)

Apparently the drafters were concerned that in a case where the duress arose from circumstances (like a natural disaster, or a shipwreck), the commission of a crime would go unpunished. Not so in the case of personal duress, where the source of the threat could be criminally liable. Is that necessarily so? Does the availability of duress to its target imply the criminal liability of its source? Cf. Model Penal Code § 212.5 (Criminal Coercion). Also, what's wrong with not punishing anyone if the only person involved acted under duress? Do other defenses face similar limitations? Do we have to abandon the defense of insanity because we cannot punish anyone for the acts committed by the criminally insane?

The distinction between personal and situational duress—and the recognition of one, but not the other—has been widely criticized. Here is a recent attempt to justify it:

> Conventional defenses of duress ... derive validity from features of human psychology that attribute a distinctive exculpatory force to threats that possess the three characteristic features of conventional duress, namely, (a) that the threats are *manmade*, (b) that the threats are *unlawful*, and (c) that the treats are *purposefully coercive*. Psychological experiments show that, everything else being equal, people tend to regard misfortunes that are natural in origin as more acceptable, more tolerable, than misfortunes which are manmade.
>
> Conversely, people tend to regard misfortunes that are manmade as more fearsome than misfortunes that are natural in origin. This intuition as to the relative fearsomeness of misfortunes that are manmade may be irrational and, hence, it may not in theory justify differences in legal treatment. Nevertheless, it may help explain why conventional defenses of duress give greater leeway to victims of manmade threats than defenses of necessity give victims of natural threats....
>
> Finally, and perhaps most importantly, experiments suggest that the presence of purposeful coercion tends to affect whether people regard an actor's harmful conduct as truly *his* as opposed to his *coercer's*. That is, the presence of the third party who is characteristic of relationships of duress, i.e., the presence of a coercer, tends to cause people to conclude that the one who is really harming the victim is not the coerced actor himself but the non-privileged aggressor who is applying the coercion—at least with respect to harms that, for those who are coerced into inflicting them, are not grossly unacceptable under the circumstances.

Peter Westen & James Mangiafico, "The Criminal Defense of Duress: A Justification, Not an Excuse—And Why It Matters," 6 Buff. Crim. L. Rev. 833, 937–39 (2003).

3. Distinguish duress from necessity and self-defense, under the Model Penal Code and under *Bailey* and *Toscano*. Can you account for the differences?

4. Why should duress be limited to threats that "a person of reasonable firmness in [the actor's] situation" couldn't withstand? Why not simply limit the defense to threats of death or (serious) physical injury?

5. Is the reasonableness test in duress the same as the reasonableness test in self-defense? In necessity? Why should only "stark, tangible factors" matter? What *is* a stark, tangible factor? Does it matter whether the person under duress is an ordinary citizen, a police officer, a CIA operative, a member of the President's Secret Service contingent, the victim's father? See, e.g., Penal Law of Israel § 34O ("The provisions of sections 34K and 34L [situational and personal duress] shall not apply where the person concerned is required by law or by virtue of his office to face the threat of danger."); German Penal Code § 35 (necessity as excuse only available "if

the perpetrator was not required to assume the risk with respect to a special legal relationship").

6. Should the duress defense be available in the case of threats to a third party who is not a member of the defendant's family? Should it be limited to cases where the defendant stands in some other special relationship of responsibility to the threatened party (parent-child, captain-crew)? Is a contractual relationship enough? Does it make sense to expand the scope of duress to cover threats to any third party whatsoever if American criminal law recognizes no similarly general duty to aid? (On omission liability, see supra ch. 4.)

7. Why should duress not be available as a defense to certain crimes? Murder? Treason? Assuming the threat is great enough, what difference does it make *what* offense I am forced to commit? In answering this question, does it matter whether duress is thought of as an element-negating defense, an excuse or a justification? Should duress be a defense to manslaughter, or other nonintentional crimes? Compare *People v. McManus*, supra part B (self-defense).

8. As with other mitigating considerations, an alternative (or supplement) to recognizing duress as an outright defense is to consider it at sentencing.

U.S. Sentencing Guidelines § 5K2.12. Coercion and Duress (Policy Statement).

If the defendant committed the offense because of serious coercion, blackmail or duress, under circumstances not amounting to a complete defense, the court may decrease the sentence below the applicable guideline range. The extent of the decrease ordinarily should depend on the reasonableness of the defendant's actions and on the extent to which the conduct would have been less harmful under the circumstances as the defendant believed them to be. Ordinarily coercion will be sufficiently serious to warrant departure only when it involves a threat of physical injury, substantial damage to property or similar injury resulting from the unlawful action of a third party or from a natural emergency. The Commission considered the relevance of economic hardship and determined that personal financial difficulties and economic pressures upon a trade or business do not warrant a decrease in sentence.

Courts are generally reluctant to grant downward departures based on duress. See, e.g., United States v. Keller, 376 F.3d 713 (7th Cir. 2004) (no duress departure from 18 U.S.C. § 922(g) felon-in-possession sentence for defendant who, after having been shot in the face, targeted in a drive-by shooting, and robbed at gunpoint, armed himself in fear of further gang-related violence).

9. *Escapes*. *Bailey* is only one in a long line of American cases exploring the duress defense—and the difference between duress and necessity—in prison escape cases. In some cases, courts permitted defendants to raise either necessity or compulsion (duress) defenses under fairly open-ended standards. See, e.g., People v. Unger, 66 Ill.2d 333, 362 N.E.2d 319 (1977). In still other cases, the court set out specific requirements that

the defendant must meet, such as the list of defense elements found in the leading case of People v. Lovercamp, 43 Cal.App.3d 823, 118 Cal.Rptr. 110 (1974), in which the defendants had been sexually threatened by fellow inmates over a period of several months:

> (1) The prisoner is faced with a specific threat of death, forcible sexual attack or substantial bodily injury in the immediate future;
>
> (2) There is no time for a complaint to the authorities or there exists a history of futile complaints which make any result from such complaints illusory;
>
> (3) There is no time or opportunity to resort to the courts;
>
> (4) There is no evidence of force or violence used towards prison personnel or other "innocent" persons in the escape; and
>
> (5) The prisoner immediately reports to the proper authorities when he has attained a position of safety from the immediate threat.

Note the resemblance between the strategy the court uses in *Lovercamp* and the strategy we noted that courts may use in "proximate cause" cases (see ch. 6 supra). While the Model Penal Code's general "rule" to deal with proximate cause is a vague standard (the defendant is causally responsible if the result is not too remote as to have a just bearing on liability), courts have worked out something a bit closer to narrower, more formally realizable rules to deal with the prototypical situations that most frequently arise (in causation cases, for instance, medical interveners or victim risk-taking; in necessity or duress cases, prison escapes motivated by fear of rape).

Do these *Lovercamp* elements make out a justification or an excuse, or some combination of the two? Why do we need a special test for escape cases—wouldn't the general necessity or duress defenses be enough? Then again, why should there ever be a defense to escape? Isn't the proper remedy for prison conditions—and *past* deprivations—prison reform, including beefing up internal administrative review of prisoner complaints, reducing overcrowding, improving staff training, etc.? Cf. People v. Brown, 70 Misc.2d 224 (N.Y. Sup. Ct. 1972). Doesn't pretty much every prisoner experience an often overwhelming urge to avoid the hardships of prison life by escaping? Should it matter whether the source of the duress is "ordinary" features of prison life vs. threats by fellow inmates vs. threats by prison staff vs. threats by outsiders? Or is the desire to escape so strong, so inevitable, and so universal that escape shouldn't be a crime in the first place?

10. In the typical duress or compulsion case, the defendant does something another human actor wants him to do. In the prison escape cases, of course, the would-be rapists don't force (or want) the defendants to escape custody (and thus end their availability as victims). Does this make the escape cases more like situational duress than personal duress? Or is the fact that we might punish those who threaten violence as accomplices to the escapee of a personally excused principal (see more in ch. 8) sufficient to differentiate the cases? Reconsider the Model Penal Code's "unlawfulness" element of duress in this context.

G. ENTRAPMENT

People v. Calvano

Court of Appeals of New York.
30 N.Y.2d 199, 282 N.E.2d 322, 331 N.Y.S.2d 430 (1972).

■ GIBSON, JUDGE.

The alleged commission by the defendant on November 15, 1968 of criminal acts unrelated to those for which he was on trial was proven by the People, who seek to justify the production of this ordinarily irrelevant evidence (1) as probative of disposition refuting the defense of entrapment, interposed to a charge of crime committed prior thereto, on November 11, 1968; and (2) as countering the defense of duress, interposed to a charge of crime committed thereafter, on November 19, 1968. . . .

Through the efforts of undercover police officers, aided by an informer, the defendant was indicted, and subsequently arrested and tried, upon charges of criminal possession of . . . and criminally selling a dangerous drug . . ., each committed on November 11, 1968, and with like possession and sale . . ., each committed on November 19, 1968. Defendant was, by verdict of a jury, acquitted of the . . . November 11 [charges] and convicted of the . . . November 19 [charges].

As to the November 11 transaction, involving a sale of heroin to the undercover officers, after they had been introduced to defendant by their informer, defendant . . . assert[ed] that he had been framed by the informer, . . . interpos[ing] the defense of entrapment.

As to the November 19 transaction, another sale to the same undercover officers was involved. Defendant, having interposed the defense of duress, testified that, following threats and physical compulsion by the officers, he gave to his friend, subsequently identified as an informer, $28 which the officers had given him and accompanied the informer to an unfamiliar area where the latter entered a house and returned with an envelope which defendant later gave to the officers.

On cross-examination bearing upon both the November 11 and November 19 transactions, defendant was asked whether, on November 15, 1968, he had possessed and had sold to these same officers a substance which he represented to be heroin, and this he categorically denied. Thereafter, the People recalled one of the detectives, who testified that on November 15 defendant sold to him and to the other detective envelopes containing a white powder, [which turned out not to be heroin]. . . . There was and is no suggestion that any conviction followed and ordinarily, of course, the People would be bound by defendant's denials on cross-examination and would not be permitted to produce proof in contradiction. The People . . . contend that it 'was properly admitted to establish the defendant's intent relative to the sales of heroin charged, after the element of intent was placed squarely in issue by the defenses of entrapment and duress.'

... Section 40.05 of the Penal Law provides for [the defense of entrapment], as follows: "In any prosecution for an offense, it is an affirmative defense that the defendant engaged in the proscribed conduct because he was induced or encouraged to do so by a public servant, or by a person acting in cooperation with a public servant, seeking to obtain evidence against him for the purpose of criminal prosecution, and when the methods used to obtain such evidence were such as to create a substantial risk that the offense would be committed by a person not otherwise disposed to commit it. Inducement or encouragement to commit an offense means active inducement or encouragement. Conduct merely affording a person an opportunity to commit an offense does not constitute entrapment."

Duress is also designated a defense, and section 40.00 of the Penal Law, defining it, provides, so far as here pertinent: "In any prosecution for an offense, it is an affirmative defense that the defendant engaged in the proscribed conduct because he was coerced to do so by the use or threatened imminent use of unlawful physical force upon him or a third person, which force or threatened force a person of reasonable firmness in his situation would have been unable to resist."

It is provided by section 25.00 (subd. 2) of the Penal Law that when an affirmative defense is raised, "the defendant has the burden of establishing such defense by a preponderance of the evidence" and we have recently found unwarranted the "(c)oncern (that) has been expressed whether constitutional due process limitations are invaded by placing the burden of persuasion on a defendant with respect to the defense of entrapment".

Thus, the defendant was under the burden of proving entrapment by showing that he was "a person not ... disposed to commit" the drug crimes charged, and of proving duress by satisfying the jury that he was coerced to commit them by the use or threat of force overcoming his will; and the People ... were, therefore, entitled to refute his proof by evidence of his intent or disposition to commit criminal acts of that nature. * * *

The People contend that proof of another crime is proper to rebut the defense of duress for the same reason that renders it competent to refute the claim of entrapment, that is, to rebut the denial, implicit in each defense, of any criminal intent. Concluding, as we have, that proof of other sales would be competent to rebut the entrapment defense interposed in a narcotics prosecution, it is rather clear that parity of reasoning compels the same conclusion with respect to the duress defense. Under each defense there is asserted, and a defendant may prima facie prove, absence of the criminal intent ordinarily inferable from the admitted acts of commission; under one he asserts that he was persuaded, under the other that he was coerced, i.e., "induced or encouraged" in one case (entrapment) or "coerced" in the other (duress). Indeed, the terms "induced" and "coerced" differ only in respect of the pressures exerted; so that, if prior criminal acts of the same nature may properly be proved to rebut the defense that defendant was 'coerced' into the transgression, like proof may properly be received in refutation of a claim that he was "induced or encouraged" to transgress. In one case, as in the other, his intent—meaning his will and volition—is overcome by force or by persuasion, as the case may be, exerted by another. And thus, because—and only because—defendant tenders the issue of innocent intent which his admitted acts would otherwise belie, the People should be permitted, in respect of each defense, to prove a disposition inconsistent with an intent or disposition free of criminality. * * *

Appellant contends, however, that insofar as the proof of his acts of November 15 was tendered to refute his defense of entrapment asserted against the charges of crime committed November 11, the evidence was not relevant—that 'predisposition' may not be shown by proof of subsequent acts. Ordinarily, of course, the statutory test of whether a defendant was not "disposed to commit" a drug offense would look to prior acts; but that is not to say that acts subsequently occurring or physical conditions existing as of a later time may not in some cases reflect a disposition or condition antedating the criminal act charged; and certainly they may have that effect when shown as part of a continuing transaction or a chain of events initiated before and continuing after the offense in issue. In other cases, a subsequent incident alone may sometimes be of such a nature and so related to disposition as to render proof of the incident relevant.... In this case, clearly, proof of defendant's alleged criminal acts intermediate the November 11 and November 19 incidents was, under the circumstances, relevant to the jury's consideration of defendant's disposition and volition....

Jacobson v. United States

Supreme Court of the United States.
503 U.S. 540, 112 S.Ct. 1535 (1992).

■ JUSTICE WHITE delivered the opinion of the Court.

In February 1984, petitioner, a 56–year-old veteran-turned-farmer who supported his elderly father in Nebraska, ordered two magazines and a brochure from a California adult bookstore. The magazines, entitled Bare Boys I and Bare Boys II, contained photographs of nude preteen and teenage boys.... The young men depicted in the magazines were not engaged in sexual activity, and petitioner's receipt of the magazines was legal under both federal and Nebraska law.

Within three months, the law with respect to child pornography changed; Congress passed the Act illegalizing the receipt through the mails of sexually explicit depictions of children. In the very month that the new provision became law, postal inspectors found petitioner's name on the mailing list of the California bookstore that had mailed him Bare Boys I and II. There followed over the next 2 1/2 years repeated efforts by two Government agencies, through five fictitious organizations and a bogus pen pal, to explore petitioner's willingness to break the new law by ordering sexually explicit photographs of children through the mail. * * *

[Eventually, petitioner ordered a pornographic magazine depicting young boys engaged in various sexual activities.] [He] was arrested after a controlled delivery of a photocopy of the magazine....

Petitioner was indicted for violating 18 U.S.C. § 2252(a)(2)(A)[, which criminalizes the knowing receipt through the mails of a "visual depiction [that] involves the use of a minor engaging in sexually explicit conduct...."] The trial court instructed the jury on the petitioner's entrapment defense, [and] petitioner was convicted. * * *

.... Where the Government has induced an individual to break the law and the defense of entrapment is at issue, as it was in this case, the prosecution must prove beyond reasonable doubt that the defendant was disposed to commit the criminal act prior to first being approached by Government agents.

.... [A]n agent deployed to stop the traffic in illegal drugs may offer the opportunity to buy or sell drugs and, if the offer is accepted, make an arrest on the spot or later. In such a typical case, or in a more elaborate "sting" operation involving government-sponsored fencing where the defendant is simply provided with the opportunity to commit a crime, the entrapment defense is of little use because the ready commission of the criminal act amply demonstrates the defendant's predisposition. Had the agents in this case simply offered petitioner the opportunity to order child pornography through the mails, and petitioner—who must be presumed to know the law—had promptly availed himself of this criminal opportunity, it is unlikely that his entrapment defense would have warranted a jury instruction.

But that is not what happened here. By the time petitioner finally placed his order, he had already been the target of 26 months of repeated mailings and communications from Government agents and fictitious organizations. Therefore, although he had become predisposed to break the law by May 1987, it is our view that the Government did not prove that this predisposition was independent and not the product of the attention that the Government had directed at petitioner since January 1985. * * *

... [B]y waving the banner of individual rights and disparaging the legitimacy and constitutionality of efforts to restrict the availability of sexually explicit materials, the Government not only excited petitioner's interest in sexually explicit materials banned by law but also exerted substantial pressure on petitioner to obtain and read such material as part of a fight against censorship and the infringement of individual rights. For instance, HINT[, "Heartland Institute for a New Tomorrow," a fictitious group set up by the Government], described itself as "an organization founded to protect and promote sexual freedom and freedom of choice" and stated that "the most appropriate means to accomplish [its] objectives is to promote honest dialogue among concerned individuals and to continue its lobbying efforts with State Legislators." These lobbying efforts were to be financed through catalog sales. ...

Similarly, ... two solicitations in the spring of 1987 raised the spectre of censorship while suggesting that petitioner ought to be allowed to do what he had been solicited to do. [A] mailing from the Customs Service referred to "the worldwide ban and intense enforcement on this type of material," observed that "what was legal and commonplace is now an 'underground' and secretive service," and emphasized that "[t]his environment forces us to take extreme measures" to ensure delivery. [A] Postal

Service solicitation described the concern about child pornography as "hysterical nonsense," decried "international censorship," and assured petitioner, based on consultation with "American solicitors," that an order that had been posted could not be opened for inspection without authorization of a judge. It further asked petitioner to affirm that he was not a Government agent attempting to entrap the mail order company or its customers. In these particulars, both Government solicitations suggested that receiving this material was something that petitioner ought to be allowed to do.

Petitioner's ready response to these solicitations cannot be enough to establish beyond reasonable doubt that he was predisposed, prior to the Government acts intended to create predisposition, to commit the crime of receiving child pornography through the mails. The evidence that petitioner was ready and willing to commit the offense came only after the Government had devoted 2 1/2 years to convincing him that he had or should have the right to engage in the very behavior proscribed by law. Rational jurors could not say beyond a reasonable doubt that petitioner possessed the requisite predisposition prior to the Government's investigation and that it existed independent of the Government's many and varied approaches to petitioner.

.... When the Government's quest for convictions leads to the apprehension of an otherwise law-abiding citizen who, if left to his own devices, likely would have never run afoul of the law, the courts should intervene.

Because we conclude that this is such a case and that the prosecution failed, as a matter of law, to adduce evidence to support the jury verdict that petitioner was predisposed, independent of the Government's acts and beyond a reasonable doubt, to violate the law by receiving child pornography through the mails, we reverse the Court of Appeals' judgment affirming the conviction of Keith Jacobson.

Model Penal Code § 2.13. Entrapment.

(1) A public law enforcement official or a person acting in cooperation with such an official perpetrates an entrapment if for the purpose of obtaining evidence of the commission of an offense, he induces or encourages another person to engage in conduct constituting such offense by either:

(a) making knowingly false representations designed to induce the belief that such conduct is not prohibited; or

(b) employing methods of persuasion or inducement which create a substantial risk that such an offense will be committed by persons other than those who are ready to commit it.

(2) Except as provided in Subsection (3) of this Section, a person prosecuted for an offense shall be acquitted if he proves by a preponderance of evidence that his conduct occurred in response to an entrapment. The issue of entrapment shall be tried by the Court in the absence of the jury.

(3) The defense afforded by this Section is unavailable when causing or threatening bodily injury is an element of the offense charged and the

prosecution is based on conduct causing or threatening such injury to a person other than the person perpetrating the entrapment.

QUESTIONS AND COMMENTS

1. In *Jacobson, Calvano,* and the Model Penal Code, is entrapment best thought of as an element-negating defense or an excuse? Is the point that the entrapped actor doesn't commit a crime, or that she couldn't help *but* commit a crime, or that the reason she committed a crime exculpates her? Under the various views of entrapment, what is the significance of "predisposition"? Is predisposition a type of motive? Of character? Of mens rea? Of dangerousness? In some states, the defendant may be required to admit to the crime in order to raise the entrapment defense. See, e.g., People v. Hendrickson, 45 P.3d 786 (Colo. App. 2001). Is this rule more consistent with entrapment as element-negating or as excusing?

Consider in this regard the Seventh Circuit's reading of *Jacobson*, in United States v. Hollingsworth, 27 F.3d 1196 (7th Cir. 1994) (en banc):

> We do not suggest that *Jacobson* adds a new element to the entrapment defense—"readiness" or "ability" or "dangerousness" on top of inducement and, most important, predisposition. ([I]nducement is significant chiefly as evidence bearing on predisposition: the greater the inducement, the weaker the inference that in yielding to it the defendant demonstrated that he was predisposed to commit the crime in question.) Rather, the Court clarified the meaning of predisposition. Predisposition is not a purely mental state, the state of being willing to swallow the government's bait. It has positional as well as dispositional force. The dictionary definitions of the word include "tendency" as well as "inclination." The defendant must be so situated by reason of previous training or experience or occupation or acquaintances that it is likely that if the government had not induced him to commit the crime some criminal would have done so; only then does a sting or other arranged crime take a dangerous person out of circulation. A public official is in a position to take bribes; a drug addict to deal drugs; a gun dealer to engage in illegal gun sales. For these and other traditional targets of stings all that must be shown to establish predisposition and thus defeat the defense of entrapment is willingness to violate the law without extraordinary inducements; ability can be presumed. It is different when the defendant is not in a position without the government's help to become involved in illegal activity. [To illustrate the point, consider the following hypothetical.] Suppose the government went to someone and asked him whether he would like to make money as a counterfeiter, and the reply was, "Sure, but I don't know anything about counterfeiting." Suppose the government then bought him a printer, paper, and ink, showed him how to make the counterfeit money, hired a staff for him, and got everything set up so that all he had to do was press a button to print the money; and then offered him $10,000 for some quantity of counterfeit bills.

2. For the entrapment defense to succeed, must the government's behavior be the sole cause of the defendant's criminal conduct? (And would

we accept the notion that the government is the *sole* cause unless we believed—rather mysteriously—that everyone in the defendant's position would have violated the law? Would we need entrapment to supplement duress if that were the case?) How about a contributing cause? The primary cause? In light of *Jacobson*, at what point must predisposition be present—when government officials first contact a suspect or when they first suggest the commission of a crime? Does it matter how much time separates the initial contact from the suggestion of criminal conduct?

Is it enough that the government has set up a situation so different than the situations the defendant would face in his ordinary life that we can't be certain what he would have done had he simply been *observed* in that life? Do the police "entrap" robbers preying on the homeless, then, if a police decoy lies on a street corner with $100 hanging out of his pocket, when most of the victims would have had less? How about $10,000? Should undercover police, as a matter of policy, if not of entrapment law, try only to recreate "real life" temptations? Is the point of undercover work simply to observe what we generally don't have the chance to observe, not to try to spot people willing to commit crimes in some situations?

Does the mental state of the *entrapper* matter? Do the general rules of causation apply (including foreseeability)? Is the entrapper criminally liable if the entrapped has a valid entrapment defense? Compare the approach to entrapment in civil law countries:

> In the United States, but almost nowhere else, entrapment is a defense wholly relieving the defendant from liability. Most Western European legal systems instead treat entrapment as a mode of complicity that fails to excuse the target but implicates the investigator in the crime. Defining entrapment subjectively rather than objectively, the American test largely focuses on the offender's predisposition. Even powerful inducements will fall short of entrapment if the offender is predisposed to commit the crime. By contrast, the offender's predispositions are less important to European legal systems that focus on the undercover agent's complicity. Suppose an agent offered a suspect too tempting an opportunity to commit a crime—securing, for instance, essential resources such as hard-to-get ingredients for a bomb or criminal contacts that the offender would not have been likely to locate on his own. If so, the agent may be complicit in the attempted crime, despite the target's subjective willingness to commit it. Even if the investigator has not entrapped the target, he may himself have engaged in illegal conduct by handling contraband, transferring funds, or using false documents. European legal systems treat such conduct as criminal unless a law expressly exempts the investigator from liability for specified acts. . . .
>
> Agents incur a risk of criminal liability not only by participating in crimes undercover, but also by postponing the arrest of targets until the conclusion of the covert investigation. . . . If a country lacks prosecutorial discretion and requires prosecution of all apparent offenses committed by police officials and civilians alike, undercover operatives may face a very real danger of punishment unless they confine their activities within legislatively defined bounds.

Jacqueline E. Ross, "Tradeoffs in Undercover Investigations: A Comparative Perspective," 69 U. Chi. L. Rev. 1501 (2002).

3. How important is character to the availability of an entrapment defense? See United States v. Mendoza–Prado, 314 F.3d 1099 (9th Cir. 2002) (reviewing admission of evidence of prior bad acts to prove predisposition and noting that "[t]he character of the defendant is one of the elements—indeed, it is an essential element—to be considered in determining predisposition"). Should "criminals" be entitled to the defense? Any criminal? Serious criminals? Persons convicted of (charged with? suspected of?) offenses similar (identical?) to the one they are charged with? Convicted within the last two months, three years, no matter when? Consider the following case (People v. Missrie, 300 A.D.2d 35, 751 N.Y.S.2d 16 (2002)):

> Defendant was [convicted of] conspiracy in the second degree and attempted kidnaping in the first degree stemming from conversations he had with an informant for the District Attorney's office.... At the trial, defendant asserted the affirmative defense of entrapment....
>
> [T]he court instructed the jury as follows: "In general the purpose of the defense of entrapment is to prevent a conviction of persons who although not criminals or predisposed to become criminals, nevertheless commit a crime because induced or encouraged to do so by pressure exerted by the police or people acting in cooperation with them." Counsel objected to this instruction on the ground that "it suggests that someone who is a criminal is not entitled to an entrapment defense. And a juror might infer because Isaac Missrie is a convicted felon, which he is, that he is a criminal and, therefore, not entitled to an entrapment defense." * * *
>
> We have held that the inclusion of the "although not criminals" phrase in a charge on the entrapment defense leaves the jury with the erroneous impression that the defense is available to "non-criminals" only and thus strips a defendant with a criminal record of the benefit of the defense as a matter of law.... A defendant's criminal record is only one factor to be considered by the jury in assessing his predisposition; an instruction that renders the entrapment defense unavailable to a defendant with a criminal record precludes the jury from considering any other factor.
>
> [Reversed.]

4. *Subjective vs. Objective Entrapment.* Two versions of the entrapment defense can be distinguished. Subjective entrapment focuses on the defendant; if she was "predisposed" to commit the offense, state inducement makes no difference. Objective entrapment focuses on the state; even a "predisposed" defendant can be entrapped provided the law enforcement tactics are unacceptably intrusive and overbearing.

Compare the Model Penal Code provision with the New York Penal Law provision, reproduced in *Calvano.* The Model Penal Code provision was meant to "represent[] an objective standard." Model Penal Code Commentaries § 2.13, at 411; see also id. at 406–07 (purpose of entrapment provision is not to safeguard "innocence of the defendant" but "to deter wrongful conduct on the part of the government"). Does it? The New York statute, though it follows the Model Penal Code version in many respects, is, by contrast, regarded as a *subjective* entrapment statute (as *Calvano* makes clear). Do you see the difference?

From the perspective of objective entrapment, it makes no sense to limit entrapment to "innocent" defendants, as the Model Penal Code drafters pointed out, quoting Justice Felix Frankfurter:

> Permissible police activity does not vary according to the particular defendant concerned; surely if two suspects have been solicited at the same time in the same manner, one should not go to jail simply because he has been convicted before and is said to have a criminal predisposition.

Id. at 412 (quoting Sherman v. United States, 356 U.S. 369, 383 (1958) (Frankfurter, J., concurring)).

Many jurisdictions that favor a subjective entrapment defense—including New York and federal law—also recognize a *constitutional* defense of objective entrapment, which goes by the name of "outrageous government (mis)conduct." First mentioned in Supreme Court dictum, United States v. Russell, 411 U.S. 423, 93 S.Ct. 1637 (1973) ("[W]e may some day be presented with a situation in which the conduct of law enforcement agents is so outrageous that due process principles would absolutely bar the government from invoking judicial processes to obtain a conviction."), the defense has been so unsuccessful in federal cases that it has been declared "moribund," United States v. Santana, 6 F.3d 1 (1st Cir. 1993), and even "stillborn," United States v. Boyd, 55 F.3d 239 (7th Cir. 1995). It has fared slightly better in state courts. See generally State v. Vallejos, 123 N.M. 739, 945 P.2d 957 (1997) (objective entrapment present if "police conduct created a substantial risk that an ordinary person would have been caused to commit the crime" and "police conduct exceeded the standards of proper investigation"); see also State v. Lively, 130 Wash.2d 1, 921 P.2d 1035 (1996) (successful invocation of outrageous government conduct defense).

A leading case is People v. Isaacson, 44 N.Y.2d 511 (1978), in which the New York Court of Appeals overturned the drug conviction of a defendant described as a "graduate student and teacher at Penn State University, on the brink of receiving his doctoral degree in plant physiology and biochemistry" with "no prior criminal record":

> The events leading to defendant's conviction trace back to December 5, 1974 when J. D. Breniman, a young man with an unsavory drug history, was arrested by the New York State Police in Steuben County for possession of a controlled substance in the second degree, a class A–2 felony punishable by a 15–year to life term. . . .
>
> Breniman . . . was interviewed after his arrest on December 5, 1974 at the New York State Police substation at Painted Post. [D]uring this questioning, an investigator of the New York State Police struck Breniman with such force as to knock him out of a chair, then kicked him, resulting in a cutting of his mouth and forehead, and shortly thereafter threatened to shoot him. . . .
>
> . . . Breniman agreed to assist the State Police as an informant. . . . Breniman began his informant activities by telephoning

various persons indiscriminately for the purpose of setting up drug sales in which the police would arrest the sellers. He made "collect" calls and one of the individuals contacted was defendant, whom he had known for two years through a mutual friend at State College. Defendant's version of the conversations is that Breniman cried and sobbed on the phone, relating that he was facing 15 years to life in Attica, that his parents had effectively cast him from the family home, that he was running out of friends, and that he was looking for ways to make money to hire a decent lawyer. . . .

Between December 24, 1974 and January 4, 1975, Breniman made seven phone calls to defendant before finally arranging a sale. Initially, he sought to buy heroin, but defendant flatly refused. As to cocaine, defendant tried to put him off by saying that there was nothing worthwhile, but Breniman persisted in his efforts to get defendant to make a sale.

. . . . Defendant's studies and his teaching responsibilities required him to work 12 to 14 hours a day. He did not have access to someone who could supply him with the cocaine the two ounces worth $3,800 which Breniman was seeking but Denise Marcon, [his roommate,] did. She called a girl friend who gave her a number at which to contact a man known as "Zorch". . . .

The sale was scheduled for January 4, 1975. . . . Defendant feared New York's drug laws and did not want to enter the State, but the investigator instructed Breniman that the transaction must take place in New York where he had authority to make an arrest. To cause defendant to sell drugs in this State, Breniman cleverly kept changing the destination, progressively northward, culminating in an arrangement by which defendant would make a three-or four-hour trip to meet at a place near the Pennsylvania–New York border, at a spot where it would be difficult for defendant to ascertain his location. . . .

The meeting place finally settled upon was the Whiffle Tree Bar, which Breniman told defendant was in Lawrenceville[, Pennsylvania]. What Breniman did know, and defendant did not, was that the bar was actually in the Town of Lindley, Steuben County, New York. Traveling north on Route 15 in Pennsylvania toward Lawrenceville, the only clear indication a motorist might have that he is leaving Pennsylvania is a sign adjacent to the southerly approach of a bridge spanning the Cowanesque River and welcoming the traveler to New York State. Actually, the State line is several hundred yards southerly of the bridge and is designated by a stone marker, which at the time of defendant's visit had crumbled and was obscured in the vegetation alongside the road. The Whiffle Tree Bar is situated between the hidden stone marker and the bridge sign and thus is located in the Town of Lindley in New York State, rather than in Lawrenceville, Pennsylvania, as defendant had been led to believe. . . .

Defendant engaged in a rather elaborate method of delivering the cocaine, including an arrangement to have Denise Marcon drive along in a separate vehicle conveying the contraband and the toting beneath his shirt of a plastic bag containing a nonnarcotic substance with a cocaine appearance to be turned over in the event of a "rip-off". He testified these precautions were suggested by Zorch, the supplier....

Defendant's precautions notwithstanding, he was arrested in the course of the transaction outside of the Whiffle Tree Bar....

In reversing the conviction, the court set out four much-cited "illustrative" factors to test an outrageous conduct defense: "(1) whether the police manufactured a crime which otherwise would not likely have occurred, or merely involved themselves in an ongoing criminal activity; (2) whether the police themselves engaged in criminal or improper conduct repugnant to a sense of justice; (3) whether the defendant's reluctance to commit the crime is overcome by appeals to humanitarian instincts such as sympathy or past friendship, by temptation of exorbitant gain, or by persistent solicitation in the face of unwillingness; and (4) whether the record reveals simply a desire to obtain a conviction with no reading that the police motive is to prevent further crime or protect the populace."

What does objective entrapment have to do with the question of the defendant's criminal liability? Assuming the defendant was ready to commit the crime, what difference does it make how outrageous the government's conduct was? Under any of the traditional rationales of punishment? Do we bar conviction in such cases because we see no other good ways of deterring the police conduct? (Think about evidentiary exclusionary rules for, say, coerced confessions or unreasonable searches.) Do we bar convictions because courts should not be complicit in any way, with grievous wrongdoers, and should dissociate themselves from government misconduct?

Does the distinction between subjective and objective entrapment make much practical difference? Could *Jacobson* have been decided as an objective entrapment case? Was the problem that Jacobson wasn't interested in ordering illegal pornography or that the government's efforts to foster and exploit that interest were beyond the pale (wasteful? disproportionate to the seriousness of the offense?)? Could *Isaacson* have been decided on subjective entrapment grounds? If *Jacobson* is a subjective entrapment case, why isn't *Isaacson*?

5. *Sentencing Entrapment.* A defendant who is predisposed to commit a crime—and therefore would not qualify for an outright acquittal under a subjective theory of entrapment—may be able to avoid conviction of a greater crime by arguing "sentencing entrapment." This defense is particularly useful—at least potentially—in drug cases. For instance, a defendant may argue that while she was predisposed to possess a quantity of drugs that would expose her to liability for simple drug possession, law enforcement officers entrapped her into possessing a larger quantity of drugs that exposed her to liability for the greater crime of possession with intent to distribute. See, e.g., Leech v. State, 66 P.3d 987 (Okla. Crim. App. 2003). Or a defendant might have offered to sell an undercover agent marijuana, who then induced her to sell him crack cocaine instead (thus manipulating the identity, rather than the quantity of the drug). Sentencing enhancement arguments—if they are accepted by courts at all—rarely succeed. Why do you think that is?

6. *Duress*. Compare entrapment to duress. Is *Calvano* right to treat them as two sides of the same coin? Should entrapment be limited to inducements by government agents? Why would entrapment not apply to every type of offense (see MPC § 2.13(3))?

7. *Entrapment by Estoppel*. Compare § 2.13(1)(a) with the defense of ignorance of law (see, e.g., MPC § 2.04(3)). (Could *Jacobson* make a mistake of law argument?) For a case discussing the constitutional defense of "entrapment by estoppel," see United States v. Nichols, 21 F.3d 1016, 1018 (10th Cir. 1994) ("The defense of entrapment by estoppel is implicated where an agent of the government affirmatively misleads a party as to the state of the law and that party proceeds to act on the misrepresentation so that criminal prosecution of the actor implicates due process concerns.... [T]he defendant's reliance must be reasonable in light of the identity of the agent, the point of law misrepresented, and the substance of the misrepresentation."). What's the connection between this defense and the principle of legality (see ch. 2)?

What if the defendant followed a specific order by a police officer to engage in the conduct that gives rise to the charges against him? Does it matter whether the officer giving the order knew (intended, or suspected, or should have suspected) that the defendant would engage in criminal (or unlawful) conduct pursuant to her order? Does the *defendant* have to know he is being ordered to commit a crime? See, e.g., State v. Fogarty, 128 N.J. 59 (1992) (upholding DWI conviction in a case where the intoxicated defendant had been ordered to drive off by a police officer trying to break up a parking lot scuffle); cf. Penal Law of Israel § 34M(2) ("A person shall bear no criminal liability for an act done by him [when] he does it on the order of a competent authority while bound under law to obey such authority, save where the order is manifestly unlawful.").

What if the defendant is a soldier following orders? See, e.g., United States v. Calley, 22 U.S.C.M.A. 534 (1973) (My Lai case) ("The acts of a subordinate done in compliance with an unlawful order given him by his superior are excused and impose no criminal liability upon him unless the superior's order is one which a man of ordinary sense and understanding would, under the circumstances, know to be unlawful, or if the order in question is actually known to the accused to be unlawful."); see also Model Penal Code § 2.10 ("It is an affirmative defense that the actor, in engaging in the conduct charged to constitute an offense, does no more than execute an order of his superior in the armed services which he does not know to be unlawful."). How does the superior orders defense differ from entrapment by estoppel? Some regard the superior orders defense as necessary for the proper functioning of the armed forces, particularly in times of war. Others focus on the extraordinary power military superiors hold over subordinates. Under either view, would superior orders constitute a justification or an excuse? Should a version of the superior orders defense be available outside the military context? Consider the following case:

> A woman who nursed her infant while driving 65 mph on the Ohio Turnpike was found innocent Friday of child endangerment but convicted of three other charges.

> Catherine Nicole Donkers, 29, was found guilty of violating child-restraint laws, driving without a valid driver's license and fleeing police.
>
> She said her husband, Brad Lee Barnhill, ordered her by cell phone to breast-feed the baby while she drove from Pennsylvania to Michigan in May.
>
> Police stopped Donkers after a trucker called 911 to report he had seen a woman driver holding a baby on her lap. Donkers refused to pull over for three miles as a state trooper pursued her. . . .
>
> Donkers, who represented herself, said she did nothing wrong and was following her husband's orders. The two belong to the First Christian Fellowship for Eternal Sovereignty. . . .

"Nursing Driver Innocent of Endangerment," N.Y. Times, Aug. 8, 2003.

Note that traditionally a wife could raise duress as a defense if she acted on her husband's orders. But see Model Penal Code § 2.09(3) ("It is not a defense that a woman acted on the command of her husband. . . . [The presumption that a woman, acting in the presence of her husband, is coerced is abolished.]")

H. Mental Disease or Defect (Insanity and Immaturity)

M'Naghten's Case

House of Lords.
10 Clark & F. 200, 2 Eng. Rep. 718 (1843).

[Daniel M'Naghten killed the Prime Minister's Secretary, Edward Drummond, under an insane belief that the government was persecuting him, having mistaken Drummond for the Prime Minister. He was found not guilty on the ground of insanity.]

This verdict, and the question of the nature and extent of the unsoundness of mind which would excuse the commission of a felony of this sort, having been made the subject of debate in the House of Lords, it was determined to take the opinion of the Judges on the law governing such cases. Accordingly, [o]n the 19th of June, 1843, the Judges . . . attended the House of Lords; when (no argument having been had) the following questions of law were propounded to them:—

> . . . .
>
> 2d. What are the proper questions to be submitted to the jury, when a person alleged to be afflicted with insane delusion respecting one or more particular subjects or persons, is charged with the commission of a crime (murder, for example), and insanity is set up as a defence?
>
> 3d. In what terms ought the question to be left to the jury, as to the prisoner's state of mind at the time when the act was committed?

. . . .

Lord Chief Justice Tindal:—My Lords, Her Majesty's Judges, in answering the questions proposed to them by your Lordships' House, think it right, in the first place, to state that they have forborne entering into any particular discussion upon these questions, from the extreme and almost insuperable difficulty of applying those answers to cases in which the facts are not brought judicially before them. The facts of each particular case must of necessity present themselves with endless variety, and with every shade of difference in each case; and as it is their duty to declare the law upon each particular case, on facts proved before them, and after hearing argument of counsel thereon, they deem it at once impracticable, and at the same time dangerous to the administration of justice, if it were practicable, to attempt to make minute applications of the principles involved in the answers given by them to your Lordships' questions. * * *

. . . . [A]s these two questions appear to us to be more conveniently answered together, we have to submit our opinion to be, that the jurors ought to be told in all cases that every man is to be presumed to be sane, and to possess a sufficient degree of reason to be responsible for his crimes, until the contrary be proved to their satisfaction; and that to establish a defence on the ground of insanity, it must be clearly proved that, at the time of the committing of the act, the party accused was labouring under such a defect of reason, from disease of the mind, as not to know the nature and quality of the act he was doing; or, if he did know it, that he did not know he was doing what was wrong. . . .

People v. Schmidt

Court of Appeals of New York.
216 N.Y. 324 (1915).

■ CARDOZO, J.

[The defendant confessed to the murder of Anna Aumuller.] He told the physicians who examined him that he had heard the voice of God calling upon him to kill the woman as a sacrifice and atonement. . . . [A jury] found him guilty of murder in the first degree [and he was subsequently sentenced to death.] * * *

The defendant [argues that the trial judge's instruction on the insanity defense was in error.] The rule of our statute is that "a person is not excused from criminal liability as an idiot, imbecile, lunatic or insane person, except upon proof that, at the time of committing the alleged criminal act, he was laboring under such a defect of reason as: (1) not to know the nature and quality of the act he was doing; or (2) not to know that the act was wrong" (Penal Law, § 1120). The learned trial judge said to the jury that "wrong" in this definition means "contrary to the law of the state." The jury was instructed in pointed and impressive terms, that even if the defendant believed in good faith that God had appeared to him and commanded the sacrifice of Anna Aumuller, and this belief was a delusion, the result of a defect of reason, the defendant must none the less answer to the law if he knew the nature and quality of the act, and knew that it was wrong, in the sense that it was forbidden by the law of the state. . . .

We are unable to accept the view that the word "wrong" in the statutory definition is to receive so narrow a construction. We must interpret the rule in the light of its history. That history has been often sketched. In the beginning of our law the madman charged with murder was not acquitted. A special verdict was given that he was mad, and then the king pardoned him. There was the same need of the royal pardon for homicide by misadventure or in self-defense. "The man who commits homicide by misadventure or self defense deserves but needs a pardon". "If the justices have before them a man who, as a verdict declares, has done a deed of this kind, they do not acquit him, nor can they pardon him, they bid him hope for the king's mercy". Then came the age of what has become known as the "wild beast test." The law of that age and of later days has been adequately stated by Judge Doe in State v. Pike (49 N. H. 399) and by Judge Ladd, writing for the same court, in State v. Jones (50 N. H. 369). "The defendant was not excused unless he was totally deprived of his reason, understanding and memory, and did not know what he was doing any more than a wild beast" (Arnold's Case, 16 Howell's State Trials, 764). As late as 1800, in Hadfield's Case (27 St. Tr. 1288), that test was announced as law. The first departure from the ancient rule came in 1812. The capacity to distinguish right from wrong was then put forward as another test. As propounded in these cases, it meant a capacity to distinguish right from wrong, not with reference to the particular act, but generally or in the abstract. Sometimes it was spoken of as a capacity to distinguish between "good and evil". Wrong was conceived of as synonymous not with legal but rather with moral wrong. Lord Mansfield told the jury in Bellingham's case: "It must be proved beyond all doubt that at the time he committed the atrocious act, he did not consider that murder was a crime against the laws of God and nature." That became for many years the classic definition. . . .

Then in 1843 came the famous decision of the House of Lords in M'Naghten's Case (10 Cl. & F. 200). It is idle to look to this decision for precise and scientific statement. The judges passed, not on a concrete case, but on hypothetical questions addressed to them by the lords. * * *

The definition . . . propounded [in M'Naghten's Case] is the one that has been carried forward into our statute. The judges expressly held that a defendant who knew nothing of the law would none the less be responsible if he knew that the act was wrong, by which, therefore, they must have meant, if he knew that it was morally wrong. Whether he would also be responsible if he knew that it was against the law, but did not know it to be morally wrong, is a question that was not considered. In most cases, of course, knowledge that an act is illegal will justify the inference of knowledge that it is wrong. But none the less it is the knowledge of wrong, conceived of as moral wrong, that seems to have been established by that decision as the controlling test. * * *

In the light of all [the relevant] precedents, it is impossible, we think, to say that there is any decisive adjudication which limits the word "wrong" in the statutory definition to legal as opposed to moral wrong. . . .

We must, therefore, give that construction to the statute which seems to us most consonant with reason and justice. . . . We must not . . . exaggerate the rigor of the rule by giving the word "wrong" a strained interpretation, at war with its broad and primary meaning, and least of all, if in so doing, we rob the rule of all relation to the mental health and true capacity of the criminal. The interpretation placed upon the statute by the trial judge may be tested by its consequences. A mother kills her infant child to whom she has been devotedly attached. She knows the nature and quality of the act; she knows that the law condemns it; but she is inspired by an insane delusion that God has appeared to her and ordained the sacrifice. It seems a mockery to say that, within the meaning of the statute, she knows that the act is wrong. If the definition propounded by the trial judge is right, it would be the duty of a jury to hold her responsible for the crime. We find nothing either in the history of the rule, or in its reason and purpose, or in judicial exposition of its meaning, to justify a conclusion so abhorrent. No jury would be likely to find a defendant responsible in such a case, whatever a judge might tell them. But we cannot bring ourselves to believe that in declining to yield to such a construction of the statute, they would violate the law.

We hold, therefore, that there are times and circumstances in which the word "wrong" as used in the statutory test of responsibility ought not to be limited to legal wrong. . . . Knowledge that an act is forbidden by law will in most cases permit the inference of knowledge that, according to the accepted standards of mankind, it is also condemned as an offense against good morals. Obedience to the law is itself a moral duty. If, however, there is an insane delusion that God has appeared to the defendant and ordained the commission of a crime, we think it cannot be said of the offender that he knows the act to be wrong. It is not enough, to relieve from criminal liability, that the prisoner is morally depraved. It is not enough that he has views of right and wrong at variance with those that find expression in the law. The variance must have its origin in some disease of the mind. The anarchist is not at liberty to break the law because he reasons that all government is wrong. The devotee of a religious cult that enjoins polygamy or human sacrifice as a duty is not thereby relieved from responsibility before the law. In such cases the belief, however false according to our own standards, is not the product of disease. Cases will doubtless arise where criminals will take shelter behind a professed belief that their crime was ordained by God, just as this defendant attempted to shelter himself behind that belief. We can safely leave such fabrications to the common sense of juries.

We have considered the charge of the trial judge upon the subject of insanity [and] hold that there was error in the charge. [Nonetheless,] we think the error does not require us to disturb the judgment of conviction. It is of no importance now whether the trial judge charged the jury correctly upon the question of insanity, because in the record before us the defendant himself concedes that he is sane, and that everything which he said to the contrary was a fraud upon the court. . . . We hold, therefore, that the defendant has forfeited the right to avail himself of the error in the charge. . . . [W]e will not aid the defendant in his effort to gain the benefit of a fraudulent defense.

The judgment of conviction should be affirmed.

United States v. Brawner

United States Court of Appeals, District of Columbia Circuit.
471 F.2d 969 (1972) (en banc).

■ LEVENTHAL, CIRCUIT JUDGE.

The principal issues raised on this appeal from a conviction for second degree murder and carrying a dangerous weapon relate to appellant's defense of insanity. After the case was argued to a division of the court, the court sua sponte ordered rehearing en banc. We identified our intention to reconsider the appropriate standard for the insanity defense. * * *

We have stretched our canvas wide; and the focal point of the landscape before us is the formulation of the American Law Institute. The ALI's primary provision is stated thus in its Model Penal Code, see § 4.01(1).

Section 4.01 Mental Disease or Defect Excluding Responsibility.

> (1) A person is not responsible for criminal conduct if at the time of such conduct as a result of mental disease or defect he lacks substantial capacity either to appreciate the criminality [wrongfulness] of his conduct or to conform his conduct to the requirements of the law.

We have decided to adopt the ALI rule as the doctrine excluding responsibility for mental disease or defect. * * *

The landmark opinion [on the insanity defense in our jurisdiction] was written by Judge Bazelon in Durham v. United States, 94 U.S.App.D.C. 228, 214 F.2d 862 (1954). Prior to Durham the law of the District of Columbia was established by United States v. Lee, 15 D.C. (4 Mackey) 489, 496 (1886) and Smith v. United States, 59 App.D.C. 144, 36 F.2d 548 (1929), which, taken together, stated a traditional test of insanity, in terms of right and wrong[2] and irresistible impulse.[3] Durham adopted the "product rule," pioneered in State v. Pike, 49 N. H. 399, 402 (1869–70), and exculpated from criminal responsibility those whose forbidden acts were the product of a mental disease or defect.

Few cases have evoked as much comment as Durham. It has sparked widespread interest in the legal-judicial community and focused attention on the profound problems involved in defining legal responsibility in case of mental illness....

2. United States v. Lee, 15 D.C. 489, 496 (1886):

> The rule of law is very plain that in order that the plea of insanity shall prevail, there must have been that mental condition of the party which disabled him from distinguishing between right and wrong in respect of the act committed.

3. Smith v. United States, 59 App.D.C. 144, 145, 36 F.2d 548, 549 (1929):

> [it must be found that defendant's] reasoning powers were so far dethroned by his diseased mental condition as to deprive him of the will power to resist the insane impulse to perpetrate the deed, though knowing it to be wrong.

The first of these was a problem of language which raised an important symbolic issue in the law. We felt that the language of the old right-wrong/irresistible impulse rule for insanity was antiquated, no longer reflecting the community's judgment as to who ought to be held criminally liable for socially destructive acts. We considered the rule as restated to have more fruitful, accurate and considered reflection of the sensibilities of the community as revised and expanded in the light of continued study of abnormal human behavior.

The second vexing problem that Durham was designed to reach related to the concern of the psychiatrists called as expert witnesses for their special knowledge of the problem of insanity, who often and typically felt that they were obliged to reach outside of their professional expertise when they were asked, under the traditional insanity rule established in 1843 by M'Naghten's Case, whether the defendant knew right from wrong. They further felt that the narrowness of the traditional test, which framed the issue of responsibility solely in terms of cognitive impairment, made it impossible to convey to the judge and jury the full range of information material to an assessment of defendant's responsibility.

Discerning scholarship now available asserts that the experts' fears and concerns reflected a misapprehension as to the impact of the traditional standard in terms of excluding relevant evidence.... Wigmore states the rule to be that when insanity is in issue, "any and all conduct of the person is admissible in evidence." And the cases support Wigmore's view. The almost unvarying policy of the courts has been to admit any evidence of aberrational behavior so long as it is probative of the defendant's mental condition, without regard to the supposed restrictions of the test used to define insanity for the jury.

Moreover if the term "know" in the traditional test of "know right from wrong" is taken as denoting affective knowledge, rather than merely cognitive knowledge, it yields a rule of greater flexibility than was widely supposed to exist. Livermore and Meehl, The Virtues of M'Naghten, 51 Minn.L.Rev. 789, 800–08 (1967).

... In any event, [t]he rule as reformulated in Durham permitted medical experts to testify on medical matters properly put before the jury for its consideration, and to do so without the confusion that many, perhaps most, experts experienced from testimony structured under the M'Naghten rule. That was a positive contribution to jurisprudence—and one that was retained when the American Law Institute undertook to analyze the problem and proposed a different formulation.

A difficulty arose under the Durham rule in application. The rule was devised to facilitate the giving of testimony by medical experts in the context of a legal rule, with the jury called upon to reach a composite conclusion that had medical, legal and moral components. However the pristine statement of the Durham rule opened the door to "trial by label." Durham did distinguish between "disease," as used "in the sense of a condition which is considered capable of either improving or deteriorating," and "defect," as referring to a condition not capable of such change "and which may be either congenital or the result of injury, or the residual effect of a physical or mental disease." But the court failed to explicate what abnormality of mind was an essential ingredient of these concepts. In the absence of a definition of "mental disease or defect," medical experts attached to them the meanings which would naturally occur to them—medical meanings—and gave testimony accordingly. The problem was dramatically highlighted by the weekend flip flop case, In re Rosenfield, 157 F.Supp. 18 (D.D.C.1957). The petitioner was described as a sociopath. A St. Elizabeth's psychiatrist testified that a person with a sociopathic personality was not suffering from a mental disease. That was Friday afternoon. On Monday morning, through a policy change at St. Elizabeth's Hospital, it was determined as an administrative matter that the state of a psychopathic or sociopathic personality did constitute a mental disease.

The concern that medical terminology not control legal outcomes culminated in McDonald v. United States, 114 U.S.App. D.C. 120, 312 F.2d 847, 851 (en banc, 1962), where this court recognized that the term, mental disease or defect, ... means one thing to a physician bent on treatment, but something different, if somewhat overlapping, to a court of law. We provided a legal definition of mental disease or defect, and held that it included "any abnormal condition of the mind which substantially affects mental or emotional processes and substantially impairs behavior controls." ...

The Durham rule also required explication along other lines, notably the resolution of the ambiguity inherent in the formulation concerning actions that were the "product" of mental illness. It was supplemented in Carter v. United States, 102 U.S.App.D.C. 227 at 234, 235, 252 F.2d 608 at 615–616 (1957):

> The simple fact that a person has a mental disease or defect is not enough to relieve him of responsibility for a crime. There must be a relationship between the disease and the criminal act; and the relationship must be such as to justify a reasonable inference that the act would not have been committed if the person had not been suffering from the disease.

Thus Carter clarified that the mental illness must not merely have entered into the production of the act, but must have played a necessary role. Carter identified the "product" element of the rule with the "but for" variety of causation. * * *

As early as Carter, we had warned that the function of an expert was to explain the origin, development and manifestations of mental disorders, in terms that would be coherent and meaningful to the jury. "Unexplained medical labels ... are not enough." (102 U.S.App.D.C. at 236, 252 F.2d at 617). [Nonetheless,] we continued to see cases where the testimony of the experts was limited to the use of conclusory labels, without the explication of the underlying analysis....

The American Law Institute's Model Penal Code expressed a rule which has become the dominant force in the law pertaining to the defense of insanity. The ALI rule is eclectic in spirit, partaking of the moral focus of M'Naghten, the practical accommodation of the "control rules" (a term more exact and less susceptible of misunderstanding than "irresistible impulse" terminology), and responsive, at the same time, to a relatively modern, forward-looking view of what is encompassed in "knowledge." * * *

The core rule of the ALI has been adopted, with variations, by all save one of the federal circuit courts of appeals, and by all that have come to reconsider the doctrine providing exculpation for mental illness. * * *

A principal reason for our decision to depart from the Durham rule is the undesirable characteristic ... of undue dominance by the experts giving testimony.... The difficulty is rooted in the circumstance that there is no generally accepted understanding, either in the jury or the community it represents, of the concept requiring that the crime be the "product" of the mental disease. * * *

The experts have meaningful information to impart, not only on the existence of mental illness or not, but also on its relationship to the incident charged as an offense. In the interest of justice this valued information should be available, and should not be lost or blocked by requirements that unnaturally restrict communication between the experts and the jury. The more we have pondered the problem the more convinced we have become that the sound solution lies not in further shaping of the Durham "product" approach in more refined molds, but in adopting the ALI's formulation as the linchpin of our jurisprudence.

The ALI's formulation retains the core requirement of a meaningful relationship between the mental illness and the incident charged. The language in the ALI rule is sufficiently in the common ken that its use in the courtroom, or in preparation for trial, permits a reasonable three-way communication—between (a) the law-trained, judges and lawyers; (b) the experts and (c) the jurymen—without insisting on a vocabulary that is either stilted or stultified, or conducive to a testimonial mystique permitting expert dominance and encroachment on the jury's function....

Our ruling today includes our decision that in the ALI rule as adopted by this court the term "mental disease or defect" includes the definition of that term provided in our 1962 en banc McDonald opinion, as follows:

> [A] mental disease or defect includes any abnormal condition of the mind which substantially affects mental or emotional processes and substantially impairs behavior controls.

McDonald v. United States, 114 U.S.App. D.C. 120, 312 F.2d 847, 851 (en banc, 1962). * * *

A number of proposals in the journals recommend that the insanity defense be abolished altogether. This is advocated in the amicus brief of the National District Attorneys Association as both desirable and lawful.[17] The amicus brief of American Psychiatric Association concludes it would be desirable, with appropriate safeguards, but would require a constitutional amendment....

This proposal has been put forward by responsible judges for consideration, with the objective of reserving psychiatric overview for the phase of

17. It suggests that a mental condition be exculpatory solely as it negatives mens rea.

the criminal process concerned with disposition of the person determined to have been the actor....

.... Criminal responsibility is assessed when through "free will" a man elects to do evil. And while ... the legislature has dispensed with the mental element in some statutory offenses, in furtherance of a paramount need of the community, these instances mark the exception and not the rule, and only in the most limited instances has the mental element been omitted by the legislature as a requisite for an offense that was a crime at common law.

The concept of lack of "free will" is both the root of origin of the insanity defense and the line of its growth. This cherished principle is not undercut by difficulties, or differences of view, as to how best to express the free will concept in the light of the expansion of medical knowledge. We do not concur in the view of the National District Attorneys Association that the insanity defense should be abandoned judicially, either because it is at too great a variance with popular conceptions of guilt or fails "to show proper respect for the personality of the criminal [who] is liable to resent pathology more than punishment."[22] * * *

To obviate any misunderstanding from our rejection of the recommendation of those proposing judicial abolition of the insanity defense, we expressly commend their emphasis on the need for improvement of dispositional resources and programs. The defense focuses on the kind of impairment that warrants exculpation, and necessarily assigns to the prison walls many men who have serious mental impairments and difficulties. The needs of society—rooted not only in humanity but in practical need for attempting to break the recidivist cycles, and halt the spread of deviant behavior—call for the provision of psychiatrists, psychologists and counselors to help men with these mental afflictions and difficulties, as part of a total effort toward a readjustment that will permit re-integration in society.

We have also pondered the suggestion that the jury be instructed that the defendant lacks criminal responsibility if the jury finds that the defendant's mental disease impairs his capacity or controls to such an extent that he cannot "justly be held responsible."

This was the view ... proposed in 1955 by Professor Wechsler, the distinguished Reporter for the ALI's Model Penal Code, and sustained by some, albeit a minority, of the members of the ALI's Council.[24] In the ALI, the contrary view prevailed because of a concern over presenting to the jury questions put primarily in the form of "justice."

22. Citing Harris, Respect for Persons in Ethics and Society 129–130 (R. De George ed. 1966).

24. The minority, together with the Reporter for the Model Penal Code (Professor Herbert Wechsler), proposed the following test of insanity:

> A person is not responsible for criminal conduct if at the time of such conduct as a result of mental disease or defect his capacity either to appreciate the criminality of his conduct or to conform his conduct to the requirements of law is so substantially impaired that he cannot justly be held responsible.

This proposal appears as alternative (a) to paragraph (1) of Model Penal Code § 4.01 (Tent. Draft No. 4, 1955).

The proposal is not to be condemned out of hand as a suggestion that the jury be informed of an absolute prerogative that it can only exercise by flatly disregarding the applicable rule of law.... However, there is a substantial concern that an instruction overtly cast in terms of "justice" cannot feasibly be restricted to the ambit of what may properly be taken into account but will splash with unconfinable and malign consequences. The Government cautions that "explicit appeals to 'justice' will result in litigation of extraneous issues and will encourage improper arguments to the jury phrased solely in terms of 'sympathy' and 'prejudice.' "

Nor is this solely a prosecutor's concern. Mr. Flynn, counsel appointed to represent defendant, puts it that even though the jury is applying community concepts of blameworthiness "the jury should not be left at large, or asked to find out for itself what those concepts are." * * *

We are impressed by the observation of Professor Abraham S. Goldstein, one of the most careful students of the problem:

> [The] overly general standard may place too great a burden upon the jury. If the law provides no standard, members of the jury are placed in the difficult position of having to find a man responsible for no other reason than their personal feeling about him. Whether the psyches of individual jurors are strong enough to make that decision, or whether the "law" should put that obligation on them, is open to serious question. It is far easier for them to perform the role assigned to them by legislature and courts if they know-or are able to rationalize-that their verdicts are "required" by law.

A. Goldstein, The Insanity Defense 81–82 (1967). * * *

It is the sense of justice propounded by those charged with making and declaring the law—legislatures and courts—that lays down the rule that persons without substantial capacity to know or control the act shall be excused. The jury is concerned with applying the community understanding of this broad rule to particular lay and medical facts. Where the matter is unclear it naturally will call on its own sense of justice to help it determine the matter. There is wisdom in the view that a jury generally understands well enough that an instruction composed in flexible terms gives it sufficient latitude so that, without disregarding the instruction, it can provide that application of the instruction which harmonizes with its sense of justice.... It is one thing, however, to tolerate and even welcome the jury's sense of equity as a force that affects its application of instructions which state the legal rules that crystallize the requirements of justice as determined by the lawmakers of the community. It is quite another to set the jury at large, without such crystallization, to evolve its own legal rules and standards of justice. It would likely be counter-productive and contrary to the larger interest of justice to become so explicit—in an effort to hammer the point home to the very occasional jury that would otherwise be too rigid—that one puts serious strains on the normal operation of the system of criminal justice.

Taking all these considerations into account we conclude that the ALI rule as announced is not productive of injustice, and we decline to proclaim the broad "justly responsible" standard. * * *

The case is remanded for further consideration by the District Court in accordance with this opinion.

So ordered.

QUESTIONS AND COMMENTS

1. The two prongs of the Model Penal Code insanity test are often labeled *cognitive* and *volitional*, referring to a cognitive capacity to know (or "appreciate") the difference between right and wrong and to a volitional capacity to exercise one's free will to act according to one's appreciation of that difference. The volitional prong evolved from "irresistible impulse" instructions given in an effort to expand the scope of *M'Naghten* beyond cognitive defects.

Is insanity—cognitive or volitional—an element-negating defense or an excuse? Could it ever be a justification? Why? What elements could evidence of insanity negate—actus reus, mens rea? If insanity is an excuse, what is the basis for not holding an insane defendant responsible for her concededly criminal and unjustifiable act? That she couldn't help herself? That she lacked free will? In general? In the particular case? Under what theory of punishment?

2. From the perspectives of the various rationales for punishment, does evidence of insanity necessarily exculpate? Might it aggravate, rather than mitigate, punishment?

3. Compare the insanity defense to other defenses:

How does insanity relate to the voluntariness component of the act requirement? See, e.g., People v. Grant, 46 Ill.App.3d 125, 360 N.E.2d 809, 4 Ill.Dec. 696 (1977) (epileptic seizure).

The intoxication defense? See, e.g., Model Penal Code § 2.08(3) ("Intoxication does not, in itself, constitute mental disease."), (4)(a) ("Intoxication which (a) is not self-induced or (b) is pathological is an affirmative defense if by reason of such intoxication the actor at the time of his conduct lacks substantial capacity either to appreciate its criminality [wrongfulness] or to conform his conduct to the requirements of law."), (5)(a) ("intoxication" defined as "disturbance of mental or physical capacities resulting from the introduction of substances into the body"). Note that the diagnosis of pathological (or "idiosyncratic") intoxication—defined as marked behavioral change, usually aggressiveness, following the ingestion of a relatively small amount of alcohol—is no longer included in the most recent edition of the standard psychiatric reference work, the Diagnostic and Statistical Manual of Mental Disorders (DSM).

Mistake of law? See, e.g., Model Penal Code § 2.04(3). What does a defendant who raises an insanity defense claim to be mistaken about? Is she making a mistake of fact, of legal fact, or of (governing?) law? Does it make sense to think of a person suffering from a mental disease or defect as making a mistake?

Necessity (balance of evils)? Can the issues in *M'Naghten* and *Schmidt* be reframed in necessity terms? Is (cognitive) insanity a mistake about the conditions of necessity?

Provocation? See, e.g., Model Penal Code § 210.3(1)(b) ("extreme *mental* or emotional disturbance for which there is reasonable explanation or excuse").

More generally, is insanity an excuse in the same sense that, say, duress is, or entrapment? Does it make sense to distinguish between insanity as an *incapacity* defense and duress as an *inability* defense, insofar as insanity involves the lack of some fundamental capacity—cognitive or volitional—and duress the inability to exercise that capacity in particular circumstances (a threat, an enticement)? Or do they all share a common characteristic, like unavoidability, or irresponsibility? Note that some criminal codes draw a clear distinction between insanity (and immaturity) and other excuses; others do not. Contrast Model Penal Code art. 4 ("responsibility," including insanity and immaturity) with N.Y. Penal Law art. 40 ("other defenses involving lack of culpability," including duress, entrapment, and insanity) and Tex. Penal Code ch. 8 ("general defenses to criminal responsibility," including insanity, duress, and entrapment).

4. *Mens Rea.* As *Brawner* points out, those who call for the abandonment of the insanity defense do not call for the rejection of evidence of insanity for any purpose. In particular, critics of the insanity defense often are quick to point out that evidence of insanity could always be used to negate any mental state required in the definition of the statute. See, e.g., Model Penal Code § 4.02(1). What difference does it make whether there is a separate defense of insanity or not? What about strict liability offenses (elements)? What would be the verdict if a defendant succeeded in negating mens rea on the basis of insanity evidence? Do the statutes abandoning the insanity defense imply that insanity would be irrelevant for purposes of the voluntariness requirement or provocation?

5. In recent decades, several states have curtailed the insanity defense. They did so in various ways. Some "abandoned" the defense altogether, restricting evidence of insanity to mens rea. See, e.g., Kan. Stat. Ann. § 22–3220 ("It is a defense to a prosecution under any statute that the defendant, as a result of mental disease or defect, lacked the mental state required as an element of the offense charged. Mental disease or defect is not otherwise a defense."); Idaho Code Ann. § 18–207; Mont. Code Ann. § 46–14–102; Utah Code Ann. § 76–2–305.

Or they limited insanity to cognitive incapacity. That's what Congress did in the Insanity Defense Reform Act of 1984, following John Hinckley's acquittal two years before on volitional incapacity grounds, of all charges stemming from his attempt on President Reagan's life. 18 U.S.C. § 17 ("It is an affirmative defense to a prosecution under any Federal statute that, at the time of the commission of the acts constituting the offense, the defendant, as a result of a severe mental disease or defect, was unable to appreciate the nature and quality or the wrongfulness of his acts. Mental disease or defect does not otherwise constitute a defense."); on the Hinckley case and its legislative aftermath, see generally Peter W. Low, John C.

Jeffries, Jr., & Richard J. Bonnie, The Trial of John W. Hinckley, Jr.: A Case Study in the Insanity Defense (1986). (Note that this statutory reform superseded *Brawner*, which was decided at a time when the federal insanity test wasn't codified. Today federal courts are limited to interpreting 18 U.S.C. § 17, rather than choosing among various possible insanity tests. Is that a good thing?)

Yet other jurisdictions retained their insanity test, but shifted the burden of proving insanity onto the defendant. See, e.g., People v. Kohl, 72 N.Y.2d 191 (1988) (1984 reform of N.Y. Penal Law).

Some jurisdictions, including some that did away with volitional insanity, created a novel verdict of "guilty but mentally ill." A guilty but mentally ill verdict results in commitment to a prison hospital, provided that—and only as long as—the convicted person is in need of psychological treatment. If it is determined that he no longer needs the treatment, he is not released, but instead is transferred to an ordinary prison to serve out the remainder of his sentence. Consider, for instance, the Alaska insanity scheme:

Alaska Stat. § 12.47.010. Insanity as affirmative defense.

(a) In a prosecution for a crime, it is an affirmative defense that when the defendant engaged in the criminal conduct, the defendant was unable, as a result of a mental disease or defect, to appreciate the nature and quality of that conduct.

§ 12.47.020. Mental disease or defect negating culpable mental state.

(a) Evidence that the defendant suffered from a mental disease or defect is admissible whenever it is relevant to prove that the defendant did or did not have a culpable mental state which is an element of the crime.

§ 12.47.030. Guilty but mentally ill.

(a) A defendant is guilty but mentally ill if, when the defendant engaged in the criminal conduct, the defendant lacked, as a result of a mental disease or defect, the substantial capacity either to appreciate the wrongfulness of that conduct or to conform that conduct to the requirements of law.

6. The *Brawner* court reasoned that *courts* could not do away with insanity as a separate defense. Could a legislature? Does a defendant have a constitutional right to raise an insanity defense? Compare Finger v. State, 27 P.3d 66 (Nev. 2001) (yes) with State v. Korell, 213 Mont. 316, 690 P.2d 992 (1984) (no), Potter v. State, 114 Idaho 612, 759 P.2d 903 (Ct. App. 1988) (same). What about a right to introduce insanity evidence to negative an offense element? Compare *Montana v. Egelhoff,* supra ch. 5 (intoxication).

Or does a defendant have a right *not* to be treated as "insane," i.e., as someone who lacks the basic capacity to tell right from wrong, or to control her actions? Is the insanity defense itself a violation of the defendant's right to be treated as a person?

7. What happens to defendants who successfully raise an insanity defense of the traditional (non-mens rea) type? See, e.g., 18 U.S.C. § 4243 (creating comprehensive civil commitment procedure, according to which defendant found not guilty by reason of insanity is held in custody pending a court hearing about his hospitalization); cf. United States v. Weed, 389 F.3d 1060 (10th Cir. 2004) (rejecting due process attack on requirement that insanity acquittees in cases "involving bodily injury to, or serious damage to the property of, another person, or involving a substantial risk of such injury or damage" prove by clear and convincing evidence that their release into the community will not lead to a "substantial risk of bodily injury to another person," while those acquitted of a lesser offense must prove eligibility by a preponderance of the evidence). If the result of an insanity acquittal is *indefinite* commitment in a penal institution—even if it is in its hospital wing—what's the point of raising an insanity defense in the first place?

Still, indefinite isn't infinite. An insanity acquittee can, in theory, be released once he no longer suffers from the mental illness that caused his exonerating incapacity. Consider the following excerpt from the perspective of the various traditional rationales for punishment:

> On March 30, 1981 [John W. Hinkley, Jr.] awakened at the Park Central Hotel in Washington. He got breakfast from McDonald's. He left behind a note in his hotel room, addressed to [Jodie] Foster. " 'Jodie,' he pleaded, 'I'm asking you to please look into your heart and at least give me the chance, with this historical deed, to gain your respect and love.' " At 2:25 p.m., as President Ronald Reagan walked to his limousine after delivering a speech at the Washington Hilton, Hinckley fired six shots with a .22–caliber pistol that wounded four people and cast him, forever, as an American pariah.
>
> One bullet lodged inches from Reagan's heart. Another struck his press secretary, James Brady, and ravaged his brain.
>
> Fifteen months after the shooting, at the end of a seven-week trial, a jury in Washington rendered its verdict on John Hinckley: not guilty by reason of insanity. . . . Hinckley was 27 years old when he entered St. Elizabeths Hospital in Washington on June 22, 1982, the day after the verdict. He is 48 now. The law is clear on what should happen at the point Hinckley is judged to be sane. When he is no longer a danger to himself or to others, he is to be set free.
>
> This week, a hearing is scheduled to begin on Hinckley's petition for a "limited conditional release." If it is granted, he will be permitted a series of visits off the hospital grounds with his parents—and without hospital staff. These will be day outings, and if all goes well, overnight visits will follow.
>
> When he entered St. Elizabeths, Hinckley was given a diagnosis of two major psychological maladies—psychosis and major depression. According to his doctors, both are now in "full remission." In fact, his treatment team began saying that as far back as 1985.
>
> In his motion to the United States District Court, Hinckley's lawyer, Barry Levine, called the conditional release "the appropriate

next step in Mr. Hinckley's treatment." The hospital also supported Hinckley's conditional release, while recommending a more phased-in series of visits.

The government opposes any release, because the incremental steps lead ultimately to his full freedom. That Hinckley could live outside a prison or a locked hospital ward is, for many, a profoundly uncomfortable thought. He tried to kill the president. He had an attraction to Nazism and an affinity for Charles Manson. . . .

For 21 years now, Hinckley has lived on a ward inside the John Howard Pavilion, a five-story structure that houses the N.G.I.'s, as those who are found not guilty by reason of insanity are called at St. Elizabeths. His room is small, about 10 feet by 15 feet. It is furnished with a bed, a nightstand, a small dresser and little else. . . .

Since 1999, Hinckley has participated in recreational trips off the hospital grounds, accompanied by staff members—he has gone to bowling alleys, restaurants, bookstores, movies and the beach. The Secret Service tails him on these occasions. When he visited the bookstore, agents got close enough to ascertain what books caught his interest. It also observes him on the grounds of St. Elizabeths and, though the Secret Service refused to comment on this, will presumably shadow him for life, in or out of the hospital. . . .

"What people do not understand," Levine, his lawyer, told me, "is how painful the process of getting well is for someone like John. He was delusional. He did not understand the wrongfulness of what he did. Acquiring insight into his conduct, truly understanding what he did, was a difficult and terrifying experience. That's when he became aware of the unspeakable horror of what he had done." . . .

The insanity defense in United States law was broadened over time to include defendants whose acts were the "product" of mental disease, who may have known they were committing a crime but were driven by some irresistible impulse or delusion. In the Hinckley trial, Federal District Judge Barrington Parker instructed the jury to acquit Hinckley if they found his actions were related to "any abnormal condition of the mind, regardless of its medical label, which substantially affects mental or emotional processes and substantially impairs his behavior controls." The instruction was straightforward; the jury's task was anything but. Rather than making a finding of fact, the jury had to determine what was in Hinckley's mind.

That Hinckley was fairly well kempt and able to make his way around the country—to get on airplanes and check in and out of hotels, to insert exploding "Devastator" bullets into his gun rather than the more conventional ammunition he also carried—struck many as signs of his sanity. His bizarre belief that he could actually win the heart of a famous actress by shooting Ronald Reagan was powerful evidence of his insanity.

The diagnosis that Hinckley was given after he entered St. Elizabeths—psychosis, N.O.S. (meaning "not otherwise specified")—was an indication that he did not present classic or stereotypical signs of schizophrenia. The designation does not mean that the diagnosis is in doubt, but rather that it does not precisely match any of the definitions in the Diagnostic and Statistical Manual of Mental Disorders.

"Psychosis usually means you are having hallucinations or delusions; you're out of touch with reality," says E. Fuller Torrey, a prominent psychiatrist who worked at St. Elizabeths in the early 1980's and examined Hinckley. "To a lay person, John Hinckley didn't look like the raving maniac you usually think of. But to those of us in the business who looked at some of the things he was writing and saying, there was no question he was delusional."

The hearing set to begin on Monday will not involve a jury; the decision will rest solely with Federal District Judge Paul Friedman, a former president of the District of Columbia Bar who was appointed to the bench in 1994 by President Clinton. The previous judge, June L. Green, ruled consistently for the government. (She heard cases until a month before her death, in 2001, at age 87.) This will be Friedman's first chance to make a major ruling in the case, and both sides see it as a critical moment. Instead of looking at the reasons Hinckley acted, as the jury did in 1982, Friedman will have to make an equally difficult judgment: what is Hinckley likely, or not likely, to do in the future?

Hinckley's I.Q. has been measured at 113, which is considered "bright normal." He's not a genius, and should not be able, at least in theory, to fool his highly trained doctors and a hospital staff that has custody of him 24 hours a day. When they say, plainly, that he is not a danger to himself or others, they presumably are in a position to know....

"He didn't have a political fantasy and think he was saving the world by shooting my father and all the other people he shot," Ron Reagan Jr., the former president's son, says to me. "He was just trying to impress a girl, and I don't think that's changed. I think he's still the grown baby that he was. If he doesn't think he's getting his due, all the attention he wants, then he could still be a danger to people."

Ron Reagan says that his father long ago forgave Hinckley. "He made peace with it. He forgave this crazy young man. Maybe I'm just not the forgiving type, but I don't trust Mr. Hinckley. He wanted to be pen pals with Ted Bundy. Who the hell writes to Ted Bundy?" He adds: "An attack on the president or other leading members of the government is an attack on the nation itself. You can't get a free pass on that."....

Hinckley's hearing before Judge Friedman could last for more than a week. Most of it will consist of testimony by psychiatrists, including Hinckley's treatment team, and two psychiatrists chosen by prosecutors. As there was at his 1982 trial, there is likely to be disagreement among the experts, conflicting views of what Hinckley's mental state might hold for the future.

The government will argue that he is simply too dangerous and unpredictable to be trusted. Hinckley's lawyers will counter that the 1981 shootings came from a particularly dire "confluence" of psychological conditions, and that if his mental state starts to decline, there will be plenty of advance warning before he becomes dangerous. Hinckley himself is not expected to testify; taking the stand could expose him to days of cross-examination, much of it focused on what transpired when he was a young man....

Michael Sokolove, "Should John Hinckley Go Free?," N.Y. Times, Nov. 16, 2003, at 54. (Hinckley's petition was granted. Michael Janofsky, "Man Who Shot Reagan Allowed To Visit Parents Unsupervised," N.Y. Times, Dec. 18, 2003, at A1, col. 1.)

What role should the nature of the offense play in decisions about the release of insanity acquittees? Are there some offenses so heinous, so inexplicable, so indicative of dangerousness—or of "wickedness"—that their perpetrators should never be released from commitment? Cf. In re Albert F., 5 A.D.3d 5, 774 N.Y.S.2d 65 (N.Y. App. Div. 2004) (considering continued commitment of insanity acquittee who, 25 years earlier, had "lured a teenage boy into the basement of his home, restrained him at gunpoint, sodomized him, amputated his genitalia, shot him in the head, and then cannibalized the victim's sexual organs").

Should the victim's willingness to forgive play a role in making decisions regarding continued commitment? Are the theories of punishment even relevant to the question of whether—and when—to release an insanity acquittee?

8. Insanity pleas are very rare—and insanity acquittals are even rarer. A major study of indictments in four states found that insanity pleas were entered in 0.9% of cases. Henry J. Steadman et al., Before and After Hinckley: Evaluating Insanity Defense Reform 28 (1993) (California, Georgia, Montana, New York); cf. Lisa A. Callahan et al., "The Volume and Characteristics of Insanity Defense Pleas: An Eight–State Study," Bulletin Am. Acad. Psychiatry & L. 19 (1991) (1.5%). That study also found that the defense was successful in roughly a quarter of cases in which it was raised, amounting to less than one fourth of one percent of all cases. The attention the insanity defense continues to attract in American criminal law thus stands in no relation to the actual number of cases in which it is an issue. *Brawner* speaks of "an important symbolic issue in the law." What is the symbolic significance of the insanity defense? What's at stake in discussions about the insanity defense? For that matter, what is the symbolic significance of reforms of the defense in the wake of unpopular insanity acquittals?

9. Notwithstanding the arguments set out in considerable detail in *Brawner*, many jurisdictions continue to adhere to the cognitive *M'Naghten* standard. These jurisdictions have been content to revise *M'Naghten*, rather than rejecting it. Consider, for instance, the New York insanity provision, which replaced "the total impairment required for exculpation under [*M'Naghten*]" with "the more realistic standard of lack of substantial capacity." People v. Westergard, 113 A.D.2d 640, 497 N.Y.S.2d 65 (N.Y. App. Div. 1985).

Do you think it makes much of a difference in real cases whether the jury is told to acquit when the defendant suffers from a substantial incapacity, rather than a total incapacity, to tell right from wrong? What would it *mean* to be substantially, but not entirely, incapable of distinguishing right from wrong? And what's the difference between knowing that difference, and appreciating it? Can you know it without appreciating it? Vice versa?

10. *Diminished Capacity.* Some jurisdictions recognize a defense of diminished capacity (or diminished responsibility). As the California Supreme Court explained in People v. Henderson, 60 Cal.2d 482, 35 Cal.Rptr. 77, 386 P.2d 677 (1963):

> [T]he defense of mental illness not amounting to legal insanity is a "significant issue" in any case in which it is raised by substantial evidence. Its purpose and effect are to ameliorate the law governing criminal responsibility prescribed by the *M'Naghten* rule. Under that rule a defendant is not insane in the eyes of the law if at the time of the crime he knew what he was doing and that it was wrong. Under the ... rule of diminished responsibility even though a defendant be legally sane according to the *M'Naghten* test, if he was suffering from a mental illness that prevented his acting with a malice aforethought or with premeditation and deliberation, he cannot be convicted of murder of the first degree.

In this version, diminished capacity—like provocation—serves to mitigate liability for intentional homicide from murder to manslaughter. This rule has been widely criticized, and has been rejected by several courts. See, e.g., People v. Westergard, 113 A.D.2d 640, 497 N.Y.S.2d 65 (N.Y. App. Div. 1985) (no need for diminished capacity rule since New York has already "ameliorate[d]" *M'Naghten* rule by defining insanity in terms of substantial, rather than complete, incapacity).

In another version, the diminished capacity rule merely reemphasizes that evidence of mental illness may be relevant to mens rea. See, e.g., Model Penal Code § 4.02(1); State v. Breakiron, 108 N.J. 591, 532 A.2d 199 (1987) ("For the purpose of determining criminal guilt, diminished capacity either negates the state of mind required for a particular offense, if successful, or it does not."). If the defendant was incapable of forming the required mental state, then she didn't form it in fact, and therefore didn't meet every element of the offense, and therefore must be acquitted. This version of diminished capacity is not limited to murder, nor to "specific intent" crimes, but applies to all (non-strict liability) crimes. No matter how straightforward it might appear, it has been rejected in many jurisdictions. Is there any principled reason for limiting the defense to particular offenses, and murder in particular?

Finally, the Model Penal Code makes room for the consideration of mental illness—without the cognitive (or volitional) incapacity required for full-fledged insanity—in its provocation provision. See ch. 10 infra. The defendant's mental illness may be relevant if it contributed to the "extreme *mental* or emotional disturbance," provided that disturbance was reasonable under the circumstances (where of course the question arises whether mental illness can ever enter an assessment of reasonableness in the first place). Model Penal Code § 210.3(1)(b).

How would you classify these varieties of diminished capacity? Excuse or element-negating? See generally Stephen J. Morse, "Undiminished Confusion in Diminished Capacity," 75 J. Crim. L. & Criminology 1 (1984).

Many courts—and legislatures—are very wary of the diminished capacity defense. California, for one, has recently "abolished" the "defense of diminished capacity," Cal. Penal Code § 25(a), while at the same time permitting "evidence of mental disease, mental defect, or mental disorder . . . on the issue of whether or not the accused actually formed a required specific intent, premeditated, deliberated, or harbored malice aforethought, when a specific intent crime is charged," Cal. Penal Code § 28(a). Cf. Miguel A. Mendez, "Diminished Capacity in California: Premature Reports of its Demise," 3 Stan. L. & Pol'y Rev. 216 (1991). What might they be concerned about? Consider the recent reforms of the insanity defense and the role of experts explored in *Brawner*. Could a legislature constitutionally "abolish" the diminished capacity defense? Or even shift the burden of proof on the question of diminished capacity onto the defendant?

11. *Brawner* mentions another possible approach to the question of insanity: don't treat it as a defense, but consider it at the dispositional stage, i.e., at sentencing. What do you think of this solution? Who should decide the insanity question? Judges, jurors, experts? Wardens, parole board members, governors? Also consider the following compromise position:

German Penal Code § 20. Incapacity for Guilt due to Psychological Disorders.

Whoever during the commission of the act is incapable of appreciating the wrongfulness [illegality] of the act or acting in accordance with this appreciation due to a pathological psychological disorder, profound consciousness disorder, mental defect or any other serious psychological abnormality, acts without guilt.

German Penal Code § 21. Diminished Capacity for Guilt.

If the capacity of the perpetrator to appreciate the wrongfulness [illegality] of the act or to act in accordance with this appreciation is substantially diminished during the commission of the act due to one of the reasons indicated in Section 20, then the punishment may be mitigated. . . .

The U.S. Sentencing Guidelines take a very cautious approach to the consideration of mental incapacity in sentencing, except for purposes of determining the quality, rather than the quantity, of the sanction.

U.S. Sentencing Guidelines § 5H1.3. Mental and Emotional Conditions (Policy Statement).

Mental and emotional conditions are not ordinarily relevant in determining whether a sentence should be outside the applicable guideline range, except as provided in [§ 5K2.13].

Mental and emotional conditions may be relevant in determining the conditions of probation or supervised release; e.g., participation in a mental health program.

U.S. Sentencing Guidelines § 5K2.13. Diminished Capacity (Policy Statement).

If the defendant committed a non-violent offense while suffering from significantly reduced mental capacity not resulting from voluntary use of drugs or other intoxicants, a lower sentence may be warranted to reflect the extent to which reduced mental capacity contributed to the commission of the offense, provided that the defendant's criminal history does not indicate a need for incarceration to protect the public.

Recall the narrowing of the federal insanity test in the wake of Hinckley's acquittal at his trial for trying to assassinate President Reagan.

12. *Civil Liability.* Traditionally, insanity is no defense in a tort action. The following excerpt explains why (see also Restatement (Second) of Torts § 895J).

Restatement (Second) of Torts § 283B. Mental Deficiency.

Unless the actor is a child, his insanity or other mental deficiency does not relieve the actor from liability for conduct which does not conform to the standard of a reasonable man under like circumstances.

Comment:

b. The rule that a mentally deficient adult is liable for his torts is an old one, dating back at least to 1616, at a time when the action for trespass rested upon the older basis of strict liability, without regard to any fault of the individual. Apart from mere historical survival, its persistence in modern law has been explained on a number of different grounds. These are as follows:

1. The difficulty of drawing any satisfactory line between mental deficiency and those variations of temperament, intellect, and emotional balance which cannot, as a practical matter, be taken into account in imposing liability for damage done.

2. The unsatisfactory character of the evidence of mental deficiency in many cases, together with the ease with which it can be feigned, the difficulties which the triers of fact must encounter in determining its existence, nature, degree, and effect; and some fear of introducing into the law of torts the confusion which has surrounded such a defense in the criminal law [!]. Although this factor may be of decreasing importance with the continued development of medical and psychiatric science, it remains at the present time a major obstacle to any allowance for mental deficiency.

3. The feeling that if mental defectives are to live in the world they should pay for the damage they do, and that it is better that their wealth, if any, should be used to compensate innocent victims than that it should remain in their hands.

4. The belief that their liability will mean that those who have charge of them or their estates will be stimulated to look after them, keep them in order, and see that they do not do harm.

> c..... As to mental deficiency falling short of insanity, as in the case of stupidity, lack of intelligence, excitability, or proneness to accident, no allowance is made, and the actor is held to the standard of conduct of a reasonable man who is not mentally deficient, even though it is in fact beyond his capacity to conform to it.

But why should insanity count as a defense to crime, but not to a tort (even an intentional one)? And why should infancy count as a defense, but *not* insanity?

13. *Incompetence.* "Insanity" is not to be confused with "incompetence." To be competent to be tried, an accused must—at the time of trial, rather than at the time of the offense—be able to understand the nature and seriousness of the charges against her and to cooperate with her attorneys—rather than to tell right from wrong or to control her actions. See, e.g., Tex. Code Crim. Pro. § 46.02 ("A person is not competent to stand trial if the person does not have: (a) sufficient present ability to consult with the person's lawyer with a reasonable degree of rational understanding; or (b) a rational as well as factual understanding of the proceedings against the person.").

What's more, a convicted defendant must be competent to be *punished*, at least when it comes to the death penalty. See, e.g., Ill. Rev. Stat., ch. 38, § 1005–2–3(a) ("A person is unfit to be executed if because of a mental condition he is unable to understand the nature and purpose of such sentence."); Miss. Code Ann. 99–19–57(2)(b) (convict must "have sufficient intelligence to understand the nature of the proceedings against him, what he was tried for, the purpose of his punishment, the impending fate which awaits him, and a sufficient understanding to know any fact which might exist which would make his punishment unjust or unlawful and the intelligence requisite to convey such information to his attorney or the court"); see generally Ford v. Wainwright, 477 U.S. 399 (1986) (execution of incompetent person cruel and unusual punishment).

Defendants who qualify as "mentally retarded" may no longer be sentenced to death. Atkins v. Virginia, 536 U.S. 304 (2002). According to *Atkins*, though mentally retarded individuals may not qualify for the insanity defense, "[b]ecause of their disabilities in areas of reasoning, judgment, and control of their impulses ... they do not act with the level of moral culpability that characterizes the most serious adult criminal conduct." Mentally retarded persons here are thought of as displaying "subaverage intellectual functioning" and "diminished capacities to understand and process information, to communicate, to abstract from mistakes and learn from experience, to engage in logical reasoning, to control impulses, and to understand the reactions of others." Is it any less troubling to sentence a mentally retarded person suffering from these incapacities to life imprisonment than it is to sentence her to death?

14. *Infancy.* Traditionally, infancy was simply another incapacity defense. The infant, along with the "idiot" or "lunatic," were exempt from criminal liability because they were not among the "persons capable of committing crimes." 4 William Blackstone, Commentaries on the Laws of England ch. 2 (1769). Modern criminal law, by contrast, treats infancy (or "immaturity") as a procedural matter, rather than as a substantive de-

fense. Defendants below a certain age are ordinarily "transferred" to another ("juvenile") court, rather than tried in criminal court and then acquitted if the infancy defense succeeds (or punished if it doesn't). In juvenile court, the juvenile is not a "defendant," nor is he subject to "conviction," but to an order of "delinquency," and not to "punishment," but to "treatment," not in a "prison," but in a juvenile facility such as a "detention home."

There has been a strong trend, however, to try—and even to punish—juveniles as adults, particularly if they stand accused of serious offenses. See, e.g., N.Y. Penal Law § 30.00 (providing that, in general, "a person less than sixteen years old is not criminally responsible for conduct," but also that a person as young as thirteen *is* criminally responsible for murder, and fourteen-year-olds for various violent offenses, including kidnapping, arson, aggravated assault, manslaughter, rape, burglary, and robbery, along with several weapons possession offenses and attempted murder and kidnapping); see generally Simon Singer, Recriminalizing Delinquency: Violent Juvenile Crime and Juvenile Justice Reform (1996); Barry C. Feld, Bad Kids: Race and the Transformation of the Juvenile Court (1999).

What does the seriousness of an offense have to do with the incapacities of infancy? What's the connection between infancy and insanity? And could insanity be handled in the same, procedural, fashion, with a prior determination of insanity, followed by a transfer to a special court?

CHAPTER 8

GROUP CRIMINALITY: COMPLICITY, CONSPIRACY, RICO, AND CORPORATE LIABILITY

So far, we have concerned ourselves with the question of when an individual can be held criminally liable for her own conduct. Answering that question has proven difficult enough. And things don't get any easier when we're faced with the question of when *several* persons can be held criminally liable for conduct they commit, or at least plan, together. What should be my criminal liability, say, if I don't break into your garden shed by myself, but instead tell Joe, a friend of mine but not of yours, that you never lock your shed, that you keep your $1,500 snowblower in there, along with five bikes, a lawnmower, and a leafblower, and then offer to lure you away one Saturday morning so that Joe can commit the burglary in peace and quiet? Up to this point in the book, we have focused on *Joe's* criminal liability. Only he satisfies the elements of burglary—by breaking into your shed with the intent to commit theft. Under what circumstances should *I* be held liable for *his* burglary? Even though I didn't satisfy the elements of the offense through my own conduct, under what circumstances should I be held accountable for Joe's conduct, since I, after all, was the one who put him up to it, and helped him commit the crime? These are the sorts of questions that the law of *complicity* addresses. See part A.

Let's say Joe doesn't go through with the burglary, after initially agreeing to do it and even taking a quick stroll through your neighborhood to get a sense of the place. Should I (and he) be liable for entering into the agreement in the first place? Now assume that Joe does commit the burglary as planned. Should he be punished for entering into the agreement *and* for committing the burglary? Should I be punished for both the agreement *and* for inciting and helping him to commit it? This is the domain of the law of *conspiracy*. See part B.

Conspiracies, however, aren't just agreements; they are also the organizations that are bound together by more or less complex and dense webs of agreements. Many conspiracies, after all, not only involve more than two people, but also have objectives more ambitious than stealing gardening equipment. Nothing highlights the organizational aspect of conspiracy better than the federal Racketeer Influenced and Corrupt Organizations Act of 1970, better known as RICO. RICO aims to put criminal organizations—or "enterprises"—out of business. It is primarily focused on the group, rather than on the individual. Individuals are brought within its sweep in order to bring the organization they are part of to its knees. See part C.

Finally, there is the criminal liability of the organization itself. Corporate criminal liability targets the enterprise directly. The corporate structure not only dramatically simplifies the imputation of one person's conduct to another higher up in the organizational chart; more important, the corporation itself is held criminally liable for acts of its agents. But when is this imputation appropriate, and what does it mean for a corporation to have the actus reus and mens rea required for criminal liability? See part D.

By the end of this chapter, we will have a come a long way, from the criminal liability of a person who aids and abets another person in engaging in conduct that matches the elements of an offense, to the criminal liability of an institution.

A. COMPLICITY

1. INTRODUCTION

Standefer v. United States, 447 U.S. 10, 100 S.Ct. 1999 (1980)

At common law, the subject of principals and accessories was riddled with"intricate" distinctions. 2 J. Stephen, A History of the Criminal Law of England 231 (1883). In felony cases, parties to a crime were divided into four distinct categories: (1) principals in the first degree who actually perpetrated the offense; (2) principals in the second degree who were actually or constructively present at the scene of the crime and aided or abetted its commission; (3) accessories before the fact who aided or abetted the crime, but were not present at its commission; and (4) accessories after the fact who rendered assistance after the crime was complete. By contrast, misdemeanor cases "d[id] not admit of accessories either before or after the fact," United States v. Hartwell, 26 F.Cas. No. 15, 318, pp. 196, 199 (CC Mass.1869); instead, all parties to a misdemeanor, whatever their roles, were principals.

State v. Tally, 15 So. 722 (Ala. 1894)

A principal in [the second] degree is one who is present at the commission of a felony by the hand of the principal in the first degree, and who, being thus present, aids or abets, or aids and abets, the latter therein. The presence which this definition requires need not be actual, physical juxtaposition in respect of the personal perpetrator of the crime. It is enough, so far as presence is concerned, for the principal in the second degree to be in a position to aid the commission of the crime by others. It is enough if he stands guard while the act is being perpetrated by others to prevent interference with them, or to warn them of the approach of danger; and it is immaterial how distant from the scene of the crime his vigil is maintained, provided it gives some promise of protection to those engaged in its active commission. At whatever distance he may be, he is present in legal contemplation if he is at the time performing any act in furtherance of the crime, or is in a position to give information to the principal which would be helpful to the end in view, or to prevent others from doing any act, by way of warning the intended victim or otherwise, which would be but an obstacle in the way of the consummation of the crime, or render its accomplishment more difficult. This is well illustrated by the case of State v. Hamilton, 13 Nev. 386, in which a plan was arranged between Laurie and others to rob the treasure of Wells, Fargo & Co. on the road between Eureka and some point in Nye county. Laurie was to ascertain when the treasure left Eureka, and signal his confederates by building a fire on the top of a mountain in Eureka county, which could be seen by them in Nye county, 30 or 40 miles distant. This signal was given by him, and his confederates, advised by it, met the stage, attacked and attempted to rob it, and in the attempt killed one of the guards. Laurie was indicted with the rest for murder.... He was constructively present though 30 or 40 miles away, and he was guilty as a principal in the second degree in that from and across this distance he aided and abetted his confederates by the beacon lights which he set upon a hill. It was as if he had been endowed with a voice to compass the intervening space, and to advise his accomplices of the approach of the treasure, or as if his words had been transmitted over a telephone or a telegraph line to the ears of his distant confederates.

Model Penal Code § 2.06. Liability for Conduct of Another; Complicity.

(1) A person is guilty of an offense if it is committed by his own conduct or by the conduct of another person for which he is legally accountable, or both.

(2) A person is legally accountable for the conduct of another person when:

(a) acting with the kind of culpability that is sufficient for the commission of the offense, he causes an innocent or irresponsible person to engage in such conduct; or

(b) he is made accountable for the conduct of such other person by the Code or by the law defining the offense; or

(c) he is an accomplice of such other person in the commission of the offense.

(3) A person is an accomplice of another person in the commission of an offense if:

(a) with the purpose of promoting or facilitating the commission of the offense, he

(i) solicits such other person to commit it; or

(ii) aids or agrees or attempts to aid such other person in planning or committing it; or

(iii) having a legal duty to prevent the commission of the offense, fails to make proper effort so to do....

(4) When causing a particular result is an element of an offense, an accomplice in the conduct causing such result is an accomplice in the commission of that offense, if he acts with the kind of culpability, if any, with respect to that result that is sufficient for the commission of the offense.

(5) A person who is legally incapable of committing a particular offense himself may be guilty thereof if it is committed by the conduct of another person for which he is legally accountable, unless such liability is inconsistent with the purpose of the provision establishing his incapacity.

(6) Unless otherwise provided by the Code or by the law defining the offense, a person is not an accomplice in an offense committed by another person if:

(a) he is a victim of that offense; or

(b) the offense is so defined that his conduct is inevitably incident to its commission; or

(c) he terminates his complicity prior to the commission of the offense and

(i) wholly deprives it of effectiveness in the commission of the offense; or

(ii) gives timely warning to the law enforcement authorities or otherwise makes proper effort to prevent the commission of the offense.

(7) An accomplice may be convicted on proof of the commission of the offense and of his complicity therein, though the person claimed to have committed the offense has not been prosecuted or convicted or has been convicted of a different offense or degree of offense or has an immunity to prosecution or conviction or has been acquitted.

QUESTIONS AND COMMENTS

1. Consider the structure of Model Penal Code § 2.06. Complicity is but one way in which the conduct of one person is imputed to another. Subsection (1) begins by stating the obvious, that I am always liable for my "own conduct." To be liable for *another* person's conduct, I must be "legally accountable" for that conduct. Subsection (2)(a) mentions a seemingly straightforward way of treating another person's conduct as my own—if I "cause" an "innocent or irresponsible person" to commit the criminal act in my stead.

But what might "cause" mean in this context? Factual or proximate cause? Contributory cause? Can one "cause" another person to act in the way one can cause a rock one throws to hit its target? Presumably, § 2.06(2)(a) contemplates *more* than battery cases in which the defendant hurls a human object at the victim.

And how about "innocent or irresponsible"? Does "irresponsible" mean that the person I am using as a means to my criminal end have available to herself a justification defense? An excuse defense? Must she be irresponsible in the (narrower) Model Penal Code sense of insanity or infancy (see Model Penal Code art. 4)? To be "innocent," must the person have acted "involuntarily" or without the requisite mental state, or without some "criminal" motive?

2. Complicity is the most indirect—and most difficult—way of holding me liable for another's conduct. Why is that? What distinguishes my

helping another person to engage in criminal conduct from my using another person to that end? Does the person I'm aiding or abetting have a defense based on my aiding or abetting?

3. The Model Penal Code—along with the majority of jurisdictions—abandoned the common law's distinctions between principals and accessories. (Why? Is it because of the notion of "constructive" presence? But isn't complicity all about constructive *conduct*, by treating me *as if* I had engaged in another person's—the principal's—conduct?) The focus has shifted from persons to conduct; accessories are no longer punished for aiding principals, but one person is held legally accountable for another's conduct.

How does this modern approach to accomplice liability fit with the various traditional rationales for punishment, and with the Model Penal Code's treatmentism (see ch. 3, supra)? Does the common law scheme capture relevant distinctions of blameworthiness—or dangerousness—that the Model Penal Code scheme cannot accommodate? Are there even some cases where the aider or abettor is so pushy and dominant that he is "really" the principal?

Or are these matters of differentiation best left for sentencing? The United States Sentencing Guidelines include several adjustments based on the defendant's "role in the offense." The penalty is increased if the defendant qualifies as an "organizer, leader, manager, or supervisor," and decreased if she was a "minor" or even a "minimal" participant. U.S.S.G. §§ 3B1.1 & 3B1.2. These provisions reflect the judgment that organizers bear greater "responsibility" for the crime, "tend to profit more from it, present a greater danger to the public, and/or are more likely to recidivate." U.S.S.G. § 3B1.1 cmt. A sentence enhancement also applies if the defendant "used or attempted to use a person less than eighteen years of age to commit the offense or assist in avoiding detection of, or apprehension for, the offense," where using or attempting to use includes "directing, commanding, encouraging, intimidating, counseling, training, procuring, recruiting, or soliciting." U.S.S.G. § 3B1.4.

4. Traditionally, not only was the accomplice punished less severely, he could not be convicted until after the principal had been convicted.

Under the Model Penal Code scheme, by contrast, the aider can plainly be convicted even if the principal has been *acquitted*. (Note, however, that acquittal of a person charged as the principal doesn't necessarily mean that the accomplice can be convicted without a finding that *someone* has engaged in the criminal conduct that is imputed to him. See United States v. Horton, 847 F.2d 313, 322 (6th Cir. 1988).) Does that make sense? From the perspective of the traditional rationales for punishment, and the Model Penal Code's treatmentism in particular? Is it consistent with the view of complicity liability as one way in which I can be "legally accountable for the conduct of another person," Model Penal Code § 2.06(1)?

Note that the Model Penal Code, in fact, goes further. According to the Code's attempt provision, if the defendant *would have been* an accomplice to another's crime had that person attempted or committed a crime, she will be convicted (of attempt) notwithstanding the fact that the person she would have aided, or tried to aid, neither attempted nor committed any offense. § 5.01(3); cf. § 5.02 (solicitation). (For a discussion of § 5.01(3) in the context of undercover investigations, see *United States v. Washington*, infra p. 681.) Can this provision be squared with the idea that an accomplice is a party to whom liability is *imputed*, a party who is fundamentally *derivatively* liable? Or does Model Penal Code § 5.01(3) suggest instead that helping, or trying to help, someone commit a crime is itself one way of manifesting the sort of anti-social disposition that calls for correction, that "helping" is conduct no less reprehensible than committing the crime directly, in the way the most responsible actor might?

How could the Model Penal Code—which is so relentless, generally, in focusing solely on the degree to which an actor's conduct reveals *that actor's* anti-social disposition (and need for peno-correctional treatment)—care at all about any actor's conduct but the defendant's? Does the "imputation" theory of accomplice liability blur that focus on the defendant's own conduct?

There is a distinction between being indifferent as to whether the principal committed or attempted an offense (as in § 5.01(3)) and being indifferent as to whether the principal has been convicted of an offense. Acquittal doesn't mean innocence, it is said, for juries may "acquit out of compassion or compromise or because of 'their assumption of a power which they had no right to exercise, but to which they were disposed through lenity.' " Standefer v. United States, 447 U.S. 10, 100 S.Ct. 1999 (1980). Besides jury mercy and even nullification, there is the exclusionary rule, which may result in an acquittal by "bar[ring] the Government from introducing evidence against one defendant because that evidence was obtained in violation of his constitutional rights." More generally:

> [T]he purpose of a criminal court is not to provide a forum for the ascertainment of private rights. Rather it is to vindicate the public interest in the enforcement of the criminal law while at the same time safeguarding the rights of the individual defendant. The public interest in the accuracy and justice of criminal results is greater than the concern for judicial economy professed in civil cases and we are thus inclined to reject, at least as a general matter, a rule that would spread the effect of an erroneous acquittal to all those who participated in a particular criminal transaction.

Id. at 25.

What about spreading the effect of an erroneous *conviction*?

5. At any rate, even if the principal is punished, an accomplice today can be punished *more* severely than the principal, depending on his mental state with respect to the other, non-conduct, elements of the offense in question. So if it turns out, for instance, that I thought there was a good chance the principal's conduct would result in the victim's death, I will be guilty of manslaughter, even if the principal's liability is limited to negligent homicide because she was culpably unaware of that risk. (A classic example is a drag race.) See Pendry v. State, 367 A.2d 627 (Del. 1976) (accomplice convicted of murder, having presented no evidence that he personally suffered from the extreme emotional disturbance that reduced

the principal's crime from murder to manslaughter). In Regina v. Howe, [1987] 1 App. Cas. 417, 85 Crim. App. 32, the House of Lords considered the following hypothetical:

> A hands a gun to D informing him that it is loaded with blank ammunition only and telling him to go and scare X by discharging it. The ammunition is in fact live (as A knows) and X is killed. D is convicted only of manslaughter, as he might be on those facts. It would seem absurd that A should thereby escape conviction for murder.

The California Supreme Court affirmed this reasoning in People v. McCoy, 25 Cal.4th 1111, 24 P.3d 1210, 108 Cal.Rptr.2d 188 (2001) ("Aider and abettor liability is premised on the . . . act[] of . . . the principal[], but on the aider and abettor's own mens rea. If the mens rea of the aider and abettor is more culpable than the actual perpetrator's, the aider and abettor may be guilty of a more serious crime than the actual perpetrator."). Note also that, on this reasoning, I can be an accomplice to a crime I couldn't have committed myself—say, to misconduct in office even though I'm not an officeholder. See Model Penal Code § 2.06(5).

6. For purposes of deciding accomplice liability, should it matter *why* the principal is not punishable, so that some acquittals preclude complicity, but not others? What if he is acquitted because he has not committed a crime, i.e., his conduct didn't match the definition of an offense (perhaps because he lacked the requisite mens rea)? What if he is justified? Or merely excused? Must the accomplice *know* that the principal is justified, or excused? Consider the following case.

> Tomika T. Taylor ("appellant") appeals her conviction as a principal in the second degree for abduction in violation of Code § 18.2–47. She contends the evidence was legally insufficient to support her conviction because the person she aided in committing the abduction was the natural father of the child abducted. She argues that the father's legal justification in taking the child precludes her conviction. A panel of this Court reversed appellant's conviction on that ground. Upon rehearing en banc, we affirm appellant's conviction.
>
> At approximately 1:00 a.m. on December 26, 1996, appellant and her fiancé, Avery Moore, arrived at the home of Meshia Powell, ostensibly to see the ten-month-old son of Powell and Moore. . . . No custody order was in effect and no proceeding was pending. [After arriving at Powell's Virginia home, Moore grabbed the child, got in the car, and appellant drove away. Police arrested Moore and appellant in Georgia a week later, and retrieved the child.]
>
> [The abduction statute] exempts three persons from liability: (1) individuals who are legally justified, (2) individuals who are legally excused, and (3) any law-enforcement officer acting in the performance of his or her duty. Only the second exemption, "legal excuse," is raised by the contentions in this case.
>
> While the terms, "legal justification," and "excuse" are often used interchangeably, they are distinct legal concepts. See, e.g., George P. Fletcher, Rethinking Criminal Law 759–817 (1978). While the scholarly works written on the subject underscore the difficulties encountered in

defining the principles which comprise and underlie the theories of justification and excuse and in developing a generally accepted body of law setting forth the applicability of each defense in various contexts, some distillation of the relevant principles is possible.

As to the concept of excuse, there appears to be general agreement with the proposition that "excuses, in contrast [to justifications], are always personal to the actor...." Fletcher, supra, at 762. Excuses rest on the presence within the actor of a condition or status that exculpates him or her from culpability for otherwise criminal conduct. See Robert F. Schopp, Justification Defenses and Just Convictions, 24 Pac. L.J. 1233, 1238 (1993) ("Excuses are specific to defendants because they exculpate these individuals for their criminal conduct due to disabilities, such as infancy or psychological disorder, that undermine the attribution of culpability for this particular conduct to these defendants."). Because excuses relate to a condition that is peculiar to the actor, such defenses are generally considered to be non-delegable and, thus, unavailable to an accomplice. Justification defenses, on the other hand, "appeal to the special circumstances in which the ordinarily criminal conduct was performed, and they exonerate the defendant because the conduct was socially acceptable under these conditions." Schopp, supra, at 1238. The defense of justification, unlike that of excuse, generally provides a right to persons other than the primary actor to assist, or to directly defend the interests of, the primary actor because a third party is in the same position as the primary actor to evaluate the circumstances warranting the conduct in question. Claims of justification include the defenses of "consent, lesser evils, self-defense, defense of others, defense of property and habitation, self-help in recapturing chattels, the use of force in effecting arrests and executing legal judgments, as well as superior orders." Fletcher, supra, at 769.

Based on the foregoing principles, even were we to conclude that Moore's abduction of the child was excused by his parental relationship to the child, appellant's "accessorial liability would not be undercut by [Moore's] personal excuse." Fletcher, supra, at 62. [Although excused, an offense is nonetheless committed.] In short, the defense of "legal excuse," is personal to Moore and unavailable to appellant.

Taylor v. Commonwealth, 31 Va.App. 54, 521 S.E.2d 293 (1999); see also Farnsworth v. Zerbst, 98 F.2d 541 (5th Cir. 1938) (accomplice can be convicted though principal is diplomatically immune); United States v. Azadian, 436 F.2d 81 (9th Cir. 1971) (accomplice can be convicted though principal cannot, because the principal, though not the accomplice, was entrapped).

Ascertaining whether a given principal enjoys a personal immunity (or excuse) that precludes punishment, or whether instead she has committed no crime at all, given her status, may be difficult. In People v. Eberhardt, 169 Cal.App.3d 292, 215 Cal.Rptr. 161 (1985), the defendant conspired with his wife to use gill nets to catch fish. As a Native American, his wife was immune from prosecution for the use of such nets. Is she personally immunized from prosecution or does she enjoy a more robust legal privilege to fish in this way? Is he entitled to help her exercise this privilege?

Assume that you are in a jurisdiction in which the accomplice cannot be convicted of a crime unless the principal committed the actus reus of that crime (contra Model Penal Code § 5.01(3)) but that the accomplice can still be convicted (a) if the principal does not have as culpable a mental state as is required to be convicted of the offense with which the accomplice is charged or (b) if the principal merely has a personal excuse or immunity. Consider Regina v. Richards, [1974] Q.B. 776: The defendant hired two men to beat up her husband, stating that she "wanted them to beat him up bad enough to put him in the hospital for a month." Had they done so, she would plainly have been guilty as an accessory to felonious assault, defined as an assault with the intent to cause grievous bodily harm. However, when they accosted the husband, he escaped without serious injury. Should her liability be limited to misdemeanor assault, requiring merely the intent to cause harm? On appeal, the court reversed her conviction of felonious assault, stating:

> [The prosecution] says that here one can properly look at the actus reus, that is the physical blows struck upon Mr. Richards, and separately the intention with which the blows were struck.... [But] if there is only one offense committed, and that is the offense of [misdemeanor assault], then the person who has requested that offense to be committed ... cannot be guilty of a graver offense than that in fact which was committed.

Are the two offenses distinguished only by mental state (in the way murder and manslaughter are)? Or are the acts that predicate felonious assault (subtly) distinct from those that predicate misdemeanor assault? (Does the felonious assailant hit harder, or with weapons, or strike different parts of the body?) If the offenses are distinguished only by mental state, can the appellate court's decision be defended? Imagine that the parties Mrs. Richards had hired to rough up her husband were categorically irresponsible (because of insanity or youth): which crime would she have been convicted of then? See Glanville Williams, Criminal Law: The General Part 391 (2d ed. 1961) (arguing that if a person can act through a completely innocent agent, there is no reason why he shouldn't be responsible for acting through a "semi-innocent" agent).

7. What's the point of the termination defense? See Model Penal Code § 2.02(6)(c). What constitutes a "proper effort" to prevent commission of a crime that I incited? Should the degree of my participation in a crime affect what efforts I have to undertake to prevent its commission? If I incited a crime, should it be enough if I deprive my abetting of "effectiveness"? Am I less blameworthy or dangerous if I change my mind before the crime is committed? Or is it simply a matter of deterrence?

And is termination an element-negating defense, a justification, or an excuse? What element would it be negating—actus reus or mens rea? Cf. N.Y. Penal Law § 40.10 ("voluntary and complete renunciation of ... criminal purpose").

8. *Accomplice Testimony.* In many jurisdictions, "a defendant may not be convicted of any offense upon the testimony of an accomplice unsupported by corroborative evidence tending to connect the defendant with the commission of such offense." N.Y. Crim. Proc. Law § 60.22(1). (Others provide for instructions advising jurors to view accomplice testimony with "care and caution." People v. Guiuan, 18 Cal.4th 558, 957 P.2d 928, 76 Cal.Rptr.2d 239 (1998).) This procedural "accomplice rule," however, doesn't necessarily employ the same concept of complicity as the substantive criminal law. Consider the following case.

> After a jury trial appellant was convicted of petit larceny for the theft of jewelry taken from a residence in the Woodsburgh section of Woodmere, Long Island. At the trial one Lo Monaco, a known receiver of stolen goods or 'fence', to whom the police had been led by a confidential informer, appeared as a witness for the prosecution in exchange for a promise that he would not be prosecuted. He testified that in response to a telephone call concerning stolen property he went to appellant's apartment where he purchased some jewelry from appellant....
>
> The evidence disclosed that Lo Monaco had known appellant for about a year and had been to his apartment on 10 or 20 occasions. Lo Monaco admitted that he had bought jewelry from appellant more than once. He had no agreement with appellant, however, but if the latter had something he would contact Lo Monaco, who would buy it. Lo Monaco testified that he had no prior knowledge that this particular theft was going to be committed or that he was going to get this lot of jewelry.
>
> Appellant urges that the trial court committed reversible error in denying his request to charge that the jury could find that the witness Lo Monaco was an accomplice.
>
> Crim. Proc. Law § 60.22(2) provides as follows:
>
> An "accomplice" means a witness in a criminal action who, according to evidence adduced in such action, may reasonably be considered to have participated in:
>
> (a) The offense charged; or
>
> (b) An offense based upon the same or some of the same facts or conduct which constitute the offense charged.
>
> This definition replaced the previous judicially formulated rule under which the test was "whether an alleged accomplice was so connected with the crime that he could have been convicted as a principal or as an accessory before the fact". The consequence of the adoption of this statutory definition is to "broaden the definition of an accomplice as the term is applied to witnesses, in order to provide a more equitable, operable and consistent standard for the courts in determining when the requirement of corroboration is applicable".
>
> Turning then to the application of the statutory definition to the facts of this case we first note that Lo Monaco was not an accomplice under paragraph (a); he could not reasonably be considered to have

> participated in the theft of the jewelry. The issue is whether he could be found to fall within the ambit of paragraph (b). We observe that perhaps in a mechanical, literal sense Lo Monaco might be said to be an accomplice within the language of paragraph (b). That is, he might be considered to have participated in an offense, criminal possession of stolen property, one material element of which would have been the theft of the jewelry by appellant. We are satisfied, however, that in view of the history of our statutes no such result was ever intended. As Mr. Justice Learned Hand wrote in other contexts, "There is no surer way to misread any document than to read it literally" (Guiseppi v. Walling, 2 Cir.,144 F.2d 608, 624). * * *
>
> We cannot agree ... with the proposition urged on us that Crim. Proc. Law § 60.22(2)(b) automatically makes every receiver an accomplice of the thief notwithstanding the absence of proof that the receiver procured or otherwise aided or abetted the thief in the commission of the larceny. Consideration of an instance in which stolen securities after perhaps several months of total concealment are disposed of through a fence theretofore completely unaware of the larceny, emphasizes the essential separateness of the two crimes.... Had there been any evidence here of a prior agreement or arrangement between appellant and Lo Monaco or any evidence that Lo Monaco was otherwise criminally implicated in the larceny, the result would be different.

People v. Brooks, 34 N.Y.2d 475 (1974).

Would Lo Monaco qualify as an accomplice under the traditional common law scheme of principals and accessories (see *Standefer*, supra; see also 18 U.S.C. § 3)? Under the Model Penal Code scheme? What do you think of the court's exercise in statutory interpretation? What practical considerations might have influenced the court's decision?

2. Actus Reus

a. Varieties of Imputation

Commonwealth v. Tavares

Superior Court of Pennsylvania.
382 Pa. Super. 317, 555 A.2d 199 (1989).

■ Beck, Judge.

Joseph ... Tavares, an attendant at Inglis House, a home for handicapped persons, entered the room of David Savage, a nineteen year old resident with cerebral palsy. David was talking with another resident, Michael Panunto, who also has cerebral palsy and who was sitting in his wheelchair next to David's bed. Tavares asked the two if they wanted to have sex. Thinking he meant "with a girl, not with a man" David said yes. Michael, who communicates through the use of a speak-and-spell word board, indicated, "No." Tavares pushed David's wheelchair against the door to hold it closed. He pulled down David's bedsheet, removed his bed bag, and placed Michael's hand on David's penis. David said "knock it the fuck off, Joe" and Michael removed his hand. ...

The episode ended when David's father knocked on the door and an attendant brought in lunch trays. ...

Tavares was convicted in a non-jury trial of attempted involuntary deviate sexual intercourse (IDSI), indecent assault, and unlawful restraint....

Tavares contends that the trial court erred in convicting him of attempted IDSI and indecent assault as he did not engage in the proscribed conduct with either of the complainants. ...

Although Tavares did not himself have indecent contact with the complainants, criminal liability was extended to him under the statute relating to liability for the conduct of another, 18 Pa. Cons. Stat. Ann. § 306....

Section 306 was derived verbatim from the Model Penal Code. The Official Comment to the Model Penal Code explains that this particular provision restates the "universally acknowledged principle that one is no less guilty of the commission of a crime because he uses the overt conduct of an innocent or irresponsible agent." Model Penal Code § 2.06(2)(a), Comment at 300 (Official Draft, 1985). Furthermore, the Official Comment points out that this provision "determine[s] liability by the culpability and state of mind of the defendant, coupled with his own overt conduct and the conduct in which he caused another to engage." Id.

We note in passing that other states have acknowledged criminal liability of a third party who has caused two innocent victims to engage in proscribed conduct. For example, the California Court of Appeals, in Commonwealth v. Hernandez, 18 Cal.App.3d 651, 96 Cal Rptr. 71 (1971), sustained the conviction of a woman who compelled her husband, at gunpoint, to have sex with another, nonconsenting woman. Applying what it termed the "innocent conduit theory" the court noted that without this theory "the laws ... would create a crime without a punishable perpetrator."

b. Causation and Attempted Complicity

State v. Tally

Supreme Court of Alabama.
15 So. 722 (1894).

■ McCLELLAN, J.

John B. Tally, as judge of the ninth judicial circuit, is charged with complicity in the murder of R.C. Ross by the hands of Robert, John, James, and Walter Skelton. Tally was a brother-in-law to ... the Skeltons ..., having married their sister.... The grievance they had against Ross lay in the fact that the latter had seduced, or been criminally intimate with a sister of ... them and of Mrs. Tally. * * *

[On Sunday, February 4th, 1894,] Ross left his house in Scottsboro surreptitiously under and because of an apprehension that his life was in imminent peril at the hands of the Skeltons. He ... left Scottsboro, in a hack, for Stevenson, 18 miles distant, intending to catch a train there on another road, and go on to Chattanooga. With him were [three other men]. All of the party were armed. ... They arrived in Stevenson about 10:45 that morning, and driving to a point in a public road or street midway between an hotel and the passenger station of the two railroads that connect, or rather unite, there, and 30 or 40 yards from each, all the party alighted from the vehicle, except the driver, and took out their arms and baggage, the latter consisting of three valises. A person, William Tally [the respondent's brother], passing at the time from the hotel to the station, walked around the hack, which had stopped immediately in front of him, and met, shook hands, and passed the usual salutations with Ross, who had gotten out on the side next the station. Tally then turned away, and started on towards the station. Just at this juncture a shot was fired ... from behind the depot platform. This was followed by another from the same place, and then by other shots from two guns behind the platform, and from a pile of telegraph poles a little way down the road, in the direction from which the hack had come. Some one or more of these succeeding shots took effect in Ross' legs, and he fell. ... Ross managed to get to the side of a small oil house, a short distance beyond where the hack had stopped, and took a position affording some shelter from persons behind the platform and telegraph poles. While standing there with his gun in his hand, and looking in the direction of the telegraph poles, a man came to the corner of the house behind him, and shot him with a Winchester rifle through the head from back to front. He fell in the throes of death, and died. Then another man came up from behind the platform, and, approaching closely, also shot him through the head with a Winchester rifle. The man who fired the first and two or three other shots from behind the platform was Robert Skelton. The man who fired the other shots from that position was James Skelton. The man who fired from the telegraph poles was Walter Skelton. John Skelton it was who reached the corner of the oil house behind Ross, shot him in the back of the head, and killed him. And it was Robert who came up after he was dead, and again shot him in the head. * * *

After the killing of Ross, Robert Skelton sent a telegram to the respondent, at Scottsboro, informing him that Ross was dead, and that none of the Skeltons were hurt; and they all surrendered themselves to Huddleston, who was mayor of Stevenson, and were taken back to Scottsboro, and confined in jail. * * *

What connection had the respondent with [this] murder? [D]id he himself participate in the deed, by commanding, directing, counseling, or encouraging the Skeltons to its execution, or by aiding and abetting them in its commission? ... As has been seen, Judge Tally was the brother-in-law of Robert, James, and Walter Skelton, and of Miss Annie Skelton, the wronged girl. It may be supposed, therefore, that he shared with the Skeltons—in some degree, at least—the shame and mortification which had come upon them through Ross, and that the grievance against Ross was common to them all. It was shown that he knew all the facts known to the Skeltons, and came to his knowledge of them soon after they did. * * *

The flight of Ross and the pursuit of the Skeltons at once became generally known in the town of Scottsboro, and was well nigh the sole topic of conversation that Sunday morning. Everybody knew it. Everybody talked only about it. Everybody was impressed with the probability of a terrible tragedy to be enacted on the road to Stevenson, or at the latter point.

The respondent was soon abroad. He went to the depot, where the telegraph office was. He remained about there most of that morning. . . . E. H. Ross, a kinsman of the Ross who had fled, and was being pursued, meeting the telegraph operator, Whitner, at the passenger station, walked with him down to the freight depot, where the telegraph office was. Judge Tally followed them. They went into the telegraph office, and so did he. Ross was sitting at a table, writing a message. It was addressed to R. C. Ross, Stevenson, Ala. Its contents were: "Four men on horseback with guns following. Look out." Ross handed it to the operator to be sent. Tally either saw this message, or in some way accurately divined its contents. He called for paper, and immediately wrote a message himself, "Do not let the party warned get away," [addressed to William Huddleston, mayor of Stevenson and a lifelong friend of Tally's.].... The respondent then handed this telegram to the operator, remarking to him, "This message has something to do with that one you just received;" said he wanted it sent, and paid for it. He then started towards the door, but turned to the operator, and said: "Just add to that message, 'say nothing.'" Tally left the office. This message was sent just after that of E. H. Ross to R. C. Ross. . . . Tally then, his watch to prevent the sending or delivery of a telegram to R. C. Ross being over, went home. * * *

.... Being without conviction that Tally knew of the Skeltons' intention to take Ross' life until after they had departed on their errand of death, and there being no evidence or pretense that between this time and the homicide any communication passed between them and Tally, we reach and declare the conclusion that the respondent did not command, direct, counsel, instigate, or encourage the Skeltons to take the life of Ross, and that, in whatever and all that was done by them and him, respectively, there was no understanding, preconcert, or conspiracy between them and him.

This narrows the issues to three inquiries—two of fact and one of law: First (a question of fact), did Judge Tally, on Sunday, February 4, 1894, knowing the intention of the Skeltons to take the life of Ross, and after they had gone in pursuit of him, do any act intended to further their design, and aid them in the taking of his life? If he did, then, second (a question of law), is it essential to his guilt that his act should have contributed to the effectuation of their design—to the death of Ross? And, if so, third (another inquiry of fact), did his act contribute to the death of Ross?

There can be no reasonable doubt that Judge Tally knew, soon after the Skeltons had departed, that they had gone in pursuit of Ross, and that they intended to take his life. Within a few minutes, he was informed by his wife that Ross had fled, and that the four Skeltons were pursuing him. He had seen three of them mounted and heavily armed. He knew the fourth, even keener on the trail than these, had gone on before. He knew their grievance. The fact that they intended to wreak vengeance, in the way they did, upon overtaking Ross, was known to all men in Scottsboro, as soon as the flight and pursuit became known. * * *

[As to the first inquiry,] we therefore find and hold that John B. Tally, with full knowledge that the Skeltons were in pursuit of Ross with the intent to take his life, committed acts, namely, kept watch at Scottsboro to prevent warning of danger being sent to Ross, and, with like purpose, sent the message to Huddleston, which were calculated to aid, and were committed by him with the intent to aid, the said Skeltons to take the life of Ross under the circumstances which rendered them guilty of murder.

[W]e are next to consider and determine the second inquiry.... We have already stated our conclusion, and the considerations which led us to it, that Judge Tally did not command, direct, incite, counsel, or encourage the Skeltons to the murder of Ross.... It is said ... that "the words 'aid' and 'abet' are pretty much the synonyms of each other;" and this has doubtless come to be true in the law, though originally a different meaning attached to each. The legal definition of "aid" is not different from its meaning in common parlance. It means "to assist," "to supplement the efforts of another." "Abet" is a French word, compounded of the two words "a" and "beter,"-"to bait or excite an animal;" ... "To abet is to incite or encourage a person to commit a crime. An abettor is a person who, being present or in the neighborhood, incites another to commit a crime, and thus becomes a principal in the offense." ... [T]o be an aider or abettor when no assistance is given or word uttered, the person so charged must have been present by preconcert, special or general, or at least to the knowledge of the principal, with the intent to aid him....

We are therefore clear to the conclusion that, before Judge Tally can be found guilty of aiding and abetting the Skeltons to kill Ross, it must appear that his vigil at Scottsboro to prevent Ross from being warned of his danger was by preconcert with them, or at least known to them, whereby they would naturally be incited, encouraged, and emboldened—"given confidence"—to the deed, or that he aided them to kill Ross, contributed to Ross' death, in point of physical fact, by means of the telegram he sent to Huddleston. The assistance given, however, need not contribute to the criminal result in the sense that but for it the result would not have ensued. It is quite sufficient if it facilitated a result that would have transpired without it. It is quite enough if the aid merely rendered it easier for the principal actor to accomplish the end intended by him and the aider and abettor, though in all human probability the end would have been attained without it. If the aid in homicide can be shown to have put the deceased at a disadvantage, to have deprived him of a single chance of life which but for it he would have had, he who furnishes such aid is guilty, though it cannot be known or shown that the dead man, in the absence thereof, would have availed himself of that chance. * * *

[A]nd so we are come to a consideration of the effect, if any, produced upon the situation at Stevenson by the message of Judge Tally to Huddleston. Its effect upon the situation could only have been through Huddleston, and upon his action in respect of the delivery to Ross of the message of warning sent by Ed Ross. This latter message reached Huddleston ..., we suppose, about five minutes—certainly not more than ten minutes—before Ross arrived at Stevenson. Immediately upon the heels of it, substantially at the same time, Tally's message to Huddleston was received by the latter. Ed Ross' message imported extreme urgency in its delivery, ... and it was the manifest duty of Huddleston to deliver it at the earliest practicable moment of time.

Huddleston appears to have appreciated the urgency of the case, and at first to have intended doing his duty. Upon receiving the two messages, he went at once without waiting, to copy them, to the Stevenson Hotel, which is located very near the telegraph office, in quest of Ross, upon the idea that he might have already arrived.... Not finding him there (for he had not yet reached Stevenson), Huddleston returned to the door of the depot, upstairs, in which was the telegraph office. By this time the command which Judge Tally had laid upon him had overmastered his sense of duty, and diverted him from his purpose to deliver Ed Ross' message to Robert. Standing there at the door, he saw a hack approaching from the direction of Scottsboro. He said then that he supposed Ross was in that hack....

[I]t was Huddleston's duty to go out to the road along which the hack was being driven, at a point opposite his own position at the depot, and near to it, and there and then have delivered the message or made known its contents to Ross.... He did not warn Ross, because he did not want Ross to get away, and this because Judge Tally had asked him not to let Ross get away.... So he sends a man in search of the marshal, whose whereabouts, and, of consequence, the time necessary to find and bring whom to the station, were unknown; beckons to William Tally to come to him; then turns and goes upstairs into the telegraph office.... [I]t cannot, we think, be doubted that he then had no purpose whatever of apprising Ross of the contents of the message, if ever, until he had had this conference with the brother of the man who had asked him not to deliver it at all. That this delay was to conserve such ulterior purpose as might be born of this conference, was wholly unwarranted, and was caused by the telegram of Judge Tally to Huddleston, we believe beyond a reasonable doubt.

It remains to be determined whether the unwarranted delay in the delivery of the message to Ross, or in advising him of its contents, thus caused by Judge Tally, with intent thereby to aid the Skeltons to kill Ross, did, in fact, aid them or contribute to the death of Ross. * * *

Can it be doubted that Ross' utter ignorance of John Skelton's presence with the others at Stevenson made it easier for John Skelton to take his life? Can it be doubted that his ignorance of the presence of all four Skeltons when the first gun was fired by Robert Skelton at Bloodwood, when, had he known it, he could have fled in the appreciable time between the time of the firing of the first and other shots-the next one being fired by the same man,-made it easier for them to take his life? Can it be doubted in any case that murder by lying in wait is facilitated by the unconsciousness of the victim? Or in any case that the chances of the intended victim would be improved, and his death rendered more difficult of accomplishment, if the first unfruitful shot apprises him of the number and the identity of his assailants, and the full scope and measure of their motive and purposes? We cannot believe otherwise.

It is inconceivable to us after the maturest consideration, reflection, and discussion, but that Ross' predicament was rendered infinitely more desperate, his escape more difficult, and his death of much more easy and certain accomplishment by the withholding from him of the message of Ed Ross. This withholding was the work of Judge Tally. An intent to aid the Skeltons to take the life of Ross actuated him to it. The intent was effectuated. They thereby were enabled to take him unawares, and to send him to his death without, we doubt not, his ever actually knowing who sought his life, or being able to raise a hand in defense, or to take an advised step in retreat.

[W]e are impelled to find that John B. Tally aided and abetted the murder of Robert C. Ross . . . and to adjudge that he is . . . guilty of murder . . .; and judgment deposing him from office will be entered on the records of this court.

c. Reciprocal Conduct

People v. Manini

Court of Appeals of New York.
79 N.Y.2d 561 (1992).

■ ALEXANDER, JUDGE.

The indictments in [these] cases resulted from investigations of the New York State Organized Crime Task Force (OCTF) into the importation of drugs into New York. In *Manini*, the investigation began in December 1987, and focused on drug trafficking in Onondaga and Cayuga Counties. In the course of its investigation, the OCTF discovered that Manini, an unindicted co-conspirator, Sanford Paige, and codefendant Vincent DeTomaso, along with several other parties, were involved in the importation into and distribution of drugs within New York. Operating out of California, Manini provided Paige and DeTomaso with cocaine on two separate occasions: in April of 1988 he flew to Buffalo from California with one kilogram of cocaine and sold it to Paige; in late June of 1988, Paige obtained nine ounces of cocaine from defendant "on credit" in California. Thereafter, on June 29, 1988, Paige flew from California to Rochester, New York, carrying almost four ounces of cocaine. He was met at the Rochester Airport by DeTomaso. They left the airport together and were both arrested and the cocaine seized. A 38–count indictment resulted; six of the charges related to Manini, including criminal possession in the second and third degrees for the possession by Paige of the almost four ounces of cocaine on June 29, 1988.

Defendant's motion to dismiss the indictment on the ground that the evidence presented to the Grand Jury was legally insufficient was granted by the trial court. . . . The Appellate Division affirmed. . . .

In People v. Fuente, the investigation leading to defendant's arrest and indictment began in the summer of 1988, and focused on cocaine trafficking by various individuals in the Monroe County area. [O]n November 19, 1988 the police observed [a] blue van driven by [codefendants Disnardo Carballo and Luz Martinez] pulling into [a] driveway.... About 30 seconds later Fuente, driving his own car, also pulled into the driveway. Both vehicles pulled into a parking area behind the house and remained there for about 10 minutes. The police then observed the vehicles pull out of the driveway and head down the street. When the van turned the corner and pulled into another driveway the police blocked the driveway with two police vehicles, and searched the van pursuant to a search warrant. Approximately one kilogram of cocaine was seized from the van.... Fuente was stopped at a different location nearby and also arrested. * * *

Under section 20.00 of the Penal Law, a defendant is accessorially liable for a criminal offense committed by another when he "solicits, requests, commands, importunes, or intentionally aids" another to engage in the offense, and when the defendant does so "with the mental culpability required for the commission" of the offense (Penal Law § 20.00). The People argue that inasmuch as defendant Manini "intentionally aided" Paige to commit the offense of criminal possession of a controlled substance when he sold him the drugs "on credit", and defendant Fuente "aided and abetted" his codefendants Carballo and Martinez in their possession of a controlled substance because they procured the drugs under his direction and on his behalf, the courts below erred in dismissing the possession counts against these defendants.

Penal Law § 20.10 provides, however, that a person is not criminally liable for an offense committed by another "when his own conduct, though causing or aiding the commission of such offense, is of a kind that is necessarily incidental [to the commission of the offense]" (see, Penal Law § 20.10). If the conduct of the person sought to be held liable as an accomplice constitutes a related but separate offense, that person is liable only for his/her own offense, and not for the offense committed by the principal (see, Penal Law § 20.10). Thus, if a person's conduct is of a kind that is "necessarily incidental" to the commission of the other person's offense that person is exempt from accomplice liability, and is criminally liable only for his or her own conduct if it constitutes a related but separate offense.

The People contend, however, that Penal Law § 20.10 does not prohibit assessing accessorial liability against Manini and Fuente for possession of cocaine by others because their conduct was not "necessarily incidental" to that possession within the meaning of the statute. They argue that the plain language of the statute and its legislative history indicate that the prohibition against accomplice liability is only applicable if the definition and nature of the principal's crime is such that, in all circumstances, not just in those presented in the particular case, the crime could not have been committed without the participation of the accessory. The People point out that a person may possess drugs without there ever being a seller, i.e., where the drugs were stolen or found, or even grown or manufactured directly by the possessor. Since the offense of criminal possession of a controlled substance does not contemplate or require, in all circumstances, the participation of another, the argument goes, defendants' conduct in either "intentionally aiding" (Manini) or "aiding or abetting" (Fuente) another to possess drugs is not "of a kind" that is "necessarily incidental" thereto, and thus section 20.10 is not applicable.

We do not believe, however, that the statute should be so narrowly interpreted. ... The underlying purpose of the statute appears to have been to prevent unnecessary prosecutions in cases where "ordinarily each culprit in such a reciprocal situation [would be] prosecuted for his particular offense" such that there would be "no need for torturing [the putative accessory's] conduct into accessorial guilt of the correlative offense".

Under the former Penal Law, "a fairly logical if strained" argument could be made that a person guilty of bribe giving was also guilty of bribe receiving. Although a literal reading of section 20.00 might support the same contention, section 20.10 would in fact preclude prosecution of the bribe giver for the crime of bribe receiving.

While, as the People point out, there may be situations in which a person may come into possession of illegal drugs by finding, stealing or manufacturing them, it is far more likely that the purchaser's possession resulted from a sale.[5] Thus, in the vast majority of cases, a "sale" is "necessarily incidental" to the possession of narcotics. In the typical drug transaction scenario, the seller will continue to be liable for his own actual possession and sale, and in some cases for conspiracy to commit narcotics offenses.

Viewed in this light, it seems unlikely that in enacting section 20.10, the Legislature intended that the typical drug transaction was not to be included as one of the "kinds of reciprocal conduct and offenses" covered by the statute. Indeed, while it is conceivable that a purchaser of narcotics could be convicted of criminal sale of a controlled substance as an accessory under section 20.00, application of section 20.10 limits his culpability to that resulting from his own conduct, i.e., possession. We do not perceive any reason, nor has any been advanced by the People to demonstrate why, where a purchaser obtains drugs from a seller, section 20.10 should not similarly preclude prosecution of the seller as an accessory to the resulting possession by the purchaser, especially since he remains liable for his own conduct: his possession and sale. * * *

We therefore conclude that in both *Manini* and *Fuente*, the evidence presented to the Grand Jury was legally insufficient, as a matter of law, to the extent that evidence tended to establish accessorial liability since Penal Law § 20.10 precludes prosecution of these defendants for criminal possession of a controlled substance where the possession was solely that of another.

QUESTIONS AND COMMENTS

1. In *Tavares*, what defense(s) might David and Michael raise? Were David and Michael "innocent" or "irresponsible," or both? Could Tavares have been convicted under a different theory?

5. The term "sell" is broadly defined in the Penal Law to include any form of transfer of a controlled substance from one person to another, and means "to sell, exchange, give or dispose of to another, or to offer or agree to do the same" (see, Penal Law § 220.00).

2. Contrast *Tally* with the Model Penal Code on the question of causation. What sort of causal connection, if any, does the Model Penal Code require for complicity liability? How, in other words, does the Model Penal Code answer the second inquiry in *Tally*? Why would the Model Penal Code drafters think that "attempted complicity ought to be criminal, and to distinguish it from effective complicity appears unnecessary where the crime has been committed," Model Penal Code Commentaries § 2.06, at 314? Do you agree? Why doesn't the *Tally* court require but-for causation? Would we ever be certain that a person who encouraged another to act criminally was a but-for cause of the principal's crime? Is it appropriate to think of people as "causing" others to act in a certain way? The standard (negative) answer is defended by Sanford Kadish. See, e.g., Sanford H. Kadish, Blame and Punishment: Essays in the Criminal Law 140–45 (1987) & Sanford H. Kadish, "A Theory of Complicity," in Issues in Contemporary Legal Philosophy: The Influence of H.L.A. Hart (Ruth Gavison ed., 1987).

At any rate, is the required causal connection between my act and the criminal act that is imputed to me the same, regardless of what theory of imputation is used (innocent/irresponsible agent vs. complicity)?

3. What's wrong with extending accomplice liability to "necessarily incidental" conduct, provided the defendant meets all the requirements for accomplice liability? What if, unlike in *Manini*, the necessarily incident conduct does *not* constitute criminal conduct in itself? What if the distribution of drugs were not a crime, say? Or the giving of a bribe? Are pledges accomplices in their own hazing? See, e.g., People v. Lenti, 46 Misc.2d 682, 260 N.Y.S.2d 284 (N.Y. County Ct. 1965). Assume that a legislature explicitly decriminalizes the possession of small quantities of marijuana (or punishes such possession as a mere "violation"). Would it make sense to punish someone who purchases a small amount of marijuana as an accomplice to the (serious) crime of selling or distributing marijuana, or would that undercut the legislature's attempt to decriminalize possession?

Relatedly, why shouldn't a "victim" be held liable as an accomplice? How can you be a victim and an accomplice at the same time?

4. *Complicity by Omission.* In State v. Jackson, 137 Wash.2d 712, 976 P.2d 1229 (1999), the Washington Supreme Court held accomplice liability does not reach a defendant who aids or abets the principal through inaction. The court pointed out that Washington's complicity statute, though otherwise modeled on the Model Penal Code provision, lacked an analogue to MPC § 2.06(3)(a)(iii). That subsection had been rejected by the legislative drafting commission because "the language is over-broad and might be held to encompass situations where accessorial liability should not attach" and "the rest of the section will cover all situations to which the excluded subdivision was addressed without raising the above-stated objection." The Model Penal Code drafters had in mind "[t]he policeman or the watchman who closes his eyes to a robbery or burglary [and thereby] fails to present an obstacle to its commission that he is obliged to interpose." Model Penal Code Commentaries § 2.06, at 320. Assuming they have the proper purpose to aid or abet, and a duty (toward whom—the victim or the principal?) why shouldn't they be held liable as accomplices? (Think about

Huddleston in *Tally*, supra.) Is A's duty to prevent B from committing an offense against C really the same as A's duty to prevent C from suffering harm not caused by a third person's criminal (illegal, immoral) conduct? Does the right to use force to prevent an offense imply a legal (criminally sanctioned?) duty to prevent the offense? See *Backun v. United States*, section 3 infra.

Can we adequately distinguish omissions from acts in this context? Do bar patrons who watch a gang rape without protesting or intervening *encourage* the rape by staying silent in a situation in which the perpetrators might expect disapproval, or do they act only if they use words to egg the principals on? Don't we communicate with one another through the selective use of silence as well as words? If the henchman asks the proverbial "Mob Boss" whether it would be better if a would-be informant never troubled him again and the "Boss" remained silent, would he have directed or encouraged the criminal homicide or simply failed to prevent it?

5. *Constructive Possession and Accomplice Liability.* In *Manini*, the prosecution tried another theory, with more success (at least with respect to Fuente). Instead of complicity, they argued constructive possession; compare and contrast the function and operation of constructive possession and accomplice liability. (For more on constructive possession, see supra ch. 4.)

> The People acknowledge in *Manini* that constructive possession is usually established by showing that a defendant exercised dominion and control over the place where contraband was seized or over the person who actually possessed the property. They argue, however, that a defendant's constructive possession may also be established by showing that he retained a "continuing possessory interest" in the contraband sufficient to give him the requisite dominion and control. They rely principally on United States v. Burroughs, 11th Cir., 830 F.2d 1574, where the defendant was charged with possession with intent to distribute, based on the actual possession of narcotics by others. Burroughs sold heroin "on credit" in New York to various individuals who ultimately possessed and sold the drugs in Jacksonville, Florida. Finding that he had a financial stake in the ultimate sale of the heroin in Florida, the court deemed Burroughs to have had constructive possession of the drugs seized from persons in Florida until he received payment, even though he relinquished physical possession of the drugs in New York.
>
> We have never adopted such a broad definition of constructive possession in this State, and are not persuaded that we should do so now. In New York, the rule has long been that to support a charge that a defendant was in constructive possession of tangible property, the People must show that the defendant exercised "dominion or control" over the property by a sufficient level of control over the area in which the contraband is found or over the person from whom the contraband is seized....
>
> Applying these principles to the facts in *Manini*, we conclude that the evidence was insufficient to establish the requisite level of control or authority by Manini over Paige to support a finding that Manini was

in constructive possession of the drugs seized from Paige in New York. The record does not reflect that any evidence was presented to the Grand Jury that Manini, in California, exercised any type of authority over Paige while Paige was in New York in possession of the cocaine. To the contrary, the record evidence is that Manini gave Paige the drugs "on credit" and fully expected to receive payment for them. In order to insure payment on the debt, Manini demanded and received "collateral" from Paige as security. Rather than establishing any continuing dominion and control over the cocaine, it is clear that Manini relinquished dominion and control over the drugs by selling them to Paige, albeit "on credit". There is no indication that Manini was involved in Paige's subsequent distribution or had any authority over what Paige did with the drugs after receiving them. Thus, the evidence presented was legally insufficient to establish that Manini was in constructive possession of the cocaine. The evidence presented in *Fuente*, however, compels a different result. Viewing that evidence, as we must, in the light most favorable to the People, we conclude that it was legally sufficient to establish defendant's liability, under a theory of constructive possession, for the actual possession of the kilogram of cocaine seized from the van occupied by codefendants Carballo and Martinez.

A defendant may constructively possess property if he has dominion and control over the drugs as a result of his authority over the person who actually possesses them, rather than through his access to or control over the place where the drugs are kept (see, e.g., People v. Rivera, 77 A.D.2d 538, 430 N.Y.S.2d 88 [supra ch. 4]). Here, there was evidence from the extensive intercepted telephone conversations that the cocaine seized from the van occupied by Carballo and Martinez had been obtained for resale to defendant's customers and was being transported on defendant's behalf and at his direction. Moreover, in contrast to the situation in *Manini*, Fuente, although not in physical possession of the narcotics, retained a level of control over the drugs sufficient to support a finding of constructive possession. Minutes before the seizure of the cocaine, he was observed following closely behind the van in his own car, and both vehicles stopped together for several minutes in the parking area of [a] driveway . . . before continuing their progress. Fuente was subsequently apprehended in his own car only a short distance from where the van was stopped.

* * *

Problem

For purposes of this Problem, ignore any possible issues of conspiracy; focus solely on traditional accomplice liability:

Peter Prince is a salesman at a store in a suburban mall that sells high price audio equipment. Late one afternoon, his boss tells him that he will have to leave early that day, due to his wife's illness, and he asks Peter to stay till closing time (an hour after Peter usually leaves) and to close up the store. When his boss leaves, Peter decides he will steal a large amount of expensive, but relatively portable equipment that is on display and in the small storage room right off one of the demo rooms. He has no key to get into the warehouse in back of the store. He believes he can readily find buyers for the stolen equipment back in Portland, Oregon where he'd lived till three months earlier.

Peter telephones his friend Alicia and tells her of his plan. He asks her to come by the mall, park her car opposite the store and watch out for the security guard who patrols the mall after its 6 o'clock closing time. He asks her to warn him with hand signals if she sees the security guard approach. He then calls his friends Bart (who lives down the street) and Carlotta (back in Portland); he asks Bart to do just what he asked Alicia to do, and asks Carlotta if he can stay with her in Portland until he sells the stolen equipment.

At 6:15, Alicia shows up at the mall. Though Bart agreed to come when Peter phoned him, Bart never shows up at all. At 6:20, Peter begins to place a number of expensive items in a large garbage bag, trying to look as if he's just taking out the trash. Dean, who works at an ice cream store in the same mall, notices what Peter's doing, and believes that Peter will share some of the proceeds of the larceny with him if he helps him out in some way, so *he* starts looking out for the security guard, unaware that Alicia's already doing just that.

At 6:23, Dean's girlfriend Ellen arrives to pick him up; he runs over to her car to tell him that he's busy for a few more minutes and that she should park across the street and wait for him. He explains to her that she should be available to drive this guy who's stealing stereo equipment away, should he need to ditch his own car, and she agrees to do that. By 6:25, the time Dean returns to the area just outside the store, Peter's already out the back door with his garbage bags full of audio equipment, but Dean does not see that Peter's gone. Alicia's gone home too, never having had to shout or signal, since the security guard has not come by. At 6:27, the security guard comes by, and Dean shouts, "Here he comes!" though Peter does not hear this, since he is already gone. The security guard approaches Dean to ask him what he's shouting about; when Ellen sees this, she drives away. Though Dean doesn't really answer him, the guard checks inside the audio store and sees that some equipment is almost surely missing.

Assess whether Alicia, Bart, Carlotta, Dean and/or Ellen are accomplices to Peter's crime.

Assume now, too, that Alicia had done precisely what she did, but that Peter had had a change of heart and taken nothing from the store. Assess her liability in that case.

Does it matter in assessing Carlotta's liability as an accomplice whether she actually puts him up in Portland when he gets there? If so, how?

In thinking about these questions, consider whether the answers are different if you are in a jurisdiction that has adopted the Model Penal Code or in a jurisdiction following the more traditional complicity rules.

3. Mens Rea

a. Purpose vs. Knowledge to Facilitate or Encourage Proscribed Conduct

United States v. Peoni

United States Circuit Court of Appeals for the Second Circuit.
100 F.2d 401 (1938).

■ Learned Hand, Circuit Judge.

Peoni was indicted in the Eastern District of New York upon three counts for possessing counterfeit money.... The jury convicted him on all counts, and the only question we need consider is whether the evidence was enough to sustain the verdict. It was this. In the Borough of the Bronx Peoni sold counterfeit bills to one, Regno; and Regno sold the same bills to one, Dorsey, also in the Bronx. All three knew that the bills were counterfeit, and Dorsey was arrested while trying to pass them in the Borough of Brooklyn. The question is whether Peoni was guilty as an accessory to Dorsey's possession....

The prosecution's argument is that, as Peoni put the bills in circulation and knew that Regno would be likely, not to pass them himself, but to sell them to another guilty possessor, the possession of the second buyer was a natural consequence of Peoni's original act, with which he might be charged. If this were a civil case, that would be true; an innocent buyer from Dorsey could sue Peoni and get judgment against him for his loss. But the rule of criminal liability is not the same; since Dorsey's possession was not de facto Peoni's, and since Dorsey was not Peoni's agent, Peoni can be liable only as an accessory to Dorsey's act of possession. The test of that must be found in the appropriate federal statute (18 U.S.C.A. § 550[a]). The first statute dealing with the matter was passed in 1790 and made those accessories who should "aid and assist, procure, command, counsel or advise", murder or robbery on land or sea, or piracy at sea. This was broadened in 1870 to include any felony, and by it an accessory was anyone who "counsels, advises or procures" the crime; this phrase was probably regarded as an equivalent of the first. Both those statutes were repealed in 1909 by Sec. 341 of the Criminal Code, and supplanted by Sec. 332 of that act, which like Sec. 550 of Title 18 U.S. Code, 18 U.S.C.A. § 550, read as follows: "aids, abets, counsels, commands, induces, or procures". The substance of that formula goes back a long way. Pollock & Maitland, Vol. II, p. 507, in speaking of the English law at the beginning of the 14th Century, say that already "the law of homicide is quite wide enough to comprise * * * those who have 'procured, counselled, commanded or abetted' the felony".... In The Case of Macdaniel & others, 1755, Foster, 125, the question was bruited whether one might be an accessory at one remove, and it was said, though obiter, that he might, for "whoever procured a felony to be committed though it be by the intervention of a third person is an accessory * * * For what is there in the notion of commanding, hiring,

a. Now codified at 18 U.S.C. § 2.—Eds.

counselling, aiding or abetting which may not be effected by the intervention of a third person." Blackstone, 1768, Book IV, pp. 36 & 37, described an accessory as "he who in any wise commands or counsels another to commit an unlawful act"....

It will be observed that all these definitions have nothing whatever to do with the probability that the forbidden result would follow upon the accessory's conduct; and that they all demand that he in some sort associate himself with the venture, that he participate in it as in something that he wishes to bring about, that he seek by his action to make it succeed. All the words used—even the most colorless, "abet"—carry an implication of purposive attitude towards it. So understood, Peoni was not an accessory to Dorsey's possession; his connection with the business ended when he got his money from Regno, who might dispose of the bills as he chose; it was of no moment to him whether Regno passed them himself, and so ended the possibility of further guilty possession, or whether he sold them to a second possible passer. His utterance of the bills was indeed a step in the causal chain which ended in Dorsey's possession, but that was all. Perhaps he was Regno's accessory. ... Be that as it may, nobody, so far as we can find, has ever held that a contract is criminal, because the seller has reason to know, not that the buyer will use the goods unlawfully, but that some one further down the line may do so. Nor is it at all desirable that the seller should be held indefinitely. The real gravamen of the charge against him is his utterance of the bills; and he ought not to be tried for that wherever the prosecution may pick up any guilty possessor—perhaps thousands of miles away....

Backun v. United States

United States Circuit Court of Appeals for the Fourth Circuit.
112 F.2d 635 (1940).

■ PARKER, CIRCUIT JUDGE.

This is an appeal from a conviction and sentence under an indictment charging the appellant Backun and one Zucker with the crime of transporting stolen merchandise of a value in excess of $5,000 in interstate commerce, knowing it to have been stolen, in violation of the National Stolen Property Act, 18 U.S.C.A. § 415. Zucker pleaded guilty and testified for the prosecution. There was evidence to the effect that he was apprehended at a pawnshop in Charlotte, N.C., in possession of a large quantity of silverware, a portion of which was shown to have been stolen a short while before. He testified that he purchased all of the silverware from Backun in New York; that the purchase was partly on credit; that Backun had the silverware concealed in a closet and in the cellar of his residence; that there was no sale for second hand silverware in New York but a good market for it in the South; that Backun knew of Zucker's custom to travel in the South and was told by Zucker that he wished to take the silverware on the road with him; and that Backun sold to him for $1,400 silverware which was shown by other witnesses to be of a much greater value. A part of the silverware was wrapped in a laundry bag which was identified by means of a laundry ticket as having been in the possession of Backun. As bearing upon

Backun's knowledge that the stolen silverware was to be transported by Zucker in interstate commerce, the following quotation from the testimony of Zucker is pertinent, viz.:

> "Q. And you didn't discuss with him what you were going to do with it? A. He knows I go on the road.
>
> "Q. You didn't discuss with him where you were going? A. I told him I wanted to go on the road with it. He knew that. That is the reason he wanted to sell it to me.
>
> "Mr. Jones: I ask Your Honor to strike that out.
>
> "Q. Did you discuss with him and tell him where you were going? A. Yes sir."

There is no serious controversy as to the evidence being sufficient to show that Backun sold the property to Zucker knowing it to have been stolen. It is contended, however, . . . that there is no evidence that Backun had anything to do with the transportation in interstate commerce. . . .

[T]he case presented is not that of a mere seller of merchandise, who knows that the buyer intends to put it to an unlawful use, but who cannot be said in anywise to will the unlawful use by the buyer. It is the case of a sale of stolen property by a guilty possessor who knows that the buyer will transport it in interstate commerce in violation of law and who desires to sell it to him for that reason. The stolen property was not salable in New York. Backun knew that Zucker could dispose of it on his visits to the Southern pawnbrokers and would take it with him on his trips to the South. The sale was made at a grossly inadequate price and Zucker was credited for a part even of that. While there was no express contract that Zucker was to carry the property out of the state, Backun knew that he would do so; and, by making the sale to him, caused the transportation in interstate commerce just as certainly as if that transportation had been a term of the contract of sale. . . . His guilt as a principal is fixed by section 332 of the Criminal Code, 18 U.S.C.A. § 550, which provides that one who "aids, abets, counsels, commands, induces, or procures" the commission of an offense is guilty as a principal, as well as by the terms of the Stolen Property Act itself which make it a crime to cause stolen property to be transported in interstate commerce.

Whether one who sells property to another knowing that the buyer intends to use it for the commission of a felony renders himself criminally liable as aiding and abetting in its commission, is a question as to which there is some conflict of authority. [S]ince it is elementary that every citizen is under moral obligation to prevent the commission of felony, if possible, and has the legal right to use force to prevent its commission and to arrest the perpetrator without warrant, it is difficult to see why, in selling goods which he knows will make its perpetration possible with knowledge that they are to be used for that purpose, he is not aiding and abetting in its commission within any fair meaning of those terms. Undoubtedly he would be guilty, were he to give to the felon the goods which make the perpetration of the felony possible with knowledge that they would be used for that purpose. . . .

Guilt as an accessory depends, not on "having a stake" in the outcome of crime, . . . but on aiding and assisting the perpetrators; and those who make a profit by furnishing to criminals, whether by sale or otherwise, the means to carry on their nefarious undertakings aid them just as truly as if they were actual partners with them, having a stake in the fruits of their enterprise. To say that the sale of goods is a normally lawful transaction is beside the point. The seller may not ignore the purpose for which the purchase is made if he is advised of that purpose, or wash his hands of the aid that he has given the perpetrator of a felony by the plea that he has merely made a sale of merchandise. One who sells a gun to another knowing that he is buying it to commit a murder, would hardly escape conviction as an accessory to the murder by showing that he received full price for the gun; and no difference in principle can be drawn between such a case and any other case of a seller who knows that the purchaser intends to use the goods which he is purchasing in the commission of felony. In any such case, not only does the act of the seller assist in the commission of the felony, but his will assents to its commission, since he could refuse to give the assistance by refusing to make the sale. * * *

But even if the view be taken that aiding and abetting is not to be predicated of an ordinary sale made with knowledge that the purchaser intends to use the goods purchased in the commission of felony, we think that the circumstances relied on by the government here are sufficient to establish the guilt of Backun. The sale here was not of a mere instrumentality to be used in the commission of felony, but of the very goods which were to be feloniously transported. Backun knew not only that the commission of felony was contemplated by Zucker with respect to such goods, but also that the felony could not be committed by Zucker unless the sale were made to him. The sale thus made possible the commission of the felony by Zucker; and, if Zucker is to be believed, the commission of the felony was one of the purposes which Backun had in mind in making the sale. After testifying that he had told Backun that he wished to go on the road with the silverware (i.e. transport it in interstate commerce), he says "He (Backun) knew that. That is the reason he wanted to sell it to me." There can be no question, therefore, but that the evidence sustains the view that the felony committed by Zucker flowed from the will of Backun as well as from his own will, and that Backun aided its commission by making the sale. There was thus evidence of direct participation of Backun in the criminal purpose of Zucker; and whatever view be taken as to the case of a mere sale, certainly such evidence is sufficient to establish guilt. . . .

b. Criminal Facilitation Statutes

People v. Gordon

Court of Appeals of New York.
32 N.Y.2d 62 (1973).

■ FULD, CHIEF JUDGE.

The defendant stands convicted of the crime of criminal facilitation in the second degree, a class A misdemeanor, in violation of section 115.00 of the Penal Law. A person is guilty of the crime, that section provides, "when, believing it probable that he is rendering aid to a person who intends to commit a crime, he engages in conduct which provides such person with means or opportunity for the commission thereof and which in fact aids such person to commit a felony."

Richard Cryan, a trooper with the State Police, worked as an undercover agent investigating the sale of narcotics and dangerous drugs in the City of Batavia in up-state New York. On May 1, 1969, he met a Larry Hicks, a police informer, and went with him to a restaurant in that city where they joined several men, one of whom was the defendant, at a table. The defendant, learning from Cryan that he was interested in buying marijuana—referred to as "grass" or "hash"—told the trooper that "a fellow by the name of Craig, who lives in the apartment on 110 Bank Street, deals quite heavily in narcotics" and suggested that he, Cryan, should go to that address and "attempt to effect a narcotics purchase." The defendant, at the trooper's request, gave him directions how to get to 110 Bank Street. Cryan and Hicks then left the restaurant and proceeded to that address.

Upon arriving there, Trooper Cryan knocked on the door and Craig Newlon responded. The undercover agent said that he wanted to "cop"—i.e., purchase—marijuana and Newlon invited the two men inside. After some bargaining, he sold the officer $20 worth of marijuana.

As indicated, the defendant was subsequently indicted. Accusing him of criminal facilitation, the indictment, in effect, charged that he aided Newlon in committing a felony—namely, the sale of marijuana to the undercover agent Cryan—by providing the latter with information to enable Newlon to sell him a quantity of marijuana. The defendant, following a jury trial, was convicted and, on appeal, the judgment of conviction was unanimously affirmed.

Section 115.00 of the Penal Law, as well as the indictment, requires proof that the defendant believed it "probable" that, when he acted, he was rendering aid to a person who then "intends" to commit a crime. The type of situation contemplated and envisaged by the section is clearly one involving assistance, of the indicated nature, by the defendant to a person who, at the time of such assistance or facilitation, not only intends to commit a crime but who subsequently does commit it in a felonious form.

As the Practice Commentary suggests, section 115.00 was designed to cover cases such as these: (1) a person "sells a gun to a man who he knows intends to use it to kill his wife" or (2) the telephone company "provides telephone service to a person with knowledge that he intends to use it for bookmaking purposes" or (3) a night watchman for a warehouse "looks the other way when he sees his burglar friend about to break into the warehouse." Here, on the contrary, although the defendant may have believed it probable that Cryan intended to commit a crime (of possessing a dangerous drug) and that he was aiding him to do so, he may not be adjudged guilty of facilitation on that basis—and, indeed, the indictment is not predicated on any such hypothesis—since Cryan did not commit any felony: it is enough to note that the possession of a dangerous drug, in the absence of aggravating circumstances, is a misdemeanor and not a felony (Penal Law, § 220.05).

Under no circumstances, however, can a conviction of criminal facilitation be based upon the unusual theory, here advanced, that the defendant aided Newlon to commit the crime of selling drugs to Cryan. The conduct relied upon as constituting the alleged facilitation consisted of the defendant's declaration to Cryan that Newlon sold drugs and suggesting that Cryan visit him in order to "attempt to effect a narcotics purchase." The statute, as we have already noted, expressly requires that the defendant-facilitator believe that he is rendering aid to a person who "intends to commit a crime". In this case, it is indisputable that, at the time the defendant had his conversation with Cryan, Newlon, who had never even heard of that individual, could not possibly have "intended" to commit the crime of selling marijuana to him. And it follows, therefore, that the defendant could not possibly have "believed" it probable that Newlon intended to commit that crime. Thus, as is manifest, one of the basic elements required by the statute, namely, the element of intent, was missing.

To stretch this offense beyond its normal and intended scope to cover a case of this nature would extend it beyond its plainly circumscribed boundaries and might well lead to further abuse in its construction and application.

In the view which we have taken, we have put off for another day and for a more appropriate case consideration of the defendant's contention that there is a distinction between "conduct"—as used in section 115.00—and 'speech' and that, consequently, conviction under the statute requires proof of more than words.

The order appealed from should be reversed and the indictment dismissed.

QUESTIONS AND COMMENTS

1. The big mens rea issue in the law of complicity is the question of whether knowledge that one's behavior facilitates someone else's criminal conduct is enough, or whether purpose should be required. The Model Penal Code drafters were divided on the issue. The main proponent of the knowledge test was the main drafter of the Code, Herbert Wechsler (along with various commentators and judges, including the judge who wrote *Backun*). The main proponent of the contrary view was Judge Learned Hand, the author of *Peoni*.

Hand's faction won—an unusual feat since Wechsler ordinarily got his way. The original draft of the complicity section, as proposed by Wechsler, contained the following provision, later omitted:

> (3) A person is an accomplice of another person in commission of a crime if:
>
> > (b) acting with knowledge that such other person was committing or had the purpose of committing the crime, he knowingly, substantially facilitated its commission; or
> >
> > [Alternate: (b) acting with knowledge that such other person was committing or had the purpose of committing the crime, he

knowingly provided means or opportunity for the commission of the crime, substantially facilitating its commission.]

Most jurisdictions agreed with Hand and require purpose. But what about the cases that wouldn't be covered by a purposeful complicity provision—the ones the facilitation statute in *Gordon* was designed to capture (see also Model Penal Code Commentaries § 2.06, at 316)? Should someone who "sells a gun to a man who he knows intends to use it to kill his wife" really escape criminal liability? Why do we hesitate to punish knowing complicity, particularly given that purpose may be difficult to prove, absent an outright confession on the part of the defendant? Then again, why should it matter how difficult it is to prove purpose? Is this difficulty unique to the law of complicity? Should we lighten the prosecution's burden in cases of serious crime, so that complicity in murder, for instance, would require only knowledge, but complicity in shoplifting required purpose?

2. How would you describe the mental state Hand rejects as insufficient in *Peoni*—knowledge or recklessness? Is the reason why Hand rejects it that it considers probabilities, rather than objectives, or that the probabilities of which the accomplice must be aware are insufficiently high (so that requiring knowledge rather than purpose might satisfy Hand after all)? From Hand's perspective, does it make a difference whether Peoni knows for certain, or is merely pretty sure, that someone will end up possessing the counterfeit money he is distributing? And what does Hand mean when he speaks of requiring that the defendant associate himself with the principal's venture or share a true purpose to achieve the principal's criminal ends? There are certainly easy cases when the object of the crime is financial: The defendant has a true purpose that the principal succeed if he gets a percentage of the principal's take. But what about more "expressive crimes" (assault, vandalism)? What about financial crimes in which the defendant's claims are less explicitly tied to the success of the particular venture?

3. How useful is the broad distinction between purpose and knowledge in differentiating between punishable and nonpunishable assistance? Consider the following scenarios.

A sells P a car knowing that P intends to use it to smuggle, but it's just a regular old car sold at regular market price.

B sells P a car knowing that P will use it to smuggle. He also knows it is particularly well-suited to that end, but the sale is at regular market price for cars of that original price and age, commanding no premium because of its unusual suitability for smuggling. Such cars, however, are not easy to obtain.

C builds P a smuggling compartment in the car and gets paid exceedingly well to do it, considerably more than laborers would be able to charge for equally skilled work, in part because few mechanics want to get mixed up with people like P, and perhaps also because he is expected to be quiet about the smuggling plan. C detests P and sincerely hopes he will get caught. Moreover, he knows no details of the smuggling plan and gets no more money from P if and when the plan succeeds. (That is to say, he's fully paid upon completion of his work; he does not, *ex post*, "split the loot.")

What is the argument that A is guilty under *neither* the Hand nor the Parker test? What is the (trickier?) argument that C is guilty under both? If it is indeed true that the tests are most likely to affect liability in B's case, should we consider how common (or significant) cases "like" this one would be? Can you think of other fact patterns in which the use of one test rather than the other will be outcome-determinative?

On what grounds might we distinguish between A, B, and C? Blameworthiness? Dangerousness?

If knowledge is enough for accomplice liability, is "willful blindness" enough as well? Is it enough to show that the defendant *should have known* that he was aiding a crime? Why not require recklessness (or even "believing it probable" that I'm aiding or abetting)? Why not grade accomplice liability by the specific mental state I have with respect to my action aiding or abetting another's criminal conduct, so that we have purposeful complicity, knowing complicity, and so on? Why do we need an on-off switch in complicity law when it comes to mens rea?

Can we escape the difficulties of mens rea in complicity cases by turning to an objective test—by asking, for instance, whether "in the ordinary course of things [the crime] was the natural or probable consequence" of my aiding or abetting? See Sharma v. State, 56 P.3d 868 (Nev. 2002) (abandoning this approach because "it permits conviction without proof that the accused possessed the state of mind required by the statutory definition of the crime").

4. What, exactly, is the question that the doctrine of complicity tries to answer? "When are those who supply 'goods or services' to offenders criminally liable?" Or, "When am I legally accountable for another's criminal conduct?" Or, "When am I sufficiently involved in some criminal enterprise to warrant punishment?" Or, "When am I so closely associated with another person that I am liable for whatever that person does?" Is the accomplice aiding a crime, or is she aiding a criminal? Is the disagreement about the various prerequisites for accomplice liability a function of a disagreement about the point of accomplice liability? In other words, are the different tests answering different questions?

Consider the (presumably common) case in which an accused accessory gives the principal his car (his weapon, his burglar's tools). The alleged accomplice might know little about the principal's precise plans. He may or may not be (implicitly? explicitly?) compensated more if the principal uses the car more often, or in a more lucrative (but dangerous?) burglary. Should the alleged accomplice be responsible for each and every crime the principal commits using the car (weapon, tools)? Is it fair if the punishment an accomplice receives turns entirely on a fact utterly outside his control—the behavior of a principal he does not direct or even consult with?

There is some disagreement on the question of whether—and under what circumstances—a defendant-accomplice can be liable for offenses committed by the principal other than those he explicitly intended to aid or abet. For instance, should the defendant-accomplice who intends to aid the principal in battering a victim be liable for homicide (murder or manslaughter) if he simply *should have known* that the principal might kill? The Model Penal Code and some jurisdictions say no. Model Penal Code § 2.06(3) & Commentaries § 2.06(3), at 310–13. Other jurisdictions disagree. See, e.g., People v. Prettyman, 14 Cal.4th 248, 926 P.2d 1013, 58 Cal.Rptr.2d 827 (1996) (defendant-accomplice liable for principal's crimes that were "natural and probable consequence" of the crime originally aided or abetted); People v. Croy, 41 Cal.3d 1, 12 n.5, 221 Cal.Rptr. 592, 710 P.2d 392 (1985) (defendant-accomplice liable for principal's crimes that were "reasonably foreseeable" consequence of the crime originally aided or abetted); see also Kan. Stat. Ann. § 21–3205(2) (accomplice "also liable for any other crime committed in pursuance of the intended crime if reasonably foreseeable by such person as a probable consequence of committing or attempting to commit the crime intended"). Assume (for argument's sake) that we reject the Model Penal Code's position and are willing to convict people of aiding a serious crime when they intend only to aid a less serious one: Isn't there still a (significant) distinction between crimes that are reasonably foreseeable and those that are probable? Can't we foresee many events we think are unlikely to occur?

In People v. Luparello, 187 Cal.App.3d 410, 231 Cal.Rptr. 832 (1986), the defendant asked a group of men to extract information from Mark Martin "at any cost." When they showed up at Martin's house armed with a collection of weapons, Martin was killed by an unidentified shooter. Luparello was convicted of murder under an accomplice theory on the ground that Martin's death was reasonably foreseeable. The majority affirmed. Judge Wiener concurred in the result, but laid out a comprehensive critique of the doctrine that an accomplice is liable for the foreseeable consequences of the principal's conduct he intended to aid or abet:

> The major fallacy I see in the "foreseeable consequence" doctrine is not so much that it attributes an unintended *act* to the accomplice but rather that it assesses the degree of his culpability for that act not by his own mental state but rather by the mental state of the perpetrator and/or the circumstances of the crime. The present case provides an appropriate example. The assault on Mark Martin ... involved a foreseeable risk of death or serious injury. We can assume ... that Luparello was criminally negligent in failing to appreciate the degree of risk. Under usual circumstances, a person negligently causing the death of another is guilty, at most, of involuntary manslaughter. Here, however, Luparello's liability is not based on his individual mental state but instead turns on the jury's finding that the unidentified shooter intentionally killed Martin while lying in wait. Thus, Luparello is guilty of first degree murder. If the circumstances of Luparello's participation were exactly the same but the shooter did not "lie in wait," Luparello could only be convicted of second degree murder. I am intrigued by the notion that if unknown to Luparello, the shooter ingested drugs and/or alcohol to the point where he did not in fact harbor the requisite malice, Luparello would presumably be guilty only of voluntary manslaughter. And to take it a step further, if it turned out the shooter was insane, would Luparello have no liability at all for Martin's homicide? ... I find such fortuity of result irrational.

So too, apparently, do Professors LaFave and Scott in their treatise on criminal law: "The 'natural and probable consequence' rule of accomplice liability, if viewed as a broad generalization, is inconsistent with more fundamental principles of our system of criminal law. It would permit liability to be predicated upon negligence even when the crime involved requires a different state of mind. Such is not possible as to one who has personally committed a crime, and should likewise not be the case as to those who have given aid or counsel." (LaFave & Scott, Handbook on Criminal Law (1972 ed.) p. 516.)

The drafters of the Model Penal Code reached a similar conclusion. Section 2.06(3)(a) establishes a standard for accomplice liability which ... requires that the accomplice act "with the purpose of promoting or facilitating the commission of the offense." Missing from the Model Penal Code, however, is any reference to the "foreseeable consequence" doctrine. The Comment to the section addresses the issue as follows: "[The accomplice] must have the purpose to promote or facilitate the particular conduct that forms the basis for the charge, and thus he will not be liable for conduct that does not fall within this purpose. This does not mean, of course, that the precise means used in the commission of the crime must have been fixed or contemplated or, when they have been, that liability is limited to their employment. One who solicits an end, or aids or agrees to aid in its achievement, is an accomplice in whatever means may be employed, insofar as they constitute or commit an offense fairly envisaged in the purposes of the association. *But when a wholly different crime has been committed, thus involving conduct not within the conscious objectives of the accomplice, he is not liable for it....*" (Model Pen. Code & Commentaries, com. 6(b) to § 2.06, pp. 310–311, italics added.)....

[T]he "foreseeable consequence" doctrine [is] founded on the ... outmoded and logically indefensible proposition that if a person exhibits some intent to violate the law, we need not be terribly concerned that the contemplated crime was far less serious than the crime which actually took place....

.... The artificial imputation of stepped-up intent ... is inconsistent with the "universal and persistent" notion that criminal punishment must be proportional to the defendant's culpable mental state. Justice Mosk's dissent in *Taylor* v. *Superior Court* (1970) 3 Cal.3d 578, 593 [91 Cal.Rptr. 275, 477 P.2d 131] expressed it well: "Fundamental principles of criminal responsibility dictate that the defendant be subject to a greater penalty only when he has demonstrated a greater degree of culpability. To ignore that rule is at best to frustrate the deterrent purpose of punishment, and at worst to risk constitutional invalidation on the ground of invidious discrimination." The fact that the accomplice ... intended to facilitate some less serious criminal act does not render these fundamental principles inapplicable.... "Under our system of criminal justice even a thief is entitled to complain that he has been unconstitutionally convicted and imprisoned as a burglar." (*Jackson* v. *Virginia* (1979) 443 U.S. 307, 323–324 [61 L.Ed.2d 560, 576–577, 99 S.Ct. 2781].)

.... Here ... Luparello has been convicted of first degree murder under circumstances where, in the absence of the "foreseeable consequence" doctrine, he would be guilty at most of involuntary manslaughter.

Can the foreseeable consequences doctrine be defended (in light of the traditional rationales of punishment)? An English commentator suggests that "the person who embarks on a joint enterprise knowing that his confederate may intentionally kill is taking a deliberate risk of assisting or encouraging not merely killing but murder." John C. Smith, Case and Comment, 1991 Crim. L. Rev. 134. Is this true in every case? Would this observation lend support to the foreseeable consequences doctrine? Would it support Luparello's murder conviction?

What is perhaps more troublesome is what to do in cases in which the defendant-accomplice clearly intends to aid a principal in achieving a *range* of possible criminal goals. See, e.g., Director of Public Prosecutions for Northern Ireland v. Maxwell, [1978] 3 All. E.R. 1140 (defendants knew that the principals in the Irish Republican Army they have aided are planning "a military operation," but are not certain precisely what crime they plan). These are neither cases in which the principal has clearly done something worse than the defendant-accomplice intended to aid her in doing, nor are they cases in which the defendant-accomplice had a clear purpose to aid or facilitate the precise conduct the principal engaged in or to help achieve the result she desired.

5. Consider alternatives to accomplice liability. A general facilitation statute (like the one in New York) is an obvious example. (What's the mens rea of facilitation in New York?) Would it matter, under such a statute, whether the defendant is facilitating the felony that the principal ends up committing in fact? What if I believe I'm probably facilitating a drug sale on day 1, but I end up facilitating it on day 2? To another purchaser? Of a different drug? Of a different quantity? On this point, compare *Gordon* with the following facts, which were held to constitute facilitation:

> [Billy Ron Adams, David Bennett, and George Leschorn were convicted of burglary and grand larceny in connection with a break-in at Ray Dann's Town and Country Trading Post, where they stole cigarettes, a small amount of cash, food stamps, and six shotguns.] [O]n the night of the burglary [Leschorn's wife and Bennett's girlfriend] went to [Adams's] home so they could babysit his six children while he went somewhere with Bennett and Leschorn. While Leschorn's wife testified that the men never mentioned that they were planning to burglarize anything or where they were going and that she would not have babysat for defendant had she known of such plans, she also testified that she thought that her husband and Bennett were going to raid drug houses for money that night, she knew they intended to commit a crime, and she knew that by babysitting for defendant he would be free to go out and do "bad things" with the two other men.
>
> Bennett's girlfriend testified that the men never mentioned stealing anything that night, they did not discuss their plans for the evening because she did not want to know, and Bennett specifically

> would not tell her what he was doing in order to protect her. She also testified that she was present in the car on a previous occasion when Bennett and defendant burglarized a home, she knew that when they said they were going to "make money" they planned to do something illegal, the men stated that night that they were going to "make money," she babysat for defendant's children that night so he would be available to go with the other two men, and she knew they were probably going to commit a crime that night. Although the women were unaware of what establishment the men intended to burglarize, the men themselves were uncertain where they would be fortunate enough to "make money" that night.

People v. Adams, 307 A.D.2d 475, 763 N.Y.S.2d 347 (N.Y. App. Div. 2003).

6. Alternatively, we might regulate—prospectively—certain activities which we know *generally* bear a certain connection to criminal conduct, without resting criminal liability on the connection between the defendant's conduct and that of a particular principal. For instance, we might forbid the sale of drug paraphernalia, enact laws against the sale of radar detection devices, or proscribe the distribution of contraceptives to minors, rather than punish the seller or distributor for complicity in drug possession, speeding, and statutory rape, respectively.

Presumably, sellers dispense a number of items that are routinely used in crimes (most obviously guns). Does it make sense for the legislature to enact a precise code, detailing when one can and cannot sell guns with or without certain background checks or mandated waiting periods, rather than relying on either conventional accomplice liability (with a "knowledge" mental state) or facilitation statutes? Cf. Robert Weisberg, "Reappraising Complicity," 4 Buff. Crim. L. Rev. 271 (2000). What is the argument that we need to retain at least a residual role for accomplice liability in these cases? Is it possible for a legislature to enumerate (and proscribe) all the precise ways that people might employ to aid someone in meeting a criminal objective?

Are these types of prospective, anticipatory, regulation preferable to a complicity regime that derives liability from criminal conduct that has actually occurred? How close must the connection be between "facilitating" conduct and "real" criminal conduct? Should the *absence* of intent to facilitate criminal conduct count as a defense in these cases? How many of these specific prohibitions would we need to cover the ground of a general complicity proscription?

7. *Mistakes*. What if I am completely unaware of the fact that I am assisting another person in committing a crime? Assume my friend asks me if he can borrow my shotgun so that he can shoot up his old t.v. set in his backyard, just for laughs. What if it turns out the t.v. was not his after all? Am I liable as an accomplice in criminal mischief (Model Penal Code § 220.3)?

Now assume that my friend told me that he planned to use my shotgun to shoot up his roommate's t.v. I lend him the gun, but he instead uses it to rob a bank. Am I an accomplice in a bank robbery? What if I think I'm aiding one crime, but actually end up aiding another?

Now assume that my friend does use my shotgun to blow up his very own t.v., but I think that criminal mischief criminalizes destroying anyone's property, including one's own. What if I think I'm aiding a crime, but it turns out the conduct isn't criminal? Conversely, what if my friend told me that he planned to use my shotgun to destroy his roommate's broken t.v., but I believe that destroying another's worthless property is not a crime?

In each of these scenarios, does it matter whether the principal deceived me—or whether I was mistaken for some other reason?

8. *Purpose vs. Motive*. X decides to help P commit a burglary; he assists him in disabling an alarm system so he can enter a store. His sole aim, though, is to get P in trouble, and he calls the police to tell them that P is in the store. See Wilson v. People, 103 Colo. 441, 87 P.2d 5 (1939) (reversing a conviction in a similar case). Think, too, about a case in which Y hands P a loaded gun that P uses to kill V: is Y an accomplice to murder, even if her only goal were to insure that P winds up in jail? Compare Y with Z, who hands P an *unloaded* gun: when P "fires" at V, he is guilty of attempted murder, but is Z guilty as an accomplice in the crime, though he does not intend that V die? Do we ever care about motive, or do we think instead that, at least as to explicit preparatory crimes (attempts) or implicit ones (burglary), certain defendants lack the purpose that the consummated crime actually occur? Should Wilson have been exonerated had he aided the principal not in breaking in to steal property that would be immediately restored to the owner, but in breaking in to vandalize the premises? Even if his underlying motivation, in both cases, was identical: to see the principal punished?

c. Complicity in Nonintentional Result Crimes?

People v. Flayhart

Court of Appeals of New York.
72 N.Y.2d 737 (1988).

■ TITONE, JUDGE.

Defendants Richard and Beatrice Flayhart, who are husband and wife, were charged with reckless manslaughter and criminally negligent homicide on the theory that, acting together and with the requisite culpable mental states, they engaged in conduct that brought about the death of Richard's brother, Terry Flayhart. Terry, who lived with defendants during the last period of his life, was mentally retarded and afflicted with a number of ailments, including cerebral palsy and epilepsy. The People's case against defendants was based on the premise that Terry, who weighed approximately 75 pounds just before his death, had died of neglect while he was living in defendants' home and was totally dependent upon their care.

At the close of the evidence, the trial court submitted the charged counts to the jury, along with an instruction on accomplice liability under Penal Law § 20.00. The jury found defendants guilty of criminally negligent homicide, and each defendant was sentenced to a term of imprisonment. . . .

Defendants' primary contention on their appeals to this court is that the convictions cannot be sustained because it is logically impossible to "aid and abet" criminally negligent homicide, an unintentional crime. Specifically, they contend that the crime of which they were convicted is nonexistent because one cannot "intentionally aid" another to "fail to perceive a substantial and unjustifiable risk" of death, the requisite mental state for criminally negligent homicide (see, Penal Law § 15.05; § 20.00).

However, Penal Law § 20.00 imposes accessorial liability on an accomplice not for aiding or encouraging another to reach a particular mental state, but rather for intentionally aiding another to engage in conduct which constitutes the charged offense while himself "acting with the mental culpability required for the commission" of that offense. Thus, defendants were convicted because the jury found that each of them, while "fail[ing] to perceive a substantial and unjustifiable risk" of death, intentionally aided the other to engage in certain conduct, such as failure to provide food and medical care, which ultimately brought about Terry Flayhart's death. There is no logical or conceptual difficulty with such convictions.

d. "Shared Intent" and Stings

United States v. Washington

United States Court of Appeals for the District of Columbia Circuit.
106 F.3d 983 (1997).

In these consolidated appeals, appellants are three officers of the Metropolitan Police Department ("MPD"), who, with others, were caught in a reverse-sting operation. [They agreed to provide protection to undercover FBI Agent José Olivier, posing as a member of a Miami-based narcotics organization, for his illegal narcotics activities while in the District of Columbia.] * * *

Appellants ... challenge their convictions for attempted possession of cocaine with intent to distribute.... The record contains no evidence that appellants themselves attempted to possess the cocaine that was being transported by the undercover officers. Rather, the evidence ... showed that appellants willingly and knowingly helped Olivier, whom they believed to be a drug dealer, in what they believed to be his possession of cocaine with intent to distribute. Consistent with these facts, the prosecution put forth its charge of attempted possession on an aiding and abetting theory. In support of the proposed charge, the prosecution explained:

> The fact that [appellant] Harmon never touched the suitcase [containing the drugs], never touched any drugs is irrelevant under the government's theory of aiding and abetting the possession with intent to distribute cocaine. What he did was *take a substantial step in furtherance of his intended purpose to aid* José Olivier in the transportation of [the drugs].

.... Appellants now claim that there was insufficient evidence to convict them under an aiding and abetting theory because they did not possess "the same criminal intent as the principals." *United States v. North,* 285 U.S. App. D.C. 343, 910 F.2d 843, 881 n.11 (D.C. Cir. 1990). They argue that their convictions must be reversed because the undercover FBI agents participating in Operation Broken Faith, who were the so-called "principals" to the attempted possession crime, had no criminal intent whatsoever. The government, on the other hand, argues that the "shared intent" requirement of accomplice liability refers not to the fact that the accomplice and the principal must have the same intent, but rather to the fact that "the accomplice must have some criminal purpose in mind."

It is true that in order to convict an accomplice of a completed substantive crime (rather than a mere attempt), "there must be a guilty principal before there can be an aider and abettor," and the accomplice and the principal must have a "shared intent." *United States v. Walker,* 321 U.S. App. D.C. 300, 99 F.3d 439, 442 (D.C. Cir. 1996).[32] In *United States v. Raper,* we set forth the specific requirements for convicting an accomplice:

> The elements of aiding or abetting an offense are (1) the specific intent to facilitate the commission of a crime by another; (2) guilty knowledge on the part of the accused; (3) that *an offense was being committed by someone;* and (4) that the accused assisted or participated in the commission of the offense.

219 U.S. App. D.C. 243, 676 F.2d 841, 849 (D.C. Cir. 1982) (emphasis added). In purported reliance on these principles, appellants here claim that they could not legitimately be convicted of aiding and abetting attempted possession of drugs with intent to distribute because there was no guilty principal, and because there was no "shared intent" between the "principals" and the accessories (because the government agents, unlike the appellants, were only pretending to be drug dealers and therefore did not have the necessary *mens rea* for the offense). Whatever merit such arguments might have in another context, appellants' reliance on these principles here is entirely misplaced—because they were not charged or convicted of the completed substantive crime, but only of an *attempt.*

The Model Penal Code has expressly addressed the question we face here. In a section on the law of criminal attempt, it states:

> Section 5.01. Criminal Attempt.
>
> ....
>
> (3) Conduct Designed to Aid Another in Commission of a Crime. A person who engages in conduct designed to aid another to commit a crime that would establish his complicity under Section 2.06 if the

32. However, in *Walker* and our earlier decision in *Edmond,* we emphasized that the aider and abettor need not have the exact same intent as the principal. Rather, a finding of overlapping intent between accomplice and principal is sufficient to establish liability. *See Walker,* 99 F.3d at 442 ("The intent of the aider and abettor must be shown, in crucial respects, to overlap with (but not necessarily match) the criminal intent of the principal"); *United States v. Edmond,* 288 U.S. App. D.C. 17, 924 F.2d 261, 266, 267 (D.C. Cir. 1991) (holding that, although "the government must prove the criminal act the defendant is accused of abetting," a jury "could consistently convict the [defendant-]abettor of first-degree murder while finding the actual perpetrator guilty only of the lesser offense" because "the *degree* of murder in each case depends on the mens rea of the defendant who is on trial.") (emphasis added).

crime were committed by such other person, is guilty of an attempt to commit the crime, although the crime is not committed or attempted by such other person.

Model Penal Code and Commentaries (Official Draft and Revised Comments), Part I, § 5.01(3) (A.L.I. 1985). In an explanatory note, the Code identifies the purpose behind subsection (3):

> Subsection (3) fills what would otherwise be a gap in complicity liability. Section 2.06 [of the Model Penal Code] covers accomplice liability in situations where the principal actor actually commits the offense. In cases where the principal actor does not commit an offense, however, it is provided here that the accomplice will be liable if he engaged in conduct that would have established his complicity had the crime been committed.

Id. at 297–98 (explanatory note to § 5.01(3)). It is important to highlight the fact that this passage does not describe an offense of aiding and abetting an *attempted* crime (in that case, there would be a guilty principal and an offense, thus posing no problem under the traditional aiding-and-abetting framework), but rather refers to *attempting* to aid and abet a crime (an offense for which there may not be a guilty principal). But in either case, paradoxically, the crime ultimately charged is the same. If the principal had actually attempted to commit a crime but had failed, the aider and abettor would be charged with the same offense as the principal (attempt to commit the crime). If (as here), the principal had only pretended to commit the crime, and the accomplice attempted to aid the principal by "engaging in conduct that would have established his complicity had the crime been committed," the accomplice may also be charged with an attempt to commit the crime.

In the latter scenario, however, the prosecution need not show that an offense was actually committed, nor that the principal and accomplice had a "shared intent." As with other attempt crimes, the focus of the court's analysis shifts away from external circumstances to an examination of the defendant's intent and actions in furtherance of that intent. Thus, the prosecution must show that the defendant "acted with the kind of culpability otherwise required for the commission of the crime which he is charged with attempting," and that he "engaged in conduct which constitutes a substantial step toward the commission of the crime.". . . . The court looks . . . to the question of whether, if the facts had been as the accomplice believed them, the principal would have been guilty. As with other attempt crimes, permitting convictions on the basis of the "attempt to aid and abet" theory is justified because, even if an offense was not actually committed, the defendant "manifests the same dangerousness of character as the actor who himself attempts to commit the offense." Model Penal Code, *supra,* at 356.

QUESTIONS AND COMMENTS

1. If purpose is "the mens rea" of complicity, can I be held liable as an accomplice for a crime that requires less than purpose for conviction?

How can I purposefully aid or abet a crime that requires knowledge, or recklessness, or even negligence?

In *Flayhart*, the crime at issue (homicide) required less than purpose with respect to the result element (death). What if the offense required less than purpose with respect to the *conduct* element? Assume two drag racers are screaming down a residential street. Can one be charged as an accomplice in the reckless driving of the other (as opposed to homicide, should a fatal accident occur)? Cf. People v. Abbott, 84 A.D.2d 11, 445 N.Y.S.2d 344 (N.Y. App. Div. 1981).

What about *attendant circumstances*? Assume arson (starting a fire with the purpose of destroying an occupied structure of another, MPC § 220.1(1)(a)) requires recklessness with respect to the element of "occupied building of another." Can I be an accomplice in arson—say, by supplying the principal with matches and lighter fluid—if I am less than certain that the building the principal is setting on fire is not his own?

2. In *Flayhart*, assume that Richard, while encouraging Beatrice to neglect Terry, didn't realize—but should have—that Terry would die from starvation. Beatrice, by contrast, wanted Terry dead so she could get to his life insurance money. Could Richard be convicted of negligent homicide, and Beatrice of murder? Would that have presented a "logical or conceptual" difficulty? Or must the two have a "shared intent," bound together as accomplice and principal in a common criminal endeavor?

3. Most, but not all, courts interpreting statutes that resemble Model Penal Code § 2.06(4) have found that a defendant-accomplice can be guilty of manslaughter or negligent homicide provided he intentionally aids the principal to commit the proscribed act, and is reckless or negligent as to the result of the act. Compare Riley v. State, 60 P.3d 204 (Ct. App. Alaska 2002) (upholding convictions for first-degree assault—defined as "recklessly caus[ing] serious physical injury to another by means of a dangerous instrument"—even though prosecutors couldn't establish which of the defendants' guns shot which bullets into a crowd, so long as each defendant intended to promote or facilitate another's act of shooting into the crowd, and was reckless as to the possibility that this conduct would cause serious injury) with State v. Etzweiler, 125 N.H. 57, 480 A.2d 870 (1984) (defendant could not be convicted for negligent homicide when he lent his car to a drunk friend who drove recklessly and killed two passengers in another car because his acts were not designed to aid the principal in committing negligent homicide).

In jurisdictions that follow the "rule" in *Riley*, convictions are less problematic when the defendant-accomplice has procured, aided, or ordered the *precise* acts that caused injury or death. (The *Riley* defendants encouraged *shooting*.) Similarly, in State v. McVay, 47 R.I. 292, 132 A. 436 (1926), the defendant-accomplice ordered the principals (captain and engineer) to start up the ferry, negligent that doing so would result in a boiler explosion. But what about drag racers? Does the "encouraging" drag racer really encourage the *precise* reckless deed that actually kills (the last second swerve, the final fatal acceleration, etc.)? Or is he taking a chance that by encouraging another to *race*, the fellow racer will choose to do something more particular that is more dangerous still than (generic) racing? When the defendant-accomplice is merely reckless that what he does will lead to the principal's *precise* act—and "second order" reckless in that sense as to whether death will ultimately result from the course of conduct he has helped set off—it may be harder to hold him accountable than if he purposely aids (and associates herself) with the very deed that we find blameworthy.

The analytics behind this position are not entirely clear: if I take a one in ten chance that by doing X, I will encourage you to do Y, and doing Y has a one in ten chance of causing death, is it as appropriate to say that I am taking a one in a hundred chance of causing death as it would be if I absolutely and unequivocally aid you to do Y and Y has a one in one hundred chance of causing death? Are the cases distinct (even if each defendant took steps that increase the background risk in the world that a victim will die by the same amount) because we cannot impute a fatal *act* to the defendant-accomplice unless she wanted that act to occur (or at least knew that it would)? Perhaps imputation is as much about image as analytics anyway. Note, in this regard, that defendant-accomplices who are physically present at the scene of the principal's crime seem to be convicted more readily than those who provide means of harm that the principal uses *later*. Compare State v. Ayers, 478 N.W.2d 606 (Iowa 1991) (defendant sold a gun to a 15–year-old who later shot his girlfriend; conviction for aiding and abetting involuntary manslaughter reversed because the parties were not "assembled or combined together") with State v. Travis, 497 N.W.2d 905 (Iowa App. 1993) (defendant gave a malfunctioning motorcycle to his 15–year-old friend who caused a fatal accident, failed to give the friend driving lessons, and rode on the back of the cycle; conviction for aiding and abetting involuntary manslaughter affirmed). Travis might be described—like Ayers—as someone who (merely?) was reckless as to the possibility that his friend would behave recklessly. What drives the court's decision to characterize him as someone who "intentionally direct[ed] and counsel[ed]" his friend to drive recklessly?

4. *Attempts, once more*. What if I assist someone who only pretends to intend to engage in criminal conduct? See *Washington*. What, in other words, if I attempt to aid or abet, but fail, though this time not because my actions do nothing to facilitate the crime committed by the principal (see *Tally*, supra), but the principal doesn't (can't?) commit the crime because he never intended to do so? Does it make a difference whether the principal is a police officer or a private individual? (If she is a police officer, there may be an entrapment issue. See supra ch. 7.)

What if the principal did intend to commit it, but then changes her mind?

Alternatively, what if she did intend to commit the crime and attempted, but failed, to consummate it? How can conduct be imputed to me that never occurred?

5. The *Washington* court relies heavily on the Model Penal Code to conclude that in this particular *attempt* case "the prosecution need not show ... that the principal and accomplice had a 'shared intent.'" But does the Model Penal Code *ever* require "shared intent" for accomplice liability—even in cases where the principal does commit the crime? Does

the MPC provision quoted by the court (§ 5.01(3)) even apply to the case before it? Is it true that "the principal actor [did] not commit an offense" in this case? Or did the undercover officers engage in the proscribed conduct (possession), but lacked the intent to distribute (though they presumably did have the requisite mental state—if any—regarding their conduct, possession, and the items they were possessing, unless the drugs were fake)? Similarly, is it true that the undercover officers "had no criminal intent whatsoever," other than in the sense that they had no intent to commit a crime (but since when does intent encompass not only the elements of the proscribed conduct but also the fact that the conduct is proscribed)? Does it (should it) matter *why* the undercover officers are not criminally liable: because they are among the persons statutorily exempted from the criminal prohibition of drug possession (along with certain physicians and researchers), because they are eligible for a necessity defense (justification), because they lack the mental state regarding some offense element (lack of mens rea), because they don't do what they told their "accomplices" they would do (lack of actus reus)? Cf. Model Penal Code § 2.06(7).

* * *

Problem

Title 18, section 1503 of the United States Criminal Code reads in pertinent part: "Any person who corruptly influences, intimidates or impedes the due administration of justice [shall be guilty of a felony.]" Assume (contrary to fact), for purposes of this Problem, that there are no other germane substantive criminal sections applicable to this fact situation, and that federal complicity law precisely parallels the Model Penal Code's complicity law.

Alison Applegate is the founder, board chair and majority shareholder of the Applegate Corporation, which sells equipment to the U.S. Department of Defense. Since 1999, federal investigators have suspected that the Applegate Corporation falsified its financial records in the mid–1990s in order to defraud the government. (The company was paid, on some occasions, on what amounted to a complex form of a cost-plus basis and federal investigators believe that the company overstated its costs. Investigators suspect that Applegate directed Betty Bonilla, the corporation's chief financial officer, second largest stockholder and highest paid employee to falsify cost records, and that Bonilla did so with the aid of Charles Cunningham, an accountant who worked directly under Bonilla as a salaried employee.) Donald Dahl, Cunningham's secretary (also a salaried employee) physically prepared the documents that were submitted to the Defense Department.

A federal grand jury was convened in 2000 to determine whether to indict the corporation as an entity, Applegate as an individual, Bonilla as an individual, Cunningham as an individual and/or Dahl as an individual.

Ignore whether any or all of these individuals or the corporate entity has committed any offense in defrauding the government or conspiring to do so. Instead, focus upon the following:

On January 3, 2000, Bonilla was called before the grand jury. She was asked general questions about the company's financial practices and cost accounting procedures as well as more focused questions about documents that auditors now suspect were fraudulent. Each time she was asked a substantive question relating to the investigation, she invoked her constitutionally guaranteed Fifth Amendment privilege against self-incrimination ("I refuse to answer that question on the ground that the answer might incriminate me.") You should assume that it would have materially facilitated the investigation if she had answered the questions posed to her, and that the grand jury's investigative task was substantially impeded by her failure to respond. While Susan Boise, the United States Attorney presenting the case to the grand jury, considered granting Bonilla immunity from prosecution, which would have made it impermissible for Bonilla to "take the Fifth" (since no answer could then incriminate her), she decided that Bonilla was too central and culpable a figure to be granted immunity.

Cunningham was called before the grand jury on January 4 and like Bonilla, refused to answer all germane questions. Dahl did the same on January 5.

In late January, Boise learned that Applegate had met with Bonilla on December 28, 1999 and urged her to take the Fifth Amendment if asked any questions pertaining in any way to the corporation's cost reports. Applegate said, in relevant part, "Even if you cut some kind of deal for yourself, or somehow minimize your own role in all this, the company will fold if there's even an indictment here. And let's face it, you're not going to find any other job paying you close to what you've been making with me if that happens."

Boise also learned that Applegate had met with Cunningham on December 29, 1999 and told him that if he did not take the Fifth each time he was asked a question pertaining in any way to the company's cost reports he would be fired. She learned that Applegate had met with Dahl on December 30 and offered him $25,000 to take the Fifth if asked any questions.

Is Applegate liable—as accomplice and/or as principal—for violating section 1503? Analyze her liability in relationship to Bonilla, Cunningham and Dahl. Does it make sense to hold her liable (and if so, why)? What arguments would you make against holding her liable? What if Bonilla's best friend, Jay Neukom, had made the precise same statements to Bonilla that Applegate did: should Neukom be liable under section 1503?

B. CONSPIRACY

1. INTRODUCTION

Pinkerton v. United States

Supreme Court of the United States.
328 U.S. 640, 66 S.Ct. 1180 (1946).

A conspiracy is a partnership in crime. It has ingredients, as well as implications, distinct from the completion of the unlawful project. As stated in United States v. Rabinowich, 238 U.S. 78, 88, 35 S.Ct. 682, 684, 685:

"For two or more to confederate and combine together to commit or cause to be committed a breach of the criminal laws is an offense of the gravest character, sometimes quite outweighing, in injury to the public, the mere commission of the contemplated crime. It involves deliberate plotting to subvert the laws, educating and preparing the conspirators for further and habitual criminal practices. And it is characterized by secrecy, rendering it difficult of detection, requiring more time for its discovery, and adding to the importance of punishing it when discovered."

Moreover, it is not material that overt acts charged in the conspiracy counts were also charged and proved as substantive offenses. "If the overt act be the offense which was the object of the conspiracy, and is also punished, there is not a double punishment of it." The agreement to do an unlawful act is even then distinct from the doing of the act.

Callanan v. United States

Supreme Court of the United States.
364 U.S. 587, 81 S.Ct. 321 (1961).

Under the early common law, a conspiracy—which constituted a misdemeanor—was said to merge with the completed felony which was its object. This rule, however, was based upon significant procedural distinctions between misdemeanors and felonies. The defendant in a misdemeanor trial was entitled to counsel and a copy of the indictment; these advantages were unavailable on trial for a felony. Therefore no conviction was permitted of a constituent misdemeanor upon an indictment for the felony. When the substantive crime was also a misdemeanor, or when the conspiracy was defined by statute as a felony, merger did not obtain. As these common-law procedural niceties disappeared, the merger concept lost significance, and today it has been abandoned. * * *

The distinctiveness between a substantive offense and a conspiracy to commit it is a postulate of our law. . . . Over the years, this distinction has been applied in various situations. For example, in Clune v. United States, 159 U.S. 590, 16 S.Ct. 125, the Court upheld a two-year sentence for conspiracy over the objection that the crime which was the object of the unlawful agreement could only be punished by a $100 fine. The same result was reached when, as in the present case, both offenses were described within the same statute. In Carter v. McClaughry, 183 U.S. 365, 22 S.Ct. 181, cumulative sentences for conspiracy to defraud and fraud were upheld. "Cumulative sentences," the Court pronounced, "are not cumulative punishments, and a single sentence for several offenses, in excess of that prescribed for one offense, may be authorized to statute."

This settled principle derives from the reason of things in dealing with socially reprehensible conduct: collective criminal agreement—partnership in crime—presents a greater potential threat to the public than individual delicts. Concerted action both increases the likelihood that the criminal object will be successfully attained and decreases the probability that the individuals involved will depart from their path of criminality. Group association for criminal purposes often, if not normally, makes possible the attainment of ends more complex than those which one criminal could accomplish. Nor is the danger of a conspiratorial group limited to the particular end toward which it has embarked. Combination in crime makes more likely the commission of crimes unrelated to the original purpose for which the group was formed. In sum, the danger which a conspiracy generates is not confined to the substantive offense which is the immediate aim of the enterprise.

Model Penal Code § 5.03. Criminal Conspiracy.

(1) *Definition of Conspiracy.* A person is guilty of conspiracy with another person or persons to commit a crime if with the purpose of promoting or facilitating its commission he:

(a) agrees with such other person or persons that they or one or more of them will engage in conduct which constitutes such crime or an attempt or solicitation to commit such crime; or

(b) agrees to aid such other person or persons in the planning or commission of such crime or of an attempt or solicitation to commit such crime.

. . . .

(5) *Overt Act.* No person may be convicted of conspiracy to commit a crime, other than a felony of the first or second degree, unless an overt act in pursuance of such conspiracy is alleged and proved to have been done by him or by a person with whom he conspired.

(6) *Renunciation of Criminal Purpose.* It is an affirmative defense that the actor, after conspiring to commit a crime, thwarted the success of the conspiracy, under circumstances manifesting a complete and voluntary renunciation of his criminal purpose.

QUESTIONS AND COMMENTS

1. *Actus Reus.* The actus reus of conspiracy is an agreement or, in some cases, an agreement plus an "overt act" in furtherance of it. The "crux" of conspiracy, however, is the agreement. Cf. United States v. Crochiere, 129 F.3d 233 (1st Cir. 1997) (conspiracy to violate civil rights, 18 U.S.C. § 241, requires no overt act); United States v. Shabani, 513 U.S. 10, 115 S.Ct. 382 (1994) (same for conspiracy to distribute cocaine, 21 U.S.C. § 846). (For a detailed discussion of what constitutes an agreement for purposes of criminal conspiracy, see section 3 infra.)

Focusing on the overt act may confuse matters. To begin with, the "overt act" in conspiracy may be confused with the "substantial step" in attempt. While every substantial step is an overt act, the converse is not true:

[A]n act which would support a conspiracy conviction would not necessarily be sufficient to support an attempt conviction....

The primary focus of the crime of conspiracy is the agreement itself, the collusion, the secrecy and the resulting threat to society that such criminal liaisons create. The act is required as a method of showing that some step has been taken toward executing the illicit agreement. Any action sufficient to corroborate the existence of the agreement and to show that it is being put into effect is sufficient to support the conspiracy. In contrast, the crime of attempt focuses more directly upon the unequivocal nature of the steps taken toward consummating the intended crime. In attempt, the act for which the defendant is held criminally responsible, must be more than preparatory. Perkins, in his treatise on criminal law, concludes that the "overt act" in a conspiracy "need not amount to an attempt to commit the crime which is the object of the combination." Perkins, Criminal Law, 618 (2d ed. 1968).

"Care must be taken not to equate the overt act required by conspiracy with the overt act required in the crime of attempt. Whereas under the crime of attempt, mere preparation does not constitute an overt act, this is not true when dealing with the overt act required by conspiracy. The overt act may be merely a part of preliminary arrangements for commission of the ultimate crime. It need amount to no more than an act showing that the conspiracy has gone beyond a mere meeting of the minds upon the attainment of an unlawful object and that action between conspirators as such has begun."

Perkins explains further:

"The function of the 'overt act' is quite different in the two offenses. In the case of attempt the act must go beyond preparation because the attempt is deemed a punishable segment of the crime intended. But if the statute requires an 'overt act' for conviction of conspiracy, whether such act is held to be a part of the conspiracy or only required evidence thereof, the purpose of the requirement is merely to afford 'a locus poenitentiae, so that before the act done one or more of the parties may abandon their design, and thus avoid the penalty prescribed by the statute.' "

State v. Verive, 128 Ariz. 570, 627 P.2d 721 (Ariz. App. 1981).

The substantial step in attempt *is* the actus reus of attempt, whereas the actus reus of conspiracy is not whatever overt act might be required, but the agreement it furthers. And so any act, no matter how trivial, that is undertaken to put the conspiratorial agreement into action—buying a map, making a phone call, renting an apartment—will do.

Why should conspirators be punished at a stage less proximate to the consummation of an offense than an individual acting on his own would be punished? Is it (merely) because creating a "criminal organization" is bad, regardless of the risk of consummating the offense? (Isn't that what justifies the *Callanan* rule on cumulative sentencing?) Or is it because the risk of consummating the offense is higher at an earlier stage when multiple parties are involved? (Is the notion that an individual perpetrator can turn back readily, without disappointing others, while once a group forms, members "egg each other on"?)

More troubling, the overt act in conspiracy may be confused with the object of the conspiracy, or with some other substantive offense. Certainly robbing a bank is an overt act in furtherance of a conspiracy to commit bank robbery. But does that mean that every co-conspirator will be liable both for the conspiracy *and* for the bank robbery?

2. *Mens Rea.* The Model Penal Code identifies "purpose" as the mens rea for conspiracy. As one might expect, however, the question of mens rea in conspiracy raises very much the same issues as the question of mens rea in complicity, discussed in the previous section. Here too, there was a debate among those who preferred knowledge and those who favored purpose, which once again was resolved in favor of the latter. The Commentaries simply remark that "[t]he case for this position seems an even stronger one with respect to the inchoate crime." Model Penal Code Commentaries § 5.03, at 406. Why is that?

And, as in the case of complicity, one might wonder just what difference the adoption of a purpose standard makes, given that courts have never had much difficulty inferring purpose "from such circumstances as, for example, quantity of sales, the seller's initiative or encouragement, continuity of the relationship, and the contraband nature of the materials sold." Id. at 404; see also People v. Lauria, 251 Cal.App.2d 471, 59 Cal.Rptr. 628 (1967).

Then there is the question—which arises not only in complicity, but also in other purpose-requiring inchoate crimes like attempt and solicitation—of whether it is "logically impossible" to conspire to commit a *nonintentional* crime. Can I enter into an agreement to commit a crime "with the purpose of promoting or facilitating its commission" if that crime requires less than purpose for its commission? Assuming manslaughter is defined as reckless homicide, can I conspire to commit manslaughter? Cf. Mitchell v. State, 363 Md. 130, 767 A.2d 844 (2001) (conspiracy to commit second degree murder). If two people agree to engage in certain conduct—say, drag racing—that results in death, can one be punished for conspiracy to commit reckless homicide (assuming she was aware of the risk of death, but went ahead anyway) and the other for conspiracy to commit negligent homicide (because he wasn't aware of the risk, but should have been)?

Think about the two key functional features of conspiracy law that we have already touched upon: First, looked at as inchoate criminals, conspirators can typically be punished at a stage far less proximate to the consummation of the offense than those acting on their own (reaching an agreement plus engaging in any overt act is generally enough, and they need not take a substantial step that strongly corroborates criminal intent). Second, according to *Callanan*, a conspiracy conviction (unlike one for attempt) does not merge into the conviction of the substantive offense. Instead, the defendant may be sentenced both for the substantive offense *and* for the creation of the conspiracy. The creation of the criminal group is thought to merit punishment independently. In the "drag racing" conspiracy, though, the inchoacy rules would plainly not apply: we could not *label* this a conspiracy to commit reckless homicide *until* the victim died (though it might be a conspiracy to *drive* recklessly). Moreover, whatever one makes of arguments supporting the *Callanan* rule that all "criminal groups" are both harder to police and more prone to offend further, the argument appears especially tenuous in relationship to "organizations" that have not sought to achieve any particular evil aims at all.

What about attendant circumstances? To be liable for conspiracy to sell alcohol to minors, must I have the conscious objective of selling to minors, or is it enough that I suspect that some (all?) customers will be underage? What if the mental state attaching to the attendant circumstance of the purchaser's age is recklessness? Strict liability?

3. Imagine that two alleged conspirators, X and Y, make a mistake of governing law: They agree, for instance, to make a contribution to a candidate that violates campaign finance laws, though they do not know it does. Traditionally, of course, such mistakes of governing law would generally not exonerate individuals (see ch. 5); they *would*, however, have precluded conviction for conspiracy, given what is generally known as the "corrupt motive" (or "evil purpose") doctrine. In People v. Powell, 63 N.Y. 88 (1875), the court held that

> to make an agreement between two or more persons to do an act innocent in itself a criminal conspiracy, it is not enough that it appears that the act which was the object of the agreement was prohibited. The confederation must be corrupt. The agreement must have been entered into with an evil purpose, as distinguished from a purpose simply to do the act prohibited in ignorance of the prohibition.

The Model Penal Code is typical in rejecting the traditional *Powell* doctrine (see Model Penal Code Commentaries § 5.03, at 417–18), believing that the maxim "ignorance of the law is no excuse" is no less (or more) applicable to conspiracy than individual perpetration cases. Is the Model Penal Code's position valid?

We punish conspirators at a stage far less proximate to the consummation of an offense in significant part because we believe that once a group is formed, the risk of consummation is atypically high. Could we make a serious argument that people who do not yet know that what they have agreed to do is criminal (illegal?) will, if they learn it is criminal, fail to desist in the (potentially substantial) period between the time liability attaches for the conspiracy and the time the object offense is committed? We also punish conspirators (both earlier and more harshly) because "criminal organizations" are purportedly dangerous. Can we really say that people who've never agreed to do anything they know is criminal have formed the sort of criminal organization—apt not only to consummate the particular object offense but to continue offending—that the Court in *Callanan* worries about?

4. As an inchoate offense, conspiracy—like attempt—raises questions of factual and legal impossibility. If there is no way we could have succeeded in implementing our criminal plan, should we be punished just for making the plan? The U.S. Supreme Court has rejected the impossibility defense for federal criminal law, on the (now familiar) ground that " 'an agreement to commit an unlawful act' . . . is 'a distinct evil,' which 'may exist and be punished whether or not the substantive crime ensues.' " United States v. Jimenez Recio, 537 U.S. 270, 123 S.Ct. 819 (2003). The Model Penal Code likewise rejects the defense on the ground that the act of

joining an agreement to engage in criminal conduct signals sufficient dangerousness to warrant criminal intervention. Recall that the Model Code, for similar reasons, did away with the impossibility defense in the law of attempt. Why is impossibility even less likely to be accepted as a defense to conspiracy? What about cases of "pure legal impossibility," when conspirators plan to a engage in conduct that turns out not to be criminal at all? See ch. 6.

5. Does conspiracy punish an act at all? Or does it punish merely the *intent* to commit some criminal act in the future? Cf. Krulewitch v. United States, 336 U.S. 440 (1949) (Jackson, J., concurring) (conspiracy "predominantly mental in composition because it consists primarily of a meeting of minds and an intent").

Or does conspiracy punish a *status*, e.g., membership in an "organization," "enterprise," "confederation," or "combination"? Cf. *Robinson v. California*, ch. 4, supra.

6. Alternatively, does conspiracy criminalize the group—the "conspiracy"—itself, with the liability of its constituents derived from the criminality of the whole? If so, is that a bad thing? Neal Katyal doesn't think so; he calls for "mak[ing] conspiracies operate less efficiently" by "reverse-engineering" psychologists' "advances in understanding the ways in which people in groups act differently than they do as individuals" and economists' "sophisticated explanations for why firms promote efficiency." Along the way he develops a "functional justification for punishing conspiracy" that explicitly focuses on group, rather than individual, behavior. He sees

> two reasons why conspiracies are harmful: the specialization of labor/economies of scale and the development of a pernicious group identity. The former is easily understood by thinking about how difficult it is for an individual to rob a bank alone. Several individuals are needed to carry weapons and provide firepower (economies of scale), someone needs to be the "brains behind the operation" (a form of specialization of labor), and another should serve as a lookout (specialization again)....
>
> What are somewhat less obvious, but at least as important, are psychological accounts of the dangers of group activity. Advances in psychology over the past thirty years have demonstrated that groups cultivate a special social identity. This identity often encourages risky behavior, leads individuals to behave against their self-interest, solidifies loyalty, and facilitates harm against nonmembers. The psychological and economic accounts explain why law treats conspiracy in a distinctive way. The law focuses on "agreement" because that decision has drastic consequences. The law seeks to attach a broad and potentially uncognizable set of penalties at this early stage to deter many from becoming conspirators.

Neal Kumar Katyal, "Conspiracy Theory," 112 Yale L.J. 1307, 1309–12 (2003).

While this focus on "group dynamics" may explain why—and how—punishing conspiracy helps prevent crime, can it help us decide whether punishing conspiracy (in whatever form) is legitimate? In analytic terms, how useful is this approach in the case of small conspiracies with limited scope and duration?

At least in the case of large, sophisticated, and continuing criminal conspiracies—many of which are regulated more by RICO (see part C infra) than by conventional conspiracy law—it might be helpful to think about assessing (personal) criminal liability in economic organizational terms. On one end of the spectrum, there is the "ideal type" conspiracy as a thoroughly vertically integrated hierarchical organization. Presumably, such organizations are most likely to have the economic and psychological characteristics Katyal is wary of. At the other end is a world of individuals acting in "markets" with new people dealing with them each time. The reality of most (noncriminal and criminal) enterprises, however, falls somewhere in the middle. There is a continuum between "markets" and "enterprises," with repeat dealing being the phenomenon that blurs the distinction between the two. Each time a particular shipment of drugs enters the country, and winds up in the hands of a dealer who sells it on the street, we can imagine that all of those who handled the drug (grower, smuggler, processor, middleman, dealer) have conspired with one another. See, e.g., United States v. Bruno, 105 F.2d 921 (2d Cir.), rev'd on other grounds, 308 U.S. 287 (1939). In some cases, all these parties would in fact be integrated parts of a disciplined organization. In others, though, a smuggler might deal with different middlemen each time he brought drugs in, and be indifferent to the fate of the drugs once they left his hand. Or, he might deal with a small group of middlemen over and over again.

Moreover, in thinking about (noncriminal and criminal) organizations, it is often hard to distinguish between single "enterprises" and commonly held "holding" companies. A central figure organizes many individual property owners to defraud the Federal Housing Administration, each of whom knows (broadly) about the others' existence. See Kotteakos v. United States, 328 U.S. 750 (1946). Is there a single organization or does the central character simply own a string of smaller businesses? Does it matter if there are (substantial?) scale economies (e.g., if the pay-off one has to offer a realtor to take the risk of going to jail when she misappraises properties can be spread out over a larger number of deals)? Even if we decide that what we are dealing with is a single integrated enterprise (rather than either a market or a holding company), which people who work under the enterprise's umbrella are "responsible" for its existence?

In every enterprise, there is a distinction between managers/equity holders and employees, and we are generally inclined to hold only the former responsible for the existence of a criminal organization (or, more problematically, for criminal aspects of an otherwise straight organization). But again, there is a continuum. How, for instance, are we to deal with employees who have profit-sharing agreements, or are overpaid by market standards because of the specific features of the organizations for which they work? In *Kotteakos*, the organizer, Simon Brown, may well have earned all the residual profits; each purported co-conspirator may have gained no more if the other fraudulent loans netted more profit than they would have without the conspiracy. But that may not be strictly true either; their "cut" may be formally or subtly influenced by their bosses' success.

7. Should it matter how sophisticated a "criminal combination" is, or is an agreement between two people sufficient evidence of exceptional dangerousness to warrant punishment? Should conspiracy, rather than functioning as a general inchoate offense that could attach itself to any substantive crime, no matter how insignificant, be defined as a separate offense? Consider the following provision in the German Penal Code, which is representative of the approach to conspiracy in civil law countries (see generally Wienczyslaw J. Wagner, "Conspiracy in Civil Law Countries," 42 J. Crim. L. & Criminology 171 (1951)).

German Penal Code § 129. Formation of Criminal Organizations.

(1) Whoever forms an organization, the objectives or activity of which are directed towards the commission of crimes, or whoever participates in such an organization as a member, recruits for it or supports it, shall be punished with imprisonment for not more than five years or a fine.

(2) Subsection (2) shall not be applied:

1. if the organization is a political party . . .; [or]

2. if the commission of crimes is only an objective or activity of minor significance. . . .

(4) If the perpetrator is one of the ringleaders or supporters or there exists an especially serious case, then imprisonment from six months to five years shall be imposed.

(5) The court may dispense with punishment . . . in the case of participants whose guilt is slight or whose involvement is of minor significance.

"Criminal organization" has been interpreted to mean an "organizational combination established for a specific duration by at least three persons, who are subordinating their individual will to the will of the group for the purpose of pursuing common ends and stand in such a relation to one another that they consider themselves as a uniform association." Strafgesetzbuch § 129, at 807 (Herbert Tröndle & Thomas Fischer 49th ed., 1999).

The distinction between the concept of conspiracy in common law and civil law countries played a central role in the Allied preparations for the Nuremberg War Crimes Tribunal at the end of World War II:

> During much of the discussion, the Russians and French seemed unable to grasp all the implications of the concept; when they finally did grasp it, they were genuinely shocked. The French viewed it entirely as a barbarous legal mechanism unworthy of modern law, while the Soviets seemed to have shaken their head in wonderment—a reaction, some cynics may believe, prompted by envy. But the main point of the Soviet attack on conspiracy was that it was too vague and so unfamiliar to the French and themselves, as well as to the Germans, that it would lead to endless confusion.

Stanislaw Pomorski, "Conspiracy and Criminal Organizations," in The Nuremberg Trial and International Law 213, 218–19 (quoting Bradley F. Smith, Reaching Judgment at Nuremberg 51 (1977)).

In fact, none other than Herbert Wechsler, who served as Assistant Attorney General at the time and went on to draft the Model Penal Code, cautioned against relying on the traditional common law notion of conspiracy:

> [T]he principal difficulty is the fact that some of the elements of the conspiracy charged, notably violation of treaties, atrocities committed upon German nationals on racial, religious, and political grounds, and atrocities committed prior to the state of war, are not embraced within the ordinary concept of crimes punishable as violations of the laws of war.... The theory of conspiracy affords a proper basis for reaching a large number of people, no one of whom engaged in all of the criminal conduct, but it is an error to designate as conspiracy the crime itself, the more so since the common-law conception of the criminality of an unexecuted plan is not universally accepted in the civilized world.

Id. at 217 (quoting Herbert Wechsler, Memorandum for the Attorney General, Dec. 29, 1944 (Doc. 27), in The American Road to Nuremberg: The Documentary Record 1944–1945, at 84, 86–87 (Bradley F. Smith ed., 1982)).

In the end, the Anglo–American view prevailed. The Tribunal's Charter provided (in ch. 6) that:

> The following acts, or any of them, are crimes within the jurisdiction of the Tribunal for which there shall be individual responsibility:
>
> (a) Crimes Against Peace: namely, planning, preparation, initiation or waging of a war of aggression, or a war in violation of international treaties, ties, agreements or assurance, or *participation in a common plan or conspiracy* for the accomplishment of any of the foregoing: ...
>
> Leaders, organizers, instigators and accomplices participating in the formulation or execution of a common plan or conspiracy to commit any of the foregoing crimes are responsible for all acts performed by any persons in execution of such plan (emphasis added).

8. *Inchoacy.* Conspiracy is an agreement (plus overt act), and nothing more. It makes no difference for purposes of conspiracy liability whether anyone ever bothered to carry out its objective. The agreement is enough. We punish conspiracy because conspiracies (or conspirators?) are exceptionally—and inherently—dangerous, as *Pinkerton* and *Callanan* explain. Are you convinced by the Supreme Court's evocation of the special perils of criminal association?

Assuming conspiracies are as dangerous as the Court makes them out to be, should mere dangerousness be enough, without anyone having engaged in a single substantive offense? Without anyone having inflicted any harm? Without anyone even having come close—or at least close enough for purposes of attempt—to committing an offense?

Note also that, as an inchoate crime, conspiracy is always a conspiracy to commit some (other) crime. This was not always so. Traditionally, conspiracy was punishable even if its object was not itself a crime:

> In order that a combination may be punishable it must be formed to do either an unlawful act or a lawful act by criminal or unlawful means. * * * It is not essential, however, to criminal liability that the acts contemplated should constitute a criminal offense for which, without the elements of conspiracy, one alone could be indicted. It is an offense independent of the crime or unlawful act which is its purpose; and *it will be enough if the acts contemplated are corrupt, dishonest, fraudulent, or immoral, and in that sense illegal.* A conspiracy will be indictable, if the end proposed or the means to be employed are, by reason of the combination, particularly dangerous to the public interests, or particularly injurious to some individual, although not criminal.

State v. Kemp, 126 Conn. 60, 77–78 (1939) (emphasis added).

Does that make sense? If we punish conspiracies because they are, in and of themselves, dangerous to public interests, why shouldn't we punish conspiracies that don't have as their object conduct that happens to be criminalized (or is only the *criminal* law concerned with protecting public interests)? If conspiracies are as dangerous as the Supreme Court suggests, why should this distinction, between technically criminal and otherwise unlawful objectives, make a difference? Why should we have to wait until a merely unlawful objective has transformed itself into a criminal one? If evidence of a "pernicious group identity" has been unearthed before the commission of a substantive crime, why shouldn't the criminal law interfere at that point? Why should one type of evidence of the dangerousness of a group be privileged over another? See United States v. Ballistrea, 101 F.3d 827, 832 (2d Cir. 1996) ("so long as deceitful or dishonest means are employed," conspiracy "to defraud the United States, or any agency thereof in any manner or for any purpose" under 18 U.S.C. § 371 "need not involve the violation of a separate statute").

9. What if the danger inherent in a conspiracy becomes reality? Should we still punish the conspirators for having posed that very danger, or is it enough that we punish them for manifesting the danger in a criminal act? Should we punish them both for being dangerous *and* for causing the harm they threatened to cause? The Model Penal Code says no. § 1.07(b) ("When the same conduct of a defendant may establish the commission of more than one offense, the defendant may be prosecuted for each such offense. He may not, however, be convicted of more than one offense if . . . one offense consists only of a conspiracy or other form of preparation to commit the other."). The Model Penal Code Commentaries argue that "[w]hen a conspiracy is declared criminal because its object is a crime, it is entirely meaningless to say that the preliminary combination is more dangerous than the forbidden consummation; the measure of its danger is the risk of such a culmination." § 5.03, at 390. What if the conspiracy encompasses objectives other than the crimes that have been committed in furtherance of it? (In that case, the Model Penal Code *does*

permit cumulative punishment of conspiracy and consummated crimes.) What incentive does the conspirator have *not* to commit the object offense?

Assume a jurisdiction considering whether it is apt to impose cumulative sentences for conspiracy and the criminal act that was the object of the conspiracy. It could adopt one of two simple "rules": always impose cumulative sentences or never impose cumulative sentences. The "always" cumulate rule seems overinclusive; not every agreement between two people to commit a crime establishes a dangerous ongoing *organization*. The "never" cumulate rule seems underinclusive, though, if there is any good reason to worry about the sorts of concerns Katyal raises, though. The Model Penal Code's "standard"—cumulate when you think the people have formed an ongoing group that poses prospective dangers beyond the consummation of the object offense but don't cumulate if you think they haven't—seems to pose considerable problems of its own. It may well be enforced prejudicially (how likely were *these* defendants to stop with the one crime rather than some defendants we find more sympathetic), may be enforced on the basis of procedurally suspect information (is a prosecutor's unproven allegation that the defendants may have committed other offenses sufficient to make us think they have established an ongoing organization?), and may, surreptitiously, punish "criminal *status*" rather than a discernible *act*.

10. *Jurisdiction*. According to the traditional rule, a state did not have criminal jurisdiction over a conspiracy if the agreement was made within its borders, but the object crime was to be committed elsewhere, unless acts in furtherance of the conspiracy were committed within the state and amounted at least to an attempt to commit the object offense. More recently courts—and the Model Penal Code—have abandoned this rule in light of "the principles that define the crime of conspiracy and the rationale for punishing the commission of that offense" as well as the "pragmatic needs of law enforcement." People v. Morante, 20 Cal.4th 403, 975 P.2d 1071, 84 Cal.Rptr.2d 665 (1999) ("if the state may seek the prosecution and punishment of an agreement and overt act (coupled with the requisite intent) amounting to conspiracy *regardless* whether the crime that is the object of the conspiracy is completed, it is not apparent why we should ... require, at the same time, that the location of the intended crime be within the state"); cf. Model Penal Code § 1.03(1)(d).

11. *Renunciation*. Traditionally renunciation was not a defense to conspiracy. If the agreement is the "crux" of conspiracy, than what does it matter whether the conspirator gets cold feet later on? Assuming an overt act is required, should the renunciation defense be available only *before* an overt act has been committed (by anyone, by the person raising the renunciation defense)? In jurisdictions that do not recognize a defense of renunciation to conspiracy, renunciation nonetheless has considerable procedural significance. For instance, it may bar the imputation of (former) coconspirators' acts to the defendant or it may form the basis for a statute-of-limitations defense (the statute of limitations runs with the defendant's withdrawal, so that the conspiracy prosecution may be time barred). See, e.g., United States v. Grimmett, 236 F.3d 452 (8th Cir. 2001) ("making

clean breast" to authorities constitutes withdrawal for purposes of statute-of-limitations defense).

The Model Penal Code does recognize a "renunciation of criminal purpose" defense to the conspiracy charge itself: "It is an affirmative defense that the actor, after conspiring to commit a crime, thwarted the success of the conspiracy, under circumstances manifesting a complete and voluntary renunciation of his criminal purpose." § 5.03(6); see also German Penal Code § 129(6) ("court may in its discretion mitigate the punishment . . . or dispense with punishment under these provisions if the perpetrator (1) voluntarily and earnestly makes efforts to prevent the continued existence of the organization or the commission of a crime consistent with its goals; or (2) voluntarily discloses his knowledge to a government agency in time, so that crimes, the planning of which he is aware, may still be prevented; if the perpetrator attains his goal of preventing the continued existence of the organization or if it is attained without his efforts, then he shall not be punished").

What is the status of this defense? Is it element-negating, or is it a justification or an excuse? If the point of the defense is renunciation of *purpose*, the mens rea of conspiracy, how can it be an *affirmative* defense? Recall that affirmative defenses in the Model Penal Code shift only the burden of production onto the defendant, not the burden of persuasion, which remains on the state. § 1.12. What if the defendant also bore the burden of persuasion? See, e.g., N.Y. Penal Law § 40.10; cf. N.Y. Penal Law §§ 25.00(2).

In fact, the New York provision on renunciation is worth a closer look, because it attempts to combine, under one roof, renunciation defenses for complicity, conspiracy, solicitation, and facilitation:

1. In any prosecution for an offense, other than an attempt to commit a crime, in which the defendant's guilt depends upon his criminal liability for the conduct of another person pursuant to section 20.00 [accomplice liability], it is an affirmative defense that, under circumstances manifesting a voluntary and complete renunciation of his criminal purpose, the defendant withdrew from participation in such offense prior to the commission thereof and made a substantial effort to prevent the commission thereof.
2. In any prosecution for criminal facilitation . . ., it is an affirmative defense that, prior to the commission of the felony which he facilitated, the defendant made a substantial effort to prevent the commission of such felony.
3. In any prosecution . . . for an attempt to commit a crime, it is an affirmative defense that, under circumstances manifesting a voluntary and complete renunciation of his criminal purpose, the defendant avoided the commission of the crime attempted by abandoning his criminal effort and, if mere abandonment was insufficient to accomplish such avoidance, by taking further and affirmative steps which prevented the commission thereof.
4. In any prosecution for criminal solicitation . . . or for conspiracy . . . in which the crime solicited or the crime contemplated by the

conspiracy was not in fact committed, it is an affirmative defense that, under circumstances manifesting a voluntary and complete renunciation of his criminal purpose, the defendant prevented the commission of such crime.

5. A renunciation is not "voluntary and complete" within the meaning of this section if it is motivated in whole or in part by (a) a belief that circumstances exist which increase the probability of detection or apprehension of the defendant or another participant in the criminal enterprise, or which render more difficult the accomplishment of the criminal purpose, or (b) a decision to postpone the criminal conduct until another time or to transfer the criminal effort to another victim or another but similar objective.

N.Y. Penal Law § 40.10.

Could these provisions be replaced by a single one? Or are the differences among the various versions of renunciation worth preserving? Why?

12. *Punishment.* How should we punish the agreement to commit a crime? *Callanan* clarified not only that conspiracy can be punished in addition to the crime that was its object (no merger), but that there was also nothing wrong with punishing the conspiracy *more harshly* than its object crime. See also United States v. Rabinowich, 238 U.S. 78, 88 (1915) (conspiracy more dangerous than "the mere commission of the contemplated crime"). Does this make any sense?

The Model Penal Code provides that conspiracy is a crime "of the same grade and degree as the most serious offenses which ... is an object of the conspiracy," except for conspiracies to commit a first degree felony, which are graded as second degree felonies. § 5.05(1). Why this different treatment of conspiracies to commit the most serious offenses? Shouldn't we punish posing a danger of harm less harshly than causing the harm, as is commonly the case in American criminal law?

2. Conspiracy vs. Complicity: The *Pinkerton* Rule

Pinkerton v. United States

Supreme Court of the United States.
328 U.S. 640 (1946).

■ Mr. Justice Douglas delivered the opinion of the Court.

Walter and Daniel Pinkerton are brothers who live a short distance from each other on Daniel's farm. They were indicted for violations of the Internal Revenue Code.[a] The indictment contained ten substantive counts and one conspiracy count. The jury found Walter guilty on nine of the

a. The indictment alleged that "the appellants did unlawfully remove, deposit and conceal certain commodities, namely, a large quantity of distilled spirits, ... whereof a tax was then and there imposed by the laws of the United States, with intent then and there to defraud the United States of such tax." Pinkerton v. United States, 151 F.2d 499, 500 (5th Cir. 1945).—Eds.

substantive counts and on the conspiracy count. It found Daniel guilty on six of the substantive counts and on the conspiracy count. * * *

There is ... no evidence to show that Daniel[, who was in prison at the time,] participated directly in the commission of the substantive offenses on which his conviction has been sustained, although there was evidence to show that these substantive offenses were in fact committed by Walter in furtherance of the unlawful agreement or conspiracy existing between the brothers. The question was submitted to the jury on the theory that each petitioner could be found guilty of the substantive offenses, if it was found at the time those offenses were committed petitioners were parties to an unlawful conspiracy and the substantive offenses charged were in fact committed in furtherance of it.

.... We have here a continuous conspiracy. There is here no evidence of the affirmative action on the part of Daniel which is necessary to establish his withdrawal from it.... [S]o long as the partnership in crime continues, the partners act for each other in carrying it forward. It is settled that "an overt act of one partner may be the act of all without any new agreement specifically directed to that act." Motive or intent may be proved by the acts or declarations of some of the conspirators in furtherance of the common objective.

.... The criminal intent to do the act is established by the formation of the conspiracy. Each conspirator instigated the commission of the crime. The unlawful agreement contemplated precisely what was done. It was formed for the purpose. The act done was in execution of the enterprise. The rule which holds responsible one who counsels, procures, or commands another to commit a crime is founded on the same principle. That principle is recognized in the law of conspiracy when the overt act of one partner in crime is attributable to all. An overt act is an essential ingredient of the crime of conspiracy.... If that can be supplied by the act of one conspirator, we fail to see why the same or other acts in furtherance of the conspiracy are likewise not attributable to the others for the purpose of holding them responsible for the substantive offense.

A different case would arise if the substantive offense committed by one of the conspirators was not in fact done in furtherance of the conspiracy, did not fall within the scope of the unlawful project, or was merely a part of the ramifications of the plan which could not be reasonably foreseen as a necessary or natural consequence of the unlawful agreement. But as we read this record, that is not this case.

Affirmed.

People v. McGee

Court of Appeals of New York.
49 N.Y.2d 48 (1979).

■ COOKE, CHIEF JUDGE.

Two trials are considered here. Out of one evolve appeals by defendants McGee, Edwards and Tolliver, who were convicted, after a jury trial, of one count of conspiracy in the third degree and 28 counts of bribery in the second degree. From the other arise appeals by defendants Quamina and Waters, who were convicted, upon a jury verdict, of one count of conspiracy in the third degree and 10 counts of bribery in the second degree.

[T]he People's theory was that the defendants proposed an arrangement whereby Rochester Police Officers Gerald Luciano and Gustave J. D'Aprile, members of the Vice Squad, would be paid to prevent the arrest of defendants' gambling associates while enforcing the law against competitors.... The officers were offered monetary and other benefits in exchange for their assistance. * * *

[In late 1973 and early 1974, Quamina and Waters met with the officers on several occasions.] Defendants McGee, Edwards and Tolliver were later brought into the operation.... On November 13, [1974] there was a meeting with Edwards and McGee at which the group discussed the scope of police activity, as well as weekly payments to the police. No payments were made at that meeting.... At various intervals during the ensuing months, Edwards made payments to the officers. * * *

McGee argues that the Trial Judge erred in charging the jury that he could be found guilty of the substantive offense of bribery by virtue of his status as a conspirator. After determining that there was sufficient evidence of an agreement among the defendants to go to the jury on the conspiracy count, the court charged that each conspirator could be convicted of bribery on the basis of acts of any one of the coconspirators committed in furtherance of the conspiracy (see Pinkerton v. United States, 328 U.S. 640, 66 S.Ct. 1180). The court also charged that McGee alone could be convicted of the bribery if he solicited, requested, commanded, importuned or intentionally aided another to engage in that offense (see Penal Law, § 20.00). McGee is correct in his contention that the portion of the charge concerning conspirator liability was erroneous. It is held that liability for the substantive offense may not be independently predicated upon defendant's participation in an underlying conspiracy. As there was no evidence of McGee's complicity in the bribery counts submitted to the jury,[1] and thus no basis for accomplice liability, there must be a reversal of the conviction of bribery and a dismissal of the indictment as to those counts.

In rejecting the notion that one's status as a conspirator standing alone is sufficient to support a conviction for a substantive offense committed by a coconspirator, it is noted that the Legislature has defined the conduct that will render a person criminally responsible for the act of another. Conspicuously absent from section 20.00 of the Penal Law is reference to one who conspires to commit an offense. That omission cannot be supplied by construction. Conduct that will support a conviction for conspiracy will not perforce give rise to accessorial liability. True, a conspirator's conduct in many instances will suffice to establish liability as an accomplice, but the concepts are, in reality, analytically distinct. To

1. The trial court dismissed two bribery counts on the ground that there was no agreement on November 13 to pay the specific amount of $50 to each officer as charged in the indictment. The court determined, however, that there was sufficient evidence of an agreement among defendants and the remaining counts were submitted to the jury.

permit mere guilt of conspiracy to establish the defendant's guilt of the substantive crime without any evidence of further action on the part of the defendant, would be to expand the basis of accomplice liability beyond the legislative design.

The crime of conspiracy is an offense separate from the crime that is the object of the conspiracy. Once an illicit agreement is shown, the overt act of any conspirator may be attributed to other conspirators to establish the offense of conspiracy and that act may be the object crime. But the overt act itself is not the crime in a conspiracy prosecution; it is merely an element of the crime that has as its basis the agreement. It is not offensive to permit a conviction of conspiracy to stand on the overt act committed by another, for the act merely provides corroboration of the existence of the agreement and indicates that the agreement has reached a point where it poses a sufficient threat to society to impose sanctions. But it is repugnant to our system of jurisprudence, where guilt is generally personal to the defendant, to impose punishment, not for the socially harmful agreement to which the defendant is a party, but for substantive offenses in which he did not participate.

We refuse to sanction such a result and thus decline to follow the rule adopted for Federal prosecutions in Pinkerton v. United States, 328 U.S. 640, 66 S.Ct. 1180. Accessorial conduct may not be equated with mere membership in a conspiracy and the State may not rely solely on the latter to prove guilt of the substantive offense.

QUESTIONS AND COMMENTS

1. In thinking about *Pinkerton* and *McGee*, it might be useful to keep some differences between complicity and conspiracy in mind.

Complicity and conspiracy are most easily distinguished if we think of complicity as a doctrinal tool for imputing the conduct of one person (the principal) to another (the accomplice). It's not the only method of imputation—using a person as an unwilling or unwitting instrument is another. See Model Penal Code § 2.06(2)(a). Complicity is not an offense; the accomplice is not convicted of complicity, but of the offense he aided or abetted—murder, say. Accomplice liability may be based on an agreement between accomplice and principal—if that agreement facilitates or encourages the principal's criminal conduct. But it need not be. Any sort of facilitation or encouragement—with or without an agreement—suffices.

Conspiracy, by contrast, *is* an offense (albeit an inchoate one that—ordinarily—derives its criminality from its object, another—substantive—offense). The conspirator *is* convicted of conspiracy, though—ordinarily—of a conspiracy to commit some other offense. Conspiracy doesn't just require an agreement; it is an agreement. It may also require an overt act. That overt act, however, needn't be a crime, nor need it be the crime that is the object of the conspiracy.

2. Consider the U.S. Supreme Court's justification of the *Pinkerton* rule, which treats all co-conspirators as accomplices in each others' reasonably foreseeable crimes in furtherance of the conspiracy. Since an overt act

in furtherance of the conspiracy by one co-conspirator can be imputed to any other, the Court argues, any act should be similarly imputable, including those that constitute separate offenses. How does *McGee* respond to this argument? Does *McGee* dispute that overt acts are imputable from one co-conspirator to another? What, according to *McGee*, is the function of the overt act requirement? And what, therefore, is the effect of imputing one co-conspirator's overt act to another?

3. *McGee* rejects the *Pinkerton* rule on the ground that "it is repugnant to our system of jurisprudence, where guilt is generally personal to the defendant, to impose punishment, not for the socially harmful agreement to which the defendant is a party, but for substantive offenses in which he did not participate."

Are you satisfied with this explanation? If guilt is "generally" personal in American criminal law, how can I ever be held liable for the conduct of another person? Is accomplice liability consistent with this principle of the personalness of guilt? Where does this principle come from? Is it of constitutional origin?

4. *McGee* insists on differentiating between liability for a conspiracy and for an offense committed in furtherance of it. But how significant is that distinction, and therefore *McGee's* rejection of *Pinkerton*? How likely is it that proof of a conspiracy will not also constitute proof of complicity in crimes committed in furtherance of it? Is *Pinkerton* anything more than an evidentiary shortcut?

In *McGee* itself, the court declares that there was "no evidence of McGee's complicity in the bribery counts submitted to the jury," so that McGee's liability for the substantive bribery counts could only have been based on a *Pinkerton* theory. What would McGee have to have done to be legally accountable for the payment of the bribe, other than paying the bribe himself?

Does the distinction between "expansive" conspiracy-complicity doctrine and the (purported) defendant-protectiveness of conventional complicity law disappear even more clearly in jurisdictions that hold an accomplice responsible for all crimes the principal commits that were "reasonably foreseeable" at the time she gave aid to the principal? See People v. Luparello, 187 Cal.App.3d 410, 231 Cal.Rptr. 832 (1986).

5. Note that *Pinkerton* itself recognizes a limitation on the general rule that conspiracy implies complicity—"reasonable foreseeability." Does this proviso make the rule less objectionable? Is *Pinkerton* problematic because it circumvents the actus reus of complicity, or its mens rea?

6. Pinkerton's *Limits*. Despite much criticism—and rejection by the Model Penal Code drafters—the *Pinkerton* rule lives on in federal criminal law, as well as in some state jurisdictions. See, e.g., State v. Walton, 227 Conn. 32, 630 A.2d 990 (1993). Some federal courts, however, have begun hinting at constitutional limitations on the reach of the *Pinkerton* rule. "Several circuits ... recognize that due process constrains the application of *Pinkerton* where the relationship between the defendant and the substantive offense is slight." United States v. Castaneda, 9 F.3d 761, 766 (9th Cir. 1993). Courts have had a hard time specifying these constraints other

than to say that they examine whether a particular application of *Pinkerton* "extends the concept of foreseeability, the touchstone of co-conspirator liability, beyond the limits of fundamental fairness." Id. at 765. Recently, courts have balked at applying *Pinkerton* in certain federal weapons possession cases:

> Sharee S. Williams ... attacks her conviction for possession of a firearm as a felon under 18 U.S.C. § 922(g)(1).[a] In order to obtain a conviction for felon-in-possession under that provision, the government must establish beyond a reasonable doubt that (1) the defendant had a previous felony conviction, (2) the defendant possessed a firearm, and (3) the firearm had traveled in or affected interstate commerce.... [T]he government ... sought to prove the element of possession under a theory of vicarious liability premised on the Supreme Court's decision in *Pinkerton v. United States,* 328 U.S. 640, 66 S.Ct. 1180 (1946). Under that theory, Williams could be found guilty of possessing the firearm as a felon even if she lacked either actual or constructive possession, as long as another member of the conspiracy possessed a gun. The government made no real effort to produce any evidence regarding the co-conspirator who possessed the firearm. Williams' defense theory, however, appeared to be that Samuel Simmons ... was the one involved in the drug dealing and that she was unaware of it. The government presumably proffered the *Pinkerton* instruction for the proposition that if Williams did not possess the gun found in her apartment, then her roommate, Samuel Simmons, must have possessed it and that he was a co-conspirator because she attributed the drugs to him....
>
> In order to properly determine the applicability of *Pinkerton* to this case, we must examine the basis for the *Pinkerton* ruling.... The Court ... considered whether a conspirator could be found guilty of the substantive offense committed by a co-conspirator in furtherance of the conspiracy. It held that the governing principle should be the same where the overt acts in the conspiracy constitute a substantive offense, and that a conspirator could be convicted of the substantive offense committed by a co-conspirator as long as the offense was committed in furtherance of the conspiracy, fell within the scope of the unlawful project, and was reasonably foreseeable as a necessary or natural consequence of the unlawful agreement....
>
> .... The government's use of *Pinkerton* in this case takes this one step farther in that it seeks *Pinkerton* liability based in part upon acts by a co-conspirator that did not constitute the crime. There are no allegations that a co-conspirator was guilty of violating § 922(g)(1). Instead, the government uses a cut-and-paste approach, taking the firearm possession by one conspirator, adding it to the felon status of another conspirator, and thereby creating a substantive offense for

a. Firearms possession by a person "who has a been convicted in any court of a crime punishable by imprisonment for a term exceeding one year" is punishable by ten years' imprisonment, 18 U.S.C. § 924(a)(2), or, if the defendant has three prior convictions of a violent felony or a serious drug offense, by a minimum of fifteen years' imprisonment, id. § 924(e)(1).—EDS.

> that second conspirator. It is a significant expansion of the *Pinkerton* doctrine that appears to be difficult to limit.
>
> For instance, under such a use of *Pinkerton,* even lawful possession of a firearm by a conspirator could presumably be used to establish a § 922(g)(1) violation for a co-conspirator who is a felon. Moreover, one can easily imagine a large-scale conspiracy, in which a conspirator's possession of a firearm in California is used to obtain a felon-in-possession conviction of a co-conspirator in Illinois. This seems far afield from the purpose of the felon-in-possession prohibition, which is to "keep firearms away from the persons Congress classified as potentially irresponsible and dangerous." It is an unwarranted, and possibly unconstitutional, expansion of the *Pinkerton* doctrine. * * *
>
> Theoretically, the application of *Pinkerton* here would ... invite the future inverse use of the doctrine to attribute a felon's possession of a firearm to his non-felon co-conspirator. A non-felon could be deemed guilty of being a felon in possession of a firearm. That ridiculous prospect reveals the fundamental problem with extending *Pinkerton* liability to the felon-in-possession statute. Because § 922(g)(1) defines the offense in terms of the status of the individual possessing the firearm, the vicarious liability provisions of *Pinkerton* are inappropriate for such an offense. Accordingly, the district court erred in submitting the *Pinkerton* instruction to the jury on the § 922(g)(1) charge. * * *
>
> The firearm was found in a dresser drawer that arguably contained only men's clothing in a bedroom shared by Samuel Simmons.... No evidence was introduced that linked Williams to that firearm. For instance, no testimony was introduced that the gun was ever displayed in Williams' presence or that she ever mentioned its existence, and no fingerprint or other evidence tied her to it....

United States v. Walls, 225 F.3d 858 (7th Cir. 2000).

Is *Pinkerton* the problem in this case, or is it the felon-in-possession statute? Can *Pinkerton* never be applied to possession offenses? Any offense defined in terms of the status of the offender? For that matter, how can I be an *accomplice* to such a status crime? What conduct would be imputed to me?

7. The *Pinkerton* rule is hardly self-executing. Co-conspirators are responsible for all reasonably foreseeable crimes committed by confederates in furtherance of "the conspiracy." But what is "the conspiracy"? Revisit Kotteakos v. United States, 328 U.S. 750 (1946), p. 694, supra. Assume one of the parties Brown works with in defrauding the FHA bribes an investigating officer. It is certainly foreseeable that people may bribe the impediments to their white collar crime schemes. But is there *one* conspiracy to defraud the FHA or multiple conspiracies between Brown and his posse of defrauders to commit distinct multiple crimes? Are all of the defrauders confederates in a single conspiracy at all?

Moreover, federal courts have plainly balked at the idea that every minor participant in "an enterprise" is responsible for everything the other participants do, so long as it serves general enterprise ends (making more money?) and is foreseeable. A whole slew of petty numbers runners, prostitutes, and drug couriers may know they work for the same "crime boss" but it's hard to imagine that the courts would tolerate punishing each prostitute for all the drug sales, beatings, bribes, and killings that she knows or should know "members of her organization" commit in furtherance of the general profit-maximizing aims of the group. Some of this hesitancy is articulated in dicta in United States v. Alvarez, 755 F.2d 830 (11th Cir. 1985) (noting "potential due process limitations on the *Pinkerton* doctrine in cases involving attenuated relationships between the conspirator and the substantive crime," rejecting the argument that "prosecutorial discretion would protect truly 'minor' participants ... from liability for the far more serious crimes committed by their coconspirators," and insisting that "the liability of such 'minor' participants must rest on a more substantial foundation than the mere whim of the prosecutor").

8. The distinction between conspiracy and complicity also arises in cases where the defendant is charged with conspiring to aid and abet. Consider the following case.

> We now turn to the issue at hand—the constituents of the crime of "conspiracy to aid and abet the manufacture of marijuana." [The government argues that] it need not charge and prove the [manufacture of marijuana] to bring the instant charge.... We agree with the government that the operative charge here is conspiracy and that the essence of conspiracy is an agreement to commit an illegal act, not its accomplishment. In other words, the conspiracy itself is a complete offense....
>
> The illegal act to which defendants have allegedly conspired, the "unlawful object of the conspiracy," is "aiding and abetting the manufacture of marijuana." The aiding and abetting statute under which defendants are charged, provides:
>
> > (a) Whoever commits an offense against the United States or aids, abets, counsels, commands, induces or procures its commission is punishable as a principal.
>
> 18 U.S.C. § 2(a). The section does not create a separate crime, but rather abolishes the common law distinction between principals and accessories....
>
> The problem here is how to logically combine the crime of conspiracy, which does not require proof of the underlying substantive offense, with an aiding and abetting offense, which doesn't exist without one. If the charge were merely "conspiracy to manufacture marijuana," the government would have to prove only an agreement between defendants and their customers to manufacture marijuana. Had defendants been charged with "aiding and abetting the manufacture of marijuana," the government would not have to prove any agreement between defendants and their customers, but would have to prove that defendants knew their customers were manufacturing marijuana or intended to, and intended to assist in the unlawful act. It seems to us then that in order to conspire or agree to assist "X" in the manufacture of marijuana, "Y and Z" have to know that "X" is manufacturing

marijuana or planning to. Otherwise, all "Y and Z" are agreeing to do is to aid and abet a "possibility," or a "criminal wish"; which simply isn't a crime.

It is for this reason that we find the government's reasoning specious. Absent an awareness that their customers are manufacturing marijuana, defendants cannot have the requisite criminal intent to conspire to aid and abet them. Without the underlying crime, there can be no knowledge or intent to further it. The necessary and inescapable conclusion then is that the occurrence of the underlying crime has to be an essential element of such a charge because otherwise the requisite knowledge and intent to further the substantive offense cannot exist.

United States v. Superior Growers Supply, 982 F.2d 173 (6th Cir. 1992).

3. Agreement

People v. Berkowitz

Court of Appeals of New York.
50 N.Y.2d 333 (1980).

■ Gabrielli, Judge.

Defendant was convicted of conspiring with one Diane Alvarez to commit certain drug related ... felonies. * * * Alvarez, who was charged with several counts, was acquitted of conspiracy but was convicted of criminal sale of a controlled substance in the second degree.[3]

On defendant's appeal, the Appellate Division reversed the judgment of conviction on the law alone and dismissed the indictment. Correctly noting that any statements made by Alvarez and acts performed by her during and in furtherance of the alleged conspiracy could not be admitted into evidence against defendant unless the People first established a prima facie case of conspiracy without such evidence, the Appellate Division then found that the People in this case had failed, as a matter of law, to establish a prima facie case of conspiracy. Accordingly, the Appellate Division concluded that the People had failed to prove defendant's guilt beyond a reasonable doubt. We disagree.

Initially, we note that the principles of law applicable to this case are well settled.... Where two or more persons have entered into an illicit agreement to commit a crime, each of them to some extent may be deemed to speak as an agent for the others.... Thus, ... "(o)nce an illicit agreement is shown, the overt act of any conspirator may be attributed to other conspirators to establish the offense of conspiracy"....

3. Alvarez' conviction was subsequently reversed by the Appellate Division on an appeal raising issues unrelated to those involved on defendant's appeal. We note that unlike defendant, who did not testify at his trial, Alvarez testified on her own behalf at her trial, and also raised the affirmative defenses of duress and entrapment. Alvarez did not testify at defendant's trial.

. . . Defendant's involvement in the plan to sell drugs to [Detective Robert Wainen, an undercover agent of the Drug Enforcement Administration,] was evidenced by his significant connections with the transaction: there was evidence indicating that from the very beginning, it was defendant whom Wainen was to meet on December 13, not Alvarez. . . . Similarly, once the informant and Officer Wainen arrived at the apartment, the transaction was delayed until defendant made his appearance. While the actual sale was conducted by Alvarez, the details of that transaction . . . lead inexorably to the conclusion that defendant was involved. . . . In short, although it might well be that absent the incriminatory statements and actions of Alvarez there would be insufficient evidence to prove defendant's guilt beyond a reasonable doubt, the introduction into evidence of those statements and acts requires only the establishment of a prima facie case. We find that the evidence as to the statements and actions of defendant alone sufficed to establish a prima facie case, and thus the statements made by Alvarez and the overt acts performed by her were properly admitted against defendant. . . .

This does not end the matter, however, for defendant also contends that the acquittal of Alvarez served as a bar to the subsequent trial of defendant for conspiracy, pursuant to established rules of collateral estoppel or issue preclusion. . . . Initially, defendant argues that the crime of conspiracy necessarily requires at least two conspirators since it is premised upon an agreement between at least two persons. In the instant case, the only alleged conspirators were Alvarez and defendant, and thus, according to defendant, if Alvarez is not a conspirator, neither is he. Finally, according to defendant, since Alvarez has been acquitted of participation in this conspiracy, the People are estopped from contending at his subsequent trial that he and she entered into an illicit agreement. Thus, it is claimed that since the People are supposedly precluded from proving the existence of any illicit agreement between Alvarez and defendant, they must of necessity be precluded from prosecuting defendant as a conspirator.

Insofar as defendant's argument is premised upon the belief that there must exist at least two criminally culpable persons for there to be a conspiracy, it must be rejected as an attempt to return to the traditional "bilateral" theory of conspiracy, which is no longer the law in this State as a result of the Legislature's decision to adopt a "unilateral" theory of liability for conspiracy. Under the unilateral theory of conspiracy as it exists in this State, a defendant may be convicted of conspiracy even though all other parties to the illicit agreement are not criminally liable due to age, lack of intent, or some similar impediment (see Penal Law § 105.30). Thus, the fact that Alvarez, as a result of her acquittal, must be deemed not to be criminally liable as a conspirator, does not alone bar prosecution of defendant even though he is the only other alleged conspirator.

This does not completely dispose of defendant's contentions, however, since regardless whether a unilateral or bilateral approach to conspiracy be involved, it is fundamental that no one can be convicted of conspiracy if there exists no illicit agreement. In the instant case, defendant contends that Alvarez' acquittal on the conspiracy count, when viewed together with her conviction for sale of a controlled substance, mandates the conclusion that the acquittal for conspiracy was premised not on a lack of intent or any similar impediment, but rather on the absence of any illicit agreement between her and defendant. Defendant argues strenuously that since Alvarez was convicted of the sale charge stemming from her dealings with Wainen, the jury could not have concluded that she lacked intent or any other mental element necessary to show a conspiracy. And finally, in this connection, defendant contends that pursuant to traditional principles of collateral estoppel, the purported finding by the jury in the Alvarez prosecution that there was no agreement precludes prosecution of this defendant for a conspiracy premised upon that same agreement. * * *

It is now well settled that the doctrine of collateral estoppel is applicable to criminal as well as civil matters, and exists independent of the prohibition against double jeopardy. As we have previously noted, "(c)ollateral estoppel, as distinguished from the principle of double jeopardy, arises not so much from concern for the peace of mind of the defendant as from a long-recognized equitable reaction against allowing a party to relitigate issues which have already been decided against him". Nonetheless, it has long been recognized that neither the doctrine of collateral estoppel nor the principles of res judicata from which it has developed should be applied "to criminal prosecutions in quite the same way as that body of doctrine is applicable to civil cases"....

.... [I]n the criminal law, in contrast to civil litigation, society has an overwhelming interest in ensuring not merely that the determination of guilt or innocence be made, but that it be made correctly. While the correct resolution of civil disputes is indeed an important goal of our legal system, it may fairly be said that society's primary interest in the resolution of civil disputes is that they be settled in a peaceful, orderly, and impartial manner. Since this is so, it is appropriate that litigation-limiting devices such as the doctrine of collateral estoppel be liberally applied in civil litigation.

In contradistinction, it is the correctness of the result which is of preeminent concern in a criminal prosecution, for the major function of a criminal proceeding is the conviction of the guilty and the acquittal of the innocent, not the swift resolution of some private dispute between the prosecutor and the accused. Hence, the civil doctrine of collateral estoppel, which accepts the occasional enthronement of erroneous findings of fact as a necessary cost of conserving the time and resources of the parties and the courts, is of less relevance in the criminal law.

Of considerable significance is the fact that in criminal law, unlike civil litigation, defendants are, to a great extent, protected from burdensome and repetitious prosecution by the constitutional and statutory prohibitions against double jeopardy. Thus, the doctrines of collateral estoppel and res judicata are somewhat less needed in the criminal law....

There exist several other persuasive reasons not to apply principles of collateral estoppel so as to allow the acquittal of one defendant to ever serve as a bar to the prosecution of another. In most cases there will be significant disparities in the proof which is available against each of two defendants. For example, one defendant may make admissions which can be used against him at his trial, but which could not be introduced at the trial of a codefendant. To suggest that the People had a fair opportunity to litigate the issue of the confessing defendant's guilt at the trial of the nonconfessing defendant would result in an absurdity. While this example is perhaps rather extreme, it is certainly not uncommon, and the vagaries of the complex rules of evidence applicable to criminal trials will in most cases result in the existence of evidence which may be used against only one of several persons accused of the same crimes. This is especially significant in light of the fact that the People must meet the high burden of proving guilt beyond a reasonable doubt in a criminal prosecution. Hence, the acquittal of one of two defendants means merely that the People were unable to prove his guilt beyond a reasonable doubt; it does not mean that the People will necessarily be unable to prove the guilt of the other defendant beyond a reasonable doubt. We see no reason to forbid an attempt to do so.

Additionally, it will normally be impossible to ascertain the exact import of a verdict of acquittal in a criminal trial. It may well be that the acquittal of one defendant is based on some factor which is not relevant to the guilt or innocence of the other defendant. For example, there exist several defenses and affirmative defenses which are personal to a particular defendant and would not affect the guilt or innocence of another person accused of the same crime. Moreover, there always exists the possibility that the jury in the first case will have exercised its so-called "mercy" function despite instructions to the contrary, especially in a case involving multiple crimes arising from the same transaction.

For all these reasons, we conclude that a defendant whose own interests were not put directly in issue at the prior trial may not utilize the doctrine of collateral estoppel as a bar to his own prosecution. This is so because the doctrine of collateral estoppel may be used only against a party who has had a full and fair opportunity to previously litigate that same issue, and the People simply do not have a full and fair opportunity to contest the guilt of one defendant at the trial of another defendant.

Model Penal Code § 5.04. Incapacity, Irresponsibility or Immunity of Party to Solicitation or Conspiracy.

(1) [I]t is immaterial to the liability of a person who solicits or conspires with another to commit a crime that:

(a) he or the person whom he solicits or with whom he conspires does not occupy a particular position or have a particular characteristic which is an element of such crime, if he believes that one of them does; or

(b) the person whom he solicits or with whom he conspires is irresponsible or has an immunity to prosecution or conviction for the commission of the crime.

QUESTIONS AND COMMENTS

1. *Unilateral Conspiracy*. How can there be an agreement between fewer than two people? Why is an "agreement" with an undercover agent a

conspiracy, rather than an attempted conspiracy? Or is punishing an attempted conspiracy (i.e., a double inchoate crime) more troubling than punishing an agreement of one?

Why adopt the unilateral approach? Does effective law enforcement require it? What would happen to undercover police work if the unilateral approach were abandoned? Or is it simply a matter of diagnosing dangerousness? See Miller v. State, 955 P.2d 892 (Wyo. 1998) ("A person who believes he is conspiring with another to commit a crime is a danger to the public regardless of whether the other person in fact has agreed to commit the crime."). But isn't it the conspiracy that poses the exceptional danger which warrants state interference, rather than any one (would-be) conspirator? United States v. Escobar de Bright, 742 F.2d 1196 (9th Cir. 1984) ("Criminal conspiracy is an offense separate from the actual criminal act because of the perception 'that collective action toward an antisocial end involves a greater risk to society than individual action toward the same end.' In part, this view is based on the perception that group activity increases the likelihood of success of the criminal act and of future criminal activity by members of the group, and is difficult for law enforcement officers to detect.... Such dangers, however, are nonexistent when a person 'conspires' only with a government agent.").

2. Federal criminal law is among the jurisdictions that continue to adhere to a bilateral view of conspiracy. Note, however, that while federal law defines an agreement more narrowly than, say, the Model Penal Code, it then provides for harsher punishment of a conspiracy, once it has been proven. Recall that federal criminal law—unlike the Model Penal Code and the jurisdictions that follow it—also features the *Pinkerton* rule (which quickly turns conspiracy into complicity), provides for the cumulative punishment of the conspiracy and its object offense, and—depending on the statute—punishes the conspiracy more harshly than its object offense.

3. Judge Learned Hand is often quoted as saying that conspiracy is "the darling of the modern prosecutor's nursery." Harrison v. United States, 7 F.2d 259 (2d Cir. 1925). Much of this popularity stems from its vagueness, which may be attributed both to its *object* and the concept of *agreement*. The former source of vagueness today is less significant than it was in 1925, as the conspiratorial object has generally been limited to crimes, as opposed to any type of unlawful, corrupt, or otherwise objectionable conduct, though here too federal conspiracy law, thanks in large part to the "defraud" clause of the general federal conspiracy statute, 18 U.S.C. § 371, remains open-ended. The concept of agreement has remained conveniently broad to this day; it need be neither written nor explicit, but "can instead be inferred from the facts and circumstances of the case." Iannelli v. United States, 420 U.S. 770 (1975).

But there are other conveniences as well that mark conspiracy statutes as prime crime fighting tools. *Pinkerton* and *McGee* mention that the overt act requirement—should there be any—can be fulfilled by the act of any conspirator, which is then attributed to all the others. Likewise, since those who enter into "an illicit agreement" are deemed each other's "agents" (see *Berkowitz*), each conspirator's out-of-court statements may be used against any of her co-conspirators, provided independent evidence of the conspiracy has been introduced:

Fed. Rules Evid. 801. Definitions.

(c) Hearsay.

"Hearsay" is a statement, other than one made by the declarant while testifying at the trial or hearing, offered in evidence to prove the truth of the matter asserted.

(d) Statements which are not hearsay.

A statement is not hearsay if—

(2) Admission by party-opponent. The statement is offered against a party and is (A) the party's own statement in either an individual or a representative capacity or (B) a statement of which the party has manifested an adoption or belief in its truth, or (C) a statement by a person authorized by the party to make a statement concerning the subject, or (D) a statement by the party's agent or servant concerning a matter within the scope of the agency or employment, made during the existence of the relationship, or (E) a statement by a coconspirator of a party during the course and in furtherance of the conspiracy.

Federal prosecutors in particular benefit from another procedural feature of the law of conspiracy: venue. They have unusually wide latitude in choosing where to prosecute a conspiracy case since venue lies not only where the agreement was made, but also wherever any of the overt acts by any of the conspirators occurred. Particularly in complex cases involving allegations of far flung criminal networks, this rule may provide prosecutors with an opportunity to move the case to a remote and inhospitable district. Justice Jackson's concurrence in Krulewitch v. United States, 336 U.S. 440 (1949), paints a vivid picture of the dire straits faced by a defendant who finds himself the subject of a conspiracy prosecution, particularly in federal court:

> An accused, under the Sixth Amendment, has the right to trial "by an impartial jury of the State and district wherein the crime shall have been committed." The leverage of a conspiracy charge lifts this limitation from the prosecution and reduces its protection to a phantom, for the crime is considered so vagrant as to have been committed in any district where any one of the conspirators did any one of the acts, however innocent, intended to accomplish its object. The Government may, and often does, compel one to defend at a great distance from any place he ever did any act because some accused confederate did some trivial and by itself innocent act in the chosen district. . . .
>
> When the trial starts, the accused feels the full impact of the conspiracy strategy. Strictly, the prosecution should first establish prima facie the conspiracy and identify the conspirators, after which evidence of acts and declarations of each in the course of its execution are admissible against all. But the order of proof of so sprawling a charge is difficult for a judge to control. As a practical matter, the

accused often is confronted with a hodgepodge of acts and statements by others which he may never have authorized or intended or even known about, but which help to persuade the jury of existence of the conspiracy itself. In other words, a conspiracy often is proved by evidence that is admissible only upon assumption that conspiracy existed. The naive assumption that prejudicial effects can be overcome by instructions to the jury, all practicing lawyers know to be unmitigated fiction.

The trial of a conspiracy charge doubtless imposes a heavy burden on the prosecution, but it is an especially difficult situation for the defendant. The hazard from loose application of rules of evidence is aggravated where the Government institutes mass trials. Moreover, in federal practice there is no rule preventing conviction on uncorroborated testimony of accomplices, as there are in many jurisdictions, and the most comfort a defendant can expect is that the court can be induced to follow the "practice" and caution the jury against "too much reliance upon the testimony of accomplices."

A co-defendant in a conspiracy trial occupies an uneasy seat. There generally will be evidence of wrongdoing by somebody. It is difficult for the individual to make his own case stand on its own merits in the minds of jurors who are ready to believe that birds of a feather are flocked together. If he is silent, he is taken to admit it and if, as often happens, co-defendants can be prodded into accusing or contradicting each other, they convict each other.

4. *Acquittal of Co-conspirator.* The court in *Berkowitz* stressed that New York punished unilateral conspiracies. Does acquittal of one conspirator imply acquittal of the other in *bilateral* conspiracy jurisdictions? See State v. Colon, 257 Conn. 587, 778 A.2d 875 (2001) (no).

5. *Berkowitz* insists that even under a unilateral theory of conspiracy, proof of an agreement is still required. In other words, even if the other conspirator lacked the requisite mens rea (purpose) for conspiracy liability so that there is no such thing as a "meeting of the minds," the actus reus of conspiracy (the agreement) must be present. (What if the co-conspirator is exculpated not because she lacks mens rea, but because she is excused, or justified?) But does it make sense to speak of an agreement between two people if one of them has no intention of carrying it out? In what sense is an agreement an *act* separate from the intent of those who enter into it?

6. Obviously, the requirement of an agreement is not limited to jurisdictions that adhere to the unilateral theory of conspiracy. The state's burden of proving an agreement, however, is lightened considerably by the oft-repeated rule that "a tacit understanding is sufficient." United States v. Burns, 162 F.3d 840, 849 (5th Cir. 1998). Consider the following case.

Richard Perry ("Victim") drove to the Mt. Zion area of Lexington County in order to purchase drugs. As he entered the neighborhood, three individuals approached his car and offered to sell him crack cocaine. Rodney Mouzon was standing some distance away from Victim's vehicle. There was testimony that the deal did not go through, that there was an argument between the parties, that Victim's car door slammed, and that Victim tried to leave the area.... Someone yelled that Victim was trying to "jack," meaning that he was trying to run away with the drugs. Everyone scattered, trying to find bottles and other objects to throw at the car. Mouzon ran behind his house to a location where he kept a gun, and he returned to the spot where he was previously standing. As Victim drove past the individuals who had approached him, two shots were fired, one of which struck Victim in his back. One witness, who was himself throwing a bottle at the car, heard a shot, looked up, and saw Mouzon "coming back down with the revolver in his hand." Victim was able to drive himself to a hospital, but died the following day as a result of bleeding caused by the gunshot.

Rodney Mouzon was indicted for murder, conspiracy to distribute crack cocaine, and possession of a firearm during the commission of a violent crime.... He was acquitted on the murder charge, but convicted on the latter two offenses. He was sentenced to twenty-five years' imprisonment and fined $50,000 for conspiracy to distribute crack cocaine, and sentenced to five years, consecutive, for possession of a firearm during the commission of a violent crime. * * *

The State argues the Court of Appeals erred when it determined that the trial court should have directed a verdict of acquittal based upon insufficient evidence of conspiracy to distribute crack cocaine. We disagree....

What is required [for a conspiracy] is a shared, single criminal objective, not just similar or parallel objectives between similarly situated people.... It is not enough that a group of people separately intend to distribute drugs in a single area, nor enough that their activities occasionally or sporadically place them in contact with each other. People in the same industry in the same locale (even competitors) can occasionally be expected to interact with each other without thereby becoming coconspirators. What is needed is proof they intended to act together for their shared mutual benefit within the scope of the conspiracy charged. * * *

The dealers tried to muscle each other out of the way to try to get up to the car to sell the drugs. Such evidence reveals not an agreement on a shared objective, but parallel and competing objectives.

The State posits that persons in the neighborhood would throw bottles and bricks at cars which attempted to leave when a deal went bad. This fact, it argues, demonstrates the existence of a tacit agreement by the drug dealers to act for the shared mutual benefit of enforcing payment and protecting each other in drug transactions. Accordingly, it asserts, there was evidence that Mouzon was engaged in conspiracy to distribute crack cocaine.

.... In order to establish the logical nexus between the evidence (of participants throwing objects at vehicles trying to get away) and the conclusion (that this is a conspiracy to distribute crack cocaine), certain assumptions have to be made. Among these assumptions are that (1) the participants were, in throwing bottles and bricks, trying to

> extract payment for crack cocaine, and not simply trying to inflict injury (or effect street justice) upon those who have not paid for their drugs; and (2) all the participants were acting in concert, and not independently of one another. This argument assumes the very conclusion it is seeking to establish.

State v. Mouzon, 326 S.C. 199, 485 S.E.2d 918 (1997).

Is the problem with Mouzon's conviction of conspiracy to distribute crack cocaine the absence of proof of a *conspiracy* or the absence of proof of a conspiracy *to distribute crack cocaine*? Did the evidence support a conviction of conspiracy to commit assault? Do you agree with the court that there was no evidence of even a tacit agreement among the bottle throwers? Even if they competed for drug sales, didn't they share a common interest in preventing customers from running off with the merchandise, perhaps to send a message to potential *customers* that this sort of behavior would not be tolerated in their sales location, or to communicate their willingness to resort to violence to potential *competitors* operating elsewhere who might be tempted to drive them out of business by force? Can competitors never conspire? Where would that leave antitrust laws, which—among other things—prohibit competitors from conspiring, say, to fix prices? What would it have taken for the state to prove a tacit agreement in this case?

Courts often treat coordinated behavior as *evidence* of an (unobserved) explicit agreement. As we noted, criminal conspirators, after all, would not likely have drafted contracts and kept them on file, so we'd expect that we would use circumstantial evidence to infer the fact of (even the most explicit) agreement. Still other times, the courts plainly assume that no such explicit (if unobserved) formal agreement was reached, but the courts still believe the parties *communicated* an intention to agree (without words). In that sense, of course, a tacit agreement is not circumstantial evidence of an overt agreement, but the court still plainly believes the parties have communicated their intention to be bound to a common objective. But there is a third possibility: the parties simply never agreed (in words or winks), but they engage in a certain form of conscious parallelism of conduct. In these cases, we may well be asking whether parties who engage in certain forms of self-interested parallel action are conspirators so long as they recognize that their action is self-interested only so long as others follow the same script. (One might say they have grown into an agreement in such a case.) In Interstate Circuit v. United States, 306 U.S. 208 (1939), Interstate Circuit and Texas Consolidated Theaters entered agreements with eight distributors to distribute films. To form this agreement, they sent a letter to all the distributors demanding that prices be set at a certain price that was higher than the going rate. The letter was addressed so that each distributor knew that the other distributors were getting the same letter. The question was whether the distributors knew that the other distributors had agreed to the price fixing scheme and so could be said to have conspired with each other to unlawfully restrain trade.

The evidence in *Interstate Circuit* could support an inference that the distributors actually spoke to one another and agreed to act in common.

However, the court noted that a spoken or express agreement is not necessary. Thus, it is not necessary to prove that there was communication or an express agreement provided that there is a tacit agreement reached without communication. ("It is elementary that an unlawful conspiracy may be and often is formed without simultaneous action or agreement on the part of the conspirators.") The distributors in *Interstate Circuit* are liable because they "knew that cooperation was essential to successful operation of the plan" and acted accordingly. They certainly would not be liable if they merely acted in parallel without that knowledge: the Court seems to believe, though, that acting with that knowledge is tantamount to reaching a tacit agreement.

What if defendants are members of a gang and engage in a good deal of parallel action ("talking smack" to rivals; coming armed to confrontations and drawing weapons simultaneously)? What if the actions taken by each gang member are considerably more likely to be taken if each gang member knows others in the gang are likely to be (if not formally committed to) doing the same thing? The Ninth Circuit, in United States v. Garcia, 151 F.3d 1243 (9th Cir. 1998), reversed conspiracy convictions in such a case: "The facts establish only that . . . an ongoing gang-related dispute [between the Crips and Bloods] erupted into shooting. The government points to expert testimony . . . that generally gang members have a 'basic agreement' to back one another up in fights. . . . This testimony . . . at most establishes one of the characteristics of gangs but not a specific objective of a particular gang—let alone a specific agreement on the part of its members to accomplish an illegal objective. . . . [T]he fact that more than one member of the Bloods was shooting at rival[s] does not prove a pre-arrangement—the Crips, too, were able to pull out their guns almost immediately, suggesting that readiness for a gunfight requires no prior agreement. Such readiness may be a sad commentary on the state of mind of many of the nation's youth, but it is not indicative of a criminal conspiracy."

7. In People v. Lauria, 251 Cal.App.2d 471, 59 Cal.Rptr. 628 (1967), the defendant provided phone answering services—in the pre-cell phone, pre-answering machine era—to a group of "call girls" (prostitutes). The case is widely cited for the proposition that a defendant cannot be convicted for conspiracy to commit a (relatively) "minor offense" (like prostitution) unless he has a true *purpose* to achieve the criminal end. The court notes along the way that a defendant might be guilty of conspiracy if he merely *knew* (as Lauria did) that he was helping others achieve a criminal end, provided the object of the conspiracy was a more serious crime. In fact, in United States v. Fountain, 768 F.2d 790 (7th Cir. 1985), Judge Posner picks up on this aspect of *Lauria* and finds, in a conventional accomplice liability case, that "aiding and abetting murder is established by proof beyond a reasonable doubt that the supplier of the murder weapon knew the purpose for which it would be used." (Can adopting different mens rea requirements depending on the severity of the object offense be justified (from the perspectives of the various traditional theories of punishment))? Reconsider *Commonwealth v. Kennedy* (differentiating between preparation and attempt based in part on severity of object offense), supra ch. 6.

But what if we set aside the question of whether Lauria should be convicted of conspiracy to commit prostitution if he merely knew that furnishing phone services helped the "call girls" break the law but lacked a stake in the venture. Isn't there a prior issue, though, that the court evades? In what sense have the call girls and Lauria made an *agreement*, even a tacit one? One might imagine that if two (or more) people agree to do something, there is some way in which each could breach his promise. But what have Lauria and the "call girls" promised one another? Would Lauria disappoint some expectation that "call girls" have if he stopped furnishing them with phone-answering services? Would they disappoint some expectation he has if they stopped working as prostitutes? Would they even disappoint some expectation he has if they failed to use *his* answering service so long as they worked as call girls?

Consider, too, the following case:

> [Kolda testified that he regularly got marijuana from another dealer and sold it in small quantities on credit to his roommates, Defendant Desantos and Perrault. He kept the marijuana in a safe in the basement of the house the roommates shared. While Desantos lived with Kolda and Perrault, Kolda testified that he saw Desantos selling small quantities of the drugs he bought to his friends in order to pay Kolda for it.]
>
> The state need not show direct contact or an explicit agreement between all the conspirators.... It is sufficient to show that each knew or had reason to know of the conspiracy's scope and that the defendant had reason to believe that his own benefits were dependent upon the success of the entire venture.
>
> .... A reasonable jury could find that Desantos, Kolda, and Perrault shared the common goal of maintaining a marijuana inventory for distribution. It also could have found that Desantos and Perrault tacitly agreed with Kolda to use their residence as a storage place for the marijuana inventory [and that] Kolda, Desantos, and Perrault benefited from their cooperative group activity because it helped finance a continuous and convenient marijuana supply for their own use.
>
> The record permitted a finding that over the course of thirty-five weeks, Kolda distributed approximately sixty pounds of marijuana with the help of Desantos, Perrault, and others. Thus, the evidence permitted the jury to reasonably conclude that Desantos tacitly agreed with Kolda to participate in a group that distributed more than 2500 grams of marijuana.

State v. Desantos, 233 Wis.2d 274, 610 N.W.2d 230 (Wis. Ct. App. 2000).

What does the court think Desantos (implicitly) agreed to do? What might have he done that would have breached the implicit agreement, or disappointed Kolda's expectations of him? Is there any reason to believe that Kolda would have felt betrayed by Desantos had he merely passively watched him continue to engage in drug dealing?

4. SOLICITATION

Benson v. People

Supreme Court of California.
57 Cal.2d 240 (1962).

■ TRAYNOR, J.

Petitioner seeks a writ of prohibition to restrain the Superior Court of Los Angeles County from taking further proceedings against him under a count of an indictment charging him with soliciting perjured testimony in violation of Penal Code section 653f.*

The Department of Social Welfare had been conducting an investigation of adoption practices in Los Angeles County. Mrs. Evelyn Scheingold, an investigator, visited petitioner, an attorney, and told him that she was pregnant, that she wished to have the child adopted, and that the child's father was unknown, since she had been living with her husband and another man. The husband's consent would normally be necessary for an adoption, for a legitimate child "cannot be adopted without the consent of its parents. . . ." (Civ. Code, §§ 224, 226.) To make the husband's consent unnecessary, the wife must show that she is not cohabiting with him and must rebut the statutory presumptions favoring the child's legitimacy. In a custody proceeding the wife may present testimony establishing that she has lived apart from her husband for a sufficient length of time to rebut the presumptions that the husband is the child's father.

Mrs. Scheingold testified before the grand jury that in contemplation of a custody proceeding petitioner said to her: " 'There are ways of getting around the law, and I'm the only lawyer in town who knows how to do it.' He said, 'I will help you get a witness to establish that your husband could not have been the father. I know how to get around these Courts.' " She testified further: "I said, 'Mr. Benson, my big problem is how I am going to get a witness to testify that I have not been with my husband for a period of time.'

"He said, 'You have a girl friend here, haven't you?'

"I said, 'Yes, but I am afraid she may say the wrong things. She's pretty nervous.'

"Mr. Benson said, 'Don't worry. I'll talk to her. She will say the right things.' "

Subsequently, Mrs. Scheingold introduced Miss Terri Pallato, a fellow investigator, to petitioner as a friend. Mrs. Scheingold testified that Miss Pallato, "told Mr. Benson that she had never seen my husband," that she

* Section 653f of the Penal Code provides: "Every person who solicits another . . . to commit or join in the commission of . . . perjury . . . is punishable by imprisonment in the county jail not longer than one year or in the state prison not longer than five years, or by a fine of not more than five thousand dollars. Such offense must be proved by the testimony of two witnesses, or of one witness and corroborating circumstances."

did not know him, that she did not know whether or not this was his baby, but she was willing to swear in the affirmative to both of these points. . . .

"Mr. Benson assured her that there was nothing to it. He said that Terri and I would go into the Judge's chambers and he would ask whether or not she knew my husband and whether or not this could be his baby, and she would answer that this could not be his baby."

"Mr. Benson said that Terri should say that she knew my husband, but that I had been living out here in Los Angeles for over 11 months and this could not be his child."

Miss Pallato testified: "He said, 'All we do is we three, you, her and me, will walk into the Judge's chambers and he will ask you those two questions.'

"Now, he didn't repeat the questions, but he meant, 'Do you know Evelyn's husband' and 'Do you know that this is not his baby?'

"And he said, 'All you do is answer yes to both those questions.'

"So I said, 'Well, I'm terribly nervous about it, Mr. Benson.' I said, 'I don't do this every day of my life. . . .'

"He said, 'Look, there's absolutely nothing to it.' ". . . .

Petitioner contends, however, that he could not have committed the crime of solicitation since the perjury would not have occurred because the fact that Mrs. Scheingold was an investigator who was not even pregnant would have precluded a custody proceeding. Petitioner's alleged acts nevertheless fall clearly within Penal Code section 653f.

That section is designed not only to prevent solicitations from resulting in the commission of the crimes solicited, but to protect "inhabitants of this state from being exposed to inducement to commit or join in the commission of the crimes specified. . . ." "Purposeful solicitation presents dangers calling for preventive intervention and is sufficiently indicative of a disposition towards criminal activity to call for liability. Moreover, the fortuity that the person solicited does not agree to commit the incited crime plainly should not relieve the solicitor of liability. . . ." (Model Penal Code, § 5.02, comment [Tent. Draft No. 10, 1960] 82.)

The act solicited must, of course, be criminal. If the solicitor believes that the act can be committed "it is immaterial that the crime urged is not possible of fulfilment at the time when the words are spoken" or becomes impossible at a later time. This rule was clearly enunciated as early as 1864 in Commonwealth v. Jacobs, 91 Mass. (9 Allen) 274, 275. In that case a statute made criminal the solicitation of another to leave the state to offer himself as a draft substitute for the solicitor. The court rejected defendant's contention that since the person solicited, without the solicitor's knowledge, had been rejected as physically unfit by the army before the solicitation, the impossibility of completing the act barred a conviction.

Solicitation itself is the evil prohibited by the Legislature, and prosecution therefor is particularly appropriate for the very case in which the crime solicited does not take place.

People v. Lubow

Court of Appeals of New York.
29 N.Y.2d 58 (1971).

■ BERGAN, JUDGE.

The basic statutory definition of criminal solicitation is that with intent that another person shall "engage in conduct constituting a crime" the accused "solicits, requests, commands, importunes or otherwise attempts to cause such other person to engage in such conduct". . . . [N]othing need be done under the statute in furtherance of the communication ("solicits, commands, importunes") to constitute the offense. The communication itself with intent the other person engage in the unlawful conduct is enough. It needs no corroboration.

And an attempt at communication which fails to reach the other person may also constitute the offense for the concluding clause "or otherwise attempts to cause such other person to engage in such conduct" would seem literally to embrace as an attempt an undelivered letter or message initiated with the necessary intent. * * *

The evidence showed that complainant Silverman and both defendants were engaged in the jewelry business. It could be found that defendant Lubow owed Silverman $30,000 for diamonds on notes which were unpaid; that Lubow had told Silverman he was associated with a big operator interested in buying diamonds and introduced him to defendant Gissinger.

It could also be found that in October, 1967, Silverman met the two defendants together at their office, demanded his money, and said that because of the amount owed him he was being forced into bankruptcy.

Silverman testified in response to this Lubow said "Well, let's make it a big one, a big bankruptcy", and Gissinger said this was a good idea. When Silverman asked "how it is done" he testified that Lubow, with Gissinger participating, outlined a method by which diamonds would be purchased partly on credit, sold for less than cost, with the proceeds pyramided to boost Silverman's credit rating until very substantial amounts came in, when there was to be a bankruptcy with Silverman explaining that he had lost the cash gambling in Puerto Rico and Las Vegas. The cash would be divided among the three men. The gambling explanation for the disappearance of cash would be made to seem believable by producing credit cards for Puerto Rico and Las Vegas. Silverman testified that Lubow said "we would eventually wind up with a quarter of a million dollars each" and that Gissinger said "maybe millions".

Silverman reported this proposal to the District Attorney in October, 1967 and the following month a police detective equipped Silverman with a tape recorder concealed on his person which was in operation during conversations with defendants on November 16 and which tends to substantiate the charge. The reel was received in evidence on concession that it was taken from the machine Silverman wore November 16.

A police detective testified as an expert that a "bust out operation" is a"pyramiding of credit by rapid purchasing of merchandise, and the rapid selling of the same merchandise sometimes 10 and 20 per cent the cost of the merchandise itself, and they keep selling and buying until they establish such a credit rating that they are able to purchase a large order at the end of their operation, and at this time they go into bankruptcy or they just leave". * * *

Commentators closely associated with the drafting of the Model Penal Code of the American Law Institute, from which the New York solicitation statute stems, have observed: "Purposeful solicitation presents dangers calling for preventive intervention and is sufficiently indicative of a disposition towards criminal activity to call for liability. Moreover, the fortuity that the person solicited does not agree to commit or attempt to commit the incited crime plainly should not relieve the solicitor of liability, when otherwise he would be a conspirator or an accomplice."[1]

Solicitation to commit a felony was a misdemeanor at common law. Summarizing this historical fact Judge Cardozo observed: "So at common law, incitement to a felony, when it did not reach the stage of an attempt, was itself a separate crime, and like conspiracy, which it resembled, was a misdemeanor, not a felony" (People v. Werblow, 241 N.Y. 55, 66, 148 N.E. 786, 791, citing Higgins and Rex v. Gregory, L.R. 1 C.C.R. 77).

But as People v. Bush, 4 Hill 133, demonstrates, the solicitation in early New York cases was treated as closely related to an attempt. There defendant asked another to burn a barn and gave him a match for that purpose. This principle was followed to some extent but there were fundamental difficulties with it under the concept of attempt and it seems not to have been followed....

In commenting on the criminal solicitation enactment of article 100, two lawyers who were active in the work of the State Commission on Revision of the Penal Law and Criminal Code which prepared the present statute observed that article 100 "closes that gap" for those who believe, as apparently the commission and the American Law Institute did, that "solicitation to commit a crime involves sufficient culpability to warrant criminal sanctions".

There are, however, potential difficulties inherent in this penal provision.... One, of course, is the absence of any need for corroboration.... Extraordinary care might be required in deciding when to prosecute; in determining the truth; and in appellate review of the factual decision.

One example would be the suggestion of one person to another that he commit a sexual offense; another is the suggestion that he commit perjury. The Model Penal Code did not require corroboration; but ... there are dangers in the misinterpretation of innuendos or remarks which could be taken as invitations to commit sexual offenses. These are discussed by Wechsler–Jones–Korn (61 Col.L.Rev., p. 623, *supra* n. 1) with the comment that "it is a risk implicit in the punishment of almost all inchoate crimes". * * *

Another potential problem with the statute is that it includes an attempt to commit unlawful solicitation, i.e., solicits, etc., "or otherwise attempts to cause" the conduct. This has the same effect as the Model

1. Herbert Wechsler, Chief Reporter, Model Penal Code; William Kenneth Jones, Special Consultant, Model Penal Code, and Harold L. Korn, Special Consultant, Model Penal Code, The Treatment of Inchoate Crimes in the Model Penal Code of the American Law Institute: Attempt, Solicitation, and Conspiracy, 61 Col.L.Rev. 571, 622.

Penal Code, but the language there is different. The code spells the purpose out more specifically that: "It is immaterial that the actor fails to communicate with the person he solicits to commit a crime if his conduct was designed to effect such communication" (Model Penal Code, § 5.02(2), Tent. Draft No. 10). This could be an attempt in the classic sense and might be committed by a telephone message initiated but never delivered. The present Penal Law, stated in different language, has the same effect. * * *

The judgment should be affirmed.

Model Penal Code § 5.02. Criminal Solicitation.

(1) *Definition of Solicitation.* A person is guilty of solicitation to commit a crime if with the purpose of promoting or facilitating its commission he commands, encourages or requests another person to engage in specific conduct which would constitute such crime or an attempt to commit such crime or which would establish his complicity in its commission or attempted commission.

(2) *Uncommunicated Solicitation.* It is immaterial under Subsection (1) of this Section that the actor fails to communicate with the person he solicits to commit a crime if his conduct was designed to effect such communication.

(3) *Renunciation of Criminal Purpose.* It is an affirmative defense that the actor, after soliciting another person to commit a crime, persuaded him not to do so or otherwise prevented the commission of the crime, under circumstances manifesting a complete and voluntary renunciation of his criminal purpose.

QUESTIONS AND COMMENTS

1. Consider the connection between solicitation, conspiracy, and attempt. According to the Model Penal Code Commentaries, solicitation "may, indeed, be thought of as an attempt to conspire." Commentaries § 5.02, at 365–66. But then why do we need a separate offense of solicitation? Or is there something troubling about the notion of an inchoate inchoate offense (like an attempted conspiracy), one that punishes preparing to prepare to commit a crime, or anticipating to anticipating committing one? The Model Penal Commentaries also set out the now standard justification of solicitation statutes: "Purposeful solicitation presents dangers calling for preventive intervention and is sufficiently indicative of a disposition towards criminal activity to call for liability." Do you agree? Is it the "purpose," once again, that marks otherwise noncriminal preparatory conduct as criminal?

What conduct is covered by solicitation that isn't covered by the law of attempt? Does this conduct deserve punishment? Where do we draw the line between conduct that indicates dangerousness and conduct that indicates dangerousness but lies beyond the reach of criminal law?

2. Now consider the connection between solicitation and complicity. One way of having another person's (the principal's) conduct imputed to me is, "with the purpose of promoting or facilitating the commission of the

offense," to "solicit[] such other person to commit it." Model Penal Code § 2.06(3)(a)(i). So what do we need a solicitation statute for? Cf. Model Penal Code § 5.01(3) (attempted aiding)?

3. *Benson* rejects the defendant's attempt to raise an impossibility defense as beside the point. Yet at the same time it insists that the "act solicited must, of course, be criminal." What if the solicitor thinks—incorrectly—that the act is criminal (assuming no mental defect amounting to insanity)? If the point of the offense of solicitation is to identify and incapacitate dangerous individuals, why should it matter whether they are right about the criminality of the behavior they're soliciting? Are they any less dangerous if they make a mistake of law? Cf. the discussion of impossibility in the context of the law of attempt, ch. 6.

C. RICO

United States v. Elliott et al.

United States Court of Appeals for the Fifth Circuit.
571 F.2d 880 (1978).

■ SIMPSON, CIRCUIT JUDGE.

In this case we deal with the question of whether and, if so, how a free society can protect itself when groups of people, through division of labor, specialization, diversification, complexity of organization, and the accumulation of capital, turn crime into an ongoing business. Congress fired a telling shot at organized crime when it passed the Racketeer Influenced and Corrupt Organizations Act of 1970, popularly known as RICO. 18 U.S.C. §§ 1961 et seq. (1970). Since the enactment of RICO, the federal courts, guided by constitutional and legislative dictates, have been responsible for perfecting the weapons in society's arsenal against criminal confederacies.

Today we review the convictions of six persons accused of conspiring to violate the RICO statute, two of whom were also accused and convicted of substantive RICO violations. The government admits that in this prosecution it has attempted to achieve a broader application of RICO than has heretofore been sanctioned. Predictably, the government and the defendants differ as to what this case is about. According to the defendants, what we are dealing with is a leg, a tail, a trunk, an ear—separate entities unaffected by RICO proscriptions. The government, on the other hand, asserts that we have come eyeball to eyeball with a single creature of behemoth proportions, securely within RICO's grasp. . . .

I. THE FACTS

Simply stated, this is a case involving a group of persons informally associated with the purpose of profiting from criminal activity. The facts giving rise to this generalization, however, are considerably more complex. Evidence presented during the 12 day trial implicated the six defendants and 37 unindicted co-conspirators in more than 20 different criminal endeavors....

II. THE INDICTMENT

The eight count indictment in this case ... charged the following:

COUNT ONE: Conspiracy to Violate RICO: All six defendants, James Alford Elliott, Jr., Robert Ervin Delph, Jr., William Marion Foster, Recea Howell Hawkins, John Clayburn Hawkins, Jr. a/k/a J. C., and John Frank Taylor, were named in Count One as having conspired ... with each other, with 37 unindicted co-conspirators, and with "others to the grand jury known and unknown" to violate a substantive provision of the RICO statute, 18 U.S.C. § 1962(c), in violation of 18 U.S.C. § 1962(d).[15] The essence of the conspiracy charge was that the defendants agreed to participate, directly and indirectly, in the conduct of the affairs of an "enterprise" whose purposes were to commit thefts, "fence" stolen property, illegally traffic in narcotics, obstruct justice, and engage in "other criminal activities". The indictment listed 25 overt acts, beginning with the burning of the [Sparta] Community Convalescent Nursing Home in 1970 and culminating with ... [the possession and distribution of several hundred pounds of] marihuana ... in the spring of 1976.

COUNT TWO: The Substantive RICO Charge: J. C. and Recea Hawkins only were charged with a substantive violation of the RICO statute, 18 U.S.C. § 1962(c), in that they conducted and participated, directly and indirectly, in the conduct of the affairs of an enterprise through a pattern of racketeering activity. The crimes alleged to satisfy the statutory requirements for "a pattern of racketeering activity" included those charged in Counts Three through Six and Count Eight, as well as the possession and sale of Ritalin and the distribution of MDA on three occasions, all in violation of 21 U.S.C. § 841, the murder of Jimmy Reeves, in violation of Ga. Code Ann. § 26–1101, and the burning of the Community Convalescent Nursing Home, in violation of Ga. Code Ann. § 26–1401.

COUNT THREE: J. C. Hawkins was charged with violating 18 U.S.C. §§ 659 and 2 in that he possessed and concealed with the intent to convert to his own use a stolen interstate shipment of Hormel meat valued in excess of $100.

COUNT FOUR: J. C. Hawkins and James Elliott were charged with violating 18 U.S.C. §§ 1503 and 2 in that they corruptly endeavored to obstruct justice by "hanging" the jury in the trial of Rudolph Flanders for the possession and concealment of the stolen Hormel meat. [Elliott was the lone holdout for acquittal on the jury, thus causing a mistrial.]

COUNT FIVE: J. C. Hawkins and William Marion Foster were charged with violating 18 U.S.C. §§ 659 and 2 in that they possessed and concealed with the intent to convert to their own use a stolen interstate shipment of Swift Premium meat and dairy products valued in excess of $100.

15. The defendants were not charged under the general conspiracy statute, 18 U.S.C. § 371, which carries a maximum penalty less severe than does the specific RICO conspiracy provision.

COUNT SIX: J. C. Hawkins, Recea Hawkins and Foster were charged with violating 18 U.S.C. §§ 659 and 2 in that they possessed and concealed with the intent to convert to their own use a stolen interstate shipment of "Career Club" shirts valued in excess of $100.

COUNT SEVEN: James Elliott was charged with violating 18 U.S.C. § 1503 in that he corruptly endeavored to obstruct justice by encouraging Joe Fuchs to lie to a federal grand jury "investigating theft from interstate shipment of [Hormel] Premium boxed beef". . . .

COUNT EIGHT: J. C. Hawkins was charged with violating 18 U.S.C. § 2315 in that he knowingly received and disposed of a counterfeit security, a Georgia State Certificate of Title, moving in interstate commerce.

At the close of the government's case, the trial judge directed a verdict of acquittal on Count Four in favor of James Elliott. The jury acquitted J. C. Hawkins on Count Four and Elliott on Count Seven, thus eliminating all substantive obstruction of justice charges from the case. All remaining defendants were found guilty as charged by the jury under Counts One, Two, Three, Five, Six, and Eight, were adjudged guilty, and received the following sentences: J. C. Hawkins, 80 years imprisonment; Recea Hawkins, 50 years imprisonment; Delph and Taylor, each 10 years, with parole eligibility in 24 months; Foster, one year imprisonment, five years probation; James Elliott, five years probation.

III. THE SUBSTANTIVE RICO VIOLATION

J. C. and Recea Hawkins contend that their acts, while arguably violative of other criminal statutes, are not proscribed by the substantive RICO provision under which they were charged, 18 U.S.C. § 1962(c), in that they were not committed in furtherance of the affairs of an "enterprise" as required by the Act. At best, they say, the facts disclosed that two brothers confederated to commit a few, isolated criminal acts over a period of six years. . . .

. . . . Section 1962(c) provides:

> It shall be unlawful for any person employed by or associated with any enterprise engaged in, or the activities of which affect, interstate or foreign commerce, to conduct or participate, directly or indirectly, in the conduct of such enterprise's affairs through a pattern of racketeering activity or collection of unlawful debt.

This section must be read in the context of the statutory definitions of its key terms. "Enterprise", as used in the Act, "includes any individual, partnership, corporation, association, or other legal entity, and any union or group of individuals associated in fact although not a legal entity". 18 U.S.C. § 1961(4). As relevant to this case, a "pattern of racketeering activity" simply requires at least two acts of "racketeering activity" committed within ten years of each other. 18 U.S.C. § 1961(5). "Racketeering activity" includes three broad categories of crimes: (A) any of several specified "act[s] or threat[s] . . . chargeable under State law and punishable by imprisonment for more than one year", including, as relevant here, murder and arson, (B) any act which is indictable under any of several specified sections of Title 18, U.S.C., including, as relevant here, § 659 (felonious theft from interstate shipment), § 1503 (obstruction of justice), and § 2315 (interstate shipment of stolen or counterfeit securities) or (C) federal offenses involving narcotics or other dangerous drugs. 18 U.S.C. § 1961(1).

Reduced to its bare essentials, the charge against J. C. and Recea may be restated as follows:

> Being associated with a group of individuals who were associated in fact, J. C. and Recea Hawkins each directly and indirectly participated in the group's affairs through the commission of two or more predicate crimes.

The gist of J. C.'s and Recea's objection to their conviction . . . is that there was no group of individuals associated in fact—no enterprise—in whose affairs they could have participated, directly or indirectly. . . .

In *United States v. Hawes*, 529 F.2d 472, 479 (5th Cir. 1976), we noted that "Congress gave the term 'enterprise' a very broad meaning". On its face and in light of its legislative history, the Act clearly encompasses "not only legitimate businesses but also enterprises which are from their inception organized for illicit purposes".[a] Similarly, we are persuaded that "enterprise" includes an informal, de facto association such as that involved in this case. In defining "enterprise", Congress made clear that the statute extended beyond conventional business organizations to reach "*any* . . . group of individuals" whose association, however loose or informal, furnishes a vehicle for the commission of two or more predicate crimes. The statute demands only that there be association "in fact" when it cannot be implied in law. There is no distinction, for "enterprise" purposes, between a duly formed corporation that elects officers and holds annual meetings and an amoeba-like infra-structure that controls a secret criminal network.

Here, the government proved beyond a reasonable doubt the existence of an enterprise comprised of at least five of the defendants.[18] This enterprise can best be analogized to a large business conglomerate. Metaphorically speaking, J. C. Hawkins was the chairman of the board, functioning as the chief executive officer and overseeing the operations of many separate branches of the corporation. An executive committee in charge of the "Counterfeit Title, Stolen Car, and Amphetamine Sales Department" was comprised of J. C., Delph, and Taylor, who supervised the operations of lower level employees such as Farr, the printer, and Green, Boyd, and

a. The Supreme Court since has agreed. United States v. Turkette, 452 U.S. 576, 101 S. Ct. 2524 (1981) (RICO not "intended solely to protect legitimate business enterprises from infiltration by racketeers," but also reaches "participation in an association which performs only illegal acts and which has not infiltrated or attempted to infiltrate a legitimate enterprise").—Eds.

18. . . . . The number of persons making up an enterprise is irrelevant . . . in that even a single individual may be considered an "enterprise" under the statutory definition. 18 U.S.C. § 1961(4). Thus, under the facts of this case, we could view J. C. Hawkins as the enterprise and the other defendants as persons merely "employed by or associated with" the enterprise. 18 U.S.C. § 1962(c). We treat the enterprise in this case as a group of people in light of the government's admission that its "theory of the case from beginning to end has been that the 'enterprise' in this case was comprised of all six appellants as a group of individuals associated in fact". The indictment charged only that each defendant was associated with the enterprise.

Jackson, the car thieves. Another executive committee, comprised of J. C., Recea and Foster, controlled the "Thefts From Interstate Commerce Department", arranging the purchase, concealment, and distribution of such commodities as meat, dairy products, "Career Club" shirts, and heavy construction equipment. An offshoot of this department handled subsidiary activities, such as murder and obstruction of justice, intended to facilitate the smooth operation of its primary activities. Each member of the conglomerate, with the exception of Foster, was responsible for procuring and wholesaling whatever narcotics could be obtained. The thread tying all of these departments, activities, and individuals together was the desire to make money. J. C. might have been voicing the corporation's motto when he told Bob Day ["a pilot and an old friend" who was recording their conversation for the Georgia Bureau of Investigation], in May, 1976, "if it ain't a pretty damn good bit of money, I ain't going to fuck with it".

A jury is entitled to infer the existence of an enterprise on the basis of largely or wholly circumstantial evidence. Like a criminal conspiracy, a RICO enterprise cannot be expected to maintain a high profile in the community. Its affairs are likely to be conducted in secrecy and to involve a minimal amount of necessary contact between participants. Thus, direct evidence of association may be difficult to obtain; a jury should be permitted to draw the natural inference arising from circumstantial evidence of association.[19] In this case, persuasive circumstantial evidence of association was buttressed by direct evidence tending to prove the existence of an enterprise. According to Boyd, defendant Delph stated that "he had a truck that he was running for J. C. and that they was partners in the deal or some kind of operation or setup." William Martin [a minor participant in the car theft ring who was cooperating with the Drug Enforcement Agency] described defendant Taylor's admission that he and others "had just gotten through purchasing an airplane for $102,000 to bring heroin into this country", and J. C. told Day that he had virtually bankrupted himself by spending money on airplanes to import drugs. Leon Averett, in the course of selling a trailer load of stolen shirts, stated that his associates had a warehouse in Atlanta big enough to handle several tractor-trailers.

Additionally, although the target of the RICO statute is not "sporadic activity", we find nothing in the Act excluding from its ambit an enterprise engaged in diversified activity. Indeed, Congress expressly stated that the purpose of the Act was "to seek the eradication of organized crime", which it described as a "highly sophisticated, diversified, and widespread activity that annually drains billions of dollars from America's economy by unlawful conduct. . . ." Pub.L. 91–452, § 1, 84 Stat. 922 (1970). To this end, it directed that "the provisions of this title shall be liberally construed to effectuate its remedial purposes". Id., § 904. While earlier cases have considered enterprises engaged in only one type of prohibited activity, a single enterprise engaged in diversified activities fits comfortably within the proscriptions of the statute and the dictates of common sense:

19. In conspiracy cases, we allow the jury to infer agreement on the basis of "the acts and conduct of the alleged conspirators themselves". *United States v. Morado,* 454 F.2d 167, 174 (5th Cir. 1972). In this case, it is apparent that the enterprise operated in a manner calculated to minimize direct evidence of association.

> As in a firm with a real estate department and an insurance department, the fact that partners bring in two kinds of business on the basis of their different skills and connections does not affect the fact that they are partners in a more general business venture.

United States v. Mallah, 503 F.2d 971, 976 (2d Cir. 1974), cert. denied, 420 U.S. 995, 95 S. Ct. 1425 (1975). We would deny society the protection intended by Congress were we to hold that the Act does not reach those enterprises nefarious enough to diversify their criminal activity.

The evidence in this case demonstrated the existence of an enterprise—a myriopod criminal network, loosely connected but connected nonetheless. By committing arson, actively assisting a car theft ring, fencing thousands of dollars worth of goods stolen from interstate commerce, murdering a key witness, and dealing in narcotics, J. C. and Recea Hawkins directly and indirectly participated in the enterprise's affairs through a pattern, indeed a plethora, of racketeering activity .....

IV. THE RICO CONSPIRACY COUNT

All six defendants were convicted under 18 U.S.C. § 1962(d) of having conspired to violate a substantive RICO provision, § 1962(c). In this appeal, all defendants ... argue that while the indictment alleged but one conspiracy, the government's evidence at trial proved the existence of several conspiracies, resulting in a variance which substantially prejudiced their rights and requires reversal, citing *Kotteakos v. United States*, 328 U.S. 750, 66 S. Ct. 1239 (1946). Prior to the enactment of the RICO statute, this argument would have been more persuasive. However, as we explain below, RICO has displaced many of the legal precepts traditionally applied to concerted criminal activity. Its effect in this case is to free the government from the strictures of the multiple conspiracy doctrine and to allow the joint trial of many persons accused of diversified crimes.

A. *Prior Law: Wheels and Chains*

1. Kotteakos *and the Wheel Conspiracy Rationale*: The Court in *Kotteakos* held that proof of multiple conspiracies under an indictment alleging a single conspiracy constituted a material variance requiring reversal where a defendant's substantial rights had been affected. At issue was "the right not to be tried *en masse* for the conglomeration of distinct and separate offenses committed by others". *Kotteakos* thus protects against the "spill-over effect", the transference of guilt from members of one conspiracy to members of another.

The facts of *Kotteakos* have been summarized by this court as follows:

> In that case, one where the indictment charged but one overall conspiracy, the government's proof at trial, by its own admission, showed that there were eight separate conspiracies involving some thirty-two persons. The key figure in the scheme, which involved the obtaining of government loans by making fraudulent representations, was a man named Brown, who was a part of, and directed each of the eight conspiracies. Brown was the only element common to the eight otherwise completely separate undertakings, no other person taking part in, nor having knowledge of the other conspiracies. Though each

> of the conspiracies had similar illegal objects, none depended upon, was aided by, or had any interest in the success of the others.

United States v. Perez, 489 F.2d 51, 60 (5th Cir. 1973). These facts led the Court to speak in terms of a "wheel conspiracy", in which one person, the "hub" of the wheel, was accused of conspiring with several others, the "spokes" of the wheel. As we explained in *United States v. Levine*, 546 F.2d 658, 663 (5th Cir. 1977):

> For a [single] wheel conspiracy to exist those people who form the wheel's spokes must have been aware of each other and must do something in furtherance of some single, illegal enterprise. Otherwise the conspiracy lacks "the rim of the wheel to enclose the spokes." If there is not some interaction between those conspirators who form the spokes of the wheel as to at least one common illegal object, the "wheel" is incomplete, and two conspiracies rather than one are charged.

2. Blumenthal *and the Chain Conspiracy Rationale*: The impact of *Kotteakos* was soon limited by the Court in *Blumenthal v. United States*, 332 U.S. 539, 68 S. Ct. 248 (1947), where the indictment charged a single conspiracy to sell whiskey at prices above the ceiling set by the Office of Price Administration. The owner of the whiskey, through a series of middlemen, had devised an intricate scheme to conceal the true amount he was charging for the whiskey. Although some of the middlemen had no contact with each other and did not know the identity of the owner, they had to have realized that they were indispensable cogs in the machinery through which this illegal scheme was effectuated. The Court concluded that "in every practical sense the unique facts of this case reveal a single conspiracy of which the several agreements were essential and integral steps". Thus the "chain conspiracy" rationale evolved.

The essential element of a chain conspiracy—allowing persons unknown to each other and never before in contact to be jointly prosecuted as co-conspirators—is interdependence. The scheme which is the object of the conspiracy must depend on the successful operation of each link in the chain. "An individual associating himself with a 'chain' conspiracy knows that it has a 'scope' and that for its success it requires an organization wider than may be disclosed by his personal participation". *United States v. Agueci*, 310 F.2d 817, 827 (2d Cir. 1962). "Thus, in a 'chain' conspiracy prosecution, the requisite element—knowledge of the existence of remote links—may be inferred solely from the nature of the enterprise." *United States v. Perez, supra*, 489 F.2d at 59 n. 10.[24]

24. Although *Perez* was a hybrid case, involving a wheel conspiracy in which each spoke was itself a chain conspiracy, we applied the interdependence rationale to find a single, overall conspiracy. Perez involved a series of fraudulent insurance claims based on several staged car accidents involving different groups of people, with minimal overlap among the groups. The scheme could not be described as a "chain" in the ordinary sense, but we noted that each participant had to realize that the single fraudulent claim in which he or she was involved could not be profitable unless it was one of multiple claims and that, in turn, multiple claims could not be successfully made unless they involved many different people and accidents in different locations across the state.

3. *Limits of the Chain Conspiracy Rationale*: The rationale of *Blumenthal* applies only insofar as the alleged agreement has "a common end or single unified purpose". Generally, where the government has shown that a number of otherwise diverse activities were performed to achieve a single goal, courts have been willing to find a single conspiracy. This "common objective" test has most often been used to connect the many facets of drug importation and distribution schemes. The rationale falls apart, however, where the remote members of the alleged conspiracy are not truly interdependent or where the various activities sought to be tied together cannot reasonably be said to constitute a unified scheme. In *United States v. Miley*, 513 F.2d 1191, 1207 (2d Cir. 1975), for example, the Second Circuit held that the value and quantity of drugs sold by the defendant-suppliers was insufficient to justify the inference that each knew his supplies were only a small part of the drugs handled by a larger operation. Similarly, in *United States v. Bertolotti,* 529 F.2d 149, 156 (2d Cir. 1975), the same Court focused on an alleged narcotics conspiracy that bore little resemblance to "the orthodox business operation" found to exist in other drug cases; many of the "narcotics transactions" involved amounted to "little more than simple cash thefts" in which no drugs changed hands. The only factor that tied several isolated transactions together, the Court noted, was the presence of two of the defendants, Rossi and Coralluzzo, in each. In effect, "the scope of the operation was defined only by Rossi's resourcefulness in devising new methods to make money". Under these circumstances, the Court held that the government had failed to prove the existence of a single conspiracy.

Applying pre-RICO conspiracy concepts to the facts of this case, we doubt that a single conspiracy could be demonstrated. Foster had no contact with Delph and Taylor during the life of the alleged conspiracy. Delph and Taylor, so far as the evidence revealed, had no contact with Recea Hawkins. The activities allegedly embraced by the illegal agreement in this case are simply too diverse to be tied together on the theory that participation in one activity necessarily implied awareness of others. Even viewing the "common objective" of the conspiracy as the raising of revenue through criminal activity, we could not say, for example, that Foster, when he helped to conceal stolen meat, had to know that J.C. was selling drugs to persons unknown to Foster, or that Delph and Taylor, when they furnished counterfeit titles to a car theft ring, had to know that the man supplying the titles was also stealing goods out of interstate commerce. The enterprise involved in this case probably could not have been successfully prosecuted as a single conspiracy under the general federal conspiracy statute, 18 U.S.C. § 371.

B. *RICO to the Rescue: The Enterprise Conspiracy*

In enacting RICO, Congress found that "organized crime continues to grow" in part "because the sanctions and remedies available to the Government are unnecessarily limited in scope and impact". Thus, one of the express purposes of the Act was "to seek the eradication of organized crime ... by establishing new penal prohibitions, and by providing enhanced sanctions and new remedies to deal with the unlawful activities of those engaged in organized crime". Pub.L. 91–452, § 1, 84 Stat. 922 (1970).

Against this background, we are convinced that, through RICO, Congress intended to authorize the single prosecution of a multi-faceted, diversified conspiracy by replacing the inadequate "wheel" and "chain" rationales with a new statutory concept: the enterprise.

To achieve this result, Congress acted against the backdrop of hornbook conspiracy law. Under the general federal conspiracy statute,

> the precise nature and extent of the conspiracy must be determined by reference to the agreement which embraces and defines its objects. Whether the object of a single agreement is to commit one or many crimes, it is in either case that agreement which constitutes the conspiracy which the statute punishes.

Braverman v. United States, 317 U.S. 49, 53, 63 S. Ct. 99, 102 (1942).

In the context of organized crime, this principle inhibited mass prosecutions because a single agreement or "common objective" cannot be inferred from the commission of highly diverse crimes by apparently unrelated individuals. RICO helps to eliminate this problem by creating a substantive offense which ties together these diverse parties and crimes. Thus, the object of a RICO conspiracy is to violate a substantive RICO provision—here, to conduct or participate in the affairs of an enterprise through a pattern of racketeering activity—and not merely to commit each of the predicate crimes necessary to demonstrate a pattern of racketeering activity. The gravamen of the conspiracy charge in this case is not that each defendant agreed to commit arson, to steal goods from interstate commerce, to obstruct justice, and to sell narcotics; rather, it is that each agreed to participate, directly and indirectly, in the affairs of the enterprise by committing two or more predicate crimes. Under the statute, it is irrelevant that each defendant participated in the enterprise's affairs through different, even unrelated crimes, so long as we may reasonably infer that each crime was intended to further the enterprise's affairs. To find a single conspiracy, we still must look for agreement on an overall objective. What Congress did was to define that objective through the substantive provisions of the Act.

C. *Constitutional Considerations*

The "enterprise conspiracy" is a legislative innovation in the realm of individual liability for group crime. We need to consider whether this innovation comports with the fundamental demand of due process that guilt remain "individual and personal". *Kotteakos, supra*, 328 U.S. at 772, 66 S. Ct. at 1252.

The substantive proscriptions of the RICO statute apply to insiders *and outsiders*—those merely "associated with" an enterprise—who participate directly *and indirectly* in the enterprise's affairs through a pattern of racketeering activity. 18 U.S.C. § 1962(c). Thus, the RICO net is woven tightly to trap even the smallest fish, those peripherally involved with the enterprise. This effect is enhanced by principles of conspiracy law also developed to facilitate prosecution of conspirators at all levels. Direct evidence of agreement is unnecessary: "proof of such an agreement may rest upon inferences drawn from relevant and competent circumstantial evidence—ordinarily the acts and conduct of the alleged conspirators themselves". Additionally, once the conspiracy has been established, the government need show only "slight evidence" that a particular person was a member of the conspiracy. Of course, "a party to a conspiracy need not know the identity, or even the number, of his confederates".

Undeniably, then, under the RICO conspiracy provision, remote associates of an enterprise may be convicted as conspirators on the basis of purely circumstantial evidence. We cannot say, however, that this section of the statute demands inferences that cannot reasonably be drawn from circumstantial evidence or that it otherwise offends the rule that guilt be individual and personal. The Act does not authorize that individuals "be tried *en masse* for the conglomeration of distinct and separate offenses committed by others". *Kotteakos, supra*. Nor does it punish mere association with conspirators or knowledge of illegal activity; its proscriptions are directed against conduct, not status. To be convicted as a member of an enterprise conspiracy, an individual, by his words or actions, must have objectively manifested an agreement to participate, directly or indirectly, in the affairs of an enterprise *through the commission of two or more predicate crimes*. One whose agreement with the members of an enterprise did not include this vital element cannot be convicted under the Act. Where, as here, the evidence establishes that each defendant, over a period of years, committed several acts of racketeering activity in furtherance of the enterprise's affairs, the inference of an agreement to do so is unmistakable.

It is well established that "the government is not required to prove that a conspirator had full knowledge of all the details of the conspiracy; knowledge of the essential nature of the plan is sufficient". *United States v. Brasseaux*, 509 F.2d 157, 160 n. 3 (5th Cir. 1975). The Supreme Court explained the policy behind this rule in *Blumenthal v. United States, supra*, 332 U.S. at 556–57, 68 S. Ct. at 256:

> For it is most often true, especially in broad schemes calling for the aid of many persons, that after discovery of enough to show clearly the essence of the scheme and the identity of a number participating, the identity and the fact of participation of others remain undiscovered and undiscoverable. Secrecy and concealment are essential features of successful conspiracy. The more completely they are achieved, the more successful the crime. Hence the law rightly gives room for allowing the conviction of those discovered upon showing sufficiently the essential nature of the plan and their connections with it, without requiring evidence of knowledge of all its details or of the participation of others. Otherwise the difficulties, not only of discovery, but of certainty in proof and of correlating proof with pleading would become insuperable, and conspirators would go free by their very ingenuity.

In the instant case, it is clear that "the essential nature of the plan" was to associate for the purpose of making money from repeated criminal activity. Defendant Foster, for example, hired J. C. Hawkins to commit arson, helped him to conceal large quantities of meat and shirts stolen from interstate commerce, and bought a stolen forklift from him. It would be "a perversion of natural thought and of natural language" to deny that these facts give rise to the inference that Foster knew he was directly involved in an enterprise whose purpose was to profit from crime. As we noted in *United States v. Gonzalez*, 491 F.2d 1202, 1206 (5th Cir. 1974), "persons so associating and forming organizations for furthering such illicit purposes do not normally conceive of the association as engaging in one unlawful transaction and then disbanding. Rather the nature of such organizations seems to be an ongoing operation . . ." Foster also had to know that the enterprise was bigger than his role in it, and that others unknown to him were participating in its affairs. He may have been unaware that others who had agreed to participate in the enterprise's affairs did so by selling drugs and murdering a key witness. That, however, is irrelevant to his own liability, for he is charged with agreeing *to participate* in the enterprise through his own crimes, not with agreeing *to commit* each of the crimes through which the overall affairs of the enterprise were conducted. We perceive in this no significant extension of a co-conspirator's liability. When a person "embarks upon a criminal venture of indefinite outline, he takes his chances as to its content and membership, so be it that they fall within the common purposes as he understands them".[31]

Our society disdains mass prosecutions because we abhor the totalitarian doctrine of mass guilt. We nevertheless punish conspiracy as a distinct offense because we recognize that collective action toward an illegal end

31. Although the evidence here supports the inference that each remote member of this enterprise knew he was a part of a much larger criminal venture, we do not wish to imply that each "department" of the enterprise was wholly independent of the others. A close look at the *modus operandi* of the enterprise reveals a pattern of interdependence which bolsters our conclusion that the functions of each "department" directly contributed to the success of the overall operation. Many of the enterprise's practices were analogous to those common in legitimate businesses:

—*Investment Capital*: Most of the enterprise's activities depended upon the ready availability of investment capital, or "front money", to finance the purchase of stolen goods and narcotics for eventual resale at a profit. In this sense, money brought in from one project could be used to purchase goods in another unrelated project.

—"Good Will": Part of the value of a business is the reputation it has established in the community, its "good will". The enterprise here benefited from a negative form of "good will". For example, Foster and J.C. exploited their cooperation in the . . . nursing home arson to gain the confidence of James Gunnells when they needed his help in concealing stolen meat; that earlier endeavor furnished proof that Foster and J.C. could be trusted in criminal pursuits. Similarly, J.C.'s threats of physical harm to many of those involved with the enterprise helped to build a fear in the community which deterred potential witnesses from going to the police. In this way, each successful criminal act and each threat contributed to the success of the enterprise as a whole.

—*Arrangements to Limit Liability*: Like most large business organizations, this enterprise conducted its affairs in a manner calculated to limit its liability for the acts of its agents. J.C. erroneously believed that he could limit each person's liability by keeping him as isolated from the others as possible—in other words, that it would be safer to have the affairs of the enterprise conducted through chains composed of many persons playing limited roles than through a small circle of individuals performing many functions. Where overlap was unavoidable, the enterprise's ongoing operations depended upon each member's confidence that the others would remain silent. When J.C. spoke to Joe Fuchs in January, 1976, for example, he expressed confidence that the government could never make a case against his enterprise. He was certain that James Elliott would not talk because "James is scared". He also assured Fuchs that he, J.C., and Scooter Herring would say nothing; as for Recea, "that's plum out of the question, you can eliminate that". Thus, he concluded, the only other persons who might implicate Fuchs could provide only uncorroborated accounts which would "mean nothing" in court.

involves a greater risk to society than individual action toward the same end. That risk is greatly compounded when the conspirators contemplate not a single crime but a career of crime. "There are times when of necessity, because of the nature and scope of the particular federation, large numbers of persons taking part must be tried together or perhaps not at all.... When many conspire, they invite mass trial by their conduct". *Kotteakos, supra*, 328 U.S. at 773, 66 S. Ct. at 1252.

We do not lightly dismiss the fact that under this statute four defendants who did not commit murder have been forced to stand trial jointly with, and as confederates of, two others who did. Prejudice inheres in such a trial; great Neptune's ocean could not purge its taint.[33] But the Constitution does not guarantee a trial free from the prejudice that inevitably accompanies any charge of heinous group crime; it demands only that the potential for transference of guilt be minimized to the extent possible under the circumstances in order "to individualize each defendant in his relation to the mass". *Kotteakos, supra*, 328 U.S. at 773, 66 S. Ct. at 1252. The RICO statute does not offend this principle. Congress, in a proper exercise of its legislative power, has decided that murder, like thefts from interstate commerce and the counterfeiting of securities, qualifies as racketeering activity. This, of course, ups the ante for RICO violators who personally would not contemplate taking a human life. Whether there is a moral imbalance in the equation of thieves and counterfeiters with murderers is a question whose answer lies in the halls of Congress, not in the judicial conscience. * * *

D. *[Sufficiency of the Evidence as to James Elliott]*

The evidence relevant to James Elliott as we view the record, was not sufficient to permit the jury to conclude that he conspired with the other five defendants to violate the RICO statute. Accordingly, his conviction under Count One must be reversed.

We recognize "that once a conspiracy is shown to exist, slight evidence is all that is required to connect a particular defendant with the conspiracy". The proof, however, must be individual and personal and the government must prove beyond a reasonable doubt that each member of the conspiracy had the deliberate, knowing, and specific intent to join the conspiracy. Mere association with conspirators or knowledge of the illegal activity is not sufficient.

Where the government, as here, relies mainly upon circumstantial evidence to establish a defendant's guilt, we test the sufficiency of the evidence by asking whether the jury might reasonably have concluded that the evidence fails to exclude every reasonable hypothesis but that of guilt. Viewed in a light most favorable to the government, the evidence against Elliott proved the following:

(1) Early in the spring of 1971, Joe Fuchs gave Elliott a bottle of 500 amphetamine capsules without a prescription.

(2) Shortly thereafter, Elliott negotiated a deal with Fuchs for Joe Breland to build an enclosed porch and for Fuchs to repay Elliot and

33. Cf. Shakespeare, Macbeth, Act III, Scene I.

Breland with amphetamine pills. During the next year, Fuchs delivered the pills in installments of 400.

(3) In April, 1972, Elliott, apparently as a favor for J.C., either sold or gave to Fuchs a 50 pound piece of stolen Hormel meat.

(4) In May, 1973, Elliott, serving as a juror in the trial of Rudolph Flanders for possession of meat from the same stolen shipment, held out for acquittal, causing a mistrial. No evidence was presented that Elliott had been contacted in advance about how he would vote in the Flanders case, although J.C. had told others that he felt Elliott would cooperate.

(5) In January, 1976, Elliott encouraged Fuchs to lie to a federal grand jury about how he acquired the stolen meat given to him by Elliott in 1972.

This evidence could not be taken to support, to the exclusion of all other reasonable hypotheses, a conclusion by the jury that Elliott agreed to participate, directly or indirectly, in the affairs of an enterprise through a pattern of racketeering activity. At best, this evidence discloses that Elliott used a close friend, Joe Fuchs, as a personal source of amphetamines and that he became peripherally involved in a stolen meat deal, an involvement he later attempted to conceal. The government failed to prove that Elliott's amphetamine transactions with Fuchs were in any way connected with the affairs of the enterprise. The Hormel meat, on the other hand, undeniably was acquired as a result of enterprise activity, but Elliott's cooperation with J. C. Hawkins in disposing of a small portion of the meat is insufficient to prove beyond a reasonable doubt that Elliott knowingly and intentionally joined the broad conspiracy to violate RICO. Elliott's acts are equally consistent with the hypothesis that he conspired with J.C. and Fuchs for the limited purpose of aiding in the distribution of stolen meat, an offense with which he was not charged in this case. Under this hypothesis, Elliott agreed to participate in the affairs of the enterprise, but not through a *pattern* of racketeering activity, hence, not in violation of the Act. Similarly, Elliott's two subsequent attempts to cover up the facts in the Hormel meat case are subject to two interpretations: (1) as possible overt acts in furtherance of an agreement to participate in the enterprise's affairs through a pattern of racketeering activity, or (2) as efforts at concealment undertaken after the object of his more limited conspiracy with J.C. and Fuchs had been accomplished, on the theory that "every conspiracy will inevitably be followed by actions taken to cover the conspirators' traces". To allow these predictable acts of concealment to be construed as independent evidence that Elliott agreed to conduct a pattern of racketeering activity would unjustifiably broaden the already pervasive scope of the RICO statute. We hold, then, that the more reasonable conclusion dictated by these facts is that, while Elliott may have conspired to distribute stolen meat, the jury could not reasonably conclude that he conspired to violate RICO.

.... We are convinced that Elliott "associated with the wrong people and was convicted because of guilt by association only". We thus reverse his conviction under Count One. * * *

VII. CONCLUSION

Through RICO, Congress defined a new separate crime to help snare those who make careers of crime. Participation in the affairs of an enterprise through the commission of two or more predicate crimes is now an offense separate and distinct from those predicate crimes. So too is conspiracy to commit this new offense a crime separate and distinct from conspiracy to commit the predicate crimes. The necessity which mothered this statutory invention was caused by the inability of the traditional criminal law to punish and deter organized crime.

The realistic view of group crime which inspired Congress to enact RICO should also guide the courts in construing RICO. Thus, in this case, we are satisfied that the evidence, circumstantial and indirect though it largely was, proved the existence of both an enterprise committed to profiting from criminal activity and an agreement among five of the defendants to participate in the affairs of the enterprise through a pattern of racketeering activity.

People v. Capaldo

Supreme Court of New York, New York County.
151 Misc.2d 114, 572 N.Y.S.2d 989 (1991).

■ FRANKLIN R. WEISSBERG, JUSTICE OF THE SUPREME COURT.

This case arises out of a well-publicized investigation into the activities of various union officials, painting contractors and alleged organized crime members of the Luchese crime family during the period December 1978 until June, 1990. In essence it is alleged that a criminal enterprise existed in New York City and Long Island to control and corrupt the affairs of District Council No. 9 of the International Brotherhood of Painters and Allied Trades ("Painters Union").

The indictment which resulted from the investigation accuses eight defendants and contains 153 counts. Seven of the eight defendants were officials of various District Councils of the Painters Union during the period in question. The eighth defendant, Daniel Rech, was employed by a painting contractor. All eight defendants are charged in the first count of the indictment with Enterprise Corruption, in violation of Penal Law Section 460.20....

Each of the defendants has moved to dismiss the Enterprise Corruption charge contained in Count One, claiming that the Penal Law Article upon which the charge is grounded is unconstitutionally vague....

Article 460 of the Penal Law, part of the New York "Organized Crime Control Act" ("OCCA"), is a progeny of the federal "Racketeer Influenced and Corrupt Organizations" Law ("RICO"). Like RICO, the article is designed to "thwart the activities of organized crime activity". Although OCCA is based upon RICO, it is clear from both the language of OCCA and the legislative history that the New York State Legislature intended to draft a narrower and more precise statute than RICO. The legislature was aware of and sought to avoid the wide scope and sweep of RICO.

That scope is extremely broad. 18 USC 1962(c) makes it unlawful "for any person employed by or associated with any enterprise engaged in or the activities of which affect, interstate or foreign commerce to conduct or participate, directly or indirectly, in the conduct of such enterprise's affairs through a pattern of racketeering activity ..." There is no requirement that the "enterprise" be criminal in nature. As a result RICO has spawned substantial civil and criminal litigation having nothing to do with organized crime.

The drafters of OCCA were also concerned about what they regarded as vague language in RICO. For example, the term "enterprise" is not defined in RICO. "Pattern of racketeering activity" is defined merely as "requiring at least two acts of racketeering activity." Because of RICO's vagueness, there have been suggestions that the law may be vulnerable to constitutional attack.

The failure of the RICO statute to precisely define "enterprise" has not prevented courts from concluding that use of that term therein is constitutional. Indeed, the use of that undefined term has been defended as "necessary in view of the fluid nature of criminal associations." United States v. Swiderski, 593 F.2d 1246, 1249 (D.C. Cir. 1978), cert. denied, 441 U.S. 933 (1979).

The term "pattern of racketeering activity" has also found judicial approval. Racketeering activity means any offense from an extensive list of federal and state crimes listed in the statute. 18 U.S.C 1961. The limited definition of "pattern" contained in RICO has also survived challenges that it is too vague. See, United States v. Angiulo, 897 F.2d 1169, 1179 (1st Cir. 1990), in which the court declined to invalidate the statute as vague "simply because potential uncertainty exists regarding the precise reach of the statute in marginal fact situations. . . ."

The United States Supreme Court has on occasion had difficulty discerning what Congress intended a RICO "pattern" to involve. In Sedima, S.P.R.L. v. Imrex Co., 473 U.S. 479 (1985), the Court expressed dismay that Congress had failed to properly define the term at all but had simply required that a "pattern" include at least two acts of racketeering activity. The court concluded that "pattern" involved something more than two acts, and after examining RICO's legislative history, settled on "continuity plus relationship" as the additional requirement.

Almost five years later, in H. J. Inc. v. The Northwestern Bell Tel. Co., 109 S. Ct. 2893 (1989), the Court conceded that "continuity plus relationship" meant different things to different circuits. Nevertheless, it held firm to the Sedima requirement that, in order to establish a RICO pattern, the government had to show "that the racketeering predicates are related, and that they amount to or pose a threat of continued criminal activity." H.J. Inc., supra at 2900 (emphasis in original).

Justice Scalia, in a concurring opinion in which three other justices joined, derided the "relationship" requirement as not "much more helpful [to the lower courts] than telling them to look for a pattern—which is what the statute already says". As for the continuity requirement, Justice Scalia wrote:

> "Today's opinion has added nothing to improve our prior guidance, which has created a kaleidoscope of circuit positions, except to clarify

that RICO may in addition be violated when there is a 'threat of continuity.' It seems to me this increases rather than removes the vagueness. There is no reason to believe that the Courts of Appeals will be any more unified in the future, than they have in the past, regarding the content of this law."

Despite these criticisms, no challenge to RICO's constitutionality has ever succeeded in federal court.

Aware of the controversies and ambiguities surrounding RICO, the OCCA drafters sought to limit the statute's applicability and enact "more rigorous definitions." Legislative findings, § 460.00. For example, the OCCA statute, unlike RICO, requires that there be a "criminal enterprise." That phrase is defined in Penal Law Section 460.10(3):

> "Criminal Enterprise" means a group of persons sharing a common purpose of engaging in criminal conduct, associated in an ascertainable structure distinct from a pattern of criminal activity, and with a continuity of existence, structure and criminal purpose beyond the scope of individual criminal incidents.

The limiting nature of this phase was described by Assemblyman Melvin H. Miller, one of the authors of OCCA, in a letter dated July 16, 1986 to the Governor's Counsel urging adoption of the legislation:

> "The most fundamental difference between the measure approved by the Assembly and all prior versions is the requirement of each defendant's association with a criminal enterprise. Other proposals would have permitted, as does federal law, prosecution of individuals who engage in a pattern of criminal activity without further proof that the criminal activity was accomplished for the purpose of participating in or advancing the affairs of a criminal enterprise with a separate, distinct and ascertainable structure and a continuity of existence and purpose beyond the scope of the pattern itself.
>
> The members of the Codes Committees felt that the extraordinary sanctions allowed under the Act should be reserved for those who not only commit crimes but do so as part of an organized criminal enterprise. Present law is adequate to punish ordinary white-collar crime ... For that reason, it was not the sponsors' intent to redefine or sanction anew conduct already punishable under current law. Similarly, mere corruption of a legitimate enterprise by a pattern of criminal activity is insufficient to justify prosecution under this Act. Since the pattern of criminal activity is separately prosecutable there is no need to further prosecute the same conduct merely because the defendant is associated with a legitimate enterprise. Rather, the bill now requires association with an ascertainably distinct criminal enterprise in addition to corruption of a legitimate enterprise by criminal activity. In this way we are assured that the Act will only be applied to those who knowingly and voluntarily seek to advance an organized criminal enterprise by their misconduct."

The OCCA drafters also crafted a very specific description of what constitutes a "pattern of criminal activity." Penal Law Section 460.10 reads:

4. "Pattern of criminal activity" means conduct engaged in by persons charged in an enterprise corruption count constituting three or more criminal acts that:

"(a) were committed within ten years of the commencement of the criminal action:

(b) are neither isolated incidents, nor so closely related and connected in point of time or circumstance of commission as to constitute a criminal offense or criminal transaction, as those terms are defined in section 40.10 of the criminal procedure law; and

(c) are either: (i) related to one another through a common scheme or plan or (ii) were committed, solicited, requested, importuned or intentionally aided by persons acting with the mental culpability required for the commission thereof and associated with or in the criminal enterprise."

The resultant statutory scheme is significantly clearer and more limited than RICO. The complaint of vagueness lacks merit with respect to OCCA. The definitional requirements for a criminal enterprise emphasize a group structure distinct from the criminal acts committed, and it is difficult to perceive how a member of such a criminal organization can profess ignorance that he was violating OCCA.

As noted, RICO has survived all constitutional attacks based on vagueness and over-broadness. The drafters of OCCA, who had the benefit of the federal experience, drafted a narrower and more precise statute.... Therefore, the motion to dismiss Count One of the indictment on constitutional grounds is denied.

QUESTIONS AND COMMENTS

1. If conspiracy is "the darling of the modern prosecutor's nursery," Harrison v. United States, 7 F.2d 259 (2d Cir. 1925) (Learned Hand, J.), what is RICO? Consider the various ways in which RICO is designed to expand the scope of what the *Elliott* court calls "individual liability for group crime" and, more specifically, the scope of conspiratorial liability.

2. What constraints can the principle of legality (and particularly the principle of specificity) place on a statute which contains an instruction by the legislature to the courts that it "shall be liberally construed to effectuate its remedial purposes"?

What about the rule of lenity? Shouldn't the rule of lenity place some limitations on the scope of RICO? No, courts say, because RICO may be broad, but it isn't ambiguous. Congress was very clear not only about RICO's breadth, but also about courts' obligation to interpret it broadly:

> [T]he rule of lenity applies only when an ambiguity is present; " 'it is not used to beget one.... The rule comes into operation at the end of the process of construing what Congress has expressed, not at the beginning as an overriding consideration of being lenient to wrongdoers.' " We simply do not think there is an ambiguity here which would suffice to invoke the rule of lenity. " 'The fact that RICO has

> been applied in situations not expressly anticipated by Congress does not demonstrate ambiguity. It demonstrates breadth.' "

NOW v. Scheidler, 510 U.S. 249, 114 S.Ct. 798 (1994).

More generally, what constitutional constraints of any kind can (should?) there be on a criminal statute that "seek[s] the eradication of organized crime," which is said to "annually drain[] billions of dollars from America's economy"? What happens to judicial review of legislation when courts view their role in RICO cases as "perfecting the weapons in society's arsenal against criminal confederacies"?

3. Courts, and the Supreme Court in particular, have followed the legislative instruction to "liberally construe" RICO on many occasions. Here are some examples.

RICO is not limited to "criminal enterprises," nor is it limited to "legitimate enterprises" that have been infiltrated by "criminal elements." See United States v. Turkette, 452 U.S. 576, 101 S.Ct. 2524 (1981) (criminal enterprise involved in drug trafficking, arson, insurance fraud, and bribery): Just because "primary purpose of RICO is to cope with the infiltration of legitimate businesses" doesn't mean that it can't also be applied it to criminal organizations, thereby "attack[ing] their source of economic power itself."

Nor is it limited to "organized crime." See H. J. Inc. v. Northwestern Bell Telephone Co., 492 U.S. 229, 109 S.Ct. 2893 (1989) (phone company's efforts to get a state utility commission to set inflated rates): "The occasion for Congress' action was the perceived need to combat organized crime. But Congress for cogent reasons chose to enact a more general statute, one which, although it had organized crime as its focus, was not limited in application to organized crime."

Nor is it limited to enterprises or racketeering activities motivated by an economic purpose. See NOW v. Scheidler, 510 U.S. 249, 114 S.Ct. 798 (1994) (abortion protesters' effort to "shut down [abortion] clinics and persuade women not to have abortions"): "An enterprise can . . . have a detrimental influence on interstate or foreign commerce without having its own profit-seeking motive" and, though not financially benefiting its members, "still may drain money from the economy by harming businesses."

4. The court in *Elliott* reads RICO as an attempt to "free the government from the strictures of the multiple conspiracy doctrine" of wheels and chains, and combinations thereof, stating clearly that "[t]he enterprise involved in this case probably could not have been successfully prosecuted as a single conspiracy under the general federal conspiracy statute." It insists, however, that even RICO requires that conspirators be aware at least of "the essential nature of the plan." Does "associat[ing] for the purpose of making money from repeated criminal activity" qualify as "the essential nature" of a conspiratorial plan? How does this requirement differ from that of a "common objective" in chain conspiracy cases, if that objective can consist of something like "the raising of revenue through criminal activity"?

5. Does RICO criminalize an act? Or a status? Note that the RICO conspiracy statute, unlike the general federal conspiracy statute (18 U.S.C.

§ 371), doesn't require an overt act. Salinas v. United States, 522 U.S. 52, 118 S.Ct. 469 (1997) (RICO conspiracy, by not requiring overt act, "even more comprehensive than the general conspiracy provision applicable to federal crimes"). Consider the following excerpt from Gerard Lynch's much-cited article on RICO:

> The notion that a defendant is being punished merely for his character or status, or for the danger that he potentially represents, is often said to be offensive to our concepts of fairness. A person may be a seething mass of antisocial ideas, repulsive character traits, dangerous tendencies, and even concrete evil plans, but he is neither a criminal nor subject to punishment until he commits specific proscribed acts. Even if society might gain by engaging in preemptive strikes against such villains, it is essential to the liberty and security of ordinary citizens that government not be permitted to deprive them of freedom unless they violate clearly defined norms. "Character" or "predicted danger" are flexible and unpredictable standards of decision, too easily used as tools of oppression.
>
> These substantive concerns, however, are not directly violated by RICO. Although the distinguishing features of RICO are its somewhat amorphous associational and course of conduct elements, a fundamental prerequisite of a substantive RICO violation is the commission of particular criminal acts. These predicate racketeering acts are themselves conventional, transactionally defined crimes, requiring the commission of particular conduct for their violation. RICO does not permit a person to be convicted on the basis of his thoughts, tendencies, intentions, or character alone; defined and concrete antisocial acts are a part of the definition of the crime. It is not a crime under section 1962(c) to have the character or status of a racketeer, but to be a racketeer who commits acts of racketeering.... To the extent that the elements of association with an illicit enterprise and pattern of criminal conduct define a "status" of "racketeer," that "status" is neither passive (unlike addiction, it cannot be acquired in utero or by medical treatment) nor uncontrollable (unlike addiction, continued involvement in the criminal enterprise is not the product of physiological compulsion).
>
> Nevertheless, RICO does make aspects of a defendant's background and associations an aggravating factor in a defined crime. But our law has never held that such factors are irrelevant to the quantum of punishment that can be administered to one who has violated concrete norms. The practical operation of law enforcement, in fact, frequently aims to do precisely what a purely retributive model of criminal law tells us is illegitimate: to punish based on character and propensity rather than on the condemnation of specific actions. Considerations of "character" and "danger to the community," often said to be banished from the definition of criminal conduct, pervade the critical discretionary decisions of all three of the agencies responsible for applying those definitions: prosecutors, juries, and sentencing judges.

Gerard E. Lynch, "RICO: The Crime of Being a Criminal," 87 Colum. L. Rev. 920, 955–56 (1987).

6. As *Elliott* points out, RICO pulls in "remote associates of an enterprise," punishing them for conspiracy along with more central figures. There are some formal limits on liability for lower-level employees, but these limits are, to put it kindly, difficult to interpret. In a civil RICO case, Reves v. Ernst & Young, 507 U.S. 170 (1993), the Court restricts vulnerability even to civil liability to those who have "*some* part in directing the enterprise's affairs." But since the Court goes on to note that an enterprise is " 'operated' not just by upper management but also by lower rung participants in the enterprise who are under the direction of upper management," the liability restrictions appear quite fuzzy.

Because low-level employees are (at least theoretically) vulnerable to extensive liability, they have a strong incentive to strike deals in exchange for their testimony against higher ups. What do you think of this use of a substantive rule of liability to facilitate law enforcement? What are the limits on this strategy? Does there come a point where a person's connection to a criminal "enterprise" is so attenuated that it would be improper to expose her to potential criminal liability for the sake of collecting evidence against others? Does it help to say that prosecutors are "not really interested" in "remote associates," and care only about the "big fish"? Note that for this strategy to work, the threat of punishment must be real; otherwise no one would have an incentive to turn state's evidence.

Since RICO remains silent on these—and many other issues—should courts take into account prosecutorial guidelines regarding the choice of what RICO covers, whom to pursue, how, when and for what purpose (e.g., to get evidence on others or to punish)? Should prosecutors' offices be required to set up guidelines of this sort in the first place? If they are not followed, what should be the remedy? Dismissing the case? Disciplining the prosecutor? Here is an excerpt from the U.S. Justice Department's RICO Guidelines:

> No RICO criminal indictment or information or civil complaint shall be filed, and no civil investigative demand shall be issued, without the prior approval of the Criminal Division
>
> .... The decision to institute a federal criminal prosecution involves balancing society's interest in effective law enforcement against the consequences for the accused. Utilization of the RICO statute, more so than most other federal criminal sanctions, requires particularly careful and reasoned application, because, among other things, RICO incorporates certain state crimes. One purpose of these guidelines is to reemphasize the principle that the primary responsibility for enforcing state laws rests with the state concerned. Despite the broad statutory language of RICO and the legislative intent that the statute " ... shall be liberally construed to effectuate its remedial purpose," it is the policy of the Criminal Division that RICO be selectively and uniformly used. [N]ot every proposed RICO charge that meets the technical requirements of a RICO violation will be approved. Further, the Criminal Division will not approve "imaginative" prosecutions under RICO which are far afield from the congressional purpose of the

RICO statute. A RICO count which merely duplicates the elements of proof of traditional Hobbs Act, Travel Act, mail fraud, wire fraud, gambling or controlled substances cases, will not be approved unless it serves some special RICO purpose. Only in exceptional circumstances will approval be granted when RICO is sought merely to serve some evidentiary purpose.

These guidelines provide only internal Department of Justice guidance. They are not intended to, do not, and may not be relied upon to create any rights, substantive or procedural, enforceable at law by any party in any matter civil or criminal. Nor are any limitations hereby placed on otherwise lawful litigative prerogatives of the Department of Justice.

U.S. Attorneys' Manual § 9–110.101 & .200.

7. Does New York's OCCA cure RICO's problems? Why do states need RICO-type statutes of their own if the federal RICO is so broadly framed?

8. *Capaldo* questions the need for criminalizing conduct under a RICO-type statute if that conduct is already criminal in its own right. Note that RICO reaches not only conduct that is already criminal under federal law, but conduct that is criminal (only) under state law as well. RICO, in other words, turns many a state offense into a federal crime. This federal encroachment into state law has raised concerns; even if RICO's expansion of federal criminal law is unobjectionable as a general matter, it has been argued, courts should hesitate to further widen its scope through statutory interpretation. The Supreme Court, though otherwise quite protective of states' rights, has been unmoved by these concerns:

[I]t is urged that the interpretation of RICO to include both legitimate and illegitimate enterprises will substantially alter the balance between federal and state enforcement of criminal law. This is particularly true, so the argument goes, since included within the definition of racketeering activity are a significant number of acts made criminal under state law. [18 U.S.C. § 1961(1)(a) (" 'racketeering activity' means . . . any act or threat involving murder, kidnapping, gambling, arson, robbery, bribery, extortion, dealing in obscene matter, or dealing in a controlled substance . . ., which is chargeable under State law and punishable by imprisonment for more than one year").]

But even assuming that the more inclusive definition of enterprise will have the effect suggested, the language of the statute and its legislative history indicate that Congress was well aware that it was entering a new domain of federal involvement through the enactment of this measure. [RICO imposes no restrictions upon the criminal justice systems of the States. See 84 Stat. 947 ("Nothing in this title shall supersede any provision of Federal, State, or other law imposing criminal penalties or affording civil remedies in addition to those provided for in this title"). Thus, under RICO, the States remain free to exercise their police powers to the fullest constitutional extent in defining and prosecuting crimes within their respective jurisdictions.]

That some of those crimes may also constitute predicate acts of racketeering under RICO, is no restriction on the separate administration of criminal justice by the States. Indeed, the very purpose of the Organized Crime Control Act of 1970 was to enable the Federal Government to address a large and seemingly neglected problem. The view was that existing law, state and federal, was not adequate to address the problem, which was of national dimensions. That Congress included within the definition of racketeering activities a number of state crimes strongly indicates that RICO criminalized conduct that was also criminal under state law, at least when the requisite elements of a RICO offense are present.

As the hearings and legislative debates reveal, Congress was well aware of the fear that RICO would "[move] large substantive areas formerly totally within the police power of the State into the Federal realm." In the face of these objections, Congress nonetheless proceeded to enact the measure, knowing that it would alter somewhat the role of the Federal Government in the war against organized crime and that the alteration would entail prosecutions involving acts of racketeering that are also crimes under state law.

United States v. Turkette, 452 U.S. 576, 101 S.Ct. 2524 (1981).

10. *Forfeiture.* RICO "seek[s] the eradication of organized crime" not only by creating a crime above and beyond the crimes that constitute its "prohibited activities," and thereby—often significantly—increasing the maximum available prison sentence for "racketeers." It also includes a broad, and automatic, criminal forfeiture provision:

18 U.S.C. § 1963. Criminal penalties.

(a) Whoever violates any provision of section 1962 . . . shall forfeit to the United States . . .

(1) any interest the person has acquired or maintained in violation of section 1962;

(2) any—

(A) interest in;

(B) security of;

(C) claim against; or

(D) property or contractual right of any kind affording a source of influence over;

any enterprise which the person has established, operated, controlled, conducted, or participated in the conduct of, in violation of section 1962; and

(3) any property constituting, or derived from, any proceeds which the person obtained, directly or indirectly, from racketeering activity or unlawful debt collection in violation of section 1962 . . . . .

(b) Property subject to criminal forfeiture under this section includes—

(1) real property, including things growing on, affixed to, and found in land; and

(2) tangible and intangible personal property, including rights, privileges, interests, claims, and securities.

Note the scope of RICO forfeiture. It is "not limited to those assets of a RICO enterprise that are *tainted by use* in connection with racketeering activity, but rather extends to the convicted person's entire interest in the enterprise." United States v. Busher, 817 F.2d 1409, 1413 (9th Cir. 1987) (emphasis added); see also United States v. Cauble, 706 F.2d 1322, 1350 (5th Cir. 1983) ("property forfeited under RICO need not be 'guilty' "). The point of RICO, after all, is to destroy criminal enterprises; it's no surprise, then, that its criminal forfeiture component would not rely on the traditional justification for ("in rem") forfeiture, that the thing itself became "tainted"—or even "guilty"—by having been used in some criminal activity or other.

11. *Civil vs. Criminal*. Under 18 U.S.C. § 1964, "[a]ny person injured in his business or property by reason of a violation of section 1962 of this chapter [setting out 'prohibited activities' under RICO] may sue therefor in any appropriate United States district court and shall recover threefold the damages he sustains and the cost of the suit, including a reasonable attorney's fee. . . ." A civil RICO claim thus requires a showing of both that the defendant has engaged in a RICO violation (and therefore would be criminally liable, provided the higher burden of proof in a criminal case, beyond a reasonable doubt, is met) and that the plaintiff has been injured by that violation. Civil RICO has become so popular that "there is now . . . a 'RICO bar' which specializes in bringing or defending RICO claims," whose members "have found, as would appear obvious, that the stigma associated with the label 'racketeering' is a good settlement weapon." Sedima, S.P.R.L. v. Imrex Co., 741 F.2d 482 (2d Cir. 1984). In the Supreme Court's view, however, the widespread use of civil RICO is merely further evidence of its intended scope and effectiveness: "Instead of being used against mobsters and organized criminals, [civil RICO] has become a tool for everyday fraud cases brought against 'respected and legitimate' enterprises. Yet Congress wanted to reach both 'legitimate' and 'illegitimate' enterprises. The former enjoy neither an inherent incapacity for criminal activity nor immunity from its consequences." Sedima, S.P.R.L. v. Imrex Co., 473 U.S. 479, 105 S.Ct. 3275 (1985).

12. RICO was specifically designed to provide the federal government with more effective tools for the war against organized crime. Even if we disregard the use of RICO against enterprises far outside the paradigm of organized crime, can RICO be justified? What were RICO "racketeers" doing that wasn't already subject to (often severe) criminal penalties? (The list of RICO predicate offenses includes, after all and among many others, murder, kidnapping, gambling, arson, robbery, bribery, extortion, and drug dealing, all of which are felonies, and some of which are punishable by life imprisonment or even death. 18 U.S.C. § 1961(1)(A).) If the point of RICO isn't punishing otherwise noncriminal conduct, or even to severely punish already severely punished conduct, what is it? Is it to induce underlings to flip by threatening them with exorbitant punishment? If so, why not

torture them? What's the real difference? Isn't the real problem in fighting organized crime *evidentiary*, not substantive? And how does RICO solve the evidence problem but for its unprincipled threats directed at minor participants in "enterprises"?

D. CORPORATE LIABILITY

1. INTRODUCTION

N.Y. Central & Hudson River Railroad Co. v. United States

Supreme Court of the United States.
212 U.S. 481, 29 S.Ct. 304 (1909).

■ MR. JUSTICE DAY delivered the opinion of the Court.

[The railroad company and its assistant traffic manager were convicted of paying rebates to sugar companies, by charging them less than the published rate in order to prevent them from shipping sugar from New York City to Detroit by water rather than by train, in violation of the Elkins Act.]

The principal attack in this court is upon the constitutional validity of certain features of the Elkins act. 32 Stat. 847. That act, among other things, provides:

> "(1) That anything done or omitted to be done by a corporation common carrier subject to the act to regulate commerce, and the acts amendatory thereof, which, if done or omitted to be done by any director or officer thereof, or any receiver, trustee, lessee, agent or person acting for or employed by such corporation, would constitute a misdemeanor under said acts, or under this act, shall also be held to be a misdemeanor committed by such corporation, and upon conviction thereof it shall be subject to like penalties as are prescribed in said acts, or by this act, with reference to such persons, except as such penalties are herein changed.
>
> * * *
>
> "In construing and enforcing the provisions of this section, the act, omission or failure of any officer, agent or other person acting for or employed by any common carrier, acting within the scope of his employment, shall in every case be also deemed to be the act, omission or failure of such carrier, as well as of that person."

It is contended that these provisions of the law are unconstitutional because Congress has no authority to impute to a corporation the commission of criminal offenses, or to subject a corporation to a criminal prosecution by reason of the things charged. The argument is that to thus punish the corporation is in reality to punish the innocent stockholders, and to deprive them of their property without opportunity to be heard, consequently without due process of law.... It is urged that ... owing to the nature and character of its organization and the extent of its power and authority, a corporation cannot commit a crime of the nature charged in this case.

Some of the earlier writers on common law held the law to be that a corporation could not commit a crime. It is said to have been held by Lord Chief Justice Holt that "a corporation is not indictable, although the particular members of it are." In Blackstone's Commentaries, chapter 18, § 12, we find it stated: "A corporation cannot commit treason, or felony, or other crime in its corporate capacity, though its members may in their distinct individual capacities." The modern authority, universally, so far as we know, is the other way. In considering the subject, Bishop's New Criminal Law, § 417, devotes a chapter to the capacity of corporations to commit crime, and states the law to be: "Since a corporation acts by its officers and agents their purposes, motives, and intent are just as much those of the corporation as are the things done. If, for example, the invisible, intangible essence of air, which we term a corporation, can level mountains, fill up valleys, lay down iron tracks, and run railroad cars on them, it can intend to do it, and can act therein as well viciously as virtuously." [In] Telegram Newspaper Company v. Commonwealth, 172 Massachusetts, 294, ... Mr. Chief Justice Field said: "We think that a corporation may be liable criminally for certain offenses of which a specific intent may be a necessary element. There is no more difficulty in imputing to a corporation a specific intent in criminal proceedings than in civil. A corporation cannot be arrested and imprisoned in either civil or criminal proceedings, but its property may be taken either as compensation for a private wrong or as punishment for a public wrong." It is held in England that corporations may be criminally prosecuted for acts of misfeasance as well as nonfeasance.

It is now well established that in actions for tort the corporation may be held responsible for damages for the acts of its agent within the scope of his employment. * * *

In this case we are to consider the criminal responsibility of a corporation for an act done while an authorized agent of the company is exercising the authority conferred upon him.... Applying the principle governing civil liability, we go only a step farther in holding that the act of the agent, while exercising the authority delegated to him to make rates for transportation, may be controlled, in the interest of public policy, by imputing his act to his employer and imposing penalties upon the corporation for which he is acting in the premises.

It is true that there are some crimes, which in their nature cannot be committed by corporations. But there is a large class of offenses ..., wherein the crime consists in purposely doing the things prohibited by statute. In that class of crimes we see no good reason why corporations may not be held responsible for and charged with the knowledge and purposes of their agents, acting within the authority conferred upon them. If it were not so, many offenses might go unpunished and acts be committed in violation of law, where, as in the present case, the statute requires all persons, corporate or private, to refrain from certain practices forbidden in the interest of public policy. * * *

.... While the law should have regard to the rights of all, and to those of corporations no less than to those of individuals, it cannot shut its eyes to the fact that the great majority of business transactions in modern times are conducted through these bodies, and particularly that interstate commerce is almost entirely in their hands, and to give them immunity from all punishment because of the old and exploded doctrine that a corporation cannot commit a crime would virtually take away the only means of effectually controlling the subject-matter and correcting the abuses aimed at.

State v. Chapman Dodge Center

Supreme Court of Louisiana.
428 So.2d 413 (1983).

■ Sexton, Jr., Justice Ad Hoc.

[Defendants Chapman Dodge and John Swindle were charged with several counts of theft. With the car dealership in financial trouble, they were alleged to have kept the money they received from customers to cover the sales tax due, rather than forwarding it to the state and registering the car. Both defendants were convicted of the lesser included offense of unauthorized use of a movable.]

The evidence showed that the defendant ... was seldom at the dealership more than twice a month.... Donald Barrett ... was in charge of the daily operations of Chapman Dodge as general manager.... According to the testimony of James Duvall, Chapman Dodge's accountant, he and Barrett made the decisions as to which bills were to be paid.

Swindle testified that ... he ordered Duvall to pay all of the taxes owed.... When the dealership was closed, Swindle asked Barrett if all the taxes had been paid. The record shows that in the presence of Johnilyn Smith, an administrative assistant to Swindle, and Frank Peel, a business associate of Swindle, Barrett stated that *all* taxes had been paid....

The defendant received no indication that the sales taxes were not paid until a week or ten days after closing the dealership when the district attorney contacted Chapman Dodge's lawyer. Duvall testified that he was instructed by Donald Barrett to retain the sales tax money. Donald Barrett however testified that he had told James Duvall in June of 1980 to pay only those obligations necessary to keep the dealership open; but that he never told Duvall to retain the contracts and sales taxes on the purchased vehicles.

The question of the criminal liability of the corporate defendant in this cause is a ... difficult proposition involving fundamental issues of the nature of criminal responsibility....

The problem of what criminal liability a corporation should bear for the unauthorized acts of its officers and managers is indeed a grave and troubling one. Recent allegations of corporate responsibility for large train derailments and massive pollution of water sources underscore the importance of this troubling topic. Certainly there is civil responsibility under such circumstances. The question is whether a corporation should be criminally responsible in the absence of a specific statute which defines and describes the corporate act, prohibits that act, and establishes a specific punishment therefor.

.... Our Civil Code in Article 427 defines a corporation as:

"... an intellectual body, created by law, composed of individuals united under a common name, the members of which succeed each other, so that the body continues always the same, notwithstanding the change of the individuals which compose it, and which, for certain purposes, *is considered as a natural person*." (emphasis added).

The corporation as a fictitious person is capable of entering into contracts, owning property and making and receiving donations. In short, it is capable of doing virtually anything that a natural person is capable of doing.

A corporation by the very nature of its operation is dependent upon people to carry out its business. Some of these people may rightfully be regarded as the "mind" of the corporation. This group, known as the board of directors, is responsible for the direction that the corporation takes in its business activity. Plans for the corporation, developed by the board of directors, are transmitted to the officers of the corporation and through them to the employees. This latter group may be regarded as the "hands" of the corporation. But here our analogy to the human form must end. For unlike ordinary human hands, corporate "hands" have minds of their own and are capable of self direction.

When a corporation is accused of committing a crime which requires intent, it must be determined who within the corporate structure had the intent to commit the crime. If the crime was the product of a board of directors' resolution authorizing its employees to commit specific criminal acts, then intent on the part of the corporation is manifest. However, a more difficult question arises if the crime is actually committed by an employee of the corporation not authorized to perform such an act. Holding a corporation criminally responsible for the acts of an employee may be inconsistent with basic notions of criminal intent, since such a posture would render a corporate entity responsible for actions which it theoretically had no intent to commit.

Common law jurisdictions hold corporations criminally liable for the acts of low-ranking employees. In such jurisdictions, corporate criminal liability is based on an extension of the tort doctrine of vicarious liability. The theme of vicarious criminal liability, however, is varied. Some jurisdictions impose criminal liability where there has been an act or an authorization to act by a managerial officer, some where there has been an act committed within the scope of the actor's employment, and still others where there has been an act done which benefits the corporation. These varied applications notwithstanding, common law jurisdictions have found corporations liable for forms of homicide, theft, extortion—in short, virtually every crime other than rape....

Although this merger of tort and criminal law doctrine has found wide acceptance, it has also generated significant theoretical problems. Admittedly, tort law and criminal law are cousins, causing concern as to whether their relationship is within the prohibited degree such that a union of the two might produce unwanted offspring. It should be remembered that the main function of the law of torts is compensation and to a much lesser degree, deterrence.

Tort law attempts to distribute the loss of a harmful occurrence. Causation is the important ingredient therein. Holding a corporation vicariously liable for the torts of its employees dovetails with the idea of compensating the victim. The corporation is in a more likely position to compensate.

On the other hand, as mentioned earlier, the primary function of criminal law is to deter future criminal liability. To impose such liability on another party who had no part in the act and, as in the case of most corporate crimes, no intent to commit such an act, seems at first glance to be contrary to the purpose of our criminal legal system.

It is important to point out that while corporate criminal liability is recognized and applied in common law jurisdictions, the maxim that *societas delinquere non potest* (a corporation cannot do wrong) is still firmly recognized in the civil law.[9] Only the natural person acting for the corporation can incur criminal guilt. Courts cannot, as often occurs in common law jurisdictions, convict the corporation alone so that the individual defendant may escape punishment.

In France, . . . the courts reason that corporate criminal liability is irreconcilable with the principle of guilt. Corporate criminal liability is considered ineffective as a deterrent because it is deterrence addressed to no mind at all. The same line of thinking with no material difference is followed by virtually every other civil law country.

One of the most interesting aspects of the concept that a corporation may be guilty of an offense without specific statutory authority is the question of how one punishes a corporation. It cannot be imprisoned. Obviously it may not be sentenced to death in the sense that an individual may be. Of course, the charter may be revoked but obviously in that circumstance there would have to be a statute which authorizes this sanction.

The only method of punishing a corporation that is guilty of an offense . . . is by the imposition of a fine. Certainly it may be argued that a fine in such instances punishes those not guilty of the offense, for funds lost from the corporate treasury can be recouped either by withholding dividends from shareholders or increasing the price of the product to the consumer. On the other hand, serious fines levied against corporations can modify the behavior of corporate officers who want to keep their jobs, and the behavior of voting shareholders who will vote to elect officers that will avoid such costly fines. But obviously there are certain theoretical inconsistencies between a fine to a corporation for an offense . . . and the concept that the purpose of criminal statutes is to punish and deter. . . .

9. [U]ntil 1942, La. Rev. Civil Code of 1870, Article 443 expressly stated that a corporation could not be convicted of any crime.

The instant defendant is a closely held holding corporation which is accused of a basic "Ten Commandment Crime"—theft—and convicted of a lesser included offense[, unauthorized use of a movable.[a]] Thus the finder of fact in effect determined that the defendant corporation kept the money in question with fraudulent intent, but with the intent to eventually return the funds. The evidence further indicates that "retention" of the funds was not specifically authorized by the board of directors or by the president or any other officer of the corporation. The record does not indicate, moreover, that any of these entities had any real knowledge of that action. [In the present case,] the corporation, its board of directors, its parent corporations and its president are for all practical purposes the same entity—the individual defendant Swindle....

... [U]nder the circumstances of this case, criminal intent has not been adequately established.... [S]ince this record reveals no evidence of complicity by the officers or the board of directors, explicit or tacit, ... the actions of these managers and/or employees were insufficient to cause this corporate entity to be guilty of the offense of an unauthorized use of a movable.

We thus reverse as to both defendants and order their discharge.

QUESTIONS AND COMMENTS

1. Think about what it means for a corporation to engage in criminal conduct. Start with actus reus. Can a corporation *act*? Recall the definition of an act. See, e.g., Model Penal Code § 1.13(2) ("a bodily movement whether voluntary or involuntary"). Can a corporation act *voluntarily*? See, e.g., Model Penal Code § 2.01(2) ("The following are not voluntary acts ...: (a) a reflex or convulsion; (b) a bodily movement during unconsciousness or sleep; (c) conduct during hypnosis or resulting from hypnotic suggestion; (d) a bodily movement that otherwise is not a product of the effort or determination of the actor, either conscious or habitual."). Note that originally, corporate criminal liability was limited to omissions—like the failure to file reports, or to pay taxes. Is omission liability for corporations less problematic than commission liability?

Now mens rea. Can a corporation form a mental state? See, e.g., Model Penal Code § 2.02 ("person acts purposely when ... it is his conscious object ... to cause ... a result," knowingly when "he is aware that it is practically certain that his conduct will cause such a result," recklessly when "he consciously disregards a substantial and unjustifiable risk," negligently when "he should be aware of a substantial and unjustifiable risk"). Originally, corporations were only held criminally liable for strict liability offenses. Is it appropriate to punish an entity for a strict liability offense if it is incapable of forming a mental state?

a. LSA–R.S. § 14:68: "Unauthorized use of a movable is the intentional taking or use of a movable which belongs to another, either without the other's consent, or by means of fraudulent conduct, practices, or representations, but without any intention to deprive the other of the movable permanently."—EDS.

Now defenses. Can a corporation claim element-negating defenses, like mistake or intoxication? How about justifications, like necessity, self-defense, defense of another, defense of property, consent?

And excuses? Duress, entrapment, insanity, infancy?

2. Is corporate criminal liability consistent with the principle that "guilt is generally personal" (*People v. McGee*, supra part B) and "the fundamental demand of due process that guilt remain 'individual and personal' " (*United States v. Elliott*, supra part C)? Is it enough to point out that the legislature intended to classify corporations as "persons," or that there is no evidence that it didn't?

3. Does the possibility of civil liability imply the possibility of criminal liability? Does the fact that corporations can commit a tort, or enter into a contract, imply that they can commit a crime? Does the fact that an insane person can commit a tort imply that he can commit a crime? Does the fact that a child can enter into a contract imply that he or she can commit a crime?

4. If corporations can commit some crimes, can they commit *any* crime? Can they commit murder or assault? In *People v. Warner–Lambert*, supra ch. 6, the New York Court of Appeals laid out the competing interests: "the protection of New York residents against injury or death knowingly or recklessly inflicted and of the State against the burden of having to care for and support persons so injured or killed on the one hand, as opposed to the possible adverse effect on the State's economy of extending criminal liability to manufacturing operations on the other." Are there other factors that should be considered? Or should corporate liability extend to malum prohibitum crimes only, but not to malum in se crimes (or "Ten Commandment Crimes," as *Chapman* put it)? For the distinction between malum prohibitum and malum in se, see *Morissette v. United States*, supra ch. 5.

5. As *Chapman* indicates, American criminal law traditionally has had fewer qualms about extending criminal liability to corporations (and legal, rather, than natural persons more generally) than other legal systems. German criminal law to this day insists that corporations cannot be reached by criminal sanctions. (Contra *Chapman*, French criminal law no longer does. Eli Lederman, "Models for Imposing Corporate Criminal Liability," 4 Buff. Crim. L. Rev. 641, 645 (2000).) The consensus is that corporations are incapable of performing an act, defined as the "expression or manifestation of one's personality": "Since they lack psychic-spiritual substance, they cannot express or manifest themselves." Claus Roxin, Strafrecht: Allgemeiner Teil (Pt. 1) § 8 III (3d ed. 1997). Still, even in German law corporations *are* capable of committing noncriminal "transgressions" that are subject not to "punishment," but to noncriminal sanctions, including fines of any size. See generally Hans-Heinrich Jescheck & Thomas Weigend, Lehrbuch des Strafrechts: Allgemeiner Teil § 23 VII (5th ed. 1996); Criminal Responsibility of Legal and Collective Entities (Albin Eser et al. eds., 1999).

6. *Sentencing*. Unlike in civil law countries, debates about corporate criminal law in the U.S. have centered less on the question of the propriety

of corporate criminal liability in general than on the question of how to punish corporations convicted of criminal conduct. The U.S. Sentencing Commission found that the punishment of corporations required a separate set of sentencing guidelines. See U.S.S.G. ch. 8 ("sentencing of organizations"). The introduction to that chapter outlines the competing considerations influencing the sentencing of corporations—particularly in cases that combine corporate and individual liability—and the Commission's general approach to corporate sentencing:

> Organizations can act only through agents and, under federal criminal law, generally are vicariously liable for offenses committed by their agents. At the same time, individual agents are responsible for their own criminal conduct. Federal prosecutions of organizations therefore frequently involve individual and organizational co-defendants. Convicted individual agents of organizations are sentenced in accordance with the guidelines and policy statements in the preceding chapters. This chapter is designed so that the sanctions imposed upon organizations and their agents, taken together, will provide just punishment, adequate deterrence, and incentives for organizations to maintain internal mechanisms for preventing, detecting, and reporting criminal conduct.
>
> This chapter reflects the following general principles: First, the court must, whenever practicable, order the organization to remedy any harm caused by the offense. The resources expended to remedy the harm should not be viewed as punishment, but rather as a means of making victims whole for the harm caused. Second, if the organization operated primarily for a criminal purpose or primarily by criminal means, the fine should be set sufficiently high to divest the organization of all its assets. Third, the fine range for any other organization should be based on the seriousness of the offense and the culpability of the organization. The seriousness of the offense generally will be reflected by the highest of the pecuniary gain, the pecuniary loss, or the amount in a guideline offense level fine table. Culpability generally will be determined by the steps taken by the organization prior to the offense to prevent and detect criminal conduct, the level and extent of involvement in or tolerance of the offense by certain personnel, and the organization's actions after an offense has been committed. Fourth, probation is an appropriate sentence for an organizational defendant when needed to ensure that another sanction will be fully implemented, or to ensure that steps will be taken within the organization to reduce the likelihood of future criminal conduct.

See generally Ilene H. Nagel & Winthrop M. Swenson, "The Federal Sentencing Guidelines for Corporations: Their Development, Theoretical Underpinnings, and Some Thoughts about Their Future," 71 Wash. U. L. Q. 205 (1993).

7. Consider the question of corporate liability from the perspective of the various traditional rationales for punishment. Does it even make sense to think of sanctioning a corporation as "punishment"? Are corporations "punished" in the same way that individuals are? Does punishing a corporation and punishing an individual serve different purposes? Consider

the following comments on the federal sentencing guidelines for corporations by the chair of the federal sentencing commission:

> An organization is not the typical offender. It is therefore not surprising that the organizational guidelines have a unique approach. The guidelines for individuals, according to some commentators, focus on punishment and incapacitation. They provide a method for determining the appropriate range of imprisonment in proportion to the offense. Conversely, the organizational guidelines focus on providing restitution and an appropriate fine range for the offender organization through far reaching probation provisions. Perhaps more importantly, however, these guidelines are geared toward deterrence, and they provide sentencing benefits for organizations that have an "effective program to prevent and detect violations of law."
>
> The organizational guidelines give organizations an incentive to have in place an effective compliance program. They not only encourage corporations to exemplify "good corporate citizenship," but also provide a means to "rehabilitate" corporations that have engaged in criminal conduct by requiring them, as a term of probation, to institute and maintain effective compliance programs. The organizational guidelines provide that "the hallmark of an effective program to prevent and detect violations of law is that the organization exercised due diligence in seeking to prevent and detect criminal conduct by its employees and other agents."

Diana E. Murphy, "The Federal Sentencing Guidelines for Organizations: A Decade of Promoting Compliance and Ethics," 87 Iowa L. Rev. 697, 702–03 (2002).

Recall the rejection of rehabilitation in the federal sentencing guidelines for individuals, and in American criminal law as a whole, over the past few decades. (See supra ch. 1.) Why should we permit corporations to rehabilitate themselves, but not individuals?

8. Perhaps because there is little reason to believe (in either "expressive" or retributive terms) that corporations can be made to "suffer" in the ways individuals do (and retributivists argue, *should*) if punished, most discussions of corporate liability are at core *instrumental*, emphasizing the prospective gains that we should expect (or should despair that we will achieve) if we punish corporations. Criminal law theorists writing in the "Law and Economics" tradition have been especially active in debates over the utility of distinct forms of corporate liability.

In " 'No Soul to Damn: No Body to Kick': An Unscandalized Inquiry into the Problem of Corporate Punishment," 79 Mich. L. Rev. 386 (1981), John C. Coffee argued that conventional corporate punishment is difficult to defend. He reasoned that given the inevitably low risk of detection and apprehension, combined with the high value of committing many corporate crimes, the penalty would have to be set extremely high to deter offenses, but companies could rarely pay fines that are set at that otherwise appropriately high level. Moreover, managers will take risks if the possibility the corporation will punish them (by firing) for failing to take profit-enhancing illegal steps is higher than the possibility they'll personally face criminal penalties (most corporate penalties directly affect the shareholders, not the managers). He worried, too, that heavy sanctions don't penalize those who are actually blameworthy because cash penalties are passed on to consumers or compensated for by firing low-level employees. Coffee emphasized the need to pursue the individuals most responsible for wrongdoing, but recognized that if the firm is held liable as well, it may cause them to monitor and police employees. He proposed three approaches that would minimize perverse effects while increasing the likelihood that punished firms would monitor better: equity fines (that essentially make victim compensation funds owners of shares in the corporation), use of adverse publicity, and fuller integration of public and private enforcement. He also noted that courts can deter wrongdoing by putting the corporation on probation rather than by using cash penalties. Once a corporation is put on probation, the court can mandate measures that are typically seen in agency consent decrees: they may realign the managers' interests (e.g., make their pay subject to meeting safety measures), order a report that will expose negligence on all levels of the corporation and encourage critical evaluation of executives and fix information flow problems, and enforce the consent decree type requirements with contempt of court proceedings.

Daniel R. Fischel and Alan O. Sykes maintain in "Corporate Crime," 25 J. Legal Stud. 319 (1996), that the goal of corporate criminal liability should be to set a penalty that is equal to the social harm caused by the crimes of corporate agents, adjusted for the probability of nondetection. This will create the appropriate incentive for a firm to monitor up to the point at which the marginal cost of monitoring would exceed the marginal social gain in the form of reduced social harm from criminal activity. Where civil fines are already being assessed at that optimal level, criminal penalties added on top of the civil liability will only cause overdeterrence and excessive investment of resources in compliance. And criminal liability is not even helpful when civil liability is deficient (or as a supplement to civil liability), not only because it lacks the virtues associated with criminal punishment for individuals (individuals, but not companies, who cannot afford fines can be jailed; individuals, but not companies, might be aptly incapacitated) but because it has serious faults. In the criminal context, penalties do not take into account the actual harm caused and they allow for double penalties (assessed against both the firm and the agent). All in all, they argue, the *civil* context is the best place for penalizing corporate "crimes" and should be pursued by the government in lieu of criminal liability.

In "Corporate Control," New Palgrave Dictionary of Economics and the Law 492 (1998), Jennifer Arlen starts by noting that individual liability can efficiently deter individuals in firms from committing crimes if the individuals can pay the optimal penalty. Those agents will only commit the crimes that are socially beneficial. But where the individual wrongdoer cannot pay the fine, corporate liability may be necessary. When corporate liability is necessary, it will induce firms to take preventive measures and police their employees by monitoring and sanctioning, though she notes that corporate liability cannot inevitably deter wrongdoing by ensuring that the firm does not profit from socially undesirable crimes because individual agents can profit from wrongdoing even if the firm doesn't. Like Fischel and Sykes, she ultimately argues that civil fines dominate criminal proceedings in the bulk of cases.

2. Respondeat Superior

a. Imputation from Individual to Corporation

Commonwealth v. Penn Valley Resorts

Superior Court of Pennsylvania.
343 Pa. Super. 387, 494 A.2d 1139 (1985).

■ Hester, Judge.

On October 20, 1983, a jury convicted appellant, Penn Valley Resorts, Inc., of involuntary manslaughter,[a] reckless endangerment and two counts of furnishing liquor or malt beverages to minors and visibly intoxicated persons. Post trial motions for a new trial and in arrest of judgment were denied, and appellant was fined $10,000.00 on the involuntary manslaughter conviction and $1.00 on each count of furnishing liquor or malt beverages to minors and visibly intoxicated persons. The charge of reckless endangerment was held to merge with involuntary manslaughter for purposes of sentencing. . . .

On May 8, 1981, 60 undergraduate students from the State University of New York at Alfred, New York (hereinafter "Alfred Tech"), a two-year agricultural and technical college, drove to Genesee, Potter County, Pennsylvania for a dinner dance at appellant's resort facility. A student representative made arrangements with appellant's president, Edwin Clancy, whereby appellant agreed to provide appropriate facilities, serve dinner and furnish an open bar. The students arranged for the music for dancing.

The deceased, William Edward Frazer, Jr., a 20–year-old Alfred Tech student, attended the dinner dance. He consumed sufficient alcohol during the affair to cause him to stagger, slur his speech, quickly alternate his moods and ultimately cause a fatal automobile accident. * * *

[A]ppellant argues that without proof that Edwin Clancy's actions were "condoned, sanctioned or recklessly disregarded by the Board of Directors," it cannot be held criminally responsible for such actions.

Under § 307(a)(3) of the Crimes Code, appellant may be convicted of a crime committed by Edwin Clancy in his position as "a high managerial agent." Section 307(a)(3) sets forth that:

> A corporation may be convicted of the commission of an offense if . . . . the commission of the offense was authorized, requested, commanded, performed or recklessly tolerated by the board of directors or by a high managerial agent acting in behalf of the corporation within the scope of his office or employment.

a. § 2504. Involuntary manslaughter.

(a) A person is guilty of involuntary manslaughter when as a direct result of the doing of an unlawful act in a reckless or grossly negligent manner, or the doing of a lawful act in a reckless or grossly negligent manner, he causes the death of another person.—Eds.

. . . .

There is no requirement in § 307(a)(3) that the criminal action must be "condoned, sanctioned or recklessly disregarded" by the Board of Directors. Corporations are criminally accountable for the actions of a "high managerial agent" who commits a wrongdoing in the scope of his office. This corporate accountability is based upon a simple principal/agency relationship and not upon a corporation affirming the officer's act. Appellant concedes that Edwin Clancy, acting as president, was its high managerial agent.

[Clancy tended the open bar, which closed at 10:30 P.M.] Frazer drank double shots of whiskey and a sloe gin fizz. It was not known how many drinks he consumed from the open bar . . .; nevertheless, Frazer's behavior reflected significant drinking. . . .

After the open bar was closed, Frazer went to the public bar. When he complained about the amount of whiskey poured into a double shot glass at 1:00 A.M., Edwin Clancy intervened. In an effort to temper Frazer, Clancy poured more whiskey into the glass. Immediately thereafter, Clancy allowed Frazer to order another drink. As Frazer drank, Clancy remarked that Frazer obviously had a problem with excessive alcohol consumption.

Frazer would not leave, so Clancy presented a challenge in hope of compelling him to leave. The challenge was Clancy's placing a cocktail on the bar and instructing Frazer that if he were not an alcoholic, Frazer could leave without drinking the cocktail. Frazer drank it and finally walked to the parking lot with his friends.

Once outside, Frazer's friends pleaded with him to allow someone to drive his car. When Frazer locked himself in the car, James Corriveau returned to appellant's facility to call the police. Clancy prevented Corriveau from calling the police; instead, Clancy tried to settle the matter himself. He walked to the parking lot and challenged Frazer to a fight to get Frazer to step from his car. When Frazer emerged, two friends locked the car doors, and Clancy retreated to his facility instructing the friends to resolve the problem themselves.

As the parking lot confrontation continued, Frazer's friends left, except Phillip Knapp, who remained to prevent Frazer from driving. When Knapp wrestled the car keys from him, Frazer ran to appellant's facility, where Clancy and other employees were preparing to leave. Knapp followed and attempted to call the police.

Clancy prevented Knapp from calling by pushing him outside. Clancy then acquired the keys from Knapp and promptly handed them to Frazer. This evidence supports the inference that Clancy had grown weary of Frazer's temper and obstreperous conduct. Fearing dire consequences to his business and liquor license if the police were summoned, Clancy subdued Frazer by opting for the only available alternative of giving him his car keys.

After Clancy and his employees departed, Knapp was left alone with Frazer. [A]fter Knapp wrestled the keys from Frazer a second time, Frazer searched his car for a gun and Knapp released the keys. Frazer then drove away and was killed shortly thereafter. * * *

Judgment of sentence affirmed.

United States v. Bank of New England

United States Court of Appeals for the First Circuit.
821 F.2d 844 (1987).

■ BOWNES, CIRCUIT JUDGE.

The Bank of New England appeals a jury verdict convicting it of thirty-one violations of the Currency Transaction Reporting Act (the Act). 31 U.S.C. §§ 5311–22 (1982). Department of Treasury regulations promulgated under the Act require banks to file Currency Transaction Reports (CTRs) within fifteen days of customer currency transactions exceeding $10,000. 31 C.F.R. § 103.22 (1986). The Act imposes felony liability when a bank willfully fails to file such reports "as part of a pattern of illegal activity involving transactions of more than $100,000 in a twelve-month period...." 31 U.S.C. § 5322(b).

The Bank was found guilty of having failed to file CTRs on cash withdrawals made by James McDonough. It is undisputed that on thirty-one separate occasions between May 1983 and July 1984, McDonough withdrew from the Prudential Branch of the Bank more than $10,000 in cash by using multiple checks—each one individually under $10,000—presented simultaneously to a single bank teller.... The Bank ... argues that the trial judge's instructions on willfulness were fatally flawed. * * *

Criminal liability under 31 U.S.C. § 5322 only attaches when a financial institution "willfully" violates the CTR filing requirement. A finding of willfulness under the Reporting Act must be supported by "proof of the defendant's knowledge of the reporting requirements and his specific intent to commit the crime." Willfulness can rarely be proven by direct evidence, since it is a state of mind; it is usually established by drawing reasonable inferences from the available facts.

The Bank contends that the trial court's instructions on knowledge and specific intent effectively relieved the government of its responsibility to prove that the Bank acted willfully. The trial judge began her instructions on this element by outlining generally the concepts of knowledge and willfulness:

> Knowingly simply means voluntarily and intentionally. It's designed to exclude a failure that is done by mistake or accident, or for some other innocent reason. Willfully means voluntarily, intentionally, and with a specific intent to disregard, to disobey the law, with a bad purpose to violate the law.

The trial judge properly instructed the jury that it could infer knowledge if a defendant consciously avoided learning about the reporting requirements. The court then focused on the kind of proof that would establish the Bank's knowledge of its filing obligations. The judge instructed that the knowledge of individual employees acting within the scope of their employment is imputed to the Bank. She told the jury that "if any employee knew that multiple checks would require the filing of reports, the bank knew it, provided the employee knew it within the scope of his employment,. . . ."

The trial judge then focused on the issue of "collective knowledge":

> In addition, however, you have to look at the bank as an institution. As such, its knowledge is the sum of the knowledge of all of the employees. That is, the bank's knowledge is the totality of what all of the employees know within the scope of their employment. So, if Employee A knows one facet of the currency reporting requirement, B knows another facet of it, and C a third facet of it, the bank knows them all. So if you find that an employee within the scope of his employment knew that CTRs had to be filed, even if multiple checks are used, the bank is deemed to know it. The bank is also deemed to know it if each of several employees knew a part of that requirement and the sum of what the separate employees knew amounted to knowledge that such a requirement existed.

After discussing the two modes of establishing knowledge—via either knowledge of one of its individual employees or the aggregate knowledge of all its employees—the trial judge turned to the issue of specific intent:

> There is a similar double business with respect to the concept of willfulness with respect to the bank. In deciding whether the bank acted willfully, again you have to look first at the conduct of all employees and officers, and, second, at what the bank did or did not do as an institution. The bank is deemed to have acted willfully if one of its employees in the scope of his employment acted willfully. So, if you find that an employee willfully failed to do what was necessary to file these reports, then that is deemed to be the act of the bank, and the bank is deemed to have willfully failed to file.
>
> . . . .
>
> Alternatively, the bank as an institution has certain responsibilities; as an organization, it has certain responsibilities. And you will have to determine whether the bank as an organization consciously avoided learning about and observing CTR requirements. The Government to prove the bank guilty on this theory, has to show that its failure to file was the result of some flagrant organizational indifference. In this connection, you should look at the evidence as to the bank's effort, if any, to inform its employees of the law; its effort to check on their compliance; . . .; its policies, and how it carried out its stated policies.
>
> . . . .
>
> If you find that the Government has proven with respect to any transaction either that an employee within the scope of his employment willfully failed to file a required report or that the bank was flagrantly indifferent to its obligations, then you may find that the bank has willfully failed to file the required reports.

The Bank contends that the trial court's instructions regarding knowledge were defective because they eliminated the requirement that it be proven that the Bank violated a known legal duty. It avers that the knowledge instruction invited the jury to convict the Bank for negligently maintaining a poor communications network that prevented the consolidation of the information held by its various employees. The Bank argues that it is error to find that a corporation possesses a particular item of knowledge if one part of the corporation has half the information making up the item, and another part of the entity has the other half.

A collective knowledge instruction is entirely appropriate in the context of corporate criminal liability. The acts of a corporation are, after all, simply the acts of all of its employees operating within the scope of their employment. Similarly, the knowledge obtained by corporate employees acting within the scope of their employment is imputed to the corporation. Corporations compartmentalize knowledge, subdividing the elements of specific duties and operations into smaller components. The aggregate of those components constitutes the corporation's knowledge of a particular operation. It is irrelevant whether employees administering one component of an operation know the specific activities of employees administering another aspect of the operation.... Since the Bank had the compartmentalized structure common to all large corporations, the court's collective knowledge instruction was not only proper but necessary.

Nor do we find any defects in the trial court's instructions on specific intent. The court told the jury that the concept of willfulness entails a voluntary, intentional, and bad purpose to disobey the law. Her instructions on this element, when viewed as a whole, directed the jury not to convict for accidental, mistaken or inadvertent acts or omissions. It is urged that the court erroneously charged that willfulness could be found via flagrant indifference by the Bank toward its reporting obligations. With respect to federal regulatory statutes, the Supreme Court has endorsed defining willfulness, in both civil and criminal contexts, as "a disregard for the governing statute and an indifference to its requirements." *Trans World Airlines, Inc. v. Thurston*, 469 U.S. 111, 127 & n.20, S. Ct. 613 (1985). Accordingly, we find no error in the court's instruction on willfulness.

Model Penal Code § 2.07. Liability of Corporations, Unincorporated Associations and Persons Acting, or Under a Duty to Act, in Their Behalf.

(1) A corporation may be convicted of the commission of an offense if:

(a) the offense is a violation or the offense is defined by a statute other than the Code in which a legislative purpose to impose liability on corporations plainly appears and the conduct is performed by an agent of the corporation acting in behalf of the corporation within the scope of his office or employment, except that if the law defining the offense designates the agents for whose conduct the corporation is accountable or the circumstances under which it is accountable, such provisions shall apply; or

(b) the offense consists of an omission to discharge a specific duty of affirmative performance imposed on corporations by law; or

(c) the commission of the offense was authorized, requested, commanded, performed or recklessly tolerated by the board of directors or by a high managerial agent acting in behalf of the corporation within the scope of his office or employment.

(2) When absolute liability is imposed for the commission of an offense, a legislative purpose to impose liability on a corporation shall be assumed, unless the contrary plainly appears.

. . . .

(4) As used in this Section:

(a) "corporation" does not include an entity organized as or by a governmental agency for the execution of a governmental program;

(b) "agent" means any director, officer, servant, employee or other person authorized to act in behalf of the corporation or association and, in the case of an unincorporated association, a member of such association;

(c) "high managerial agent" means an officer of a corporation or an unincorporated association, or, in the case of a partnership, a partner, or any other agent of a corporation or association having duties of such responsibility that his conduct may fairly be assumed to represent the policy of the corporation or association.

(5) In any prosecution of a corporation or an unincorporated association for the commission of an offense included within the terms of Subsection (1)(a) . . . of this Section, other than an offense for which absolute liability has been imposed, it shall be a defense if the defendant proves by a preponderance of evidence that the high managerial agent having supervisory responsibility over the subject matter of the offense employed due diligence to prevent its commission. This paragraph shall not apply if it is plainly inconsistent with the legislative purpose in defining the particular offense.

QUESTIONS AND COMMENTS

1. Compare corporate liability with traditional principles of complicity liability. Is an employee's conduct imputed to the corporation, or is the employee's conduct evidence of the corporation's conduct—or intent? Is the corporation the accomplice or the principal? If it is to be an accomplice—i.e., the entity to whom another's conduct is imputed—does it need the purpose to aid or abet? Is there such a thing as corporate conduct beyond the conduct of one—all, most—of its constituents? Could the corporation act in any other way than through its members?

2. Is only conduct imputed to the corporation, or is another (natural) person's *mens rea* imputed to it as well? What is corporate mens rea, and how does one go about determining it in a particular case? Does corporate mens rea exist independently of the mens rea of any—some, all—of the human constituents of the corporation? If there is to be a "brains" of the corporation, made up of one (or more?) person(s) (who set policy? who sit on its board? who bear the title "chief executive"?), shouldn't her (their?) mens rea count as the corporation's? Does the "collective" mens rea in *Bank of New England* add up to a corporate mens rea?

3. In the face of difficulties raised by the notion—and the discovery—of corporate conduct and mens rea, some scholars have proposed a new approach to the problem. Rather than piece together scraps of mental states from among various persons who constitute the corporation, they suggest we treat the corporation as an independent entity, whose conduct or mens rea is then assessed in very much the same way as we might assess the conduct or mens rea of an individual. Pamela Bucy, for one, has "propose[d] a standard of corporate criminal liability that uses a new conceptual paradigm for identifying and proving corporate intent":

> This standard assumes that each corporate entity has a distinct and identifiable personality or "ethos." The government can convict a corporation under this standard only if it proves that the corporate ethos encouraged agents of the corporation to commit the criminal act. Central to this approach is the assumption that organizations possess an identity that is independent of specific individuals who control or work for the organization. This corporate identity, or "ethos," results from the dynamic of many individuals working together toward corporate goals. The living cell provides an apt analogy: Just as a living cell has an identity separate from the activities of its constituent molecules, a corporation has an identity separate from its individual agents.
>
> In a sense, this corporate ethos standard takes its cue from notions of intent developed in the context of individual liability. When considering whether an individual should be held criminally liable we ask, did this person commit this act accidentally or purposely. If the individual committed the act purposely, we consider it to be a crime, while if the individual committed the act accidentally, we do not. Similarly, the standard proposed herein imposes criminal liability on a corporation only if the corporation encouraged the criminal conduct at issue. If it did, the criminal conduct is not an accident or the unpredictable act of a maverick employee. Instead, the criminal conduct is predictable and consistent with corporate goals, policies, and ethos. In the context of a fictional entity, this translates into intention.
>
> This proposed standard offers the following four advantages over the current standards of liability. To the extent that historical and current standards of corporate criminal liability allow criminal convictions without proof of the corporation's intent, they encourage the blurring of criminal and civil liability. This blurring dilutes the impact of a criminal conviction, ultimately, erodes the power of the criminal law. The theoretical and practical framework of the corporate ethos standard provides a method for identifying and proving the intent of corporate actors. This is its first and major advantage.
>
> The second advantage of the corporate ethos standard is that it distinguishes among diverse corporations. The current standards of corporate criminal liability often treat all corporations alike by imposing criminal liability on corporations for the acts of their individual agents, regardless of the circumstances within a particular corporation. From Bentham on, scholars and practitioners have recognized that a fundamental requirement for any criminal justice system is that the system treat like actors alike and different actors differently. Anyone,

from the average person on the street to the most respected scholar in organizational behavior, recognizes that no two corporations are alike. Our criminal justice system should not treat them as if they were.

The third advantage of the corporate ethos standard is that it rewards those corporations that make efforts to educate and motivate their employees to follow the letter and spirit of the law. This encourages responsible corporate behavior. This advantage is in sharp contrast to the Model Penal Code's standard of liability that discourages higher echelon employees from properly supervising lower echelon employees. This advantage also contrasts with the minimal deterrence achieved by imposing criminal liability on individuals within the corporation. Convicting individual agents and employees of a corporation does not stop other corporate employees from committing future criminal acts if sufficient internal corporate pressure to violate the law continues to exist. In such an environment, the agents are cogs in a wheel. Those convicted are simply replaced by others whose original propensity to obey the law is similarly overcome by a corporate ethos that encourages illegal acts. Unless inside or outside forces change the lawless ethos, it will corrupt each generation of corporate agents. The proposed standard of liability addresses this problem by punishing any corporation that establishes a lawless ethos which overcomes its employees' propensity to obey the law.

The last advantage of the corporate ethos standard is that it is practical, workable, and provable, from concrete information already available in grand jury investigations of corporate crime. To ascertain the ethos of a corporation, and to determine if this ethos encouraged the criminal conduct at issue, the factfinder should examine: the corporate hierarchy, the corporate goals and policies, the corporation's historical treatment of prior offenses, the corporation's efforts to educate and monitor employees' compliance with the law, and the corporation's compensation scheme, especially its policy on indemnification of corporate employees. These facts are typically, or easily, examined in any criminal investigation of corporate misdeeds and are subject to proof in a courtroom.

Pamela H. Bucy, "Corporate Ethos: A Standard for Imposing Corporate Criminal Liability," 75 Minn. L. Rev. 1095, 1099 (1991).

Does "assuming" that a corporation has a "distinct and identifiable personality or 'ethos'" make it so? Or is a counterfactual assumption acceptable given the need to address the problem of corporate criminality? Would it be appropriate to punish the "distinct and identifiable personality" of an *individual*? If not, what's different about a corporate defendant, i.e., a legal person, rather than a natural one?

b. Imputation from Individual to Individual

United States v. Dotterweich

Supreme Court of the United States.
320 U.S. 277, 64 S.Ct. 134 (1943).

■ MR. JUSTICE FRANKFURTER delivered the opinion of the Court.

This was a prosecution begun by two informations, consolidated for trial, charging Buffalo Pharmacal Company, Inc., and Dotterweich, its president and general manager, with violations of the Act of Congress of June 25, 1938, c. 675, 52 Stat. 1040, 21 U.S.C. §§ 301–392, known as the Federal Food, Drug, and Cosmetic Act. The Company, a jobber in drugs, purchased them from their manufacturers and shipped them, repacked under its own label, in interstate commerce.... The informations were based on § 301 of that Act, 21 U.S.C. § 331, paragraph (a) of which prohibits "The introduction or delivery for introduction into interstate commerce of any * * * drug * * * that is adulterated or misbranded". "Any person" violating this provision is, by paragraph (a) of § 303, 21 U.S.C. § 333, made "guilty of a misdemeanor". Three counts went to the jury—two, for shipping misbranded drugs in interstate commerce, and a third, for so shipping an adulterated drug.[a] The jury disagreed as to the corporation and found Dotterweich guilty on all three counts. [Dotterweich was sentenced to pay a fine and to probation for 60 days. The statute provided for punishment of up to one year's imprisonment.]

.... [T]he claim of Dotterweich that, having failed to find the corporation guilty, the jury could not find him guilty[, is baseless]. Whether the jury's verdict was the result of carelessness or compromise or a belief that the responsible individual should suffer the penalty instead of merely increasing, as it were, the cost of running the business of the corporation, is immaterial. Juries may indulge in precisely such motives or vagaries. * * *

The prosecution to which Dotterweich was subjected is based on a now familiar type of legislation whereby penalties serve as effective means of regulation. Such legislation dispenses with the conventional requirement for criminal conduct—awareness of some wrongdoing. In the interest of the larger good it puts the burden of acting at hazard upon a person otherwise innocent but standing in responsible relation to a public danger. And so it is clear that shipments like those now in issue are "punished by the statute if the article is misbranded (or adulterated), and that the article may be misbranded (or adulterated) without any conscious fraud at all. It was

a. The first count was based on an interstate shipment on October 2, 1939, of a bottle of cascara compound which was charged to be misbranded; the other two counts related to an interstate shipment on January 9, 1940, of a bottle of digitalis tablets, one of the counts charging adulteration, and the other misbranding. Each of the shipments was made in filling an order received through the mails by Buffalo Pharmacal Company from a physician resident in a state other than New York. The corporation had purchased the drugs from a wholesale manufacturer; it repackaged them for the shipments under attack. The appellant Dotterweich had no personal connection with either shipment, but he was in general charge of the corporation's business and had given general instructions to its employees to fill orders received from physicians.... The bottle of cascara compound carried a label reading "1000 Tablets Cascara Compound * * * (Hinkle)," followed by a list of the ingredients, one of which was strychnine sulphate. The charge of misbranding was based on the fact that this ingredient had been removed from the formula for Hinkle pills stated in the official National Formulary promulgated January 1, 1939.... The label on the bottle of digitalis tablets represented that each tablet possessed a potency of one U.S.P. unit of digitalis, whereas in fact analysis proved that the tablets were less than one-half of the represented potency.

United States v. Buffalo Pharmacal Co., 131 F.2d 500 (2d Cir. 1942).—EDS.

natural enough to throw this risk on shippers with regard to the identity of their wares. . . ." * * *

It would be too treacherous to define or even to indicate by way of illustration the class of employees which stands in such a responsible relation. To attempt a formula embracing the variety of conduct whereby persons may responsibly contribute in furthering a transaction forbidden by an Act of Congress, to wit, to send illicit goods across state lines, would be mischievous futility. In such matters the good sense of prosecutors, the wise guidance of trial judges, and the ultimate judgment of juries must be trusted. Our system of criminal justice necessarily depends on "conscience and circumspection in prosecuting officers," even when the consequences are far more drastic than they are under the provision of law before us. See United States v. Balint, 258 U.S. 250, 42 S.Ct. 301 (involving a maximum sentence of five years).

United States v. Park

Supreme Court of the United States.
421 U.S. 658, 95 S.Ct. 1903 (1975).

■ MR. CHIEF JUSTICE BURGER delivered the opinion of the Court.

Acme Markets, Inc., is a national retail food chain with approximately 36,000 employees, 874 retail outlets, 12 general warehouses, and four special warehouses. Its headquarters, including the office of the president, respondent Park, who is chief executive officer of the corporation, are located in Philadelphia, Pa. In a five-count information filed in the United States District Court for the District of Maryland, the Government charged Acme and respondent with violations of the Federal Food, Drug and Cosmetic Act (the Act). Each count of the information alleged that the defendants had received food that had been shipped in interstate commerce and that, while the food was being held for sale in Acme's Baltimore warehouse following shipment in interstate commerce, they caused it to be held in a building accessible to rodents and to be exposed to contamination by rodents. These acts were alleged to have resulted in the food's being adulterated within the meaning of 21 U.S.C. §§ 342(a)(3) and (4), in violation of 21 U.S.C. § 331(k).

Acme pleaded guilty to each count of the information. Respondent pleaded not guilty. The evidence at trial demonstrated that in April 1970 the Food and Drug Administration (FDA) advised respondent by letter of insanitary conditions in Acme's Philadelphia warehouse. In 1971 the FDA found that similar conditions existed in the firm's Baltimore warehouse. An FDA consumer safety officer testified concerning evidence of rodent infestation and other insanitary conditions discovered during a 12–day inspection of the Baltimore warehouse in November and December 1971. He also related that a second inspection of the warehouse had been conducted in March 1972. On that occasion the inspectors found that there had been improvement in the sanitary conditions, but that "there was still evidence of rodent activity in the building and in the warehouses and we found some rodent-contaminated lots of food items."

The Government also presented testimony by the Chief of Compliance of the FDA's Baltimore office, who informed respondent by letter of the conditions at the Baltimore warehouse after the first inspection. There was testimony by Acme's Baltimore division vice president, who had responded to the letter on behalf of Acme and respondent and who described the steps taken to remedy the insanitary conditions discovered by both inspections. The Government's final witness, Acme's vice president for legal affairs and assistant secretary, identified respondent as the president and chief executive officer of the company and read a bylaw prescribing the duties of the chief executive officer.[7] . . .

At the close of the Government's case in chief, respondent moved for a judgment of acquittal on the ground that "the evidence in chief has shown that Mr. Park is not personally concerned in this Food and Drug violation." The trial judge denied the motion, stating that United States v. Dotterweich, 320 U.S. 277, 64 S.Ct. 134 (1943), was controlling.

Respondent was the only defense witness. He testified that, although all of Acme's employees were in a sense under his general direction, the company had an "organizational structure for responsibilities for certain functions" according to which different phases of its operation were "assigned to individuals who, in turn, have staff and departments under them." He identified those individuals responsible for sanitation, and related that upon receipt of the January 1972 FDA letter, he had conferred with the vice president for legal affairs, who informed him that the Baltimore division vice president "was investigating the situation immediately and would be taking corrective action and would be preparing a summary of the corrective action to reply to the letter." Respondent stated that he did not "believe there was anything (he) could have done more constructively than what (he) found was being done." * * *

The relevant portion of the trial judge's instructions to the jury challenged by respondent is set out in the margin.[9] Respondent's counsel

7. The bylaw provided in pertinent part:

"The Chairman of the board of directors or the president shall be the chief executive officer of the company as the board of directors may from time to time determine. He shall, subject to the board of directors, have general and active supervision of the affairs, business, offices and employees of the company. . . .

"He shall, from time to time, in his discretion or at the order of the board, report the operations and affairs of the company. He shall also perform such other duties and have such other powers as may be assigned to him from time to time by the board of directors."

9. "In order to find the Defendant guilty on any count of the Information, you must find beyond a reasonable doubt on each count. . . .

"Thirdly, that John R. Park held a position of authority in the operation of the business of Acme Markets, Incorporated.

"However, you need not concern yourselves with the first two elements of the case. The main issue for your determination is only with the third element, whether the Defendant held a position of authority and responsibility in the business of Acme Markets.

"The statute makes individuals, as well as corporations, liable for violations. An individual is liable if it is clear, beyond a reasonable doubt, that the elements of the adulteration of the food as to travel in interstate commerce are present. As I have instructed you in this case, they are, and that the individual had a responsible relation to the situation, even though he may not have participated personally.

objected to the instructions on the ground that they failed fairly to reflect our decision in United States v. Dotterweich, supra, and to define "responsible relationship." The trial judge overruled the objection. The jury found respondent guilty on all counts of the information, and he was subsequently sentenced to pay a fine of $50 on each count. * * *

The Act does not, as we observed in Dotterweich, make criminal liability turn on "awareness of some wrongdoing" or "conscious fraud." The duty imposed by Congress on responsible corporate agents is, we emphasize, one that requires the highest standard of foresight and vigilance, but the Act, in its criminal aspect, does not require that which is objectively impossible. The theory upon which responsible corporate agents are held criminally accountable for "causing" violations of the Act permits a claim that a defendant was "powerless" to prevent or correct the violation to "be raised defensively at a trial on the merits." If such a claim is made, the defendant has the burden of coming forward with evidence, but this does not alter the Government's ultimate burden of proving beyond a reasonable doubt the defendant's guilt, including his power, in light of the duty imposed by the Act, to prevent or correct the prohibited condition. Congress has seen fit to enforce the accountability of responsible corporate agents dealing with products which may affect the health of consumers by penal sanctions cast in rigorous terms, and the obligation of the courts is to give them effect so long as they do not violate the Constitution.

We cannot agree with the Court of Appeals that it was incumbent upon the District Court to instruct the jury that the Government had the burden of establishing "wrongful action".... The concept of a "responsible relationship" to, or a "responsible share" in, a violation of the Act indeed imports some measure of blameworthiness; but it is equally clear that the Government establishes a prima facie case when it introduces evidence sufficient to warrant a finding by the trier of the facts that the defendant had, by reason of his position in the corporation, responsibility and authority either to prevent in the first instance, or promptly to correct, the violation complained of, and that he failed to do so. The failure thus to fulfill the duty imposed by the interaction of the corporate agent's authority and the statute furnishes a sufficient causal link. The considerations which prompted the imposition of this duty, and the scope of the duty, provide the measure of culpability.

Turning to the jury charge in this case, ... we conclude that, viewed as a whole and in the context of the trial, the charge was not misleading and contained an adequate statement of the law to guide the jury's determination.

"The individual is or could be liable under the statute, even if he did not consciously do wrong. However, the fact that the Defendant is president and is a chief executive officer of the Acme Markets does not require a finding of guilt. Though, he need not have personally participated in the situation, he must have had a responsible relationship to the issue. The issue is, in this case, whether the Defendant, John R. Park, by virtue of his position in the company, had a position of authority and responsibility in the situation out of which these charges arose."

Commonwealth v. Koczwara

Supreme Court of Pennsylvania.
397 Pa. 575, 155 A.2d 825 (1959).

■ Cohen, Justice.

John Koczwara, the defendant, is the licensee and operator of an establishment on Jackson Street in the City of Scranton known as J. K.'s Tavern. At that place he had a restaurant liquor license issued by the Pennsylvania Liquor Control Board. The Lackawanna County Grand Jury indicted the defendant on [four] counts for violations of the Liquor Code. * * *

At the conclusion of the Commonwealth's evidence, count three of the indictment, charging the sale by the defendant personally to minors, was removed from the jury's consideration by the trial judge on the ground that there was no evidence that the defendant had personally participated in the sale or was present in the tavern when sales to minors took place. . . . [T]he jury returned a verdict of guilty as to each of the remaining three counts: two counts of permitting minors to frequent the licensed premises without parental or other supervision, and the count of permitting sales to minors.

. . . Judge Hoban . . . sentenced the defendant to pay the costs of prosecution, a fine of five hundred dollars and to undergo imprisonment in the Lackawanna County Jail for three months. . . .

Defendant . . . question[s] whether the undisputed facts of this case support the judgment and sentence imposed by the Quarter Sessions Court. Judge Hoban found as fact that "in every instance the purchase [by minors] was made from a bartender, not identified by name, and service to the boys was made by the bartender. There was no evidence that the defendant was present on any one of the occasions testified to by these witnesses, nor that he had any personal knowledge of the sales to them or to other persons on the premises." We, therefore, must determine the criminal responsibility of a licensee of the Liquor Control Board for acts committed by his employees upon his premises, without his personal knowledge, participation, or presence, which acts violate a valid regulatory statute passed under the Commonwealth's police power.

While an employer in almost all cases is not criminally responsible for the unlawful acts of his employees, unless he consents to, approves, or participates in such acts, courts all over the nation have struggled for years in applying this rule within the framework of "controlling the sale of intoxicating liquor." At common law, any attempt to invoke the doctrine of respondeat superior in a criminal case would have run afoul of our deeply ingrained notions of criminal jurisprudence that guilt must be personal and individual.[1] In recent decades, however, many states have enacted detailed

1. The distinction between respondeat superior in tort law and its application to the criminal law is obvious. In tort law, the doctrine is employed for the purpose of settling the incidence of loss upon the party who can best bear such loss. But the criminal law is supported by totally different concepts. We impose penal treatment upon those who injure or menace social interests, partly in order to reform, partly to prevent the continua-

regulatory provisions in fields which are essentially noncriminal, e.g., pure food and drug acts, speeding ordinances, building regulations, and child labor, minimum wage and maximum hour legislation. Such statutes are generally enforceable by light penalties, and although violations are labelled crimes, the considerations applicable to them are totally different from those applicable to true crimes, which involve moral delinquency and which are punishable by imprisonment or another serious penalty. Such so-called statutory crimes are in reality an attempt to utilize the machinery of criminal administration as an enforcing arm for social regulations of a purely civil nature, with the punishment totally unrelated to questions of moral wrongdoing or guilt. It is here that the social interest in the general well-being and security of the populace has been held to outweigh the individual interest of the particular defendant....

Not the least of the legitimate police power areas of the legislature is the control of intoxicating liquor. ... Because of the peculiar nature of this business, one who applies for and receives permission from the Commonwealth to carry on the liquor trade assumes the highest degree of responsibility to his fellow citizens. As the licensee of the Board, he is under a duty not only to regulate his own personal conduct in a manner consistent with the permit he has received, but also to control the acts and conduct of any employee to whom he entrusts the sale of liquor. Such fealty is the quid pro quo which the Commonwealth demands in return for the privilege of entering the highly restricted and, what is more important, the highly dangerous business of selling intoxicating liquor.

.... The question here raised is whether the legislature intended to impose vicarious criminal liability on the licensee-principal for acts committed on his premises without his presence, participation or knowledge. * * *

As the defendant has pointed out, there is a distinction between the requirement of a mens rea and the imposition of vicarious absolute liability for the acts of another. It may be that the courts below, in relying on prior authority, have failed to make such a distinction.[5] In any case, we fully recognize it. Moreover, we find that the intent of the legislature in enacting this Code was not only to eliminate the common law requirement of a mens rea, but also to place a very high degree of responsibility upon the holder of a liquor license to make certain that neither he nor anyone in his employ commit any of the prohibited acts upon the licensed premises. Such a burden of care is imposed upon the licensee in order to protect the public from the potentially noxious effects of an inherently dangerous business. We, of course, express no opinion as to the wisdom of the legislature's imposing vicarious responsibility under certain sections of the Liquor Code. There may or may not be an economic-sociological justification for such liability on a theory of deterrence. Such determination is for the legislature to make, so long as the constitutional requirements are met.

tion of the anti-social activity and partly to deter others. If a defendant has personally lived up to the social standards of the criminal law and has not menaced or injured anyone, why impose penal treatment?

5. We must also be extremely careful to distinguish the present situation from the question of corporate criminal liability....

Can the legislature, consistent with the requirements of due process, thus establish absolute criminal liability? Were this the defendant's first violation of the Code, and the penalty solely a minor fine of from $100–$300, we would have no hesitation in upholding such a judgment. Defendant, by accepting a liquor license, must bear this financial risk. Because of a prior conviction for violations of the Code, however, the trial judge felt compelled under the mandatory language of the statute, Section 494(a), to impose not only an increased fine of five hundred dollars, but also a three month sentence of imprisonment. Such sentence of imprisonment in a case where liability is imposed vicariously cannot be sanctioned by this Court consistently with the law of the land clause of Section 9, Article I of the Constitution of the Commonwealth of Pennsylvania., P.S.[7]

The Courts of the Commonwealth have already strained to permit the legislature to carry over the civil doctrine of respondeat superior and to apply it as a means of enforcing the regulatory scheme that covers the liquor trade. We have done so on the theory that the Code established petty misdemeanors involving only light monetary fines. It would be unthinkable to impose vicarious criminal responsibility in cases involving true crimes. Although to hold a principal criminally liable might possibly be an effective means of enforcing law and order, it would do violence to our more sophisticated modern-day concepts of justice. Liability for all true crimes, wherein an offense carries with it a jail sentence, must be based exclusively upon personal causation. It can be readily imagined that even a licensee who is meticulously careful in the choice of his employees cannot supervise every single act of the subordinates. A man's liberty cannot rest on so frail a reed as whether his employee will commit a mistake in judgment.

* * *

Judgment, as modified, is affirmed.

QUESTIONS AND COMMENTS

1. Would Dotterweich, Park, or Koczwara be liable under traditional complicity doctrine? (Conspiracy? Facilitation?) From the perspective of complicity, are they best thought of as accomplices or as principals?

2. How is a superior held liable for her subordinate's conduct? Is his conduct imputed to her? His mens rea? Is vicarious liability less troubling in cases of strict liability crime—as in *Dotterweich, Park,* and *Koczwara*? Or is the problem, once again, that guilt is supposed to be "personal"? Or is the "superior" not held liable as the supervisor of a subordinate but as a representative of the corporation? Or is the superior's liability grounded on his own behavior, because he has failed to discipline and/or supervise his underlings in a fashion that would preclude the agency he manages from engaging in the conduct that the statute proscribes? Is such "bad supervision" an act or an omission? If an omission, does the defendant have a duty to act?

7. Sec. 9. "* * * nor can he be deprived of his life, liberty or property, unless by the judgment of his peers or the law of the land."

3. Is the concern in *Koczwara* over the imputation of an employee's *act* or over the unproven supposition that the license-holder/supervisor should have been able to prevent his subordinate's misconduct? Is the problem strict liability or imputation of acts? The statute mandates imprisonment on the second offense: what if, instead, it mandated imprisonment on the twentieth (and multiple offenses were extremely rare)? If we were satisfied that the supervisor did not take reasonable steps to stop violations—either because a jury engaged in particularistic fact-finding and decided *this* supervisor was negligent in his supervision or because we believe that it is appropriate to presume conclusively that if there have been (enough) multiple violations, he *must* have been negligent (see ch. 5, on strict liability)—would we find punishing Koczwara less bothersome?

4. Should the principle of respondeat superior be expanded to other relationships, including that between parent and child, teacher and student, passenger and captain, warden and prisoner? To any relationship that gives rise to a duty to aid—and criminal omission liability for the failure to do so? (See supra ch. 4.) To any situation in which we want to encourage a person of authority to prevent criminal conduct by those within her charge? Does an expansion of the duty to aid—and the attendant omission liability—imply an expansion of respondeat superior in criminal law?

5. *Dotterweich* and *Park* are now seen as the origins of the "responsible corporate officer" doctrine, which bases vicarious criminal liability of an officer of corporation on her "responsible relation" to the conduct that actually constitutes a violation of the criminal statute in question. What does this doctrine mean? Is it shorthand for negligence? Is it, perhaps, a type of (targeted) negligence standard, one that asks what officers in corporations can be expected to do? Or does it refer to the absence of defenses based on the lack of responsibility—excuses like duress or insanity (how would they apply to a corporation?)? Alternatively, does it stake out an area of institutional competence, focusing on the act performed (or not), rather than on any mental state that might be accompanying it?

Assuming we know what the responsible officer doctrine means, where does it come from? Is it a constitutional requirement (based on what constitutional principle?)? Or is it simply a result of statutory interpretation, an inquiry into (federal) legislative intent?

6. Does the responsible corporate officer doctrine apply even in cases involving non-strict liability statutes? More specifically, does the officer's responsible relation permit the imputation not only of conduct, but of mens rea as well? Consider the following application of the responsible corporate officer doctrine to the Clean Water Act, which threatens anyone "who willfully or negligently" violates its provisions with criminal punishment:

> Congress intended, with the [Clean Water] Act, "to restore and maintain the chemical, physical, and biological integrity of the Nation's waters ... [and that] the discharge of pollutants into the navigable waters be eliminated by 1985." 33 U.S.C. § 1251(a). We think that Congress perceived this objective to outweigh hardships suffered by "responsible corporate officers" who are held criminally liable in spite of their lack of "consciousness of wrong-doing.".... [A] "responsible corporate officer," to be held criminally liable, would not have to

> "willfully or negligently" cause a permit violation. Instead, the willfulness or negligence of the actor would be imputed to him by virtue of his position of responsibility.

United States v. Brittain, 931 F.2d 1413, 1419 (10th Cir. 1991).

Does restoring and maintaining the integrity of the Nation's waters justify the imposition of strict and vicarious criminal liability, even in the case of statutes that nominally require mens rea?

7. The *Koczwara* court makes a point of saying that it didn't disregard "the distinction between the requirement of a mens rea and the imposition of vicarious absolute liability for the acts of another." What is that distinction? The offense in *Dotterweich* was one of strict liability (liability didn't require that the mislabeler knew or even suspected or should have suspected that he was mislabeling drugs). Commentators have chided the *Dotterweich* Court for confusing the question of strict liability with that of vicarious liability. Why are courts more likely to embrace vicarious liability in cases involving crimes that do not require mens rea? What if the offense in *Koczwara* (or in *Dotterweich*) had not been one of strict liability?

The *Koczwara* court reminds itself to "be extremely careful to distinguish the present situation from the question of corporate criminal liability." What is *that* distinction?

CHAPTER 9

RAPE

A. INTRODUCTION

1. A SURVIVOR'S EXPERIENCE

Lynne Henderson, "Review Essay: What Makes Rape a Crime?," 3 Berkeley Women's L.J. 193 (1988)

Although five and a half years have passed since I was raped, it takes but a moment to remember the forty-five minutes of terror and horror of the event and the aftermath of guilt, shame, fury, and isolation. I was asleep in my bed, when I awoke to find a man on top of me. I struggled to get up; "what are *you* doing here," I demanded. "I'm going to fuck you," was the response. "The hell you are," was mine. In the brief struggle, I told myself, "look, look at everything so you can remember, so you can describe." He hit my face repeatedly; I felt nothing except pressure. It seemed clear to me that this was a battle I wouldn't win; I turned my head and thought "oh God, this *is* really happening." . . . At some point, I realized he might very well kill me if I did not cooperate, and if he killed me, I would not live to "get him." . . . I left my body but I didn't; I remember thinking how can something so beautiful be so horrible? . . .

I really have no complaints about the actors in the criminal justice system; other than the [police] dispatcher's initial incredulity, they were all sensitive and non-sexist. . . . The district attorney met with me, stayed in touch, and asked if I wanted to continue at each new stage in the proceeding. The police officers worked long hours to "make" the case. The defense lawyer never hinted at my foibles or my sexual history. . . . The jury did not take much time to come back with a guilty verdict. . . . Perfect, right?

Well, yes and no. Many people, men and women, were kind, but many men I knew could not handle the rape at all. Subtle messages of blame, denial—believe it or not, *prurience*, snuck through. . . . Three weeks after the assault, and only one week after the cast was taken off my nose, [the man I was dating] said irritably, "Why are you still so angry?" I was scared—at the least little noise I would jump and sometimes scream; I was in pain; I was furious at men and my vulnerability; I was in mourning. I never thought I would recover—at times I thought I was losing my mind. I had nightmares. . . .

For a year, I did not get over a kind of perpetual state of panic—a state not helped, perhaps, by the prospect of testifying against the rapist in another case, frighteningly similar to my own, that fortunately settled. It took three years to get over the "anniversary" nightmares. It took two years of my life to get over my absolute fear and distrust of men, and yet more time to overcome occasional flashbacks. And all the time I tried to act normally—work, function, and rebuild. I remember—what a triumph!—the first night I was able to go alone to a friend's house for dinner, stay, and come home without absolutely panicking.

2. THE DIMENSIONS OF THE PROBLEM OF SEXUAL VIOLENCE

It is difficult to know the precise frequency of rape. This is in part a function of some of the definitional problems we will deal with in this chapter: Is it rape if a man has intercourse with a woman who had gotten drunk and was still able to make some decisions but was markedly impaired in her judgment? Is it rape if a supervisor refuses to promote a woman who merits a promotion unless she has sex with him? Is it rape if a woman says she doesn't want to have sex but the man persistently keeps touching her and hounding her "to change her mind," though he never verbally threatens to hurt her if she doesn't acquiesce to his repeated attempts to have intercourse with her? It is also in substantial part a function of the fact that victims underreport even the most unambiguous instances of the crime, not only to police but to surveyors, particularly when the assailant is someone known to the victim. The U.S. Department of Justice, Bureau of Justice Statistics, Criminal Victimization in the United States, 2002 reports more than 167,000 rapes and attempted rapes in 2002, a rate of roughly 700/100,000 women, and another 80,000 or so sexual assaults other than rapes (table 1). Roughly two thirds of rape and sexual assault victims questioned in this survey were victimized by men who are known to them, not strangers (table 27). Other surveys suggest that sexual assault is even more likely to be perpetrated by a person known to the victim. See Crime Victims Research and Treatment Center, Rape in America 4 (1992) (only 22% victimized by total or virtual strangers, 9% by husbands or ex-husbands, 10% by boyfriends or ex-boyfriends, 11% by fathers or stepfathers, and 29% by neighbors or other acquaintances).

Some researchers believe that rates of sexual victimization are quite a bit higher, especially among college women. One study found that 27% of college women had been victims of rape or attempted rape since they were fourteen. See Mary P. Koss, Christine A. Gidycz & Nadine Wisniewski, "The Scope of Rape: Incidence and Prevalence of Sexual Aggression and Victimization in a National Sample of Higher Education Students," 55 J. Consulting & Clinical Psych. 162 (1987). Similarly, a 1999 Justice Department survey reported that 2.8% of college women had experienced a completed or attempted rape during the past six months, implying a victimization rate of nearly 5,600/100,000 within this group. There are debates about how to interpret these far higher numbers, debates that might both inform and be informed by our discussions of the legal elements of rape. A good summary of the most skeptical responses to these higher estimates can be found in Neil Gilbert, "The Phantom Epidemic of Sexual Assault," Pub. Interest 54 (Spring 1991). First, those skeptical of the figures note that campus police receive next to no reports of completed rapes, let alone reports from 2.8% of college women each six months. But some would argue that this is a function of both accurately perceived systemic indifference to acquaintance rape allegations and the socially constructed tendency of victims to blame themselves for the incidents. Second, critics note that 42% of those whom the survey defined as rape victims in the Koss et al. survey subsequently dated and had voluntary sexual relations with the men they had described as having done things that the surveyors interpreted as meaning that these men had raped them. This, critics suggest, implies that the women themselves did not think they were dealing with especially blameworthy people, let alone horrific criminals.

It is difficult as well to say with confidence precisely what social impact the *fear* of rape has on women's lives. There are certainly obvious "practical" effects—in terms of women's freedom to move about freely, to take certain jobs that might leave them especially vulnerable to sexual violence etc.—and certainly effects on their overall sense of security and well-being, but quantifying these effects is hardly easy (as is true of criminal victimization in general). For a discussion of these issues, see Margaret T. Gordon & Stephanie Riger, The Female Fear: The Social Cost of Rape (1991).

3. An Introduction to the Legal Issues

State v. Rusk

Court of Appeals of Maryland.
289 Md. 230, 424 A.2d 720 (1981).

■ Murphy, C.J.

Edward Rusk was found guilty by a jury of second degree rape in violation of Maryland Code, Art. 27, sec. 463(a)(1), which provides in pertinent part:

"A person is guilty of rape in the second degree if the person engages in vaginal intercourse with another person:

(1) By force or threat of force against the will and without the consent of the other person."

On appeal, the Court of Special Appeals, sitting en banc, reversed the conviction; it concluded . . . that in view of the prevailing law as set forth in *Hazel v. State*, 221 Md. 464, 157 A.2d 922 (1960), insufficient evidence of Rusk's guilt had been adduced at trial to permit the case to go the jury. . . .

At the trial, the 21–year-old prosecuting witness, Pat, testified that on the evening of September 21, 1977, she attended a high school alumnae meeting where she met a girl friend, Terry. After the meeting, Terry and Pat agreed to drive in their respective cars to Fells Point to have a few drinks. . . . Rusk approached them [at a bar] and said "hello" to Terry. Terry, who was then conversing with another individual, momentarily interrupted her conversation and said "Hi, Eddie." Rusk then began talking with Pat and during their conversation both of them acknowledged being separated from their respective spouses and having a child. Pat told Rusk that she had to go home early because it was a weeknight. . . .

Rusk asked Pat the direction in which she was driving and after she responded, Rusk requested a ride to his apartment. Although Pat did not know Rusk, she thought that Terry knew him. She thereafter agreed to give him a ride. Pat cautioned Rusk on the way to the car that "I'm just giving a ride home, you know, as a friend, not anything to be, you know, thought of other than a ride;" and he said, "Oh, okay." ...

After a twenty-minute drive, they arrived at Rusk's apartment. Pat testified she was totally unfamiliar with the neighborhood. She parked the car at the curb on the opposite side of the street from Rusk's apartment but left the engine running. Rusk asked Pat to come in, but she refused. He invited her again, and she again declined. She told Rusk that she could not go in even if she wanted to because she was separated from her husband and a detective could be observing her movements.... Notwithstanding her repeated refusals, Pat testified that Rusk reached over and turned off the ignition to her car and took her car keys. He got out of the car, walked over to her side, opened the door and said, "Now, will you come up?" Pat explained her subsequent actions:

> "At that point, because I was scared, because he had my car keys, I didn't know what to do. I was someplace I didn't even know where I was ... I didn't know whether to run. I really didn't think at that point, what to do.
>
> Now, I know that I should have blown the horn. I should have run. There were a million things I could have done. I was scared, at that point, and I didn't do any of them."

Pat testified that at this moment she feared that Rusk would rape her. She said, "[I]t was the way he looked at me, and said 'Come on up, come on up;' and when he took the keys, I knew that was wrong."

It was then about 1 a.m. Pat accompanied Rusk across the street into a totally dark house. She followed him up two flights of stairs. She neither saw nor heard anyone in the building.... Rusk unlocked the door to his one-room apartment, and turned on the light. According to Pat, he told her to sit down. She sat in a chair beside the bed. Rusk sat on the bed. After Rusk talked for a few minutes, he left the room for about one to five minutes. Pat remained seated on the chair. She made no noise and did not attempt to leave. She said that she did not notice a telephone in the room. When Rusk returned, he turned off the light, and sat down on the bed. Pat asked if she could leave; she told him that she wanted to go home and "didn't want to come up." She said, "Now [that] I came up, can I go?" Rusk, who was still in possession of her car keys, said he wanted her to stay.

Rusk then asked Pat to get on the bed with him. He pulled her by the arms to the bed and began to undress her, removing her blouse and bra. He unzipped her slacks and she took them off after he told her to do so. Pat removed the rest of her clothing, and then removed Rusk's pants because "he asked me to do it." After they were both undressed Rusk started kissing Pat as she was lying on her back. Pat explained what happened next:

> "I was still begging him to please, you know, let me leave. I said, 'you can get a lot of other girls, down there, for what you want,' and he just kept saying, 'no'; and then I was really scared, because I can't describe,

> you know what was said. It was more the look in his eyes, and I said, at that point—I didn't know what to say; and I said, 'If I do what you want, will you let me go without killing me?' Because I didn't know, at that point, what he was going to do; and I started to cry; and when I did, he put his hands on my throat, and started lightly to choke me; and I said, 'If I do what you want, will you let me go?' And he said, yes, and at that time, I proceeded to do what he wanted me to do."

Pat testified that Rusk made her perform oral sex and then vaginal intercourse.

Immediately after the intercourse, Pat asked if she could leave. She testified that Rusk said, "Yes," after which she got up and got dressed and Rusk returned her car keys. She said that Rusk then "walked me to my car, and asked if he could see me again; and said, 'Yes'; and he asked me for my telephone number; and I said, 'No, I'll see you down Fells Point sometime,' just so I could leave."...

She reported the incident to the police at about 3:15 a.m. ...

[Rusk's friend David Carroll testified on the defendant's behalf, saying that when Rusk had left the bar at which he had met Pat, he] saw Rusk walking down the street arm-in-arm with a woman. He said "[s]he was kind of like, you know, snuggling up to him like.... She was hanging all over him then." Carroll was fairly certain that Pat was the woman....

According to Rusk, when they arrived in front of his apartment Pat parked the car and turned the engine off. They sat for several minutes "petting each other." Rusk denied switching off the ignition and removing the keys.... Rusk testified that Pat came willingly to his room and that at no time did he make threatening facial expressions.... Rusk explained that after the intercourse, Pat "got uptight."

> "Well, she started to cry. She said that—she said, 'You guys are all alike,' she says, 'just out for,' you know, 'one thing.' ..."

Rusk denied placing his hands on Pat's throat or attempting to strangle her. He also denied using force or threats of force to get Pat to have intercourse with him.

In reversing Rusk's second degree rape conviction, the Court of Special Appeals [noted that] *Hazel* ... recognized that force and lack of consent are distinct elements of the crime of rape. It said:

> "Force is an essential element of the crime and to justify a conviction, the evidence must warrant a conclusion either that the victim resisted and her resistance was overcome by force or that she was prevented from resisting by threats to her safety.... If the acts and threats of the defendant were reasonably calculated to create in the mind of the victim—having regard to the circumstances in which she was placed—a real apprehension, due to fear, of imminent bodily harm, serious enough to impair or overcome her will to resist, then such acts or threats are the equivalent of force." ...

Hazel did not expressly determine whether the victim's fear must be "reasonable." ... The vast majority of jurisdictions have required that the victim's fear be reasonably grounded in order to obviate the need for either proof of actual force on the part of the assailant or physical resistance on the part of the victim. We think that, generally, this is the correct standard....

We think the reversal of Rusk's conviction by the Court of Special Appeals was in error [for the reason that it] "trampled upon the first principle of appellate restraint ... [because it] substituted [its] own view of the evidence ... for that of the judge and jury ..." In view of the evidence adduced at the trial, the reasonableness of Pat's apprehension and fear was plainly a question of fact for the jury to determine....

Just where persuasion ends and force begins in cases like the present is fundamentally a factual issue.... Considering all the evidence in the case, with particular focus upon the actual force applied by Rusk to Pat's neck, we conclude that the jury could rationally find that the essential elements of second degree rape had been established....

■ COLE, J. dissenting:

I agree with the Court of Special Appeals that the evidence ... was insufficient to convict....

While courts no longer require a female to resist to the utmost or to resist where resistance would be foolhardy, they do require her acquiescence in the act of intercourse to stem from fear generated by something of substance. She may not simply say, "I was really scared," and thereby transform consent or mere unwillingness into submission by force. These words do not transform a seducer into a rapist. She must follow the instinct of every proud female to resist, by more than mere words, the violation of her person by a stranger or an unwelcomed friend. She must make it plain that she regards such sexual acts as abhorrent and repugnant to her natural sense of pride. She must resist unless the defendant has objectively manifested his intent to use physical force to accomplish his purpose. The law regards rape as a crime of violence. The majority today attenuates this proposition. It declares the innocence of an at best distraught young woman. It does not demonstrate the defendant's guilt of the crime of rape....

I find it incredible for the majority to conclude that on these facts, without more, a woman was *forced* to commit oral sex upon the defendant and then to engage in vaginal intercourse. In the absence of any verbal threats to do her grievous bodily harm or the display of any weapon and threat to use it, I find it difficult to understand how a victim could participate in these activities and not be willing....

This was a married woman with children.... He had not forced his way into her car; he had not taken advantage of a difference in years or a state of intoxication or mental or physical incapacity on her part. He did not grapple with her. She got out of the car, *walked with him* across the street and *followed* him up the stairs to his room. She certainly had to realize they were not going upstairs to play *Scrabble*.

Once in the room she waited while he went to the bathroom where he stayed for five minutes. In his absence, the room was lighted but she did not seek a means of escape....

Upon his return, he turned off the lights and pulled her on to the bed. There is no suggestion or inference to be drawn from her testimony that he yanked her on the bed or in any manner physically abused her by this conduct. As a matter of fact there is no suggestion by her that he bruised her or hurt her in any manner, or that the "choking" was intended to be disabling....

He did not rip her clothes off or use any greater force than was necessary to unfasten her garments....

In my judgment the State failed to prove the essential element of force beyond a reasonable doubt....

QUESTIONS AND COMMENTS

1. In thinking about the rape cases that we read it is important to separate out three distinct concerns:

First, how should we define the *act* that is criminally proscribed? Is there a distinction between criminally proscribed rape and sex that ought to be morally deplored and condemned because the person who feels victimized deeply did not want to have sex? Why might someone have unwanted sex unless she was either forced to or threatened with physical harm if she did not acquiesce? The dissenting judge in *Rusk* assumes that if Pat was not raped, she was "willing." Whether or not you believe that Pat was raped, is the dissenting judge's assumption valid that all sex that is not rape is properly described as "willing sex"?

Reflect, in this regard, on the following comments: "[W]omen are socialized to passive receptivity; may have or perceive no alternative to acquiescence; may prefer it to the escalated risk of injury and the humiliation of a lost fight; submit to survive ... Sexual intercourse may be deeply unwanted, the woman would never have initiated it, yet no force may be present." Catharine A. MacKinnon, Toward a Feminist Theory of the State 172 (1989).

Second, can the defendant be exonerated, even if he has performed the proscribed act, if he has made a *mistake of fact* (a *mental state* or *mens rea* defense), if he is unaware that he performed the proscribed act? Can he be exonerated only if his mistake of fact is reasonable, and, if so, how do we decide what sorts of mistakes *are* reasonable? Or should no mistake, however reasonable a jury might believe it to be, pose a barrier to conviction? If such "strict liability" is appropriate, is it appropriate only when the proscribed act is defined (unduly?) restrictively—e.g., as sex accomplished despite the utmost physical resistance by the victim—so that it is difficult to imagine that the defendant *could* claim he made a reasonable mistake about the victim's non-consent? (Applying the Model Penal Code rules regarding the interpretation of statutory mens rea requirements, see ch. 5, which mental state, if any, would attach to the non-consent element in the statute at issue in *Rusk*?)

The question of how to deal with mistakes regarding the presence of consent is not limited to rape cases, but arises whenever a defendant raises a consent defense. (On consent as a defense, see ch. 7.) Should it make a difference whether consent in rape cases negates an offense element or makes out a separate (justification) defense? Compare the statute at issue in *Rusk* (sexual intercourse "by force or threat of force against the will and without the consent of the other person") with Model Penal Code § 213.1(1) (sexual intercourse "by force or by threat of imminent death, serious bodily injury, extreme pain or kidnapping, to be inflicted on anyone"). According to the Model Penal Code's general consent provision, consent is a defense if it "negatives an element of the offense or precludes the infliction of the harm or evil sought to be prevented by the law defining the offense." § 2.11(1). What is the harm or evil sought to be prevented by the offense of rape?

In rape cases, should we treat mistakes regarding consent differently than mistakes regarding other offense elements? (Perhaps because we think of consent as a separate justification defense (or an excuse, if the perpetrator was reasonably mistaken about consent) upon which the defendant may have to carry the burden of proof, rather than thinking of *non*consent as an offense element that must be proved by the prosecution, and thus could be negatived?) Should we treat mistakes regarding consent in rape cases differently than in other cases—because rape is a more serious offense, because consent is more central to the wrong of rape, because consent is more difficult to determine in rape cases?

Third, how will we sort out *evidentiary* conflicts that so often arise in these cases? No matter how we define the act or the culpable mental state, witness testimony will often conflict. We will consider the first two issues (act and mental state) in detail, and consider evidentiary issues to a limited extent at the end of the chapter. But let's first highlight how these issues arise in *Rusk*.

2. *Act*. What does the majority in *Rusk* hold? That a defendant is not guilty of rape unless the victim (physically?) resists or is prevented from (physically) resisting by force or threat of physical violence? That a defendant is not guilty of rape unless the victim acquiesces only because the defendant has done things that would make a reasonable person afraid? Are these standards the same, and if not, why not? Should a defendant who threatened a woman with grievous bodily harm unless she had sexual relations with him be exonerated if he can convince the jury that she would not have physically resisted his advances—but "merely" protested instead—even if she were unafraid of violence?

Why does it matter if a reasonable woman (or most women) would be afraid in Pat's situation? Assume, simply for argument's sake, that Pat was more scared of the defendant than many other women would have been in the same situation. That *might* (in some cases? in this case?) be relevant to *his* mental state—should he have known that she submitted because she was afraid if her fear were indeed atypical—but how is it relevant to the question of whether he has committed the proscribed act? If she submitted to his sexual demands because *she* was afraid, wasn't she raped?

Why does the majority state that it is particularly important to focus on the choking? If we believe Pat had been forced to do sexual things that she would not have consented to do absent her fear of the defendant (like undressing the defendant) *before* the choking, don't we need to figure out what Rusk did to *force* (or *threaten*) her to do those things? Isn't the choking relevant at all only to corroborate her testimony that he was "scary" in ways that are not entirely easily communicated by pointing to any of his particular acts or words?

Would it be sufficient, given the Maryland statute, to convict Rusk simply because Pat expressed her desire to be taken home and her desire not to have sex many times over the course of the evening? *Should* it be sufficient? Or is Rusk entitled to "hit on" Pat persistently (at least in the sense that he won't be criminally punished if he does so and she ultimately submits to having sex), hoping she will "change her mind," so long as he doesn't either force her to do something that she does not want to do (in the sense that she literally cannot physically prevent penetration) or threaten her with violence so that she thinks it is her better, safer option to be cooperative than to continue to say "no"? At the (very narrow) moment she "chooses" to have sex, even someone threatened with a gun might be exercising her autonomous will—but isn't a person who "chooses" to have sex injured by the defendant when her option set is restricted to the choice between having unwanted sex or facing other sorts of physical harm? Compare the excuse of duress (ch. 7).

The Maryland statute in *Rusk* (and other rape statutes as well) provides that the intercourse be "against the will and without the consent of the other person"? What's the difference between these two clauses? What is consent other than concurrence of the will? Does consent here refer to an *expression* of consent so that sexual intercourse is rape if that expression is absent (either because non-consent has been expressed, or because consent hasn't been)?

3. Historically, many states convicted defendants only if the victim "resisted to the utmost" or "resisted earnestly." These sorts of formal, physical resistance requirements have all but disappeared. For a good discussion of California's legislative abolition of the resistance requirement, see People v. Barnes, 42 Cal.3d 284, 228 Cal.Rptr. 228, 721 P.2d 110 (1986) (noting, among other things, that requiring resistance might subject victims to the risk of further violence from their attackers and that resistance is an imperfect proxy for nonconsent, noting that "the presence of resistance may well be probative on the issue of force or nonconsent [but] its absence may not [be]"). Nonetheless, implicit expectations about (physical) resistance may still affect practice: victims may be more likely to report, prosecutors may well be far more prone to prosecute and juries far more likely to convict when there is (physical) resistance.

Note, though, that if one believes Pat's account of their encounter, she clearly *has* resisted having sex in any number of ways, even if she has not fought. In the car, she does so in a way that she doubtless feels is least likely to anger a man she doesn't know well, but might be dangerous if angry: she tells him that she *couldn't* go to his apartment even if she wanted to, given her marital situation. In the apartment, she asks him to let her go home any number of times. There is a good deal of evidence that physical resistance can be an effective strategy—and may well be less risky in terms of inducing higher levels of brutal violence by rapists than is commonly thought. For a summary of this evidence, see Michelle Anderson,

"Reviving Resistance in Rape Law," 1998 U. Ill. L. Rev. 953. Still, there is little doubt that the sorts of verbal strategies Pat employed may be effective as well, at least on some occasions.

4. Distinct act requirements may be linked to distinct conceptions of *provable* mens rea. Thus, one could imagine defending the historical requirement that defendants have not committed a culpable act unless they overcome the victim's resistance by arguing that one cannot be sure beyond a reasonable doubt that the defendant knew or should have known that the victim did not consent to sex unless she resisted: If that were the case, the "real" proscribed act would be nonconsensual sex, not sex achieved by overcoming resistance, but worries about proof of mental state would lead us to narrow the definition. Similarly, one might defend still-common requirements that only sex achieved through force or threats of violence is rape by arguing that it is only in those situations that we can establish that the defendant made no reasonable mistakes of fact about non-consent.

On the other hand, one could imagine arguing that the defendant should be guilty of rape unless sex follows an explicit verbal permission to have sex even though we might believe, substantively, that some sexual encounters are perfectly consensual even though the woman did not verbally assent to sex. (Thus, just as demanding resistance is *underinclusive* if our real substantive goal is to punish *all* non-consensual sex, punishing all sex that occurs without explicit formal verbal assent is *overinclusive* if our goal is to punish *only* nonconsensual sex.) But we might argue that unless they learn (by threat of criminal sanction) to get formal verbal assent, men will never really know what women want: only this standard will adequately diminish mistakes of fact. Naturally, we would assume that women who did not feel violated—even though they had not formally verbally assented to sex—would not (typically? ever?) bring complaints to the authorities. Is that answer good enough? (Of course, as we will note later, it is possible to mix-and-match these theories: one might instruct fact finders to convict only if they believe that the sex is nonconsensual and *then* to reject any mental state/mistake of fact defenses unless the defendant received explicit verbal assent to his sexual demands. This is part of the problem we need to deal with in the section on mental state: if only reasonable mistakes of fact exculpate, how do we *define* a reasonable mistake?)

Furthermore, one might believe, substantively, that a man rapes a woman if he has sex that she does not affirmatively desire, but believe that it would not be feasible to have trials that could resolve defendant claims that they were unaware—and reasonably unaware—of the woman's actual distaste.

5. In his dissent, Judge Cole remarks, sarcastically, that a grown woman would know that if one goes to a man's apartment late at night, one isn't going there "to play *Scrabble*." Assume, just for argument's sake, that Pat chose, without constraint, to accompany the defendant to his apartment, and that she in no way did so because she was afraid not to. What is Judge Cole's point? That going to a man's apartment is a conventional social signal of willingness to have sex? That might well be *descriptively* wrong—and might be even more blatantly descriptively wrong in some sub-

cultural settings than others (e.g., among late adolescents and young adults living at colleges with coed dorms)—but what if it were descriptively right? Is Judge Cole suggesting that one forfeits the right to the criminal law's protection from forced sex once one has signaled, at some point, that one is (likely) willing to have sex? That the defendant could not possibly know, or be reasonably expected to realize, that a woman is unwilling to have sex if she has given some prior signal of willingness? That men are so sexually out-of-control that once they expect to have sexual relations in a given evening, it is unfair to expect them to stop themselves?

6. *Mens Rea.* Glanville Williams, among others, has argued that it will rarely matter whether we require that a defendant be consciously aware that the victim is not consenting or allow conviction instead upon a finding that a reasonable person *should have been aware* of the victim's nonconsent, except in cases in which the defendant is either extremely cognitively impaired or inebriated (so that he misunderstands what Williams imagines to be inevitably clear signals of nonconsent). See Glanville Williams, Letter to The Times (London), May 8, 1975. This may be true in the classic "stranger-jumping-out-of-the-bushes" rape, but is it true in cases like *Rusk*? What evidence is there that Rusk himself is not subjectively aware that Pat did not consent to sex, even assuming that you believe that a reasonable person would have been?

Assume instead that you were defending Rusk in a jurisdiction in which only a reasonable mistake of fact suffices to exculpate: what evidence would you point to if you wanted to claim that Rusk was reasonable in mistakenly believing that Pat did not submit to oral sex and intercourse because she was afraid? If you were prosecuting the case, what evidence would you point to in saying that he was unreasonable?

7. One might defend the substantive requirement articulated in *Rusk*—that the defendant is not guilty unless he took steps that would put a reasonable woman in fear—by reference to provable mental states: our best default assumption, in many cases, might be that a reasonable defendant assumes that what is in the victim's mind is what would be in most women's minds. But isn't that assumption manifestly false in *Rusk*, at least if we credit Pat's testimony? Doesn't Rusk know things about what *Pat* is thinking, without having to infer that she must be thinking what other women would typically think? See in this regard, the (rather atypical) holding in People v. Iniguez, 872 P.2d 1183 (Cal. 1994) (rape conviction can be sustained even if the victim's fear is unreasonable so long as "the perpetrator knew of the victim's subjective fear and took advantage of it").

8. It might seem, at first blush, that no defendant could make a mistake—much less a reasonable one—about whether he had forced a woman to have sex or threatened her with physical violence. If that were the case, it might seem sensible that rape would be a "strict liability crime" (at least if the act requirement includes the presence of force or physical threat). Look carefully at *Rusk*, though: what act do you believe is *really* the most threatening act that the defendant took (particularly if one is skeptical of the majority's conclusion that it is "choking")? Is it possible that Rusk did not know that *this* act was threatening? That a reasonable person in his position might not have known that it was threatening, either

in this case, or more abstractly, in some other case, in which the woman's subsequent conduct revealed less fear than Pat claims to have revealed?

9. What significance should be attached to the *victim's* state of mind? Is it rape if the victim perceives the sexual encounter as rape? What if the defendant's actions could not reasonably be perceived as amounting to "forcible compulsion"? What if the defendant didn't intend them to be so perceived?

On this point, compare People v. Evans, 85 Misc.2d 1088 (N.Y. Sup. Ct. 1975), with People v. Thompson, 72 N.Y.2d 410 (1988). In *Evans*, the defendant ("a bachelor of approximately thirty-seven years of age, aptly described in the testimony as 'glib' ") used various false pretenses (most importantly, the claim that he was a psychologist doing interviews for a magazine article) to induce the victim ("a twenty-year-old petite, attractive second-year student at Wellesley College, an unworldly girl, evidently unacquainted with New York City and the sophisticated city ways, a girl who proved to be, as indicated by the testimony, incredibly gullible, trusting and naïve") to enter a New York City apartment, where the following occurred:

> She had been there for one to two hours when the defendant made his move and pulled her on to the opened sofa-bed in the living room of that apartment and attempted to disrobe her. She resisted that.... At that point, the defendant's tactics, according to her testimony, appeared to have changed. First, he informed her of his disappointment that she had failed the test, that this was all part of his psychological experiment, that, in fact, this was a way in which he was trying to reach her innermost consciousness, one of the ways in which that could be done. Then, after expressing disappointment in the failure of this psychological experiment, he took steps to cause doubt and fear to arise in the mind of Miss Peterson. He said, 'Look where you are. You are in the apartment of a strange man. How do you know that I am really who I say I am? How do you know that I am really a psychologist?' Then, he went on and said, "I could kill you. I could rape you. I could hurt you physically."
>
> Miss Peterson testified that at that point she became extremely frightened, that she realized, indeed, how vulnerable she was. The defendant did not strike her, did not beat her, he exhibited no weapons at the time, but he made the statement, "I could kill you; I could rape you."
>
> Then there was yelling and screaming, ... and then an abrupt switch in which the defendant attempted to play on the sympathy of Miss Peterson by telling her a story about his lost love, how Miss Peterson had reminded him of her, and the hurt that he had sustained when she had driven her car off a cliff. Obviously, Miss Peterson's sympathy was engaged, and at that time acting instinctively, she took a step forward and reached out for him and put her hand on his shoulders, and then he grabbed her and said, "You're mine, you are mine." There thereupon followed an act of sexual intercourse, an act of oral-genital contact; a half-hour later a second act of sexual inter-

course, and then, before she left, about seven o'clock that morning, an additional act.

The court acquitted the defendant after a bench trial on the following grounds:

> Of course, it is entirely possible that Miss Peterson, who heard the statements, construed that as a threat, even though it may not have been intended as such by the person who uttered those words. The question arises as to which is the controlling state of mind—that of a person who hears the words and interprets them as a threat, or the state of mind of the person who utters such words. It appears to the Court that the controlling state of mind must be that of the speaker. She, the hearer, may, in fact, take the words as a threat and be terrified by them. . . . But this being a criminal trial, it is basic that the criminal intent of the defendant must be shown beyond a reasonable doubt. It is his intent when he acts, his intent when he speaks, which must therefore be controlling. And so, if he utters words which are taken as a threat by the person who hears them, but are not intended as a threat by the person who utters them, there would be no basis for finding the necessary criminal intent to establish culpability under the law.
>
> So where a statement is ambiguous, where the words and the acts which purport to constitute force or threats are susceptible of diverse interpretations, which may be consistent with either guilt or innocence, the Court, as the trier of the facts, cannot say beyond a reasonable doubt that the guilt of the defendant has been established with respect to the crime of rape.

In *Thompson,* decided thirteen years later, the court upheld the conviction in a prison rape case under the following facts:

> The defendant, a 35-year-old male, was housed in one of the adult tiers. . . . [The victim was only 16 years old and a novice to the world of incarceration.] The victim testified that he was about five feet, six inches tall and weighed approximately 120 pounds. He estimated that defendant was six feet tall and weighed about 180 pounds.
>
> Defendant called to the victim through the bars separating the catwalk from the rest of the tier. The victim exited his cell and approached the bars. Defendant then stated that he wanted the victim to perform an act of oral sex. When the victim refused, defendant issued the threats which are the focus of this appeal. According to the victim:
>
> "[H]e started to threaten me and say he could have people kick my ass if I didn't do it. He told me that anything could happen to me if I walked off the tier. It could happen anywhere, he said. I could get beat up anywhere, it could even be somebody on the tier if he wanted to. He said that he could put the word out on me if he wanted to and he could have anybody kick my ass. [H]e said it was a matter of trusting him and if I did it with him I wouldn't have to worry about it. I wouldn't have to be worried about being bothered again and if I didn't do it, that, you know, the same thing would happen. He would make sure I would have a rough time while I was there."

> Following these threats, the victim complied with defendant's requests.... During the entire incident the two remained on opposite sides of the bars of the catwalk.

In affirming the conviction, the court explained that

> [t]he impossibility or improbability of the defendant's assertions may be relevant considerations for the fact finder in determining whether the victim was actually placed in fear or whether the defendant intended such an effect. But the fact that a court may, in hindsight, determine that the threats were incapable of being executed cannot transform the victim's submission to them into consent. As the drafters of the Model Penal Code noted, "It seems clear * * * that one who takes advantage of [a victim's] unreasonable fears of violence should not escape punishment any more than a swindler who cheats gullible people by false statements which they should have found incredible. Neither the blameworthiness of the actor nor the gravity of the insult to the victim is ameliorated by a finding that the threat was implausible or that the actor lacked capacity to carry it out" (ALI, Model Penal Code and Commentaries § 213.1, at 310). ... Thus, the proper question is not whether the defendant was capable of carrying out his threats, but rather whether the jury could reasonably infer that those threats placed the victim in fear of "immediate death or serious physical injury".

Can *Thompson* be squared with *Evans*?

10. *Evidence*. Note that in *Rusk* there are many clashes in the testimony over both unquestionably relevant facts—for example, did Rusk remove the keys from the car or not?—as well as facts that might be probative of the credibility of testimony over obviously material facts—for instance, did the defendant and Pat engage in "heavy petting" in the car?

Factual controversies are obviously present outside the context of rape cases as well, but, historically, there seemed to be more (undue?) worry about the problem of mistaken convictions in this area than others. For instance, rape prosecutions could be defeated if the prosecutrix did not complain promptly. See, e.g., State v. Anderson, 137 N.W.2d 781 (Minn. 1965). Pat, the victim in *Rusk*, did report the incident to the police immediately, but should that matter?

B. SUBSTANTIVE ISSUES: THE PROSCRIBED ACT

1. VARIETIES OF "COERCIVE" SEX

a. Force or Fear of Violence vs. Nonconsensual Sex vs. Sex Without Affirmative Consent

Commonwealth v. Berkowitz

Supreme Court of Pennsylvania.
537 Pa. 143, 641 A.2d 1161 (1994).

■ CAPPY, J.

The complainant, a female college student, left her class, went to her dormitory room where she drank a martini, and then went to a lounge to await her boyfriend. When her boyfriend failed to appear, she went to another dormitory to find a friend.... She knocked on the door, but received no answer ... entered the room and discovered a man [she originally believed to be her friend, but who turned out to be Appellee] asleep on the bed. Appellee asked her to stay for a while and she agreed. He requested a back-rub and she declined. He suggested that she sit on the bed, but she declined and sat on the floor.

Appellee then moved to the floor beside her, lifted up her shirt and bra and massaged her breasts.... They both stood up, and he locked the door. He returned to push her onto the bed, and removed her undergarments from one leg. He then penetrated her.... [Afterward] he stated, "Wow, I guess we just got carried away," to which she responded, "No, we didn't get carried away, you got carried away."

The crime of rape is defined as follows:

§ 3121. Rape

A person commits a felony of the first degree when he engages in sexual intercourse with another person not one's spouse: (1) by forcible compulsion; [or] (2) by threat of forcible compulsion that would prevent resistance by a person of reasonable resolution....

The victim of rape need not resist. "The force necessary to support a conviction of rape ... need only be such as to establish lack of consent and to induce the [victim] to submit without additional resistance." ... Commonwealth v. Rhodes, 510 A.2d 1217 (1986).

In regard to the issue of forcible compulsion, the complainant's testimony is devoid of any statement which clearly or adequately describes the use of force or the threat of force against her.... When asked, "Is it possible that [Appellee] was not making any physical contact with you ... aside from attempting to untie the knot [in the drawstrings of complainant's sweatpants]," she answered, "It's possible." She testified that "He put me down on the bed. It was kind of like—He didn't throw me down on the bed," ... and further detailed that their movement to the bed "wasn't slow like a romantic kind of thing, but it wasn't a fast shove either. It was kind of in the middle." She agreed that Appellee's hands were not restraining her in any manner during the actual penetration, and that the weight of his body on top of her was the only force applied. She testified that at no time did Appellee verbally threaten her. The complainant did testify that she sought to leave the room, and said "no" throughout the encounter. As to the complainant's desire to leave the room, the record clearly demonstrates that the door could be unlocked quite easily from the inside, that she was aware of this fact, but that she never attempted to go to the door or unlock it.

As to the complainant's testimony that she stated "no" throughout the encounter with Appellee, we point out that, while such an allegation of fact would be relevant to the issue of consent, it is not relevant to the issue of force....

[W]e find it instructive that in defining the related but distinct crime of "indecent assault" under 18 Pa. Cons. Stat. § 3126, the Legislature did not employ the phrase "forcible compulsion" but rather chose to define indecent assault as "indecent contact with another ... without the consent of the other person." ...

The evidence described above is clearly sufficient to support the jury's conviction of indecent assault....

[T]he order of the Superior Court reversing the rape conviction is affirmed.

State in the Interest of M.T.S.

New Jersey Supreme Court.
129 N.J. 422, 609 A.2d 1266 (1992).

■ HANDLER, J.

Under New Jersey law a person who commits an act of sexual penetration using physical force or coercion is guilty of second-degree sexual assault. The sexual assault statute does not define the words "physical force." The question posed by this appeal is whether the element of "physical force" is met simply by an act of non-consensual penetration involving no more force than necessary to accomplish that result.

That issue is presented in the context of what is often referred to as "acquaintance rape." The record in the case discloses that the juvenile, a seventeen-year-old boy, engaged in consensual kissing and heavy petting with a fifteen-year-old girl and thereafter engaged in actual sexual penetration of the girl to which she had not consented. There was no evidence of suggestion that the juvenile used any unusual or extra force or threats to accomplish the acts of penetration. The trial court determined that the juvenile was delinquent for committing a sexual assault. The Appellate Division reversed the disposition of delinquency, concluding that non-consensual penetration does not constitute sexual assault unless it is accompanied by some level of force more than that necessary to accomplish the penetration....

... C.G. testified that she awoke [on the night of the incident] at approximately 1:30 A.M. and saw M.T.S. fully clothed, standing in her doorway. According to C.G., M.T.S. said, "he was going to tease [her] a little bit." C.G. testified that she "didn't think anything of it"; she used the bathroom and returned to bed, falling into a "heavy" sleep within fifteen minutes. The next event C.G. claimed to recall was waking up with M.T.S. on top of her, her underpants and shorts removed. She said "his penis was [inside her vagina]." As soon as C.G. realized what had happened, she said, she immediately slapped M.T.S. once in the face, then "told him to get off, and get out." She did not scream or cry out. She testified that M.T.S. complied in less than one minute after being struck....

M.T.S. testified that at exactly 1:15 A.M. on May 22, he entered C.G.'s bedroom as she was walking to the bathroom. He said C.G. soon returned from the bathroom, and the two began "kissing and all," eventually moving to the bed. Once they were in bed, they undressed each other and proceeded to engage in sexual intercourse. According to M.T.S. "[he thrust] three times, and then the fourth time ... that's when [she] pulled [him] off of her." M.T.S. said that as C.G. pushed him off, she said, "stop, get off," and he "hopped off right away." ...

[The trial judge] concluded that the victim had consented to a session of kissing and heavy petting with M.T.S. The trial court did not find that C.G. had been sleeping at the time of penetration, but nevertheless found that she had not consented to the actual sexual act....

N.J. Stat. Ann. § 2C:14–2c(1) defines "sexual assault as the commission of 'sexual penetration' with the use of 'physical force or coercion.'[1] Both the act of 'sexual penetration' and the use of 'physical force or coercion' are separate and distinct elements of the offense ..."

The parties offer two alternative understandings of the concept of "physical force" as it is used in the statute. The State would read "physical force" to entail any amount of sexual touching brought about involuntarily. A showing of sexual penetration coupled with a lack of consent would satisfy the elements of the statute. The Public Defender urges an interpretation of "physical force" to mean force "used to overcome lack of consent." That definition equates force with violence and leads to the conclusion that sexual assault requires the application of some amount of force in addition to the act of penetration....

The Legislature's concept of sexual assault and the role of force was significantly colored by its understanding of the law of assault and battery.... Thus, just as any unauthorized touching is a crime under traditional laws of assault and battery, so is any unauthorized sexual contact a crime under the reformed law of criminal sexual contact, and so is any unauthorized sexual penetration a crime under the reformed law of sexual assault.

The understanding of sexual assault as a criminal battery, albeit one with especially serious consequences, follows necessarily from the Legislature's decision to eliminate non-consent and resistance from the substantive definition of the offense. Under the new law, the victim no longer is required to resist and therefore need not have said or done anything in order for the sexual penetration to be unlawful.... [A]n interpretation of the statutory crime of sexual assault to require physical force in addition to that entailed in an act of involuntary or unwanted sexual penetration would be fundamentally inconsistent with the legislative purpose to eliminate any consideration of whether the victim resisted or expressed non-consent ...

We conclude, therefore, that any act of sexual penetration engaged in by the defendant without the affirmative and freely-given permission of the victim to the specific act of penetration constitutes the offense of sexual assault ... Under the reformed statute, permission to engage in sexual

1. The sexual assault statute ... reads as follows:

c. An actor is guilty of sexual assault if he commits an act of sexual penetration with another person under any one of the following circumstances:

(1) The actor *uses physical force or coercion*, but the victim does not sustain severe personal injuries....

penetration must be affirmative and it must be given freely, but that permission may be inferred either from acts or statements reasonably viewed in light of the surrounding circumstances. Persons need not, of course, expressly announce their consent to engage in intercourse for there to be affirmative permission. Permission to engage in an act of sexual penetration can be and often is indicated through physical actions rather than words. Permission is demonstrated when the evidence, in whatever form, is sufficient to demonstrate that a reasonable person would have believed that the alleged victim had affirmatively and freely given authorization to the act.

... Although it is possible to imagine a set of rules in which persons must demonstrate affirmatively that sexual contact is unwanted or not permitted, such a regime would be inconsistent with modern principles of personal autonomy.

... The decision to engage in sexual relations with another person is one of the most private and intimate decisions a person can make. Each person has the right not only to decide whether to engage in sexual contact with another, but also to control the circumstances and character of that contact....

In a case such as this one, in which the State does not allege violence or force extrinsic to the act of penetration, the factfinder must decide whether the defendant's act of penetration was undertaken in circumstances that led the defendant reasonably to believe that the alleged victim had freely given affirmative permission to the specific act of sexual penetration.... [T]he law places no burden on the alleged victim to have expressed non-consent or to have denied permission, and no inquiry is made into what he or she thought or desired or why he or she did not resist or protest.

We acknowledge that cases such as this are inherently fact sensitive.... We conclude that the record provides reasonable support for the trial court's disposition.

b. Non-Violent Threats and the Threat/Offer Line

Commonwealth v. Mlinarich

Supreme Court of Pennsylvania.
518 Pa. 247, 542 A.2d 1335 (1988).

■ NIX, C.J.

In the instant appeal we have agreed to consider the Commonwealth's contention that the threats made by an adult guardian to a fourteen-year-old girl to cause her to be recommitted to a juvenile detention facility supplies the "forcible compulsion" elements of the crime of rape. For the reasons that follow, we are constrained to conclude that they do not....

... There has never been any question that the gravamen of the crimes of rape and the later statutory offense of involuntary deviate sexual intercourse was their non-volitional quality.... [T]he adjective "forceful" was employed to establish that the assault must be upon the will.... The critical distinction is where the compulsion overcomes the will of the victim in contrast to a situation where the victim can make a deliberate choice to avoid the encounter even though the alternative may be an undesirable one. Indeed, the victim in this instance apparently found the prospect of being returned to the detention home a repugnant one. Notwithstanding she was left with a choice and therefore the submission was a result of a deliberate choice and was not an involuntary act. This is not in any way to deny the despicable nature of the appellee's conduct or even to suggest that it was not criminal. We are merely constrained to recognize that it does not meet the test of "forcible compulsion" set forth in ... [section 3121 (quoted in *Berkowitz*, supra)]....

In reaching its conclusion that the charges of rape and attempted rape were not established, the majority of the Superior Court erroneously inferred that the term "forcible compulsion" required physical violence. As we have indicated, the term "forcible compulsion" was employed to convey that the result produced must be non-voluntary rather than to describe the character of force itself. Certainly, psychological coercion can be applied with such intensity that it may overpower the will to resist as effectively as physical force.... [D]ifficult choices have a coercive effect but the result is the product of the reason, albeit unpleasant and reluctantly made. The fact cannot be escaped that the victim has made the choice and the act is not involuntary....

■ LARSEN, J., dissenting.

Threatening to have her placed in physical confinement unless she complied with his demands, Joseph Mlinarich, at sixty-three years of age, engaged in sustained, systematic sexual abuse of a fourteen-year-old child with low mental abilities, despite her continual crying, her pain and her pleading with him to stop.... The jury called these acts rape and attempted rape. The Opinion in Support of Affirmance says the jury was wrong because a person of reasonable resolution would have withstood Mlinarich's threats and advances, and would hold that this fourteen-year-old child voluntarily consented to have sexual intercourse with the sixty-three-year-old Mlinarich of her own free will and volition.

... Has civilization fallen so far, have our values become so distorted and misplaced, as to leave a fourteen-year-old child without protection when she is forced to make such an awful "choice"? ...

One wonders what is the "prescribed level of intensity designed to have an effect upon the will of the victim" ... that will satisfy the criteria of those who would affirm the Superior Court.... If a male judge calls a female litigant into his chambers, and tells her that he will find her in contempt of court and have her thrown in jail unless she has intercourse with him, and she complies, would such compulsion reach the majority's "prescribed level of intensity"? ...

Model Penal Code § 213.1(2). Gross Sexual Imposition.

A male who has sexual intercourse with a female not his wife commits a felony of the third degree if: (a) he compels her to submit by any threat that would prevent resistance by a woman of ordinary resolution....

Model Penal Code § 213.1(1). Rape.

A male who has sexual intercourse with a female ... is guilty of rape if:

(a) he compels her to submit by force or by threat of imminent death, serious bodily injury, extreme pain or kidnapping, to be inflicted on anyone....

Rape is a felony of the second degree unless (i) in the course thereof the actor inflicts serious bodily injury upon anyone, or (ii) the victim was not a voluntary social companion of the actor upon the occasion of the crime and had not previously permitted him sexual liberties, in which cases the offense is a felony of the first degree.

State v. Hilton, 1991 WL 168608 (Tenn. Crim. App. 1991).

[The court reversed a conviction for rape. The prosecutor had argued that the defendant had demanded that his seventeen-year-old adopted stepdaughter have sex with him in exchange "for permission to go places, to do things, or get things." The court noted that the Tennessee rape statute plainly permitted convictions of defendants who used coercion, including extortion, to accomplish sexual penetration but stated that she had not been coerced by a threat. Instead ...] "she wanted the defendant to buy her something. [S]ex was the price she paid for receiving things which her sisters did not have."

c. Problems of Application: Applying Existing Law, Thinking about "Ideal" Law, and Considering Alternatives to the Use of the Criminal Sanction

In looking at the following Problem, set aside issues of evidence (treat everything the narrator says as absolutely accurate) and set aside issues of mental state or mistake as well (assume that the person with whom the narrator had sexual contact knew everything that the narrator felt). Focus solely on questions of whether the act would be proscribed, or should be.

Problem

"I was going to a party at a fraternity. One of my girl friends had gone to high school with one of the guys from the frat, though they barely knew each other, and she had set it up that he'd be my escort for before the party. We got along fine, but truth is, we didn't really get to know each other all that well. Before the "real" party, we were drinking champagne with a big group of friends and weren't that focused on each other. Then, at the party, for the first half of the evening, I didn't even see him.

I don't even remember exactly how it is that I got back in touch with him. But I remember that we were dancing at some point, probably about midnight. Then he kissed me. I was uncomfortable because we were on the dance floor, but everyone was really drunk, and no one really seemed to notice. Also, I was happy because I felt social and attractive and because I'm quiet, I usually don't meet guys at parties. We went outside and were kissing. Then we went to his room.

As soon as I got there, I felt a little uncomfortable. I wasn't sure I wanted to be there. I was attracted to him, and I basically liked his personality. I did want to keep kissing him, but I felt kind of slutty being in this frat guy's bed. Then things started moving faster and that was okay. But in a sense I didn't want to be there anymore, though I felt obligated. I didn't feel like I could just stop things. Then he got up and went to his dresser—I assume to get a condom. I told him I didn't want things to go too far. That was fine. We started talking then, about how we had gotten in such a situation ... that we had both been drunk.... We started talking and finally got to know a little more about each other; where we came from, what classes we liked and disliked, that kind of stuff. I did think he was interesting, attractive etc.

Still though, I was looking for a way out. I said I wanted to go home but he suggested we take a nap. I just wanted to get out of there, but I could hear his roommate moving around in the outside room, and I didn't want anyone to know I was there. We fell asleep for a while, then when I woke up he had an erection. I indicated I wanted to go home, but he kept kissing me. I felt worn down, that I could only resist so long. I knew I should just say stop and leave, but I just couldn't. I didn't know him. I ended up giving him a blow job because I knew the situation would just be prolonged until he came. Then he walked me home."

Assume that the standards for sexual battery and rape—in terms of consent, force, etc.—are precisely parallel. (Thus, the fact that there was oral sex rather than intercourse, and hence that this would not be rape, on that account alone, in most, but not all, jurisdictions, shouldn't end your inquiry as to whether a crime occurred here. For instance, § 750.520a(o) of the Michigan Penal Code states that " 'Sexual penetration' means sexual intercourse, cunnilingus, fellatio, anal intercourse, or any other intrusion, however slight, of any part of a person's body or of any object into the genital or anal openings of another person's body, but emission of semen is not required.")

Would the case get to the jury under the standard articulated in *Berkowitz*?

Would the case get to the jury under the standard articulated in *M.T.S.*?

Should the case get to the jury in your view? If you were a juror, how would you be predisposed to decide the case?

Assume, at least for purposes of this last set of questions, that you think this is not a case of sexual battery (or rape). How can you define sexual battery/rape so as to exclude this case while including other cases you think ought to be included? For instance, if you were to try to draw a line that exonerated the defendant in this case but convicted given the trial court's version of the facts in *M.T.S.*, how might one draw it? What sorts of jury instructions do you think would be appropriate?

If this conduct isn't criminal, is it nonetheless problematic? Should it be dealt with through civil suits? Techniques other than formal sanctions of any kind? If the victim has been, in some sense "coerced," why isn't it criminal? If she hasn't been "coerced," why isn't this interaction perfectly fine? Is the concept of "coercion" really useful? Are questions about whether the narrator had "free will" useful? Questions about whether she was adequately empowered? Questions about whether this event injured her?

QUESTIONS AND COMMENTS

1. Look at how the courts interpreted their state's rape statutes in *Berkowitz* and *M.T.S.* Are you persuaded by the Pennsylvania court's inference in *Berkowitz* that "mere nonconsent" was insufficient to predicate conviction under the rape statute because the indecent assault statute makes no reference to forcible compulsion? Why do you believe there is no force requirement in the indecent assault statement? Is that statute likely a product of feminist reform, or does it simply contemplate factual scenarios in which force is unlikely to be an issue?

How about the New Jersey court's efforts at statutory interpretation in *M.T.S.?* If the judges are correct that the only force that must be proven in New Jersey is the force inherent in penetration, isn't the statute that they cite hopelessly jumbled and redundant? Why would the legislature say that a person is guilty of sexual assault when he commits an act of sexual penetration under the circumstance that he uses physical force (or coercion) if he is always using physical force whenever he commits an act of sexual penetration?

2. The court in *M.T.S.* may or may not be reading statutory *language* in a strained way, but the judges are also attempting to read statutory *purpose*: they appear both to be making an effort to effectuate the legislature's intent to protect sexual autonomy to the maximum degree possible and to align rape law with traditional battery law. In doing so, the opinion emphasizes two (quite distinct) points. First, the complainant must *manifest consent* (either in words or in acts). Second, even if she manifests consent at some point before the moment of sexual penetration, the consent must be "freely given."

The *M.T.S.* court doesn't get to the second issue, because it affirms the trial court's finding that the complainant did not manifest consent in words or deeds. (Would we have to face that second issue in our Problem? Why?) Does the court give us adequate guidance as to how fact finders should make such judgments? Obviously, if we demanded verbal assent, we could (given ordinary limits on our capacity to judge witness credibility) *know* whether the victim had consented. And we could know that she did *not* manifest consent "through her deeds" if she were physically precluded from preventing sexual penetration. But does the court give enough guidance for cases (like *M.T.S.*?) in which the complainant could (alternatively) be described as physically "acquiescent," passively resistant, or cooperative but unengaged? Do rape law reforms nominally abolishing the force requirement in favor of a nonconsent requirement mean anything if (some? all?) fact finders believe that women manifest consent in deeds by acquiescing in their penetration *unless* the woman is physically constrained or threatened with violence?

Would it be sufficient to say that at least so long as the woman *says* "no," it is rape if the man persists in his efforts to have sexual relations? But isn't there a time frame problem: what if the complainant says "no" at midnight and the sex occurs at one in the morning? Doesn't she have the right to "change her mind"? Might the *M.T.S.* court have held that while assent in "deed" may be sufficient if there's *never* been a verbal no, that once a woman has *said* no, she can only "undo" the effect of that "no" through a verbal yes. Consider in this regard Robin Weiner's comments:

> The woman, who believes that she *has* conveyed her lack of consent, may interpret the man's persistence as an indication that he does not care if she objects and plans to have sex despite her lack of consent. She may then feel frightened by the man's persistence, and may submit against her will.

See Robin D. Weiner, "Shifting the Communication Burden: A Meaningful Consent Standard in Rape," 6 Harv. Women's L.J. 143, 149 (1983).

What if the court had decided that the complainant *had* manifested consent? Is there anything in the *M.T.S.* opinion that would help us decide whether the assent was freely given? Does *M.T.S.* have any implications for cases like *Mlinarich*? What if the girl in *Mlinarich* had not cried or protested but cooperated physically, keeping her suffering, pain and revulsion hidden?

3. One can certainly imagine requiring that consent must be manifest in words (for all partners? for those who have not had prior voluntary sexual relations?).

Look, for instance, at the Antioch College Sexual Offense Prevention Policy (SOPP):

> "Consent" is defined as the act of willingly and verbally agreeing to engage in specific sexual conduct. Previously agreed upon forms of non-verbal communication are appropriate methods for expressing consent.... The person who initiates sexual conduct is responsible for verbally asking for the "consent" of the individual(s) involved. "Consent" must be obtained with each new level of sexual conduct. The person with whom sexual conduct is initiated must verbally express "consent" or lack of "consent." Silence conveys a lack of consent. If at any time consent is withdrawn, the conduct must stop immediately.

Would women, as a matter of substance, be substantially more empowered in heterosexual relationships if such verbal formality were required? Would the narrator in the Problem have been more likely to avoid an unwanted sexual contact if the young man had had to ask her explicitly what she wanted to do and wait for her to *say* that she wanted (or was willing to engage in?) a particular sexual contact? Or would we demand verbally explicit assent only to reduce the occasions on which men mistakenly believed that women were consenting to sex when they weren't?

Presumably, even if the criminal law *seems* to *demand* that all sexual partners wait for verbal assent, some (many?) won't; many of those who don't, though, won't seem the least bit like rapists. (The woman might have welcomed the sexual overture or the physical contact might have been mutually initiated.) Is that troublesome only if some women (in bad faith?

to vindicate the norm demanding verbal explicitness even though they did not follow it themselves?) bring charges in situations in which they were perfectly willing to have sex? Or is it problematic even if literally every woman is in perfectly good faith and complains to the authorities *only* in situations in which she had sex against her desires at the time? Is there a difference between liability for acts that meet the definition of rape and liability for "being a rapist"? Is "being a rapist" an additional prerequisite for criminal liability, or an independent ground for punishment?

4. Judge Larsen, dissenting in *Mlinarich*, makes reference to a hypothetical trial court judge who threatens a woman with (presumably unjustified) jail time unless she has sex with him. Should it make any difference if imposing the jail time were legally justified, but within his discretionary power to withhold? Note that the defendant in *Mlinarich* was under no legal obligation to continue to act as the victim's foster parent; as a matter of fact, she would indeed go back to the juvenile detention center if he (and his wife) stopped serving as her guardian, but it is not clear that it would be apt to say that the defendant had the power to "send" her to detention.

Some argue that the concept of "coercion" is parasitic on conceptions of prior entitlement: a person, in that view, is coerced if (and only if) forced to elect between an unwanted outcome and the violation of a prior right. If this were an adequate account of our intuitions about coercion—and if intuitions about coercion explained all of our intuitions about rape, or about the distinction between welcome and unwelcome sex—then it might matter a great deal if the woman chose between sex and a deserved prison term or sex and an *undeserved* one.

Letting *everything* turn on rights violations will plainly be overinclusive, though: we would not think a person had been coerced (in ways relevant either to extortion law or rape) if someone said, for instance, "Give me your money (have sex with me) or I will trespass on your property for ten seconds."

Far more important, focusing on rights violations might be underinclusive as well. A heroin addict goes to her usual dealer: he says that he will not sell her the drugs he typically sells her unless she has intercourse with him. Plainly, she is not legally *entitled* to the drugs. Has he nonetheless done something the dissenters in *Mlinarich* would describe as rape if she submits to his sexual demands?

Men aggressively seeking sex may well tell the women they are dating that their refusal to have sex belies their "immaturity," or "prudishness," or the fact that they are "teases." It is possible to interpret the men's behavior in terms of threats and offers—"sleep with me or I will call you a tease" sounds like a threat under some conceptions, "sleep with me and I will not call you a tease" sounds like an offer under some conceptions—but it is not clear that men in these situations are really putting women to that sort of explicit election (in the way the defendant in *Mlinarich* put the complainant to an election between two bad outcomes). But, if she finds his taunts unpleasant, he has plainly changed the "desirability" of acquiescing to his sexual demands compared to how desirable acquiescence would be if he had desisted from taunting. Of course, it is *worse* to be physically injured than taunted if one sticks to one's predisposition to refuse demands for undesired sexual intimacy, but why should the criminal law not protect women against facing *any* needless bad consequences from acting on their sexual principles and desires?

5. Figuring out precisely when it is appropriate to describe people as coerced is one of the most challenging topics in both philosophy and law. It is of great moment not only in criminal law (most obviously in relationship to the offenses of extortion and rape, but also to the *defense* of duress), but in *contract law* as well. Ascertaining when an agreement is or is not a product of "duress" is central not only to the project of distinguishing enforceable from non-enforceable promises but justifying a regime in which we support the practice of making agreements because exchange ostensibly benefits both contracting parties. For an excellent general discussion of the difficulties of defining coercion, see Alan Wertheimer, Coercion 192–241 (1987). Here is Barbara Fried's summary of the conventional Legal Realist position, most forcefully articulated by Robert Hale, on the inevitability of "coercion" in seemingly "voluntary" exchanges:

> When [traditional economists] extolled the market as a sphere of freedom, they focused only on the moment of choice, embodied in the contract, to give up what one already had in favor of a greater advantage to be secured by trade. But from that vantage point, the choice of the slave to work rather than to starve or be beaten; the choice of the victim to hand over money rather than to be killed; the choice to work and remit a portion of one's earning to the government as tribute rather than not to work at all, were equally voluntary choices to improve one's position over what it would have been in the absence of that choice. Once one understands that coercion operated as background constraints on socially available choices, not as the deprivation of all choice, Hale argued, it would be evident that the sphere of so-called voluntary market exchanges ... was really a complicated network of mutual coercion, in which the "choice" to accede to the other side's terms was coerced by the fact that the money, goods, or services that one obtained in exchange were unavailable on more favorable terms. The reason that they were unavailable ... was not natural necessity. Instead, it was the state itself, which, through its law of liberty, property, and contract, gave owners the right to withhold property and services from others absolutely, and the power to waive that right upon payment of the price demanded.

Barbara Fried, The Progressive Assault on Laissez Faire 49–50 (1998).

For discussions of the issue that focus on coercion especially in the context of choices that women make in relationship to sex, see Peter Westen, The Logic of Consent: The Diversity and Deceptiveness of Consent as a Defense in Criminal Law (2004); Alan Wertheimer, Consent to Sexual Relations (2003); Kimberly A. Yuracko, Perfectionism and Contemporary Feminist Values 51–75 (2003); Stephen J. Schulhofer, Unwanted Sex 114–67 (1998).

Some argue that certain forms of both "persistent offers" and "seductive offers" are problematic in much the same way that more obvious coercion is problematic. Others argue that so long as one is free to reject an offer, an offer cannot possibly make the offeree worse off (except to the degree, not especially relevant for these purposes, that processing offers is a time-consuming, and in that sense, costly activity).

Think first about persistence: Isn't the narrator in our Problem, supra, worse off if she receives more (and more) "offers" (each of which we might assume, at least for argument's sake, she is free to reject) to have sex over the course of the night? If she ultimately accedes, do we think that signals her *desire* to have sex? Does the fact that she has no formal entitlement to be free from any particular number of "requests" (in the way she has a separate entitlement to be free from a violent attack) mean that she hasn't been harmed by the persistence of the person(s) making the "requests"?

Think, too, about a "seductive offer" of the form, "I will reduce the amount of jail time you'd otherwise get if you have sex." (Is the defendant in *Mlinarich* making a "threat" if he hadn't otherwise considered discontinuing his guardianship, but making an "offer" if he had? Can we let so much turn on the defendant's collateral intentions, even though the victim's perception of constraint does not depend on these intentions?) Obviously, the judge may be breaching his obligations to citizens generally to make legal judgments for relevant reasons, but might he also be said to harm the person he is making the "offer" to? Should she be protected from deciding to have sex for certain sorts of reasons? Why? Why not? Does the fact that a woman might "choose" to have sex with a man for so many distinct reasons that might seem to have little to do with either romance or passion (to be popular, to impress her girl friends, to be taken care of materially, because she thinks she is obliged by social custom given their past dealings) make it impossible to say that some reasons (besides discrete threats) are "out of bounds"? Look, in this regard, at Kimberly Yuracko's comments:

> The term "seductive offer" typically and intuitively describes offers of the form "do X and you will get Y." However, I am also using "seductive offer" to describe proposals that take the form of a threat, "do X or I will do Y to you," where Y does not involve a threatened rights violation.... [M]ost threats that do not involve rights violations can also be framed as seductive offers and vice versa. "Have sex with me or else I'll break up with you," [can be framed] as "Have sex with me and I'll continue to date you." ... For both seductive offers and non-rights-violating threats, what makes the choice set coercive is something about how the two options interact with each other and whether one option, Y, is a reasonable basis for choosing the other option, X. In both cases, what is "coercive" about the proposal is not the prospect of either option taken by itself but the interplay of the two options. Certain choices should not be made for certain reasons....
>
> If ... what determines whether a particular choice constitutes a problematic autonomy infringement is the individual's preference never to have been faced with a choice at all, then autonomy violations become purely subject-dependent. This subjectivity may be less problematic with respect to threats because of the assumption that people uniformly prefer not to be faced with threats to their person and their property. This subjectivity constraint is a bigger problem with respect to seductive offers. Women would probably disagree about whether

> they prefer to be presented with seductive choice sets. Some eighteen-year-old female students might prefer to have the option to have sex with their professors as a way to raise their grades while others would hate being encouraged to think of themselves and their sexuality as objects for exchange and would strongly prefer never to have the option....
>
> What is problematic about these choices can only be understood by resorting to the perfectionist idea that individuals should not be presented with certain choices and trade-offs because they should not be encouraged to think about their characteristics and attributes in certain ways.

Kimberly A. Yuracko, Perfectionism and Contemporary Feminist Values 66, 70 (2003).

Outside the context of criminal law, in the commercial arena we ordinarily think about in contract law, do sellers who persistently approach a potential customer with "offers" harm the would-be customers? How? What if the sellers make it socially awkward to turn them down: for instance, car salesmen may pretend to go out of their way to "bargain for you" with (real or imaginary) supervisors, before "offering" you a final price, or an extended warranty so that you will feel you must reciprocate their "kindness"? Have they coerced you? Do we believe that if you make the deal they are offering that you will be "better off" than you'd have been if you hadn't made it? For an excellent discussion of the myriad ways in which commercial actors and those seeking political support or charitable contributions induce others to do things they might otherwise have been predisposed not to do, see Robert B. Cialdini, Influence: The Psychology of Persuasion (rev. ed. 1993).

Outside the context of sex, but within the domain of the criminal law, we must decide when transfers of money or other things of value are a product of the sorts of coercive pressure that makes extortion charges appropriate. Note, first, though, that in some jurisdictions in which statutory language plainly precludes finding defendants guilty of rape if they "merely" threaten such things as economic harm or threats to reputation, courts will find that sex is a "thing of value" so that those who induce "its" transfer by threat are guilty of extortion. Compare in that regard United States v. Hicks, 24 M.J. 3 (C.M.A. 1987) (finding that so long as the defendant found some "value" or "advantage" in the thing sought, he could be guilty of extortion) with State v. Stockton, 97 Wash.2d 528, 647 P.2d 21 (1982) (finding that sex was neither property nor the sort of service contemplated by the extortion statute). The larger question, though, is why we would convict someone of extortion if, for instance, he obtained money by threatening to ruin his victim's reputation, but not convict him of rape if he forced her to elect between having sex and having her reputation ruined.

Consider, in this regard, the argument by Anne Coughlin that, historically, many of the apparently anomalous limits on the reach of rape law can best be understood if we see the woman as defending herself against criminal charges of fornication (i.e., nonmarital sex) by arguing that she was raped. The definition of rape, given that view, is coextensive with the excuse defenses that the woman could raise to fornication accusations: for instance, that she was subject to duress (but only if a reasonably firm person would have disobeyed the law given the presence of imminent threats). See Anne Coughlin, "Sex and Guilt," 84 Va. L. Rev. 1 (1998). Coughlin's argument is not simply about technical limits on the reach of rape law. She notes that in a regime in which adultery and fornication are criminal, we do not highly value "sexual autonomy" (or the capacity to control one's own body); rather, in such a regime, certain exercises of sexual autonomy are criminalized unless the actor could be relieved of responsibility for the offense. We return to this argument when we discuss sex induced by fraudulent misrepresentation.

6. A woman may feel afraid of violence on a particular occasion because the man aggressively seeking sex has physically harmed her in the past. Should a defendant who has physically abused the complainant over a long period of time be convicted of rape even in a jurisdiction that requires force, rather than "mere" nonconsent, if he does not use explicit force or threats on the particular occasion at issue in the trial?

The North Carolina Supreme Court reversed a rape conviction in a case with facts that were in some ways even less favorable to the defendant than these (not only had the defendant abused the victim for six months, he threatened to hit her when he confronted her at her school before taking her to a friend's house, where he pulled her up from a chair and pushed her legs apart when she said she did not want to have sex with him). See State v. Alston, 310 N.C. 399, 312 S.E.2d 470 (1984). The court stated that the prosecutrix Brown "specifically stated that her fear of the defendant was based on an experience with him prior to June 15 [the day of the alleged rape] and that on June 15 he did not hold her down or threaten her with what would happen if she refused to submit to him.... Although Brown's general fear of the defendant may have been justified by his conduct on prior occasions, absent evidence that the defendant used force or threats to overcome the will of the victim to *resist the sexual intercourse alleged to have been rape*, such general fear was not sufficient to show that the defendant used the force required to support a conviction of rape."

Why is a pattern of violence not a threat? If a school child beat up another child each day for a month and took his lunch money, would we think the child was robbed once more if on the last day of the month, the bully merely said, "Hand over your money, okay?"

7. Even if valid consent is present, questions regarding its duration and scope remain. (To what has the victim consented and how long does the consent remain valid?, etc.) In rape cases, however, courts have struggled even with the apparently much simpler question of the effects of an unequivocal *withdrawal* of consent. As recently as 1985, a California appellate court rejected a withdrawal of consent as irrelevant on the ground that

> the essence of the crime of rape is the outrage to the person and feelings of the female resulting from the nonconsensual violation of her womanhood. When a female willingly consents to an act of sexual intercourse, the penetration by the male cannot constitute a violation of her womanhood nor cause outrage to her person and feelings. If she

> withdraws consent during the act of sexual intercourse and the male forcibly continues the act without interruption, the female may certainly feel outrage because of the force applied or because the male ignores her wishes, but the sense of outrage to her person and feelings could hardly be of the same magnitude as that resulting from an initial nonconsensual violation of her womanhood. It would seem, therefore, that the essential guilt of rape ... is lacking in the withdrawn consent scenario.

People v. Vela, 172 Cal.App.3d 237, 243 (1985), rev'd sub nom. In re Z., 29 Cal. 4th 756, 60 P.3d 183, 128 Cal.Rptr.2d 783 (2003) ("while outrage of the victim may be the cause for criminalizing and severely punishing forcible rape, outrage by the victim is not an element of forcible rape").

Other courts explicitly declare that a defendant is guilty of rape if the woman has withdrawn consent. See, e.g., State v. Siering, 35 Conn.App. 173, 644 A.2d 958 (1994).

8. Historically, husbands who committed acts that would otherwise constitute rape were immune from prosecution. The Model Penal Code's act definition was typical: Section 213.1 begins: "A male who has sexual intercourse *with a female not his wife* is guilty of rape if ..." (emphasis added).

As of 2003, only one state—Kentucky—retained unqualified spousal immunity from rape prosecutions (until the spouses are not merely factually but legally separated), and another—Alaska—backed away in 2002 from its 1989 decision to eliminate spousal immunity entirely so that it now prohibits prosecutions of husbands unless the complainant had filed for legal separation or divorce, prior to prosecution, but either before or after the alleged assault. See Alaska Stat. § 11.41.432(a)(2). Thirty-one jurisdictions had abolished conventional spousal immunity altogether, but there were many remnants of the traditional position in a substantial minority of jurisdictions. For instance, some jurisdictions (e.g., California, Arizona) punish spousal rape less severely and others (e.g., Virginia, Nevada) punish only the most extrinsically violent forms of spousal rape, rather than all the varieties of coercive sex that they ordinarily punish. Others (e.g., South Carolina, Maryland) make distinctions between cohabiting and non-cohabiting spouses. Moreover, there is reason to believe that prosecutors remain reluctant to charge husbands with rape, except when they use a great deal of extrinsic violent force.

The New York Court of Appeals, in People v. Liberta, 64 N.Y.2d 152, 474 N.E.2d 567 (1984), explains the rejection of the traditional doctrine of spousal immunity well:

> We find that there is no rational basis for distinguishing between marital rape and non-marital rape. The various rationales which have been asserted in defense of the exemption are either based upon archaic notions about the consent and property rights incident to marriage or are simply unable to withstand the slightest scrutiny.
>
> Lord Hale's notion of an irrevocable implied consent by a married woman to sexual intercourse has been cited most frequently in support of the marital exemption.... Other than in the context of rape

statutes, marriage has never been viewed as giving the husband the right to coerced intercourse on demand.... A married woman has the same right to control her own body as does an unmarried woman....

The other traditional justifications for the marital exemption were the common law doctrines that a woman was the property of her husband and that the legal existence of the woman was "incorporated and consolidated into that of the husband." ... Both these doctrines, of course, have long been rejected in this state....

Because the traditional justifications for the marital exemption no longer have any validity, other arguments have been advanced in its defense. The first ... is that the marital exemption protects against government intrusion into marital privacy and promotes reconciliation of the spouses, and thus the elimination of the exemption would be disruptive to marriages. While protecting marital privacy and encouraging reconciliation are legitimate state interests, there is no rational relationship between allowing a husband to forcibly rape his wife and these interests.... [The] right of privacy protects consensual acts, not violent sexual assaults....

Similarly ... it is the violent act of rape and not the subsequent attempt of the wife to seek protection through the criminal justice system which "disrupts" a marriage. Moreover, if the marriage has already reached the point where intercourse is accomplished by violent assault it is doubtful that there is anything left to reconcile.

Another rationale sometimes advanced in support of the marital exemption is that marital rape would be a difficult crime to prove.... The criminal justice system, with all of its built-in safeguards, is presumed to be capable of handling any false complaints....

The final argument in defense of the marital exemption is that marital rape is not as serious an offense as other rape.... The fact that rape statutes exist, however, is a recognition that the harm caused by a forcible rape is different, and more severe, than the harm caused by an ordinary assault.... [T]here is no evidence to support the argument that marital rape has less severe consequences than other rape. On the contrary, numerous studies have shown that marital rape is frequently quite violent and generally has *more* severe traumatic effects on the victim than other rape.

9. Note that in *Berkowitz* the Pennsylvania Supreme Court reverses the rape conviction, but not that for indecent assault, a crime that requires nonconsent, but not forcible compulsion. This distinction between rape and lesser sexual offenses is now fairly common in American criminal codes. See also N.Y. Penal Law § 130.35 (defining first-degree rape as "engag[ing] in sexual intercourse with another person ... [b]y forcible compulsion") & id. § 130.20(1) (defining "sexual misconduct" as "engag[ing] in sexual intercourse with another person without such person's consent"). These lesser offenses, however, tend to be very much lesser indeed. In Pennsylvania, for instance, rape is a first-degree felony, punishable by up to 20 years' imprisonment; indecent assault, by contrast, is a second-degree misdemeanor, punishable by up to 2 years' imprisonment. See also N.Y. Penal Law

§ 130.35 (classifying first-degree rape as a class B felony, punishable by up to 25 years' imprisonment) & id. § 130.20(1) (classifying sexual misconduct as a class A misdemeanor, punishable by up to 1 year's imprisonment). Which view of the gist of rape might account for this dramatic punishment differential?

2. FRAUD

Model Penal Code § 213.1(2). Gross Sexual Imposition.

A male who has sexual intercourse with a female ... commits a felony of the third degree if:

(c) he knows that she is unaware that a sexual act is being committed upon her or that she submits because she mistakenly supposes that he is her husband.

Boro v. People

California Court of Appeal.
163 Cal.App.3d 1224, 210 Cal.Rptr. 122 (1985).

■ NEWSOM, ASSOCIATE JUSTICE.

... Ms. R, the rape victim ... received a telephone call from a person who identified himself as "Dr. Stevens" and said he worked at Peninsula Hospital.

"Dr. Stevens" told Ms. R. that he had results of her blood test and that she had contracted a dangerous, highly infectious and perhaps fatal disease....

"Dr. Stevens" further explained that there were only two ways to treat the disease. The first was a painful surgical procedure—graphically described—costing $9,000 and requiring her uninsured hospitalization for six weeks. A second alternative ... was to have sexual intercourse with an anonymous donor who had been injected with a serum which would cure the disease. The latter, nonsurgical procedure would only cost $4,500. When the victim replied that she lacked sufficient funds, the "doctor" suggested that $1,000 would suffice as a down payment. The victim thereupon agreed to the nonsurgical alternative.... [Shortly thereafter the victim checked into a hotel room as instructed by petitioner, where] the "donor," petitioner, after urging her to relax, had sexual intercourse with her.

The People's position is stated concisely: "We contend, quite simply, that at the time of the intercourse, Ms. R., the victim, was 'unconscious of the nature of the act': because of [petitioner's] misrepresentation she believed it was in the nature of a medical treatment...." Petitioner, on the other hand, stresses that the victim was plainly aware of the *nature* of the act in which she voluntarily engaged, so that her motivation in doing so ... is irrelevant....

... In People v. Minkowski (1962) 204 Cal. App. 2d 832, 23 Cal. Rptr. 92 the defendant was a physician who "treated" several victims for menstrual cramps. Each victim testified that she was treated in a position with her back to the doctor, bent over a table, with feet apart, in a dressing gown. And in each case the "treatment" consisted of the defendant first inserting a metal instrument, then substituting an instrument which "felt different"—the victims not realizing that the second instrument was in fact the doctor's penis....

... [A]s a leading authority has written, "if deception causes a misunderstanding as to the fact itself (fraud in the *factum*) there is no legally-recognized consent because what happened is not that for which consent was given, whereas consent induced by fraud is as effective as any other consent, so far as direct and immediate legal consequences are concerned, if the deception relates not to the thing done but merely to some collateral matter (fraud in the inducement)." ...

The victims in *Minkowski* consented, not to sexual intercourse, but to an act of an altogether different nature, penetration by medical instrument....

Another relatively common situation ... is the fraudulent obtaining of consent by impersonating a spouse.... [Some, but not all] courts hold such a mistake to be rape on the theory that it involves fraud in the *factum*, since the woman's consent is to the innocent act of marital intercourse while what is actually perpetrated is an act of adultery....

... [Ms. R.] precisely understood the "nature of her act", but motivated by fear of disease, and death, succumbed to petitioner's fraudulent blandishments.

To so conclude is not to vitiate the heartless cruelty of petitioner's scheme, but to say that it comprised crimes of a different order, than a violation of the [rape statute.][a]

United States v. Hughes

U.S. Court of Appeals for the Armed Forces.
48 M.J. 214 (1998).

■ GIERKE, J.

Private First Class (PFC) B had been drinking and was asleep in her barracks room at Camp Hovey, Korea. She left the door unlocked so that her boyfriend, Sergeant (SGT) R, could enter. At some time during the night, appellant entered her barracks and had intercourse with PFC B. She was not fully awake and called out SGT R's name several times during the intercourse. After the intercourse was completed, PFC B got out of bed, went to the bathroom, and then noticed that appellant and not SGT R was sitting on her bunk....

Article 120 defines rape as "an act of sexual intercourse, by force and without consent." Paragraph 45c(1)(b), Part IV, Manual for Courts–Martial

a. The California legislature subsequently amended the statute, explicitly overturning the ruling in *Boro*. See Cal. Penal Code § 266(c). Boro himself was subsequently prosecuted in 1987 under the revised statute for engaging in the same sort of conduct he had engaged in with Ms. R. See Patricia Falk, "Rape by Fraud and Rape by Coercion," 64 Brooklyn L. Rev. 1, 57 (1998).—EDS.

(1995), provides that, "if there is actual consent, although obtained by fraud, the act is not rape." The distinction involved in this case is between fraud in the inducement and fraud in the *factum*. The former applies to situations where consent is obtained by misrepresentations ("No, I'm not married."); the latter applies to misrepresentations about the nature of the act itself.

The Government relies on this Court's opinions in United States v. Traylor, 40 M.J. 248 (C.M.A. 1994), and United States v. Booker, 25 M.J. 114, 116 (C.M.A. 1987), for the proposition that PFC B did not consent to intercourse with appellant and, thus, her purported consent was invalid because it was obtained by fraud in the *factum*.

In *Booker*, then-Judge Cox recognized that "[t]here are differences in opinion as to whether 'consent' relates only to the act or also to the actor".... Writing the lead opinion ... Judge Cox opined that actual consent means that "a woman must be agreeable to the penetration of her body by ... a particular male sex organ."

Appellant argues that *Traylor* is distinguishable from this case because, in *Traylor*, the victim protested as soon as she realized that the second male had penetrated her. We reject appellant's argument. In *Traylor* we held that the victim's retroactive consent or lack thereof "has no effect on the accused's guilt" because the offense was completed at the moment of penetration.

Applying the principles articulated in *Traylor* and *Booker*, we hold that there was sufficient evidence of record to show that PFC B did not consent to being penetrated by appellant. Accordingly, we hold that the military judge did not err by denying the motion for a finding of not guilty....

QUESTIONS AND COMMENTS

1. Boro could plainly be convicted of some form of larceny in connection with the receipt of $1,000 from Ms. R.; she transferred the money solely as a result of a material misrepresentation (that she would receive genuine medical treatment in exchange for the money). He did not, in fact, contest the theft-related indictments. Should it be any more difficult to convict him of rape, and if so, why?

2. In United States v. Booker, 25 M.J. 114 (C.A.A.F. 1987), the U.S. Court of Appeals for the Armed Forces noted: "Clearly, fraud in the inducement includes such general knavery as: 'No, I'm not married'; 'Of course I'll respect you in the morning'; 'We'll get married as soon as ...'; 'I'll pay you [ ] dollars'; and so on. Whatever else such tactics amount to, they are not rape."

Why not? In a violent stranger rape in which a woman decides to cooperate with her attacker because he threatens her with death or grievous injury if she does not, the victim would plainly recognize that she would not have had sex but-for the threatened violation of her rights (to be free from violence). In these "fraud in the inducement" cases, the woman might note, similarly, that she would not have had sex but-for the violation of her right not to be misled about facts material to her decision to engage in sex with the particular person. Are the violations of autonomy similar?

Consider the following comments by Stephen Schulhofer:

> When a woman submits to a sexual demand because of physical force or non-violent coercion (for example, a threat to fire her from her job), she endures sex she knows she doesn't want. That experience is unlikely to give her physical pleasure, and it may cause lasting physical and emotional harm. When her consent is given under false pretenses, in contrast, the psychological experience is different, because the encounter is one—*at the time*—she believes she wants....
>
> When the woman discovers the misrepresentations later, she will very likely feel cheated and used. The impact could be devastating, but it might not be.... In any case, the harm will differ from that of sex that a woman knows at the time she doesn't want. And the injury will also differ from the harm caused by misrepresentation in a property case, where the deception (if it is material at all) will typically go to the heart of the value of the transaction....
>
> Another difficulty affecting both marital and nonmarital relationships arises from the elusive nature of "truth" and the complex role of emotional imagination in sexual encounters. What a date or sexual partner says about his feelings of attraction, future plans, or commitment to the relationship may be disbelieved, half-believed, or believed but not relied upon....

Stephen J. Schulhofer, Unwanted Sex 156–58 (1998).

3. Recall Anne Coughlin's insight in "Sex and Guilt" that we might best understand, if not justify, the historical limits on the reach of rape law by thinking of the limits on prosecuting male defendants as corresponding to the claims that female "victims" might make in articulating defenses to charges of adultery or fornication. Think about *Hughes* in this regard: a woman *does* have a mistake of fact defense to a fornication charge if she reasonably believes that she is having sex with her husband (though in fact he is not), but would have no such defense if she mistakenly believed she was having sex with her boyfriend. Think too about why the California court distinguished the culpable defendant in *Minkowski* from the exonerated defendant in *Boro*: the victim does not know that she is committing fornication if she thinks she is being penetrated by a medical instrument but does know that she is committing fornication—though she might, with some difficulty, present a justification defense—in a situation in which she is having sex as a medical procedure. Recall, too, the court's holding in *Rusk*: the court's decision that the defendant cannot be convicted of rape unless he caused fear in a "reasonable person" might reflect the fact that only a reasonably firm victim could claim duress as a defense to a charge of fornication.

From the vantage point of those concerned with safeguarding not only the sexual autonomy to refuse unwanted sex but the power to engage in desired sexual relations, these distinctions may seem preposterous. As the court in *Booker* noted: "[W]hile it is arguable that there may be people who are willing to hop into bed with absolutely anyone, we take it that even the most uninhibited people ordinarily make some assessment of a potential sexual partner and exercise some modicum of discretion before consenting to sexual intercourse. Thus, consent to the act is based on the identity of the prospective partner."

Coughlin's point may not be entirely historical. Even though we no longer treat fornication as criminal (and many don't even view it as wrongful),[a] many of us may still believe, more or less consciously, that the capacity to make the decision not to have sex at all, except under highly delimited conditions, is worthier of protection than the capacity to be fully informed about the qualities of each of one's partners. Though rape law reform (particularly evidence law reform that we return to in part D, infra) has ostensibly removed any focus on victim virginity, fraudulent inducement doctrine suggests to some degree that significant numbers of actors with legal authority *still* think women who are tricked into having non-marital sex with a particular person, though manifestly willing to have it more generally, are less injured (or worthy of protection) than those who are tricked into having non-marital sex altogether.

4. Can *Boro* be classified as a fraud in the factum case because Ms. R. consented to an act of sexual intercourse (1) with an anonymous donor, not with Dr. Stevens, and certainly not with Boro and (2) with someone who had been injected with a special serum, not with Boro, who had not? If the identity—and characteristics—of the perpetrator are irrelevant, why is *Hughes* a fraud in the factum case? What distinguishes "the thing done" from "some collateral matter"? Can a case of fraudulent consent involve neither a fraud in the factum nor a fraud in the inducement? What was the fraudulent misrepresentation in *Hughes*? What if the perpetrator makes no effort to mislead the victim? What if he merely fails to correct a mistake on the part of the victim?

Is the distinction between fraud in the factum and fraud in the inducement worth preserving? See Model Penal Code § 2.11(3)(d) ("[A]ssent does not constitute consent if ... it is induced by force, duress or deception of a kind sought to be prevented by the law defining the offense."). How would *Boro* and *Hughes* be resolved under the Model Penal Code? Or is the relevant distinction that between misrepresentations affecting the victim's consent to each element in the definition of an offense and those affecting her reasons for giving the consent? How would *Boro* and *Hughes* come out under this approach?

3. Incapacity to Consent

a. Traditional Law on Intoxication

McKinney v. State

Court of Appeals of Texas.
825 S.W.2d 238 (1992).

■ Meyers, J.

Appellant, Brandon McKinney, appeals from a conviction by the jury of sexual assault. See Tex. Penal Code Ann. § 22.011(a)(1)(A)[a] & (b)(3).

a. Note, however, that sexual offenses other than rape (and adultery in particular) are substantially more likely to be prosecuted under military criminal law than under civilian criminal law. Though rarely enforced, adultery statutes remain in the criminal codes of many states. See, e.g., N.Y. Penal Law § 255.17.—Eds.

Punishment was assessed by the jury at five years confinement, probated for five years, and a $5,000.00 fine. . . .

On November 19, 1989, K.H., a nineteen-year-old female, was with McKinney and some other friends on a road trip to Denton. When they arrived in Denton, they picked up some beer and went to a local park to drink it. . . . While en route to a friend's house, McKinney and another passenger were sniffing paint in the back seat. They arrived at the friend's house and smoked some marihuana. After they finished smoking the "joint" they continued driving out into the country towards Navo. While out in the country, K.H. was sexually assaulted by McKinney and two other men. . . .

McKinney was convicted under Tex. Penal Code Ann. § 22.011(b)(3). A sexual assault is without the consent of the other person if:

(3) the other person has not consented and the actor knows the other person is unconscious or physically unable to resist. . . .

We begin our sufficiency review by considering the evidence that supports the jury's finding McKinney knew K.H. was physically unable to resist. First, McKinney testified that he knew "[s]he wasn't feeling very good." He also testified that when the other men were raping her "it almost made [him] throw up." Secondly, K.H. testified that she had a buzz and was intoxicated from the combined effects of the beer, the marihuana, and the paint fumes. Additionally, she testified she did not resist because "there was [sic] three of them and one of me," and that she was "afraid they'd try to kill me." Lastly, she testified that when McKinney got into the back of the car she sat up and asked, "Why are you doing this to me?"

Under the facts of this case, a reasonable trier of fact could have found McKinney guilty of section 22.011(b)(1) (the actor compels the person to participate by use of force) or subsection (b)(2) (the actor compels the other person to participate by threatening to use force), or even subsection (b)(4) (as a result of mental defect the person is incapable of resisting). However, after viewing the evidence a reasonable trier of fact could not have found beyond a reasonable doubt that K.H. was physically unable to resist, as subsection (b)(3) is contemplated by the Penal Code. . . .

In the present case, K.H. never testified she was unconscious or physically unable to resist. On the contrary, she testified that she *was* physically able to resist. And further, that she was physically able to speak and move her arms and body. After viewing the evidence in the light most favorable to the verdict, we find a rational trier of fact could not have found the victim was physically unable to resist. . . .

Judgment is reversed, and an acquittal ordered.

a. Tex. Penal Code Ann. § 22.011. Sexual Assault

(a) A person commits an offense if the person:

(1) intentionally or knowingly:

(A) causes the penetration of the anus or sexual organ of another person by any means, without that person's consent. . . .—Eds.

Model Penal Code § 213.1(1). Rape.

A male who has sexual intercourse with a female ... is guilty of rape if:

(b) he has substantially impaired her power to appraise or control her conduct by administering or employing without her knowledge drugs, intoxicants or other means for the purpose of preventing resistance; or

(c) the female is unconscious....

Model Penal Code § 2.11(3). Ineffective Consent.

[A]ssent does not constitute consent if:

(b) it is given by a person who by reason of youth, mental disease or defect or intoxication is manifestly unable or known by the actor to be unable to make a reasonable judgment as to the nature or harmfulness of the conduct charged to constitute the offense....

b. Norms that Would Define Rape or Impermissible Sexual Conduct More Inclusively

Antioch College Survival Guide 2002–2003: Sexual Offense Prevention Policy (SOPP)

In 1991, a group of Antioch students began creating this policy which would alter the culture of an entire community. This policy is the embodiment of Antioch College's commitment to ending sexual violence and fostering a culture of consensual sexuality. It governs the Antioch College Community by working with existing staff and faculty policies. It now exists as a piece of a larger educational framework charged with furthering these goals. The intent of the document is not to replace existing ... laws....

"Consent" is defined as the act of willingly and verbally agreeing to engage in specific sexual conduct.... In order for "consent" to be valid, all parties must have unimpaired judgment and a shared understanding of the nature of the act to which they are consenting including safer sex practices.

Remedies for violation of the policy include mediation, mandatory sexual offense therapy, mandatory substance abuse therapy, public apology, community service, loss of on-campus housing, suspension, and expulsion.

In "Rule by Myth: The Social and Legal Dynamics Governing Alcohol–Related Acquaintance Rapes," 47 Stan. L. Rev. 115 (1994), Karen Kramer proposes a model rape statute which includes the following provision:

Presumptively, no consent is obtained where ...

d) the complainant's ability to affirmatively communicate willingness or unwillingness to engage in the act is hindered by reason of intoxication with alcohol or other substances substantially enough to cause observable physical weakening or impaired verbal ability.

QUESTIONS AND COMMENTS

1. In *McKinney,* if sexual assault is defined as sexual intercourse "without consent," what's the point of *defining* "without consent" as lack

of consent *plus* unconsciousness or inability to resist? What does inability to resist have to do with lack of consent? If resistance is no longer required for rape liability, what relevance does the inability to resist have?

Compare the Texas statute in *McKinney* with the Model Penal Code statute (§ 213.1(1)). What considerations does each reflect? Is the Model Penal Code provision best thought of as a fraud—rather than as an incapacity—provision?

2. Would McKinney have been able to raise an intoxication defense on the issue of inability to resist or incapacity to consent? Under the Texas statute? Under the Model Penal Code? Under Kramer's model rape statute?

3. *Other Forms of Incapacity to Consent: Unconsciousness and Mental Incapacity.* Defendants may be criminally punished if they have sexual relations with people who are sleeping, unconscious, or otherwise incapacitated so that they could not resist or give consent. For a discussion, see State v. Moorman, 358 S.E.2d 502 (N.C. 1987).

It is similarly criminal to have sexual relations with a person who, by reason of mental incapacity, lacks the ability to give meaningful consent. Naturally, there are difficult line-drawing problems. In State v. Olivio, 123 N.J. 550, 589 A.2d 597 (1991), for instance, the defendant challenged the trial court's determination that the person with whom he had sex was mentally defective under the Code. The dilemma faced by the court was straightforward:

> "The difficulty in making that determination inheres in its implications for both mentally-defective persons who are vulnerable and need the special protection of our laws from the sexual intrusions of others and persons whose mental deficiencies need not be an impediment to the enjoyment of a reasonably normal life, including consensual sexual relations." The court held "that a person is mentally defective ... if, at the time of the sexual activity, he or she is unable to comprehend the distinctively sexual nature of the conduct or is incapable of understanding or exercising the right to refuse to engage in such conduct with another." At the same time, the court rejected suggestions—embodied in other state court opinions—that would make it criminal to have sexual relations with someone who did not have an "understanding [of] 'the moral quality' of the conduct 'in the framework of the societal environment and taboos to which a person will be exposed' " or to have sex with a person who did not "[understand] the 'consequences' as well as the 'nature' of sex" or "specifically understand that sex can lead to pregnancy and sexually-transmitted disease."

Could someone who is considered "mentally defective" under *Olivio* be criminally liable as a perpetrator of rape? Does sex between two mentally defective individuals pose the same dilemma as sex when only one of the partners is mentally defective?

Is the prohibition on sex with mentally defective persons compatible with the substantive due process right to private consensual sex that the Supreme Court created in *Lawrence v. Texas* (ch. 7, supra)? In her partial concurrence and partial dissent in Anderson v. Morrow, 371 F. 3d 1027 (9th Cir. 2004), Judge Berzon raises the following issues:

> It is true that *Lawrence* did not involve a case where consent was in doubt. But that distinction does not conclusively decide this case. * * *
>
> At the time of the sexual encounter for which Anderson was prosecuted, JH was 26 years old and lived with her mother. She is 4′7″ tall, has the emotional maturity of a 6 to 8-year-old child, and is moderately mentally retarded. She has "a little" vision in one eye, and "fairly good" vision in the other. She also has a hearing deficiency but does not always wear a hearing aid. It is difficult to understand her speech.
>
> As an adult, JH has had at least two boyfriends with whom she had sexual relationships. After both relationships had ended, with one boyfriend she "continued a sexual relationship . . . a couple of times a year." She has also received counseling at the Benton County Mental Health Center, where she learned about using condoms. Prosecution experts testified that, "She understands that a man is on top and the woman is on the bottom and the penis is inserted into the vagina," and that she understands the health and pregnancy risks of not using condoms, but that she does not understand dating norms, such as the circumstances in which kissing or holding hands is appropriate dating behavior. * * *
>
> Also, Tina Pahre, an acquaintance of Anderson's, testified that in 1992 she had frequently seen JH at Pahre's apartment complex. JH's apparent purpose was to visit a man named Jim, who "[s]he seemed to really, really like." According to Pahr, even when Jim was not there, JH would visit other men at the apartment complex, "follow them up to their apartment . . . [e]ven if they didn't want her there . . . and flirt with them." * * *
>
> Additionally, Anderson testified at trial about a 1989 consensual sexual encounter with JH, for which he was not prosecuted.
>
> The 1992 sexual encounter for which Anderson was prosecuted began when Anderson saw JH as he was driving home from work. JH was walking home from a bar where she had been dancing, an activity in which she regularly engaged, and drinking. Anderson claimed that she accepted a ride with him and that they proceeded to a secluded parking lot. According to him, they conversed about their previous intimate relationships. While he suspected she might be deaf, he maintained that he did not realize that she was mentally retarded. Anderson claims that JH initiated the consensual sexual encounter that followed. * * *
>
> The jury acquitted him of [kidnapping, forcible rape, and forcible sodomy]. Thus, the jury *rejected* JH's version of the incident, as it concluded there was no forcible rape or sodomy. Instead, the basis for Anderson's conviction was non-forcible sexual activity with a person legally incapable of consent. * * *

The question, then, is whether the sexual liberty interest outlined in *Lawrence* regulates the manner in which a state drafts and applies its statutory rape law as applied to adult victims. I believe it does.

Before proceeding, it is crucial to note the interrelationship between JH's sexual liberty interest and Anderson's: If JH has, in certain circumstances, a constitutionally protected right to consent to sex and she does in fact consent, then there is no constitutionally legitimate basis, under *Lawrence*, to preclude Anderson from having sex with her *in those circumstances*.* * *

As written and as read to the jury at Anderson's trial, the language of section 163.305(3)[5] is susceptible to at least two constructions that could . . . impermissibly limit JH's ability to consent to sex: (1) the construction, ultimately proffered by the prosecution in this case after some wavering, that JH is *never* able legally to consent to sex; and (2) a construction that invites law enforcement, including police officers, prosecutors, judges, and juries, to impose its own sexual mores upon JH when deciding whether her consent was valid. * * *

The first reason why section 163.305(3), as written and as read to the jury at Anderson's trial, could implicate constitutionally protected conduct is that is susceptible to a construction that JH will *never* be able legally to consent to sex. The jury could have easily interpreted the phrase "*incapable* of appraising the nature of the conduct" to mean that either JH is always capable of consenting to sex or she never is. This binary view of mentally retarded individuals generally and JH in particular might well be an unconstitutional imposition on their sexual liberty. * * * [T]here is clear consensus among experts in the field of mental retardation that mentally retarded individuals experience sexual desire and can meaningfully consent to sex in *some* situations. The prosecution expert witness conceded as much at trial.

Moreover, JH has evidently engaged in voluntary sexual intercourse on a number of occasions in a manner that offended neither her mother nor the state. Given the general clinical belief that mentally retarded individuals desire and can "ethically" consent to sex, as well as JH's own desire and demonstrated capacity to understand and appreciate sexual contact, it could well be unconstitutional for Oregon law to hold that JH can *never* legally consent to sex. * * *

[T]he statutory provision alternatively invites those applying the law to invoke their own sexual mores and override JH's sexual choice when deciding whether JH is capable of consent in a particular instance. During the pre-trial hearing, the prosecutor first interpreted the statutory scheme in precisely this contextual manner. The prosecution's initial attempt at interpreting the statute was to propose a rule that JH's mother could provide consent on JH's behalf. Realizing the

5. Or. Rev. Stat. § 163.375(1)(d) states that a person who has sexual intercourse with another person is guilty of first degree rape if "the victim is incapable of consent by reason of mental defect, mental incapacitation or physical helplessness." Or. Rev. Stat. § 163.305(3) states: " 'Mentally defective' means that a person suffers from a mental disease or defect that renders the person incapable of appraising the nature of the conduct of the person . . ."

problem with this interpretation, the prosecution suggested that JH's consent would be legally valid in the context of a "boyfriend-girlfriend" relationship. * * *

Expert testimony at trial also suggested an invitation to apply one's own moral framework to JH's sexual choice. In explaining why JH's consent was not valid, the prosecution's non-medical expert on sexually abused, mentally retarded individuals testified that whereas JH sees "sex" as merely a physical act, "If you ask, you know, anyone else what sex was or what intercourse is you see an entire picture. You see the candles, the wine, the dating, you know, whatever else goes on. With her sex is just one quick spur of the moment thing."

That the state may not burden a particular sexual choice out of distaste or disagreement is the central holding of *Lawrence*. * * *

[W]hile the state surely has a very strong, legitimate interest in ensuring that the consent of a mentally disabled individual is knowledgeable and truly voluntary, and in disregarding that consent in situations where the alleged victim does not understand either the circumstances and consequences of sexual conduct or the extent of her ability to refuse sex, the state has no legitimate interest in imposing sexual mores on retarded individuals or their consensual partners. When considering how to construct a regime that both respects the sexual choice of the mentally retarded and protects them from predation, others have recognized this distinction between an appropriate voluntariness inquiry and inappropriate moralizing.

Would Judge Berzon's concerns be satisfied if the state argued that JH lacks knowledge (or true understanding) of the emotional consequences of the decision to have sex *in certain circumstances*? What if the state argues that she is cognitively capable of figuring out what certain sexual contacts have meant to her in the past, but incapable of understanding that *this* contact might be different than the others have been? What if she is incapable of "reading" whether her sexual partner thinks of her as an appealing person or merely as a dupe who is sexually "available"? If she doesn't know her sexual partner thinks she is a "dupe," does it matter if we believe that *she* would be upset if she knew how she were viewed? Do we really purport to know the answer to that question or is Judge Berzon correct to suspect that we inevitably focus on our own distaste at seeing someone have sex with someone because he thinks she doesn't know that she is, in some senses, being mocked or "used"?

4. *Other Forms of Incapacity to Consent: Underage Sex.* Girls (and in many states boys as well) below particular ages are legally incapable of giving consent, either to any person or to persons who are markedly older than they are. Such "statutory rape" laws may well be used largely to prosecute cases in which the defendant has committed some other crime—for instance, nonconsensual rape, domestic abuse, or incest—in situations in which the District Attorney wants to protect the victim against the trauma of testifying or in which proving the criminal conduct might appear difficult. Arguably, too, they have been used more recently to deter teen pregnancy on the (contestable) assumption that sexual demands by substantially older men on teenage girls has been a major cause of the "teen

pregnancy problem." There are concerns, of course, about whether such selective enforcement practices are desirable. See, in this regard, Rigel Oliveri, "Statutory Rape Law and Enforcement in the Wake of Welfare Reform," 52 Stan. L. Rev. 463 (2000).

In Jones v. State, 640 So.2d 1084 (Fla. 1994), two male defendants aged nineteen and twenty were convicted of statutory rape in a situation in which the relatives of the "victims" initiated prosecution over the fourteen-year-old girls' objections. The defendants argued that the statute, which proscribed sexual intercourse with "any child under the age of 16 years" (Fla. Stat. § 800.04), was unconstitutional as applied because it prevented no harm and restricted the capacity of the girls to enter relationships that they desired. The Florida Supreme Court rejected their contentions, noting that, "sexual activity with a child opens the door to sexual exploitation, physical harm, and sometimes psychological damage, regardless of the child's maturity or lack of chastity."

However, in B.B. v. State, 659 So.2d 256 (Fla. 1995), the court held that a statute proscribing "unlawful carnal intercourse with any unmarried person, of previous chaste character, who at the time of such intercourse is under the age of 18 years" (Fla. Stat. § 794.05) could not constitutionally be applied to sexual intercourse between a 16–year-old boy and a 16–year-old girl. Citing the right to privacy under the state constitution, the court held that the state's genuine interest in "protecting children from sexual activity before their minds and bodies have sufficiently matured to make it appropriate, safe, and healthy for them" was not, unlike the interest in avoiding exploitation, sufficient to justify the use of criminal sanctions as a means to meet that interest, rather than a less intrusive means. Such constitutional claims, though, have been widely rejected elsewhere. See, e.g., People v. T.A.J., 62 Cal.App.4th 1350, 73 Cal.Rptr.2d 331 (1998).

Couldn't statutory rape laws be justified on the ground that individuals below a certain age are incapable of consenting, perhaps using a test based on *Olivio*—inability to comprehend the sexual (and procreative) nature of the conduct or to understand or exercise one's right to refuse consent? Compare the defense of immaturity, which operates in analogy to the defense of insanity (i.e., incapacity due to mental disease or defect). See ch. 7.

To what degree might (or should) we extend the laws that protect young people from sexual exploitation by adults to other situations in which we might believe that power disparities lead to systematic exploitation: for instance, would it be a good idea to criminalize sexual relationships between teachers and (late adolescent and adult) students? Psychotherapists and patients? Prison guards and inmates? Does it matter whether we believe ostensible consent is problematic because of either *fear* or physical dependency (the prison guard case) or psychological factors (the psychotherapist case)? If this distinction matters, what do we do about the teacher/student case? Do we look, in particular cases, to ascertain whether the "victim" is motivated by something more like fear of losing academic support or more like a desire for the approval of an authority figure? Why should victim motive matter if defendant motive doesn't (on the irrelevance of motive, see ch. 5)?

5. Should statutory rape laws apply only to males who have sex with females? While all sex crimes were originally limited to male offenders and female victims ("a male who has sexual intercourse with a female ..."), there has been a growing trend to render them gender neutral ("whoever has sexual intercourse with another person...."). Not so for statutory rape. Why? Consider the following case.

People v. Whidden
Court of Appeals of New York.
51 N.Y.2d 457 (1980).

■ WACHTLER, JUDGE.

The State has advanced three distinct legislative justifications for penalizing males for the commission of acts which would not be criminal if committed by a similarly situated woman: preventing psychological injury to emotionally immature girls, preventing physical damage and, finally, preventing the deleterious consequences of pregnancy in minors. The first of these claimed justifications, protecting young females from psychological harm, must be rejected as a suitable ground ... since it is rooted in the unfounded assumption that underage women are more vulnerable to emotional harm than are their male counterparts. Such an "archaic and overbroad generalization," which is evidently grounded in long-standing stereotypical notions of the differences between the sexes, simply cannot serve as a legitimate rationale for a penal provision that is addressed only to adult males.

On the other hand, the problem of early pregnancy provides an ample justification for the Legislature's decision to deter sexual contact between older males and teen-age girls by imposing criminal sanctions.... Of course, it may be argued that [the statutory rape law] is underinclusive in that it does not penalize sexual contact between young females and teen-age boys, although such contact is just as likely to lead to unwanted pregnancy as is the prohibited conduct. This obvious underinclusiveness, however, is not objectionable in the present case, since it may be justified as a societal decision not to impose penal sanction upon those who are not yet capable of exercising mature judgment.

■ MEYER, JUDGE (dissenting).

[To uphold the statutory rape law] is, in effect, to embrace the moral viewpoint that girls, but not boys, need to be protected from their own inclination to enter into consensual sexual relationships with adults of the opposite sex. Yet this very day we have declared, "(I)t is not the function of the Penal Law in our governmental polity to provide either a medium for the articulation or the apparatus for the intended enforcement of moral or theological values" (People v. Onofre, 51 N.Y.2d 476 (1980) [striking down statute criminalizing consensual sodomy]).

.... In the absence of any data indicating that teenage pregnancy results to a significant extent from sexual liaisons between young girls

> and older men, rather than between young girls and their teenage contemporaries, it cannot be maintained that the imposition of felony punishment upon a limited class of older males meets the [constitutional] requirement[s]. The majority's assumption that such a demonstration is unnecessary in effect, once again, expresses a moral point of view.

More generally, does the recasting of sexual offenses obscure the nature of rape as a form of male-female aggression? If so, what about male homosexual rape? Are doctrinal rules from cases of male homosexual rape applicable in cases of male-female heterosexual rape? See People v. Thompson, 72 N.Y.2d 410 (1988) ("forcible compulsion" in a male homosexual rape case); see generally Tatjana Hörnle, "Penal Law and Sexuality: Recent Reforms in German Criminal Law," 3 Buff. Crim. L. Rev. 369 (2000) (discussing recent reform of German law of "crimes against sexual autonomy," abandoning distinction between male-female and other sexual assaults, as well as another distinction still found in American criminal codes, that between sexual intercourse and " 'deviate' sexual intercourse").

6. Those who endorse punishing sex with intoxicated persons in a wider range of circumstances than the law conventionally did (compare the Antioch Policy and the Kramer proposal) often rely on the notion that rape law will not adequately protect personal autonomy if it permits bodily invasions to occur when they are not "authorized" by a fully competent person. J.H. Bogart's remarks in this regard are representative:

> What is the nature of the acts necessary for a rape to occur? What are the elements of the wrong of rape?
>
> ... [W]henever sexual intercourse is not consented to, it is rape .... [C]onsent requires fully voluntary and informed agreement by an agent of appropriate actual present capacities.... For there to be valid consent, the agent must have a reasonably full understanding of the proposed course of conduct, both as to the nature of the acts and their import. Further, the agent's reasoning abilities must be relatively unimpaired....
>
> With respect to rape, [victims] suffer ... a violation of autonomy....
>
> Autonomy is not simply a more formal term for self-control or bodily integrity. An autonomous agent is self-determining, but not merely. Autonomy requires the agent's choices to be consonant with and expressive of a rational and reasonable personality. An autonomous agent, for example, is not merely subject to her desires and preferences, but is able to shape those desires and preferences....
>
> Under the present account, where there is intoxication, the capacity to give valid consent is compromised....

See J.H. Bogart, "Reconsidering Rape: Rethinking the Conceptual Foundations of Rape Law," 8 Can. J.L. & Jurisprudence 159 (1995).

Is the concept of *autonomy* that Bogart is using here meaningful? Helpful? Or, should we prohibit sex with inebriated people only if we believe that they will typically (unduly frequently?) regret it, or be substantially unhappier, over the course of their lives, if they have engaged in it than if they didn't?

The notion that invoking the "ideal of autonomy" may do little in these cases (at least without a fuller account of the impact intoxication may have on autonomy—how intoxicated must the person be? how does intoxication affect one's ability to choose?) is suggested by reflecting on the following: First, we must recognize, and try to explain, the fact that there is a "restricted domain" in which we worry that the choices intoxicated people make are "non-autonomous." (Compare, for instance, the limited significance of intoxication as a *defense* to criminal conduct. Would the intoxicated would-be rapist be exonerated for having sex with an intoxicated person?) While one could *imagine* sticking to a principle that inebriated people are simply not rational agents, capable of making choices that express their will as persons, the account is inconsistent with the fact that we recognize that an inebriated woman makes many choices that we would plainly respect. An intoxicated person whose judgment is "hindered" may well be capable of entertaining the thought that she should say "no" not only to the particular sexual proposition but would also plainly be able to evaluate and then reject a wide range of other non-sexual options. We recognize that she is making many choices we have no reason to question (not only can she choose which snack to eat for instance, she can choose to go out dancing, though in her ordinary sober state, she is far too shy to dance in front of others). Why, then, are we worried about her choices only in the sexual domain?

There is a second problem as well, a familiar one for those who have dealt with the thorny question of whether those who assume risks, *ex ante*, can be thought (at least in some sense) to consent to bad *ex post* outcomes or at least to be bound to accept them as having been an imbedded aspect of their chosen, autonomous life plan. Assume, for argument's sake, that women who voluntarily choose to become inebriated know pretty much what we, as policymakers attempting to assess the legal (or moral) propriety of having sex with intoxicated women, know: they are more likely to have sex if they get drunk around men, and they are more likely to regret the sex they have. How should we interpret the fact that they nonetheless decide to get drunk (recalling that we are excepting cases in which the intoxicant is *administered* to the woman without her knowledge or agreement)?

In one view, it would be paternalistic (and in this sense disrespectful towards, though doubtless not a legal *violation* of, the woman's autonomy) for the man to *refuse* to have sex with her, if she assented to do so once drunk, for her sake. Arguably, the person best qualified to judge whether she prefers a life of drinking or drug-taking, having somewhat more sex, and a higher risk of regretted sex, is the woman herself. Here the woman can be seen as making an initial autonomous decision to render herself less capable of making what are, *arguendo*, less fully autonomous decisions at some later time. By contrast, women who believe that their "expected utility" (in relationship to sex) will be negative if they drink (they will regret more than they enjoy) decide not to drink, or not to drink around men who might initiate sex with them (at least unless the separate gains from drinking in those settings are high enough, a situation that raises the second "assumption of risk" concern we will return to). Certainly, if a woman has sex while intoxicated a *second* time, having had the chance not only to reflect on general facts about women's experience but to experience regret in her own particular case, a non-paternalist will be prone to respect her decision to, in a sense, probabilistically pre-commit (or "bind herself to the mast") by getting drunk, knowing that she will later (at least be more likely to) have sex that she would resist if not drunk.

The fact that the woman does not (by hypothesis) control her sexuality at the moment sex occurs is of little moment in the limiting case: one in which she is certain (and correct) that the only way she can have her most enjoyable sexual experience is to intoxicate herself so that her capacity to choose sex—though not her capacity to enjoy (or even recall enjoying) it—is obliterated. A person chooses to sky dive, and we (ordinarily) let her (at least if she is informed about the physical and psychological perils), even though as soon as she exits the plane, she will have absolutely *no* control over whether she is sky diving (or plummeting toward the ground). We can plainly make autonomous choices to be powerless at some later time. Whether this is one of those situations in which a choice to be (relatively) powerless later should be respected seemingly depends, at core, on our view of its projected impact on her long-term well-being, not on its formal characteristic as autonomous or not.

Outside the limiting case, though, claims that one "consents" to an injury so long as one is aware of the *risk* that the injury might occur and chooses to run that risk (presumably because one gains something from running the risk) are problematic. Would we say, for instance, that a person consented to have his house burglarized if he moved into a neighborhood in which the risk of burglary was especially high, in part because housing prices were lower there?

C. SUBSTANTIVE ISSUES: MENTAL STATE

1. DECISIONS REQUIRING SUBJECTIVE AWARENESS BY THE DEFENDANT

Regina v. Morgan, [1976] A.C. 182

[The defendants had sexual relations with the wife of their commanding officer and drinking companion. The victim was awakened from a fast sleep and held by each of her limbs while the men had intercourse with her. The woman testified that she had made her nonconsent manifest; the defendants claimed, though, that they mistakenly believed she was consenting because her husband had not only suggested that they have intercourse with her, but "told them that they must not be surprised if [she] struggled a bit, since she was 'kinky' and this was the only way in which she could get 'turned on.'" On appeal, the House of Lords refused to reverse the conviction of rape, defined as "unlawful sexual intercourse with a woman without her consent and by force," arguing that the trial court's failure to instruct the jury that they should convict only if they believed the defendants were subjectively aware of the victim's nonconsent was, in essence, harmless error. But the Court agreed with the appellant's contention that, as a general matter, an honest belief in consent ought to suffice to exonerate.]

No doubt a defendant will wish to raise argument or lead evidence to show that this [honest] belief was reasonable, since this will support its honesty. No doubt the prosecution will seek to cross-examine or raise arguments or adduce evidence to undermine the contention that the belief is reasonable, because, in the nature of the case, the fact that a belief cannot reasonably be held is a strong ground for saying that it was not in fact held honestly at all. Nonetheless ... the fact to be refuted by the prosecution is honesty and not honesty plus reasonableness....

[T]he prohibited act is and always has been intercourse without consent of the victim and the mental element is and always has been the intention to commit that act, or the equivalent intention of having intercourse willy-nilly not caring whether the victim consents or not.

Reynolds v. State, 664 P.2d 621 (Alaska App. 1983)

[The defendant was convicted of first degree sexual assault under Alaska Stat. § 11.41.410(a)(1) ("An offender commits the crime of sexual assault in the first degree if ... the offender engages in sexual penetration with another person without consent of that person."). The victim, J.D., testified that the defendant, a voluntary social companion whom she had not previously dated "had intercourse with her against her will and restrained her at [his] apartment until morning at which time he accepted her request to drive her home. She concedes that her objections were verbal, that she never forcibly resisted Reynolds and that Reynolds never threatened her or struck her." The defendant testified that the sex was consensual and that "he did not notice anything about her behavior or demeanor which would indicate that she did not wish to have intercourse with him." The court went on to state:]

At common law ... [r]ape was a general intent crime. The state was required to prove that the defendant intentionally engaged in the prohibited conduct, i.e., sexual intercourse to which the complaining witness had not consented. However, it was not necessary for the state to prove that the defendant knew or should have known that the victim did not consent. The potential harshness of this rule was mitigated by the common law requirement that in order for the state to prove the absence of consent, it must show that the victim "resisted to the utmost." ...

[T]he legislature has substantially enhanced the risk of conviction in ambiguous circumstances by eliminating the requirement that the state prove "resistance" and by substantially broadening the definitions of "force" [Alaska Stat. § 11.81.900(b)(22) ("any bodily impact, restraint, or confinement or the threat of imminent bodily impact, restraint, or confinement")] and "physical injury" [§ 11.81.900(b)(40) ("physical pain or an impairment of physical condition")]. We are satisfied, however, that the legislature counteracted this risk through its treatment of mens rea. It did this by shifting the focus of the jury's attention from the victim's resistance or actions to the defendant's understanding of the totality of the circumstances. Lack of consent is a "surrounding circumstance" which under the Revised Code, requires a complementary mental state as well as conduct to constitute a crime. No specific mental state is mentioned in Alaska Stat. § 11.41.410(a)(1) governing the surrounding circumstance of "consent." Therefore, the state must prove that the defendant acted "recklessly" regarding his putative victim's lack of consent.

2. DECISIONS PERMITTING CONVICTION OF DEFENDANTS WHO MAKE UNREASONABLE MISTAKES OF FACT

People v. Williams

Supreme Court of California.
4 Cal.4th 354, 841 P.2d 961, 14 Cal.Rptr.2d 441 (1992).

■ ARABIAN, J.

On Saturday, November 4, 1989, Deborah S. and her sister Jenny S. were staying at the Episcopal Sanctuary homeless shelter.... They had arrived in San Francisco from Wichita, Kansas approximately two weeks earlier. Deborah and Jenny returned to the shelter mid-Saturday morning after completing some errands. Jenny entered the shelter, and Deborah waited outside.

Shortly after Jenny's departure, Deborah was approached by defendant Wash Jones Williams. Deborah had not met Williams before, and he did not introduce himself. Williams was an electrician, and a volunteer and resident at the shelter....

Williams asked if Deborah would like to get some coffee, "no strings attached." Williams and Deborah agree that for the remainder of the morning they walked, engaged in conversation, and ate some food....

Deborah testified ... Williams asked her if she would like to watch television. Deborah said the only place she knew of to watch television for free was the Osmond Center, located next door to the shelter. Williams later told her the place he was talking about to watch television was not far away.

Deborah and Williams walked towards Turk Street. Williams purchased a bracelet from a street vendor for Deborah. The area was unfamiliar to her.... Williams mentioned nothing about sex, and in fact led Deborah to believe he was not interested in sex because he mentioned that he had a daughter about Deborah's age.

They stopped at a building with a gate across the front, and Williams rang a buzzer. While Deborah did not see a sign in front of the building, the building was later identified as the Dahlia Hotel. Once inside, Williams rented a room, and asked the clerk for a sheet. At this point Deborah realized they were in a hotel....

Deborah walked into the room ahead of Williams. She noticed that there was no television. When Williams arrived, she asked him how it was that he wanted to watch television when there was no television in the room. He lay down on the bed and said he wanted Deborah to lie down beside him. Deborah went to the door to let herself out, but was unable to release the bolt lock. Williams came up behind her, and put his hand on the door.... He "hollered" at her that "he didn't spend $20.00 for nothing." He punched her in the left eye. He said he wanted her "over there in the bed." She said "no," so he pushed her down on the bed....

Williams told Deborah to take off her pants. She asked "Why do I need to take off my pants?" He repeated his demand that she take off her pants, and said that he did not like to hurt people. She was scared so she removed her pants. He took off his clothes, got on top of her, and ... engaged in sexual intercourse for approximately 10 to 15 minutes. She screamed and tried to push him off, but because of the disparity in their size, her efforts were unsuccessful.

Once Williams had ejaculated, he allowed Deborah to get up and get dressed. He offered her $50, but she said she was not a prostitute and did not want the money. She threw the bracelet at him....

The examining nurse and doctor testified that the injury to the eye was more consistent with a punch than a slap.... The doctor testified that Deborah appeared scared, and that the examination was consistent with her complaint of sexual assault.

Williams gave a dramatically different account of the encounter. He testified that prior to entering the hotel room, he neither wanted nor expected to have sex. However, when he entered the room, Deborah hugged and kissed him and began to remove her clothes, whereupon Williams also began to remove his clothes. Williams asserted that he is diabetic and almost impotent, and therefore Deborah had to fondle his genitals for 10 to 15 minutes before helping him to insert his penis into her vagina....

After intercourse, Deborah told Williams she needed $50 because her sister was moving in with her boyfriend and she was not sure if she would fit in. He told her he did not "turn tricks" and refused to give her the money. She became hostile and ... threatened to create a problem for him by telling Father Nunn and her sister if he did not give her the money. Williams said he did not care whom she told, that she had come to the room voluntarily, and "we made love." Deborah called Williams a "welching Nigger," and said she knew how to "fix" him, since her father ... had previously raped her. Angry at these remarks, Williams slapped her hard on the right, not the left, side of her face....

A jury found Williams guilty of two counts of forcible rape (Pen. Code § 261, now subd. (a)(2) ("Rape is an act of sexual intercourse accomplished with a person not the spouse of the perpetrator ... [w]here it is accomplished against a person's will by means of force, violence, duress, menace, or fear of immediate and unlawful bodily injury on the person or another."))....

In *People v. Mayberry*, 15 Cal.3d 143, 125 Cal.Rptr. 745, 542 P.2d 1337 (1975), this court held that a defendant's reasonable and good faith mistake of fact regarding a person's consent to sexual intercourse is a defense to rape....

The *Mayberry* defense has two components, one subjective and one objective. The subjective component asks whether the defendant honestly and in good faith, albeit mistakenly, believed that the victim consented to sexual intercourse. . . .

In addition, the defendant must satisfy the objective component, which asks whether the defendant's mistake regarding consent was reasonable under the circumstances. Thus, regardless of how strongly a defendant may subjectively believe a person has consented to sexual intercourse, that belief must be formed under circumstances society will tolerate as reasonable in order for the defendant to have adduced substantial evidence giving rise to a *Mayberry* instruction. . . .

In *Mayberry*, we held that a requested instruction regarding mistake of fact was required when "some evidence 'deserving of ... consideration' " existed to support that contention. . . .

Thus, because the *Mayberry* instruction is premised on mistake of fact, the instruction should not be given absent substantial evidence of equivocal conduct that would have led a defendant to reasonably and in good faith believe consent existed where it did not. As one author has explained, under the reasonable mistake defense, "a woman is raped but not by a rapist." (Berliner, Rethinking the Reasonable Belief Defense to Rape (1991) 100 Yale L.J. 2687, 2695, fn. 56.) . . .

Here, there was no substantial evidence supporting a *Mayberry* instruction. Williams testified that Deborah initiated sexual contact, fondled him to overcome his impotence, and inserted his penis inside herself. This testimony, if believed, established actual consent. In contrast, Deborah testified that the sexual encounter occurred only after Williams blocked her attempt to leave, punched her in the eye, pushed her onto the bed, and ordered her to take her clothes off, warning her that he did not like to hurt people. This testimony, if believed, would preclude any reasonable belief of consent. These wholly divergent accounts create no middle ground from which Williams could argue he reasonably misinterpreted Deborah's conduct. . . .

In finding substantial evidence to support a *Mayberry* instruction, the Court of Appeal relied primarily on three circumstances. First, it noted that Deborah "willingly accompanied [Williams] to the hotel ... [and] that she did not object when the hotel clerk handed him a bedsheet." The relevant inquiry under *Mayberry*, however, is whether Williams believed Deborah consented to have intercourse, not whether she consented to spend time with him. To characterize the latter circumstance alone as a basis for a reasonable and good faith but mistaken belief in consent to intercourse is, as noted by Presiding Justice Low's dissent in the Court of Appeal, to "revive the obsolete and repugnant idea that a woman loses her right to refuse sexual consent if she accompanied a man alone to a private place. This is an especially cruel assumption here, where the victim, a homeless woman, may well have wanted nothing more than the relative quiet and comfort of a private room in which to relax and watch television."

Second, the Court of Appeal relied on Williams's testimony; [however] this testimony of Deborah's unequivocal behavior was evidence of actual consent, not reasonable and good faith mistake as to consent.

Finally, the Court of Appeal cited the fact that "during the hour they were inside the room the hotel clerk did not hear any screams or other sounds indicating physical violence." ... [T]he clerk's failure to hear Deborah's screams or struggling sheds no light on Williams's state of mind....

We note for the guidance of the lower courts [that a defendant may not] ... assert a claim of reasonable and good faith but mistaken belief in consent based on the victim's behavior *after* the defendant had exercised or threatened "force, violence, duress, menace, or fear of immediate and unlawful bodily injury ..." However, a trier of fact is permitted to credit some portions of a witness's testimony, and not credit others. Since a trial judge cannot predict which evidence the jury will find credible, he or she must give the *Mayberry* instruction whenever there is substantial evidence of equivocal conduct that could be reasonably and in good faith relied on to form a mistaken belief of consent, despite the alleged temporal context in which that equivocal conduct occurred. The jury should, however, be further instructed, if appropriate, that a reasonable mistake of fact may not be found if the jury finds that such equivocal conduct on the part of the victim was the product of "force, violence, duress, menace, or fear of immediate and unlawful bodily injury ..."

■ MOSK, J., concurring.

I concur in the judgment. The Court of Appeal ... concluded that the superior court prejudicially erred when it refused to instruct on the defense of reasonable and honest belief by the defendant regarding the complainant's consent. As will appear, that conclusion was itself erroneous; there was error at trial but no prejudice. Consequently, the judgment must be reversed.

I cannot concur, however, in the majority opinion. Its analysis does not go deep enough. And to the depth it does go, it is unsound....

A jury could have credited [Williams's] testimony. Had it done so, it could have found that defendant had a reasonable and honest belief in consent....

First, and more generally, the majority assert that the reasonable-and-honest-belief defense involves only a *mistaken* belief. *Mayberry*, however, does not so limit the defense ... Neither does logic limit the defense. It is not a *mistaken* belief that negatives the requisite "wrongful intent," but simply the belief itself....

Further, a "mistake" limitation would lead to untenable results. It would effectively prohibit the defendant to attempt to raise a reasonable doubt about the intent element of rape unless he concedes the no-consent element. In other words, to offer the defense he would have to take the position that he was *mistaken* about the complainant's consent—and thereby admit, at least by implication, that the complainant did not in fact consent. That is illogical. Consent by the complainant and a reasonable and honest belief by the defendant in that consent are altogether compatible....

To the extent that the majority imply that the evidence is insufficient as a matter of law when the defendant testifies to consent and the complainant testifies to no consent, they are also wrong. Their premise is that, in a credibility contest between the defendant and the complainant, the jury must accept in toto the testimony of one and reject in toto the testimony of the other. Such a view is without basis in logic or experience.... Here ... the jury could have inferred that once inside the hotel room, the complainant became apprehensive about the situation in which she found herself; she thought her only "choice" was sexual intercourse with great bodily injury if she actively resisted *or* sexual intercourse without such injury if she did not; as a consequence, she engaged in conduct that could have supported a reasonable and honest belief in consent; but she did not, in fact, consent.

I now turn from the fact of error to the consequences. The question, of course, is this: Does the superior court's erroneous refusal of an instruction on the defense of reasonable and honest belief by the defendant regarding the complainant's consent require reversal of the judgment? The answer ... is in the negative.

... [T]he superior court properly instructed the jury as follows. Rape requires "a union or joint operation of act or conduct and a general criminal intent ... When a person intentionally does that which the law declares to be a crime, he is acting with general criminal intent ..." What "the law declares to be a crime" insofar as rape is concerned is "an act of sexual intercourse with a female person who is not the spouse of the perpetrator accomplished against such person[']s will by means of force, violence or fear of immediate and unlawful bodily injury to such person ..."

... In returning a verdict of guilty on each of the two counts of rape, the jury necessarily found under the proper instructions quoted above that defendant intentionally engaged in an act of sexual intercourse that was in fact unconsented and forcible. By implication, it necessarily found that he acted at least recklessly as to consent and force.... When, as here, under proper instructions the jury necessarily and soundly makes a finding adverse to the defendant on an issue erroneously omitted from the instructions, there is no prejudice arising from the omission....

3. STRICT LIABILITY?

Commonwealth v. Lopez

Supreme Court of Massachusetts.
433 Mass. 722, 745 N.E.2d 961 (2001).

■ SPINA, J.

The defendant, Kenny Lopez, was convicted on two indictments charging rape....

Before the jury retired, defense counsel requested a mistake of fact instruction as to consent. The judge declined to give the instruction, saying that, based "both on the law, as well as on the facts, that instruction is not warranted." Because the defendant's theory at trial was that the victim actually consented and not that the defendant was "confused, misled, or mistaken" as to the victim's willingness to engage in sexual intercourse, the judge concluded that the ultimate question for the jury was simply whether they believed the victim's or the defendant's version of the encounter. The decision not to give the instruction provides the basis for this appeal. . . .

The defendant . . . was not entitled to this instruction. In Commonwealth v. Ascolillo, 405 Mass. 456, 541 N.E.2d 570 (1989), we held that the defendant was not entitled to a mistake of fact instruction and declined to adopt a rule that "in order to establish the crime of rape the Commonwealth must prove *in every case* not only that the defendant intended intercourse but also that he did the act pursuant to an honest and reasonable belief that the victim consented" (emphasis added). Neither the plain language of our rape statute nor the court's decisions prior to the *Ascolillo* decision warrant a different result. . . .

. . . In determining whether the defendant's honest and reasonable belief as to the victim's consent would relieve him of culpability, it is necessary to review the required elements of the crime of rape. . . .

At common law, rape was defined as "the carnal knowledge of a woman forcibly and against her will." 4 W. Blackstone, Commentaries 210. Since 1642, rape has been proscribed by statute in this Commonwealth. While there have been several revisions to this statute, the definition and the required elements of the crime have remained essentially unchanged since its original enactment. The current rape statute, Mass. Gen. Laws ch. 265, § 22(b), provides in pertinent part:

> Whoever has sexual intercourse or unnatural sexual intercourse with a person and compels such person to submit by force and against his will, or compels such person to submit by threat of bodily injury, shall be punished by imprisonment in the state prison for not more than twenty years.

This statute follows the common-law definition of rape, and requires the Commonwealth to prove beyond a reasonable doubt that the defendant committed (1) sexual intercourse (2) by force or threat of force and against the will of the victim.

. . . . We have construed the element, "by force and against his will," as truly encompassing two separate elements each of which must independently be satisfied. Therefore, the Commonwealth must demonstrate beyond a reasonable doubt that the defendant committed sexual intercourse (1) by means of physical force, nonphysical, constructive force, or threats of bodily harm, either explicit or implicit, and (2) at the time of penetration, there was no consent.

Although the Commonwealth must prove lack of consent, the "elements necessary for rape do not require that the defendant intend the intercourse be without consent." Historically, the relevant inquiry has been limited to consent in fact, and no mens rea or knowledge as to the lack of consent has ever been required.

A mistake of fact as to consent, therefore, has very little application to our rape statute. . . .

This is not say, contrary to the defendant's suggestion, that the absence of any *mens rea* as to the consent element transforms rape into a strict liability crime. It does not. Rape, at common law and pursuant to Mass. Gen. Laws ch. 265, § 22 is a general intent crime, and proof that a defendant intended sexual intercourse by force coupled with proof that the victim did not in fact consent is sufficient to maintain a conviction....

We also have concerns that the mistake of fact defense would tend to eviscerate the long-standing rule in this Commonwealth that victims need not use any force to resist an attack. A shift in focus from the victim's to the defendant's state of mind might require victims to use physical force in order to communicate an unqualified lack of consent to defeat any honest and reasonable belief as to consent. The mistake of fact defense is incompatible with the evolution of our jurisprudence with respect to the crime of rape....

In the present case, there was no evidence of equivocal conduct. The complaining witness testified that she had told the defendant, repeatedly and explicitly, that she did not want any form of sexual contact, that she tried to get away from the defendant, and that she cried during the forced intercourse. The defendant testified that the complaining witness was the one to initiate intimate contact; that she participated actively; and that she suggested they get together again later that evening....

This case does not persuade us that we should recognize a mistake of fact as to consent as a defense to rape in all cases. Whether such a defense might, in some circumstances, be appropriate is a difficult question that we may consider in a future case where a defendant's claim of reasonable mistake of fact is at least arguably supported by the evidence. This is not such a case.

QUESTIONS AND COMMENTS

1. Under *Morgan, Reynolds, Williams,* and *Lopez,* what mental state—if any—is attached to the element of nonconsent, and why?

2. According to Justice Mosk's concurrence in *Williams,* would a defendant raising a mistake (or, a "reasonable and honest belief") defense ever be entitled to a specific instruction on that defense? Or would it be enough to instruct on mens rea with respect to each element of rape? Is the disagreement in *Williams* about the need to give instructions spelling out a mistake of fact defense or about the mens rea attaching to the nonconsent element of rape?

3. The *Lopez* court insists that rape is not a strict liability crime in Massachusetts. But is nonconsent a strict liability *element*? Compare *Regina v. Prince,* ch. 5. The court regards the recognition of a mistake of fact defense on the nonconsent element as a novel development that would eviscerate long-standing rules and would be incompatible with "the evolution of our jurisprudence with respect to the crime of rape." At the same time, it appears to leave open the possibility that a mistake of fact claim might, after all, be relevant in some future case. What role does the state's rape statute play in the court's analysis? (Compare *Lopez* to *Reynolds* and

Williams on this point.) Does the court's analysis raise concerns in light of the various aspects of the principle of legality (legislativity, specificity, lenity, prospectivity, publicity)?

4. *Mistakes of Fact other than Mistakes about Consent.* Naturally, defendants could assert that they did not have a blameworthy mental state as to any element of a sex crime: thus, for instance, if the defendant is accused of rape because he had sexual relations with a woman deemed incapable of consenting because of mental incapacity, we must assess whether he should be exonerated if he did not know that she lacked such capacity.

This issue has attracted particular attention in relationship to mistakes about the victim's age in the statutory rape context. Historically, one of the most significant pockets of "strict liability" in the criminal law was the refusal by most courts to permit defendants to defend against statutory rape charges by claiming that they had made such a reasonable mistake of fact. For a typical holding, see Commonwealth v. Murphy, 165 Mass. 66, 42 N.E. 504 (1896).

The traditional rule was subject to the usual attacks on strict liability—courts following this rule were said to treat some people as felons who had not been shown to have acted with the requisite "consciousness of wrongdoing"—and a number of courts altered the traditional rule. See, e.g., People v. Hernandez, 393 P.2d 673 (Cal. 1964); State v. Guest, 583 P.2d 836 (Alaska 1978).

Mark Kelman treats the traditional rule as defensible, if not necessarily correct. In his view, strict liability does not dispense with blameworthiness, it merely removes from the jury the capacity to make a *particularized* decision that the defendant made reasonable efforts to ascertain the girl's age. Removing this decision from the jury is a more sensible strategy if we simultaneously believe that: 1) left to their own devices, jurors are unduly likely to believe that defendants made reasonable efforts to ascertain age if they relied on appearances or statements by their sexual partner, even if instructed by judges that such steps are not sufficient, and 2) if those who had sex with young women even remotely close to the age of consent took steps to avoid making mistakes that the legislature believes a man they would *define* as reasonable would take (checking photo IDs, asking her parents or guardians etc.), then there would effectively be no or nearly no mistakes of age. Those few truly reasonable mistakes (by the legislature's lights) that existed (for instance, in situations in which the "victim" set up the defendant with an elaborate scheme to hide her age) might better be handled by informal discretionary means (e.g., prosecutorial decisions not to prosecute). See Mark Kelman, "Interpretive Construction in Substantive Criminal Law," 33 Stan. L. Rev. 591, 606–11 (1980).

Richard Posner notes that we should be reluctant to make defendants strictly liable only when we worry about "chilling" nearby activity. Since, he says, we have no interest in facilitating sexual activity with young women very close to the age of consent, we needn't worry that men will be held liable if they reasonably think they're engaging in (barely) protected activity: we would be perfectly happy if they foreswore sex with women young enough for there to be any appreciable risk that the sex turns out to be statutory rape. See Richard Posner, "An Economic Theory of the Criminal Law," 85 Colum. L. Rev. 1193, 1222 (1985).

5. Proponents of using a *negligence* standard must defend their choice both against those who advocate requiring subjective awareness and those who believe that the defendant's beliefs, however reasonable, are irrelevant. The argument against requiring subjective awareness is explained succinctly by Susan Estrich:

> It is not unfair ... to demand that men behave "reasonably" and to impose criminal penalties on them when they do not....
>
> If inaccuracy or indifference to consent is "the best that this man can do" because he lacks the capacity to act reasonably, then it might well be unjust and ineffective to punish him for it. But such men will be rare, at least so long as voluntary drunkenness is not equated with inherent lack of capacity. More common is the case of the man who could have done better but did not; could have paid attention, but did not; heard her refusal or saw her tears, but decided to ignore them. The man who has the inherent capacity to act reasonably but fails to has, through that failure, made a blameworthy choice for which he can justly be punished.

Susan Estrich, Real Rape 97–98 (1987).

The arguments against employing strict liability are, at core, double-edged: the first focuses on fairness to defendants while the second focuses on the risk of unduly restricting the act definition if we dispense with mens rea entirely. On the first point, see the Pennsylvania legislative subcommittee report cited in Commonwealth v. Fischer, 721 A.2d 1111, 1117–18 (Pa.Super. 1998):

> [T]here may be cases [now that the Pennsylvania Supreme Court] has extended the definition of force to psychological, moral, and intellectual force, where a defendant might non-recklessly or even reasonably, but wrongly, believe that his words and conduct do not constitute force or the threat of force and that a non-resisting female is consenting. An example might be "date rape" resulting from mutual misunderstanding. The boy does not intend or suspect the intimidating potential of his vigorous wooing. The girl, misjudging the boy's character, believes he will become violent if thwarted; she feigns willingness, even some pleasure. In our opinion, the defendant in such a case ought not to be convicted of rape.

On the second point, Estrich again expresses the position concisely:

> [B]y ignoring mens rea, American courts and legislators have imposed limits on the fair expansion of our understanding of rape. As long as the law holds that mens rea is not required, and that no instructions on intent need be given, pressure will exist to retain some form of resistance requirement and to insist on force as conventionally defined in order to protect men against conviction for "sex." Using resistance as a substitute for mens rea unnecessarily and unfairly immunizes those men whose victims are afraid enough, or intimidated enough ... not to take the risk of resisting physically.

See Susan Estrich, "Rape," 95 Yale L.J. 1087, 1100–01 (1986).

6. If we use a negligence standard, though, how will we give it content? When is a *false* belief in the victim's consent nonetheless reasonable? Is it helpful at all to say that "under the reasonable mistake defense, 'a woman is raped but not by a rapist?' " (See *Williams*.) Is being a criminal a prerequisite for criminal liability apart from (in addition to?) engaging in criminal conduct?

There are two critical issues. First, we must always decide in defining a negligent mistake whether to compare the defendant to "all people" or to a group of people with his more particular infirmities of judgment. Right off the bat, we face a thorny issue: if *women* are systematically more sensitive to manifestations of nonconsent than men, is it appropriate to ask whether reasonable *people* (the weighted average of women and men?) would have been aware of the victim's nonconsent or to ask only if reasonable men would have been? Can the defendant ask to be compared to members of sub-groups of men of which he is a member who are less sensitive still to women's expressions of subjectivity, more prone to treat certain behavior as signaling sexual availability?

Second, we must decide how much guidance to give juries. The negligence standard could be vague and open-ended: instruct the jury to convict only if a reasonable person in defendant's position would have been aware of the substantial and unjustifiable risk that the victim had not consented. (Is there reason to believe that vague standards in rape cases might pose dangers not present, or not present to the same degree, in other cases?) Or, we could add cautionary instructions to counteract prevalent "rape myths" that we believe some jurors will hold: the judge could tell the jurors *not* to consider how the victim was dressed, whether she had accompanied the defendant to his room voluntarily, etc., in deciding whether the defendant's belief in consent was reasonable. Some states, by statute, radically restrict the admissibility of evidence about dress, fearing that jurors will believe that dress signals actual consent or that it makes a man's error about consent reasonable. See, e.g., Ala. Code § 12–21–203(a)(3).

Or, we could establish more rigid rules that define when a mistake is unreasonable: the rules could be exclusive and mandatory (unless the defendant followed a particular, defined mode of insuring that the victim consented, his belief in consent is unreasonable) or a "safe harbor" (his belief is *per se* reasonable if he followed certain rules for ascertaining consent but the jury may find him to have been reasonable even if he didn't follow the "rules").

One obvious *rule* that we might use is that the defendant will not be deemed to have made a reasonable mistake if the woman has said "no" or manifested her desire not to have sex in some other way (for instance, by crying). Is this sort of rule appropriate? Is it *always* unreasonable for a man to believe a woman is consenting to sex if she says "no"? Consider in this regard a survey of female undergraduates in which 39% of the surveyed group, and 61% of the sexually active group, reported that they had said "no" when they meant "yes"; the overwhelming majority of those who did so said they had done so out of fear of appearing promiscuous, and many others either wanted to have their dates "talk [them] into it" or "be more physically aggressive." See Charlene L. Muehlenhard & Lisa C. Hollabaugh, "Do Women Sometimes Say No When They Mean Yes?," 54 J. Personality & Soc. Psych. 872 (1988). Might it not be unreasonable for the defendant to act on the supposition that "no" means "yes"—even if it is sometimes *true*—because the *risk* that the defendant is badly harming the woman if he is wrong is too high to be justifiable? Don't we hold drivers who kill responsible for negligent manslaughter when they drive in a fashion that *often* would prove harmless?

Another obvious rule one might use instead is that the defendant is unreasonable in believing the woman has consented unless he is relying on explicit verbal permission. (Recall the Antioch Sexual Offense Prevention Policy's *substantive* definition of consent in this regard.) Naturally, he may *still* be unreasonable in believing the woman has consented to sexual relations even if the victim has explicitly said "yes" if she has done so because of impermissible coercive pressures, and he should have known that she said "yes" for that reason. The question then is simply whether it is a necessary, though not sufficient, condition to form a *reasonable* belief that the victim has consented, that the woman *say* she is assenting.

7. California seems to permit rape defendants to be exonerated if they reasonably believed the defendant consented to the sexual contact; Massachusetts apparently does not permit defendants to raise such a defense. Look carefully at *Lopez* and *Williams*, though: how distinct are the rules that are actually in force in the two jurisdictions? What does this say, generally, about the distinction between strict liability and negligence? (See ch. 5.)

D. NOTES ON EVIDENCE ISSUES

1. TRADITIONAL LAW AND ATTITUDES SUSPICIOUS OF THE COMPLAINANT'S TESTIMONY

Davis v. State, 120 Ga. 433, 48 S.E. 180 (1904)

The law is well-established ... that a man shall not be convicted of rape on the testimony of the woman alone, unless there are some concurrent circumstances which tend to corroborate her evidence. The offense of rape seems to be an exceptional one in this regard. The accused should not be convicted upon the woman's testimony alone, however positive it may be, unless she made some outcry or told of the injury promptly, or her clothing was torn or disarranged, or her person showed signs of violence, or there were some other circumstances which tend to corroborate her story. This rule appears to be a sound one. Without it, every man is in danger of being prosecuted and convicted on the testimony of a base woman in whose testimony there is no truth.

Model Penal Code § 213.6(5). Testimony of Complainants

... In any prosecution before a jury for a [sexual] offense, the jury shall be instructed to evaluate the testimony of a victim or complaining witness with special care in view of the emotional involvement of the witness and the difficulty of determining the truth with respect to alleged sexual activities carried out in private.

Glanville Williams, "Corroboration—Sexual Cases," 1962 Crim. L. Rev. 662

[S]exual cases are particularly subject to the danger of deliberately false charges, resulting from sexual neurosis, phantasy, jealousy, spite, or simply a girl's refusal to admit that she consented to an act of which she is now ashamed.

State v. Wood, 59 Ariz. 48, 122 P.2d 416 (1942)

If consent be a defense to the charge [of rape], then certainly any evidence which reasonably tends to show consent is relevant and material, and common experience teaches us that the woman who has once departed from the paths of virtue is far more apt to consent to another lapse than is the one who has never stepped aside from that path.

2. Reform: Prompt Report and Corroboration

Pa. Crim. Code § 3105. Prompt Complaint

Prompt reporting to public authority is not required in a prosecution under this chapter. Provided, however, that nothing in this section shall be construed to prohibit a defendant from introducing evidence of the complainant's failure to promptly report the crime if such evidence would be admissible pursuant to the rules of evidence.

Pa. Crim. Code § 3106. Testimony of Complainants

The credibility of a complainant of [a sexual offense] shall be determined by the same standard as the credibility of a complainant of any other crime. The testimony of a complainant need not be corroborated in prosecutions under this chapter. No instructions shall be given cautioning the jury to view the complainant's testimony in any other way than that in which all complainants' testimony is viewed.

3. Reform: Rape Shield Laws

People v. Jovanovic

Supreme Court of New York, Appellate Division, First Department.
263 A.D.2d 182, 700 N.Y.S.2d 156 (1999)

■ Saxe, J.

On this appeal of his conviction for ... sexual abuse[a] ..., defendant Oliver Jovanovic asks us to examine certain issues regarding the application of the Rape Shield Law (Crim. Proc. L. § 60.42)....

The People's case against Jovanovic was primarily founded upon the testimony of the complainant. She told a detailed story of becoming

a. N.Y. Penal Law § 130.65 (Sexual abuse in the first degree): A person is guilty of sexual abuse in the first degree when he or she subjects another person to sexual contact [b]y forcible compulsion.—Eds.

acquainted with Jovanovic through communications over the Internet, both by e-mail and by so-called "instant messages," as well as in a number of lengthy telephone conversations.

Their first contact took place during the summer of 1996. The complainant, a Barnard undergraduate who was home for the summer in Salamanca, a small town in upstate New York, went on-line and logged onto a "chat room" called "Manhattan," hoping to find other Columbia students there. In the course of a general discussion, she received an "instant message" from Jovanovic, and embarked upon a long, "instant message" private conversation with him. Their first conversation quickly took on an intimate tone; for instance, in response to Jovanovic's information that he studied molecular genetics and computational biology at Columbia and ran a small multimedia design firm with his brother, the complainant said "I may love you, hold a sec while I check the profile." When they shortly discovered that they both spent a lot of time in a particular building at Columbia, the complainant referred to "destiny" and asked "want to have coffee?"

In this first conversation, Jovanovic indicated his interest in the grotesque, the bizarre, and the occult. He mentioned Joel–Peter Witkin, explaining that Witkin creates photographs using corpses....

Then, on October 9, 1996, the complainant sent Jovanovic an e-mail reminding him of their previous conversation.... He responded by e-mail (from Seattle) the next day, and she e-mailed back immediately. His next e-mail was on October 16, 1996, by which time he had returned to New York. She responded right away, continuing the tone of her earlier correspondence with him ("bring me anything back from Seattle?"). He did not write again until October 20, 1996. When she responded that evening, she (among other remarks) asked how tall he was.

He did not reply until November 10, 1996, when he asked "As for my height, why? Are you looking to be dismembered by a tall, dark stranger, or something of that sort? I'm sometimes strange and dark, but of average height, so perhaps you should look elsewhere. <g>"[2] [T]he complainant responded that same day.... Their exchange of e-mail [until] November 14, 1996 continued discussing ... the complainant's purported interest in what she termed "a tall dark dismember-er."

[Their e-mail exchanges resumed on November 17. On November 20, the complainant] asked "So Oliver, you keep mentioning film after film, but where pray tell am I supposed to find them?" She also indicated an intense desire to know more about him, and spoke of "too many taboos surrounding the questions I want to ask." Two hours later he replied "Taboos are meant to be broken.... You'll simply have to ask more questions. Of course, that way lies dismemberment." Soon after that, still on November 20, 1996, she e-mailed back, "I think you may just be toying with the idea of dismemberment" and told him that she has to push herself, see how far she can take it, testing her limits. She also warned, "arms and legs are not toys" and that "It could get sick. And just may."

2. <g> is used to mean "grin" in on-line shorthand.

After more e-mails back and forth during the late night/early morning hours of November 21, 1996, at about 2:30 a.m., the complainant referred to things getting "kind of intimate," and then, at about 5:00 a.m., Jovanovic ended his message with "Should I call you, or you call me." That afternoon her e-mail message included her phone number, with the message that she would be home around 3:00 that night.

He called at about 3:00 a.m. on November 22nd, and they spoke for approximately four hours. According to the complainant's trial testimony, Jovanovic invited her to see a movie with him that night, and she gave him the address of her dormitory.

Jovanovic arrived at 8:30 p.m. on November 22, and suggested that they get something to eat. When they finished dinner at around 10:15, he said it was too late for the movie they had agreed upon, and asked if she wanted to see a video at his apartment instead. She said "I don't know"—explaining in her testimony that although she did not want to, she has trouble being assertive. Finally she agreed. He drove to three video rental outlets, but did not find what he wanted. He said he had some videos at his apartment, which was located in Washington Heights, and they proceeded to drive there, arriving at about 11:30 p.m.

Jovanovic gave her some tea ... and a book of photographs by Joel–Peter Witkin, depicting corpses placed in grotesque poses. They watched a video entitled "Meet the Feebles," in which Muppet-like characters engage in sexual or violent behavior....

When the movie was over, she said it was getting late and she should go, but they began a conversation that ranged from the subjects of East Timor, media control of the news, and religion, to the subject of people with multiple personalities....

When [Jovanovic] introduced the subject of good and evil, the complainant told him that she did not believe that evil existed. He looked stern, and in a voice she also characterized as "stern," told her to take off her sweater. He then repeated this directive in a louder voice. The complainant testified that she did not know what to do, thought it was a joke, but nevertheless removed her sweater. Then he told her to take off her pants, and she complied. [S]he explained that she did not protest because she did not know what to think.

[According to the complainant's testimony, Jovanovic then proceeded to hold her captive for 20 hours during which time, over her repeated objections, he tied her up, bit her, dropped hot wax on her skin and molested her with a baton.]

The complainant's next memory was of waking some time on Saturday, November 23, 1996.... [She] found that she was able to untie her legs, and stood up.... At this point, although she said he still sought to restrain her, she continued to run and to fight him off, ... unlocking the apartment door and finally escaping.

.... On Sunday night, November 24, 1996, [the complainant] logged on to the computer at her school library and retrieved an e-mail message sent by Jovanovic the night before at 10:35 p.m. In it, he said she had forgotten her gold chain when she left the apartment, and that he could mail it if she gave him her zip code, or he could drop it off. He also said, "I have a feeling the experience may not have done you as much good as I'd hoped, because you weren't acting much smarter at the end than you were at the beginning." He closed with the words, "I hope you managed to get back all right." . . . .

The Redacted Statements

[The trial court ruled that certain statements made by the complainant in e-mails sent to Jovanovic were inadmissible under the Rape Shield Law.] The following discussion sets forth the portions of the complainant's e-mails to defendant that were subject to the court's preclusion order.

[First] Redacted E–Mail

[O]n November 19th, the complainant sent Jovanovic a long message relating how she became involved with [one] Luke. She told of "fingering"[3] Luke to chat with, and how Luke's "x-intrest," Karen, was unhappy about the complainant's new friendship with Luke and sent the complainant an e-mail warning her to stay away from him. The court deleted from this e-mail the following paragraphs . . . (with misspellings and other errors left intact).

> "the boy calls, tells lots and lots of a life led like burroughs: heroin addicted, bisexual atheist. My kinda comrad. so he seduced me. come to Ufm, I did[,] come to my appartment, I did[,] then he got me.
>
> "Oh he sighed and pulled out an agonized tale of being young in Edinborough and on a field trip for highschool . . . there were 'very nice boys' (according to the chaperons) who worked at the hotel, so said chaperons let luke and his teen friends hang out with the big boys for a night on the town. Unfortunately for poor luke, one took a liking to him, (this is liking with twisted glint in the eye mind you). yes yes, so young man took young boy (luke) to empty hotel room [where he raped him].
>
> " 'oh wow' I perked up [and] presented offer of assistance. Luke said sure, then told me more, about his old boyfriend gillian, what he taught him. and about ginger and this one dominatrix who lives on the 10th floor."
>
> [Second] Redacted E–Mail

Jovanovic answered, shortly thereafter on November 19th, "[t]hen he got you? How suspenseful," although the court precluded the first four words, "[t]hen he got you?" The complainant's response on November 20th, contained a further personal confession that the court also deleted from the evidence, in which the complainant had replied, "No duh, there's more, more interesting than sex, yes he did catch me, no sex, but he was a sadomasochist and now I'm his slave and its painful, but the fun of telling my friends 'hey I'm a sadomasochist' more than outweighs the torment."

3. The complainant used the word "fingered" to indicate initiating an on-line conversation with a person she didn't previously know, whose user ID she obtained from a Columbia on-line ID directory.

[Third] Redacted E–Mail

Jovanovic's responsive e-mail on November 20th said, "You're submissive sometimes? Should have told me earlier." The complainant's next message in reply, also on November 20th included the following ... information, which was also redacted: "and yes, I'm what those happy pain fiends at the Vault call a 'pushy bottom'."[4]

.... These messages were ruled inadmissible on the ground that they were covered by the protection of the Rape Shield Law (Crim. Proc. L. § 60.42), in that they constituted evidence of the complainant's prior sexual conduct, having the effect of demonstrating her "unchastity." In addition to the messages themselves, based upon the trial court's understanding of the Rape Shield Law, Jovanovic was precluded from questioning either the complainant or Luke as to whether the two had mutually engaged in consensual sadomasochism....

The Rape Shield Law represents a rejection of the centuries-old legal tradition holding that, as Professor Wigmore stated, "the character of a woman as to chastity is of considerable probative value in judging the likelihood of [her] consent". No longer does our society generally accept the premise that a woman who is "unchaste," i.e., unmarried and sexually active, is more likely than a "chaste" woman to consent to the sexual advances of any man. It is because society now views such evidence as generally irrelevant that the Legislature enacted a law prohibiting the use of such evidence: the law "bar[s] harassment of victims and confusion of issues through raising matters relating to the victims' sexual conduct that have *no proper bearing* upon the defendant's guilt or innocence" (Preiser, Practice Commentaries, McKinneys Cons. Laws of N.Y., Book 11A, Crim. Proc. L. § 60.42, at 9 [emphasis added]). Thus, it is critical to the theory behind the Rape Shield Law that evidence of the victim's character for chastity is generally irrelevant to a rape prosecution.

In accordance with this premise, Crim. Proc. L. § 60.42 provides that, "Evidence of a victim's *sexual conduct* shall not be admissible in the prosecution for [a sex] offense or an attempt to commit [a sex] offense unless such evidence:

"1. proves or tends to prove specific instances of the victim's prior sexual conduct with the accused; or

"2. proves or tends to prove that the victim has been convicted of [prostitution] within three years prior to the sex offense which is the subject of the prosecution; or

"3. rebuts evidence introduced by the people of the victim's failure to engage in sexual intercourse, deviate sexual intercourse or sexual contact during a given period of time; or

"4. rebuts evidence introduced by the people which proves or tends to prove that the accused is the cause of pregnancy or disease of the victim, or the source of semen found in the victim; or

4. The defense explains that The Vault is a club catering to sadomasochists, and a "pushy bottom" is a submissive partner who pushes the dominant partner to inflict greater pain.

"5. is determined by the court after an offer of proof by the accused outside the hearing of the jury, or such hearing as the court may require, and a statement by the court of its findings of fact essential to its determination, to be relevant and admissible in the interests of justice" (emphasis added).

Initially, we hold that the redacted e-mail messages were not subject to the Rape Shield Law because they did not constitute evidence of the sexual *conduct* of the complainant. Rather, they were merely evidence of *statements* made by the complainant about herself to Jovanovic.

The distinction between evidence of prior sexual *conduct* (to which the statute expressly applies), and evidence of *statements concerning* prior sexual conduct, is more than merely semantic. Direct evidence of the complainant's *conduct* with others would generally be introduced (if admissible) as a basis to infer that she had voluntarily behaved in such a way on prior occasions with others. In contrast, the use of a statement is not so straightforward. It is frequently relevant not to prove the truth of the matter stated, but rather, for the fact that the speaker made the statement. That is, a statement may be relevant as proof of the speaker's, or the listener's, state of mind.

For instance, here, the complainant's statement to Jovanovic regarding sadomasochism were not necessarily offered to prove the truth of what she said, i.e., that she actually was a sadomasochist. Rather, much of their importance lay in the fact that she chose to say these things to Jovanovic in the context of her electronic, on-line conversation with him, so as to convey to him another message, namely, her interest in exploring the subject of such activities with him. . . .

However, even assuming, arguendo, that no distinction could properly be made between prior conduct and statements *about* prior conduct, we would still hold that the Rape Shield Law does not support the preclusion of the e-mails at issue, because we conclude that these statements fall within a number of the exceptions set forth within the statute. . . .

[T]he inclusion of exceptions within Crim. Proc. L. § 60.42 is due to our Legislature's recognition of the possibility that certain types of sexual history evidence will be relevant. The bill was specifically drafted "to strike a reasonable balance between protection of a victim's privacy and reputation while not infringing on the defendant's right to a fair trial based on the presumption of innocence". . . .

First, given the highly intimate nature of some of this information, the statements, as a practical matter, should be viewed as the equivalent of "prior sexual conduct with the accused" (subd [1]). These statements, made to Jovanovic in the context of a relationship being developed on-line, as part and parcel of the ongoing conversation that led up to their in-person encounter, are really part of the complainant's verbal repartee with him, in which each participant tells the other of their interests and preferences. Viewed with the purpose of her statements in mind, . . . the redacted statements should therefore have been held to be admissible as falling within the first exception to the Rape Shield Law (Crim. Proc. L. § 60.42 [1]).

The exception for past conduct with the accused is included in the statute because a "history of intimacies" would "tend to bolster a claim of consent". The statements here, especially in view of their intimate nature, have the same sort of potential of shedding light on the motive, intent, and state of mind of these two people in their subsequent encounter. * * *

[Second], given the relevance of the redacted statements to the issues presented to the jury, even if none of the statute's other exceptions covered the complainant's statements to Jovanovic, the "interests of justice" exception of Crim. Proc. L. § 60.42 (5) would be applicable. That exception was included in order to give courts discretion to admit what was otherwise excludable under the statute, where it is determined that the evidence is relevant.

[T]he precluded communications from the complainant to Jovanovic were highly relevant. The defense did not seek to introduce them to demonstrate the complainant's "unchastity" and thereby impugn her character or her honesty. Instead, the fact that the complainant made these statements to Jovanovic is relevant to establish that she purposefully conveyed to Jovanovic an interest in engaging in consensual sadomasochism with him.

Because the jury could have inferred from the redacted e-mail messages that the complainant had shown an interest in participating in sadomasochism with Jovanovic, this evidence is clearly central to the question of whether she consented to the charged ... sexual abuse. The People emphasize that it is not whether she initially consented that is relevant, but whether she withdrew her consent and whether defendant continued to act despite the withdrawal of consent. However, the strength of the evidence as to the extent to which the complainant initially indicated to Jovanovic an interest in participating in sadomasochism with him *is* relevant to a determination of whether that consent was withdrawn.

Furthermore, the e-mails Jovanovic received from the complainant, particularly her statements, "now I'm his slave and its painful, but the fun of telling my friends 'hey I'm a sadomasochist' more than outweighs the torment," and "yes, I'm what those happy pain fiends at the Vault call a 'pushy bottom,' " could illuminate Jovanovic's understanding and beliefs as to the complainant's willingness to participate in sadomasochism with him, and, as such, are also relevant to Jovanovic's state of mind....

We conclude that the trial court's rulings erroneously withheld from the jury a substantial amount of highly relevant, admissible evidence....

Accordingly, the judgment of the Supreme Court, New York County ... convicting defendant, after a jury trial, of ... sexual abuse in the first degree ... should be reversed ... and the matter remanded for a new trial.

■ MAZZARELLI, J.P. (concurring in part and dissenting in part).

While I agree with the majority's conclusion that a new trial is required because the trial court misapplied the Rape Shield Law when it precluded material evidence which may have affected the conviction on the kidnapping and sex abuse counts, a different perspective informs my analysis....

With respect to the redacted e-mails, I would also find that the complainant's statements concerning her interest in sadomasochistic practices should have been admitted, because the Rape Shield Law, which is designed to preclude introduction of "[e]vidence of a victim's sexual conduct," is not meant to exclude statements of interest in sex....

However, ... I would ... find that the [second] redacted November 20th e-mail was properly redacted because it concerned a direct statement relating to the complainant's prior conduct, her sadomasochistic relationship with her boyfriend. This redaction was also appropriate because the transmission described behavior which would serve only to disparage the complaining witness's reputation....

Unlike the majority, I would not find the [second] redacted November 20th e-mail admissible under ... the interest of justice exception to the Rape Shield Law. Since Crim. Proc. L. § 60.42 (5) is designed to allow the introduction of material which has been deemed presumptively inadmissible, the proffered evidence merits careful scrutiny. Given the complainant's right to sexual self-determination, I would find that the inflammatory nature of the evidence of her prior sexual conduct would, in the eyes of the jury, outweigh the probative value of this evidence. Presenting this information could mislead the jury to conclude that the complainant was more likely to consent to the charged sexual offenses because she had previously consented to similar, violent acts....

The Rape Shield Law was expressly drafted for the purpose of protecting those persons who are sexually active outside a legally sanctioned relationship. It serves the very important policy objective of removing certain impediments to the reporting of sex crimes. Specifically, the law was drafted to encourage victims of sex offenses to prosecute their attackers without fear that their own prior sexual activities, regardless of their nature, could be used against them at trial. In enacting the Rape Shield Law, the Legislature sought to prevent muddling the trial with matters relating to a victim's prior sexual conduct which have no proper bearing on the defendant's guilt or innocence, but only serve to impugn the character of the complainant and to prejudice the jury. To limit its applicability and protections as the majority holds would only serve to turn the clock back to the days when the main defense to any such charge was to malign the complainant. Here, where a victim's sexual preferences are widely disapproved, it is crucial that evidentiary determinations be made with heightened concern that a jury may act on the very prejudices that the statute seeks to exclude.

QUESTIONS AND COMMENTS

1. To what degree do the traditional defendant-protective rules depend on the notion that women either fantasize rapes or make false charges, whether out of malice or the desire to cover up (for instance, from boyfriends and parents) and evade responsibility for their decisions to have engaged in non-coercive sex? To what degree do they depend on the assumption that juries are especially bad in sex crime cases at assessing witness credibility, or that juries are particularly unlikely to acquit in (at

least certain) rape cases? (Reconsider *McQuirter*, ch. 6.) Note that the Model Penal Code's draftsmen tried to defend variants of the traditional rules without recourse to these assumptions:

> In no other context is felony liability premised on conduct that under other circumstances may be welcomed by the "victim." The difference between criminal and non-criminal conduct depends ultimately on a question of attitude. Proof of this elusive issue often boils down to a confrontation of conflicting accounts. The corroboration requirement is an attempt to skew resolution of such disputes in favor of the defendant. It does not, or it at least need not, rest on the assertion that one person's testimony is inherently more deserving of credence than another's. It certainly is not dependent on allegations that women generally fabricate such charges or that judges and juries regularly favor complaining witnesses at the expense of justice. It is, rather, a determination to favor justice to the defendant, even at some cost to societal interest in effective law enforcement and to the personal demand of the victim for redress.

Model Penal Code Commentaries § 213.6, at 428–29. Why isn't the rape defendant protected adequately by the general requirement that he should not be convicted absent "proof beyond a reasonable doubt"? What if it turns out that juries in rape cases are more *acquittal*-prone than in other cases?

2. What is the source of jury prejudice in admitting evidence of past voluntary sexual behavior by the victim: is it (dominantly) the fear that jurors will overestimate the probability that the victim consented to sex with this defendant on this occasion because she had consented to sex with other men, or is it the fear that they simply will not *care* that she's been raped because the rape could not have deprived her of a valuable reputation for chastity? If the latter, can the perception of the harm of rape that it reflects be corrected through evidentiary rules?

3. In *Jovanovic*, the dissenter accuses the majority of "turn[ing] the clock back to the days when the main defense to [a rape] charge was to malign the complainant." Do you agree? Compare the majority opinion in *Jovanovic* with the dissent in *Rusk*, supra. Do they reflect similar attitudes toward women who file rape complaints?

The majority makes much of the distinction between statements about one's sex life as statements about sexual interest, on one hand, and as statements about the sexual past, on the other. Do you find this distinction to be "more than merely semantic"? If the point of rape shield laws is not to confuse juries, do you think jurors would be able to draw this distinction? In general? In this particular case? Who should shoulder the risk of jurors' inability to keep this distinction in mind as they deliberate—the defendant or the complainant?

More generally, to what extent does *Jovanovic* (both the majority opinion and the dissent) turn on the particular nature of the sexual conduct involved? What difference does it (should it?) make whether "the victim's [how about the defendant's?] sexual preferences are widely disapproved"?

4. Some rape shield laws reaffirm what would plainly be the case even in the absence of statute: the rape shield laws cannot deprive defendants of their Sixth Amendment right to confront witnesses. See, e.g., Federal Rule of Evidence 412(b)(3) (evidence of the complainant's past sexual behavior admissible "where exclusion of the evidence would violate the constitutional rights of the defendant"). In Michigan v. Lucas, 500 U.S. 145 (1991), the Supreme Court held that the federal rape shield law did not *per se* violate the Sixth Amendment. But there is a rich case law (involving both state and federal constitutional arguments) adjudicating claims that particular *applications* of the shield laws deprive defendants of their right to confront witnesses.

In State v. Sheline, 955 S.W.2d 42 (Tenn. 1997), the court upheld the constitutionality of the trial court's refusal to admit, first, testimony of the victim's prior voluntary sexual contacts with a male friend under circumstances that were (very broadly) similar to the circumstances at issue in the present trial (in both cases, the victim and the man had been drinking at a bar and returned to her apartment where they engaged in oral sex and then intercourse). Second, they upheld the refusal to accept testimony that the victim had first kissed and then asked another man at the same bar where she met the defendant to come home with her on the evening of the alleged rape. In State v. Jalo, 27 Or.App. 845, 557 P.2d 1359 (1976), however, the appeals court reversed a trial judge who had refused to allow the defendant to present evidence that he had threatened to tell the complainant's parents about her sexual activity with others; the appeals court held that this refusal unconstitutionally deprived the defendant of the right to show that the victim had a motive (falsely) to accuse him of rape.

The court in State v. Pulizzano, 155 Wis.2d 633, 456 N.W.2d 325 (1990), articulated a five-factor test to determine whether in a specific case there is a constitutional right to present evidence otherwise excluded by a state evidentiary rule. The factors are: 1) whether there is a clear showing that the complainant committed the prior acts; 2) whether the circumstances of the prior acts closely resemble those of the present case; 3) whether the prior acts are clearly relevant to a material issue, such as identity, intent or bias; 4) whether the evidence is necessary to the defendant's case; and 5) whether the probative value of the evidence outweighs its prejudicial effect. Is this multi-factor balancing test usable or helpful?

5. There is also controversy over the use of two distinct forms of psychiatric testimony.

On the one hand, the *prosecution* may seek to introduce evidence that the victim suffers from Rape Trauma Syndrome or some other form of Post–Traumatic Stress Disorder (or, more interestingly, Battered Woman Syndrome, see People v. White, 4 Misc. 3d 797, 780 N.Y.S. 2d 727 (N.Y. Dist. Ct. 2004)), to bolster the victim's claim that the sex was non-consensual or to explain a recantation or a delay in reporting the crime. Most, but not all, courts have been wary about admitting such testimony, especially when the experts describe the victim as suffering from Rape Trauma Syndrome, rather than more general Post–Traumatic Stress Disorder, since the expert then appears to have made a judgment about the ultimate fact that the jury is asked to determine. Compare, for instance, State v. Heath, 316 N.C. 337, 341 S.E.2d 565 (1986) (holding that experts could not testify as to their opinion on the complainant's credibility) and Commonwealth v. Garcia, 403 Pa.Super. 280, 588 A.2d 951 (1991) (experts cannot even testify that it is common for young sexual assault victims to delay reporting abuse, because it improperly bolsters the credibility of complainants) with State v. Allewalt, 308 Md. 89, 517 A.2d 741 (1986) (trial court judge did not abuse his discretion in permitting a psychiatric expert to testify that complainant suffered from "post traumatic stress disorder" and that, in his opinion, the cause of the disorder was the rape, particularly because he did not directly comment on the credibility of the complainant nor use the term "rape trauma syndrome").

On the other hand, the *defendant* may seek a complainant's psychiatric records or seek to have a psychiatrist examine the complainant to determine whether she might be psychologically predisposed to fabricate charges. Appellate courts have, on some occasions, reversed convictions in which the trial court has refused to allow the defendant to gain professional information about the complainant's psychological state. See, e.g., Commonwealth v. Stockhammer, 409 Mass. 867, 570 N.E.2d 992 (1991). More typically, though, courts hold that the same sorts of interests that justify the enactment of the rape shield laws—a desire to preserve complainants' privacy, a desire to insure that complainants are not subject to public harassment and humiliation, both to protect them as individuals and to encourage higher rates of reporting—justify great wariness in ordering either mandatory examinations or disclosure of psychiatric records. See, e.g., United States v. Benn, 476 F.2d 1127 (D.C. Cir. 1972).

CHAPTER 10

Homicide

A. Varieties of Homicide

1. Traditional Scheme (California Penal Code)

§ 187. (a) Murder is the unlawful killing of a human being, or a fetus, with malice aforethought. . . .

§ 188. Such malice may be express or implied. It is express when there is manifested a deliberate intention unlawfully to take away the life of a fellow creature. It is implied, when no considerable provocation appears, or when the circumstances attending the killing show an abandoned and malignant heart. . . .

§ 189. All murder which is perpetrated by . . . willful, deliberate, and premeditated killing, or which is committed in the perpetration of, or attempt to perpetrate, arson, rape, carjacking, robbery, burglary, mayhem, kidnapping, train wrecking, or any act punishable under Section 206 [torture], 286 [sodomy], 288 [statutory rape], 288a [oral copulation], or 289 [rape], . . . is murder of the first degree. All other kinds of murders are of the second degree.

§ 192. Manslaughter is the unlawful killing of a human being without malice. It is of three kinds:

(a) Voluntary—upon a sudden quarrel or heat of passion.

(b) Involuntary—in the commission of an unlawful act, not amounting to felony; or in the commission of a lawful act which might produce death, in an unlawful manner, or without due caution and circumspection. . . .

Punishment: First degree murder is punishable by death, life imprisonment without the possibility of parole, or imprisonment for 25 years to life, and second degree murder by imprisonment for 15 years to life. Cal. Penal Code § 190. Voluntary manslaughter is punishable by imprisonment for three, six, or eleven years, and involuntary manslaughter by imprisonment for two, three, or four years. Id. § 193.

2. Model Penal Code

§ 210.1. Criminal Homicide.

(1) A person is guilty of criminal homicide if he purposely, knowingly, recklessly or negligently causes the death of another human being.

(2) Criminal homicide is murder, manslaughter or negligent homicide.

§ 210.2. Murder.

(1) Except as provided in Section 210.3(1)(b), criminal homicide constitutes murder when:

(a) it is committed purposely or knowingly; or

(b) it is committed recklessly under circumstances manifesting extreme indifference to the value of human life. Such recklessness and indifference are presumed if the actor is engaged or is an accomplice in the commission of, or an attempt to commit, or flight after committing or attempting to commit robbery, rape or deviate sexual intercourse by force or threat of force, arson, burglary, kidnapping or felonious escape.

§ 210.3. Manslaughter.

(1) Criminal homicide constitutes manslaughter when:

(a) it is committed recklessly; or

(b) a homicide which would otherwise be murder is committed under the influence of extreme mental or emotional disturbance for which there is reasonable explanation or excuse. The reasonableness of such explanation or excuse shall be determined from the viewpoint of a person in the actor's situation under the circumstances as he believes them to be.

§ 210.4. Negligent Homicide.

(1) Criminal homicide constitutes negligent homicide when it is committed negligently.

Punishment: Murder is punishable by imprisonment for a minimum of no less than one year and no more than ten years and a maximum of life; manslaughter by imprisonment for a minimum of no less than one year and no more than three years and a maximum of ten years; and negligent homicide by imprisonment of no less than one year and no more than two years and a maximum of five years. Model Penal Code § 6.06.

3. New York Penal Law

§ 125.10 Criminally negligent homicide.

A person is guilty of criminally negligent homicide when, with criminal negligence, he causes the death of another person.

§ 125.15 Manslaughter in the second degree.

A person is guilty of manslaughter in the second degree when:

1. He recklessly causes the death of another person. . . .

§ 125.20 Manslaughter in the first degree.

A person is guilty of manslaughter in the first degree when:. . . .

1. With intent to cause serious physical injury to another person, he causes the death of such person or of a third person; or

2. With intent to cause the death of another person, he causes the death of such person or of a third person under circumstances which do not constitute murder because he acts under the influence of extreme emotion-

al disturbance, as defined in paragraph (a) of subdivision one of section 125.25....

§ 125.25 Murder in the second degree.

A person is guilty of murder in the second degree when:

1. With intent to cause the death of another person, he causes the death of such person or of a third person; except that in any prosecution under this subdivision, it is an affirmative defense that:

(a) The defendant acted under the influence of extreme emotional disturbance for which there was a reasonable explanation or excuse, the reasonableness of which is to be determined from the viewpoint of a person in the defendant's situation under the circumstances as the defendant believed them to be ...; or

....

2. Under circumstances evincing a depraved indifference to human life, he recklessly engages in conduct which creates a grave risk of death to another person, and thereby causes the death of another person; or

3. Acting either alone or with one or more other persons, he commits or attempts to commit robbery, burglary, kidnapping, arson, rape in the first degree, sodomy in the first degree, sexual abuse in the first degree, aggravated sexual abuse, escape in the first degree, or escape in the second degree, and, in the course of and in furtherance of such crime or of immediate flight therefrom, he, or another participant, if there be any, causes the death of a person other than one of the participants....

§ 125.27 Murder in the first degree.

A person is guilty of murder in the first degree when:

1. With intent to cause the death of another person, he causes the death of such person or of a third person; and [certain special circumstances are present; see infra section B.4 (capital murder)].

Punishment: The various types of homicide in New York are punishable (roughly) as follows. First degree murder: death, life imprisonment without parole, or imprisonment for a minimum between twenty and twenty-five years and a maximum of life. N.Y. Penal Law §§ 60.06, 70.00. Second degree murder: imprisonment for a minimum between fifteen and twenty-five years and a maximum of life. Id. § 70.00. First degree manslaughter: imprisonment for between five and twenty-five years. Id. Second degree manslaughter: imprisonment for between one and fifteen years. Id. Criminally negligent homicide: imprisonment for between less than one year and four years, probation, or fine. Id. §§ 60.01, 70.00.

QUESTIONS AND COMMENTS

1. *Homicide in Context.* It's useful to get a sense of homicide's place within the special part of American criminal law. Empirically speaking, homicides are extremely rare, though obviously their consequence is enormous. In 2002, there were 16,204 murders or nonnegligent homicide

committed in the United States, a rate of 5.6 per 100,000 residents. By comparison, here are the numbers for some other crimes: rape (95,136/33.0), robbery (420,637/145.9), aggravated assault (894,348/310.1), car theft (1,246,096/432.1), burglary (2,151,875/746.2), and larceny (7,052,922/2,445.8).

Homicide traditionally has attracted the lion's share of doctrinal attention in American criminal law scholarship and teaching. Many of what we now think of as general principles of criminal law were developed within the context of homicide law. For instance, much of the law of mens rea was the law of malice aforethought—the mens rea of common law murder—and self-defense was homicide *se defendendo*. More recently, the main drafter of the Model Penal Code originally laid out his scheme for the reform of American criminal law in an article on the law of homicide. See Jerome Michael & Herbert Wechsler, "A Rationale of the Law of Homicide (Parts I & II)," 37 Colum. L. Rev. 701, 1261 (1937). What effect might this focus on homicide have had on the development of American criminal law doctrine?

Within the special part of American criminal law, homicide is one of the crimes against the person. Unlike assault, another crime against the person, homicide is defined in terms of "death," rather than of "injury." See, e.g., Model Penal Code § 211.1(a) ("person is guilty of assault if he ... purposely, knowingly or recklessly causes bodily injury to another"). On the meaning of "death," see, e.g., People v. Eulo, 63 N.Y. 2d 341 (1984) (defining "death" as "an irreversible cessation of breathing and heartbeat or, when these functions are artificially maintained, an irreversible cessation of the functioning of the entire brain"). In many jurisdictions, homicide differs from abortion in that it requires causing the death of a "person," where "person" is defined as "a human being who has been born and is alive." See, e.g., N.Y. Penal Law § 125.05(1). Note, however, that the California Penal Code defines murder as "the unlawful killing of a human being, *or a fetus*." Cal. Penal Code § 187 (emphasis added). Originally Cal. Penal Code § 187 defined murder as "the unlawful killing of a human being." The clause "or a fetus" was added after the California Supreme Court held in Keeler v. Superior Court, 2 Cal.3d 619, 470 P.2d 617, 87 Cal.Rptr. 481 (1970), that the legislature did not intend the murder provision in its original version to cover the killing of a fetus.

2. *Result vs. Conduct*. Homicide is the quintessential result offense. Its central and distinguishing element is the proscribed result—death of another human being. In its most basic form, homicide does not specify any particular conduct as a result of which death occurs. It is defined, simply, as "caus[ing] the death of another person." Besides the basic forms of homicide, which differ largely in the mental state that attaches to the result element of death, modern American criminal codes also contain quite a few definitions of homicide that define the conduct element in greater detail. Good examples are vehicular homicide statutes that aggravate homicides committed while intoxicated:

N.Y. Penal Law § 125.12 Vehicular manslaughter in the second degree

A person is guilty of vehicular manslaughter in the second degree when he:

(1) commits the crime of criminally negligent homicide . . ., and

(2) causes the death of such other person by operation of a vehicle [while intoxicated].

Vehicular manslaughter in the second degree is a class D felony. [Criminally negligent homicide is otherwise a class E felony.]

§ 125.13 Vehicular manslaughter in the first degree

A person is guilty of vehicular manslaughter in the first degree when he:

(1) commits the crime of vehicular manslaughter in the second degree as defined in section 125.12, and

(2) commits such crime while knowing or having reason to know that . . . his license or his privilege of operating a motor vehicle . . . is suspended or revoked and such suspension or revocation is based upon a conviction [for driving while intoxicated].

Vehicular manslaughter in the first degree is a class C felony.

3. *Types of Homicide.* While all American jurisdictions punish homicide, they have developed a fairly complex classification of types of homicide. To start with, there is the basic distinction between murder and manslaughter. The line between the two is as important as it may be difficult to draw, as we shall see—murder is punished considerably more harshly than is manslaughter.

A more recent distinction is that between first degree and second degree murder, which was introduced in late 18th century American criminal law to differentiate between capital and noncapital murder. The point of limiting capital punishment to first degree murder was to limit the scope of capital punishment, without eliminating it altogether.

Independent of the distinction between first and second degree murder, most states continue to provide for the death penalty as a possible punishment for some sub-set of homicides. Capital murder is murder plus one or more of a set of statutorily defined "aggravating" or "special" circumstances, including—among others—murder of a police officer, "heinous" murder, murder by a prison inmate, or murder during the perpetration of a felony. (Note, however, that the punishment for capital murder is not necessarily capital. Conviction of capital murder is a necessary but not a sufficient condition for imposition of the death penalty, insofar as the sentencer—a jury or, if the defendant waives a jury, a judge—may decide against capital punishment on the basis of mitigating circumstances.)

Another common distinction among different varieties of murder, besides those between first and second degree, and between capital and noncapital murder, is that between intentional and "gross recklessness" (or "deliberate indifference") murder. (Since reckless homicide is a type of *manslaughter*, rather than of murder, the line between gross recklessness murder and recklessness manslaughter can be difficult to discern.)

A final variety of murder that deserves mention here is felony murder, which punishes a homicide as murder without any need to show an intent to kill as long as the homicide occurred during the commission of a felony.

This doctrine has come under heavy criticism for some time on the ground that it permits harsh punishment for a strict liability crime. Felony murder should be distinguished from capital felony murder; only the former does without the requirement of an intent to kill.

As to manslaughter, we've already mentioned the reckless homicide variety, also known as "involuntary" manslaughter. "Voluntary" manslaughter, by contrast, is homicide that would qualify as murder—given the intent to kill—but is partially excused on the ground of provocation.

Finally, there is negligent homicide. (Note that, in the Model Penal Code, the default mental state is recklessness. The Code includes only three offenses that explicitly impose criminal liability for negligent conduct: homicide, assault (§ 211.1), and criminal mischief (§ 220.3).) Traditionally negligent homicide was considered a type of involuntary manslaughter, as courts did not carefully differentiate between negligence and recklessness. The Model Penal Code strove to clarify the distinction between the two, on one hand, and between criminal and civil negligence on the other.

4. While all types of homicide contain the result element of death of another person, not all require that the actor *intend* to cause death—or have some other mental state regarding the death. Felony murder is the prime example. Another is intent-to-injure homicide (murder in some jurisdictions, manslaughter in New York), which requires an intent "to cause serious physical injury," but not death. Depending on how one defines "serious physical injury," there may not be much difference between this type of homicide and ordinary involuntary manslaughter. (New York defines it as "physical injury which creates a substantial risk of death, or which causes death or serious and protracted disfigurement, protracted impairment of health or protracted loss or impairment of the function of any bodily organ." N.Y. Penal Law § 10.00(10)). This type of homicide, however, should be distinguished from assault with intent to kill. There the intent to kill is present, but the result element of death is not.

5. Homicide is generally considered to be the most serious offense. Why? Who is the victim of a homicide? Note that tort law originally did not permit recovery for wrongful death. Even today, wrongful death statutes do not permit recovery for the decedent's pain and suffering. See Markus Dirk Dubber, Victims in the War on Crime: The Use and Abuse of Victims' Rights 179–80 (2003).

B. Murder

1. First Degree vs. Second Degree Murder

Watson v. United States

District of Columbia Court of Appeals.
501 A.2d 791 (1985).

■ Rogers, Associate Judge:

First degree murder is a calculated and planned killing while second degree murder is unplanned or impulsive. The government must therefore prove beyond a reasonable doubt that the accused acted with premeditation and deliberation, the thought processes necessary to distinguish first degree murder from second degree. "To prove premeditation, the government must show that a defendant gave 'thought before acting to the idea of taking a human life and [reached] a definite decision to kill.' " Deliberation is proved by demonstrating that the accused acted with "consideration and reflection upon the preconceived design to kill; turning it over in the mind, giving it second thought." Although no specific amount of time is necessary to demonstrate premeditation and deliberation, the evidence must demonstrate that the accused did not kill impulsively, in the heat of passion, or in an orgy of frenzied activity.

"[S]ome appreciable time must elapse" between the formation of design to kill and actual execution of the design to establish that reflection and consideration amounted to deliberation. The time need not be long. Thus, the government is not required to show that there was a "lapse of days or hours, or even minutes," and the time involved may be as brief as a few seconds. Although reflection and consideration, and not lapse of time, are determinative of deliberation, "[l]apse of time is important because of the opportunity which it affords for deliberation." . . .

Viewing the evidence most favorably to the government, the government's case-in-chief showed that during the investigation of a stolen car, two police officers saw the stolen car pull into the parking lot of 3729 Jay Street, N.E. They ordered the driver to stop by shouting, "Police. Hold it." The driver of the car, appellant, jumped out, looked at the officers, and ran toward an apartment complex; Officer Lunning, with his gun drawn, pursued. Appellant ran through the archway of 3749 Jay Street, N.E. and then through the open door of the Davis' apartment at 3712–A Hayes Street, N.E. Three young girls, ages approximately 14, 13 and 9, were sitting at a table doing their homework. Appellant asked to use the telephone, and after dialing, he asked the responding party "[Are] they still out there?" He sat down at the table, where the girls were sitting, and held his head in his hands.

Officer Lunning entered the open door of the apartment holding his gun in front of him and told appellant "Police, you are under arrest." Appellant asked, "For what?" When appellant refused to cooperate with being handcuffed, the officer said, "Do you want me to blow your m——— f———head off?" Appellant stood up. As the officer reached for his hand to put on the handcuffs, appellant said, "You are not going to put those things on me." Appellant grabbed the officer in a bear hug around the waist. Eventually the two men fell over a table. The officer's gun, which had been pointed downwards as he had tried to handcuff appellant, dropped onto the floor.

The two men scuffled, rolling over each other, until appellant had the officer in a position where he could not move: appellant had his knee in the officer's chest and, with his hands, held down the officer's hands. At this point, according to two of the girls, the officer told appellant, "It wasn't worth it." Then, with the officer still flat on his back, appellant reached out and grabbed the loose gun. He proceeded to hold the gun to the officer's chest. The officer now repeated, "It wasn't worth it." One of the girls then ran back to the back of the apartment, a distance of approximately twenty feet. She was inside the bathroom when, within seconds, she heard a shot. Another girl ran from the apartment, approximately sixteen feet, and heard a shot while outside. She next saw appellant coming down the steps as he was leaving the apartment complex holding the gun in his hand. The officer followed shortly, holding his chest and eventually fell to the ground.

The gun was fired approximately thirty to thirty-six inches from Officer Lunning's body while he was lying on the floor. The bullet entered at the midline of the top of the officer's abdomen on the right side. Appellant was uninjured when he was arrested at the scene, suffering only scrapes on his kneecap. Appellant was six feet four inches tall and weighed 218 pounds. Officer Lunning was five feet nine inches tall and weighed approximately 220 pounds.

A neighbor testified that when appellant ran into 3694 Hayes Street, N.E. and asked to use her sister's telephone, she heard him say into the telephone, "I just shot the police; could you come and get me." He also said he "had something on him and the police were chasing him so he hit [the officer] with the gun." The sister who lived in the apartment corroborated this testimony, and also testified that appellant told her he was carrying drugs and offered her money if she would hide him.

"Premeditation and deliberation may be inferred from sufficiently probative facts and circumstances." In the instant case the jury could reasonably find that when appellant sat at the table, after making the telephone call, he was anticipating the officer's arrival and planning how to escape. He knew the officer had drawn his gun, and a juror could infer that appellant realized he would have to disarm the officer in order to escape. Appellant, who was five inches taller, and described by one of the girls as much larger than the officer, initiated the struggle while the officer was pointing his gun at him. He struggled with the officer and caused him to drop his gun. He then continued to struggle with the officer until he gained complete physical control of the officer. One of the girls testified that the officer did not have a chance to get the loose gun. A juror could reasonably find that when the officer said, "It wasn't worth it," and appellant grabbed the gun, the officer was pleading for his life or at least suggesting to appellant that avoiding arrest for stealing a car was not worth assaulting an officer. Since there was nothing blocking appellant's escape from the apartment, a juror could further infer that by grabbing the loose gun and holding it to the officer's chest instead of fleeing, appellant had made the decision to kill the officer.

Before a shot was fired, however, the officer had time to repeat, "It wasn't worth it." Two of the girls also had time to run from the room into another part of the apartment or outside of the apartment building. In addition, appellant rose up and stood over the officer. At no time was anything or anyone impeding appellant's escape from the apartment. Considering the lapse of time before appellant fired the gun, a juror could reasonably infer from all the circumstances that the officer's second plea was asking appellant to reconsider the decision to kill him, and that appellant had sufficient time to, and did reaffirm his decision to kill the officer. Although these events occurred within a short period of time, there was evidence before the jury from which it could find that there were two significant pauses in the action—when appellant had immobilized the officer and when the officer repeated his plea—which afforded appellant time to premeditate and deliberate. * * *

The government's evidence showed that although he was facing an officer with a drawn gun, appellant, having waited for the officer to arrive, initiated the physical struggle with him. Even after he had immobilized the officer and had grabbed the gun, appellant did not shoot immediately, but held the gun in the officer's chest. When he fired the gun he did not fire a series of shots, as though in a panic, but a single shot, which went directly into the right side of the officer's chest. Combined with the evidence of appellant's motive to escape, these circumstances could cause a reasonable juror to conclude that appellant did not shoot in a panic but acted with deliberation, having decided to kill the officer in order to assure his escape, and that he reflected upon his decision before pulling the trigger. * * *

Affirmed.

State v. Thompson

Supreme Court of Arizona.
204 Ariz. 471, 65 P.3d 420 (2003).

■ BERCH, JUSTICE.

On May 17, 1999, Thompson shot and killed his wife, Roberta Palma. Several days before the shooting, Palma had filed for divorce, and Thompson had discovered that she was seeing someone else. Just a week before the shooting, Thompson moved out of the couple's home. As he did so, Thompson threatened Palma that, "if you divorce me, I will kill you."

Thompson returned to the couple's neighborhood the morning of May 17.... That same morning, police received and recorded a 9–1–1 call from the house. The tape recorded a woman's screams and four gunshots. The four gunshots span nearly twenty-seven seconds. Nine seconds elapse between the first shot and the third, and there is an eighteen-second delay between the third shot and the fourth....

At trial, Thompson did not deny killing his wife, but claimed that he did so in the heat of passion, making the killing manslaughter or, at most, second degree murder. During closing arguments, Thompson's counsel argued that ... Thompson had "simply snapped." ...

The jury found Thompson guilty of first degree murder and the judge sentenced him to life in prison without the possibility of parole....

... Arizona's first degree murder statute, provides that "[a] person commits first degree murder if ... intending or knowing that the person's conduct will cause death, the person causes the death of another *with* premeditation." Ariz. Rev. Stat. § 13–1105(A)(1) (2001) (emphasis added). Thompson challenges the constitutionality of the statute, arguing that it renders first degree murder indistinguishable from second degree murder.

A person commits second degree murder in Arizona "if *without* premeditation ... such person intentionally causes the death of another person." Ariz. Rev. Stat. § 13–1104(A)(1) (2001) (emphasis added).

According to the definition adopted by the legislature,

> "premeditation" means that the defendant acts with either the intention or the knowledge that he will kill another human being, when such intention or knowledge precedes the killing by any length of time to permit reflection. *Proof of actual reflection is not required,* but an act is not done with premeditation if it is the instant effect of a sudden quarrel or heat of passion.

Ariz. Rev. Stat. § 13–1101(1) (emphasis added).

The question before us is whether this definition of premeditation abolishes the requirement of actual reflection altogether, whether it eliminates the requirement of direct proof of actual reflection, or whether it substitutes for the necessary proof of actual reflection the mere passage of enough time to permit reflection. The State asserts the third interpretation, that the legislature intended to relieve the State of the burden of proving a defendant's hidden thought processes, and that this definition of premeditation establishes that the passage of time may serve as a proxy for reflection. The court of appeals agreed with this interpretation.

Thompson maintains that reducing premeditation to the mere passage of time renders the statute vague and unenforceable because courts have held that actual reflection can occur as quickly as "successive thoughts of the mind." Thus, he argues and the court of appeals agreed, the difference between first and second degree murder has been eliminated....

For most of this state's history, first degree murder explicitly required proof of "premeditation," or actual reflection by the defendant. Because premeditation involves a defendant's thought processes, the question arose how to prove that a defendant had reflected on the decision to kill. Courts responded by allowing the issue to be proved by circumstantial evidence. Indeed, at one time, the murder statute set forth fact patterns that suggested premeditation: "poison, lying in wait, torture, or when the killing is done in the perpetration or attempt to perpetrate certain felonies. If none of these elements appear, the evidence must show in some manner that the killing was 'wilful, deliberate and premeditated.' "

In 1978, however, premeditation was redefined to mean

> that the defendant acts with either the intention or the knowledge that he will kill another human being, when such intention or knowledge precedes the killing by a length of time to permit reflection. An act is not done with premeditation if it is the instant effect of a sudden quarrel or heat of passion.

Ariz. Rev. Stat. § 13–1101(1) (1978). This definition highlights the time element, speaking, as it does, in terms of intention or knowledge that precedes the killing by enough time to allow reflection and excluding killings that occur as a result of a sudden quarrel....

To ... clarify the distinction between first and second degree murder, the legislature amended the definition of premeditation in 1998 to include the clause "proof of actual reflection is not required." ...

We conclude ... that if the only difference between first and second degree murder is the mere passage of time, and that length of time can be "as instantaneous as successive thoughts of the mind," then there is no meaningful distinction between first and second degree murder. Such an interpretation would relieve the state of its burden to prove actual reflection and would render the first degree murder statute impermissibly vague and therefore unconstitutional under the United States and Arizona Constitutions.

We are, however, mindful of our duty to construe this statute, if possible, in a way that not only gives effect to the legislature's intent, but also in a way that maintains its constitutionality. As a starting point, we note that the words chosen by the legislature do not say that actual reflection is no longer required to distinguish first from second degree murder. Rather, the legislature provided that "*proof of* actual reflection is not required." Ariz. Rev. Stat. § 13–1101 (1) (emphasis added). Recognizing that direct proof of a defendant's intent to kill often does not exist, the legislature sought to relieve the state of the often impossible burden of proving premeditation through direct evidence. But by this act the legislature did not intend to eliminate the requirement of reflection altogether or to allow the state to substitute the mere passing of time for the element of premeditation.[6] ...

Our decision today distinguishes the *element* of premeditation from the *evidence* that might establish that element. Although the mere passage of time suggests that a defendant premeditated—and the state might be able to convince a jury to make that inference—the passage of time is not, in and of itself, premeditation. To allow the state to establish the element of premeditation by merely proving that sufficient time passed to permit reflection would be to essentially relieve the state of its burden to establish the sole element that distinguishes between first and second degree murder....

As we noted earlier, only in rare situations will a defendant's reflection be established by direct evidence such as diary entries or statements to others. But the state may use all the circumstantial evidence at its disposal in a case to prove premeditation. Such evidence might include, among other things, threats made by the defendant to the victim, a pattern of escalating violence between the defendant and the victim, or the acquisition of a weapon by the defendant before the killing. In short, the passage of time is but one factor that can show that the defendant actually reflected. The key is that the evidence, whether direct or circumstantial, must convince a jury beyond a reasonable doubt that the defendant actually reflected.

6. .... To redefine the mental state as a moment of time that may be "instantaneous" ... allows a defendant's culpability to turn "on the ticking of a clock, and not on any differential act, omission, or accompanying mental state." An offense so defined does not "give fair warning" whether conduct will be punished as first degree murder rather than second, nor does it "differentiate on reasonable grounds between [first and second degree murder]." Such a chance result does not satisfy the requirements of due process.

[P]remeditation should be defined for the jury. But we also recognize that the statutory definition of premeditation may not explain it in an easily understandable way and, indeed, might mislead the jury. Thus, we disapprove of the use of the phrase "proof of actual reflection is not required" in a jury instruction.... [T]rial judges should, in future cases, instruct juries as follows:

> "Premeditation" means that the defendant intended to kill another human being [knew he/she would kill another human being], and that after forming that intent [knowledge], reflected on the decision before killing. It is this reflection, regardless of the length of time in which it occurs, that distinguishes first degree murder from second degree murder. An act is not done with premeditation if it is the instant effect of a sudden quarrel or heat of passion.

. . . .

In the case before us, the jury was instructed that "proof of actual reflection is not required." We hold that, without further clarification, this instruction was erroneous.... However, the jury was not instructed that actual reflection can occur as instantaneously as successive thoughts of the mind. Moreover, the State presented overwhelming evidence that Thompson actually reflected on his decision to kill his wife, including evidence of threats to kill her a week before the murder, the time that elapsed between each gunshot, and the victim's screams as recorded on the 9–1–1 tape between each gunshot. We conclude beyond a reasonable doubt that the flawed jury instruction ... did not affect the jury's verdict, and we will not overturn Thompson's conviction and sentence.

■ RYAN, JUSTICE, concurring in part and dissenting in part.

[The definition of premeditation as statutorily defined is not unconstitutionally vague.] The conclusion I reach in this case is one of long standing. In *Commonwealth v. Drum,* 58 Pa. 9, 16 (1868), the court explained the interplay between the speed at which premeditation can occur and the requirement that the defendant not be under the influence of a sudden quarrel or heat of passion:

> *No* time is too short for a wicked man to frame in his mind his scheme of murder, and to contrive the means of accomplishing it. But this expression must be qualified, lest it mislead. It is true that such is the swiftness of human thought, that no time is so short in which a wicked man may not form a design to kill ... yet this suddenness is opposed to premeditation, and a jury must be well convinced upon the evidence that there was time to deliberate and premeditate. The law regards, and the jury must find, the actual intent; that is to say the fully formed purpose to kill, with so much time for deliberation and premeditation, as to convince them that this purpose is not the immediate offspring of rashness and impetuous temper, and that the mind has become fully conscious of its own design.

Perhaps as one commentator contends, premeditation fails "as the dividing line between degrees of murder." Matthew A. Pauley, *Murder by Premeditation,* 36 Am. Crim. L. Rev. 145, 169 (1999). Nonetheless, our legislature has chosen to use premeditation as that dividing line. By using the passage of time as a substitute for actual reflection, while at the same time requiring that a killing not be "the instant effect of a sudden quarrel or heat of passion," Ariz. Rev. Stat. section 13–1101(1), the legislature has drawn a discernible line between intentional or knowing first degree murder and intentional or knowing second degree murder. That is all the constitution requires.

QUESTIONS AND COMMENTS

1. The court in *Watson* decides that the evidence of premeditation was not so insufficient as to require a reversal of the first-degree murder conviction on appeal. Imagine yourself as Watson's attorney at trial. What arguments might you make that the state has not established beyond a reasonable doubt that Watson acted with premeditation? (Try to steer clear of arguments that would support a conviction of manslaughter, rather than of second-degree murder.)

2. What's left of the distinction between first and second degree murder if "lapse of time" isn't determinative, and "premeditation and deliberation" can occur within seconds (or yet smaller units of time)? Does abandoning a temporal distinction leave the fact finder with sufficient guidance on the distinction between first and second degree murder? What is the danger of not providing that guidance, particularly in homicide cases? (Do you think jurors understand the difference between not requiring *proof* of reflection and not requiring proof of *reflection*?) Would it be preferable to reintroduce detailed rules about the presence of premeditation (lying in wait, etc.)?

What exactly is the vagueness problem in *Thompson*? Recall that void-for-vagueness analysis has two prongs—fair notice and arbitrary enforcement. What's the arbitrary enforcement problem in a case like *Thompson*? What's the fair notice problem? Compare *Thompson* to the vagueness cases discussed in ch. 2.

3. What's the use of a temporal distinction that's defined in terms of "reasonableness" or other "sufficiency"? Is it better to retain a vague temporal distinction between first and degree murder or to focus the fact finder's attention squarely onto the issue at hand: reflection?

4. Why should reflection matter, even if we *could* discover its presence or absence? Is an actor who kills upon reflection more dangerous than one who kills without reflection? Might reflection indicate hesitation (a conscience? empathy? a sense of justice?) that is otherwise absent? If so, does the hesitating killer deserve more or less punishment than the nonhesitating one? Who has the worse character? Should it matter?

5. Is the distinction between first and second degree murder captured by the Model Penal Code's distinction between purpose and knowledge? Or does it take into account factors the Model Code's distinction doesn't? Is that a good thing? If the line between purpose and knowledge does match that between first and second degree murder, is it appropriate for the Model Code to treat purposeful and knowing homicide as one crime, subject to the same penalty?

6. The Model Penal Code, and many jurisdictions following it, did away with premeditation as the distinguishing feature of first degree murder. The comments of the commission that revised the New York Penal Law are representative:

> [The new murder provision] defines the basic crime as intentional killing, making no mention of premeditation and deliberation, which were, of course, elements of the former first degree offense and the factors which differentiated it from second degree murder. If those words denoted planning or preparation to kill formulated over a considerable period of time, there might be validity to the distinction drawn between intentional homicides of a premeditated and of an unpremeditated character. The inherent difficulty of precise definition, however, has produced a judicial construction of "premeditation" so broad that it includes a determination to kill formed a fleeting second before the homicidal act. Under that formulation—almost inevitable because of the impossibility of a definition based upon length of time—the determination of whether premeditation has occurred in a particular instance frequently amounted to no more than an exercise in semantics, and a jury's decision . . . turned upon an issue which not even experienced attorneys truly understand.

Proposed New York Penal Law, Commission Staff Notes § 130.25 (1964).

2. Intentional vs. Depraved Indifference Murder

Robinson v. State

Court of Appeals of Maryland.
307 Md. 738, 517 A.2d 94 (1986).

■ Adkins, Judge.

On 3 September 1984 appellant, Jacqueline Camille Robinson, and her lover, Henry Garvey, were alone in Robinson's apartment. An altercation occurred. Robinson shot Garvey in the thigh; the bullet travelled upwards and lodged in his abdomen. A jury sitting in the Circuit Court for Prince George's County convicted her of, among other things, assault with intent to disable. It acquitted her of assault with intent to murder. . . .

Shortly after Robinson's trial Garvey died. She was then charged with second degree murder. She moved to dismiss the indictment on various grounds, including collateral estoppel. [She now appeals from the denial of her motion to dismiss.] * * *

[H]er argument is essentially this: She was convicted of assaulting Garvey with intent to disable him. The conviction established as a fact that this was her only intent, especially in view of her acquittal of assault with intent to murder, which established the fact that she did not intend to murder her lover. "Depraved heart" murder does not require any specific intent to kill or injure. Moreover, "depraved heart" murder must be based on general recklessness; the act on which the charge is based must be dangerous to a number of persons, but not directed at any particular person. Robinson concludes that "[b]ecause a jury has established the fact that [she] is guilty of a deliberate intent to disable a specific individual, the doctrine of collateral estoppel bars the State from arguing that the same act also gives rise to a finding of a wanton and reckless disregard for human life." ...

.... The intent element of assault with intent to disable is a specific intent to do just that, and is inconsistent with an intent to [kill].... Intent to disable[, however,] is in no way inconsistent with the intent element of "depraved heart" murder.

That offense does not require an intent to kill, which would be inconsistent with an intent to disable. It is one of the "unintentional murders," that is punishable as murder because another element of blameworthiness fills the place of intent to kill. As Judge Moylan explained in *Debettencourt v. State*, 48 Md.App. 522, 530, 428 A.2d 479, 484 (1981):

> "It ['depraved heart' murder] is the form [of murder] that establishes that the wilful doing of a dangerous and reckless act with wanton indifference to the consequences and perils involved, is just as blameworthy, and just as worthy of punishment, when the harmful result ensues, as is the express intent to kill itself.... It involves ... the deliberate perpetration of a knowingly dangerous act with reckless and wanton unconcern and indifference as to whether anyone is harmed or not. The common law treats such a state of mind as just as blameworthy, just as anti-social and, therefore, just as truly murderous as the specific intents to kill and to harm."

Robinson seizes upon the last sentence we have just quoted and argues that "depraved heart" murder does not exist if there is a specific intent to harm. *See also Lindsay v. State*, 8 Md.App. 100, 104, 258 A.2d 760, 763 (1969) ("depraved heart" murder exists where, "conceding that there was no actual intent to injure, an act was done or duty omitted wilfully, the natural tendency of which was to cause death or great bodily harm"); R. Perkins, *Criminal Law* at 36 (2d ed. 1969) (" ... even if there is no actual intent to kill or injure"). But these authorities say no more than that the crime may be committed absent intent to injure. They do not hold that the crime is not committed if there is an intent to injure.

.... The critical feature of "depraved heart" murder is that the act in question be committed "under circumstances manifesting extreme indifference to the value of human life." The terms "recklessness" or "indifference," often used to define the crime, do not preclude an act of intentional injury. They refer to "recklessness" or "indifference" to the ultimate consequence of the act—death—not to the act that produces that result. "That the actor intended to cause injury of a particular nature or gravity is, of course, a relevant consideration in determining whether he acted with 'extreme indifference to the value of human life....'" *See Model Penal Code* § 210.2 comment at 28–29 (1980).

It would be strange, indeed, if unintended death resulting from an intentionally-inflicted injury were deemed less blameworthy than unintended death resulting from an injury not so inflicted.... We hold, therefore, that when injury is intentionally inflicted, without intent to kill, and the victim subsequently dies as the result of the injury, the assailant may be guilty of "depraved heart" murder, if no excuse, justification, or mitigation is present, and if the circumstances are such as to demonstrate the requisite element of depravity. Accordingly, Robinson's conviction of assault with intent to disable does not collaterally estop the State from prosecuting her for "depraved heart" murder because of the finding of intent to injure necessarily inherent in that conviction.

This leaves for consideration Robinson's argument that "depraved heart" murder requires a showing of universal malice—an act imminently dangerous to more than just the person who was killed. She contends that her conviction of assault with intent to disable Garvey, when they were alone in her apartment, establishes conclusively that she could not have harbored the requisite universal malice. We believe, however, that universal malice, while it is a proper basis for "depraved heart" murder, is not the only basis for the offense.

There are, to be sure, decisions that support Robinson's position. The leading one is *Darry v. People*, 10 N.Y. 120 (1854). Darry beat his wife; she died as a result, although he had not intended that outcome. In that case the New York Court of Appeals had before it a statute designed to improve the common law. The statute defined as murder the killing of a human being "unless it be manslaughter, or excusable or justifiable homicide, . . . [w]hen perpetrated by an act imminently dangerous *to others*, and evincing a depraved mind, regardless of human life, although without any premeditated design to effect the death of any particular individual." *Id.* at 153 [emphasis supplied]. The *Darry* court examined legislative intent. It concluded that at common law he would have been guilty of murder, but that he was not guilty under the statute because it did not extend to a case in which only a particular victim was involved. Rather, the imminently dangerous act had to be dangerous to *others*. The court reasoned that a brutal assault on an individual might evince a "depraved heart," but it could not "be evidence of a recklessness and disregard of human life generally."

.... On the other hand, two courts faced with a statute like the one involved in *Darry* have read legislative intent otherwise. In *State v. Lowe*, 68 N.W. 1094 (Minn.1896), the Supreme Court of Minnesota expressly disagreed with *Darry*. Looking to Minnesota legislative intent, the court thought it was not "necessary that more than one person was or might have been put in jeopardy by [the imminently dangerous] act." And in *Hogan v. State*, 36 Wis. 226 (1874), the Supreme Court of Wisconsin held that the statutory phrase "dangerous to others" did not mean "dangerous to several" but rather "that the act shall be dangerous to other or others, that is to say, than the person committing it."

Still other courts, construing other statutes, have found no need for universal malice. New York, the home of *Darry*, later amended its "depraved heart" law to make a person guilty of murder when "[u]nder circumstances evincing a depraved indifference to human life, he recklessly engages in conduct which creates a grave risk of death to another person, and thereby causes the death of another person." N.Y. Penal Law § 125.25 subd. 2. The New York Court of Appeals noted that this statute (unlike the one in *Darry*) no longer required a threat of danger to more than one person. *People v. Poplis,* 30 N.Y.2d 85, 89, 330 N.Y.S.2d 365, 367, 281 N.E.2d 167, 168 (1972).

All of these cases involved particular statutes and frequently an analysis of particular legislative intent. Except to the extent they show that legislative intent can be read quite differently, even in the face of identical statutory language, they are of little help to us. Maryland has no "depraved heart" murder statute. By virtue of Code, Art. 27, § 411, "all . . . kinds of murders [other than those defined in §§ 407–410] shall be deemed murder in the second degree." These statutes do not create a new statutory crime of murder, but merely divide the crime into degrees, leaving the common law concept of murder unimpaired. What, then, was the common law concept of "depraved heart" murder, so far as universal malice is concerned?

Lord Coke gives an example:

> "If a man knowing that many people come in the street from a sermon, throw a stone over a wall, intending only to feare them, or to give them a light hurt, and thereupon one is killed, this is murder; for he had an ill intent, though that intent extended not to death, and though he knew not the party slaine."

Coke, Third Inst. 56 (1797 ed.). This passage suggests that universal malice is required, for the "ill intent" of the stone-thrower was not directed at any one of the people, but at "them." Sir William Blackstone, on the other hand, seems to see the possibility of universal malice being directed at an individual only:

> "Also, even if upon a sudden provocation one beats another in a cruel and unusual manner, so that he dies, though he did not intend his death, yet he is guilty of murder by express malice; that is, by an express evil design, the genuine sense of *malitia.* As when a park-keeper tied a boy, that was stealing wood, to a horse's tail, and dragged him along the park; when a master corrected his servant with an iron bar, and a schoolmaster stamped on his scholar's belly; so that each of the sufferers died; these were justly held to be murders, because the correction being excessive, and such as could not proceed but from a bad heart, it was equivalent to a deliberate act of slaughter. Neither shall he be guilty of a less crime, who kills another in consequence of such a wilful act, as shews him to be an enemy to all mankind in general; as going deliberately with a horse used to strike, or discharging a gun, among a multitude of people. So if a man resolves to kill the next man he meets, and does kill him, it is murder, although he knew him not; for this is universal malice."

4 Bl.Comm. 199–200 (1769).

The last act Blackstone refers to as denoting "universal malice" is the killing of a single individual who is not "among a multitude of people." Noteworthy, too, is his lumping of "intent-to-commit-grievous-bodily-harm" murder (often listed as a separate category from "depraved heart" murder) with the latter. The reason appears to be that both involve "a bad heart" which is to say the depravity, the reckless indifference to value of human life, that we associate with "depraved heart" murder. If, as we have seen, extreme blameworthiness is the basis for establishing a killing as "depraved heart" murder, despite a lack of intent to kill, this treatment is logical. One who indifferently fires into a crowd has one sort of depraved mental state; one who deliberately injures another with reckless unconcern for the likely fatal consequences has another; but both are worthy of severe blame, as Blackstone recognizes.

What the common law of England understands "universal malice" to be, in the context of "depraved heart" murder, may not be entirely clear. It is difficult to say what the position was in 1776, when that common law was preserved for the benefit of the "Inhabitants of Maryland...." Decl. of Rights, Art. 5. No Maryland appellate court has directly addressed this issue. But this Court is authorized to adapt and modify the common law to meet modern day demands and needs. We hold that under the common law of Maryland "depraved heart" murder does not require that more than one life be placed in imminent danger by an assailant's life-threatening act, although the offense clearly is committed if, under appropriate circumstance, several lives are threatened. The requisite disregard for human life, or as Professor Perkins says, the "man-endangering-state-of-mind," Perkins, *supra*, at 46, may be found in either case.

We reach this conclusion because of what we have already said about the blameworthiness of an act that, without intent to kill, nevertheless produces that result because of the actor's reckless disregard for the likely fatal consequences of the act. We are not persuaded that such an act is punishable as second degree murder only when several potential victims are involved. As we have seen, Blackstone seems to place on a par the evil mental states required for "intent-to-commit-grievous-bodily-harm" murder and for "depraved heart" murder. Indeed, he may regard them both as springing from the same root. The American Law Institute follows a similar analysis. Its *Model Penal Code* § 210.2 provides (subject to an exception not here pertinent):

> "(1) ... criminal homicide constitutes murder when:
>
> (b) it is committed recklessly under circumstances manifesting extreme indifference to the value of human life."

According to the ALI, this provision encompasses both "intent-to-cause-grievous-bodily-harm" murder and "depraved heart" murder. *Id.*, comment at 22, 28. The critical factor in either case is not the number of persons whose lives are threatened but whether the assailant acted with extreme indifference to the value of any human life.

As a consequence, the fact that Robinson's pistol shot was directed only at Garvey, and not at a group of people, does not bar her prosecution for "depraved heart" murder. Her conviction of assault with intent to disable Garvey does not, therefore, establish any fact that collaterally estops the State so far as the instant case is concerned.[6] Whether the assault was committed under circumstances manifesting sufficiently de-

6. Nor does her acquittal of assault with intent to murder create collateral estoppel. The fact that Robinson did not intend to murder Garvey would not be a defense to "depraved heart" murder, which does not require the presence of such an intent.

praved conduct (extreme indifference to the value of human life) to support a conviction for "depraved heart" murder is, of course, not before us.

QUESTIONS AND COMMENTS

1. The *Robinson* court concludes that it is "not persuaded" by the defendant's restrictive interpretation of depraved heart murder. Given that there is considerable support for the defendant's position, why doesn't she win under the rule of lenity (see ch. 2 supra)? And is the court's authority "to adapt and modify the common law to meet modern day demands and needs" consistent with the principle of legality?

2. The distinction between intentional and grossly reckless murder, unlike that between first and second degree murder, generally does not imply a difference in criminal liability. Grossly reckless homicide is just as much murder as is intentional homicide. See, e.g., N.Y. Penal Law § 125.25. (That's not to say that the difference between the two may not play a role in specific cases, particularly when a defendant is acquitted of one (usually intentional murder) but convicted of the other (usually gross recklessness murder). See, e.g., People v. Gonzalez, 1 N.Y.3d 464 (2004).) The distinction between gross recklessness murder and "ordinary" recklessness *manslaughter* will be taken up below.

Still, even though intentional and grossly reckless homicides are treated as the same *offense* (murder), they differ in the *defenses* that may be available. So intoxication or provocation (extreme emotional disturbance) may be a defense to intentional, but not to grossly reckless homicide (on the theory that these defenses negative intention, not recklessness). Cf. People v. Register, 60 N.Y. 2d 270 (1983) (intoxication); People v. Fardan, 82 N.Y.2d 638 (1993) (provocation).

3. Is the law right not to differentiate between the punishment for intentional and grossly reckless homicide, or even to treat grossly reckless homicide *more harshly* than intentional homicide, by limiting certain (partial) defenses (like intoxication and provocation) to intentional homicide? Is someone who merely accepts a serious chance that his actions may result in death truly as dangerous, or as blameworthy, as someone who sets out to kill?

The U.S. Sentencing Guidelines for murder make room for a downward departure in cases where the defendant "did not cause the death intentionally or knowingly . . . based upon the defendant's state of mind . . ., the degree of risk inherent in the conduct, and the nature of the underlying offense conduct." U.S.S.G. § 2A1.1 cmt. Is it enough to leave the differentiation among types of murder to the sentencing judge?

4. *Malice and Depravity*. Grossly reckless homicide statutes often use terms like "depravity" and "malignancy." See, e.g., N.Y. Penal Law § 125.25(2) ("depraved indifference to human life"); Miss. Code Ann. § 97–3–19(1)(b) ("depraved heart, regardless of human life"); Cal. Penal Code § 188 ("abandoned and malignant heart"). Note, however, that this depravity was not a distinguishing feature of depraved heart murder, but of murder generally speaking. Each of these colorful terms boiled down to the

concept that traditionally has unified all types of murder (intentional and nonintentional): "malice." If the defendant intended to cause death, that malice was "express," and if he didn't, then it was merely "implied." He committed murder either way.

The term "malice" was abandoned by the Model Penal Code, and by many jurisdictions as vague and moralistic. (The Code also rejected "depravity," though many codes retained this term. Is "depravity" preferable to "malice"?) But then what do all varieties of murder share in common now? Didn't the Model Penal Code simply replace "malice" with "extreme indifference to human life"? And is that any less vague, and for that matter, moralistic? Did the Model Penal Code replace the search for evidence of "malice" with the search for evidence of extraordinary dangerousness? What is won, and lost, along the way?

If the point of murder law is to spot depravity and malignancy, doesn't that amount to punishing someone's character? Does it matter, in that case, whether the person is responsible for that character? How would we find that out? And is only the person who commits murder (the "murderer") depraved, or are other "felons" depraved as well?

5. The defendant in Smallwood v. State, 343 Md. 97, 680 A.2d 512 (1996) (ch. 6, supra), was convicted of attempted murder for knowingly exposing another to risk of HIV-infection (though the conviction was overturned on appeal). Imagine that Smallwood's victim had actually died and that we could causally attribute the death, beyond a reasonable doubt, to the defendant (causation proof problems might well disappear if, for instance, the victim had had no other sexual contacts, nor blood transfusions, nor contact with potentially contaminated needles). Note further that the knowing transfer of HIV to another is criminalized (in the public health code) and punishable by up to three years' imprisonment. Md. Code Ann., Health–Gen. §§ 18–601.1.

Would it be problematic to convict such a person of murder (or at least voluntary manslaughter), even though he may well have engaged in conduct with the sort of risk, and subjective awareness of risk, of causing death that would ordinarily justify a murder conviction? Do "residual" duties not to risk others' death kick in only when people engage in death-risking conduct that hasn't been more directly regulated and/or anticipated by a legislature, presumably with full knowledge of the trade-offs between permitting health risk and avoiding stigmatizing quarantine?

Is there some reason why we wouldn't want particular prosecutors to indict, and particular juries to convict, cigarette manufacturers, or even sellers, of murder if a particular jury decides that they have consciously taken unduly substantial and unjustified risks that they are killing others? See "Law Professor Calls for Homicide Prosecution of Tobacco Companies, Executives," Corp. Crime Rep., vol.17, no. 2, Mar. 24, 2003, at 1, 3. How about tunnel builders (if we know with statistical certainty that some workers will die building tunnels, even if all safety regulations are complied with, and the worker's consent would not be a defense)?

Perhaps, though, there are *distinctions* among HIV+ persons' sexual conduct that suggest it is appropriate to think some, but not others, have taken *undue* risks and that particularized jury judgments of recklessness are thus appropriate. The legislature may have decided that it is not appropriate to ban sexual activity by HIV+ persons generally, despite the health risks (just as it has decided to tolerate "properly regulated" cigarette sale, tunnel-building, gun sale, etc.), but it might still be the case that a sub-class of HIV+ persons engage in sex that the legislature did not intend to immunize. Is it all right to rely on prosecutorial discretion to prosecute HIV+ rapists or needle jabbers for (attempted) homicide? What about the selective prosecution of those who are (merely?) promiscuous? See, e.g., Michael Cooper, "Drifter Says He Had Sex With Up to 300," N.Y. Times, July 29, 1999, at B5, col. 4 (case of Nushawn Williams, an HIV+ man from New York City, convicted of reckless endangerment for infecting young women and girls in upstate New York).

3. FELONY MURDER

a. Introduction

Cal. Penal Code § 189. All murder ... which is committed in the perpetration of, or attempt to perpetrate, arson, rape, carjacking, robbery, burglary, mayhem, kidnapping, train wrecking, or any act punishable under Section 206 [torture], 286 [sodomy], 288 [statutory rape], 288a [oral copulation], or 289 [rape], ... is murder of the first degree. All other kinds of murders are of the second degree.

"A homicide that is a direct causal result of the commission of a felony inherently dangerous to human life (other than the ... felonies enumerated in Pen. Code, § 189) constitutes at least second degree murder." People v. Ford, 60 Cal.2d 772, 795 (1964).

Model Penal Code § 210.2. Murder.

(1) [C]riminal homicide constitutes murder when:

(b) it is committed recklessly under circumstances manifesting extreme indifference to the value of human life. Such recklessness and indifference are presumed if the actor is engaged or is an accomplice in the commission of, or an attempt to commit, or flight after committing or attempting to commit robbery, rape or deviate sexual intercourse by force or threat of force, arson, burglary, kidnapping or felonious escape.

N.Y. Penal Law § 125.25 Murder in the second degree.

A person is guilty of murder in the second degree when: ...

2. Under circumstances evincing a depraved indifference to human life, he recklessly engages in conduct which creates a grave risk of death to another person, and thereby causes the death of another person; or

3. Acting either alone or with one or more other persons, he commits or attempts to commit robbery, burglary, kidnapping, arson, rape ..., sodomy ..., sexual abuse ..., ... or escape ..., and, in the course of and in furtherance of such crime or of immediate flight therefrom, he, or another participant, if there be any, causes the death of a person other than one of the participants; except that in any prosecution under this

subdivision, in which the defendant was not the only participant in the underlying crime, it is an affirmative defense that the defendant:

(a) Did not commit the homicidal act or in any way solicit, request, command, importune, cause or aid the commission thereof; and

(b) Was not armed with a deadly weapon, or any instrument, article or substance readily capable of causing death or serious physical injury and of a sort not ordinarily carried in public places by law-abiding persons; and

(c) Had no reasonable ground to believe that any other participant was armed with such a weapon, instrument, article or substance; and

(d) Had no reasonable ground to believe that any other participant intended to engage in conduct likely to result in death or serious physical injury....

b. Predicate Felonies

People v. Burroughs

Supreme Court of California.
35 Cal.3d 824, 678 P.2d 894, 201 Cal.Rptr. 319 (1984).

■ GRODIN, J.

Defendant Burroughs, a 77–year-old self-styled "healer," appeals from a judgment convicting him of unlawfully selling drugs, compounds, or devices for alleviation or cure of cancer (Health & Saf. Code, § 1707.1); felony practicing medicine without a license (Bus. & Prof. Code, § 2141.5, now § 2053); and second degree felony murder (Pen. Code, § 187) in the treatment and death of Lee Swatsenbarg.

Burroughs challenges his second degree murder conviction by contending the felonious unlicensed practice of medicine is not an "inherently dangerous" felony, as that term has been used in our previous decisions to describe and limit the kinds of offenses which will support application of the felony-murder rule. We conclude that while the felonious unlicensed practice of medicine can, in many circumstances, pose a threat to the health of the individual being treated, commission of that crime as defined by statute does not inevitably pose danger to human life. Under well-established principles it cannot, therefore, be made the predicate for a finding of murder, absent proof of malice. As a consequence, we must reverse defendant's second degree felony-murder conviction....

Lee Swatsenbarg had been diagnosed by the family physician as suffering from terminal leukemia. Unable to accept impending death, the 24–year-old Swatsenbarg unsuccessfully sought treatment from a variety of traditional medical sources. He and his wife then began to participate in Bible study, hoping that through faith Lee might be cured. Finally, on the advice of a mutual acquaintance who had heard of defendant's ostensible successes in healing others, Lee turned to defendant for treatment.

During the first meeting between Lee and defendant, the latter described his method of curing cancer. This method included consumption of a unique "lemonade," exposure to colored lights, and a brand of vigorous massage administered by defendant. Defendant remarked that he had successfully treated "thousands" of people, including a number of physicians. He suggested the Swatsenbargs purchase a copy of his book, *Healing for the Age of Enlightenment*. If after reading the book Lee wished to begin defendant's unorthodox treatment, defendant would commence caring for Lee immediately. During the 30 days designated for the treatment, Lee would have to avoid contact with his physician.

Lee read the book, submitted to the conditions delineated by defendant, and placed himself under defendant's care. Defendant instructed Lee to drink the lemonade, salt water, and herb tea, but consume nothing more for the ensuing 30 days. At defendant's behest, the Swatsenbargs bought a lamp equipped with some colored plastic sheets, to bathe Lee in various tints of light. Defendant also agreed to massage Lee from time to time, for an additional fee per session.

Rather than improve, within two weeks Lee's condition began rapidly to deteriorate. He developed a fever, and was growing progressively weaker. Defendant counseled Lee that all was proceeding according to plan, and convinced the young man to postpone a bone marrow test urged by his doctor.

During the next week Lee became increasingly ill. He was experiencing severe pain in several areas, including his abdomen, and vomiting frequently. Defendant administered "deep" abdominal massages on two successive days, each time telling Lee he would soon recuperate.

Lee did not recover as defendant expected, however, and the patient began to suffer from convulsions and excruciating pain. He vomited with increasing frequency. Despite defendant's constant attempts at reassurance, the Swatsenbargs began to panic when Lee convulsed for a third time after the latest abdominal massage. Three and a half weeks into the treatment, the couple spent the night at defendant's house, where Lee died of a massive hemorrhage of the mesentary in the abdomen. The evidence presented at trial strongly suggested the hemorrhage was the direct result of the massages performed by defendant.

Defendant's conviction of second degree felony murder arose out of the jury's determination that Lee Swatsenbarg's death was a homicide committed by defendant while he was engaged in the felonious unlicensed practice of medicine. The trial court ruled that an underlying felony of unlicensed practice of medicine could support a felony-murder conviction because such practice was a felony "inherently dangerous to human life."[1] Consequently, the trial judge instructed the jury that if the homicide resulted directly

1. Felony practicing medicine without a license violates section 2053 of the Business and Professions Code (formerly § 2141.5) which states: "Any person who willfully, under circumstances or conditions which cause or create a risk of great bodily harm, serious physical or mental illness, or death, practices or attempts to practice, or advertises or holds himself or herself out as practicing, any system or mode of treating the sick or afflicted in this state, or diagnoses, treats, operates for, or prescribes for any ailment, blemish, deformity, disease, disfigurement, disorder, injury, or other physical or mental condition of any person, without having at the time of so doing a valid, unrevoked or suspended certificate as provided in this chapter, or without being authorized to perform such act pursuant to a certificate obtained in accordance with some other provision of law, is punishable by imprisonment in the county jail for not exceeding one year or in the state prison."

from the commission of this felony, the homicide was felony murder of the second degree.[2] This instruction was erroneous as a matter of law.

When an individual causes the death of another in furtherance of the perpetration of a felony, the resulting offense may be felony murder. This court has long held the felony-murder rule in disfavor. "We have repeatedly stated that felony murder is a 'highly artificial concept' which 'deserves no extension beyond its required application.'" (*People* v. *Dillon* (1983) 34 Cal.3d 441, 462–463 [194 Cal.Rptr. 390, 668 P.2d 697]) For the reasons stated below, we hold that to apply the felony-murder rule to the facts of the instant case would be an unwarranted extension of this highly "anachronistic"[3] notion.

At the outset we must determine whether the underlying felony is "inherently dangerous to human life." We formulated this standard because "[if] the felony is not inherently dangerous, it is highly improbable that the potential felon will be deterred; he will not anticipate that any injury or death might arise solely from the fact that he will commit the felony."

In assessing whether the felony is inherently dangerous to human life, "we look to the elements of the felony in the abstract, not the particular 'facts' of the case." This form of analysis is compelled because there is a killing in every case where the rule might potentially be applied. If in such circumstances a court were to examine the particular facts of the case prior to establishing whether the underlying felony is inherently dangerous, the court might well be led to conclude the rule applicable despite any unfairness which might redound to the defendant by so broad an application: the existence of the dead victim might appear to lead inexorably to the conclusion that the underlying felony is exceptionally hazardous. We continue to resist such unjustifiable bootstrapping.

In our application of the second degree felony-murder analysis we are guided by the bipartite standard articulated by this court in *People* v. *Henderson,* 19 Cal.3d 86. In *Henderson*, we stated a reviewing court should look first to the primary element of the offense at issue, then to the "factors elevating the offense to a felony," to determine whether the felony,

2. Second degree felony murder was defined for the jury as, "The unlawful killing of a human being, whether intentional, unintentional or accidental, which occurs as a direct causal result of the commission of or attempt to commit a felony inherently dangerous to human life, namely, the crime of practicing medicine without a license under circumstances or conditions which cause or create risk of great bodily harm, serious mental or physical illness, or death, and where there was in the mind of the perpetrator the specific intent to commit such crime, is murder of the second degree. The specific intent to commit such felony, i.e., practicing medicine without a license under circumstances or conditions which cause or create risk of great bodily harm, serious mental or physical illness, or death, and the commission of or attempt to commit such crime must be proved beyond any doubt." (CALJIC No. 8.32.)

3. .... In *People* v. *Dillon,* 34 Cal.3d 441, 462–472, we reaffirmed the first degree felony-murder rule despite serious reservations as to its rationality and moral vitality, because we regarded ourselves bound by the explicit statutory provision (Pen. Code, § 189) from which that rule derived. The second degree felony-murder rule, by contrast, is a creature of judicial invention, and as the Chief Justice's concurring opinion suggests the time may be ripe to reconsider its continued vitality. We decline to do so here, however, since that issue has not been raised, briefed, or argued.

taken in the abstract, is inherently dangerous to human life, or whether it possibly could be committed without creating such peril. In this examination we are required to view the statutory definition of the offense as a whole, taking into account even nonhazardous ways of violating the provisions of the law which do not necessarily pose a threat to human life.

The primary element of the offense in question here is the practice of medicine without a license. The statute defines such practice as "treating the sick or afflicted." One can certainly conceive of treatment of the sick or afflicted which has quite innocuous results—the affliction at stake could be a common cold, or a sprained finger, and the form of treatment an admonition to rest in bed and drink fluids or the application of ice to mild swelling. Thus, we do not find inherent dangerousness at this stage of our investigation.

The next level of analysis takes us to consideration of the factors which elevate the unlicensed practice of medicine to a felony: "circumstances or conditions which cause or create a risk of great bodily harm, serious mental or physical illness, *or death*." That the Legislature referred to "death" as a separate risk, and in the disjunctive, strongly suggests the Legislature perceived that one may violate the proscription against the felonious practice of medicine without a license and yet not necessarily endanger human life....

The statute at issue can also be violated by administering to an individual in a manner which threatens risk of serious mental or physical illness. Whether risk of serious physical illness is inherently dangerous to life is a question we do not reach; however, we believe the existence of the category of risk of serious mental illness also renders a breach of the statute's prohibitions potentially less than inherently dangerous to life....

While conceding ... the possibility that mental illness may be inherently dangerous, we note ... there are occasions when this need not be the case. It is not difficult, for example, to envision one who suffers from delusions of grandeur, believing himself to be the President of the United States. An individual who purports without the proper license to be able to treat such a person need not be placing the patient's life in jeopardy, though such treatment, if conducted, for example, without expertise, may lead to the need for more serious psychiatric attention.

Consequently, we are disinclined to rule today that the risks set forth in section 2053 are so critical as to render commission of this felony of necessity inherently dangerous to human life. Indeed, were we to interpret either the risk of great bodily harm or serious mental illness as being synonymous with the risk of death for purposes of the felony-murder rule, we would be according those terms a more restrictive meaning than that which the Legislature obviously meant them to have in the definition of the felony itself. Such a reading would require that an unlicensed practitioner of medicine actually perform treatment under circumstances or conditions which necessarily place the very life of the patient in jeopardy before such a practitioner could be susceptible to a conviction for *felonious* unlicensed practice. We possess grave doubts that the Legislature intended such a result.

Moreover, our analysis of precedent in this area reveals that the few times we have found an underlying felony inherently dangerous (so that it would support a conviction of felony murder), the offense has been tinged with malevolence totally absent from the facts of this case. In *People* v. *Mattison* (1971) 4 Cal.3d 177 [93 Cal.Rptr. 185, 481 P.2d 193], we held that poisoning food, drink, or medicine with intent to injure was inherently dangerous. The wilful and malicious burning of an automobile (located in a garage beneath an occupied home) was ruled inherently dangerous in *People* v. *Nichols* (1970) 3 Cal.3d 150, 162–163 [89 Cal.Rptr. 721, 474 P.2d 673]. Finally, we held kidnaping to be such an offense in *People* v. *Ford,* 60 Cal.2d 772, 795.

To hold, as we do today, that a violation of section 2053 is not inherently so dangerous that by its very nature, it cannot be committed without creating a substantial risk that someone will be killed, is consistent with our previous decisions in which the underlying felony has been held not inherently hazardous. We have so held where the underlying felony was felony false imprisonment, possession of a concealable firearm by an ex-felon, escape from a city or county penal facility, and in other, less potentially threatening circumstances.

Finally, the underlying purpose of the felony-murder rule, to encourage felons to commit their offenses without perpetrating unnecessary violence which might result in a homicide, would not be served by applying the rule to the facts of this case. Defendant was or should have been aware he was committing a crime by treating Swatsenbarg in the first place.[5] Yet, it is unlikely he would have been deterred from administering to Lee in the manner in which he did for fear of a prosecution for murder, given his published beliefs on the efficacy of massage in the curing of cancer. Indeed, nowhere is it claimed that defendant attempted to perform any action with respect to Swatsenbarg other than to heal him—and earn a fee for doing so.

This clearly is a case in which conviction of felony murder is contrary to our settled law, as well as inappropriate as a matter of sound judicial policy. The instruction regarding felony murder was erroneous. Accordingly, defendant's second degree murder conviction is reversed.

In addition to asserting the felonious unlicensed practice of medicine will not provide the predicate for a felony-murder conviction because felonious unlicensed medical practice is not inherently dangerous to human life, Burroughs claims the trial court erroneously refused to give an instruction, requested by defendant, on the purportedly lesser included offense of involuntary manslaughter. [W]hile there was no evidence to suggest Swatsenbarg's demise was the intended consequence of Burroughs' treatment of the decedent, there was substantial evidence that this treatment, the administering of "deep abdominal massages" in particular, was performed "without due caution and circumspection," and was the proximate cause of Lee Swatsenbarg's death. Thus, on the evidence presented, Burroughs was susceptible to a possible conviction of involuntary manslaughter, and the jury should have been so instructed. * * *

■ BIRD, C.J., concurring.

5. He had been convicted of practicing medicine without a license in 1960.

The majority reverse appellant's second degree felony-murder conviction on the ground that practicing medicine without a license is not an inherently dangerous felony. I agree with that conclusion, as well as with the directions that on retrial appellant may be prosecuted for involuntary manslaughter. However, I would rest the reversal on a broader ground. The time has come for this court to discard the artificial and court-created offense of second degree felony murder.

.... Felony murder has been described as "a highly artificial concept that deserves no extension beyond its required application." "[The] rule is much censured 'because it anachronistically resurrects from a bygone age a 'barbaric' concept that has been discarded in the place of its origin' ... and because 'in almost all cases in which it is applied it is unnecessary' and 'it erodes the relation between criminal liability and moral culpability'...."

.... The second degree felony-murder rule is, "as it has been since 1872, a judge-made doctrine without any express basis in the Penal Code." Therefore, the power to do away "with ... the 'barbaric' anachronism which we are responsible for creating" lies with this court....

Accordingly, this court should take the long-overdue step and eliminate the second degree felony-murder rule.[2] * * *

The history of the felony-murder rule is in reality a history of limitation. [After a series of cases limiting the doctrine beginning in the nineteenth century, it was abandoned in England] by the Homicide Act of 1957. Section 1 of the act provided in relevant part: "Where a person kills another in the course or furtherance of some other offence, the killing shall not amount to murder unless done with the same malice aforethought (express or implied) as is required for a killing to amount to murder when not done in the course or furtherance of another offense."[16]

In the United States, the rule has followed a somewhat similar path. Since the state of English common law in 1776 served as the basis for the development of American jurisprudence, Blackstone's version of the felony-murder rule[17] became an integral part of the common law of the first 13 states. Not surprisingly, the Atlantic separation did nothing to reduce the amount of criticism to which the doctrine has been subjected. As early as 1854, this criticism appears to have resulted in the statutory abolition of the felony-murder rule in Ohio.

2. This court would not be the first to take such a step. In *People* v. *Aaron* (1980) 409 Mich. 672 [299 N.W.2d 304], the Michigan Supreme Court ... reviewed the common law doctrine of felony murder and concluded that "it violates the basic premise of individual moral culpability upon which our criminal law is based." As a result, the court abolished the felony-murder rule in Michigan....

16. Criticism of the felony-murder rule and the concept of presumed or constructive malice appears in virtually every country whose legal system, based on the tradition of English common law, is "blessed" with this relic of our medieval heritage. India abolished the felony-murder rule by statute in 1951. None of the nations of continental Europe has a concept of criminal law analogous to the felony-murder rule.

17. "[When] an involuntary killing happens in consequence of an unlawful act, it will be either murder or manslaughter according to the nature of the act which occasioned it. If it be in prosecution of a felonious intent, or in it's [*sic*] consequences naturally tended to bloodshed, it will be murder; but if no more was intended than a mere civil trespass, it will only amount to manslaughter."

Oliver Wendell Holmes questioned the rule's deterrent effect in 1881. "[If] a man does an act with intent to commit a felony, and thereby accidentally kills another, ... [the] fact that the shooting is felonious does not make it any more likely to kill people. If the object of the rule is to prevent such accidents, it should make accidental killing with firearms murder, not accidental killing in the effort to steal; while, if its object is to prevent stealing, it would do better to hang one thief in every thousand by lot." (Holmes, The Common Law (1881) pp. 57–58.)

Two states, Hawaii and Kentucky, have followed Ohio in abolishing the felony-murder rule by statute. The comment to the Hawaii statute is instructive.

> "Even in its limited formulation the felony-murder rule is still objectionable. It is not sound principle to convert an accidental, negligent, or reckless homicide into a murder simply because, without more, the killing was in furtherance of a criminal objective of some defined class. Engaging in certain penally-prohibited behavior may, of course, evidence a recklessness sufficient to establish manslaughter, or a practical certainty or intent, with respect to causing death, sufficient to establish murder, but such a finding is an independent determination which must rest on the facts of each case....
>
> "In recognition of the trend toward, and the substantial body of criticism supporting, the abolition of the felony-murder rule, and because of the extremely questionable results which the rule has worked in other jurisdictions, the Code has eliminated from our law the felony-murder rule."

The drafters of the Model Penal Code concluded that the felony-murder rule should be abandoned. (Model Pen. Code, § 201.2, com. 4 (Tent. Draft No. 9, 1959) p. 33) However, concern over possible political opposition to the idea led them to insert a provision in section 201.2(b)'s definition of reckless murder, to the effect that "recklessness and [extreme] indifference [to the value of human life] are [rebuttably] presumed if the actor is engaged or is an accomplice in the commission of, or an attempt to commit or flight after committing or attempting to commit [one of seven enumerated felonies]." (see Model Pen. Code, § 210.2, subd. (1)(b))

While New Hampshire is the only state to have adopted the Model Penal Code formulation, several other states require that the accused exhibit a mens rea above and beyond the mere intent to commit a felony. Arkansas requires that the defendant cause death "under circumstances manifesting extreme indifference to the value of human life." (Ark. Stat. Ann., § 41.1502.) The Texas Penal Code provides that the act causing death must be "clearly dangerous to human life." (Tex. Pen. Code Ann., § 19.02(a)(3).) The Delaware first degree murder statute mandates that the accused at least have acted with criminal negligence in the course of committing certain enumerated felonies or recklessly in the course of committing nonenumerated felonies. (Del. Code, tit. 11, § 636(a)(2), (6) (1979).) ...

Perhaps the most objectionable and often criticized feature of the felony-murder rule involves its vicarious application to accomplices who did not participate in the acts which caused the victim's death. Accordingly, legislatures in 10 states have adopted statutes which provide an affirmative defense for such persons in certain limited circumstances.[22]

.... In 1959 the drafters of the Model Penal Code listed seven major limitations which had been imposed by various state courts.[24] The intervening 25 years have done little to reduce the need for or number of limitations on the rule. The most important of these include requirements that the underlying felony be inherently dangerous, that the killing be committed by one of the felons, that the duration of the felony be strictly construed, and that the purpose of the underlying felony be independent of the killing.

California's approach to the rule mirrors these developments.... The reasons for limiting the rule were well summarized over a decade ago in *People* v. *Satchell,* 6 Cal.3d 28. This court observed that the felony-murder rule is "usually unnecessary for conviction...." In almost all cases in which the rule is applied, conviction "can be predicated on the normal rules as to murder and as to accomplice liability...." If the defendant commits the felony in a highly reckless manner, he can be convicted of second degree murder independently of the shortcut of the felony-murder rule. Under California's interpretation of the implied malice provision of the Penal Code [§ 188], proof of conduct evidencing extreme or wanton recklessness establishes the element of malice aforethought required for a second degree murder conviction.... [In cases where the facts suggested such a theory], the prosecutions would be free to prove the extreme recklessness of the conduct. The jury would decide whether the evidence, including the defendant's conduct and inferences rising from it, established the requisite malice aforethought.... In the "small residuum" of cases where the "normal rules" of murder would not apply, " 'there may be a substantial question whether the rule reaches a rational result or does not at least distract attention from more relevant criteria.' "

In keeping with this view of the rule, the limitations on its application have been extensive. This court has "refused to apply the doctrine in cases wherein the killing is committed by persons other than the defendant or an accomplice acting in furtherance of a common felonious design ...; in cases wherein the operation of the doctrine depends upon 'a felony which is an integral part of the homicide and which the evidence produced by the prosecution shows to be an offense included *in fact* within the offense charged' ...; and in cases wherein the underlying felony is not one of the six enumerated in section 189 of the Penal Code and is not inherently dangerous to human life....".....

Even today's majority recognize that appellant would most likely not have been deterred by the possibility that his actions could have subjected

22. The New York statute (N.Y. Pen. L., § 125.25(3)) is typical.

24. (1) The felonious act must be dangerous to life. (2) The homicide must be a natural and probable consequence of the felonious act. (3) Death must be 'proximately' caused. (4) The felony must be *malum in se.* (5) The act must be a common law felony. (6) The period during which the felony is in the process of commission must be narrowly construed. (7) The underlying felony must be "independent" of the homicide. Model Penal Code § 201.2, comment 4 (Tent. Draft No. 9, 1959) at 37.

him to a murder conviction, since his "published beliefs on the efficacy of massage in the curing of cancer" were firmly entrenched and for well over two decades formed the basis for his "medical practice."

As the list of limitations and modifications grows longer, the California second degree felony-murder rule bears less and less resemblance to Blackstone's simple statement that "when an involuntary killing happens ... in prosecution of a felonious intent ... it will be murder." As the [Michigan Supreme Court noted in *People v. Aaron* (1980) 409 Mich. 672 (299 N.W.2d 304)], "[to] the extent that these modifications reduce the scope and significance of the common-law doctrine, they also call into question the continued existence of the doctrine itself." In sum—and particularly in light of the fact that this court has sole responsibility for the creation of the rule—the viability of it is a question that can no longer be ignored.

The second degree felony-murder rule erodes the important relationship between criminal liability and an accused's mental state. That relationship has been described as "the most basic principle of the criminal law." ... Not only does it obliterate the distinction between intended and unintended homicides, but it seeks to apply the same ponderous sanction to any participant in the criminal conspiracy or enterprise from which a death results. Thus, the doctrine has been applied where a codefendant served only in a getaway driver capacity, where the codefendant was present at the scene of the killing but did not fire the fatal shot, and where the victim died from a heart attack precipitated by the fright induced by commission of the felony.

Legal commentators have been virtually unanimous in their condemnation of the felony-murder rule because it ignores the significance of the actor's mental state in determining his criminal liability. As the drafters of the Model Penal Code concluded in 1959, "principled argument in ... defense [of the felony-murder rule] is hard to find." (Model Pen. Code, § 201.2, com. 4.)

As noted earlier, the rule is perhaps the last vestige of an archaic and indiscriminate philosophy still present in our modern system of criminal law.[30] "The rationale of the doctrine is that one who commits a felony is a bad person with a bad state of mind, and he has caused a bad result, so that we should not worry too much about the fact that the fatal result he accomplished was quite different and a good deal worse than the bad result he intended. Yet it is a general principle of criminal law that one is not ordinarily criminally liable for bad results which differ greatly from intended results." (LaFave & Scott, Criminal Law (1972) p. 560.)

.... [T]he harshness of the rule, which leads some juries to disregard the law and others to follow it only with great reluctance, results in haphazard application of the criminal sanction. As the Ohio Supreme Court concluded more than a century ago in deciding to abandon the felony-

30. As Professor Hall has noted, "[the] underlying rationale of the felony-murder doctrine—that the offender has shown himself to be a 'bad actor,' and that this is enough to exclude the niceties bearing on the gravity of the harm actually committed—might have been defensible in early law. The survival of the felony-murder doctrine is a tribute to the tenacity of legal conceptions rooted in simple moral attitudes." (Hall, General Principles of Criminal Law (1947) p. 455).

murder rule, "crime is more effectually prevented by the *certainty* than by any unreasonable *severity* of punishment disproportionate to the turpitude and danger of the offense." In my view, it is far preferable to do away with an irrational doctrine than to permit it to be applied in an irrational manner. * * *

As Holmes so eloquently stated, "It is revolting to have no better reason for a rule of law than that so it was laid down in the time of Henry IV. It is still more revolting if the grounds upon which it was laid down have vanished long since, and the rule simply persists from blind imitation of the past." (Holmes, Collected Legal Papers (1920) p. 187.) It is time this court laid this ill-conceived rule to rest.

■ RICHARDSON, J. (dissenting)

I respectfully dissent. In my view, the unauthorized practice of medicine "under circumstances or conditions which cause or create a risk of great bodily harm, serious physical or mental illness, or death" (Bus. & Prof. Code, § 2053) fully supports application of the second degree felony-murder rule.

Relying on hypertechnical and irrelevant distinctions between great bodily harm, serious physical and mental injury, and the risk of death, the majority ignores the "rational function that [the felony-murder rule] is designed to serve." As we have frequently reiterated, that purpose "is to deter those engaged in felonies from killing negligently or accidentally." * * *

[In] *People* v. *Taylor* (1970) 11 Cal.App.3d 57 [89 Cal.Rptr. 697], . . . the Court of Appeal upheld a second degree murder conviction under the felony-murder rule when the underlying felony was furnishing of heroin to the victim. "In other words the felony was not done with the intent to commit injury which would cause death. Giving a felony-murder instruction in such a situation serves rather than subverts the purpose of the rule. 'While the felony-murder rule can hardly be much of a deterrent to a defendant who has decided to assault his victim with a deadly weapon, it seems obvious that in the situation presented in the case at bar, it does serve a rational purpose: knowledge that the death of a person to whom heroin is furnished may result in a conviction for murder should have some effect on the defendant's readiness to do the furnishing.' " Similarly, here, knowledge that the death of a "sick or afflicted" person whom the unauthorized practitioner treats, "willfully, under circumstances or conditions which cause or create a risk of great bodily harm, serious physical or mental illness, or death," may have an effect on such person's willingness to so practice.

The majority's fine distinctions become even more dubious when one considers the holding in *People* v. *Nichols* (1970) 3 Cal.3d 150 [89 Cal.Rptr. 721, 474 P.2d 673], approving a second degree murder conviction premised on the burning of an automobile. . . . How can the underlying felony at issue here be less "inherently dangerous to human life" than the burning of an automobile?

In enacting Business and Professions Code section 2053, the Legislature clearly sought to impose a greater penalty in those cases where the unauthorized practice of medicine causes significant risks that may lead to death. The use of the felony-murder rule in this context clearly furthers the goal of deterring such conduct. The underlying conduct proscribed by section 2053 is manifestly "inherently dangerous to life." Viewed in the abstract, improper treatment of the "sick and afflicted" under the dangerous circumstances and conditions specified in that section is almost synonymous with inherently dangerous conduct.

QUESTIONS AND COMMENTS

1. The Model Penal Code drafters may have been right that "principled argument in ... defense [of the felony-murder rule] is hard to find." There is, however, some support at least for some versions of the felony murder rule. Guyora Binder, for one, chides the legal academy for "eschew[ing] efforts to develop any cogent moral rationale for the felony murder rule," thereby "render[ing] itself irrelevant to its further development and reform":

> [T]he felony murder rule is not a strict liability rule, at least not in the form in which it is found in almost every American jurisdiction. [M]ost American jurisdictions condition felony murder either on a short list of inherently dangerous predicate offenses, or simply on the dangerousness of the underlying felony or the means by which it was perpetrated. [M]ost of the remaining jurisdictions condition it on some level of culpability with respect to the risk of death, or on proximate cause standards that condition liability on the foreseeability of death. When felony murder is conditioned on dangerous predicate offenses, it is not a strict liability crime, but a crime of negligence, as [Kenneth] Simons explains:
>
>> On first impression, any grading differential for which no formal culpability is required seems inconsistent with retributivism. Consider felony-murder as an example. We punish the felony at a certain level. We do not otherwise punish nonculpable homicide. Thus, adding a penalty to the felony because it resulted in death seems no more justifiable than punishing someone for an accidental, non-negligent homicide today simply because he committed a felony last year. But this analysis is incorrect. Often, culpably doing X, which happens to cause Y, amounts to negligence (or to a higher culpability, such as recklessness) as to Y. Consider a more specific felony murder example. If armed robbery is the predicate felony, then it is not difficult to conclude that an armed robber should foresee, and often does foresee, a significant risk that robbery will result in a death. Thus, the robber is ordinarily negligent and often reckless as to the risk of death.
>>
>> This analysis suggests that formal strict liability as to death (i.e. the lack of any explicit culpability requirement) can nevertheless be consistent with substantive culpability.

Guyora Binder, "Meaning and Motive in the Law of Homicide," 3 Buff. Crim. L. Rev. 755 (2000) (quoting Kenneth W. Simons, "When is Strict Liability Just?," 87 J. Crim. L. & Criminology 1075, 1121–22 (1997)).

Look again at the discussion of *Cunningham*, ch. 5, supra. If a negligent risk is one that is "substantial *and* unjustifiable," even slight risks of death may seem too high when the defendant's death-risking activity produces no legitimate benefits. Mark G. Kelman, "Interpretive Construction in the Substantive Criminal Law," 33 Stan. L. Rev. 591, 635 (1981).

In Binder's view, commentators (and judges like Chief Justice Bird in *Burroughs*) have consistently exaggerated the harshness of the felony-murder rule for polemical purposes. Not even in the nineteenth century was the rule as broad—and indefensible—as its critics would have us believe:

> Very few of these [nineteenth century] cases are likely to trouble modern readers. Nineteenth-century American felony murder convictions typically arose from the intentional shooting of a robbery victim. Often, the killing would have been murder anyway, and was aggravated to murder in the first degree because it was committed in furtherance of a particularly dangerous felony.
>
> In a handful of nineteenth-century American cases, felony murder liability was imposed for killings which most modern observers would probably grade as lesser forms of homicide. These few convictions were predicated on such dubious "felonies" as riot, consensual abortion, and suicide. It is tempting for critics to make these few cases poster children in the campaign against the felony murder rule. But such a polemical use of these cases effaces the federal structure of the American polity and the statutory basis of American criminal law. There was no unitary felony murder rule in nineteenth-century America. Instead there was a range of different rules, some better and some worse. But most of these rules were limited in scope and were applied fairly. The few exceptions are just that. They are not evidence of the common descent of all felony murder rules from a barbaric rule of strict liability for all deaths in the course of all felonies. * * *
>
> By mislabeling this unenacted doctrine as the "common law rule," legal writers falsely imply that it expresses the essential normative premises underlying the far different rules actually enacted. Yet they also imply that this harsh doctrine remains a legally binding default rule, authoritative in every American jurisdiction unless explicitly altered by legislatures or courts. Thus, in their determination to condemn modern felony murder rules as barbaric anachronisms, legal scholars actually mislead courts about the source and scope of those rules. By mischaracterizing the origins of American felony murder rules, legal scholars may actually contribute to broadening the very rules they inveigh against. In this way, the critics' cherished myth of a monstrous "common law felony murder rule" threatens to become a self-fulfilling prophecy.

Guyora Binder, "The Origins of American Felony Murder Rules," 57 Stan. L. Rev. 59, 66, 68 (2004).

2. How does the felony murder rule work? What function does the predicate felony have? Does it supply the intent that is then transferred to

the homicide? (Contrast the felony murder rule with *Regina v. Faulkner*, supra ch. 5.) Is the predicate felony an element of felony murder? If so, what if the defendant is acquitted of the predicate felony? Consider the following case.

> Defendant has been indicted for felony murder (the underlying felonies are robbery and burglary) and one count of intentional murder. Defendant's confession indicates that at the time of the homicide he was "high" on drugs. In its jury charge this court did not charge intoxication as to felony murder, but did charge intoxication as to intentional murder. The court wishes to expand on its rationale.
>
> Other states have discussed the issue of whether voluntary intoxication is a defense to felony murder. ... In ... Commonwealth v. Wooding, 355 Pa. 555, 50 A.2d 328, the Supreme Court of Pennsylvania held that neither a specific intent to kill nor premeditation to take life was an element of the crime of felony murder. Thus, the fact that defendant may have been intoxicated during the commission of the crime of felony murder "was of no legal significance ...".. . .
>
> In New York, intoxication, although not a defense to a criminal charge, may be offered by a defendant at trial "whenever it is relevant to negative an element of the crime charged" (P.L. 15.25). "[E]lements" of an offense are identified as a "culpable mental state (mens rea) and a voluntary act (actus reus) (Penal Law, § 15.10). Both are required in all but the strict liability offenses ..."
>
> In People v. Register, 60 N.Y.2d 270, 276, 469 N.Y.S.2d 599, 457 N.E.2d 704, [discussed in *People v. Sanchez*, ch. 5 supra] the Court of Appeals held that in some crimes there is an "additional requirement" which "refers to neither the mens rea nor the actus reus". This "additional requirement," Register held, "is not an element in the traditional sense but rather a definition of the factual setting in which the risk creating conduct must occur—objective circumstances which are not subject to being negatived by evidence of defendant's intoxication".
>
> The court must determine whether the underlying felony in the crime of felony murder is an element, or a "definition of the factual setting in which the risk creating conduct must occur ..." (i.e., "objective circumstances"). It has been held that in "felony murder, the underlying felony is not so much an element of the crime, but instead functions as a replacement for the mens rea or intent necessary for common-law murder ..." This legal fiction has been substituted for the intent necessary to commit common-law murder because the crime of felony murder does not have as an element an intent to kill or "malice" or "malice aforethought".
>
> This substituted intent is a general, rather than a specific intent, and cannot be negatived by intoxication. Thus, the Court of Appeals in People v. Berzups, (49 N.Y.2d 417, 427, 426 N.Y.S.2d 253, 402 N.E.2d 1155), in holding that the underlying felony "is not so much an element of the crime [of felony murder]" has recognized that the underlying felony is not an element of that crime. . . .

> As the underlying felony is not an essential element of felony murder it is possible to be found guilty of felony murder notwithstanding that the underlying felony was dismissed for legal insufficiency on that defendant was acquitted of the underlying felony. Since there can be an acquittal of the underlying felony and a conviction of felony murder also indicates that the underlying felony is not an "element" of felony murder.
>
> .... It is also noted that defenses or legal requirements of the underlying felony are not necessarily defenses or legal requirements of a felony murder based on such underlying felony. It would appear that although intoxication is a "defense" to the underlying felony, it does not apply to felony murder.
>
> The underlying felony, not being an element of felony murder can best be described as an aggravating circumstance. It describes the "factual setting in which the risk creating conduct must occur—objective circumstances ...". Such "objective circumstances" cannot be negatived by intoxication. This court therefore did not charge intoxication as to the counts alleging felony murder.

People v. Davis, 128 Misc.2d 782 (N.Y. Sup. Ct. 1985).

The general rule is that intoxication negatives specific (but not general) intent—or, in Model Penal Code terms, purpose and knowledge, but not recklessness or negligence. See ch. 5 supra. What if the predicate felony is a specific intent crime? Shouldn't intoxication be a defense to a felony murder charge then? If the predicate is a specific intent crime, does that mean that its specific intent is "transferred" to the homicide in felony murder? If so, then why shouldn't intoxication be a defense? Or does any intent, specific or general, somehow become general when it is transferred from predicate felony to homicide? Talk of transferring intent aside, is felony murder best thought of as a variety of reckless (or perhaps negligent) homicide? In that case, of course, it would make sense that intoxication wouldn't be a defense. Or is the *Davis* court saying that felony murder is a type of strict liability homicide after all, which would likewise explain why intoxication wouldn't be a defense to it?

3. Did the Model Penal Code "abandon" the felony murder rule? Does a procedural device—a rebuttable presumption of "recklessness under circumstances manifesting extreme indifference to the value of human life"—solve the rule's substantive problems? How likely is it that a defendant will succeed in rebutting the presumption? Would it be preferable to spell out in detail circumstances in which the presumption might be rebutted (e.g., the defendants were unarmed, or they reasonably believed the burglarized premises would be unoccupied)? If the legislation *lists* circumstances in which the presumption of recklessness might be rebutted, should the list be exclusive or illustrative?

4. Is the judicial creation of the crime of second-degree felony murder consistent with the legality principle (see ch. 2 supra)?

5. Who needs the felony murder rule? Note that the Model Penal Code's "felony murder" provision appears in its gross recklessness murder provision. If we already punish gross recklessness homicide as murder and

all justifiable felony murder cases qualify as grossly reckless homicide, what's the point of the felony murder rule? Prosecutorial convenience? The added deterrent effect of doctrinal constructions widely (?) known for their harshness, if not their irrationality? And even if gross recklessness murder doesn't stick, wouldn't reckless manslaughter or, at the very least, negligent homicide? Assuming causation, is the alternative to felony murder outright acquittal? What about the deterrent effect of the already substantial penalties attached to predicate felonies? As a compromise, in cases where no homicide can be proved (because causation or any mens rea, even negligence, is lacking) would it be appropriate to aggravate the punishment for the felony?

c. Merger

People v. Wilson

Supreme Court of California.
1 Cal.3d 431, 462 P.2d 22, 82 Cal.Rptr. 494 (1969).

■ MOSK, J.

Defendant Rufus Wilson was charged with the first degree murders of his wife and William Washington, and assaults with a deadly weapon with intent to murder Lewis Champion and Joe Stoglin. [A] jury found defendant guilty of murder in the first degree of his wife, murder in the second degree of Washington, and assault with a deadly weapon upon Champion. The jury fixed the penalty for the murder of defendant's wife at death; this appeal is automatic.

Prior to the events resulting in the convictions in the instant proceedings, defendant had no criminal record. He was 43 years of age and had worked for the preceding 19 years as a forklift operator for a Los Angeles firm. He was married to Ann Wilson for nine years, but she left him in January 1964 and filed for divorce. After their separation defendant attempted to effect a reconciliation and occasionally they met or talked on the telephone.

.... About 10:30 p.m. on October 14, 1964, Lewis Champion, Joe Stoglin, and William Washington accompanied defendant's wife to her apartment where they ate some food and watched television. Stoglin and Washington fell asleep in the living room, while Champion continued to watch television. There were several telephone calls within the next hour which were answered by Mrs. Wilson. Champion answered a later call from defendant, but Mrs. Wilson told him to hang up....

A few minutes later Champion saw automobile lights shining in the driveway to the apartment and immediately thereafter heard the sound of breaking glass from the window on the door at the bottom of the stairs of the building.... Defendant broke into the apartment with a shotgun in his hand and pointed it at Champion.... Champion rushed out of the building and fled. Stoglin, who had followed Champion, was shot and wounded as he descended the stairs. [Mrs. Wilson was found shot to death in the bathroom, having been shot at close range with a shotgun. Washington was found lying on the lawn outside the apartment, with several gunshot wounds; he died after surgery the next day.] * * *

The jury were instructed on a verdict of second degree murder in relevant part as follows: "[The] unlawful killing of a human being with malice aforethought is murder of the second degree in any of the following cases: . . . (3) When the killing is a direct causal result of the perpetration or the attempt to perpetrate a felony inherently dangerous to human life, such as an assault with a deadly weapon." This instruction was prejudicial error and requires reversal of defendant's conviction of the second degree murder of Washington.

Properly understood, the instruction permitted the jury to find defendant guilty of second degree murder if they found only that the homicide was committed in the perpetration of the crime of assault with a deadly weapon. The instruction is intended to relieve the jury of the necessity to make a specific finding of malice aforethought if a killing is caused by a defendant in the course of a felonious assault or other dangerous felony.

In our recent decision of *People* v. *Ireland* (1969) 70 Cal.2d 522 [75 Cal.Rptr. 188, 450 P.2d 580], we held an identical instruction to be improper on the ground that it went beyond any "rational function" that the felony-murder rule was intended to serve. "To allow such use of the felony-murder rule would effectively preclude the jury from considering the issue of malice aforethought in all cases wherein homicide has been committed as a result of a felonious assault—a category which includes the great majority of all homicides. This kind of bootstrapping finds support neither in logic nor in law. We therefore hold that a second degree felony-murder instruction may not properly be given when it is based upon a felony which is an integral part of the homicide and which the evidence produced by the prosecution shows to be an offense included in fact within the offense charged."

The instruction given in this case allowed the jury to return a verdict of second degree murder if they found that Washington was killed in the course of defendant's perpetration of an assault with a deadly weapon upon Washington. Thus, the felony-murder instruction was based on an underlying felony which was a necessary ingredient of the homicide, and converted the homicide automatically into second degree murder on a finding of the underlying felony. This "bootstrapping" was erroneous in *Ireland* and is erroneous here.

[We also reverse] defendant's conviction of first degree murder for the killing of his wife. . . . The clear purport of [the instructions that were given with respect to the first degree murder charge was] that if defendant entered his wife's apartment or any room thereof with an intent to commit an assault with a deadly weapon, he was guilty of burglary; and if in the course of such burglary he killed his wife and/or Washington, such killing was first degree murder, whether it was intentional, negligent, or accidental. * * *

[T]he reasoning and the language [in *Ireland*] are applicable to the case at bar. Here the prosecution sought to apply the felony-murder rule on the theory that the homicide occurred in the course of a burglary, but the only basis for finding a felonious entry is the intent to commit an assault with a deadly weapon. When, as here, the entry would be nonfelonious but for the intent to commit the assault, and the assault is an integral part of the homicide and is included in fact in the offense charged, utilization of the felony-murder rule extends that doctrine "beyond any rational function that it is designed to serve." . . . .

"The purpose of the felony-murder rule is to deter felons from killing negligently or accidentally by holding them strictly responsible for killings they commit." Where a person enters a building with an intent to assault his victim with a deadly weapon, he is not deterred by the felony-murder rule. That doctrine can serve its purpose only when applied to a felony independent of the homicide. In *Ireland*, we reasoned that a man assaulting another with a deadly weapon could not be deterred by the second degree felony-murder rule, since the assault was an integral part of the homicide. Here, the only distinction is that the assault and homicide occurred inside a dwelling so that the underlying felony is burglary based on an intention to assault with a deadly weapon, rather than simply assault with a deadly weapon.

We do not suggest that no relevant differences exist between crimes committed inside and outside dwellings. We have often recognized that persons within dwellings are in greater peril from intruders bent on stealing or engaging in other felonious conduct. Persons within dwellings are more likely to resist and less likely to be able to avoid the consequences of crimes committed inside their homes. However, this rationale does not justify application of the felony-murder rule to the case at bar. Where the intended felony of the burglar is an assault with a deadly weapon, the likelihood of homicide from the lethal weapon is not significantly increased by the site of the assault. Furthermore, the burglary statute in this state includes within its definition numerous structures other than dwellings as to which there can be no conceivable basis for distinguishing between an assault with a deadly weapon outdoors and a burglary in which the felonious intent is solely to assault with a deadly weapon.[3]

In *Ireland*, we rejected the bootstrap reasoning involved in taking an element of a homicide and using it as the underlying felony in a second degree felony-murder instruction. We conclude that the same bootstrapping is involved in instructing a jury that the intent to assault makes the entry burglary and that the burglary raises the homicide resulting from the assault to first degree murder without proof of malice aforethought and premeditation. To hold otherwise, we would have to declare that because burglary is not technically a lesser offense included within a charge of murder, burglary constitutes an independent felony which can support a felony-murder instruction. However, in *Ireland* itself we did not assert that assault with a deadly weapon was a lesser included offense in murder; we asserted only that it was "included in fact" in the charge of murder, in that the elements of the assault were necessary elements in the homicide. In the same sense, a burglary based on intent to assault with a deadly weapon is included in fact within a charge of murder, and cannot support a felony-murder instruction.

3. Included are any "shop, warehouse, store, mill, barn, stable, outhouse or other building, tent, vessel, railroad car, trailer coach . . ., vehicle . . ., aircraft . . ., mine or any underground portion thereof. . . ." (Pen. Code, § 459.)

We recognize that *Ireland* dealt with a court-made rule while this case involves first degree felony murder, which is statutory. However, the statutory source of the rule does not compel us to apply it in disregard of logic and reason. Indeed, a literal interpretation of section 189 would have limited the felony-murder doctrine to the role of converting all "murder" committed in the course of the perpetration of the named felonies to first degree murder. Instead, we have more broadly interpreted the word "murder" to mean "homicide" or "killings," so that the elements of the crime of murder need not be proved under the felony-murder doctrine.

QUESTIONS AND COMMENTS

1. In jurisdictions where any felony qualifies as the predicate offense for felony murder, and even in those where the predicate felony must be "inherently dangerous," courts occasionally face the question of what to do with felonies that aren't "independent" of the homicide. The most obvious example are lesser types of homicide: manslaughter or even negligent homicide. Since manslaughter and negligent homicide would qualify as (inherently dangerous) felonies during the commission of which a death occurred, the prosecution could "bootstrap" itself from any manslaughter and negligent homicide to a (felony) murder. (The problem would be the same if the prosecution presented a second degree felony murder case as an aggravated assault. Since all voluntary manslaughter cases, and many involuntary manslaughter cases, involve assaults, the prosecutor could sidestep the legislative homicide grading scheme by charging second degree felony murder.) To deal with this problem, courts developed the "merger" doctrine, which also proved convenient as a means for blunting the impact of the felony murder rule.

Does the merger doctrine serve any purpose if the predicate felonies are enumerated in the felony murder statute? Compare *Wilson* to the following case, interpreting New York's felony murder statute:

> The issue presented upon this appeal is whether a burglary based upon the crime of assault can properly serve as the predicate for a felony-murder conviction. * * *
>
> The considerations which prompted our court to announce the merger doctrine do not justify its extension here. We developed this doctrine to remedy a fundamental defect in the old felony-murder statute (Penal Law of 1909, § 1044). Under that statute, *any* felony, including assault, could be the predicate for a felony murder. Since, a fortiori, every homicide, not excusable or justifiable, occurs during the commission of assault, every homicide would constitute a felony murder.
>
> This defect was remedied by the Legislature in 1965 by including in the revised Penal Law a list of specified felonies—all involving violence or substantial risk of physical injury—as the only felonies forming a basis for felony murder. The legislative purpose for this limitation was "to exclude from felony murder, cases of accidental or not reasonably foreseeable fatality occurring in an unlikely manner in the course of a non-violent felony."

> It should be apparent that the Legislature, in including burglary as one of the enumerated felonies as a basis for felony murder, recognized that persons within domiciles are in greater peril from those entering the domicile with criminal intent, than persons on the street who are being subjected to the same criminal intent. Thus, the burglary statutes prescribe greater punishment for a criminal act committed within the domicile than for the same act committed on the street. Where, as here, the criminal act underlying the burglary is an assault with a dangerous weapon, the likelihood that the assault will culminate in a homicide is significantly increased by the situs of the assault. When the assault takes place within the domicile, the victim may be more likely to resist the assault; the victim is also less likely to be able to avoid the consequences of the assault, since his paths of retreat and escape may be barred or severely restricted by furniture, walls and other obstructions incidental to buildings. Further, it is also more likely that when the assault occurs in the victim's domicile, there will be present family or close friends who will come to the victim's aid and be killed. Since the purpose of the felony-murder statute is to reduce the disproportionate number of accidental homicides which occur during the commission of the enumerated predicate felonies by punishing the party responsible for the homicide not merely for manslaughter, but for murder (see Model Penal Code, Tent. Draft No. 9, pp. 37, 38), the Legislature, in enacting the burglary and felony-murder statutes, did not exclude from the definition of burglary, a burglary based upon the intent to assault, but intended that the definition be "satisfied if the intruder's intent, existing at the time of the unlawful entry or remaining, is to commit *any* crime".

People v. Miller, 32 N.Y.2d 157, 297 N.E.2d 85, 344 N.Y.S.2d 342 (1973).

2. Does the merger rule make any sense, except for lesser included homicide offenses like negligent homicide and manslaughter? How about assault? Isn't the whole *point* of the felony murder rule to attach murder liability to offenses that are "inherently dangerous" because they are unusually likely to result in death, accidental or not? See People v. Hansen, 9 Cal.4th 300, 885 P.2d 1022 (1994) (felony of "discharging a firearm at an inhabited dwelling house" doesn't merge with resulting homicide); see also Roary v. State, 2005 WL 321018 (Md.) (assault doesn't merge with homicide "when committed in a manner inherently dangerous to human life"; the assailants had kicked the victim on the ground and then dropped a 20-30 pound boulder on his head).

3. Two years after *Wilson,* the California Supreme Court held that the merger doctrine did *not* apply if the predicate felony is robbery, and armed robbery in particular. People v. Burton, 6 Cal.3d 375, 491 P.2d 793, 99 Cal.Rptr. 1 (1971). Here is how the Court distinguished *Wilson* and *Ireland*:

> [Burton] argues that armed robbery includes as a necessary element assault with a deadly weapon . . . : robbery "is the felonious taking of personal property in the possession of another, from his person or immediate presence, and against his will, accomplished by means of force or fear" (Pen. Code, § 211); thus robbery is assault

> (force or fear directed against a person) coupled with larceny, which when accomplished by means of a deadly weapon necessarily includes in fact assault with a deadly weapon; any charge of murder with respect to a killing arising out of armed robbery then necessarily includes in fact assault with a deadly weapon and cannot support a felony-murder instruction....
>
> In both *Ireland* and *Wilson* the purpose of the conduct which eventually resulted in a homicide was assault with a deadly weapon, namely the infliction of bodily injury upon the person of another.... Thus, there was a single course of conduct with a single purpose.
>
> However, in the case of armed robbery, as well as the other felonies enumerated in section 189 of the Penal Code [arson, rape, mayhem, robbery, burglary or lewd and lascivious acts upon the body of a child], there is an *independent felonious purpose*, namely in the case of robbery to acquire money or property belonging to another. Once a person has embarked upon a course of conduct for one of the enumerated felonious purposes, he comes directly within a clear legislative warning—if a death results from his commission of that felony it will be first degree murder, regardless of the circumstances. This court has reiterated numerous times that "The purpose of the felony-murder rule is to deter felons from killing negligently or accidentally by holding them strictly responsible for killings they commit." The Legislature has said in effect that this deterrent purpose outweighs the normal legislative policy of examining the individual state of mind of each person causing an unlawful killing to determine whether the killing was with or without malice, deliberate or accidental, and calibrating our treatment of the person accordingly. Once a person perpetrates or attempts to perpetrate one of the enumerated felonies, then in the judgment of the Legislature, he is no longer entitled to such fine judicial calibration, but will be deemed guilty of first degree murder for any homicide committed in the course thereof.

Are you convinced? What might account for the court's decision in *Burton*? Might the court have felt that it had gone too far in *Wilson*, having expanded the merger exception to the point where it threatened to swallow the felony murder rule? But what is left of the merger doctrine after *Burton* when that decision is based on a general unwillingness to engage in "fine judicial calibration" in felony murder cases? What's the point of the merger doctrine if not to refine the coarse legislative calibration that is the felony murder rule? Is the point of the felony murder rule really that we can't be bothered with investigating the homicidal intent of certain people ("felons"), or is it rather that homicidal intent is presumed if death occurs in the course of certain types of highly dangerous behavior?

* * *

Problem

Jared Jackson was married to and living with Marilyn Jackson for seven months, during which time he was frequently physically abusive.

Roughly a month ago, Marilyn left Jared and moved into a trailer with her mother, Cora.

Jared ran into a friend of Marilyn's, Amy Andrews, while shopping. Amy told him that Marilyn had "been seeing" another guy for the last week or two. Though Marilyn had filed for divorce, Jared still told Amy that Marilyn was "his woman" and that the news she'd shared with him about the new man Marilyn was seeing incensed him. He called Marilyn on the phone and demanded, first, that she stop seeing her "new boyfriend" and, second, that she give him back the wedding ring he'd given her. She said that the ring was hers, and that she had no intention of giving it back, though she was thinking about pawning it. When he insisted she give it back once again, he heard Cora shouting in the background, "Hang up on him. Hang up on the bastard." He told Marilyn he was coming over to get the ring.

On the way over, he stopped at his friend Larry's house and grabbed a (legally registered) handgun that he had lent Larry. When Larry asked him what he needed it for, he told him he was going to take the ring he'd given Marilyn and then "blow away the old bitch" (Cora) because "she's caused all the trouble between me and Marilyn anyway."

When he kicked in the door and entered Cora's trailer, he discovered that Marilyn had locked herself in the bathroom. Hiding the handgun from view, he pleaded with Marilyn to come out and give him the ring. He also started to look around the trailer for the ring, which he knew Marilyn no longer wore. Not finding it, he became more agitated and pulled the gun out, waving it at Cora. Marilyn came out from the bathroom. She saw the gun and became very alarmed. She ran out the front door of the trailer and slipped on an icy patch on the front step. When she fell, her head hit a sharp rock, and she died instantly.

What might Jared be charged with under (a) California law, (b) New York law, and (c) the Model Penal Code? What are the strengths and weaknesses in the prosecution's case (assuming no evidentiary problems)? What appears to be Jared's best defense?

d. Causation and "Agency"

People v. Lowery

Supreme Court of Illinois.
178 Ill.2d 462, 687 N.E.2d 973 (1997).

■ CHIEF JUSTICE FREEMAN delivered the opinion of the court.

Following a jury trial in the circuit court of Cook County, defendant, Antonio Lowery, was convicted of first degree murder based on the commission of a felony, attempted armed robbery and two counts of armed robbery. The trial court sentenced defendant to 35 years' imprisonment for first degree murder, 20 years for each of the two armed robberies and 12 years for attempted armed robbery, to be served concurrently. On appeal, the appellate court reversed defendant's conviction and vacated his sentence for felony murder, holding that there was insufficient evidence to support defendant's conviction. We granted the State's petition for leave to appeal and now reverse the judgment of the appellate court.

On March 20, 1993, defendant was arrested and charged with two counts of armed robbery and one count of attempt armed robbery of Maurice Moore, Marlon Moore, and Robert Thomas. Defendant was also charged with the murder of Norma Sargent. In his statement to the police officers, defendant explained that he and his companion, "Capone," planned to rob Maurice, Marlon, and Robert. As Maurice, Marlon, and Robert walked along Leland Avenue in Chicago, defendant approached them, pulled out a gun and forced Maurice into an alley. Capone remained on the sidewalk with Robert and Marlon. Once in the alley, defendant demanded Maurice's money. Maurice grabbed defendant's gun and a struggle ensued. Meanwhile, Capone fled with Robert in pursuit. Marlon ran into the alley and began hitting defendant with his fists. As defendant struggled with Maurice and Marlon, the gun discharged. The three continued to struggle onto Leland Avenue. Upon pushing Maurice down, defendant noticed that Maurice now had the gun. Defendant then ran from the place of the struggle to the corner of Leland and Magnolia Avenues, where he saw two women walking. As he ran, he heard gunshots and one of the women scream.

Defendant continued to run, and in an apparent attempt at disguise, he turned the Bulls jacket which he was wearing inside-out. He was subsequently apprehended by the police and transported to the scene of the shooting, where Maurice identified him as the man who had tried to rob him. . . .

At issue in this appeal is whether the felony-murder rule applies where the intended victim of an underlying felony, as opposed to the defendant or his accomplice, fired the fatal shot which killed an innocent bystander. To answer this question, it is necessary to discuss the theories of liability upon which a felony-murder conviction may be based. The two theories of liability are proximate cause and agency.

In considering the applicability of the felony-murder rule where the murder is committed by someone resisting the felony, Illinois follows the "proximate cause theory." Under this theory, liability attaches under the felony-murder rule for any death proximately resulting from the unlawful activity—notwithstanding the fact that the killing was by one resisting the crime.

People v. Payne, 359 Ill. 246, 194 N.E. 539 (1935), is exemplary of Illinois' first application of the proximate cause theory. In *Payne*, the armed robbers approached the home of two brothers. One of the brothers fired a gun, attempting to prevent the robbery, and one of the robbers also fired. The second brother was killed by the gunfire, but it could not be determined whether his brother or the robber fired the fatal shot. The court found this fact to be immaterial and confirmed the defendant's murder conviction, stating:

> "It reasonably might be anticipated that an attempted robbery would meet with resistance, during which the victim might be shot either by

> himself or someone else in attempting to prevent the robbery, and those attempting to perpetrate the robbery would be guilty of murder."

More recently, this court followed the reasoning of *Payne* in *People v. Hickman*, 59 Ill. 2d 89, 319 N.E.2d 511 (1974). In *Hickman*, a police officer killed another police officer while attempting to apprehend cofelons fleeing from the scene of a burglary. This court held that the shot that killed the police officer was in opposition to the escape of the fleeing burglars and was a direct and foreseeable consequence of defendant's actions.

Alternatively, the majority of jurisdictions employ an agency theory of liability. Under this theory, "the doctrine of felony murder does not extend to a killing, although growing out of the commission of the felony, if directly attributable to the act of one other than the defendant or those associated with him in the unlawful enterprise." *State v. Canola*, 73 N.J. 206, 211–12, 374 A.2d 20, 23 (1977). Thus, under the agency theory, the felony-murder rule is inapplicable where the killing is done by one resisting the felony.

Defendant offers several arguments in an attempt at avoiding application of the proximate cause theory in this case. Initially, defendant urges this court to overrule *Payne* and *Hickman*, and adopt an agency theory of felony murder. We decline to do so. We believe that the analogies between civil and criminal cases in which individuals are injured or killed are so close that the principle of proximate cause applies to both classes of cases. Causal relation is the universal factor common to all legal liability. In the law of torts, the individual who unlawfully sets in motion a chain of events which in the natural order of things results in damages to another is held to be responsible for it.

It is equally consistent with reason and sound public policy to hold that when a felon's attempt to commit a forcible felony sets in motion a chain of events which were or should have been within his contemplation when the motion was initiated, he should be held responsible for any death which by direct and almost inevitable sequence results from the initial criminal act. Thus, there is no reason why the principle underlying the doctrine of proximate cause should not apply to criminal cases. Moreover, we believe that the intent behind the felony-murder doctrine would be thwarted if we did not hold felons responsible for the foreseeable consequences of their actions. * * *

Defendant further argues that the plain and clear language of the Illinois Criminal Code of 1961 (720 Ill. Comp. Stat. 5/1–1 *et seq.* (West 1992)) requires adoption of the agency theory and that *Hickman* failed to follow the plain language of the statute in rejecting the agency theory. Defendant refers to section 9–1(a) of the Code, which states:

> "(a) A person who kills an individual without lawful justification commits first degree murder if, in performing the acts which cause the death:
>
> > (1) he either intends to kill or do great bodily harm to that individual or another, or knows that such acts will cause death to that individual or another; or

(2) he knows that such acts create a strong probability of death or great bodily harm to that individual or another; or

(3) he is attempting or committing a forcible felony other than second degree murder."

We fail to see how the plain language of the statute demonstrates legislative intent to follow the agency theory. To the contrary, the intent of the legislature is an adherence to the proximate cause theory. Citing *Payne*, the committee comments to section 9–1(a)(3) state as follows:

> "It is immaterial whether the killing in such a case is intentional or accidental, or is committed by a confederate without the connivance of the defendant * * * or even by a third person trying to prevent the commission of the felony." * * *

Defendant further argues that the plain words of the felony-murder provision demonstrate the legislature's intent that felony murder be treated like all other offenses in the Criminal Code, subject to the same defenses and limits on culpability. Again, we fail to recognize any language, express or implied, that would allow felony murder to be treated like all other offenses. It is the inherent dangerousness of forcible felonies that differentiates them from nonforcible felonies. As noted in the committee comments of the felony-murder statute, "it is well established in Illinois to the extent of recognizing the forcible felony as so inherently dangerous that a homicide occurring in the course thereof, even though accidentally, should be held without further proof to be within the 'strong probability' classification of murder." This differentiation reflects the legislature's concern for protecting the general populace and deterring criminals from acts of violence. * * *

Because we have decided to adhere to the proximate cause theory of the felony-murder rule, we must now decide whether the victim's death in this case was a direct and foreseeable consequence of defendant's armed and attempted armed robberies. The State, relying on *Hickman* and *Payne*, argues that defendant was liable for decedent's death because it was reasonably foreseeable that Marlon would retaliate against defendant. We agree. A felon is liable for those deaths which occur during a felony and which are the foreseeable consequence of his initial criminal acts.

In the present case, when defendant dropped the gun and realized that Marlon was then in possession of the weapon, he believed that Marlon would retaliate, and, therefore, he ran. If decedent's death resulted from Marlon's firing the gun as defendant attempted to flee, it was, nonetheless, defendant's action that set in motion the events leading to the victim's death. It is unimportant that defendant did not anticipate the precise sequence of events that followed his robbery attempt. We conclude that defendant's unlawful acts precipitated those events, and he is responsible for the consequences.

Incidentally, we note that the appellate court interpreted *Hickman* as limiting the use of retaliation to the conduct of a police officer acting in the line of duty. We reject the court's narrow interpretation of *Hickman*. *Hickman* clearly states that "those who commit forcible felonies know they may encounter resistance, both to their affirmative actions and to any subsequent escape." *Hickman*, 59 Ill. 2d at 94. This court did not state expressly or impliedly that a robber's expectation of retaliation should be limited to police officers....

Defendant posits several unavailing arguments. He argues first that Marlon's act was an intervening cause because it was not foreseeable that Marlon would act as a vigilante and take the law into his own hands. It is true that an intervening cause completely unrelated to the acts of the defendant does relieve a defendant of criminal liability. However, the converse of this is also true: when criminal acts of the defendant have contributed to a person's death, the defendant may be found guilty of murder. It is not the law in this state that the defendant's acts must be the sole and immediate cause of death.

Here, we do not believe that Marlon's act of firing at defendant was intervening or coincidental. Marlon's resistance was in direct response to defendant's criminal acts and did not break the causal chain between defendant's acts and decedent's death. It would defeat the purpose of the felony-murder doctrine if such resistance—an inherent danger of the forcible felony—could be considered a sufficient intervening circumstance to terminate the underlying felony or attempted felony.

Furthermore, we do not believe that Marlon acted as a vigilante, or that because of our holding, the citizenry will have license to practice vigilantism. A vigilante is defined as a member of "a group extralegally assuming authority for summary action professedly to keep order and punish crime because of the alleged lack or failure of the usual law-enforcement agencies." Webster's New World Dictionary 1583 (2d ed. 1974). Regardless of how unreasonable Marlon's conduct may, in hindsight, be perceived, his response was not based on a deliberate attempt to take the law into his own hands, but on his natural, human instincts to protect himself.

Defendant next argues that decedent's death falls outside the scope of felony murder because it did not occur during the course of defendant's armed robbery and attempted armed robbery. In support, he relies on section 7–4 of the Code, which states that justifiable use of force is not available to a person who:

> "(c) Otherwise initially provokes the use of force against himself, unless: ...
>
> > (2) In good faith, he withdraws from physical contact with the assailant and indicates clearly to the assailant that he desires to withdraw and terminate the use of force, but the assailant continues or resumes the use of force."

Defendant maintains that he had "overtly retreated" from physical contact with Marlon and that Marlon's pursuit of defendant constituted a new conflict. The State, on the other hand, argues that defendant's election to flee fell within the commission of the armed and attempted armed robberies.

We must agree with the State. This court has consistently held that when a murder is committed in the course of an escape from a robbery, each of the conspirators is guilty of murder under the felony-murder statute, inasmuch as the conspirators have not won their way to a place of safety.

Defendant asserts that he had reached a place of "legal safety" when he ran. We disagree. Defendant was attempting to escape when Marlon fired the shots at him. Apparently, defendant also did not believe he had "won a place of safety" as evidenced by his own act of turning his coat inside-out to avoid detection before the police arrested him. Therefore, decedent's death falls within the scope of the felony-murder doctrine.

Defendant's final contention that Marlon was not legally justified in firing at defendant is misplaced. There is no claim that Marlon shot at defendant in self-defense or in an attempt to arrest him. Moreover, the proper focus of this inquiry is not whether Marlon was justified in his actions, but whether defendant's actions set in motion a chain of events that ultimately caused the death of decedent. We hold that defendant's actions were the proximate cause of decedent's death and the issue of whether Marlon's conduct was justified is not before this court.

Appellate court judgment reversed; cause remanded.

People v. Hernandez

Court of Appeals of New York.
82 N.Y.2d 309 (1993).

■ SIMONS, JUDGE.

This appeal raises the question whether a conviction of felony murder under Penal Law § 125.25(3) should be sustained where the homicide victim, a police officer, was shot not by one of the defendants but by a fellow officer during a gun battle following defendants' attempted robbery. . . .

Defendants Santana and Hernandez conspired to ambush and rob a man who was coming to a New York City apartment building to buy drugs. The plan was to have Santana lure him into the building stairwell where Hernandez waited with a gun. In fact, the man was an undercover State Trooper, wearing a transmitter, and backed up by fellow officers.

Once the Trooper was inside the building, Hernandez accosted him and pointed a gun at his head. A fight ensued during which the officer announced that he was a policeman, pulled out his service revolver and began firing. In the confusion, Hernandez, still armed, ran from the building into a courtyard where he encountered members of the police back-up unit. They ordered him to halt. Instead, he aimed his gun at one of the officers and moved toward him. The officers began firing, and one, Trooper Joseph Aversa, was fatally shot in the head. His body was found near the area where Hernandez was apprehended after being wounded. Santana was arrested inside the building.

The evidence at trial did not establish who killed Aversa, but the People concede that it effectively eliminated the possibility that either defendant was the shooter. Separate juries were empaneled for the two cases, and both defendants were convicted of felony murder and other charges.

On appeal, defendants contend that the felony murder charges should have been dismissed because neither one of them fired the fatal shot. The Appellate Division rejected that argument. Even though a fellow officer shot Aversa, the Court concluded that defendants were properly held responsible for felony murder because their conduct "unquestionably 'forged' a critical link in the chain of events that led to Trooper Aversa's death".

Some 30 years ago, this Court affirmed the dismissal of a felony murder charge on the grounds that neither the defendant nor a cofelon had fired the weapon that caused the deaths (People v. Wood, 8 N.Y.2d 48, 201 N.Y.S.2d 328, 167 N.E.2d 736). In Wood, the defendant and his companions were escaping from a fight outside a tavern when the tavern owner, attempting to aid police, fatally shot a bystander and one of defendant's companions. Defendant was charged with assault and felony murder. At the time, the relevant provision of section 1044 of the former Penal Law defined murder in the first degree as "[t]he killing of a human being * * * without a design to effect death, by a person engaged in the commission of, or in an attempt to commit a felony" (§ 1044[2]). We concluded that by the plain terms of the statute defendant could not be liable for murder, for the killing of the two men was not committed by a person "engaged in the commission of" a felony or a felony attempt. . . . The Wood case acknowledged that other jurisdictions differed on whether to apply a proximate cause theory under which felons could be held responsible for homicides committed by nonparticipants or an agency theory under which felons would be responsible only if they committed the final, fatal act.

In 1965, the Legislature revised the felony murder statute by removing the language that had been dispositive in Wood and replacing it with a provision holding a person culpable for felony murder when, during the commission of an enumerated felony or attempt, either the defendant or an accomplice "causes the death of a person other than one of the participants" (Penal Law § 125.25[3]). Thus, this appeal raises the question of whether Wood remains good law despite the recasting of the Penal Law. The question is one of first impression for this Court, although some Appellate Division panels have continued to adhere to the Wood rule that the shooter must be a participant in the underlying felony.

The People believe those Appellate Division decisions to be in error. They premise their argument on the established construction of the term "causes the death", which is now the operative language in the Penal Law. That term is used consistently throughout article 125 and has been construed to mean that homicide is properly charged when the defendant's culpable act is "a sufficiently direct cause" of the death so that the fatal result was reasonably foreseeable (People v. Kibbe, 35 N.Y.2d 407, 412, 362 N.Y.S.2d 848, 321 N.E.2d 773 [supra ch. 6]). In the People's view the evidence here meets that standard. They contend that it was highly foreseeable that someone would be killed in a shootout when Hernandez refused to put down his gun and instead persisted in threatening the life of one of the back-up officers. Thus, under the People's theory, Hernandez "caused the death" of Aversa. Because his attempt to avoid arrest was in furtherance of a common criminal objective shared with Santana, the People contend that the murder was properly attributed to Santana as well as under principles of accomplice liability.

In response, defendants assert that People v. Wood, though decided on narrow statutory grounds, states a rule that was followed for centuries at common law and one that has been embraced by a significant number of jurisdictions. The rationale for requiring that one of the cofelons be the shooter (or, more broadly, the person who commits the final, fatal act) has been framed in several ways. Some courts have held that when the victim or a police officer or a bystander shoots and kills, it cannot be said that the killing was in furtherance of a common criminal objective (State v. Severs, 759 S.W.2d 935, 938 [Tenn.Crim.App.]).

Others have concluded that under such circumstances the necessary malice or intent is missing (Wooden v. Commonwealth, 222 Va. 758, 284 S.E.2d 811). Under the traditional felony murder doctrine, the malice necessary to make the killing murder was constructively imputed from the mens rea incidental to perpetration of the underlying felony (Commonwealth v. Redline, 391 Pa. 486, 493–494, 137 A.2d 472, 475; IV Blackstone, Commentaries, at 200–201). Thus, in Wooden, the Virginia Supreme Court concluded that where a nonparticipant in the felony is the shooter, there can be no imputation of the necessary malice to him, and no party in the causal chain has both the requisite mens rea and culpability for the actus reus.

Still other courts have expressed policy concerns about extending felony murder liability. They have asserted that no deterrence value attaches when the felon is not the person immediately responsible for the death, or have contended that an expansive felony murder rule might unreasonably hold the felons responsible for the acts of others—for instance, when an unarmed felon is fleeing the scene and a bystander is hit by the bad aim of the armed victim (see, People v. Washington, 62 Cal.2d 777, 781–782, 44 Cal.Rptr. 442, 446, 402 P.2d 130, 134).

Analysis begins with the statute. The causal language used in our felony murder provision and elsewhere in the homicide statutes has consistently been construed by this Court according to the rule in People v. Kibbe (35 N.Y.2d 407, 362 N.Y.S.2d 848, 321 N.E.2d 773), where we held that the accused need not commit the final, fatal act to be culpable for causing death. To accept defendants' analysis would require that we hold that the phrase "causes the death" in subdivision (3), the felony murder paragraph of section 125.25, means something entirely different than it does in subdivisions (1) and (2) of the very same section. That is contrary to the normal rules of statutory construction.

That rule of construction must bend, of course, if in fact the Legislature intended the language to have a unique meaning within the context of the felony murder provision, but the legislative history of the 1965 revision reveals nothing about whether the Legislature intended to overturn People v. Wood. Defendants read that silence to mean that no such substantive change in the law was envisioned by the Legislature, and they urge us to reaffirm the common law as it applied to felony murder to limit liability when a nonparticipant is the killer.

Defendants' position is problematic for several reasons. First, it asks us to find in the ambiguous silence of the legislative record grounds for contradicting the unambiguous language of the statute. Second, it assumes that the Legislature intended an unusually narrow construction of the word "causes" even though New York homicide decisions had defined causality more expansively (see, e.g., People v. Kane, 213 N.Y. 260, 270, 107 N.E. 655 [error in medical treatment provided to victim does not relieve attacker of liability]).... The Legislature could easily have written into subdivision (3) the limitation endorsed by defendants—as it did with the limitation applying to the death of a cofelon—but it chose not to do so.

Third and more serious, defendants' argument is premised on the assumption that the relevant common law pertaining to felony murder was uniform and unambiguous at the time the Legislature acted in 1965. In fact, the leading American case for limiting felony murder liability, Commonwealth v. Redline, 391 Pa. 486, 137 A.2d 472, which was decided shortly before People v. Wood, overturned prior case law in Pennsylvania. Variations on the felony murder doctrine were widespread in American jurisprudence, with liability turning on such factors as whether the victim was one of the felons, whether the felons initiated the gun battle and whether the deceased had been used as a shield by defendant.

Nor can it be contended that the limited view of felony murder liability was clearly the law in New York at the time the Legislature acted. In People v. Wood, we noted that two of our decisions had incidentally endorsed the idea that the felon must be the killer, but we expressly left open questions concerning "the application of the rules of causation and foreseeability". ...

In light of the statutory language and the case law prior to the revision, we conclude that the Legislature intended what appears obvious from the face of the statute: that "causes" in the felony murder provision should be accorded the same meaning it is given in subdivisions (1) and (2) of section 125.25 of the Penal Law.

Unlike defendants and those courts adopting the so-called agency theory, we believe New York's view of causality, based on a proximate cause theory, to be consistent with fundamental principles of criminal law. Advocates of the agency theory suggest that no culpable party has the requisite mens rea when a nonparticipant is the shooter. We disagree. The basic tenet of felony murder liability is that the mens rea of the underlying felony is imputed to the participant responsible for the killing. By operation of that legal fiction, the transferred intent allows the law to characterize a homicide, though unintended and not in the common design of the felons, as an intentional killing. Thus, the presence or absence of the requisite mens rea is an issue turning on whether the felon is acting in furtherance of the underlying crime at the time of the homicide, not on the proximity or attenuation of the death resulting from the felon's acts. Whether the death is an immediate result or an attenuated one, the necessary mens rea is present if the causal act is part of the felonious conduct.

No more persuasive is the argument that the proximate cause view will extend criminal liability unreasonably. First, New York law is clear that felony murder does not embrace any killing that is coincidental with the felony but instead is limited to those deaths caused by one of the felons in furtherance of their crime. More than civil tort liability must be established; criminal liability will adhere only when the felons' acts are a sufficiently direct cause of the death. When the intervening acts of another party are supervening or unforeseeable, the necessary causal chain is broken, and there is no liability for the felons. Where a victim, a police officer or other third party shoots and kills, the prosecution faces a significant obstacle in proving beyond a reasonable doubt to a jury that the felons should be held responsible for causing the death.

Second, the New York felony murder statute spells out the affirmative defense available to the accomplice who does not cause the death (see, Penal Law § 125.25[3][a]-[d]). Defendants assert that our construction of the statute's causality language will mean that an accomplice whose partner is the shooter will have a defense but one whose unarmed partner causes the death will not. The plain language of the statute does not support that proposition. The statutory defense is available to the accomplice who (a) does not cause the death, (b) is unarmed, (c) has no reason to believe that the cofelon is armed and (d) has no reason to believe that the cofelon will "engage in conduct likely to result in death or serious physical injury". Thus, by its terms, the defense is not limited to situations where the cofelon kills with a weapon; it applies as well to instances where some other "conduct likely to result in death" is not within the contemplation of the accomplice.

In short, our established common-law rules governing determinations of causality and the availability of the statutory defense provide adequate boundaries to felony murder liability. The language of Penal Law § 125.25(3) evinces the Legislature's desire to extend liability broadly to those who commit serious crimes in ways that endanger the lives of others. That other States choose more narrow approaches is of no moment to our statutory scheme. Our Legislature has chosen not to write those limitations into our law, and we are bound by that legislative determination.

Finally, we conclude that there was no error in the court's instructions on defendant Santana's culpability. The jury was properly charged that more than "but for" causation was required; that it must find the fatal result was the sufficiently direct and foreseeable result of Hernandez's acts.

The evidence established that Hernandez, when confronted by the officers in the courtyard, refused to surrender and continued to move toward one officer with his gun drawn. Immediate flight and attempts to thwart apprehension are patently within the furtherance of the cofelons' criminal objective. Moreover, it was highly foreseeable that when Hernandez continued toward the officer with his gun drawn that shots would be fired and someone might be hit. Foreseeability does not mean that the result must be the most likely event. Undoubtedly, in planning the robbery, defendants did not anticipate that their victim would be a State Trooper or that a back-up unit would be on the scene. Yet, it was foreseeable that police would try to thwart crime, and Hernandez was aware that police were on the scene at the point he resisted arrest and remained armed. As the Appellate Division concluded, it is simply implausible for defendants to claim that defendants could not have foreseen a bullet going astray when Hernandez provoked a gun battle outside a residential building in an urban area.

Accordingly, the order of the Appellate Division should be affirmed.

QUESTIONS AND COMMENTS

1. Both *Lowery* and *Hernandez* favor the "proximate cause" theory, the former because felony murder *should not* be "treated like all other offenses," the latter because felony murder *should* be treated just like all other offenses. How—and why—does *Lowery* treat felony murder differently? How—and why—does *Hernandez* treat it the same?

2. What does it mean to adopt the agency theory over the proximate cause theory? Does it mean that felony murder is not subject to ordinary causation requirements? Conversely, does adopting the proximate cause theory imply denying the relevance of "agency," or "intervening causes"? Is there any difference between these two "theories" other than that one results in a more expansive application of the felony murder rule than the other?

Can a case be made that felony murder requires a showing only of factual, but not of proximate, causation? See *People v. Stamp*, ch. 6 supra ("As long as the homicide is the direct causal result of the [predicate felony] the felony-murder rule applies whether or not the death was a natural or probable consequence of the [felony]."). Or that it requires civil causation, not criminal causation? See *Lowery*.

More specifically, is a showing of proximate cause unnecessary because felony murder is a strict liability crime? (Cf. Model Penal Code § 2.03(4).) Put another way, would a requirement of proximate cause circumvent the felony murder doctrine by smuggling in a mens rea requirement with respect to the resulting death? Does this depend on whether we view "proximate causation" as fundamentally about foreseeability—so that inquiries into causation closely resemble inquiries into the negligence or recklessness of the defendant—or whether we view "causation" as a look *backward* from the dead body? (See ch. 6.)

Plainly, a defendant (outside the felony-murder context as well as within it) may foresee that his conduct will cause death—and thus be reckless—but argue that the death that occurred was not proximately caused by his conduct. The defendant in a robbery-murder case like *Stamp* may recognize, ex ante, that the risk of *deaths* occurring during robberies is substantial and unjustifiable, but still argue that *his* victim's death was not a result of the robbery, but the victim's wholly separate health status. A driver who leads the police on a high speed chase may recognize that he is reckless as to someone dying, but still argue that when police helicopters above him crash because of pilot error, he is not responsible for *that* death. See People v. Acosta, 232 Cal.App.3d 1375, 284 Cal.Rptr. 117 (Cal. Ct. App. 1991).

3. Note that the New York Penal Law—but not the Illinois Criminal Code—explicitly precludes the application of felony murder liability to the death of a "cofelon." (What exactly is a cofelon? A conspirator, an accomplice? An unwilling, or even unwitting, participant?) What's the justification for this exemption? Is taking the life of a person engaged in crime (in a felony? in a violent felony?) not homicide? Does it matter why and how the cofelon was killed? What if one of two robbers had stayed behind to attend to the injuries of their robbery victim, and then is shot by a police officer as he attempts to flee?

4. Should felony murder defendants be entitled to raise a justification defense like self-defense? The *Lowery* court dismisses the defendant's retreat argument as beside the point. But if Lowery is treated as though he had fired the fatal shot, why shouldn't he be allowed to justify his constructive conduct? Could any act sever the causal connection between a felon and a death occurring during, or in furtherance of, or in flight from, his felony? What if the robbery victim had intentionally killed a bystander?

e. Group Liability

Enmund v. Florida

Supreme Court of the United States.
458 U.S. 782, 102 S.Ct. 3368 (1982).

■ JUSTICE WHITE delivered the opinion of the Court.

The facts of this case, taken principally from the opinion of the Florida Supreme Court, are as follows. On April 1, 1975, at approximately 7:45 a.m., Thomas and Eunice Kersey, aged 86 and 74, were robbed and fatally shot at their farmhouse in central Florida. The evidence showed that Sampson and Jeanette Armstrong had gone to the back door of the Kersey house and asked for water for an overheated car. When Mr. Kersey came out of the house, Sampson Armstrong grabbed him, pointed a gun at him, and told Jeanette Armstrong to take his money. Mr. Kersey cried for help, and his wife came out of the house with a gun and shot Jeanette Armstrong, wounding her. Sampson Armstrong, and perhaps Jeanette Armstrong, then shot and killed both of the Kerseys, dragged them into the kitchen, and took their money and fled.

Two witnesses testified that they drove past the Kersey house between 7:30 and 7:40 a.m. and saw a large cream-or yellow-colored car parked beside the road about 200 yards from the house and that a man was sitting in the car. Another witness testified that at approximately 6:45 a.m. he saw Ida Jean Shaw, petitioner's common-law wife and Jeanette Armstrong's mother, driving a yellow Buick with a vinyl top which belonged to her and petitioner Earl Enmund. Enmund was a passenger in the car along with an unidentified woman. At about 8 a.m. the same witness saw the car return at a high rate of speed. Enmund was driving, Ida Jean Shaw was in the front seat, and one of the other two people in the car was lying down across the back seat.

Enmund, Sampson Armstrong, and Jeanette Armstrong were indicted for the first-degree murder and robbery of the Kerseys. Enmund and Sampson Armstrong were tried together.[1] The prosecutor maintained in his closing argument that "Sampson Armstrong killed the old people."....

The jury found both Enmund and Sampson Armstrong guilty of two counts of first-degree murder and one count of robbery. A separate sentencing hearing was held and the jury recommended the death penalty for both defendants under the Florida procedure whereby the jury advises the trial judge whether to impose the death penalty. The trial judge then sentenced Enmund to death on the two counts of first-degree murder....

The trial judge found four statutory aggravating circumstances[, including that] the capital felony was committed while Enmund was engaged in or was an accomplice in the commission of an armed robbery. * * *

The Florida Supreme Court affirmed Enmund's conviction and sentences. * * * [It] held that the record supported no more than the inference that Enmund was the person in the car by the side of the road at the time of the killings, waiting to help the robbers escape. This was enough under Florida law to make Enmund a constructive aider and abettor and hence a principal in first-degree murder upon whom the death penalty could be imposed. It was thus irrelevant to Enmund's challenge to the death sentence that he did not himself kill and was not present at the killings; also beside the point was whether he intended that the Kerseys be killed or anticipated that lethal force would or might be used if necessary to effectuate the robbery or a safe escape. We have concluded that imposition of the death penalty in these circumstances is inconsistent with the Eighth and Fourteenth Amendments.

The Cruel and Unusual Punishments Clause of the Eighth Amendment is directed, in part, " 'against all punishments which by their excessive length or severity are greatly disproportioned to the offenses charged.' " * * *

[O]nly a small minority of jurisdictions—eight—allow the death penalty to be imposed solely because the defendant somehow participated in a robbery in the course of which a murder was committed.... Society's rejection of the death penalty for accomplice liability in felony murders is also indicated by the sentencing decisions that juries have made.... The evidence is overwhelming that American juries have repudiated imposition of the death penalty for crimes such as petitioner's. * * *

Although the judgments of legislatures, juries, and prosecutors weigh heavily in the balance, it is for us ultimately to judge whether the Eighth Amendment permits imposition of the death penalty on one such as Enmund who aids and abets a felony in the course of which a murder is committed by others but who does not himself kill, attempt to kill, or intend that a killing take place or that lethal force will be employed. We have concluded, along with most legislatures and juries, that it does not. * * *

1. Jeanette Armstrong's trial was severed and she was convicted of two counts of second-degree murder and one count of robbery and sentenced to three consecutive life sentences.

Here the robbers did commit murder; but they were subjected to the death penalty only because they killed as well as robbed. The question before us is not the disproportionality of death as a penalty for murder, but rather the validity of capital punishment for Enmund's own conduct. The focus must be on *his* culpability, not on that of those who committed the robbery and shot the victims.... Enmund himself did not kill or attempt to kill; and, as construed by the Florida Supreme Court, the record before us does not warrant a finding that Enmund had any intention of participating in or facilitating a murder. Yet under Florida law death was an authorized penalty because Enmund aided and abetted a robbery in the course of which murder was committed. It is fundamental that "causing harm intentionally must be punished more severely than causing the same harm unintentionally." H. Hart, Punishment and Responsibility 162 (1968). Enmund did not kill or intend to kill and thus his culpability is plainly different from that of the robbers who killed; yet the State treated them alike and attributed to Enmund the culpability of those who killed the Kerseys. This was impermissible under the Eighth Amendment.

In *Gregg v. Georgia*, 428 U.S. 153 (1976), the opinion announcing the judgment observed that "[the] death penalty is said to serve two principal social purposes: retribution and deterrence of capital crimes by prospective offenders." Unless the death penalty when applied to those in Enmund's position measurably contributes to one or both of these goals, it "is nothing more than the purposeless and needless imposition of pain and suffering," and hence an unconstitutional punishment. We are quite unconvinced, however, that the threat that the death penalty will be imposed for murder will measurably deter one who does not kill and has no intention or purpose that life will be taken. Instead, it seems likely that "capital punishment can serve as a deterrent only when murder is the result of premeditation and deliberation," for if a person does not intend that life be taken or contemplate that lethal force will be employed by others, the possibility that the death penalty will be imposed for vicarious felony murder will not "enter into the cold calculus that precedes the decision to act."

It would be very different if the likelihood of a killing in the course of a robbery were so substantial that one should share the blame for the killing if he somehow participated in the felony. But competent observers have concluded that there is no basis in experience for the notion that death so frequently occurs in the course of a felony for which killing is not an essential ingredient that the death penalty should be considered as a justifiable deterrent to the felony itself. Model Penal Code § 210.2, Comment, p. 38, and n. 96. This conclusion was based on three comparisons of robbery statistics, each of which showed that only about one-half of one percent of robberies resulted in homicide.[23] The most recent national crime

23. The statistics relied upon by the American Law Institute may be summarized as follows:

Date & Location	No. of Robberies	Robberies Accompanied by Homicide	%
Cook County, Ill. 1926–1927	14,392 (est.)	71	.49
Philadelphia, Pa. 1948–1952	16,432	38	.59
New Jersey 1975	16,273	66	.41

statistics strongly support this conclusion.[24] In addition to the evidence that killings only rarely occur during robberies is the fact, already noted, that however often death occurs in the course of a felony such as robbery, the death penalty is rarely imposed on one only vicariously guilty of the murder, a fact which further attenuates its possible utility as an effective deterrence.

As for retribution as a justification for executing Enmund, we think this very much depends on the degree of Enmund's culpability—what Enmund's intentions, expectations, and actions were. American criminal law has long considered a defendant's intention—and therefore his moral guilt—to be critical to "the degree of [his] criminal culpability," and the Court has found criminal penalties to be unconstitutionally excessive in the absence of intentional wrongdoing. In *Robinson v. California*, 370 U.S. 660, 667 (1962), a statute making narcotics addiction a crime, even though such addiction "is apparently an illness which may be contracted innocently or involuntarily," was struck down under the Eighth Amendment. Similarly, in *Weems v. United States*, 217 U.S. 349 (1910), the Court invalidated a statute making it a crime for a public official to make a false entry in a public record but not requiring the offender to "[injure] any one by his act or [intend] to injure any one."....

For purposes of imposing the death penalty, Enmund's criminal culpability must be limited to his participation in the robbery, and his punishment must be tailored to his personal responsibility and moral guilt. Putting Enmund to death to avenge two killings that he did not commit and had no intention of committing or causing does not measurably contribute to the retributive end of ensuring that the criminal gets his just deserts. This is the judgment of most of the legislatures that have recently addressed the matter, and we have no reason to disagree with that judgment for purposes of construing and applying the Eighth Amendment.

Because the Florida Supreme Court affirmed the death penalty in this case in the absence of proof that Enmund killed or attempted to kill, and regardless of whether Enmund intended or contemplated that life would be taken, we reverse the judgment upholding the death penalty and remand for further proceedings not inconsistent with this opinion.

QUESTIONS AND COMMENTS

1. The *Enmund* court deals only with capital felony murder. It says nothing about the propriety of convicting an accomplice in the predicate felony who doesn't "intentionally" cause death of *noncapital* felony murder. What would be surprising, after all, about convicting an accomplice in

24. An estimated total of 548,809 robberies occurred in the United States in 1980. U.S. Dept. of Justice, Federal Bureau of Investigation, Uniform Crime Reports 17 (1981). Approximately 2,361 persons were murdered in the United States in 1980 in connection with robberies, *id.*, at 13, and thus only about 0.43% of robberies in the United States in 1980 resulted in homicide. See also Cook, The Effect of Gun Availability on Robbery and Robbery Murder, in 3 R. Haveman & B. Zellner, Policy Studies Review Annual 743, 747 (1980) (0.48% of all robberies result in murder).

the underlying felony of a death caused by a fellow accomplice, given that deaths caused by the *victim* of the felony or by *police officers* are attributable to her as well? (Or is there a difference, possibly based on the "innocence" of the perpetrators of the homicide?) Still, are the statistics cited and the distinctions drawn in *Enmund* entirely without significance regarding the advisability, if not the constitutionality, of the felony murder doctrine as a whole?

Then again, why *would* an accomplice (or conspirator) in the underlying felony necessarily be an accomplice (or conspirator) in the homicide? Wouldn't he need to have *intended* the result element of the homicide (death)? Or is it enough that he had the mental state required in the definition of the offense (in the case of felony murder, wouldn't that be none)?

2. In a subsequent case, the Supreme Court clarified that *Enmund* did not hold that capital felony murder be limited to those who acted with an "intent to kill," since "reckless indifference to the value of human life may be every bit as shocking to the moral sense as an 'intent to kill.'" Tison v. Arizona, 481 U.S. 137, 157, 107 S.Ct. 1676 (1987). The Court argues in *Enmund* that the risk of death during robberies is not so substantial as to make it just to blame all robbery participants for the (rare) deaths that do occur. Is a 1 in 200 rate really, as the Court implies, very low? Assume the typical robbery takes five minutes. If what we ordinarily did in our lives risked killing others to the degree robbing them does, we would kill someone roughly once every seventeen hours. Does it manifest "reckless indifference to the value of human life" to engage in an activity that would, if engaged in continuously, kill someone more than once a day?

3. How often do *unintentional* killings occur during robberies? Is robbery best described as "risky" (in the way driving recklessly is risky) or is it better described as a setting in which intentional killings occur? Is the real point of the felony murder rule to relieve the prosecution of the need to *prove* that felony murder defendants (mostly robbers) shot their victims intentionally, in situations in which ballistics evidence will often be insufficient to refute defendant claims that guns went off accidentally?

4. Some jurisdictions provide accomplices with a limited defense in *noncapital* felony murder cases:

> [I]n any prosecution under this subdivision, in which the defendant was not the only participant in the underlying crime, it is an affirmative defense that the defendant:
>
> (a) Did not commit the homicidal act or in any way solicit, request, command, importune, cause or aid the commission thereof; and
>
> (b) Was not armed with a deadly weapon, or any instrument, article or substance readily capable of causing death or serious physical injury and of a sort not ordinarily carried in public places by law-abiding persons; and
>
> (c) Had no reasonable ground to believe that any other participant was armed with such a weapon, instrument, article or substance; and

(d) Had no reasonable ground to believe that any other participant intended to engage in conduct likely to result in death or serious physical injury. . . .

N.Y. Penal Law § 125.25(4).

This provision was meant to "extend[] a defendant an opportunity to fight his way out of a felony murder charge by persuading a jury, by way of affirmative defense, that he not only had nothing to do with the killing itself but was unarmed and had no idea that any of his confederates were armed or intended to engage in any conduct dangerous to life." It "is based upon the theory that the felony murder doctrine, in its rigid automatic envelopment of all participants in the underlying felony, may be unduly harsh in particular instances; and that some cases do arise, rare though they may be, where it would be just and desirable to allow a nonkiller defendant of relatively minor culpability a chance of extricating himself from liability for murder—though not, of course, from liability for the underlying felony." What do you think are the chances of succeeding on this defense? What type of defense is this anyway? A justification, an excuse, or is it element-negating? (Note that, in New York, a defendant bears the burden of production and persuasion on an affirmative defense.) Cf. People v. Bornholdt, 33 N.Y.2d 75, 305 N.E.2d 461, 350 N.Y.S.2d 369 (1973).

5. Who counts as a "participant" for purpose of vicarious felony murder liability? See, e.g., N.Y. Penal Law § 125.25(3). Must I be an accomplice, or is it enough if I am merely a conspirator (and the crime occurs in a jurisdiction that doesn't follow *Pinkerton*, see ch. 8, in assuming that conspirators aid and abet all of one another's substantive offenses that are foreseeable and in furtherance of the conspiracy)? Let's say I conspire with two other people to rob a bank; they go and commit the actual bank robbery, during which a teller drops dead of a heart attack. Am I guilty of felony murder?

6. In *Enmund's* wake, capital felony murder survives, but now requires a showing of homicidal intent (or gross recklessness). That the intentional homicide was committed in the course of some other felony is an aggravating factor that elevates noncapital to capital murder. The New York Penal Law, once again, provides an example:

§ 125.27 Murder in the first degree.

A person is guilty of murder in the first degree when:

1. With intent to cause the death of another person, he causes the death of such person or of a third person; and

(a)(vii) the victim was killed while the defendant was in the course of committing or attempting to commit and in furtherance of robbery, burglary . . ., kidnapping . . ., arson . . ., rape . . . or escape . . ., or in the course of and furtherance of immediate flight after committing or attempting to commit any such crime or in the course of and furtherance of immediate flight after attempting to commit the crime of murder in the second degree; provided however, the victim is not a participant in one of the aforementioned crimes and, provided further that, unless the defendant's criminal liability under this subparagraph is based upon the defendant having commanded another person to cause the death of the victim or intended victim pursuant to section 20.00 of this chapter [complicity], this subparagraph shall not apply where the defendant's criminal liability is based upon the conduct of another pursuant to section 20.00 of this chapter....

4. Capital Murder

Gregg v. Georgia

Supreme Court of the United States.
428 U.S. 153, 96 S.Ct. 2909 (1976).

■ Justice Stewart.

[U]ntil Furman v. Georgia, 408 U.S. 238, 92 S.Ct. 2726 (1972), the Court never confronted squarely the fundamental claim that the punishment of death always, regardless of the enormity of the offense or the procedure followed in imposing the sentence, is cruel and unusual punishment in violation of the Constitution. Although this issue was presented and addressed in Furman, it was not resolved by the Court. Four Justices would have held that capital punishment is not unconstitutional per se; two Justices would have reached the opposite conclusion; and three Justices, while agreeing that the statutes then before the Court were invalid as applied, left open the question whether such punishment may ever be imposed. We now hold that the punishment of death does not invariably violate the Constitution.

The history of the prohibition of "cruel and unusual" punishment already has been reviewed at length. The phrase first appeared in the English Bill of Rights of 1689, which was drafted by Parliament at the accession of William and Mary. See Granucci, "Nor Cruel and Unusual Punishments Inflicted: The Original Meaning," 57 Calif.L.Rev. 839, 852–853 (1969). The English version appears to have been directed against punishments unauthorized by statute and beyond the jurisdiction of the sentencing court, as well as those disproportionate to the offense involved. The American draftsmen, who adopted the English phrasing in drafting the Eighth Amendment, were primarily concerned, however, with proscribing "tortures" and other "barbarous" methods of punishment.

In the earliest cases raising Eighth Amendment claims, the Court focused on particular methods of execution to determine whether they were too cruel to pass constitutional muster. The constitutionality of the sentence of death itself was not at issue, and the criterion used to evaluate the mode of execution was its similarity to "torture" and other "barbarous" methods. See Louisiana ex rel. Francis v. Resweber, 329 U.S. 459, 464, 67 S.Ct. 374, 376 (1947) (second attempt at electrocution found not to violate Eighth Amendment, since failure of initial execution attempt was "an unforeseeable accident" and "(t)here was no purpose to inflict unnecessary pain nor any unnecessary pain involved in the proposed execution").

But the Court has not confined the prohibition embodied in the Eighth Amendment to "barbarous" methods that were generally outlawed in the 18th century. Instead, the Amendment has been interpreted in a flexible and dynamic manner. * * * As Mr. Chief Justice Warren said, in an oft-quoted phrase, "(t)he Amendment must draw its meaning from the evolving standards of decency that mark the progress of a maturing society." Trop v. Dulles, 356 U.S. 86, 101, 78 S.Ct. 590, 598 (1958). Thus, an assessment of contemporary values concerning the infliction of a challenged sanction is relevant to the application of the Eighth Amendment. [T]his assessment does not call for a subjective judgment. It requires, rather, that we look to objective indicia that reflect the public attitude toward a given sanction.

But our cases also make clear that public perceptions of standards of decency with respect to criminal sanctions are not conclusive. A penalty also must accord with "the dignity of man," which is the "basic concept underlying the Eighth Amendment." Trop v. Dulles, supra, 356 U.S., at 100, 78 S.Ct., at 597 (plurality opinion). This means, at least, that the punishment not be "excessive." When a form of punishment in the abstract (in this case, whether capital punishment may ever be imposed as a sanction for murder) rather than in the particular (the propriety of death as a penalty to be applied to a specific defendant for a specific crime) is under consideration, the inquiry into "excessiveness" has two aspects. First, the punishment must not involve the unnecessary and wanton infliction of pain. Second, the punishment must not be grossly out of proportion to the severity of the crime.

* * * [I]n assessing a punishment selected by a democratically elected legislature against the constitutional measure, we presume its validity. We may not require the legislature to select the least severe penalty possible so long as the penalty selected is not cruelly inhumane or disproportionate to the crime involved. And a heavy burden rests on those who would attack the judgment of the representatives of the people.

This is true in part because the constitutional test is intertwined with an assessment of contemporary standards and the legislative judgment weighs heavily in ascertaining such standards. "(I)n a democratic society legislatures, not courts, are constituted to respond to the will and consequently the moral values of the people." The deference we owe to the decisions of the state legislatures under our federal system is enhanced where the specification of punishments is concerned, for "these are peculiarly questions of legislative policy." . . .

In the discussion to this point we have sought to identify the principles and considerations that guide a court in addressing an Eighth Amendment claim. We now consider specifically whether the sentence of death for the crime of murder is a per se violation of the Eighth and Fourteenth Amendments to the Constitution. We note first that history and precedent strongly support a negative answer to this question.

The imposition of the death penalty for the crime of murder has a long history of acceptance both in the United States and in England. The common-law rule imposed a mandatory death sentence on all convicted murderers. And the penalty continued to be used into the 20th century by most American States, although the breadth of the common-law rule was diminished, initially by narrowing the class of murders to be punished by death and subsequently by widespread adoption of laws expressly granting juries the discretion to recommend mercy.

It is apparent from the text of the Constitution itself that the existence of capital punishment was accepted by the Framers. At the time the Eighth Amendment was ratified, capital punishment was a common sanction in every State. Indeed, the First Congress of the United States enacted legislation providing death as the penalty for specified crimes. C. 9, 1 Stat. 112 (1790). The Fifth Amendment, adopted at the same time as the Eighth, contemplated the continued existence of the capital sanction by imposing certain limits on the prosecution of capital cases:

"No person shall be held to answer for a capital, or otherwise infamous crime, unless on a presentment or indictment of a Grand Jury . . .; nor shall any person be subject for the same offense to be twice put in jeopardy of life or limb; . . . nor be deprived of life, liberty, or property, without due process of law. . . ."

And the Fourteenth Amendment, adopted over three-quarters of a century later, similarly contemplates the existence of the capital sanction in providing that no State shall deprive any person of "life, liberty, or property" without due process of law. * * *

Four years ago, the petitioners in Furman and its companion cases predicated their argument primarily upon the asserted proposition that standards of decency had evolved to the point where capital punishment no longer could be tolerated. The petitioners in those cases said, in effect, that the evolutionary process had come to an end, and that standards of decency required that the Eighth Amendment be construed finally as prohibiting capital punishment for any crime regardless of its depravity and impact on society. This view was accepted by two Justices. Three other Justices were unwilling to go so far; focusing on the procedures by which convicted defendants were selected for the death penalty rather than on the actual punishment inflicted, they joined in the conclusion that the statutes before the Court were constitutionally invalid.

The petitioners in the capital cases before the Court today renew the "standards of decency" argument, but developments during the four years since Furman have undercut substantially the assumptions upon which their argument rested. Despite the continuing debate, dating back to the 19th century, over the morality and utility of capital punishment, it is now evident that a large proportion of American society continues to regard it as an appropriate and necessary criminal sanction.

The most marked indication of society's endorsement of the death penalty for murder is the legislative response to Furman. The legislatures of at least 35 States have enacted new statutes that provide for the death penalty for at least some crimes that result in the death of another person. . . . [A]ll of the post-Furman Statutes make clear that capital punishment itself has not been rejected by the elected representatives of the people.

The jury also is a significant and reliable objective index of contemporary values because it is so directly involved. The Court has said that "one of the most important functions any jury can perform in making ... a selection (between life imprisonment and death for a defendant convicted in a capital case) is to maintain a link between contemporary community values and the penal system." It may be true that evolving standards have influenced juries in recent decades to be more discriminating in imposing the sentence of death. But the relative infrequency of jury verdicts imposing the death sentence does not indicate rejection of capital punishment per se. Rather, the reluctance of juries in many cases to impose the sentence may well reflect the humane feeling that this most irrevocable of sanctions should be reserved for a small number of extreme cases. Indeed, the actions of juries in many States since Furman are fully compatible with the legislative judgments, reflected in the new statutes, as to the continued utility and necessity of capital punishment in appropriate cases. At the close of 1974 at least 254 persons had been sentenced to death since Furman, and by the end of March 1976, more than 460 persons were subject to death sentences.

As we have seen, however, the Eighth Amendment demands more than that a challenged punishment be acceptable to contemporary society. The Court also must ask whether it comports with the basic concept of human dignity at the core of the Amendment. Trop v. Dulles, 356 U.S., at 100, 78 S.Ct., at 597 (plurality opinion). Although we cannot "invalidate a category of penalties because we deem less severe penalties adequate to serve the ends of penology," the sanction imposed cannot be so totally without penological justification that it results in the gratuitous infliction of suffering.

The death penalty is said to serve two principal social purposes: retribution and deterrence of capital crimes by prospective offenders.[28] In part, capital punishment is an expression of society's moral outrage at particularly offensive conduct. This function may be unappealing to many, but it is essential in an ordered society that asks its citizens to rely on legal processes rather than self-help to vindicate their wrongs.

[Retribution is not] a forbidden objective nor one inconsistent with our respect for the dignity of men. Indeed, the decision that capital punishment may be the appropriate sanction in extreme cases is an expression of the community's belief that certain crimes are themselves so grievous an affront to humanity that the only adequate response may be the penalty of death.

Statistical attempts to evaluate the worth of the death penalty as a deterrent to crimes by potential offenders have occasioned a great deal of debate. The results simply have been inconclusive. As one opponent of capital punishment has said:

"(A)fter all possible inquiry, including the probing of all possible methods of inquiry, we do not know, and for systematic and easily visible

28. Another purpose that has been discussed is the incapacitation of dangerous criminals and the consequent prevention of crimes that they may otherwise commit in the future.

reasons cannot know, what the truth about this 'deterrent' effect may be. . . .

"The inescapable flaw is . . . that social conditions in any state are not constant through time, and that social conditions are not the same in any two states. If an effect were observed (and the observed effects, one way or another, are not large) then one could not at all tell whether any of this effect is attributable to the presence or absence of capital punishment. A 'scientific' that is to say, a soundly based conclusion is simply impossible, and no methodological path out of this tangle suggests itself." C. Black, Capital Punishment: The Inevitability of Caprice and Mistake 25–26 (1974).

Although some of the studies suggest that the death penalty may not function as a significantly greater deterrent than lesser penalties, there is no convincing empirical evidence either supporting or refuting this view. We may nevertheless assume safely that there are murderers, such as those who act in passion, for whom the threat of death has little or no deterrent effect. But for many others, the death penalty undoubtedly is a significant deterrent. There are carefully contemplated murders, such as murder for hire, where the possible penalty of death may well enter into the cold calculus that precedes the decision to act. And there are some categories of murder, such as murder by a life prisoner, where other sanctions may not be adequate.

The value of capital punishment as a deterrent of crime is a complex factual issue the resolution of which properly rests with the legislatures, which can evaluate the results of statistical studies in terms of their own local conditions and with a flexibility of approach that is not available to the courts. Indeed, many of the post-Furman statutes reflect just such a responsible effort to define those crimes and those criminals for which capital punishment is most probably an effective deterrent.

In sum, we cannot say that the judgment of the Georgia Legislature that capital punishment may be necessary in some cases is clearly wrong. Considerations of federalism, as well as respect for the ability of a legislature to evaluate, in terms of its particular State, the moral consensus concerning the death penalty and its social utility as a sanction, require us to conclude, in the absence of more convincing evidence, that the infliction of death as a punishment for murder is not without justification and thus is not unconstitutionally severe.

Finally, we must consider whether the punishment of death is disproportionate in relation to the crime for which it is imposed. There is no question that death as a punishment is unique in its severity and irrevocability. When a defendant's life is at stake, the Court has been particularly sensitive to insure that every safeguard is observed. But we are concerned here only with the imposition of capital punishment for the crime of murder, and when a life has been taken deliberately by the offender,[35] we

35. We do not address here the question whether the taking of the criminal's life is a proportionate sanction where no victim has been deprived of life for example, when capital punishment is imposed for rape, kidnaping, or armed robbery that does not result in the death of any human being.

cannot say that the punishment is invariably disproportionate to the crime. It is an extreme sanction, suitable to the most extreme of crimes.

We hold that the death penalty is not a form of punishment that may never be imposed, regardless of the circumstances of the offense, regardless of the character of the offender, and regardless of the procedure followed in reaching the decision to impose it.

QUESTIONS AND COMMENTS

1. In an effort to prevent the arbitrary application of the death penalty, the U.S. Supreme Court has insisted that states guide the sentencer's discretion by identifying a series of aggravating factors that differentiate capital from run-of-the-mill murder. The lists of aggravating factors found in death penalty statutes throughout the country generally derive from the Model Penal Code (which is ironic given the Code drafters' ambivalence regarding, if not outright disapproval of, capital punishment).

Model Penal Code § 210.6(3). Aggravating Circumstances.

(a) The murder was committed by a convict under sentence of imprisonment.

(b) The defendant was previously convicted of another murder or of a felony involving the use or threat of violence to the person.

(c) At the time the murder was committed the defendant also committed another murder.

(d) The defendant knowingly created a great risk of death to many persons.

(e) The murder was committed while the defendant was engaged or was an accomplice in the commission of, or an attempt to commit, or flight after committing or attempting to commit robbery, rape or deviate sexual intercourse by force or threat of force, arson, burglary or kidnapping.

(f) The murder was committed for the purpose of avoiding or preventing a lawful arrest or effecting an escape from lawful custody.

(g) The murder was committed for pecuniary gain.

(h) The murder was especially heinous, atrocious or cruel, manifesting exceptional depravity.

Another popular aggravating factor is based on the status of the victim; if the murder victim was a police officer, or other government official (or witness or juror):

Cal. Penal Code § 190.2(a)(7).

The victim was a peace officer, ... who, while engaged in the course of the performance of his or her duties, was intentionally killed, and the defendant knew, or reasonably should have known, that the victim was a peace officer engaged in the performance of his or her duties; or the victim was a peace officer ... or a former peace officer

... and was intentionally killed in retaliation for the performance of his or her official duties

To be weighed against these aggravating factors, are several mitigating circumstances:

Model Penal Code § 210.3(4). Mitigating Circumstances.

(a) The defendant has no significant history of prior criminal activity.

(b) The murder was committed while the defendant was under the influence of extreme mental or emotional disturbance.

(c) The victim was a participant in the defendant's homicidal conduct or consented to the homicidal act.

(d) The murder was committed under circumstances which the defendant believed to provide a moral justification or extenuation for his conduct.

(e) The defendant was an accomplice in a murder committed by another person and his participation in the homicidal act was relatively minor.

(f) The defendant acted under duress or under the domination of another person.

(g) At the time of the murder, the capacity of the defendant to appreciate the criminality [wrongfulness] of his conduct or to conform his conduct to the requirements of law was impaired as a result of mental disease or defect or intoxication.

(h) The youth of the defendant at the time of the crime.

How do the various aggravating and mitigating circumstances fit with the rationales for capital punishment discussed in *Gregg*? Do they provide meaningful guidance to sentencers (almost always a jury)? Do they capture significant (legitimate) distinctions between capital and noncapital murder? Do they simply rehash issues already resolved at the guilt phase of the trial—in favor of the prosecution?

2. The Supreme Court in *Gregg* addresses only the constitutionality of capital punishment. It does not address its wisdom, or appropriateness. Assuming its constitutionality *arguendo*, should the state threaten, impose, and inflict capital punishment?

Does the crime of taking life require the punishment of taking life? Is homicide sufficiently unique to require the unique punishment of death? Is the punishment of death sufficiently unique to require a unique justification? May life imprisonment without the possibility of parole be a harsher punishment in some cases? (What if the *defendant* thinks life in prison in worse than death?)

Who bears the burden of proving the deterrent effect of capital punishment? If capital punishment is rejected because its deterrent effect is inconclusive, must all criminal punishment be rejected?

Or is incapacitation the most potent justification for capital punishment? From an incapacitative standpoint, are there preferable alternatives to capital punishment? Mutilation? Branding? Transportation? If permanent incarceration is the answer, what about the risk of escape? Also, is it fair to impose the risk of victimization on fellow prison inmates and prison guards, rather than on the public at large? Are prison inmates truly (sufficiently) incapacitated?

As you think about these questions, consider the following exchange between Ernest van den Haag and Hugo Bedau.

Ernest van den Haag, "The Death Penalty Once More," 18 U.C. Davis L. Rev. 957, 964–71 (1985):

> *Is the Death Penalty More Deterrent Than Other Punishments?*
>
> Whether or not the death penalty deters the crimes it punishes more than alternative penalties—in this case life imprisonment with or without parole—has been widely debated since Isaac Ehrlich broke the abolitionist ranks by finding that from 1933–65 "an additional execution per year ... may have resulted on the average in seven or eight fewer murders."[14] Since his article appeared, a whole cottage industry devoted to refuting his findings has arisen. Ehrlich, no slouch, has been refuting those who refuted him. The result seems inconclusive. Statistics have not proved conclusively that the death penalty does or does not deter murder more than other penalties.... I myself have no contribution to make to the mathematical analyses of deterrent effects. Perhaps this is why I have come to believe that they may becloud the issue, leading us to rely on demonstrable deterrence as though decisive....
>
> .... I should favor the death penalty for murderers, if probably deterrent, or even just possibly deterrent. To me, the life of any innocent victim who might be spared has great value; the life of a convicted murderer does not....
>
> Even though statistical demonstrations are not conclusive, and perhaps cannot be, I believe that capital punishment is likely to deter more than other punishments because people fear death more than anything else. They fear most death deliberately inflicted by law and scheduled by the courts. Whatever people fear more is likely to deter most.... And surely the death penalty is the only penalty that could deter prisoners already serving a life sentence and tempted to kill a guard, or offenders about to be arrested and facing a life sentence....
>
> Many murders are "crimes of passion" that, perhaps, cannot be deterred by any threat. Whether or not they can be would depend on the degree of passion; it is unlikely to be always so extreme as to make the person seized by it totally undeterrable.... Almost all convicted murderers try to avoid the death penalty by appeals for commutation to life imprisonment. However, a minuscule proportion of convicted murderers prefer execution. It is sometimes argued that they murdered for the sake of being executed, of committing suicide via execution. More likely, they prefer execution to life imprisonment. Although

14. Isaac Ehrlich, "The Deterrent Effect of Capital Punishment: A Question of Life and Death," 65 Am. Econ. Rev. 397, 414 (1975).

shared by few, this preference is not irrational per se. It is also possible that these convicts accept the verdict of the court, and feel that they deserve the death penalty for the crimes they committed, although the modern mind finds it hard to imagine such feelings....

Because those sentenced to death tend to sedulously appeal the verdict of the trial courts, executions are correctly said to be costly.... But even if execution were more costly than life imprisonment, it should not be abandoned if it is just. If unjust, execution should not occur, even if it were cheap and imprisonment costly....

Is the Death Penalty Moral?

Miscarriages

Miscarriages of justice are rare, but do occur. Over a long enough time they lead to the execution of some innocents. Does this make irrevocable punishments morally wrong? Hardly. Our government employs trucks. They run over innocent bystanders more frequently than courts sentence innocents to death. We do not give up trucks because the benefits they produce outweigh the harm, including the death of innocents. Many human activities, even quite trivial ones, foreseeably cause wrongful deaths....

Vengeance

Some abolitionists feel that the motive for the death penalty is an ... unacceptable desire for vengeance. But though vengeance is the motive, it is not the purpose of the death penalty. Doing justice and deterring crime are the purposes, whatever the motive. Purpose (let alone effect) and motive are not the same....

Human Dignity

.... Many abolitionists believe that capital punishment is "degrading to human dignity".... Why would execution degrade human dignity more than life imprisonment? One may prefer the latter; but it seems at least as degrading as execution. [N]o one has explained why capital punishment degrades. Apparently those who argue that it does degrade dignity simply define the death penalty as degrading....

Writers, such as Albert Camus, have suggested that murderers have a miserable time waiting for execution and anticipating it. I do not doubt that. But punishments are not meant to be pleasant. Other people suffer greatly waiting for the end, in hospitals, under circumstances that, I am afraid, are at least as degrading to their dignity as execution....

Lex Talionis

Some writers insist that the suffering the death penalty imposes on murderers exceeds the suffering of their victims. This is hard to determine, but probably true in some cases and not in other cases. However, the comparison is irrelevant. Murderers are punished, as are all offenders, not just for the suffering they caused their victims, but for the harm they do to society by making life insecure, by threatening everyone, and by requiring protective measures. Punishment, ultimately, is a vindication for the moral and legal order of society and not limited by the Lex Talionis, meant to limit private retaliation for harms originally regarded as private.

Severity

Is the death penalty too severe? It stands in a class by itself. But so does murder. Execution is irreparable. So is murder. In contrast, all other crimes and punishments are, at least partly or potentially, reparable. The death penalty thus is congruous with the moral and material gravity of the crime it punishes.

Still, is it repulsive? Torture, however well deserved, now is repulsive to us. But torture is an artifact. Death is not, since nature has placed us all under sentence of death. Capital punishment, in John Stuart Mill's phrase, only "hastens death" which is what the murderer did to his victim. I find nothing repulsive in hastening the murderer's death, provided it be done in a nontorturous manner. Had he wished to be secure in his life, he could have avoided murder.

To believe that capital punishment is too severe for any act, one must believe that there can be no act horrible enough to deserve death. I find this belief difficult to understand. I should readily impose the death penalty on a Hitler or a Stalin, or on anyone who does what they did, albeit on a smaller scale.

H.A. Bedau, "A Reply to van den Haag," in The Death Penalty in America: Current Controversies 457, 461–69 (Hugo Adam Bedau ed., 1997):

Van den Haag [begins by] address[ing] deterrence and the empirical research on which judgments of deterrence are and ought to be made. Oddly, he says nothing explicit about incapacitation, although the special incapacitative effects of the death penalty are usually touted by those of its defenders who attach importance to deterrence. He ... insists that despite the lack of empirical evidence he still believes the death penalty is a better deterrent. Why? "[B]ecause people fear death more than anything else." Perhaps they would say they do, if they were asked to answer the question, which do you fear more, a death penalty or life in prison? But armed robbers, gangland hit men, kids in cars hell-bent on drive-by shootings, and other persons really interested in murdering someone are not thinking about that question. They are thinking instead about this question: "What's the best way for me to commit the crime and not get caught?"

Van den Haag also argues that the death penalty must be a better deterrent because death row convicts would rather have their sentences commuted to life in prison. This preference tends to show that life imprisonment is believed to be a less severe punishment than death. It does not show that death is a better deterrent—unless you accept as an axiom that the more severe a punishment is thought to be, the better a deterrent it is. The truth of that belief matters not at all if rational people will be deterred from murder as well by a long prison sentence as by a death sentence....

Throughout his discussion of deterrence, van den Haag fails to address a crucial question: If the death penalty is to be defended on grounds of its superior deterrence (or incapacitation), what stops us from defending even more savage penalties if they prove (or seem likely to prove) to be an even better deterrent than the death penalty as currently used?....

In the final and most important ... part of his argument, van den Haag raises ... issues [related to the] morality of the death penalty. On the first of these, miscarriages of justice, he concedes that in the long run the death penalty "leads to the execution of some innocents." ... But these losses are rare and worth it, he argues, because of the offsetting advantages that only the death penalty provides—[particularly] the deterrent superiority of the death penalty. As for his analogy (we tolerate high-speed highways despite our knowledge that they increase traffic deaths), all one can say is that there is no analogy between a morally defensive practice in which lethal accidents do occur that take statistical lives and a morally dubious practice in which lethal events are designed for particular individuals in the mistaken belief that they deserve it.

Van den Haag turns next to the role of "vengeance." ... I am troubled by van den Haag's endorsement of vengeance as a legitimate "motive" for the death penalty, even if not its real "purpose". [V]engeance is too eruptive and violent an emotion to encourage in ourselves and others. It cannot be confined and channeled to tolerate, much less support, due process of law in punishment, and is likely to spill over into private violence....

Van den Haag next tackles the concept and role of "human dignity" and denies that there is any mileage for abolitionists to be gained by invoking this value.... In an essay published some years after his ..., I [used] the four principles Justice Brennan introduced in his concurring opinion in Furman v. Georgia, 408 U.S. 238 (1972), in order to explain why the death penalty was an affront to human dignity ...:

> .... First, it is an affront to the dignity of a person to be forced to undergo catastrophic harm at the hands of another when, before the harm is imposed, the former is entirely at the mercy of the latter, as is always the case with legal punishments. Second, it offends the dignity of a person who is punished according to the will of a punisher free to pick and choose arbitrarily among offenders so that only a few are punished very severely when all deserve the same severe punishment if any do. Third, it offends the dignity of a person to be subjected to a severe punishment when society shows by its actual conduct in sentencing that it no longer regards this severe punishment as appropriate. Finally, it is an affront to human dignity to impose a very severe punishment on an offender when it is known that a less severe punishment will achieve all the purposes it is appropriate to try to achieve by punishing anyone in any manner whatsoever.

> .... Respect for the autonomy of rational creatures forbids its needless curtailment in the course of deserved punishment. Respect for the equal worth of persons forbids inequitable punishments of convicted offenders equally guilty. The fundamental equal rights of persons, including convicted offenders, precludes treating some offenders as if they had ceased to be persons.

Van den Haag turns to the law of retaliation, *lex talionis*, only to reject its authority. This is another important concession because it deprives him of arguing from this general principle of retaliatory punishments to the special case of the death penalty for murder, in which we take "a life for a life." (Of course, his disavowal of *lex talionis* also spares him the embarrassment of trying to cope with the inapplicability and absurdity of this law for a wide range of crimes, just as it frees him to defend the death penalty, should he wish to, for crimes that include no murder.) Instead, he argues that "punishment, ultimately, is a vindication of the moral and legal order of society." No doubt it ought to be, although it behooves those who would defend punishment in these terms to convince us that the current moral and legal order is sufficiently just to warrant our punitive practices. But of course one can grant van den Haag's claim about the nature or ultimate purpose of state punishment without for one moment suggesting that law and moral order can be vindicated *only* or *best* by the use of death penalties or any other unnecessary punishment....

Before turning to the next of van den Haag's moral considerations, we should notice how the fundamental principle of much of his overall argument is badly neglected. He makes it clear in passing that murderers *deserve* to die, and that the principal justification of the death penalty is *justice.* (Notice, by the way, that van den Haag nowhere claims that when society uses the death penalty, it does so in self-defense. Perhaps he would grant that this is an implausible claim for defenders of the death penalty to advance, because nowhere in Europe today, or in Michigan for a century and a half, to cite but one local example, has social defense required reliance on the death penalty.) He seems to believe that *desert* tells us *whom* to punish (guilty criminals), *what* they deserve as their punishment (murderers deserve death), and *why* this is what they deserve (justice). Yet his position on these issues is incomplete and unsatisfactory, for at least two reasons. First, he does not defend a mandatory death penalty; in principle that ought to prevent the arbitrariness, which he concedes, of our current discretionary death penalty, just as it ought to increase deterrence and retribution....

Second, what are we to make of his fundamental proposition that murderers deserve the death penalty? Is it supposed to be a necessary moral truth that anyone can see to be true simply by understanding the concepts used to express it, an analytic a priori proposition? [Instead t]his proposition must be somehow established by derivation from more fundamental norms. What are they? Since he has rejected *lex talionis*—the obvious if unsatisfactory answer—and supplied no alternative, we are left to guess....

Finally, van den Haag turns to the question whether the death penalty is "too severe" and concludes that it is not. [W]hether the death penalty is too severe depends on what one thinks the purpose and rationale of its severity is. Whatever that purpose or rationale, I think it is unnecessary for deterrence or incapacitation, arbitrary and discriminatory in the retribution it inflicts, and therefore an affront to our civilized sensibilities.

As to whether the death penalty is repulsive, [consider] what happens during a typical electrocution—a pretty ugly affair at best.... [Perhaps] the physical act of execution by lethal injection is not repulsive typically or necessarily—no doubt, a widely shared belief and a significant factor in explaining the popularity of lethal injection with American legislatures during the past twenty years. But this emphasis on the details of particular executions or on techniques for carrying out the death penalty obscures what is arguably repulsive about executions as such: It is not only that the prisoner dies, or dies in agony, or dies with ugly disfigurement, but the lethal act itself is the result of calculated planning by the impersonal state in which the state's overwhelming power is on display against the helplessness of the prisoner.

When van den Haag reminds us that death is inevitable in the nature of things, he does not make a very persuasive point. Human disappointment, pain, loneliness, bereavement, and other forms of misery and suffering are part of the human condition and virtually inevitable for each of us. Yet is that a good reason for complacency in their face if it is within our power to remedy or mitigate, even if only briefly or slightly, these inevitabilities? ...

As for Hitler and Stalin, they are often the trump card used by modern defenders of the death penalty who cannot believe that anyone really would oppose *all* executions. The trouble is that appealing to Hitler and Stalin sheds no light on whether to execute all or some or none of the more than three thousand prisoners on American death rows today. For myself, I would be glad to make an exception to my absolute rejection of the death penalty by permitting van den Haag to destroy tyrants such as these if he would give me the lives of those actually under sentence of death today, whose crimes are pathetically insignificant if measured against genocide, aggressive warfare, and the other crimes against humanity of which these dictators and their henchmen were guilty.

3. One of the reasons the U.S. Supreme Court—and others—believe that "death is different" is that capital punishment is uniquely irrevocable. How great must the likelihood of error be in capital cases to affect the constitutionality—or appropriateness—of capital punishment? Over a 23-year period ending in 1995, almost seven in ten death sentences were reversed on appeal. James S. Liebman, Jeffrey Fagan & Valerie West, A Broken System: Error Rates in Capital Cases, 1973–1995 (2000), http://justice.policy.net/cjedfund/jpreport/ (accessed Feb. 27, 2004). While the errors in these cases need have nothing to do with the defendant's substantive innocence of the crime of conviction (or even "innocence" of the death

penalty, i.e., the justification of capital punishment given his guilt of the underlying crime), several death row inmates have been exonerated and released, many on the basis of DNA testing. Cf. Death Penalty Information Center, Cases of Innocence 1973–Present, http://www.deathpenaltyinfo.org/ (accessed Feb. 27, 2004) (listing "111 people in 25 states who have been released from death row with evidence of their innocence" since 1973; list includes defendants who "had been convicted and sentenced to death, and subsequently either a) their conviction was overturned and they were acquitted at a re-trial, or all charges were dropped; or b) they were given an absolute pardon by the governor based on new evidence of innocence").

4. Having decided that capital punishment is not per se unconstitutional, the Supreme Court has devoted considerable effort to the task of setting up a procedure that minimizes the risk of unconstitutional *application*. The result has been a complex set of procedural requirements that are often contradictory—most importantly, the demand that the sentencing process be both consistent *and* tailored to the specific characteristics of each crime, offender, and victim. For general assessments of the Supreme Court's procedural capital punishment jurisprudence, see Carol S. Steiker & Jordan M. Steiker, "Sober Second Thoughts: Reflections on Two Decades of Constitutional Regulation of Capital Punishment," 109 Harv. L. Rev. 355 (1995) ("aura of science and shared responsibility" legitimates capital punishment); Markus Dirk Dubber, "The Pain of Punishment," 44 Buff. L. Rev. 545 (1996) (attempt to dissipate responsibility for the infliction of death).

The process of imposing a death sentence in a proceeding according to the Supreme Court's specifications, however, is nowhere near as complex and protracted as the process of checking and rechecking its results. Once a death sentence has been imposed, cases spend years on state and federal appeals. The average time between death sentence and execution is between eleven and twelve years. U.S. Dep't Justice, Bureau of Justice Statistics Bulletin, T. Snell, Capital Punishment 2000, at 12 (Dec. 2001). So long is the wait for execution in some cases, that death row inmates have begun arguing that the delay itself constitutes cruel and unusual punishment. See, e.g., Foster v. Florida, 537 U.S. 990 (2002) (Breyer, J., dissenting from denial of certiorari) (petitioner had spent 27 years on death row).

5. What does individualized sentencing mean? The U.S. Supreme Court has held that "the decision to impose [the death sentence] had to be guided by standards so that the sentencing authority would focus on the particularized circumstances of the crime and the defendant." Gregg v. Georgia, 428 U.S. 153, 199 (1976). What about the particularized circumstances of the victim? What, in other words, is the harm of capital murder? Is it the death of a particular person in a particular way? Or is it the death of a "person" in the abstract? In Payne v. Tennessee, 501 U.S. 808, 111 S.Ct. 2597 (1991), the U.S. Supreme Court overturned its decision, reached only four years earlier, to exclude victim impact evidence from capital sentencing hearings:

> [Our decision in *Booth* v. *Maryland*, 482 U.S. 496, 107 S.Ct. 2529 (1987), was] based on two premises: that evidence relating to a particular victim or to the harm that a capital defendant causes a victim's

family do not in general reflect on the defendant's "blameworthiness," and that only evidence relating to "blameworthiness" is relevant to the capital sentencing decision. However, the assessment of harm caused by the defendant as a result of the crime charged has understandably been an important concern of the criminal law, both in determining the elements of the offense and in determining the appropriate punishment. Thus, two equally blameworthy criminal defendants may be guilty of different offenses solely because their acts cause differing amounts of harm. "If a bank robber aims his gun at a guard, pulls the trigger, and kills his target, he may be put to death. If the gun unexpectedly misfires, he may not. His moral guilt in both cases is identical, but his responsibility in the former is greater."

* * * "The first significance of harm in Anglo–American jurisprudence is, then, as a prerequisite to the criminal sanction. The second significance of harm—one no less important to judges—is as a measure of the seriousness of the offense and therefore as a standard for determining the severity of the sentence that will be meted out." S. Wheeler, K. Mann, & A. Sarat, Sitting in Judgment: The Sentencing of White–Collar Criminals 56 (1988).

* * * We have held that a State cannot preclude the sentencer from considering "any relevant mitigating evidence" that the defendant proffers in support of a sentence less than death. Thus we have ... required that the capital defendant be treated as a "uniquely individual human being.".... *Booth* has, we think, unfairly weighted the scales in a capital trial; while virtually no limits are placed on the relevant mitigating evidence a capital defendant may introduce concerning his own circumstances, the State is barred from either offering "a quick glimpse of the life" which a defendant "chose to extinguish," or demonstrating the loss to the victim's family and to society which has resulted from the defendant's homicide.

The *Booth* Court reasoned that victim impact evidence must be excluded because it would be difficult, if not impossible, for the defendant to rebut such evidence without shifting the focus of the sentencing hearing away from the defendant, thus creating a " 'mini-trial' on the victim's character." ...

Payne echoes the concern voiced in *Booth*'s case that the admission of victim impact evidence permits a jury to find that defendants whose victims were assets to their community are more deserving of punishment than those whose victims are perceived to be less worthy. As a general matter, however, victim impact evidence is not offered to encourage comparative judgments of this kind—for instance, that the killer of a hardworking, devoted parent deserves the death penalty, but that the murderer of a reprobate does not. It is designed to show instead *each* victim's "uniqueness as an individual human being," whatever the jury might think the loss to the community resulting from his death might be....

* * * "Within the constitutional limitations defined by our cases, the States enjoy their traditional latitude to prescribe the method by which those who commit murder shall be punished." The States

> remain free, in capital cases, as well as others, to devise new procedures and new remedies to meet felt needs. Victim impact evidence is simply another form or method of informing the sentencing authority about the specific harm caused by the crime in question, evidence of a general type long considered by sentencing authorities. We think the *Booth* Court was wrong in stating that this kind of evidence leads to the arbitrary imposition of the death penalty.... Courts have always taken into consideration the harm done by the defendant in imposing sentence. * * *
>
> We thus hold that if the State chooses to permit the admission of victim impact evidence and prosecutorial argument on that subject, the Eighth Amendment erects no *per se* bar. A State may legitimately conclude that evidence about the victim and about the impact of the murder on the victim's family is relevant to the jury's decision as to whether or not the death penalty should be imposed....

Should it matter whether the defendant was aware of—or should (or could) at least have foreseen—the victim's characteristics? Of the person or persons who would be affected by her death? Of the nature and extent of their suffering? Should the victim's—as opposed to the offender's—characteristics make the difference between ordinary and capital murder?

6. Victim impact statements are not alone in drawing distinctions among murder victims; such distinctions are also common in capital murder statutes. Should it matter whether the victim was a police officer, or some other government official? The following excerpt considers the propriety of victim impact evidence and of distinctions among types of victims from the perspective of the various punishment theories said by the Supreme Court to justify capital punishment:

> Over the course of capital jurisprudence since *Furman*, the Court has settled on a generally retributive approach to capital sentencing. According to the standard retributive theory underlying the Court's capital jurisprudence, retributive desert falls into two components: moral culpability and harm. Much of the Court's capital jurisprudence has focused on ensuring that the capital sentencer has an opportunity to properly assess the defendant's degree of culpability. The victim impact evidence cases raise the question of how a capital sentencing scheme should take into account the harm element of retributive desert....
>
> The relationship between deterrence, incapacitation, and retribution in the Court's capital jurisprudence remains sketchy. As capital jurisprudence has tended to focus on the moral culpability element of the retributive desert determination, the Court has had little occasion to consider the place of deterrence and incapacitation, neither of which concerns itself with the question of accountability. Retributive desert, however, clearly serves at least as a limiting principle in the Court's capital jurisprudence. This means that no defendant may receive the death penalty unless the sentencer has determined that the defendant possessed the requisite level of culpability to deserve the death penalty....

As a deontological theory, retribution assigns desert irrespective of any benefit a particular community—be it the victim's family, the victim's favorite charity, or society at large—might have derived or would have continued to derive from the victim. From a retributive standpoint, the taker of human life is no more deserving of death because the victim happened to be a proud father of five and a pillar of the community, or because one victim is ... "more unique" than another. The Court's retributive approach to capital jurisprudence therefore prohibits consideration of the victim's societal worth at sentencing.

That is not to say, however, that retributive capital punishment schemes may not in other ways reflect the harm caused by the offense. First, the legislature considers the qualitatively different harm of a person's death in designating certain crimes as capital. According to retributive theory, the taking of human life, and only the taking of human life, deserves the imposition of the death penalty.

Second, the sentencer arguably may consider the specific nature of the harm caused by the defendant during the commission of the crime. All other things being equal, a person who causes another's slow and painful death may be said to deserve greater moral blame than a person who causes another's quick and painless death. Capital sentencing schemes accordingly list the exceptionally brutal commission of a crime as an aggravating factor....

It may be argued, however, that the details of a crime do not affect retributive desert in the capital sentencing context because retributive theory, as applied to the death penalty, recognizes only one type of harm, the qualitatively unique taking of a human life. The violent transformation of a human being possessed of the unique quality of life into a faceless quantity, this "ultimate act of depersonalization," this "desecration of the human and divine realms," is the only harm that can expose an offender to the "ultimate act of depersonalization" in return....

Limiting harm assessments to the legislative aspect of capital punishment schemes obviously does not exclude harm considerations from capital punishment. [The argument] that criminal sentencing has considered and should continue to consider harm, therefore misses the point. While harm plays a crucial role in the legislature's definition of capital crimes and aggravating circumstances, harm differentiation is irrelevant for the sentencer's decision whether a particular offender possesses the requisite moral culpability to die....

Even if we assume that ... value differentiations between persons are not offensive, but only irrelevant, to the retributive desert assessment, deterrence and incapacitation would still not permit these distinctions. Incapacitation looks only to the likelihood that an offender will commit a (capital) crime in the future. According to incapacitation theory, the death penalty serves to incapacitate offenders who are likely to commit other (capital) crimes, because only execution incapacitates completely. The harm caused by the present offense does not affect an offender's recidivist potential, and it is therefore irrelevant for incapacitative purposes.

Similarly, the deterrent effect of a given penalty does not depend on the harm caused by the offense. Deterrence looks to the effect that the threat of imposition of a certain punishment will have on potential offenders in the future. Relevant deterrence considerations in a capital sentencing hearing therefore include the relative deterrent effects on this particular offender of imposing the death sentence or a life sentence on that offender (specific deterrence) and the relative deterrent effects on other potential offenders of imposing the death sentence or a life sentence on this particular offender (general deterrence). The societal cost of the victim's death does not influence the specific or general deterrent effect of imposing a particular sentence on the person responsible for her death. The only relevant harm for deterrent purposes is not the harm caused by the present offense, but the potential harm caused by offenses not yet committed or the harm likely to be caused by the sentencer's failure to impose one sentence rather than another. Unlike a retributive desert assessment, a deterrence calculus therefore does not consider harm that has already resulted from the commission of the present offense.

This is not to say that the legislature may not, within certain limits, base its definitions of capital murder or of aggravating circumstances on a consideration of potential societal harm. The legislature, after all, makes exclusively prospective judgments—at least in the criminal law field, where retroactive laws are frowned upon—in that it establishes rules designed to affect future behavior, both on the part of the potential offenders (by deterring them from crime) and on the part of capital sentencers (by guiding their discretion). [T]here exists an important distinction between justifying a death penalty statute and justifying a particular death sentence. While the legislature, in considering a death penalty statute, may well be entitled to consider the benefit derived by society from a certain class of persons, say police officers, firefighters, or Vice Presidents, it does not follow that the sentencer may consider that benefit in imposing the death sentence on a particular offender.

In a nutshell, the potential societal cost resulting from the future death of a person within a given class of persons may be relevant to the legislature's definition of a capital crime or of an aggravating factor. The actual societal cost created by the victim's past death, however, is irrelevant to the sentencer's decision about the relative deterrent effects of imposing a life sentence or the death penalty on a particular offender.

[L]et us turn briefly to the legislative consideration of the victim's identity in defining capital murder or aggravating circumstances. While, for the reasons outlined above, the bar against considering the victim's societal worth at sentencing does not automatically prohibit the legislature from classifying the murder of one person as more egregious than the murder of another person, this "seriousness ranking" of murders nevertheless gives rise to concern. Initially, there remains something deeply disturbing about distinguishing between the seriousness of murders based on the victim's position in life. In response, one may suggest that the legislative choice to threaten the death penalty for the murder of a police officer but not for the murder of a high school teacher does not reflect a legislative judgment that the life of a detective is worth more than that of a math instructor. Instead, one may argue, the legislature finds both murders equally morally reprehensible, and distinguishes between a police officer and a teacher only on the utilitarian ground that the murder of the former results in a greater cost to society than the murder of the latter. The murder of a police officer, one might say, would not only have the immediate effect of leaving an important societal function unattended, but would also discourage others from serving a similar function.

Assuming for the sake of argument that legislative distinctions between murders based on the victim's identity do not reflect a distinction between different levels of moral wrongdoing, distinctions drawn on the basis of the victim's societal worth will nevertheless seem dubious even to the most hardened utilitarian theorist. Moreover, societal worth estimations cannot fully explain the ranking of murder victims in death penalty statutes. If societal worth were the determinative ranking factor, it is unclear why a legislature does not define capital murder as the murder of a nurse, a priest, or a grandmother of three. Society does not necessarily derive a greater benefit from a pencil pushing deputy than from a neurosurgeon. Legislatures do not threaten the death penalty for the murder of a person who performs a vital societal function but who is not a State official of some sort. The protected class instead includes members of Congress, Supreme Court Justices, Presidents, district attorneys, police officers, corrections employees, and firefighters. Perhaps it is thought that the murder of a firefighter or a district attorney shakes the public's confidence in the State's authority and therefore generates an additional, indirect societal cost which the murder of a neurosurgeon would not create.

It is more plausible that societal worth alone cannot explain the distinction between classes of persons in death penalty statutes.... The limitation of the protected class to State officials may instead derive from a self-protective, if not retaliatory, impulse on the part of the State. The definition of capital murder and aggravating factors makes sense if one views State officials as seeking to protect one another, much like the members of some other social unit would do. Consider, for example, the deep retaliatory desires that the murder of a fellow judge, police officer, or prosecutor unleashes among State officials. However understandable these retaliatory desires are, it is questionable whether the members of one social unit should be permitted to act upon such desires while the members of other social units may not. The superior power of State officials suggests that the imposition of greater, rather than lesser, restraints on their ability to implement their retaliatory desires would be appropriate.

Markus Dirk Dubber, "Regulating the Tender Heart When the Axe Is Ready to Strike," 41 Buff. L. Rev. 85, 131–43 (1993).

7. The distinction between noncapital and capital (or, in some jurisdictions, between second and first degree) murder raises nonconstitutional questions as well, as courts have been called upon to interpret statutory aggravating factors. See, e.g., People v. Cahill, 2 N.Y.3d 14, 809 N.E.2d 561, 777 N.Y.S.2d 332 (2003) (witness elimination purpose must be "substantial factor" in, but need not be sole purpose of, murder). In many cases, however, this exercise in statutory interpretation takes place against the backdrop of the stricter constitutional scrutiny applied to capital cases. See, e.g., Proffitt v. Florida, 428 U.S. 242 (1976) (upholding Florida's "especially heinous, atrocious or cruel" circumstance as interpreted to include only "the conscienceless or pitiless crime which is unnecessarily torturous to the victim").

8. What distinguishes capital murder, not from ordinary murder, but from other serious crimes? *Enmund* explores the constitutional minimum of culpability. Coker v. Georgia, 433 U.S. 584 (1977), addresses the constitutional minimum of *harm*:

> We do not discount the seriousness of rape as a crime. It is highly reprehensible, both in a moral sense and in its almost total contempt for the personal integrity and autonomy of the female victim and for the latter's privilege of choosing those with whom intimate relationships are to be established. Short of homicide, it is the "ultimate violation of self." It is also a violent crime because it normally involves force, or the threat of force or intimidation, to overcome the will and the capacity of the victim to resist. Rape is very often accompanied by physical injury to the female and can also inflict mental and psychological damage. Because it undermines the community's sense of security, there is public injury as well.
>
> Rape is without doubt deserving of serious punishment; but in terms of moral depravity and of the injury to the person and to the public, it does not compare with murder, which does involve the unjustified taking of human life. Although it may be accompanied by another crime, rape by definition does not include the death of or even the serious injury to another person. The murderer kills; the rapist, if no more than that, does not. Life is over for the victim of the murderer; for the rape victim, life may not be nearly so happy as it was, but it is not over and normally is not beyond repair. We have the abiding conviction that the death penalty, which "is unique in its severity and irrevocability," is an excessive penalty for the rapist who, as such, does not take human life.

Coker v. Georgia, 433 U.S. 584, 597–98 (1977).

Coker dealt with the rape of an adult woman. Would the following aggravated rape statute pass constitutional muster?

La. Rev. Stat. § 14:42. Aggravated Rape.

(A) Aggravated rape is a rape committed upon a person sixty-five years of age or older or where the anal, oral, or vaginal sexual intercourse is deemed to be without lawful consent of the victim because it is committed under any one or more of the following circumstances:

(1) When the victim resists the act to the utmost, but whose resistance is overcome by force.

(2) When the victim is prevented from resisting the act by threats of great and immediate bodily harm, accompanied by apparent power of execution.

(3) When the victim is prevented from resisting the act because the offender is armed with a dangerous weapon.

(4) When the victim is under the age of twelve years. Lack of knowledge of the victim's age shall not be a defense.

(5) When two or more offenders participated in the act.

(6) When the victim is prevented from resisting the act because the victim suffers from a physical or mental infirmity preventing such resistance.

. . . .

(D)(2) [I]f the victim was under the age of twelve years . . . :

(a) And if the district attorney seeks a capital verdict, the offender shall be punished by death or life imprisonment at hard labor without benefit of parole, probation, or suspension of sentence. . . .

9. *Race*. The role of race in the administration of the death penalty in the United States continues to attract attention. See generally David C. Baldus & George Woodworth, "Race Discrimination and the Death Penalty: An Empirical and Legal Overview," in America's Experiment with Capital Punishment 385 (James C. Acker et al. eds. 1998). In McCleskey v. Kemp, 481 U.S. 279 (1987), the U.S. Supreme Court considered—and rejected—a racial discrimination challenge to the administration of capital punishment in Georgia. The decision was widely criticized, including by Randall Kennedy:

> In 1978, Warren McCleskey, a young black man, was convicted in Fulton County, Georgia, of robbing a furniture store and killing Frank Schlatt, a white police officer. A jury composed of eleven whites and one black sentenced McCleskey to life imprisonment for the robbery and death for the murder. His subsequent appeals followed the normal, dreary route of post-conviction proceedings in capital cases. When McCleskey sought habeas corpus relief from the federal district court, however, his conventional struggle against execution was transformed into an extraordinary challenge to the entire system of capital punishment in Georgia. Supported by the most comprehensive statistical analysis ever done on the racial demographics of capital sentencing in a single state, McCleskey argued that his sentence should be nullified because, among other things, there existed a constitutionally impermissible risk that both his race and that of his victim played a significant role in the decision to sentence him to death. His arguments were rejected at every level of the federal judiciary. Even though the Supreme Court assumed the validity of statistics indicating that murderers of whites are four times more likely to be sentenced to death than murderers of blacks, it nonetheless held against the petitioner.

> .... I shall focus almost exclusively on the equal protection aspect of the case. More specifically, I shall elaborate a claim that has largely been ignored: the right of black victims or potential victims of murder to a response on the part of the state that is equally as vigorous as that which follows the murder of whites. McCleskey asserted two very different equal protection theories. The first, a theory of race-of-the-defendant discrimination, maintains that sentencing in Georgia is improperly influenced by the race of the defendant; the second, a theory of race-of-the-victim discrimination, maintains that sentencing is improperly influenced by the race of the victim. It now appears that even on the basis of the very studies on which McCleskey relied, there existed no statewide, statistically significant evidence to support his allegation of race-of-the-defendant discrimination.... A different problem is posed by the race-of-the-victim theory that McCleskey asserts. He claims that race-of-the-victim discrimination deprived him of rights protected by the equal protection clause by increasing the likelihood that he would be sentenced to death. He emphasizes the unfairness that race-of-the-victim discrimination visits upon those who happen to murder whites. I emphasize, by contrast, the unfairness that race-of-the-victim discrimination visits upon the black community by denying it equal treatment with respect to those who kill its members. McCleskey's theory is defendant-oriented while mine is community-oriented.... Georgia's race-of-the-victim disparities indicate a devaluation of black victims: put bluntly, officials in Georgia "place[] a higher value on the lives of whites than blacks."

Randall L. Kennedy, "*McCleskey v. Kemp*: Race, Capital Punishment, and the Supreme Court," 101 Harv. L. Rev. 1388, 1388–91 (1988).

C. MANSLAUGHTER

1. MURDER VS. INVOLUNTARY MANSLAUGHTER

Commonwealth v. Malone

Supreme Court of Pennsylvania.
354 Pa. 180 (1946).

■ MAXEY, C.J.

This is an appeal from the judgment and sentence under a conviction of murder in the second degree. William H. Long, age 13 years, was killed by a shot from a 32–caliber revolver held against his right side by the defendant, then aged 17 years. These youths were on friendly terms at the time of the homicide....

On the evening of February 26, 1945, when the defendant went to a moving picture theater, he carried in the pocket of his raincoat a revolver which he had obtained at the home of his uncle on the preceding day. In the afternoon preceding the shooting, the decedent procured a cartridge from his father's room and he and the defendant placed it in the revolver.

After leaving the theater, the defendant went to a dairy store and there met the decedent. Both youths sat in the rear of the store ten minutes, during which period the defendant took the gun out of his pocket and loaded the chamber to the right of the firing pin and then closed the gun. A few minutes later, both youths sat on stools in front of the lunch counter and ate some food. The defendant suggested to the decedent that they play "Russian Poker".[1] Long replied: "I don't care; go ahead". The defendant then placed the revolver against the right side of Long and pulled the trigger three times. The third pull resulted in a fatal wound to Long. The latter jumped off the stool and cried: "Oh! Oh! Oh!" and Malone said: "Did I hit you, Billy? Gee, Kid, I'm sorry." Long died from the wounds two days later.

The defendant testified that the gun chamber he loaded was the first one to the right of the firing chamber and that when he pulled the trigger he did not "expect to have the gun go off". He declared he had no intention of harming Long, who was his friend and companion. The defendant was indicted for murder, tried and found guilty of murder in the second degree and sentenced to a term in the penitentiary for a period not less than five years and not exceeding ten years. . . .

Appellant alleges certain errors in the charge of the court and also contends that the facts did not justify a conviction for any form of homicide except involuntary manslaughter. This contention we overrule. A specific intent to take life is, under our law, an essential ingredient of murder in the first degree. At common law, the "grand criterion" which "distinguished murder from other killing" was malice on the part of the killer and this malice was not necessarily "malevolent to the deceased particularly" but "any evil design in general; the dictate of a wicked, depraved and malignant heart": 4 Blackstone 199. Among the examples that Blackstone cites of murder is "coolly discharging a gun among a multitude of people", causing the death of someone of the multitude.

In Pennsylvania, the common law crime of murder is divided into two degrees, and murder of the second degree includes every element which enters into first degree murder except the intention to kill. When an individual commits an act of gross recklessness for which he must reasonably anticipate that death to another is likely to result, he exhibits that "wickedness of disposition; hardness of heart; cruelty; recklessness of consequences and a mind regardless of social duty" which proved that there was at that time in him "that state or frame of mind termed malice". . . .

The trial judge . . . erred in charging that "A person on trial for murder cannot be convicted of any offense if the testimony shows that the death was accidental". Death may be accidental though it resulted from a malicious act intentionally committed. In such a case the means were not accidental; the result was.[3] In the instant case if the defendant had by some

1. It has been explained that "Russian poker" is a game in which the participants, in turn, place a single cartridge in one of the five chambers of a revolver cylinder, give the latter a quick twirl, place the muzzle of the gun against the temple and pull the trigger, leaving it to chance whether or not death results to the trigger puller.

3. If A maliciously beats B intending to do him enormous bodily harm without killing

negligent, unintentional act, caused Long to fall off the stool at which he was sitting in the store and if, as a result of that fall, Long had sustained a fatal injury, both the initial act and the death might be correctly characterized as accidental. But when the defendant knowing that a revolver had at least one loaded cartridge in it, pressed the muzzle of that revolver to the side of Long and pulled the trigger three times, his act cannot be characterized as accidental, even if his statement that he had no intention to kill Long is accepted (as the jury accepted it). The way the trial judge used the word "accidental" throughout the charge must have been confusing to the jury and might easily have misled it into acquitting the accused on the theory that since the death of Long was accidental, "the defendant cannot be convicted of any offense", (as the trial judge said). The latter should have made it clear to the jury that even though Long's death might have been unintended and, therefore, accidental, the evidence showed that the act which caused the victim's death was not accidental. This was the view the jury took of the case despite the court's instructions.... Of such and similar errors, the appellant cannot complain; they were prejudicial only to the Commonwealth. * * *

The killing of William H. Long by this defendant resulted from an act intentionally done by the latter, in reckless and wanton disregard of the consequences which were at least sixty per cent certain from his thrice attempted discharge of a gun known to contain one bullet and aimed at a vital part of Long's body. This killing was, therefore, murder, for malice in the sense of a wicked disposition is evidenced by the intentional doing of an uncalled-for act in callous disregard of its likely harmful effects on others. The fact that there was no motive for this homicide does not exculpate the accused. In a trial for murder proof of motive is always relevant but never necessary.

QUESTIONS AND COMMENTS

1. The difficulty of distinguishing murder from manslaughter is—mainly—the difficulty of distinguishing deliberate indifference (or "implied malice") murder from reckless (or "involuntary") manslaughter. Traditionally that distinction was clear enough—at least in theory. Murder required malice, manslaughter did not. In what sense did Malone act with malice since he had no intention of killing, or even harming, Long? He might have been careless, but was he malicious?

Note that the distinction between murder and involuntary manslaughter is not of mere academic interest. Involuntary manslaughter is punished far less severely than is murder. In Pennsylvania, for instance, involuntary manslaughter is a first-degree misdemeanor, punishable by up to five years in prison, Pa. Cons. Stat. §§ 2504, 1104(1); third-degree (nonintentional) murder is a first-degree felony, punishable by up to 40 years, id. §§ 2502(c), 1102(d). Intentional murder is punishable by life imprisonment or death. Id. § 1102.

him and B dies as result of the beating, A can be found guilty of murder in the second degree, though death was "accidental" in the sense that it was not intended by A.

2. Having done away with malice, the Model Penal Code needed another way of differentiating murder from manslaughter. Once again, the distinction between intentional murder and manslaughter was unproblematic—intentional murder required purpose or knowledge with respect to the result element of homicide (death), while manslaughter required only recklessness. But what was to be the difference between gross recklessness murder and recklessness manslaughter? What distinguishes homicide "committed recklessly under circumstances manifesting extreme indifference to the value of human life" (§ 210.2(1)(b)) from homicide just "committed recklessly" (§ 210.3(1)(a))? Was the difference only in the degree of risk (gross recklessness vs. recklessness) or the extent of the indifference (given that simple recklessness already requires "conscious disregard," § 2.02(2)(c))? Was the indifference to the value of human life something altogether different than the indifference to the value of physical integrity presumably manifested by an assault or the indifference to the value of personal property in theft?

3. Many of the jurisdictions that followed the Model Penal Code in rejecting malice as the distinguishing characteristic felt the need to draw a clearer line between gross recklessness murder and recklessness manslaughter. New York is one example. There gross recklessness murder is committed by a person who "[u]nder circumstances evincing a depraved indifference to human life, ... recklessly engages in conduct which creates a grave risk of death to another person, and thereby causes the death of another person." N.Y. Penal Law § 125.25(2). Commenting on the difference between murder and manslaughter the New York Court of Appeals explained that, in the case of depraved indifference murder, "the focus of the offense is not upon the subjective intent of the defendant, as it is with intentional murder, but rather upon an objective assessment of the degree of risk presented by defendant's reckless conduct." People v. Register, 60 N.Y.2d 270(1983). Unlike ordinary recklessness, which is defined in terms of a "substantial" risk, the recklessness of depraved indifference murder requires a "grave" risk. Does this distinction between murder and manslaughter provide better guidance to factfinders than the traditional one based on the concept of malice? If Malone had pulled the trigger once, would it have been manslaughter? Twice? Spun the chamber before the first pull? Between the first and the second squeeze? If he did in fact load the chamber to the right of the pin, did he really ignore a "substantial" risk, never mind a "grave" one? Do you think he would have gone ahead had he been aware of the fact that he might end up killing Billy? Isn't this a case of negligence, then, not of recklessness, let alone gross recklessness?

Appellate courts have struggled with "the challenging task of articulating the distinction between the crimes of depraved indifference murder and reckless manslaughter." People v. Hartman, 772 N.Y.S.2d 396 (App. Div. 2004). If appellate courts have trouble with this distinction, will juries (or trial judges, for that matter) find it any easier to grasp?

Note that the New York Court of Appeals rejected a reading of the New York depraved indifference statute that would have required a mens rea "more vicious than recklessness but less so than intent": "A person acts with depraved indifference ... when he engages in conduct whereby he does not intend to kill but is so indifferent to the consequences, which he knows with substantial certainty will result in the death of another, as to be willing to kill." *Register*, 60 N.Y.2d at 285 (Jansen, J., dissenting). Is a focus on indifference, and depravity, more helpful than a focus on the degree of risk?

2. Voluntary Manslaughter (Provocation/Extreme Emotional Disturbance)

a. Introduction

Cal. Penal Code § 192. Manslaughter is the unlawful killing of a human being without malice. It is of three kinds:

(a) Voluntary—upon a sudden quarrel or heat of passion....

The punishment for voluntary manslaughter is between three and eleven years' imprisonment. Cal. Penal Code § 193. The punishment for murder is death, life imprisonment without possibility of parole, or 25 years to life in prison (for first-degree murder), or 15 years to life (for second-degree murder). § 190.

Model Penal Code § 210.3. Manslaughter.

Criminal homicide constitutes manslaughter when: ...

(b) a homicide which would otherwise be murder is committed under the influence of extreme mental or emotional disturbance for which there is reasonable explanation or excuse. The reasonableness of such explanation or excuse shall be determined from the viewpoint of a person in the actor's situation under the circumstances as he believes them to be.

The maximum sentence is ten years in prison for voluntary manslaughter, and life imprisonment for murder. Model Penal Code § 6.06.

N.Y. Penal Law § 125.20. Manslaughter in the first degree.

A person is guilty of manslaughter in the first degree when:....

2. With intent to cause the death of another person, he causes the death of such person or of a third person under circumstances which do not constitute murder because he acts under the influence of extreme emotional disturbance [for which there was a reasonable explanation or excuse, the reasonableness of which is to be determined from the viewpoint of a person in the defendant's situation under the circumstances as the defendant believed them to be].

Voluntary manslaughter is punishable by between five and 25 years' imprisonment. Murder is punishable by between 20 years and death (first-degree) and by between 15 years and life (second-degree). N.Y. Penal Law §§ 60.06, 70.00.

State v. Gounagias, 88 Wash. 304, 153 P. 9 (1915)

The doctrine of mitigation is briefly this: That if the act of killing, though intentional, be committed under the influence of sudden, intense anger, or heat of blood, obscuring the reason, produced by an adequate or reasonable provocation, and before sufficient time has elapsed for the blood to cool and reason to reassert itself, so that the killing is the result of temporary excitement rather than wickedness of heart or innate recklessness of disposition, then the law, recognizing the standard of human conduct as that of the ordinary or average man, regards the offense so committed as of less heinous character than premeditated or deliberate murder. Measured as it must be by the conduct of the average man, what constitutes adequate cause is incapable of strict definition.

QUESTIONS AND COMMENTS

1. Homicidal acts that might otherwise constitute murder will be punished more leniently if done in certain circumstances, circumstances that are thought to make it more difficult for the defendant to exercise self-control. (Voluntary manslaughter, however, is punished more harshly than *involuntary* manslaughter. Does that make sense? See Cal. Pen. Code § 193(b) (2 to 4 years for involuntary manslaughter).)

Broadly speaking, one must consider how the legal system distinguishes circumstances worthy of a certain degree of mitigating mercy from those in which the defendant will receive the full punishment ordinarily imposed on intentional killers: We might confine the defense to those who kill only in response to a particular, named set of provocative situations or grant the fact finder more discretion in determining whether the defendant has responded to atypical stressors; we might mitigate (solely? more readily?) in situations in which the source of the stress is the (somewhat) blameworthy action of the victim (arguably partially justifying the defendant's actions) or simply focus on the fact that the defendant found himself faced by the sorts of atypical pressures, no matter who or what the cause, that lead us to believe that his conduct is in significant part a product of the unusual circumstances, not just his wicked character (arguably, then, partially *excusing* the homicide); we might, or might not, confine the defense to those who kill without delay in response to the stress-inducing, provocative incident; we might, or might not, confine the defense to those who kill the source of the provocative situation (or accidentally kill a third party while trying to kill the person who provoked them or caused their extreme emotional disturbance).

In looking at the materials to follow, it is vital to think both about the wisdom of each particular limitation on the defense—does it, for instance, make sense to *specify* a short list of stressors that might reduce murder to manslaughter or is it sensible to give fact finders broader discretion—*and* to consider what it might mean to drop *all* the limitations on the defense at once. Also keep in mind that, even though voluntary manslaughter is punished less severely than murder, it remains a serious felony subject to substantial punishment. "Success" in the following cases thus doesn't mean acquittal, but liability for one (lesser) type of homicide rather than another.

2. The court in *Gounagias* notes that people may kill when subject to intense anger that "obscures the reason." What could that mean? How does that standard compare with the California Penal Code and the Model Penal Code?

3. A deterrence-oriented theorist might agree that there are situations in which it is atypically *tempting* to kill: wouldn't such a theorist,

though, be prone to urge us to punish killers *more*, not less, when it is atypically tempting to kill if we are to prevent these unjustifiable homicides? Or do we (partially) excuse some killers because they are, in one variety of retributive terms, simply less blameworthy: acts taken in certain circumstances reveal less about what the *Gounagias* court calls the defendant's "wickedness of heart or innate recklessness of disposition"? Can another variety of retributivists—those who urge us to exact punishment commensurate with the offender's violation, rather than character—explain or justify why we would punish one set of deliberate killers less harshly than another? Or do we simply believe, instead, that those who kill when severely stressed have revealed less about their prospective dangerousness: all we have learned in these voluntary manslaughter cases, as incapacitationists, is that the defendant might kill if faced by atypical (and therefore unlikely to recur?) stressors. We punish *some*, nonetheless, rather than excuse entirely, both because we are unsure that the defendant's dangerousness is actually confined to these stressful settings (or doubt that these stressful settings are so idiosyncratic) and because our punishment views may *blend* incapacitationist with deterrence and blame-centered theories.

4. Assume that we must try to ascertain whether the defendant in succumbing to pressures was reasonable enough to warrant having his punishment mitigated. Do we mean to say that his conduct (killing) was reasonable in the same way that we believe an exonerated self-defender might most typically be described as reasonable? If we believed that *most* people should (or, to put it in somewhat weaker excuse terms, at least *would*) kill in the defendant's situation, would we exonerate him, rather than mitigate punishment? Assuming we are trying to ascertain when it is reasonable that the defendant found it especially hard to maintain his ordinary self-control, should we account for the defendant's particular features or simply, instead, ask whether some generic, average "reasonable man" would have found it atypically difficult to maintain his self-control? This problem is especially thorny if we do not have a pre-specified list of "provocative incidents" to constrain our judgment: it might even be hard to *name* the stressor without regard to the defendant's particular identity. (Can we even specify what happened to an African–American subjected to charged racial epithets without talking about the reactions of those in his cultural group to such epithets?)

b. Historical Categorical Rules and the Open–Ended Model Penal Code System

(i) Precipitating Incidents

a. THE TRADITIONAL APPROACH

Girouard v. State

Court of Appeals of Maryland.
321 Md. 532, 583 A.2d 718 (1991).

■ COLE, JUDGE.

In this case we are asked to reconsider whether the types of provocation sufficient to mitigate the crime of murder to manslaughter should be limited to the categories we have heretofore recognized, or whether the sufficiency of the provocation should be decided by the factfinder on a case-by-case basis. Specifically, we must determine whether words alone are provocation adequate to justify a conviction of manslaughter rather than one of second degree murder.

The Petitioner, Steven S. Girouard, and the deceased, Joyce M. Girouard, had been married for about two months on . . . the night of Joyce's death. . . . The evidence at trial indicated that the marriage was often tense and strained, and there was some evidence that after marrying Steven, Joyce had resumed a relationship with her old boyfriend, Wayne.

On the night of Joyce's death, Steven overheard her talking on the telephone to her friend, whereupon she told the friend . . . that Steven did not love her anymore. Steven went into the living room . . . and asked what she meant by her comments; she responded, "nothing." Angered by her lack of response, Steven kicked away the plate of food Joyce had in front of her. He then went to lie down in the bedroom.

Joyce followed him into the bedroom, stepped up onto the bed and onto Steven's back, pulled his hair and said, "What are you going to do, hit me?" She continued to taunt him by saying, "I never did want to marry you and you are a lousy fuck and you remind me of my dad [who had evidently sexually abused her as a child]." The barrage of insults continued with her telling Steven that she wanted a divorce. [She also lied and told him that she had filed abuse charges with the Judge Advocate General's Office so that he would be court-martialed.]

When she was through, Steven asked her if she had really done all these things, and she responded in the affirmative. He left the bedroom with his pillow in his arms and proceeded to the kitchen where he procured a long handled kitchen knife. He returned to . . . the bedroom. He testified that he was enraged and that he kept waiting for Joyce to say she was kidding, but Joyce continued talking. She said she had learned a lot from the marriage and that it had been a mistake. She also told him she would remain in their apartment after he moved out. When he questioned how she would afford it, she told him she would claim her brain-damaged sister as a dependent and have the sister move in. . . .

After pausing for a moment, Joyce asked Steven what he was going to do. What he did was lunge at her with the kitchen knife . . . and stab her 19 times. . . . Feeling like he wanted to die, Steven . . . slit his own wrists.

At trial, [a defense psychologist] testified . . . that Steven had "basically reach[ed] the limit of his ability to swallow his anger, to rationalize his wife's behavior. . . . He essentially went over the limit of his ability to bottle up those strong emotions. What ensued was a very extreme explosion of rage that was intermingled with a great deal of panic." Another defense . . . psychiatrist . . . testified that Joyce had a "compulsive need to provoke jealousy so that she's always asking for love and at the same time destroying and undermining any chance that she might really have to establish any kind of mature love with anybody."

Steven Girouard was convicted . . . of second degree murder.

Petitioner relies primarily on out of state cases to provide support for his argument that the provocation to mitigate murder to manslaughter should not be limited only to the traditional circumstances of extreme assault or battery upon the defendant; mutual combat; defendant's illegal arrest; injury or serious abuse of a close relative of the defendant's; or the sudden discovery of a spouse's adultery. Petitioner argues that manslaughter is a catchall for homicides which are criminal but lack the malice essential for a conviction of murder. Stephen argues that the trial judge did find provocation (although he held it inadequate to mitigate murder) and that the categories of provocation adequate to mitigate should be broadened to include factual situations such as this one.

The State counters by stating that although there is no finite list of legally adequate provocations, the common law has developed to a point at which it may be said that there are some concededly provocative acts that society is not prepared to recognize as reasonable. Words spoken by the victim, no matter how abusive or taunting, fall into a category society should not accept as adequate provocation. . . .

There are certain facts that may mitigate what would normally be murder to manslaughter [adultery; mutual combat; assault and battery; injury to a relative and illegal arrest]. . . . These acts mitigate homicide to manslaughter because they create passion in the defendant and are not considered the product of free will. . . .

. . . Although a psychologist testified to Steven's mental problems . . . the standard is one of reasonableness; it does not and should not focus on the peculiar frailties of mind of the Petitioner. That standard of reasonableness has not been met here. We cannot in good conscience countenance holding that a verbal domestic argument ending in the death of one spouse can result in a conviction of manslaughter. We agree with the trial judge that social necessity dictates our holding. Domestic arguments easily escalate into furious fights. We perceive no reason for a holding in favor of those who find the easiest way to end a domestic dispute is by killing the offending spouse.

We will leave to another day the possibility of expansion of the categories of adequate provocation. . . . The facts of this case do not warrant the broadening of the categories recognized thus far.

b. *THE MODEL PENAL CODE APPROACH*

People v. Shelton

Supreme Court of New York, New York County.
385 N.Y.S.2d 708, 88 Misc.2d 136 (1976).

■ KASSAL, JUSTICE.

The defendant, a narcotics counsellor at a public school, shortly after noon, smoked a couple of joints in his car with the deceased [a fourteen-year-old girl]. They drove around until she asked to buy some marijuana from him. Upon being refused, she threatened to report him which he felt would cause him to lose his job.... He tried to dissuade her.... At about 6:00 P.M. when he found she was not being swayed, he parked ..., and tied her hands in front of her ..., finally dropped a large rock on her head, saw she was still alive and talking to him and dropped it a second time. [He then stabbed her throat with a pick from an Afro-comb and began to stab her with a piece of auto stripping.] ...

[To make out an affirmative defense to second degree murder under the New York statute, patterned in this regard after the Model Penal Code, a defendant who intentionally causes the death of another human being must show that he acted ... "under the influence of extreme emotional disturbance"; and ... there must be "a reasonable explanation or excuse." N.Y. Penal Law §§ 125.20, 125.25.]

[Extreme] emotional disturbance is the emotional state of an individual, who:

(a) has no mental disease or defect....

(b) is exposed to an extremely unusual and overwhelming stress; and

(c) has an extreme emotional reaction to it, as a result of which there is a loss of self-control and reason is overborne by intense feelings, such as passion, anger, distress, grief, excessive agitation, or other similar emotions. In evaluating this, consideration is given to whether the actor is able to reflect dispassionately, the time interval between the provocation and the acts and whether the intensity of these feelings are such that his usual intellectual controls fail and the normal rational thinking for that individual no longer prevail at the time of the act....

I find as follows:

(a) The defendant had no mental disease or defect....

(b) Although the defendant was exposed to an unusual stress, the People have established that it was neither extremely unusual nor overwhelming.

The stress asserted here was that Nilda Cruz threatened to tell his superiors that defendant, a narcotics counsellor, used marijuana and consequently, he might lose his position, which concededly was of importance to him in terms of status and money. On the other hand, it was proved that the defendant, as he described himself, had always been very "cool" and in the last analysis, he knew it was his word against hers, a 14 year old student....

(c) The defendant had no loss of self-control....

There was a period of at least four to five hours that he was aware of Nilda Cruz's threat to report him. The parties drove around and "rapped," with the defendant trying to dissuade her from reporting him.

The following statements by the defendant support this conclusion....

> "It's not really anger ... you can call it anger. Just something that you want to try and convince the kid.... I pulled off the highway.... It could be seen but it's off enough where it's not noticeable. And then I still rapped. We sit down for a little while.... So she said well I don't care but somebody is going to find out what's happening. And from

there I said well, you're not going to squeal on me. So I tied her hands up with a rag and then She start copping a plea after that.... It wasn't intentionally (trying to kill her). But that's how it worked out.... If somebody put you in a bind and you know, you're going to blow your job, no telling when you're going to get any more money anytime soon. Maybe you might try, if you think you can get away with it.... I had to do something to finish her off because she won't bear witness against me...."

Since the second element of the defense ... the reasonableness of the excuse or explanation, presumes a finding of extreme emotional disturbance, that element is not reached here....

People v. Casassa

Court of Appeals of New York.
49 N.Y.2d 668, 427 N.Y.S.2d 769, 404 N.E.2d 1310 (1980).

■ JASEN, JUDGE.

The significant issue on this appeal is whether the defendant, in a murder prosecution, established the affirmative defense of "extreme emotional disturbance" which would have reduced the crime to manslaughter in the first degree.

... Defendant Victor Casassa and Miss Lo Consolo had been acquainted for some time prior to the latter's tragic death. They met in August 1976 ... [and] apparently dated casually ... until November, 1976 when Miss Lo Consolo informed defendant that she was not "falling in love" with him. Defendant claims that Miss Lo Consolo's candid statement of her feelings "devastated him."

Miss Lo Consolo's rejection of defendant's advances also precipitated a bizarre series of actions on the part of defendant, which, he asserts, demonstrate the existence of extreme emotional disturbance.... [On] one occasion, he broke into Miss Lo Consolo's apartment while she was out. Defendant took nothing, but, instead, observed the apartment, disrobed and lay for a time in Miss Lo Consolo's bed. During the break-in, defendant was armed with a knife which, he later told police, he carried "because he knew that he was either going to hurt Victoria or Victoria was going to cause him to commit suicide."

Defendant's final visit to his victim's apartment occurred on February 28, 1977. Defendant brought several bottles of wine and liquor with him to offer as a gift. Upon Miss Lo Consolo's rejection of this offering, defendant ... stabbed Miss Lo Consolo several times in the throat, dragged her body to the bathroom and submerged it in a bathtub full of water to "make sure she was dead." ...

On this appeal defendant contends that the trial court erred in failing to afford him the benefit of the affirmative defense of "extreme emotional disturbance." ...

Consideration of the comments to the Model Penal Code, from which the New York statute was drawn, is instructive. The defense of "extreme emotional disturbance" has two principal components—(i) the particular defendant must have "acted under the influence of extreme emotional disturbance" and (ii) there must have been "a reasonable explanation or excuse" for such extreme emotional disturbance, the "reasonableness of which is to be determined from the viewpoint of a person in the defendant's situation under the circumstances as the defendant believed them to be." The first requirement is wholly subjective—i.e. it involves a determination that the particular defendant did in fact act under extreme emotional disturbance, that the claimed explanation as to the cause of the action is not contrived or sham.

The second component is more difficult to describe—i.e. whether there was a reasonable explanation or excuse for the emotional disturbance. It was designed to sweep away "the rigid rules that have developed with respect to the sufficiency of particular types of provocation," . . . "The ultimate test, however, is objective. . . ." [We] conclude that the determination whether there was reasonable explanation or excuse for a particular emotional disturbance should be made by viewing the subjective, internal situation in which the defendant found himself and the external circumstances as he perceived them at the time, however inaccurate that perception may have been, and assessing from that standpoint whether the explanation or excuse for his emotional disturbance was reasonable. . . .

In the end, we believe that what the Legislature intended in enacting the statute was to allow the finder of fact the discretionary power to mitigate the penalty when presented with a situation which, under the circumstances, appears to them to have caused an understandable weakness in one of their fellows. . . .

We conclude that the trial court . . . properly applied the statute. The court apparently accepted, as a factual matter, that defendant killed Miss Lo Consolo while under the influence of "extreme emotional disturbance," a threshold question which must be answered in the affirmative before any test of reasonableness is required. The court, however, also recognized that in exercising its function as a trier of fact, it must make a further inquiry into the reasonableness of the disturbance. In this regard, the court . . . found that the excuse offered by the defendant was so peculiar to him that it was unworthy of mitigation. The court obviously made a sincere effort to understand defendant's "situation" and "the circumstances as defendant believed them to be," but concluded that the murder in this case was the result of defendant's malevolence rather than an understandable human response deserving of mercy. . . .

(ii) "Cooling Off": A Bar to the Defense, a Bar Absent "Rekindling," a "Factor" to Be Weighed

People v. Ashland, 128 P. 798 (Cal. Dist. Ct. App. 1912)

[The defendant's wife informed the defendant that the victim had raped her. Defendant promptly went out to search for the victim, who had returned to his home. The defendant took a train to the city where the victim lived. He found him some seventeen hours after the initial conversation with his wife and immediately shot him. The court upheld the trial court's refusal to instruct the jury on voluntary manslaughter....] [The] law will not permit the defendant to deliberate upon his wrong and, avenging it by killing the wrongdoer, set up the plea that his act was committed in the heat of passion.

In re Fraley, 3 Okla.Crim. 719, 109 P. 295 (1910)

It was stated by counsel for the petitioner ... that the deceased, some nine or ten months previously, had shot and killed the son of the petitioner ... and it is urged here that when the petitioner saw the deceased ... the recollection of that event must have engendered within him a passion which overcame him.... To this we cannot assent.... [The] question is not alone whether the defendant's passion in fact cooled, but also was there sufficient time in which the passion of a reasonable man would cool. If in fact the defendant's passion did cool, which may be shown by circumstances, such as the transaction of other business in the meantime, rational conversations upon other subjects, evidence of preparation for the killing etc. then the length of time is immaterial. But if it in fact did not cool yet if such time intervened between the provocation and the killing that the passion of the average man would have cooled ... then there still is no reduction of the homicide to manslaughter.

State v. Flory, 40 Wyo. 184, 276 P. 458 (1929)

[The deceased was the long-estranged father of defendant's wife. In December of 1927, the deceased stayed at the home of defendant and his wife and during that time, the deceased "made indecent proposals ... and raped her and committed incest upon her." Defendant did not learn of the rapes till January of 1928. He went to see his wife's father, carrying a gun "because I knew he was stouter than I and I knew he could handle me. I had no intentions when I went in of killing the man at all ... I said, 'What made you rape [my wife] Daisy' ... and I says to him, 'Charley, do you know you just about ruined my home?' and he says, 'I will keep the girl' and when he said that, I says, 'You are a pretty son of a bitch to keep your daughter.' " The defendant claimed he shot Charley when Charley came at him, but the court rejected the legal sufficiency of the self-defense claim. In addition, the defendant urged on appeal that murder might be mitigated to manslaughter. The court agreed:] The defendant contends that the information given him by his wife as to the rape and incest committed upon her ... so aroused his passions ... that his act cannot be held to be murder.... The state contends that the testimony was not admissible ... because ample time—at least a day and probably longer—had elapsed after the defendant had been informed of the acts of decedent ... [and that] defendant's own testimony shows ... his blood had cooled ... The crime of deceased ... was most heinous and was calculated to create a most violent passion in the mind of the defendant, and it is hardly to be expected that it would, as a matter of law, subside within so short a time, especially when, as testified, a situation arose by which past facts were clearly recalled.

People v. Patterson, 39 N.Y.2d 288, 383 N.Y.S.2d 573, 347 N.E.2d 898 (1976)

An action influenced by an extreme emotional disturbance is not one that is necessarily so spontaneously undertaken. Rather, it may be that a significant mental trauma has affected a defendant's mind for a substantial period of time, simmering in the unknowing subconscious and then inexplicably coming to the fore. The differences between the present New York statute and its predecessor ... can be explained by the tremendous advances made in psychology since 1881 and a willingness on the part of the courts, legislators, and the public to reduce the level of responsibility imposed on those whose capacity has been diminished by mental trauma.

People v. Berry, 18 Cal.3d 509, 134 Cal.Rptr. 415, 556 P.2d 777 (1976)

[Defendant killed his wife Rachel after a ten-day period during which she taunted him with the fact that she was sexually attracted to, and having relations with, another man. On one occasion, she insisted on having sexual relations with the defendant in the car, but upon returning home, she stated that she still loved the other man and would not have sex with defendant again. Three days before the killing, the defendant and Rachel engaged in heavy petting at a movie; later, at home, Rachel announced that she had intended to have sex with the defendant but changed her mind because she was saving herself for the other man. Defendant started to leave; Rachel kept screaming at him. He choked her into unconsciousness, but did not kill her. He took her to the hospital. The victim reported the incident to the police and obtained a warrant for his arrest. A day later, defendant came to the apartment to talk to Rachel. He waited for twenty hours for her to return home. When she returned, she said, "I suppose you have come here to kill me." His response was ambiguous; she started to scream at him again. Defendant grabbed her by the shoulder and tried to stop her screaming. She persisted. He strangled her to death with a telephone cord. The defense introduced psychiatric testimony that "Rachel was a depressed, suicidally inclined girl and this suicidal impulse led her to involve herself even more deeply in a dangerous situation with defendant. She did this by sexually arousing him and taunting him into jealous rages in an unconscious desire to provoke him into killing her." He further testified that as a result of this cumulative series of provocations, "defendant at the time he fatally strangled Rachel was in a state of uncontrollable rage, completely under the sway of passion." The court reversed Berry's conviction:] The Attorney General contends that the killing could not have been done in the heat of passion because there was a cooling off period, defendant having waited in the apartment for 20 hours. However, the long course of provocatory conduct, which had resulted in intermittent outbreaks of rage under specific provocation in the past, reached its final culmination in the apartment when Rachel began screaming....

(iii) Must the Defendant (Intend to) Kill the "Source" of the "Provocation" or "Emotional Disturbance"?

a. INTENTIONALLY KILLING THOSE WHO ARE NOT THE SOURCE OF PROVOCATION

State v. Follin, 263 Kan. 28, 947 P.2d 8 (1997)

[Defendant, having listened to a tape recording in which his wife told someone he presumed to be her lover "how much she missed him," killed the couple's two infant daughters some hours later before attempting suicide. The court affirmed the trial court's refusal to instruct the jury on voluntary manslaughter, not only because they thought the evidence insufficient to show that he had acted in a heat of passion but also because ...] Follin's murdering his children rather than his wife or her lover removes any possibility that the offenses could be voluntary manslaughter rather than murder. The point is that the murderous actions were directed against persons innocent of any responsibility for provoking defendant ... The courts have quite consistently held that the killing [of an innocent bystander] does not qualify as manslaughter, apparently upon the assumption that a reasonable man would never be so greatly provoked as to strike out in blind anger at an innocent person.

Simpson v. United States, 632 A.2d 374 (D.C. Ct. App. 1993)

[The defendant killed his two sons, and then stabbed himself. Both boys had cerebral palsy. Neither child could feed, dress, or bathe himself. Dwayne spoke only a few words, and never learned to walk independently, but was always smiling.... The boys shared one wheelchair, as the family could not afford to purchase another.... Defendant's relationship with the boy's mother, Venita Barnes, was "plagued by her drug addiction." In order to support her drug habit, she sold the boys' diapers and clothing.... She prostituted herself in the room ... while the boys were present and left the boys unattended for long periods of time.... On the afternoon of January 5, Barnes returned briefly with one check and drugs, then left again promising to return to pick up the children's dinner.... As hour after hour passed, Simpson realized that Ms. Barnes was not coming back. Pacing the floor he felt himself losing control. When the children fell asleep, he stabbed them and then himself. The trial court refused to give a voluntary manslaughter instruction.

The appeals court reversed on other grounds but noted that were it the case that the District of Columbia adopted the Model Penal Code position on manslaughter, the defendant might well be entitled to have the jury consider that "the despair and frustration" that he felt (as a result of unemployment, homelessness, two handicapped sons, a long-standing relationship with their mother addicted to drugs) would provoke a reasonable person to suddenly lose control and kill without deliberation and without malice....]

Judge Terry, concurring, stated: "I would flatly reject appellant's argument and hold, as the government argues, that the provocation must come from the victim, or at least from someone associated with the victim. I find no merit whatever in appellant's argument that the harsh circumstances or 'personal tragedies' of his daily life could constitute mitigation...."

Model Penal Code Commentaries § 210.3, at 60–61

[T]he Code does not require that the actor's emotional distress arise from some injury, affront, or other provocative acts perpetrated upon him by the deceased.

b. ACCIDENTALLY KILLING SOMEONE WHO WAS NOT THE SOURCE OF PROVOCATION

Consider as well the following scenarios in light of the Texas and Pennsylvania statutes below: "If A has been reasonably provoked and believes that B is the person ... responsible for the provoking conduct, then the killing of B in a heat of passion is manslaughter even if it turns out that C and not B was the provoking party. Likewise, if A, who has been reasonably and actually provoked by B into a passion to kill B, shoots at B but instead hits and kills innocent bystander C, A's crime is voluntary manslaughter." Wayne R. LaFave, Criminal Law § 7.10(g) (3d ed. 2000).

Texas Penal Code § 19.02(a). Murder.

(2) "Sudden passion" means passion directly caused by and arising out of provocation by the individual killed or another acting with the person killed....

Pa. Crim. Code § 2503(a). Voluntary Manslaughter.

A person who kills an individual without lawful justification commits voluntary manslaughter if at the time of the killing he is acting under a sudden and intense passion resulting from serious provocation by:

1. the individual killed; or

2. another whom the actor endeavors to kill, but he negligently or accidentally causes the death of the individual killed.

QUESTIONS AND COMMENTS

1. There are long-standing debates both about whether *any* intentional killings should receive lesser punishment, and if so, whether those who are "provoked" are partly *justified* or partly *excused*. Lucid statements of these alternative accounts of the defense can be found in A.J. Ashworth, "The Doctrine of Provocation," 35 Camb. L.J. 292 (1976) (urging that the defense must be grounded to a limited degree in the idea that defendants were partly *entitled* to attack their provokers) and Joshua Dressler, "Rethinking Heat of Passion: A Defense in Search of a Rationale," 73 J. Crim. L. & Criminology 421 (1982) (concluding that mitigation derives entirely from the ethics of excuse).

It is somewhat hard to see precisely what commentators who believe that provoked defendants are partly justified *mean*: they plainly don't think that the benefits of killing the particular victims in these cases outweigh the cost of disobeying the ordinary norms against homicide but don't do so clearly and substantially enough to support a full-blown justification defense. If what lies at the core of the ordinary justification defense is the recognition that defendants may commit acts that are generally undesirable (and therefore defined as crimes) in unusual situations in which those same acts are affirmatively good, then these cases hardly seem to be about justification: it is in no way *affirmatively good* that these victims are killed, given the defendant's option set. Instead, in some vaguer way, proponents of the "partial justification" view believe that provocative victims are somewhat more responsible for their own deaths than typical victims (a factual statement that may well be true), and that, *normatively*, we should (therefore?) be *somewhat* less protective of their lives than we would be of the lives of ordinary victims. Is this view convincing? Acceptable? Might this view be grounded in the incentives-based thinking that characterizes deterrence theory generally? If we let provocative victims know that their potential killers won't be as deterred by criminal sanctions as they would be if they'd just stop doing provocative things, perhaps they will recognize that if they're to avoid getting killed, they should rely on a form of self-help—avoid provocation—rather than the state. Do the ways in which many jurisdictions *restrict* the defense suggest they might be influenced by the partial justification view? Think especially of restricting the defense to those who kill the source of the provocation.

Of course, it is plausible that *excuses* are valid only in situations in which the excuse is in some sense "warranted." See, in this regard, the normative aspect of the argument in Victoria Nourse, "Passion's Progress: Modern Law Reform and the Provocation Defense," 106 Yale L.J. 1331 (1997). In her view, the focus in these cases should remain on excusing the defendant, not blaming the victim or lauding the defendant's actions. We attend at core to whether the defendant lost control for a good reason, not whether the victim in some sense forfeited her full rights to be protected against homicide. But a *good* reason, in Nourse's view, is not simply a commonplace explanation or cause for the individual defendant's loss of self-control: thus, the fact that many men may indeed become angry and agitated when their wives or lovers dump them does not mean that men who kill those who reject them should be partly excused. Only if the defendant can gain not only our sympathy—our understanding that he was indeed out of control and was out of control for a reason we understand—but our legally sanctioned concurrence to the moral view that precipitated his action should he be partly exonerated. Of course, an excuse can be *warranted*, in this sense, because the defendant is reacting to wrongdoing by the victim (in which case Nourse is arguably, in essence, restating the partial justification view, in effect, without succumbing to the idea that these killings may not be entirely bad *outcomes*), but presumably too, hard-to-control anger could be warranted at circumstances that are not authored by the victim. The key, at core, for Nourse is that it is especially morally problematic and socially destructive to lose control over some of life's setbacks, even when it is commonplace to do so (see sexual rejection and separation), while it is less troublesome to lose control when confronted with other sorts of stress (see, perhaps, assaults, long-term abuse).

In thinking about whether it is sufficient for mitigating punishment to find that rage is a (reasonably) *commonplace* reaction to a certain set of events, even when the reaction is "unwarranted," consider cases in which a (self-described) "straight" male defendant kills another man who sexually propositioned him. Should it matter if we think of the defendant as "suffering" from "homosexual *panic*" or think of him as acting out of unbridled homophobic *rage*? Or is it sufficient simply to observe that significant numbers of men in this culture, for whatever reason, become agitated when other men "come on" to them, just as many men, for whatever reason, become agitated in the face of infidelity? Some appellate courts have flatly rejected the use of the provocation defense in situations in which the defendant is responding to a nonviolent homosexual advance. See, e.g., People v. Page, 193 Ill.2d 120 (2000) ("even if evidence that [the deceased] made a sexual advance toward defendant on the night of the murder had been admitted at trial, this evidence would not have entitled defendant to a voluntary manslaughter instruction").

If, though, one takes the view that it is acceptable (in some sense) to devalue the lives of some class of victims who did something morally problematic that angered the defendant, one still must look at what sorts of conduct courts think merit that sort of devaluation. Look first at the core of the traditional defense—defendants are reasonably provoked when responding to serious assaults. In this class of cases, the partial justification view is a bit easier to swallow. Most "voluntary manslaughter" cases, under this rubric, are at core cases in which the defendant is likely to make a self-defense claim, but fails to prevail because he continues to attack after he is out of danger or because he responds disproportionately to non-deadly force.

But what about adultery, looked at from a partial justification viewpoint? There is a question whether witnessing or discovering adultery ought to be deemed a partial excuse, because, rightly or wholly wrongly, (especially male) defendants get so upset by witnessing or learning of it. Can we countenance the idea that a person who is sexually unfaithful has (even partly) forfeited the law's protection? Does it matter that adultery is rather commonplace: while survey data on sexual behavior is notoriously imprecise, it is instructive to note that the University of Chicago's National Opinion Research Center reported in 1996 that 24% of married men, and 14% of married women had committed adultery. (The range of findings in this area is startlingly high, though: another survey found that more than one third of married men and one quarter of married women had committed adultery. See Samuel Janus & Cynthia Janus, The Janus Report on Sexual Behavior 169 (1993).)

Note that in a number of the cases that we looked at (see *Casassa*, see *Berry*) the defense proffered what might be termed a "psychiatric autopsy" of the (not coincidentally?) female victim, arguing in essence that the homicides were "victim precipitated" by masochistic women who challenged men to hurt or kill them. Naturally, there are serious questions about the accuracy of these post-mortem diagnoses, but what if they were factually right? Are they *relevant*? Assume, for instance, that you would advise any of your female friends that it's *risky* and *dangerous* to say, as the victims in these cases purportedly did, things like, "Are you going to hit me?" or "Have you come to kill me?" (especially if you have reason to believe you are saying that to a man who could be described as "insecure," obsessed with "masculinity" or easily enraged). Doing so—especially in a taunting way—may indeed increase the probability that one will be assaulted or killed and may even, at least arguably, be morally suspect in some fashion or other. But does the fact that one might have increased the chances that one would be victimized *justify* (even partially) the defendant's conduct? Cars are more likely to be stolen when left with the keys in them, or even left in isolated places. And, once more, one might counsel a friend not to leave a car in an isolated place (especially if it is in an isolated place in which car thefts are atypically common). Could we imagine, though, describing the person who stole an isolated car as "partly justified"? If the focus, instead, moves completely away from the *causal* relevance of the victim's conduct to its moral quality, isn't there a substantial distinction between assault and adultery? Are there further lines between adultery and simply rejecting the defendant's advances (consider *Casassa*), "flirting" with another man, or "taunting" men about their sexual inadequacy? For an excellent discussion of the degree to which provocation law has embodied a strongly patriarchal perspective on these issues, see Donna A. Coker, "Heat of Passion and Wife Killing: Men Who Batter/Men Who Kill," 2 So. Cal. Rev. L. & Women's Stud. 71 (1992).

2. The more facially plausible premise underlying provocation and extreme emotional disturbance doctrine is that those who kill under certain circumstances are partly *excused*—that their conduct, though abhorrent, reveals less about the deficiencies in their moral character than would killing in distinct circumstances. See Model Penal Code § 210.3 ("disturbance for which there is reasonable explanation or excuse"). It is hardly uncontroversial, though, to conclude that any intentional killers should be partly excused. Compare these comments:

> Other things being equal, the greater the provocation ... the more ground there is for attributing the intensity of the actor's passions and his lack of self-control ... to the extraordinary character of the situation in which he was placed rather than to any extraordinary deficiency in his own character. While it is true, it is also beside the point, that most men do not kill even on the gravest provocation; the point is that the more strongly they would be moved to kill by circumstances of the sort which provoked the actor ... and the more difficulty they would experience in resisting the impulse to which he yielded, the less does his succumbing serve to differentiate his character from theirs.

Jerome Michael & Herbert Wechsler, "A Rationale of the Law of Homicide," 37 Colum. L. Rev. 1261, 1281–82 (1937).

> Reasonable people do not kill no matter how much they are provoked, and even enraged people generally retain the capacity to control homicidal ... desire. We cheapen both life and our conception of responsibility by maintaining the provocation/passion mitigation.... As virtually every human being knows because we have all been enraged, it is easy not to kill, even when one is enraged.

Stephen J. Morse, "Undiminished Confusion in Diminished Capacity," 75 J. Crim. L. & Criminology 1, 33–34 (1984).

3. But why must provocation be either a justification or an excuse? Why can't it be a failure-of-proof (or level-one) "defense" that negates an offense element, and more specifically the mens rea of murder (be it premeditation, malice, intent, purpose, or knowledge)? (See *Patterson v. New York*, ch. 4, supra.) Does viewing the defense in this way depend on the particular jurisdiction's statutory structure? Is it plausible to take this view in a jurisdiction using the Model Penal Code's provisions on homicide? And is it reasonable to reconceive of the defense depending (so much) on

statutory *language*? Does extreme emotional disturbance play a different *substantive* role in the Model Penal Code than malice-negating "provocation" does in traditional state codes?

Why, though, if it is a (partial) justification or an excuse, does it apply *only* to murder? However the defense is classified, why would an "emotionally disturbed" or "provoked" assailant or arsonist not deserve the same mitigation of punishment, and on the same grounds, as the murderer who lost his cool? It is worth considering that even the emotionally disturbed *manslaughterer* who aims not at the heart, but at the legs of his provoker, seeking to maim but not to kill, is not formally entitled to mitigation. Why is provocation a defense only to one type of homicide, murder? What is left of provocation once one abandons the view that there is no such thing as a special mens rea for murder (malice aforethought) that could be negated without any implication for other crimes?

But perhaps provoked assailants and arsonists *do* receive lower penalties. Historically, they might have done so because judges, exercising their considerable sentencing discretion, accounted for provocative victims. Note that today's Federal Sentencing Guidelines provide for a downward sentencing departure "[i]f the victim's wrongful conduct contributed significantly to provoking the offense behavior." § 5K2.10. For an application of the provision, see United States v. Yellow Earrings, 891 F.2d 650 (8th Cir. 1989) (granting downward departure for defendant who pled guilty to assault because victim had pushed, verbally abused and "publicly humiliated" the defendant).

Arguably, then, we developed a highly detailed law of provocation to mitigate punishment for murder (but not other offenses) largely because the sentences for murder were (uniquely) so high that it seemed inappropriate to allow judges to engage in what would amount to truly massive downward departures without formal and limited definitions of the situations in which such leniency was merited.

4. The argument behind the Model Penal Code's refusal to restrict the possibility of mitigation to those who had responded to a pre-defined list of stressors is perfectly consistent with typical arguments against the use of rigid rules. Such rules may well be over-inclusive (that is, in this case, the use of the rules will lead us to judge *more* crimes to be manslaughter than the policymaker would prefer). We would worry about over-inclusiveness to the degree that fact finders come to *assume* that the defendant has a good mitigating defense if he has killed in one of the typical provocative circumstances, whether or not the situation is really as stressful as similar situations are. More significantly, the rule will be dramatically under-inclusive since it *bars* the fact finder from considering whether the defendant found himself under enormous stress unless he was in one of the listed stressful situations.

Advocates of the Model Penal Code's position will emphasize that there is little reason to believe we can specify in advance all the circumstances in which people will find it especially difficult to retain self-control: it is hardly obvious, for instance, that it is harder to retain self-control when one learns of a spouse's infidelity (in an already souring marriage? when one might have suspected it for a long while?) than when a supervisor taunts an employee that he is powerless to prevent him from getting the employee fired by filing a false and vindictive job evaluation or when one loses custody of one's child because of one's spouse's ongoing drug use. (The variations are endless; in a sense, that is the point ...) In a similar manner, traditional provocation doctrine generally, though not invariably, assumes—too narrowly?—that what we need to do is explain the defendant's anger or rage, but it is not clear that people might not kill, unjustifiably, when overcome by panic or fear, a quite different sort of extreme emotional disturbance. See People v. Tapia, 204 Cal.App.3d 1055, 251 Cal.Rptr. 823 (1988) (permitting a heat of passion defense in a situation in which the defendants feared the victim, a heroin supplier who'd threatened and beaten them over a long period.)

Moreover, those who are suspicious of the use of rules in this—and other—contexts will typically note that the "rules" are less clear and self-enforcing than those who like to believe that the use of rules will restrain unwanted discretion imagine. Thus, we know that an assault can be sufficient provocation under the traditional system, but how severe must the assault be? In *Girouard*, for instance, the victim *does* physically attack the defendant (she jumps on his back and pulls his hair), but the court assumes that the defendant is responding to her taunting words, not the assault. Bedder v. Director of Public Prosecutions, [1954] 1 W.L.R. 119, is best known for holding that fact finders should not consider whether the defendant's emotionally disturbed reaction to a prostitute's taunts about his impotence was a reasonable reaction for the class of impotent men, but rather should consider whether it was a reasonable reaction to such taunts by people more generally, but the court assumes, again with little explanation, that he was *not* responding to her physical assaults (she had slapped him in the face and punched him in the stomach; when he pushed her in response, she kicked him in the groin).

The attack on the use of the vague Model Penal Code standard—there is little to guide jurors trying to figure out precisely when there is a *reasonable* explanation or excuse for the defendant's emotional disturbance—is also fairly typical of the arguments against the use of vague standards. Giving fact finders high levels of discretion arguably leads to unpredictable and inexplicably inconsistent judgments across cases. It may also permit jurors to manifest either personal bias (favoring defendants they find more appealing, perhaps because they seem more similar to the jurors) or a sort of ideological bias that the legislature did not intend to delegate to juries (forgiving, for instance, men who kill when they feel wounded by non-compliant women more than they forgive women lashing out at long-term abuse). Note that four of the fourteen states (Maine, Ohio, Washington, and Wisconsin) that initially adopted the Model Penal Code approach returned to the common law formulations.

In this regard, too, it is interesting to note that Victoria Nourse discovered that jurors in Model Penal Code and what she called "mixed" jurisdictions, compared to more traditional jurisdictions, rather substantially altered traditional law. Punishment was frequently mitigated in situations in which the deceased had simply left (or was trying to leave) the killer (a defense that *never* worked in traditional jurisdictions) and was more frequently mitigated in situations in which a separated spouse's infidelity is discovered. At the same time, jurors are less likely to partially excuse those who react to physical violence in MPC jurisdictions than in traditional jurisdictions, where it remains the dominant successful defense. See Victoria Nourse, "Passion's Progress: Modern Law Reform and the Provocation Defense," 106 Yale L.J. 1331 (1997).

5. It may well be the case that even if the "official," above-board version of the defense focuses on partly excusing the defendant for his frailty, rather than rewarding him (relative to the punishment he'd otherwise have received) for getting rid of a bad actor, the sub-text at trials in which provocation or extreme emotional disturbance defenses are raised will nonetheless "blame the victim." It may well be true in self-defense cases as well that the precise formal contours of the defense—those demanding no more than proportional responses to ongoing imminent threats—are obscured if the jurors are led to focus on the malevolence of the ultimate victim, so that they will feel, at worst, indifferent that the victim died. Think in this regard of the epigram attributed to a prominent defense lawyer who had tried innumerable homicide cases: "The issue in every murder case is the same: why does the bag of shit in the morgue deserve to be there and why was my client the right man to put him there?"

6. It is vital to distinguish incapacitationist from character-focused retributivist accounts of the defense, looked at as a partial excuse. For the incapacitationist, at core, what makes the existence of provocation germane is that "provocative circumstances" are (by hypothesis?) unusual and therefore unlikely to recur. What we (claim to) know about the defendant is that he will kill in *these* circumstances, but we have little reason to believe that he is a likely recidivist. For the character-focused retributivist, what makes the existence of provocation germane is that the person who kills under stress does not reveal his *true individuating character*, but only something that might be thought of as his situation-sensitive *behavior* or some unduly contingent character.

There are practical implications to this distinction. First, and most salient, imagine that we abolish *all* the limitations (finite list of stressors, cooling off periods, restriction on appropriate intended victims) at once (as the Model Penal Code arguably does): a person is guilty of manslaughter, not murder, if he is highly agitated when he kills, and he is agitated for a good reason. It doesn't matter whom he kills; it doesn't matter whether the reason is an event (or events) that just happened, or one that happened in his distant past. Arguably, all intentional killers are in a rage when they kill whomever they kill, and there is generally some (plausible) explanation for that rage (e.g., the unloving, abusive home they grew up in). For the incapacitationist, the fact that the killing might not reveal some "true, non-contingent character"—do we *really* know if the defendant would have killed but-for the particular history of abuse and other life-altering experiences he had?—is plainly beside the point. Globally angry people—however well they can *explain* their anger and cause us to wonder, at a minimum, whether they are distinct in disposition or distinct in experience from those of us who sit in judgment upon them—are likely to kill again.

Second, we might need to distinguish more carefully between *recurring* situations that are indeed very upsetting and (arguably) non-recurring ones, if we treat the defense as reflecting an incapacitationist's views: it *may* be very hard to contain anger when one is romantically rejected, but our intuition may be that people get rejected often. They may not witness adultery in progress nearly so often. (Of course, the incapacitationist must *categorize* the stressor: is our intuition that the person who kills his cheating spouse will contain himself unless he witnesses adultery or is it that he is readily upset by all assertions of female autonomy, or perceived "slights" to his manhood? If we think adultery is a sub-set of "assertiveness," then the defendant *is* likely to confront the same stress again.)

7. The Model Penal Code—explicitly—as well as more traditional jurisdictions—more implicitly—demand that the actor in fact be in a state of passion or emotional disturbance. What factors persuaded the trial court judge that the defendant in *Shelton* was *not* in a state of extreme emotional disturbance? What do we *mean* when we say someone is (or isn't) in such a state? Do we focus (unduly) on agitation rather than other perturbed emotional states?

8. Assume that the trial court judge in *Shelton* had decided that the defendant was in fact extremely emotionally disturbed when he killed the victim. Assume, too, that the victim's threat to get him fired might be a reasonable explanation or excuse for the defendant's disturbance.

Think about the following: Or. Rev. Stat. § 163.135(1) (1995) states that extreme emotional disturbance is not a defense when it is "the result of the person's own intentional, knowing, reckless or criminally negligent act." Plainly, the statute is meant to strip a defendant of the provocation defense if he is responding to a victim's assault in situations in which the defendant himself initiated the fight. Is it meant to apply to a situation like that in *Shelton* in which the defendant made himself vulnerable to the victim's threats by using illegal drugs in the first instance? What if the defendant had engaged in *noncriminal* conduct? Toward a third party? With, or without, awareness—or purpose—that the eventual victim would be affected?

Think generally about how far back in time we should go before we cut off a defendant's narrative, or the prosecutor's. Generally, in criminal law, we believe we can learn everything we need to know to render judgment from the criminal incident itself. It is generally defendants who want to go back in time to "explain" the criminal behavior that on its face bespeaks bad character. But once defendants can go back in time to introduce "determinist excuses"—like provocation, like duress—it appears that prosecutors are often entitled to respond that the defendant *intentionally* placed herself in the position in which she'd later be subject to constraint. Thus, a person may not be able to claim he was acting under duress when he joined a gang that put him under that duress. Similarly, the defendant in *Decina* (ch. 4 supra) might not be able to claim that he did not act voluntarily, though he was unconscious when his car actually struck the victims, because he took earlier steps that put him at risk of "not acting" later. Think about this issue in relation to battered wives' self-defense claims (ch. 7 supra): to the degree that a particular defendant's "objectively mistaken" apprehension of imminent danger is "caused" by her status as a long-term domestic abuse victim, should she be held responsible for *becoming* a long-term abuse victim, because she (voluntarily?) stayed with an abuser?

9. Notice that many of the defendants in these cases attempted suicide at the same time they killed their victims, or at least made extremely serious suicidal gestures. (See *Girouard*, *Fallin*, *Simpson*.) What does this suggest about the degree to which their crimes might have been deterred by the promise of certain punishment? About the degree to which they are morally blameworthy?

c. The Sub–Group Question: Would the Precipitating Incident Have Agitated People (Generally) or People More Precisely like the Defendant?

Keenan v. Commonwealth, 44 Pa. 55, 58 (1863)

[The defendant was somewhat intoxicated when he entered the passenger car of a railroad. He and his companions "behaved badly and noisily, and used very profane language." The conductor twice requested them to be quiet; when he refused and continued to be abusive, the conductor "took him by the lapel of his coat, and was proceeding to put him out, when he struck the conductor and was struck in return." He stabbed and mortally wounded the conductor in the ensuing scuffle. The court rejected his provocation defense, in part because he had set off the chain of events that resulted in the mortal struggle. But the court also dealt with his contention that the question of whether he was reasonably provoked should be answered by reference to the reactions of intoxicated people, stating:]

[M]easured by [the rule the defendant urges], the crimes of a proud, or captious, or selfish, or habitually ill-natured man ... or of one who is habitually quarrelsome ... or who, by any sort of indulgence, fault, or vice, renders himself very easily excitable, or very subject to temptation, are much less criminal than those of a moderate, well-tempered and ordinary citizen, because to the former a very small provocation or temptation becomes adequate to excuse or palliate any crime. If such were the rule, a defendant would be much more likely to injure than to benefit his case by showing a good character, and the law would present no inducement to men to try to rise to the standard of even ordinary social morality.... [In addition], no judicial tribunal can have time or competence for such a thorough investigation of the special character or state of each individual mind....

State v. Felton, 329 N.W.2d 161 (Wis. 1983)

[The defendant killed her sleeping husband, who had subjected her to years of abuse. Her attorney claimed that the question of whether her homicidal response to long-term abuse was "reasonable" should be judged from the vantage point of battered women. The court agreed noting ...] [The court below] appeared to think that it would have been erroneous to consider how others of a similar background ... would have reacted, but only to consider whether a person ordinarily constituted would have acted in the heat of passion in response to the immediate provocation. It declined to consider how an ordinarily constituted person who was a battered spouse would have reacted to the provocation. [This constitutes error.] [A] defendant's background is not in general relevant to the objective test for heat of passion, the question is how an ordinary person faced with a similar provocation would react. The provocation can consist, as it did here, of a long history of abuse. It is proper in applying the objective test, therefore, to consider how other persons, similarly situated with respect to that type, or that history, of provocation, would react.

QUESTIONS AND COMMENTS

1. On the one hand, it seems plain that we will not say that a person reacted reasonably if her reactions were simply the reactions of someone as unreasonably hotheaded and intemperate as she was, even if we viewed such hot-headedness as one of the defendant's persistent "traits." The criminal law, generally, seeks to deter and blame people for being hotheaded; more obviously, it would seek to incapacitate them. But what if we describe "hot-headedness" in psychiatric diagnostic terms—the defendant reacted in the way those with borderline personality disorders react? And what if we compare the defendant to others not in terms of their intemperance but in terms of some other trait that *causes* intemperance? It is plain in *Bedder* (p. 942, supra) that we don't *blame* Bedder for his impotence (or try to deter it) in the way that we might blame him or try to deter hot-headedness. But what if the impotent, as a matter of fact, are atypically quick to lose self-control in a variety of recurring situations? Would we compare *Bedder* to other impotent men only if we thought that their reactions were very situation-specific? Would we compare Felton's reactions to the reactions of other battered women (assuming, as the defense counsel must assume if it seems worthwhile to seek the proffered jury instructions, that such battered women lose their self-control in the situation the defendant faced more readily than most people would) only if we believed such women were prone to atypical anger only in atypical circumstances? If so, does that suggest, once again, that the defense at core is not about mercy and blame, but about predicting dangerousness?

2. How do we *describe* certain precipitating incidents without making reference to the defendant's sub-group? Do we describe a history of domestic abuse accurately if we break it back down into a discrete series of assaults, and ask how "people" respond to such a series of assaults? Is it sensible to ask how "people" react to racial epithets? Would we ask in that regard in a trial of an African–American how those of all races react to the particular derogatory epithet most commonly used in the United States for African–Americans? Or how, say, whites would react to the rather rarer epithets—like "Honky"—directed at them? Do *any* epithets directed at majority group members have the same social meaning that epithets directed at members of historically subordinated groups have?

Reconsider this question in looking at the Problem, p. 948, below. How would we *describe* the "precipitating incident" *without* reference to the defendant's sub-group? Is such a description satisfactory?

3. Consider the relationship between the law of "diminished responsibility" or "diminished capacity" and the law of provocation/extreme emotional disturbance.

The 1957 reform of homicide law in the United Kingdom (see Homicide Act, 1957, 5 & 6 Eliz. 2, c. 11, sec. 2) provided as follows:

> Persons suffering from diminished responsibility:
>
> (1) Where a person kills ... he shall not be convicted of murder if he was suffering from such abnormality of mind (whether arising from a condition of arrested or retarded development of mind or any inherent causes or induced by disease or injury) as substantially impaired his mental responsibility for his acts and omissions in doing or being a party to the killing.

Prior to its (formal) abolition, first by legislation and then by popular initiative in the early 1980s, California law was similar. In People v. Conley, 64 Cal.2d 310, 411 P.2d 911 (1966), the California Supreme Court held that a defendant did not have the "malice" needed to sustain a murder conviction unless he had the capacity "to comprehend his duty to govern his actions in accordance with the duty imposed by law." Evidence of psychological disorder and voluntary intoxication could be used to rebut the existence of malice.

One might, of course, reach a somewhat similar result, without formally establishing a diminished capacity defense, if one permits a defendant to argue that his emotional disturbance was responsive to pressures that would cause people as psychologically impaired, or as intoxicated, as he was to lose self-control (even if the pressures would not cause most people to suffer extreme disturbance.) Recall that the Model Penal Code instructs jurors to determine if there is a reasonable explanation or excuse for the defendant's "extreme mental or emotional disturbance" given the "actor's situation." Model Penal Code § 210.3. As the Code's reporters noted (Model Penal Commentaries, § 210.3 at 72–73 (1980)):

> The term "situation" ... is designedly ambiguous and is plainly flexible enough to allow the law to grow in the direction of taking account of mental abnormalities that have been recognized in the developing law of diminished responsibility.

At the same time, however, the Commentaries hint at "justice" limits on the relevance of a "mental disturbance":

> Mental disorder clearly does not preclude moral depravity, and there surely will be cases where the actor's mental condition, although recognized as disturbed or abnormal should be regarded as having no just bearing on his liability for intentional homicide.

American case law overwhelmingly rejects the relevance of a defendant's claim that as a result of his atypical psychiatric profile, he is vulnerable to becoming extremely disturbed in situations in which more typical people would not. For a thorough review of the case law, see Taylor v. State, 452 So.2d 441 (Miss. 1984). The rule that diminished capacity mitigates homicide liability from murder to manslaughter (like provocation and, at least in some jurisdictions, "imperfect" self-defense) has been widely discredited. Note, however, that evidence of diminished capacity (or "diminished responsibility" as the Model Penal Code prefers to call it) in the sense of mental disorder short of insanity remains relevant insofar as it negates an element of any offense (not only murder), most particularly mens rea. See Model Penal Code § 4.02; State v. Breakiron, 108 N.J. 591, 532 A.2d 199 (1987).

4. What about more widely shared, cultural dispositions to react to certain particular forms of stress, rather than more idiosyncratic personal dispositions? Consider the following Problem.

* * *

Problem

The defendant, Abbas El–Gabir, is twenty-three years old. His sister, Sahar, whom he shot and killed under circumstances about to be detailed, was nineteen. They were born in a very traditional village in rural Algeria. His mother died of natural causes when he was eleven. His father, a political opponent of the Algerian regime, died when Abbas was fourteen while in the custody of Algerian state officials. Upon his father's death, he and his sister left Algeria, joining an uncle and aunt (who had themselves left Algeria several years earlier) in Jordan. Abbas and Sahar lived in Jordan till Abbas turned twenty-one and Sahar seventeen, at which time they both came to the United States, to live with yet another uncle and aunt, who had emigrated from Algeria to the United States in the early 1980s.

Abbas has lived all of his life in extremely traditional communities, though he has obviously had some casual contact, (e.g., in shops, on buses, etc.) with more secular, anti-traditional Algerians and Jordanians as well as people coming from even more distinct cultural backgrounds (e.g., persons of European, sub-Saharan African, Latin American, and Asian descent in the United States). But even in the United States, he rarely ventured outside the small neighborhood in which he lived, a community consisting almost entirely of quite traditional recent immigrants from rural and urban working class backgrounds in the Middle East, except to go to work. He worked for a small office cleaning service owned by his uncle that employed only other recent émigrés from Algeria, all of whom shared their customs.

Abbas, like most of the men with whom he had ever had extensive social contact, deeply believed that it was the duty of a woman's father or brother (and to a lesser extent, her husband) to strictly enforce certain norms of sexual purity. Thus, historically, fathers or brothers would sometimes kill their daughters or sisters who (deeply) dishonored the family: the paradigmatic "crime of honor" is the killing of a woman by her father or brother when she is discovered by her husband not to be a virgin on her wedding night, but Abbas witnessed two other "crimes of honor" growing up. (One unmarried young woman was killed by her father when seen conversing with a man behind a fence in rural Algeria. Another young woman, in urban Jordan, was killed by her brother when he saw her leave the car of a male university classmate.) "Honor crimes" are not at all unusual; Jordanian police estimated that in 1991, slightly less than a third of the killings in Jordan were "crimes of honor." You should recognize, though, that aggregate rates of *lethal* violence against women are certainly not atypically high in these traditional communities, compared to rates in the United States among those of European descent, though the *pattern* of violence (who the killer is, what explanations he gives for his violence) may be different. Furthermore, rates of *sexual* violence (rape, sexual battery) against women are almost surely *lower* in these traditional communities.

The legal treatment of these crimes in Abbas's countries of origin (Algeria, Jordan) is not straightforward:

The Algerian Code, perhaps the least "traditional" criminal code in the Middle East, treats "crimes of passion" in much the way they are treated in most American jurisdictions that allow a provocation defense: a husband (or wife) who catches his (or her) spouse in the course of committing adultery will receive a reduction in penalty if he (or she) kills the other or the other's lover.

The Jordanian Code (and practice) is a fair bit more complex. Article 340 of the Jordanian Penal Code reads as follows:

> 1) He who catches his wife, or one of his female unlawfuls,[1] committing adultery with another, and he kills, wounds, or injures one or both of them is exempt from any penalty.[2]
>
> 2) He who catches his wife, or one of his female ascendants or descendants or sisters, with another in an unlawful bed[3] and he kills or wounds or injures one or both of them benefits from a reduction in penalty.

From the early 1950s until the mid–1960s, only "crimes of honor" covered under Article 340 were treated differently from any other killings. But starting in the mid–1960s, Jordanian courts applied a broader, more general mitigating principle (encoded in Article 98 of the Penal Code) to certain other "crimes of honor" to which Article 340 would not apply. (For example, a father learning of his daughter's pregnancy outside of marriage would not be entitled to exemption from punishment or mitigation of punishment under Article 340, but the case was deemed appropriate for mitigation under Article 98.) Article 98 reads:

> He who commits a crime in a fit of fury caused by an unrightful and dangerous act on the part of the victim benefits from a reduction in penalty.

1. A "female unlawful" is any woman a man cannot lawfully marry. What this phrase means, then, is that all those persons who would be barred from marrying the woman by prohibitions against "incest" are in the same position as the woman's husband. The "incest" prohibitions are broader and more inclusive than American incest prohibitions (e.g., by including relatives by marriage) but would certainly, like American incest rules, include a brother.

2. Note that there is no distinction between what most Americans would label adultery, i.e., sex between a wife and someone not her husband, and pre-marital sex in interpreting the Code.

3. The "unlawful bed" phrase is generally interpreted to mean that the killer sees the woman in some place that strongly suggests she is having an adulterous or pre-marital sexual relationship, not just the literal bed of her lover.

In the middle 1960s, for the first time, the Jordanian courts reversed prior practice and declared that sexual misconduct was "an unrightful act" within the terms of Article 98.

When Abbas's sister Sahar first arrived in America, at the age of seventeen, she remained faithful to the traditions of her cultural community for roughly a year. For instance, she covered her hair with a scarf, as was the custom of all of the women in her extended family, whenever she was outside the exclusive company of women, as she was almost daily (since she worked as an orderly at a care-taking facility for the elderly with both male and female workers and clients). Roughly a year after arriving in the United States, though, her behavior changed, unbeknownst to her brother. She would leave their uncle's house in what would have been deemed appropriately modest attire (including the scarf), but would change at a girl friend's house, a block away from her workplace, into far less modest Westernized clothes, and put on a good deal of make-up as well. (The girl friend was an American of European descent.) At the end of the workday, she would return to her friend's home, change back into more traditional dress, cover her hair with the scarf she had removed earlier in the day, and clean off her make-up.

By the time she was nineteen, a month before her death, Sahar would often join (male and female) co-workers at a bar after work, though she never drank anything alcoholic. (She lied to her brother about how long it took to make bus connections to explain her relatively late arrival home.) Though she remained a virgin, she did, on one occasion, "make out" with Zeid, a first generation immigrant from Lebanon, whom she had met many times at the bar.

The day before her death, her uncle Rachid spotted Sahar leaving the bar, dressed in her Westernized clothes. Her "boyfriend" Zeid touched her shoulder saying goodbye to her. Later that night, Rachid told Abbas what he had seen. Before Abbas went to sleep that night, Rachid entered his room and said, "You know what your father would do, now, don't you? Go see yourself, she'll be at this place at 5:30."

The next day, Abbas went to the bar, bringing a gun. He saw Sahar, for the first time, in Western clothes, wearing make-up. She was sitting next to Zeid and was holding his hand, giggling. Abbas began to shake and cry. Sahar saw her brother, and saw also that he was reaching for a gun. She got up screaming and tried to run. Abbas shot her once, wounding her badly. As she struggled to escape, Abbas was able to shoot Sahar a second time, less than ten seconds later, and this second shot killed her.

Assume, first, that the jurisdiction in which these events occurred observes all the traditional limits on the provocation defense. Could Abbas raise a successful provocation defense in such a jurisdiction?

Assume, now, instead, that the jurisdiction has adopted Model Penal Code § 210.3. How could Abbas best frame his case that he ought to be guilty of manslaughter only? What arguments would you expect the District Attorney to use to counter the defendant's claims?

Finally, think back to the material on "cultural defenses" and mistake of law (ch. 5, supra). Assume, now, that Abbas offers to prove that he was completely unfamiliar with the American legal treatment of "crimes of honor," and that he believed he was not only entitled, but duty-bound, to kill his sister in these circumstances. Assume instead he offered to persuade us that his actions, if criminal, would not have been murder in any culture whose norms he was familiar with. Assess in detail the relevance of these sorts of "cultural defenses" in this context.

In thinking about this Problem, you should consider the possibility that Western observers may overestimate the distinction between the "crimes of honor" that might well be treated too leniently in a number of non-Western countries, and "crimes of passion" committed by American males against wives and girlfriends who "cheat" on them or leave them. You should consider how different (and how similar) these crimes are, both in terms of the stresses that the defendants might or might not face, the degree to which each defendant, while claiming "partial excuse" may actually *feel* that he is (to some extent) *justified,* and the degree to which each practice can be thought of as protecting patriarchal prerogatives. (Should the *defendant's* perception of the justifiability, or excusability, of his conduct, make a difference?) For an illuminating discussion of these issues, including an excellent summary of the comparative law issues, see Lama Abu–Odeh, "The 'Honor' of the 'East' and the 'Passion' of the 'West,' " 1997 Utah L. Rev. 287.

D. NEGLIGENT HOMICIDE

People v. Beiter

Supreme Court of New York, Appellate Division, Fourth Department.
77 A.D.2d 214, 432 N.Y.S.2d 947 (1980).

■ SIMONS, JUSTICE.

The issue on this appeal is the sufficiency of the People's evidence to sustain the jury's finding that defendant was guilty of criminal negligence in causing the death of David A. Schifano in a motor vehicle accident (Penal Law, § 125.10).

The accident happened at about 2:00 a.m. on December 4, 1977. Defendant had been working the previous evening as a waitress in the Country House Restaurant in East Rochester. At about 11:00 p.m., after completing work, she went to a discotheque on the floor below the restaurant and there she visited with friends until she left between 1:30 a.m. and 2:00 a.m. to drive home alone in her 1968 Chevrolet sedan. While at the discotheque, she had two or three "Singapore Slings."

The accident occurred on Plank Road in Penfield, New York, near the Landmark Inn. Plank Road is a two-lane paved highway, straight and level for a considerable distance from the scene of the accident in both directions. On the night of the accident, the weather was clear and the road was dry. Defendant had entered Plank Road by turning right from an intersecting highway about .2 of a mile west of the scene and she was proceeding east when the accident occurred. There was no street lighting in the area at the time but there was some illumination of the road from a neon beverage sign in the window of the Inn and lights in the parking lot behind it. Three or four vehicles were parked on the shoulder of the road near the Inn.

Immediately before the accident, decedent and his companion, Leonard Colantoni, left the Landmark Inn to go home. They started across Plank Road walking north to south to enter Colantoni's van which was parked on the south side of the road.

When Colantoni was in the road, about 10 feet ahead of decedent, he observed the headlights of defendant's car to the west. He watched the car as it approached them and then yelled to decedent to hurry because the car was traveling fast. After reaching the side of the road, Colantoni heard a loud noise, saw broken glass and saw something fly and hit the road as the car continued on without stopping. Colantoni estimated defendant's speed at 60 miles per hour, "maybe more."

After the accident, Colantoni found articles of decedent's clothing in the road, his body in a ditch approximately 141 feet from the point of impact and decedent's severed leg about 20 feet from the body. Decedent apparently was killed instantly by the impact. The pathologist testified that there were several major injuries and that decedent's blood alcohol level was .11 per cent by weight.

The only other witness to the accident was defendant. She testified that she was proceeding easterly on Plank Road at 40 miles per hour, that there was no other traffic on the highway and that just after passing the Inn she saw two men about 40 feet in front of her, one off the road to her right, and the other just behind him. As she approached, she drove her car slightly to the left to avoid them. She did not realize that she had hit anyone but she slowed down after noticing that her radio went off and her windshield was cracked. Nevertheless, she drove on home and it was there, after examining the damage to her car, that she realized that she had hit someone and called the police. Colantoni had testified that defendant did not apply her brakes and that he did not hear a horn at any time. Defendant admitted that she did not apply her brakes and she could not recall sounding her horn. Defendant took a breathalyzer test at 4:50 a.m. and it resulted in a reading of .07 per cent.

Defendant was indicted on three counts: Criminal Negligence; Leaving the Scene of an Incident; and Operating a Motor Vehicle under the influence of Alcohol or Drugs. The criminal negligence count charged defendant with causing decedent's death "by operating a motor vehicle while under the influence of alcohol at an excessive rate of speed on a straight level road and thereby failing to observe" decedent, although there was no obstruction to her vision. The jury convicted defendant of criminal negligence and leaving the scene but acquitted her of driving while under the influence of alcohol.

Section 125.10 of the Penal Law provides that "(a) person is guilty of criminally negligent homicide when, with criminal negligence, he causes the death of another person." A person acts with criminal negligence with respect to a result or circumstance "when he fails to perceive a substantial and unjustifiable risk that such result will occur or that such circumstance exists. The risk must be of such nature and degree that the failure to perceive it constitutes a gross deviation from the standard of care that a reasonable person would observe in the situation''.

Considering the evidence in the light most favorable to the People, as we must, the proof established that defendant was operating her automobile at night on a straight and level rural road, partially illuminated by the lights of a nearby tavern, at a speed of 60 miles per hour in a 40 mile-per-hour zone, at a time when there were three or four other cars parked in the vicinity on the shoulder of the highway; that she saw two men when they were approximately 40 feet in front of her, swerved slightly to the left to avoid hitting them but struck one man, damaging the right headlight, right front fender and right side of the windshield of the car. We do not think that this evidence establishes a ''gross deviation'' from the standard of care of a reasonable person under the circumstances.

The People place considerable emphasis on defendant's failure to sound her horn or apply her brakes after she observed the pedestrians. Defendant was confronted suddenly by an unanticipated situation, however, and even if her spontaneous reaction to the emergency was wrong, it did not constitute a gross deviation from the standard of reasonable care. Under familiar rules, if an emergency is the result of defendant's own inattention it may not serve as an excuse for her negligent conduct. But the existence of the emergency situation does provide a different standard of reasonableness for judging her actions after the emergency was created. ''It is . . . not the conduct after the emergency has arisen which is *not* excused, but the prior negligence'' (Prosser, Torts (4th ed.), § 33, p. 170 (emphasis added)). Thus, although defendant may have failed to exercise the required care before she observed the pedestrians, her failure to sound her horn or brake after being confronted with the emergency cannot serve to magnify her criminal culpability and it is at least arguable that her swerve to the left to avoid striking Schifano was the most reasonable course of action under the conditions.

The issue, then, is whether defendant's illegal speed and her failure to perceive the danger, considering the traffic, road conditions and lighting conditions existing that night constituted criminal negligence.

In People v. Haney, 30 N.Y.2d 328, 333 N.Y.S.2d 403, 284 N.E.2d 564, the Court of Appeals, recognizing the difficulty of clarifying the elements necessary to establish criminal negligence, observed that ''two main considerations should be emphasized. Firstly, criminal liability cannot be predicated upon every careless act merely because its carelessness results in another's death; and, secondly, the elements of the crime 'preclude the proper condemnation of inadvertent risk creation unless 'the significance of the circumstances of fact would be apparent to one who shares the community's general sense of right and wrong' '' (Model Penal Code, Tent. Draft No. 9, at p. 53). The court noted that the quantum of proof required for criminal negligence is ''appreciably greater than that required for ordinary civil negligence by virtue of the 'substantial and unjustifiable' character of the risk involved and the factor of 'gross deviation' from the ordinary standard of care'' (Commission Staff Notes, Gilbert Criminal Code and Penal Law (1971), p. 2–248; cf. Prosser, Law of Torts (4th ed.), § 31; Restatement, Torts, § 282).

In *Haney* the Court of Appeals tested the legal sufficiency of an indictment, not the evidence after trial. Defendant Haney was accused of striking and killing a pedestrian in mid-intersection while driving an automobile through a red light on a city street at a speed of 52 miles per hour during daylight hours. The court held the indictment sufficient and stated that it was for the trier of the facts to evaluate defendant's conduct and his failure of perception and to determine whether defendant's conduct constituted a gross deviation from the standard of reasonable care.

By contrast, this defendant was driving down a straight and level highway in a sparsely populated area with her lights on. The area was dark and the road free of other traffic, circumstances in which she could reasonably expect that anyone crossing the road would see her headlights and conduct themselves accordingly. Seeing the victim from 40 feet away, she swerved, albeit not enough, to avoid striking him. Such conduct does not constitute a gross deviation from the ordinary standard of care held by those who share "the community's general sense of right and wrong".

The judgment should be modified by reversing the conviction for criminal negligence, dismissing the first count of the indictment charging that crime and vacating the sentence and as so modified the judgment should be affirmed.

■ HANCOCK, JUSTICE (dissenting).

In my opinion, there is in this record ample evidence from which a jury could have concluded that defendant, after consuming alcoholic beverages, drove her automobile at night at a dangerously high rate of speed and without keeping a careful lookout past a lighted restaurant the glare from which impaired her vision and where there was a likelihood of pedestrian traffic, and that by doing so she created a substantial and unjustifiable risk; that defendant failed to perceive that risk; and that the failure to perceive it constituted a gross deviation from the standard of care that a reasonable person would have observed in the situation.

To support a finding of excessive speed by the defendant, the jury had before it not only the testimony of the eye witness that defendant's car was "hauling ass" and going "60 miles an hour, maybe more" but the physical evidence of high speed from the substantial damage to the automobile and the multiple fractures and massive injuries to the deceased resulting from an impact of such force as to sever the aorta in three places, wrench the right leg completely away from the pelvis and propel deceased's body a distance of 141 feet from the point of impact, as well as defendant's admissions on cross-examination and in her statement to the police that she was in a hurry and that she did not know how fast she was traveling. Based on defendant's own statements, the jury could have inferred that from her frequent trips past the restaurant she was either aware or should have been aware of the facts that the glare from the restaurant would reduce her ability to see and that there was a likelihood that there would be parked cars and pedestrian traffic on the highway in front of the restaurant. Further, defendant's testimony that she did not see the cars which were parked on the highway, did not observe the two pedestrians until she was 40 feet away, heard no noise from the impact, saw nothing hit the windshield despite the extensive damage it sustained, and that she was not immediately aware that she had hit someone would, taken together, support a conclusion by a trier of the facts either that defendant's senses and powers of observation were impaired or that she was not paying attention and keeping a careful lookout.

The jury could have inferred solely from defendant's conduct under the circumstances that she must have been oblivious to the substantial risks she was creating by driving her automobile in the manner described. There is, moreover, direct evidence that defendant failed to perceive these risks; i.e., her testimony that she saw no "problem at all in getting by" the pedestrians when she saw them for the first time in front of her car at a distance of 40 feet and that she did not sound her horn or apply her brakes but "just swerved over a little bit" to the left. I cannot agree with the majority that, as a matter of law, defendant's failure to perceive the risks did not constitute a gross deviation from the ordinary standard of care held by one who shares the community's general sense of right and wrong. In my opinion, it was for the jury to " 'evaluate the actor's failure of perception and determine whether, under all the circumstances, it was serious enough to be condemned.' " (Model Penal Code, Tent. Draft No. 4, (April 25, 1955), p. 126).

QUESTIONS AND COMMENTS

1. The distinction between manslaughter and negligent homicide is the familiar one between recklessness and negligence. See *People v. Strong*, supra ch. 5 ("The essential distinction between the crimes of manslaughter, second degree, and criminally negligent homicide is the mental state of the defendant at the time the crime was committed. In one, the actor perceives the risk, but consciously disregards it. In the other, he negligently fails to perceive the risk."). The distinction between reckless and negligent homicide has considerable practical significance. In New York, for instance, reckless homicide is punishable by up to fifteen years' imprisonment, and negligent homicide by no more than four years in prison and as little as probation or a fine. N.Y. Penal Law §§ 60.01, 70.00. On the difficulty of differentiating between recklessness and negligence (and therefore also between reckless and negligent homicide, which traditionally were simply thought of as instances of involuntary homicide), see ch. 5 supra.

2. Trickier, and more significant, still is the distinction between criminal and civil negligence. Courts have had a hard time telling the two apart. When the New York legislature, following the Model Penal Code, adopted a negligent homicide statute, trial courts often balked at the prospect of converting every fatal car accident into a negligent homicide case. For instance, in *People v. Haney*, discussed in *Beiter*, supra, the trial court dismissed the negligent homicide charge. The Court of Appeals reversed, explaining that "criminally negligent homicide is one of general application, encompassing an infinite variety of conduct":

> It should be abundantly clear that [Haney's] conduct cannot be characterized as mere carelessness, sufficient only to establish liability for ordinary civil negligence. Rather, from this evidence, and the reasonable inferences to be drawn therefrom, a jury could find the defendant guilty of criminally negligent homicide.... To hold otherwise, and excuse the flagrant disregard manifested here, would sanction conduct at which the statute was clearly aimed, and, in effect, abolish the crime of criminally negligent homicide in all homicides resulting from a misuse of a motor vehicle.

But isn't "flagrant disregard" supposed to be hallmark of recklessness, not negligence? And what is the difference between "mere carelessness" sufficient for "ordinary civil negligence" and the aggravated (?) carelessness required for criminal negligence? Does it help to tell the jury it should punish only (and all?) defendants whose behavior indicates that they don't share "the community's general sense of right and wrong"? Assume Beiter was on a cell phone at the time of the accident, but had not had any Singapore Slings. What is your (*your* community's, or *the* community's) sense as to the rightness or wrongness of her behavior? Did Beiter share that sense? If she didn't, should she be punished for homicide? Does it matter that use of a handheld cell phone while driving is prohibited, N.Y. Veh. & Traf. L. § 1225–c ($100 fine)? That this prohibition is widely ignored? Rarely enforced?

3. What explains the decision in *Beiter*? Does the court pay sufficient attention to the distinction between criminal and civil negligence? Is it possible that Beiter was criminally, but not civilly, negligent? But shouldn't it be the other way around—shouldn't it be *harder* to establish criminal negligence?

What possible relevance does the victim's behavior—or alcohol level—have for purposes of determining the defendant's criminal negligence? Is Beiter acquitted because her victim was contributorily negligent?

The court discusses another tort doctrine, the so-called "emergency rule." ("[W]hen confronted with an emergency through no negligence of his own, a driver will not be found negligent for failing to choose the best or safest course of action." Berg v. Nelson, 559 N.W.2d 722, 724 (Minn. App. 1997).) What does this rule have to do with the facts of the case? (See Restatement of Torts (Second) § 296(2) ("The fact that the actor is not negligent after the emergency has arisen does not preclude his liability for his tortious conduct which has produced the emergency.")) Should a defendant accused of *criminally* negligent homicide be entitled to rely on her nonnegligent response to an emergency which is attributable to her negligence? Compare the defense of necessity (balance of evils). E.g., Model Penal Code § 3.02(2).

CHAPTER 11

White Collar Crimes: Larceny, Mail Fraud, Money Laundering

The category of "white collar crime" is ill-defined. The term was coined in 1940 by Edwin Sutherland, an American criminologist who urged his colleagues to expand their conception of crime, and therefore of their discipline, to include "the criminal behavior of business and professional men." Eager to challenge the received wisdom that crime is "caused by poverty or by personal and social characteristics believed to be associated statistically with poverty, including feeblemindedness, psychopathic deviations, slum neighborhoods, and 'deteriorated' families," Sutherland called attention to a wide array of criminal behavior that had until then escaped the attention of criminologists:

> White-collar criminality in business is expressed in the form of misrepresentation in financial statements of corporations, manipulation in the stock exchange, commercial bribery, bribery of public officials directly or indirectly in order to secure favorable contracts and legislation, misrepresentation in advertising and salesmanship, embezzlement and misapplication of funds, short weights and measures and misgrading of commodities, tax frauds, misapplication of funds in receiverships and bankruptcies. These are what Al Capone called "the legitimate rackets." These and many others are found in abundance in the business world....
>
> These varied types of white-collar crimes in business and the professions consist principally of violation of delegated or implied trust, and many of them can be reduced to two categories: misrepresentation of asset values and duplicity in the manipulation of power. The first is approximately the same as fraud or swindling: the second is similar to the double-cross. The latter is illustrated by the corporation director who, acting on inside information, purchases land which the corporation will need and sells it at a fantastic profit to his corporation. The principle of duplicity is that the offender holds two antagonistic positions, one of which is a position of trust, which is violated, generally by misapplication of funds, in the interest of the other position.

Edwin H. Sutherland, "White Collar Criminality," 5 Am. Soc. Rev. 1 (1940).

Insofar as white collar crime is defined in significant part in terms of those who commit it ("a person of respectability and high social status in the course of his occupation"), rather than exclusively in terms of the criminal acts they commit, it is not only difficult to quantify, but also hard to define as a matter of criminal law, which generally classifies criminality solely in terms of acts, rather than actors: Criminal codes today contain lists of crimes, rather than of criminals. (This wasn't always so. See, e.g., Papachristou v. Jacksonville, 405 U.S. 156 (1972) (reviewing the following vagrancy statute, whose origins can be traced back to the 14th century: "Rogues and vagabonds, ... common gamblers, ... common drunkards, common night walkers, thieves, pilferers or pickpockets, ... lewd, wanton and lascivious persons, ... common railers and brawlers, ... habitual loafers, disorderly persons, ... shall be deemed vagrants.").)

For that reason, the category of white collar crime is also controversial. Although Sutherland's point was to emphasize that not only poor people violate the criminal law, the concept of *white collar* crime itself appears to cement the very distinction between "the criminal behavior of business and professional men" and other crime that he ostensibly sought to undermine. What, then, is that crime which is *not* white collar? Ordinary? Real? True? Blue collar? (Note that the concept of white collar crime is unique to Anglo–American law. In civil law countries, there is such a thing as "business crime" or "economic crime," but no overarching category of criminal behavior defined by social status. Cf. Stuart P. Green, "The Concept of White Collar Crime in Law and Legal Theory," 8 Buff. Crim. L. Rev. 1 (2005).) Does it help to retain the concept of white collar crime, but then define it in terms of acts? See, e.g., the definition of white collar crime favored by the U.S. Justice Department: "White-collar offenses shall constitute those classes of non-violent illegal activities which principally involve traditional notions of deceit, deception, concealment, manipulation, breach of trust, subterfuge or illegal circumvention." U.S. Dep't of Justice, National Priorities for White–Collar Crime 5 (1977). For a discussion of the various definitions of white collar crime that have been proposed over the years, see David T. Johnson & Richard A. Leo, "The Yale White–Collar Crime Project: A Review and Critique," 17 L. & Soc. Inquiry 63 (1993).

Despite these limitations, the concept of white collar crime has become a fixture of American criminal law. Law schools offer courses on white collar crime (with accompanying casebooks), attorneys general (and presidents) set up white collar crime task forces, criminal defense attorneys specialize in white collar criminal defense, and academics (legal and otherwise) study it.

What's more, Sutherland's instinct was right, even in the context of a basic criminal law course. Whatever white collar crime may be, exactly, it is important to recognize that crimes are committed, on a regular basis, by those who qualify as white collar workers, including—among others—lawyers. More generally, crime is not limited to violent crime (such as rape or homicide) or public "street crime." There is more to modern criminal law than homicide, rape, and armed robbery.

Still, this being a book on criminal law rather than on criminology, we will focus on the "crime"—rather than the "white collar"—in white collar crime. More specifically, we will highlight nonviolent crimes against property and, more specifically yet, the category of crimes Sutherland grouped under "fraud or swindling." The modern white collar crime of *mail fraud*, we will see, is best understood against the backdrop of the age-old crime of larceny. The history of the law of larceny is the history of the continuing effort, first by courts and then also by legislatures, to close perceived "gaps" in the law proscribing non-consensual property transfers exploited by the ingenuity of the criminal mind. The crime of mail fraud, in the end, is designed as "a first line of defense" against the crafty trickster: "When a 'new' fraud develops—as constantly happens—the mail fraud statute becomes a stopgap device to deal on a temporary basis with the new phenomenon, until particularized legislation can be developed and passed to deal directly with the evil." United States v. Maze, 414 U.S. 395, 405, 94 S.Ct. 645 (1974) (Burger, C.J., dissenting).

Given the longstanding effort to use the criminal law to protect property interests, it is easy to forget that thefts, frauds, and "swindles" constitute not only criminal, but civil wrongs as well. In fact, the history of larceny and fraud is also the history of supplementing civil actions with criminal punishment. What was once a contract breach, or perhaps (also) a tort, may now very well be a crime. It is plainly important, though, to recognize that (and explain why) not every breach of contract is a crime, even though the breaching party might (at least if the breach is not apparent?) deprive the promisee of something valuable she was entitled to receive.

Furthermore, the phenomenon of white collar crime cannot be divorced from the rise of federal criminal law. Mail fraud is a federal crime; in fact, it was one of the first federal crimes to make significant inroads into the traditional realm of state criminal law. As a result, what was once a state crime may now very well (also) be a federal crime.

Finally, we will turn our attention to money laundering, a federal crime of more recent origin and broader sweep than mail fraud. Money laundering occurs whenever "dirty" money is "cleansed" through the concealment of its criminal origin; it is not limited to any one type of lucrative criminal conduct. (Instead, the statute provides an extensive list of offenses that give rise to the taint that money laundering removes.) The crime of money laundering doesn't appear to protect a particular interest, as larceny and mail fraud arguably do; it instead seeks to interfere with a wide range of criminal conduct without any readily discernible commonality.

A. LARCENY

People v. Olivo

Court of Appeals of New York.
52 N.Y.2d 309, 420 N.E.2d 40, 438 N.Y.S.2d 242 (1981).

■ COOKE, CHIEF JUDGE.

These cases present a recurring question in this era of the self-service store . . .: may a person be convicted of larceny for shoplifting if the person is caught with goods while still inside the store?. . . .

In People v. Olivo, defendant was observed by a security guard in the hardware area of a department store. Initially conversing with another person, defendant began to look around furtively when his acquaintance departed. The security agent continued to observe and saw defendant assume a crouching position, take a set of wrenches and secret it in his clothes. After again looking around, defendant began walking toward an exit, passing a number of cash registers en route. When defendant did not stop to pay for the merchandise, the officer accosted him a few feet from the exit. . . .

In People v. Gasparik, defendant was in a department store trying on a leather jacket. Two store detectives observed him tear off the price tag and remove a "sensormatic" device designed to set off an alarm if the jacket were carried through a detection machine. There was at least one such machine at the exit of each floor. Defendant placed the tag and the device in the pocket of another jacket on the merchandise rack. He took his own jacket, which he had been carrying with him, and placed it on a table. Leaving his own jacket, defendant put on the leather jacket and walked through the store, still on the same floor, by passing several cash registers. When he headed for the exit from that floor, in the direction of the main floor, he was apprehended by security personnel. . . .

In People v. Spatzier, defendant entered a bookstore on Fulton Street in Hempstead carrying an attaché case. The two co-owners of the store observed the defendant in a ceiling mirror as he browsed through the store. They watched defendant remove a book from the shelf, look up and down the aisle, and place the book in his case. He then placed the case at his feet and continued to browse. . . .

The primary issue in each case is whether the evidence, viewed in the light most favorable to the prosecution, was sufficient to establish the elements of larceny as defined by the Penal Law. . . .

Larceny at common law was defined as a trespassory taking and carrying away of the property of another with intent to steal it. The early common-law courts apparently viewed larceny as defending society against breach of the peace, rather than protecting individual property rights, and therefore placed heavy emphasis upon the requirement of a trespassory taking. . . .

Gradually, the courts began to expand the reach of the offense, initially by subtle alterations in the common-law concept of possession. Thus, for instance, it became a general rule that goods entrusted to an employee were not deemed to be in his possession, but were only considered to be in his custody, so long as he remained on the employer's premises. And, in the case of Chisser (83 Eng.Rep. 142 [1678]), it was held that a shop owner retained legal possession of merchandise being examined by a prospective customer until the actual sale was made. In these situations, the employee and the customer would not have been guilty of larceny if they had first obtained lawful possession of the property from the owner. By holding that they had not acquired possession, but merely custody, the court was able to sustain a larceny conviction.

As the reach of larceny expanded, the intent element of the crime became of increasing importance, while the requirement of a trespassory taking became less significant. As a result, the bar against convicting a person who had initially obtained lawful possession of property faded. In

King v. Pear (168 Eng.Rep. 208 [1779]), for instance, a defendant who had lied about his address and ultimate destination when renting a horse was found guilty of larceny for later converting the horse. Because of the fraudulent misrepresentation, the court reasoned, the defendant had never obtained legal possession. Thus, "larceny by trick" was born.

Later cases went even further, often ignoring the fact that a defendant had initially obtained possession lawfully, and instead focused upon his later intent. The crime of larceny then encompassed, not only situations where the defendant initially obtained property by a trespassory taking, but many situations where an individual, possessing the requisite intent, exercised control over property inconsistent with the continued rights of the owner. During this evolutionary process, the purpose served by the crime of larceny obviously shifted from protecting society's peace to general protection of property rights.[4]

Modern penal statutes generally have incorporated these developments under a unified definition of larceny (see e.g., American Law Institute, Model Penal Code [Tent. Draft No. 1], § 206.1 [theft is appropriation of property of another, which includes unauthorized exercise of control]). Case law, too, now tends to focus upon the actor's intent and the exercise of dominion and control over the property. Indeed, this court has recognized, in construing the New York Penal Law,[5] that the "ancient common-law concepts of larceny" no longer strictly apply.

This evolution is particularly relevant to thefts occurring in modern self-service stores. In stores of that type, customers are impliedly invited to examine, try on, and carry about the merchandise on display. Thus in a sense, the owner has consented to the customer's possession of the goods for a limited purpose. That the owner has consented to that possession does not, however, preclude a conviction for larceny. If the customer exercises dominion and control wholly inconsistent with the continued rights of the owner, and the other elements of the crime are present, a larceny has occurred.[6] Such conduct on the part of a customer satisfies the "taking" element of the crime.

4. One commentator has argued that the concept of possessorial immunity—i.e., that one who obtains possession of property by delivery from the owner cannot be guilty of larceny—stems from a general reluctance of the early common law to criminalize acts arising out of private relationships (Fletcher, Metamorphosis of Larceny, 89 Harv.L.Rev. 469, 472–476). Thus, although an owner deprived of property by a bailee could seek a civil remedy in detinue and later trover, the harm was deemed private and not a matter for societal intervention. Over time, the public-private dichotomy waned and the criminal law increasingly was viewed as an instrument for protecting certain interests and controlling social behavior. As a concomitant development, the criminal law changed its main focus from the objective behavior of the defendant to his subjective intent.

5. Section 155.05 of the Penal Law defines larceny: "1. A person steals property and commits larceny when, with intent to deprive another of property or to appropriate the same to himself or to a third person, he wrongfully takes, obtains, or withholds such property from an owner thereof. 2. Larceny includes a wrongful taking, obtaining or withholding of another's property, with the intent prescribed in subdivision one of this section, committed in any of the following ways: (a) By conduct heretofore defined or known as common law larceny by trespassory taking, common law larceny by trick, embezzlement, or obtaining property by false pretenses."

6. Also, required, of course, is the intent prescribed by subdivision 1 of section 155.05 of the Penal Law, and some move-

It is this element that forms the core of the controversy in these cases. The defendants argue, in essence, that the crime is not established, as a matter of law, unless there is evidence that the customer departed the shop without paying for the merchandise.

Although this court has not addressed the issue, case law from other jurisdictions seems unanimous in holding that a shoplifter need not leave the store to be guilty of larceny. This is because a shopper may treat merchandise in a manner inconsistent with the owner's continued rights—and in a manner not in accord with that of a prospective purchaser—without actually walking out of the store. Indeed, depending upon the circumstances of each case, a variety of conduct may be sufficient to allow the trier of fact to find a taking. It would be well-nigh impossible, and unwise, to attempt to delineate all the situations which would establish a taking. But it is possible to identify some of the factors used in determining whether the evidence is sufficient to be submitted to the fact finder.

In many cases, it will be particularly relevant that defendant concealed the goods under clothing or in a container. Such conduct is not generally expected in a self-service store and may in a proper case be deemed an exercise of dominion and control inconsistent with the store's continued rights. Other furtive or unusual behavior on the part of the defendant should also be weighed. Thus, if the defendant surveys the area while secreting the merchandise or abandoned his or her own property in exchange for the concealed goods, this may evince larcenous rather than innocent behavior. Relevant too is the customer's proximity to or movement towards one of the store's exits. Certainly it is highly probative of guilt that the customer was in possession of secreted goods just a few short steps from the door or moving in that direction. Finally, possession of a known shoplifting device actually used to conceal merchandise, such as a specially designed outer garment or false bottomed carrying case, would be all but decisive.

Of course, in a particular case, any one or any combination of these factors may take on special significance. And there may be other considerations, not now identified, which should be examined. So long as its bears upon the principal issue—whether the shopper exercised control wholly inconsistent with the owner's continued rights—any attending circumstance is relevant and may be taken into account.

Under these principles, there was ample evidence in each case to raise a factual question as to the defendants' guilt. In People v. Olivo, defendant not only concealed goods in his clothing, but he did so in a particularly suspicious manner. And, when defendant was stopped, he was moving towards the door, just three feet short of exiting the store. It cannot be said as a matter of law that these circumstances failed to establish a taking.[8]

ment when property other than an automobile is involved. As a practical matter in shoplifting cases the same evidence which proves the taking will usually involve movement. The movement, or asportation requirement has traditionally been satisfied by a slight moving of the property. This accords with the purpose of the asportation element which is to show that the thief had indeed gained possession and control of the property.

8. As discussed, the same evidence which establishes dominion and control in these circumstances will often establish

In People v. Gasparik, defendant removed the price tag and sensor device from a jacket, abandoned his own garment, put the jacket on and ultimately headed for the main floor of the store. Removal of the price tag and sensor device, and careful concealment of those items, is highly unusual and suspicious conduct for a shopper. Coupled with defendant's abandonment of his own coat and his attempt to leave the floor, those factors were sufficient to make out a prima facie case of a taking.

In People v. Spatzier, defendant concealed a book in an attaché case. Unaware that he was being observed in an overhead mirror, defendant looked furtively up and down an aisle before secreting the book. In these circumstances, given the manner in which defendant concealed the book and his suspicious behavior, the evidence was not insufficient as a matter of law.

In sum, in view of the modern definition of the crime of larceny, and its purpose of protecting individual property rights, a taking of property in the self-service store context can be established by evidence that a customer exercised control over merchandise wholly inconsistent with the store's continued rights. Quite simply, a customer who crosses the line between the limited right he or she has to deal with merchandise and the store owner's rights may be subject to prosecution for larceny. Such a rule should foster the legitimate interests and continued operation of self-service shops, a convenience which most members of the society enjoy.

Accordingly, in each case, the order of the Appellate Term should be affirmed.

People v. Norman

Court of Appeals of New York.
85 N.Y.2d 609, 650 N.E.2d 1303, 627 N.Y.S.2d 302 (1995).

■ TITONE, J.

In each of these cases, the defendants were convicted of larceny after selling goods to customers, taking the customers' money and then failing to deliver the promised goods. Their appeals from the judgments of conviction require us to revisit the specialized requirements for the crimes that were known as larceny by false promise and larceny by false pretenses before the adoption of the Penal Law.

I.

People v Norman

In 1989, according to the trial evidence, defendant entered into a one-year lease on an old sawmill in South Colton, New York, opened a business office in the City of Watertown and began selling kits to individuals wishing to build their own log homes. In June of 1990, Joseph and Sharon Gana,

movement of the property. And, the requisite intent generally may be inferred from all the surrounding circumstances. It would be the rare case indeed in which the evidence establishes all the other elements of the crime but would be insufficient to give rise to an inference of intent.

responding to a newspaper advertisement, contacted defendant and expressed an interest in purchasing one of his log home kits. During their discussions, defendant offered the Ganas the opportunity to become dealers for his product. As dealers, the Ganas would be responsible for allowing prospective customers to see their own log home and would receive a 15% commission on any home they sold or on any sale defendant made as a result of their referral.

On July 19, 1990, the Ganas signed a contract to purchase a log home kit for $20,325. The delivery date was left open because the Ganas needed to dig a foundation before they would be ready to receive their logs. Payment was to be made upon delivery, which, according to defendant, would occur within two weeks of the Ganas' request.

Approximately three weeks after the Ganas signed their contract, defendant called them and stated that he had another couple from their area, the Mikels, who were interested in a dealership. Defendant was prepared to give the Ganas' dealership to this couple unless the Ganas paid for the log home kit by August 9th. According to Sharon Gana, defendant was quite insistent on that date. Anxious not to lose their dealership opportunity, the Ganas obtained a loan and wired defendant the full amount of the purchase price on August 8, 1990. No arrangements for delivery were made at that time, since the Ganas' foundation was still not ready.

In mid-September of 1990, the Ganas told defendant that they were ready for their kit, but, despite defendant's promise to deliver at least part of the material, several weeks passed without a delivery. In the ensuing weeks, defendant offered the Ganas a series of excuses for his failure to deliver, including problems with truckers, problems with the mill, a death in the family, a need for new equipment and a claim that the logs milled for the Ganas had turned black. In the end, the Ganas travelled to defendant's office, arriving just in time to see him packing up his telephone, office items and books. At that point, defendant told the Ganas that he had spent their money and was unable to obtain further materials or supplies without new financing.

A subsequent investigation revealed that defendant's bank account had been overdrawn during the first week in August and that he had used the Ganas' money to pay his personal bills and overdue business debts. Defendant admitted to investigators that none of the money had been used to purchase materials for the Ganas' log home kit.

When asked whether he intended to compensate the Ganas, defendant first told investigators that he was trying to obtain financing based on the equity he had in the mill. He said nothing further on this subject, however, when confronted with the fact that he did not have an ownership interest in the mill.

In addition to the testimony of the Ganas and several investigators, the People elicited testimony from other customers who had purchased log home kits from defendant and had had similarly unsatisfactory experiences. The evidence furnished by these witnesses, which was admitted primarily on the question of defendant's larcenous intent, demonstrated that defendant had several other unfilled orders outstanding at the time he accepted the Ganas' money. It was undisputed that defendant had laid off all of his mill workers and had "shut down" operations at the mill some two weeks before he asked for the Ganas' money.

.... The jury ... found defendant guilty of third degree grand larceny (Penal Law § 155.35).... On defendant's appeal from the judgment of conviction, however, the Appellate Division reversed and dismissed the indictment, holding that the evidence had been insufficient "to show guilty intent on the part of defendant." In so ruling, the Court stressed that defendant's intent not to keep his promise "may not be inferred from the mere nonperformance of the promise" (see, Penal Law § 155.05[2][d]). The People now appeal from that Court's order.

People v King

The incident out of which the charges against defendant King arose began when defendant, who owned a used car business, engaged in a conversation with Carol Bondy, a local print shop owner with whom he had dealt on several occasions. According to the People's trial evidence, Bondy expressed an interest in buying a small Bronco or Jeep for her son, who would soon be returning home after a stint with the Marines. Within a month, defendant called Bondy to tell her that he had seen a Bronco and planned to acquire it for her at an auction. A few weeks later, defendant drove a two-tone Bronco to Bondy's shop and offered to sell it to her. With defendant's permission, Bondy's boyfriend, Karl Rohrbaugh, took the vehicle for a test drive and pronounced it sound. Bondy then agreed to pay $4,977.50 for the vehicle and gave defendant a $2,000 down payment....

The following week, defendant told Bondy that he would need the rest of the money for the Bronco "to get the title processed." Bondy met with defendant and, in Rohrbaugh's presence, gave him the additional $2,977.50. Papers, including one for the Department of Motor Vehicles, were signed.

Despite repeated inquiries, defendant failed to deliver the Bronco to Bondy, instead giving her and Rohrbaugh a series of excuses over the course of some 25 conversations. Finally, approximately four months after Bondy had paid defendant for the car, Rohrbaugh confronted him, demanding that he either deliver the vehicle or return the purchase price. At that point, defendant denied having received the full $4,977.50 from Bondy.... Subsequent investigation revealed that no vehicle meeting the description of the two-tone Bronco was ever registered or titled to defendant....

At the close of the evidence, defense counsel argued that the jury should be instructed on the elements of larceny by false promise. The prosecutor opposed this request, stressing that the People were alleging that defendant was guilty of larceny by false pretenses. In view of the People's position, the trial court charged the jury only on the elements of the latter crime. The jury ultimately found defendant guilty of third degree grand larceny. The Appellate Division upheld the resulting judgment of conviction....

II.

On this appeal, defendant Norman argues that the trial evidence established that he was guilty of no more than an ordinary civil breach of contract and that the exacting requirements for proving criminal larceny by false promise were not satisfied. Defendant King . . . contends that the case against him was erroneously submitted as a larceny by false pretenses rather than a larceny by false promise and that, accordingly, he was wrongly deprived of the benefit of the higher burden of proof that is required in connection with the latter crime. . . .

Historically, the crime of larceny, which was created by English Judges rather than Parliament, was narrowly circumscribed to encompass only trespassory takings, most of which entailed some threat to the public peace. As trade and business expanded, however, the English legal system became more sensitive to the need to protect property owners' interests in personalty. As a consequence, the courts began to create legal fictions which treated certain types of takings as "trespassory" even though the owner had voluntarily relinquished actual physical possession of the property.[1]

For example, a bailee who opened closed bales and misappropriated some or all of the contents was deemed to have committed a "trespassory" taking either because the bailee's possessory right terminated upon the "breaking of the bulk" or because the package's contents, as distinguished from its covering, were deemed to continue in the possession of the bailor. A second category of fictitious "trespassory" takings involved situations in which property that had been entrusted to a person in a special relationship to the owner was nonetheless deemed to have constructively remained in the owner's possession (cf., 39 Geo III, ch 85 [1799] [creating crime of embezzlement]).

The third historical category of larceny, larceny by false pretenses, was originally created as a matter of legislative decree rather than judicial prescription (30 Geo II, ch 24 [1757]).[2] The gravamen of that offense was obtaining property, with the intent permanently to deprive the owner, by fraudulently inducing the owner to part with both possession and title through the use of false statements about some prior or existing facts.[3] As adopted in New York and many other jurisdictions, the crime of larceny by false pretenses did not apply to the act of obtaining money or property by a false promise to do something (such as repaying a loan or delivering goods) in the future. Although a promise accompanied by an intention not to perform could theoretically have been viewed as a false statement of an

1. It has been suggested that the early treatment of all felonies as capital offenses was responsible, at least in part, for the English courts' confinement of the crime of larceny to a relatively narrow class of cases.

2. This shift in the law-making initiative from the judiciary to the legislative body occurred as part of an over-all trend that arose toward the end of the 18th century as a result of a number of factors, including the expansion of the prestige and power of Parliament and a change in the perceived role of Judges from policy-makers to interpreters of "natural law" (see, ALI, Model Penal Code § 223.1, Commentary, at 128–129 [1980]).

3. The common-law crime of "larceny by trick," which had been created by the courts at an earlier point in history, was limited to situations in which possession of, but not title to, the property had been obtained by the wrongdoer's false statements. [See *People v. Olivo*, supra.]

existing fact, most courts, including this one, took the narrowest possible view and held that such conduct did not constitute the crime of larceny by false pretenses. The judicial reluctance to criminalize such conduct was principally derived in concerns about jailing individuals for mere nonpayment of debt and in the courts' sensitivity to the potential chilling effect that criminalizing such conduct might have on business.

It was not until 1965, when the present Penal Law was adopted, that this State recognized the making of a dishonest promise as a crime (Penal Law § 155.05[2][d]). Since that time, the statute defining the crime of larceny has criminalized both wrongful takings by "false promises" and wrongful takings by "false pretenses" (Penal Law § 155.05[2][a], [d]).

With regard to larceny by false pretenses, the Penal Law incorporates the historical elements that were applied at common law, i.e., a false material statement about a past or presently existing fact (Penal Law § 155.05[2][a]). With regard to larceny by false promises, Penal Law § 155.05(2)(d) provides that the crime occurs "when, pursuant to a scheme to defraud, [a person] obtains property of another by means of a representation, express or implied, that he ... will in the future engage in particular conduct, and when he does not intend to engage in such conduct." Thus, as adopted in New York, the crime of larceny by false promise is limited to situations in which an individual has made a promise while harboring a present intention not to perform.

While the two crimes have considerable overlap, it is important not to lose sight of the distinction between them, particularly in light of the special burden of proof that the Legislature has imposed in prosecutions for larceny by false promise. Because of continuing concerns about the need to avoid prosecution for conduct constituting only civil breach of contract, the Legislature has specifically provided that the inference of guilty intent may not be drawn solely from the fact that the defendant's promise was not performed (Penal Law § 155.05[2][d]). Moreover, the Legislature has provided that a conviction of larceny by false promise "may be based only upon evidence establishing that the facts and circumstances of the case are wholly consistent with guilty intent or belief and wholly inconsistent with innocent intent or belief, and excluding to a moral certainty every hypothesis except that of the defendant's intention or belief that the promise would not be performed" (Penal Law § 155.05[2][d]). * * *

IV.

People v Norman

[T]he evidence against this defendant was sufficient to establish his guilt of larceny by false promise on the theory that he took the Ganas' money at a time when he had no intention of delivering the log cabin kit he had promised them. The jury was entitled to believe the evidence that defendant had pressured the Ganas into giving him the full purchase price of the kit they had ordered and had then spent all of their money on past-due personal and business bills without using any of it to purchase materials for their kit. There was also evidence that defendant had laid off his mill workers approximately one week before he took the Ganas' money, that he had closed his bank account shortly after paying his bills and that he was unable to obtain more suppliers or services without new financing. This evidence that, at the time he took the Ganas' money, defendant lacked the wherewithal to perform and had no realistic prospect of changing the situation in the near future provided ample ground for a jury to "[exclude] to a moral certainty every hypothesis except that of defendant's intention or belief that [his] promise would not be performed" (Penal Law § 155.05[2][d]).

The additional evidence that defendant had offered a series of dubious excuses for failing to deliver the victims' logs, that he had business dealings with other customers with similar results and that he had been caught packing up his office equipment when the Ganas went to his office to confront him lent further support to the inference that defendant had intended to bilk the Ganas from the outset. Finally, defendant's patently false statement to investigating officers that he planned to compensate the Ganas by using his equity in the mill—a property he did not own—furnished additional circumstantial proof of his criminal intent at the time he took the Ganas' payment.

.... Accordingly, the Appellate Division erred in holding that defendant's conviction for larceny by false promise should be vacated.

People v King

Defendant King ... seeks to capitalize on the similarity between the crimes of larceny by false pretenses and larceny by false promise. [He] argues that the People's case against him was actually one for larceny by false promise rather than larceny by false pretenses and that the former crime should have been submitted to the jury in place of the latter. The erroneous refusal to submit the case as a larceny by false promise prosecution was highly prejudicial, defendant contends, because it deprived him of the opportunity to have the jury consider the evidence of his intent under the far more exacting standard of proof prescribed for that crime (see, Penal Law § 155.05[2][d]).

[T]his claim ... is utterly lacking in merit. In addition to showing that defendant had made an unfulfilled promise to deliver a particular car, the trial evidence supported the inference that defendant had made a material misrepresentation of fact to Bondy, namely that he owned the vehicle in question and therefore had the power to sell it to her. While defendant never made a specific oral claim that the bronze and beige Bronco was his to sell, his conduct conveyed as surely as a direct statement that he had an interest in the Bronco sufficient to enable him to transfer ownership to her. This conduct included his first telling Bondy that he had seen a particular Bronco and planned to acquire it for her at auction and then bringing a Bronco to Bondy's shop for a test drive. It also included his telling Bondy he needed the rest of her money "to get the title processed" and giving her Department of Motor Vehicle forms to sign.

In sum, there was more to the case against defendant King than a simple false promise made with an intent not to perform. Accordingly, the prosecution was entitled to choose to prosecute him for larceny by false pretenses rather than for larceny by false promise. The fact that the evidence might have also supported a false promise theory is of no moment, since, as long as their theory was supported by the adduced facts, the People had the right to have the case submitted to the jury under the Penal Law subdivision they had chosen.

Accordingly, in People v Norman, the order of the Appellate Division should be reversed and the case remitted to that Court for a review of the facts; in People v King, the order of the Appellate Division should be affirmed.

■ BELLACOSA, J. (Dissenting).

The controlling guidepost for these cases should be the recognition of the steadfast reluctance, resistance and barriers established by the Legislature and the courts against authorizing the transmutation of civil mishaps into felonious inflations. To obscure the central demarcation, that for centuries has marked the boundary between civil and criminal matters in the myriad of ordinary commercial transactions, trivializes true criminality, diverts attention and resources away from victims of true crimes against "the People," and engenders opportunistic manipulation of the criminal processes by unhappy civil suitors for redress of private wrongs and harms. * * *

In formulating the modern, non-common-law brand of larceny by false promise provision, the Commission on Revision of the Penal Law warned "that an unqualified larceny by false promise 'might result in an avalanche of criminal prosecutions based upon conduct essentially civil in character and constituting little more than breach of contract' ". * * *

[I]n my view, these cases ... do not merit prosecutorial cognizance in the criminal hemisphere.

QUESTIONS AND COMMENTS

1. What legal right or interest does the law of larceny protect? *Olivo* and *Norman* explore the origins of larceny in the king's interest in protecting the royal peace, which eventually evolved into the state's interest in protecting the public peace. If today the law of larceny is concerned with protecting individual property rights, what is the function of the "taking" element of larceny? In fact, what function does the conduct element serve in general? Is it mere evidence of larcenous intent? Perhaps it's helpful to think of modern larceny as an (adverse) possession offense: The thief exercises dominion and control (i.e., possession) over an item that once was in the possession of another, with no intention of relinquishing that possession.

2. The story of the metamorphosis of larceny from protecting the peace to protecting individual rights, as recounted in *Olivo* and *Norman*, is now standard (as evidenced by its appearance in judicial opinions). But does contemporary criminal law necessarily treat property as an individual right? Is larceny about protecting an individual's right over a particular item, or is it about protecting the "property system" in general? See Model Penal Code Commentaries § 223.1, at 157. What is the significance of consent? If I give you permission to take an item in my possession—if I give you a birthday present, say—do you escape criminal liability for larceny (a)

because you didn't "take" anything from me, (b) because I can decide to waive my personal right over the item, or (c) because a consensual taking is far less likely to cause a breach of the peace than a nonconsensual one?

What is a breach of peace anyway? Are we worried that an "owner" is more likely in a conventional trespassory taking case to use violence to avert the taking? Is that an empirical claim and if so, how would we know if it were a *true* empirical claim? Or is it that the trespassory taking itself is "violent" or "socially disruptive"? Surely, if one saw a film of a conventional trespassory taking, one would intuit the presence of wrong-doing, while if one saw a film of the money transfer in *Norman*, all one would see is a peaceful, conventional commercial transaction. Does this matter? And if it does, where on the continuum would *Olivo* fit? Note, too, that in *both* the larceny by false pretenses cases (with their rather substantial historical pedigree) and the more recent, more troublesome larceny by false promise cases, the transaction seems, *at the time*, non-disruptive and unexceptional. Recall Stephen Schulhofer's comments on sex induced by fraud, rather than violence (ch. 9): he notes that the victim of sex induced by fraud only discovers *retrospectively* that she has been injured. Should we reserve criminal punishment for situations in which the victim knows that she is being harmed at the moment property is transferred, or *would* know she is being harmed if she knew that her property were being transferred? Why?

3. If larceny is indeed about protecting an individual's possessory interest, then why shouldn't it be limited to a civil action (a tort)? Does the shift from protecting the public peace to protecting individual property rights imply a shift from criminal to civil law, and thereby draw into question the criminalization of larceny? Can the interests and rights affected by larceny be vindicated through civil suits brought against the perpetrator? Contrast larceny with assault, or rape, or homicide. Is the most significant interest we should concern ourselves with in responding to an assault the interest of the victim in bodily integrity or avoiding injury? Why can't *that* interest be vindicated by civil suit? Can the interest of the state in incapacitating those who have shown themselves likely to steal be met without imprisonment? Should the objective of public enforcement of laws against larceny be compensation, rather than punishment? What are the interests of victims of larceny—that they recover their property and/or receive compensation for their loss, or that the thief be punished? See generally Markus Dirk Dubber, Victims in the War on Crime: The Use and Abuse of Victims' Rights pt. II (2002) (outlining a law of victim compensation paralleling the conventional law of offender punishment).

Think about shoplifting. Each of the defendants in *Olivo* was caught before leaving the store. The store suffered no harm. Even if they had succeeded, the financial loss would have been minimal. What is the public interest in prosecuting these cases? What is the victim's interest?

Does it matter if storeowners generally expend (substantial?) resources protecting themselves against shoplifting, or that other shoppers pay higher prices because shoplifters raise costs (both by increasing precautionary expenditures and by diverting otherwise sellable inventory)? What makes theft *inefficient*, from an economist's vantage point, rather than *wrong*, from a moralist's, is that preventing it wastes real resources; the mere transfer from "owner" to "thief" is not in and of itself "inefficient," since the stolen resources are still used by *someone*, but resources expended solely to insure that a particular party maintains control of a resource could better be spent satisfying a demand to consume. This economic view of the harm of theft was forcefully presented by Gordon Tullock, "The Welfare Costs of Tariffs, Monopolies and Theft," 5 W. Econ. J. 224, 228–32 (1967).

4. Now consider larceny by false promise in particular. Why do we need to invoke the criminal law in these cases if we have the law of contracts? Courts tend to stress the distinction between punishing someone for making a promise that she never intended to honor and punishing her for making a promise that she didn't honor. The former is supposed to be a crime, and the latter (merely) a breach of contract. Does this distinction hold water, given that the best evidence of (present) intent not to perform is the fact of (future) nonperformance? Does an instruction that mere nonperformance is, by itself, insufficient evidence of the lack of an intent to perform satisfy your concerns? What about a heightened standard of proof (moral certainty)? Can a substantive weakness—particularly serious questions about criminalization, as in the case of larceny by false promise—be overcome by procedural means? Or do unusually high procedural hurdles suggest that the conduct shouldn't be a crime in the first place?

Then again, why should it matter when I decide not to deliver on a promise—before, while, or after making it? Isn't the victim harmed either way? Does it matter if the defendant attempted to evade a breach of contract suit by *hiding* her breach, or absenting herself from possible service of process? Why might we need the criminal law to deal with a carpenter who (secretly) uses inferior materials that are difficult to discover in building the high-price desk she has promised to make you but not to deal with a carpenter who fails to deliver the desk at all, forcing the buyer to turn to another seller who might cost more? Presumably, some breaches are efficient—it is better for *both* parties if the seller does not perform, at least so long as she pays expectations damages. Assume the carpenter with whom you've contracted promised to build a desk for $1,000 but can't do so without losing $600 on the deal and that you must now pay $1,500 for a desk of the quality she promised (including the cost of locating and contracting with a second cabinetmaker). You will be just as well off if given $500 as you'd be if the promise were kept, and she'd be *better* off; presumably, too, we would collectively prefer that you get an identical desk at a resource cost of $1,500, not $1,600. And so long as she discloses her intention to breach, it is possible that prior to suit, the parties will negotiate a deal that insures *both* parties are better off as a result of breach. (They will somehow split the $100 surplus that results from breach.) Are there any *secret* breaches, though, that benefit both parties (or at least leave both parties uninjured)?

5. What's left of the conduct element in larceny after *Olivo*? The *Olivo* court insists that "some movement" of the property is still required, but then goes on to point out that this so-called asportation requirement has "traditionally been satisfied by a slight moving of the property," in keeping with "the purpose of the asportation element which is to show that

the thief had indeed gained possession and control of the property." In an earlier decision the court had decided that the asportation requirement didn't apply *at all* to car theft:

> A wallet, or a diamond ring, or a safe are totally inert objects susceptible of movement only by physical lifting or shoving by the thief. An automobile, however, is itself an instrument of transportation and when activated comes within the total possession and control of the operator. In this situation movement or motion is not essential to control. Absent any evidence that the vehicle is somehow fastened or immovable because of a mechanical defect, the thief has taken command of the object of the larceny. He has ... wrongfully "taken" the property from its owner....
>
> Consistency is always desirable in the application of the various laws.... An established line of authority ... holds that for purposes of offenses for driving while intoxicated ..., operation of the vehicle is established on proof that the defendant was merely behind the wheel with the engine running without need for proof that defendant was observed driving the car, i.e., operating it so as to put it in motion.... It would be difficult to understand how a person who is operating a car, as defendant was under the authority just discussed, could be said nevertheless not to be in possession and control of that car.

People v. Alamo, 34 N.Y.2d 453, 315 N.E.2d 446 (1974).

Other courts stress the distinction between offenses that contain an element of "taking" and those that are defined in terms of "carrying away," and hold that only the latter require asportation, on the ground that "the plain meaning of 'taking' does not necessarily impute an asportation requirement." See, e.g., People v. Lopez, 31 Cal.4th 1051, 79 P.3d 548, 6 Cal.Rptr.3d 432 (2003) (carjacking); cf. Carter v. United States, 530 U.S. 255, 272 (2000) (comparing 18 U.S.C. § 2113(a) ("takes") with 18 U.S.C. § 2113(b) ("takes and carries away")). Do you agree?

In *Alamo*, the defendant was observed in the car, which was in the right lane, with its headlights on and the motor running. The wheels were pointing to the left and the car was "inching out" into the street. Why isn't he (and the defendants in *Olivo*) guilty of attempted larceny, but not of consummated larceny? And what relevance does the interpretation of the term "operate" in a DWI statute in the traffic code have for the interpretation of the term "take" in a larceny statute in the criminal code?

If asportation is merely evidence of possession, why don't we just abandon the asportation as an element of larceny and define it exclusively in terms of possession? See Model Penal Code § 223.2(1) ("A person is guilty of theft if he unlawfully takes, *or exercises unlawful control over*, movable property of another with purpose to deprive him thereof."). If the legislature doesn't do away with asportation, is a court entitled to do so (for all larcenies, for only some)?

6. What's left of the mens rea of larceny after *Olivo*? Having relegated the actus reus of larceny to a supporting (evidentiary) role, the court holds that "the requisite intent generally may be inferred from all the surrounding circumstances." But it's these same circumstances that, ac-

cording to the court, establish asportation and, by implication, possession. Is possession of another's property in suspicious circumstances enough for larceny liability?

7. *Olivo* and *Norman* illustrate three common varieties of larceny (trespassory taking, larceny by false pretenses and by false promise) and mention several others (embezzlement and larceny by trick). The New York criminal jury instructions try to capture the distinctions among these offenses:

> Larceny by Trespassory Taking
>
> A person steals property and commits larceny when, with the intent to deprive another of property or to appropriate the same to himself or herself [*or* to a third person], such person wrongfully takes, obtains, or withholds such property from an owner of the property.
>
> A person wrongfully takes, obtains or withholds property from an owner when that person takes, obtains or withholds property without an owner's consent, and exercises dominion and control over that property for a period of time, however temporary, in a manner wholly inconsistent with the owner's rights.
>
> Larceny by Embezzlement
>
> A person [also] wrongfully takes, obtains, or withholds property from an owner when, having been entrusted to hold such property on behalf of the owner, such person thereafter, without the permission or authority of the owner, intentionally exercises control over it in a manner inconsistent with the continued rights of the owner, knowing that he has no permission or authority to do so.
>
> Larceny by Trick
>
> A person [also] wrongfully takes, obtains, or withholds property from an owner when that person engages in some trick, fraudulent device, or artifice, and thereby obtains possession of the property, and exercises possession over that property for a period of time, however temporary, in a manner inconsistent with the continued rights of the owner.
>
> Larceny by False Pretense
>
> A person [also] wrongfully takes, obtains or withholds property from an owner when that person makes a false representation of a past or existing fact while aware that such representation is false, and obtains possession and title to the property as a result of the owner's reliance upon such representation.
>
> Larceny by False Promise
>
> A person [also] wrongfully takes, obtains, or withholds property when, pursuant to a scheme to defraud, he obtains property of another by means of a representation, express or implied, that he or she or a third person will in the future engage in particular conduct, and when he does not intend to engage in such conduct or, as the case may be, does not believe that the third person intends to engage in such conduct.

CJI2d [NY] Penal Law art. 155 (http://www.nycourts.gov/cji/3–Penal-Law/155/art155hp.htm).

It is not always easy to distinguish between the above types of larceny. (For instance, what's the difference between larceny by trick and larceny by false pretenses?) As the court in *Norman* points out, a larceny by false promise can be construed as a larceny by false pretenses since "a promise accompanied by an intention not to perform could theoretically have been viewed as a false statement of an existing fact," namely that I have no intention to perform as promised. See United States v. Shah, 44 F.3d 285 (5th Cir. 1995) ("a false promise fraudulently given amounts to a false statement of an existing intent"). Then what's the point of having a crime of larceny by false promise at all? Should the decision about which type of larceny to charge be left up to prosecutors, especially if one type of larceny is more difficult to prove than another (as in *Norman*)? Why don't we simply set out a broad definition of larceny (taking another's property with the intent to deprive him thereof permanently) and then let prosecutors decide how best to convince a jury (or a judge, in a bench trial) that each of the elements of larceny have been satisfied, instead of adhering to an outdated taxonomy of larceny? But see People v. Foster, 73 N.Y.2d 596 (1989) (rejecting prosecution's attempt to prove larceny on a theory not explicitly enumerated in criminal code, "wrongful taking of property through a deliberate and deceitful misuse of the judicial process"; the defendants-lawyers were charged with having executed upon a default judgment against a former client that they knew to have been obtained by improper service).

As a classification exercise, consider the following provision on gas station "drive-offs" (a.k.a. "gas-and-dashes"):

N.C. Gen. Stat. § 14–72.5. Larceny of Motor Fuel.

(a) If any person shall take and carry away motor fuel valued at less than one thousand dollars ($1,000) from an establishment where motor fuel is offered for retail sale with the intent to steal the motor fuel, that person shall be guilty of a . . . misdemeanor.

(c) Conviction Report Sent to Division of Motor Vehicles.

The court shall report final convictions of violations of this section to the Division of Motor Vehicles. The Division of Motor Vehicles shall revoke a person's drivers license for a second or subsequent conviction under this section. . . .

Under the N.Y. larceny scheme, would this provision be necessary or could drive-offs be prosecuted under the existing larceny provisions?

8. Some other types of larceny deserve mention as well. One is *larceny by acquiring lost property*. If I find someone else's wallet on the sidewalk and pick it up with no intention of returning it, or if UPS mistakenly drops off my neighbor's package at my house, I wouldn't qualify for traditional larceny, since I wouldn't have "taken" the wallet—or the package—out of another's possession. The wallet, after all, was no longer in anyone's possession when I picked it up, and the package's possessor simply gave me the package. The modern law of larceny, however, fills this perceived gap in criminalization by creating another type of larceny: "A

person acquires lost property when he exercises control over property of another which he knows to have been lost or mislaid, or to have been delivered under a mistake as to the identity of the recipient or the nature or amount of the property, without taking reasonable measures to return such property to the owner." N.Y. Penal Law § 155.05(2)(b). But why should it be my job to make up for another's mistakes or simple carelessness? I might have a moral obligation to do so, but do I have a legal duty? If so, should this duty be *criminally* enforced? Should I be punished as a thief for not dropping off a pair of sunglasses at the Lost and Found? For not returning the extra CD that amazon.com sent me by mistake? Compare the scope of this type of larceny with the scope of omission liability in general. See ch. 4.

Issuing a bad check may also be treated as larceny. See, e.g., N.Y. Penal Law § 155.05(2)(c). Writing a rubber check is a crime in and of itself, but if it results in my obtaining another's property in exchange for the bad check, then I may well be guilty of larceny. (Why do we need this crime if we already criminalize larceny by false pretense and by false promise?) In a typical version of a bad check statute, I must know that I don't have enough money in my bank account to cover the check at the time I'm making it out, plus I have to intend or at least believe that the bank won't cash it, and the bank must in fact refuse the check when it is presented. N.Y. Penal Law § 190.05. These requirements may sound demanding. The prosecution, however, gets to invoke a number of presumptions to lighten its burden of proof, including that I'm presumed to *know* I don't have sufficient funds to cover the check if I in fact did not have sufficient funds. Id. § 190.10. (Is that a defensible presumption? See ch. 4.)

Finally, there is *larceny by extortion*, as defined (again quite typically) in the New York Penal Law:

> A person obtains property by extortion when he compels or induces another person to deliver such property to himself or to a third person by means of instilling in him a fear that, if the property is not so delivered, the actor or another will:
>
> (i) Cause physical injury to some person in the future; or
>
> (ii) Cause damage to property; or
>
> (iii) Engage in other conduct constituting a crime; or
>
> (iv) Accuse some person of a crime or cause criminal charges to be instituted against him; or
>
> (v) Expose a secret or publicize an asserted fact, whether true or false, tending to subject some person to hatred, contempt or ridicule; or . . .
>
> (ix) Perform any other act which would not in itself materially benefit the actor but which is calculated to harm another person materially with respect to his health, safety, business, calling, career, financial condition, reputation or personal relationships.

N.Y. Penal Law § 155.05(2)(e).

Extortion differs from the other varieties of larceny in that it involves compulsion of one sort or another. (Note that it requires the threat, not the infliction, of harm. Would you classify extortion as a violent crime, then? As a crime against the person?) Then again, it too criminalizes taking possession of another's possession. In fact, why do we even need extortion as a separate crime? Isn't extortion simply one way in which the possessor's consent to my taking possession of his property is absent, or at least ineffective? Does it matter whether my consent is obtained through fraud or through compulsion? See the discussion of consent in ch. 7.

Think of extortion as larceny plus coercion. Coercion is compelling another "to engage in conduct which the latter has a legal right to abstain from engaging in ... by means of instilling in him a fear that" he will suffer physical injury to his person or damage to his property. See N.Y. Penal Law § 135.60. Extortion then is coercion used to extract property. People v. Eboli, 34 N.Y.2d 281 (1974).

One variety of extortion, "blackmail," has befuddled commentators for some time. See, e.g., James Lindgren, "Unraveling the Paradox of Blackmail," 84 Colum. L. Rev. 670 (1984). Here I am not threatening you with violence (or other criminal conduct), but with conduct that is, by itself, not criminal at all. N.Y. Penal Law § 155.05(2)(e)(iv), (v), & (ix). There is nothing obviously criminal about "[a]ccus[ing] some person of a crime or caus[ing] criminal charges to be instituted against him," nor about "[e]xpos[ing] a secret or publiciz[ing] an asserted fact, whether true or false, tending to subject some person to hatred, contempt or ridicule." Note that, on the face of the statute, it makes no difference whether the accusation is true, or even whether I believe it to be true.

Why shouldn't I be permitted to threaten a thief with reporting him to the police, in the hope of getting him to return my laptop? (Thieves can be the victims of larceny. Larceny from the outset has protected possessory, not ownership, interests. See 2 Frederick Pollock & Frederic William Maitland, The History of English Law Before the Time of Edward I, at 498 (2d ed. 1898) (" 'larceny' involves a violation of possession; it is an offence against a possessor"). As long as the thief is in possession of a thing, it can be stolen from her.)

And may it not be good negotiation strategy to threaten the person across the table with acts that might harm her "business, calling, career, financial condition, reputation or personal relationships," even if I don't "materially benefit" from these acts themselves? Where does forceful bargaining end, and criminal blackmail begin? And why shouldn't a victim of blackmail be expected to simply refuse payment, even if she might be exposed to "ridicule" as a result? Why should the blackmailer have to keep a dirty secret? Or is compulsion always criminal, provided it forces a person to do (or not do) something against her will? Recall the discussion of coercion in the context of rape (see ch. 9). Is it possible to distinguish situations in which a party is subject to compulsion from situations in which she is "free"? So long as our choice sets are limited, aren't we always subject to some degree of compulsion?

Rather than doing away with the crime of blackmail altogether, legislatures instead have tried to carve out limited defenses to it. For instance, the New York Penal Law provides that "[i]n any prosecution for larceny by extortion committed by instilling in the victim a fear that he or another person would be charged with a crime, it is an affirmative defense that the defendant reasonably believed the threatened charge to be true and that his sole purpose was to compel or induce the victim to take reasonable action to make good the wrong which was the subject of such threatened charge." N.Y. Penal Law § 155.15(2). Here the drafters had in mind the car owner who uses the threat of a criminal complaint to encourage the recalcitrant neighborhood kid to repair the car mirror he broke off throwing around a football in the street. (What if he merely threatens to tell the boy's mother?) How would you classify this defense? If it is a justification, why do we need it at all? Could a broadly conceived necessity (consent?) defense cover the relevant situations?

9. In the face of the cornucopia of larcenies, it might be useful to think about how larceny in general differs from other, related, offenses. Larceny requires an intent to permanently deprive another of possession (the *animus furandi*). The offense of *joyriding* does not. Taking your neighbor's new car for a spin around the block—without getting permission first—doesn't amount to larceny, as long as you always intended to put it back where you found it. That's not to say, however, that you didn't commit a (lesser) crime, just that you didn't commit a full-blown larceny. See, e.g., N.Y. Penal Law § 165.05 (unauthorized use of a vehicle).

Robbery, like larceny, requires *animus furandi*, but, unlike larceny, also requires the use or threatened use of physical force. It requires not just stealing, but *forcible* stealing. See, e.g., N.Y. Penal Law § 160.00 ("A person forcibly steals property and commits robbery when, in the course of committing a larceny, he uses or threatens the immediate use of physical force upon another person for the purpose of (1) [p]reventing or overcoming resistance to the taking of the property or to the retention thereof immediately after the taking; or (2) [c]ompelling the owner of such property or another person to deliver up the property or to engage in other conduct which aids in the commission of the larceny."). What's the difference between larceny by extortion and robbery, then? Why is robbery conventionally punished so much more harshly?

Once again, cars don't quite fit the mold. We've already noted that many courts do away with the asportation element in ordinary car thefts. When it comes to car *robbery*, legislatures have minted an entirely separate offense, *carjacking*. Carjacking, unlike traditional robbery and larceny, however, requires no *animus furandi*. This omission was intentional; legislatures felt the need for a carjacking statute partly because "many carjackings cannot be charged as robbery because it is difficult to prove the intent required of a robbery offense (to permanently deprive one of the car) since many of these gang carjackings are thrill seeking thefts." See People v. Lopez, 6 Cal.Rptr.3d 432, 79 P.3d 548 (2003) (quoting legislative history). The California Penal Code, then, defines carjacking as "the felonious taking of a motor vehicle in the possession of another, from his or her person or immediate presence ... against his or her will and with the intent to either permanently or temporarily deprive the person in possession of the motor vehicle of his or her possession, accomplished by means of force or fear." Cal. Penal Code § 215(a).

Another crime that has much in common with larceny is *burglary*. Burglary, like larceny, traditionally has required a "trespass," though in the case of burglary the trespass was upon a piece of real—rather than of personal—property. The classical definition of burglary is "breaking and entering" a building with the intent to commit a crime therein. But just as larceny no longer looks to concepts such as "breaking bulk," burglary too has moved away from the once crucial element of "breaking in" (like smashing a window, or prying open a locked door).

Interestingly, as the trespassory element of larceny has been watered down, so the trespassory element of modern burglary law no longer requires creating a breach or opening, no matter how small—as opposed to, say, simply slipping through an open door. Not even an unlawful *entry* may be required, as "remain[ing] unlawfully" in the building may suffice. See, e.g., N.Y. Penal Law § 140.20; cf. People v. Gaines, 74 N.Y.2d 358 (1989) ("remaining unlawful" clause designed to reach not unlawful entry, but "unauthorized remaining in a building after lawful entry (as a shoplifter who remains on store premises after closing," i.e., after termination of the "license or privilege" to enter)). (Another element of burglary that has faded away is the requirement that the break-in occur at night. But see State v. Cox, 280 N.C. 689, 187 S.E.2d 1 (1972) (holding that, even though state burglary statute makes no reference to the time of commission, "the common law required the felonious breaking and entering to occur in the nighttime, and this common law requirement is still the law in North Carolina"). Predictably, the definition of "night" has proved somewhat difficult. Compare State v. Frank, 284 N.C. 137, 200 S.E.2d 169 (1973) ("the law considers it to be nighttime when it is so dark that a man's face cannot be identified except by artificial light or moonlight") with Model Penal Code § 221.0(2) (defining "night," for purposes of burglary, as "the period between thirty minutes past sunset and thirty minutes before sunrise"); see also State v. Squalls, 65 N.C.App. 599, 309 S.E.2d 558 (1983) (evidence that defendant loaded up his car with a t.v. at 9 p.m. suffices for burglary charge "since 9 o'clock at night in January in this longitude is two hours or more after darkness begins"). In some, but not all, jurisdictions, a defendant can be guilty of burglary if he enters a store, generally open to the public, intending to steal. See, e.g., People v. Wilson, 160 Cal.App.2d 606, 325 P.2d 106 (1958) (affirming burglary conviction for shoplifting on the ground that "[o]ne who enters a store with the intent of committing larceny is guilty of burglary although the entry was made through the public entrance during business hours"). Given these developments, can classical and modern burglary be said to protect the same interests?

Burglary is related to larceny in another sense; the crime the burglar intended to commit once inside tended to be larceny. The definition of burglary, however, is generally not limited to larcenous intent. Procedurally speaking, it's enough if the state can prove that the defendant intended to commit *some* crime inside the building. Cf. People v. Mackey, 49 N.Y.2d 274 (1980) (no need to specify which crime was intended).

Unlike larceny, burglary does not require an actual taking of property; trespassing with the *intent* to steal suffices. And yet burglary is punished more harshly than "mere" larceny. Why do you think that is? And why do we need a crime of burglary at all? Why don't we just punish the illegal entry, plus whatever other crimes are committed inside the house? And if I get caught before I can commit the crime I planned to commit inside, why isn't it enough to punish me for an attempt to commit that crime, in addition to the illegal entry?

The emergence of the offense of burglary as an independent felony (as opposed to the combination of trespass and another offense, most often larceny) has been attributed to perceived "deficiencies in the early law of attempt: that an attempt could not be penalized until the last act short of completion had occurred, and that the conduct was in any event punishable only as a misdemeanor." *Gaines*, supra. Under the modern law of attempt, which follows the Model Penal Code in expanding attempt liability beyond the last proximate act to any "substantial step" and in punishing attempts (almost) as harshly as consummated offenses, what's the point of burglary? See ch. 6. (For another offense that constitutes an inchoate form of larceny, see N.Y. Penal Law § 165.25 (jostling)).

10. *Claim of Right*. The law of larceny early on developed an offense-specific defense, "claim of right." (Compare the offense-specific defenses in the traditional law of homicide. See ch. 10.) It still appears in modern criminal codes. See, e.g., Model Penal Code § 223.1(3) ("It is an affirmative defense to prosecution for theft that the actor: (a) was unaware that the property or service was that of another; or (b) acted under an honest claim of right to the property or service involved or that he had a right to acquire or dispose of it as he did; or (c) took property exposed for sale, intending to purchase and pay for it promptly, or reasonably believing that the owner, if present, would have consented."). But what is the status of the claim of right defense? Is it anything other than an element-negating mistake defense? But then how can it be an *affirmative* defense, given that the state is constitutionally required to prove every offense element? And why do we need it in the first place, given the law of mistake? Consider the following case.

> In 1969 Local 246 of the Journeymen Barbers' International Union of America of Rochester embarked on the construction of an apartment house project to be located in the Town of Greece in Monroe County. Barbers Realty and Holding Corporation was formed as the corporate vehicle for the project. Vincent A. Verrone, business agent for the union, became the corporate president and Vincent J. Rallo was appointed secretary. After another law firm had been legal counsel for the project for a year and a half, when additional financing was needed the corporation retained the law firm of which defendant Lawrence D. Chesler was a partner. Inasmuch as defendant customarily handled the firm's commercial transactions, he was assigned to work with the new client.
>
> On August 17, 1971 the corporation obtained a building loan from a New York City lender in the amount of $3,440,000. Defendant's law firm represented the corporate borrower on the closing and arranged for the deposit of a portion, said to be $190,109.45, of the proceeds of the construction loan in the law firm's special trust account for the purpose of paying certain creditors. Thereafter defendant, assertedly at

the direction of Verrone or Rallo, drew checks on the account to a number of creditors and on occasion to Verrone and Rallo, allegedly as repayment of funds they were said to have advanced on behalf of the corporation.

Defendant was indicted [and convicted] ... for larceny in violation of section 79–a of the Lien Law. * * * That section provides as follows:

"§ 79–a. Misappropriation of funds of trust

"1. Any trustee of a trust ... who applies ... trust funds ... for any purpose other than the trust purposes of that trust, ... is guilty of larceny and punishable as provided in the penal law....

"2. Notwithstanding subdivision one of this section, if the application of trust funds for a purpose other than the trust purposes of the trust is a repayment to another person of advances made by such other person to the trustee ... and the advances so repaid were actually applied for the purposes of the trust ..., such application ... shall be deemed justifiable and the trustee ... shall not be deemed guilty of larceny by reason of such application...."

Initially it must be noted that nothing in this statute suggests that the Legislature intended therein to create a "strict liability" offense, i.e., that for a conviction the prosecutor is not required to prove any culpable mental state on the part of the defendant. Subdivision 2 of section 15.15 of the Penal Law is pertinent. It provides: "2. Although no culpable mental state is expressly designated in a statute defining an offense, a culpable mental state may nevertheless be required for the commission of such offense, or with respect to some or all of the material elements thereof, if the proscribed conduct necessarily involves such culpable mental state. A statute defining a crime, unless clearly indicating a legislative intent to impose strict liability, should be construed as defining a crime of mental culpability. This subdivision applies to offenses defined both in and outside this chapter." Indeed, "larceny", the crime of which violation of subdivision 1 of section 79–a is explicitly made a particular instance, is defined as requiring on the part of the defendant the "intent to deprive another of property or to appropriate the same to himself or to a third person" (Penal Law, § 155.05, subd. 1). Thus, to obtain a conviction the burden is unmistakably on the prosecutor to prove the requisite criminal intent beyond a reasonable doubt.

There can be no doubt in this instance that an assertion that the payments were made in good faith by defendant from the law firm's special trust account to those whom he believed to be creditors who had advanced funds for construction of the project is the obverse of the contention that the payments were made with intent to deprive another of property and to appropriate it to a third person. Then to apply section 155.15, which explicitly makes it an affirmative defense "that the property was appropriated under a claim of right made in good faith" thus, in consequence of subdivision 2 of section 25.00, placing the burden of proof on the defendant to establish such defense by a preponderance of the evidence would be to prescribe a constitutionally

> impermissible shift in that burden in this instance. Such a shift in burden of proof is precisely what the Supreme Court of the United States has struck down (Mullaney v. Wilbur, 421 U.S. 684, 95 S.Ct. 1881; Matter of Winship, 397 U.S. 358, 90 S.Ct. 1068).

People v. Chesler, 50 N.Y.2d 203 (1980).

If claim of right is—as *Chesler* holds—but a particular instance of a mistake defense that negatives an offense element—the *animus furandi*, say—then one would expect that it would be available as a defense to any offense that contains that offense element. That is not so, however. The New York Penal Law limits the claim of right defense to larceny by trespassory taking or embezzlement. N.Y. Penal Law § 155.15(1). Why? (No similar limitation appears in the Model Penal Code version of the defense.) The defense has also been held inapplicable to robbery:

> Defendant Edward Reid was [convicted of] three counts of robbery in the first degree [and] one count of criminal possession of a weapon in the third degree.... The convictions stem from defendant's forcible taking of money from three others. The evidence established that defendant and his stepbrother, Andre McLean, approached Arthur Taylor, Donnie Peterson and Donald Thompson, while the three men were standing on a street corner in The Bronx. Defendant and McLean were holding pistols when defendant demanded that the three men hand over money "that belonged to him," apparently referring to money owed him as the result of prior drug transactions....
>
> Defendant Walter Riddles was indicted for robbery in the second degree and assault in the second degree. He was convicted after a bench trial of robbery in the third degree for forcibly taking money from Genevieve Bellamy on November 10, 1982.... [Riddles] testified that he knew Bellamy prior to the incident and that she owed him $25. He stated that he met her on the evening of November 10 and she offered to pay him $15 toward her debt if he drove her downtown so she could pick up a package. Defendant maintained that he took Bellamy downtown, as she asked, but that she was unable to obtain her package so he drove her back uptown. Defendant testified that during the return trip, Bellamy again offered to pay him $15 toward her debt, but upon seeing her counting a large sum of money, he took the full amount she owed him, $25, and no more....
>
> Since a good-faith claim of right is a defense to larceny, and because robbery is defined as forcible larceny, defendants contend that claim of right is also a defense to robbery. They concede the culpability of their forcible conduct, but maintain that because they acted under a claim of right to recover their own property, they were not guilty of robbery, but only some lesser crime, such as assault or unlawful possession of a weapon. Defendants' general contention is not without support. Several jurisdictions have held that one who acts under a claim of right lacks the intent to steal and should not be convicted of robbery. That logic is tenable when a person seeks to recover a specific chattel. It is less so when asserted under the circumstances presented in these two cases: in Reid to recover the proceeds of crime, and in Riddles, to recover cash to satisfy a debt.

> [W]e conclude that the claim of right defense is not available in these cases. We need not decide the quite different question of whether an individual who uses force to recover a specific chattel which he owns may be convicted of robbery. It should be noted, however, that because taking property "from an owner thereof" is an element of robbery, a person who recovers property which is his own (as compared to the fungible cash taken to satisfy a claimed debt in the cases before us) may not be guilty of robbery (see Penal Law § 35.25 [indicating that a person would be justified in using nondeadly force to prevent an apparent larcenist from taking his property]).
>
> The claim of right defense is found in the larceny article of the Penal Law, which provides that a good-faith claim of right is a defense to trespassory larceny or embezzlement. The defense does not apply to all forms of larceny. For example, extortion is a form of larceny, but the Legislature, consistent with a prior decision of this court, has not authorized a claim of right defense to extortion. The exception is significant for extortion entails the threat of actual or potential force or some form of coercion....
>
> Our decision also rests upon policy considerations against expanding the area of permissible self-help. Manifestly, a larceny, in which the accused reacquires property belonging to him without using force, differs from a robbery in which the defendant obtains money allegedly owed to him by threatening or using force. "The former is an instance of mistake, not subjected to penal sanctions because the threat to private property is not so serious as to warrant intervention by the criminal law. The latter is a species of self help and whether or not the exponent of force or threats is correct in estimating his rights, he is resorting to extra-judicial means in order to protect a property interest" (Note, A Rationale of the Law of Aggravated Theft, 54 Colum.L.Rev. 84, 98 [1954]). Since such forcible conduct is not merely a transgression against property, but also entails the risk of physical or mental injury to individuals, it should be subjected to criminal sanctions.

People v. Reid, 69 N.Y.2d 469 (1987).

Contrast the claim of right defense with the defense of property, discussed in ch. 7. As the court explains, New York law authorizes the use of nondeadly force to prevent or terminate a larceny. See also Model Penal Code § 3.06(1). In fact, New York even authorizes the use of *deadly* force to prevent or terminate a burglary. N.Y. Penal Law § 35.20(3). The defense of property is generally classified as a justification. Why would the attempt to prevent a larceny provide a justification, and the attempt to recover stolen property negate an offense element? Does the use of force explain the difference? In general, shouldn't claim of right count as a justification, insofar as it is based on a claim that the defendant "had a *right* to acquire" the property? See Model Penal Code § 223.1(3)(b) (emphasis added).

Could we do away with the claim of right defense if we turned to the law of mistake (see Model Penal Code § 223.1(3)(a)), the law of necessity and defense of property (id. § 223.1(3)(b)), and the law of consent (id. § 223.1(3)(c))? Or is the entire claim of right defense simply a collection of mistakes, regarding various offense elements and the availability of various (justification) defense elements? If we think about claim of right as a question of the justification of necessity, would *Reid* come out differently? Would it be sufficient to punish the defendant in *Reid* for aggravated assault, rather than robbery, if he indeed could not be convicted of larceny, given his claim of right?

B. MAIL FRAUD

1. SCOPE AND RELATION TO LARCENY

United States v. Handakas

United States Court of Appeals for the Second Circuit.
286 F.3d 92 (2002).

■ DENNIS JACOBS, CIRCUIT JUDGE.

Vassilios K. Handakas appeals from the judgment of conviction and sentence entered in the United States District Court for the Eastern District of New York, following his conviction by a jury of (inter alia) conspiracy to commit mail fraud by depriving the New York City School Construction Authority ("SCA") of its "intangible right of honest services"....

The mail fraud conspiracy count arises out of work done for the SCA by a Handakas-owned construction company and the violation of [1] the "prevailing rate of wage" contract provision required by New York's "Little Davis–Bacon Act," and [2] other certification and reporting requirements in the construction contracts. The government's deprivation of "honest services" theory was all that was left of the mail fraud charge after a special jury verdict absolved Handakas of the alternative theory that Handakas conspired to defraud the SCA of its "money or property."

On appeal, Handakas ... argues ... that his mail fraud conviction cannot stand because the "honest services" provision of the mail fraud statute is unconstitutionally vague....

Handakas, in his capacity as president and sole shareholder of Astro Waterproofing Restoration Company ("Astro"), submitted a number of successful general contracting bids to the SCA, a public benefit corporation that oversees construction projects performed on New York City schools. The mail fraud conviction arises out of his wilful breach of certain contractual obligations undertaken by Astro.

In awarding its contracts, the SCA follows state law mandating that, inter alia: [1] the SCA award all contracts to the lowest qualified bidder, see N.Y. Pub. Auth. Law § 1734; and [2] the successful bidder pay project workers "prevailing rate of wages," and submit certified payroll records that so certify as a condition of receiving payment. N.Y. Lab. Law § 220, et seq. Under § 220, "any person or corporation that wilfully pays ... less than [the] stipulated wage scale ... shall be guilty of a misdemeanor and

. . . shall be punished for such first offense by a fine of five hundred dollars or by imprisonment for not more than thirty days. . . ."

In the course of the projects, Handakas submitted certified payroll records that reflected compliance with the prevailing rate of wage requirement. Handakas, in fact, paid his workers substantially less than half the prevailing rate of wage.

Additionally, there was evidence that Handakas left certain workers's names off the payroll and fraudulently substituted other names, that he manipulated the record of the number of hours worked, and that the SCA paid Handakas based upon his false submissions. It is, however, doubtful that the government is entitled to the benefit of findings and inferences based on this evidence, which bears upon possible financial harm to the SCA. Although the government argued to the jury that the SCA suffered financial loss, i.e., that the SCA was deprived of money or property as well as "honest services," the jury found by special verdict that Handakas was guilty of mail fraud only on the ground that he deprived the SCA of its "intangible right of honest services"—and not on the ground that the SCA was deprived of money or property. * * *

The elements of mail fraud are: [1] "a scheme or artifice to defraud," [2] furthered by the use of interstate mail, [3] to deprive another of money, property, or "the intangible right of honest services." 18 U.S.C. §§ 1341, 1346. The first element requires: [i] the existence of a scheme to defraud, [ii] specific intent to defraud on the part of the defendant, and [iii] material misrepresentations. The second element is satisfied if the mail is used or if its use is reasonably foreseeable. The first two elements are easily satisfied on this record.

As to the third element, the statutory wording requires that there be a deprivation of money, property, or "the intangible right of honest services." 18 U.S.C. §§ 1341, 1346. At trial, the government contended that the SCA suffered loss on all three scores. The theory of "honest services" argued to the jury by the government was that "the SCA had a right to determine how its contracts would be fulfilled," and that Handakas "took away that right."

As to whether the SCA was deprived of "money or property," conflicting evidence was adduced at trial. That question was then decided via a special verdict form, supplied by the district court, which separately asked whether the SCA was deprived [i] of money or property, or [ii] of "honest services." The jury checked off only that the SCA was deprived of "honest services." The district court thus carefully assured that each theory of the prosecution would be separately considered and decided. As a result, this case compels us to review in isolation a conviction for theft of "honest services." * * *

The Due Process Clauses of the Fifth and Fourteenth Amendments require the legislature to specify the elements of criminal offenses. "There are no constructive offenses; and, before one can be punished, it must be shown that his case is plainly within the statute." Fasulo v. United States, 272 U.S. 620, 629, 47 S. Ct. 200 (1926). A criminal statute is void for vagueness if it fails to give notice of the conduct prohibited or fails to channel the discretion of the prosecution....

The doctrine of "honest services" was originally judge-made law. Courts construed the term "any scheme or artifice to defraud" to include schemes to deprive another of "the intangible right of honest services."

Over time, the "honest services" doctrine became applicable to four general categories of defendants: [1] government officials who defraud the public of their own honest services; [2] elected officials and campaign workers who falsify votes and thereby defraud the electorate of the right to an honest election; [3] private actors who abuse fiduciary duties by, for example, taking bribes; and [4] private actors who defraud others of certain intangible rights, such as privacy. McNally v. United States, 483 U.S. 350, 362–64 n.1, 107 S. Ct. 2875–84 (1987) (Stevens, J., dissenting) (surveying the pre-*McNally* scope of the doctrine).

Within these four categories, the doctrine grew in an "uneven" way, case-by-case and circuit-by-circuit; and court after court warned of prosecutorial abuse. United States v. Lemire, 720 F.2d 1327, 1336 n.11 (D.C. Cir. 1983) ("If merely depriving the victim of the loyalty and faithful service of his fiduciary constitutes criminal fraud ... disloyalty alone becomes the crime, [and] little remains before every civil wrong is potentially indictable."); Geraldine Szott Moohr, Mail Fraud and the Intangible Rights Doctrine: Someone to Watch over Us, 31 Harvard J. on Legis. 153, 179 (1994) ("Incremental progression of ... the intangible rights doctrine ... is an excellent example of judicial crime creation. Prosecutors ... bring previously undefined conduct to trial in the hope that the court will criminalize it.").

Until 1987, courts continued to uphold convictions for theft of "honest services," relying on a 1909 Congressional amendment to § 1341 which supposedly expanded the statute's scope beyond deprivations of money or property. In 1987, however, the Supreme Court held that the amendment actually was intended only to codify an earlier Supreme Court holding (which had done no more than expand the definition of "property" in § 1341); mail fraud prosecutions were therefore limited by the Court to deprivations of money or property. *McNally*, 483 U.S. at 358, 360. Citing principles of federalism and separation of powers, *McNally* reasoned that it was wrong for the federal judiciary to "set[] standards of disclosure and good government for local and state officials."

McNally declared that "if Congress desires to go further, it must speak more clearly than it has." *McNally*, 483 U.S. at 360. One question presented by the conviction of Handakas is whether the statute adopted by Congress a year later (18 U.S.C. § 1346) speaks with clarity sufficient to satisfy the Court's command.

Section 1346 (an amendment to the Anti–Drug Abuse Act of 1988) defines "scheme or artifice to defraud" to include "a scheme or artifice to deprive another of the intangible right of honest services." According to one Senator, the intent was "to reinstate all of the pre-McNally caselaw pertaining to the mail and wire fraud statutes without change." 134 Cong. Rec. S17360–02 (daily ed. Nov. 10, 1988) (statement of Sen. Biden).

Some circuits have implemented § 1346 by resurrecting pre-*McNally* law. Thus, the Sixth Circuit has held that "§ 1346 has restored the mail fraud statute to its pre-McNally scope." United States v. Frost, 125 F.3d 346, 364 (6th Cir. 1997). And the Fifth Circuit, after noting that "Congress could not have intended to bless each and every pre-McNally lower court 'honest services' opinion," observed that "Congress ... has set us back on a course of defining 'honest services' "; and that Court has "turned to that task." 116 F.3d 728, 733 (5th Cir. 1997) (en banc). However, one of these approaches simply reinstates the entire, dissonant body of prior circuit precedent, while the other invites the creation out of whole cloth of new judicial interpretations of "honest services"—interpretations that will undoubtedly vary from circuit to circuit. The result is "a truly extraordinary statute, in which the substantive force of the statute varies in each judicial circuit." United States v. Brumley, 116 F.3d 728, 743 n.6 (5th Cir. 1997) (Jolly, J., dissenting).

.... In deciding whether the revised statute provides [1] notice, and [2] limits on prosecutorial discretion, we are ... left (where we start) with the statutory wording: "the intangible right of honest services."

The first inquiry that bears on vagueness—the sufficiency of notice—is whether the statute, as it is written, provides notice sufficient to alert "ordinary people [to] what conduct is prohibited." Kolender v. Lawson, 461 U.S. 352, 357, 103 S. Ct. 1855 (1983). Notice is essentially a definitional requirement: a penal statute must speak for itself so that a lay person can understand the prohibition. It is not enough to say that judges can intuit the scope of the prohibition if Handakas could not.

If we were the first panel attempting to discern the meaning of the phrase "honest services" in § 1346, we would likely find that part of the statute so vague as to be unconstitutional on its face. Section 1346 specifies that a "scheme to defraud" includes the deprivation of another's "intangible right of honest services," and in that way expresses legislative intent to expand the offense beyond deprivations of money or property; but it does not say what "honest services" may be, or when they are withheld deceitfully.

The plain meaning of "honest services" in the text of § 1346 simply provides no clue to the public or the courts as to what conduct is prohibited under the statute. Judge Jolly observed in 1997 that the terms "intangible right" and "honest services" cannot be found in Black's Law Dictionary, the United States Code, or (for that matter) any federal statute other than § 1346. *Brumley*, 116 F.3d at 742 (Jolly, J., dissenting). That observation remains accurate today. Clearly, " 'honest services' has not achieved the status of a commonly accepted and recognized term of art which Congress could have been relying upon in using these words.... The phrase is ... inherently undefined and ambiguous." Id. at 742, 746 (Jolly, J. dissenting).

Nor is this "a case where further precision in the statutory language is either impossible or impractical." *Kolender*, 461 U.S. at 361. Congress contemplated (but ultimately rejected) more determinate versions of § 1346. For instance, Senate Bill 2793, entitled the "Anti-Corruption Act of 1988," was passed by the Senate on October 14, 1988. However, the

House later deleted the text of the bill, and replaced it with the text of § 1346.[3]

Congress wrestled with the vagueness problem. At a hearing on the proposed addition of § 1346, the following exchange ensued between Ronald Stroman, assistant counsel for the subcommittee, and John C. Keeney, Acting Assistant Attorney General:

> Mr. STROMAN: Well, honest services of [a] public official, do you think that is [] specific? I mean what does "honest services" mean? Certainly if I am a public official—
>
> Mr. KEENEY: Well, it means that—it means what the circuit courts of appeals have been saying for years that when a Mandel or a Kerner corruptly uses his office he is depriving the citizens of that State of his honest services.
>
> Mr. STROMAN: I would wholeheartedly agree with that, but certainly the concept of intangible rights has been interpreted by a whole host of cases as well. To use the term "honest government" and say that is more specific than intangible rights when you have got the same history of case law, quite frankly I do not see the distinction. If I am an official in the Government and I see the term "honest government," that certainly does not alert me anymore than the existing statute as to what you are trying to cover. I do not know what that means. I would have to read the cases that you referred to. If I read the mail fraud statute, the same situation applies. I would have to read the cases to specifically understand what the statute is attempting to get at. And my point is that if you say that what you are trying to do is create a new statute because it is more specific, quite frankly it is not anymore [sic] specific.

Mail Fraud: Hearing Before the Subcomm. on Criminal Justice of the House Comm. on the Judiciary, 100th Cong., 2d Sess. 7, at 48–49 (1988).

We have held that an administrative prison rule was unconstitutionally vague as applied where its prohibition could be understood only through "the lawyer-like task of statutory interpretation. . . ." Chatin v. Coombe, 186 F.3d 82, 89 (2d Cir. 1999). Similarly, here, no one can know what is forbidden by § 1346 without undertaking the "lawyer-like task" of answering the following questions: [1] Can pre-McNally case law be consulted to illuminate the wording of § 1346? [2] Can any meaning be drawn from the case law, either the uneven pre-McNally cases or the few cases decided post-§ 1346? [3] Is one to be guided only by case law within one's own circuit, or by the law of the circuits taken together (if that is possible)? A "[lay-] individual of ordinary intelligence" in Handakas's position would not know where to begin. . . .

3. Senate Bill 2793 would have criminalized:

(a) depriving or defrauding the inhabitants of a state or a political subdivision of a state of the honest services of an official or employee of such state or subdivision and (b) depriving or defrauding the inhabitants of a state or political subdivision of a state of a fair and impartially conducted election process in any primary, runoff, special or general election.

We are not, however, the first panel of our court to consider the meaning of "honest services" in § 1346. In United States v. Sancho, 157 F.3d 918 (2d Cir. 1998), the defendant argued that his conduct did not fall within the "honest services" provision, primarily on the grounds that the "consultant" he bribed did not owe the intended victim a fiduciary duty. The panel rejected that argument, which was based on pre-McNally case law, holding that such cases are "not pertinent" to interpretation of "honest services" in § 1346. It stated that there was "no doubt" that the "consultant" was under a legal duty to inform the intended victim of the bribe, and that there was also "no doubt" that the duty fell within the meaning of "honest services" in § 1346. The cases the panel cited in support of its analysis were all cases involving a duty of disclosure enforceable by an action in tort. See Fund of Funds, Ltd. v. Arthur Andersen & Co., 545 F. Supp. 1314, 1360 (S.D.N.Y. 1982) (duty to disclose was part of common law professional duties); Maritime Fish Prods., Inc. v. World-Wide Fish Prods., Inc., 100 A.D.2d 81, 474 N.Y.S.2d 281, 285 (1st Dep't 1984) (duty to disclose by virtue of employment or agency relationship); Aaron Ferer & Sons Ltd. v. Chase Manhattan Bank, 731 F.2d 112, 123 (2d Cir. 1984) (duty to disclose by virtue of superior knowledge).

In *Sancho's* only progeny, United States v. Middlemiss, 217 F.3d 112 (2d Cir. 2000), the panel, relying on *Sancho*, upheld a conviction for mail fraud involving a scheme that deprived the defendant's employer of "all the services that a totally faithful employee would have provided" and in furtherance of which the defendant acted contrary to the best interest of his employer. Thus, *Middlemiss* also involved the breach of a duty enforceable by an action in tort. Together, then, *Sancho* and *Middlemiss* appear to stand for the proposition that a scheme to harm another by the breach of a duty enforceable by an action in tort may support a conviction for a scheme to defraud another of "honest services."

Neither *Sancho* nor *Middlemiss* provides a meaning of "honest services" that controls this case or saves this prosecution. The prosecution of Handakas arises out of his violation of the duties imposed by Article 1, § 17 of the New York State Constitution and § 220 of the New York State Labor Law, duties that are not enforceable by an action in tort. For present purposes, we see no principled distinction between the duties breached by Handakas and the garden-variety contractual duties usually collected under the rubric of "representations and warranties." For the wrongs committed by Handakas, New York law prescribes criminal penalties and may afford contract remedies, but does not afford an action in tort. New York law endeavors to maintain the distinction between contract and tort remedies, and generally bars an action in tort for a breach of contract. Pilewski v. Solymosy, 266 A.D.2d 83, 698 N.Y.S.2d 660, 662 (1st Dep't 1999) ("The law generally does not permit recovery in tort where the complaint states a legally sufficient claim sounding in contract.").

In *Middlemiss*, a company seeking a food-concession license at the offices of a public authority conveyed a secret corporate interest to an employee of the authority, who was convicted both of extorting payments from the licensee and of (simultaneously) committing mail fraud by the theft of his "honest services." Even if the "honest services" clause could be read to prohibit such conduct, it still would fail to give the slightest notice that breach of contract could subject one to a mail fraud conviction.[7]

If we were to affirm Handakas's mail fraud conviction on the grounds that he violated a state-mandated undertaking to pay "prevailing rate of wages," or to furnish accurate reports of work performed, we would effect a breathtaking expansion of mail fraud. Every breach of a contract or state law (committed in the vicinity of a telephone) and every false state tax return (sent by mail) would become punishable as a felony in federal court.

The government's summation on the subject of "honest services" focused entirely on the deprivation of the SCA's contractual rights. Even someone fully familiar with §§ 1341 and 1346, and our cases, would lack any comprehensible notice that federal law has criminalized breaches of contract. Accordingly, application of those criminal statutes to Handakas violates the due process guarantee of fair notice.

The second vagueness inquiry (and "the more important" of the two) is whether the "statutory language [is] of such a standardless sweep [that it] allows policemen, prosecutors, and juries to pursue their personal predilections." Smith v. Goguen, 415 U.S. 566, 575, 94 S. Ct. 1242 (1974). "An enactment fails to provide sufficiently explicit standards for those who apply it when it 'impermissibly delegates basic policy matters to policemen, judges and juries for resolution on an ad hoc and subjective basis.' " Chatin v. Coombe, 186 F.3d 82, 89 (2d Cir. 1999).

An indefinite criminal statute creates opportunity for the misuse of government power. To appropriate Judge Winter's phrase, the honest services doctrine renders mail fraud "a catch-all ... which has no use but misuse." See United States v. Margiotta, 688 F.2d 108, 144 (2d Cir. 1982) (Winter, J., dissenting) (explaining that "when the first corrupt prosecutor prosecutes a political enemy for mail fraud," talk of honest services and "good government will ring hollow indeed").

.... Even without the overlay provided by the amendment on "honest services," the mail fraud statute has been aptly described as an all-purpose prosecutorial expedient.[9] By invoking § 1346, prosecutors are free to invite juries "to apply a legal standard which amounts to little more than the rhetoric of sixth grade civics classes." *Margiotta*, 688 F.2d at 142 (Winter, J., dissenting). If the "honest services" clause can be used to punish a

7. If, instead, *Middlemiss* had affirmed the conviction of the cafeteria operator, for serving ordinary tuna fish notwithstanding a contract term requiring that all tuna be netted dolphin-free, *Middlemiss* might be precedent militating in favor of affirmance in this case.

9. See *Margiotta*, 688 F.2d at 143 (Winter, J., dissenting) ("What profoundly troubles me is the potential for abuse through selective prosecution and the degree of raw political power the freeswinging club of mail fraud affords federal prosecutors."); John C. Coffee, Jr., The Metastasis of Mail Fraud: The Continuing Story of the "Evolution" of a White–Collar Crime, 21 Am. Crim. L. Rev. 1, 3 (1983) (arguing that mail fraud statute "seems destined to provide the federal prosecutor with what Archimedes long sought—a simple fulcrum from which one can move the world"); Roger J. Miner, Federal Courts, Federal Crimes, and Federalism, 10 Harv. J.L. & Pub. Pol'y 117, 121 (1987) (arguing that judicial interpretation of the mail fraud statute has converted mail fraud statute into a "vehicle for the prosecution of an almost unlimited number of offenses bearing very little connection to the mails").

failure to honor the SCA's insistence on the payment of prevailing rate of wages, it could make a criminal out of anyone who breaches any contractual representation: that tuna was netted dolphin-free; that stationery is made of recycled paper; that sneakers or T-shirts are not made by child workers; that grapes are picked by union labor—in sum so called consumer protection law and far more.

At trial, the government thought it sufficient to argue that Handakas was guilty of conspiracy to commit mail fraud simply by violating his non-fiduciary contractual obligation to pay his workers the prevailing rate of wages. That is what the prosecutor argued to the jury:

> Sometimes you care about how things are done, and if you spell that out in a contract and you make it clear to the people you are dealing with, as the SCA did here, that not only do you want something but you want it done a certain way, you have a right to that, and that's what's at issue here. The SCA had a right to determine how its contracts would be fulfilled....
>
> The SCA had a property right in its contract.... [Handakas] took away that right ... to decide how the SCA had its contract performed.... The defendant owes a duty of honest services. There is a contract here....
>
> That's exactly the point. There was a relationship ... defined by a contract....
>
> There can be no doubt that what the defendant did here was intentionally seek to deprive the SCA of this contract right, the right not just to determine what work gets done, but how it gets done.

These arguments prove too much, however, as the government apparently realized on appeal. By the time the government filed its post-argument supplemental brief on this subject, it was back-peddling and conceded that it "misspoke" during oral argument when it suggested that a duty of "honest services" arises in connection with the performance of all contracts and is violated by any contract breach. The government's improved appellate theory of this prosecution is that the "honest services" clause may have its limits, but that Handakas's conduct falls within those limits because of a supposed "agency" relationship between Handakas and the SCA. However, there is no reference to agency (or fiduciary relationships) in the indictment, or in the charge, or in the summations, or in the government's brief in chief on appeal. The government's summation on the subject of "honest services" was focused on the contract right to compliance with representations and warranties:

> There are times when there are things more important than price. We are probably all familiar with instances where you ... have decided not to buy a particular product because you don't like ... the way workers are treated. Years ago there was a boycott of grapes because the workers who picked it weren't being treated fairly. You read all the time about people who won't buy certain clothing because it's made in sweatshops in Asia.

The contract argument was thus cast in terms of social conscience and treated "honest services" as a concept without boundary or standard.

Even the circuits that have reinstated pre-*McNally* law recognize that ad hoc parameters are needed to give the statute shape. See United States v. Frost, 125 F.3d 346, 368 (6th Cir. 1997) ("[Our] refusal to carry the intangible rights doctrine to its logical extreme stems from a need to avoid the over-criminalization of private relationships: 'If merely depriving the victim of the loyalty and faithful service of his fiduciary constitutes mail fraud ... disloyalty alone becomes the crime, little remains before every civil wrong is potentially indictable.' "); United States v. Cochran, 109 F.3d 660, 667 (10th Cir. 1997) ("It would give us great pause if a right to honest services is violated by every breach of contract or every misstatement made in the course of dealing.").

If the words of a criminal statute insufficiently define the offense, it is no part of deference to Congress for us to intuit or invent the crime. *Smith*, 415 U.S. at 574–75; United States v. Reese, 92 U.S. 214, 221 (1875) (mem.) ("It would certainly be dangerous if the legislature could set a net large enough to catch all possible offenders, and leave it to the courts to step inside and say who could be rightfully detained, and who should be set at large. This would, to some extent, substitute the judicial for the legislative department of government.").

The absence of discernible standards in the "honest services" doctrine implicates principles of federalism. As the government's summation demonstrates, this prosecution was driven by a conception formed by federal prosecutors that certain New York laws appeal so strongly to the social conscience that violation should be treated as felonious under federal law. New York's interest in the payment of prevailing rate of wages is secured and enforced by state laws deemed sufficient by the state. Under § 220 of the New York State Labor Law, the comptroller of the City of New York is empowered to make findings of fact and enforce a judgment against contractors who fail to pay prevailing rate of wages. Additionally, the statute provides that willful violation constitutes a misdemeanor. Prosecutorial discretion has been exercised here to sharpen the penalty for the violation of certain state laws that, in the estimation of a federal prosecutor, are insufficiently policed or punished by the state itself. This is particularly dubious where interstate commerce is at best tangentially implicated. Cf. United States v. Lopez, 514 U.S. 549, 115 S.Ct. 1624 (1995) (holding Federal Gun Free School Zone Act unconstitutional, because criminal statute exceeded Congress's commerce clause authority; reasoning that possession of gun in school zone was not economic activity that substantially affected interstate commerce). * * *

■ FEINBERG, CIRCUIT JUDGE (dissenting).

I dissent from the holding that 18 U.S.C. § 1346 is unconstitutional as applied in this case....

It is true that Handakas was under a contractual duty to refrain from falsifying payroll records and paying sub-standard rates. It may also be true, as the majority points out, that there is a question whether a contractual duty alone should be enough to allow a conviction. But ... there were duties other than simply contractual ones imposed on Handakas. Article 1, Section 17 of the New York State Constitution, for example, prohibits any "laborer, workman or mechanic in the employ of a contractor or subcontractor engaged in the performance of any public work" from being "paid less than the rate" of the prevailing wage. That constitutional mandate is implemented by New York Labor Law § 220, which imposes duties upon various entities to enforce the prevailing wage requirement.

The majority points out that paying sub-standard wages is a criminal misdemeanor under N.Y. Lab. Law § 220. But state law imposes even more extensive duties on contractors such as Handakas. For instance, under N.Y. Lab. Law § 220(3–a. a.), contractors "shall keep original payrolls or transcripts thereof, subscribed and affirmed by him as true under the penalties of perjury," showing the "hours and days worked by" and "hourly wage rate paid" to each "workman, laborer or mechanic." Another section of the statute further extends the criminal penalties for false statements. It is therefore a state felony to submit falsified material information on any filing required by the labor statute. See N.Y. Penal Law § 210.10 (perjury)....

The majority attempts to distinguish United States v. Sancho, 157 F.3d 918 (2d Cir. 1998), and "*Sancho's* only progeny," United States v. Middlemiss, 217 F.3d 112 (2d Cir. 2000), on the dubious ground that those cases limited the state law duties that, when breached, may support a conviction for a scheme to defraud another of "honest services" to duties actionable only in tort. However, nowhere in *Sancho* or *Middlemiss* is there such a limiting principle. Rather, each case looked only to whether there was a legal duty to provide honest services, without imposing any requirements on the nature of that duty.... In any event, Handakas violated both contractual and criminal state law duties, as the majority acknowledges. A defendant has more notice that his behavior violated § 1346, and there is less risk of an abuse of prosecutorial discretion, when that behavior also constitutes a state crime rather than simply a tort.

QUESTIONS AND COMMENTS

1. What does *Handakas* hold? That a contract breach does not constitute a deprivation of honest services under 18 U.S.C. § 1346? That punishing Handakas's contract breach as an instance of honest services fraud would be unconstitutional? Under *Handakas*, could any contract breach (in the Second Circuit?) amount to honest services fraud?

2. *Handakas* involved 18 U.S.C. § 1346, the most controversial—and most recent—version of federal mail fraud: honest services fraud. The denial of honest services itself, without any financial loss, is punished. See, e.g., United States v. Rybicki, 287 F.3d 257 (2d Cir. 2002) (lawyers guilty of mail fraud for paying insurance company adjusters to expedite settlements of personal injury claims, even though the prosecution had presented no evidence that the claims were settled for inflated value). Why would someone "bribe" adjusters to expedite settlements unless there was some gain in getting claims settled quickly? And if the "bribing" party *gains* something (of value) must not *someone* else lose something? Is the problem in *Rybicki* the absence of a concrete victim or the (relatively) trivial level of harm compared to the punishment? Or is the biggest problem that U.S. Attorneys bring these cases when they *believe* they are dealing with very

bad actors (for instance, believe that the lawyers' payments did lead to excessive settlements) but needn't bother to *prove* that their suspicions are correct?

Consider, too, United States v. Alfisi, 308 F.3d 144 (2d Cir. 2002). The defendants there were indicted not for mail fraud, but bribery, under 18 U.S.C. § 201(b)(1)(A). Nonetheless, the case is instructive. The defendants in the case claimed that they paid government inspectors at the Hunts Point Market in New York City, the world's largest wholesale produce market, simply to do their jobs properly; they paid them not to insure that the products receive any particular USDA "grade" but paid them simply to be graded. Their convictions were sustained in an opinion by Judge Winter, over a caustic dissent by Judge Sack. It is not clear that Judge Winter relies exclusively on the notion that the bribery statute, on its face, proscribes *all* payments "to influence any official act" and that these payments clearly *do* influence an official act. He notes as well that defendants were entitled to raise an affirmative defense that they were subject to economic coercion—in essence, that they were the *victims* of official extortion, not the perpetrators of bribery—and that the jury rejected that defense. But what if this were not a shakedown by inspectors who demanded money to do their jobs? What if the inspectors were just lazy? Is anyone materially injured by the payments if the inspectors were simply sitting around and chatting with one another till "bribed"? Reconsider *Rybicki*: Should it matter if the lawyers helped their clients to jump a queue? And even if paying money to jump a queue is wrong, is it *criminal*? And even if it is criminal, is it properly subject to substantial terms of imprisonment? Would a person who jumped the queue by telling the insurance adjuster a compelling tale of his urgent need to receive the insurance check due to him *now* be acting wrongfully? Criminally? Would a person violate the sorts of norms the criminal law should be used to vindicate if he got served first (at a store, at a restaurant) because he was whinier, more boorish, cuter, or more famous than those around him waiting in line? Because he offers an explicit bribe? Big tips? The promise of atypically high levels of repeat business?

The mail fraud statute, in 18 U.S.C. § 1341, also reaches, more straightforwardly, "scheme[s] or artifice[s] to defraud, or for obtaining money or property." Note, however, that no matter what the interest or right protected, the statute does not require an actual deprivation of that interest or right. It applies to anyone who, "having devised or intending to devise any scheme or artifice to defraud," uses the mails "for the purpose of executing such scheme or artifice or attempting so to do." Not only is mail fraud not limited to the infliction of financial harm; it covers cases where the intended injury (financial harm or loss of honest services) is not inflicted in fact.

The definition of mail fraud thus is considerably broader than that of common law fraud. As the Supreme Court explained, in Neder v. United States, 527 U.S. 1, 119 S.Ct. 1827 (1999): "The common-law requirements of 'justifiable reliance' and 'damages' ... plainly have no place in the federal fraud statutes." See, e.g., United States v. Stewart, 872 F.2d 957, 960 (10th Cir. 1989) ("[Under the mail fraud statute,] the government does not have to prove actual reliance upon the defendant's misrepresentations."); United States v. Rowe, 56 F.2d 747, 749 (2d Cir. 1932) (L. Hand, J.) ("Civilly of course the [mail fraud statute] would fail without proof of damage, but that has no application to criminal liability.") Here is one fairly typical list of the elements of common law fraud:

> (1) a representation of an existing fact, (2) its materiality, (3) its falsity, (4) the speaker's knowledge of its falsity or ignorance of its truth, (5) his intent that it should be acted on by the person to whom it is made, (6) ignorance of its falsity on the part of the person to whom it is made, (7) the latter's reliance on the truth of the representation, (8) his right to rely upon it, and (9) his consequent damage.

Pedersen v. Bibioff, 64 Wash.App. 710, 723, 828 P.2d 1113 (1992).

Does it make sense that the prerequisites for civil liability are more demanding than those for criminal liability? Wouldn't you expect the opposite, given the criminal penalties for mail fraud (fine or up to five years' imprisonment; if the fraud affects a financial institution, up to $1,000,000 fine or 30 years' imprisonment)? What view of criminal law (and what theory of punishment) would be most consistent with abandoning reliance and damages in particular? Could the issue of reliance (or gullibility) be introduced into the analysis under the doctrine of consent? What's the point of requiring a "scheme" to defraud? Is it an indicator of the exceptional dangerousness of the "schemer" (or "artificer")? If so, can it make up for the absence of a requirement of actual damages, or justifiable reliance? Or is the point merely to place some, any, limits on the scope of criminal fraud?

3. Now compare mail fraud to larceny by false pretenses and by false promise. Like civil common-law fraud, larceny requires an actual interference with another's property interest, rather than a mere *scheme* to interfere. Note, in fact, that mail fraud requires not even a scheme to defraud; an *intent* to devise such a scheme will do. Note also that the statute covers not only "executing such scheme or artifice" but also "attempting so to do." (Where does that leave the law of attempt as applied to criminal mail fraud? See ch. 6.) Contrast N.Y. Penal Law § 190.60 (defining crime of "scheme to defraud" as "engag[ing] in a scheme constituting a systematic ongoing course of conduct with intent to defraud more than one person or to obtain property from more than one person by false or fraudulent pretenses, representations or promises, and *so obtains property from one or more of such persons*") (emphasis added); People v. Taylor, 304 A.D.2d 434, 758 N.Y.S.2d 634 (N.Y. App. Div. 2003) (§ 190.60 derived from federal mail fraud statute).

Federal mail fraud expanded criminal liability to false promises long before (some) state jurisdictions did so with considerable reluctance, as *Norman* illustrates. In fact, the distinction between false pretenses and false promise disappears entirely in light of the congressional effort to "protect[] the public against all . . . intentional efforts to despoil":

> [In] *Durland* v. *United States*, 161 U.S. 306, 16 S.Ct. 508 (1896), our first decision construing the mail fraud statute, . . . the defendant, who had used the mails to sell bonds he did not intend to honor, argued that he could not be held criminally liable because his conduct did not

> fall within the scope of the common-law crime of "false pretenses." We rejected the argument that "the statute reaches only such cases as, at common law, would come within the definition of 'false pretenses,' in order to make out which there must be a misrepresentation as to some existing fact and not a mere promise as to the future." Instead, we construed the statute to "include everything designed to defraud by representations as to the past or present, or suggestions and promises as to the future." ...

Neder v. United States, 527 U.S. 1, 119 S.Ct. 1827 (1999).

Note that, once again unlike state efforts to criminalize larceny by false promise, the federal mail fraud statute does not provide for any additional safeguards to prevent the conversion of ordinary contract actions into criminal cases (such as the "moral certainty" standard).

4. *Claim of Right.* The defense of claim of right is not available in mail fraud cases. In United States v. Gole, 158 F.3d 166 (2d Cir. 1998), the defendant was a New York firefighter who had retired after being injured on the job. He under-reported his income to receive his full pension, which would have been reduced had his income exceeded a certain amount. The court rejected Gole's argument that he "did not intend to harm the NYCFD Pension Fund because he had a claim-of-right to the pension overpayments" on the ground that claim of right was no defense to mail fraud. While it was indeed a defense to "the traditional common law crime of false pretenses, the mail fraud statute does not mention this as a defense and the Supreme Court long ago rejected the argument that the mail fraud statute 'reaches only such cases as, at common law, would come within the definition of false pretences.' " Plus,

> common sense commands us to reject the purported defense. If Gole's theory of self-help were the law, anyone who believed that he was legally entitled to benefits from a pension plan, or an insurance policy, or a government program, but who was concerned that he or she might nevertheless be denied such benefits, would be given carte blanche simply to lie to obtain those benefits. Such a course of action would often be much easier than pursuing legal remedies through civil actions in court, and would guarantee success as long as the misrepresentation remained undiscovered. We will not encourage people to lie to obtain benefits rather than pursue their rights in civil actions. Such controversies may be resolved by civil suit or settlement, but cannot be won by using lies and deception.

Can I ever use "lies and deception" and claim a right to the property at the same time, particularly if the "victim" is the state?

5. *Federalism.* Federal mail fraud converts not only civil wrongs (torts, breaches of contract, violations of fiduciary duty) into criminal ones; it also converts *state* offenses into federal ones. The *Handakas* majority complains that "[p]rosecutorial discretion has been exercised here to sharpen the penalty for the violation of certain state laws that, in the estimation of a federal prosecutor, are insufficiently policed or punished by the state itself." This passage raises two critiques, it seems. As a matter of federalism, the court suggests, it is problematic that a *federal* prosecutor should

sit in judgment over matters of state criminal law. And as a matter of separation of powers, it is questionable that an (unelected) member of the executive—a federal *prosecutor*—should wield the power to second-guess the state legislature. Would the court direct the same criticism at a federal prosecutor's decision to seek a conviction under federal civil rights law of a white Southern defendant accused of a racist murder, motivated, for instance, by a desire to intimidate African–Americans seeking to exercise the franchise, who has escaped punishment only due to the less than enthusiastic enforcement effort exerted by the state prosecutor to pursue a conviction under the state murder statute or perhaps the unwillingness of all-white juries to return a guilty verdict despite overwhelming evidence of guilt? If a state does not criminalize certain conduct, or does not enforce its own criminal statutes, should the federal government be entitled to step in, by converting that conduct into a federal crime, rather than criminalizing it directly?

6. The Second Circuit, in a decision rendered shortly after *Handakas*, attempted to deal with what it called the "virtually limitless" reach of the federal honest services statute not by finding it unconstitutionally vague, but by adopting a "prudential limitation" on the statute's reach:

> As we have noted, "not every breach of an employee's fiduciary duty to his employer constitutes mail or wire fraud." For example, a customer who importunes an employee to allow her to use the company's telephone access code to make an important long-distance telephone call, in the face of a written company policy expressly prohibiting non-employees from using the access code, could conceivably fall within the scope of the statute if read literally. So too could an employee's use of his company's letterhead to lend authority to a letter of complaint mailed to the employee's landlord in disregard of the company's code of conduct prohibiting the use of the company's letterhead for non-company business.
>
> Several circuits, addressing this concern, have interpreted "scheme or artifice to deprive another of the intangible right of honest services" in such a way as to properly curtail the statute's reach. Some courts have imposed a requirement that the misrepresentation or omission at issue be "material," such that "an employee has reason to believe the information would lead a reasonable employer to change its business conduct." [S]everal [other] circuits have adopted a requirement that it must have been reasonably foreseeable to the defendant that the scheme at issue could have resulted in some economic or pecuniary harm to the victim.
>
> [W]e believe the "reasonably foreseeable harm" standard to be superior because ... it focuses the inquiry on whether the scheme at issue created a foreseeable risk of economic or pecuniary harm to the victim, which is consistent with traditional notions of fraud and fraudulent harm. In addition, the "reasonably foreseeable harm" test has the virtue of being capable of straightforward and consistent application, while at the same time placing a reasonable boundary around what is otherwise so boundless a concept as to be a suitable candidate for a finding of unconstitutional vagueness. We hasten to

> add, however, that the foreseeable economic or pecuniary harm must be more than *de minimis*, in order to establish a minimum threshold that will exclude cases, such as the two hypothetical ones discussed above, that could result in some slight economic harm—such as the cost of stationery or a single phone call.

United States v. Rybicki, 287 F.3d 257, 264–66 (2d Cir. 2002).

Is it the courts' business to place "prudential limitations" on statutes? See also United States v. Frost, 125 F.3d 346, 368 (6th Cir. 1997) (although mail fraud statute's "literal terms suggest that dishonesty by an employee, standing alone, is a crime," courts "have refused to interpret the doctrine so broadly"). What is the basis for the limitation adopted in *Rybicki*? Statutory interpretation? Legislative intent? Constitutional law? Consider *Rybicki* in light of the various aspects of the principle of legality.

The *Rybicki* limitation itself was rejected on rehearing en banc as "something of an ipse dixit designed simply to limit the scope of section 1346." The en banc Second Circuit, in *Rybicki II*, instead "prefer[red] the 'materiality' test because it has the virtue of arising out of fundamental principles of the law of fraud: A material misrepresentation is an element of the crime." 354 F.3d 124, 146 (2d Cir. 2003) (en banc). (The en banc court also limits *Handakas* to its facts.) But if materiality is an element of the crime, then how does requiring materiality *limit* the scope of crime of mail fraud? And what does this trio of Second Circuit opinions—*Handakas, Rybicki,* and *Rybicki II*—issued within the space of two years tell you about the specificity—constitutionality, propriety—of the federal mail fraud statute? (*Rybicki II's* response: "Disparity does not establish vagueness.")

7. Should it make any difference, for purposes of defining the scope of mail fraud, whether the criminal fraud also amounts to a tort, or a breach of contract, or perhaps some other duty defined elsewhere, by statute, or by judicial opinion? (Cf. Major League Baseball Uniform Player's Contract § 3(a) ("Loyalty"): "The player agrees to perform his services hereunder diligently and faithfully, to keep himself in first-class physical condition and to obey the club's training rules, and pledges himself to the American public and to the club to conform to high standards of personal conduct, fair play and good sportsmanship.") The *Handakas* majority argues that converting a breach of contract into federal mail fraud "would effect a breathtaking expansion of mail fraud." That may be so. But hasn't that expansion already occurred? Doesn't applying section 1346 to violations of an employee's *tort* duties toward her employer convert labor law into a species of federal mail fraud?

Compare the search for a duty in the law of mail fraud with the search for a duty in the law of omissions. Should there be any limitation on the nature and source of the duty? Why? Or is federal mail fraud best thought of as a general means for identifying those individuals whose callous disregard for others' entitlements and for their own obligations marks them as so dangerous as to warrant criminal punishment?

Then again, why should the violation of a noncriminal duty, or of a contractual obligation, be punishable in the first place? What justifies the use of the criminal sanction in these cases? Compare the law of mail fraud with the law of conspiracy. (See ch. 8.) Why should conspiracy, but not mail fraud, be limited to otherwise *criminal* objectives? Or should prosecutors be entitled to select the proper state response to a particular behavior from a range of possible criminal—and civil—sanctions, with few restrictions so as to give them the greatest possible flexibility? What view of the relationship among the various branches of government—legislature, judiciary, executive—underlies federal mail fraud? Is this division of labor among the branches of government intended, constitutional, desirable, inevitable? Consider the following excerpts:

> For over a generation, the mail and wire fraud statutes have provided federal prosecutors with a residual catch-all that was available when nothing else in their arsenal seemed likely to work.... At first glance, [the federal mail fraud statute] may seem intended only to protect the integrity of a federally administered service, the post office. Yet its key phrase, "scheme ... to defraud" ... has long served instead as a charter of authority for courts to decide, retroactively, what forms of unfair or questionable conduct in commercial, public and even private life should be deemed criminal. In so doing, this phrase has provided more expansive interpretations from prosecutors and judges than probably any other phrase in federal criminal law.

John C. Coffee, Jr. & Charles K. Whitehead, "The Federalization of Fraud: Mail and Wire Fraud Statutes," in 1 Otto G. Obermaier & Robert G. Morvillo, White Collar Crime: Business and Regulatory Offenses § 9.01 (2003).

> [F]ederal criminal law consists of a muscular corpus of judge-made doctrine stretched out over a skeletal statutory frame. Take the federal criminal law of "fraud" as an example. By incorporating "fraud" and its cognates into a host of important statutory offenses—including conspiracy to defraud, and mail and wire fraud—Congress all but guaranteed a central role for courts in constructing federal criminal law. At common law, fraud was understood to be less a legal rule in its own right than a license to courts to devise new rules on an ad hoc basis. And that's exactly the function that the concept has played in federal criminal law.

Dan M. Kahan, "Three Conceptions of Federal Criminal–Lawmaking," 1 Buff. Crim. L. Rev. 5 (1997).

2. THE PROTECTED INTEREST AND JUSTIFICATIONS FOR FEDERAL JURISDICTION

What exactly is the federal interest the crime of mail fraud protects? Unlike the states, the federal government does not enjoy a general "police power" to criminalize conduct it considers a threat to the public welfare. Its authority is, at least in theory, limited to certain powers enumerated in the federal constitution. But see Ernst Freund, The Police Power: Public Policy and Constitutional Rights 63 (1904) (pointing out federal government's de facto police power). Among them is the power to regulate international and interstate commerce. Much, probably most, of federal criminal law is derived from the federal government's commerce power.

Until fairly recently, the U.S. Supreme Court granted the Congress virtually unlimited discretion in passing criminal legislation under the commerce clause. In United States v. Lopez, 514 U.S. 549, 115 S.Ct. 1624 (1995), however, the Supreme Court reversed course and struck down a federal statute that criminalized gun possession near schools, holding that the proscribed activity was insufficiently related to interstate commerce. The mail fraud statute now is in a privileged position as it can draw on another constitutional source, the power "to establish post offices and post roads," also to be found in art. I, § 8 of the federal constitution. (Its offspring, the wire fraud statute, 18 U.S.C. § 1343, which is virtually identical to the mail fraud statute, 18 U.S.C. § 1341, except that it proscribes use of "wire, radio, or television communication," rather than of the mail isn't so lucky. It must rely on the commerce clause. The same presumably would hold for mail fraud committed through the fraudulent use of a "private or commercial interstate carrier." 18 U.S.C. § 1341.) But what exactly is it about the post office—as opposed to postal employees, say—that requires invoking criminal sanctions? Its integrity, its proper functioning, its efficiency? Whatever the federal government's postal interest might be, how central must the use of the postal service be to the operation of the fraudulent scheme? Consider the following case.

Schmuck v. United States

Supreme Court of the United State.
489 U.S. 705 , 109 S.Ct. 1443 (1989).

■ JUSTICE BLACKMUN delivered the opinion of the Court.

In August 1983, petitioner Wayne T. Schmuck, a used-car distributor, was indicted in the United States District Court for the Western District of Wisconsin on 12 counts of mail fraud, in violation of 18 U.S.C. §§ 1341 and 1342.

The alleged fraud was a common and straightforward one. Schmuck purchased used cars, rolled back their odometers, and then sold the automobiles to Wisconsin retail dealers for prices artificially inflated because of the low-mileage readings. These unwitting car dealers, relying on the altered odometer figures, then resold the cars to customers, who in turn paid prices reflecting Schmuck's fraud. To complete the resale of each automobile, the dealer who purchased it from Schmuck would submit a title-application form to the Wisconsin Department of Transportation on behalf of his retail customer. The receipt of a Wisconsin title was a prerequisite for completing the resale; without it, the dealer could not transfer title to the customer and the customer could not obtain Wisconsin tags. The submission of the title-application form supplied the mailing element of each of the alleged mail frauds.

Before trial, Schmuck moved to dismiss the indictment on the ground that the mailings at issue—the submissions of the title-application forms by the automobile dealers—were not in furtherance of the fraudulent scheme and, thus, did not satisfy the mailing element of the crime of mail fraud.... The District Court denied both motions. After trial, the jury returned guilty verdicts on all 12 counts. * * *

"The federal mail fraud statute does not purport to reach all frauds, but only those limited instances in which the use of the mails is a part of the execution of the fraud, leaving all other cases to be dealt with by appropriate state law." *Kann* v. *United States*, 323 U.S. 88, 95 (1944).[6] To be part of the execution of the fraud, however, the use of the mails need not be an essential element of the scheme. *Pereira* v. *United States*, 347 U.S. 1, 8 (1954). It is sufficient for the mailing to be "incident to an essential part of the scheme," *ibid.*, or "a step in [the] plot," *Badders* v. *United States*, 240 U.S. 391, 394 (1916).

Schmuck, relying principally on this Court's decisions in *Kann, supra, Parr* v. *United States*, 363 U.S. 370 (1960), and *United States* v. *Maze*, 414 U.S. 395 (1974), argues that mail fraud can be predicated only on a mailing that affirmatively assists the perpetrator in carrying out his fraudulent scheme. The mailing element of the offense, he contends, cannot be satisfied by a mailing, such as those at issue here, that is routine and innocent in and of itself, and that, far from furthering the execution of the fraud, occurs after the fraud has come to fruition, is merely tangentially related to the fraud, and is counterproductive in that it creates a "paper trail" from which the fraud may be discovered....

We begin by considering the scope of Schmuck's fraudulent scheme.... Schmuck's was not a "one-shot" operation in which he sold a single car to an isolated dealer. His was an ongoing fraudulent venture. A rational jury could have concluded that the success of Schmuck's venture depended upon his continued harmonious relations with, and good reputation among, retail dealers, which in turn required the smooth flow of cars from the dealers to their Wisconsin customers.

Under these circumstances, we believe that a rational jury could have found that the title-registration mailings were part of the execution of the fraudulent scheme, a scheme which did not reach fruition until the retail dealers resold the cars and effected transfers of title. Schmuck's scheme would have come to an abrupt halt if the dealers either had lost faith in Schmuck or had not been able to resell the cars obtained from him. These resales and Schmuck's relationships with the retail dealers naturally depended on the successful passage of title among the various parties. Thus, although the registration-form mailings may not have contributed directly to the duping of either the retail dealers or the customers, they were necessary to the passage of title, which in turn was essential to the perpetuation of Schmuck's scheme....

Once the full flavor of Schmuck's scheme is appreciated, the critical distinctions between this case and the three cases in which this Court has delimited the reach of the mail fraud statute—*Kann, Parr*, and *Maze*—are

6. The statute provides in relevant part:

"Whoever, having devised or intending to devise any scheme or artifice to defraud, or for obtaining money or property by means of false or fraudulent pretenses, representations, or promises ... for the purpose of executing such scheme or artifice or attempting so to do ... knowingly causes to be delivered by mail according to the direction thereon, or at the place at which it is directed to be delivered by the person to whom it is addressed, any such matter or thing, shall be fined not more than $1,000 or imprisoned not more than five years, or both." 18 U.S.C. § 1341.

readily apparent. The defendants in *Kann* were corporate officers and directors accused of setting up a dummy corporation through which to divert profits into their own pockets. As part of this fraudulent scheme, the defendants caused the corporation to issue two checks payable to them. The defendants cashed these checks at local banks, which then mailed the checks to the drawee banks for collection. This Court held that the mailing of the cashed checks to the drawee banks could not supply the mailing element of the mail fraud charges. The defendants' fraudulent scheme had reached fruition. "It was immaterial to them, or to any consummation of the scheme, how the bank which paid or credited the check would collect from the drawee bank."

In *Parr*, several defendants were charged, *inter alia*, with having fraudulently obtained gasoline and a variety of other products and services through the unauthorized use of a credit card issued to the school district which employed them. The mailing element of the mail fraud charges in *Parr* was purportedly satisfied when the oil company which issued the credit card mailed invoices to the school district for payment, and when the district mailed payment in the form of a check. Relying on *Kann*, this Court held that these mailings were not in execution of the scheme as required by the statute because it was immaterial to the defendants how the oil company went about collecting its payment.

Later, in *Maze*, the defendant allegedly stole his roommate's credit card, headed south on a winter jaunt, and obtained food and lodging at motels along the route by placing the charges on the stolen card. The mailing element of the mail fraud charge was supplied by the fact that the defendant knew that each motel proprietor would mail an invoice to the bank that had issued the credit card, which in turn would mail a bill to the card owner for payment. The Court found that these mailings could not support mail fraud charges because the defendant's scheme had reached fruition when he checked out of each motel. The success of his scheme in no way depended on the mailings; they merely determined which of his victims would ultimately bear the loss.

The title-registration mailings at issue here served a function different from the mailings in *Kann, Parr*, and *Maze*. The intrabank mailings in *Kann* and the credit card invoice mailings in *Parr* and *Maze* involved little more than post-fraud accounting among the potential victims of the various schemes, and the long-term success of the fraud did not turn on which of the potential victims bore the ultimate loss. Here, in contrast, a jury rationally could have found that Schmuck by no means was indifferent to the fact of who bore the loss. The mailing of the title-registration forms was an essential step in the successful passage of title to the retail purchasers. Moreover, a failure of this passage of title would have jeopardized Schmuck's relationship of trust and goodwill with the retail dealers upon whose unwitting cooperation his scheme depended. Schmuck's reliance on our prior cases limiting the reach of the mail fraud statute is simply misplaced.

To the extent that Schmuck would draw from these previous cases a general rule that routine mailings that are innocent in themselves cannot supply the mailing element of the mail fraud offense, he misapprehends this Court's precedents.... We also reject Schmuck's contention that mailings that someday may contribute to the uncovering of a fraudulent scheme cannot supply the mailing element of the mail fraud offense. The relevant question at all times is whether the mailing is part of the execution of the scheme as conceived by the perpetrator at the time, regardless of whether the mailing later, through hindsight, may prove to have been counterproductive and return to haunt the perpetrator of the fraud. The mail fraud statute includes no guarantee that the use of the mails for the purpose of executing a fraudulent scheme will be risk free. Those who use the mails to defraud proceed at their peril. * * *

■ JUSTICE SCALIA, with whom JUSTICE BRENNAN, JUSTICE MARSHALL, and JUSTICE O'CONNOR join, dissenting.

The purpose of the mail fraud statute is "to prevent the post office from being used to carry [fraudulent schemes] into effect." *Durland* v. *United States*, 161 U.S. 306, 314 (1896); *Parr* v. *United States*, 363 U.S. 370, 389 (1960). The law does not establish a general federal remedy against fraudulent conduct, with use of the mails as the jurisdictional hook, but reaches only "those limited instances in which the use of the mails is *a part of the execution of the fraud*, leaving all other cases to be dealt with by appropriate state law." *Kann* v. *United States*, 323 U.S. 88, 95 (1944) (emphasis added). In other words, it is mail fraud, not mail and fraud, that incurs liability. This federal statute is not violated by a fraudulent scheme in which, at some point, a mailing happens to occur—nor even by one in which a mailing predictably and necessarily occurs. The mailing must be in furtherance of the fraud.

In *Kann* v. *United States*, we concluded that even though defendants who cashed checks obtained as part of a fraudulent scheme knew that the bank cashing the checks would send them by mail to a drawee bank for collection, they did not thereby violate the mail fraud statute, because upon their receipt of the cash "[t]he scheme ... had reached fruition," and the mailing was "immaterial ... to any consummation of the scheme." We held to the same effect in *United States* v. *Maze*, 414 U.S. 395, 400–402 (1974), declining to find that credit card fraud was converted into mail fraud by the certainty that, after the wrongdoer had fraudulently received his goods and services from the merchants, they would forward the credit charges by mail for payment. These cases are squarely in point here. For though the Government chose to charge a defrauding of retail customers (to whom the innocent dealers resold the cars), it is obvious that, regardless of who the ultimate victim of the fraud may have been, the fraud was complete with respect to each car when petitioner pocketed the dealer's money. As far as each particular transaction was concerned, it was as inconsequential to him whether the dealer resold the car as it was inconsequential to the defendant in *Maze* whether the defrauded merchant ever forwarded the charges to the credit card company.

Nor can the force of our cases be avoided by combining all of the individual transactions into a single scheme, and saying, as the Court does, that if the dealers' mailings obtaining title for each retail purchaser had not occurred then the dealers would have stopped trusting petitioner for future transactions. (That conclusion seems to me a non sequitur, but I accept it for the sake of argument.) This establishes, at most, that the scheme could not technically have been consummated if the mechanical step of the mailings to obtain conveyance of title had not occurred. But we have held that the indispensability of such mechanical mailings, not strictly in furtherance of the fraud, is not enough to invoke the statute. * * *

QUESTIONS AND COMMENTS

1. Federal mail fraud threatens with serious punishment anyone who "for the purpose of executing [a fraudulent] scheme . . ., places in any post office . . . any matter or thing whatever to be sent . . . by the Postal Service. . . ." Federal mail fraud, in other words, criminalizes the use of the mails for fraudulent ends. It does not criminalize the fraudulent end, but the means toward that end. The use of the mails thus not only accounts for the "federal" in mail fraud, but constitutes the central conduct element of the offense. After *Schmuck*, is the federal mail fraud statute anything other than a federal fraud statute? What mental state—if any—attaches to the element of use of the mails? If the federal mail fraud statute is not about preventing fraud, but about preventing abuses of the mails, does it make sense to protect the integrity of the Postal Service by punishing violators with up to 30 years in prison?

Why would we care *at all* that the Post Office is used to implement a fraudulent scheme, rather than face-to-face blandishments or rumor? Is it that we believe that no one who fails to use a federally proscribed means (like the mails or phone) could pull off the sorts of frauds that would actually compromise commerce? Or is this really about the "purity" of a federal institution? If we most typically defend the use of federal criminal authority in situations in which we despair that states will lack either the motivation or expertise to combat a problem, is there any reason to believe that states would be atypically inept (or inept at all) in dealing with fraud cases in which the defendant used the mails? Is there, instead, any reason to believe that federalization is appropriate in these cases because there is, in fact, substantial disparity across states in the treatment of fraud and that such disparity, if it exists, is undesirable?

2. The mail fraud statute in 1994 was amended to include the use of "any private or commercial interstate carrier." Violent Crime Control and Law Enforcement Act of 1994, Pub. L. No. 103–322, § 250006, 108 Stat. 1796, 2087 (1994). Courts have held that the statute applies even to *intra*state mailings through private carriers:

> Gil contends that the 1994 amendment exceeded the scope of Congress's authority to legislate under the Commerce Clause, U.S. Const. Art. I, § 8 ["The Congress shall have power . . . [t]o regulate commerce with foreign nations, and among the several states, and with the Indian tribes"], because it criminalizes conduct that takes place entirely intrastate and that has no substantial effect on interstate commerce. On that ground, he seeks reversal of his convictions . . ., which charge mail fraud effected by intrastate mailings via Federal Express. . . .

In United States v. Lopez, 514 U.S. 549, 115 S.Ct. 1624 (1995), the Supreme Court categorizes the activities that Congress may regulate under the Commerce Clause:

> First, Congress may regulate the use of the channels of interstate commerce. Second, Congress is empowered to regulate and protect the instrumentalities of interstate commerce, or persons or things in interstate commerce, even though the threat may come only from intrastate activities. Finally, Congress' commerce authority includes the power to regulate those activities having a substantial relation to interstate commerce, i.e., those activities that substantially affect interstate commerce.

Id. at 558–59. A showing that a regulated activity substantially affects interstate commerce (as required for the third category) is not needed when Congress regulates activity in the first two categories.

We conclude that private and commercial interstate carriers, which carry mailings between and among states and countries, are instrumentalities of interstate commerce, notwithstanding the fact that they also deliver mailings intrastate. Shreveport Rate Cases, 234 U.S. 342, 351, 34 S.Ct. 833 (1914) ("The fact that carriers are instruments of intrastate commerce, as well as of interstate commerce, does not derogate from the complete and paramount authority of Congress over the latter, or preclude the Federal power from being exerted to prevent the intrastate operations of such carriers from being made a means of injury to that which has been confided to Federal care.").

United States v. Gil, 297 F.3d 93, 99–100 (2d Cir. 2002). See also Peter J. Henning, "Maybe it Should Just be Called Federal Fraud: The Changing Nature of the Mail Fraud Statute," 36 B.C.L. Rev. 435 (1995).

C. MONEY LAUNDERING

Federal mail fraud is often regarded as a modern expansion of traditional crimes like larceny by false pretenses (and false promise) and, of course, common law fraud. The original federal mail fraud statute, however, is older than one might suspect, given mail fraud's central role in contemporary federal criminal law. It was passed in 1872, at a time when federal criminal law was still in its infancy. Since there wasn't much federal criminal law, the mail fraud statute would have had a very narrow scope had it been limited to objectives that constituted a federal crime. Rather than criminalizing the fraudulent objective—thereby creating a federal criminal law of frauds duplicative of existing state laws—the Congress instead criminalized uses of the mails to further fraudulent ends, be they criminal (under state or federal law) or not.

Money laundering, by contrast, is an invention of the late twentieth century. See Money Laundering Control Act of 1986, Pub. L. No. 99–570. Federal mail fraud ostensibly criminalizes not the fraud, but the use of a particular means to commit it, specifically the use of the federal (and eventually also private) mail service. Money laundering criminalizes neither fraud, nor the use of certain means to commit it, but concealing the fruits of criminal activity (fraudulent or not). See President's Comm'n on Organized Crime, The Cash Connection: Organized Crime, Financial Institutions, and Money Laundering 7 (1984) (defining money laundering as "the process by which one conceals the existence, illegal source, or illegal application of income, and disguises that income to make it appear legitimate"). Money laundering is a popular offense among federal prosecutors, though just how its popularity compares with that of mail fraud—and perhaps RICO—is unclear. Compare Elkan Abramowitz, "Money Laundering: The New RICO?," N.Y.L.J., Sept. 1, 1992, at 3, and G. Richard Strafer, "Money Laundering: The Crime of the '90's," 27 Am. Crim. L. Rev. 149 (1989) with John C. Coffee, Jr., "From Tort to Crime: Some Reflections on the Criminalization of Fiduciary Breaches and the Problematic Line Between Law and Ethics," 19 Am. Crim. L. Rev. 117, 129 (1981) (quoting federal prosecutors' maxim, "when in doubt, charge mail fraud") and Jed S. Rakoff, "The Federal Mail Fraud Statute (Part I)," 18 Duq. L. Rev. 771, 771–72 (1980) ("the mail fraud statute is our Stradivarius, our Colt 45, our Louisville Slugger, our Cuisinart").

Ostensibly targeted at major drug traffickers, federal money laundering sweeps far more broadly, applying to any "financial transaction which . . . involves the proceeds of specified unlawful activity." 18 U.S.C. § 1956(a)(1). And "specified unlawful activity" is broadly defined to include, among others, RICO violations, major drug crimes, destroying aircraft, coercing federal officials, concealing assets, false claims, bribery, federal assassinations, counterfeiting, smuggling, theft, embezzlement, espionage, arms trafficking, bank fraud, computer fraud, murder, kidnapping, hostage taking, destruction of federal property, bank robbery, copyright infringement, trafficking in counterfeit goods, terrorism, food stamp fraud, environmental crimes, and health care offenses. Id. (c)(7). A sizeable proportion of money laundering cases thus do not involve drug trafficking. Robert G. Morvillo & Barry A. Bohrer,"Checking the Balance: Prosecutorial Power in an Age of Expansive Legislation," 32 Am. Crim. L. Rev. 137, 145 & n.41 (1995) (40%).

There are two federal money laundering statutes, 18 U.S.C. §§ 1956 and 1957, partially reproduced below.

§ 1956(a). Laundering of monetary instruments

(1) Whoever, knowing that the property involved in a financial transaction represents the proceeds of some form of unlawful activity, conducts or attempts to conduct such a financial transaction which in fact involves the proceeds of specified unlawful activity—

(A) (i) with the intent to promote the carrying on of specified unlawful activity; or

(ii) with intent to engage in conduct constituting a violation of section 7201 or 7206 of the Internal Revenue Code of 1986;[a] or

(B) knowing that the transaction is designed in whole or in part—

a. Tax evasion or tax fraud.—Eds.

(i) to conceal or disguise the nature, the location, the source, the ownership, or the control of the proceeds of specified unlawful activity; or

(ii) to avoid a transaction reporting requirement under State or Federal law,[b] shall be sentenced to a fine of not more than $500,000 or twice the value of the property involved in the transaction, whichever is greater, or imprisonment for not more than twenty years, or both.

(2) Whoever transports, transmits, or transfers, or attempts to transport, transmit, or transfer a monetary instrument or funds from a place in the United States to or through a place outside the United States or to a place in the United States from or through a place outside the United States—

(A) with the intent to promote the carrying on of specified unlawful activity; or

(B) knowing that the monetary instrument or funds involved in the transportation represent the proceeds of some form of unlawful activity and knowing that such transportation, transmission, or transfer is designed in whole or in part—

(i) to conceal or disguise the nature, the location, the source, the ownership, or the control of the proceeds of specified unlawful activity; or

(ii) to avoid a transaction reporting requirement under State or Federal law, shall be sentenced to a fine of not more than $500,000 or twice the value of the monetary instrument or funds involved in the transportation, transmission, or transfer, whichever is greater, or imprisonment for not more than twenty years, or both. . . .

(3) Whoever, with the intent—

(A) to promote the carrying on of specified unlawful activity;

(B) to conceal or disguise the nature, location, source, ownership, or control of property believed to be the proceeds of specified unlawful activity; or

(C) to avoid a transaction reporting requirement under State or Federal law, conducts or attempts to conduct a financial transaction involving property represented to be the proceeds of specified unlawful activity, or property used to conduct or facilitate specified unlawful activity, shall be fined under this title or imprisoned for not more than 20 years, or both. . . .

b. Federal law requires the reporting of various monetary transactions in excess of $10,000. (For instance, financial institutions are obligated to report cash transactions exceeding $10,000. 31 U.S.C. § 5313; C.F.R. § 103.11.) Failure to comply with these requirements is criminal, and so is their wilful circumvention. See, e.g., Ratzlaf v. United States, 510 U.S. 135 (1994) (applying 31 U.S.C. §§ 5322(a) & 5324).—EDS.

§ 1957. Engaging in monetary transactions in property derived from specified unlawful activity

(a) Whoever ... knowingly engages or attempts to engage in a monetary transaction in criminally derived property that is of a value greater than $10,000 and is derived from specified unlawful activity, shall be punished as provided in subsection (b).

(b) [T]he punishment for an offense under this section is a fine under title 18, United States Code, or imprisonment for not more than ten years or both....

(c) In a prosecution for an offense under this section, the Government is not required to prove the defendant knew that the offense from which the criminally derived property was derived was specified unlawful activity....

(f) As used in this section—

(1) the term "monetary transaction" means the deposit, withdrawal, transfer, or exchange, in or affecting interstate or foreign commerce, of funds or a monetary instrument by, through, or to a financial institution, ... but such term does not include any transaction necessary to preserve a person's right to representation as guaranteed by the sixth amendment to the Constitution....

United States v. Campbell

United States Court of Appeals for the Fourth Circuit.
977 F.2d 854 (1992).

■ Ervin, Chief Judge.

The United States appeals from the district court's grant of Ellen Campbell's motion for judgment of acquittal on charges of money laundering, 18 U.S.C. § 1956(a)(1)(B)(i), and engaging in a transaction in criminally derived property, 18 U.S.C. § 1957(a)....

In the summer of 1989, Ellen Campbell was a licensed real estate agent working at Lake Norman Realty in Mooresville, North Carolina. During the same period, Mark Lawing was a drug dealer in Kannapolis, North Carolina. Lawing decided to buy a house on Lake Norman....

Lawing represented himself to Campbell as the owner of a legitimate business, L & N Autocraft, which purportedly performed automobile customizing services. When meeting with Campbell, Lawing would travel in either a red Porsche he owned or a gold Porsche owned by a fellow drug dealer, Randy Sweatt, who would usually accompany Lawing. During the trips to look at houses, which occurred during normal business hours, Lawing would bring his cellular phone and would often consume food and beer with Sweatt. At one point, Lawing brought a briefcase containing $20,000 in cash, showing the money to Campbell to demonstrate his ability to purchase a house.

Lawing eventually settled upon a house listed for $191,000 and owned by Edward and Nancy Guy Fortier.... After negotiations, Lawing and the

Fortiers agreed on a price of $182,500, and entered into a written contract. Lawing was unable to secure a loan and decided to ask the Fortiers to accept $60,000 under the table in cash and to lower the contract price to $122,500.[1] ... The Fortiers agreed....

Thereafter Lawing met the Fortiers ... and Campbell in the Mooresville sales office with $60,000 in cash. The money was wrapped in small bundles and carried in a brown paper grocery bag. The money was counted, and a new contract was executed reflecting a sales price of $122,500. Lawing tipped ... Campbell with "a couple of hundred dollars." ...

The money laundering statute under which Campbell was charged applies to any person who:

> knowing that the property involved in a financial transaction represents the proceeds of some form of unlawful activity, conducts or attempts to conduct such a financial transaction which in fact involves the proceeds of specified unlawful activity ... knowing that the transaction is designed in whole or in part ... to conceal or disguise the nature, the location, the source, the ownership, or the control of the proceeds of specified unlawful activity....

18 U.S.C. § 1956(a)(1). The district court found, and Campbell does not dispute, that there was adequate evidence for the jury to find that Campbell conducted a financial transaction which in fact involved the proceeds of Lawing's illegal drug activities. The central issue in contention is whether there was sufficient evidence for the jury to find that Campbell possessed the knowledge that: (1) Lawing's funds were the proceeds of illegal activity, and (2) the transaction was designed to disguise the nature of those proceeds.

In assessing Campbell's culpability, it must be noted that the statute requires actual subjective knowledge. Campbell cannot be convicted on what she objectively should have known. However, this requirement is softened somewhat by the doctrine of willful blindness. In this case, the jury was instructed that:

> The element of knowledge may be satisfied by inferences drawn from proof that a defendant deliberately closed her eyes to what would otherwise have been obvious to her. A finding beyond a reasonable doubt of a conscious purpose to avoid enlightenment would permit an inference of knowledge. Stated another way, a defendant's knowledge of a fact may be inferred upon willful blindness to the existence of a fact.
>
> It is entirely up to you as to whether you find any deliberate closing of the eyes and inferences to be drawn from any evidence. A showing of negligence is not sufficient to support a finding of willfulness or knowledge.

1. Lawing's explanation to Campbell of this unorthodox arrangement was that the lower purchase price would allow Lawing's parents to qualify for a mortgage. Lawing would then make the mortgage payments on his parent's behalf. Lawing justified the secrecy of the arrangement by explaining that his parents had to remain unaware of the $60,000 payment because the only way he could induce their involvement was to convince them he was getting an excellent bargain on the real estate.

I caution you that the willful blindness charge does not authorize you to find that the defendant acted knowingly because she should have known what was occurring when the property at 763 Sundown Road was being sold, or that in the exercise of hindsight she should have known what was occurring or because she was negligent in failing to recognize what was occurring or even because she was reckless or foolish in failing to recognize what was occurring.

Instead, the Government must prove beyond a reasonable doubt that the defendant purposely and deliberately contrived to avoid learning all of the facts.

As outlined above, a money laundering conviction under section 1956(a)(1)(B)(i) requires proof of the defendant's knowledge of two separate facts: (1) that the funds involved in the transaction were the proceeds of illegal activity; and (2) that the transaction was designed to conceal the nature of the proceeds. In its opinion supporting the entry of the judgment of acquittal, the district court erred in interpreting the elements of the offense. After correctly reciting the elements of the statute, the court stated, "in a prosecution against a party other than the drug dealer," the Government must show "a purpose of concealment" and "knowledge of the drug dealer's activities." This assertion misstates the Government's burden. The Government need not prove that the defendant had the purpose of concealing the proceeds of illegal activity. Instead, as the plain language of the statute suggests, the Government must only show that the defendant possessed the knowledge that the transaction was designed to conceal illegal proceeds. This distinction is critical in cases such as the present one, in which the defendant is a person other than the individual who is the source of the tainted money. It is clear from the record that Campbell herself did not act with the purpose of concealing drug proceeds. Her motive, without question, was to close the real estate deal and collect the resulting commission, without regard to the source of the money or the effect of the transaction in concealing a portion of the purchase price. However, Campbell's motivations are irrelevant. Under the terms of the statute, the relevant question is not Campbell's purpose, but rather her knowledge of Lawing's purpose.[4]

The sufficiency of evidence regarding Campbell's knowledge of Lawing's purpose depends on whether Campbell was aware of Lawing's status as a drug dealer. Assuming for the moment that Campbell knew that Lawing's funds were derived from illegal activity, then the under the table transfer of $60,000 in cash would have been sufficient, by itself, to allow the jury to find that Campbell knew, or was willfully blind to the fact, that the transaction was designed for an illicit purpose. Only if Campbell was

4. We have no difficulty in finding that Lawing's purpose satisfied the statutory requirement that the transaction be "designed in whole or in part ... to conceal or disguise the nature, the location, the source, the ownership, or the control of the proceeds of specified unlawful activity...." 18 U.S.C. § 1956(a)(1)(B). The omission of $60,000 from all documentation regarding the sales price of the property clearly satisfies this standard—concealing both the nature and the location of Lawing's illegally derived funds. Accordingly, we need not address the Government's alternative argument that Lawing concealed ownership of the funds by placing title to the Lake Norman property in the name of his parents.

oblivious to the illicit nature of Lawing's funds could she credibly argue that she believed Lawing's explanation of the under the table transfer of cash and was unaware of the money laundering potential of the transaction. In short, the fraudulent nature of the transaction itself provides a sufficient basis from which a jury could infer Campbell's knowledge of the transaction's purpose, if, as assumed above, Campbell also knew of the illegal source of Lawing's money.[5] As a result, we find that, in this case, the knowledge components of the money laundering statute collapse into a single inquiry: Did Campbell know that Lawing's funds were derived from an illegal source?

The Government emphasizes that the district court misstated the Government's burden on this point as well, by holding that the Government must show Campbell's "knowledge of the drug dealer's activities." As the text of the statute indicates, the Government need only show knowledge that the funds represented "the proceeds of some form of unlawful activity." 18 U.S.C. § 1956(a)(1). Practically, this distinction makes little difference. All of the Government's evidence was designed to show that Campbell knew that Lawing was a drug dealer. There is no indication that the jury could have believed that Lawing was involved in some form of criminal activity other than drug dealing. As a result, the district court's misstatement on this point is of little consequence.

The evidence pointing to Campbell's knowledge of Lawing's illegal activities is not overwhelming. First, we find that the district court correctly excluded from consideration testimony by Sweatt that Lawing was a "known" drug dealer. Kannapolis, where Lawing's operations were located, is approximately fifteen miles from Mooresville, where Campbell lived and worked, and, as the district court pointed out, there was no indication that Lawing's reputation extended over such an extensive "community."

However, the district court also downplayed evidence that we find to be highly relevant. [T]he Government presented extensive evidence regarding Lawing's lifestyle. This evidence showed that Lawing and his companion both drove new Porsches, and that Lawing carried a cellular phone, flashed vast amounts of cash, and was able to be away from his purportedly legitimate business for long stretches of time during normal working hours. The district court conceded that this evidence "is not wholely [sic] irrelevant" to Campbell's knowledge of Lawing's true occupation, but noted that Lawing's lifestyle was not inconsistent with that of many of the other inhabitants of the affluent Lake Norman area who were not drug dealers.

5. In this respect the present case is completely distinguishable from the principal case relied upon by the district court, United States v. Sanders, 929 F.2d 1466 (10th Cir. 1991). In that case, the court overturned two money laundering convictions of a defendant who, with funds admittedly derived from an illegal source, had purchased two automobiles. Unlike the present case, there was nothing irregular about the transactions themselves. The court found the transactions to be devoid of any attempt "to conceal or disguise the source or nature of the proceeds" and found that application of the money laundering statute to "ordinary commercial transactions" would "turn the money laundering statute into a 'money spending statute,' " a result clearly not intended by Congress. The present case, by contrast, presents a highly irregular financial transaction which, by its very structure, was designed to mislead onlookers as to the amount of money involved in the transaction.

Again, we find that the district court has drawn inferences from the evidence which, while possibly well-founded, are not the only inferences that can be drawn. It should have been left to the jury to decide whether or not the Government's evidence of Lawing's lifestyle was sufficient to negate the credibility of Campbell's assertion that she believed Lawing to be a legitimate businessman.

The statute under which Campbell was charged in Count 2 provides:

> Whoever ... knowingly engages or attempts to engage in a monetary transaction in criminally derived property that is of a value greater than $10,000 and is derived from specified unlawful activity, shall be punished as provided in subsection (b).

18 U.S.C. § 1957(a). The parties do not dispute that Campbell engaged in a monetary transaction in property of a value in excess of $10,000 or that the property was derived from "specified unlawful activity" as defined by the statute. Once again, the dispositive question is whether Campbell knew that Lawing's funds were the proceeds of criminal activity. As such, the discussion above with regard to the money laundering charge is completely applicable here. Because a jury could reasonably find that Campbell knew of, or was willfully blind to, Lawing's true occupation, it was error for the district court to grant a judgment of acquittal on this count as well....

QUESTIONS AND COMMENTS

1. Read sections 1956 and 1957 carefully to identify the elements of the various offenses they define, including attaching mental states, if any. You may find the following excerpt from the U.S. Attorney's Manual (the guidebook for federal prosecutors) helpful:

> Section 1956(a) defines three types of criminal conduct: domestic money laundering transactions (§ 1956(a)(1)); international money laundering transactions (§ 1956(a)(2)); and undercover "sting" money laundering transactions (§ 1956(a)(3)).
>
> To be criminally culpable under 18 U.S.C. § 1956(a)(1), a defendant must conduct or attempt to conduct a financial transaction, knowing that the property involved in the financial transaction represents the proceeds of some unlawful activity, with one of the four specific intents discussed below, and the property must *in fact* be derived from a specified unlawful activity.
>
> The actual source of the funds must be one of the specified forms of criminal activity.... [P]roceeds of certain crimes committed in another country may constitute proceeds of a specified unlawful activity for purposes of the money laundering statutes.
>
> To prove a violation of § 1956(a)(1), the prosecutor must prove, either by direct or circumstantial evidence, that the defendant knew that the property involved was the proceeds of any felony under State, Federal or foreign law. The prosecutor need not show that the defendant knew the specific crime from which the proceeds were derived; the prosecutor must prove only that the defendant knew that the property was illegally derived in some way.

The prosecutor must also prove that the defendant initiated or concluded, or participated in initiating or concluding, a financial transaction. A "transaction" is defined in § 1956(c)(3) as a purchase, sale, loan, pledge, gift, transfer, delivery, other disposition, and with respect to a financial institution, a deposit, withdrawal, transfer between accounts, loan, exchange of currency, extension of credit, purchase or sale of any stock, bond, certificate of deposit, or other monetary instrument, use of a safe-deposit box, or any other payment, transfer or delivery by, through or to a financial institution.

A "financial transaction" is defined in § 1956(c)(4) as a transaction which affects interstate or foreign commerce and: (1) involves the movement of funds by wire or by other means; (2) involves the use of a monetary instrument; or (3) involves the transfer of title to real property, a vehicle, a vessel or an aircraft; or (4) involves the use of a financial institution which is engaged in, or the activities of which affect, interstate or foreign commerce. * * *

In conducting the financial transaction, the defendant must have acted with one of the following four specific intents:

§ 1956(a)(1)(A)(i): intent to promote the carrying on of specified unlawful activity;

§ 1956(a)(1)(A)(ii): intent to engage in tax evasion or tax fraud;

§ 1956(a)(1)(B)(i): knowledge that the transaction was designed to conceal or disguise the nature, location, source, ownership or control of proceeds of the specified unlawful activity; or

§ 1956(a)(1)(B)(ii): knowledge that the transaction was designed to avoid a transaction reporting requirement under State or Federal law.

Prosecutions pursuant to 18 U.S.C. § 1956(a)(2) arise when monetary instruments or funds are transported, transmitted or transferred internationally, and the defendant acted with one of the requisite criminal intents (i.e., promoting, concealing, or avoiding reporting requirements). The intent to engage in tax violations is not included in § 1956(a)(2). * * *

Section 1956(a)(3) relates to undercover operations where the financial transaction involves property represented to be proceeds of specified unlawful activity. The proceeds in § 1956(a)(3) cases are not actually derived from a real crime; they are undercover funds supplied by the Government. The representation must be made by or authorized by a Federal officer with authority to investigate or prosecute money laundering violations. The representation may also be made by another at the direction of or approval of a Federal officer. It should be noted that the specific intent provisions in § 1956(a)(3) are slightly different from those in § 1956(a)(1). First, the intent to violate the tax laws is *not* included in this subsection. Second, subsections 1956(a)(3)(B) and (C) require that the transaction be conducted with the *intent* to conceal or disguise the nature, location, source, ownership or control of the property or to avoid a transaction reporting requirement, respectively, in contrast to subsections 1956(a)(1)(B)(i) and (ii), which only require that defendant *know* that the transaction is designed, in whole or in part, to accomplish one of those ends....

Prosecutions under 18 U.S.C. § 1957 arise when the defendant knowingly conducts a *monetary* transaction in criminally derived property in an amount greater than $10,000, which is in fact proceeds of a specified unlawful activity. Section 1957(f)(1) defines a monetary transaction as a "deposit, withdrawal, transfer, or exchange, in or affecting interstate or foreign commerce, of funds or a monetary instrument ... by, through, or to a financial institution (as defined in section 1956 of this title), including any transaction that would be a financial transaction under section 1956(c)(4)(B)...." ...

The most significant difference from § 1956 prosecutions is the intent requirement. Under § 1957, the four intents have been replaced with a $10,000 threshold amount for each non-aggregated transaction and the requirement that a financial institution be involved in the transaction. Although the prosecutor need not prove any intent to promote, conceal or avoid the reporting requirements, it still must be shown that the defendant knew the property was derived from some criminal activity and that the funds were in fact derived from a specified unlawful activity....

Sections 1956 and 1957 include "attempts" as well as completed offenses. Conspiracies are indictable under 18 U.S.C. § 1956(h)....

U.S. Dep't of Justice, U.S. Attorneys Manual, Criminal Resource Manual § 2101.

2. Compare sections 1956 and 1957—in form, substance, and function—with the federal mail fraud statute. Do they face similar vagueness problems? Problems with other aspects of the principle of legality (ch. 2)? Note that in *Blarek* (supra ch. 1), the defendants argued on appeal that the money laundering statute (section 1957(a), to be precise) was unconstitutionally vague as applied to them. In particular, they argued that the phrase "criminally derived property" failed to provide them with adequate notice. The Second Circuit disagreed, noting that, while the phrase "might be vague as applied to extreme situations," the specific defendants had sufficient notice that the money they laundered was in fact "criminally derived." United States v. Blarek, 166 F.3d 1202 (2d Cir. 1998). See generally D. Randall Johnson, "The Criminally Derived Property Statute: Constitutional and Interpretive Issues Raised by 18 U.S.C. § 1957," 34 Wm. & Mary L. Rev. 1291 (1993).

3. To get a sense of the scope of section 1956, consider that "financial transaction" has been interpreted by courts to mean "a transaction involving the movement of funds involving one or more monetary instruments," including, e.g., writing a personal check, buying a money order, buying or selling a car, arranging a sham purchase of a car, accepting a cashier's check, as well as mailing or transporting cash (in a car, say). "Financial institutions" include not only banks but also car dealerships, travel agencies, and casinos. See 1 Otto G. Obermaier & Robert G. Morvillo, White Collar Crime: Business and Regulatory Offenses § 2A.02[1][a] (2003).

4. Why is money laundering a crime? In the case of mail fraud, though not in it its inchoate version (attempt or conspiracy), it is often not difficult to identify a personal victim who has been defrauded and thus has experienced an interference with her property interests. (That the discovery of a personal victim is not required for conviction of federal mail fraud, because the victim of this offense is in fact *not* the fraud victim but the U.S. Postal Service and therefore ultimately the federal government, is another matter. See supra part B.)

Who, then, is the victim of money laundering? The judge in the *Blarek* case—against two interior decorators who were charged with laundering a drug lord's money by decorating his homes (supra ch. 1)—tries to answer that question:

> While listening to a defendant's descriptions of the embellished bedrooms and recreation areas created for the children of José Santacruz, and how much fun they would provide for these young people, the jury could not help but reflect on the thousands of teens whose lives had been ruined by Cali cartel drugs sold for the cash used to pay for Santacruz's extravagant lifestyle.

United States v. Blarek, 7 F.Supp.2d 192, 196 (E.D.N.Y.1998).

Peter Alldridge has compiled a more comprehensive list of rationales:

> 1. Laundering Removes the Incentive to Commit Predicate Offenses
>
> 2. Laundering is a Form of Complicity in Predicate Offenses
>
> 3. Laundering "Gets the Real Criminals" (i.e., Upper–Level Offenders)
>
> 4. Laundering Corrupts Professionals (e.g., Lawyers, Bankers, Accountants)
>
> 5. Laundering Jeopardizes Confidence in the Banking System

"The Moral Limits of the Crime of Money Laundering," 5 Buff. Crim. L. Rev. 279 (2001).

Alldridge finds these rationales unconvincing. Do you? Is it sufficient justification for a criminal offense—and one that carries significant penalties—that it drains some otherwise criminal activity of its "life blood" or, more generally, that it disrupts "criminal finance"? See generally Mariano–Florentino Cuéllar, "The Tenuous Relationship Between the Fight Against Money Laundering and the Disruption of Criminal Finance," 93 J. Crim. L. & Criminology 311 (2003). How far removed may the definition of a criminal offense be from the conduct it is designed to prevent and prohibit, and the interests it is designed to protect?

5. Imagine that we charged Campbell with aiding and abetting Lawing's drug sales *or* with aiding and abetting *his* money laundering. What problems would the prosecutor face, using traditional complicity law, with each charge? Focus primarily on whether she is aiding the drug sales themselves. Would it be (more?) legitimate to charge Campbell as an accomplice to the sales if Lawing had told her, "I'll have $60,000 in cash for you next week"? Can she be an accomplice to sales that already occurred,

though she did not promise Lawing at the time of the sales that she would take his cash? Would agreeing to take cash in the future take care of the "act" requirement for complicity? How about the mental state requirement for complicity, though? Does it matter if we believe Campbell will make more money on this sale than she'd otherwise make selling to a different buyer because she is willing to accommodate his desire to unload lots of cash? Recall the discussion of whether (or when) there is a genuine distinction between requiring that an accomplice have a true purpose to aid the principal's crime and requiring merely that she knew that she is facilitating the crime, so long as the facilitation is substantial (and the crime is serious?). See ch. 8.

Recall, too, the discussion of whether (or when) it might be more appropriate to proscribe (relatively?) specific behavior thought to contribute to perpetrators' criminal ventures *rather* than to assess whether an actor had aided and abetted a particular crime (or a particular criminal performing a range of criminal actions). We assessed, for instance, the wisdom of proscribing the sale of radar detector devices rather than punishing the sellers as accomplices to speeding. Are the rules against "money laundering" that apply to those other than the original criminals who are trying to conceal the proceeds of their offenses sensible, specific conduct restrictions? Are punishment levels for this sort of conduct set too high, though, even if one believes the conduct facilitates criminal behavior to some extent?

Would it be more sensible to forbid (very large) cash transactions across the board, without regard to the seller's direct knowledge or willful ignorance of the source of cash, or to require that *all* such transactions be reported, not just the sub-set that gives rise to the reporting requirements now? (Revisit *Ratzlaf*, ch. 5.) Would it be sensible instead (or in addition) to remove large (hundred dollar) bills from circulation altogether to try to make the use of cash more difficult? To bar cash altogether and use a (government-subsidized) electronic money system? Or are the rules in this area not so much premised on the notion that sellers who take large quantities of cash (unduly) facilitate the initial crimes as they are premised on the idea that we will be able to *locate* criminals better if they can't secret the cash? In this sense, do we punish those who might accept cash in order to force the initial criminal to use entities (like banks) to dispose of cash that can be monitored, thus revealing criminal identity?

In either case, does applying the money-laundering rules to sellers violate either the spirit or letter of our principles against punishing omissions? (See ch. 4.) Or does thinking about whether the seller is "acting" or "failing to act" simply expose the difficulty of drawing stable act/omission lines? In any case, is it fair to enlist sellers in the war on crime by asking them to turn away buyers? Would it be any fairer if we believed sellers (almost) always receive (at least some) premium when they accept large quantities of cash, so that we might think of them as splitting some of the gains from the initial criminal transaction? (In *Campbell*, did the Fortiers commit money laundering?)

6. Note that money laundering is "a separate crime distinct from the underlying offense that generated the money to be laundered." United

States v. Edgmon, 952 F.2d 1206, 1213 (10th Cir. 1991). But, in the case of defendants who are charged with both the underlying offense and with laundering the proceeds of the offense, does money laundering amount to more than enhancing the punishment for the underlying offense?

7. Why is money laundering a *federal* crime? Unlike mail fraud (but like wire fraud), money laundering cannot rely on the federal government's "postal power." It rests on the commerce power instead. Hence section 1956(c)(4), which requires that to qualify as money laundering a financial transaction must "affect[] interstate or foreign commerce." Courts, however, have been quick to point out that the impact on commerce need only be "de minimis." Cf. United States v. Leslie, 103 F.3d 1093 (2d Cir. 1997) (involvement of "a bank" in transaction not enough to establish impact on interstate commerce, unless the word "Federal" appears in bank's name).

8. Reconsider *Blarek* in light of *Campbell* and *Sanders* (discussed in *Campbell* n. 5). What's the difference between "money laundering" and "money spending"? Is money spending always money laundering if I know (or willfully ignored) that the money is "dirty"? At any rate, isn't section 1957 in fact a money spending statute? The Sanders were prosecuted under section 1956; what if they had been prosecuted under section 1957 instead (assuming the cars cost more than $10,000)? Is there any reason why Congress—or any state legislature—could not simply criminalize spending dirty money (or receiving it in exchange for goods), no matter what the amount and no matter in what form, by what means, and to what end?

9. *Lawyers and Money Laundering*. If interior decorators (*Blarek*) and real estate agents (*Campbell*) can be guilty of money laundering, what about lawyers (not to mention the local grocery store owner)? Since 1994, Section 1957 (but not § 1956—why?) now includes the following proviso: " 'monetary transaction'. . . . does not include any transaction necessary to preserve a person's right to representation as guaranteed by the sixth amendment to the Constitution. . . ." 18 U.S.C. § 1957(f)(1). That is not to say, however, that defendants are free to pay their attorneys with "dirty" money, nor that defense attorneys don't fear—or face—prosecution for money laundering. Consider the following news story.

> [C]riminal defense attorney Neil Taylor is now on trial in U.S. District Court in Miami on charges of money laundering, conspiracy to obstruct justice and filing false tax returns in connection with accepting legal fees to represent an accused drug dealer. Taylor is charged with taking more than $1 million in illicit fees from accused drug lords Willie Falcon and Sal Magluta, in violation of a restraining order that froze the two men's assets, then hiding the source of the money on his tax forms.
>
> When accepting payments of more than $10,000, all businesses, including law firms, are required to file Internal Revenue Service forms detailing names and full identification of those paying. Taylor, say prosecutors, conspired with the accused drug traffickers to make up a phony name and driver license for Wilfredo Alvarez, who was a courier for Falcon and Magluta, and who allegedly paid Taylor's fee. Taylor's

attorney, Robert Josefsberg, a partner at Podhurst Orseck Josefsberg in Miami, denies the charges.

Prosecutors have accused Falcon and Magluta in court of operating a $2 billion drug trafficking business. They allegedly spent $25 million on attorneys' fees through the 1990s. They were acquitted in 1996, but a jury foreman was later charged with taking a bribe in that trial. Falcon and Magluta, who remain behind bars, are facing a new federal indictment alleging conspiracy to intimidate and bribe witnesses.

Taylor . . . is the fourth lawyer—out of nearly 40 who represented Falcon and Magluta—to be prosecuted by the U.S. Attorney's office in Miami. The other three—Don Ferguson, Leonard Mark Dachs and Richard Martinez—all were convicted. "This has had a chilling effect on criminal defense lawyers," says Richard Sharpstein, another criminal defense attorney who used to specialize in drug cases. "I and most lawyers will not go near cases where the fees are questionable, 'cause they're absolutely not worth it."

The U.S. Department of Justice started clamping down on lawyers who represent alleged drug dealers in the early 1980s by seizing their fees as forfeiture funds. The crackdown was prompted by fear among tough-on-drugs politicians and law enforcement officials that the government was losing the war on illegal narcotics because cocaine and marijuana kingpins were hiring high-priced lawyers and winning acquittals.

In the mid–1980s, Congress passed tough money laundering laws, . . . which gave federal prosecutors powerful new weapons in the narcotics war. It enabled them to put anyone who took money originating from drug trafficking or other illegal activities in prison.

But some defense attorneys say these statutes were never intended to be used against attorneys representing defendants in these cases. They point to an amendment, passed by Congress in 1994 after heavy lobbying by criminal defense lawyers, that excludes funds used "for the right to representation as guaranteed by the Sixth Amendment" from consideration in money laundering cases. . . .

A broader problem, according to the South Florida defense bar, is that the government also is scrutinizing legal fees paid by those charged with white-collar crimes such as health care fraud and securities fraud. . . .

Reuben Cahn, chief assistant to the federal public defender in Miami, angrily argues that the U.S. Attorney's pre-conviction seizure of defendants' assets and its targeting of defense attorneys essentially is forcing wealthy defendants to turn to public defenders for representation. The problem, he says, is that the P.D.'s office is supposed to represent the indigent and already is stretched thin.

"It's galling," Cahn says. "The U.S. Attorney's office has 221 regular attorneys and 40 special attorneys. We have 49 lawyers. It's a struggle to provide good representation to everyone."

> To make sure the feds won't object to their collecting legal fees from "hot" clients, several criminal defense attorneys say they routinely meet with the line prosecutor in the case before accepting the client. But that is no guarantee of safe passage. In his opening statement, prosecutor Rubino acknowledged that Neil Taylor had met beforehand with the prosecutor in the Falcon/Magluta case to discuss his fees before taking on representation of the two defendants. But Taylor still was prosecuted. . . .

Julie Kay, "Heat is on Attorneys in Drug Trafficking Cases: Florida Lawyer Is Accused of Taking 'Dirty Money,' " Miami Daily Bus. Rev., May 25, 2001. [Taylor's trial ended in a mistrial. After his second trial also ended in a mistrial, he accepted a misdemeanor plea (relating to the reporting requirement) with a sentence of one year's probation. Barry Tarlow, "Column: RICO Report," 26 Champion 51 (2002).]

Apart from criminal liability for money laundering, defense attorneys who are paid with dirty money may find that their fees are subject to forfeiture. Caplin & Drysdale v. United States, 491 U.S. 617 (1989) (rejecting sixth amendment challenge to attorneys' fees forfeiture under 21 U.S.C. § 853 on the ground that defendants may still "be able to find lawyers willing to represent them, hoping that their fees will be paid in the event of acquittal, or via some other means that a defendant might come by in the future"). In fact, federal prosecutors have argued that the Sixth Amendment exception to § 1957 is meaningless in light of *Caplin & Drysdale*. Consider the following case, which rejects this reading of the exception but ultimately interprets it as an affirmative defense:

> In this case of first impression, the United States brings a criminal prosecution against a former criminal defense attorney for money laundering in violation of 18 U.S.C. § 1957. . . . Salvador Magluta, on four separate occasions, purportedly transferred large sums of cash, totaling $566,400.00, to Defendant, who deposited these monies into his trust accounts, ostensibly as payment for Benjamin Kramer's criminal defense. [At the time of the charged offenses, Magluta had been indicted in a massive drug conspiracy case in this district. Kramer was facing state murder charges.]
>
> The United States asserts that, by accepting and then depositing these payments, Defendant violated § 1957, a broadly worded statute that criminalizes a wide range of financial transactions involving criminal proceeds. . . .
>
> Defendant's motion to dismiss centers on the statutory exception for payments necessary to preserve an individual's Sixth Amendment right to counsel. . . .
>
> . . . . Defendant argues that because he received the funds from Magluta to pay for Kramer's criminal defense, he cannot be prosecuted under § 1957, due to the statutory exception. . . . The United States counters that the Supreme Court's decisions holding that the Sixth Amendment right to counsel provides no defense to federal forfeiture actions has severely limited, if not completely eviscerated, the exception contained in § 1957(f). The United States reasons that, since the

Sixth Amendment does not preclude the forfeiture of assets transferred by a criminal defendant to his attorney, § 1957(f)'s exception cannot sanitize otherwise culpable transactions on the basis that they constitute payment for criminal defense work. . . .

At oral argument, Defendant's counsel articulated his broad interpretation of § 1957(f)'s Sixth Amendment exception as one that "does not permit prosecution of a criminal defense attorney for receipt of fees for legal representation." As the Seventh Circuit recently explained, such an expansive reading of the exception is untenable [because] "every defendant charged with money laundering under 18 U.S.C. § 1957 could, *at any time*, beat the charge by funneling the proceeds which constituted the initial, illegal transaction toward their defense. . . . Correctly read, the statute offers a defense where a defendant engages in a transaction underlying a money laundering charge with the present intent of exercising Sixth Amendment rights." United States v. Hoogenboom, 209 F.3d 665, 669 (7th Cir. 2000) (emphasis supplied). . . .

On the other hand, it cannot be deduced that § 1957(f)'s exception effectively has no teeth, as the United States argues. The United States' position relies upon . . . Caplin & Drysdale, Chartered v. United States, 491 U.S. 617, 109 S.Ct. 2646 (1989). The United States' analysis, however, is basically flawed because the federal forfeiture statutes do not include a parallel exception to the one contained in § 1957(f). Thus, the Supreme Court's decision [was] limited to whether the Sixth Amendment, in and of itself, prohibited the forfeiture of criminal proceeds paid to attorneys. . . . The Supreme Court's determination that assets paid to criminal defense attorneys can be subject to forfeiture was necessitated by its construction of the federal forfeiture statutes. Absent a statutory exception, the Supreme Court reasoned the Sixth Amendment could not protect assets from forfeiture because they were never rightfully the defendant's to transfer to his attorney in the first instance. Drug proceeds, like the loot from a bank robbery, are not excluded from the reach of the federal forfeiture statutes simply because they are used to pay for a criminal defendant's legal fees. Congress could have statutorily excluded such transactions from the federal forfeiture statutes, but chose not to.

. . . . If § 1957 were construed in the manner that the United States urges, the exception for transactions necessary to protect an individual's Sixth Amendment rights would amount to no exception at all. . . . [R]equiring the forfeiture of assets received by a criminal defense attorney for his services is far less draconian than making the attorney a criminal for receiving such assets for his services. . . .

Having determined that the § 1957 exception is neither an absolute bar to Defendant's prosecution, nor a nullity, the Court [considers] whether § 1957(f)'s exception is (1) an element of the money laundering offense, which the Government has the burden of negating, or (2) an affirmative defense, which Defendant has the burden of proving. This distinction is of importance at the motion to dismiss stage, because if the exception is considered an element of the offense, the

Government would be required to aver in the indictment that the transactions were not necessary to protect a person's Sixth Amendment rights. In that event, the failure to aver in the indictment that the transactions were necessary to protect a person's Sixth Amendment rights would constitute a "legal infirmity." Here, the superseding indictment contains no such averments.

However, the Court concludes that § 1957(f)'s Sixth Amendment exception is an affirmative defense, the merits of which must be assessed based upon the evidence adduced at trial. From the face of § 1957, it is not obvious whether Congress intended § 1957(f)'s exception to be an element of the offense or an affirmative defense. On the one hand, reading § 1957(f) naturally, the exception appears to be part of the statutory definition of prohibited "monetary transactions," which would support the exception being an element of the money laundering crime. On the other hand, weighing heavily in favor of construing the exception as an affirmative defense is the process by which the exception was adopted. The exception was added to the statute two years after its enactment, in order to prevent criminalizing the legitimate dealings of defense attorneys with drug dealing clients. "Without the amendment a drug dealer's check to his lawyer might have constituted a new federal felony." [United States v. Rutgard, 116 F.3d 1270, 1291 (9th Cir. 1997).] Through the exception Congress created a safe harbor for legitimate criminal defense expenses; it did not alter the substantive elements of money laundering under § 1957....

With the exception correctly viewed as an affirmative defense, it is clear that Defendant's motion to dismiss is premature.... Defendant's argument is that he is innocent in light of § 1957(f)'s exception; however, "guilt or innocence is a decision which may properly be reached only after a trial on the merits and not before." To bring § 1957(f)'s affirmative defense before the jury, Defendant must come forward with credible evidence at trial that the subject transactions were "necessary to preserve a person's right to representation as guaranteed by the sixth amendment to the Constitution." If he does so, he will be entitled to a jury instruction on the affirmative defense created by § 1957(f). If he fails to come forward with such evidence, the case will be given to the jury as a straight § 1957 money laundering case.

United States v. Ferguson, 142 F.Supp.2d 1350 (S.D. Fla. 2000). [Having lost his motion to dismiss, Ferguson, a former federal prosecutor, pled guilty to a lesser charge.]

Under the court's analysis in *Ferguson*, what (more?) could the legislature have done to communicate its intent to classify the clause as an element of the offense? If it's an affirmative defense, what type of affirmative defense is it supposed to be? A justification, an excuse? Or does it perhaps disprove an offense element ("monetary transaction")? (In that case, shouldn't the prosecution bear the burden of proof?)

APPENDIX
MODEL PENAL CODE

Table of Contents

PART I. GENERAL PROVISIONS

ARTICLE 1. PRELIMINARY

ARTICLE 2. GENERAL PRINCIPLES OF LIABILITY

ARTICLE 7. AUTHORITY OF COURT IN SENTENCING

PART II. DEFINITION OF SPECIFIC CRIMES

OFFENSES AGAINST EXISTENCE OR STABILITY OF THE STATE

ARTICLE 200. OFFENSES AGAINST EXISTANCE OR STABILITY OF THE STATE

OFFENSES INVOLVING DANGER TO THE PERSON

ARTICLE 210. CRIMINAL HOMICIDE

ARTICLE 211. ASSAULT; RECKLESS ENDANGERING; THREATS

ARTICLE 243. ABUSE OF OFFICE

OFFENSES AGAINST PUBLIC ORDER AND DECENCY

ARTICLE 250. RIOT, DISORDERLY CONDUCT, AND RELATED OFFENSES

ARTICLE 251. PUBLIC INDECENCY

ADDITIONAL ARTICLES

PART III. TREATMENT AND CORRECTION—TABLE OF CONTENTS AND SELECTED PROVISIONS

ARTICLE 301. SUSPENSION OF SENTENCE; PROBATION

ARTICLE 302. FINES

ARTICLE 303. SHORT–TERM IMPRISONMENT

ARTICLE 304. LONG–TERM IMPRISONMENT

ARTICLE 305. RELEASE ON PAROLE

ARTICLE 306. LOSS AND RESTORATION OF RIGHTS INCIDENT TO CONVICTION OR IMPRISONMENT

PART IV. ORGANIZATION OF CORRECTION—TABLE OF CONTENTS

ARTICLE 401. DEPARTMENT OF CORRECTION

ARTICLE 402. BOARD OF PAROLE

ARTICLE 403. ADMINISTRATION OF INSTITUTIONS

ARTICLE 404. DIVISION OF PAROLE

ALTERNATIVE ARTICLE 404. DIVISION OF PROBATION AND PAROLE

ARTICLE 405. DIVISION OF PROBATION

PART I. GENERAL PROVISIONS

ARTICLE 1. PRELIMINARY

Section 1.01. Title and Effective Date.

(1) This Act is called the Penal and Correctional Code and may be cited as P.C.C. It shall become effective on ___.

(2) Except as provided in Subsections (3) and (4) of this Section, the Code does not apply to offenses committed prior to its effective date and prosecutions for such offenses shall be governed by the prior law, which is continued in effect for that purpose, as if this Code were not in force. For the purposes of this Section, an offense was committed prior to the effective date of the Code if any of the elements of the offense occurred prior thereto.

(3) In any case pending on or after the effective date of the Code, involving an offense committed prior to such date:

(a) procedural provisions of the Code shall govern, insofar as they are justly applicable and their application does not introduce confusion or delay;

(b) provisions of the Code according a defense or mitigation shall apply, with the consent of the defendant;

(c) the Court, with the consent of the defendant, may impose sentence under the provisions of the Code applicable to the offense and the offender.

(4) Provisions of the Code governing the treatment and the release or discharge of prisoners, probationers and parolees shall apply to persons under sentence for offenses committed prior to the effective date of the Code, except that the minimum or maximum period of their detention or supervision shall in no case be increased.

Section 1.02. Purposes; Principles of Construction.

(1) The general purposes of the provisions governing the definition of offenses are:

(a) to forbid and prevent conduct that unjustifiably and inexcusably inflicts or threatens substantial harm to individual or public interests;

(b) to subject to public control persons whose conduct indicates that they are disposed to commit crimes;

(c) to safeguard conduct that is without fault from condemnation as criminal;

(d) to give fair warning of the nature of the conduct declared to constitute an offense;

(e) to differentiate on reasonable grounds between serious and minor offenses.

(2) The general purposes of the provisions governing the sentencing and treatment of offenders are:

(a) to prevent the commission of offenses;

(b) to promote the correction and rehabilitation of offenders;

(c) to safeguard offenders against excessive, disproportionate or arbitrary punishment;

(d) to give fair warning of the nature of the sentences that may be imposed on conviction of an offense;

(e) to differentiate among offenders with a view to a just individualization in their treatment;

(f) to define, coordinate and harmonize the powers, duties and functions of the courts and of administrative officers and agencies responsible for dealing with offenders;

(g) to advance the use of generally accepted scientific methods and knowledge in the sentencing and treatment of offenders;

(h) to integrate responsibility for the administration of the correctional system in a State Department of Correction [or other single department or agency].

(3) The provisions of the Code shall be construed according to the fair import of their terms but when the language is susceptible of differing constructions it shall be interpreted to further the general purposes stated in this Section and the special purposes of the particular provision involved. The discretionary powers conferred by the Code shall be exercised in accordance with the criteria stated in the Code and, insofar as such criteria are not decisive, to further the general purposes stated in this Section.

Section 1.03. Territorial Applicability.

(1) Except as otherwise provided in this Section, a person may be convicted under the law of this State of an offense committed by his own conduct or the conduct of another for which he is legally accountable if:

(a) either the conduct which is an element of the offense or the result which is such an element occurs within this State; or

(b) conduct occurring outside the State is sufficient under the law of this State to constitute an attempt to commit an offense within the State; or

(c) conduct occurring outside the State is sufficient under the law of this State to constitute a conspiracy to commit an offense within the State and an overt act in furtherance of such conspiracy occurs within the State; or

(d) conduct occurring within the State establishes complicity in the commission of, or an attempt, solicitation or conspiracy to commit, an offense in another jurisdiction which also is an offense under the law of this State; or

(e) the offense consists of the omission to perform a legal duty imposed by the law of the State with respect to domicile, residence or a relationship to a person, thing or transaction in the State; or

(f) the offense is based on a statute of this State which expressly prohibits conduct outside the State, when the conduct bears a reasonable relation to a legitimate interest of this State and the actor knows or should know that his conduct is likely to affect that interest.

(2) Subsection (1)(a) does not apply when either causing a specified result or a purpose to cause or danger of causing such a result is an element of an offense and the result occurs or is designed or likely to occur only in another jurisdiction where the conduct charged would not constitute an offense, unless a legislative purpose plainly appears to declare the conduct criminal regardless of the place of the result.

(3) Subsection (1)(a) does not apply when causing a particular result is an element of an offense and the result is caused by conduct occurring outside the State which would not constitute an offense if the result had occurred there, unless the actor purposely or knowingly caused the result within the State.

(4) When the offense is homicide, either the death of the victim or the bodily impact causing death constitutes a "result," within the meaning of Subsection (1)(a) and if the body of a homicide victim is found within the State, it is presumed that such result occurred within the State.

(5) This State includes the land and water and the air space above such land and water with respect to which the State has legislative jurisdiction.

Section 1.04. Classes of Crimes; Violations.

(1) An offense defined by this Code or by any other statute of this State, for which a sentence of [death or of] imprisonment is authorized, constitutes a crime. Crimes are classified as felonies, misdemeanors or petty misdemeanors.

(2) A crime is a felony if it is so designated in this Code or if persons convicted thereof may be sentenced [to death or] to imprisonment for a term which, apart from an extended term, is in excess of one year.

(3) A crime is a misdemeanor if it is so designated in this Code or in a statute other than this Code enacted subsequent thereto.

(4) A crime is a petty misdemeanor if it is so designated in this Code or in a statute other than this Code enacted subsequent thereto or if it is defined by a statute other than this Code which now provides that persons convicted thereof may be sentenced to imprisonment for a term of which the maximum is less than one year.

(5) An offense defined by this Code or by any other statute of this State constitutes a violation if it is so designated in this Code or in the law defining the offense or if no other sentence than a fine, or fine and forfeiture or other civil penalty is authorized upon conviction or if it is defined by a statute other than this Code which now provides that the offense shall not constitute a crime. A violation does not constitute a crime and conviction of a violation shall not give rise to any disability or legal disadvantage based on conviction of a criminal offense.

(6) Any offense declared by law to constitute a crime, without specification of the grade thereof or of the sentence authorized upon conviction, is a misdemeanor.

(7) An offense defined by any statute of this State other than this Code shall be classified as provided in this Section and the sentence that may be imposed upon conviction thereof shall hereafter be governed by this Code.

Section 1.05. All Offenses Defined by Statute; Application of General Provisions of the Code.

(1) No conduct constitutes an offense unless it is a crime or violation under this Code or another statute of this State.

(2) The provisions of Part I of the Code are applicable to offenses defined by other statutes, unless the Code otherwise provides.

(3) This Section does not affect the power of a court to punish for contempt or to employ any sanction authorized by law for the enforcement of an order or a civil judgment or decree.

Section 1.06. Time Limitations.

(1) A prosecution for murder may be commenced at any time.

(2) Except as otherwise provided in this Section, prosecutions for other offenses are subject to the following periods of limitation:

(a) a prosecution for a felony of the first degree must be commenced within six years after it is committed;

(b) a prosecution for any other felony must be commenced within three years after it is committed;

(c) a prosecution for a misdemeanor must be commenced within two years after it is committed;

(d) a prosecution for a petty misdemeanor or a violation must be commenced within six months after it is committed.

(3) If the period prescribed in Subsection (2) has expired, a prosecution may nevertheless be commenced for:

(a) any offense a material element of which is either fraud or a breach of fiduciary obligation within one year after discovery of the offense by an aggrieved party or by a person who has legal duty to represent an aggrieved party and who is himself not a party to the offense, but in no case shall this provision extend the period of limitation otherwise applicable by more than three years; and

(b) any offense based upon misconduct in office by a public officer or employee at any time when the defendant is in public office or employment or within two years thereafter, but in no case shall this provision extend the period of limitation otherwise applicable by more than three years.

(4) An offense is committed either when every element occurs, or, if a legislative purpose to prohibit a continuing course of conduct plainly appears, at the time when the course of conduct or the defendant's complicity therein is terminated. Time starts to run on the day after the offense is committed.

(5) A prosecution is commenced either when an indictment is found [or an information filed] or when a warrant or other process is issued, provided that such warrant or process is executed without unreasonable delay.

(6) The period of limitation does not run:

(a) during any time when the accused is continuously absent from the State or has no reasonably ascertainable place of abode or work within the State, but in no case shall this provision extend the period of limitation otherwise applicable by more than three years; or

(b) during any time when a prosecution against the accused for the same conduct is pending in this State.

Section 1.07. Method of Prosecution When Conduct Constitutes More Than One Offense.

(1) *Prosecution for Multiple Offenses; Limitation on Convictions.* When the same conduct of a defendant may establish the commission of more than one offense, the defendant may be prosecuted for each such offense. He may not, however, be convicted of more than one offense if:

(a) one offense is included in the other, as defined in Subsection (4) of this Section; or

(b) one offense consists only of a conspiracy or other form of preparation to commit the other; or

(c) inconsistent findings of fact are required to establish the commission of the offenses; or

(d) the offenses differ only in that one is defined to prohibit a designated kind of conduct generally and the other to prohibit a specific instance of such conduct; or

(e) the offense is defined as a continuing course of conduct and the defendant's course of conduct was uninterrupted, unless the law provides that specific periods of such conduct constitute separate offenses.

(2) *Limitation on Separate Trials for Multiple Offenses.* Except as provided in Subsection (3) of this Section, a defendant shall not be subject to separate trials for multiple offenses based on the same conduct or arising from the same criminal episode, if such offenses are known to the appropriate prosecuting officer at the

time of the commencement of the first trial and are within the jurisdiction of a single court.

(3) *Authority of Court to Order Separate Trials.* When a defendant is charged with two or more offenses based on the same conduct or arising from the same criminal episode, the Court, on application of the prosecuting attorney or of the defendant, may order any such charge to be tried separately, if it is satisfied that justice so requires.

(4) *Conviction of Included Offense Permitted.* A defendant may be convicted of an offense included in an offense charged in the indictment [or the information]. An offense is so included when:

(a) it is established by proof of the same or less than all the facts required to establish the commission of the offense charged; or

(b) it consists of an attempt or solicitation to commit the offense charged or to commit an offense otherwise included therein; or

(c) it differs from the offense charged only in the respect that a less serious injury or risk of injury to the same person, property or public interest or a lesser kind of culpability suffices to establish its commission.

(5) *Submission of Included Offense to Jury.* The Court shall not be obligated to charge the jury with respect to an included offense unless there is a rational basis for a verdict acquitting the defendant of the offense charged and convicting him of the included offense.

Section 1.08. When Prosecution Barred by Former Prosecution for the Same Offense.

When a prosecution is for a violation of the same provision of the statutes and is based upon the same facts as a former prosecution, it is barred by such former prosecution under the following circumstances:

(1) The former prosecution resulted in an acquittal. There is an acquittal if the prosecution resulted in a finding of not guilty by the trier of fact or in a determination that there was insufficient evidence to warrant a conviction. A finding of guilty of a lesser included offense is an acquittal of the greater inclusive offense, although the conviction is subsequently set aside.

(2) The former prosecution was terminated, after the information had been filed or the indictment found, by a final order or judgment for the defendant, which has not been set aside, reversed, or vacated and which necessarily required a determination inconsistent with a fact or a legal proposition that must be established for conviction of the offense.

(3) The former prosecution resulted in a conviction. There is a conviction if the prosecution resulted in a judgment of conviction which has not been reversed or vacated, a verdict of guilty which has not been set aside and which is capable of supporting a judgment, or a plea of guilty accepted by the Court. In the latter two cases failure to enter judgment must be for a reason other than a motion of the defendant.

(4) The former prosecution was improperly terminated. Except as provided in this Subsection, there is an improper termination of a prosecution if the termination is for reasons not amounting to an acquittal, and it takes place after the first witness is sworn but before verdict. Termination under any of the following circumstances is not improper:

(a) The defendant consents to the termination or waives, by motion to dismiss or otherwise, his right to object to the termination.

(b) The trial court finds that the termination is necessary because:

(1) it is physically impossible to proceed with the trial in conformity with law; or

(2) there is a legal defect in the proceedings which would make any judgment entered upon a verdict reversible as a matter of law; or

(3) prejudicial conduct, in or outside the courtroom, makes it impossible to proceed with the trial without injustice to either the defendant or the State; or

(4) the jury is unable to agree upon a verdict; or

(5) false statements of a juror on voir dire prevent a fair trial.

Section 1.09. When Prosecution Barred by Former Prosecution for Different Offense.

Although a prosecution is for a violation of a different provision of the statutes than a former prosecution or is based on different facts, it is barred by such former prosecution under the following circumstances:

(1) The former prosecution resulted in an acquittal or in a conviction as defined in Section 1.08 and the subsequent prosecution is for:

(a) any offense of which the defendant could have been convicted on the first prosecution; or

(b) any offense for which the defendant should have been tried on the first prosecution under Section 1.07, unless the Court ordered a separate trial of the charge of such offense; or

(c) the same conduct, unless (i) the offense of which the defendant was formerly convicted or acquitted and the offense for which he is subsequently prosecuted each requires proof of a fact not required by the other and the law defining each of such offenses is intended to prevent a substantially different harm or evil, or (ii) the second offense was not consummated when the former trial began.

(2) The former prosecution was terminated, after the information was filed or the indictment found, by an acquittal or by a final order or judgment for the defendant which has not been set aside, reversed or vacated and which acquittal, final order or judgment necessarily required a determination inconsistent with a fact which must be established for conviction of the second offense.

(3) The former prosecution was improperly terminated, as improper termination is defined in Section 1.08, and the subsequent prosecution is for an offense of which the defendant could have been convicted had the former prosecution not been improperly terminated.

Section 1.10. Former Prosecution in Another Jurisdiction: When a Bar.

When conduct constitutes an offense within the concurrent jurisdiction of this State and of the United States or another State, a prosecution in any such other jurisdiction is a bar to a subsequent prosecution in this State under the following circumstances:

(1) The first prosecution resulted in an acquittal or in a conviction as defined in Section 1.08 and the subsequent prosecution is based on the same conduct, unless (a) the offense of which the defendant was formerly convicted or acquitted and the offense for which he is subsequently prosecuted each requires proof of a fact not required by the other and the law defining each of such offenses is intended to

prevent a substantially different harm or evil or (b) the second offense was not consummated when the former trial began; or

(2) The former prosecution was terminated, after the information was filed or the indictment found, by an acquittal or by a final order or judgment for the defendant which has not been set aside, reversed or vacated and which acquittal, final order or judgment necessarily required a determination inconsistent with a fact which must be established for conviction of the offense of which the defendant is subsequently prosecuted.

Section 1.11. Former Prosecution Before Court Lacking Jurisdiction or When Fraudulently Procured by the Defendant.

A prosecution is not a bar within the meaning of Sections 1.08, 1.09 and 1.10 under any of the following circumstances:

(1) The former prosecution was before a court which lacked jurisdiction over the defendant or the offense; or

(2) The former prosecution was procured by the defendant without the knowledge of the appropriate prosecuting officer and with the purpose of avoiding the sentence which might otherwise be imposed; or

(3) The former prosecution resulted in a judgment of conviction which was held invalid in a subsequent proceeding on a writ of habeas corpus, coram nobis or similar process.

Section 1.12. Proof Beyond a Reasonable Doubt; Affirmative Defenses; Burden of Proving Fact When Not an Element of an Offense; Presumptions.

(1) No person may be convicted of an offense unless each element of such offense is proved beyond a reasonable doubt. In the absence of such proof, the innocence of the defendant is assumed.

(2) Subsection (1) of this Section does not:

(a) require the disproof of an affirmative defense unless and until there is evidence supporting such defense; or

(b) apply to any defense which the Code or another statute plainly requires the defendant to prove by a preponderance of evidence.

(3) A ground of defense is affirmative, within the meaning of Subsection (2)(a) of this Section, when:

(a) it arises under a section of the Code which so provides; or

(b) it relates to an offense defined by a statute other than the Code and such statute so provides; or

(c) it involves a matter of excuse or justification peculiarly within the knowledge of the defendant on which he can fairly be required to adduce supporting evidence.

(4) When the application of the Code depends upon the finding of a fact which is not an element of an offense, unless the Code otherwise provides:

(a) the burden of proving the fact is on the prosecution or defendant, depending on whose interest or contention will be furthered if the finding should be made; and

(b) the fact must be proved to the satisfaction of the Court or jury, as the case may be.

(5) When the Code establishes a presumption with respect to any fact which is an element of an offense, it has the following consequences:

(a) when there is evidence of the facts which give rise to the presumption, the issue of the existence of the presumed fact must be submitted to the jury, unless the Court is satisfied that the evidence as a whole clearly negatives the presumed fact; and

(b) when the issue of the existence of the presumed fact is submitted to the jury, the Court shall charge that while the presumed fact must, on all the evidence, be proved beyond a reasonable doubt, the law declares that the jury may regard the facts giving rise to the presumption as sufficient evidence of the presumed fact.

(6) A presumption not established by the Code or inconsistent with it has the consequences otherwise accorded it by law.

Section 1.13. General Definitions.

In this Code, unless a different meaning plainly is required:

(1) "statute" includes the Constitution and a local law or ordinance of a political subdivision of the State;

(2) "act" or "action" means a bodily movement whether voluntary or involuntary;

(3) "voluntary" has the meaning specified in Section 2.01;

(4) "omission" means a failure to act;

(5) "conduct" means an action or omission and its accompanying state of mind, or, where relevant, a series of acts and omissions;

(6) "actor" includes, where relevant, a person guilty of an omission;

(7) "acted" includes, where relevant, "omitted to act";

(8) "person," "he" and "actor" include any natural person and, where relevant, a corporation or an unincorporated association;

(9) "element of an offense" means (i) such conduct or (ii) such attendant circumstances or (iii) such a result of conduct as

(a) is included in the description of the forbidden conduct in the definition of the offense; or

(b) establishes the required kind of culpability; or

(c) negatives an excuse or justification for such conduct; or

(d) negatives a defense under the statute of limitations; or

(e) establishes jurisdiction or venue;

(10) "material element of an offense" means an element that does not relate exclusively to the statute of limitations, jurisdiction, venue or to any other matter similarly unconnected with (i) the harm or evil, incident to conduct, sought to be prevented by the law defining the offense, or (ii) the existence of a justification or excuse for such conduct;

(11) "purposely" has the meaning specified in Section 2.02 and equivalent terms such as "with purpose," "designed" or "with design" have the same meaning;

(12) "intentionally" or "with intent" means purposely;

(13) "knowingly" has the meaning specified in Section 2.02 and equivalent terms such as "knowing" or "with knowledge" have the same meaning;

(14) "recklessly" has the meaning specified in Section 2.02 and equivalent terms such as "recklessness" or "with recklessness" have the same meaning;

(15) "negligently" has the meaning specified in Section 2.02 and equivalent terms such as "negligence' " or "with negligence" have the same meaning;

(16) "reasonably believes" or "reasonable belief" designates a belief which the actor is not reckless or negligent in holding.

ARTICLE 2. GENERAL PRINCIPLES OF LIABILITY

Section 2.01. Requirement of Voluntary Act; Omission as Basis of Liability; Possession as an Act.

(1) A person is not guilty of an offense unless his liability is based on conduct which includes a voluntary act or the omission to perform an act of which he is physically capable.

(2) The following are not voluntary acts within the meaning of this Section:

(a) a reflex or convulsion;

(b) a bodily movement during unconsciousness or sleep;

(c) conduct during hypnosis or resulting from hypnotic suggestion;

(d) a bodily movement that otherwise is not a product of the effort or determination of the actor, either conscious or habitual.

(3) Liability for the commission of an offense may not be based on an omission unaccompanied by action unless:

(a) the omission is expressly made sufficient by the law defining the offense; or

(b) a duty to perform the omitted act is otherwise imposed by law.

(4) Possession is an act, within the meaning of this Section, if the possessor knowingly procured or received the thing possessed or was aware of his control thereof for a sufficient period to have been able to terminate his possession.

Section 2.02. General Requirements of Culpability.

(1) *Minimum Requirements of Culpability.* Except as provided in Section 2.05, a person is not guilty of an offense unless he acted purposely, knowingly, recklessly or negligently, as the law may require, with respect to each material element of the offense.

(2) *Kinds of Culpability Defined.*

(a) *Purposely.*

A person acts purposely with respect to a material element of an offense when:

(i) if the element involves the nature of his conduct or a result thereof, it is his conscious object to engage in conduct of that nature or to cause such a result; and

(ii) if the element involves the attendant circumstances, he is aware of the existence of such circumstances or he believes or hopes that they exist.

(b) *Knowingly.*

A person acts knowingly with respect to a material element of an offense when:

(i) if the element involves the nature of his conduct or the attendant circumstances, he is aware that his conduct is of that nature or that such circumstances exist; and

(ii) if the element involves a result of his conduct, he is aware that it is practically certain that his conduct will cause such a result.

(c) *Recklessly.*

A person acts recklessly with respect to a material element of an offense when he consciously disregards a substantial and unjustifiable risk that the material element exists or will result from his conduct. The risk must be of such a nature and degree that, considering the nature and purpose of the actor's conduct and the circumstances known to him, its disregard involves a gross deviation from the standard of conduct that a law-abiding person would observe in the actor's situation.

(d) *Negligently.*

A person acts negligently with respect to a material element of an offense when he should be aware of a substantial and unjustifiable risk that the material element exists or will result from his conduct. The risk must be of such a nature and degree that the actor's failure to perceive it, considering the nature and purpose of his conduct and the circumstances known to him, involves a gross deviation from the standard of care that a reasonable person would observe in the actor's situation.

(3) *Culpability Required Unless Otherwise Provided.* When the culpability sufficient to establish a material element of an offense is not prescribed by law, such element is established if a person acts purposely, knowingly or recklessly with respect thereto.

(4) *Prescribed Culpability Requirement Applies to All Material Elements.* When the law defining an offense prescribes the kind of culpability that is sufficient for the commission of an offense, without distinguishing among the material elements thereof, such provision shall apply to all the material elements of the offense, unless a contrary purpose plainly appears.

(5) *Substitutes for Negligence, Recklessness and Knowledge.* When the law provides that negligence suffices to establish an element of an offense, such element also is established if a person acts purposely, knowingly or recklessly. When recklessness suffices to establish an element, such element also is established if a person acts purposely or knowingly. When acting knowingly suffices to establish an element, such element also is established if a person acts purposely.

(6) *Requirement of Purpose Satisfied if Purpose Is Conditional.* When a particular purpose is an element of an offense, the element is established although such purpose is conditional, unless the condition negatives the harm or evil sought to be prevented by the law defining the offense.

(7) *Requirement of Knowledge Satisfied by Knowledge of High Probability.* When knowledge of the existence of a particular fact is an element of an offense, such knowledge is established if a person is aware of a high probability of its existence, unless he actually believes that it does not exist.

(8) *Requirement of Wilfulness Satisfied by Acting Knowingly.* A requirement that an offense be committed wilfully is satisfied if a person acts knowingly with respect to the material elements of the offense, unless a purpose to impose further requirements appears.

(9) *Culpability as to Illegality of Conduct.* Neither knowledge nor recklessness or negligence as to whether conduct constitutes an offense or as to the existence,

meaning or application of the law determining the elements of an offense is an element of such offense, unless the definition of the offense or the Code so provides.

(10) *Culpability as Determinant of Grade of Offense.* When the grade or degree of an offense depends on whether the offense is committed purposely, knowingly, recklessly or negligently, its grade or degree shall be the lowest for which the determinative kind of culpability is established with respect to any material element of the offense.

Section 2.03. Causal Relationship Between Conduct and Result; Divergence Between Result Designed or Contemplated and Actual Result or Between Probable and Actual Result.

(1) Conduct is the cause of a result when:

(a) it is an antecedent but for which the result in question would not have occurred; and

(b) the relationship between the conduct and result satisfies any additional causal requirements imposed by the Code or by the law defining the offense.

(2) When purposely or knowingly causing a particular result is an element of an offense, the element is not established if the actual result is not within the purpose or the contemplation of the actor unless:

(a) the actual result differs from that designed or contemplated, as the case may be, only in the respect that a different person or different property is injured or affected or that the injury or harm designed or contemplated would have been more serious or more extensive than that caused; or

(b) the actual result involves the same kind of injury or harm as that designed or contemplated and is not too remote or accidental in its occurrence to have a [just] bearing on the actor's liability or on the gravity of his offense.

(3) When recklessly or negligently causing a particular result is an element of an offense, the element is not established if the actual result is not within the risk of which the actor is aware or, in the case of negligence, of which he should be aware unless:

(a) the actual result differs from the probable result only in the respect that a different person or different property is injured or affected or that the probable injury or harm would have been more serious or more extensive than that caused; or

(b) the actual result involves the same kind of injury or harm as the probable result and is not too remote or accidental in its occurrence to have a [just] bearing on the actor's liability or on the gravity of his offense.

(4) When causing a particular result is a material element of an offense for which absolute liability is imposed by law, the element is not established unless the actual result is a probable consequence of the actor's conduct.

Section 2.04. Ignorance or Mistake.

(1) Ignorance or mistake as to a matter of fact or law is a defense if:

(a) the ignorance or mistake negatives the purpose, knowledge, belief, recklessness or negligence required to establish a material element of the offense; or

(b) the law provides that the state of mind established by such ignorance or mistake constitutes a defense.

(2) Although ignorance or mistake would otherwise afford a defense to the offense charged, the defense is not available if the defendant would be guilty of

another offense had the situation been as he supposed. In such case, however, the ignorance or mistake of the defendant shall reduce the grade and degree of the offense of which he may be convicted to those of the offense of which he would be guilty had the situation been as he supposed.

(3) A belief that conduct does not legally constitute an offense is a defense to a prosecution for that offense based upon such conduct when:

(a) the statute or other enactment defining the offense is not known to the actor and has not been published or otherwise reasonably made available prior to the conduct alleged; or

(b) he acts in reasonable reliance upon an official statement of the law, afterward determined to be invalid or erroneous, contained in (i) a statute or other enactment; (ii) a judicial decision, opinion or judgment; (iii) an administrative order or grant of permission; or (iv) an official interpretation of the public officer or body charged by law with responsibility for the interpretation, administration or enforcement of the law defining the offense.

(4) The defendant must prove a defense arising under Subsection (3) of this Section by a preponderance of evidence.

Section 2.05. When Culpability Requirements Are Inapplicable to Violations and to Offenses Defined by Other Statutes; Effect of Absolute Liability in Reducing Grade of Offense to Violation.

(1) The requirements of culpability prescribed by Sections 2.01 and 2.02 do not apply to:

(a) offenses which constitute violations, unless the requirement involved is included in the definition of the offense or the Court determines that its application is consistent with effective enforcement of the law defining the offense; or

(b) offenses defined by statutes other than the Code, insofar as a legislative purpose to impose absolute liability for such offenses or with respect to any material element thereof plainly appears.

(2) Notwithstanding any other provision of existing law and unless a subsequent statute otherwise provides:

(a) when absolute liability is imposed with respect to any material element of an offense defined by a statute other than the Code and a conviction is based upon such liability, the offense constitutes a violation; and

(b) although absolute liability is imposed by law with respect to one or more of the material elements of an offense defined by a statute other than the Code, the culpable commission of the offense may be charged and proved, in which event negligence with respect to such elements constitutes sufficient culpability and the classification of the offense and the sentence that may be imposed therefor upon conviction are determined by Section 1.04 and Article 6 of the Code.

Section 2.06. Liability for Conduct of Another; Complicity.

(1) A person is guilty of an offense if it is committed by his own conduct or by the conduct of another person for which he is legally accountable, or both.

(2) A person is legally accountable for the conduct of another person when:

(a) acting with the kind of culpability that is sufficient for the commission of the offense, he causes an innocent or irresponsible person to engage in such conduct; or

(b) he is made accountable for the conduct of such other person by the Code or by the law defining the offense; or

(c) he is an accomplice of such other person in the commission of the offense.

(3) A person is an accomplice of another person in the commission of an offense if:

(a) with the purpose of promoting or facilitating the commission of the offense, he

(i) solicits such other person to commit it; or

(ii) aids or agrees or attempts to aid such other person in planning or committing it; or

(iii) having a legal duty to prevent the commission of the offense, fails to make proper effort so to do; or

(b) his conduct is expressly declared by law to establish his complicity.

(4) When causing a particular result is an element of an offense, an accomplice in the conduct causing such result is an accomplice in the commission of that offense, if he acts with the kind of culpability, if any, with respect to that result that is sufficient for the commission of the offense.

(5) A person who is legally incapable of committing a particular offense himself may be guilty thereof if it is committed by the conduct of another person for which he is legally accountable, unless such liability is inconsistent with the purpose of the provision establishing his incapacity.

(6) Unless otherwise provided by the Code or by the law defining the offense, a person is not an accomplice in an offense committed by another person if:

(a) he is a victim of that offense; or

(b) the offense is so defined that his conduct is inevitably incident to its commission; or

(c) he terminates his complicity prior to the commission of the offense and

(i) wholly deprives it of effectiveness in the commission of the offense; or

(ii) gives timely warning to the law enforcement authorities or otherwise makes proper effort to prevent the commission of the offense.

(7) An accomplice may be convicted on proof of the commission of the offense and of his complicity therein, though the person claimed to have committed the offense has not been prosecuted or convicted or has been convicted of a different offense or degree of offense or has an immunity to prosecution or conviction or has been acquitted.

Section 2.07. Liability of Corporations, Unincorporated Associations and Persons Acting, or Under a Duty to Act, in Their Behalf.

(1) A corporation may be convicted of the commission of an offense if:

(a) the offense is a violation or the offense is defined by a statute other than the Code in which a legislative purpose to impose liability on corporations plainly appears and the conduct is performed by an agent of the corporation acting in behalf of the corporation within the scope of his office or employment, except that if the law defining the offense designates the agents for whose conduct the corporation is accountable or the circumstances under which it is accountable, such provisions shall apply; or

(b) the offense consists of an omission to discharge a specific duty of affirmative performance imposed on corporations by law; or

(c) the commission of the offense was authorized, requested, commanded, performed or recklessly tolerated by the board of directors or by a high managerial agent acting in behalf of the corporation within the scope of his office or employment.

(2) When absolute liability is imposed for the commission of an offense, a legislative purpose to impose liability on a corporation shall be assumed, unless the contrary plainly appears.

(3) An unincorporated association may be convicted of the commission of an offense if:

(a) the offense is defined by a statute other than the Code which expressly provides for the liability of such an association and the conduct is performed by an agent of the association acting in behalf of the association within the scope of his office or employment, except that if the law defining the offense designates the agents for whose conduct the association is accountable or the circumstances under which it is accountable, such provisions shall apply; or

(b) the offense consists of an omission to discharge a specific duty of affirmative performance imposed on associations by law.

(4) As used in this Section:

(a) "corporation" does not include an entity organized as or by a governmental agency for the execution of a governmental program;

(b) "agent" means any director, officer, servant, employee or other person authorized to act in behalf of the corporation or association and, in the case of an unincorporated association, a member of such association;

(c) "high managerial agent" means an officer of a corporation or an unincorporated association, or, in the case of a partnership, a partner, or any other agent of a corporation or association having duties of such responsibility that his conduct may fairly be assumed to represent the policy of the corporation or association.

(5) In any prosecution of a corporation or an unincorporated association for the commission of an offense included within the terms of Subsection (1)(a) or Subsection (3)(a) of this Section, other than an offense for which absolute liability has been imposed, it shall be a defense if the defendant proves by a preponderance of evidence that the high managerial agent having supervisory responsibility over the subject matter of the offense employed due diligence to prevent its commission. This paragraph shall not apply if it is plainly inconsistent with the legislative purpose in defining the particular offense.

(6)(a) A person is legally accountable for any conduct he performs or causes to be performed in the name of the corporation or an unincorporated association or in its behalf to the same extent as if it were performed in his own name or behalf.

(b) Whenever a duty to act is imposed by law upon a corporation or an unincorporated association, any agent of the corporation or association having primary responsibility for the discharge of the duty is legally accountable for a reckless omission to perform the required act to the same extent as if the duty were imposed by law directly upon himself.

(c) When a person is convicted of an offense by reason of his legal accountability for the conduct of a corporation or an unincorporated association, he is subject to the sentence authorized by law when a natural person is convicted of an offense of the grade and the degree involved.

Section 2.08. Intoxication.

(1) Except as provided in Subsection (4) of this Section, intoxication of the actor is not a defense unless it negatives an element of the offense.

(2) When recklessness establishes an element of the offense, if the actor, due to self-induced intoxication, is unaware of a risk of which he would have been aware had he been sober, such unawareness is immaterial.

(3) Intoxication does not, in itself, constitute mental disease within the meaning of Section 4.01.

(4) Intoxication which (a) is not self-induced or (b) is pathological is an affirmative defense if by reason of such intoxication the actor at the time of his conduct lacks substantial capacity either to appreciate its criminality [wrongfulness] or to conform his conduct to the requirements of law.

(5) *Definitions.* In this Section unless a different meaning plainly is required:

(a) "intoxication" means a disturbance of mental or physical capacities resulting from the introduction of substances into the body;

(b) "self-induced intoxication" means intoxication caused by substances which the actor knowingly introduces into his body, the tendency of which to cause intoxication he knows or ought to know, unless he introduces them pursuant to medical advice or under such circumstances as would afford a defense to a charge of crime;

(c) "pathological intoxication" means intoxication grossly excessive in degree, given the amount of the intoxicant, to which the actor does not know he is susceptible.

Section 2.09. Duress.

(1) It is an affirmative defense that the actor engaged in the conduct charged to constitute an offense because he was coerced to do so by the use of, or a threat to use, unlawful force against his person or the person of another, which a person of reasonable firmness in his situation would have been unable to resist.

(2) The defense provided by this Section is unavailable if the actor recklessly placed himself in a situation in which it was probable that he would be subjected to duress. The defense is also unavailable if he was negligent in placing himself in such a situation, whenever negligence suffices to establish culpability for the offense charged.

(3) It is not a defense that a woman acted on the command of her husband, unless she acted under such coercion as would establish a defense under this Section. [The presumption that a woman, acting in the presence of her husband, is coerced is abolished.]

(4) When the conduct of the actor would otherwise be justifiable under Section 3.02, this Section does not preclude such defense.

Section 2.10. Military Orders.

It is an affirmative defense that the actor, in engaging in the conduct charged to constitute an offense, does no more than execute an order of his superior in the armed services which he does not know to be unlawful.

Section 2.11. Consent.

(1) *In General.* The consent of the victim to conduct charged to constitute an offense or to the result thereof is a defense if such consent negatives an element of the offense or precludes the infliction of the harm or evil sought to be prevented by the law defining the offense.

(2) *Consent to Bodily Harm.* When conduct is charged to constitute an offense because it causes or threatens bodily harm, consent to such conduct or to the infliction of such harm is a defense if:

(a) the bodily harm consented to or threatened by the conduct consented to is not serious; or

(b) the conduct and the harm are reasonably foreseeable hazards of joint participation in a lawful athletic contest or competitive sport; or

(c) the consent establishes a justification for the conduct under Article 3 of the Code.

(3) *Ineffective Consent.* Unless otherwise provided by the Code or by the law defining the offense, assent does not constitute consent if:

(a) it is given by a person who is legally incompetent to authorize the conduct charged to constitute the offense; or

(b) it is given by a person who by reason of youth, mental disease or defect or intoxication is manifestly unable or known by the actor to be unable to make a reasonable judgment as to the nature or harmfulness of the conduct charged to constitute the offense; or

(c) it is given by a person whose improvident consent is sought to be prevented by the law defining the offense; or

(d) it is induced by force, duress or deception of a kind sought to be prevented by the law defining the offense.

Section 2.12. De Minimis Infractions.

The Court shall dismiss a prosecution if, having regard to the nature of the conduct charged to constitute an offense and the nature of the attendant circumstances, it finds that the defendant's conduct:

(1) was within a customary license or tolerance, neither expressly negatived by the person whose interest was infringed nor inconsistent with the purpose of the law defining the offense; or

(2) did not actually cause or threaten the harm or evil sought to be prevented by the law defining the offense or did so only to an extent too trivial to warrant the condemnation of conviction; or

(3) presents such other extenuations that it cannot reasonably be regarded as envisaged by the legislature in forbidding the offense.

The Court shall not dismiss a prosecution under Subsection (3) of this Section without filing a written statement of its reasons.

Section 2.13. Entrapment.

(1) A public law enforcement official or a person acting in cooperation with such an official perpetrates an entrapment if for the purpose of obtaining evidence of the commission of an offense, he induces or encourages another person to engage in conduct constituting such offense by either:

(a) making knowingly false representations designed to induce the belief that such conduct is not prohibited; or

(b) employing methods of persuasion or inducement which create a substantial risk that such an offense will be committed by persons other than those who are ready to commit it.

(2) Except as provided in Subsection (3) of this Section, a person prosecuted for an offense shall be acquitted if he proves by a preponderance of evidence that his conduct occurred in response to an entrapment. The issue of entrapment shall be tried by the Court in the absence of the jury.

(3) The defense afforded by this Section is unavailable when causing or threatening bodily injury is an element of the offense charged and the prosecution is based on conduct causing or threatening such injury to a person other than the person perpetrating the entrapment.

ARTICLE 3. GENERAL PRINCIPLES OF JUSTIFICATION

Section 3.01. Justification an Affirmative Defense; Civil Remedies Unaffected.

(1) In any prosecution based on conduct which is justifiable under this Article, justification is an affirmative defense.

(2) The fact that conduct is justifiable under this Article does not abolish or impair any remedy for such conduct which is available in any civil action.

Section 3.02. Justification Generally: Choice of Evils.

(1) Conduct which the actor believes to be necessary to avoid a harm or evil to himself or to another is justifiable, provided that:

(a) the harm or evil sought to be avoided by such conduct is greater than that sought to be prevented by the law defining the offense charged; and

(b) neither the Code nor other law defining the offense provides exceptions or defenses dealing with the specific situation involved; and

(c) a legislative purpose to exclude the justification claimed does not otherwise plainly appear.

(2) When the actor was reckless or negligent in bringing about the situation requiring a choice of harms or evils or in appraising the necessity for his conduct, the justification afforded by this Section is unavailable in a prosecution for any offense for which recklessness or negligence, as the case may be, suffices to establish culpability.

Section 3.03. Execution of Public Duty.

(1) Except as provided in Subsection (2) of this Section, conduct is justifiable when it is required or authorized by:

(a) the law defining the duties or functions of a public officer or the assistance to be rendered to such officer in the performance of his duties; or

(b) the law governing the execution of legal process; or

(c) the judgment or order of a competent court or tribunal; or

(d) the law governing the armed services or the lawful conduct of war; or

(e) any other provision of law imposing a public duty.

(2) The other sections of this Article apply to:

(a) the use of force upon or toward the person of another for any of the purposes dealt with in such sections; and

(b) the use of deadly force for any purpose, unless the use of such force is otherwise expressly authorized by law or occurs in the lawful conduct of war.

(3) The justification afforded by Subsection (1) of this Section applies:

(a) when the actor believes his conduct to be required or authorized by the judgment or direction of a competent court or tribunal or in the lawful execution of legal process, notwithstanding lack of jurisdiction of the court or defect in the legal process; and

(b) when the actor believes his conduct to be required or authorized to assist a public officer in the performance of his duties, notwithstanding that the officer exceeded his legal authority.

Section 3.04. Use of Force in Self–Protection.

(1) *Use of Force Justifiable for Protection of the Person.* Subject to the provisions of this Section and of Section 3.09, the use of force upon or toward another person is justifiable when the actor believes that such force is immediately necessary for the purpose of protecting himself against the use of unlawful force by such other person on the present occasion.

(2) *Limitations on Justifying Necessity for Use of Force.*

(a) The use of force is not justifiable under this Section:

(i) to resist an arrest which the actor knows is being made by a peace officer, although the arrest is unlawful; or

(ii) to resist force used by the occupier or possessor of property or by another person on his behalf, where the actor knows that the person using the force is doing so under a claim of right to protect the property, except that this limitation shall not apply if:

(1) the actor is a public officer acting in the performance of his duties or a person lawfully assisting him therein or a person making or assisting in a lawful arrest; or

(2) the actor has been unlawfully dispossessed of the property and is making a re-entry or recaption justified by Section 3.06; or

(3) the actor believes that such force is necessary to protect himself against death or serious bodily harm.

(b) The use of deadly force is not justifiable under this Section unless the actor believes that such force is necessary to protect himself against death, serious bodily harm, kidnapping or sexual intercourse compelled by force or threat; nor is it justifiable if:

(i) the actor, with the purpose of causing death or serious bodily harm, provoked the use of force against himself in the same encounter; or

(ii) the actor knows that he can avoid the necessity of using such force with complete safety by retreating or by surrendering possession of a thing to a person asserting a claim of right thereto or by complying with a demand that he abstain from any action which he has no duty to take, except that:

(1) the actor is not obliged to retreat from his dwelling or place of work, unless he was the initial aggressor or is assailed in his place of work by another person whose place of work the actor knows it to be; and

(2) a public officer justified in using force in the performance of his duties or a person justified in using force in his assistance or a

person justified in using force in making an arrest or preventing an escape is not obliged to desist from efforts to perform such duty, effect such arrest or prevent such escape because of resistance or threatened resistance by or on behalf of the person against whom such action is directed.

(c) Except as required by paragraphs (a) and (b) of this Subsection, a person employing protective force may estimate the necessity thereof under the circumstances as he believes them to be when the force is used, without retreating, surrendering possession, doing any other act which he has no legal duty to do or abstaining from any lawful action.

(3) *Use of Confinement as Protective Force.* The justification afforded by this Section extends to the use of confinement as protective force only if the actor takes all reasonable measures to terminate the confinement as soon as he knows that he safely can, unless the person confined has been arrested on a charge of crime.

Section 3.05. Use of Force for the Protection of Other Persons.

(1) Subject to the provisions of this Section and of Section 3.09, the use of force upon or toward the person of another is justifiable to protect a third person when:

(a) the actor would be justified under Section 3.04 in using such force to protect himself against the injury he believes to be threatened to the person whom he seeks to protect; and

(b) under the circumstances as the actor believes them to be, the person whom he seeks to protect would be justified in using such protective force; and

(c) the actor believes that his intervention is necessary for the protection of such other person.

(2) Notwithstanding Subsection (1) of this Section:

(a) when the actor would be obliged under Section 3.04 to retreat, to surrender the possession of a thing or to comply with a demand before using force in self-protection, he is not obliged to do so before using force for the protection of another person, unless he knows that he can thereby secure the complete safety of such other person; and

(b) when the person whom the actor seeks to protect would be obliged under Section 3.04 to retreat, to surrender the possession of a thing or to comply with a demand if he knew that he could obtain complete safety by so doing, the actor is obliged to try to cause him to do so before using force in his protection if the actor knows that he can obtain complete safety in that way; and

(c) neither the actor nor the person whom he seeks to protect is obliged to retreat when in the other's dwelling or place of work to any greater extent than in his own.

Section 3.06. Use of Force for the Protection of Property.

(1) *Use of Force Justifiable for Protection of Property.* Subject to the provisions of this Section and of Section 3.09, the use of force upon or toward the person of another is justifiable when the actor believes that such force is immediately necessary:

(a) to prevent or terminate an unlawful entry or other trespass upon land or a trespass against or the unlawful carrying away of tangible, movable property, provided that such land or movable property is, or is believed by the actor to be, in his possession or in the possession of another person for whose protection he acts; or

(b) to effect an entry or re-entry upon land or to retake tangible movable property, provided that the actor believes that he or the person by whose authority he acts or a person from whom he or such other person derives title was unlawfully dispossessed of such land or movable property and is entitled to possession, and provided, further, that:

(i) the force is used immediately or on fresh pursuit after such dispossession; or

(ii) the actor believes that the person against whom he uses force has no claim of right to the possession of the property and, in the case of land, the circumstances, as the actor believes them to be, are of such urgency that it would be an exceptional hardship to postpone the entry or re-entry until a court order is obtained.

(2) *Meaning of Possession.* For the purposes of Subsection (1) of this Section:

(a) a person who has parted with the custody of property to another who refuses to restore it to him is no longer in possession, unless the property is movable and was and still is located on land in his possession;

(b) a person who has been dispossessed of land does not regain possession thereof merely by setting foot thereon;

(c) a person who has a license to use or occupy real property is deemed to be in possession thereof except against the licensor acting under claim of right.

(3) *Limitations on Justifiable Use of Force.*

(a) *Request to Desist.* The use of force is justifiable under this Section only if the actor first requests the person against whom such force is used to desist from his interference with the property, unless the actor believes that:

(i) such request would be useless; or

(ii) it would be dangerous to himself or another person to make the request; or

(iii) substantial harm will be done to the physical condition of the property which is sought to be protected before the request can effectively be made.

(b) *Exclusion of Trespasser.* The use of force to prevent or terminate a trespass is not justifiable under this Section if the actor knows that the exclusion of the trespasser will expose him to substantial danger of serious bodily harm.

(c) *Resistance of Lawful Re-entry or Recaption.* The use of force to prevent an entry or re-entry upon land or the recaption of movable property is not justifiable under this Section, although the actor believes that such re-entry or recaption is unlawful, if:

(i) the re-entry or recaption is made by or on behalf of a person who was actually dispossessed of the property; and

(ii) it is otherwise justifiable under paragraph (1)(b) of this Section.

(d) *Use of Deadly Force.* The use of deadly force is not justifiable under this Section unless the actor believes that:

(i) the person against whom the force is used is attempting to dispossess him of his dwelling otherwise than under a claim of right to its possession; or

(ii) the person against whom the force is used is attempting to commit or consummate arson, burglary, robbery or other felonious theft or property destruction and either:

(1) has employed or threatened deadly force against or in the presence of the actor; or

(2) the use of force other than deadly force to prevent the commission or the consummation of the crime would expose the actor or another in his presence to substantial danger of serious bodily harm.

(4) *Use of Confinement as Protective Force.* The justification afforded by this Section extends to the use of confinement as protective force only if the actor takes all reasonable measures to terminate the confinement as soon as he knows that he can do so with safety to the property, unless the person confined has been arrested on a charge of crime.

(5) *Use of Device to Protect Property.* The justification afforded by this Section extends to the use of a device for the purpose of protecting property only if:

(a) the device is not designed to cause or known to create a substantial risk of causing death or serious bodily harm; and

(b) the use of the particular device to protect the property from entry or trespass is reasonable under the circumstances, as the actor believes them to be; and

(c) the device is one customarily used for such a purpose or reasonable care is taken to make known to probable intruders the fact that it is used.

(6) *Use of Force to Pass Wrongful Obstructor.* The use of force to pass a person whom the actor believes to be purposely or knowingly and unjustifiably obstructing the actor from going to a place to which he may lawfully go is justifiable, provided that:

(a) the actor believes that the person against whom he uses force has no claim of right to obstruct the actor; and

(b) the actor is not being obstructed from entry or movement on land which he knows to be in the possession or custody of the person obstructing him, or in the possession or custody of another person by whose authority the obstructor acts, unless the circumstances, as the actor believes them to be, are of such urgency that it would not be reasonable to postpone the entry or movement on such land until a court order is obtained; and

(c) the force used is not greater than would be justifiable if the person obstructing the actor were using force against him to prevent his passage.

Section 3.07. Use of Force in Law Enforcement.

(1) *Use of Force Justifiable to Effect an Arrest.* Subject to the provisions of this Section and of Section 3.09, the use of force upon or toward the person of another is justifiable when the actor is making or assisting in making an arrest and the actor believes that such force is immediately necessary to effect a lawful arrest.

(2) *Limitations on the Use of Force.*

(a) The use of force is not justifiable under this Section unless:

(i) the actor makes known the purpose of the arrest or believes that it is otherwise known by or cannot reasonably be made known to the person to be arrested; and

(ii) when the arrest is made under a warrant, the warrant is valid or believed by the actor to be valid.

(b) The use of deadly force is not justifiable under this Section unless:

(i) the arrest is for a felony; and

(ii) the person effecting the arrest is authorized to act as a peace officer or is assisting a person whom he believes to be authorized to act as a peace officer; and

(iii) the actor believes that the force employed creates no substantial risk of injury to innocent persons; and

(iv) the actor believes that:

(1) the crime for which the arrest is made involved conduct including the use or threatened use of deadly force; or

(2) there is a substantial risk that the person to be arrested will cause death or serious bodily harm if his apprehension is delayed.

(3) *Use of Force to Prevent Escape from Custody.* The use of force to prevent the escape of an arrested person from custody is justifiable when the force could justifiably have been employed to effect the arrest under which the person is in custody, except that a guard or other person authorized to act as a peace officer is justified in using any force, including deadly force, which he believes to be immediately necessary to prevent the escape of a person from a jail, prison, or other institution for the detention of persons charged with or convicted of a crime.

(4) *Use of Force by Private Person Assisting an Unlawful Arrest.*

(a) A private person who is summoned by a peace officer to assist in effecting an unlawful arrest, is justified in using any force which he would be justified in using if the arrest were lawful, provided that he does not believe the arrest is unlawful.

(b) A private person who assists another private person in effecting an unlawful arrest, or who, not being summoned, assists a peace officer in effecting an unlawful arrest, is justified in using any force which he would be justified in using if the arrest were lawful, provided that (i) he believes the arrest is lawful, and (ii) the arrest would be lawful if the facts were as he believes them to be.

(5) *Use of Force to Prevent Suicide or the Commission of a Crime.*

(a) The use of force upon or toward the person of another is justifiable when the actor believes that such force is immediately necessary to prevent such other person from committing suicide, inflicting serious bodily harm upon himself, committing or consummating the commission of a crime involving or threatening bodily harm, damage to or loss of property or a breach of the peace, except that:

(i) any limitations imposed by the other provisions of this Article on the justifiable use of force in self-protection, for the protection of others, the protection of property, the effectuation of an arrest or the prevention of an escape from custody shall apply notwithstanding the criminality of the conduct against which such force is used; and

(ii) the use of deadly force is not in any event justifiable under this Subsection unless:

(1) the actor believes that there is a substantial risk that the person whom he seeks to prevent from committing a crime will cause death or serious bodily harm to another unless the commission or the consummation of the crime is prevented and that the use of such force presents no substantial risk of injury to innocent persons; or

(2) the actor believes that the use of such force is necessary to suppress a riot or mutiny after the rioters or mutineers have been ordered to disperse and warned, in any particular manner that the law may require, that such force will be used if they do not obey.

(b) The justification afforded by this Subsection extends to the use of confinement as preventive force only if the actor takes all reasonable measures to terminate the confinement as soon as he knows that he safely can, unless the person confined has been arrested on a charge of crime.

Section 3.08. Use of Force by Persons with Special Responsibility for Care, Discipline or Safety of Others.

The use of force upon or toward the person of another is justifiable if:

(1) the actor is the parent or guardian or other person similarly responsible for the general care and supervision of a minor or a person acting at the request of such parent, guardian or other responsible person and:

(a) the force is used for the purpose of safeguarding or promoting the welfare of the minor, including the prevention or punishment of his misconduct; and

(b) the force used is not designed to cause or known to create a substantial risk of causing death, serious bodily harm, disfigurement, extreme pain or mental distress or gross degradation; or

(2) the actor is a teacher or a person otherwise entrusted with the care or supervision for a special purpose of a minor and:

(a) the actor believes that the force used is necessary to further such special purpose, including the maintenance of reasonable discipline in a school, class or other group, and that the use of such force is consistent with the welfare of the minor; and

(b) the degree of force, if it had been used by the parent or guardian of the minor, would not be unjustifiable under Subsection (1)(b) of this Section; or

(3) the actor is the guardian or other person similarly responsible for the general care and supervision of an incompetent person; and:

(a) the force is used for the purpose of safeguarding or promoting the welfare of the incompetent person, including the prevention of his misconduct, or, when such incompetent person is in a hospital or other institution for his care and custody, for the maintenance of reasonable discipline in such institution; and

(b) the force used is not designed to cause or known to create a substantial risk of causing death, serious bodily harm, disfigurement, extreme or unnecessary pain, mental distress, or humiliation; or

(4) the actor is a doctor or other therapist or a person assisting him at his direction, and:

(a) the force is used for the purpose of administering a recognized form of treatment which the actor believes to be adapted to promoting the physical or mental health of the patient; and

(b) the treatment is administered with the consent of the patient or, if the patient is a minor or an incompetent person, with the consent of his parent or guardian or other person legally competent to consent in his behalf, or the treatment is administered in an emergency when the actor believes that no one competent to consent can be consulted and that a reasonable person, wishing to safeguard the welfare of the patient, would consent; or

(5) the actor is a warden or other authorized official of a correctional institution, and:

(a) he believes that the force used is necessary for the purpose of enforcing the lawful rules or procedures of the institution, unless his belief in the lawfulness of the rule or procedure sought to be enforced is erroneous and his error is due to ignorance or mistake as to the provisions of the Code, any other provision of the criminal law or the law governing the administration of the institution; and

(b) the nature or degree of force used is not forbidden by Article 303 or 304 of the Code; and

(c) if deadly force is used, its use is otherwise justifiable under this Article; or

(6) the actor is a person responsible for the safety of a vessel or an aircraft or a person acting at his direction, and

(a) he believes that the force used is necessary to prevent interference with the operation of the vessel or aircraft or obstruction of the execution of a lawful order, unless his belief in the lawfulness of the order is erroneous and his error is due to ignorance or mistake as to the law defining his authority; and

(b) if deadly force is used, its use is otherwise justifiable under this Article; or

(7) the actor is a person who is authorized or required by law to maintain order or decorum in a vehicle, train or other carrier or in a place where others are assembled, and:

(a) he believes that the force used is necessary for such purpose; and

(b) the force used is not designed to cause or known to create a substantial risk of causing death, bodily harm, or extreme mental distress.

Section 3.09. Mistake of Law as to Unlawfulness of Force or Legality of Arrest; Reckless or Negligent Use of Otherwise Justifiable Force; Reckless or Negligent Injury or Risk of Injury to Innocent Persons.

(1) The justification afforded by Sections 3.04 to 3.07, inclusive, is unavailable when:

(a) the actor's belief in the unlawfulness of the force or conduct against which he employs protective force or his belief in the lawfulness of an arrest which he endeavors to effect by force is erroneous; and

(b) his error is due to ignorance or mistake as to the provisions of the Code, any other provision of the criminal law or the law governing the legality of an arrest or search.

(2) When the actor believes that the use of force upon or toward the person of another is necessary for any of the purposes for which such belief would establish a justification under Sections 3.03 to 3.08 but the actor is reckless or negligent in having such belief or in acquiring or failing to acquire any knowledge or belief which is material to the justifiability of his use of force, the justification afforded by those Sections is unavailable in a prosecution for an offense for which recklessness or negligence, as the case may be, suffices to establish culpability.

(3) When the actor is justified under Sections 3.03 to 3.08 in using force upon or toward the person of another but he recklessly or negligently injures or creates a risk of injury to innocent persons, the justification afforded by those Sections is

unavailable in a prosecution for such recklessness or negligence towards innocent persons.

Section 3.10. Justification in Property Crimes.

Conduct involving the appropriation, seizure or destruction of, damage to, intrusion on or interference with property is justifiable under circumstances which would establish a defense of privilege in a civil action based thereon, unless:

(1) the Code or the law defining the offense deals with the specific situation involved; or

(2) a legislative purpose to exclude the justification claimed otherwise plainly appears.

Section 3.11. Definitions.

In this Article, unless a different meaning plainly is required:

(1) "unlawful force" means force, including confinement, which is employed without the consent of the person against whom it is directed and the employment of which constitutes an offense or actionable tort or would constitute such offense or tort except for a defense (such as the absence of intent, negligence, or mental capacity; duress; youth; or diplomatic status) not amounting to a privilege to use the force. Assent constitutes consent, within the meaning of this Section, whether or not it otherwise is legally effective, except assent to the infliction of death or serious bodily harm.

(2) "deadly force" means force which the actor uses with the purpose of causing or which he knows to create a substantial risk of causing death or serious bodily harm. Purposely firing a firearm in the direction of another person or at a vehicle in which another person is believed to be constitutes deadly force. A threat to cause death or serious bodily harm, by the production of a weapon or otherwise, so long as the actor's purpose is limited to creating an apprehension that he will use deadly force if necessary, does not constitute deadly force;

(3) "dwelling" means any building or structure, though movable or temporary, or a portion thereof, which is for the time being the actor's home or place of lodging.

ARTICLE 4. RESPONSIBILITY

Section 4.01. Mental Disease or Defect Excluding Responsibility.

(1) A person is not responsible for criminal conduct if at the time of such conduct as a result of mental disease or defect he lacks substantial capacity either to appreciate the criminality [wrongfulness] of his conduct or to conform his conduct to the requirements of law.

(2) As used in this Article, the terms "mental disease or defect" do not include an abnormality manifested only by repeated criminal or otherwise anti-social conduct.

Section 4.02. Evidence of Mental Disease or Defect Admissible When Relevant to Element of the Offense; [Mental Disease or Defect Impairing Capacity as Ground for Mitigation of Punishment in Capital Cases].

(1) Evidence that the defendant suffered from a mental disease or defect is admissible whenever it is relevant to prove that the defendant did or did not have a state of mind which is an element of the offense.

[(2) Whenever the jury or the Court is authorized to determine or to recommend whether or not the defendant shall be sentenced to death or imprisonment upon conviction, evidence that the capacity of the defendant to appreciate the criminality [wrongfulness] of his conduct or to conform his conduct to the requirements of law was impaired as a result of mental disease or defect is admissible in favor of sentence of imprisonment.]

Section 4.03. Mental Disease or Defect Excluding Responsibility Is Affirmative Defense; Requirement of Notice; Form of Verdict and Judgment When Finding of Irresponsibility Is Made.

(1) Mental disease or defect excluding responsibility is an affirmative defense.

(2) Evidence of mental disease or defect excluding responsibility is not admissible unless the defendant, at the time of entering his plea of not guilty or within ten days thereafter or at such later time as the Court may for good cause permit, files a written notice of his purpose to rely on such defense.

(3) When the defendant is acquitted on the ground of mental disease or defect excluding responsibility, the verdict and the judgment shall so state.

Section 4.04. Mental Disease or Defect Excluding Fitness to Proceed.

No person who as a result of mental disease or defect lacks capacity to understand the proceedings against him or to assist in his own defense shall be tried, convicted or sentenced for the commission of an offense so long as such incapacity endures.

Section 4.05. Psychiatric Examination of Defendant with Respect to Mental Disease or Defect.

(1) Whenever the defendant has filed a notice of intention to rely on the defense of mental disease or defect excluding responsibility, or there is reason to doubt his fitness to proceed, or reason to believe that mental disease or defect of the defendant will otherwise become an issue in the cause, the Court shall appoint at least one qualified psychiatrist or shall request the Superintendent of the ___ Hospital to designate at least one qualified psychiatrist, which designation may be or include himself, to examine and report upon the mental condition of the defendant. The Court may order the defendant to be committed to a hospital or other suitable facility for the purpose of the examination for a period of not exceeding sixty days or such longer period as the Court determines to be necessary for the purpose and may direct that a qualified psychiatrist retained by the defendant be permitted to witness and participate in the examination.

(2) In such examination any method may be employed which is accepted by the medical profession for the examination of those alleged to be suffering from mental disease or defect.

(3) The report of the examination shall include the following: (a) a description of the nature of the examination; (b) a diagnosis of the mental condition of the defendant; (c) if the defendant suffers from a mental disease or defect, an opinion as to his capacity to understand the proceedings against him and to assist in his own defense; (d) when a notice of intention to rely on the defense of irresponsibility has been filed, an opinion as to the extent, if any, to which the capacity of the defendant to appreciate the criminality [wrongfulness] of his conduct or to conform his conduct to the requirements of law was impaired at the time of the criminal conduct charged; and (e) when directed by the Court, an opinion as to the capacity of the defendant to have a particular state of mind which is an element of the offense charged.

If the examination can not be conducted by reason of the unwillingness of the defendant to participate therein, the report shall so state and shall include, if possible, an opinion as to whether such unwillingness of the defendant was the result of mental disease or defect.

The report of the examination shall be filed [in triplicate] with the clerk of the Court, who shall cause copies to be delivered to the district attorney and to counsel for the defendant.

Section 4.06. Determination of Fitness to Proceed; Effect of Finding of Unfitness; Proceedings if Fitness is Regained [; Post-Commitment Hearing].

(1) When the defendant's fitness to proceed is drawn in question, the issue shall be determined by the Court. If neither the prosecuting attorney nor counsel for the defendant contests the finding of the report filed pursuant to Section 4.05, the Court may make the determination on the basis of such report. If the finding is contested, the Court shall hold a hearing on the issue. If the report is received in evidence upon such hearing, the party who contests the finding thereof shall have the right to summon and to cross-examine the psychiatrists who joined in the report and to offer evidence upon the issue.

(2) If the Court determines that the defendant lacks fitness to proceed, the proceeding against him shall be suspended, except as provided in Subsection (3) [Subsections (3) and (4)] of this Section, and the Court shall commit him to the custody of the Commissioner of Mental Hygiene [Public Health or Correction] to be placed in an appropriate institution of the Department of Mental Hygiene [Public Health or Correction] for so long as such unfitness shall endure. When the Court, on its own motion or upon the application of the Commissioner of Mental Hygiene [Public Health or Correction] or the prosecuting attorney, determines, after a hearing if a hearing is requested, that the defendant has regained fitness to proceed, the proceeding shall be resumed. If, however, the Court is of the view that so much time has elapsed since the commitment of the defendant that it would be unjust to resume the criminal proceeding, the Court may dismiss the charge and may order the defendant to be discharged or, subject to the law governing the civil commitment of persons suffering from mental disease or defect, order the defendant to be committed to an appropriate institution of the Department of Mental Hygiene [Public Health].

(3) The fact that the defendant is unfit to proceed does not preclude any legal objection to the prosecution which is susceptible of fair determination prior to trial and without the personal participation of the defendant.

[Alternative: (3) At any time within ninety days after commitment as provided in Subsection (2) of this Section, or at any later time with permission of the Court granted for good cause, the defendant or his counsel or the Commissioner of Mental Hygiene [Public Health or Correction] may apply for a special post-commitment hearing. If the application is made by or on behalf of a defendant not represented by counsel, he shall be afforded a reasonable opportunity to obtain counsel, and if he lacks funds to do so, counsel shall be assigned by the Court. The application shall be granted only if the counsel for the defendant satisfies the Court by affidavit or otherwise that as an attorney he has reasonable grounds for a good faith belief that his client has, on the facts and the law, a defense to the charge other than mental disease or defect excluding responsibility.]

[(4) If the motion for a special post-commitment hearing is granted, the hearing shall be by the Court without a jury. No evidence shall be offered at the hearing by either party on the issue of mental disease or defect as a defense to, or in mitigation of, the crime charged. After hearing, the Court may in an appropriate case quash the indictment or other charge, or find it to be defective or insufficient, or determine that it is not proved beyond a reasonable doubt by the evidence, or otherwise terminate the proceedings on the evidence or the law. In any such case, unless all defects in the proceedings are promptly cured, the Court shall terminate the commitment ordered under Subsection (2) of this Section and order the defendant to be discharged or, subject to the law governing the civil commitment of persons suffering from mental disease or defect, order the defendant to be committed to an appropriate institution of the Department of Mental Hygiene [Public Health].]

Section 4.07. Determination of Irresponsibility on Basis of Report; Access to Defendant by Psychiatrist of His Own Choice; Form of Expert Testimony When Issue of Responsibility Is Tried.

(1) If the report filed pursuant to Section 4.05 finds that the defendant at the time of the criminal conduct charged suffered from a mental disease or defect which substantially impaired his capacity to appreciate the criminality [wrongfulness] of his conduct or to conform his conduct to the requirements of law, and the Court, after a hearing if a hearing is requested by the prosecuting attorney or the defendant, is satisfied that such impairment was sufficient to exclude responsibility, the Court on motion of the defendant shall enter judgment of acquittal on the ground of mental disease or defect excluding responsibility.

(2) When, notwithstanding the report filed pursuant to Section 4.05, the defendant wishes to be examined by a qualified psychiatrist or other expert of his own choice, such examiner shall be permitted to have reasonable access to the defendant for the purposes of such examination.

(3) Upon the trial, the psychiatrists who reported pursuant to Section 4.05 may be called as witnesses by the prosecution, the defendant or the Court. If the issue is being tried before a jury, the jury may be informed that the psychiatrists were designated by the Court or by the Superintendent of the ___ Hospital at the request of the Court, as the case may be. If called by the Court, the witness shall be subject to cross-examination by the prosecution and by the defendant. Both the prosecution and the defendant may summon any other qualified psychiatrist or other expert to testify, but no one who has not examined the defendant shall be competent to testify to an expert opinion with respect to the mental condition or responsibility of the defendant, as distinguished from the validity of the procedure followed by, or the general scientific propositions stated by, another witness.

(4) When a psychiatrist or other expert who has examined the defendant testifies concerning his mental condition, he shall be permitted to make a statement as to the nature of his examination, his diagnosis of the mental condition of the defendant at the time of the commission of the offense charged and his opinion as to the extent, if any, to which the capacity of the defendant to appreciate the criminality [wrongfulness] of his conduct or to conform his conduct to the requirements of law or to have a particular state of mind which is an element of the offense charged was impaired as a result of mental disease or defect at that time. He shall be permitted to make any explanation reasonably serving to clarify his diagnosis and opinion and may be cross-examined as to any matter bearing on his competency or credibility or the validity of his diagnosis or opinion.

Section 4.08. Legal Effect of Acquittal on the Ground of Mental Disease or Defect Excluding Responsibility; Commitment; Release or Discharge.

(1) When a defendant is acquitted on the ground of mental disease or defect excluding responsibility, the Court shall order him to be committed to the custody

of the Commissioner of Mental Hygiene [Public Health] to be placed in an appropriate institution for custody, care and treatment.

(2) If the Commissioner of Mental Hygiene [Public Health] is of the view that a person committed to his custody, pursuant to paragraph (1) of this Section, may be discharged or released on condition without danger to himself or to others, he shall make application for the discharge or release of such person in a report to the Court by which such person was committed and shall transmit a copy of such application and report to the prosecuting attorney of the county [parish] from which the defendant was committed. The Court shall thereupon appoint at least two qualified psychiatrists to examine such person and to report within sixty days, or such longer period as the Court determines to be necessary for the purpose, their opinion as to his mental condition. To facilitate such examination and the proceedings thereon, the Court may cause such person to be confined in any institution located near the place where the Court sits, which may hereafter be designated by the Commissioner of Mental Hygiene [Public Health] as suitable for the temporary detention of irresponsible persons.

(3) If the Court is satisfied by the report filed pursuant to paragraph (2) of this Section and such testimony of the reporting psychiatrists as the Court deems necessary that the committed person may be discharged or released on condition without danger to himself or others, the Court shall order his discharge or his release on such conditions as the Court determines to be necessary. If the Court is not so satisfied, it shall promptly order a hearing to determine whether such person may safely be discharged or released. Any such hearing shall be deemed a civil proceeding and the burden shall be upon the committed person to prove that he may safely be discharged or released. According to the determination of the Court upon the hearing, the committed person shall thereupon be discharged or released on such conditions as the Court determines to be necessary, or shall be recommitted to the custody of the Commissioner of Mental Hygiene [Public Health], subject to discharge or release only in accordance with the procedure prescribed above for a first hearing.

(4) If, within [five] years after the conditional release of a committed person, the Court shall determine, after hearing evidence, that the conditions of release have not been fulfilled and that for the safety of such person or for the safety of others his conditional release should be revoked, the Court shall forthwith order him to be recommitted to the Commissioner of Mental Hygiene [Public Health], subject to discharge or release only in accordance with the procedure prescribed above for a first hearing.

(5) A committed person may make application for his discharge or release to the Court by which he was committed, and the procedure to be followed upon such application shall be the same as that prescribed above in the case of an application by the Commissioner of Mental Hygiene [Public Health]. However, no such application by a committed person need be considered until he has been confined for a period of not less than [six months] from the date of the order of commitment, and if the determination of the Court be adverse to the application, such person shall not be permitted to file a further application until [one year] has elapsed from the date of any preceding hearing on an application for his release or discharge.

Section 4.09. Statements for Purposes of Examination or Treatment Inadmissible Except on Issue of Mental Condition.

A statement made by a person subjected to psychiatric examination or treatment pursuant to Sections 4.05, 4.06 or 4.08 for the purposes of such examination or treatment shall not be admissible in evidence against him in any criminal proceeding on any issue other than that of his mental condition but it shall be admissible upon that issue, whether or not it would otherwise be deemed a privileged communication [, unless such statement constitutes an admission of guilt of the crime charged].

Section 4.10. Immaturity Excluding Criminal Convictions; Transfer of Proceedings to Juvenile Court.

(1) A person shall not be tried for or convicted of an offense if:

(a) at the time of the conduct charged to constitute the offense he was less than sixteen years of age [, in which case the Juvenile Court shall have exclusive jurisdiction*]; or

(b) at the time of the conduct charged to constitute the offense he was sixteen or seventeen years of age, unless:

(i) the Juvenile Court has no jurisdiction over him, or,

(ii) the Juvenile Court has entered an order waiving jurisdiction and consenting to the institution of criminal proceedings against him.

(2) No court shall have jurisdiction to try or convict a person of an offense if criminal proceedings against him are barred by Subsection (1) of this Section. When it appears that a person charged with the commission of an offense may be of such an age that criminal proceedings may be barred under Subsection (1) of this Section, the Court shall hold a hearing thereon, and the burden shall be on the prosecution to establish to the satisfaction of the Court that the criminal proceeding is not barred upon such grounds. If the Court determines that the proceeding is barred, custody of the person charged shall be surrendered to the Juvenile Court, and the case, including all papers and processes relating thereto, shall be transferred.

* The bracketed words are unnecessary if the Juvenile Court Act so provides or is amended accordingly.

ARTICLE 5. INCHOATE CRIMES

Section 5.01. Criminal Attempt.

(1) *Definition of Attempt.* A person is guilty of an attempt to commit a crime if, acting with the kind of culpability otherwise required for commission of the crime, he:

(a) purposely engages in conduct which would constitute the crime if the attendant circumstances were as he believes them to be; or

(b) when causing a particular result is an element of the crime, does or omits to do anything with the purpose of causing or with the belief that it will cause such result without further conduct on his part; or

(c) purposely does or omits to do anything which, under the circumstances as he believes them to be, is an act or omission constituting a substantial step in a course of conduct planned to culminate in his commission of the crime.

(2) *Conduct Which May Be Held Substantial Step Under Subsection (1)(c).* Conduct shall not be held to constitute a substantial step under Subsection (1)(c) of this Section unless it is strongly corroborative of the actor's criminal purpose. Without negativing the sufficiency of other conduct, the following, if strongly corroborative of the actor's criminal purpose, shall not be held insufficient as a matter of law:

(a) lying in wait, searching for or following the contemplated victim of the crime;

(b) enticing or seeking to entice the contemplated victim of the crime to go to the place contemplated for its commission;

(c) reconnoitering the place contemplated for the commission of the crime;

(d) unlawful entry of a structure, vehicle or enclosure in which it is contemplated that the crime will be committed;

(e) possession of materials to be employed in the commission of the crime, which are specially designed for such unlawful use or which can serve no lawful purpose of the actor under the circumstances;

(f) possession, collection or fabrication of materials to be employed in the commission of the crime, at or near the place contemplated for its commission, where such possession, collection or fabrication serves no lawful purpose of the actor under the circumstances;

(g) soliciting an innocent agent to engage in conduct constituting an element of the crime.

(3) *Conduct Designed to Aid Another in Commission of a Crime.* A person who engages in conduct designed to aid another to commit a crime which would establish his complicity under Section 2.06 if the crime were committed by such other person, is guilty of an attempt to commit the crime, although the crime is not committed or attempted by such other person.

(4) *Renunciation of Criminal Purpose.* When the actor's conduct would otherwise constitute an attempt under Subsection (1)(b) or (1)(c) of this Section, it is an affirmative defense that he abandoned his effort to commit the crime or otherwise prevented its commission, under circumstances manifesting a complete and voluntary renunciation of his criminal purpose. The establishment of such defense does not, however, affect the liability of an accomplice who did not join in such abandonment or prevention.

Within the meaning of this Article, renunciation of criminal purpose is not voluntary if it is motivated, in whole or in part, by circumstances, not present or apparent at the inception of the actor's course of conduct, which increase the probability of detection or apprehension or which make more difficult the accomplishment of the criminal purpose. Renunciation is not complete if it is motivated by a decision to postpone the criminal conduct until a more advantageous time or to transfer the criminal effort to another but similar objective or victim.

Section 5.02. Criminal Solicitation.

(1) *Definition of Solicitation.* A person is guilty of solicitation to commit a crime if with the purpose of promoting or facilitating its commission he commands, encourages or requests another person to engage in specific conduct which would constitute such crime or an attempt to commit such crime or which would establish his complicity in its commission or attempted commission.

(2) *Uncommunicated Solicitation.* It is immaterial under Subsection (1) of this Section that the actor fails to communicate with the person he solicits to commit a crime if his conduct was designed to effect such communication.

(3) *Renunciation of Criminal Purpose.* It is an affirmative defense that the actor, after soliciting another person to commit a crime, persuaded him not to do so or otherwise prevented the commission of the crime, under circumstances manifesting a complete and voluntary renunciation of his criminal purpose.

Section 5.03. Criminal Conspiracy.

(1) *Definition of Conspiracy.* A person is guilty of conspiracy with another person or persons to commit a crime if with the purpose of promoting or facilitating its commission he:

(a) agrees with such other person or persons that they or one or more of them will engage in conduct which constitutes such crime or an attempt or solicitation to commit such crime; or

(b) agrees to aid such other person or persons in the planning or commission of such crime or of an attempt or solicitation to commit such crime.

(2) *Scope of Conspiratorial Relationship.* If a person guilty of conspiracy, as defined by Subsection (1) of this Section, knows that a person with whom he conspires to commit a crime has conspired with another person or persons to commit the same crime, he is guilty of conspiring with such other person or persons, whether or not he knows their identity, to commit such crime.

(3) *Conspiracy With Multiple Criminal Objectives.* If a person conspires to commit a number of crimes, he is guilty of only one conspiracy so long as such multiple crimes are the object of the same agreement or continuous conspiratorial relationship.

(4) *Joinder and Venue in Conspiracy Prosecutions.*

(a) Subject to the provisions of paragraph (b) of this Subsection, two or more persons charged with criminal conspiracy may be prosecuted jointly if:

(i) they are charged with conspiring with one another; or

(ii) the conspiracies alleged, whether they have the same or different parties, are so related that they constitute different aspects of a scheme of organized criminal conduct.

(b) In any joint prosecution under paragraph (a) of this Subsection:

(i) no defendant shall be charged with a conspiracy in any county [parish or district] other than one in which he entered into such conspiracy or in which an overt act pursuant to such conspiracy was done by him or by a person with whom he conspired; and

(ii) neither the liability of any defendant nor the admissibility against him of evidence of acts or declarations of another shall be enlarged by such joinder; and

(iii) the Court shall order a severance or take a special verdict as to any defendant who so requests, if it deems it necessary or appropriate to promote the fair determination of his guilt or innocence, and shall take any other proper measures to protect the fairness of the trial.

(5) *Overt Act.* No person may be convicted of conspiracy to commit a crime, other than a felony of the first or second degree, unless an overt act in pursuance of such conspiracy is alleged and proved to have been done by him or by a person with whom he conspired.

(6) *Renunciation of Criminal Purpose.* It is an affirmative defense that the actor, after conspiring to commit a crime, thwarted the success of the conspiracy, under circumstances manifesting a complete and voluntary renunciation of his criminal purpose.

(7) *Duration of Conspiracy.* For purposes of Section 1.06(4):

(a) conspiracy is a continuing course of conduct which terminates when the crime or crimes which are its object are committed or the agreement that they be committed is abandoned by the defendant and by those with whom he conspired; and

(b) such abandonment is presumed if neither the defendant nor anyone with whom he conspired does any overt act in pursuance of the conspiracy during the applicable period of limitation; and

(c) if an individual abandons the agreement, the conspiracy is terminated as to him only if and when he advises those with whom he conspired of his abandonment or he informs the law enforcement authorities of the existence of the conspiracy and of his participation therein.

Section 5.04. Incapacity, Irresponsibility or Immunity of Party to Solicitation or Conspiracy.

(1) Except as provided in Subsection (2) of this Section, it is immaterial to the liability of a person who solicits or conspires with another to commit a crime that:

(a) he or the person whom he solicits or with whom he conspires does not occupy a particular position or have a particular characteristic which is an element of such crime, if he believes that one of them does; or

(b) the person whom he solicits or with whom he conspires is irresponsible or has an immunity to prosecution or conviction for the commission of the crime.

(2) It is a defense to a charge of solicitation or conspiracy to commit a crime that if the criminal object were achieved, the actor would not be guilty of a crime under the law defining the offense or as an accomplice under Section 2.06(5) or 2.06(6)(a) or (b).

Section 5.05. Grading of Criminal Attempt, Solicitation and Conspiracy; Mitigation in Cases of Lesser Danger; Multiple Convictions Barred.

(1) *Grading.* Except as otherwise provided in this Section, attempt, solicitation and conspiracy are crimes of the same grade and degree as the most serious offense which is attempted or solicited or is an object of the conspiracy. An attempt, solicitation or conspiracy to commit a [capital crime or a] felony of the first degree is a felony of the second degree.

(2) *Mitigation.* If the particular conduct charged to constitute a criminal attempt, solicitation or conspiracy is so inherently unlikely to result or culminate in the commission of a crime that neither such conduct nor the actor presents a public danger warranting the grading of such offense under this Section, the Court shall exercise its power under Section 6.12 to enter judgment and impose sentence for a crime of lower grade or degree or, in extreme cases, may dismiss the prosecution.

(3) *Multiple Convictions.* A person may not be convicted of more than one offense defined by this Article for conduct designed to commit or to culminate in the commission of the same crime.

Section 5.06. Possessing Instruments of Crime; Weapons.

(1) *Criminal Instruments Generally.* A person commits a misdemeanor if he possesses any instrument of crime with purpose to employ it criminally. "Instrument of crime" means:

(a) anything specially made or specially adapted for criminal use; or

(b) anything commonly used for criminal purposes and possessed by the actor under circumstances which do not negative unlawful purpose.

(2) *Presumption of Criminal Purpose from Possession of Weapon.* If a person possesses a firearm or other weapon on or about his person, in a vehicle occupied by him, or otherwise readily available for use, it is presumed that he had the purpose to employ it criminally, unless:

(a) the weapon is possessed in the actor's home or place of business;

(b) the actor is licensed or otherwise authorized by law to possess such weapon; or

(c) the weapon is of a type commonly used in lawful sport.

"Weapon" means anything readily capable of lethal use and possessed under circumstances not manifestly appropriate for lawful uses which it may have; the term includes a firearm which is not loaded or lacks a clip or other component to render it immediately operable, and components which can readily be assembled into a weapon.

(3) *Presumptions as to Possession of Criminal Instruments in Automobiles.* Where a weapon or other instrument of crime is found in an automobile, it shall be presumed to be in the possession of the occupant if there is but one. If there is more than one occupant, it shall be presumed to be in the possession of all, except under the following circumstances:

(a) where it is found upon the person of one of the occupants;

(b) where the automobile is not a stolen one and the weapon or instrument is found out of view in a glove compartment, car trunk, or other enclosed customary depository, in which case it shall be presumed to be in the possession of the occupant or occupants who own or have authority to operate the automobile;

(c) in the case of a taxicab, a weapon or instrument found in the passengers' portion of the vehicle shall be presumed to be in the possession of all the passengers, if there are any, and, if not, in the possession of the driver.

Section 5.07. Prohibited Offensive Weapons.

A person commits a misdemeanor if, except as authorized by law, he makes, repairs, sells, or otherwise deals in, uses, or possesses any offensive weapon. "Offensive weapon" means any bomb, machine gun, sawed-off shotgun, firearm specially made or specially adapted for concealment or silent discharge, any blackjack, sandbag, metal knuckles, dagger, or other implement for the infliction of serious bodily injury which serves no common lawful purpose. It is a defense under this Section for the defendant to prove by a preponderance of evidence that he possessed or dealt with the weapon solely as a curio or in a dramatic performance, or that he possessed it briefly in consequence of having found it or taken it from an aggressor, or under circumstances similarly negativing any purpose or likelihood that the weapon would be used unlawfully. The presumptions provided in Section 5.06(3) are applicable to prosecutions under this Section.

ARTICLE 6. AUTHORIZED DISPOSITION OF OFFENDERS

Section 6.01. Degrees of Felonies.

(1) Felonies defined by this Code are classified, for the purpose of sentence, into three degrees, as follows:

(a) felonies of the first degree;

(b) felonies of the second degree;

(c) felonies of the third degree.

A felony is of the first or second degree when it is so designated by the Code. A crime declared to be a felony, without specification of degree, is of the third degree.

(2) Notwithstanding any other provision of law, a felony defined by any statute of this State other than this Code shall constitute for the purpose of sentence a felony of the third degree.

Section 6.02. Sentence in Accordance with Code; Authorized Dispositions.

(1) No person convicted of an offense shall be sentenced otherwise than in accordance with this Article.

[(2) The Court shall sentence a person who has been convicted of murder to death or imprisonment, in accordance with Section 210.6.]

(3) Except as provided in Subsection (2) of this Section and subject to the applicable provisions of the Code, the Court may suspend the imposition of sentence on a person who has been convicted of a crime, may order him to be committed in lieu of sentence, in accordance with Section 6.13, or may sentence him as follows:

(a) to pay a fine authorized by Section 6.03; or

(b) to be placed on probation [, and, in the case of a person convicted of a felony or misdemeanor to imprisonment for a term fixed by the Court not exceeding thirty days to be served as a condition of probation]; or

(c) to imprisonment for a term authorized by Sections 6.05, 6.06, 6.07, 6.08, 6.09, or 7.06; or

(d) to fine and probation or fine and imprisonment, but not to probation and imprisonment [, except as authorized in paragraph (b) of this Subsection].

(4) The Court may suspend the imposition of sentence on a person who has been convicted of a violation or may sentence him to pay a fine authorized by Section 6.03.

(5) This Article does not deprive the Court of any authority conferred by law to decree a forfeiture of property, suspend or cancel a license, remove a person from office, or impose any other civil penalty. Such a judgment or order may be included in the sentence.

Section 6.03. Fines.

A person who has been convicted of an offense may be sentenced to pay a fine not exceeding:

(1) $10,000, when the conviction is of a felony of the first or second degree;

(2) $5,000, when the conviction is of a felony of the third degree;

(3) $1,000, when the conviction is of a misdemeanor;

(4) $500, when the conviction is of a petty misdemeanor or a violation;

(5) any higher amount equal to double the pecuniary gain derived from the offense by the offender;

(6) any higher amount specifically authorized by statute.

Section 6.04. Penalties Against Corporations and Unincorporated Association; Forfeiture of Corporate Charter or Revocation of Certificate Authorizing Foreign Corporation to Do Business in the State.

(1) The Court may suspend the sentence of a corporation or an unincorporated association which has been convicted of an offense or may sentence it to pay a fine authorized by Section 6.03.

(2)(a) The [prosecuting attorney] is authorized to institute civil proceedings in the appropriate court of general jurisdiction to forfeit the charter of a corporation organized under the laws of this State or to revoke the certificate authorizing a foreign corporation to conduct business in this State. The Court may order the charter forfeited or the certificate revoked upon finding (i) that the board of directors or a high managerial agent acting in behalf of the corporation has, in conducting the corporation's affairs, purposely engaged in a persistent course of criminal conduct and (ii) that for the prevention of future criminal conduct of the same character, the public interest requires the charter of the corporation to be forfeited and the corporation to be dissolved or the certificate to be revoked.

(b) When a corporation is convicted of a crime or a high managerial agent of a corporation, as defined in Section 2.07, is convicted of a crime committed in the conduct of the affairs of the corporation, the Court, in sentencing the corporation or the agent, may direct the [prosecuting attorney] to institute proceedings authorized by paragraph (a) of this Subsection.

(c) The proceedings authorized by paragraph (a) of this Subsection shall be conducted in accordance with the procedures authorized by law for the involuntary dissolution of a corporation or the revocation of the certificate authorizing a foreign corporation to conduct business in this State. Such proceedings shall be deemed additional to any other proceedings authorized by law for the purpose of forfeiting the charter of a corporation or revoking the certificate of a foreign corporation.

Section 6.05. Young Adult Offenders.

(1) *Specialized Correctional Treatment.* A young adult offender is a person convicted of a crime who, at the time of sentencing, is sixteen but less than twenty-two years of age. A young adult offender who is sentenced to a term of imprisonment which may exceed thirty days [alternatives: (1) ninety days; (2) one year] shall be committed to the custody of the Division of Young Adult Correction of the Department of Correction, and shall receive, as far as practicable, such special and individualized correctional and rehabilitative treatment as may be appropriate to his needs.

(2) *Special Term.* A young adult offender convicted of a felony may, in lieu of any other sentence of imprisonment authorized by this Article, be sentenced to a special term of imprisonment without a minimum and with a maximum of four years, regardless of the degree of the felony involved, if the Court is of the opinion that such special term is adequate for his correction and rehabilitation and will not jeopardize the protection of the public.

[(3) *Removal of Disabilities; Vacation of Conviction.*

(a) In sentencing a young adult offender to the special term provided by this Section or to any sentence other than one of imprisonment, the Court may order that so long as he is not convicted of another felony, the judgment shall not constitute a conviction for the purposes of any disqualification or disability imposed by law upon conviction of a crime.

(b) When any young adult offender is unconditionally discharged from probation or parole before the expiration of the maximum term thereof, the Court may enter an order vacating the judgment of conviction.]

[(4) *Commitment for Observation.* If, after pre-sentence investigation, the Court desires additional information concerning a young adult offender before imposing sentence, it may order that he be committed, for a period not exceeding ninety days, to the custody of the Division of Young Adult Correction of the Department of Correction for observation and study at an appropriate reception or classification center. Such Division of the Department of Correction and the [Young Adult Division of the] Board of Parole shall advise the Court of their findings and recommendations on or before the expiration of such ninety-day period.]

Section 6.06. Sentence of Imprisonment for Felony; Ordinary Terms.

A person who has been convicted of a felony may be sentenced to imprisonment, as follows:

(1) in the case of a felony of the first degree, for a term the minimum of which shall be fixed by the Court at not less than one year nor more than ten years, and the maximum of which shall be life imprisonment;

(2) in the case of a felony of the second degree, for a term the minimum of which shall be fixed by the Court at not less than one year nor more than three years, and the maximum of which shall be ten years;

(3) in the case of a felony of the third degree, for a term the minimum of which shall be fixed by the Court at not less than one year nor more than two years, and the maximum of which shall be five years.

Alternate Section 6.06. Sentence of Imprisonment for Felony; Ordinary Terms.

A person who has been convicted of a felony may be sentenced to imprisonment, as follows:

(1) in the case of a felony of the first degree, for a term the minimum of which shall be fixed by the Court at not less than one year nor more than ten years, and the maximum at not more than twenty years or at life imprisonment;

(2) in the case of a felony of the second degree, for a term the minimum of which shall be fixed by the Court at not less than one year nor more than three years, and the maximum at not more than ten years;

(3) in the case of a felony of the third degree, for a term the minimum of which shall be fixed by the Court at not less than one year nor more than two years, and the maximum at not more than five years.

No sentence shall be imposed under this Section of which the minimum is longer than one-half the maximum, or, when the maximum is life imprisonment, longer than ten years.

Section 6.07. Sentence of Imprisonment for Felony; Extended Terms.

In the cases designated in Section 7.03, a person who has been convicted of a felony may be sentenced to an extended term of imprisonment, as follows:

(1) in the case of a felony of the first degree, for a term the minimum of which shall be fixed by the Court at not less than five years nor more than ten years, and the maximum of which shall be life imprisonment;

(2) in the case of a felony of the second degree, for a term the minimum of which shall be fixed by the Court at not less than one year nor more than five years, and the maximum of which shall be fixed by the Court at not less than ten nor more than twenty years;

(3) in the case of a felony of the third degree, for a term the minimum of which shall be fixed by the Court at not less than one year nor more than three years, and the maximum of which shall be fixed by the Court at not less than five nor more than ten years.

Section 6.08. Sentence of Imprisonment for Misdemeanors and Petty Misdemeanors; Ordinary Terms.

A person who has been convicted of a misdemeanor or a petty misdemeanor may be sentenced to imprisonment for a definite term which shall be fixed by the

Court and shall not exceed one year in the case of a misdemeanor or thirty days in the case of a petty misdemeanor.

Section 6.09. Sentence of Imprisonment for Misdemeanors and Petty Misdemeanors; Extended Terms.

(1) In the cases designated in Section 7.04, a person who has been convicted of a misdemeanor or a petty misdemeanor may be sentenced to an extended term of imprisonment, as follows:

(a) in the case of a misdemeanor, for a term the minimum of which shall be fixed by the Court at not more than one year and the maximum of which shall be three years;

(b) in the case of a petty misdemeanor, for a term the minimum of which shall be fixed by the Court at not more than six months and the maximum of which shall be two years.

(2) No such sentence for an extended term shall be imposed unless:

(a) the Director of Correction has certified that there is an institution in the Department of Correction, or in a county, city [or other appropriate political subdivision of the State] which is appropriate for the detention and correctional treatment of such misdemeanants or petty misdemeanants, and that such institution is available to receive such commitments; and

(b) the [Board of Parole] [Parole Administrator] has certified that the Board of Parole is able to visit such institution and to assume responsibility for the release of such prisoners on parole and for their parole supervision.

Section 6.10. First Release of All Offenders on Parole; Sentence of Imprisonment Includes Separate Parole Term; Length of Parole Term; Length of Recommitment and Reparole After Revocation of Parole; Final Unconditional Release.

(1) *First Release of All Offenders on Parole.* An offender sentenced to an indefinite term of imprisonment in excess of one year under Section 6.05, 6.06, 6.07, 6.09 or 7.06 shall be released conditionally on parole at or before the expiration of the maximum of such term, in accordance with Article 305.

(2) *Sentence of Imprisonment Includes Separate Parole Term; Length of Parole Term.* A sentence to an indefinite term of imprisonment in excess of one year under Section 6.05, 6.06, 6.07, 6.09 or 7.06 includes as a separate portion of the sentence a term of parole or of recommitment for violation of the conditions of parole which governs the duration of parole or recommitment after the offender's first conditional release on parole. The minimum of such term is one year and the maximum is five years, unless the sentence was imposed under Section 6.05(2) or Section 6.09, in which case the maximum is two years.

(3) *Length of Recommitment and Reparole After Revocation of Parole.* If an offender is recommitted upon revocation of his parole, the term of further imprisonment upon such recommitment and of any subsequent reparole or recommitment under the same sentence shall be fixed by the Board of Parole but shall not exceed in aggregate length the unserved balance of the maximum parole term provided by Subsection (2) of this Section.

(4) *Final Unconditional Release.* When the maximum of his parole term has expired or he has been sooner discharged from parole under Section 305.12, an offender shall be deemed to have served his sentence and shall be released unconditionally.

Section 6.11. Place of imprisonment.

(1) When a person is sentenced to imprisonment for an indefinite term with a maximum in excess of one year, the Court shall commit him to the custody of the Department of Correction [or other single department or agency] for the term of his sentence and until released in accordance with law.

(2) When a person is sentenced to imprisonment for a definite term, the Court shall designate the institution or agency to which he is committed for the term of his sentence and until released in accordance with law.

Section 6.12. Reduction of Conviction by Court to Lesser Degree of Felony or to Misdemeanor.

If, when a person has been convicted of a felony, the Court, having regard to the nature and circumstances of the crime and to the history and character of the defendant, is of the view that it would be unduly harsh to sentence the offender in accordance with the Code, the Court may enter judgment of conviction for a lesser degree of felony or for a misdemeanor and impose sentence accordingly.

Section 6.13. Civil Commitment in Lieu of Prosecution or of Sentence.

(1) When a person prosecuted for a [felony of the third degree,] misdemeanor or petty misdemeanor is a chronic alcoholic, narcotic addict [or prostitute] or person suffering from mental abnormality and the Court is authorized by law to order the civil commitment of such person to a hospital or other institution for medical, psychiatric or other rehabilitative treatment, the Court may order such commitment and dismiss the prosecution.

The order of commitment may be made after conviction, in which event the Court may set aside the verdict or judgment of conviction and dismiss the prosecution.

(2) The Court shall not make an order under Subsection (1) of this Section unless it is of the view that it will substantially further the rehabilitation of the defendant and will not jeopardize the protection of the public.

ARTICLE 7. AUTHORITY OF COURT IN SENTENCING

Section 7.01. Criteria for Withholding Sentence of Imprisonment and for Placing Defendant on Probation.

(1) The Court shall deal with a person who has been convicted of a crime without imposing sentence of imprisonment unless, having regard to the nature and circumstances of the crime and the history, character and condition of the defendant, it is of the opinion that his imprisonment is necessary for protection of the public because:

(a) there is undue risk that during the period of a suspended sentence or probation the defendant will commit another crime; or

(b) the defendant is in need of correctional treatment that can be provided most effectively by his commitment to an institution; or

(c) a lesser sentence will depreciate the seriousness of the defendant's crime.

(2) The following grounds, while not controlling the discretion of the Court, shall be accorded weight in favor of withholding sentence of imprisonment:

(a) the defendant's criminal conduct neither caused nor threatened serious harm;

(b) the defendant did not contemplate that his criminal conduct would cause or threaten serious harm;

(c) the defendant acted under a strong provocation;

(d) there were substantial grounds tending to excuse or justify the defendant's criminal conduct, though failing to establish a defense;

(e) the victim of the defendant's criminal conduct induced or facilitated its commission;

(f) the defendant has compensated or will compensate the victim of his criminal conduct for the damage or injury that he sustained;

(g) the defendant has no history of prior delinquency or criminal activity or has led a law-abiding life for a substantial period of time before the commission of the present crime;

(h) the defendant's criminal conduct was the result of circumstances unlikely to recur;

(i) the character and attitudes of the defendant indicate that he is unlikely to commit another crime;

(j) the defendant is particularly likely to respond affirmatively to probationary treatment;

(k) the imprisonment of the defendant would entail excessive hardship to himself or his dependents.

(3) When a person who has been convicted of a crime is not sentenced to imprisonment, the Court shall place him on probation if he is in need of the supervision, guidance, assistance or direction that the probation service can provide.

Section 7.02. Criteria for Imposing Fines.

(1) The Court shall not sentence a defendant only to pay a fine, when any other disposition is authorized by law, unless having regard to the nature and circumstances of the crime and to the history and character of the defendant, it is of the opinion that the fine alone suffices for protection of the public.

(2) The Court shall not sentence a defendant to pay a fine in addition to a sentence of imprisonment or probation unless:

(a) the defendant has derived a pecuniary gain from the crime; or

(b) the Court is of opinion that a fine is specially adapted to deterrence of the crime involved or to the correction of the offender.

(3) The Court shall not sentence a defendant to pay a fine unless:

(a) the defendant is or will be able to pay the fine; and

(b) the fine will not prevent the defendant from making restitution or reparation to the victim of the crime.

(4) In determining the amount and method of payment of a fine, the Court shall take into account the financial resources of the defendant and the nature of the burden that its payment will impose.

Section 7.03. Criteria for Sentence of Extended Term of Imprisonment; Felonies.

The Court may sentence a person who has been convicted of a felony to an extended term of imprisonment if it finds one or more of the grounds specified in this Section. The finding of the Court shall be incorporated in the record.

(1) The defendant is a persistent offender whose commitment for an extended term is necessary for protection of the public.

The Court shall not make such a finding unless the defendant is over twenty-one years of age and has previously been convicted of two felonies or of one felony and two misdemeanors, committed at different times when he was over [insert Juvenile Court age] years of age.

(2) The defendant is a professional criminal whose commitment for an extended term is necessary for protection of the public.

The Court shall not make such a finding unless the defendant is over twenty-one years of age and:

(a) the circumstances of the crime show that the defendant has knowingly devoted himself to criminal activity as a major source of livelihood; or

(b) the defendant has substantial income or resources not explained to be derived from a source other than criminal activity.

(3) The defendant is a dangerous, mentally abnormal person whose commitment for an extended term is necessary for protection of the public.

The Court shall not make such a finding unless the defendant has been subjected to a psychiatric examination resulting in the conclusions that his mental condition is gravely abnormal; that his criminal conduct has been characterized by a pattern of repetitive or compulsive behavior or by persistent aggressive behavior with heedless indifference to consequences; and that such condition makes him a serious danger to others.

(4) The defendant is a multiple offender whose criminality was so extensive that a sentence of imprisonment for an extended term is warranted.

The Court shall not make such a finding unless:

(a) the defendant is being sentenced for two or more felonies, or is already under sentence of imprisonment for felony, and the sentences of imprisonment involved will run concurrently under Section 7.06; or

(b) the defendant admits in open court the commission of one or more other felonies and asks that they be taken into account when he is sentenced; and

(c) the longest sentences of imprisonment authorized for each of the defendant's crimes, including admitted crimes taken into account, if made to run consecutively would exceed in length the minimum and maximum of the extended term imposed.

Section 7.04. Criteria for Sentence of Extended Term of Imprisonment; Misdemeanors and Petty Misdemeanors.

The Court may sentence a person who has been convicted of a misdemeanor or petty misdemeanor to an extended term of imprisonment if it finds one or more of the grounds specified in this Section. The finding of the Court shall be incorporated in the record.

(1) The defendant is a persistent offender whose commitment for an extended term is necessary for protection of the public.

The Court shall not make such a finding unless the defendant has previously been convicted of two crimes, committed at different times when he was over [insert Juvenile Court age] years of age.

(2) The defendant is a professional criminal whose commitment for an extended term is necessary for protection of the public.

The Court shall not make such a finding unless:

(a) the circumstances of the crime show that the defendant has knowingly devoted himself to criminal activity as a major source of livelihood; or

(b) the defendant has substantial income or resources not explained to be derived from a source other than criminal activity.

(3) The defendant is a chronic alcoholic, narcotic addict, prostitute or person of abnormal mental condition who requires rehabilitative treatment for a substantial period of time.

The Court shall not make such a finding unless, with respect to the particular category to which the defendant belongs, the Director of Correction has certified that there is a specialized institution or facility which is satisfactory for the rehabilitative treatment of such persons and which otherwise meets the requirements of Section 6.09, Subsection (2).

(4) The defendant is a multiple offender whose criminality was so extensive that a sentence of imprisonment for an extended term is warranted.

The Court shall not make such a finding unless:

(a) the defendant is being sentenced for a number of misdemeanors or petty misdemeanors or is already under sentence of imprisonment for crime of such grades, or admits in open court the commission of one or more such crimes and asks that they be taken into account when he is sentenced; and

(b) maximum fixed sentences of imprisonment for each of the defendant's crimes, including admitted crimes taken into account, if made to run consecutively, would exceed in length the maximum period of the extended term imposed.

Section 7.05. Former Conviction in Another Jurisdiction; Definition and Proof of Conviction; Sentence Taking Into Account Admitted Crimes Bars Subsequent Conviction for Such Crimes.

(1) For purposes of paragraph (1) of Section 7.03 or 7.04, a conviction of the commission of a crime in another jurisdiction shall constitute a previous conviction. Such conviction shall be deemed to have been of a felony if sentence of death or of imprisonment in excess of one year was authorized under the law of such other jurisdiction, of a misdemeanor if sentence of imprisonment in excess of thirty days but not in excess of a year was authorized and of a petty misdemeanor if sentence of imprisonment for not more than thirty days was authorized.

(2) An adjudication by a court of competent jurisdiction that the defendant committed a crime constitutes a conviction for purposes of Sections 7.03 to 7.05 inclusive, although sentence or the execution thereof was suspended, provided that the time to appeal has expired and that the defendant was not pardoned on the ground of innocence.

(3) Prior conviction may be proved by any evidence, including fingerprint records made in connection with arrest, conviction or imprisonment, that reasonably satisfies the Court that the defendant was convicted.

(4) When the defendant has asked that other crimes admitted in open court be taken into account when he is sentenced and the Court has not rejected such request, the sentence shall bar the prosecution or conviction of the defendant in this State for any such admitted crime.

Section 7.06. Multiple Sentences; Concurrent and Consecutive Terms.

(1) *Sentences of Imprisonment for More Than One Crime.* When multiple sentences of imprisonment are imposed on a defendant for more than one crime, including a crime for which a previous suspended sentence or sentence of probation has been revoked, such multiple sentences shall run concurrently or consecutively as the Court determines at the time of sentence, except that:

(a) a definite and an indefinite term shall run concurrently and both sentences shall be satisfied by service of the indefinite term; and

(b) the aggregate of consecutive definite terms shall not exceed one year; and

(c) the aggregate of consecutive indefinite terms shall not exceed in minimum or maximum length the longest extended term authorized for the highest grade and degree of crime for which any of the sentences was imposed; and

(d) not more than one sentence for an extended term shall be imposed.

(2) *Sentences of Imprisonment Imposed at Different Times.* When a defendant who has previously been sentenced to imprisonment is subsequently sentenced to another term for a crime committed prior to the former sentence, other than a crime committed while in custody:

(a) the multiple sentences imposed shall so far as possible conform to Subsection (1) of this Section; and

(b) whether the Court determines that the terms shall run concurrently or consecutively, the defendant shall be credited with time served in imprisonment on the prior sentence in determining the permissible aggregate length of the term or terms remaining to be served; and

(c) when a new sentence is imposed on a prisoner who is on parole, the balance of the parole term on the former sentence shall be deemed to run during the period of the new imprisonment.

(3) *Sentence of Imprisonment for Crime Committed While on Parole.* When a defendant is sentenced to imprisonment for a crime committed while on parole in this State, such term of imprisonment and any period of reimprisonment that the Board of Parole may require the defendant to serve upon the revocation of his parole shall run concurrently, unless the Court orders them to run consecutively.

(4) *Multiple Sentences of Imprisonment in Other Cases.* Except as otherwise provided in this Section, multiple terms of imprisonment shall run concurrently or consecutively as the Court determines when the second or subsequent sentence is imposed.

(5) *Calculation of Concurrent and Consecutive Terms of Imprisonment.*

(a) When indefinite terms run concurrently, the shorter minimum terms merge in and are satisfied by serving the longest minimum term and the shorter maximum terms merge in and are satisfied by discharge of the longest maximum term.

(b) When indefinite terms run consecutively, the minimum terms are added to arrive at an aggregate minimum to be served equal to the sum of all minimum terms and the maximum terms are added to arrive at an aggregate maximum equal to the sum of all maximum terms.

(c) When a definite and an indefinite term run consecutively, the period of the definite term is added to both the minimum and maximum of the indefinite term and both sentences are satisfied by serving the indefinite term.

(6) *Suspension of Sentence or Probation and Imprisonment; Multiple Terms of Suspension and Probation.* When a defendant is sentenced for more than one offense or a defendant already under sentence is sentenced for another offense committed prior to the former sentence:

(a) the Court shall not sentence to probation a defendant who is under sentence of imprisonment [with more than thirty days to run] or impose a sentence of probation and a sentence of imprisonment [, except as authorized by Section 6.02(3)(b)]; and

(b) multiple periods of suspension or probation shall run concurrently from the date of the first such disposition; and

(c) when a sentence of imprisonment is imposed for an indefinite term, the service of such sentence shall satisfy a suspended sentence on another count or a prior suspended sentence or sentence to probation; and

(d) when a sentence of imprisonment is imposed for a definite term, the period of a suspended sentence on another count or a prior suspended sentence or sentence to probation shall run during the period of such imprisonment.

(7) *Offense Committed While Under Suspension of Sentence or Probation.* When a defendant is convicted of an offense committed while under suspension of sentence or on probation and such suspension or probation is not revoked:

(a) if the defendant is sentenced to imprisonment for an indefinite term, the service of such sentence shall satisfy the prior suspended sentence or sentence to probation; and

(b) if the defendant is sentenced to imprisonment for a definite term, the period of the suspension or probation shall not run during the period of such imprisonment; and

(c) if sentence is suspended or the defendant is sentenced to probation, the period of such suspension or probation shall run concurrently with or consecutively to the remainder of the prior periods, as the Court determines at the time of sentence.

Section 7.07. Procedure on Sentence; Pre-sentence Investigation and Report; Remand for Psychiatric Examination; Transmission of Records to Department of Correction.

(1) The Court shall not impose sentence without first ordering a pre-sentence investigation of the defendant and according due consideration to a written report of such investigation where:

(a) the defendant has been convicted of a felony; or

(b) the defendant is less than twenty-two years of age and has been convicted of a crime; or

(c) the defendant will be [placed on probation or] sentenced to imprisonment for an extended term.

(2) The Court may order a pre-sentence investigation in any other case.

(3) The pre-sentence investigation shall include an analysis of the circumstances attending the commission of the crime, the defendant's history of delinquency or criminality, physical and mental condition, family situation and background, economic status, education, occupation and personal habits and any other matters that the probation officer deems relevant or the Court directs to be included.

(4) Before imposing sentence, the Court may order the defendant to submit to psychiatric observation and examination for a period of not exceeding sixty days or such longer period as the Court determines to be necessary for the purpose. The defendant may be remanded for this purpose to any available clinic or mental hospital or the Court may appoint a qualified psychiatrist to make the examination. The report of the examination shall be submitted to the Court.

(5) Before imposing sentence, the Court shall advise the defendant or his counsel of the factual contents and the conclusions of any pre-sentence investigation or psychiatric examination and afford fair opportunity, if the defendant so requests, to controvert them. The sources of confidential information need not, however, be disclosed.

(6) The Court shall not impose a sentence of imprisonment for an extended term unless the ground therefor has been established at a hearing after the conviction of the defendant and on written notice to him of the ground proposed. Subject to the limitation of Subsection (5) of this Section, the defendant shall have the right to hear and controvert the evidence against him and to offer evidence upon the issue.

(7) If the defendant is sentenced to imprisonment, a copy of the report of any pre-sentence investigation or psychiatric examination shall be transmitted forthwith to the Department of Correction [or other state department or agency] or, when the defendant is committed to the custody of a specific institution, to such institution.

Section 7.08. Commitment for Observation; Sentence of Imprisonment for Felony Deemed Tentative for Period of One Year; Re-sentence on Petition of Commissioner of Correction.

(1) If, after pre-sentence investigation, the Court desires additional information concerning an offender convicted of a felony or misdemeanor before imposing sentence, it may order that he be committed, for a period not exceeding ninety days, to the custody of the Department of Correction, or, in the case of a young adult offender, to the custody of the Division of Young Adult Correction, for observation and study at an appropriate reception or classification center. The Department and the Board of Parole, or the Young Adult Divisions thereof, shall advise the Court of their findings and recommendations on or before the expiration of such ninety-day period. If the offender is thereafter sentenced to imprisonment, the period of such commitment for observation shall be deducted from the maximum term and from the minimum, if any, of such sentence.

(2) When a person has been sentenced to imprisonment upon conviction of a felony, whether for an ordinary or extended term, the sentence shall be deemed tentative, to the extent provided in this Section, for the period of one year following the date when the offender is received in custody by the Department of Correction [or other state department or agency].

(3) If, as a result of the examination and classification by the Department of Correction [or other state department or agency] of a person under sentence of imprisonment upon conviction of a felony, the Commissioner of Correction [or other department head] is satisfied that the sentence of the Court may have been based upon a misapprehension as to the history, character or physical or mental condition of the offender, the Commissioner, during the period when the offender's sentence is deemed tentative under Subsection (2) of this Section shall file in the sentencing Court a petition to re-sentence the offender. The petition shall set forth the information as to the offender that is deemed to warrant his re-sentence and may include a recommendation as to the sentence to be imposed.

(4) The Court may dismiss a petition filed under Subsection (3) of this Section without a hearing if it deems the information set forth insufficient to warrant reconsideration of the sentence. If the Court is of the view that the petition warrants such reconsideration, a copy of the petition shall be served on the offender, who shall have the right to be heard on the issue and to be represented by counsel.

(5) When the Court grants a petition filed under Subsection (3) of this Section, it shall re-sentence the offender and may impose any sentence that might have been imposed originally for the felony of which the defendant was convicted. The period of his imprisonment prior to re-sentence and any reduction for good behavior to which he is entitled shall be applied in satisfaction of the final sentence.

(6) For all purposes other than this Section, a sentence of imprisonment has the same finality when it is imposed that it would have if this Section were not in force.

(7) Nothing in this Section shall alter the remedies provided by law for vacating or correcting an illegal sentence.

Section 7.09. Credit for Time of Detention Prior to Sentence; Credit for Imprisonment Under Earlier Sentence for the Same Crime.

(1) When a defendant who is sentenced to imprisonment has previously been detained in any state or local correctional or other institution following his [conviction of] [arrest for] the crime for which such sentence is imposed, such period of detention following his [conviction] [arrest] shall be deducted from the maximum term, and from the minimum, if any, of such sentence. The officer having custody of the defendant shall furnish a certificate to the Court at the time of sentence, showing the length of such detention of the defendant prior to sentence in any state or local correctional or other institution, and the certificate shall be annexed to the official records of the defendant's commitment.

(2) When a judgment of conviction is vacated and a new sentence is thereafter imposed upon the defendant for the same crime, the period of detention and imprisonment theretofore served shall be deducted from the maximum term, and from the minimum, if any, of the new sentence. The officer having custody of the defendant shall furnish a certificate to the Court at the time of sentence, showing the period of imprisonment served under the original sentence, and the certificate shall be annexed to the official records of the defendant's new commitment.

PART II. DEFINITION OF SPECIFIC CRIMES

OFFENSES AGAINST EXISTENCE OR STABILITY OF THE STATE[a]

[This category of offenses, including treason, sedition, espionage and like crimes, was excluded from the scope of the Model Penal Code. These offenses are peculiarly the concern of the federal government. The Constitution itself defines treason: "Treason against the United States shall consist of levying War against them, or in adhering to their Enemies, giving the Aid and Comfort. . . ." Article III, Section 3; cf. Pennsylvania v. Nelson, 350 U.S. 497 (supersession of state sedition legislation by federal law). Also, the definition of offenses against the stability of the state is inevitably affected by special political considerations. These factors militated against the use of the Institute's limited resources to attempt to draft "model" provisions in this area. However we provide at this point in the Plan of the Model Penal Code for an Article 200, where definitions of offenses against the existence of stability of the state may be incorporated.]

OFFENSES INVOLVING DANGER TO THE PERSON

ARTICLE 210. CRIMINAL HOMICIDE

Section 210.0. Definitions.

In Articles 210–213, unless a different meaning plainly is required:

(1) "human being" means a person who has been born and is alive;

(2) "bodily injury" means physical pain, illness or any impairment of physical condition;

(3) "serious bodily injury" means bodily injury which creates a substantial risk of death or which causes serious, permanent disfigurement, or protracted loss or impairment of the function of any bodily member or organ;

(4) "deadly weapon" means any firearm, or other weapon, device, instrument, material or substance, whether animate or inanimate, which in the manner it is used or is intended to be used is known to be capable of producing death or serious bodily injury.

Section 210.1. Criminal Homicide.

(1) A person is guilty of criminal homicide if he purposely, knowingly, recklessly or negligently causes the death of another human being.

(2) Criminal homicide is murder, manslaughter or negligent homicide.

Section 210.2. Murder.

(1) Except as provided in Section 210.3(1)(b), criminal homicide constitutes murder when:

(a) it is committed purposely or knowingly; or

(b) it is committed recklessly under circumstances manifesting extreme indifference to the value of human life. Such recklessness and indifference are presumed if the actor is engaged or is an accomplice in the commission of, or an attempt to commit, or flight after committing or attempting to commit robbery, rape or deviate sexual intercourse by force or threat of force, arson, burglary, kidnapping or felonious escape.

a. Model Penal Code 123 (Proposed Official Draft 1962).—EDS.

(2) Murder is a felony of the first degree [but a person convicted of murder may be sentenced to death, as provided in Section 210.6].

Section 210.3. Manslaughter.

(1) Criminal homicide constitutes manslaughter when:

(a) it is committed recklessly; or

(b) a homicide which would otherwise be murder is committed under the influence of extreme mental or emotional disturbance for which there is reasonable explanation or excuse. The reasonableness of such explanation or excuse shall be determined from the viewpoint of a person in the actor's situation under the circumstances as he believes them to be.

(2) Manslaughter is a felony of the second degree.

Section 210.4. Negligent Homicide.

(1) Criminal homicide constitutes negligent homicide when it is committed negligently.

(2) Negligent homicide is a felony of the third degree.

Section 210.5. Causing or Aiding Suicide.

(1) *Causing Suicide as Criminal Homicide.* A person may be convicted of criminal homicide for causing another to commit suicide only if he purposely causes such suicide by force, duress or deception.

(2) *Aiding or Soliciting Suicide as an Independent Offense.* A person who purposely aids or solicits another to commit suicide is guilty of a felony of the second degree if his conduct causes such suicide or an attempted suicide, and otherwise of a misdemeanor.

[Section 210.6. Sentence of Death for Murder; Further Proceedings to Determine Sentence].

(1) *Death Sentence Excluded.* When a defendant is found guilty of murder, the Court shall impose sentence for a felony of the first degree if it is satisfied that:

(a) none of the aggravating circumstances enumerated in Subsection (3) of this Section was established by the evidence at the trial or will be established if further proceedings are initiated under Subsection (2) of this Section; or

(b) substantial mitigating circumstances, established by the evidence at the trial, call for leniency; or

(c) the defendant, with the consent of the prosecuting attorney and the approval of the Court, pleaded guilty to murder as a felony of the first degree; or

(d) the defendant was under 18 years of age at the time of the commission of the crime; or

(e) the defendant's physical or mental condition calls for leniency; or

(f) although the evidence suffices to sustain the verdict, it does not foreclose all doubt respecting the defendant's guilt.

(2) *Determination by Court or by Court and Jury.* Unless the Court imposes sentence under Subsection (1) of this Section, it shall conduct a separate proceeding to determine whether the defendant should be sentenced for a felony of the first degree or sentenced to death. The proceeding shall be conducted before the Court alone if the defendant was convicted by a Court sitting without a jury or upon his

plea of guilty or if the prosecuting attorney and the defendant waive a jury with respect to sentence. In other cases it shall be conducted before the Court sitting with the jury which determined the defendant's guilt or, if the Court for good cause shown discharges that jury, with a new jury empanelled for the purpose.

In the proceeding, evidence may be presented as to any matter that the Court deems relevant to sentence, including but not limited to the nature and circumstances of the crime, the defendant's character, background, history, mental and physical condition and any of the aggravating or mitigating circumstances enumerated in Subsections (3) and (4) of this Section. Any such evidence, not legally privileged, which the Court deems to have probative force, may be received, regardless of its admissibility under the exclusionary rules of evidence, provided that the defendant's counsel is accorded a fair opportunity to rebut such evidence. The prosecuting attorney and the defendant or his counsel shall be permitted to present argument for or against sentence of death.

The determination whether sentence of death shall be imposed shall be in the discretion of the Court, except that when the proceeding is conducted before the Court sitting with a jury, the Court shall not impose sentence of death unless it submits to the jury the issue whether the defendant should be sentenced to death or to imprisonment and the jury returns a verdict that the sentence should be death. If the jury is unable to reach a unanimous verdict, the Court shall dismiss the jury and impose sentence for a felony of the first degree.

The Court, in exercising its discretion as to sentence, and the jury, in determining upon its verdict, shall take into account the aggravating and mitigating circumstances enumerated in Subsections (3) and (4) and any other facts that it deems relevant, but it shall not impose or recommend sentence of death unless it finds one of the aggravating circumstances enumerated in Subsection (3) and further finds that there are no mitigating circumstances sufficiently substantial to call for leniency. When the issue is submitted to the jury, the Court shall so instruct and also shall inform the jury of the nature of the sentence of imprisonment that may be imposed, including its implication with respect to possible release upon parole, if the jury verdict is against sentence of death.

Alternative formulation of Subsection (2):

(2) *Determination by Court.* Unless the Court imposes sentence under Subsection (1) of this Section, it shall conduct a separate proceeding to determine whether the defendant should be sentenced for a felony of the first degree or sentenced to death. In the proceeding, the Court, in accordance with Section 7.07, shall consider the report of the pre-sentence investigation and, if a psychiatric examination has been ordered, the report of such examination. In addition, evidence may be presented as to any matter that the Court deems relevant to sentence, including but not limited to the nature and circumstances of the crime, the defendant's character, background, history, mental and physical condition and any of the aggravating or mitigating circumstances enumerated in Subsections (3) and (4) of this Section. Any such evidence, not legally privileged, which the Court deems to have probative force, may be received, regardless of its admissibility under the exclusionary rules of evidence, provided that the defendant's counsel is accorded a fair opportunity to rebut such evidence. The prosecuting attorney and the defendant or his counsel shall be permitted to present argument for or against sentence of death.

The determination whether sentence of death shall be imposed shall be in the discretion of the Court. In exercising such discretion, the Court shall take into account the aggravating and mitigating circumstances enumerated in Subsections (3) and (4) and any other facts that it deems relevant but shall not impose sentence of death unless it finds one of the aggravating circumstances enumerated in

Subsection (3) and further finds that there are no mitigating circumstances sufficiently substantial to call for leniency.

(3) *Aggravating Circumstances.*

(a) The murder was committed by a convict under sentence of imprisonment.

(b) The defendant was previously convicted of another murder or of a felony involving the use or threat of violence to the person.

(c) At the time the murder was committed the defendant also committed another murder.

(d) The defendant knowingly created a great risk of death to many persons.

(e) The murder was committed while the defendant was engaged or was an accomplice in the commission of, or an attempt to commit, or flight after committing or attempting to commit robbery, rape or deviate sexual intercourse by force or threat of force, arson, burglary or kidnapping.

(f) The murder was committed for the purpose of avoiding or preventing a lawful arrest or effecting an escape from lawful custody.

(g) The murder was committed for pecuniary gain.

(h) The murder was especially heinous, atrocious or cruel, manifesting exceptional depravity.

(4) *Mitigating Circumstances.*

(a) The defendant has no significant history of prior criminal activity.

(b) The murder was committed while the defendant was under the influence of extreme mental or emotional disturbance.

(c) The victim was a participant in the defendant's homicidal conduct or consented to the homicidal act.

(d) The murder was committed under circumstances which the defendant believed to provide a moral justification or extenuation for his conduct.

(e) The defendant was an accomplice in a murder committed by another person and his participation in the homicidal act was relatively minor.

(f) The defendant acted under duress or under the domination of another person.

(g) At the time of the murder, the capacity of the defendant to appreciate the criminality [wrongfulness] of his conduct or to conform his conduct to the requirements of law was impaired as a result of mental disease or defect or intoxication.

(h) The youth of the defendant at the time of the crime.]

ARTICLE 211. ASSAULT; RECKLESS ENDANGERING; THREATS

Section 211.0. Definitions.

In this Article, the definitions given in Section 210.0 apply unless a different meaning plainly is required.

Section 211.1. Assault.

(1) *Simple Assault.* A person is guilty of assault if he:

(a) attempts to cause or purposely, knowingly or recklessly causes bodily injury to another; or

(b) negligently causes bodily injury to another with a deadly weapon; or

(c) attempts by physical menace to put another in fear of imminent serious bodily injury.

Simple assault is a misdemeanor unless committed in a fight or scuffle entered into by mutual consent, in which case it is a petty misdemeanor.

(2) *Aggravated Assault.* A person is guilty of aggravated assault if he:

(a) attempts to cause serious bodily injury to another, or causes such injury purposely, knowingly or recklessly under circumstances manifesting extreme indifference to the value of human life; or

(b) attempts to cause or purposely or knowingly causes bodily injury to another with a deadly weapon.

Aggravated assault under paragraph (a) is a felony of the second degree; aggravated assault under paragraph (b) is a felony of the third degree.

Section 211.2. Recklessly Endangering Another Person.

A person commits a misdemeanor if he recklessly engages in conduct which places or may place another person in danger of death or serious bodily injury. Recklessness and danger shall be presumed where a person knowingly points a firearm at or in the direction of another, whether or not the actor believed the firearm to be loaded.

Section 211.3. Terroristic Threats.

A person is guilty of a felony of the third degree if he threatens to commit any crime of violence with purpose to terrorize another or to cause evacuation of a building, place of assembly, or facility of public transportation, or otherwise to cause serious public inconvenience, or in reckless disregard of the risk of causing such terror or inconvenience.

ARTICLE 212. KIDNAPPING AND RELATED OFFENSES; COERCION

Section 212.0. Definitions.

In this Article, the definitions given in Section 210.0 apply unless a different meaning plainly is required.

Section 212.1. Kidnapping.

A person is guilty of kidnapping if he unlawfully removes another from his place of residence or business, or a substantial distance from the vicinity where he is found, or if he unlawfully confines another for a substantial period in a place of isolation, with any of the following purposes:

(a) to hold for ransom or reward, or as a shield or hostage; or

(b) to facilitate commission of any felony or flight thereafter; or

(c) to inflict bodily injury on or to terrorize the victim or another; or

(d) to interfere with the performance of any governmental or political function.

Kidnapping is a felony of the first degree unless the actor voluntarily releases the victim alive and in a safe place prior to trial, in which case it is a felony of the second degree. A removal or confinement is unlawful within the meaning of this Section if it is accomplished by force, threat or deception, or, in the case of a person who is under the age of 14 or incompetent, if it is accomplished without the consent of a parent, guardian or other person responsible for general supervision of his welfare.

Section 212.2. Felonious Restraint.

A person commits a felony of the third degree if he knowingly:

(a) restrains another unlawfully in circumstances exposing him to risk of serious bodily injury; or

(b) holds another in a condition of involuntary servitude.

Section 212.3. False Imprisonment.

A person commits a misdemeanor if he knowingly restrains another unlawfully so as to interfere substantially with his liberty.

Section 212.4. Interference with Custody.

(1) *Custody of Children.* A person commits an offense if he knowingly or recklessly takes or entices any child under the age of 18 from the custody of its parent, guardian or other lawful custodian, when he has no privilege to do so. It is an affirmative defense that:

(a) the actor believed that his action was necessary to preserve the child from danger to its welfare; or

(b) the child, being at the time not less than 14 years old, was taken away at its own instigation without enticement and without purpose to commit a criminal offense with or against the child.

Proof that the child was below the critical age gives rise to a presumption that the actor knew the child's age or acted in reckless disregard thereof. The offense is a misdemeanor unless the actor, not being a parent or person in equivalent relation to the child, acted with knowledge that his conduct would cause serious alarm for the child's safety, or in reckless disregard of a likelihood of causing such alarm, in which case the offense is a felony of the third degree.

(2) *Custody of Committed Persons.* A person is guilty of a misdemeanor if he knowingly or recklessly takes or entices any committed person away from lawful custody when he is not privileged to do so. "Committed person" means, in addition to anyone committed under judicial warrant, any orphan, neglected or delinquent child, mentally defective or insane person, or other dependent or incompetent person entrusted to another's custody by or through a recognized social agency or otherwise by authority of law.

Section 212.5. Criminal Coercion.

(1) *Offense Defined.* A person is guilty of criminal coercion if, with purpose unlawfully to restrict another's freedom of action to his detriment, he threatens to:

(a) commit any criminal offense; or

(b) accuse anyone of a criminal offense; or

(c) expose any secret tending to subject any person to hatred, contempt or ridicule, or to impair his credit or business repute; or

(d) take or withhold action as an official, or cause an official to take or withhold action.

It is an affirmative defense to prosecution based on paragraphs (b), (c) or (d) that the actor believed the accusation or secret to be true or the proposed official action justified and that his purpose was limited to compelling the other to behave in a way reasonably related to the circumstances which were the subject of the accusation, exposure or proposed official action, as by desisting from further misbehavior, making good a wrong done, refraining from taking any action or responsibility for which the actor believes the other disqualified.

(2) *Grading.* Criminal coercion is a misdemeanor unless the threat is to commit a felony or the actor's purpose is felonious, in which cases the offense is a felony of the third degree.

ARTICLE 213. SEXUAL OFFENSES

Section 213.0. Definitions.

In this Article, unless a different meaning plainly is required:

(1) the definitions given in Section 210.0 apply;

(2) "Sexual intercourse" includes intercourse per os or per anus, with some penetration however slight; emission is not required;

(3) "Deviate sexual intercourse" means sexual intercourse per os or per anus between human beings who are not husband and wife, and any form of sexual intercourse with an animal.

Section 213.1. Rape and Related Offenses.

(1) *Rape.* A male who has sexual intercourse with a female not his wife is guilty of rape if:

(a) he compels her to submit by force or by threat of imminent death, serious bodily injury, extreme pain or kidnapping, to be inflicted on anyone; or

(b) he has substantially impaired her power to appraise or control her conduct by administering or employing without her knowledge drugs, intoxicants or other means for the purpose of preventing resistance; or

(c) the female is unconscious; or

(d) the female is less than 10 years old.

Rape is a felony of the second degree unless (i) in the course thereof the actor inflicts serious bodily injury upon anyone, or (ii) the victim was not a voluntary social companion of the actor upon the occasion of the crime and had not previously permitted him sexual liberties, in which cases the offense is a felony of the first degree.

(2) *Gross Sexual Imposition.* A male who has sexual intercourse with a female not his wife commits a felony of the third degree if:

(a) he compels her to submit by any threat that would prevent resistance by a woman of ordinary resolution; or

(b) he knows that she suffers from a mental disease or defect which renders her incapable of appraising the nature of her conduct; or

(c) he knows that she is unaware that a sexual act is being committed upon her or that she submits because she mistakenly supposes that he is her husband.

Section 213.2. Deviate Sexual Intercourse by Force or Imposition.

(1) *By Force or Its Equivalent.* A person who engages in deviate sexual intercourse with another person, or who causes another to engage in deviate sexual intercourse, commits a felony of the second degree if:

(a) he compels the other person to participate by force or by threat of imminent death, serious bodily injury, extreme pain or kidnapping, to be inflicted on anyone; or

(b) he has substantially impaired the other person's power to appraise or control his conduct, by administering or employing without the knowledge of the other person drugs, intoxicants or other means for the purpose of preventing resistance; or

(c) the other person is unconscious; or

(d) the other person is less than 10 years old.

(2) *By Other Imposition.* A person who engages in deviate sexual intercourse with another person, or who causes another to engage in deviate sexual intercourse, commits a felony of the third degree if:

(a) he compels the other person to participate by any threat that would prevent resistance by a person of ordinary resolution; or

(b) he knows that the other person suffers from a mental disease or defect which renders him incapable of appraising the nature of his conduct; or

(c) he knows that the other person submits because he is unaware that a sexual act is being committed upon him.

Section 213.3. Corruption of Minors and Seduction.

(1) *Offense Defined.* A male who has sexual intercourse with a female not his wife, or any person who engages in deviate sexual intercourse or causes another to engage in deviate sexual intercourse, is guilty of an offense if:

(a) the other person is less than [16] years old and the actor is at least [4] years older than the other person; or

(b) the other person is less than 21 years old and the actor is his guardian or otherwise responsible for general supervision of his welfare; or

(c) the other person is in custody of law or detained in a hospital or other institution and the actor has supervisory or disciplinary authority over him; or

(d) the other person is a female who is induced to participate by a promise of marriage which the actor does not mean to perform.

(2) *Grading.* An offense under paragraph (a) of Subsection (1) is a felony of the third degree. Otherwise an offense under this section is a misdemeanor.

Section 213.4. Sexual Assault.

A person who has sexual contact with another not his spouse, or causes such other to have sexual contact with him, is guilty of sexual assault, a misdemeanor, if:

(1) he knows that the contact is offensive to the other person; or

(2) he knows that the other person suffers from a mental disease or defect which renders him or her incapable of appraising the nature of his or her conduct; or

(3) he knows that the other person is unaware that a sexual act is being committed; or

(4) the other person is less than 10 years old; or

(5) he has substantially impaired the other person's power to appraise or control his or her conduct, by administering or employing without the other's knowledge drugs, intoxicants or other means for the purpose of preventing resistance; or

(6) the other person is less than [16] years old and the actor is at least [4] years older than the other person; or

(7) the other person is less than 21 years old and the actor is his guardian or otherwise responsible for general supervision of his welfare; or

(8) the other person is in custody of law or detained in a hospital or other institution and the actor has supervisory or disciplinary authority over him.

Sexual contact is any touching of the sexual or other intimate parts of the person for the purpose of arousing or gratifying sexual desire.

Section 213.5. Indecent Exposure.

A person commits a misdemeanor if, for the purpose of arousing or gratifying sexual desire of himself or of any person other than his spouse, he exposes his genitals under circumstances in which he knows his conduct is likely to cause affront or alarm.

Section 213.6. Provisions Generally Applicable to Article 213.

(1) *Mistake as to Age.* Whenever in this Article the criminality of conduct depends on a child's being below the age of 10, it is no defense that the actor did not know the child's age, or reasonably believed the child to be older than 10. When criminality depends on the child's being below a critical age other than 10, it is a defense for the actor to prove by a preponderance of the evidence that he reasonably believed the child to be above the critical age.

(2) *Spouse Relationships.* Whenever in this Article the definition of an offense excludes conduct with a spouse, the exclusion shall be deemed to extend to persons living as man and wife, regardless of the legal status of their relationship. The exclusion shall be inoperative as respects spouses living apart under a decree of judicial separation. Where the definition of an offense excludes conduct with a spouse or conduct by a woman, this shall not preclude conviction of a spouse or woman as accomplice in a sexual act which he or she causes another person, not within the exclusion, to perform.

(3) *Sexually Promiscuous Complainants.* It is a defense to prosecution under Section 213.3 and paragraphs (6), (7) and (8) of Section 213.4 for the actor to prove by a preponderance of the evidence that the alleged victim had, prior to the time of the offense charged, engaged promiscuously in sexual relations with others.

(4) *Prompt Complaint.* No prosecution may be instituted or maintained under this Article unless the alleged offense was brought to the notice of public authority within [3] months of its occurrence or, where the alleged victim was less than [16] years old or otherwise incompetent to make complaint, within [3] months after a parent, guardian or other competent person specially interested in the victim learns of the offense.

(5) *Testimony of Complainants.* No person shall be convicted of any felony under this Article upon the uncorroborated testimony of the alleged victim. Corroboration may be circumstantial. In any prosecution before a jury for an offense under this Article, the jury shall be instructed to evaluate the testimony of a victim or complaining witness with special care in view of the emotional involvement of the witness and the difficulty of determining the truth with respect to alleged sexual activities carried out in private.

OFFENSES AGAINST PROPERTY

ARTICLE 220. ARSON, CRIMINAL MISCHIEF, AND OTHER PROPERTY DESTRUCTION

Section 220.1. Arson and Related Offenses.

(1) *Arson.* A person is guilty of arson, a felony of the second degree, if he starts a fire or causes an explosion with the purpose of:

(a) destroying a building or occupied structure of another; or

(b) destroying or damaging any property, whether his own or another's, to collect insurance for such loss. It shall be an affirmative defense to prosecution under this paragraph that the actor's conduct did not recklessly endanger any building or occupied structure of another or place any other person in danger of death or bodily injury.

(2) *Reckless Burning or Exploding.* A person commits a felony of the third degree if he purposely starts a fire or causes an explosion, whether on his own property or another's, and thereby recklessly:

(a) places another person in danger of death or bodily injury; or

(b) places a building or occupied structure of another in danger of damage or destruction.

(3) *Failure to Control or Report Dangerous Fire.* A person who knows that a fire is endangering life or a substantial amount of property of another and fails to take reasonable measures to put out or control the fire, when he can do so without substantial risk to himself, or to give a prompt fire alarm, commits a misdemeanor if:

(a) he knows that he is under an official, contractual, or other legal duty to prevent or combat the fire; or

(b) the fire was started, albeit lawfully, by him or with his assent, or on property in his custody or control.

(4) *Definitions.* "Occupied structure" means any structure, vehicle or place adapted for overnight accommodation of persons, or for carrying on business therein, whether or not a person is actually present. Property is that of another, for the purposes of this section, if anyone other than the actor has a possessory or proprietary interest therein. If a building or structure is divided into separately occupied units, any unit not occupied by the actor is an occupied structure of another.

Section 220.2. Causing or Risking Catastrophe.

(1) *Causing Catastrophe.* A person who causes a catastrophe by explosion, fire, flood, avalanche, collapse of building, release of poison gas, radioactive material or other harmful or destructive force or substance, or by any other means of causing potentially widespread injury or damage, commits a felony of the second degree if he does so purposely or knowingly, or a felony of the third degree if he does so recklessly.

(2) *Risking Catastrophe.* A person is guilty of a misdemeanor if he recklessly creates a risk of catastrophe in the employment of fire, explosives or other dangerous means listed in Subsection (1).

(3) *Failure to Prevent Catastrophe.* A person who knowingly or recklessly fails to take reasonable measures to prevent or mitigate a catastrophe commits a misdemeanor if:

(a) he knows that he is under an official, contractual or other legal duty to take such measures; or

(b) he did or assented to the act causing or threatening the catastrophe.

Section 220.3. Criminal Mischief.

(1) *Offense Defined.* A person is guilty of criminal mischief if he:

(a) damages tangible property of another purposely, recklessly, or by negligence in the employment of fire, explosives, or other dangerous means listed in Section 220.2(1); or

(b) purposely or recklessly tampers with tangible property of another so as to endanger person or property; or

(c) purposely or recklessly causes another to suffer pecuniary loss by deception or threat.

(2) *Grading.* Criminal mischief is a felony of the third degree if the actor purposely causes pecuniary loss in excess of $5,000, or a substantial interruption or impairment of public communication, transportation, supply of water, gas or power, or other public service. It is a misdemeanor if the actor purposely causes pecuniary loss in excess of $100, or a petty misdemeanor if he purposely or recklessly causes pecuniary loss in excess of $25. Otherwise criminal mischief is a violation.

ARTICLE 221. BURGLARY AND OTHER CRIMINAL INTRUSION

Section 221.0. Definitions.

In this Article, unless a different meaning plainly is required:

(1) "occupied structure" means any structure, vehicle or place adapted for overnight accommodation of persons, or for carrying on business therein, whether or not a person is actually present.

(2) "night" means the period between thirty minutes past sunset and thirty minutes before sunrise.

Section 221.1. Burglary.

(1) *Burglary Defined.* A person is guilty of burglary if he enters a building or occupied structure, or separately secured or occupied portion thereof, with purpose to commit a crime therein, unless the premises are at the time open to the public or the actor is licensed or privileged to enter. It is an affirmative defense to prosecution for burglary that the building or structure was abandoned.

(2) *Grading.* Burglary is a felony of the second degree if it is perpetrated in the dwelling of another at night, or if, in the course of committing the offense, the actor:

(a) purposely, knowingly or recklessly inflicts or attempts to inflict bodily injury on anyone; or

(b) is armed with explosives or a deadly weapon.

Otherwise, burglary is a felony of the third degree. An act shall be deemed "in the course of committing" an offense if it occurs in an attempt to commit the offense or in flight after the attempt or commission.

(3) *Multiple Convictions.* A person may not be convicted both for burglary and for the offense which it was his purpose to commit after the burglarious entry or for an attempt to commit that offense, unless the additional offense constitutes a felony of the first or second degree.

Section 221.2. Criminal Trespass.

(1) *Buildings and Occupied Structures.* A person commits an offense if, knowing that he is not licensed or privileged to do so, he enters or surreptitiously remains in any building or occupied structure, or separately secured or occupied portion thereof. An offense under this Subsection is a misdemeanor if it is committed in a dwelling at night. Otherwise it is a petty misdemeanor.

(2) *Defiant Trespasser.* A person commits an offense if, knowing that he is not licensed or privileged to do so, he enters or remains in any place as to which notice against trespass is given by:

(a) actual communication to the actor; or

(b) posting in a manner prescribed by law or reasonably likely to come to the attention of intruders; or

(c) fencing or other enclosure manifestly designed to exclude intruders.

An offense under this Subsection constitutes a petty misdemeanor if the offender defies an order to leave personally communicated to him by the owner of the premises or other authorized person. Otherwise it is a violation.

(3) *Defenses.* It is an affirmative defense to prosecution under this Section that:

(a) a building or occupied structure involved in an offense under Subsection (1) was abandoned; or

(b) the premises were at the time open to members of the public and the actor complied with all lawful conditions imposed on access to or remaining in the premises; or

(c) the actor reasonably believed that the owner of the premises, or other person empowered to license access thereto, would have licensed him to enter or remain.

ARTICLE 222. ROBBERY

Section 222.1. Robbery.

(1) *Robbery Defined.* A person is guilty of robbery if, in the course of committing a theft, he:

(a) inflicts serious bodily injury upon another; or

(b) threatens another with or purposely puts him in fear of immediate serious bodily injury; or

(c) commits or threatens immediately to commit any felony of the first or second degree.

An act shall be deemed "in the course of committing a theft" if it occurs in an attempt to commit theft or in flight after the attempt or commission.

(2) *Grading.* Robbery is a felony of the second degree, except that it is a felony of the first degree if in the course of committing the theft the actor attempts to kill anyone, or purposely inflicts or attempts to inflict serious bodily injury.

ARTICLE 223. THEFT AND RELATED OFFENSES

Section 223.0. Definitions.

In this Article, unless a different meaning plainly is required:

(1) "deprive" means: (a) to withhold property of another permanently or for so extended a period as to appropriate a major portion of its economic value, or with intent to restore only upon payment of reward or other compensation; or (b) to dispose of the property so as to make it unlikely that the owner will recover it.

(2) "financial institution" means a bank, insurance company, credit union, building and loan association, investment trust or other organization held out to the public as a place of deposit of funds or medium of savings or collective investment.

(3) "government" means the United States, any State, county, municipality, or other political unit, or any department, agency or subdivision of any of the

foregoing, or any corporation or other association carrying out the functions of government.

(4) "movable property" means property the location of which can be changed, including things growing on, affixed to, or found in land, and documents although the rights represented thereby have no physical location. "Immovable property" is all other property.

(5) "obtain" means: (a) in relation to property, to bring about a transfer or purported transfer of a legal interest in the property, whether to the obtainer or another; or (b) in relation to labor or service, to secure performance thereof.

(6) "property" means anything of value, including real estate, tangible and intangible personal property, contract rights, choses-in-action and other interests in or claims to wealth, admission or transportation tickets, captured or domestic animals, food and drink, electric or other power.

(7) "property of another" includes property in which any person other than the actor has an interest which the actor is not privileged to infringe, regardless of the fact that the actor also has an interest in the property and regardless of the fact that the other person might be precluded from civil recovery because the property was used in an unlawful transaction or was subject to forfeiture as contraband. Property in possession of the actor shall not be deemed property of another who has only a security interest therein, even if legal title is in the creditor pursuant to a conditional sales contract or other security agreement.

Section 223.1. Consolidation of Theft Offenses; Grading; Provisions Applicable to Theft Generally.

(1) *Consolidation of Theft Offenses.* Conduct denominated theft in this Article constitutes a single offense. An accusation of theft may be supported by evidence that it was committed in any manner that would be theft under this Article, notwithstanding the specification of a different manner in the indictment or information, subject only to the power of the Court to ensure fair trial by granting a continuance or other appropriate relief where the conduct of the defense would be prejudiced by lack of fair notice or by surprise.

(2) *Grading of Theft Offenses.*

(a) Theft constitutes a felony of the third degree if the amount involved exceeds $500, or if the property stolen is a firearm, automobile, airplane, motorcycle, motor boat, or other motor-propelled vehicle, or in the case of theft by receiving stolen property, if the receiver is in the business of buying or selling stolen property.

(b) Theft not within the preceding paragraph constitutes a misdemeanor, except that if the property was not taken from the person or by threat, or in breach of a fiduciary obligation, and the actor proves by a preponderance of the evidence that the amount involved was less than $50, the offense constitutes a petty misdemeanor.

(c) The amount involved in a theft shall be deemed to be the highest value, by any reasonable standard, of the property or services which the actor stole or attempted to steal. Amounts involved in thefts committed pursuant to one scheme or course of conduct, whether from the same person or several persons, may be aggregated in determining the grade of the offense.

(3) *Claim of Right.* It is an affirmative defense to prosecution for theft that the actor:

(a) was unaware that the property or service was that of another; or

(b) acted under an honest claim of right to the property or service involved or that he had a right to acquire or dispose of it as he did; or

(c) took property exposed for sale, intending to purchase and pay for it promptly, or reasonably believing that the owner, if present, would have consented.

(4) *Theft from Spouse.* It is no defense that theft was from the actor's spouse, except that misappropriation of household and personal effects, or other property normally accessible to both spouses, is theft only if it occurs after the parties have ceased living together.

Section 223.2. Theft by Unlawful Taking or Disposition.

(1) *Movable Property.* A person is guilty of theft if he unlawfully takes, or exercises unlawful control over, movable property of another with purpose to deprive him thereof.

(2) *Immovable Property.* A person is guilty of theft if he unlawfully transfers immovable property of another or any interest therein with purpose to benefit himself or another not entitled thereto.

Section 223.3. Theft by Deception.

A person is guilty of theft if he purposely obtains property of another by deception. A person deceives if he purposely:

(1) creates or reinforces a false impression, including false impressions as to law, value, intention or other state of mind; but deception as to a person's intention to perform a promise shall not be inferred from the fact alone that he did not subsequently perform the promise; or

(2) prevents another from acquiring information which would affect his judgment of a transaction; or

(3) fails to correct a false impression which the deceiver previously created or reinforced, or which the deceiver knows to be influencing another to whom he stands in a fiduciary or confidential relationship; or

(4) fails to disclose a known lien, adverse claim or other legal impediment to the enjoyment of property which he transfers or encumbers in consideration for the property obtained, whether such impediment is or is not valid, or is or is not a matter of official record.

The term "deceive" does not, however, include falsity as to matters having no pecuniary significance, or puffing by statements unlikely to deceive ordinary persons in the group addressed.

Section 223.4. Theft by Extortion.

A person is guilty of theft if he purposely obtains property of another by threatening to:

(1) inflict bodily injury on anyone or commit any other criminal offense; or

(2) accuse anyone of a criminal offense; or

(3) expose any secret tending to subject any person to hatred, contempt or ridicule, or to impair his credit or business repute; or

(4) take or withhold action as an official, or cause an official to take or withhold action; or

(5) bring about or continue a strike, boycott or other collective unofficial action, if the property is not demanded or received for the benefit of the group in whose interest the actor purports to act; or

(6) testify or provide information or withhold testimony or information with respect to another's legal claim or defense; or

(7) inflict any other harm which would not benefit the actor.

It is an affirmative defense to prosecution based on paragraphs (2), (3) or (4) that the property obtained by threat of accusation, exposure, lawsuit or other invocation of official action was honestly claimed as restitution or indemnification for harm done in the circumstances to which such accusation, exposure, lawsuit or other official action relates, or as compensation for property or lawful services.

Section 223.5. Theft of Property Lost, Mislaid, or Delivered by Mistake.

A person who comes into control of property of another that he knows to have been lost, mislaid, or delivered under a mistake as to the nature or amount of the property or the identity of the recipient is guilty of theft if, with purpose to deprive the owner thereof, he fails to take reasonable measures to restore the property to a person entitled to have it.

Section 223.6. Receiving Stolen Property.

(1) *Receiving.* A person is guilty of theft if he purposely receives, retains, or disposes of movable property of another knowing that it has been stolen, or believing that it has probably been stolen, unless the property is received, retained, or disposed with purpose to restore it to the owner. "Receiving" means acquiring possession, control or title, or lending on the security of the property.

(2) *Presumption of Knowledge.* The requisite knowledge or belief is presumed in the case of a dealer who:

(a) is found in possession or control of property stolen from two or more persons on separate occasions; or

(b) has received stolen property in another transaction within the year preceding the transaction charged; or

(c) being a dealer in property of the sort received, acquires it for a consideration which he knows is far below its reasonable value.

"Dealer" means a person in the business of buying or selling goods including a pawnbroker.

Section 223.7. Theft of Services.

(1) A person is guilty of theft is he purposely obtains services which he knows are available only for compensation, by deception or threat, or by false token or other means to avoid payment for the service. "Services" includes labor, professional service, transportation, telephone or other public service, accommodation in hotels, restaurants or elsewhere, admission to exhibitions, use of vehicles or other movable property. Where compensation for service is ordinarily paid immediately upon the rendering of such service, as in the case of hotels and restaurants, refusal to pay or absconding without payment or offer to pay gives rise to a presumption that the service was obtained by deception as to intention to pay.

(2) A person commits theft if, having control over the disposition of services of others, to which he is not entitled, he knowingly diverts such services to his own benefit or to the benefit of another not entitled thereto.

Section 223.8. Theft by Failure to Make Required Disposition of Funds Received.

A person who purposely obtains property upon agreement, or subject to a known legal obligation, to make specified payment or other disposition, whether from such property or its proceeds or from his own property to be reserved in equivalent amount, is guilty of theft if he deals with the property obtained as his own and fails to make the required payment or disposition. The foregoing applies notwithstanding that it may be impossible to identify particular property as belonging to the victim at the time of the actor's failure to make the required payment or disposition. An officer or employee of the government or of a financial institution is presumed: (i) to know any legal obligation relevant to his criminal liability under this Section, and (ii) to have dealt with the property as his own if he fails to pay or account upon lawful demand, or if an audit reveals a shortage or falsification of accounts.

Section 223.9. Unauthorized Use of Automobiles and Other Vehicles.

A person commits a misdemeanor if he operates another's automobile, airplane, motorcycle, motorboat, or other motor-propelled vehicle without consent of the owner. It is an affirmative defense to prosecution under this Section that the actor reasonably believed that the owner would have consented to the operation had he known of it.

ARTICLE 224. FORGERY AND FRAUDULENT PRACTICES

Section 224.0. Definitions.

In this Article, the definitions given in Section 223.0 apply unless a different meaning plainly is required.

Section 224.1. Forgery.

(1) *Definition.* A person is guilty of forgery if, with purpose to defraud or injure anyone, or with knowledge that he is facilitating a fraud or injury to be perpetrated by anyone, the actor:

(a) alters any writing of another without his authority; or

(b) makes, completes, executes, authenticates, issues or transfers any writing so that it purports to be the act of another who did not authorize that act, or to have been executed at a time or place or in a numbered sequence other than was in fact the case, or to be a copy of an original when no such original existed; or

(c) utters any writing which he knows to be forged in a manner specified in paragraphs (a) or (b).

"Writing" includes printing or any other method of recording information, money, coins, tokens, stamps, seals, credit cards, badges, trade-marks, and other symbols of value, right, privilege, or identification.

(2) *Grading.* Forgery is a felony of the second degree if the writing is or purports to be part of an issue of money, securities, postage or revenue stamps, or other instruments issued by the government, or part of an issue of stock, bonds or other instruments representing interests in or claims against any property or enterprise. Forgery is a felony of the third degree if the writing is or purports to be a will, deed, contract, release, commercial instrument, or other document evidencing, creating, transferring, altering, terminating, or otherwise affecting legal relations. Otherwise forgery is a misdemeanor.

Section 224.2. Simulating Objects of Antiquity, Rarity, Etc.

A person commits a misdemeanor if, with purpose to defraud anyone or with knowledge that he is facilitating a fraud to be perpetrated by anyone, he makes, alters or utters any object so that it appears to have value because of antiquity, rarity, source, or authorship which it does not possess.

Section 224.3. Fraudulent Destruction, Removal or Concealment of Recordable Instruments.

A person commits a felony of the third degree if, with purpose to deceive or injure anyone, he destroys, removes or conceals any will, deed, mortgage, security instrument or other writing for which the law provides public recording.

Section 224.4. Tampering with Records.

A person commits a misdemeanor if, knowing that he has no privilege to do so, he falsifies, destroys, removes or conceals any writing or record, with purpose to deceive or injure anyone or to conceal any wrongdoing.

Section 224.5. Bad Checks.

A person who issues or passes a check or similar sight order for the payment of money, knowing that it will not be honored by the drawee, commits a misdemeanor. For the purposes of this Section as well as in any prosecution for theft committed by means of a bad check, an issuer is presumed to know that the check or order (other than a postdated check or order) would not be paid, if:

(1) the issuer had no account with the drawee at the time the check or order was issued; or

(2) payment was refused by the drawee for lack of funds, upon presentation within 30 days after issue, and the issuer failed to make good within 10 days after receiving notice of that refusal.

Section 224.6. Credit Cards.

A person commits an offense if he uses a credit card for the purpose of obtaining property or services with knowledge that:

(1) the card is stolen or forged; or

(2) the card has been revoked or cancelled; or

(3) for any other reason his use of the card is unauthorized by the issuer.

It is an affirmative defense to prosecution under paragraph (3) if the actor proves by a preponderance of the evidence that he had the purpose and ability to meet all obligations to the issuer arising out of his use of the card. "Credit card" means a writing or other evidence of an undertaking to pay for property or services delivered or rendered to or upon the order of a designated person or bearer. An offense under this Section is a felony of the third degree if the value of the property or services secured or sought to be secured by means of the credit card exceeds $500; otherwise it is a misdemeanor.

Section 224.7. Deceptive Business Practices.

A person commits a misdemeanor if in the course of business he:

(1) uses or possesses for use a false weight or measure, or any other device for falsely determining or recording any quality or quantity; or

(2) sells, offers or exposes for sale, or delivers less than the represented quantity of any commodity or service; or

(3) takes or attempts to take more than the represented quantity of any commodity or service when as buyer he furnishes the weight or measure; or

(4) sells, offers or exposes for sale adulterated or mislabeled commodities. "Adulterated" means varying from the standard of composition or quality prescribed by or pursuant to any statute providing criminal penalties for such variance, or set by established commercial usage. "Mislabeled" means varying from the standard of truth or disclosure in labeling prescribed by or pursuant to any statute providing criminal penalties for such variance, or set by established commercial usage; or

(5) makes a false or misleading statement in any advertisement addressed to the public or to a substantial segment thereof for the purpose of promoting the purchase or sale of property or services; or

(6) makes a false or misleading written statement for the purpose of obtaining property or credit; or

(7) makes a false or misleading written statement for the purpose of promoting the sale of securities, or omits information required by law to be disclosed in written documents relating to securities.

It is an affirmative defense to prosecution under this Section if the defendant proves by a preponderance of the evidence that his conduct was not knowingly or recklessly deceptive.

Section 224.8. Commercial Bribery and Breach of Duty to Act Disinterestedly.

(1) A person commits a misdemeanor if he solicits, accepts or agrees to accept any benefit as consideration for knowingly violating or agreeing to violate a duty of fidelity to which he is subject as:

(a) partner, agent or employee of another;

(b) trustee, guardian, or other fiduciary;

(c) lawyer, physician, accountant, appraiser, or other professional adviser or informant;

(d) officer, director, manager or other participant in the direction of the affairs of an incorporated or unincorporated association; or

(e) arbitrator or other purportedly disinterested adjudicator or referee.

(2) A person who holds himself out to the public as being engaged in the business of making disinterested selection, appraisal, or criticism of commodities or services commits a misdemeanor if he solicits, accepts or agrees to accept any benefit to influence his selection, appraisal or criticism.

(3) A person commits a misdemeanor if he confers, or offers or agrees to confer, any benefit the acceptance of which would be criminal under this Section.

Section 224.9. Rigging Publicly Exhibited Contest.

(1) A person commits a misdemeanor if, with purpose to prevent a publicly exhibited contest from being conducted in accordance with the rules and usages purporting to govern it, he:

(a) confers or offers or agrees to confer any benefit upon, or threatens any injury to a participant, official or other person associated with the contest or exhibition; or

(b) tampers with any person, animal or thing.

(2) *Soliciting or Accepting Benefit for Rigging.* A person commits a misdemeanor if he knowingly solicits, accepts or agrees to accept any benefit the giving of which would be criminal under Subsection (1).

(3) *Participation in Rigged Contest.* A person commits a misdemeanor if he knowingly engages in, sponsors, produces, judges, or otherwise participates in a publicly exhibited contest knowing that the contest is not being conducted in compliance with the rules and usages purporting to govern it, by reason of conduct which would be criminal under this Section.

Section 224.10. Defrauding Secured Creditors.

A person commits a misdemeanor if he destroys, removes, conceals, encumbers, transfers or otherwise deals with property subject to a security interest with purpose to hinder enforcement of that interest.

Section 224.11. Fraud in Insolvency.

A person commits a misdemeanor if, knowing that proceedings have been or are about to be instituted for the appointment of a receiver or other person entitled to administer property for the benefit of creditors, or that any other composition or liquidation for the benefit of creditors has been or is about to made, he:

(a) destroys, removes, conceals, encumbers, transfers, or otherwise deals with any property with purpose to defeat or obstruct the claim of any creditor, or otherwise to obstruct the operation of any law relating to administration of property for the benefit of creditors; or

(b) knowingly falsifies any writing or record relating to the property; or

(c) knowingly misrepresents or refuses to disclose to a receiver or other person entitled to administer property for the benefit of creditors, the existence, amount or location of the property, or any other information which the actor could be legally required to furnish in relation to such administration.

Section 224.12. Receiving Deposits in a Failing Financial Institution.

An officer, manager or other person directing or participating in the direction of a financial institution commits a misdemeanor if he receives or permits the receipt of a deposit, premium payment or other investment in the institution knowing that:

(1) due to financial difficulties the institution is about to suspend operations or go into receivership or reorganization; and

(2) the person making the deposit or other payment is unaware of the precarious situation of the institution.

Section 224.13. Misapplication of Entrusted Property and Property of Government or Financial Institution.

A person commits an offense if he applies or disposes of property that has been entrusted to him as a fiduciary, or property of the government or of a financial institution, in a manner which he knows is unlawful and involves substantial risk of loss or detriment to the owner of the property or to a person for whose benefit the property was entrusted. The offense is a misdemeanor if the amount involved exceeds $50; otherwise it is a petty misdemeanor. "Fiduciary" includes trustee, guardian, executor, administrator, receiver and any person carrying on fiduciary functions on behalf of a corporation or other organization which is a fiduciary.

Section 224.14. Securing Execution of Documents by Deception.

A person commits a misdemeanor if by deception he causes another to execute any instrument affecting or purporting to affect or likely to affect the pecuniary interest of any person.

OFFENSES AGAINST THE FAMILY

ARTICLE 230. OFFENSES AGAINST THE FAMILY

Section 230.1. Bigamy and Polygamy.

(1) *Bigamy.* A married person is guilty of bigamy, a misdemeanor, if he contracts or purports to contract another marriage, unless at the time of the subsequent marriage:

(a) the actor believes that the prior spouse is dead; or

(b) the actor and the prior spouse have been living apart for five consecutive years throughout which the prior spouse was not known by the actor to be alive; or

(c) a Court has entered a judgment purporting to terminate or annul any prior disqualifying marriage, and the actor does not know that judgment to be invalid; or

(d) the actor reasonably believes that he is legally eligible to remarry.

(2) *Polygamy.* A person is guilty of polygamy, a felony of the third degree, if he marries or cohabits with more than one spouse at a time in purported exercise of the right of plural marriage. The offense is a continuing one until all cohabitation and claim of marriage with more than one spouse terminates. This section does not apply to parties to a polygamous marriage, lawful in the country of which they are residents or nationals, while they are in transit through or temporarily visiting this State.

(3) *Other Party to Bigamous or Polygamous Marriage.* A person is guilty of bigamy or polygamy, as the case may be, if he contracts or purports to contract marriage with another knowing that the other is thereby committing bigamy or polygamy.

Section 230.2. Incest.

A person is guilty of incest, a felony of the third degree, if he knowingly marries or cohabits or has sexual intercourse with an ancestor or descendant, a brother or sister of the whole or half blood [or an uncle, aunt, nephew or niece of the whole blood]. "Cohabit" means to live together under the representation or appearance of being married. The relationships referred to herein include blood relationships without regard to legitimacy, and relationship of parent and child by adoption.

Section 230.3. Abortion.

(1) *Unjustified Abortion.* A person who purposely and unjustifiably terminates the pregnancy of another otherwise than by a live birth commits a felony of the third degree or, where the pregnancy has continued beyond the twenty-sixth week, a felony of the second degree.

(2) *Justifiable Abortion.* A licensed physician is justified in terminating a pregnancy if he believes there is substantial risk that continuance of the pregnancy would gravely impair the physical or mental health of the mother or that the child would be born with grave physical or mental defect, or that the pregnancy resulted from rape, incest, or other felonious intercourse. All illicit intercourse with a girl below the age of 16 shall be deemed felonious for purposes of this subsection.

Justifiable abortions shall be performed only in a licensed hospital except in case of emergency when hospital facilities are unavailable. [Additional exceptions from the requirement of hospitalization may be incorporated here to take account of situations in sparsely settled areas where hospitals are not generally accessible.]

(3) *Physicians' Certificates; Presumption from Non–Compliance.* No abortion shall be performed unless two physicians, one of whom may be the person performing the abortion, shall have certified in writing the circumstances which they believe to justify the abortion. Such certificate shall be submitted before the abortion to the hospital where it is to be performed and, in the case of abortion following felonious intercourse, to the prosecuting attorney or the police. Failure to comply with any of the requirements of this Subsection gives rise to a presumption that the abortion was unjustified.

(4) *Self-Abortion.* A woman whose pregnancy has continued beyond the twenty-sixth week commits a felony of the third degree if she purposely terminates her own pregnancy otherwise than by a live birth, or if she uses instruments, drugs or violence upon herself for that purpose. Except as justified under Subsection (2), a person who induces or knowingly aids a woman to use instruments, drugs or violence upon herself for the purpose of terminating her pregnancy otherwise than by a live birth commits a felony of the third degree whether or not the pregnancy has continued beyond the twenty-sixth week.

(5) *Pretended Abortion.* A person commits a felony of the third degree if, representing that it is his purpose to perform an abortion, he does an act adapted to cause abortion in a pregnant woman although the woman is in fact not pregnant, or the actor does not believe she is. A person charged with unjustified abortion under Subsection (1) or an attempt to commit that offense may be convicted thereof upon proof of conduct prohibited by this Subsection.

(6) *Distribution of Abortifacients.* A person who sells, offers to sell, possesses with intent to sell, advertises, or displays for sale anything specially designed to terminate a pregnancy, or held out by the actor as useful for that purpose, commits a misdemeanor, unless:

(a) the sale, offer or display is to a physician or druggist or to an intermediary in a chain of distribution to physicians or druggists; or

(b) the sale is made upon prescription or order of a physician; or

(c) the possession is with intent to sell as authorized in paragraphs (a) and (b); or

(d) the advertising is addressed to persons named in paragraph (a) and confined to trade or professional channels not likely to reach the general public.

(7) *Section Inapplicable to Prevention of Pregnancy.* Nothing in this Section shall be deemed applicable to the prescription, administration or distribution of drugs or other substances for avoiding pregnancy, whether by preventing implantation of a fertilized ovum or by any other method that operates before, at or immediately after fertilization.

Section 230.4. Endangering Welfare of Children.

A parent, guardian, or other person supervising the welfare of a child under 18 commits a misdemeanor if he knowingly endangers the child's welfare by violating a duty of care, protection or support.

Section 230.5. Persistent Non–Support.

A person commits a misdemeanor if he persistently fails to provide support which he can provide and which he knows he is legally obliged to provide to a spouse, child or other dependent.

OFFENSES AGAINST PUBLIC ADMINISTRATION

ARTICLE 240. BRIBERY AND CORRUPT INFLUENCE

Section 240.0. Definitions.

In Articles 240–243, unless a different meaning plainly is required:

(1) "benefit" means gain or advantage, or anything regarded by the beneficiary as gain or advantage, including benefit to any other person or entity in whose welfare he is interested, but not an advantage promised generally to a group or class of voters as a consequence of public measures which a candidate engages to support or oppose;

(2) "government" includes any branch, subdivision or agency of the government of the State or any locality within it;

(3) "harm" means loss, disadvantage or injury, or anything so regarded by the person affected, including loss, disadvantage or injury to any other person or entity in whose welfare he is interested;

(4) "official proceeding" means a proceeding heard or which may be heard before any legislative, judicial, administrative or other governmental agency or official authorized to take evidence under oath, including any referee, hearing examiner, commissioner, notary or other person taking testimony or deposition in connection with any such proceeding;

(5) "party official" means a person who holds an elective or appointive post in a political party in the United States by virtue of which he directs or conducts, or participates in directing or conducting party affairs at any level of responsibility;

(6) "pecuniary benefit" is benefit in the form of money, property, commercial interests or anything else the primary significance of which is economic gain;

(7) "public servant" means any officer or employee of government, including legislators and judges, and any person participating as juror, advisor, consultant or otherwise, in performing a governmental function; but the term does not include witnesses;

(8) "administrative proceeding" means any proceeding, other than a judicial proceeding, the outcome of which is required to be based on a record or documentation prescribed by law, or in which law or regulation is particularized in application to individuals.

Section 240.1. Bribery in Official and Political Matters.

A person is guilty of bribery, a felony of the third degree, if he offers, confers or agrees to confer upon another, or solicits, accepts or agrees to accept from another:

(1) any pecuniary benefit as consideration for the recipient's decision, opinion, recommendation, vote or other exercise of discretion as a public servant, party official or voter; or

(2) any benefit as consideration for the recipient's decision, vote, recommendation or other exercise of official discretion in a judicial or administrative proceeding; or

(3) any benefit as consideration for a violation of a known legal duty as public servant or party official.

It is no defense to prosecution under this section that a person whom the actor sought to influence was not qualified to act in the desired way whether because he had not yet assumed office, or lacked jurisdiction, or for any other reason.

Section 240.2. Threats and Other Improper Influence in Official and Political Matters.

(1) *Offenses Defined.* A person commits an offense if he:

(a) threatens unlawful harm to any person with purpose to influence his decision, opinion, recommendation, vote or other exercise of discretion as a public servant, party official or voter; or

(b) threatens harm to any public servant with purpose to influence his decision, opinion, recommendation, vote or other exercise of discretion in a judicial or administrative proceeding; or

(c) threatens harm to any public servant or party official with purpose to influence him to violate his known legal duty; or

(d) privately addresses to any public servant who has or will have an official discretion in a judicial or administrative proceeding any representation, entreaty, argument or other communication with purpose to influence the outcome on the basis of considerations other than those authorized by law.

It is no defense to prosecution under this Section that a person whom the actor sought to influence was not qualified to act in the desired way, whether because he had not yet assumed office, or lacked jurisdiction, or for any other reason.

(2) *Grading.* An offense under this Section is a misdemeanor unless the actor threatened to commit a crime or made a threat with purpose to influence a judicial or administrative proceeding, in which cases the offense is a felony of the third degree.

Section 240.3. Compensation for Past Official Action.

A person commits a misdemeanor if he solicits, accepts or agrees to accept any pecuniary benefit as compensation for having, as public servant, given a decision, opinion, recommendation or vote favorable to another, or for having otherwise exercised a discretion in his favor, or for having violated his duty. A person commits a misdemeanor if he offers, confers or agrees to confer compensation acceptance of which is prohibited by this Section.

Section 240.4. Retaliation for Past Official Action.

A person commits a misdemeanor if he harms another by any unlawful act in retaliation for anything lawfully done by the latter in the capacity of public servant.

Section 240.5. Gifts to Public Servants by Persons Subject to Their Jurisdiction.

(1) *Regulatory and Law Enforcement Officials.* No public servant in any department or agency exercising regulatory functions, or conducting inspections or investigations, or carrying on civil or criminal litigation on behalf of the government, or having custody of prisoners, shall solicit, accept or agree to accept any pecuniary benefit from a person known to be subject to such regulation, inspection, investigation or custody, or against whom such litigation is known to be pending or contemplated.

(2) *Officials Concerned with Government Contracts and Pecuniary Transactions.* No public servant having any discretionary function to perform in connection with contracts, purchases, payments, claims or other pecuniary transactions of the government shall solicit, accept or agree to accept any pecuniary benefit from any person known to be interested in or likely to become interested in any such contract, purchase, payment, claim or transaction.

(3) *Judicial and Administrative Officials.* No public servant having judicial or administrative authority and no public servant employed by or in a court or other tribunal having such authority, or participating in the enforcement of its decisions, shall solicit, accept or agree to accept any pecuniary benefit from a person known to be interested in or likely to become interested in any matter before such public servant or a tribunal with which he is associated.

(4) *Legislative Officials.* No legislator or public servant employed by the legislature or by any committee or agency thereof shall solicit, accept or agree to accept any pecuniary benefit from any person known to be interested in a bill, transaction or proceeding, pending or contemplated, before the legislature or any committee or agency thereof.

(5) *Exceptions.* This Section shall not apply to:

(a) fees prescribed by law to be received by a public servant, or any other benefit for which the recipient gives legitimate consideration or to which he is otherwise legally entitled; or

(b) gifts or other benefits conferred on account of kinship or other personal, professional or business relationship independent of the official status of the receiver; or

(c) trivial benefits incidental to personal, professional or business contacts and involving no substantial risk of undermining official impartiality.

(6) *Offering Benefits Prohibited.* No person shall knowingly confer, or offer or agree to confer, any benefit prohibited by the foregoing Subsections.

(7) *Grade of Offense.* An offense under this Section is a misdemeanor.

Section 240.6. Compensating Public Servant for Assisting Private Interests in Relation to Matters Before Him.

(1) *Receiving Compensation.* A public servant commits a misdemeanor if he solicits, accepts or agrees to accept compensation for advice or other assistance in preparing or promoting a bill, contract, claim, or other transaction or proposal as to which he knows that he has or is likely to have an official discretion to exercise.

(2) *Paying Compensation.* A person commits a misdemeanor if he pays or offers or agrees to pay compensation to a public servant with knowledge that acceptance by the public servant is unlawful.

Section 240.7. Selling Political Endorsement; Special Influence.

(1) *Selling Political Endorsement.* A person commits a misdemeanor if he solicits, receives, agrees to receive, or agrees that any political party or other person shall receive, any pecuniary benefit as consideration for approval or disapproval of an appointment or advancement in public service, or for approval or disapproval of any person or transaction for any benefit conferred by an official or agency of government. "Approval" includes recommendation, failure to disapprove, or any other manifestation of favor or acquiescence. "Disapproval" includes failure to approve, or any other manifestation of disfavor or nonacquiescence.

(2) *Other Trading in Special Influence.* A person commits a misdemeanor if he solicits, receives or agrees to receive any pecuniary benefit as consideration for exerting special influence upon a public servant or procuring another to do so. "Special influence" means power to influence through kinship, friendship or other relationship, apart from the merits of the transaction.

(3) *Paying for Endorsement or Special Influence.* A person commits a misdemeanor if he offers, confers or agrees to confer any pecuniary benefit receipt of which is prohibited by this Section.

ARTICLE 241. PERJURY AND OTHER FALSIFICATION IN OFFICIAL MATTERS

Section 241.0. Definitions.

In this Article, unless a different meaning plainly is required:

(1) the definitions given in Section 240.0 apply; and

(2) "statement" means any representation, but includes a representation of opinion, belief or other state of mind only if the representation clearly relates to state of mind apart from or in addition to any facts which are the subject of the representation.

Section 241.1. Perjury.

(1) *Offense Defined.* A person is guilty of perjury, a felony of the third degree, if in any official proceeding he makes a false statement under oath or equivalent affirmation, or swears or affirms the truth of a statement previously made, when the statement is material and he does not believe it to be true.

(2) *Materiality.* Falsification is material, regardless of the admissibility of the statement under rules of evidence, if it could have affected the course or outcome of the proceeding. It is no defense that the declarant mistakenly believed the falsification to be immaterial. Whether a falsification is material in a given factual situation is a question of law.

(3) *Irregularities No Defense.* It is not a defense to prosecution under this Section that the oath or affirmation was administered or taken in an irregular manner or that the declarant was not competent to make the statement. A document purporting to be made upon oath or affirmation at any time when the actor presents it as being so verified shall be deemed to have been duly sworn or affirmed.

(4) *Retraction.* No person shall be guilty of an offense under this Section if he retracted the falsification in the course of the proceeding in which it was made before it became manifest that the falsification was or would be exposed and before the falsification substantially affected the proceeding.

(5) *Inconsistent Statements.* Where the defendant made inconsistent statements under oath or equivalent affirmation, both having been made within the period of the statute of limitations, the prosecution may proceed by setting forth the inconsistent statements in a single count alleging in the alternative that one or the other was false and not believed by the defendant. In such case it shall not be necessary for the prosecution to prove which statement was false but only that one or the other was false and not believed by the defendant to be true.

(6) *Corroboration.* No person shall be convicted of an offense under this Section where proof of falsity rests solely upon contradiction by testimony of a single person other than the defendant.

Section 241.2. False Swearing.

(1) *False Swearing in Official Matters.* A person who makes a false statement under oath or equivalent affirmation, or swears or affirms the truth of such a statement previously made, when he does not believe the statement to be true, is guilty of a misdemeanor if:

(a) the falsification occurs in an official proceeding; or

(b) the falsification is intended to mislead a public servant in performing his official function.

(2) *Other False Swearing.* A person who makes a false statement under oath or equivalent affirmation, or swears or affirms the truth of such a statement previously made, when he does not believe the statement to be true, is guilty of a petty misdemeanor, if the statement is one which is required by law to be sworn or affirmed before a notary or other person authorized to administer oaths.

(3) *Perjury Provisions Applicable.* Subsections (3) to (6) of Section 241.1 apply to the present Section.

Section 241.3. Unsworn Falsification to Authorities.

(1) *In General.* A person commits a misdemeanor if, with purpose to mislead a public servant in performing his official function, he:

(a) makes any written false statement which he does not believe to be true; or

(b) purposely creates a false impression in a written application for any pecuniary or other benefit, by omitting information necessary to prevent statements therein from being misleading; or

(c) submits or invites reliance on any writing which he knows to be forged, altered or otherwise lacking in authenticity; or

(d) submits or invites reliance on any sample, specimen, map, boundary-mark, or other object which he knows to be false.

(2) *Statements "Under Penalty."* A person commits a petty misdemeanor if he makes a written false statement which he does not believe to be true, on or pursuant to a form bearing notice, authorized by law, to the effect that false statements made therein are punishable.

(3) *Perjury Provisions Applicable.* Subsections (3) to (6) of Section 241.1 apply to the present section.

Section 241.4. False Alarms to Agencies of Public Safety.

A person who knowingly causes a false alarm of fire or other emergency to be transmitted to or within any organization, official or volunteer, for dealing with emergencies involving danger to life or property commits a misdemeanor.

Section 241.5. False Reports to Law Enforcement Authorities.

(1) *Falsely Incriminating Another.* A person who knowingly gives false information to any law enforcement officer with purpose to implicate another commits a misdemeanor.

(2) *Fictitious Reports.* A person commits a petty misdemeanor if he:

(a) reports to law enforcement authorities an offense or other incident within their concern knowing that it did not occur; or

(b) pretends to furnish such authorities with information relating to an offense or incident when he knows he has no information relating to such offense or incident.

Section 241.6. Tampering With Witnesses and Informants; Retaliation Against Them.

(1) *Tampering.* A person commits an offense if, believing that an official proceeding or investigation is pending or about to be instituted, he attempts to induce or otherwise cause a witness or informant to:

(a) testify or inform falsely; or

(b) withhold any testimony, information, document or thing; or

(c) elude legal process summoning him to testify or supply evidence; or

(d) absent himself from any proceeding or investigation to which he has been legally summoned.

The offense is a felony of the third degree if the actor employs force, deception, threat or offer of pecuniary benefit. Otherwise it is a misdemeanor.

(2) *Retaliation Against Witness or Informant.* A person commits a misdemeanor if he harms another by any unlawful act in retaliation for anything lawfully done in the capacity of witness or informant.

(3) *Witness or Informant Taking Bribe.* A person commits a felony of the third degree if he solicits, accepts or agrees to accept any benefit in consideration of his doing any of the things specified in clauses (a) to (d) of Subsection (1).

Section 241.7. Tampering with or Fabricating Physical Evidence.

A person commits a misdemeanor if, believing that an official proceeding or investigation is pending or about to be instituted, he:

(1) alters, destroys, conceals or removes any record, document or thing with purpose to impair its verity or availability in such proceeding or investigation; or

(2) makes, presents or uses any record, document or thing knowing it to be false and with purpose to mislead a public servant who is or may be engaged in such proceeding or investigation.

Section 241.8. Tampering With Public Records or Information.

(1) *Offense Defined.* A person commits an offense if he:

(a) knowingly makes a false entry in, or false alteration of, any record, document or thing belonging to, or received or kept by, the government for information or record, or required by law to be kept by others for information of the government; or

(b) makes, presents or uses any record, document or thing knowing it to be false, and with purpose that it be taken as a genuine part of information or records referred to in paragraph (a); or

(c) purposely and unlawfully destroys, conceals, removes or otherwise impairs the verity or availability of any such record, document or thing.

(2) *Grading.* An offense under this Section is a misdemeanor unless the actor's purpose is to defraud or injure anyone, in which case the offense is a felony of the third degree.

Section 241.9. Impersonating a Public Servant.

A person commits a misdemeanor if he falsely pretends to hold a position in the public service with purpose to induce another to submit to such pretended official authority or otherwise to act in reliance upon that pretense to his prejudice.

ARTICLE 242. OBSTRUCTING GOVERNMENTAL OPERATIONS; ESCAPES

Section 242.0. Definitions.

In this Article, unless another meaning plainly is required, the definitions given in Section 240.0 apply.

Section 242.1. Obstructing Administration of Law or Other Governmental Function.

A person commits a misdemeanor if he purposely obstructs, impairs or perverts the administration of law or other governmental function by force, violence, physical interference or obstacle, breach of official duty, or any other unlawful act, except that this Section does not apply to flight by a person charged with crime, refusal to submit to arrest, failure to perform a legal duty other than an official duty, or any other means of avoiding compliance with law without affirmative interference with governmental functions.

Section 242.2. Resisting Arrest or Other Law Enforcement.

A person commits a misdemeanor if, for the purpose of preventing a public servant from effecting a lawful arrest or discharging any other duty, the person creates a substantial risk of bodily injury to the public servant or anyone else, or employs means justifying or requiring substantial force to overcome the resistance.

Section 242.3. Hindering Apprehension or Prosecution.

A person commits an offense if, with purpose to hinder the apprehension, prosecution, conviction or punishment of another for crime, he:

(1) harbors or conceals the other; or

(2) provides or aids in providing a weapon, transportation, disguise or other means of avoiding apprehension or effecting escape; or

(3) conceals or destroys evidence of the crime, or tampers with a witness, informant, document or other source of information, regardless of its admissibility in evidence; or

(4) warns the other of impending discovery or apprehension, except that this paragraph does not apply to a warning given in connection with an effort to bring another into compliance with law; or

(5) volunteers false information to a law enforcement officer.

The offense is a felony of the third degree if the conduct which the actor knows has been charged or is liable to be charged against the person aided would constitute a felony of the first or second degree. Otherwise it is a misdemeanor.

Section 242.4. Aiding Consummation of Crime.

A person commits an offense if he purposely aids another to accomplish an unlawful object of a crime, as by safeguarding the proceeds thereof or converting the proceeds into negotiable funds. The offense is a felony of the third degree if the principal offense was a felony of the first or second degree. Otherwise it is a misdemeanor.

Section 242.5. Compounding.

A person commits a misdemeanor if he accepts or agrees to accept any pecuniary benefit in consideration of refraining from reporting to law enforcement authorities the commission or suspected commission of any offense or information relating to an offense. It is an affirmative defense to prosecution under this Section that the pecuniary benefit did not exceed an amount which the actor believed to be due as restitution or indemnification for harm caused by the offense.

Section 242.6. Escape.

(1) *Escape.* A person commits an offense if he unlawfully removes himself from official detention or fails to return to official detention following temporary leave

granted for a specific purpose or limited period. "Official detention" means arrest, detention in any facility for custody of persons under charge or conviction of crime or alleged or found to be delinquent, detention for extradition or deportation, or any other detention for law enforcement purposes; but "official detention" does not include supervision of probation or parole, or constraint incidental to release on bail.

(2) *Permitting or Facilitating Escape.* A public servant concerned in detention commits an offense if he knowingly or recklessly permits an escape. Any person who knowingly causes or facilitates an escape commits an offense.

(3) *Effect of Legal Irregularity in Detention.* Irregularity in bringing about or maintaining detention, or lack of jurisdiction of the committing or detaining authority, shall not be a defense to prosecution under this Section if the escape is from a prison or other custodial facility or from detention pursuant to commitment by official proceedings. In the case of other detentions, irregularity or lack of jurisdiction shall be a defense only if:

(a) the escape involved no substantial risk of harm to the person or property of anyone other than the detainee; or

(b) the detaining authority did not act in good faith under color of law.

(4) *Grading of Offenses.* An offense under this Section is a felony of the third degree where:

(a) the actor was under arrest for or detained on a charge of felony or following conviction of crime; or

(b) the actor employs force, threat, deadly weapon or other dangerous instrumentality to effect the escape; or

(c) a public servant concerned in detention of persons convicted of crime purposely facilitates or permits an escape from a detention facility.

Otherwise an offense under this section is a misdemeanor.

Section 242.7. Implements for Escape; Other Contraband.

(1) *Escape Implements.* A person commits a misdemeanor if he unlawfully introduces within a detention facility, or unlawfully provides an inmate with, any weapon, tool or other thing which may be useful for escape. An inmate commits a misdemeanor if he unlawfully procures, makes, or otherwise provides himself with, or has in his possession, any such implement of escape. "Unlawfully" means surreptitiously or contrary to law, regulation or order of the detaining authority.

(2) *Other Contraband.* A person commits a petty misdemeanor if he provides an inmate with anything which the actor knows it is unlawful for the inmate to possess.

Section 242.8. Bail Jumping; Default in Required Appearance.

A person set at liberty by court order, with or without bail, upon condition that he will subsequently appear at a specified time and place, commits a misdemeanor if, without lawful excuse, he fails to appear at that time and place. The offense constitutes a felony of the third degree where the required appearance was to answer to a charge of felony, or for disposition of any such charge, and the actor took flight or went into hiding to avoid apprehension, trial or punishment. This Section does not apply to obligations to appear incident to release under suspended sentence or on probation or parole.

ARTICLE 243. ABUSE OF OFFICE

Section 243.0. Definitions.

In this Article, unless a different meaning plainly is required, the definitions given in Section 240.0 apply.

Section 243.1. Official Oppression.

A person acting or purporting to act in an official capacity or taking advantage of such actual or purported capacity commits a misdemeanor if, knowing that his conduct is illegal, he:

(a) subjects another to arrest, detention, search, seizure, mistreatment, dispossession, assessment, lien or other infringement of personal or property rights; or

(b) denies or impedes another in the exercise or enjoyment of any right, privilege, power or immunity.

Section 243.2. Speculating or Wagering on Official Action or Information.

A public servant commits a misdemeanor if, in contemplation of official action by himself or by a governmental unit with which he is associated, or in reliance on information to which he has access in his official capacity and which has not been made public, he:

(1) acquires a pecuniary interest in any property, transaction or enterprise which may be affected by such information or official action; or

(2) speculates or wagers on the basis of such information or official action; or

(3) aids another to do any of the foregoing.

OFFENSES AGAINST PUBLIC ORDER AND DECENCY

ARTICLE 250. RIOT, DISORDERLY CONDUCT, AND RELATED OFFENSES

Section 250.1. Riot; Failure to Disperse.

(1) *Riot.* A person is guilty of riot, a felony of the third degree, if he participates with [two] or more others in a course of disorderly conduct:

(a) with purpose to commit or facilitate the commission of a felony or misdemeanor;

(b) with purpose to prevent or coerce official action; or

(c) when the actor or any other participant to the knowledge of the actor uses or plans to use a firearm or other deadly weapon.

(2) *Failure of Disorderly Persons to Disperse Upon Official Order.* Where [three] or more persons are participating in a course of disorderly conduct likely to cause substantial harm or serious inconvenience, annoyance or alarm, a peace officer or other public servant engaged in executing or enforcing the law may order the participants and others in the immediate vicinity to disperse. A person who refuses or knowingly fails to obey such an order commits a misdemeanor.

Section 250.2. Disorderly Conduct.

(1) *Offense Defined.* A person is guilty of disorderly conduct if, with purpose to cause public inconvenience, annoyance or alarm, or recklessly creating a risk thereof, he:

(a) engages in fighting or threatening, or in violent or tumultuous behavior; or

(b) makes unreasonable noise or offensively coarse utterance, gesture or display, or addresses abusive language to any person present; or

(c) creates a hazardous or physically offensive condition by any act which serves no legitimate purpose of the actor.

"Public" means affecting or likely to affect persons in a place to which the public or a substantial group has access; among the places included are highways, transport facilities, schools, prisons, apartment houses, places of business or amusement, or any neighborhood.

(2) *Grading.* An offense under this section is a petty misdemeanor if the actor's purpose is to cause substantial harm or serious inconvenience, or if he persists in disorderly conduct after reasonable warning or request to desist. Otherwise disorderly conduct is a violation.

Section 250.3. False Public Alarms.

A person is guilty of a misdemeanor if he initiates or circulates a report or warning of an impending bombing or other crime or catastrophe, knowing that the report or warning is false or baseless and that it is likely to cause evacuation of a building, place of assembly, or facility of public transport, or to cause public inconvenience or alarm.

Section 250.4. Harassment.

A person commits a petty misdemeanor if, with purpose to harass another, he:

(1) makes a telephone call without purpose of legitimate communication; or

(2) insults, taunts or challenges another in a manner likely to provoke violent or disorderly response; or

(3) makes repeated communications anonymously or at extremely inconvenient hours, or in offensively coarse language; or

(4) subjects another to an offensive touching; or

(5) engages in any other course of alarming conduct serving no legitimate purpose of the actor.

Section 250.5. Public Drunkenness; Drug Incapacitation.

A person is guilty of an offense if he appears in any public place manifestly under the influence of alcohol, narcotics or other drug, not therapeutically administered, to the degree that he may endanger himself or other persons or property, or annoy persons in his vicinity. An offense under this Section constitutes a petty misdemeanor if the actor has been convicted hereunder twice before within a period of one year. Otherwise the offense constitutes a violation.

Section 250.6. Loitering or Prowling.

A person commits a violation if he loiters or prowls in a place, at a time, or in a manner not usual for law-abiding individuals under circumstances that warrant alarm for the safety of persons or property in the vicinity. Among the circumstances which may be considered in determining whether such alarm is warranted is the fact that the actor takes flight upon appearance of a peace officer, refuses to identify himself, or manifestly endeavors to conceal himself or any object. Unless flight by the actor or other circumstance makes it impracticable, a peace officer shall prior to any arrest for an offense under this section afford the actor an opportunity to dispel any alarm which would otherwise be warranted, by requesting him to identify himself and explain his presence and conduct. No person shall be convicted of an offense under this Section if the peace officer did not comply with the preceding sentence, or if it appears at trial that the explanation given by the actor was true and, if believed by the peace officer at the time, would have dispelled the alarm.

Section 250.7. Obstructing Highways and Other Public Passages.

(1) A person, who, having no legal privilege to do so, purposely or recklessly obstructs any highway or other public passage, whether alone or with others, commits a violation, or, in case he persists after warning by a law officer, a petty misdemeanor. "Obstructs" means renders impassable without unreasonable inconvenience or hazard. No person shall be deemed guilty of recklessly obstructing in violation of this Subsection solely because of a gathering of persons to hear him speak or otherwise communicate, or solely because of being a member of such a gathering.

(2) A person in a gathering commits a violation if he refuses to obey a reasonable official request or order to move:

(a) to prevent obstruction of a highway or other public passage; or

(b) to maintain public safety by dispersing those gathered in dangerous proximity to a fire or other hazard.

An order to move, addressed to a person whose speech or other lawful behavior attracts an obstructing audience, shall not be deemed reasonable if the obstruction can be readily remedied by police control of the size or location of the gathering.

Section 250.8. Disrupting Meetings and Processions.

A person commits a misdemeanor if, with purpose to prevent or disrupt a lawful meeting, procession or gathering, he does any act tending to obstruct or interfere with it physically, or makes any utterance, gesture or display designed to outrage the sensibilities of the group.

Section 250.9. Desecration of Venerated Objects.

A person commits a misdemeanor if he purposely desecrates any public monument or structure, or place of worship or burial, or if he purposely desecrates the national flag or any other object of veneration by the public or a substantial segment thereof in any public place. "Desecrate" means defacing, damaging, polluting or otherwise physically mistreating in a way that the actor knows will outrage the sensibilities of persons likely to observe or discover his action.

Section 250.10. Abuse of Corpse.

Except as authorized by law, a person who treats a corpse in a way that he knows would outrage ordinary family sensibilities commits a misdemeanor.

Section 250.11. Cruelty to Animals.

A person commits a misdemeanor if he purposely or recklessly:

(1) subjects any animal to cruel mistreatment; or

(2) subjects any animal in his custody to cruel neglect; or

(3) kills or injures any animal belonging to another without legal privilege or consent of the owner.

Subsections (1) and (2) shall not be deemed applicable to accepted veterinary practices and activities carried on for scientific research.

Section 250.12. Violation of Privacy.

(1) *Unlawful Eavesdropping or Surveillance.* A person commits a misdemeanor if, except as authorized by law, he:

(a) trespasses on property with purpose to subject anyone to eavesdropping or other surveillance in a private place; or

(b) installs in any private place, without the consent of the person or persons entitled to privacy there, any device for observing, photographing, recording, amplifying or broadcasting sounds or events in such place, or uses any such unauthorized installation; or

(c) installs or uses outside a private place any device for hearing, recording, amplifying or broadcasting sounds originating in such place which would not ordinarily be audible or comprehensible outside, without the consent of the person or persons entitled to privacy there.

"Private place" means a place where one may reasonably expect to be safe from casual or hostile intrusion or surveillance, but does not include a place to which the public or a substantial group thereof has access.

(2) *Other Breach of Privacy of Messages.* A person commits a misdemeanor if, except as authorized by law, he:

(a) intercepts without the consent of the sender or receiver a message by telephone, telegraph, letter or other means of communicating privately; but this paragraph does not extend to (i) overhearing of messages through a regularly installed instrument on a telephone party line or on an extension, or (ii) interception by the telephone company or subscriber incident to enforcement of regulations limiting use of the facilities or incident to other normal operation and use; or

(b) divulges without the consent of the sender or receiver the existence or contents of any such message if the actor knows that the message was illegally intercepted, or if he learned of the message in the course of employment with an agency engaged in transmitting it.

ARTICLE 251. PUBLIC INDECENCY

Section 251.1. Open Lewdness.

A person commits a petty misdemeanor if he does any lewd act which he knows is likely to be observed by others who would be affronted or alarmed.

Section 251.2. Prostitution and Related Offenses.

(1) *Prostitution.* A person is guilty of prostitution, a petty misdemeanor, if he or she:

(a) is an inmate of a house of prostitution or otherwise engages in sexual activity as a business; or

(b) loiters in or within view of any public place for the purpose of being hired to engage in sexual activity.

"Sexual activity" includes homosexual and other deviate sexual relations. A "house of prostitution" is any place where prostitution or promotion of prostitution is regularly carried on by one person under the control, management or supervision of another. An "inmate" is a person who engages in prostitution in or through the agency of a house of prostitution. "Public place" means any place to which the public or any substantial group thereof has access.

(2) *Promoting Prostitution.* A person who knowingly promotes prostitution of another commits a misdemeanor or felony as provided in Subsection (3). The following acts shall, without limitation of the foregoing, constitute promoting prostitution:

(a) owning, controlling, managing, supervising or otherwise keeping, alone or in association with others, a house of prostitution or a prostitution business; or

(b) procuring an inmate for a house of prostitution or a place in a house of prostitution for one who would be an inmate; or

(c) encouraging, inducing, or otherwise purposely causing another to become or remain a prostitute; or

(d) soliciting a person to patronize a prostitute; or

(e) procuring a prostitute for a patron; or

(f) transporting a person into or within this state with purpose to promote that person's engaging in prostitution, or procuring or paying for transportation with that purpose; or

(g) leasing or otherwise permitting a place controlled by the actor, alone or in association with others, to be regularly used for prostitution or the promotion of prostitution, or failure to make reasonable effort to abate such use by ejecting the tenant, notifying law enforcement authorities, or other legally available means; or

(h) soliciting, receiving, or agreeing to receive any benefit for doing or agreeing to do anything forbidden by this Subsection.

(3) *Grading of Offenses Under Subsection (2).* An offense under Subsection (2) constitutes a felony of the third degree if:

(a) the offense falls within paragraph (a), (b) or (c) of Subsection (2); or

(b) the actor compels another to engage in or promote prostitution; or

(c) the actor promotes prostitution of a child under 16, whether or not he is aware of the child's age; or

(d) the actor promotes prostitution of his wife, child, ward or any person for whose care, protection or support he is responsible.

Otherwise the offense is a misdemeanor.

(4) *Presumption from Living off Prostitutes.* A person, other than the prostitute or the prostitute's minor child or other legal dependent incapable of self-support, who is supported in whole or substantial part by the proceeds of prostitution is presumed to be knowingly promoting prostitution in violation of Subsection (2).

(5) *Patronizing Prostitutes.* A person commits a violation if he hires a prostitute to engage in sexual activity with him, or if he enters or remains in a house of prostitution for the purpose of engaging in sexual activity.

(6) *Evidence.* On the issue whether a place is a house of prostitution the following shall be admissible evidence: its general repute; the repute of the persons who reside in or frequent the place; the frequency, timing and duration of visits by non-residents. Testimony of a person against his spouse shall be admissible to prove offenses under this Section.

Section 251.3. Loitering to Solicit Deviate Sexual Relations.

A person is guilty of a petty misdemeanor if he loiters in or near any public place for the purpose of soliciting or being solicited to engage in deviate sexual relations.

Section 251.4. Obscenity.

(1) *Obscene Defined.* Material is obscene if, considered as a whole, its predominant appeal is to prurient interest, that is, a shameful or morbid interest, in nudity, sex or excretion, and if in addition it goes substantially beyond customary limits of candor in describing or representing such matters. Predominant appeal shall be judged with reference to ordinary adults unless it appears from the character of the material or the circumstances of its dissemination to be designed for children or other specially susceptible audience. Undeveloped photographs, molds, printing plates, and the like, shall be deemed obscene notwithstanding that processing or other acts may be required to make the obscenity patent or to disseminate it.

(2) *Offenses.* Subject to the affirmative defense provided in Subsection (3), a person commits a misdemeanor if he knowingly or recklessly:

(a) sells, delivers or provides, or offers or agrees to sell, deliver or provide, any obscene writing, picture, record or other representation or embodiment of the obscene; or

(b) presents or directs an obscene play, dance or performance, or participates in that portion thereof which makes it obscene; or

(c) publishes, exhibits or otherwise makes available any obscene material; or

(d) possesses any obscene material for purposes of sale or other commercial dissemination; or

(e) sells, advertises or otherwise commercially disseminates material, whether or not obscene, by representing or suggesting that it is obscene.

A person who disseminates or possesses obscene material in the course of his business is presumed to do so knowingly or recklessly.

(3) *Justifiable and Non–Commercial Private Dissemination.* It is an affirmative defense to prosecution under this Section that dissemination was restricted to:

(a) institutions or persons having scientific, educational, governmental or other similar justification for possessing obscene material; or

(b) non-commercial dissemination to personal associates of the actor.

(4) *Evidence; Adjudication of Obscenity.* In any prosecution under this Section evidence shall be admissible to show:

(a) the character of the audience for which the material was designed or to which it was directed;

(b) what the predominant appeal of the material would be for ordinary adults or any special audience to which it was directed, and what effect, if any, it would probably have on conduct of such people;

(c) artistic, literary, scientific, educational or other merits of the material;

(d) the degree of public acceptance of the material in the United States;

(e) appeal to prurient interest, or absence thereof, in advertising or other promotion of the material; and

(f) the good repute of the author, creator, publisher or other person from whom the material originated.

Expert testimony and testimony of the author, creator, publisher or other person from whom the material originated, relating to factors entering into the determination of the issue of obscenity, shall be admissible. The Court shall dismiss a prosecution for obscenity if it is satisfied that the material is not obscene.

ADDITIONAL ARTICLES[a]

[At this point, a State enacting a new Penal Code may insert additional Articles dealing with special topics such as narcotics, alcoholic beverages, gambling and offenses against tax and trade laws. The Model Penal Code project did not extend to these, partly because a higher priority on limited time and resources was accorded to branches of the penal law which have not received close legislative scrutiny. Also, in legislation dealing with narcotics, liquor, tax evasion, and the like, penal provisions have been so intermingled with regulatory and procedural provisions that the task of segregating one group from the other presents special difficulty for model legislation.]

a. Model Penal Code 241 (Proposed Official Draft 1962).—Eds.

INDEX

References are to pages.

†

What is the sequence of events in the criminal justice system?

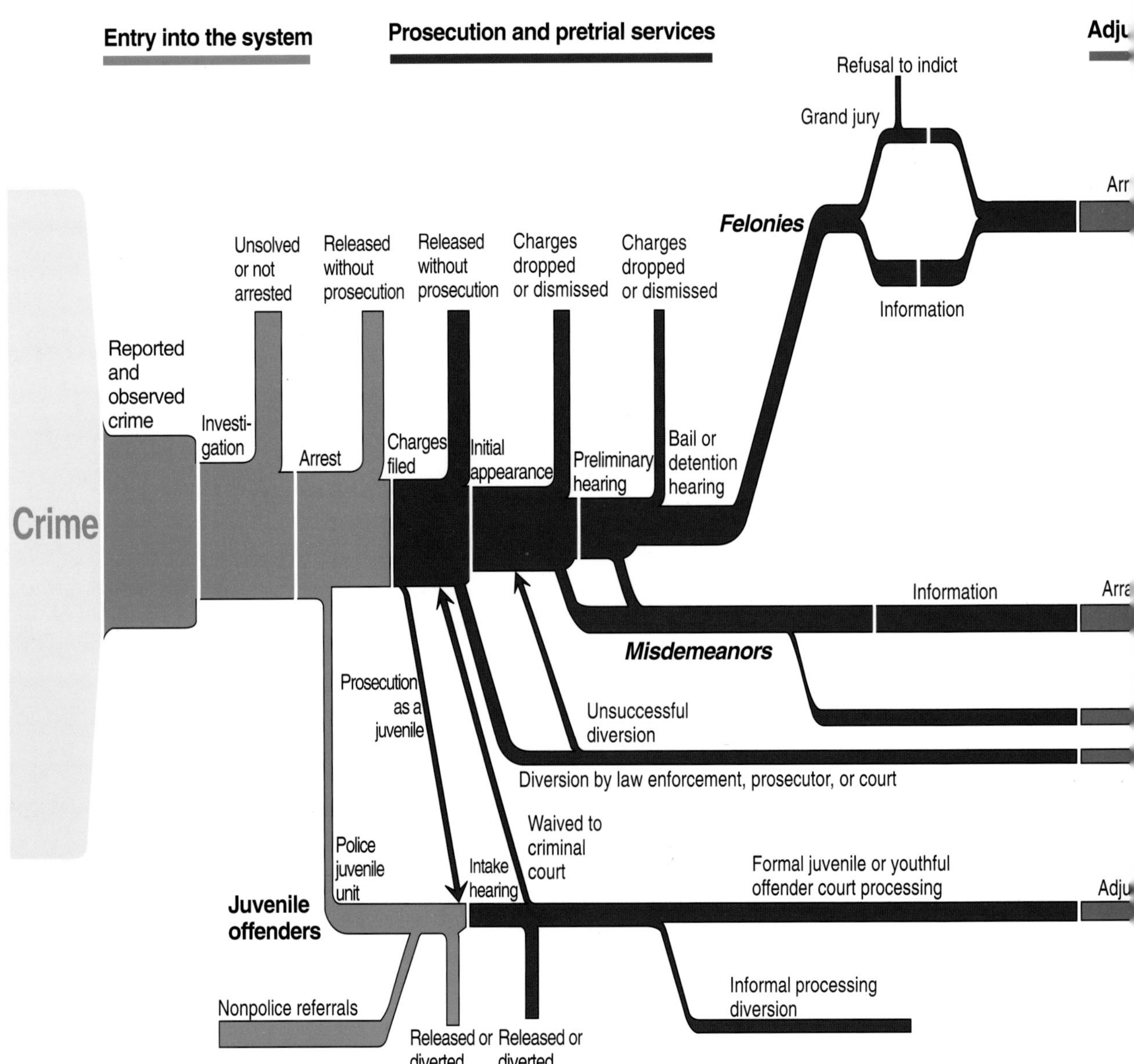

Note: This chart gives a simplified view of caseflow through the criminal justice system. Procedures vary among jurisdictions. The weights of the lines are not intended to show actual size of caseloads.

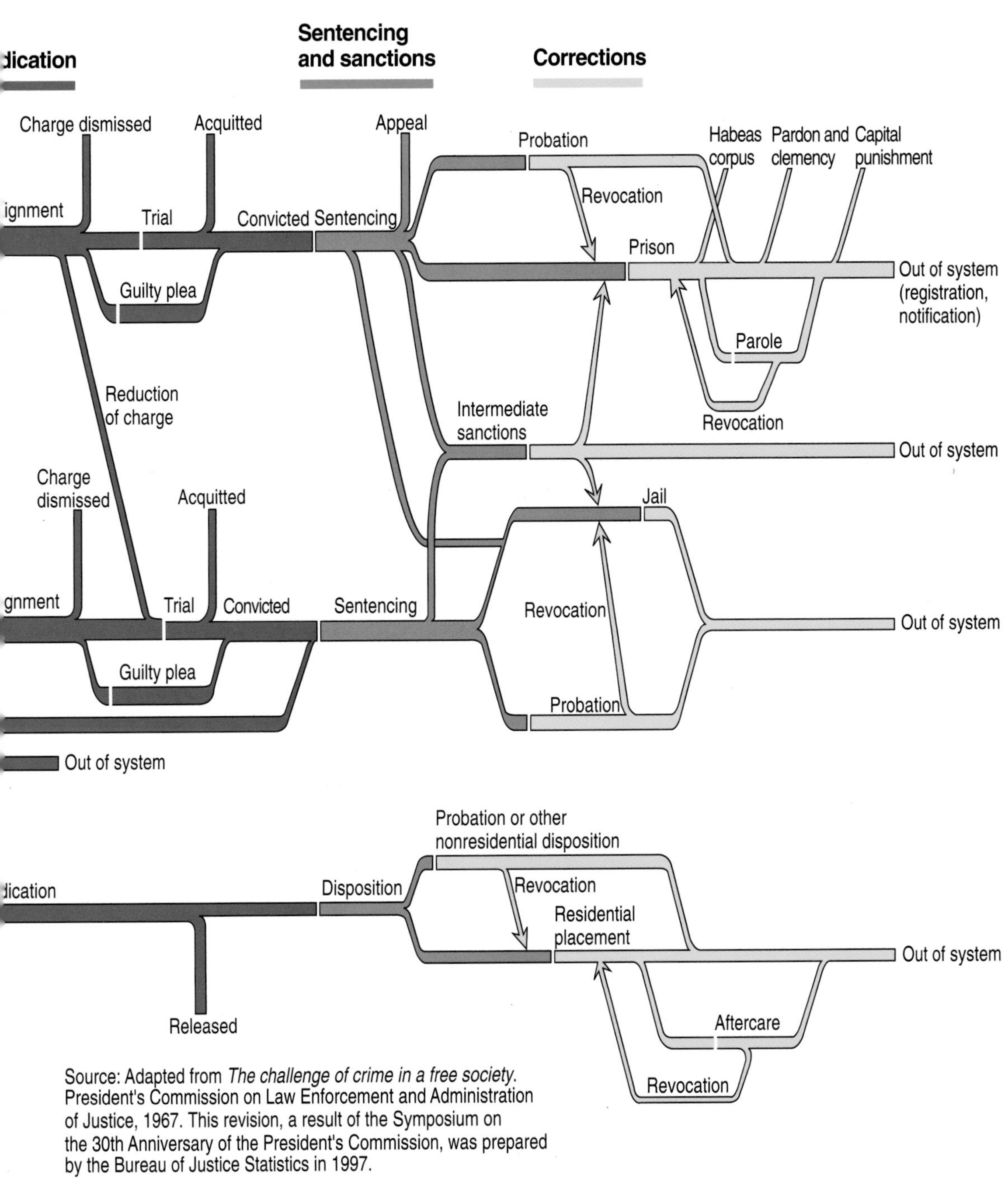

Source: Adapted from *The challenge of crime in a free society*. President's Commission on Law Enforcement and Administration of Justice, 1967. This revision, a result of the Symposium on the 30th Anniversary of the President's Commission, was prepared by the Bureau of Justice Statistics in 1997.